SISTERS, SEEDS, & CEDARS

SISTERS, SEEDS, & CEDARS

Rediscovering Nineteenth-Century Life
Through Correspondence
from Rural Arkansas and Alabama

Edited and Annotated by
Sarah M. Fountain

UCA Press
Conway, AR
1995

Library of Congress Cataloging-in-Publication Data

Sisters, seeds, and cedars : rediscovering nineteenth-century life through correspondence from rural Arkansas and Alabama / edited and annotated by Sarah M. Fountain.
728p. 25.5 cm.
  Includes bibliographical references and index.
  ISBN 0-944436-14-5 : $42.95
    1. Country life--Arkansas--History--19th century--Sources.
2. Country life--Alabama--History--19th century--Sources.
3. American letters--Arkansas. 4. American letters--Alabama.
5. Arkansas--Social life and customs--Sources. 6. Alabama--Social life and customs--Sources. I. Fountain, Sarah.

Illustrator: Jeff Huddleston
Designer: Robert E. Lowrey

Copyright © 1995 by UCA Press
All rights reserved
Manufactured in the United States of America

ISBN 0-944436-14-5

This book is fondly dedicated to the people of Ouachita County, past and present, to Sue Martin Russell, and especially to the memory of my dad, Charles Elijah Moseley, to whom Ouachita County was "home" for all of his 89 years.

Contents

Illustrations and Photographs   ix

Foreword by Senator Pryor   xi

Introduction   xiii

Maps   xviii-xix

Part One: *Spreading Wings and Learning to Fly* (1850-1861)   1

Cornelia Dickson and her sister Clarissa exchange letters between Mulberry and Selma in Autauga County, Alabama, sharing "girl talk" and news of the neighborhood and school. Both girls send to their father requests for shoes, writing tablets, hair ribbons, and other daughter items. Clarissa gains her independence by first changing her name to Clara and then by traveling to Arkansas with the families of her half-brother, George Boddie, and her half-sister, Fannie Rumph. Her visit west of the Mississippi becomes permanent when she marries John Dunlap and settles down in Ouachita County.

Part Two: *Clouds of War* (1861-1865)   107

The American Civil War brings considerable change to the people in Ouachita County and in Autauga County. Mail is slow and often undelivered, but letters are written, relating the difficult life which accompanies all war. George Boddie and John Dunlap join the Confederate Army and engage the enemy at various locations in Arkansas. Clara and Mollie Boddie are left alone to handle the chores until the Union soldiers take over their farms, and they are forced to move into the homes of other family members. Sis Mollie and Brother George exchange letters from the home front and the battlefield.

Part Three: *After the War* (1867-1875)   193

The war ends and life in the South is drastically different: Reconstruction brings high taxes, indebtedness, and difficult times of rebuilding. Having been left alone in Alabama after the death of her mother, Cornelia comes to Arkansas to live and to teach school when she can. When she cannot find teaching positions, "Aunt Nealy" goes from household to household helping wherever she is needed. She engages in a vigorous correspondence with friends and relatives in Alabama, keeping everyone informed of events taking place in Arkansas

Part Four: *Toward a New Century* (1876-1892)   337

The men and women who moved from Alabama to Arkansas two decades ago are growing older; their children have grown up and are beginning to leave the nest to build their futures. The community is larger and new names appear in the letters, many of which are posted to St. Louis from Mary Elizabeth Boddie to her son John Rumph Boddie. Cornelia continues to send news back to Alabama, much of it sad news as death comes to earlier letter writers.

Part Five: *The Twentieth Century Arrives* (1900-1928)   559

The second generation has taken the leadership of the community, and their horizons are much broader than those of their parents. They have the same busy lives as their parents, though not too many are farmers. They are raising their children in Camden or some other town where educational and economic opportunities are greater. "Aunt Nealie" becomes one of their responsibilities, and they tend to her needs with the same love and devotion that she showed them when they were children.

Appendices   649

Index   683

Table of Illustrations & Photographs

Part One

Mary Dickson Lanier	12
Ivy Creek Church Marker	23
Clarissa Lanier, as a girl	27
Clarissa Lanier Boddie Dickson	27
Colonel Samuel Henry Neeley Dickson	28
Colonel Dickson's Business cards	28
Thomas G. Howard, M.D.	38
Miss Rebecca Underwood	39
Leonidas Howard	39
Mary Elizabeth Gildersleeve Boddie	50
George Boddie "Brother George"	50
Dr. John Benjamin Rumph "Brother John"	51
Captain Dee Newton	54
Ora Stone Newton	55
Clara Dickson Dunlap	68
John Franklin Dunlap	69
Sallie Gildersleeve Rumph "Sis Sallie"	105
Sword awarded to S.H.N. Dickson	106

Part Two

Dick Dunlap and wife	140
General Frederick Steele and General Sterling Price	158
Map of Steele's Route in the Camden Expedition	159

Part Three

Rebecca Underwood's Note to Cornelia Dickson	204
School Flier for Camden High School for Males	214
The Cedar Tree	235
Lula Dunlap	242
Cora Lee Dunlap	243
W. G. (Dick) Love	244
Andrew J. Love	245
John R. Boddie	254
Mary E. A. Love	263
Martha Hodge "Matt" Proctor Rumph	274
Legislative letterhead, 1874	283
Sample of Mollie's upside down composition	323
Sample of Cross-writing	326

Part Four

Patrick Gaughan	350
Sarah Caroline Patterson Gaughan	351

Invitation to St. Valentine's Ball, 1876	352
John Rumph Boddie	363
Mary Elizabeth "Mamie" Boddie	384
Cornelia Kimball Smoker Boddie	433
Lula Dunlap	436
Cora Lee Dunlap	437
Frances Caroline "Carrie" Boddie	458
George Kimball Smoker Boddie, age 4	473
Mary Gaughan, "Our Baby"	483
Wedding Invitation: Florence Rumph and Edwin Clifton	488
Smoker Boddie with Dog	499
George Gildersleeve "Gilder" Boddie	507
Martha Hogue "Matt" Proctor Rumph	531
Mary Elizabeth "Sis Mollie" Boddie and Smoker Boddie, age 8	544
Hattie Murley	547
John B. Dunlap, age 14	552
The Rumph Sisters	553
Bettie Rumph	554
D. Carey and John B. Dunlap	555
Harry Fisher Moseley and baby brother George Boddie Moseley	557

Part Five

James Walter Martin	573
Cora Dunlap Martin	574
George Kimball Smoker Boddie at Vanderbilt University	577
Fred Hughes Coleman at West Point	578
Dennis LaFayette Gaughan	579
Belle Ferguson Gaughan	580
William Allis Moseley and sister	
Mary Arkansas Moseley Fisher	591
Godfrey Coleman	593
Mary Gilder Coleman Bagwell	594
Clarissa (Clara) Dickson Dunlap in later years	602
Caroline Lafayette Boddie Love	603
John Franklin Dunlap	603
Waitie Butler & Smoker Boddie	604
George Boddie Moseley, WW I	614
Group photo at T.J. Gaughan's Home	
with William Jennings Bryan	638
Thomas Joseph Gaughan	638
Lula Higgins Gaughan	638
Robert Lee "Tug" Boddie and Sallie Farley Boddie	
with Grandchildren	644
Cornelia Sanderson Dickson	646

DAVID PRYOR
ARKANSAS

Russell Senate Office Building
Washington, DC 20510
(202) 224-2353

ARKANSAS OFFICE:
3030 Federal Building
Little Rock, AR 72201
(501) 324-6336

United States Senate
WASHINGTON, DC 20510-0402

COMMITTEES:
AGRICULTURE, NUTRITION, AND FORESTRY
FINANCE
GOVERNMENTAL AFFAIRS
SPECIAL COMMITTEE ON AGING

Foreword

Our nation is much like a patchwork quilt. Each block has its own character and pattern, but every block in the quilt is dependent upon its surrounding neighbors for support. Together all the blocks form a whole quilt. This country of ours was pieced together in the same manner. Small communities sprang into existence as people collected in one area, forming their own little society, dependent upon each other for support. In time these small communities grew and increased in number. From this growth, states were born to culminate into the United States of America. Just as the patchwork quilt requires devoted effort and time-consuming discipline, so does the building of a nation. Every American knows that this country did not spring forth fully developed.

Historians have recorded the development of America in full detail, and have introduced us to the major figures of history. Statisticians have charted the numbers from the Atlantic to the Pacific and from Canada to the Gulf of Mexico. Sociologists have studied the motivations of every movement engendered by Americans. All of these efforts are necessary, of course, and quite admirable. However, the true picture of our history comes from the little people in these communities who went about the business of daily building a nation. In books such as this, we meet these simple people and share their experiences. We witness their courage, their selfless dedication to family and friends.

These particular people are especially interesting to me, for they are "my people." Their block in the patchwork quilt of America is my block. Captain Dee Newton of these letters is my great-grandfather. He was among those pioneers who came from Alabama to settle the small community of Harmony Grove and bring the Alabama pattern to the Arkansas quilt. I am proud of that. My mother, and granddaughter of Dee Newton, Susie Newton Pryor, like her forebearers, continued to work on "our" block of the quilt throughout her life, and instilled in all of her children a sense of duty to God and country. She exhibited for us the courage necessary to proceed with the "quilting." I am proud of that.

Sarah Fountain has indeed made a significant and most constructive contribution to the study of Arkansas history.

David Pryor

INTRODUCTION

"Something there is that doesn't love a wall..."
Robert Frost: "Mending Wall"

Something there is also that compels man to seek greener fields. For some it is nothing more than an inability to stay in one place, an inherent desire to just roam. For others it is a need to root themselves into a more promising locale, one that offers greater hope for the future. And there are those who move out of desperation, seeking escape from hopelessness or persecution. Our country, the United States of America, emerged from all such men: adventuresome men and women who were beckoned by the next mountain, the next river; ambitious men and women who longed for a better opportunity for themselves and their families; frightened men and women who could no longer endure the indignities of "man's inhumanity to man." These same men and women pushed the boundaries of America from the Atlantic Ocean to the Pacific Ocean, and every man and woman carried within themselves a story of courage, persistence, fortitude, and dedication to purpose.

The materials which compose this book tell the stories of these men and women who moved to alien fields and, in moving, transplanted their society, their culture, to a distant land. This transplantation of community undoubtedly occurred in many sections of America as she moved Westward. The community of our concern made its way from Autauga County, Alabama, across the Mississippi River to Ouachita County, Arkansas. Men packed their belongings, their families, their hopes and their dreams, and with their brothers, sisters, cousins, and neighbors, established a version of their Alabama society in Arkansas. They tied the two societies together with letters, holding Alabama tightly to their lives while building Arkansas, one day at a time.

There was a time when the only means of communication with persons in distant places was the written word. Handwritten letters were the links between friends and family members hundreds of miles away. Such letters were eagerly awaited and were avenues of visitation. Personal visits were few and infrequent, since modes of transportation were slow and, except for boats, were dependent upon the individual's personal carrier: a horse, a buggy, or in some cases, one's feet. It takes little imagination in these circumstances to recognize the importance of a letter. In our society, with its highly technical communication and transportation systems, the art of letter writing, lamentably, is a lost art. To visit with distant friends or relatives today, we need only pick up the telephone, jump in an automobile, or board an airplane. While these means of communication and travel are more convenient, speedier, and certainly less trouble, our use of language has suffered, as has our ability to read with subtle insight. We have no longer the luxury of reading and rereading, thereby prolonging the visit. When we hang up the telephone, the visit is over, without any record. Our recall of details is immediately diminished, or even lost. We must experience the lasting pleasure of written communication to appreciate the historic and aesthetic contribution of these and other letter writers.

In literature, the novel made some of its early appearances in what was labeled The Epistolary Style: the story told through letters. We borrow the style, but the letters presented here are not fiction. The people are real; their stories are not figments of some novelist's imagination but actual events. Through these letters, we are afforded a glimpse of nineteenth century society by those who created it. We watch as they go about their daily lives, and we are privy to their intimate thoughts and feelings. We experience their joys and their sorrows; we celebrate their victories and suffer their defeats. We come to know them as friends, not simply as people who lived in a different time. And when we come to the end, we are loath to give up the narrative.

The major figure in this narrative is Aunt Nealie—Cornelia S. Dickson. Every letter touches her; many are written by her, and those that are not have some effect upon her life and thoughts. Cornelia was an inveterate, meticulous letter-writer. Her use of language is poetic at times, and she had a remarkable ability to describe emotions. Her letters reveal a careful, thoughtful writing style. Indeed, had it not been for this care and painstaking thoughtfulness, we should not have her correspondence at all. She saved many, if not all, of the letters she received. Her own letters come down to us through her ledgers where she wrote the letters first, no doubt checking her punctuation, spelling, and syntax before transcribing them onto her writing paper for mailing. Aunt Nealie's correspondence, stored in a trunk in Cora Martin's attic and discovered by Sue Martin Russell, make this manuscript possible. From her letters, we learn of Cornelia Dickson's patient, caring, and generous character.

Two other women contribute heavily to the narrative. Clara Dickson Dunlap and Sis Mollie Boddie provide us with a broader view of the community in its earlier days. Their writing styles are similar; they both abbreviate common words like <u>received</u> and almost exclusively use the ampersand rather than writing the word <u>and</u>. Both of them rarely use a period or capital letter, inserting only a comma or a dash or nothing before beginning the next sentence. Such a style has a feel of spontaniety, of urgency, of having so much to say and so little time or space to say it. The tone is conversational, warm, and personal. The descriptive ability of Sis Mollie is particularly admirable; she paints with a full and colorful brush.

As the letters move through the years and into the second and third generations, the fabric of our narrative grows broader and more diverse. The correspondents travel in wider circles, and communication becomes more convenient. It is interesting to note, however, that regardless of distance, Aunt Nealie is still the object of concern and affection.

A close reading of the letters reveals several things about the society and the attitudes of that society. The first thing that comes to mind is the dedication to family, especially among the women. These women are strong, courageous human beings; they hold families together in extremely difficult times with a firm belief that God knows what is best, and they will accept and endure. There is a sense of faith, family responsibility, and obligation that our society in the final days of the twentieth century seems to be rapidly losing. Trouble and problems of one family member become the trouble and problems of all the family. There is a deep sense of duty to family in these people. To turn one's back on a family member in need was unthinkable. No sacrifice was too great; indeed "helping out" was not even considered a sacrifice.

Another characteristic of nineteenth-century life that is apparent in these letters is the fragile hold these people had on mortality. Death came very quickly, especially to children, and the value of human life was sacred. Every letter begins with a report on the health of various family members. Fevers, the "flux," injuries, and various other illnesses were commonplace.

Still another point of interest is the clustering of families and friends in the same location. A letter from Arkansas to Alabama could refer to people without long explanations of who those people were. The names were as familiar to the recipient in Alabama as they were to the writer in Arkansas. This indicates that groups emigrated together, forming close-knit communities carried over from one part of the country to another.

Manners of expression in these letters prove interesting also. The phrase "and to all inquiring friends" is found at the end of nearly every letter, suggesting the strength of ties to "home" and perhaps even a tinge of homesickness. The use of "cc" for "etc" is a reflection of how our language usage changes over the years. The absence of paragraphing in many instances indicates the value of writing paper; one had to use every inch of space.

The compiling of such a book as this entails considerable "housekeeping." Finding a focus is the first task. After much consideration, I decided to make Aunt Nealie the focal point. The entire collection of letters is voluminous, containing some 750 letters in the Dickson Collection alone. The Boddie Collection adds several hundred more letters. While every letter was most interesting and enlightening, to include them all would create a loose, wide range of topics whose only connecting point was chronology. By limiting my choices to the development of a narrative, I could focus on character and personality, allowing real people to emerge, while also revealing a time and place.

Editorial changes have been kept to a minimum, as I wanted these people to speak for themselves. I have changed spelling only when not to do so would cause confusion. For the same reason, I have inserted some apostrophes and commas. When only initials are used, I have included full names when I felt it necessary for proper identification; when such identification was obvious, I left only the initial. Editorial changes are placed in brackets; the parentheses appear in the original copy. Underlined words also appear as such in the original copy. Editorial comments are printed in italics. Words which are followed by (?) indicate that the original copy was unclear and the word used was inferred from the context. At all times I have tried to leave the letters exactly as they were written for fear of damaging their integrity. Because I am acutely aware of my professional duty as an editor, I have retained some terms which could offend some readers. I ask the reader to remember that these letters come from another time when such terms were commonly used and accepted. I cannot presume to rewrite for an audience of 150 years later. We must, I think, read from the past as it was written, albeit maintaining a sensitivity for today.

This project has been a most rewarding and enjoyable one for me. I have a personal interest in these collections of letters because they emanate from my home territory. I was born and raised in Camden, and many of the names are quite familiar to me. I know the families and count them among my friends. My father was a Moseley from Harmony Grove. Cornelia Dickson helped to raise my cousins George and Harry, whom I called "Cuddin George" and "Cuddin Harry." These letters have given me the opportunity to dig around in my roots, so to speak, and the experience has been exciting. I hope it will be enjoyable to the reader.

ACKNOWLEDGEMENTS

An undertaking of this kind cannot be accomplished without the help of many people to whom I am indebted. I am grateful first and foremost to Sue Martin Russell and Cora Russell Rogers of Harmony Grove for allowing me to be a part of this project. I appreciate the confidence they had in me when they turned their family history over to me. I appreciate Tom Dillard, Archivist at The University of Central Arkansas, for locating this marvelous collection and for giving me the opportunity to work with it. His encouragement and assistance has been most helpful. I am especially indebted to Ruth Boddie Farmer for the hours she spent in Torreyson Library checking the copy against the originals for discrepancies and for the tedious task of helping get the Index in order. Without her help, this manuscript would never have gotten to the printer. Many thanks to her, also, for bringing forth the Boddie Collection of letters which added immeasureably to the narrative. I appreciate the help of my independent readers, Della Curran, Olivia Smith and Nita Moseley Munoz, who read the manuscript from an objective distance and offered meaningful suggestions. We all appreciate the artistry of the geneological charts, provided by "Cuddin" Nita, who is the artist in the family. Thanks, too, to Ken Griffin and Mack Thompson in the UCA Computer Center for running the transcribed letters through the scanner and getting them on disks. And thanks to Sue and Cora for transcribing them in the first place. That saved many hours of sitting at the computer.

The definitions and explanations in the marginal notes come from a wide variety of sources: *The Random House Dictionary of the English Language*, the *Encyclopedia Britannica*, and particularly *A Dictionary of Slang and Unconventional English* by Eric Partridge (Macmillan, 1970). When these sources failed me, I turned to the specialists. Dr. Mary Harmon, Chairman of the Home Economics Dept, University of Central Arkansas, searched out fabric definitions, and Dr. Greg Urwin, Professor of History, UCA, who is a walking encyclopedia on the Civil War, helped identify Union and Confederate names and places. Ann Turney at Hendrix College supplied much needed information on Galloway College. Also, I am especially indebted to my brother, Charles Moseley of Blytheville, Arkansas who was so helpful in explaining terms of farming, particularly cotton farming. Thanks, too, to Jeff Huddleston for his artistic talent in the pen-and-ink drawings.

Clara Dunlap's War Letters are available to us through the permission of John Ferguson, Director of the Arkansas History Commission, where they reside in the Archives. The Rumph letters are used by permission of John Gildersleeve Hendricks of Decatur, Alabama. Mr. Hendricks is the great-grandson of Dr. John Benjamin Rumph. We appreciate the generosity of Dr. Ferguson and Mr. Hendricks.

As usual, Bob Lowrey at UCA Press has lent his support and encouragement as well as the hard drive computer which allowed me to work in my study at home. Kathy Hart-Sparks at the Press pulled my computer irons out of the fire on numerous occasions. Jeff Henderson, with his exceptional knowledge of language, provided suggestions of word choices when my brain simply ran out of choices. Many, many thanks, my friends. Special thanks go to Senator David Pryor for the Foreword. Since he is one of Ouachita County's favorite sons, his comments are most appropriate. Finally, I must thank my husband Bill for his encouragement and understanding when I was too busy to fix meals.

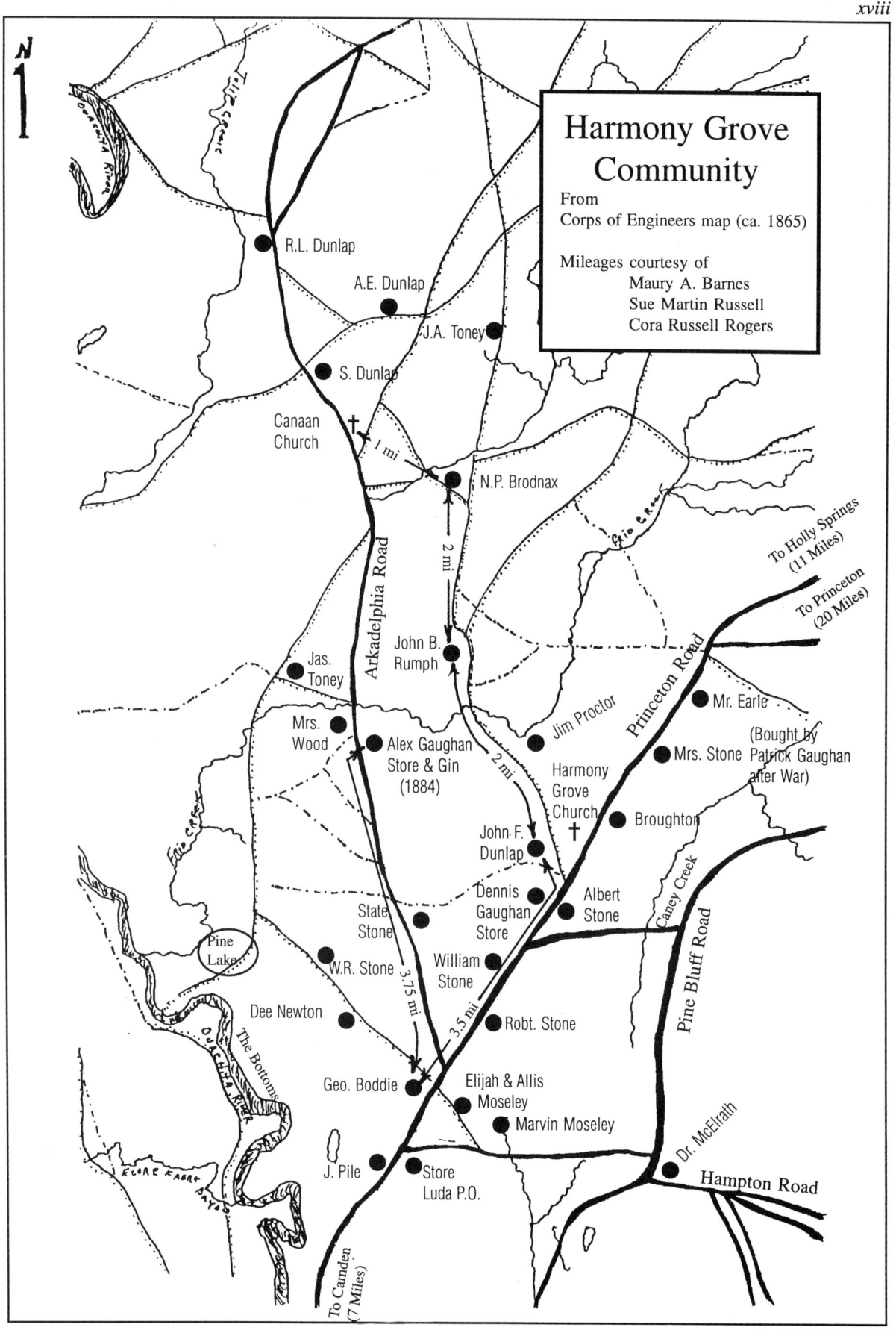

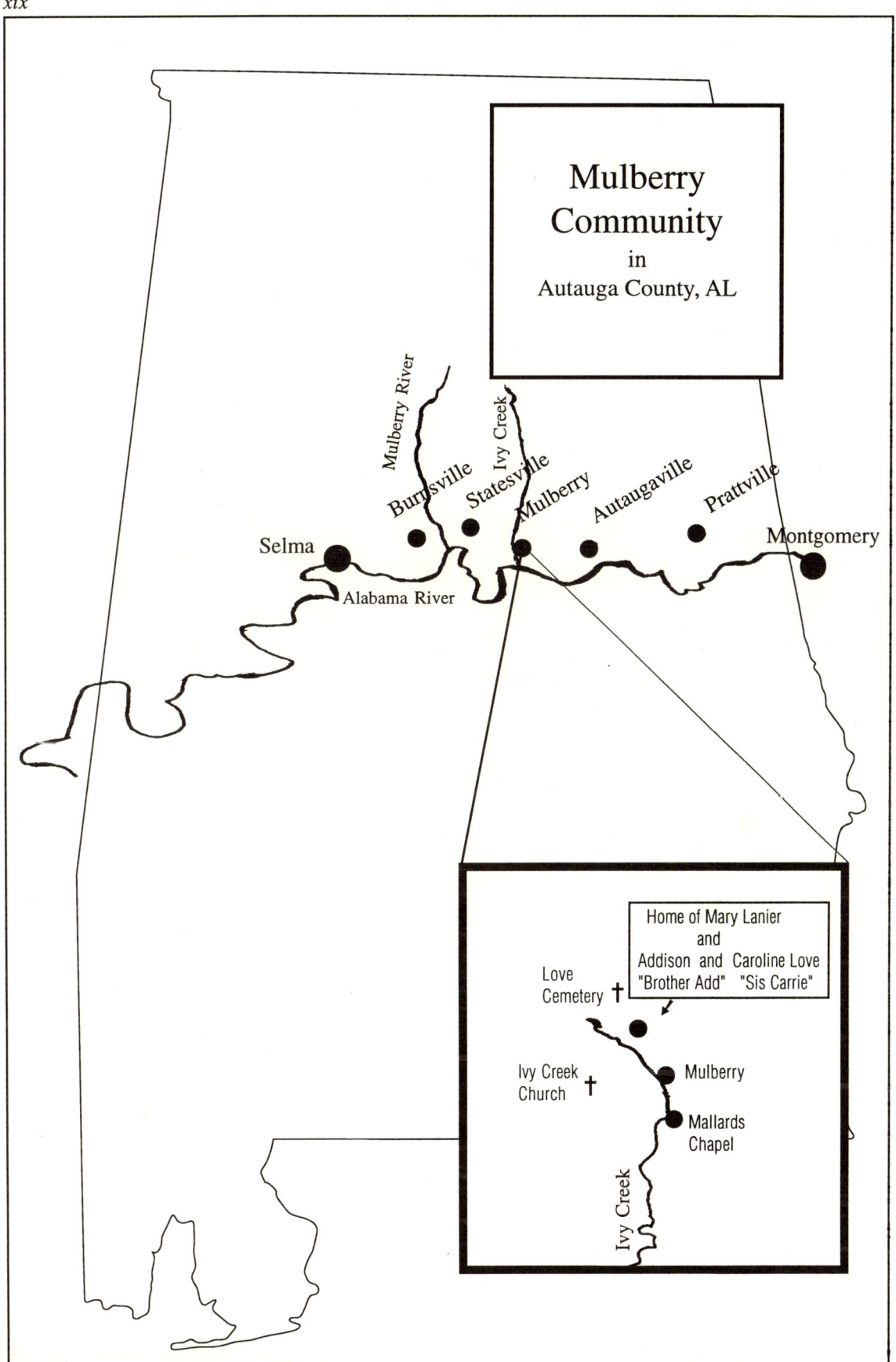

PART ONE

Spreading Wings and Learning to Fly

All narratives must have a beginning, a middle and an end. Our narrative begins with two young girls: Clarissa (later to become Clara) and Cornelia Dickson, living near Mulberry, Alabama, in 1850. We find them experiencing the notions and desires that all young girls possess. They want hair ribbons, shoes, and dresses. They are full of gossip and speculation, and life promises them adventure, romance, and success. They are anxious to grow up and meet their destinies.

Cornelia pursues her studies in Selma, Alabama, with vigor. Clarissa at times shows the normal sibling jealousy at not being allowed to attend school with her sister. There are requests to borrow clothes and to return clothes which have been borrowed. Those of us who have raised daughters find familiarity in these letters.

Unbeknownst to either girl, the foundations for their lives and characters, which we discover in the middle and end of the narrative, are being laid as they write. Cornelia emerges as a "mind" person. She enjoys learning; she reads, writes poetry, and revels in things intellectual. Clarissa is a "hands" individual and reveals early on an impatience with the "status quo." She earns a reputation as a fine seamstress and is able to "pay her way" during visits to Selma by sewing for other people. She also becomes rather adept at home nursing skills.

Cornelia will settle into the teaching profession and will remain in Alabama until after the war. Her devotion to children and education will provide her with livelihood and a special place to nieces and nephews throughout her life. Clarissa, on the other hand, eagerly takes the first opportunity to travel and see something outside of Alabama. Her skills at sewing, nursing, and household management will result in making a home in Arkansas.

Cornelia S. Dickson in Autauga County to her father, Col. S. H. N. Dickson in Mobile, Alabama.

Oct. 30th, 1850

Dear Father,

As you told me to write to you today I shall do so. We are all well and have been so since you left home. Our school is going on very well. Miss Cowan dismisses earlier than she did when you were here. I like to go to school to her better than any teacher I ever went to, if I did not have so far to walk. You must not forget to get some steal pens and me a pair of shoes. You must not forget to get the History of Marian and the Philosophy. If you get linsey*, don't get red get blue or green.

Your daughter,
Cornelia S. Dickson [11 years]

*"linsey" is a coarse fabric woven from linen warp and coarse wool felling; it is also known as linsey-woolsey.

Cornelia Dickson in Autauga County to her father, Col. S. H. N. Dickson in Mobile, Ala.

April 8th, 1851

My dear Father,

I received your letter on Friday of the 4th instant and as I had not received any letter from you in a long time, it gave me great pleasure to hear from you. We are all well. We have received the dress for Ma and the three pairs of shoes and the apron checks and the bbl [barrel] of molasses is at the landing* Clarissa's shoes are to large and they have got her name on them and she cannot get them changed. Clarissa and myself are not going to school now for Miss Cowen is very sick with the Typhoid fever, but I hope that she will get over it. I am very sory to say that Dr. Laventer is very low and is not expected to live more than two or three weeks. I suppose that you don't know that Brother George [Boddie, who is in Arkansas] has got another fine boy. Ma has got a loom and has gone to weaving. I should like to know when you are coming up. We have had a great deal of rain the last four or five days, and I expect that they have raised the river so that you can come up any time.* I have got a very pretty little puppy from Mrs. Steele. As I have no more to say, I will close my letter.

Your affectionate daughter,
Cornelia S. Dickson

*The landing would be Gaston's Landing on the Alabama River, some few miles from the home and the point at which their transportation up and down the river began.

*River traffic was totally dependent upon the water level. When the river was low, boats could not travel. Cornelia's reference to the rains explains the "they" which have raised the level.

3 Spreading Wings and Learning to Fly

This is the report card Cornelia Dickson received when she attended Mulberry Academy.

Report

Miss Cornelia Dickson is entitled to the following report of her scholarship, during the first 4 weeks, ending Apr. 18, 1851

    Number of perfect recitations 31
    imperfect 14
    Absences from recitations
    Failures in whispering 1
    General Deportment - very correct

                  A.A. Cowan, teacher
                  Mulberry Academy

Cornelia Dickson in Autauga County to her father Col. S. H. N. Dickson in Mobile, Ala.

                                            May 7th, 1851

My dear Father,

    We have received the note and the newpaper which you sent by Mr. Morton. I am very sorry to hear that you are in very bad health. I have got a very bad cold in my head. Clarissa and Ma are well. I hope that you will be up the last of this month. A great many people ask me when you will be up. I tell them that I don't know but I should like to know myself. You must send me some shoes and some blacking*. I want you to send me tolerable coarse shoes for I am tired of these little fine ones for they wear out so quick. You must send Ma some meat. School is going on very well. I believe that Miss Cowen has learned me more than any teacher I've ever went to in my life. She has thirty one scholars. As I have no more to say I shall close my letter.

                          Your affectionate daughter,
                          Cornelia

    P. S. The little copy book's that you sent are so small that we can write them threw in a little while and they would do better for composition book and I hope that you will let me get a larger one at the office*. Clarissa and myself were at the May party at Mrs. Lamar's last Saturday. There were a good many people there and we enjoyed ourselves very well. If you come up you must not forget the earrings which you promised me before you went away. Please send us up some raisons and oranges and apples.

*Blacking is a preparation for polishing shoes and stoves.

* "The office" Cornelia refers to is the Mulberry Post Office which was housed in a store.

Clarissa Dickson in Autauga County to her father Col. S. H. N. Dickson, Sweetwater P. O. in Marengo Co., Ala.

July 1st, 1851

Dear Father,

Agreeable to my promise I now seat myself with the intention of letting you know the state of affairs at home — although there is nothing of any importance occured since your late departure. *All are well.* They are taking a bee-gum tonight*

— and I have just taken a nice bite of honey, — the whitest that I most ever saw — I wish that you and Cornelia were here to get some. The small girls say they wish to see C[ornelia] very much — and are continually asking me when will she be home again. Before you left you promised me that you would look over some earrings for me at Cahawba — don't forget it, please. Well, it is late and I must think of going to bed — but before I close I will ask you one request which is if you go round by Eutaw, give my love to all my old school mates and particularly to Julia Pippin.

Good bye, your affectionate daughter,

Clarissa Dickson

> * "Taking a bee-gum" means robbing a bee hive in a gum tree.

Clarissa Dickson in Autauga County to her father Col. S. H. N. Dickson, Jefferson P. O., Marengo Co., Ala.

July 20th, 1851

Dear Father,

Mother received your letter a few minutes ago, and she would have answered it herself, but as it is night and you know she can not see well enough to write at night — and so she requested me to write in her stead.

"All are well" and have continued so since your departure. We have suffered greatly for rain — but within the last two or three days there has been a plenty for a while at least.

Our examinations came on the eleventh, all of us done very well indeed — I was head in all my classes — there were a great many people there, and we had a most excellent dinner.

I have sad news to tell you — your kind and benevolent friend Mr Underwood is dead — he departed this life on the night of the eighth of this month — and was buried at Ivy Creek Church where his first wife is & his death is a great loss to his family as you may suppose, for to most of them he was an only parent. I have spent the day at Grandmothers as Cousin Albert Pickett, his wife,* and youngest child came there yesterday morning — and started home this evening. They don't expect to get home tonight but will stay all night at Aunt Fanny's old place. They expect to spend the month of

> *Albert Pickett's wife was Frances Dickson, sister to Mary Dickson Lanier, the girls' grandmother.

5 Spreading Wings and Learning to Fly

October there and then they can come back to see us again.

I have written you before now but you may have never received my letter as you never spoke of it in your letter. I would have not been so anxious about writing tonight — but I have a convenient way of sending it soon in the morning*, and besides you wanted us to write on the 15th but we never received your letter until a few moments ago. If you pass through Luton or green County, give my love to all my friends, and connections, and particularly to Julia Pippin, and Mrs. Morgan's family. Tell Julia P_____ I wish very much to see her, and as we cannot see each other in person, we can surely correspond by letter, which is far better than being silent.

Please don't forget my earrings if you can find any that is cheap. Hoping that this letter will find you and Cornelia in good health. (We were sorry to hear that C_____ had been sick again but hope that it was of short duration). Come home anyhow by the first of September if not sooner in order to send me and C_____ to school. You have been promising me for the last two years that you would send me to Selma — now as you say that you always think it best for a person to stick up to his promise, do please don't break yours. Well it is late and so I must close. Ma and me both send our love to you and Cornelia. Good bye
Your affectionate daughter,
Clarissa Dickson

P.S. Excuse bad writing for I am so fatigued that I can scarcely write atall. CD

P.S. My shoes is worn out and I have to wear my fine ones every day. Let me know if I can't get a pair at the Post Office. CD

*Post Offices were located in the towns and rural areas had to depend upon someone going into town to mail their letters.

Clarissa Dickson in Autauga Co. to her sister Cornelia Dickson at Boarding School in Selma.

1851*

Dear Nealy,

Your letter I received yesterday morning by Pa unexpectedly though as I looked for you to come with him, but then I suppose you could enjoy yourself better in Selma with other girls. I spent my Christmas Eve delightfully at a party given by Mrs. Lasiter had a splendid supper.

I had not fixed your dress or I would send it, but intend doing so tomorrow and send it down when Ma sends Pa's bed, also your hicory nuts; Little Fanny can walk, all the children send their love to you and howdy. If you need your gingham dress, let me know and I will send it, or had you rather I would make you a sacque* for you out of it. Ma is knitting you some stockings out of fine 15 hundred factory thread only doubled once. They are beautiful, she sends her love to you, grandma does also. Little Mary says

*No other date is given on this letter.

* A sacque was a loose fitting dress which was fashionable in the late 18th century and most of the 19th century.

she wishes you to come home, for she says I never will give her any thing like you. Good bye, write soon.

Your affectionate sister,
Clarissa Dickson

P. S. I will send your bonnet by Pa.

P. S. I wish if you have the opportunity to do so to send me a pretty neck ribbon, bright lilac and white coloured, do please.

C D

Cornelia Dickson at Boarding School in Selma to her mother Mrs. Clarissa Dickson in Autauga Co., Ala.

1851*

*There is no other date on this letter.

My Dear Mother,

I have not received any letter from you since I have been down here. The reason, I suppose, why you did not write to me before now was that you thought that I did not expect you to write to me. Neither do I expect it. But I have not received any letter from home in a week or more. I should like very much to come up and see you all Friday or Saturday, but I am afraid that Pa can not get a horse and buggy, and besides that, our concert comes on Friday night.

I like Selma and the school very well so far. Friday is my composition day and I have only got half of my composition writen. The subject is (An industrious girl). The teacher gives out the subjects and then you have to tell her what one that you are going to take before leaving the room. It is now school hours while I write. Mrs. Himble one of our teachers is sick and did not come to school yesterday or today. I have to recite three lessons in the evening and as I have just recited two of them, the third one I can not recite without Mrs. Himble was here. So you see the rest of the evening I have nothing to do and I thought I would write you a few lines. I have had a very bad coal. It was so bad that I had to stay at home Friday evening, but it is now getting better and I do not cough so much as I did. There are a few flowers open in Selma, a good many hasinths and Johnquills, some roses and so fourth. Please let me [know] if there is any open at grandma's or at home. give my love to grandma and Clarissa and Sister Caroline [Boddie Love], her children, except a share for yourself. I saw Pa last Sunday he appeared to be as well as usual. I believe Mrs. S. Conway was marred to Mr. J. M. Donald of Mississippi. Ma, you must try and come down and see me and get Sister Caroline or Clarissa to come with you.

[Cornelia S. Dickson]

Spreading Wings and Learning to Fly

Eliza Stone Wood of Ouachita Co., Ark.,* to Clarissa Dickson in Autauga Co., Ala.

*The heading on this letter reads "Washita City, Arkansas."

Nov 7 1852

Dear Clarissa,

    I take my seat once more to write you a few lines. I expect you think I have forgotten you, but far from that. I have been in too much trouble since the death of my husband that I never felt like I could write to anyone, nor indeed did I have the heart to write. My life is a lonely one, I can tell you. I stay at home most of the time. I have an uncle who stays with me. He is very kind but that does not replace my all. I have been very sick. I have had chills and fever since September until yesterday, I missed it. My Negroes have all had the fever. Some days I would have only one in the field at work. I must tell you about Mollie [Boddie] and Fanny [Rumph]. They are both well at this time, but Mollie has had the chills. Your brother George [Boddie] has had the chills too, but he is well now. Fanny's John [Rumph] has gone to Little Rock. You must not look for them this winter for they both have stumbling blocks in the way, you know what I mean. They make their dresses flowing.*

*Flowing dresses were worn by pregnant women.

    Sister Lizzie and I are going down to Mollie's tomorrow to stay several days. Then I am going to stay a week with Fanny. The waters have kept me from going this week. Fanny is by herself and I think she must have the blues which I have very bad myself sometimes. Tell your sister Carrie [Love] I think a letter from her is a long time coming. Tell her Brother Albert's wife has one of the prettiest babies she ever saw. It has curly hair. She calls it Ora Eliza after sister and myself. I have more namesakes in this country than I can shake a stick at. Clarissa I expect you will get tired of this letter before you get through with it, but I must ask you to excuse the paper that it is written on for it came out of a book. I sent to Camden several times for letter paper but could not get any and I concluded to write on this. You must not let anybody see it. Tell Uncle Dick howdy for me. Tell him to write to me soon. Give my love to Mary and Carrie and to your Mother and Grandma Lanier and all my friends, and accept the greatest share for yourself,

                  From your friend, Eliza Wood

    P.S. Be sure to answer this letter as soon as you get it and write me all the news. Tell Carrie I hope she does not have her dresses flowing now. If she does not, she is out of fashion. I would like to visit you all again, but ti will be some time before I can get that far from home. You must come out this winter if you can. I must close as it is getting late. Write soon.

                    Good night,
                    Eliza

Clarissa Dickson in Autauga Co. to her sister Cornelia Dickson in Selma, Ala.

Dec. 5th, 1852

Dear Neely,

    Your letter of the 30th was received yesterday. We were glad to hear that you & Pa, reached Selma safely and that you & him are well. Ma an[d] me have been well ever since you left. Brother Add* returned home yesterday. I received a letter from <u>Ark</u> day before yesterday — stating that all were well— The letter wes from Mrs. Wm. Wood. All the families in <u>Cabinville</u> are well.

    Nealy, I wish you would beg Pa to get me a muslin delain* dress — the first opportunity you get — let it be in the brightest colors you can find [there follows a line of description which has been marred so that it cannot be read, but the word orange is discernable] — I should think you [could] get them cheap in Selma. Tell Pa I saw Mr. Morton last Wednesday who said he wished he had known that Pa was up as he was anxious to see him. Ma sends he[r] love to you & Pa. accept of mine also —

                  Your affectionate sister,
                  Clarissa

P. S. Ma says let her know whether Pa has sent the baging, and rope, or not. If he has not — she says tell [him] to please send it directly.
    C D

*Brother Add refers to Addison C. Love who married Caroline LaFayette Boddie, "Sis Carrie", half- sister to Clarissa and Cornelia.

*Muslin delain is a thin worsted fabric, often having a printed pattern.

Clarissa Dickson in Autauga Co. to her sister Cornelia at Boarding School in Selma.

Jan. (?) 1853

Dear Nealy,

    Your letter I received yesterday evning. I had just begun to think that you was never going to write — but I will excuse you as you've been busy. Neal, who do you think is married — come try to guess — Betty Lasiter and Peyton Whetstone. Are you not surprised, she didn't have much of a wedding. I was one of the candle holders & Sue Holmes the other. Preacher Foreman married them last Wednesday night.

    Nealy, would you believe me if I told you that <u>Sally Gildersleeve</u> is about to be married to Mr. James Stubs, <u>it is really so</u>.* Last Thursday night week Miss Dora Motley and Dr. Tom Davis were married — doesn't it seem that nearly every body is marrying up. There is at least half a dozen more marriages in contemplation in this neighborhood, which will no doubt come to pass e're I write again.

    Cousin Sarah Pickett, Cousin Eliza [Walker], Cousin Fanny [Baker]

*Sally Gildersleeve is the sister of Sis Mollie Boddie, wife of George Boddie. Sally evidently did not marry Mr. Stubs, for she will later become the second wife of John B. Rumph in Arkansas.

& William Darden, has just paid us a visit. Cousin Fanny left yesterday evning. Neal, tell me if you wish your pink gingham dress made into a sacque, if so, let me know the latest fashion and I'll make it. Ma is knitting you some fine Factory cotton stockings number 1500, blue and white — they are very pretty indeed. We will be glad of the flower-seed if you get an opportunity to come up to see us soon. Do so please. Irene & Mary [Love] send their love to Aunt Nealy and wish to know when she is coming home — Fanny can walk. Write soon,

Your affectionate sister,
Clarissa

Clarissa Dickson in Autauga Co. to her father, Col. S. H. N. Dickson in Selma, Ala.

Jan. 14, 1853

Dear Father,

We received your letter yesterday evening and was glad to hear from you and that you was in good health. I received a letter from Cornelia about the same time which I answered a little while ago. We received the flour and sugar ten days ago. The sugar was excelent and the flour also. Betty Lasiter was married to Peyton Whetstone last Wednesday night — no one but me knew of it until a day or two before hand. I understood yesterday that <u>Sally</u> Gildersleeve was married or about to be, to Mr. James Stubs, and on the 7th of this month Miss Dora Motley and Dr. Tom Davis were married. On the 6th, Miss. F. Kirkland to Mr. Wm. Motley. She is Perry Kirklands's daughter. Pa please let me get some paper and envelopes at the office — I haven't a single bit of paper except this sheet. Cousin Sarah Pickett, Cousin Eliza Walker, Cousin Fanny, & Wm Darden paid us a visit this week. I think Mr. D____ a very fine man. Please write soon Pa and let us know how you are. All are well.

Your ever affectionate daughter,
Clarissa Dickson [17 yrs. old]

Sally A. Gildersleeve in Marengo, Alabama, to Cornelia Dickson at Boarding School in Selma, Ala.

Jan. 15th, 1853

My afar School-mate,

  I received your most welcome epistle one or two weeks since and so glad was I to hear from you and to hear that you are going to school. I do hope that you are pleased with the school. Don't think about home and you can always get your lessons. — I expect to go off to school some time in February, and Oh, how I do dread the time to come. Cornelia, I have never told you anything about our "Candy Party" that Sister H[attie] and myself gave on Christmas Eve. There were a great many here and Oh, the fun we had was a caution. I do wish that I could have had all of my school-mates here and I could have enjoyed myself much better. We sat up until four o'clock dancing. Don't you think that was long enough? — Sister H— received a letter from Sister Mary [Mary E. Boddie, "Mollie"] the same time I received yours. They are all well in Arkansas. Sister Mary says that Mrs [Fanny] Rumph has another pet [child]. She says it is a girl not yet named. — Sister Mary says she tells Mr. Boddie that she must come this spring anyhow. Cornelia, I had almost forgot to [tell] you that we have another Teacher. He is from Marion. His name is Yarrington. He will commence his school next Monday. He would have commenced before now, but they had the school house to cover*. John will go to school to him. He is here at present, but I expect that he will board at Mrs. Houston's or Mrs. Kennedy's. — When you write home, give my love to your Mother, Clarissa, and all Autauga friends. Sister H_____ said give her love to Miss House. I have written all that I can think of at present. All's well, but Father, he has a very bad cold. — I still consider myself your friend and school mate.

       S. A. Gildersleeve
       (Write soon)

* "To cover" means to put on a new roof.

Clara [Clarissa] Dickson in Autauga Co. to her sister Cornelia at Boarding School in Selma, Ala.

June 11th, 1853

Dear Sister,

  I received your letter a few minutes ago and as I am very anxious to let you know that I am very willing to go to your examination provided Pa will come up home for me either the 20 or 21, as brother Add says that business will deter him from going to Burnsville with me. All are well. We are suffering greatly for rain haven't had a good soaking rain since the day you and Pa left. We've had one or two rains since then, — but not good ones.

Nealy, I should not like to stay a whole week at Mrs. Caters before the examination it would seem like imposing on her; would it not & besides I could have a plenty of time to make my dress if I went down on Wednesday the 22nd — that is if Pa could make it more convenient to do so. I have since heard that he intended coming up the last of next week, but would prefer his coming the 21 & go back with me the 22. Old Mr. McClain is dead, he died last Monday night. Mrs. Whetstone (Mrs. Underwood used to be) has a fine <u>son</u>. You must be sure and let Pa see this immediately on receiving it. Ma sends her love to you and Pa accept of mine also. Write soon.

      Your affectionate sister
      Clara Dickson*

*This is the first time Clarissa has used Clara as her name.

  The Wanderer's Return
  by Cornelia S. Dickson-1853

  The sails are all swelling,
  The streamers float gay,
  The anchor is rising
  And I must away.

  Adieu! ye dear mountains
  Adieu my dear home
  Adieu ye dear mountains
  Adieu my dear home

  I turn from your threshold
  Mid strangers to roam
  I turn from your threshold
  Mid strangers to roam.
  Ju vallera, ju vallera, ju vallera ju valleralle
  valera Ju vallera ju vallera juvalle valle vallera!

  The sun through the heavens
  E'er hastes to the west
  The waves of the ocean
  Are never at rest

  The bird with its pinions
  Unfettered and free
  The bird with its pinion
  Unfettered and free
  Careers in its freedom

O'er mountain and sea.
Careers in its freedom
O'er mountain and sea and sea...

Repeat Ju vallera, ju vallera ju vallevallera
Ju vallera ju vallera ju valle valle vallera.

Adieu dearest mother!
Dear sister, Adieu!
I go where the skies are
All shining and blue.
Where flowers ever blossom
Where birds ever sing
Where fruits load the branches
From harvest til spring
Where fruits load the branches
From harvest til spring .... to spring
Juvallera ju vallera ju vallevalle vallera
Juvallera ju vallera ju vallera vallera vallera

Frances Pickett Boddie Rumph [Sis Fanny] in Ouachita Co., Ark., to her grandmother Mary Dickson Lanier in Autauga Co., Ala.

March 25, 1854

Dear Grandmother,

Mary Dickson Lanier
(1776-1861)
Courtesy of Sue Martin Russell

*Coralie refers to the eldest daughter of John B. and Frances Rumph. She was born in 1850 and was called Mittie.

Well Grandma I expect you begin [to] think Fan dont intend to write me as she promised. I do feel awful lazy and averse to writing, but knowing how very anxious you all feel about us and to relieve your mind, I will summon resolution enough to let [you] know we arrived safe home — were two weeks on our journey. We did not stop at Mr Gildersleeves owing to Coralie* being very sick and twas raining very hard at the time the boat landed.

George [Boddie] and family landed

but could not get to Mr Gildersleeve's* owing to high water. We waited for them in Mobile. All went to Orleans together, could not get a boat for Camden for 3 or 4 days, there had been no boats there since we left owing to low water — but when we arrived home the whole country was overflowed, were fortunate enough to find 2 skiffs at our landing — which we freighted* and landed near George's place — found all well at G's — divided our plants and took leave next morning for home, found all well at home — The neighborhood has been very healthy since we left — no sickness except Eliza Wood I am informed was very sick during our abscence and looks quite thin. Jerry says must tell Ole Miss he much obliged for the shirt sent him means to keep it to member Ole Miss.

*Mr Gildersleeve was the father of George Boddie's wife Mary Elizabeth, called Sis Mollie.
*One definition for freighted is to load with goods.

We came up from Orleans with an old French lady named McGuire, invited Mollie and I to call and see her Garden and Birds — The boat stayed some time so we went to her house. I assure you she had a greater collection [of] plants and curiousities than I ever saw before, she has one hundred varieties of the rose, the most beautiful kinds and everything else you could think of - — she gave us some plants such as she thought would grow now and promised us a great many next winter — gave us the Purple Magnolia and snowball; Mexican lillies —

Well I believe I have written all that would interest you. The Old Sacque I suppose is laid aside for a future occasion. Tell all howdy. The children cant talk about anything but their Grandma's and the sugar they gave them — Mit begs very often to go to Grandma Dixon's. I will write again before long. You dont know [how] nice my beds look with the new counterpanes.

Your affectionate grandaughter
Fanny Rumph

Carolina Boddie Love [Sis Carrie] in Autauga Co. to her half-sister, Cornelia Dickson in Selma

April 30th 1854

Dear Sister,

I guess it will be quite unexpected to recieve a letter from me, as you never asked me to write to you, but I think enough of you to write, & want to hear from you C[ornelia] without waiting for an invitation, so I will write to you, & you must be certain to answer my letter.

We are all well and all in & about Cabinville* enjoy fine health. I spent the day with Mother last week, helped her to quilt; she and myself quilted 1 1/2 side each, pr. day, she finished it that week and was wishing for Clara to help her with her sewing very much, says she has not sewed any in so long a time, it tires her very much, I see Mother coming now so I will have

*Cabinville could be and probably is a reference to the slave quarters.

to stop writing to say howdy. Well, I seat myself to finish writing. Ma says she has not heard from you since the 1st of April, she does not know why it is that letters are so long on the way. We have had two white frosts this month, on the first of the month & one last week, our gardens look badly in the vegatable line, though we have plenty of flowers & some nice strawberries to compensate something for nothing to eat, nearly all the corn has been killed, many has had to plant over three times to get a stand. Grandma's health is something better than it was, her new roses are opening quite pretty. She has one large straw coloured rose like the Damask. I think it is the yellow tea, your Damask rose is not blooming, you injured it by dividing your garden, otherwise looks well, now dont begin to get homesick, (you know you can come home, when you cant go anywhere else) & if you do not go to school when you are young you will not like to go after a while. So you must not be homesick but apply yourself to your studdies and improve your time and learn all you can, you know you can't be too smart. I have learned to play on the organ(?), I can play anything that I can sing, and I want you to learn to sing all the new songs you can, & I will learn you to play, it is very easy(?) & very sweet music, it is particularly adapted to Sacred music, & sentimental songs, though you can play anything you fancy; I received a letter from Sister Fanny last week, they were all well, Coralie was sick going down the river*, they all went to orleans together, had to wait 3 or 4 days for a Camden boat, were two weeks on the way from here [to] home, the river* rose in the meantime, they went up to John Rumph's landing, found two skiffs, freighted them, and rowed down to George's, a distance of 6 or 7 miles through the woods, they landed very near G[eorge's] house, divided their plants and rowed for home, found all well (fine times that, was it not,) well I have written you all about the home folks. I will give you the news of the neighborhood. Dr Lasiter's improving, running all about, old Mrs Ben Davis was thrown of[f] of a buggy at Mulberry Post office and very badly bruised though none of her limbs were broken, she has since been moved to Mr Chappells. Tom _____(?) left her in a buggy at the door & stopped in the store, the horse took fright and threw her out going down that large hill. Mr T. Taylor has been very like to die with something like scarlet fever, he is better, his daughter Matilda is very low with the same disease; I shall stop my children next week from school. I believe all the children will stop for fear of takeing it. Give my love to C[lara], tell her Mrs L[asiter] says she has not treated her right, she thought she would have written her, any how she must not be in a hurry to marry, there is plenty time to get [married].

C L Love

My respects to your papa. You must write to me, if you dont I never will write to you again, Cousin Ike has gone to Florida with W. Pickett only to stay a short time. Tell C. cant she write to me. I would be glad to hear

*The "river" is the Alabama River.

*This river is the Ouachita.

*Note: This postscript was written along the left margin of page one:

*Ike could be short for Isaac. If so, this would be Isaac Lanier, grandson of Mary Dickson Lanier, Clarissa Lanier Boddie Dickson's mother.

from her. I am glad she is pleased. Mrs L. says she must take care of the boys & not fall in love yet, a lady is staying with her teaching school at the old Lamar S[chool] H[ouse], her name is Broadwell from New York.

Cornelia S. Dickson at Boarding School in Selma to her mother Mrs. Clarissa Dickson Augauga Co., Ala.

March the (?), 1854

Dear Mother,

I now take my seat to write you a few lines. We are all well. I mean Clarissa, Pa and myself. Mr. Weaver is very sick in bed and Mary has a very bad coal, something like the hooping - cough. I have not heard from home since we left. I hope you are well. Clarissa wrote to you last Sunday. She has been sewing at Mrs. Hendree's all last week, but as Mrs. Col. Weaver has come home, she thinks of going over there in the morning. I like the school very well but not as well as I did last year. I think that Mrs. Jonson is a very fine teacher. She says that she would like to see Sister Fannie and Sister Caroline very much. I have to go to school all the week including half the Saturday and write a composition every week. I had not been going to school two days, when Sarah Lamar invited me to a candy - pulling *. I went and enjoyed myself very much. Ma, please write soon, and write all about home. I remain

Your affectionate daughter,
Cornelia S. Dickson

*One of the most popular entertainments of this period was candy-pulling. Taffy, a sticky boiled syrup, was held and pulled by hand until it became cool and brittle. It was then broken into small pieces and sucked or chewed, much like pepperment candy is today.

Clarissa Dickson in Autauga Co. to her daughter Cornelia S. Dickson at Selma.

April 3, 1854

My dear daughter,

I received your letter last Monday, two weeks after you left home and one at the same time from Clarissa. I sent to the office last Saturday expecting another, but did not get any. I wrote to C[larissa] before I received her and your letters. I am pleased to hear you like your school and wish to hear from you oftener. It is 3 weeks today since you left and I have only heard once from you. Clarissa might write every week as she is not going to school. I wish you to write and let me know when Clarissa is coming home. Your Pa promised to bring her when she wanted to come. Let me know how Mr. Weaver is. You wrote that he was sick in bed, also the little girl. We are all well, have had a severe Frost to kill the potatoes and some corn is injured, also gardens damaged. Little Delassette is getting better of his broken arm.

I have not heard from George and Fanny since they left Peachtree. I am very anxious to hear if they got home safe. I have nothing to write only I wish to see you both.

Your affectionate Mother,
C[larissa]. Dickson*

*Mrs. S. H. N. Dickson

Clara [Clarissa] Dickson in Autauga Co, to Cornelia S. Dickson at Boarding School in Selma.

May 18th, 1854

Dear Nealy,

We received your letter of the 15th yesterday. We were glad to hear that you arrived safely in Selma. We have had a great deal of rain since your departure, more than enough to suffice the wants of the farmers — but it has <u>faired off</u> beautifully and turned a little cool, just enough to make it pleasant. We have had several messes of strawberries since you left, and I can get a mess today I think, and a mess of <u>rasberries,</u> too. Won't that be nice? Mr. Taylor is still mending. I have been to see Mrs. Lasiter, she was so glad to see me. Nealy, everyone is mistaking my teeth for new ones and will hardly believe me when I tell them how grateful I feel to Dr. J_____ for improving my personal appearance so much. I love to laugh now, a great deal better than formerly, particularly in company, and I try to <u>grin</u> as much as possible, why — just to show my <u>teefes</u> that's all. Tell Pa to please get me another box of that powder. I am out, & Dr. J. said I must keep useing it for a while, & please send it the first opportunity. I have not got over my nervousness yet. How were all the beauquettes [bouquets] recd? You only wrote about Mrs. Col. W[eaver]. Neal, please direct your next letter to me, as Ma says I must do the writing, & tell me all about _____. you <u>understand.</u> If you have an opportunity, send my mantilla(?)* home please. I have not recd my trunk yet. I do wish you had some nice strawberries. We got a letter from Ark yesterday. All were well. I don't know of anything more of importance to write — Oh! I saw Uncle Dick a day or so ago, he said he heard I was married and where was the <u>fellow — what had I</u> done with him. I told him I did not know, he said, oh, you are just trying to deceive me, but I'll keep my eye on your movements, Missie. Write soon, and tell me all the news, my love to Mrs. W[eaver] & to Mrs. Lyles accept a portion for yourself and believe me as ever

* There are two definitions for *mantilla*, either of which could serve here: (1) a head covering; (2) a short cape or cloak.

Your affectionate sister <u>'Clara' somebody</u>

Ma sends her love to you and Pa. All are well.

Mary Elizabeth [Sis Molly] Boddie in Ouachita Co., to her sister-in-law Carolina Boddie Love in Autauga Co.

May 20th 1854

Dear Sister Carrie,

    I seat myself to answer your letter immediately, and no excuse whatever for not having written to you from New Orleans, (as I promised) except what all lazy folks have, defer from doing their duty from day to day until too late. Home folks were by no means forgotten Carrie, they were too often the subject of our talk and thoughts. We are very glad to hear that Grandma's health has continued to improve, and dear sis if you want to regain your health and strength, just come to Arkansas, the greatest place in creation to incite one to an appetite incredible. We have wished so often since we came home, Carrie, that you were all nearer to us, and we think perhaps we may have that pleasure one of these days. I at least hope so.

    Tell Grandma that George & I have wished very often that she could walk in our garden to see the strawberry beds, for whenever we have anything to grow to such perfection we always want her to see it. I dont think Carrie finer berries, and such quantities of them were ever raised. Counted fifty ripe berries from one stool independent of the green ones on it at the time, and that was not a selected one. Had a fine mess for dinner to-day, but they are nearly done for the season. The Raspberries are ripening now in abundance. We had a party of ten, Ladies and Gentlemen from Camden to come over to dine with us and eat strawberries some three weeks since. In the evening we got Fannie seated at the piano to play for them, and such a merry dance as they had. "Old Folks at Home" is quite a favorite. Carrie and I think "Young Folks at Home" quite as pretty. Wish I could hear someone who can sing better than I play it for me. I practice a little oftener now than I used to.

    I am very sorry Carrie to hear of your unfortunate loss, Fanny has had the misfortune to lose Josephine since we came home — her clothes accidently caught fire in the field, and she ran half a mile before any of the negroes could catch her & until her clothes were burned entirely off — she died the fourth day after being so badly burned.

    I do hope in regard to your crops Carrie that so bad a beginning may end well, we too had very cool and frosty weather, but vegetation is so much later here, than with you, that it done no injury — Of fruit we will have a fine crop. Have had recently great deal of rain, & in consequence another overflow, tell Addison, but thats no <u>great objection</u> to this country, not half as much, as many to be against <u>Texas</u>.

    George's corn is growing off finely, & he is having his cotton chopped out, John R[umph] is going ahead too with his crop, you know Carrie he's trying to beat G. this year, but I tell him that's hard to do. John spent to- day with us says all are well at home. I sent your letter to Fanny for her to read, & if I had the seed you alluded to in your letter that Grandma wanted, would send them in my letter, but I cant imagine what kind it is she wanted, as we have no pink seed, but those Grandma & you sent to us from there — the pinks are blooming beautifully this Spring, some of the Italian pinks are double. Have roses in bloom now that we brought home, & the Lilies too. I am so proud that all the plants are living & doing so finely — George thinks that nearly, or all, of his hyacinths are living, & tell Grandma we are so proud of all our plants that there is no room for us to regret anything connected with our visit, save her being so ill in bed at the time. Dr. John was regretting to-day the loss of his Cherokee Roses, & George told me to ask you Carrie to send us the seed of some — there are none in this country; I would like to make a hedge of them between my front & back yard — Carrie I must tell you we have one great Shanghi chick — hatched from one of the eggs brought all the way from Ala — I set the eggs here, for Fanny, the same evening we got home — Have but few turkeys, the eggs did not hatch well this spring.

I am glad to hear that the girls are so well pleased at Selma, we saw Col Dickson when there, & he told us he intended taking them there, dont forget our love to them when you write to Clarissa. I have heard from home twice since we left. Harriet & Mr Murley have been there & spent a week with Mother. Tell Mr Davis, I think 'twas him to blame & not I, for not getting to see him, & hope he will do better the next time we go to Ala to see our friends.

Tell Uncle Clem to come on while he is in the notion, to see us at any rate, if he does not wish to live here, though there is plenty land yet to be had I expect.

Flewellen has been to see us, he is a very intelligent old gentleman, & his sons-in-law with their families are here too — Flewellen has two daughaters unmarried and three sons [who are] younger children — The old gentleman told me that his wife was almost raised with George's father and of course knew him intimately, she was a Miss Williams I believe.

Well sis Carrie 'tis so near dark I must close my letter — but not without a word to the children, bless their hearts — kiss them all for Molly & Willie sends a sweet kiss to Aunt Carrie, Mother D[ickson] and Grandma, little George Gilder too, he's so sweet, but you know, you've got a baby too. To Mary & William dont forget my love & best respects — all are well, & with love to you all I remain yours

affectionately,
Mary E. Boddie

*Note: This postscript was written on the back of the last page:

*Phillis says she's "mighty glad Miss Clarisa & Mas Clem has Jerry's children," and she would like to go back again on a visit; would like to hear how her manny is getting along now —

19 *Spreading Wings and Learning to Fly*

Clara Dickson in Autauga Co. to her sister Cornelia Dickson in Selma, Alabama

June 9th, 1854

Dear Nealy,

    I receaved a letter from you a few days ago,— but having previously written since I recd a letter from you — that I concluded to wait a while — - I expect though ere this that you have recd and answered my last — We have a very fine garden just now — but plenty <u>of grass,</u> I can tell you though

    I suppose if one grows, the other (?) grows too — Pa came up Tuesday morning and said that you were well. I intend sending you some nice apples by him, and plums too if they are not all gone and if he will carry them. Your cuttings are nearly all living. I water them daily — Those cuttings you got from grandma's last winter are blooming — at least some them are — I have some jasmine's planted and some are living. I should think you could [not] be so very lonely with two such excellent performers of music as <u>mosquitoes</u> and gnats to sing you to sleep every night — I know I should not — but which do you prefer, Nealy — or to be more explicit which of the two musicians performs best — I do wish I could go to S[elma] again — oh you can't imagine how very lonesome I am — & I do want to see <u>him</u> so very much —

    I don't think I can leave conveniently to go to the examination — I wish I could if only to see _____. Do you see Mrs. Col. Weaver nowdays. Give my love to Mrs. W_____ and Mary — I intend writing M____ a note — which you will please deliver to her. Tell Aunt H[attie] & Mary howdy for me. You ought to visit Mrs. Col. W_____ some, Neal, if only for my sake — Sis C[arrie] family are well, another letter from Sis Molly — sent her love to you and me. Pa says he has eat plums for you & him, too —

    Do you see Dr. F. nowadays (bless his soul). Ma sends her love to you. Accept the same from your

                  affectionate sister
                  Clara

Write soon

P. S. Tell Aunt H_____ I have not forgot her kindness to me while I stayed there, and think of her often — more so then she does of me I expect & write soon and get you a grass skirt before the examination and me one too please. I want one very much indeed. C.

Clara (Clarissa) Dickson in Autauga Co. to her sister Cornelia Dickson at Boarding School in Selma, Ala.

June 17th, 1854

Dear Neal,

Again I seat myself to give you a scrape or two of my pen — I can not promise you it will be long as Pa is now waiting to convey it to the office — We have not recd but one letter from you since Pa came up — and that was one written a few days after he left you. I expect though, ere now, you have recd my last — and maybe an answer is now at the office — however, I'll soon find that out — We have daily an abundance of rain, and tis raining just now — I for one would be glad to see dry weather again — Neal, you would be surprised to see how much I have fattened since I came home. I think I have gained 5 or 10 pounds at least. Mr. _____ would hardly recognize me now if I came to S_____. Do you think he would, Neal — Oh, N, I will be so glad when you come home. I am most dead with de <u>blues</u>. Your La Mark rose is full of buds. I will try and send you a bouquet by daddy, if I don't forget it. Neal, do you ever see him [these] days — if so, I envy you your good privilege. Has Mrs. Col. Weaver left Selma yet — or does she intend spending the summer there? You have a college rose & blush cluster open now (some of your cuttings from grandmas) they are very pretty — Are your <u>nightly concerts</u> continued yet — are they just as interesting as ever? The next time you see Aunt H[attie] tell her howdy for me & ask her if she has forgotten me — no not that, if she ever speaks of me— now N___, you must try <u>your best</u> to excell in the examination. I know you can if you try — and then get a premium as being the smartest girl in the school — I wish I could attend your examination, but am afraid I can't — My love to Mrs. W_____ & M____. Ma & Pa sends their love to you accept of(?) mine also please mam & believe me ever

                        your "dood" little sis
                        Clara

Neal, please get me a cake of nice soap before you leave S_____ cold cream soap if you can find any, if not, <u>brown</u> Winsor.

*Ma says ask Mrs. Col. W_____ permission to get some pretty double pinks read[y] for grandma if you please thank you as Laura used to say. Oh Neal your kitten Peggy has three little teeny kittens, I don't know when my cat will have any, if ever. Please don't forget my mantilla & underskirt Please mam if I thank you. C_____

*Do you ever see Dunk these days — please don't forget the soap dear Neal

*Note: This postscript was written at the top of page one:

*Note: This postscript was written long the side margin of the letter:

Clara Dickson in Selma to her mother Clarissa Dickson Autauga Co.
                                             Jan. 24th, 1855
Dear Ma,

I now seat myself to let you know how I am coming on, & also to deliver a message to you from Mrs. W[eaver]. I am well and enjoying myself finely. I can tell you — Mrs. _____ wishes you, if you possibly can, to send those dried apples of yours to Burnsville to the care of Warren Andrews. He will send them to her, and get pa to put her name on a card to and tack them to the bags, I told her your price was $.50 cts she does not mind the price. She says if you will be kind enough to send them, please send at the same time <u>camomile</u> and <u>thyme</u> from your's or grandma's garden. Mrs W. had a fine <u>"old folks"</u> supper the other night, & the finest doins, don't talk. Tom Dungan was discharged Monday. Col. W sent for him to assist him in hanging up meat — his <u>dung-ship</u>* refused. Col. W told him to <u>trot</u> — he did in a hurry, too. Mr. Davis came though. I think him another Mr. Terry. Tell Neal to write soon. Please try to send those apples Ma — she wants them so much. Nothing more.

*Dungship is a deraogatory term and a play on the name Dungan.

                     Your affectionate daughter,
                         Clara
It is so cold I can hardly write.

Clara Dickson in Selma to Cornelia S. Dickson in Autuaga Co.
                                             Mar 1855
Dear Sister,

I received your letter by Pa - which found me well. I was glad to hear that all were well. You wish to know the latest fashion. They wear basque's* altogether I believe. The sleaves are gathered three or four rows at the top as for bishop sleaves* (but not sewed down to anything) & left open at the bottom; but not rounded off any — have them a little longer than the common flowing sleave — & trim with braid at the bottom, have them very wide; skirt very long & full & flounced to death. I wrote you last Sunday. Every one admires my collar Ma worked me. If I had my way, Nealy, I would not come home in two months, you know when I get there, I can never go anywhere's; but Mrs. W[eaver] thinks of going to Mobile next week, and I think I shall go home unless some one else wants my assistance here, she says she will need me when she comes back, but if I can find no one that needs me while she is gone, I can not stay — I know I shall be glad enough to get home after all, for to tell the truth I am tired out — not with Selma — but sewing so steadily debilitates me so much that I am compelled to quit for a while. Tell Mammy that I am hungry for some home doins, that's cer-

*A basque is a close fitting bodice or waist of a dress that sometimes extends to cover the hips.
* Bishop sleeves are gathered full at the shoulder and taper to the wrist.

*An ashcake is a dough cake roasted in the ashes of a wood fire.

tain — for some of her good battercakes and buttermilk and ashcake *, too. (Not any beer though). I dream about you all so often. My love to Ma, accept a portion for your self and believe me as ever, your

affectionate sister,
Clara

Write soon.

Cornelia S. Dickson in Autauga Co. to her father Col. S. H. N. Dickson in Selma

March 26th 1855

Dear Father,

Clarissa arrived yesterday with Uncle Clem.* We were very agreeably surprised at her coming, for we all wanted to see her. I was very glad to hear that you were well. We are all well and hope this will find you enjoying the same blessing. C[larissa] says please send her pocket handker chief which I sent to her by you, and please buy her and me one (apiece) as she lost the only one she had coming up. I am very thankful indeed for the shoes and candy you sent me. I have the shoes on now. Ma says please get some Irish potatoes, when they get lower, also some coffee. Cousin W[illiam] Love says to let him know positively if you are going to take the school or not.* Give my love to Mrs. Weaver and Mary. My respects to Mr. Weaver and Mr. Brooks and Mrs. Jonson when you see them also to Mr. Lyles accept a share of my love for yourself,

I remain
Your affectionate daughter,
Cornelia S. Dickson

*Uncle Clem refers to Clem Lanier, brother of Clarissa Lanier Dickson, the girls' mother.

*Col. Dickson was a Commission Merchant, which means he bought and sold goods, mostly cotton, for a commission. This reference to a school evidently means that he was offered a position as a schoolmaster, but he refused it.

Cornelia S. Dickson in Autauga Co. to her father Col. S. H. N. Dickson in Selma.

April 11, 1855

Dear Father,

I wrote to you last week, but have not received any answer to it. I expect to get a letter tonight. I understand that cousin W. Love was going to Autaugaville and will get him to drop this in the office. I can't promise a very interesting letter as the times are very dull. The Ivy Creek Church is to be dedicated next Sunday. I expect to go. We had a very fine rain last Thursday which did every thing a great deal of good, we have set out a good many collard plants and our garden looks a great deal better, our English pees are in bloom, we bid fair to have a great many strawberries to judge from the blossoms. We have not received the Potatoes yet. Please, Pa, send the handkerchiefs that I mentioned in my former letter. I have no more of importance to say at the present. C[larissa] wishes to know if Mrs. Col. Weaver has returned to Selma. Give my love to Mrs. Weaver and Mary, my respects to Mr. Weaver, accept a share of my love for yourself. This leaves us all well. I remain

Your affectionate daughter,
Cornelia S. Dickson

Col. S. H. N. Dickson in Selma to his daughter Clarissa [Clara] Dickson in Autauga Co.
July 14, 1855

My dear Daughter,

I received your letter of the 8th instant and was glad to hear that all were well. I also received Cornelia's letter of the 1st instant and wrote her by Mr. Smith. My health is as good as usual. We have had very hot weather and heavy rains. Selma is quite healthy. I expected to have been up this week, but shall postpone it for at least two weeks if my health should continue good, Mr. Alexander being absent to Virginia. Mr. Weaver is yet in town. Tell Cornelia to sell the parasol for 75c, the price it cost as it will be better to do so than to return it. Tell Cornelia to write me when you receive this without fail. Give my love to all and accept a share for yourself.

Your affectionate Father,
S.H.N. Dickson

Ivy Creek Church Marker
Photo Courtesy of Cora Russell Rogers

Clarissa [Clara] Dickson in Selma to her sister Cornelia Dickson in Autauga Co.

Dec. 14, 1855

Dear Sister,

I arrived here safe yesterday evening. Mr. McCrarry met me at the depot. I found all well & most happy to see me. Dr. Fair died last night with consumption of the bowels, or bloody diarrhea. Miss Bell Porter is to be married next week to Dr. J. Philips, a brother of Col. Philips. Neal, I forgot to bring my linen underbody down, please send it by Brother Add* next week, I can't wear my gingham dress without my underbody,* also my narrow black velvet ribbon. I will write more fully next week. I am hurried just now it being night.

Your affectionate sister,
Clara

*Brother Add is Addison C. Love, husband of Carrie Boddie Love, and brother-in-law of Clara and Cornelia

*An underbody is what we call today a slip or a petticoat

Clara Dickson in Selma to her sister Cornelia Dickson in Autauga Co.

Jan. 6th, 1856

Dear Nealy,

What is the matter that you do not write? I have not received a single line from home since I came down; and the only way I can account for your not writing is that the creeks are not passable and, of course, no mail.

I have written once since I came down, and if you don't answer this, I promise you I shall not write a single line again while I remain down here. We had a most delightful time during the Christmas and New Years day's, such nice eating and so much fun. We had five weddings here the week before Christmas, all the men were widowers but one, first Miss Porter and Dr. Phillips, & old Billy Johnson and Miss Kent, & Henry Ware & Miss Sophia McNeal, & Mr. Mitchel & a dutch gal, I don't know her name; neither do I know the 5th one. Old Billy Johnson had his house newly furnished from top to bottom. I have not time to write any more news, only we have a great many new comers moving in. Be sure & write soon, my love to all my sunday school class, also all at home — I am as well contented as can be though hardly have five minutes that I can call my own.

Your affectionate sister
Clara D.

P.S. Has Betty come home?

Excuse bad writing. I haven't time to write any more. how is Mammy— if you get the chance, please send my underbody to me. good bye — C.

*Note: This postscript was written along the left margin of the paper:

*Mammy was a slave who was loved by both girls.

George Boddie in Ouachita Co. to his mother Clarissa Lanier Boddie Dickson in Autauga Co.

Feb 17th '56

Dear Mother,

    I received your welcome letter by Mr Dee Newton in due time & was glad to hear that you were all well — It had been a long time since we herd from any of you — Mary has been looking for a letter from Carolina [Sis Carrie] for some time — the last we received was dated in Nov — I expect you have heard ere this that we have a daughter — She was born on the 4th day of Dec — I have named her after her Mother* & she is perhaps the most unmanageable little thing that ever was — all from being a <u>gal</u> — The boys are hearty & grow fast —

    I dont know of any news to write that would prove interesting to you — save that we are well — making a little money — & have plenty to eat & wear — You stated that Grand Mother was indisposed from colds — I am in hopes she has recovered ere this & is in better spirits — Tell her Mittie & Will were very proud of the spoons & that we will try & make them remember who gave them — & that if Providence should so order it that we should not have the pleasure of seeing her again in this life that we will endeavour to raise our children in such a manner that she would not be ashamed of them if she were living.

    I received a message some time ago from uncle Geo Boddie requesting me to give him the Genealogy or as <u>Clem would have it</u> the Pedigree of my Mother's family — what he wants with it I cant surmise. Perhaps he thinks we havent any & is in doubt whether to claim kin with me or not — Tell Grand Mother to send me one as long as she possibly can — all the way back to old Oliver Cromwell & a little the other side if she sees proper — As I wish to astonish him — & make him think I am somebody anyhow.

    I have just seen an old acquaintance of Clems by the name of Summer — he roomed with him at some Hotel in Selma not long since — He wanted to know if Clem ever <u>drank</u> anything stronger than water & what made him keep his eyes so nearly shut —

    John, Fanny & family are well & join Mary & myself in love to you & our near relatives — I believe I can think of nothing more to write you at this time & remain

                   Yours affectionately
                   Geo Boddie

*The daughter was Mary Elizabeth Boddie, called Mamie.

Clara Dickson in Selma to her sister Cornelia in Autauga Co.

Feb. 2, 1856

Dear Sister,

    I recd your letter a few moments ago and was very glad to hear from you. I have not heard from home before in some time. I wrote you last Sunday week, & wonder why you did not receive it. My health is some better than it was, I am taking bitters* from Mr. David Weaver, which he says I greatly needed, I also got me a pair of very thick soled shoes which keep my feet warm, and tis that I expect which has helped me. I sent Uncle Clem word to call tonight and see me, & will send this letter by him. I may conclude to go up next week, but don't know how that will be until I hear from Mrs. Lapsley, which will be tonight. I will send you word by Uncle C___, if my "business" (look what a big word, will you) was arranged, I would go up with him, but not getting your letter in time, it renders it impossible for me to do so, my best love to Ella Howard, how and where is Bettie. Tell her please write me, nothing but want of time has prevented my writing to her. I have answered every letter that I recd from home since I left. I have not time C____ to write news, that is of any account. hoping this may find all well I close, my best love to Ma, accept a portion for yourself and believe me as ever

                Your affectionate sister,
                Clara D

    P. S. When is Pa coming down — please tell Ma to send to Burnsville for me Wednesday morning, & if she can borrow Uncle C[lem']s buggy, it would be better to send that, as I could then bring my trunk with me from Burnsville when I come, or if not his, get Mrs. Lasiter's, you know how inconvenient twould be to Ma to send again for my trunk. I've learned that Mrs. Lapsley won't need me since I commenced writing, is my reason for changing my mind in regard to staying longer.

                Yours truly,
                C. D.

    P. S. Mrs. W. will need me again in April & May but not before. Be sure & send Wednesday.

*Bitters was a name given to quinine.

Clara Dickson in Selma to her sister Cornelia in Autauga Co.

May 18th, 1856

Dear Sister,

    I receaved your letter last Thursday and was very glad indeed to hear that all are well, & that you were enjoying yourself, in some measure at least, at the fishing party. I expect you will have quite <u>monopolized</u> Mr. Wm. by the time I get home. Never mind, Miss, I have a dewlarkie* down here, my Dear madam, which I would not give for fifty Mr. W .... so skin your eyes as much as you please. I have been to another Fair since I wrote, that of the Cumberland Presbyterian Ladies. I enjoyed myself much better than I did to the one previously, had Mr. Edwards to promonade me up & down the Hall & treat me to strawberries & ice cream — iced lemonade & pound-cake a-hem, his wife as you must know is a very proud lady, every time we passed her, she would turn up her nose, just a little bit though; not much; I took the compliment to myself, though it might have been directed at him never the less — it did not in the least interupt our enjoyment. But oh! Dear I forgot to tell you who conducted me to the grand affair, no other than Mr. old Bob Winter — now tell Mrs. Lasiter that if you dare, Miss. When we got in the Hall, I still had Uncle Bobby's arm, but good gracious, the way the people did stretch their necks & eyes, you don't know! I felt just like I was tied to an old rhinocerous, & soon slid from his arm to the nearest seat & then Lawyer Edwards came in, (Now tell Mrs. Lasiter that about Bob my dear; won't she be mad) — I had a call from Mrs. Wiggins and Miss Hall, (alias Jinny & Amy- Jane) yesterday-week, both Ladies behaved exceedingly well, both modest & full of blushes. Twas only a fashionable call, though, of about half an hour, when they arose to leave, declared they had staied an "hour" & twas time to go, I was up at little Phil W[eaver]'s this evening and delivered your message. Mrs. W sends her love in return, so does Mary. Mr. Weaver was sick with a bad cold, — saw Mrs. Lyle this morning, inquired about you & when you would come down, & if you did, must be sure & call, sends her love. I don't know any more news, write soon, my love to all,

Your affectionate sister,
Clara

*A dewlarkie is most likely a slang word of the period for a beau.

Clarissa Lanier as a girl.
(1801-1864)
married-Thomas Hill Boddie (1821)
-Col. S.H.N. Dickson (1832)

Clarissa Lanier Boddie Dickson wife of Col. S.H.N. Dickson—mother of Clara Dunlap and C.S. Dickson who saved the letters.
Photos courtesy of Sue Martin Russell.

Sisters, Seeds, and Cedars **28**

Colonel Samuel Henry Neeley Dickson (1798-1860) Escorted Gen. Lafayette across the state of Alabama in 1825. Photo courtesy of Sue Martin Russell.

P.S. I was never more surprised in my life than to hear of Miss Broadwell's marriage, I realy think there must be some little chance for poor me now, — feel more hopefull than I have for some time past — expect I'll have to go to Ohio too, as that seems to be a lucky state for poor old ugly wretches in general. I told you half a story about Bob & I, Col W., Miss Bettie Bohanon & a Miss Ward (relation of the former) went in the carriage with us, could not have any secret talk just then. — may make it up yet though — never do to despair while there is life — the old toad looks like he tries to mean something or other — don't or can't imagine what it can be — may be, wants to get in with a certain old lady up our way — & make me his agent in the all important business, which do you think the most probable — it will have to be her at last, as I must go to Ohio,

Yours
C.D.

[1]Note: This postscript was written across the top of page 1:

[1]They wear capes with these low necked drapes. I will bring the pattern when I come home.

[2]Note: This postscript was written along the margin of page 1:

[2]Oh, for some butter milk & ashcake or lye-hominy

[3]Note: This postscript was written along the margin of page 2:

[3]Don't let anybody see this please.

THOS. ANDERSON,   S.H.N. DICKSON,   GEORGE P. KELLY

ANDERSON, DICKSON & KELLY,

COMMISSION MERCHANTS,

No. 69 Commerce Street,

MOBILE.

FACTORAGE & COMMISSION BUSINESS.

Thomas Anderson and George P. Kelly.

Having withdrawn from the firm of Anderson, Dickson & Kelly.

The undersigned, (remaining partner,) will continue the above business on his own account.

S. H. N. DICKSON.

MOBILE, May 1849.

Colonel Samuel Henry Neeley Dickson's Business Cards

Clara Dickson in Selma to Cornelia in Autauga Co.

Dec. 11th, 1856

Dear Sister,

    I would have written sooner but have been so very busy since I came down that I haven't time, am up to head & ears in <u>work</u>, work. Mrs. L. has so much work for me to do, keep me at least til' Christmas. I call[ed] on Mrs. Lockett a few minutes — found all well, you sent me the wrong head dress, I wanted the black one, please send it & a nice night cap, when Jerry* comes down. Col. W. brought me up from the depot in his buggy — had went down for Mrs. W., who had been staying at her mothers, but she did not come, & so I got a ride. This leaves all well, write soon, please get Marie to bleach my chemise* for me, tell her I will pay her well, my love to all,

                Your affectionate sister,
                Clara

*Jerry was a slave on the place in Autauga Co.

*A chemise is a loose fitting woman's undergarment, like an undershirt.

Clara Dickson in Selma to Cornelia in Autauga Co.

Jan. 1, 1857

Dear Nealy,

    I have not recd a line from you since Jerry came down, Pa's letter, I recd last week. How have you enjoyed Christmas, we had quite a merry time of it here. I took dinner at Col. W's & such a dinner! I only wish you had been there. In fact I've been living so <u>high</u> down here I don't know how I will do when I go home.

    I am well & hope this will find you all the same. Ask Ella how they are all coming on in Autaugaville & if my jew-larkie is married yet, or what is he doing, she will know who I mean, & about all the good people up there. I suppose you went to a party Christmas, how did you enjoy yourself. Be sure & inform me when brother J* comes. I will come home immediately on reception of your letter, my love to all, write soon

                Your affectionate sister,
                Clara Louise D.

    P.S. See the handle I have put to my name. As every body has a middle name, I will have one too.

                C. L. D.

*Brother J refers to John B. Rumph, husband of Francis Pickett Boddie, half-sister of Clara and Cornelia, who lived in Ouachita County, Arkansas.

Clara Dickson in Selma to Cornelia in Autauga Co.

Jan. 11th, 1857

Dear Sister,

I receaved your letter a few days since, & was glad to hear that all were well. You spoke of your party & fine eatables. I am right mad that you did not inform me of my being invited — though I could not have accepted the invitation, it being so difficult to go backwards, and forwards, from here home — As for your sylabub*, I have had that too and as for other things, I have them every day — we have nice dessert & pineapples, grated coconut, raisens, or oranges and "champaine" besides; between meals, I have nice torte, fruit cakes, iced cake, and all other nice things, — & so, no danger of my mouth watering for your Christmas doings, when I have far better every day, missee. Though I would have no doubt have enjoyed myself there, especially as some of the Autaugaville boys attended. J. Underwood can wash his goat-tee nicely I guess with 1 1/2 pounds of soap if it is good soap. As for Frank, if the assafetida* does make him sick, tell him I hope 'twont be unto death and about the seaticks*, its too cold for them to bite much this weather. Your yard & a half of moon-shine, I guess you & Cap could easily make it a mile & a half, — just give you the chance, all you & him could do would be to let loose the bridles to your tonges, — add another couple of clappers & finish matters to your own satisfaction. Ahem. I am glad as I was not present, that none of the Dutchben gents* were there as I would have been jealous. I bet they knew I was not up there & so didnot care to go. The Cone B___* hasent rolled up yet, looking out every hour for "its" appearance. I heard last week that old Louis Rumph was dead, & so brother J. will come out now, I guess —About my writing notes instead of letters, tell Ma I don't have time, & besides it's so cold. I don't go about enough to know any news. Miss Le Grand* will start next week for New Orleans. I am now at Col. W's, recd several nice presents among which is a nice gimpure* collar, a set of ornamental dress buttons, — a nice corset, & last though not least, an 8 dollar cameo breast pin. The last given me by Mrs. Col. W. Write soon, why don't brother J. come, I wonder, give my love to all, Ella Howard in particular, write soon

Your affectionate sister,
Clara Louise

I am well.

*Syllabub is a dessert dish made of whipped cream mixed with wine, cider, or the like, often sweetened and flavored. It is traditionally served in many Southern homes during Christmas.

*Assafetida is the fetid gum resin of various oriental plants of the carrot family, used in medicine as an antispasmodic.

*Seaticks most probably refers to what we call "seedticks."

*Dutch Bend is a settlement on the Alabama River.

*"Cone B___ could refer to a boat, or it might be a variation of Queen, which would indicate a bit of sarcasm in refering to a woman.

*Miss Le Grand is the name of a boat.

*A gimp is a flat trimming of silk, wool or other cord, sometimes stiffened with wire, for garments, curtains, etc. It is also a coarse thread, usually glazed, employed in lacemaking to outline designs. Either definition could be used to describe a collar.

Clara Dickson at Air Mount, Ala. to her sister Cornelia in Autauga Co.
                                              Jan 27th, 1857
   Dear Nealy,

   We arrived here safely, found all well except Sally, she was suffering very much from bad cold & sore throat, she is much better now. Mrs. G[ildersleeve] is going about, much better than when Sis Molly left her. We are all invited to a wedding next Thursday night. I enjoyed myself finely on the boat. We will probably leave here in a week or so. Nothing more
                  Yours affectionally,
                  C. L. Dickson

Clara Dickson in Mobile to Cornelia in Autauga Co.
                                              Feb.14th, 1857
   Dear Nealy,

   We arrived here safely yesterday evening, all well. Sally* is with us. Her & I both got a new bonnet, white open- work straw, trimmed with white ribbon, just alike, only mine has pink sprigs inside — hers blue ones, $8 apiece. Had my dag - type* taken, had to sit twice, — tis not a good one atall but we have not time for me to sit again, brother G[eorge] will leave it with <u>Mr. Chester</u> or Mr. Henry Brodnax one. We are staying at the Chester House, & who ever comes down will have to enquire here, if it is not here with Mr. Chester go to Mr. Brodnaxes, the boat leaves in a short time. Good bye, my love to all, write soon & let me know if any body enquires for me or wishes me back, I am enjoying myself finely
                  Your affectionate sister,
                  C.L. Dickson
   P.S. Sally and Sis Mollie send love to you all.
                  C.L.D.

*Sally Gildersleeve, sister to Sis Mollie, Mary Elizabeth Boddie

*What Clara is calling a dag-type is most certainly a daguerreotype, an obsolete photographic process

Clara Dickson at New Orleans to Cornelia in Autauga Co.
                                              Feb. 21st, 1857
   Dear Nealy,

   Well we are in the city of <u>notions</u> amid the din & confusion of carriages, omnibuses, drays and buggys. We arrived here from Mobile last Sunday morning, found that a boat had just left for Camden the evening before & that we would have to wait nearly a week for another Ouachita boat, or rather one that went up as high as Camden. The hotells & boarding houses are crowded. We tried to get rooms at Madam Oviates (the house brother

G[eorge] always stayes at while here, but twas crowded, we then went to the Citty Hotell, stayed there until Monday morning, when finding one room at Mad. Oviates vacated, brother G. [George Boddie] engaged it & we are now staying here, at the C. Hotell, you can have every thing in the way of eatibles that you call for, but here tis cooked so much better, though not quite such a variety, & tis also much cheaper here than at the C. Hotell. I tell you, Nealy, I am living as the saying is "in clover" down here, oh, such nice eating, you don't know, such nice vegetables, too cabage, lettuce, beets, radishs, potatoes, & cc,* fresh fish & oysters twice a day, & all good things imaginable, brother G. buyes us oranges apples — bananers, cc. We had a very pleasant trip across the lake, we all escaped being seasick! Tell Grandma [Mary Dickson Lanier] Sis M[ollie] says her rose cuttings are budding out & her hyscinths & tulips [are] growing finly, has them in a box, one white hyacinth is almost in bloom, looks so pretty. She sends love to all. We have been out shopping a good deal. Tell Ma I have spent all my money but a few dimes & didn't get much either, my bonnet was $8 — dagtype was $5, one pair walking shoes $1.60, one corded skirt $1.5 bits, one fine beautiful blue monoline,* 12 yds for $9.60 cts. that is all, my dag-a-type is at Henry Brodnax's, Mobile. It is not a good one, I don't think, too dark & pale for me, but I did not have time to sit again. I never told you what boats we traveled on, we went on the LeGrand at Gaston's Landing, the St. Charls at Clifton, and the Florida from Mobile to the railroad. Phillis* lost her bag of clothes, brother G. tried to find it, but failed. Little Gilder's* clothes were in the bag. Sis Molly had to get him another suit as he had none but those he wore. We arose early this morning and went to the french Market, also to the Cathedral, but was too late to hear them say mass — but the market was a curiosity itself such a variety of — oh, I don't know what, we went first in the meat market, then the fruit, & last the vegetable market, men and women were hurrying to and fro with their basketts getting their supplies for the day. Well, good bye, I don't know what else to write. My love to all, write soon & let me know all that has transpired since my absence.

       Your affectionate sister,
       C. L. Dickson

P. S. Brother G. hired a carriage Sunday to take us out to see the grave yards, we had a pleasant ride too on the shell road.
  C.L.D.

We will leave this evening, on a very fine boat, the Soverign, for Camden.

---

*cc is apparently the symbol that was commonly used for "etc".

*Monoline is obiviously some kind of fabric, but we are unable to determine exactly what kind.

*Phillis was the slave girl who traveled with them to and from Alabama.

*Little Gilder is the son of George and Mollie, and was four years old at the time.

Clara Dickson at Ouachita Co., Ark. to her sister Cornelia in Autauga Co., Ala.

March 6th, 1857

Dear Nealy,

We arrived here safely on Wednesday the 25th and found all well. The Washita* was up high, overflowing its banks. I wrote you from New Orleans. We had a very pleasant trip up to Camden, very few ladies on board, but they were all friendly and sociable. Dee N[ewton] came on board as soon as we landed. He was well & very much surprised indeed to see me there — he enquired after you all. I delivered Mrs. L[asiter]'s message; — said he was much obliged to her, but expected twould be many years before he could go back to Ala. We had some little difficulty (as the Washita had over-flowed) in getting to brother G.'s place, & I'll tell you, N., it's no story about Ark. being famous for a plenty of water, for there is a <u>plenty</u> here sure enough. It is to go two or three hundred yds & cross a long mud-hole, — then another hundred & cross a <u>little creek</u> (as they call them out here — but we would say a <u>big one</u>) then another long long strip of water & cc. It is only so when the river is up, at any other time, they say they have good roads. I have seen but little of the country as yet — but I think I shall be well pleased after all with old <u>Rac- ensack</u>.* We sent for Sis Fanny as soon as we came, she looked so young that I hardly knew her, — she is much more <u>fleshy</u> than when she was in Ala., &, of course, ready for all the good <u>nuggs</u> * brother G. brought from New O_____. She is so lonesome since brother J[ohn] left — had the blues right bad before we came, brother G. sent for her, she staied at Sis Molly's a few days & then came home, I am with her. I think she has a beautiful place, though she hasent as many near neighbours as sis M[ollie]. We are looking for brother J[ohn] every day. I was invited to a quilting yesterday but I didn't go, it was so cold and cloudy. There is a Mr. Montgomery now staying here teaching the children, brother J. employed him before he left, he took me to church last Sunday, in his buggy, <u>ahem</u>, we had tolerable good preaching, but, Neal, I couldn't help but think, while listening to the preacher, of that one we read of in the newspaper, about "<u>de harp of a thousand strings</u>," "<u>spirits of just men made perfect</u>." You remember the piece don't you. Well N. I don't know anything more to write, Sis M. wrote to sis Carry just before we arrived at Camden, sent the letter back by the boat. You must write very soon & tell me all the news & if anybody enquires after me, cc, my love to all. Hoping this finds all well I am

Your affectionate sister,
C. L. Dickson

P. S. Tom is the prettiest child Sis F[annie] has. Tell Ella Howard she must write to me. C.L.D.

P. S. My love to Amy Golson, & tell her I will write often if she will

*Ouachita was spelled Washita by many people during this period.

*"Rackensack" was a commonly used nickname for Arkansas.

*"Nuggs" is most probably a short version of "nuggets," meaning "goodies."

write me first & tell me all the news C.L.D.

[1] I would have gone to that quilting but twas to end in a dancing frolic on a puncheon* floor at that, and I did not care about that. C.L.D.

[2] It is almost too late for Jas. Golson to bust up the boats now ain't it

Clara Dickson at Camden to her sister Cornelia in Autauga Co.

April 24th 1857

Dear Nealy,

I recd your welcome letter a few days ago, I was very glad to hear from you & that all were well. I had heard of Mr. Morton's death previous to receiving your letter, it made me feel very sad to hear it. I can hardly realise the fact; he looked so well the day before we started.

I was surprised to learn that Sis C[arrie]'s baby was a girl. I had expected <u>differently</u>. You have ere this recd my last letter, the one I wrote after we arrived here. Brother J[ohn] came home about three weeks after we came, brought 8 Negroes with him, though four belonged to his sister, he would have stopped in Ala. to see you all, but was hurried so, he could not.

I was surprised at <u>some</u> of the weddings you mentioned, G. Pons among the number. Mrs. Lasiter, Bettie & Dee [Lasiter], arrived in El Dorado a few weeks ago, so I learned.<u>Dee Newton</u> went down to see them. I sent word to Bettie by him, to be sure and come to see me. (I recd your letter the day before I heard that she was in Ark). I hope she will come.

We had a severe frost a few weeks ago, which killed every <u>thing</u>, wheat included, every one seems in low spirits about it. Sis M[ollie] is more sorry about the strawberries than anything else, brother G. says it is <u>just because S[ally] & I came out here,</u> you see he has been bragging all along to us what fine nice strawberries they have every year. Sally tells him 'taint so, she don't believe one word <u>of it</u>, they just get three or four <u>little</u> berries every two or three years & that's all, brother G. declares 'taint so, but S[ally] will have it her way.

We have not seen the aligator yet, but instead have seen Old <u>Rack-en-sack</u>. We are both much pleased with Ark, brother J[ohn] & I went to church Sunday, & would you believe it I rode behind him, had a beau, too, found Sis M[ollie] and Sally there, had a very good sermon indeed; Dr. Hartwell of Camden, (but formerly of Marian, Ala) preached for us, he is a highly educated man, resembles Cousin Albert Pickett very much. Mrs. Warren Stone invited us to come & spend a day with her this week, & insisted on our naming a day, we named Tuesday, & went and enjoyed ourselves finely. I carried your letter for Sis M[ollie], S[ally] and brother G[eorge] to read, it amused them very much particulary brother G. I told him who <u>you aluded</u>

---

[1]Note: This postscript is written along the left margin of page 1:
*A puncheon is a heavy slab of timber, roughly dressed, for used as a flooring.
[2]Note: This postscript is written along the left margin of page 2:

too in speaking of a certain _____. I had to let Sis F[annie] and brother J[ohn] see it also, it tickled me not a little. I just imagined I could see you with your eyes "skinned"* (as that Indian hunter said) peeking through the crack upstairs. Brother J[ohn] laughed, too when he come to "where do you recon I was," & cc. he made me tell him who that fellow was. Tell Ma not to be uneasy I have no idea of noticing much less answering any communication from that source whatever.

*In this instance "skinned" is probably used as we sometimes use "peeled," to mean look sharp or carefully.

Brother J[ohn] has bought Sis F[annie] a fine elegant carriage, the prettiest one I ever saw. Brother G[eorge] tells him it ain't pretty a bit, got too much Ginger-bread fixins* about it, 'taint fit for rich folks (like brother J.) to ride in, recons he had better give it too some of his poor kin-folks (meaning himself) that can't do no better, told sis F[annie] (just to tease her) before brother J. came home that he [Bro. John] must be sure & give him [George] some of his niggers, asked her how many brother J. would bring, she said she didn't know, she reconed five or six, he said he must give him at least 4 any-how, he [George] has bought Sis M[ollie] a nice gentle buggy horse, so that her & Sally can go any where. I haven't been down to his house since I recd your letter, little Mollie looked just as sweet as ever the last time I saw her.

*Ginger-bread fixins most likely means fussy or overly ornamented.

Neal, would you believe it — I am getting right fleshy. I have to let out all my dresses. I think its owing to the change of water sis M[ollie] says its because I quit snuff. I gave my box away a few days after I came out here & haven't dipped since, brother J. got me a hair tooth brush & I am using "the balm of a Thousand flowers" on my teeth, it improves them very much.

We had some nice venison last week & before that some nice wild turkies. Oh, N, we have so many eggs, more than we can use. I have just counted 24 doz. to send to Camden. I tell you N. I am living high out here, don't know what it is to sit down to corn bread tell Mammy, — but stop I haven't told you the most important of all, would you believe it, sis F[annie] had another fine fat gal last Wednesday, weighed only six pounds, but 'tis a fat plump little babe though. George wanted to know of his Ma "how many more children she was going to have", she would have so many after a while that "Pa wouldn't have a nigger" a piece to give 'em all, the little rascal who would have thought he knew so much. Mittie can recolect when she was in Ala., Aunt Nealy gave her so much sugar, Bettie wants to know if Aunt N. gave her anything. I told her yes. I declare 'twas so amusing. When brother J[ohn] told Bet that he had bought a carriage, she wanted to know who would drive, he told her Dick; no, no, says Bet I want a white nigger to drive me. Dick shant.

Tell Sis Carey I haven't seen any of the bon-tons* yet but that there is a fellow up above here that has a heap of hogs. — I expect to see him once in a while, he started down here last week but meeting brother J[ohn], go-

*Bon-ton means good or elegant form or style; men of good breeding & fashionable society.

ing to a neighbors went with him. Tell Ma brother John says she must send that "feller" out here, he wants a good race with his fox dogs anyhow & wants to go <u>fox</u> hunting (he would not answer for the <u>fox</u>), & to send him along if he wants to come, she need not be afraid but what he will <u>run him off</u> with his dogs in a hurry, too.

I hope the frost has not been as bad in Ala as it has here, we would have had so many pretty flowers (roses principaly, in the yard, but the buds are all nipped, sis F[annie] has sowed seed repeatedly but to no purpose, she has no vegetables growing but peas, beans & some mustard. You must tell Mrs. Howard I miss my sunday school more than anything else, & the many pleasant hours I have spent in her society, too. I know I shall never forget her kindness, you know she (both of them) were more friendly to us than anyone else, & next to you all I want to see her & Mrs. Dr. Howard more than any body else in Ala. Give my love to both of them. Tell Ella I will write before long, she must answer my letter — Kiss her for me, I do want to see her so much. Well, Nelly, I don't know what else — oh Sally says you must write first. I tell her I don't think so & that she must write. She & sis M send love to you all. Tell Amy G[olston]. she must write to me, I have so many to write to. Give my love to all enquiring friends, Uncle Cowert, to. Tell him I try to follow his instructions. Let me know if he has taken you all into full membership yet, my love to Ma, & sis C[arrie], accept a portion for yourself, write soon. Hoping this finds you all in the enjoyment of good health & happiness. I am

        Your affectionate sister,
        C. L. Dickson

P. S. Sis F sends her love, all are well but her, she is doing as well as could be expected though.

*Note: This postscript is written along the left margin of page 1:

*Please excuse my starting on the wrong page. I did not notice what I was doing, Mrs. Peters spent the day with us a few weeks ago — She is a fine looking old lady — inquired about Ma, she said Susan Arthur (her daughter) had quit writing to Ma, couldn't find her post office. You must tell Ma to write to her, direct the letters to Holly Springs, Miss. Mrs Peters said she would like to see Ma very much.

*Note: This footnote appears at the top of page 1:

*(looking for sis M[ollie] & S[ally] tomorrow)
     C.L.D.

Clarissa Dickson in Ouachita Co. to her mother Mrs. Clarissa Dickson in Autauga Co.

June 2nd, 1857

Dear Mother,

 I recd your most welcome letter, ten days since. I would have answered it sooner, but was so busy I could not. I wrote to C[ornelia] sometime in April. I expect she recd my letter about the same time I got yours. I acnoledge I ought to write oftener, but when I tell you the reason for my not doing so, you will not blame me so much. I wrote to C — that Sis F[annie] had a fine girl, she (Sis F.) was doing very well for about two weeks, when she was taken with a very severe pain in her leg. It was all swolen up for a while & very painful indeed, she thinks it was some kind of disease (of a very lingering nature) in her leg, it lasted four or five weeks, toward the last it got up in her side & back, twas then more painful than ever, we done everything we could by constant rubbing, blistering, & keeping bags of hot salt on it, to relieve it, but to no purpose, it just gradually wore out after so long a time. I never saw or heard tell of any one suffering so much and <u>so severely</u>, it has reduced her to a mere skeleton, oh she looks so badly, though I am glad to say she is a little better, the pains have all sceased, at last, and we have got her up in a chair, once or twice Hannah and I walked each side of her, she has to limp a little as one leg is shorter than the other. Brother J[ohn] consulted some of the Dr's in Camden, when she was first taken, they said twould have to gradually ware off they said they knew of some cases that lasted five years, Sis F is rather fortunate in getting well so soon. I think it is owing to the good <u>rubbing more</u> than anything. We have to let the baby suck a bottle all the time, it looks fat & well. I think I have learned how to attend to baby's, Ma, I washed, dressed & fed the baby all the time sis F was sick. I beleave I love it better than any baby I ever saw. The children have all had the measles while sis F was sick. I gave them hot teas & a dose of salts once in a while, they are all well, brother J & I went to church Sunday, he has bought me a nice saddle, & I rode his fine riding horse to church, we took dinner at sis M[ollie]'s, she has a fine vegetable garden, though 'tis much later than usual, Philis has been very sick, looks better now, all were well, sis M, & S[ally], and brother G[eorge] have been here once every week since sis F has been sick.

 We have a fine garden, though late, peas <u>higher than my head</u>, have had five or six messes of strawberries, brother G pleagues me & tells me "he knew I'd get fat when pease come." I weighs "131". I think old Rack-en-sack agrees with me. I rarely ever have the headache now. I am so glad I came out here Ma, sister F says she don't know what she would have done without me. I carried the keys & attended to everything while she was sick.

 Tell Mrs. L[asiter] I will write to her soon when they all get entirely well, haven't time now, my love to her and Bettie. I think hard of Bettie's not writing to me. Tell Mrs. L she ought not complain, while she has old Bob Winter left. Twill never do in the world. Miss Julia Stone is not expected to live many days, all the family have gone over to see her, G[eorge]. Stone's wife lost her baby a week or two ago with scarlet fever. Well, Ma, I haven't time to write more now. I will write you a long letter soon, & tell you every thing. I intend writing every two weeks any how, when all get well. Give my love to the two Mrs. Howards & to all enquiring friends. I often think of Mrs. L. Howard & of her many little acts of kindness to me, which I will ever remember with gratitude. Sis sends love to all, hoping this may find all well I am

your affectionate daughter, Clara L. Dickson

*P.S. Please excuse this half sheet it is all I have, til Brother J goes to Camden, tell Mammy & all the negroes howdy. I was surprised to learn that Ann was married — Wish I had been there

*We haven't named the baby yet.

C.L.D.

Thomas G. Howard M.D. (Autauga Co. Ala. in the 1860s) Photo courtesy of Sue Martin Russell

*Note: This postscript was written along the left margin of page 1:

*Note: This second postscript was written at the top of page 1:

Clarissa Dickson in Ouachita Co. to her sister Cornelia Dickson in Autauga Co.

June 26, 1857

Dear Sister,

I haven't received a letter from you in several months. Ma's dated May 7, I rec'd and answered immediately. I would not be writing now, but I told Ma that I would write oftener than I had done. N[ealy], Ma reproved me for not writing oftener, and you have only written me once since I left home. Though there may now be a letter in Cam[den] for me, if so, I will answer it, when I get it, which will be next week.

I am happy to say that all are well at last, sis F__ & babe & all, sis is getting right fleshy again, & looks so well. We have to feed the baby yet some, but not much; no name yet. Brother J says tell Ma he will name it

Clarissa, after her "if" she will give it a <u>nigger</u>, but if she won't do that, he can't, as C[larissa] is too <u>ugly</u> a name, it favors him more than anyone else. S. G. [Sally Gildersleeve] thinks it is just like grandma, it has her mark down its forehead. Sis F thinks it the prettiest baby she ever had; sis M[ollie] & S[ally] spent the day with us Tuesday.

We have preaching two or three times a month at our church, (<u>Shady Grove</u>). Does Mr Cowart preach for you yet, I wish I could hear him, he is such a good old man, & preached so faithfully for us last year. I expect the sunday school is right large now, as tis summer & all can attend. How is the two Mrs. Howards & their families & Rebecca Underwood, & all the good folks; I am most afraid to hear from Ala now, it seems every letter we get announces the death of some body. Sis M[ollie] recd Reeny's letter a week or two ago.

Sis F[annie] has a very fine garden now; all kinds of nice vegetables, squashes as large as a breakfast plate, cucumbers nearly half a yard long & cc. Corn crops are looking well, but cotton crops are sorry; oh, Neal, I had some <u>bear-meat</u> the other week, one of the neighbors sent us some. I can tell you 'twas "<u>delicious</u>", better than venison. We have no fruits except plumbs & blackberries, & a few huckleberries, they eat all the better for that though.

Tell Mrs. Clark that Miss Julia Stone is dead. She died today two weeks ago, she died very willingly. Mrs Stone, Ora, and William Stone (D N's) [Dee Newton] father are going to travel, they will go up in Tennessee as W. S. has a daughter going to school & he wishes to take her along, too. Dee N. has been very sick, he is better now, & is staying out in the country at his fathers to recruit his health. How is Mrs. Lasiter and B___ give my love to both of them, tell Bettie that I think right hard of her for not writing to me, & Amy Golson — by the by — I

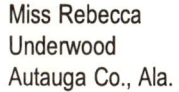

Miss Rebecca Underwood
Autauga Co., Ala.

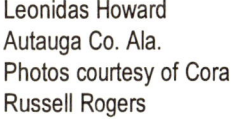

Leonidas Howard
Autauga Co. Ala.
Photos courtesy of Cora Russell Rogers

expect she is most married by this time, to W. L.

June 28th Had a fine rain yesterday. I hope you have good seasons, too, to make everything grow. How is sis C[arrie] & family & Grandma & all, Sis F sends her love & howdy [to] them & Ma & you. You must write soon, C, & write everything & write oftener. <u>Every thing</u> is interesting to me.

Give my love to Beck U[nderwood] & tell her to write to me, let me know what she has named her babe. I do want to see it so much, know its pretty, my love & a kiss for Ella Howard, tell her I'll write before long, my love to the Mrs Howards & all enquiring friends, tell all the negroes howdy, tell Mammy I know the reason she misses me, because I was so bad. I guess Ann & John have fine times don't they, during the honeymoon, be sure & write soon, my love to you all

Your affectionate sister,
Clara Louise D.

P. S. George & Mittie will start to school Monday, M. will board out
*P. S. S. S. [Sis Sally] sends love to you, says you must write.

*Note: This post script was written at the top of the page 1:

Clara Dickson in Ouachita Co. to her sister Cornelia in Autauga Co.

Aug. 1st, 1857

Dear Sister,

I received your most welcome letter of the 4th of June three or four weeks ago, the reason I did not answer it sooner was, I was taken sick immediately after with billious fever, the fever only lasted a week, but I had taken calomel*, & it staid in my system most too long, and I was badly salivated*, that lasted nearly two weeks, I have almost recovered from the effects of it now; my mouth is a little sore yet, but I can <u>eat</u> some now, all along, I lived on gruel, <u>soups</u>, & then <u>pap</u>, which last, I became quite fond of, brother J says I would have not been salivated, but my gums you know are so soft & tender, & then I had been salivated once before which made it very much against me. It tickled little George [Rumph] very much, at the idea of my eating <u>pap</u>; just like babies, he says; one thing made me hate being sick was, I had gained so much since I came out, & when I got sick I lost it all. Since I got up, brother J has killed some very fine deer; he tells me never mind I will soon make it up again, the venison is so fat & nice, oh, N, he killed the prettiest little spotted fawn; I never thought they were so pretty, & 'twas so tender and nice, I wish you had some.

Sis F[annie] & all are well, the baby grows so fast and it is so pretty. I think it prettier than any of the others, she has named it Florence. I think those names you gave were very pretty, especially Tetulia, tis a sweet name, brother J says he recons Ma will give him <u>jessy</u> when she reads in my letter, about his naming the baby after her if she would give it a nigger, he was

*Calomel is Mercurous Chloride. It is no longer used in medicine because of the mercury, but was used as a purgative and a fungacide.

*To salivate is to produce an excessive amount of saliva, resulting in a severely sore mouth and often in the loss of teeth.

only joking though. N, I wish you could see little Tom [Rumph] he is so funny, he can't talk much, says only a few words, but his motions & the way he points his little finger & shakes his head, when we pretend not to understand him, tis realy amusing. Bettie is the smartest little thing I most ever saw, can say such big words & struts about & looks so independent, whenever her Ma goes to whip her, she will get sis F[annie] a <u>big switch</u> & hold up her dress with all the gravity in the world, as much as to say, <u>if you must, you must I suppose</u>. Mittie & George are going to school. George boards at brother G[eorge]'s, Mittie boards at the Coles, it being too far for her to walk from brother G's. & Mr.Cole's is just in sight of the school-house. We have a good joke on Mittie. The first day their Pa took them down to school, Sis F[annie] filled their buckets almost entirely with nice cake & told them to be sure & give <u>John</u> & <u>Willis</u>* some, Mit sat there a little while, when so eager to tell them about it, she called oh, boys, boys, I've got so much nice cake for you all. When she went to Mr. Cole's that night she told Mrs. C that the ants got into her bucket in the morning so she set it in the "cubbord" (meaning pulpit) in the evening & the ants didn't trouble it a bit then, she didn't [know] the name of the pulpit* —she wanted to know where Mr. Marshall, (their teacher) was going to sleep she didn't see any <u>bed</u> in the <u>school-house</u>, she likes to go to school very well, so many little girls to play with. The examination in Camden came off last week, brother John had intended taking me, but my mouth was too sore then, Sally went one day. We had a quarterly meeting at Shady Grove last Sabbath. I had anticipated so much pleasure in attending, but, oh, my mouth, it made me stay home again, if it had only been a week later I could have went. [They] are going to have another big meeting up above here before long, I know I can go to that. There is a good deal of sickness now, in the neighborhood, the disease (bloody dysentry) proves very fatal, several of the neighbors have died with it, Mr. Wm Stone, (Dee's Pa), lost two or three of his negro men with it, while he was gone, too, he returned a few days ago. Aug 2. We have a fine rain today, it commenced raining about mid- night, & has been raining ever since. I know every body is so glad & every one needed rain so much, it has been cloudy and threatening rain all week, but never rained to do any good til now. I expect you all have had some good seasons lately. I recd a letter from Bettie yesterday, she spoke of having plenty of rain at that time; Oh I was so sorry to learn that Mrs. Lasiter has those spells again. I was in hopes that traveling would improve her health so much that she would miss them this summer. Give my love to her & Bettie, tell B I will write to her soon. I would do so now, but I recd your letter first, & of course must answer <u>it</u> first. How are the two Mrs. Howards. I hope they are all well. I see you have had measles to attend too, as well as myself. Tell Ella I wish to see her as bad if not worse than she wishes to see me, & that I think of her very often, & wish I could be at sunday school with her again. I think twas very kind in Mrs.

*John Rumph Boddie and Willis Boddie, first cousins of Mittie and sons of brother George and sis Mollie.

*The school was being held in the church building.

Howard to present you with such a nice bonnet. I guess you will rig out sure enough this summer, with your flounces and cc, & take all the beaus away from me before I get back, but never mind I have some out here, if they are <u>arkensaw hoosiers</u>, one especially who is not wanting in the <u>kinky head accomplishments</u> (as Mrs Dent Lamar used to say) & besides, oh N, he has so many fine fat "hogs" and cattle too, a plenty, tell Mammy if I should take a notion to grab him, she may be assured of a plenty of fat meat & greace of every description from lard down to _____ to _____ fat. He came down to go to Church with me last Sunday, but twas too cloudy & I was afraid to go as I had been salivated.

How are you all getting along with your crops & gardens, Sis Fannie has a very good garden the crops besides suffering from the effects of a cold spring, has also suffered some from want of rain, the corn will now do well though late everywhere, as we've had a general rain, the cotton is yet small, but very full of squares and 'tis thought the farmers will yet make pretty fair crops. Have you had any watermelons yet, brother John has some very fine patches, though late, he brought us in a splendid one last week, the best one I ever ate, he would have had a good many more, if he could have had rains, he says there will yet be a good many, though they will be late.

I havent seen Sally and sis Mollie in several weeks, they both came to see me when I was sick. I intended staying a week with S but was taken sick that week. I am well now & will go down in the course of a week or two. S is going to take me around to see all their neighbors & then she will come home with me & stay some. Mrs. Dupey, sis Mollie's nearest neighbor, lost her oldest son day before yesterday, with conjestive fever.

Well N I dont know what else to write. Give my love to Mrs L[eodis] Howard, tell her I do miss our sunday school <u>so much</u>, & her society too, hers & Mrs. Dr.'s too. Give my love to the latter also, tell her I will disappoint her expectation as regards my marrying; that I intend to return to Ala just as I am. My love to Rebecca Underwood, kiss her babe for me when you see it. Let me know what Mrs. L. Howard has named her babe. I do wish I could see it, too. Oh I almost forgot to tell you, I recd a long letter from Uncle Cowart a few weeks ago, tell him I thank him so much & will try to profit by his instructions, they always had more weight with me than those of any one else, & I am so sorry that it so happened he could not take me into full membership. I some how felt I would rather it would be him than anyone else. Sis Carrie wrote to sis Mollie that Pa was using the electrick fluid on his arm & it helped it so much. I am so glad. I trust twill cure his palsy. My love to him, & Ma, & Sis Carrie & family & yourself & all enquiring friends. Sis F sends her love to all of you. Write soon and write everything.

                                Goodbye, hoping I remain
                                Your affectionate sister
                                Clara L. Dickson

*Tell Ma, I will answer her letter soon. I have four more letters to answer, dont you pity me, Ma's, Betties, Mrs. Weavers & Uncle Cowarts. Tell Mammy & all the Negroes howdy. Tell Jerry I will look out for those watermelons when I come home.

*Note: This postscript was written along the left margin of page 1.

Clara Dickson in Ouachita Co. to her mother Mrs. Clarissa Dickson in Autauga Co.

Sept. 6, 1857

Dear Mother,

I receaved your letter some time ago. I should have answered it sooner, but I had recd Nealy's first & so thought 'twould be as well to answer it first, & yours afterward. I have just receaved another from N & will answer it soon. This leaves all well, though Sis F[annie] & several of the children have been quite sick with the fever. Sis was salivated too, but not as bad as I was; The baby grows very fast, & is the fattest little thing & is so pretty. I have entirely recovered, though I am not so fleshy as I was before I got sick.

Brother G[eorge] and Sis M[ollie] & Sally were up last week, all was well except Phillis, she still lingers, brother G hardly thinks she will recover. I went to see her the last time I was there, she is nothing but skin & bones. Sally is coming up next week to stay several days with me. She recd a letter from her father some time ago, he wrote he would be after her, as soon as the rivers permit. Brother J[ohn] recd a letter from Uncle Clem, last week. There has been a great deal of sickness in the neighborhood this summer, though it has abated considerably within the last two weeks, Sis F[annie] has planted beans, peas,& cc in the garden & they are growing finely, we will have nice fall vegetables if the rains continue. We have some very nice peas to eat now, they are called the wild goose pea, brother J brought them from Ala last winter. He has besides six or seven other kinds of peas, he planted & worked them all himself, last spring. The crops are pretty good, that is the corn crop, cotton is yet uncertain, though it promises to be very fair if, they have a late dry fall. We have had some very fine watermelons this summer, & will have a great many scupennong-grapes soon, old Hal Brodnax sent me word the other day that when Sally came up we must be sure & come to see him & get some of his grapes, he has more than sis F has. He says though when we come to see him he means to kiss us both, he always makes it a rule to kiss all the Autauga girls that he sees the old rascal. There has been a great revival going on in Camden for the last five or six weeks, & a great many joined the church, about 125 or 30, the meeting is still going on, tis thought twill be a great benefit to Camden, it has always been such a wicked place;-C[ornelia] wrote that you would have another protracted meeting at Ivy Creek soon. I wish I could attend. I do hope you all have such a meeting as we had last year. Sis F lost a little negro not long since Roda's second child Margaret, with <u>dropsy</u> 'twas caused from eating dirt — her youngest child is named <u>Buchanan</u>. I answered Mr Cowart's letter last week. I did not know that he thought enough of me to write me such a kind letter. I also answered Bettie's. Brother J will be out in Ala this winter, in Dec, I think, he is going to bring his mother & sister & brother out here, to live, and so you may look for me when he comes, as I shall be certain to go with him, as Sis F[annie] will have such a house full, they will live with her until Tarrant becomes of age, & then he will buy a place & Mrs.M* & Mary will live with him. Well, I don't know what else to write give my love to Mrs. L[asiter] & Bettie & to all enquiring friends. Tell Neal I will write soon, this is her <u>birthday</u>. I should have written to her today but I had your letter to answer. Sis F says tell Grandma she is saving so many nice pea & bean seed to send her this winter, some <u>Arkansas beans too</u>, you plant them in the summer (the beans) & they commence bearing when all other vegetables are gone & bear 'til frost, she got the seed from one of her neighbors, also some navy-beans they are very nice. She says she will write to grandma soon. I am going to bring you some peas & beans too, one kind, the goose pea, is very large indeed & is so richly flavored it dont take many for a mess. Sis says she has so many children that [she] can hardly come out this winter, sends her love to all, brother J says "he can't name the babe after you unless you give him a nigger <u>cash in hand!</u> as "he never goes on a <u>credit</u>" My love to Pa & Neal accept a share for yourself & beleave me as ever your affectionate daughter

C. L. Dickson

P. S. Tell the negroes howdy, tell Jerry I will look for them watermelons this winter. Write soon

C. D.

P. S. Have some very fine sweet potatoes too

*Mrs. M is Mrs Mallard, Dr. Rumph's mother.

Clara Dickson in Ouachita Co. to her sister Cornelia Dickson in Autauga Co.

Oct. 3, 1857

Dear Sister,

Your welcome epistle of Sept. 5th, I recd a few days since. I was truly glad to hear from you all, & that all are well. I should have answered your other letter, but had just written to you a short time previous; I have since then recd & answered Ma's letter. I am so glad that you are writing so often, & yet it seems a long time after getting one letter before the next one comes, Sis M[ollie] has just recd sis Carry's, in her letter she said brother Add called Sis M[ollie]'s letters <u>The London Times</u>. We call hers [Sis Carrie] <u>Brother Johnathan</u> as 'tis a little larger than sis M's. All are well at Sis M's except Bill Scott,* he has typhoid fever. Since writing the above I have learned that he is dead it is a great loss to brother G[eorge] & sis M too, as he had learned to cook & cooked much better than Julia Ann; he was so proud of it too, and tried so hard to do as he was told, sis M has had two or three fevers herself, but is much better, having missed her fever two or three days, all the rest are well; sis F[annie] was down there the other day. I stayed home with the children all well here, though the children have had a spell of the fever also. George & Mittie had to stop school, they will start again next week. They all say out here that they never have known such a year as this has been, some of the oldest settlers too, those that have been here 15 or so years. Sis F[annie]'s family is the only one that has escaped having the flux,* one or two of brother G[eorge]'s negroes had a slight attack. I think this is a year long to be remembered by all, everywhere; sis M[ollie] has just read Reeny's letter. I was surprised to hear that Grandma's house was so near done. I thought she had just begun it. I expect she will have moved into it by the time I get home, and Sis C[arrie] into hers. I am so glad of that for Sis C will have a house so much more comfortable than hers, & that reminds me, C[ornelia] that I do wish Ma would shed her house too, if 'twas only one room 'twould be so much more comfortable than just two rooms. I was so sorry to hear that Pa's palsy was worse again. I was in hopes that the Electric fluid, that he was using, would benefit him so much.

 We have fine beans now all the time; some that sis F[annie] planted in August; they bear fuller than any I ever saw, the English peas are blooming now, & I hope the frost will stay off long enough for us to have peas also. Bro. J[ohn] has oh such nice <u>taters</u>, too, the finest I ever saw, thinks to make a thousand bushels if not more; he has made fine corn also, & if frost stays off will make a fine crop of cotton. Oh I tell you Neal old <u>Rackensack</u> is a great country after all, if the farmers could only have ordinary seasons even, they would make <u>just such crops</u> almost scares one to look at em makes a body silent with wonder & amazment. Corn stalks average from two to four ears (not nubbins) per stalk. I hope Ma will make more than she thinks for, you know she always does, & then prices are so high, from 12 1/2 to 18 cts per pound. Well Neal about that hoosier fellow, you are mistaken about his being so ignorant. I can tell you, he has education a plenty, & can converse as well as anybody when he chooses, sis M[ollie] just wrote that to tease me; that was all. Do you ever do any embroidery now, I have worked sis F[annie] a beautiful collar this fall & am working one for sis M[ollie], have most finished it. I haven't embroidered much for myself, but intend doing so soon.

 Well N[eal] I don't know what else to write, Give my love to the two Mrs.Howards. Tell the Dr.'s wife I am much obliged to her, but don't intend bringing <u>any body</u> home with me either. I do want to see them all so much. I do hope we will get Mr. C. on the circuit another year. I hate so much the

* Bill Scott must refer to one of brother George's slaves.

*Flux is the word commonly used in those days for dysentery.

idea of his leaving; I think him such a good minister, better than any we've ever had at Ivy Creek, that is since I can remember. Give my love to Rebecca & Bettie & all enquiring friends, tell B ___ it is almost time for me to get another letter from her. Tell R____ to name her babe Florence, or Emma & I will embroider it a beautiful little dress next spring. Write soon & tell me all the news, my love to Ma & Pa & believe me as ever

       Your affectionate sister
       Clara

  P. S. Cousin Jim Peters I am sorry to say, has consumption very bad too, he has gone up to Kansas to a colder climate, the physicians advised him to do so; I have never seen him yet. Tell Mat Simpson, when you see her, that I have been looking for a letter from her for some time. Good bye, C. L. D.

  Sis F[annie] sends her love to all, says tell grandma she will write soon; she says Grandma has never answered her last one yet, one that she wrote two or three years ago. She says tell Ma to please send her a small sample of some of that blue checked foot valance or counterpin that she used to have long ago (before I was born I beleave) & which every one used to admire so much, it was very broad plaid, with so many little checks and stripes in it. I think Ma has the foot-valance any-how. Sis F. has learned to dye oh! such a beautiful blue, with blue-stone* & is going to have some counter-pins wove & you must send the sample in a letter, please, sis F. has dyed all the children's winter stockings with the blue stone dye. I will give you the recipe. Make a weak bath of log-wood*, into which put a little blue-stone (about a handful of log-wood to a teaspoonful of blue stone), & boil the hanks, a short time, take them out & wash them out in clear water with a little strong lye soap, which sets the color. The hanks* should be first soaked in alum water before dying which brightens the color, it is much easier than mammy's way. by the by, I dreamed about mammy the other night. I thought she looked almost as big as Aunt Rittor Morton. Tell all the negroes howdy one more adieu — my pen is so bad I scarcely can write intelligibly. C. L. D.

  Post Scripture [this was written at the bottom of the letter by Brother John B. Rumph and was most likely some kind of family joke]:

  "Give the printed scrap to A. C Love. It is a pretty good sequel to the Soda Powders." J. B. R.

---

*Blue stone is a salt occuring in large transparent deep-blue triclinic crystals.

*Logwood N. [so called from being imported in "logs"] the heartwood of a tree, a native of South America, it is red, heavy wood, and is used largely in dyeing. An extract from this wood is used in medicine as an astringent.

*Thread for weaving and embroidery was bundled in what was called "hanks."

Clara Dickson in Ouachita Co. to her sister Cornelia in Autauga Co.

Dec. 11, 1857

Dear Sister,

I receaved your most welcome & long looked for letter several days ago. I was oh so glad to hear that all were well, but words cannot express the deep regret I feel on learning that our dear friend Mrs (Dr.) H[oward] was no more, for a true friend she was indeed to us, & I know you will feel her loss most sensibly; the more so as, you and I have such few <u>friends</u>, true ones I mean in Autauga. I have almost felt of late that I never wished to live there again, so many faces missing, there'll be when I go back, & so many changes but, I am about to tell you something that will surprise you disappoint you also, brother J[ohn] recd a letter from his mother a few days ago stating that she was again "<u>married</u>" to a Dr. Harris in Macon (works 70 hands & has several children) & she could not come out here now, & so he won't go atall now he says, as the only thing that would have taken him there was to move her out, says tell Uncle Clem to be certain to come out this winter, he is looking a little now for him. Mr. G[ildersleeve] will have to come after Sally now, Sis M[ollie] had just written to him that S[ally] would return with brother J & me, but since she heard that Mrs. Mallard was married & that bro. J. won't go to Ala, says she must write to him to come or he wouldn't get Sally. I shall return with them, as brother J won't go, some time this winter, don't look for me 'til you see me. Sis F[annie], sorry to say is again in bad health she has neuralgia in her head, she was taken about a month ago with severe pains in her head, & they have continued at intervals of 24 hours or so ever since until last Sunday they came on much oftener & more severe if any thing, brother J has tried every thing he could think of but has only temporary effect, quinine I beleave does more good than any thing else, brother J sent yesterday to Cam[den] for Dr Bacon one of the best physicians there, to see if he could recommend any thing that would benefit her, the Dr is here now, but will leave in a few minutes, & so I must be as quick as possible, it is the reason I don't write any better, am in such a hurry & its so bitter cold. All the rest well, & sis M[ollie]'s family too, Lucy has another girl. I will write you a long letter next week. I hope then sis will be free from these severe pains. I do hope the Dr will cure her, she would be entirely well if it were not for that, all fall she has complained of a roaring in the head, it was the pressure of the disease. Oh it's so cold my hands are stiff. I will write a long letter next week, if Brother John had not receaved that letter from his mother we should have started on the 15th & been with you all Christmas, My love to Ma & Pa & all enquiring friends, Tell Harriet never mind. I'll be having to make nigger-gees [negliges] for her next summer. My love to Mrs.L. Howard & family, I will write to Ella in a week or so. Good bye

Your affectionate sister
Clara

Clara Dickson in Ouachita Co. to her sister Cornelia in Autauga Co.

Dec. 18, 1857

Dear Sister,

 I wrote you about ten days since, though 'twas only a few a few lines, as I didn't have time then to write more, sis F[annie] is a good deal better than she was then, but not able to be up yet, the Dr's medicine salivated her a little & she has some appetite now to eat; her desease (Neuralgea) is, I do think, the most curious desease I ever heard of, & all the remedies that brother J can think of, & all that the other physicians advise, has been tried & all afford only temporary relief; Old Mr Broadnax, said he once had it very bad & finily cured it with brandy, kept half tight all the time, we got some spirits & she tried — took enough to make her real <u>boosy</u>. It made her deathly sick, she vomited for a day or two, from the effects of it; but strange to say she has had none of those hard spells since but only light ones, that was about a week ago that they stoped. Oh when those hard pains were on her, she would scream out so many times & would get up & sit up & then lie down & cc, she couldent rest no way. I got to combing her head, just raking it with a coarse comb, right hard when the pains were on & she said I eased it more than the medicine or anything else; said it seemed like I was combing the pain out or she could feel it going out with the comb, wasent that strange. I would comb for an hour sometimes, until the pain would go entirely off. At times I thought I would rake the skin off too, but she said she hardly felt it. I do hope she won't have any more of those severe pains, she could soon get well if it were not for that, the baby is the fatest & prettiest little thing I most ever saw, & grows <u>so</u> fast, Hannah minds it all the time, sleeps right by its little cradle every night, & gives it the bottle whenever it wakes up, it is mighty good now to sleep at night, she don't get up more than once or twice during the night with it. Sis M[olly] & Sally & brother G[eorge] was up the day before yesterday, all well sis M said. She has an awful bad foot, has had risings on it for nearly six weeks, 'tis nearly well now. I was teasing her some time ago, telling her we would have to put her on a feather-bed when she started home, she can only walk on her <u>toes</u> yet. We have all had bad colds, mine is not quite well yet. I had a bad sore throat at first, but that is well. S. wrote to her mother last week telling her that brother J would not be out this winter & that her father would have to come after her. I will accompany her. If her father <u>dont</u> come, brother J. says as he will have to go to N Orleans any how on bussiness, we can go with him & he will go with us as far as Mobile, put us on a Alabama river boat, under the care of the captain, & we can sail up home <u>that way</u>. S. will get off at Clifton though & poor me will be alone then — but it is only one day & night's travel from Clifton to Gastons Landing & I won't mind that; I beleave I'll get a <u>horn</u> or trumpet in Mobile & when I arrive at the Landing

I will let you all know,* that is if I can blow loud enough, I rather think that will be the rub. Well then I'll jump on the first ole cow I meet & trot home. I think it will be a jig jig sure enough, don't you. Brother J. could go all the way but sis F. is in bad health & she is so lonesome when he goes off, & besides he has so much bussiness to attend too & 'twil only take him one day & night to cross the lake & then put us on a boat immediately (as they are always leaving Mobile, at all times I mean) & then one day & night to return to N. O. will be only two days & nights lost, & he wouldent mind that. It will be some time in Jan. & it may not be til Feb & so I can't take Christmas with you all as I anticipated. You will have to eat enough Christmas turkey for me & yourself, if you aint got no turkey, you will have to do like some of the folks out here, kill a nice fat shoat* & stuff it with possums, by the by that is what Harriet ought to have had for her supper, tell her I am mad(?) enough; she ought to have waited until I came home to fix her up. I was surprised to learn that Heely was married again so soon after his wife's death too; I had heard of M. Lamar's death, previous to getting your letter. What has become of Mat Taylor, you never write anything about her, give my love to her when you see her. I think she has treated me right shabbily since I left home. I tell you Neal this going from home tries a body's friends don't it, they can soon find out who thinks anything of them & who don't. Mat Simpson has never answered my letter yet. & I don't care much.

 Well, I don't know what to write about that would interest you, Sis F. says tell Grandma she will write as soon as she gets able, sends her love to you all. Give my love to Mrs. Howard, I do wish so much to see her & am so glad the time is so near, tell her, & to Rebecca too. Tell B[ecca?] I am going to stay with her a good deal when I come home, I want to name the baby too. Give my love to Sis Carry & family & all enquiring friends (that won't be much trouble as I've got so <u>few</u>) I have more here than I have in Ala. My love to Ma & Pa & accept a good share for yourself. Good bye. Hoping this may find you all in the enjoyment of health & happiness I am your affectionate sister

Clara

 P. S. brother J. says tell Uncle Clem he would be glad if he would come out this winter, as he can't go to Ala. Since writing my letter I have been telling him what I had written, he says if Sis F don't get a good deal better he won't go to N Orleans atall & so if Mr. G. don't come out here, good bye for this winter. Yours C. D.

*The fact that Clara can "blow a horn" at the landing and be heard at home indicates that they lived only a short distance from Gaston's Landing.

* A shoat is a young hog.

Clara Dickson in Camden, Arkansas to her sister Cornelia in Autauga Co.
Feb. 12th, 1858

Dear Sister,

I hardly know how to write to you all as I know you all are daily looking for me home. I would have written this two weeks ago, but my thumb has been so sore, I could not use it. I have had a bad rising on it & have not done anything since Christmas. & I am so sorry as I know how uneasy the delay has made you. Mr. Gildersleeve came three weeks ago yesterday stayed one week & started home with Sally. I intended all the while to go home when Sally went (as I had written you) thinking all the while that sis F's health would be so much better & that she would not need me so much, but I am sorry to say it has not, that is; not so she can attend to her housekeeping, cc though she is better now than she has been in three months, still she is not able to sew a <u>stitch</u>, nor hasent been in three or four months, & I thought she needed me so much more now than ever, having no one to keep house or sew, so I concluded to stay & come some time this summer or next fall, just the first opportunity that occurs, as brother J says when warm dry weather comes, the Neuralgea would cease entirely. I do so much hope it will. I never saw anyone suffer half so much or so <u>severely</u>. Her system is nearly worn out with suffering, her pains are in the region of the brain, she says & it is so much worse there than elsewhere & makes her foolish at times. For the last two or three weeks she is easier, but so weak & feeble as not to be able to sit up more than two or three hours at a time. I don't think Ma will blame me, for staying, under the circumstances, though I know how much she & you & Pa wanted to see me & I wanted to see you all too.

I recd your letter & Bettie's also the day before S[ally] left, & oh you can imagine how sorry I was & how surprised to learn of Ann's death, & with consumption. I

Mary Elizabeth Gildersleeve Boddie "Sis Mollie" (1824-1900)

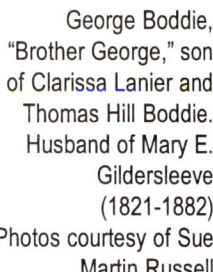

George Boddie, "Brother George," son of Clarissa Lanier and Thomas Hill Boddie. Husband of Mary E. Gildersleeve (1821-1882) Photos courtesy of Sue Martin Russell

thought she would be the last one to have it, she was so healthy & strong. I know Ma will feel her loss sensibly, but maybe 'tis all for the best though we can hardly see it now, but I feel that God knows best always, & I don't beleave he would have taken her away, if he had not saw proper to do so, & we must try to feel resigned to his decrees, severe though they be.

How have you been employing yourself this winter, it has been so wet & cold I could not do any thing but stay in the house, we had a heavy snow Christmas, the day before I mean, & another one last week, it has been raining too every other day almost for the last month, 'tis a fact, we have only two pretty fair days in a week. Brother J says ask brother Add when he is coming out, he has been looking some for him, he wrote brother J in N Orleans, to rent him a place as he was coming out this winter, & we have seen nothing of him yet, brother J says tell Uncle C[lem] he has been looking for a letter from him for some time, says he can't write, nor never will again he is afraid he has one of the worst bonefelons* on the fore finger of his right hand has had it for five weeks; thought one while he would loose two joints of his finger but he has lost only one that is bad enough, but not as bad as he feared twould be, it is getting well now, he had hard chills every night for nearly a week when it was at its worst, he is afraid 'twill always be stiff so that he can't write atall. How is Grandma & how is she getting along in her new house. I know she is disappointed in not getting her pea & bean seed. I will be certain to bring them when I do come, oh, I had almost forgot to tell you what a nice Christmas present I recd from brother J; I caught him Christmas* & the week after he presented me with a beautiful pair of ear rings with gold stone sets, they are so pretty I wish you could see them. How is our Sunday School coming on, do you attend regularly, Give my love to Mrs Howard tell her she is mistaken as to the cause of my staying here. I don't know of any one who could keep me here, that is none of the boys; not even my hoosier, as you call him; Tell her I do so much wish to see her & Ella, too. I will write to Ella when my thumb gets well. I have already inflamed it worse by writing this letter, but I thought you would all be uneasy if I did not write, you must excuse bad writing Neal this is written so very bad, but I could do no better, my thumb (it's on my right hand, too) is paining me so much. I will write again soon. Give my love to Ma & Pa, sis C[arrie] & all enquiring friends too; Good by; be a good

Dr. John Benjamin Rumph "Brother John" (1822-1886)
Photo courtesy of James Harvey Rumph

*For "bonefelon," the correct medical term is paronychia, which is an abscess or swelling around the fingernail.

*There was a custom in many families that the first person to greet a family member on Christmas morning with "Christmas Gift" would receive a gift from that family member, which explains Clara's statement about catching Brother John and receiving the ear rings.

girl, write soon, & tell Mrs. Howard I would be so proud if she would write too, sometimes only a few lines in your letter. believe me as ever,
Your affectionate Sister
Clara Dickson

Tell all the negroes howdy, what is Ann's baby name brother J says the <u>woodpile</u> has landed another "<u>cargo</u>" at the port of Boston. C. D.

Clara Dickson in Ouachita Co. to her father Col. S. H. N. Dickson in Autauga Co.

March, 1858

Dear Pa,

I receaved your letter of 11th Feb, a few days since. I was sorry that you were all so disappointed about my coming home, but was not my intention to do so when I wrote in Dec ____, but I did not think for a moment then — that Sis F's health would continue as bad as it then was, but I am sorry to say it has been the case all winter, until within the last few weeks; she has been mending slowly, & I hope when warm dry weather sets in, she will be entirely well. Oh! I never heard of anyone suffering so severly & so long as she has, all the past winter she has been unable to leave her room, more than two or three times & of course unable to attend to her housekeeping, or do a stitch of sewing — if I had not been here, I don't know what in the world she would have done, I think if you had been here & seen how low she was & how bad she looked when Mr Gildersleeve was here you could not have wished me to leave her; I should have written when sis M[ollie] wrote, but I had a severe rising on my thumb could not write atall. I wrote (or tried to write) to Neal several weeks after, but made a poor apology for a letter, 'twas all I could do — my thumb was so inflamed at the time. I told her in my letter why I remained. I could have returned if I chose to have done so when Sally did — but felt it my duty to stay — I will answer Ma's letter in a week or two. My love to all enquiring friends. Hoping this may find you <u>all</u> in the enjoyment of health, I am
your affectionate daughter,
Clara L. Dickson

P.S. brother G[eorge] & family are well, also brother J[ohn] & family, all but sis F[anny], & she is much better than she has been during the winter. My health is & has been better, much better, since I came out here, than it had been for several years before. Brother J sends his respects to you & says, any time (almost) that I wish to return home, he will take me, & says also you needn't be uneasy about me, as he has plenty of <u>hog</u> and <u>hominy</u> to feed me on, & that you must not give yourself any uneasiness about me whatever. I think so, too, Pa. You know that neither you or Ma were able to dress me when I was at home. I had to sew for it, though upon the whole, I wouldn't have stayed (let that be that it will) if Sister F's health had been good. She has been so kind & considerate toward me since I came out — it was nothing but right that I should try to be of some assistance to her in her ill health. Sis M[ollie] has just receaved a letter from sis Carry.

      Yours,
      C.L.Dickson

Clara Dickson in Ouachita Co. to CorneliaDickson in Autauga Co.
                March, 1858

Dear Sister,

 I receaved your welcome letter last week. I had just recd one from Ma & Pa the week previous — answered Pa's last Friday, & told him the reason why I did not come home, I was glad to learn from your letter that he was more reconciled to my staying, I think myself, that I was perfectly justifiable in so doing.
 Sis F is much better now, than she has been this winter, has none of those severe spells now, but says it just worry's her now all the time — says it is a strange unnatural feeling — complains of a numbness in her face, has no feeling scarcely in it, & she can't see good out of one of her eyes, but then she is willing to be patient with all that as long as she is rid of any severe pain. Old Mr Brodnax used to have it, he told her the other day when he was over here that these last symptoms of hers, was the winding up of the desease, says he has been all along there, it is in the root of her tongue now too, & she can't talk right plain, & says her tongue feels as big as her fist. Mr B. told me to rub her throat & neck with my hand & 'twould soon be well, I intend doing so as soon as I finish this letter. I have been very busy sewing since my thumb got well (I could not sew but very little all winter, which threw me back in the sewing line considerably) but am almost through — my work don't come by sprinkling like yours, it just pours down, but I sew so fast I soon get through, it never takes me long. All winter I was knitting off & on, & then I made a half barrel of <u>sour-crout</u> of the nicest white headed cabbage I ever saw we had two squares of them in the garden (besides what we ate all winter) & they had commenced running up to seed & we made sour-crout of them. I am not very fond of it, but brother J is though; I miss Sally very much indeed, I am so sorry she went home, I haven't been to sis M[ollie]'s since she left, intend going down this evening & stay a week, so much back water from the rains all winter. I could not get down there, could not get over the creek bottoms, 'twas all under water. Sis M started up after me last Saturday got as far as the creek & had to return home, — says I shall stay with her half the time now S[ally] is gone & she is so lonely.

Captain Dee Newton
(1835-1898)

George boards at sis M's & goes to school, Mitt at Dr Burford's (one of the near neighbors) & goes to school also, she is one of the smartest pupils in school, she had not been going two months before she had memorized all the boys' speeches (just from hearing them speak), she is a great fat thing & growes so fast, I can't fit any thing on her to stay so it seems like she out grows it before she wears it twice. G. is just as good a boy as I ever saw, thinks so much of the girls (the large ones) don't care about the <u>little</u> ones a bit, but is hugging around the big ones all the time - comes kisses me every night, before going to bed, (when he is at home) & little John Boddie is the same way, a young lady in the neighborhood got married last year, one that J claimed for his <u>sweetheart</u>, he was so mad, says he wouldn't speak to her again, & intended to shoot that man she married it is so amusing to hear them talk about their sweethearts the little rascals, to be talking how ever so big. Oh, I am so sorry little Ella Howard is or will be so disappointed, I do love E better than any little girl I ever saw I beleave (her Mother was always so kind to us). I intend writing her next week. I am looking every day now for a letter from her Mother. Give my love to Rebecca, tell her I love her too well to forget her but I don't think she cares much for me or she would write to me. I have so many, many letters to write or I would write to her, what is her babe named, I recon it can almost walk now.

I have not put on hoops yet, pray how do you manage to ride horse back that's what keeps me from getting one, it seems like a <u>big wind</u> would take me off the horse whether or no. When we were in New Orleans last winter, I told brother G[eorge] I intended getting one (just for fun) he said, "Wait til I get home & I'll make you one out of <u>white oak splints</u>", I read your letter to brother J[ohn], told him I beleaved I would get one any how, you spoke so highly of them; he said, "there is plenty of <u>hogs-heads</u> in the smoke house" and laughed, he knows how much I laughed at them [hoops] last year.

I have not seen Dee N[ewton] more than twice since I came out, he stays in Camden clerking all the time, his father has bought out one of the merchants there, & has commenced merchandizing, his partner is Mr J. Toney. Dee is clerking for him now. It was reported last Christmas that D[ee] & Ora Stone would marry, but I presume it is not so, as I hear nothing more of it.

Has Ma gardened any yet, I have planted mustard, radishes, lettuce, cabbage, & peas. All up & growing finely. I expect Grandma will soon have as pretty a garden as her old one, wish I had some pretty seed to sew. I wish she would write to sis F[annie], as she is not able to write to G'ma. Well Neal I don't know what else to write. You wrote that you had Ma's cotton to work, & I have some more garden seed to plant, but my letter don't resemble the London Times as much as yours, but I write oftener. I will write to Ma in a few weeks. Give my love to all enquiring friends (that is, what few I have), to Ma & Pa, & accept a share for yourself, & beleave me as ever,

Your affection-
ate sister,
Clara

P. S. Sis F sends Grandma some seed, that a friend of brother J's in Washington City sent him (the gentleman is a congressman), brother J became acquainted with him in <u>Little Rock</u>, sis is sorry that she can't send more, but twould not do to send many in a letter, you know.

I was so sorry to miss those watermelons. Tell J[erry] I won't disappoint you all next winter & he must save some more. Tell all the negroes howdy. How does Harriet come on [since] she has quit wearing flowing dresses? I tried to not get on this page, but I had to.

C. D.

*I was so sorry to hear of Mrs. Adair's death, she was such a sweet girl. Who did you write those valentines too, please tell me. I intended sending several but could not get them off in time.

Ora Stone Newton
(1838-1927)
Photos Courtesy of
Cornelia Pryor Lindsey

*Note: This postscript was written along the left margin of page 1:

Clara Dickson in Ouachita Co. to her friend Bettie Lasiter Whetstone in Autauga Co.

March 11th, 1858

Dear Bettie,

I have been wishing to write to you some time, but was unable to do so on account of my thumb; I've had a bad rising out it ever since Christmas (a long time) which has resulted in my losing the nail — have been unable to do any thing for two months & better (except knit) until lately; I did make out to answer Nealy's last, but inflamed my sore thumb by it. I thought they would be so uneasy about me, that I tried to scribble a letter, though hardly intellegable; But now I suppose you want to know the reason I did not return with Sally, I suppose , though, Neal has already informed you. I intended all the while to go when S went — but thought or rather hoped that sis F's health would be so much better that she would not need me so much; but I am sorry to say it was not; She was some better but not able to keep house or sew a stitch, nor has not been since Nov, she can knit a little & that is all. I don't think any one could blame me, under the circumstances, not even home folks, although I did disappoint them so much I know. Yet if I had went home, she would have had to hire out all her sewing. She has been better within the last two weeks, than she has, since Nov, I am so glad, brother J[ohn] says he thinks as soon as warm dry weather comes these neuralgeic pains will seacse entirely, I do hope so, oh I never heard of any one suffering so much as she does, or has. You wrote of going to several parties, I have not attended a party this winter, we have had so much rain, & consequently bad roads & besides brother J[ohn] lives between two creeks, the least wet spell causes an overflow, & of course renders travel impossible; I have enjoyed myself at home though reading & cc. It is only during the winter months, that we have these overflows; Have you gardened any yet — I've planted mustard, radishes & peas, all up & growing finely. I have found a new mode of planting Bettie, for early six-week beans (bunch) just dig a trench six inches deep, plant beans & cover the trench every cool night with wide boards or planks, don't take them off until after breakfast & then on again before sundown & by the time it is warm enough to do without the planks, the beans will be at the top of the trench, you can have them a great deal earlier; I intended planting some that way several weeks ago but could not get the seed soon enough, did not plant until last Monday. Oh, I almost forget to tell you what I have been doing this winter, learning to make <u>soft & hard soap</u>, & sour crout — we made a half barrel of the nicest white-head cabbage I ever saw, & it is splendid I assure you, about the soap, sis says, she never saw better — won't I be well posted up in the house-keeping line by the time I go home, oh! I wouldent take a pretty, for what I know already. If ever I <u>do</u> marry I will know how to keep house for my old man right at the start & make coats, pants, & cc for him, too.

  I was so sorry to learn of Ann's death (Ma's Ann) I know Ma will miss her so much, so many little ones there to work for, we could ill afford to lose her; but others have been unfortunate, some more so than us & why not we, as much so, as others. It seems to me Bettie (speaking of dying), that if twas only God's will, I would so much rather go now; than wait 'til I grow old, we see & experience so many trials & troubles in this life — I don't know whether my future will be a happy or unhappy one, probably the latter, I don't know, & if 'twas only "<u>his</u>" will (as I saw) I would go so willingly now, if no, I'll try to be resigned, hoping for the best always. You must write soon Bettie, I should have written much sooner if I could have done so, this is not written well, but I can do no better, as my thumb is very tender yet. Give my love to your mother & Dee [Lasiter] & accept a good share for yourself & beleave me as ever

         Your sincere friend
         Clara Dickson

P.S. my love to all enquiring friends. to Mary Lockett & b____ & Mrs Wiggins Tell Mary she must write to me, I will be so glad of a few lines from her.

C D

Clara Dickson in Ouachita Co. to her sister Cornelia Dickson in Autauga Co.

May 20th, 1858

Dear Sister,

I receaved your (I need not say) most welcome epistle some weeks since, and I was so busy at the time preserving rasberries, (they were so ripe that I could not put it off) that I defered writing longer than I should have done. Yours found us all well, though sis Fannie is not quite well, but mending fast, I was down at sis M[ollie]'s when your letter came — had been staying there nearly two weeks; I suppose Bettie has told you ere this of the birth of her [Sis Mollie] babe (another girl) and that she had named it <u>Sallie</u>, they intend giving it a middle name also, but have not decided what it shall be, brother G[eorge] teases Sis M about it — asks her if <u>Tabitha</u> or <u>Judy</u> ain't just pretty enough for any baby, I would have stayed with her longer, but sis F[annie]'s not being well & having the berries to preserve I had to come home, I intend going down again soon, & stay a week or two so as to divide the time between her and sis F, but will of course stay most of the time here until sis gets perfectly well, but guess who was here several weeks since, but no you couldent guess in a month, I know, why cousin Burl Lanier, in company with a Dr. Harris (a brotherinlaw of Cousin B) and a Mr Gurley, all from Madison Co Ala, they are looking for land, have been over a good portion of Ark, but are not decided yet where they will buy — think they like Clark County better than any they've seen, Cousin says when he gets settled he intends persuading brother J & G to move up near him, but I was thinking all this time that Cousin B. lived in Ark already, and didn't know any better until he came here, I don't know what made me think so but I did, I thought he came out about four or five years since. June 7th. Well Neal I had to stop writing one week, we learned that the smallpox is in Camden & Brother J said I had better defer writing until he goes to town, we've since learned that there is only one case & that is strictly guarded, & so he is going in a day or two. Well about the gardens, ours is doing finely, we have all kinds of vegetables in abundance, irish potatoes especially, they are most of them as large as teacups (beat that if you can) & then so much fine fruit coming on plumbs ripe & apples most ripe had some greenapple pies today for dinner, flavored with essence of lemon,* they were delightful I can tell you, I also preserved some cherries last week, I hope you will get some more

*Essence of lemon is probably lemon extract

from Mrs Caver & preserve for me when I come. I am so fond of them, more than of any other kind of preserve. Sis is still mending, 'tis only in wet weather that she suffers much, complains a good deal of her eyes, has not been able to see well enough to sew yet, consequently I have my hands full nearly all the time. Mit[tie] & George are still going to school to Mr. Marshal, brother G[eorge] thinks him for the best teacher they've had, Mr M told his scholars some time ago that they must study hard & the one that stayed head* two weeks at one time either in spelling or dictionary, he would present them with a prize book, John Boddie won the first one in Dictionary & Mit in spelling, everyone was so surprised, she is the youngest of the class & has been going to school but a short time. All the scholars in school, large & small, are in the class except three or four that have just started to school & more than all, Miss Mit was not content with one book, won another right after, said all the time "she was going to win one for Willis, now she had one herself" & now is studying harder than ever to win one for George, she says; brother J tells him [George] he ought to win one for himself & not let his little sister do it, but G does study as hard as any boy I ever saw, & stayed head nearly two weeks, several times, but towards the last day, he gets excited & confused & misses a word & goes down, Mr M says if G dident have the prize book in mind he wouldent miss, he is so timid, but <u>Mit</u>, you couldent <u>scare</u> into missing, too intent on being ahead of all the rest, so ambitious, Mr M says she is the most intelligent & smartest girl for her age he ever saw, but requires a very <u>strict</u> teacher, more so than any of his other pupils. He sent her books to her today, they are beautiful as well as costly, & just suits her. The teacher requires them to write a little letter once a week to somebody & hand them in Monday morning to be corrected, G's first was to Tom Love, but said he was ashamed to send it, he is now writing one to Uncle Clem & says he intends sending it. They are learning to write very fast.

Tell Grandma she has no idea what an old woman brother G has got to be, when sis M first got sick Julyann stayed in until sometime after breakfast to dress the children, make up the beds & cc, the crops got <u>grassy</u> & so one morning brother G asked sis M what Julyann had to do every morning, sis M told him, he said well, he needed her so much in the field & he could do all she had to do (sis M always done it until she got sick), & so next morning he sent J to the field, & dressed the little ones, combed their heads, made up beds, swept the floor, & cc all but <u>wash up dishes</u>; did you ever & done it all the time until sis M got well, we were right amused at him trying to make up her <u>feather</u> bed, sis M would have to tell him over again every morning, but he learned after a while, he works <u>all</u> the garden both the vegetables & flowers, plants all the seed & manures them besides, hauls the <u>manure</u> himself in a <u>wheelbarrow</u>, in short does all that a woman could do except <u>milk cows</u>, last Monday, he shouldered his hoe & went in the field

*To "stay head" evidently means to lead the class in accomplishment.

to hoeing cotton, he hoed all last week, makes all the hens' nests, chicken-coops, turkey nests & cc in short, I don't know of just such another man as that save brother C. G has a splended Garden, & had more strawberries this year than they knew what to do with, I preserved a good many for sis M when I was down there, also some rasberries, but good night, I am so sleepy I will finish writing tomorrow night, — haven't time just now, in the day time to write, I am so busy making brother J some fine shirts, little G[eorge] has been begging me to make him one <u>pleated bosom</u> shirt, & I intend doing it as soon as I finish his Pa's. I have made him (G) a pretty white linen coat & corded it all around & put some beautiful large pearl-coat buttons on it, I do wish I could send sis C[arrie] the pattern, tis the prettiest one for little boys I ever saw.

June 8 Brother J has the prettiest & finest corn of any body in the country & pretty good cotton — though the bugs & the cut worms have made their appearance in some places. I went to church last evening, had a fine sermon. How is our sunday school coming on, fine I hope. Give my love to dear Mrs Hermann & Ella & Rebecca & all other enquiring friends, we have preaching three times a month at one of our churches (Shady Grove) two Methodist & one baptist preacher, much better preachers than we had last year, especially Mr Thomas, at our other church we have preaching twice a month, well Neal I intended sending you a pretty cap-pattern and dress-sleeve pattern too, but twould make my letter too bungling. I will enclose them in an envelope in a week or so & send them to you — my love to pa & ma, accept a share for yourself, write soon — Tell all the Negroes howdy. Oh, some more about Brother G. he won't let the baby cry a minute, if sis M is too busy to attend to it, he takes it & of all the singing you ever heard, he beats all, he commences on one tune & ends on the <u>eleventh</u> almost in the same breath, of course the baby hushes, & looks amused, don't know what to make of it. I wrote to Ma some time since — but no more, good bye, write soon,

your affectionate sister
Clara

P. S. Our other church is called <u>Canian</u>.

Clara Dickson in Ouachita Co. to her sister Cornelia Dickson in Autauga Co.

Aug. 4th, 1858

Dear Sister

 I receaved your welcome epistle more than a week since; as well as the one you wrote two weeks previous. I dident answer the first as you said you had not rec'd mine, & so I waited until I rec'd the last one; Your letter found all well except sis F[annie], she is not so well as when I wrote, took a backset several weeks ago — caused I think by eating too much sour fruit, is now better, has very little pain, only weak — confined to her bed most of the time. Brother G[eorge] has had a spell of <u>fever</u>, but is nearly well, all the rest well down there. I was down twice last week to see him; we lost one of our neighbors week before last, Mr Dupey (brother G 's nearest neighbor) he was taken the same time brother G was & with the same desease, had a high fever two days & nights, on the third day his fever broke, & he felt so much better, he got up & ate watermelon, took a relapse & died in a few days, left a wife & four children. The weather is <u>very hot</u> & dry, haven't had a rain in three or four weeks, every thing drying up, gardens, crops & all. I don't know what we will do if it doesen't rain in a few days; We have a great many watermelons now the most of them very fine ones though I think we've got the last off the vines if it keeps dry. Well what do you think brother J got for me — a fine extension hoop a Short time ago, my old one kept bending & breaking & I told him, I wanted a larger one & he went & got me a fine $5 hoop, & I can extend it, or make it smaller, just as I please, & it has six hoops in it. I told him I did not want such a fine one, but he said those other kinds with or without a bustle & just two or three hoops, didn't look graceful, every one admires mine so much, all the ladies out here have commenced wearing them this spring, over in Camden, they've been wearing them a long time, mine is the only extension hoop this side of the river, you must tell Grandma that not only I but sis M[ollie] also is wearing hoops, hers has a bustle attached, says she would not be without hers for any thing, don't know how she ever done without one, don't have to wear but one or two skirts besides, says she thinks they are the most useful fashion (as well as healthy one) ever invented, I think so too. I don't know what I should do without mine. I don't wear but one skirt with it; at home I mean. C I have been attending church right often this summer, we have a singing school at one of our churches, brother J & sis F both said they wanted me to go & take the children (George, Mit & Bettie) as they never went any where & hardly knew what church was, & so I have been taking them in the carriage with me; I wish you could have heard Bet, when I first told her I was going to take her to church, she wanted to know what she would wear & cc. I told her, & she would tell every body that came here, "she was going to church (wouldn't call it a meeting house) & was going to wear her <u>speckled dress</u> & white beads & fine shoes & cc, & Dick was going to drive the carriage & cc" she would ask me every hour or two if it wasen't most sunday. I told her if she didn't behave pretty I would never take her any more, she sat still & looked at the preacher all the time, & never offered to get up, every one was praising her for behaving so pretty. I boer'd* hers & Mit's ears a week since, brother J got them some little ear-rings, though Bettie had some very pretty ones that sis M[ollie] gave her when she returned from Ala, they have pretty little coral drops attached to them; but are much too large for her to wear every day, she might break them; running & scampering about & so her Pa got some small ones. sis M got Mit some beautiful little coral beads (red and white) at the same time she got Bettie's earrings, their ears are most well now, & both very anxious to know when they can wear their earrings. I've made M[ittie] a pretty little flounced dress, pink & white, the material summer silk, (another present from sis M[ollie]). I bound the flounces with green ribbon, it looks very pretty indeed. M[ittie] don't care any thing for fine dresses, atall, thinks more of her books & then of playing & romping about; I've forgotten whether I told you about her getting two prize books at school, very fine ones too, for staying head three weeks at a time, I believe, Little Willis Boddie is in Mit's spelling class & she thinks more of him than any body else, he didën't get a prize book all last season & Mit gave him one of her pretty prize books, very generous in her, wasen't it; she is in the large spelling class also at school, where all the pupils spell, 'twas in that class that she stood head so long. Mr Marshall says she is the smartest child for her age that he ever saw but that she will always require a <u>tight</u> teacher. Brother J is going to take that (that sis C[arrie] gave Mit) to Camden the next time he goes & have it done up. Little Florence is just learning to walk, can take five or six steps; she is the tallest child of her age I ever saw, as well as the <u>sweetest,</u> is <u>so</u> good, always laughing & crowing, can say tar-tar & pap- pap she is like grandma I think; fair skin, blue eyes, & <u>white</u> curly hair, I've been thinking here lately, that the expression of her eyes resemble cousin Albert Pickett's. George [Rumph] is the greatest ladies man out, can flatter them more than a little & always waiting on them, has two or three sweethearts (grown ones though, won't have little gals), brother G[eorge] says he will be just another John Rumph when he is grown.

*Boer'd means pierced

August 7th

I had to delay my letter, brother J did not go to town as I expected, I have an opportunity today. I had almost forgot to tell you that brother J's mother is dead, or have you heard it, he rec'd the sad intelligence a few weeks since, she died very happy.

Speaking of books a while ago — I have bought me a beautiful book a religious one; <u>The Heavenly Token,</u> a gift book for Christmas, it is one of the best books I ever saw. I woulden't take $5 for it, the different subjects are, "the Love of Christ," "Christ and Him crucified," "The Wandering of a pilgrim" & "Immanual's Land." I am so sorry I disappointed you about the sleeve pattern. I did think of sending them, & then concluded 'twould be too late for your dress, thought you had made it up, I will send the cap pattern next time. Brother J says if it doesen't rain in a few days he won't make a thing, & that Ma must save all the taters, corn, & cc, that he will have to move out & live on you all another year, will starve if he stays here, sis M[ollie] is getting so fleshy, if she keeps on will be as large as cousin Mary Love, has to alter all her dresses, she is fleshyer than I ever saw her & nursing a baby too, the little thing is as fat as a pig itself, brother G[eorge] thinks it resembles Hattie. sis M[ollie] says she never intends having any more; but will fatten up & be a nice, large, fine-looking <u>old lady</u> some day. Well I don't know what else to write, Give my love to Mrs H[oward], Ella & Rebecca, & Bettie, Tell B _____ I will answer her letter soon, my love to Ma, Pa, sis C[arrie] & all enquiring friends, accept a share for yourself & beleave me as ever,

Your affectionate sister, Clara

P. S. Tell mammy Aunt Phillis died very happy — told Henry she was willing to die & was going home to Heaven, & would be at rest, Henry sends howdy to all the negroes.

C.L.D.

Clara Dickson in Ouachita Co. to her sister Cornelia Dickson in Autauga Co.

Oct. 3, 1858

Dear Sister,

I rec'd your long looked for letter a few days since, & was truly glad to learn that all were well, but am so sorry that I missed that good meeting you all had. I think it would do me more good to attend a good meeting at Ivy Creek than any thing else, was much surprised to hear that Ma had turned Methodist, as well as sis C[arrie]. I'm glad that Ma has; though, as she could not attend her own church, twas so far off. Poor Mr Nunn I am sorry he died without a change. I thought he was so long sick, he would have repented.

Sis F[annie] is no better yet, indeed we do not think she ever will, she has lingered so long, first better then worse, has been that way all summer, gradually growing weaker all the while, her mind is almost entirely gone, can't see any thing or any body as her eyesight is <u>completely</u> gone, you know I wrote you that she complained a good deal of her eyes, it has been nearly six weeks since she became blind, & now within the last week she fails to recognize even our voices, has not ate any thing in weeks except to drink a little sweet-milk, brother J keeps her stimulated with brandy & water all the time, night & day, were it not for that she would sink immediately <u>sometimes</u> as fast as he gives it, she throws it up & then begs for more, sometimes asks for water by itself, & then milk; in half an hour throws it (the milk) up as hard curd as you ever saw, consequently it don't do her any good. Oh, I am so very sorry to have such news to write you, I thought once I woulden't write the <u>worst</u>, but sis M[ollie] & brother G[eorge] said it would be best to do so or, if I diden't 'twould be giving you all reason to hope, & be thinking all the time she was getting well, brother G & sis M come nearly every week to see her; brother G told brother J several weeks ago that he (G.) had give her up months ago & told him he might as well prepare for the worst. He says she may linger all winter & then again may die any day, she is reduced <u>so much</u>, you would hardly recognize her, nothing but skin & bone, & oh, to think how I've hoped; hoped on, & continued trying to hope that she would eventually get better. & every time I've written you this year C, I've always waited (if she was very sick at the time) until she got better & never have even <u>then</u> wrote the worst, hated <u>so</u> much to make you all uneasy. but now, I think as sis M does, 'tis best to tell you <u>all</u>. Brother J looks badly, he is up nearly every night all night long with sis. Sis M rec'd a long letter from sis C[arrie], the same time I got yours; intends answering it soon though she says she hates as bad as I do, to be the writer of such sad news. Her baby is a fine, fat plump & pretty little thing, we all think it resembles Hattie Murley*. All well down there, & the children here, also, except Tommy, he had chills & fever, is getting better though, little Florence is running all about, has cut nearly all her teeth every one thinks she [is] the prettiest of the children, with her white curly head & laughing blue eyes, she has such delicate features & fair complextion. Bettie has been down to sis M's for two weeks, she likes staying there very much & sis M won't let her come home as long as she likes to stay. Do you <u>ever</u> have rain, we have not had any in two months, cotton looks badly, but turning out a little better than the farmers expected, but so dry, the ground looks like ashes. Cousin Tarrant Howard left a week ago for home, Cousin Mary Rumph* is living with brother J she is very lively, told me to send her love to you & Ma, sis F asked about you all frequently within the last few weeks, imagines she is living at Gaston's Landing, & wants to know why you all don't come to see her; then next day thinks she is on a boat, going to N Orleans, & that you all (grandma, Uncle C[lem] & all) are with her, & then she wants to know why you all got off the boat without telling her good-bye, she was so distressed one day; thought grandma & Uncle C had got off & gone home without telling her good bye, I had to tell her (just to pacify her) that grandma had just gone home to rest a while & would be back presently, she seemed satisfied then; asked brother J last week to send for Mother, he told her well; yesterday asked me if Ma haden't come yet. I told her no she haden't time to get here yet, & she seemed satisfied then, we have to let on as though she was

* Hattie Gildersleeve Murley is another of Sis Mollie's sisters.

*Cousin Mary Rumph is Dr. John Rumph's sister.

right, or it frets her & wories her so much. Oh Neal I sometimes think, what if I had returned home last winter, & knew what I do now; I never would have forgive myself for leaving her, No one to sew for the children or brother J or keep house & take care of everything & last, (though by far) not least wait on her & relieve her when I could. Oh, what would I give for that privilege now, (that of relieving her of her pain) but I can do no good now except give her water or a little brandy & water whenever she asks for it, so that brother J can rest & sleep a little in the day-time (he is up all night) I haven't left home in I don't know when, but enough, I could hardly guide my pen to write this much were it not for the faith, the confidence I have in God's promises, I would be miserable, but I know, & feel that <u>he doeth all things for the best</u>, we must try to submit to his will, hard though it seems to us. Give my love to Ma, Pa, sis C[arrie] & all enquiring friends, accept a share for yourself & beleave me as ever,

your affectionate sister
Clara Dickson

I rec'd Tom Love's letter & will answer soon

Clara Dickson in Ouachita Co. to her sister Cornelia Dickson in Autauga Co.

Nov. 20th, 1858

Dear Sister,

I receaved your welcome letter more than a week since; it found all well, I was sorry to hear that Ma was so unwell & that Pa's health was so feeble, I've been uneasy ever since & will be so glad when sis M[ollie] receaves an answer from sis C[arrie] which I hope will be soon as I shall continue to be uneasy until she does. Poor Cousin W[illiam] I had expected (from what you had written previously) to hear of his death, do hope he is better off — 'Tis so hard to suffer <u>so</u> much & so long, 'twas just a week to a day between poor dear Sis F[annie]'s & his death; Sis M[ollie] wrote to Sis C[arrie] soon after sis F died, she must have rec'd it soon after you wrote to me. Oh Neal little did I think last winter when I concluded to remain with & nurse her that it would be thus, oh I thought (as we all did) of nothing else but that she would entirely recover by warm weather & that I should return home leaving her restored to health; but oh me, how little can we fathom the future, to think instead, that I have seen her laid in the cold & silent grave, but God's will must be done, he knows best, though 'tis hard for us to feel so, when trials come upon us, all that we can do is submit obediently, or try to do so, but is it not hard though to submit, sometimes, even when we feel that <u>His hand</u> inflicts the blow. She lingered <u>so long</u> & suffered so much, no one could realize how much, (as she used to say so often to me, " Clara, you don't know how much I suffer, you <u>can't begin to know</u>, no one but <u>God alone</u>, knows how <u>very</u> much I suffer, yes he <u>only</u>) & would repeat it so often to all of us; said "she knew we were doing all we could to ease her pains & we thought we could see how she suffered but God in Heaven only <u>knew</u> the extent of her sufferings," I never heard of anyone enduring such excrutiating misery <u>so</u> long, it seems that the strongest constitution in the world would sink under it in a short time, but she lingered nearly a year, just to think of it, though towards the last her pains were not near so severe, she died very easy, just like an infant falling asleep, sis M wrote you where she was buried, brother J placed a large beautiful tombstone at her grave, at the top of the stone is a half wreath of roses & rosebuds with leaves, two roses & five buds, the two roses — her & brother J & five buds, her five little children, the stem of one of the roses is broken off, to show that she is gone, underneath her age & the time she died, brother J did not know any verses that suited him, to have engraved on it & beneath her age he had written

Heaven and I, had part in this fair woman;
Now Heaven hath all.
And all the better it is for her;
My part I could not keep from death
But Heaven keep his part in eternal life.

Oh! let us hope Nealy that she is where there is no pain & suffering. I will return home with brother John this winter, he says he cannot get off before the last of Jan, so you may look for us about the first or second week in Feb, it seems a long time though to me, I do want to see you all so bad, wish that I could be with you Christmas; I thought this time last year that I would spend last Christmas with you, but Providence ordained otherwise; what would sis Fanny & all the children have done this year if I had returned last winter; she has so often told me this year, "Clara, I don't know what in the world I should have done without you; no one to sew for the children, & keep house for me but you, & more than, so much company for me, too; how could we have got along without you." Oh, Neal, I feel <u>so</u> very thankful that I remained, much as I disappointed you all, & I know you feel so too, I never could have forgive myself had I returned home.

We have had several deaths in the neighborhood this fall; among them was that of Mr Warren Stone, (brother of Mr Wm Stone's). We've had a spell of wet weather for the last week, had a slight fall of snow last Friday night. I am at sis Molly's, been staying nearly a week, intend staying another week with her, it seems so lonely up at Brother John's now, I feel bad all the time while there. Sis M has the sweetest & prettiest, as well as the best baby I ever saw, since it turned so cold, she has a candle box which she places near the fire to put the baby in, so that it keeps warm, & just give it a bunch of keys or something of the kind & 'twill play all the time, never cries only when very hungry, she seems to know her Pa, (he says so any how) & every time he comes into the room, will turn her little head & laughs & seems like she wants to go to him. The two oldest boys are still going to school, & little George & Mittie also; sis M sends her love to all of you, Ma, Sis C[arrie], grandma, & all. She is looking for a letter from sis C, or will be looking in a week or so, do hope she will write soon, I am so anxious to hear from home again. Give my love to Ma & Pa, sis C & all enquiring friends accept a share for yourself, Hoping this may find all well I am,

      Your affectionate sister
      Clara

P. S. Write soon*

*Note: Fannie died Oct. 8, 1858. She was 35 years old and left five children: George, Coralie(Mittie), Bettie, Thomas, and Florence.

Clara Dunlap in Ouachita Co. to her mother Clarissa Dickson in Autauga Co.

Jan. 20, 1859

Dear Mother,

  I received your letter a day or two since, & was very glad to hear that all are well, but am surprised & sorry too that you were dissatisfied because I remained up here at brother John's instead of going to brother George's, it would have seemed like deserting him in the very time he needed me most — after his being so kind & taking such good care of me since I came here (more than any one else ever done) to have left him & the children when they needed my attention all the time, & besides, there was no one to keep house & take care of every thing (you know cousin Mary Rumph is no more than a child) & more than [that] the little ones had no one to sew for them but me alone nor havent had for more than a year; I think it would have seemed very ungrateful indeed on my part to have not stayed here & taken care of & nursed them when sick, & besides all that, brother G dident have room for us all either (only two rooms) he is building shed rooms now to his house for cousin M Rumph & the children when they go down there, would have had them completed by Christmas, but could not get plank for the floors & doors & cc the mill where they engaged for it got out of fix & it was some time before they could get the lumber, brother G thinks they will have them completed in a week or so, just the time that brother J wishes to start for Ala, he could have started two weeks ago but had all his bussiness to fix up & his cotton to gin & ship off (made about 70 bales) & besides had all Dr Wood's bussiness to arrange so as to be ready to settle with him when he went on to Ala. Dear Ma I know you will be very much surprised at what I am about to tell you; I am to be married this evening to Mr John Dunlap a young man that resides in our immediate neighborhood. I know you will be astonished as I've <u>never</u> written any thing about it, but I did not know it myself until this last Christmas (after I had written to Nealy & Bettie) he came over & addressed me, told me how much he loved me & had loved me a long, long time (but he was so very bashful & diffident you see) that he was almost afraid to name it then, but found out that I was getting ready to leave for Ala, he thought he would make a trial any how even if he should be rejected, yet (as he said) he couldent bear to see me leave, if any effort on his part could induce me to remain. I on my part had loved him nearly ever since I came to Ark but never revealed it to any body atall. I told him I returned his love & was willing to marry him & remain here in Ark, provided brother G & brother J was willing, that I had been placed here under their care, & he would have to consult them about it, before I could give him a definite answer; he consulted them both & both gave their consent, indeed brother J has known him intimately ever since he came to the country & never knew aught against him & says that he knew of no young man in the whole of his acquaintance that he would rather commit my happiness too than him, & he is well off to has a fine plantation & works six or eight good hands, clear of debt & all, he is real energetic persevering hard working farmer. As for brother G, he says the same that brother J does, though he has not known him quite as long, yet he says he is well enough acquainted with him to feel satisfied that he will make me a good husband & that I could hardly ever do as well again (not in Ala certain) & he has told me that he beleaves he is just the sort of man to suit you, in every particular & thinks you would feel better satisfied to know I am so well settled for life; & you know Ma that brother G is not a man to judge hastily of any one, that is he is hardly ever wrong in his judgment; he wouldent say so much in his (Mr Dunlap's) favor unless he really felt it, but brother J who will deliver this to you will tell you all the particulars about it, but oh I will feel very bad indeed if you & Pa disapprove of the step I am about to take; when you find out too that I've done so well, far better than most of the young girls do; that have neither money or good looks or accomplishments to set them off, brother J says he knows the reason Mr D fell in love with me; he always visits here a good deal (& did before I came) & seeing me stay at home so close, nursing sis F[annie] all the time, taking care of the children & every thing about the house & then doing all the sewing & cc, he of course thought I would make a good wife, if that wasent it, I dont know what else it <u>could have been,</u> as I have <u>nothing else in</u> the world to recommend me. Sis Molly came up yesterday morning & we have been baking cakes & so forth & fixing up the house & cc, we wont have a large wedding, only sis M & brother G & Mr. D's relatives. I asked him the other week if he couldent take me on when brother J went & spend a few weeks with you all, as I know you & Pa were so anxious to see me & I as much as to see you, & that you & Pa would be so disappointed if I dident go; after writing that I would come. He said if it were possible for him to leave his bussiness he would do so with pleasure, but as he had just moved on his place & had every thing to fix up (twas very much out of repair & he had just moved there a few months ago) & he said 'twould cause him to sacrefice a great deal to leave just at the time he wishes to make arrangements to make another crop, I told him if that was the case I could not reasonably insist on it, as I did not wish him to [do] any thing contrary to his interests. he says he will carry me on to see you late next fall, if nothing happens to prevent. Hoping this may find all well, I close, write again Ma & tell Nealy she must write too, & also Bettie. Give my love to sis C[arrie], Nealy, Pa, & accept a share for yourself.

Your affectionate daughter,
Clara Dunlap

Clara Dickson Dunlap, wife of John Franklin Dunlap (1836-1913) Daughter of S.H.N. Dickson and Clarissa Dickson

Jan 22 1859

Well Ma I am at home, or rather my husband's home home (it seems strange to call it mine <u>so soon</u>). I came over yesterday evening, but I have not told you what place it is. It is the one Dr Wm Wood used to live in his lifetime, Tis considered one of the most valuable in the country. There is a fine fruit orchard, near the house, & some shrubbery & bulbous in the yard & garden & I can get as many more as I wish at either brother J's or G's Ma, I would be so glad if you would pack up my bed quilts & some blankets & cc in a trunk & send them to [me] by brother J, I need them so much, & it makes me feel rather cheap to come here with nothing but my clothes, & I would be very glad indeed if you could spare me a feather bed & mattress, & some sheets, pillow cases, & such things if you have more than you need, & Ma be sure & tell Neal to put up my pretty worked basket, that I made when I went to Mrs Grey's school & <u>all</u> my books, both school books & others, also my drawings. Brother John will bring them back with him. Write soon, dear Ma. Give my love to Pa, Nealy, & all enquiring friends. Sis Molly sends her best love to you & all the family, says she will answer sis Carry's letter soon, my love to you & do Ma write soon.

Your affectionate daughter,
Clara Dunlap

*Note: This postscript is started at the top of page 1 and runs down along the left side of the page:

*P. S. Ma, you always said if I ever married any body that was <u>any account</u>, that you would give me that pretty star bed quilt that you made several years ago, & as brother J can testify to <u>that</u>, you must send it with my quilts, & if you could send me some money to buy little things that I need to keep house with (without going into debt for it) please send it or tell

brother J to get me some silver spoons in Mobile with it but you must not go in debt for it

Clara Dickson Dunlap in Ouachita Co. to her sister Cornelia Dickson in Autauga Co.

Jan 27th, 1859

John Franklin Dunlap in 1859 (1828-1898)
Photos courtesy of Sue Martin Russell

Dear Sister,

I now seat myself to answer your last letter, though I really feel at a loss to know <u>what to write</u>, as I just wrote a long letter to Ma, which I sent by brother John. I wrote a good deal in it concerning my marriage & cc & so on, but oh, don't it seem strange Nealy, to speak of my being married, & that I am <u>living</u> in <u>Ark</u> instead of Ala, it does seem <u>so</u> strange to me — I can hardly realize the fact — and yet tis so; I moved home the day after & have been here now nearly a week; I intend making a pretty home of it too, by Spring, or summer rather; Mr Dunlap (or John as I've learned to call him) says I may have as much shrubbery & flowers as I wish, he has been setting out some in the yard already & we are going down to sis M[ollie]'s soon & get some roses & cc. He is having me a garden paled* in too, so I can raise a heap of nice vegetables. I told Ma in my letter whose place this used to be (Dr Wm Woods), it is just half way between brother G's & brother J's right on the road as you go from one place to the other, & tis about three hundred yards from the public road, if the trees were only cleared up I could see every thing passing — but brother John will tell you all the particulars, & he will see you a week or more before you see this; he left last Monday night or Tues morning. I am so sorry I disappointed you all Nealy, it made me feel very bad, but then I loved <u>him too hard</u> to leave him & go back, as bad as I wanted to see you. He has told me since we married that he would have addressed me long ago — but thought that sis F[anny] needed me there, & the children, too, & he concluded to defer it, until he found out that I was getting ready to return home & he never lost a moments time before he addressed me; he was right about waiting, as nothing could have induced me to have left poor sister F while she lived, & she needed me all the while too. I wouldent have left her even for a week, while she lived. I sent him over to Cam[den] soon after we married to have his photograph taken so you could see what sort of an <u>old man</u> I have. Nealy, brother John promised me if it were possible for him to do so, that he would go by

*To pale an area is to fence it in by placing wooden planks very close together to keep the rabbits and chickens out of the garden.

Autauga, in returning home from Carolina & bring me my bed quilts, books, drawings, & cc, what-ever else Ma pleases to send me. I need a bed & bed clothes worse than any thing else, you could put the quilt & other little things in a trunk (don't forget my little paper basket that I worked under Mrs Gray). I left it in a small bandbox, you can set the bandbox in the trunk with my books & the drawings (those that I drew under Mrs Conway). Ma always said N that if I married any body that was <u>any account</u> that she would give me that pretty quilt that she made several years ago; as brother J can testify as to my marrying somebody that <u>is</u> some account, tell her she must send it now to me, I haven't but two or three & I need it any way. Tell Ma I will keep it nice & always take care of it, & tell her please mam send me those stockings that she knit last year for me, I need them, too, those that I brought out with me, have nearly all worn out. You must write soon Nealy & tell me all the news; I will find a good deal more to write about by the time I rec your next. I feel so odd & strange now; that I cant think hardly what <u>to</u> write, give my love to Betty & Mrs L[asiter] tell B I shall look for an answer now to my last. My love to Mrs H[oward], Rebecca, & all enquiring friends, to sis C[arrie] & all. Also to Ma & Pa accept a good share for yourself & beleave me as ever,

       Your affectionate sister,
       Clara Dunlap

Clara Dickson Dunlap in Ouachita Co. to her mother Clarissa Dickson in Autauga Co.

                  April 6th, 1859

  Dear Ma,

  Your most welcome letter came to hand some time since, & I've been <u>so</u> busy attending to my chickens, planting & working in the garden, that I could not well write sooner. I was as sorry as you all were at the disappointment I gave you, & would that I could have done otherwise, that is, returned home & remained until summer or fall, but I felt almost certain that Pa would never give his consent for me to leave him for good & come so far, too. I almost know I should have had to <u>run away</u> & married or not atall, & I loved John <u>too well</u> to give him up, I thought, though, that you would be willing if you knew him to be every way worthy of me he still says I shall go on in the fall or winter & remain several months with you. Brother J's overseer recd a letter from him last week, dated 4 Mar, from Carolina, he wrote as though he expected to return through Ala & remain two or three weeks, & that he would not be home before the first of May, I am so glad, as I now hope I can get my bed & bed- quilts & cc. Ma, John read your letter & (he would do it — said he was afraid you had sent him a good scolding, & that was the reason I wouluen't let him read it, & so I shewed it to him). he laughed at me for sending to you for <u>stockings</u>, says I ought to be ashamed. I told him you had always done it, as you had rather knit than do most any thing else, I told him I was going to get you to knit some for him by next winter but he said I must not do it, 'twas imposing on you too much, I then told him I was only joking; & that I intend commencing knitting him some next week (though to own the truth I had rather do most any other kind of work).

But I must tell you about my garden, I have a very forward garden I think, considering how late a start we had, have had nice mustard salad [?], radishes, & lettuce for several weeks, have 4 squares set out in collards, & would have had a square in cabbage too but our first planting did not come up, I think I will have some though in a week or two, have squashes & cucumbers up & growing fine until the last two or three days, the weather is most too cool, indeed we had a pretty smart frost last night & the night before, had to cover them up both nights, the irish potatoes are nipped badly, but about my peas, I have pea vines a knee high, but haven't bloomed yet. On the whole I have the most forward garden of any one in this neighborhood, though as you all have much earlier seasons than we do, I know you are ahead of me, I'll soon have a hundred chickens hatched out, the largest about the size of partriges, John is anxious for me to raise geese (for the feathers) & we have several ponds close by, I think they can be raised easily. I am afraid all the fruit will be killed, half is gone already, & two or three more frosts will slay the ballance. I hope you all have been more fortunate. I have not been down to sis M[ollie]'s in several weeks, when I was last there, her garden looked beautiful, so many, many pretty hyacinths, both pink & blue (have only one or two white ones) & so many pretty roses budding to bloom & some few in bloom, the children have started to school again (Bettie & little Gilder, included) it is such a relief to sis M too, (I am glad on her account); for them to be gone in the day time, gives her much more leisure time, I heard from there this morning, all well, brother J wrote to brother G to tell sis M not to let little Florence forget Papa. & sis M had learned her, every time any one askes her where Pa is, the little thing will run into sis M's spare-bedroom (where his portrait is hanging) & point up to it & laugh & clap her little hands, seems glad to see it. Sis M thinks her [little Florence] the very image of grandma; I think so to, has the prettiest hair of any child I ever saw, looks like fine white silk; I have been over to brother J's place once or twice since he left but oh every thing looked so changed, so lonely & desolate. I could not remain in one place no time it made me feel so sad, I was glad to start home. We haven't a sunday school yet, the roads have been too bad, we had one last year & I think will have one this year, as soon as the weather becomes settled. I live a mile from the church, close enough to walk, from home. I have just recd Nealy's letter, I was so glad to get it & hear all were well. Tell sis Carry to go ahead; she has almost made out her fortune-teller's dozen, only three more now, & she will be through & that she must keep her courage up.* Tell her my old man (I've no doubt) is the very sort of a one I wanted when I was a girl, plenty of cattle, all kinds, hogs, cows, sheep & cc & so on. I can grunt now at my pleasure. You must write soon Ma, tell Neal, I will answer her letter soon, give my love to her, sis Carry, Pa, & all enquiring friends. John says he intends reading this letter, but I don't intend he shall, I don't want him to see the latter part, he sends his best respects to you, & Pa, & Nealie. Accept my love, From

*Sis Carrie Boddie Love did have the dozen children, just as the "fortune teller" had told her.

Your affectionate daughter,
Clara Dunlap

Clara Dickson Dunlap in Ouachita Co. to her sister Cornelia Dickson in Autauga Co.

April 20th, 1859

Dear Sister,

Your most welcome came to hand some weeks since, but I was answering Ma's at the time & so defered writing, thinking to that as brother John would be very uneasy about his little ones, & was so rejoiced to find them well; & they were so glad to see Papa. But oh wasent I disappointed, & so badly too. I fully expected (from what he wrote to brother G while in Carolina that he would return through Ala) that he would of course go through by Ma's & bring my things with him, & then to think that he came right by Gaston's Landing & never stopped atall, he promised he would do it (go by Ma's) & he knew I needed them too, I can't help it, but I do think right hard of him, & I was so glad (until he came) to think I would have a nice bed & bed clothes, & some money to furnish my room; for I can't help, Nealy & no girl coulden't, feeling bad at not having a thing to call mine when I am home, but my clothes; 'tis too bad. But he told me as soon as he came that hearing, while in C[arolina], that his children were sick, or had been, he became so very uneasy about them that he hurried through Ala & on home as fast as he could, & besides he said, he thought I would be more apt to get to Ala next fall or winter; than if he had brought them all now; & well, maybe, tis all for the best after all, but I would much rather have had them now, I could have fixed up my house so much nicer. We have beautiful weather now, after so much rain, & oh what a nice garden I have, all my vegetables up & growing nicely; with the exception of the English peas, I have the most forward garden of any one in the neighborhood; & no body to work it but my old man, I help him, but he does the hardest part of it; you don't know how good he is about planting all my little seeds & tending the garden generally, he has planted me a large watermelon patch too, out in the field. I am so glad that he is fond of a garden & vegetables; but that reminds me Nealy of what brother G requested me to tell you for him; when I was down there the other day, he told me when I wrote to request you when you next went to grandma's to go in the garden & stick a stick by some of the prettiest tulips (those that are striped & double & diferent colors (except red & yellow) he has plenty of them but no others) & next fall you can dig down by them & get a root or two of each one; small ones, no larger than very small peas, & send them in a letter, which you can do very easily, about October I think is the time. Don't forget it, Nealy please, he is so anxious to get a variety. His garden looks beautiful now, prettier than it ever was he says, his roses & bulbus roots are growing so large, they show more. Mr Marshall, (the teacher) (who by the by was married a month or so since to a widow too; the widows can marry much faster out here than the girls Nealy, I don't know what you would do, out here, somehow they understand setting their caps better than the girls, there has been four or five widows married this last winter). Mr Marshall has a large school some four or five young ladies are attending his school this sesson, brother G & J's children are learning very fast indeed. Mit[tie] & G[eorge] shewed me their compositions (their first attempt) when I was down there last. I thought them extremely well done for such new beginners. Altogether I think their teacher the best, for little children especially; I ever saw. Nearly all the fruit was killed last week by frost, & oh I am so sorry, we had one or two light frosts the first of the month, but it didn't kill much of the fruit, but last week it played the mischief, I had to cover up all my beans, squashes, & cucumbers vines. I do hope you all were more fortunate; & speaking of fruit reminds me N, of how I was anticipating late in last fall, enjoying myself eating the fruit this year, you & I & how we would go up to Mrs Caver's & get so many cherries, & then there would be English grapes, nice apples & cc, all of which we don't have out here, I believe brother J has the only apple trees, & there are a few cherry trees (two or three) in the neighborhood, & no grapes, except the white muscadine. I haven't had a mess of cherries or grapes either since I left Ala. I do wish it was so that John & I could be with you all from May 'til July anyhow ; instead of waiting til fall or winter. N, you must go up to Mrs Caver's in cherry- time & get some more to preserve maybe I can get to eat some that way; tell Ella Howard to write first, & I'll be certain to answer her letter — I don't know her post-office yet, Give my love to Mrs Howard & Rebecca, & Mrs. L[asiter] & Bettie. Tell B she has never written yet. Give my love to Ma, Pa, sis C[arrie], Irene, & all enquiring friends & accept a good share for yourself, write soon Nealy & tell me all the news — about our sunday school & all,all everything. John sends his best respects to you & says tell you all the harm he can wish you is that you may soon marry a great fat man like him, & move out & live close by us, but he told me that laughingly, & didn't mean for me to write it down, he told me not to do it when he started off, but I told him yes I would. I know 'twill please him when I tell him I have written it. But from what brother J tells me, I would not be surprised if, when you did marry you would get just the <u>reverse</u> of an old man — one of old Hager's <u>slim shankling</u> fellows, you can guess who I mean if you try he don't live very far from the post office, rather <u>up</u> than <u>down</u> the road. Be certain when - or if - it does come off to send me a piece of the cake as I sent you some of mine, or what would be better still, wait until fall & I'll be there to assist & cc. 'til then adieu, but be certain to write soon,

Your affectionate sister,
Clara

P.S. I have written on for Peterson's Magazine for this year, I expect 'twill be very interesting, does Ma take the Lady's Book* yet? C.D.

* The "Lady's Book" undoubtedly refers to *Lady Godey's Book*, the leading popular fashion and etiquette publication of the day.

Dr. Charles M. Howard in Autauga Co. to Cornelia Dickson, also in Autauga Co., concerning the health of her father.

May 4, 1859

Miss Cornelia,

Your father was doing so well today that I scarcely think it necessary to visit him tonight. Should he suffer much pain I would give him a full dose of Elix. opium and repeat it, in 3 hours, if necessary to relieve him should there be any thing the matter, requiring attention, by letting me know I would gladly come but think he is at times disposed to attach too much importance to symptoms not at all serious. Apply mustard to the seat of pain if opium does not relieve I will come over in the morning.

Truly,
Chas. M. Howard

Clara Dunlap in Ouachita Co. to her mother Clarissa Dickson in Autauga Co.

June 10th, 1859

Dear Ma,

I receaved your most welcome a week or two since, I intended answering it immediately but have been so busy cutting out, & making up negro clothing; I am nearly through & thought I would write any-how, as brother John intends starting for Carolina in a few days, & will probably go through Ala, if so I will send this by him, I will know for certain before he leaves; I heard from Sis Molly day before yesterday; all were well, her little baby is just beginning to walk, & is certainly the prettiest & most interesting child I ever saw, sis M & brother G spent the day with me last Tuesday week, brother G went over John's crop with him, he said he (John) had the cleanest crop of any one he had seen, & the most forward & prettiest cotton, told him to come down & help <u>him</u> out, J[ohn] said he must keep his hands home to watch the grass & <u>keep</u> it out. I was down to see sis M several weeks ago & stayed a week, & assisted her about her sewing, she told John she thought it very kind in him to let me stay so long — he stayed at home by himself, too all the week. The children are still going to school & learning fast indeed; I have a very fine garden now, plenty of vegetables of all kinds, all the neighbors have good gardens this year I beleave. We've had such good seasons on them so far; we begin to need a little rain now though, on the corn especially; & to set out potatoes. I do hope you will have good seasons this year, it seems so hard to work all the year & then make nothing, & then have every thing to buy, too; it ain't like it is out here where one can raise all the meat & corn, & with only half seasons, a plenty of corn & wheat. We will have no fruit scarcely this year nearly all killed. I am so glad you are saving me so many nice little fruit trees; John says he will take a heap of pains with them, he is so fond of fruit, especially apples and pears. Out of all those Dr Wood brought out here only one or two lived & only one of them bear. I am so sorry to hear that Pa's health is so bad, it seems like he has suffered so long with that disease, & then to get so feeble & helpless. I have seen brother John since I commenced writing, he will go through Ala, but thinks he will be in too much of a hurry to stop*, I will send this by him though. I am looking for a letter from Nealy every day; I recd one from Bettie several weeks since, & will answer it soon. You must write again soon Ma & tell me all about the neighbors & all the news, Give my love to sis C[arrie] & family & all enquiring friends, to Pa & Nealy too, tell N I will tell her who that <u>boy</u> is when I write to her. My love to Mrs. Howard & Ella, accept a good share for yourself & beleave me as ever

      your affectionate daughter,
      Clara Dunlap
 P.S. John sends his best respects to you & Pa, & Nealy

*Brother John did stop in Alabama long enough to marry Sallie Gildersleeve, sister of Sis Mollie.

Clara Dunlap in Ouachita Co. to her mother Clarissa Dickson in Autauga Co.

Sept 16th, 1859

Dear Ma,

It has been some time since I recd your welcome letter. I would have answered it long since, but sickness prevented me — I have recovered from it but I'm not [as] strong as I was, I intended answering it in a week or so; as soon as I got entirely well — but brother John was over yesterday, he said sis M[ollie] had just recd a letter from Sis Carry, & that you were very uneasy about me — not having heard from me in some time, & so I concluded to write at once; He had just written to brother Add (so he told me) & told him all about my being sick cc. I have been very ill indeed, I was taken with bilious fever, which lasted a week, though in the meantime John called in a physician, but before he could break the fever, (which was very high), I had miscarried, Dr Hattox said it was a six month child with little chance that it could live, he said he hardly thought it could live more than a few days, but it might live several weeks but then would finally go off in spasms, it did live just four weeks & one day & then took hard spasms & died, day before yesterday (just the day after brother J wrote to brother Add), poor little thing, it suffered so much, I could hardly bear to look at it while the spasms were on it, (it had eight), but 'twas soon over, & I know it is better off now, I couldn't give a drop of milk for it & had to have it fed with cow's milk, diluted with warm water & sweetened, it just weighed 1 pound & a half when it was born every one said it was the smallest baby they ever saw, to be alive, it <u>was</u> really a curiosity, though it came near costing me my life twice the Dr thought I would die, first, when I was about to miscarry, & then several days after I took child-bed fever (he called it). John immediate[ly] sent for the Dr & as soon as he came he put a large blister of spanish flies* to my stomach & then a red pepper poultice on my bowels, & then gave me a little morphine to quiet my system, I soon went to sleep — when I awoke, I was entirely clear of fever & pain also, the blister had drawn as well, had just the effect he wished it to have & he came though, & continued giving me medicine for several days after; until I was entirely out of danger; The only drawback I had was, I was right badly salivated & couldn't eat any thing but a little gruel or soup for nearly two weeks, as soon as I could eat something, I began to mend right away & so fast that in less than a week, I could [sit up] & am now well but not as strong as I was, I hardly could expect it yet awhile, but about Dr Hattox, many people do beleave him to be one of the best physicians, he attended my case so closely & well, & expressed so much feeling for me when I was suffering so. Brother John couldn't come to see me atall while I was so ill — he was as low as I was all the time.

The neighbours were <u>very</u> kind though, they would come & sit up with

*Spanish flies, also called cantharides, is a preparation of powdered blister beetles, used medicinally as a skin irritant, diuretic, and aphrodisiac.

& nurse me all the while, one of them especially, Mrs. Broughton (one of my nearest neighbors) she is a Georgian, & only moved out here last winter, Ma she came day & night, while I was so bad off, & nursed & waited on me like a sister — & even after I got better, would come every day or two to see me & to wash & dress the little baby for me. I told her she was all the <u>grandma</u> it had out here, & oh she would bring me such nice little things to eat & the best light bread I most ever ate. I told her I hated to put her to so much trouble but she said 'twas none atall, but a pleasure, & that she could not think it otherwise, to visit her neighbours & do all she could for them while they were sick. I know I shall never forget her kindness.

Sis M[ollie] & Mrs. Gildersleeve was here last week, all was well at home, sis M told me I hardly looked like I had been sick atall, that is to look at my face. The children will all start to school again shortly, to the same teacher. Brother J[ohn] told me his children had all been sick but were well again. Every one is <u>busy</u> picking cotton now, John is badly behind-hand with his though; he hoped to [build a smoke]house & this summer after his crop was laid by, & then my getting sick hindered him a good deal more, his cotton commenced opening so fast he put all hands to picking last week &, hired help, or rather he hired a screw - builder* & then hired hands to put under him. Oh Ma John was <u>so kind & good</u> to me when I was sick; I can't begin to tell you how <u>good</u> he was, & then he wouleln't let me trouble a bit about the baby but would attend to having it fed himself, all night as well as day, had a negro woman to sleep in the house every night & he saw that she took good care of it, he said he was afraid for me to see to it for fear I would get worried & maybe take relapse.

*"Screw" was a word used for a carpenter.

Sept. 18

John came in day before yesterday, while I was writing & said he was going over to his brother's & as he was going right by brother John's, I was so anxious to get out once more, that I ventured to go with him that far, but it never hurt me. I came home late yesterday evening. All were well, but brother J, he had a light fever when I left. He has had sis F[annie]'s grave paled in, & nicely covered since I was there before. I do wish you could see little Florence, she is the prettiest of all the children now I think, her health has become good, & she has fattened up so much since I saw her before — has very fair beautiful skin, & such bright blue eyes, & fine silky hair. Sally* curls it every morning, it makes her look like a little wax doll, she is just beginning to talk — calls me Aunt Terra (Clara) Dunap; (can't say Dunlap) Well Ma I've written everything I can think [of], all the news I mean. You must write <u>soon</u>. I received a letter [from Bettie] while I was sick & one from sis C[arrie] just before; I will answer them back soon. Give my love to Pa, C[ornelia], sis Carry & all enquiring friends; accept a good share for yourself, & beleave me as ever

*"Sally" refers to Sally Gildersleeve Rumph, brother John's second wife.

     Your affectionate daughter
     C Dunlap

Clara Dunlap in Ouachita Co. to her sister Cornelia Dickson in Autauga Co.

Sept. 28th 1859

Dear Sister,

I now sit down to answer your welcome letter. I know you will say (it couldn't have been very welcome or you would have answered it ere now) but my letter to Ma will explain it all, my reason for not writing, I mean. I wrote to her several weeks ago, but somehow, no one would pass going to Camden (just because I was anxious to send it, I believe) so I never sent it until last Friday. I will have better luck with this one though, as 'tis court week & John is on the jury & has to attend every day. I've got right well again, & if I keep on mending I'll be so fat by next winter that you won't know me. Tell Mammy, I almost live on fat midling & greens*. It agrees with me better than anything else. John laughs & tells me he reckons I will turn to midling after a while.

I've been to see Sally since I got well. I tell you, Cornelia, she is a No. 1 housekeeper — takes so much pains with the children. She came by Sunday, going down to Sis Mollie's. Little Florence was with her, & Oh, she did look so sweet with her hair all curled ringlets all around her head. I've not been down to Sis Mollie's yet. John has been so busy.

Mrs. Gildersleeve is still out here. She likes it very well, I beleave, but would be better pleased if the people could visit more, but she came during a busy time. At least, it has been more so than usual this summer. She intends going home sometime this fall. I've been trying to persuade John to let me return with her & he could come on in December; but he says 'twill be too long for me to be gone from him, he couldn't spare me so long. He told me Monday that he wanted me to "over-see" for him this week, & he would give me half his wages. 'Twould be $2 a day, he is on the jury & besides he is a witness on some case over there & gets $4 a day this week & probably the next. He said though, I had to have so many bales of cotton out or forfeit my wages (six bales, I beleave). I knew the Negroes could pick it, & have been doing it for the past three weeks; so I told him I was not afraid of that — but as bad luck would have it, it has rained every evening this week a little, & today rained all day. But, I mean tonight when he comes I will tell him he must pay me anyhow as I couldn't help its raining. I've kept the Negroes busy anyhow, having wood & light-wood hauled, the sheep sheared, & all under the new gin house cleaned out & cc — such work as I knew he was saving for a rainy day.

Nealy, you know in your letter (in speaking of Matt Taylor's marrying) you said "of all things you thought a Methodist Preacher the last chance, & next to him, a Dr. or a widow with children." When I showed that to brother John, it plagued him right bad, for you see, you hit him there. He

*Middling is salt or smoked pork and greens has to be mustard, turnip or collard greens.

said "Tell Nealy, when you write that I bet that when she marries, she will marry, if not a preacher, a right down exhorter, & he will certainly be a widower & a house full of children, too." Brother George says that Sally used to say she would be an old maid before she would marry an old bachelor, a Dr., or a widower with children. He teases Sally now about it.

Ma spoke in her letter about making another pretty bed-quilt. Tell her to please, Mam, make me one. I have none except what John had when we married, & I have only three or four at home, you know. I would rather she would make me a thick comfort; twould be so much warmer than a quilt.

Cornelia, please tell the Negroes to save me some chestnuts. I haven't eaten one since I left Alabama. Tell Harriet, I never made any niggergees, no such thing. I only made sack-waist dresses (I suppose that was as bad though). Give my love to Mrs. Howard when you see her & to Rebecca.

John says he bets you & some of those boys you write about will marry yet, but do wait until we get there, if you do. He says he hasn't eaten any wedding cake, but once this year (when we were married) & then he had no appetite for it!

Write soon, Nealy, & write a long letter. I would write more, but having just written to Ma I am out of news, Most. Give my love to Pa & Ma, Sis Carrie & all the folks out there, accept a good share for yourself.

      Your affectionate Sister,
      Clara Dunlap

P. S. Little Florence calls me Aunt Terra Dunlap. She tries to say everything you tell her. I send you a funny little piece I cut out of a paper. C. D.

Clara Dunlap in Ouachita Co. to her mother Clarissa Dickson in Autuaga Co.

      Nov 18th 1859

Dear Mother,

Your most welcome was duly recd some two weeks since, I should have answered sooner but have been so busy making up the Negroes' winter clothing that I could not have time. You see I was so anxious to get all the sewing done, for John has given his consent for me to go with Mrs. Gildersleeve, & she intended going on the first boat & so I had to hurry. But as yet we have had no prospects of a river boat & I don't know when we will. It is very unfortunate for her, but just the reverse for me as I would have left a good part of my sewing undone. As it is I am nearly through with the exception of making a traveling dress & one or two other things. I hope the river will rise enough soon so I can be with you all by Christmas anyhow. The reason John can't go on now is that he is not near done with his cotton

& has so much other bussiness to keep him home, & would rather I go on first & stay a month or two, & then he will come after me. I had to beg a long time at first though — he said he would be so lonesome here by himself, but I told him I knew I would want to stay longer than he could leave his bussiness to stay with me. So he concluded for me to go first. Some cold morning if you happen to hear a boat coming up near the landing & giving an extra whistle or two, you may just send down the carriage or buggy (alias wagon) to the river & if I'm there I will be certain to come up home. Oh, if the river would only rise.

I was down at Sis Mollie's Sunday. All are well though little Sallie had been quite ill the week previous with sore throat & high fever. Sis Mollie & Mrs. Gildersleeve both send their love to you & Cornelia. Sally Rumph was there also. She spent the day with me Sunday before. Sis Mollie was to come that day, too, but her baby's being sick prevented her. All are well at Bro. John's also. George & Mittie stayed last night with us — both are very talkative, especially George. They seemed to enjoy themselves finely, popping corn, cc. Tell Mrs. Lasiter not to think hard of Dee Newton. He, poor fellow, has something else to think about now besides writing. His wife has a fine daughter, a beauty, they say, & Dee, of course, is nearly crazy. Tell Bettie I should certainly have written, but from what Isaac Newton told brother John, I expected all along to see them out here. Give my love to both of them. Sally Rumph sends her love to you, Nealy, & Sis Carrie.

Well, I don't know of any other news except I have had the chills this fall, not enough to hurt me much, only I've lost a good deal of my hair. Give my love to Pa & Nealy & accept a share for yourself.

From your affectionate daughter,
Clara Dunlap

Clara Dunlap at New Orleans enroute back to Arkansas to her sister Cornelia Dickson in Autauga Co.

Feb. 3, 1860

Dear Sister

*"We" refers to Clara and her husband John Dunlap, who had been visiting her family in Alabama.

We* arrived here this morning, one day later than expected, but "The King" was such a slow boat, did not get to Mobile in time to take the lake-boat & so had to remain in Mobile one night & half the next day, the boat that we've engaged passage on to go up to Camden leaves tomorrow evening, (twilight). I had a <u>hard</u> chill & high fever day before yesterday, was afraid I would have one today, but I am glad to say, I've missed it. I saw Bob Simpson in Mobile, he came aboard the lake-boat to see me. I should have went to see Mrs. S[impson] had I known where she lived, but 'twas too late when Mr. S came. I happened to see him walking near the wharf after I had went aboard of the Lake-boat, & sent John down to tell him I was there. Nealy, I left my hair-ring* near the waterpail where I had been washing my hands, & never missed it until the next day after I left, please send it to me in a letter, please write as soon as you get this. I hope Ma is well again, my love to all

*A "hair-ring was most probably what it says, a ring made of hair.

Your affectionate sister,
Clara Dunlap

P.S.I haven't taken a ride in the <u>"calabouse"</u>*yet, tell Irene.

*Calaboose is a term used for jail, but that definition doesn't fit the context of Clara's usage. Her placing the word in quotation marks implies a form of slang, but our sources do not reveal its meaning. Could she be saying that she isn't pregnant yet?

Clara Dunlap in Ouachita Co. to her sister Cornelia in Autauga Co.

Feb 7th, 1860

Dear Sister,

We arrived here (at brother George's) safe last evening, found all well, saw brother John in Cam[den]; he said all were well at home also; I wrote you from N. Orleans, we left there the next evning. I got a nice bureau, & a very nice book, Memory's Gift. I could not find one like yours, John bought one nigro girl, about 14 years old, for 12 hundred & 50 dollars. He tried to get another one, but the one he wanted he couldn't get clear title to her. He bought [a bundle] of feathers; enough to make my feather bed a large one & the rest I can put in the one we have at home, there was a Mr. Bussey & lady came up with us as far as Champanolle; Mr. B's brother married a daughter of Green Newton's: John left Mr. Mixon's letter at Wilmington, tell Mrs. Lasiter. It was one Mr. Mixon gave John to leave there. Mr. Bussey's wife is in the last stage of consumption, he had been to N Orleans with her to see if the physicians could not help her, but they could not. Sis Mollie was so glad I had come, she sends her love to you & Ma & all of them out there; Tell Reeny, brother George says he thinks her & brother Add might have come on out here as they came as far as N Orleans, Sis Mollie is very <u>much obliged</u> to you for that <u>jelly</u> & to Ma for those stockings, says they are the most acceptable present she could have sent. Sis M says there is <u>nothing to pay</u> though, but she was just wanting some <u>apple jelly</u>. I havent seen Sally yet. Tell Ma, brother George has quarreled with me already about the <u>stockings</u> & <u>socks</u> says he knows Ma sent <u>sis</u> M half of the stockings & <u>him</u> the most of the socks. I tell him no, but he says he intends to find out. Please write soon, Nealy, I am so anxious to hear from Ma; I've been uneasy ever since I left home, because she was not well when I left. Do write soon, Give my love to all at home, Ma & Pa, & accept a good share for yourself.

Your affectionate sister,
Clara Dunlap

*"Mamy" is probably Mamie, first daughter of George and Molly Boddie

P. S. My trunk's have not come yet, but I know little <u>Mamy</u>* will be glad of her doll. You must excuse me for this blotted sheet, just as I finished writing, the ink stand turned over, & spilled some on the paper.
      Good bye

Clara Dunlap in Ouachita Co. to her sister Cornelia in Autauga Co.
                Feb. 27, 1860
Dear Sister,

*"Mary" refers to Mamie, whose full name was Mary Elizabeth Boddie, after her mother Sis Mollie. Clara attempted to write Mamie, but could not settle on a spelling, so she crossed it out and wrote Mary.

 I wrote immediately on my arrival home & also in New Orleans, though only short letters just to let you know that we were safe. Sis M[ollie] was very much obliged to you for the collar & cuffs, thinks they are so pretty. The children were all pleased with the <u>chestnuts</u> said they could eat a <u>half-bushel</u>, they thought. Little Mary* thinks her doll's baby is perfection, is very anxious for her Ma to <u>dress it</u>., Sis M keeps it locked up in her dresser, says every time she goes in there, Mary has to have a look at her doll's baby, as she calls it. I sent Sally R[umph] that jelly that Sis C[arrie] sent her. I have not been over there since I came home. The creek is too high. Sis M & brother G[eorge] spent the day with me yesterday, sis M & I made an agreement that we would go over to Sallie's toward the last of this week & stay a day or two with her, brother John has gone to carry Mary Rumph to her sister's (Mrs. Jones) in Missippi. She became so dissatisfied here & wanted to go. brother J says "he will be certain to send that <u>tea-cup</u> back," tell brother Add, "by the first opportunity, or he will send it by <u>mail if brother Add will pay the postage</u>, as "he knows it is bad to have a tea-set broken". Oh, I never told you about the frollic we had coming out from Camden to Brother G's; John hired a buggy & horse from the livery stable, which was an old one as it happened, & in coming through the river bottom, the old horse stallded & would not pull a bit, John had to get down in the mud & water & carry me out in his arms, (not a very easy thing considering the mud & water was nearly knee deep). As good luck would have it, just then brother John's wagon, which had been to town to carry home some groceries came along; we got in that, right on top of the barrels & cc & came on to brother George's, John says that was <u>coming down</u> too fast, wasent it, to go all the way to Ala & back <u>dressed up</u>, & then have to take the mud & water, & worse than all, in a wagon, says next time he goes to Ala, he is going in <u>home-spun</u> & take <u>deck-passage</u> so he wont have to get down in the mud so bad; The day I came home, I planted collards & peas, & sowed mustard, all up, sowed <u>radishes,</u> beets & <u>cabbage seed</u> today. I gave brother G. over half of my hyacinths. Tell Sis C[arrie] those collard seed she gave me came in <u>very</u> well as nearly every one wanted seed, we will have preaching three times a month this year. I have heard one of our preachers & think he excells any that I've heard out here; his name is Kenerday; Several of our best neighbors moved to Texas this winter, dident have enough land. Mr. Hoge's (that one whose place John thought would suit Ma so well, that is if she ever moves out here) talks of going to Texas, lives only a mile from here. I like Mr. Macca's place best, it has a good orchard on it & richer land, lives a half mile farther from us. C, I've had several dreams about you & Ma since I left home, not bad ones though. I dreamed once that I saw you in N Orleans, & what do you think I dreamed last night — that I was in <u>Paris</u>, thought I was in a candy store, buying such pretty candies. Tell Uncle Jerry, Henry says he is very much obliged to him & Dan for those pants they sent him. Do write soon C, I havent heard from home yet. Give my love to Pa & Ma; accept a good share for your self. As ever,

      Your affectionate sister
      Clara Dunlap

 P. S. Sis M[ollie] says tell Pa she is much obliged to him for those papers.
      C.

Clara Dunlap in Ouachita Co. to her mother Clarissa Dickson in Autauga Co.

            April 6, 1860

Dear Ma,

 I intended writing to you several weeks ago, but I've been having chills & dident feel well; I am a good deal better today & am in hopes I wont have any more. I've written to Neal[y] twice since I came home, but have not received a line from her since I left Alabama. Sis Mollie recd a long letter from sis Caroline* 3 weeks since. We were all sorry to hear of Grandma's being so ill. I'm afraid she won't live much longer. Old Mr. Brodnax's three daughters were out to see him this spring. Mrs. B[rodnax] says she never saw him so over-come before, as he was when he saw them coming, had to go to bed & just laid there & cried like a child. They took one of his boys back with them. My garden is not so good as 'twas last year, those collard seed I brought home did not half of them I planted come up. I have radishes & a nice bed of mustard for salid, & peas in bloom; the red birds destroyed a good many for me, as soon as they come up the red birds would pick them off. We had several severe frosts last week; killed nearly all the peaches & plums. Tell sis Carry that jelly she sent Sallie did <u>just come in time</u>, twas <u>very</u> acceptable, S thought it <u>excellent</u>. Brother John <u>came</u> ten days ago from Carolina; has been quite sick with a bad cold; Little G[eorge] & Mittie go by to school every day on their pony, have a good school now at the church about a mile from here; We will have preaching nearly every Sunday this

*Caroline is Sis Carrie who has been referred to so often. This is the first time her full name has been used.

year, though with the exception of one, all of our preachers are quite ordinary ones.

*A scion is a shoot or twig cut for grafting or planting; a cutting.

My cuttings & scions* nearly every one lived, & some of them are growing finely, & those two Lady-banks rose bushes that sis C[arrie] gave me are living; I gave one to brother George as well as half of my white hyacinths, he has promised me some of his pink ones; Sis M[ollie] told me to tell Pa she was much obliged to him for those two papers; brother G has bought Sis M a sewing machine too. Grover & Bakers is the patent, I have not been down since he bought it, but John has; & he says brother G told him Sis M was so proud of it that she does nothing but sit & sew just for the pleasure & ease of it. John himself is so pleased with it that he wants to get one for me right away, just to see me sewing on it. But I tell him I have so little to do anyway that I would then be idle nearly all the time; The weather is fine now, though rather dry, John is very busy preparing his cotton land, his corn is doing well, says he has as good a stand as he could wish for; we planted a barrel of Irish potatoes, the frost killed them down but they are coming up again very pretty. I've had a hundred & over little chickens hatched out, the hawks though [are] hard on them this spring; last year I dont think we were troubled with a single hawk.

I was over to see Mrs. Dr. Stone the other day. I declare, Ma, she is the smartest & most energetic little woman I ever saw; has hired a negro boy about 13 or 14 years old, & he is all the one to make her crop, but the way she has him stirring, she cooks & milks herself, but between times when she is not busy sewing, tending to her chickens & cc she is out in the field working like a negro almost, her oldest son helps her a good deal, he goes around & minds the birds off of her corn nearly all day; he is a little fellow, too, & she says he seems so willing to mind her about any kind of work, but I must tell you how she planted her cotton, she had a few acres close to the house, that she wanted to plant in cotton, but had no one to lay it off, & the negro boy was not high enough to see how to plow it strait, & so she made her little son get on a horse & ride ahead (of the negro boy & his mule) as strait as he could & you would not believe it how strait & even her ground was bedded up. She had over 200 little chickens & will have a good many more, & a fine large orchard of late peach trees that she makes a good deal off of in the fall by selling them in Cam[den]. Oh she is determined to get along somehow. You must write soon, Ma. I dont know why Neal wont write to me; Give my love to all enquiring friends & accept a good share for yourself & believe me as ever,

Your affectionate daughter,
C Dunlap

P. S. John sends his respects to you, Pa, & Neal. Tell Irene [Love] to write to me & I will answer all her letters. You must excuse this paper being blotted, twas all I had. CD

Monday, 9th.

I dident seal my letter as I had no immediate chance of sending it to Cam[den], & thinking too that I might hear some other news to write about. John & I started yesterday to brother John's, but soon after starting we met them going to brother George's, & so we turned & went down with them, found all well at brother G's. Sis M's sewing machine is a beautiful one, she says she hardly wants to take time to baste her work now, can sew it <u>so much</u> fast er than she can baste it even; she says that brother G likes to sew on it better than she does, & every old piece of cloth he can get holt of, he stitches it all up in diamonds, squares, & every other shape almost he can think of. Little Bettie & Mittie were very much pleased with those stockings you sent them, but I must tell you about little Tom [Rumph]; Sally says when she was showing Mit & Bet their stockings, little Tom wanted to know where <u>his</u> was, Sallie told him you did not send him any. <u>"Well, she aint none of my grandma then, & I aint going to call her (meaning you) Grandma either, cause she knit Bettie & Mit some stockings & she wouldent send me any"</u>. We all laughed so much at Tom about talking so earnestly, but he did seem to be hurt about it sure enought, S says he often speaks of it yet. I dident think he would have noticed it. Sis M will have an abundance of strawberries this spring, I never saw vines fuller. I do hope you get this soon; brother John says he is going to town tomorrow & said he would come by & get this. no more.

C D

Clara Dunlap in Ouachita Co. to her sister Cornelia Dickson in Autauga Co.

May 17, 1860

Dear Sister,

I receaved your most welcome some time since, but having just written to Ma, I thought best to postpone writing for a while so as to find something else to write. Yours found all well, both here & at brother G[eorge]'s & brother John's, though at brother J's <u>now</u>, the children are sick with something like scarlet fever, though in a very mild form, only lasts a few days; he dont give them any medicine atall, just keeps them in the house pretty close, give them warm sage tea to drink to keep the eruption out good; & they are soon well.

I rec'd Ma's letter several days since, & was very glad indeed to get it, somehow, I get uneasy so quick this spring if I dont hear from you all often, more so than usual; & somehow I almost fear to read a letter when I recd it, I never felt so before. I recon 'twas because Grandma was sick so long. I am glad to hear that she is up again. We are having fine seasons this spring, so far, & consequently fine gardens, my garden is rather earlier than most of my neighbors on account of the light sandy soil, I suppose, the worms & bugs liked to have ate up my cabbage this spring; we had a great deal of trouble with them, had to go in there every morning soon & hunt around them for worms, sometimes find fifty every morning, but since the hot weather set in, they are growing finly. Neal, I have a new kind of English pea this year, the bunch pea, they dont grow more than knee high & bear ten times fuller than any other English pea I ever saw, we can get a good mess anytime off of half a row.

  I went to Camden this spring & bought me two very pretty new dresses, not fine ones. I thought twas useless to buy any more fine dresses & no where to wear them; & I had several very nice musline's* already, one of my new ones was pink & white brilliants* & the other one a french cambric.* I will send you a sample if I dont forget to put it in. I carried them down to sis Mollie's & got her to make them on her machine, she could <u>sew</u> so much faster than I could <u>baste</u> that it kept me busy, I can tell you; I like the work so much — so strong too, sis M is not troubled about her sewing atall now. Oh, they had such a quantity of strawberries this year, the vines bore fuller & finer berries this spring than they ever did. They are selling in Cam[den] for 25c a quart, & the people are glad to get them at <u>that</u>, chickens a little larger than partriges, 25c apiece also, did you ever; eggs 35c a doz., butter 25c a lb; I am going to begin saving my butter & eggs both to send them there. Dr. Halton came out this morning to see John on business & just begged me to sell him a dozen chickens just at my own price, he said. I told him I had so few large enough to sell, & those I wanted to eat them myself, he said he would give me as much for the small ones as if they were the larger; said they were so much sweeter, he could <u>chew up bones & all</u>. He said the people over in Cam[den] were really suffering for something to eat. They have such a sorry market there. Brother John sent over a wagon load of sweet potatoes last week, & got $2 a bushel, as soon as the wagon got in town. I do wish I could be with you all at some of your little fishing frolics. I know I could enjoy myself so well. They have a fishing party every once & awhile down to the lake, talk of having another soon, but John has been so busy with his crop, & I could not ask him for a mule to drive. He had his fine horse crippled last week, got her thigh broke, he's afraid she will die. I was so sorry; she was such a fine brood mare, too. Well C I dont know of what other news to write about just now. I will write to Ma in a week or two, & then I will have learned something else to write about. You must write soon & take time to tell me <u>all</u> the news. I have never recd your first letter yet; I do hope I may as I would be so sorry to lose that ring. Tell Rebecca I congratulate her & Tom both on their having such a <u>fine boy</u>. I just know Tom thinks there never was <u>just such a one</u>, dont he; if I was Rebecca I would be uneasy about him, for fear he would lose his crop; I dont

---

*Muslin is a plain-woven sheer to coarse cotton fabric.

*Brilliant probably refers to a light lustrous fabric similar to alpaca, usually of cotton and mohair or worsted. The term used in Webster is <u>brilliantine</u>.

*Cambric is a fine thin white linen fabric, which is named for the city of its origin Cambral, France.

expect he sees the inside of his field once a week now. Oh I just bet any thing he is in the grass,* tell him I say so too. My love to Ma & Pa, sis Carry, & Irene & all enquiring friends & accept a good share for yourself & believe me as ever your

*To be "in the grass" is a farmer's way of saying the fields are full of weeds.

Affectionate sister,
Clara Dunlap

P. S. Please excuse mistakes & bad writing it is night & I have a miserable pen; John has been asleep two hours & I can hardly hold my eyes open.

C D

Clara Dunlap in Ouachita Co. to her mother Clarissa Dickson in Autauga Co.

June 12th, 1860

Dear Ma,

Your welcome letter I receaved some time since, & I should have answered it immediately but I had just written to Neal & thought to wait awhile to find something else to write about, though I should have written a week earlier any way, but have to pick my chance of sending it to the Office & as brother John is going to Cam[den] one day this week, I thought I would write & have the letter ready for him. I rec'd Nealy's letter a few days ago & will answer it in a week or two. We are all well & have been for some time, brother John's children have been quite sick with scarlet fever, seems it takes them so long to get through with it, only one takes it at a time & then in a week or two, another one, &c, the fever itself is not so bad, but they swell up so long afterwards & have fevers. I think all of them are well now but Mitt & she is better. None of them at brother G[eorge]'s have had it yet. I was over at Sallie's two weeks ago, she is still up but wont be much longer; she is the healthiest & can stand more than any woman I ever saw to be in that situation. Sis Mollie & Mrs. Dr. Stone spent the day with me week before last; we all have good gardens now, though they came very near being burnt up by the dry hot weather, but it commenced raining about a week ago & has been raining nearly every day since — the hardest rain I most ever saw, brother John had quite a storm at his house, blowed down trees & fences like any thing, didn't do us any injury, only blowed our corn down some; by the by, John told me to tell you that he has the finest corn & cotton crop he ever had in his life, especially the <u>cotton</u>, says if the good seasons continue thinks he will make 75 bales (he has a hundred acres in cotton) & plenty of corn & some to sell, his potato crop is good too, for this season of the year, has nearly two acres planted already; sometime when we go down to brother G's, John gets to bragging so that brother G laughs & tells him that he can out-brag any man in Ouachita Co. John tells him he feels <u>so good</u> to have such a good crop that he cant help bragging, makes him feel good <u>all over</u>. All the neighbors generaly are making good crops, but is it not strange that although there was so much corn made in the county last year, & now it is selling at $2.50 a bushel in Cam[den], but John says twas the constant hauling all last fall, winter, & spring of the ox wagons all through the country, (they would come as far as sixty or seventy miles to Cam[den] with cotton & return with groceries for the up-country) & their ox-teams could eat up such a quantity of corn, much more than mule teams, that it has made corn scarce. We have a fine school in our neighborhood now, about 20 scholars, a good many of them large one. I do hope you all have had good seasons also. Tis so bad to have as much dry weather & then no crops or gardens in the summer. I was glad to hear that Grand-ma was able to be in her garden again. You must not be uneasy about my having chills anymore Ma, as they turned out to be <u>nine months chills</u> just like I had this spring was a year ago. I dont know what is the reason I always have such hard chills & fever along at first. I've quit having them some time now & enjoy very good health. I wish almost every day that I could be in Ala to eat some of them nice June apples & cherries, too, brother John has a few trees but they were nearly all killed this spring. We will have plenty of peaches, but I dont care much for them somehow now. I recon it is because we have them & no apples. John says if you dry any this summer, please dry a few for him, too; he was so fond of those I brought home last winter; & would rather eat them than most anything else I could cook for him.

  Not one of my vegetable oyster* seed came up. I was so sorry, my little jelly flowers are blooming some & the touch-me-nots, but they are all single. I have all kinds of vegetables I beleave except cucumbers & tomatoes, & will soon have them. Well I beleave I've written all the news that I can think of at present. You must write soon, Ma. I always feel so glad when I get a letter from home. Sis M & Sally request me when I wrote to give you & Neal their love, also, brother J & brother G sends their also. Give my love to Pa & Neal, & accept a good share for yourself. I remain as ever,

     Your affectionate daughter,
     Clara Dunlap

  P. S John cant wear those socks that you knit for him only [on] Sundays; says they feel better on his feet than any he ever wore in his life. Brother G asked me the other day if some of those socks of John's that I brought from Ala wasent marked <u>G. B.</u> instead of <u>J. D.</u> (wanted to claim them, you see.) I told him no that you only sent two pair for him (George) & the rest John's, said never mind, that he bet some more of them were marked <u>G. B.</u> & I wouldent let him see them. Little Tom Rumph was very proud when I told him you intended knitting him some pretty socks, says he'll be your boy when you come out here. Tell Mammy & Harriet howdy

*The oyster vegetable is a root vegetable known as salsify.

& all the negroes. Tell Harriet not to be eating all your pairs this summer, as Mammy said she ate pairs all summer before last. I would send her one of my sackque waist dresses* if I could <u>spare it</u>, but need em all myself, but no more.

>Yours & cc
>
><u>C D</u>

*Sacque waist dresses were loose-fitting dresses, used as maternity dresses.

Clara Dunlap in Ouachita Co. to her sister Cornelia Dickson in Autauga Co.

July 24, 1860

Dear Sister,

 It has been some time since I received your letter, I know you must think hard of me for not writing sooner, but when you hear my reasons you will not blame me. I intended answering your letter immediately, but sis Mollie had recd one from sis Carry previous to mine & begged me to let her write first & me write a week or two afterwards,. I agreed, when the next week John recd brother Add's letter announcing poor Pa's death, & though I had been expecting all spring to hear that he was dead when ever I recd a letter from you or Ma yet, still I wasent prepared for the sad news when it came, & it unnerved me so for several weeks that I could not write; & besides, brother Add said that you would write soon & write all the particulars, but I have not recd any further news as yet, & so I thought I would try & write any how as Ma might get uneasy not hearing from us for so long. We are all well just now. Sis M[ollie] & brother G[eorge] were up & spent the day about a week since. I was over at brother John's several days ago, Sallie has a fine son, about a week old today, a great big boy — weighed 9 1/2 lbs. the very image of brother John except its forehead which is like Sallie's. She is doing remarkably well so far; Mittie has picked out a name for it already & is begging her Pa to name it Richard LaFayette so she can call him Dicky. I dont know how she came to think of that name. John (Dunlap) told little Florence to ask her Pa if the baby wasent named <u>John Bell</u> (after the Whigg candidate for President, you know). Florence went & asked her Pa if the baby wasn't named John <u>Belly</u>; We have been suffering for rain very much indeed for three or four weeks, the corn crop is cut off nearly half & some of the neighbors cant make even half crops. John had <u>very</u> early corn which hit the seasons better, you know, than that which was later, we will make enough to do us he thinks, but if we could have had one or two good seasons in time, he says he would have made 15 hundred bushels; the drouth was not such a long one, but so intensely <u>hot</u> & at a time when frequent rains were needed most, brother John says he never knew such hot weather at this time of the year as the last three or four weeks has been, we had a good shower yesterday, for the first, which cooled the air some, but today is as hot as ever. The cotton crop has not suffered very much as yet & with moderate seasons only, those that planted early will make good crops. I expect you all are suffering too with the dry weather from what brother Add wrote. I declare it does seem disheartening to work so hard all spring & then be cut off with drouth. The gardens are nearly burnt up, too, I have Irish potatoes, tomatoes, & a few butter beans, that is all I beleave. The rest are burnt up. But I must tell you about a serious hurt John got some weeks since, a mule threw him & came very near killing him, he threw him on his head & from the way he was hurt, brother John says he must have turned a complete summer set over the mule's head, he fell on his back & was senseless for a half hour or more, there happened to be a neighbor's house near by & he managed to get there & borrow a horse to come home, was confined to the house 2 or three weeks, & of all the dreadful looking places I ever saw, his back was the worst, brother G said he never saw such a bruise, looked perfectly black & just like something mortified, the place was as large as the brim of a man's hat. I used Opodeldoc* on it which hope [helped] it more than any thing else. Oh! he would have the hottest fevers, I ever saw most; besides that John has had a good deal of bad luck this spring. First he lost his fine riding mare, then one of his best negro men ran away some six or seven weeks ago, & he has never heard from him yet, & a few days after one of his fine oxen was killed in a storm, that was such a pity too, they were by far the finest yoke of oxen in the country, he only bought them last fall from a Texas wagoner, & there is none like them in the country, he paid $80 for them. I do hope we wont have any more bad luck; surely John has had his share & a good one, too, I think, he keeps stirring as much as ever & tries not to take it hard, but you know he cant help it some. Our orchard has turned out fine this year, not with-standing the drouth, (twas well cultivated), & the peaches were very large & fine. I thought to commence drying this morning but 'tis getting so cloudy & threating rain, I gave it out & commenced making preserves. I do wish Neal, you could have been here to have enjoyed our fine early peaches. I know you never saw any so nice, for early ones I mean, they were fully as juicy as an <u>orange</u>, you could not begin to eat one without holding it over a plate or something, they are the only ones of the kind in the neighborhood. brother J & G said they were the finest peaches they ever saw. I expect your school is out by this time, & I know you feel relieved to get to rest awhile, what would I give if you could spend vacations with me, you & Irene, wouldn't I be glad. You speak of being lonesome at home now, Neal, what would you do if you were near tied & had to stay in the house all day by yourself, your old man out attending to his business; that is, if your old man was as industrious & stirring as mine is (not bragging atall , mind you), he is getting so fleshy now, though, that he cant work as hard as he used too. I know if you were to see him now, you

*Opodeldoc is any of various liniments containing soap, camphor, alcohol, etc.

would not call him <u>little</u>. I do hope he will fall off some before winter, though, or I will have to make him a new suit, out & out. He can't wear any of his Sunday now, he is having the house finished this summer, the other room at least, mine was finished when built, the yard trees are trimmed up & an avenue opened up to the public road, which improves the looks of the place so much. Tis only 2 hundreds yards to the road, & I can see all the passing now, after all Neal, I beleave 'tis better if you do have to stay in the house by yourself & have a smart old man that tends to business, even if he does stay out in the field all day, than have one so lazy you couldent move him out. I know I would soon get tired of him then, & <u>as it is</u> I never get the chance to get tired of <u>my old man</u>. By the by what has Rebecca named her boy or can Mr. Tom find a name pretty enough; by the by you may tell Bettie W. she might as well get those little shoes she promised <u>me</u> last year & send them out this fall or winter by some one passing, as from <u>appearances just now,</u> they will be needed this winter, if not a little before. I think you were saying you would be so lonesome at home this summer. I will just give you something to do, so you may go to <u>embroidering something or other</u>. I dont much care what, <u>if you please mam do,</u> I will try to return the <u>obligation some day if it is necessary.</u> But I must close as I've filled out my paper.

    Give my love to Ma, sis Carry, Irene, & all enquiring friends, especially Rebecca & Mrs. L. Howard & Mrs Lasiter & Bettie. Tell Bettie Dee Newton has lost his little <u>girl</u>. Please write soon Neal, & tell me all the news, tell <u>me how</u> Pa died, if he died easy, & if he knew you all, & if he said anything about me & cc. Give howdy to Mammy, Harriet, & Jerry. Tell H[arriet] if I had any way I'd send her some of my sacques that would fit her, too, I guess, my love to you & beleave me as ever,

                Your affectionate sister,
                <u>Clara</u>

    *P. S. Sis Mollie & Sallie send their love to you & Ma & Sis Carrie & all. July 27th still no rain & tis so warm & dry everything is burning up.
                C.D.

*Note: This postscript was written along the left margin of page 1:

William G. Hutton in Green County, Alabama, to Cornelia Dickson in Autauga Co.

                              Aug. 22, 1860

    Dear Relation,*

    I rec'd your kind epistle the 30th in due time which brought sad intelligence to me on the <u>death of your dear father</u>. I had heard some time before of his demise, but had heard he died on the 17th of June. Cousin John Dickson was at my house and informed me of it. I do truly sympathize with you in the loss you have sustained, but I beleave it is his eternal gain. You

*Cornelia's father's mother's maiden name was Barbara Hutton. The writer of this letter must be a distant cousin of Cornelia and Clara.

have lost a tender affectionate parent. One who fondly loved you and one whose anxiety for your welfare and happiness was equal to any earthly parent. I have been expecting to hear of his death some time, knowing his situation. He has had many trying scenes to encounter. I know something from what he has told me of the troubles he has experienced, but now death has relieved him of all, and no doubt his spirit is with God. Let us all endeavor to be ready to depart when the summons comes. I hope you will attend to his instructions and be ready to meet him when you shall be called to leave those low grounds of sorrow & disappointment. We had quite a pleasant trip to S. C. and we enjoyed ourselves well in the company of our relations, met with no casualty & kept well during our visit which was 6 weeks — we went & came through Selma. I shall try and convey your father's sword & belt to the person you desired. I wrote a letter today to your Uncle John, I rec'd one from him yesterday, I am glad so much is coming to you all. My family unite with me in presenting our love to you & Mother. Put your <u>trust</u> in the <u>Lord</u> & He will not <u>leave you</u> or <u>forsake you</u>. I hope the <u>Lord</u> will be with you always & <u>bless you</u> is my Sincere prayer — let me hear from you when convenient. My eldest daughter is on a visit with her children at my house, Mary Elizabeth Thacher. You will recollect her. She lives in Columbus, Miss. I conclude

      Your affectionate relation,
      William G. Hutton

Clara Dunlap in Ouachita Co. to her mother Clarissa Dickson in Autauga Co.

                Aug 27th, 1860
Dear Ma,

 Your <u>most welcome</u> letter I receaved several days since, & you dont know how <u>glad</u> I was to hear from you all. I hadent heard a word from Ala since brother Add wrote to John, & he said in his letter that Neal would write soon & tell us all the particulars of poor Pa's death (he only wrote a few lines himself). I was looking so hard for a letter from C[ornelia] & not getting one, I feared you all were sick or something. Oh, I was so very uneasy until I got yours, it relieved me so much & to learn, too, that he was so resigned & willing, & died so easy. I do hope he is better off, far better than living in so much pain, life had become no pleasure for him. Yours found all well, both here & at brother G[eorge]'s & J Rumph's, the latter & Sally & all the children spent the day with me yesterday. Sallie's baby is the largest, finest child to its age I most ever saw, resembles brother John more than any of the children; they have named him John Gildersleeve, the children were all well & lively. We have not had much sickness in the neighborhood this summer & less in our family than any in our neighborhood, we have had the worst drouth we have ever had since I've been out here this summer, not so long but so very hot & at a time when rain was needed the most, very few in the neighborhood have made corn enough to do them, & no cotton crop atall, & after having <u>such</u> fine prospects, too, tis too bad; John has made enough to do him by being saving with it, but his cotton crop wont be half what it was last year, brother John says he himself wont make more than 15 or 20 bales at the outside, brother George laughs & says he reckons he will make 2 bales & besides have to buy 400 bushels of corn. A great many havent made more than enough to do them til Christmas. It commenced raining about a week ago & has been raining ever since. I hope if it aint to late 'twil make potatoes anyhow, & turnips, John has sowed a large turnip patch, but if the rain keeps on much longer, it will ruin what little cotton <u>is</u> made. But I must tell you about that negro boy of John's that ran away early in the summer, he heard from him a few days ago, he has been taken up in the Indian Nation*, by an <u>Indian</u> at that, the gentleman that he was taken(?) to lives at the Agency (they call it) he wrote to John, that he had a negro boy in custody, who said he belonged to him & to come & get him; by some means the letter has been a long time coming; the negro was taken up on the 12th of July; it will cost John nearly $200 by the time he gets him home, you see the law allows an Indian $40 for taking up a negro & then the man has had him in custoday long enough to raise it over a $100. John's trip up there & back (its over 200 hundred miles) will be nearly if not quite $100 more, as he has to get some man that knew the boy to go with him to confirm his oath as being owner of said negro boy. Mr. Williams, one of our neighbors has promised to go with him, but says the trip itself & getting to look at the country will be pay enough for him, but I know John will pay him <u>well</u> besides, he is to be gone two weeks or more. I am going to stay with sis Mollie & Sallie together while he is gone, but aint it too bad to think John has been doing without that negro's work all summer & now have to pay so much more to get him home; he ran away twice before, but dident stay long, & begged so hard & promised so faithfully not to do so again that John let him off, the reason he ran away was, John had told him a few days previous about not plowing the cotton right, he dident plow close enough, I think, a few days after, John went into the field & the boy was plowing so <u>close</u> to the cotton that it was wilting behind him. John reproved him about it & asked him why he dident do better, Bob (thats the boys name) said he was plowing just as good as he was going to, John was going to whip him for his impudence & he sloped*, one of our negro women had a fine girl about a week ago, another will be down in a month or six weeks, dont you think we'll have <u>music</u> enough here after a while, well, I dont know what else to write except I want to see you all so bad — wish I could go to Ala again this winter, or that you all could move out here, tell Neal I wrote her some time since. You must write soon Ma, if only a page or two, it does me so much good to even

*The Indian Nation Clara refers to is most probably what we know today as Oklahoma.

*Slope, in the mid-nineteenth century, meanat to make off; run away.

hear that all are well, my love to sis Caroline, Reeny & Neal, & all enquiring friends; accept a good share yourself, & beleave me as ever,

Your affectionate daughter,
C Dunlap

Sis Mollie & Sallie send their love to you & all.
CD

Aug 28th I am at sis Mollie's today, all well

Clara Dunlap in Ouachita Co. to her sister Cornelia Dickson in Autauga Co.

Oct 2nd, 1860

Dear Sister,

Your most welcome I receaved a few days ago, & you dont know how <u>very</u> glad I was to hear from home; for with the exception of one letter from Ma, I have not heard from home since brother Add wrote to John in June, soon after Pa's death. I couldent imagine what was to pay, feared that some of you were very sick or something else. I couldent think what, but John would laugh & tell me that you were studying more about some of them <u>boys</u> than of writing to me, & that he would not be surprised at any time to hear that you were married; but I told him I knew better, though if you did I would not be much surprised after all, as you said when I married & would not tell you of it, that you intended to treat me the same way. Your letter found all of us well. I was at Sallie's last Sunday week & all were well yesterday over there, Little George has been staying here going to school for the last three weeks, as his pony['s] foot was sore & he had to quit riding him until it got better, he goes home every Friday evening though. John & Willis Boddie came home with him tonight; they wanted to gather chinquapins, & there is none down at brother G[eorge]'s place, or at brother J[ohn]'s either, & George was telling them at school today how many he gathered every evening [after] school & so they came home with him this evening to gather some, too, they have been playing <u>hull-gull</u>*, ever since supper, & then boiled their chinquapins, & have just gone to bed. They, (John & Will) said all were well at home, brother G is building him a fine new gin-house; has it almost completed; John said his Ma [Sis Mollie] would have come up this week & helped me quilt (I have one in) but his Pa was too busy to come with her & she is afraid to drive their buggy horse. Sallie Rumph's baby is named John Gildersleeve. Robert Stone (Bill Stone's son) is lying very low with something like Typhoid fever at brother John's; he went over several weeks ago to deer-hunt with brother J, took the fever & has been very sick ever since, he is very little, if any, better; there has been a good deal of sickness in the neighborhood above here, this summer, with the same fever, one of

*Hull-gull was a game played with chinquapins. One player would hold both hands behind his back and another player had to choose the hand which held the chinquapins in order to win.

John's brothers Dick Dunlap lost his wife in August. I do feel so sorry for him, she was a most excelent woman, well beloved by all who knew her; I had become so much attached to her, she seemed almost like kin-folks to me; she left two small children; poor Dick says he is broke up now. I dont think he will hardly ever get another that will suit him as well in every way as Lucy did. You spoke of having such good meetings this summer; Oh, how <u>very</u>, very much I wish I could have been there. I have never been to any good meetings since I came to Ark., the circuit riders they send us here are very ordinary ones indeed, with a <u>few</u> exceptions; & then so few of the people out here pretend to care even for preaching much less trying to have protracted meetings; sometimes I think it is right hard to be denied having any good meetings atall. Sept. 4. John went over today to brother John's, all were well. I had almost forgot to tell you about his trip to the Indian Nation, he was gone nearly two weeks, he had to pay 175 dollars to get his negro from the agent Mr. Morris, 100 to the Indian for taking him up, & 75 to Mr. Morris for keeping him nearly two months. I think it was very high, more than John expected to pay; John has built me a nice pantry and dairy both since he came home, the dairy is a large one, just like one Cousin Mary used to have with a ground floor, his cotton crop is turning out a little better than he expected it would; thinks now he will make 30 bales if the rainy weather dont injure it too much; it is pretty tight times now throughout the country, about something to eat, we have a plenty of <u>greens</u> & a few potatoes, & a fine turnip patch coming on; J[ohn] says he is going to plant a large field of wheat this fall so as to have cake anyhow next year, though he has made plenty of corn & some to sell. [Little] George says to tell Irene he will write before long, he is answering Tom's [Tom Love] letter now & says he wouldent know what to write about in <u>two letters</u>. Tell Harriet she must name her baby <u>John Bell</u>. Tell sis C[arrie] that sis Mollie was just saying a short time ago; that she bet something was <u>to pay</u> with her the reason she did not write; Neal you must tell Mrs. Wagner the next time she speaks of the Babtists gathering up <u>all</u> the grapes that I always heard that the Babtist were a <u>lazy</u> set, but dident know they had to get <u>so</u> lazy as to have the <u>Methodist</u> to <u>shake</u> their vine for them, much less help them gather up too; looks like they are willing for the Methodist to start the work & they take all the credit of it when finished, but maybe you had better not tell her Neal, she might not like my speaking so plain about the Babtist, for I do hope the good they have done will be permanent. I was glad to hear that Clem & Dee Lasiter had professed religion. Neal I am perfectly willing that brother Add should have Pa's watch as far as I am concerned, that is. I am so sorry that Ma is making such a poor crop this year, I do wish she would move out here, she could most always make enough to eat, & with good seasons so much; I do hate for her to be living on that poor land & not making half a support no year when she could be doing so much better out here. I know it is enough to keep her worried & fretted all the time, just studying how to get along. C, you <u>must</u> write me oftener. I do think right hard of you sometimes for writing so seldom when I know you have nothing to do but enjoy yourself all the time. I would so much rather hear from you oftener, if only a page or two at a time. Give my love to Mrs. L. Howard & the Dr's wife too, & to Rebecca (tell her I often wish we lived near each other) & all enquiring friends, tell Bettie I will write her as soon as I get <u>young</u> again. I am <u>old folks</u> just about now (that is in my feelings) & it tires me so to write, Sallie Rumph sends her love to you, Ma, & Sis C[arrie], & I know sis Mollie would, did she know I was writing, though she always tells me to send it anyhow if she dont happen to see me at the time of writing. Give my love to Ma & accept a good share for yourself, & beleave me as ever,

       Your affectionate sister,
       Clara Dunlap

P.S. Tell all the negroes howdy for me; Brother George's Henry enquires about them every time I see him, & always tells me to be certain & send his remembrance & love to them all, his kinfolks, that is.

Mary Elizabeth Boddie in Ouachita Co. to her sister-in-law Cornelia Dickson in Autauga Co.

              Nov 21st, 1860

  My dear Nealy,

   I must write you a few lines to-night although I find I've but a half sheet paper by me to write on & I promised Clara to write for her as twill be some time ere she can, she is very anxious to let you all at home know of her good fortune this time. John & Clara are rejoicing in the possession of the finest, <u>biggest boy</u> & I guess they think, greatest boy now in Arkansaw. I was with her Nealy, & so soon as the baby was weighed she commenced bragging over Sallie, beat her 1/2 pound, C's boy weighed 10 lbs. John is so proud of it. I guess he'll be some time selecting a name for his big boy, he was born a week ago yesterday, the 13th of Nov. Clara sits up a little now, one of her breast & nipple have been very sore, but with care now, she will have but little trouble with it, can draw the milk out easily; & with my old remedy Camphor plaster, drew all the soreness out of her breast, & dispersed the lumps. Sallie's baby has been sick with croup, but is quite well now & as fat as a little beef, the children all think there never was such babies. Mittie wants to know of every one which baby is the prettiest, her Ma's or Aunt Clara's; she wants to nurse Johnny all the time. The boys* have great times since the school session is up, they stay first with us, then at Uncle John R[umph]'s hunting, fishing & cc. They say there are not as <u>many squirrels</u> in all this country as their cousin Tom* kills. They hunt ducks now. Little

*"The boys" refers to George Rumph and John R. Boddie, both about 12 or 13 years old.

*"Cousin Tom" refers to Tom Love who lives in Alabama.

Geo. has killed two — he is here tonight, says tell his cousin Tom he will write to him in a week or two. When is Carrie ever going to write to me again? Tell her I guess she hears so often through Clara's letters to you & Mother D[ickson], she never cares to write to me. When I heard she was sick, I would excuse, & sympathize with her, too. Tell Carrie I am very busy trying to get all my work complete before I travel, I cant work long at the machine at a time now; it gives me cramps, but Geo helps me occasionally with the long seams & cc George has finished his gin house except the pick room*, & the hands are gathering cotton, his crop will be very short this year, thinks probably he will have but little corn to buy. John R[umph] has twenty bales picked, all his crop except perhaps two bales more, he will have a sufficiency of corn. John D[unlap] has not finished gathering his cotton yet. Clara says be sure & write to her, she will write to you & her Mother as soon as she can. Tell Mother D[ickson] I would be so glad if she could make us a visit. I am sure if she could only think so, she is better able to come than we are able to go to Ala, we have so many little ones to take care of now. I know she will be anxious to see her fine grandson. Little Florence is as much like Grdma Lanier as ever. Mittie & Bettie grow very fast, little Tom is little Tom yet. He & Gilder are the dumpy ones of the family, but what they lack in size, they make up in mischief. There is nothing new to speak of here, Nealy. The weather is pretty cold, & we women folk, for that reason & some other compulsory ones, have to stay within doors, & the gentle folks* have cooled down considerably since the election returns are proving so contrary to their wishes & expectations.'Tis a pity if Lincoln is to be President*, but we can only hope that all things that happen is for the best ... This leaves all well, Nealy, with my dear love to you all, I remain

yours affectionately,

Mary E. Boddie

Tell Grandma Lanier that George kills for us a brace of wild ducks every day or two, & caught a fine mess of fish this week, he has the fattest pigs & the finest turnips to eat with them of all her boys here. John R[umph] kills the most deer, but I tell him that is because Geo dont hunt deer.

*The pick room is where cotton is stored until a full bale is picked.

*It is difficult to determine who Sis Mollie refers to as "the gentle folks." Ordinarily one would think of the slaves, but it is doubtful that the election of Lincoln was contrary to their desires. She perhaps is refering to those men who opposed the election of Douglas because of his Northern leanings.

*Lincoln did not carry the popular vote, but he did finally carry the electoral college and was inaugurated on March 24, 1861.

Clara Dunlap in Ouachita Co. to her mother Clarissa Dickson in Autauga Co.

Dec. 10th, 1860

Dear Ma,

I receaved your welcome letter more than a month since, & you will know ere receaving this why I neglected writing so long as sis Mollie wrote to Neal that I had been confined, & had a fine great, big boy, weighed 10 lbs. only. I dont know, but I expect she wrote all the particulars, however, I dont suppose it will be any harm to tell them over again. I had a very hard time though not a very long one, 15 hours, it seemed so many days to me almost. I dont know who my baby favors. Sallie R[umph] thinks he resembles you some say it favors me, but I dont think so, he has very fair rosy skin, deep blue eyes, & (well to own the truth) <u>no hair</u>, his little head is nearly as bald as his face; & he has a very small mouth. I've had a time though with my breasts, one of them threatened to rise at first, but I doctored it close, & it got well, my other breast has had a lump in it, now about two weeks; brother John thinks I took cold, it is right close to the nipple, so close that the baby cant suck that breast atall, & I have to keep the milk out with a nipple glass, brother J[ohn] came over to look at it, he told me how & what to apply to it & says it may remain there several weeks yet & that I would have to take the best of care & attend to it very close to prevent its rising. I am applying a gum-camphor poultices, & bath[e] or rub it well three or four times a day with a lineament composed of turpentine, hartsthorn*, laudanum, & sweet oil. I think it is softer & better today than it has been yet, & I do hope it will not get bad again, but the worst of all yet, Ma, that I have to suffer with, is my nipples. Oh, they have been so very sore, all the time, one of them came off gradually in little plugs, & became so painful that I had to quit nursing the baby for several days so as to heal them up some, though my right breast had no nipple atall from the first, except what the baby made by sucking & you cant think how tender & sore it was; & is yet, though not as bad now; Ma I do think of all the suffering yet; having sore breasts is the hardest to bear. You have the same pain to go over again & again every time the child nurses, as I told sis Mollie the other week, as hard as it was, I beleave after all I would rather <u>have</u> a baby than suffer for weeks with such sore breasts as I've had & no relief either except to get used to it, all the remedies I've tried seemed to do no good hardly; were it not for my breasts, I would have been well in a few weeks. I felt so well & strong for any one in my situation that is, felt well enough in a week after the baby was born to go to work, but suffering so much with my breasts has weakened me down, I've had to fix a bottle for the baby as I did not give enough out of one breast to satisfy him, well Ma I cant write you much of a letter now; it hurts my breast to lean over, but I will write a long letter to you or Neal in a week or two & write all the news, but I must tell you how proud John is of his boy, he has learned more little songs to sing to it than a little, & will get up any time in the night to sing it to sleep when it wont go to sleep after nursing I know we are spoiling it bad, but I cant help it until I get entirely well, John says it is the prettiest (by far) grandchild you ever had, that none of them can begin to compare with his boy. Tell Neal she would laugh her & Irene enough if she could hear him singing or talking to it. But no more just now, my love to all accept a good share for yourself. Hoping this finds all well, I am

*Probably Clara means hartshorn, a preparation of ammonia.

Your affectionate daughter
Clara Dunlap

P. S. Excuse bad writing, brother G[eorge] was here this evening, all well at home, sis M[ollie] looking every day, brother J, Sallie, & all the children were here yesterday, all were well. Ma you must tell sis Carry I agree with her now entirely about girls not marrying until they are 22 or 23 years old, as she used to tell me I ought not marry until I was that age no how, tell her I think, indeed, I <u>know from experience now</u> that I married soon enough, <u>plenty soon</u>, but good bye again.
CD

Tell Neal she must pick out a pretty name for the baby & send it when you write, & let it be soon, as they will nick-name him if I dont name him soon, send a pretty one, tell her.

Mary Elizabeth (Mollie) Boddie in Ouachita Co. to her sister-in-law Cornelia Dickson in Autauga Co.

January 9th, 1861

Dear Nealy,

I was very glad indeed to receive a letter from you & I will answer it with pleasure, though I dont feel strong enough to write long at a time, & writing on my lap at that, for you must know, dear Nealy, I am confined to my room, & have beside me, in bed, one of the sweetest little girl baby's you ever saw. My babe was born on the 19th day of December, & this is only the fourth day that I've been up except a few minutes at a time to have my bed made. I sent your letter to Clara, & have it not by me now. I am not certain if she has written to any of you, not having seen her for some time, but hear from there every week. I am so sorry to tell you of Clara's suffering with her breast, one of them rose in two places, but 'twas nothing more than I expected, for with all our persuasions she would not let her baby nurse from it sufficiently to keep the milk out, you know how Clara is, will have her own way, although she promised so readily to let the baby suck, but she did not, because she said 'twas so painful, & she had the milk drawn every way but the right one, & in consequence 'twas not done effectively. John D[unlap] was to see us one day last week, he said Clara was better, had had her breast lanced twice, that Clara expressed herself as having had a bitter experience in letting her breast rise when she suffered ten times more than she did in letting her baby suck. John said his boy was doing finely that he would beat all the boys & gals in Arkansaw if he got plenty to eat; if C[lara] dont take care, John will be feeding him with fat meat, & potatoes & perhaps greens. John loves to brag on his boy, I assure you. Sis says, he is a very pretty baby, we think he favors his Grandma Dickson, they have not yet named him. I saw C after I wrote to you, Nealy, & she asked me if I had told you to send a name for her boy, told her no, as she had not requested me to do so, but I tell you now Nealy, do select a name, for John & C will never decide on one to suit. George has the naming of our baby, & he speaks of calling her for his sisters, Frances Caroline, if he gives her that name, which I think is a very pretty one, I shall call her Carrie. She is just three weeks old today, Nealy. Both of my breast have been very sore, one of them so that I could not turn myself in bed, but thanks to George's good nursing, they are relieved for the present, but the weather is so changeable I am in fear lest a cold should settle in the one that is so difficult to cure. When mine were so sore & threatening to rise, I had my baby & Lucy's babe both to draw them. Lucy's baby is nearly three months old, she named it for Julia Ann. While I am on the subject of babies, I might as well tell you Albert Stone's wife has one too, a girl just four days older than mine, hers is named Mary Julia. Geo[rge] S[tone]'s wife has a son, hers is nearly three months old. Geo Stone, & his brother-in-law, Silas Pope, has bought a farm on our side of the river, they have moved over with their families. Dee Newton has also bought a place over here, but 'tis off the road, & a retired place. I guess Ora & Dee will remain with the old lady in Camden, untill the place is improved before they would move to it to live. The place Dee bought, is nearly adjoining George, on the lake.

    I hope you have all spent a pleasant Christmas & may all happiness attend you through the New Year; I spent my holiday in bed you know, but was happy through the enjoyment of others, for the times here seemed so lively, the children enjoyed themselves so much . Sis [Sally] & John R[umph] with all the children were here, they came down a day or two before Christmas, as Aunt Sallie had to make all the good nogs & cc for our dear <u>old</u> men, & all the little fry. I dont know, Nealy, how you can reconcile yourself to the lonely life of ever being a <u>dear old Aunty,</u> to your numerous nephews & nieces, but I often tease Geo. & tell him I wish I had been an old maid, but 'tis only when on the eve of such an event, as has just taken place, for I do love the sweet little babies & dont mind the trouble of them afterward. I wish you could make us all a visit, & have the pleasure of attending to some of your dozen little progency in the capacity of Aunty before some of the boys put the notion of marrying in your head, for then I know all chance of your company is gone, the men are so selfish, (I'll tell you that much, Nealy), that they will not spare one out of their sight for long. I am not much surprised at anything I hear of Betty's doing; has Mrs. Nunn moved to Selma to educate her children? Mrs. Lasiter will be quite lonely, all her children gone. I suppose her son is with her yet, or is he off at school? We have no school at present, & Geo. speaks of not wishing to send his boys this year. They are at work, Willie has been sick with severe cold, all the balance well.

Friday 11th, I had company yesterday, Nealy, & will finish my letter today. I heard from Clara, too. I am so sorry to tell you she is still suffering with her breast, has had it lanced again & there is still another place to be opened yet. I do wish 'twas so I could go & see her. I know she is almost disheartened, being ill so long, but John D[unlap] said C. was up all the time, that she felt better up than in bed, but this week she is in bed with it. The baby keeps well — Sallie goes to see her every opportunity she gets to leave home, the roads are getting to be so bad through the Freeo Bottom that sis says she almost dreads a trip over there. When Sis came over before Christmas the bottom was covered with water, & every big rain we have, the slues across the bottom are swimming. I do wish John R[umph] had moved on our side of the creek, instead of selling his place over here. Mr. O'Bannon (who bought his Geo. Stone farm) has two married daughters moved out, & the third one is to come this spring. They are all much pleased with this country & his sons-in-law wish to purchase places here. The Old Lady & gentleman O'Bannon say they are settled for life. We have had a warm winter so far with occasional days of frost & ice, our river in good boating order before Christmas. Geo. will commence ginning his crop tomorrow, he is much bothered getting his meat out of the bottom, such a good range, 'tis almost impossible to get the hogs tolled home — only killed seventeen before the holidays, & he has any number of the finest kind in the bottom range if he can only get them. I have nearly a half-barrel of nice lard on hand made last year, Nealy, but I miss all my good sausage meat this year, as I am not able to attend to the making of it — Sis[Sally] said she would make some for me if I would send the meat to her, we have sausage cutters & 'tis not much trouble to prepare, but I dont care to let the negroes have the entire management of it, unless I <u>could see</u> that 'twas done nice, & cleanly Well, dear Nealy, I will run on to the last sheet of paper & writing but very little of interest to you, I guess, but I wont have the time to pester you again with such rigmarole, for when I get strong, I must go to work, patching, darning, knitting & cc is accumulating now for me, but I shall be more than pleased, dear Nealy, to have you write to me <u>very often</u>, long or short letters, any word from you all is gladly received, & George is just as anxious as I am to hear from you all, but I never can prevail on him to write, he often asks me if 'tis not time to hear from home, & why dont some of them write. Why I tell him he's no business to wonder why some of you dont write, if you don't write, for if everyone of us would do as he does, none of us would hear from you. Tell Carrie to write as soon as she can. I know well enough her situation to find some excuse for her, give her our dear love, so also every member of the family, tell Mother D[ickson] I am glad to hear she has quit the pipe, that Geo. has quit chewing tobacco, but I laugh; & tell him, he cant hold out long, I guess. We send love to Mother D, Grandma L[anier]. does Irene stay with the latter yet? I hope to hear of Grandma's health being much better, & how does Uncle Clem come on these times? Whenever you see any of my old friends, Nealy, who enquire of me remember me kindly to them. I love to hear of all my Autauga acquaintances. Write to me, Nealy, although I cant promise to write often, you shall [not] hear from Clara as long as she cant write for herself — tis her right breast I think that has troubled her so much — I am so sorry for her, for I've experienced some of what she has to suffer — my breast that rose when John was a baby was nearly three months getting well.

The children send love to you, & Grandma, & all their little cousins. All Sallie's little ones are well. Geo R[umph] was here one day last week, said his Ma was busy with her lard, & making sausage, cc. Mrs. D. Stone was to see me yesterday, she complains of getting no letters at all from her friends in Ala. The black ones here send their howdy to their kin, & all well. Well, dear Nealy, I must bid you good bye for this time. I remain,

Your affectionate sister
Mollie E. Boddie

Clara Dunlap in Ouachita Co. to her mother Clarissa Dickson in Autauga Co.

Feb 28th, 1861

Dear Ma,

I receaved your most welcome letter . . . last week & you may know I was very glad indeed to receave it, as twas the first letter I had rec'd from home since last October. I should have written to you again as I promised in my letter before Christmas, but (as you have heard ere this) I've been afflicted with the worst rising breast I recon you ever heard of, the physiscon that has attended me ever since the second week in Jan. says it is the worst, as well as most obstinate case of rising breast he ever saw & he is an old experienced physision. It hadent got to its worst the last time sis M[ollie] wrote to Neal[y]. It rose & was lanced <u>seven times</u>, & two more risings have come since, but were so near the openings where it was lanced that they broke into them & so did not have to be lanced, the Dr. once thought he would have to cut it off to save my life; it had got so bad, it threw me into high fevers & I had night sweats & a dry hacking cough, he gave me medicine, (Sassaparilla* was one thing) I dont know what else, but he put something in it which hope* or rather cured my cough but I had lost my appetite, & could not eat anything for weeks. I begged the doctor not to cut it off, told him I would submit to any remedy he saw propper rather than it cut off, it seemed like I would rather have died; than that; he said he would try blistering it, & he put a blister of iodine on; & let it remain 2 nights & a day, & oh Ma, of all the blisters I ever saw it was the worst, the little blis-

*Sarsaparilla is any of a various climbing or trailing tropical American plants of genus <u>Smilax</u>, having a root which has been used in medicine as an alterative. My grandmother called it "Sasperilla" and used it for many home remedies.

*"Hope" was frequently used to mean "help" in days past, though I tend to think that Clara simply mistakenly wrote it in her rush and agitation of the discussion.

ters about over it had even mattered; he then applied collard leaves, & kept them on for nearly two weeks; (I thought my whole breast had turned to matter, the openings ran so much) & then my breast all at once became very offensive. John went right off after the Dr. — when he came he said it was trying to mortify, & put a poultice of <u>flaxseed</u> & <u>charcoal</u>; which soon took away the offensive smell & prevented it from mortifying. But, for two weeks after it was blistered I could not raise my head, & when I was raised up to drink anything (I could not eat) I suffered so much that I would drink as fast as I could just to get to lay down, again, a little wine or buttermilk was all I lived on for several weeks. The Dr. scolded me every time he came about not eating, told John he must make me eat, but 'twas no use; the neighbors were very kind to send me so many nice things, especially Mrs. Broughton, that lady that was so kind summer before last, she would send me something nearly every day. As soon as my breast got well enough to bear it, the Dr. put strops of coal plaster as close as he could lay them on, or rather bound up my breast just as tight as I could bear them with strips of the plaster, you see, it commenced getting hard all over again & all the sound part of my breast which was underneath had two large hard lumps in it; & it was to prevent their rising by stopping the circulation in it; that he bound it up, it has been nearly three weeks since, & I am in hopes they wont rise, though they are hard yet, & one of them is paining me very much. I will have one consolation, if it can be called one, if these lumps do rise there wont be any more, for the reason that there is no place for another rising to come on that breast. It is deceased too much, all cut up with the <u>lancet</u>. Ma, did you ever know a breast after it rose & was lanced; to turn black all around the places, where it was lanced at, well, mine did, (as brother George says "as black as a hat") though 'tis hardly that black, but dark purple, & looks like the flesh is almost rotten. Dr. McElrath says 'twill all come right when it gets well, that wont be soon — three or four weeks at the farthest, he says. Oh, just think how long I've been suffering with it — 3 months — ever since I wrote to you nearly 3 months, it commenced several days after, & I have not been allowed to go out of my room until the last few days, & cant do any kind of work, not even knit, without inflaming it. I get all the good books I can & read nearly all the time, since I've got better, I've got so that I can eat now. I nurse the baby out of the other breast, (the sore one has gone dry) but do not give enough for it, & so we have to give it the bottle, too, cows milk diluted with boilling water & sweetened, the baby keeps well except a little collic once in a while & grows so fast you dont know. John says I must be certain to tell you that it can sit alone, in your lap though, has been sitting alone for two or three weeks, ain't he smart, & at night when he gets fretful sometimes John takes him in his arms & pats him to sleep. I declare it seems so strange that J should have to take care of him at night instead of me, but I am too weak to lift him at least it hurts my breast ask mammy what is good for collic in babies, her remedy I mean — every one says he is such a pretty baby, such bright blue eyes & fair skin, it seems almost transparent, has a very high forehead, & well — a fine baby every way; I know you would laugh to hear J praising to any one that comes he is so proud of him; calls him his <u>lawyer</u>.

Tell Neal I had named the baby before I rec'd your letter, & happened to pick out the same name she did, only John wanted to name him after his brother James, & so I named him <u>James Howard</u>, you must tell the Dr. & Mr[s] Howard that I named the baby after them. But Ma, why dont Neal[y] write to me. I have not receaved a line from her since Oct. I do think so <u>very</u> hard of her for not writing to me, I thought of it all the time I was suffering so much, & it made me feel so bad; I felt neglected by you all, it seemed that I could not get a letter from N, & she wrote Sis Mollie 2 long ones. I would not have treated her so (Neal, I mean) if I had been well & she sick. But I am nearly done & have not written anything hardly except my breast & the baby, but I thought you would wish to hear all about it, & I will write a more interesting letter next time; that is if my breast dont get bad again, I do hope it wont — some how it has been so long sore, that I am almost disheartened about its getting well soon. I know you will think this a very badly written letter, but Ma the Dr kept me so stimilated with morphine so much, when I was suffering <u>so much</u> that I can scarcely hold my pen sometimes, so nervous, I wanted to write to you several weeks ago, but I couldnt sit up long enough then, much less hold my pen.

I've comenced gardening; or rather John has, for me, have mustard up & peas & cabbage, have all kinds of other seeds planted, almost, that we plant at this season of the year, but none up yet. John bedded potatoes today, & commenced planting corn; he made a plenty to do him last year & two or three hundred bushels to sell & made 27 bales of cotton, sold $85 worth of fresh pork & bought pickled pork, insted, says 'tis so much fatter & will go farther than his meat would; for the negroes; he killed 2 thousand lbs. of pork besides, that with six barrels of pork (pickled) that he had bought, & a couple of fat beeves this fall will do him he says; I heard from brother John's & brother G's this week, all well, Sis Mollie's baby is the prettiest, fattest little thing; dont resemble any of her children, thinks of naming her <u>Frances Caroline</u> after sis F[rances] & sis C[arrie], but will call her <u>Carrie</u>, after sis C. well, Ma, I am so tired; I've had to stop & rest four or five times, my breast hurts so, leaning over; I will write a long letter just as soon as I get better & will try to write it better too, my love to all, & accept a good share for yourself, & beleave me as ever

your affectionate daughter
Clara Dunlap

P. S. Oh, I do wish you lived out here so John could help you some, it seems so hard that you have to buy corn & everything, when we have it to sell. I dont know what I would give if you did

*John says I must not forget to tell you, that brother George said the other day, that if Arkansas did not <u>ceecede</u> from the Union that he would sell out & move right back to Ala.

C. D.

*Note: This postscript was written at the top of page 1:

Sallie Gildersleeve Rumph
Photo courtesy of Ruth Bagwell King

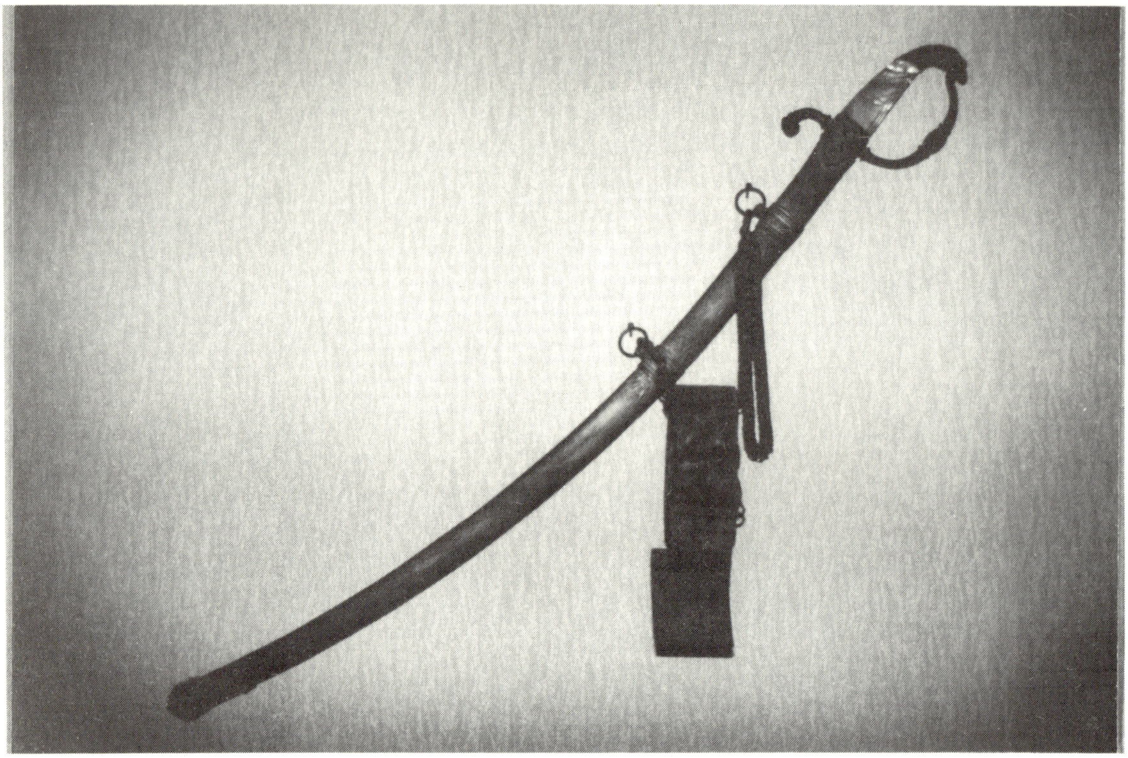

Sword awarded to S.H.N. Dickson when he was a member of the official escort for General Lafayette when he came back to the States on a visit in 1828.
Both the sword and the epauletes hang in Sue M. Russell's home. Photos courtesy of Sue Martin Russell.

PART TWO

Clouds of War

Lincoln WAS elected president, Arkansas DID secede from the Union, and the nation was embroiled in a civil war. For those of us in the 1990's, that war is distant history. But for the writers of the letters found here in Part Two, it was immediate and heartbreaking. Regardless of age, today's readers know the anguish of war, both as active participants and as keepers of the homefront. The difficulty we might have with these letters is one of perspective. We have never known anything but a unified nation, one that has warred against other nations. These letters, however, were written from those who experienced national division in its ultimate and most tragic form. Sentiments ran extremely high; there was unsuppressed anger and resentment, and people reacted violently to that which threatened them and their way of life. It is hoped that our readers will establish a high level of empathy for these writers to better understand their emotions.

The War Between the States was not felt west of the Mississippi with the actual intensity of fighting that the states east of the river experienced. The tensions, however, were great and the men were pressed into service for the Confederacy. The hardships of war became an integral part of the life they lived. Mail delivery became most uncertain, and we read of undelivered letters and of long lapses between correspondents.

Included in Part Two are letters written by and to Mary E. Boddie at home to and from George Boddie, whom we know as "brother G," who was serving with the Confederate troops. While these letters are a departure from Clara's and Cornelia's correspondence, they provide a coherent picture of both fronts, the homefront and the battlefront. And they do come from the "family" of Clara and Cornelia. The chronological order of the letters is temporarily abandoned to maintain a tighter focus.

We also include some letters from Tom Love, who was fighting east of the Mississippi, to Cornelia. The inclusion of these letters is simply to broaden the first-hand scope of the war.

THE HOMEFRONT

Clara Dunlap in Ouachita Co. to her sister Cornelia Dickson in Autauga Co.

April 17th, 1861

Dear Sister,

I receaved your most welcome letter week before last, & should have answered it immediately, but being so behind hand with my sewing (losing so much time by being sick all winter, you know) I had to sew very hard to catch up again. I commenced getting well over a month ago, but am not as strong yet as I used to be, my breast did not rise any more after I wrote to Ma; as I then thought it would, but it has gone dry & has shrunk away until it is not as large as my fist, oh I did have an <u>awful</u> time of it all winter: & really thought when it was <u>so</u> bad that I never would get over it; & C, you dont know how much I wished for you & Ma to come & see me once more; sometimes I would almost deceave myself in the belief that I should see one of you riding up some day, but you know 'twas because my mind was so weak. I could imagine almost anything then. I nurse my baby out of the other breast, but dont give enough for him, the little rascal is so hearty, he sucks me & a bottle full besides, nearly every time, & is never sick a day. I just scald his milk now, & sweeten it instead of making it half water & milk, & he thrives faster, oh C, I do so much wish you could see him now, he is such a fine pretty boy, so every one says that sees him, brother G[eorge] was up this morning, he says he is as fine a boy as he ever saw & so pretty, & thinks he will make the tallest man in the family, has such a large foot & hand & is so tall for his age & you know C, if brother G praises him so much; he must be pretty sure enough. All were well at home, he said; — has a fine garden this year, & his crop is more forward than it has been in several years, my garden is tolerable good, but late, my first planting's did not come up; we will have a great deal of fruit this year, if we have no more frost. I think 'twill be large too, John has set out a plumb nursry this winter; C, you forgot to put that little song in your letter for J[ohn] to sing to the baby, you must send it next time, he sings all kinds to him, with or without a <u>tune</u>, or words either, sometimes, just makes them as he goes — thinks there never was as fine a boy as his future <u>President</u> as he calls him, says he is too smart for any thing else. The <u>cannon</u> have been firing in Camden a great deal to-day, & I learned late this evening that the President has ordered <u>75 thousand men</u> from the <u>border States</u>, to help him fight the <u>Confederate States</u>. I guess they will show the old rascal about that though. Arkansas did not ceceede but they were going to have another election next August to determine what to do, as by that time all would know whether Lincoln would do right or not;

but as it is, I expect her & all the rest of the border Slave States will go out, & that quick as lightening, too; 'tis a great pity they did not go out when the rest did, they might have known what an old Abolitionist like Lincoln would do, but I almost forgot to say I receaved a long letter from Ma yesterday, & I was so very glad to get it, & to learn that all were well, I think it strange (dont you) that I never receaved a letter from you all winter, but the mails have been so irregular. I am so sorry Ma is so uneasy about me, I ought not to have told her how bad my breast was, I never thought how uneasy 'twould make her, as I wrote that I was getting better; tell her I will write again next week, to her, & will write oftener than I have been doing. Brother J[ohn] will start to Carolina shortly, to see about his law business there; but will go through by Memphis. I intend begging him & doing my best to get him to come back by Autauga, to see you all, if he does you can send that little dress by him. I know I will be proud of it, C.; 'twill be the first present my baby has ever got, bless his little heart, C , I do wish you could see him, tell Ma he sleeps all night long, hardly ever wakes 'til daybreak, & then he is hungry enough I can tell you, but tis the hardest matter in the world to get him to eat, he <u>will</u> spit it out & makes all kinds of faces; but dearly loves his bottle, you ought to see him how glad he looks when he sees me warming it for him, he can hold it in his little hands as tight, when sucking, but 'tis late bedtime I must close, I have told you all the news that I thought would interest you; I have not heard from brother John's in a week, the creek has been too high for passing, tell Ma I will be certain to write next week if possible, you must write again <u>soon</u> let it be, C. I am always so glad to hear from home, give my best love to Rebecca & Mrs. Howard. Tell Jimmy H[oward] I named my baby after him, my love to all enquiring friends, to sis Carrie, Irene & Mary & tell all the negroes howdy, my best love to Ma & accept a good share for yourself, & do write soon. Hoping this may find all well, I am your

Affectionate sister,
Clara Dunlap

P. S. John sends his best respects. Oh, I must tell you what brother G said about all of them weighing last week, brother J & Sally was down, & they took a notion to be weighed, Sallie weighed <u>175</u> lbs, sis Mollie <u>145</u>, brother G <u>151</u>, brother J <u>150</u>, brother G's little Mary weighed nearly 60 lbs, I did not think she would weigh so much; or sis M either.*

*Brother George probably had a cotton scale at his gin which prompted all this weighing.

Clara Dunlap in Ouachita Co. to her sister Cornelia Dickson in Autauga Co.

May 6th 1861

Dear Sister,

Yours of the 18th I receaved several days since, & I can assure you that I was truly glad to hear from you, & from home, & that all were well in the enjoyment of good health; & oh, what a real blessing it is; I never before in my life, reallized what a great blessing health was so much, as now, I am getting to beleave that every one has to be afflicted one way or another the better to appreciate it <u>fully</u> as I do now.

I am happy to say your letter found all well; I was over at brother John's yesterday, brother G[eorge] & sis M[ollie] & all their children were there; all were well; we had a nice strawberry dinner, S[ally]'s strawberry vines are doing finly this year, better than mine or brother G's either; & the finest berries I most ever saw. Sis M's baby is growing very pretty indeed, brother J thinks her the prettiest one of the children, Sallie's boy still grows, has several teeth, G recd a letter from Irene, not long since, & will answer it soon, I should like so much to see Grandma's garden just now; I know from Irene's description it must be pretty. Sis M & I were speaking of it & wondering how she can in so short a time, make such a nice garden, & to think she is now confined to her bed & cannot go to see how pretty she has made it. I am in hopes though when warm weather comes she will be able to get out. My garden is doing better, vegetable's are beginning to grow, will soon have peas, — have had one mess of Irish potato & have upwards of a hundred & fifty chickens; John has a fine stand of corn & growing very fast, cotton has come up & looks well; he has <u>185</u> acres in cultivation this year besides his potatoe patches & pea patch; you know it will keep him <u>very</u> busy, to work it well. We were all much surprised to hear of Bettie Ziglar's marrying; I did not think she was that old; I am glad to learn that Dee [Lasiter] is doing so well; if he keeps on, he will soon coin himself a <u>name</u>, though he is very young yet. I recon Mrs Lassiter won't mind it so much now, about his leaving home, as he is trying so hard to do his duty faithfully.

I think our state is arroused <u>at last</u>, to thinking of <u>war</u>. I think they have 8 or ten companies now at Little Rock, they will soon start to Virginia to assist Jeff D[avis], & <u>not</u> old Abe as he thought they would; at least he had the presumption to demand assistance from us; but I now give you our Governer's reply to Mr <u>Abraham,</u> (as they call him) in answer to his demand for troops to fight the Southern States; Governor Rector* telegraphed back to him "Go to <u>hel</u>l,God dam him", I <u>al</u>most hated to repeat it. I guess old Abe is begining to think by this time; that he might as well be <u>there</u> as here; for all the South & Ark included cares, well he deserves the worst that can

*"Governor Rector" refers to Henry M. Rector, governor of Arkansas from 1860 to 1862.

befall him. I guess he thinks we out here, are <u>hoosiers</u> sure enough; or that we have a <u>hoosier</u> Governor one, & with all that we are pretty independent in our way of speaking, & there he will think just about right. A great many of our young men in this neighborhood & in Cam[den] has gone, & a good many others speak of going in the next regiment that's formed. John is more excited than I ever saw him, speaks strongly of going in the next company that goes, so does brother G, he told sis Mollie the other day; if her father was only out here, that he would go off with those brave young men that were going to defend the country, & it made him feel so bad to stay behind. Sis M says the tears would roll down his face while he was speaking; he is <u>very</u> much excited, too; very much. brother J is more cool but determined. Oh I almost forgot brother G told me to ask you & Irene to save him some more tulip seed, if you pleased, he had some very pretty ones this year, but wants a variety. Nealy, all of my fruit trees died last summer, when we had that drouth, but have 5 cherry trees, 4 or 5 pairs, as many apples, 3 peach trees, & one little blue-plumb scion living; all the others died, all my grafts died, too, brother J told me to tell Ma she must not mind his pleagueing her & not to get mad & scold him too much & when she moves out here, he will give her one of his best cows & calves to start with, says he is always joking every body & she must not mind what he said. I told him though, I did hope she would send him a good scolding; so that he would know better next time. Sis M & S[ally] both told me to be sure & send their best love to you & Ma, G'ma, Sis C[arrie], Irene, & all enquiring friends, sis M says you must write soon. Well Neal I am writing so often now, I dont have as much news to write as I did when I wrote more seldom, you must write soon. Give my love to Ma, sis C[arrie], G'ma, & all enquiring friends. Tell Mrs Howard were I twice the distance, I could never forget the many acts of her kindness to me & you, & to you alone since I left. I think her too true a friend to forget so easily, that neither <u>time</u> nor <u>distance</u> can make me forget one who has proved so true a friend as she has to us. Give my love to her & Rebecca in particular, tell R I should like to be there to compare <u>babies</u>. Jimmy is learning to eat right well now, gets prettier every day, so <u>John</u> says. I dont think he would hardly own that there ever was a baby so pretty or so smart as <u>Papa's hoosier</u> as he calls him. Tell all the negroes howdy. Tell Laura not to name her baby (I guess she has one in this time) until I send her a name, tell Mammy my baby loves <u>biscuit</u> & <u>rice</u> & <u>flour doins</u> better than cornbread, do write soon C & tell me all the news; from

your affectionate sister,
Clara Dunlap

P.S. John sends his respect to you all. A convention of delegates met yesterday at Little Rock to pass an order on <u>ceesession</u>.

Sisters, Seeds, and Cedars **112**

Clara Dunlap in Ouachita Co. to her sister Cornelia Dickson in Autauga Co.

July 27th, 1861

Dear Sister,

I receaved your most welcome week before last, but having been quite sick since then I had to put it off, I had an attack of diarrhea & bad cold which settled on my bowels. I had very little fever though & am glad to say I am entirely well. Jimmy keeps well, is just as hearty a baby as I ever saw — never sick,— does nothing but grow, I think him very backwards about teething though — has no sign of a tooth yet, & dont try to crawl; but when I stand him up he tries his best to walk, John braggs just as much as ever; says I must tell you that Jimmy's <u>name</u> is the most <u>indiferent</u> part about him; as well as the most <u>common</u>. I saw brother John yesterday, said all kept well, he is suffering very much for rain, we've had several good rains, & at his house the dust was hardly laid, brother G[eorge] had more rain than brother J. Sis M[ollie] & Sallie spent the day here several weeks ago, S[allie] is away on the <u>road</u> to <u>Boston</u>* again; over half way, I beleave, she is fast, aint she; Our fine early peaches (that I told you about last year) have all ripened & gone; a great many of them rotted & fell off before they got ripe good, about half a dozen of our best trees broke down this last spring so heavily loaded with peaches, we have a great many fine watermelons & mushmelons now; John's corn is pretty good; will make enough to do him & some to sell, but would have made double as much almost, if he could have got one or two <u>good</u> seasons on it at the right time, his cotton is fine at present, & if the seasons continue, will make 50 or sixty bales though he hasent as much land in cotton as he had last year & year before, but the bolls & squares are so much thicker, I went with him to the watermelon patch this morning, & we passed some of the cotton in going; & I declare I never saw finer cotton; J says he thinks the <u>lice</u> helps the cotton, keeps it down until it gets the age on it, or until away in June; & then the bolls & squares come on much thicker than when it grows off rank & weedy at first. I do hope Ma has a good crop this year. I declare it seems too bad to have to live out there on that poor land & have a drouth nearly every year. I do wish you & her lived out here where you could make a living anyhow, even if you did miss several good seasons.

I was both sorry & surprised too, to hear of Grandma's death, surprised, because from what you wrote before, I thought she was getting better, I know you will all miss her so much; as regards the contents of her will, I was not at all <u>surprised</u>; as I knew <u>almost</u> (from what Bill Hall told me several years ago how the negroes were to be distributed) though, like Ma, I thought Mark & Cash <u>both</u> were for her & Robert for bro George, as you say, <u>we</u> never expected anything, as for myself, I know that John has a plenty to surport

*"On the road to Boston" is a colorful euphemism for the word <u>pregnant</u>. I have never heard that phrase before.

me comfortably & well as long as I live; but I cannot but think that Grandma did wrong to disappoint Ma in the way she did, by inducing her to beleave what she would never realize; though you know C Grandma was not so much to blame, she was old & childish & twas nothing in God's world but Mary Love's* <u>low mean contemptable lies</u> & <u>news carriaing</u> forever tattling into Grandma's ears that induced G'ma to do so — nothing else but <u>her's</u> & <u>Bill Love's</u>* mean low-life tales, against Ma & her children; Well, little the good it does <u>him</u> & maybe it may never do her any, God only knows, <u>she</u> may be taken off just as <u>he</u> was, I know C, Ma used always say that whatever anyone obtained by dishonest or unfair means would never do them any good: & I beleave it. One thing is certain, <u>I</u> wouldent have Mary L's <u>conscience</u> for five times the value of her ill-gotten property.

 You never wrote me what Sis Carrie's baby was named, Sis Mollie was up a few days ago, for a little while, & she was saying she would like to know its name & said tell Sis C to write & tell her what she had named it, says she must not think of being run out of names <u>yet</u>, says tell her she will have to commence at the first of the Bible & go through all the bible names, sis M thinks right hard of sis C for not writing all this time, she has not rec a letter from sis C since last summer, & she answered that, as soon as she recd it. I dont think I ever told you that we had a home-guard formed in our neighborhood & that they elected brother George captain and they have formed a vigilante committee. [You] have heard before this I know of two <u>great</u> battles fought in Virginia, & our troops gaining the <u>victory</u>, also of the battle in Missouri, & our troops gaining the victory there, & what a great revulsion of feeling was taking place in St. Louis, the cecessionist's were not afraid to speak out now, their real sentiments. I never could begin to beleave that we <u>could</u> ever be conquered. But I had almost forgot to give you the recipt for making that candle, when brother John was over the other day; I was speaking of it & saying I was afraid I could not make it plain enough for you to go by, Oh he says; "just tell C, to take a long str[ing] pour some wax around it; coil it up like a snake, & stick fire to one end of it." I laughed & told him that would never do, that I would have to be plainer than that, (Of course, he was joking though) & so to begin; just get one pound or a little more, of wax, melt & strain it, in a clean skillet, then get a <u>small</u> tea cup of soft white rosin; melt that & <u>strain it</u> into the wax, set your skillet in the yard, over a few coal's so as to keep the wax & rosin melted good & you would have more room out in the yard, than in the house. Have ready some thread suitable for candle wick, measure off your wicks some four or five yards in length & about double the size of common candle wick; about 6 or 7 of them will make a large candle stand (the reason you have them in so many pieces is to make it more convenient to dip them, which would be almost impossible were it all in one piece,) then take one of the wicks & pass it through the wax in the skillet, taking care to leave 2 or 3 inches at each

*Mary Love refers to Mary Rawlings Love, granddaughter of Mary Dickson Lanier, Grandma.

* Bill Love refers to Mary's husband, William G. Love, brother of Addison Love.

end to hold it by, as the hot wax would burn your fingers; To do this the best way, you must have a small forked stick, to hold the wick down good, in the wax, as it is passing through, then let one of the negroes catch hold of one end of the wick & another one the other end & stand to one side until the wax on it is cool, while this is cooling, pass another through the same way, & if you have a good many to help you, you can pass them through before you stop, but it takes two persons to each string. Then commence with the first wick & pass them all through again, let them cool a <u>second</u> time then pass them through a <u>third</u> time, that gives 3 coats of wax; & when perfectly cold <u>again</u>; your wicks are made; Then get a smooth cob about 4 inches long, trim the smallest end smooth for the top of your stand, — then commence at the top with one of your wicks & wind it around the cob close & smooth until you get to the bottom, then carry the wick up & down the cob until you get around it, commence again about half an inch from the top this time, & wind it around, (as at first), to the bottom again, in the mean-time when one wick gives out, & you have to commence with another one, take care to lap it well, then up & down length ways the cob, then around it, alternatly, until you use up all the wicks, & your stand, if made right, will be in the form of a <u>sugar-loaf</u>, not quite as tapering though, but take care always to commence <u>half an inch each time</u> from the top of the last round. When within two finger lengths of the end of your last wick stop & carry it up to the top of the stand, it will easily stick there, allowing a straight piece to stick up to be lighted like a candle, & remember C, you must be very particular not to let the wick burn down too close, or your whole stand will be in a blaze in half a minute, notice & keep the wick pulled up several inches, say 3 or 4, above the stand, it gives a beautiful light when well made; Well now I just know almost you & sis C[arrie], too, I expect, will laugh at such a <u>lengthy</u> description of a <u>candle</u> but I could not explain all the particular's in fewer words, I dont think so, at least, & I think them worth making; they are so cheap too, mine I had last year, lasted nearly six months, when you've used your candle most up, you will find the cob wont stand up as at first; then just lay it down on the table & stick the wick upwards & twill do as well as at first, maybe if you could have a small wooden stand made, twould be better than a cob. July 28th. Sis Mollie came up while I was writing this evening & she told me to give her best love to you, Ma, & Sis Carry, too, & to Irene & little Mary, brother G sends his love to you & Ma; also, brother J sends his respects to you all. All the neighbors had a meeting here yesterday, for the purpose of forming a new committe, & a Mr Arrington was here; he has been appointed <u>agent</u> to get up some subscriptions of <u>cotton</u> for the Southern Confederacy, every man of them gave <u>half</u> of their <u>cotton crops</u>; You spoke of Autauga Co sending her <u>third</u> company; our county can beat that, Neal; Ouachita has sent her <u>sixth</u> company, all large company's, too, one of them a company of cavelry, the first company was the Camden Knights No.1, 2nd City Guards; 3rd Ouachita Voligneers; 4th Ouachita Rangers (they are the horse co) & Camden Knights No.2. Well C 'tis late & I must close with love to Ma, Sis Carry, Irene, & all enquiring <u>friends</u> accept a good share for your self & beleave me as ever,

your affectionate
Clara

*This is the last good page of letter paper I have in the house, John is going to town tomorrow & I am anxious to send this letter right off, that I wont wait, so please excuse it; C.D. Tell all the negroes howdy for me; you never spoke of old Aunt Ester, C. Is she dead?

*I left out the name of one of the company's, the Ouachita Greys.

*Note: This postscript is written at the top of page 1:

*Note: This post script is written along the left margin of page 1:

Clara Dunlap in Ouachita Co. to her mother Clarissa Dickson in Autauga Co.

Aug 19th 1861

Dear Mother,

It has been a <u>long</u> time since I receaved a letter from you. C[ornelia] wrote that you would write soon, & I have been looking sometime for a letter, but not recving any, have come to the conclusion to write any-how as maybe some of you were sick; though I do hope that is not the case; This leaves all well, though we have had some sickness, (but nothing serious) this summer. Jimmy has been quite sick with fever & bad cold, he was threatened with croup every night for a week, I tried various remedies, but none seemed to relieve him, until I put a scotch snuff plaster* on his breast, which soon eased him. I dont think it was more than 20 minutes after putting on the plaster before he went to sleep & before that he seemed to be almost chokeing. His fever was caused from cutting teeth, he has only one through yet. I had no idea 'twould make him so sick, he has always been such a healthy baby. Ma you have no idea what a good nurse John is. I have no trouble atall when Jimmy gets sick. John helps me sit-up at night just like a woman, & nurses Jimmy half the night sometimes & indeed all the time Jimmy was sick; but I know you would laugh Ma to see John in his shirt-tail with Jimmy in his arms, rocking him to sleep, & singing some old Methodist tune, though it makes no diference what tune he commences with, he allways ends with "<u>On Jorden's Stormy Banks, I Stand</u>", he looks so short & duck-legged some how, it reminds me more of the picture of an old <u>Catholic priest</u> than anything else, minus the priest's robe, that is.

But I have some very sad news to tell you, Ma. Sis Mollie lost her little Sallie about two weeks ago, August 5th, she died very suddenly with conjestive fever*; John & I were down there on Saturday & she appeared as well as usual, though she has been rather delicate all summer; she was

*While none of my reference sources list "scotch snuff plaster," I am confident it is a thick mixture of snuff and scotch whiskey, used as a poultice to rub on the chest.

*Conjestive fever is most likely pneumonia.

*Calomel is a white, tasteless powder, used as a purgative.

taken sick on Sunday morning (the day after I was there), had a high fever all day, late in the evening brother G[eorge] gave her a dose of calomal*, & a dose of oil the next morning, but the medicine dident act, she had another high fever & towards evening became delirious, they sent immediately for a doctor, but it was late in the evening before he got there. As soon as he saw her, he pronounced it conjestion, & told them there was no hope; she died that night about one o'clock. The Dr said she had conjestion of the brain, lungs, bowels, & stomach. Bill came up next morning & told me the sad news. We went down & I could hardly beleave she was dead, she look[ed] like she was lying asleap, perfectly natural, & I think the prettiest corpse I ever saw. Sis M[ollie] wished her funeral preached there in the house, & brother G sent over to Cam[den] & the Rev Mr Ratcliffe of Cam, preached her funeral that evining. He read the 15th Chapt of 1st. Corinthians, the hymn he sang was "Life is a span, a fleeting hour" & cc, you can find it in the Methodist hymn book. All the neighbors attended the funeral. Poor Sis Mollie took it oh so hard, it seemed like she could not bear to give her up, & brother G too, I never saw him so affected, & how could they help it, she was such a sweet amiable child, every one loved her, little John* took her

*"Little John" refers to the dead Sally's older brother, John R. Boddie.

death harder than any of the children, she thought no one was like her <u>buddy Johnnie</u>,(as she called him), & she was his favorite, he would give up to her in every thing; she is buried near Sis Fannie; Sis Mollie told Mr. Ratcliffe (he was trying to console her about her loss) that she <u>would</u> try & live from this time forth, so as to be prepared to meet her little darling in heaven, John was down there yesterday & he says he never saw any one changed as much as she has in the last two weeks; & I know it must be hard to have children long enough to love & become attached to them & then to see them die, but God knows best, he gave & he can take away. Sis M recd a long letter from sis Carrie, she sent it up to me to read, oh Ma it makes me so uneasy to hear that you are having such severe attacks again, 'tis true you have enough to trouble you, what with Grandma's death & the way you have been slighted in her will, not because of the value of what she had, but to have given others preference over you, & you never merited one bit of it either, but as sis C says, she was influenced by M[ary] L[ove] & Bill, & I beleave she was, as regards M L, I've nothing to say (I expressed my opinion in my letter to Nealy) only that retribution will reach her some day, just as sure as there is a God in heaven. Oh Ma I would give anything if you only lived out here, near us, where we could see you often & where you would always make a plenty to live on any how, if no more; John & I went up to Holly Springs, a town above here, about twelve miles from here, this summer. About 3 miles this side of the town, there is the prettiest little place I have seen out here, with a large apple orchard, peach orchard, & one of the best springs in the country, the land is hilly, though not as rolling as where you all live, & a nice little frame house on it; John said it would just suit you, it belongs to

a Mrs White in Holly Springs, & I think she would sell it now, she has no one to work it now her boys have gone off to war, J says the land is very good indeed. I would rather, if you do move out here, have you nearer than that, but I know you would prefer a hilly place to these flat bottoms, & would it not be better Ma than to live away in Ala, where we cant see each other in two or three years, & besides if you had that place, you could be near to such good preaching every Sunday Methodist, Baptist, & Presbyterian, just which you prefer. Oh I do so much wish you were out here. Tell Nealy to hold onto that little dress, if the war ends & I get a chance to go with any one I will come after it next winter or spring, but if she gets a chance, must send it to me, as the chances are very much against the war ending. Well I have finished my paper & have hardly got through. Sis Mollie & Sally both send their love to you, Nealy, & sis Carrie, Irene, & Mary. My love to Neal, sis C, Irene, & Mary, & accept a good portion for yourself, write soon Ma, I am so uneasy about you since I heard of your sickness.
Clara D.

*I am very busy drying peaches; John has just finished me a new kitchen, a large roomy one, we needed it very much though. Ma ask sis Carrie if she heard whether Joe Brodnax (in the Selma Co.) was killed or not, his father is nearly crazy about him. C.D.

*John made 150 bushels of wheat this year and has splendid wheat too. He made enough corn to do him & right smart to spare, says if the seasons continue, he will make 50 bales of cotton, have a large turnip patch sowed — have had three messes of sweet potatoes this week, tell Jerry he cant best that I know, I think we will make a large crop this year, tell Mammy & Harriet & the other negroes howdy, brother John's Derry died the first of last week, tell Jerry. I send you a lock of little Sallie's hair. Sis Mollie requested me to do so. Tis one of her little curls, rather. C.D.

*Note: This postscript is written along the left margin of page 1:

*Note: This postscript is written across the top of page 1.

Clara Dunlap in Ouachita Co. to her sister Cornelia in Autauga Co.
Sept. 17th, 1861

Dear Sister,

Your most welcome I receaved last week & need not say I was truly glad to hear from you all & that all are well, but was much surprised indeed to learn that you had not received my letter, nor Ma either; I know that yours had been written long enough almost for me to rec' an answer; & the letter I wrote Ma about the middle of Aug as well as I can recolect, & if you or Ma have not rec'd either of them yet, <u>some one</u> has been smart enough to take them out of the post office, — if such be the case, you will have to get some one to go to the office the day the mail is expected & be the first to see the letters & cc, or you will often be disappointed in the letter-line, & I am sorry it is so & it hurts me to hear that you & Ma are uneasy about me; & I write regularly all the time, except when sickness prevents. Yours found all well, though Jimmy is not to say well, he has something like chicken-pox, though the doctor says it is not that, the sores on their first appearance resemble fever blisters more than anything else, & when the water in them breaks, they form large sores, he has had it now almost three weeks, & you know it is enough to make him cross <u>enough</u>, & then teething, too, but that would not fret him half so much as the sores, they are nearly all over him now, & it hurts him every time he is moved, he has only two teeth yet; John & I spent last Saturday & Sunday with Sallie, John & brother J went deer hunting Saturday, but never killed anything; brother J killed a large deer a few days before, says it was the fattest deer he ever saw; John went hunting week before last with some of the neighbors, he killed 3, (2 large deer & a fawn) & they killed 2, quite lucky, wasent he, all were well at brother John's, S[allie]'s baby has been quite sick but is well again, can walk a few steps. C brother J says he dident know that you were being sent for as a physician (you know what he means), pretends like he understood from your letter that you were being sent for in a <u>particular way</u> only, to women folks, & says if you are not proficient in <u>the art</u> he will <u>will</u> you some of his books when he dies; You must study up on something to <u>retaliate</u> on him good fashion, (when you write again) for joking you so, & you must not mind his jokes C, he is always joking sis M[ollie] & me about something. Brother J's Roda has another baby, a girl — makes 6 living children, besides 2 dead. I heard from brother G[eorge]'s Sunday, all well, but John [Boddie], he has fever; there is not much sickness in the neighborhood now, & what there is, is light cases, 3 of our negroes have been down with this bad sore throat, but no cases of fever in our family this year.

You wished to know what papers we all take, brother G takes the Montgomery Mail & New Orleans Delta, brother J takes the Richmond Whig & Memphis Appeal. John takes the Richmond Enquirer & New Orleans Crescent besides other papers in <u>this</u> state. John & brother G took the Eagle of Cam[den], but the editor is now fighting in Mo; brother J takes the Gazette from Little Rock, & Herald from Cam. so you see we get all the late war news. I send you a statement of the no. of troops Arkansas has furnished for the War. I cut it from the Herald. I also send you a parody on Gen Scott.* I think it pretty good & true also. & I also send a photograph of Lincoln which I think really laughable, as much so as his message, which you sent me. I am almost ashamed to say that I havent knit a single pair of socks, but I've had so much other work, what with Jimmy's being sick & my housekeeping to attend to, & I've been knitting for John, too, he was plum out of socks, but I intend commensing soon, & knit all I can. Sis M & Sallie are both ahead of me, both of them have 3 pair apiece & still knitting. The sewing society in Cam have between 2 & 3 hundred garments made to send on, &

*"Gen Scott" refers to General Winfield Scott, Commander of the Union Army at that time.

still making, they are just as busy as bee's over there. I don't think I told you that I saw John Sims some time since, going up to fight. His company are the Lisbon Invincibles, he was 3rd Lieutenant in the co; I happened to be over to Alb[ert] Stones, & they stopped to get water, he was very much surprised to see me, dident know I was out here, or married either, he said his brother Wm had gone in another co. He came back a few weeks ago as a recruiting officer, & to get up some more volunteers to fill up the regiment, as some had got sick & had returned home; which left a vacancy in the regiment, he saw brother J in Camden & was telling him all about the little events that occured up there, before the regiment was called into action, & among other things he was telling about some of the Missouri girls that he saw up there, said they wore their hoops next to the skin & went barefooted & brought the soldiers butter milk in jugs & a good many other anecdotes, brother J said he seemed to be in high spirits. C, Ark Ouachita Co has beat Autauga in sending volenteers, she has sent eleven companies, besides odd numbers that have went up & joined other companies.

 C, about those things of Pa's. I am perfectly willing they should remain at Ma's until I do come, though when that will be I cant tell. I would be afraid to start now, & venture from N Orleans to Mobile, anyhow; As to Pa's gun; Ma can keep that & I dont want her to think about paying me for it; & you wouldent either, would you? & you or her one, can keep the watch, too; I have such a good clock, I dont need it, but C, about the sword of Pa's, brother J says Pa told him, that winter he was out there, that he intended to give that & his eppilettes to John when he died; & as that is the case, I would like John to have the sword & eppilettes* both, but I dont want Ma to think about paying for the gun, that is, pay me I mean; & you could claim the watch, about the other things, I am willing they remain there till I come. Oh, I do so wish Ma could move out here & be near us. I know the society is better there, but ours is improving every year, & brother J says tell brother Add he must be sure & come out here first, to look for land; come by to see him anyhow. But C, we all were surprised to hear that G'ma had left Ike* sis Carrie's place. I thought it was the place she died at, who did she leave that to; I have written my paper up & hardly finished. Give my love to Ma, Sis C, Irene, & Mrs. Howard, Rebecca & Mrs. Lassiter & Bettie, accept a good share for yourself.

Your affectionate sister,
Clara Dunlap

 Sept 23rd. You see I've had no opportunity of sending this letter off until today & thought I would add a small postscript. John & I were down at sis Mollie's yesterday, found all well, sis M is having her children's winter clothes wove at home, or rather Mrs. Dr. Stone is weaving jeans for the boys: Sis M & her go on halves; sis M finds the loom & warp, & Mrs. Stone the filling, & weaves it, sis M is going to learn Julyann to weave the negroe

*The sword Clara speaks of was awarded to Col Dickson when he served as a member of the official escort for General Lafayette in 1828 on his visit to the U.S. The epauletes were a part of his uniform. (Photo page 106)

*"Ike" must be Isaac Lanier, son of Dickson Mann Lanier, and grandson of Mary D. Lanier, Grandma.

clothes at home, sis M told me to give her best love to you & Ma & sis Carrie, to all she said, Sallie was down there with the children, she sends her love to all, too. She said brother John had a hard chill Saturday & high fever. Neal, ask sis C what she put up grapes in several years ago before I came out here, she had some put up in saw dust, I think, but I have forgotten. I put up some in wheat bran to keep until winter, & they have rotted, ask her what kind of wild grape she put up once, & what time of the year was it, summer or fall, & if they were winter grapes or fall grapes, Jimmy has cut 2 more teeth.

C.D.

*Note: This postscript is written along the left margin of page 1 and continues all across the top of the page and some short distance down the right margin

*Be sure & let us know who G'ma left the place she was living on to; You never said whether Ma had her buggy home or not or her clock <u>either</u>. I think <u>Ike</u> is utterly devoid of principle, to act the way he has though I suppose that is his real nature. Let me know what Bettie has named her baby and recon she is very proud that it is a girl. John thinks he will make <u>50</u> bales of cotton, & C, about that little dress; just make it infant waist, & tuck the skirt, dont cut it off, maybe some chance will arise for you to send it. Tell Mammy, Harriet, & all the negroes howdy for me. I expect Ellen is most married, aint she; I do wish you could come out with brother Add this winter. I would be so glad, & S[allie] & Sis M would, too, both send their love to you all. Make the little dress body large so it will fit him next summer. I know it is pretty, & am so much obliged to you; I think Irene deserves a great deal of praise for knitting so much.

C.D.

Clara Dunlap in Ouachita Co. to her mother Clarissa Dickson in Autauga Co.

Oct 14th 1861

Dear Ma,

I receaved your most welcome letter a few days ago. I would have written immediately but wanted to see brother J[ohn] & G[eorge] before I wrote. I expect your letter must have lain in Cam[den] a week before I got it, by the date, but John dont go often now, he is so busy having his cotton gathered. I have seen Brother G & J & they both say that not knowing anything about the wording of the <u>will</u>, they could not give any correct views about it, & not knowing anything about what the laws of Ala would be, about such a case, but if it was in Ark they could tell more about it; & brother John says he wouldent for the world (by giving advice mislead you & cause you to take a step that you might afterwards regret,) for anything, but if you would go to Selma & pay a good lawyer 10 or 20 dollars to review the will & examine into it, he (the lawyer) would give his op[in]ion to you about it,

& then if he thought he could gain it for you, you could employ him to do so; & his judgement about it would be a great deal more correct than his, (brother J) or brother G either, but <u>brother J</u> did bid me tell you, Ma, that as circumstances is now it is out of his power to give you any assistance whatever, he has no money atall, neither has John; there is no specie* scarcely in the country, & paper money is not allowed to pass, anything under a $20 bill & twill soon be raised to a $50 bill; but he (brother J) told me to say to you, if circumstances got better, or if the blockades were opened so cotton could sell, that he has about $4000 due him this winter, & he could collect some of it; if not all; & he could lend you all he could spare; & you could either pay lawyers or buy a negro or land either, just as you pleased about <u>that</u>, he would lend it as soon for one thing as another & you could use your own pleasure about the disposal of it & you could pay him just when you could or when you got able. That would be sufficient, but he thought that now would be the worst time you could move, owing to the scarcity of money for one thing & then provisions of all kinds. Corn, meat, cattle, & cc command <u>cash</u>, they are not selling high, but it is impossible to get them on credit & twould be a much more favorable time to wait & move next fall or winter, the block[ades] will surely be ended in that time. But oh Ma it seems hard to have to wait so long before I can have you & Neal living near me. I never wanted to be <u>rich</u> so bad in my life as now, so that I could just buy you a place, buy John M[orton], & move you out myself, but as times is John has no money atall himself, not even enough to pay taxes next spring, if the blockades are not opened, true he is making a large crop of cotton, probably 50 bales, but it wont do him any good unless he can sell it, & he has more than enough corn to do him another year, & he would be as willing to help you as I am, if he could only sell his cotton. It would be a bad time for either of them to leave home now, brother J's health is not good this fall, he has frequent spells of sickness. All the rest of his family are well though, Sally will be down the last of this month or the first of next, & neither John or brother G[eorge] could leave their families, without leaving some man to take charge of the negroes, & all the men have gone off to war except those who have families & negroes & a good many even of them have left. But Ma about John Morton. I am perfectly willing to lend you my share of the money that Uncle Clem* has for us, & I know Neal will be quite as willing to lend her's to you. I dont know how much it is, but N[ealy] said in a letter to me that Pa did not owe much, & I think Uncle C got 500 dollars for us in Georgia, did he not? & if Pa did not owe much, what Uncle Clem has for us would be nearly enough to buy John M. Let me know how much it lacks & John says if he can sell his cotton he will furnish the ballance, & then you could let him have a hand to work long enough to pay him back, when you do move out, if he had it (the money) now & any way to send it, he would sent it, but he has not. He has over a

*Specie is coin money.

*"Uncle Clem" refers to Clement Lanier, brother of Clarissa Lanier Boddie Dickson.

*John Morton was a slave who had been sold and separated from his family. Clara as well as her mother and Cornelia are quite anxious to buy him before Mr Caver, who bought him, moves away to Texas.

thousand dollars owing him & cant collect a cent, until people can sell their cotton to pay him. I am as anxious as you are to get John M & have been ever since he was first sold,* but I have had nothing of my own to get him with, I do hope if Mr Caver goes to Texas this fall he will sell in Ala, & then we can get him anyhow, when times get better, find out Ma how much will be coming to us from Uncle Clem & how much it lacks of buying him, if <u>uncle C</u> could advance the money to Mr. Caver, & if he (Mr. Caver) would wait on us, until the blockades are raised, he may be able to get him & hold him until John could pay the ballance, after <u>his</u> cotton was sold, but if they dont raise the blockades, John wont be able you know Ma to help get him, but I freely lend you my part of what Uncle C has of ours & I hope Neal will do the same, I wish it were enough itself to get him. About that place I spoke to you of, I have not had an opportunity of finding out what it cost, but will find out in less than a week & will sit right down & write to you as soon as I learn. I will find out all about it as you said, it is not as rich land as ours down here, but it is improved & has a fine orchard & spring. I think but I dont know for certain that there is over 300 acres on it, the greater part is woodland, there is right smart cleared land, but John dont know how much until we find out, it is on the public road, has a nice little frame house, & is within 2 or 3 miles of Holly Springs, a small town up there, the owner lives in H Springs & has rented the place I spoke of out for the last 2 years & would probably rent it again, if you could rent it the first year, maybe then with help, if times got better, buy it. I dont think it would cost more than $2000, & maybe not that, I expect they would want some of it cash down. I will find out though & let you know in a week sure

C Dunlap

*Note: This postscript is written across the top of page 1.

*Give my love to sis Carrie, Irene, Mary, & all enquiring friends. Tell C I will answer her letter soon, our family are all well, my health was never better. Brother G & J's families are all well, sis Mollie & Sallie send their love to all. What does Uncle Clem think about the <u>land deed</u> does he think it can stand I do hope it may be broken.

C D

Clara Dunlap in Ouachita Co. to her sister Cornelia Dickson in Autauga Co.

Oct 22nd 1861

Dear Sister,

I wrote to Ma a week ago, & in my letter I said I would write again in a week or so as soon as I learned about that place I spoke of some time ago, (the gentleman that went up to see about the place for me; as John's going would have made them think <u>he</u> wanted it, & consequently they would have raised the price, but Mr. Houge's going & merely enquiring about it did not seem so; he is one of our neighbors, & very kindly offered to go & enquire all about it.) Well the administrator told Mr. H. that he could not sell the place atall until the old lady's son came home from war, he is off fighting in Kentucky; & he said too that they would want $3000 dollars for it then, I was astonished as I had no idea it would cost so much; there is 360 acres in the tract, & more than one third of it is cleared land, the other is woodland if it was so that Ma was able to get it, or if times or the war was ended, so that times would be better, so the[n] we could get it for her; it is one of the most desirable places in the country, & so near to good regular preaching too; but there are cheaper places than that, that are nearer here, than that, they dont offer the same advantages, but the land is some richer; oh C it does seem as if I would give every cent I had (of money) be it much or little, just to move you & Ma out, & have you near us, but times is so, John cant collect a cent that is owing him; he would be as willing as I am to help her; I wrote Ma that I would lend her all the money that Uncle Clem had of mine, & I was sure that you would do the <u>same</u>, & if the blockades are raised so that the cotton can sell, John will make up the ballance of the money. Ma said she thought John Morton could be bought for 4 or 5 hundred dollars; & C you said that Pa did not owe much, & if so, Uncle Clem has nearly enough of ours to buy him; & twould be so much better than for him to go away off to Texas, & never see Mammy, or his children any more. I wrote to Ma to let me know how much Uncle lacked of having enough & John could find the ballance, when he could sell his cotton; Ma wanted to know what corn & pork could be bought for, C tell her that corn is selling at 4 bits per bushel & pork at from 10 cents to a bit*, there has been a great deal of corn made this year & wheat too, the wheat sells at $1 per bushel. C you were writing about how the land was to be divided, & if Uncle C could settle up the estate without Ma's [sanction] or approval, brother J says he thinks if the estate is not in debt, that Uncle C could settle it up any time he wished, though he (brother J) could not advise Ma about the case, as he knew nothing about the wording of the will, or any of the particulars, or about how the law would be, on the case, as it is in Ala; & he would be afraid to advise Ma, as he <u>might</u>, by so doing, lead her to take a step, that she might afterwards regret & she would thereby loose what confidence she has in his judgement, & he would not have her to loose <u>that</u>, for any thing, by giving her wrong advice, but he bid me tell her (& I did in my letter of last week) "<u>if times got better, so he could collect what was due him, that he would lend her all the money he could spare</u>" "to do as she pleased with," & she could pay it back just when she got able;" (I am writing all this for fear Ma did not get my letter) & I wrote all of this & much more in my letter to her, he says if she would go to Selma & pay a lawyer $10 or 20 he would give her better advice, than he (brother J) could do; I do hope it will be so she can get her share

*A bit is 12 ½ cents.

yet. I was down at brother G[eorge's] Sunday. All were well. Sis M[ollie] has a loomb in her house, & is weaving her self, or learning how, as she dont understand all about it yet, she is learning July Ann how to weave, too. Mrs. Dr. Stone has woven a piece of jeans for sis M & herself, the first she has ever wove, I think she done finely, considering it was the first attempt, nearly every one is having loombs made now. John says if the war continues he will have one for <u>me</u> next year, tell Ma brother G[eorge] takes as much interest in the loomb as sis M does, & more if anything. He helps draw in the warp & cc, just like a woman, & brags on sis M's weaving, says she will make the prettiest cloth of any of the women, yet, if she keeps on; he said Sunday if Ma were here she could learn us all, as she knows all about it, they all send their love to you, Ma, & Sis Carrie. brother J & Sallie were down there too, they both send their love to you all, Sallie's little boy can walk. I know if you were to see him, you would say he is just like Mr. Gildersleeve. All the children were well, little Mary [Mamie] has knit a sock for Gilder, aint she smart, & only 5 years old. I have had a nice piece of jeans wove for John, had to hire it done, though, & just sent off my warp & filling to have the negro cloth woven. I intend trying to do that myself next year if I live. Well C do write soon & write all the news, about everybody, tell me about Betty Whetstone, & what she has named her baby, & give my best love to her & Mrs. Lasiter. Give my best love to Rebecca & Mrs Howard & Ella, & my respects to Dr & Mrs H[oward] tell the Dr that if Jimmie lives I intend sending him out to study medicine under <u>him</u> when he gets old enough. Give my love to Ma, Sis Carrie & all the children, & let me know what sis C has named <u>her</u> baby. Do C write all, everything & write soon to your

Affectionate sister,
Clara Dunlap

P. S. Tell all the Negroes howdy, tell Mammy if we dont succeed in getting John M now, I will never rest til I do get him; if its 5 years, & if I ever get able, tell Harriet I intend buying Tom Caver, too, if Bill Caver* will sell him.

*Slaves when they were sold on the block had no last names; the custom of that day was for the slaves to take the last names of their owners, thus Tom Caver was owned by Bill Caver.

Clara Dunlap in Ouachita Co. to her sister Cornelia Dickson in Autauga Co.

Dec 5th 1861

Dear Sister,

Your most welcome & long looked for letter was duly receaved a few days since, & I need not say how glad I was to receive it, especially as I had been looking several weeks for one from you, & I was more than glad to hear that all are well though you did speak of Laura's baby being sick, & in sis Carrie's letter to sis Mollie three days later, she said it was dead, I was very sorry to hear that; I dont think you ever told me its name.

I think you are all <u>very</u> deserving of credit for working so busily for the soldiers, & Irene especially, I declare she has more than done her part, & deserves an extra share of credit, & Fanny* too, has done more to her age than the married laidies out here, we have no sewing society out here in the country, but they have a large one in town, most all the laidies have contributed more or less to the society, one old lady out here spun & wove a nice piece of jeans & made 5 coats, 5 pair pants; & knit 7 pair of socks, I think she done well for an old lady. I was down at sis Mollie's day before yesterday, she was busy weaving a piece of negro cloth has woven one piece & is now most done the other. You have no idea how well she can weave, for a new beginer. I tell you she can make the shuttle fly, she is going to put in a piece of jeans (when she gets this piece out) for her boys coats, Mrs Dr Stone wove the jeans for their pants; I was at Mrs Stones a few days ago, she has another piece of jeans in, for her boys sunday suit, she said, it was both fine & pretty, a pretty jet-black. I had to hire our negroes cloth wove, & am making it up now, I lined the coats through & through, & they are so heavy to sew on, it tires me, I will have a loom next year, & then I intend learning, I've just learned that there is a man living below here, that makes <u>clock reels</u>,* I intend getting one just as soon as I get money enough to pay for it, they cost 3 dollars, it is so much trouble to count every thread as you reel it; as you have to do on a home-made reel. I got tired of it this fall, having all my woolen filling to reel myself. But I had almost forgoten to tell you that Sallie Rumph has a fine daughter, born on the 24th of October, she is not as large a baby as Johnny, but prettier, she has named her Sarah Amelia, the children call her little Sallie hard time. Sallie was telling me a funny little incident about George, the morning the baby was born (twas before breakfast) while the children were eating breakfast out in the entry, the baby squalled, all the children quit eating (but George) & looked at each other & commenced laughing & whispering; when G (with all the gravity of a judge) said "oh, <u>children</u>, do pray hush & behave yourselves aint you ashamed"; & went on with his breakfast just as though he was an old man & was trying to set an example for them. Little Johnny is running all about the yard. Jimmie has commenced crawling at last, & such crawling, twould make you laugh to see him. Sis Mollie says he looks like he is rowing a boat, he sits flat down & jumps along on his little rump & working his hands up & down just like anyone would swimming. Tell Mammy he has just begun to eat corn bread & pot liquor & greens, & he dearly loves fat meat, but I cant coax him to eat sweet potatoes, only once & a while, or butter milk either, oh he is just as fat as a little pig, & such rosy cheeks, oh C I do wish you could see him, he is so lively & playful, but I must stop or you will say I am bragging again but John says if you could only see him <u>once</u>, you never would accuse me of <u>bragging</u> never, Well C what do you all have to eat, these hard times; we have plenty of greens, turnips, potatoes, peas,& <u>pumpkins</u>,

*Susan Frances Love

*A clock reel is a machine on which yarn is wound and measured into hanks.

& fine ones too, (& would you beleave it, Jimmie cries for them whenever he sees them, I cant give him enough, he is so fond of them.) We have plenty of meat yet, to last until spring, I think. John says he will have to send down several hundred bushels of corn to New Orleans & get molasses & sugar & cc; by getting 3 or 4 barrels of molasses, we will kill enough meat to do us; every one seems to be troubled about getting coffee next year; severel of our neighbors are out & are useing parched pinders,* wheat or potatoes as a substitute for coffee; I think I would prefer parched meal coffee to any of the other substitutes, but we have enough coffee to do us another year, by close saving. The article is selling in Cam[den] at 4 bits per pound, isent that dear, I went over to Cam a few weeks ago, & among other things, I bought 4 calico dresses, enough to last me 2 years with what I have; the reason I got so many, they are getting very scarce, very few pieces in Cam in fact, & I thought I would get while I had a chance. Well C I don't know anything else to write that would be interesting. Does brother Add speak of coming out this winter yet. If so, I do wish you & Irene <u>could</u> come with him, I do want to see you all so bad, & it seems I cant get out there this winter no how, will have to hope for a better time. Give my love to Mrs H[oward], & Ella, to Rebecca & Mrs Lasiter Bettie. Tell B I think her baby has a very prettie name, it is uncommon & I like it somehow; tell her to write to me. Give my love to Ma, Sis Carrie, Irene, Mary & all enquiring friends, accept a good share for yourself & beleave me as ever

*Pindars are peanuts.

Your affectionate sister
Clara Dunlap

[1] Note: This postscript is written along the left margin of page 1.

[1] C <u>has</u> Mr Caver moved yet, & what did Ma think about getting John Morton, the way I told her to, do please write soon. You must excuse this sheet of paper, I did not know it was cut until I had nearly written a page.

[2] Note: This postscript is written across the top of page 1.

[2] Sis M sends her best love to you all, & to all enquiring friends, she rec'd a letter from her mother recently, & Mr Gildersleeve has been offered such a good price for his place that he was about to accept it, & probably would move out here, if he could find a place to suit him. Harriet Murley has a fine <u>son</u>, weighed 12 pounds. Tell all the negroes howdy for me, I want to see them all.

Clara Dunlap in Ouachita Co. to her sister Cornelia Dickson in Autauga Co.

March 12th 1862

Dear Sister,

I receaved your most welcome some weeks since, & though I cant (like you) plead the enjoyment of <u>pleasure</u> as an excuse for not sooner writing, yet I can plead house-keeping duties as partly the reason, & then, I've been gardening, have peas stuck some time, & collards, beets, radishes, lettuce up nearly a month ago, & I've been making a new flower bed in the garden, for my bulbous roots & seed flowers. My roses & other shrubery are in the yard. I think my flower bed will be beautiful in a year or two; I cut a large square into 4 three cornered bed's & bordered them all around the outside with small blue lillies & inside of the lillies with pinks, the inside <u>walks</u> are bordered with jonquils, narcissus & daffodils, the hyacinths are placed inside of them & cape jasamine & green ivy (the large kind) in the center of each bed, my other seed flowers are scattered promisciously all over the beds. I made a new strawberry bed last fall, it embraces a whole square; they are growing finly. Oh, I do wish you could come out & see our garden & cc, & stay with us a while, though I should suppose that would be right dificult these times, but it does seem strange, that I should dream so often of your coming, & diferent ways every time. I dreamed once that you & Irene came with brother Add, & we had a large party somewhere in a fine house, & brother Add danced with all the girls, & I thought he was dressed finer than I ever saw him; it seemed he had on a vest embroidered with silver & gold with pearl buttons. I dident know what to make of my dream atall, unless he is going to have some good luck, the last time I dreamed of your coming, you & Irene were in a stage, & 'twas so unexpected to me to see you, but the strangest dreams of all was about being in the presence of, & conversing with Jeff Davis & Beauregard*. I thought Jeff Davis's wife was with him & she had the prettiest little babe I ever saw, but a truce to dream's, speaking of Beauregard brings me back to thinking of the affairs of our country, the present state of affairs is not very cheering, we have met with several reverses, & if reports are true, if our Generals dont make greater exertions, we will meet with much hevier losses yet, they have bragged so long of the impregnability of Columbus [Mississippi], & now if our last news is true, our troops have evacuated it & saying they cant hold it, & cc & so on. If that is the case the enemy will soon be down to N Orleans, which I've no doubt they can take, as easy as they please, that is if our men dont rally more than they've been doing lately, & above all <u>act</u> instead of <u>talking</u> & <u>braging</u> so, for I do think C our first victories instead of stirring them up to greater deeds of daring & courage, just made perfect fools of a good many, they began to regard the yankeys as a pack of cowards whom it was nothing to whip. I recon they are beginning to find out their mistake, as brother John said about the battle of Fort Henry,* our men being accustomed to seeing the <u>yankeys run</u>, & finding they dident, were so surprised they (our men) run themselves. Our Generals may have some good motive in view for all their movements, but I confess I cant understand it. I have firmly beleaved & do now, the South will eventually gain her independence, but matters look very forbid[d]ing now, & every one seems low-spirited about it. John would be off now, & so would brother G & J if they could get some man to stay on

*Beauregard refers to Pierre Gustave Toutant de Beauregard, a Louisiana Creole, who served as a general in the Confederate Army.

*Fort Henry was a Confederate fort built on the Tennessee River just below the Kentucky line.

*General Earl Van Dorn was the Confederate general who was defeated at the Battle of Pea Ridge.

*Cotton cards were shingle-like pieces of wood with stiff wires pushed through them. They were used to comb cotton and yarn in order to remove any rubbish or knots left after the ginning.

their farms, but so many have left & still going they have not as yet found any one, there is a company made up & ready to start, in Camden now, will leave tomorrow. Gen Van Dorn's* call for 8000 & 5 hundred has been filled, but he may make another soon, & if so, it will take the last man that is capiable of bearing arms. In several counties, they have called out the malitia; One thing Ark can boast of, there hasent been a single draft sent through our part of the state, & no necessity for one, as our men go quick enough without. Sis Mollie wrote to her father to come out & stay with her & Sallie in case brother G & J went off to war. Mr. G[ildersleeve] has sold out again, & they want him to come out here & stay with them in case brother G & J goes off, it will be good protection for them, but poor me, I dont know what I will do, unless I give up housekeeping & go stay with sis M & S; C what do you all do for cotton cards to card with,* is there any in Autaugaville. They are the most scarce article in the country. A good many have none atall, I've only one pair & when they give out dont know what I will do, there hasent been a pair in Cam since last summer, in Arkadelphia they are selling for $12 a pair. Did you ever, & worst of all we cant get warp, the factories cant begin to supply the demand, I heard that there were 50 Texas wagons at the factory 70 miles above here, with gold & silver to pay for thread, of course they get the first attention when that is the case, & they get their thread at $1.25 per bunch; & we that have no gold, & only State & Confederate bonds, give $2 per bunch & scarce at that. John speaks of sending a bale or two [of cotton] to the factory & get it exchanged for thread, but they wont give but five cts per pound of cotton, & you give $1.50 per bunch in trade for thread; tis too bad, but a body cant do any better these times, & the negroes have to have clothes. I have seen some very pretty fine homespun dresses this winter, spun & woven by some of my neighbors for themselves, two prettier than any I ever saw. I went to church last Sunday 8 miles above here, & saw some of the ladies at church with very pretty fine homespun dresses, & they seemed proud of them. Ladies out here are making & wearing them that never wore them before. Sis M & S speak of wearing them, S says she would wear them in a minute, but hasent learned how to make them yet. Sis M tells her she would weave one for her if she will wear it. Sis M has woven a small piece of jeans & made brother G 1 pair pants & 2 vests, & all of her boys 2 vests, & little G Rumph a pair of pants. I think it was very pretty jeans for the first. John wants to know the reason you have changed in your notions about Howard being prettier than Jimmie.* You used to think Jimmie the sweetest of all names, but bless me, I havent mentioned the little rascal, he is running all about the yard playing with the little negroes, & calling the chickens, turkeys, pigs & every thing he can call in his way, cant talk plain yet, but makes you understand him & talks so sweet, too. I do wish you all could see him, with his bright blue eyes & red cheeks, & the fairest skin for a boy I ever saw. I tell you, C it looks like those pretty flesh-colored hyacinths grandma used to have more than anything else I can think of, his movements are so quick & changeable, always doing something all day long. Oh, I just know you would say I havent been bragging a bit & that he was your <u>beau-ideal</u> of a pretty boy — if his name is Jimmie. Be certain & send John word how come you to change your mind about Howard being a prettier name than Jimmie. Sis M & S send their love to you & Ma & Sis Carrie. Write what Sis Carrie has named her baby. C ask Ma if she knows how Aunt Fannie Pickett used to dye turkey-red thread so it would not fade. I can dye it, but mine fades. She gave me a ball of red cotton thread once. I have some of it yet & it dont fade a bit. Tell Ma, Cornelia, I think right hard of her. She has not written to me since early last fall. My love to her, Sis Carrie, & all enquiring friends. Accept a good share for yourself & write soon.

*Clara's little boy is named James Howard.

Your affectionate Sister,
Clara Dunlap

Tell all the negroes howdy.

Clara Dunlap in Ouachita Co. to her mother Clarissa Dickson in Autauga Co.

May 23rd 1862

Dear Ma,

It has been a long long time since I heard from you all, the first of Jan. I think; it <u>seems</u> even longer than that. I dont know what to make of Nealy, why she dont write once & a while at least; its true, I did not answer her letter as soon as I should, but when I did write, I told her the reason; that I had been very busy attending to my garden & planting seeds & cc, & I know she dont have anything of the kind to attend to, nothing but visit & enjoy herself; it may be wrong, but I cant but think hard of her for not writing oftener, it does me so much good to hear from you all. Sis M[ollie] rec'd a long letter from Sis Carrie in April I beleave; & answered it soon after. Sis M has been busy weaving, she wove a beautiful piece of jeans* this spring, said she was going to send a piece to sis Carrie, she has since woven a piece of plain coarse cloth for her negro woman's dresses, its dyed purple & white plaid, very pretty I think, I think she is going to weave some for her boys summer clothing next; Sallie has no loom, but is having both warp & filling spun at home, & hiring the cloth wove, says she is going to have a loom though as she is anxious to learn herself. I have a piece in my loom now, & have almost learned to weave, mend threads, & cc without assistance though my slaie* is a very inferior one; the reeds have broken in half a dozen places, but John put me new ones in, I think I will try and get a better one when I get this piece out, we have a negro woman that can weave, but she is a good

*Jeans was a strong twilled cotton fabric used to make overalls.

*A slay or batten is a part of a hand loom that supports the swing, or lay, of the loom.

field hand, & J cant spare her only on rainy days; But buying a slaie now is almost as hard to get as cotton cards. What do you suppose Ma, I give for a pair in Cam[den] last week, but I know you could not guess, $15. Dont you think that a price for cards, & common wool cards are selling for $6. I would not have bought my cotton cards, but my old ones were almost gone, & I had to give that or let the negroes go nakid, as osnaburg & any kind of domestic* selling in Cam for 50 cts a yard. John is going to buy all of the warp, but had to give 2 dollars & 50 cts per bunch for No. 5's & dident get but 5 bunches, the ballance I've had spun at home, as well as filling enough for over 100 yards, we have a woman that does nothing but spin all the time. I have a bunch of fine No. 12 for mine & Jimmie's dresses, but dont know how to dye it, if I could only see old Mrs. Cases now; I know she could tell me how to dye some pretty colours. I am having fine filling spun for them but dont know when I will attempt weaving such a fine piece, but aside from the subject, it does seem right diverting now Ma, to go visiting, & hear everyone discussing the merits of this, that, or other mode of dying, & how many cuts of such & such a No. it takes to fill in a yd of such a No. & cc & so on, but aint it so different from a few years since, when all the topic under discussion would be fashion's & cc, but what amuses me with it all is to hear those that one year ago; (dident know a bear in a harness from I dont know what;) now talking & advising as though they did it all from long experience, but aside from all joking I do think this war will be the making of a great many women; I expect you all live so near the factory you can get cloth cheap enough without weaving it. Were you not surprised to hear of the Federals having possession of N Orleans; & Jeff Davis is calling for more men, under the conscript, it will take a great many, wont it; all under 35 & over 18, but poor me, what will I do when John goes, it seems as if I cant give up every thing, to go to rack; as it surely will do if I go off & leave it, I have the promise of a young lady in our neighborhood to come & stay with me if John is called off, but if she proves to be no braver than I am, I dont know what we will do. Oh, if Nealy was only out here to stay with me I would not mind it so much, though the lady that will stay with me is a very steady, well-behaved girl, yet I would feel so much better satisfied if it was Neal. I have finished getting John's clothes ready & he would have been gone to Corinth, but orders came from Van Dorn through Gen. Rhone for all the troops that were called out, to remain in the state to defend it, & all the Texians that were on their way to Corinth, have been stoped at Little Rock. Several regiments of cavalry went through here. I like to see them coming, they are such brave fighters, so reckless as regards danger, a whole regiment camped between here & brother G[eorge]'s, one or two companies right in front of his house. Sis M says they kept her dairy empty, as well as other articles they wanted, brother G sold them a great deal of corn, but Sis

*Osnaburg is a heavy coarse cotton fabric in a plain weave, while domestic is similar fabric though not quite so heavy.

Clouds of War

M wouldent let them pay for milk & such little things as they asked for, they were well behaved & never interfered with anything, they seemed more eager to get milk than any thing else, & we heard yesterday that orders had come to Cam for all the cotton to be burned, if so, the work will soon commence, John made 60 bales last year & this winter has paid off all his store accounts with it except one account, & that aint much, it seems a pity but the good of our country demands it & I wouldent hesitate a moment, if it were 50 times as valuable, they've burnt the last lock on Arkansas & Red rivers, John, brother G ,& [brother] John have planted all corn this year, or just enough cotton to give them fresh seed another year, in case the war ends, but John says if he burns his cotton, he will plow that little cotton up & plant in peas, he is planting peas in all his corn this year, & he will have a large patch of potatoes, I have sweet potatoes to eat yet, & have sold some besides, we made so many last year. It seems as if it never will quit raining, we havent had but one little spell of dry weather since the first of April. The corn it looks fine, & so does the <u>grass</u>, though; my garden is better this spring than its been in 2 years, had a quantity of peas & will soon have a mess of beans, & everything is growing so fast. My new strawberry bed done much better than I expected, had six or seven large messes. At Sis M's & Sallie's you could almost gather them by the bushel, I never saw such beds in Ala as we can have out here. I think the land must suit them better. Those largest cherry trees you gave me bloomed full this year. I'm in hopes they'll bear next year, but speaking of gardens reminds me of something I wanted to find out about hop-vines, <u>there is no soda in Cam & we'll all have to raise hops, if we have good bread,</u> & I wanted you to ask Mrs Lasiter for a receipt for making <u>hop-cakes</u> like she used to make them. Sis M says if she had some good hop yeast-cakes to start with, she could make them, but there is no one out here, that uses them, & we were speaking of it, & I told her I would write & get a receipt from Mrs L as I knew if any one knew how to make them good, she did, tell her to please say in your letter, all about when to gather them, & cc & so on. I will be much obliged to her, I suppose Dee has gone, if so I know she must be very uneasy about him. Give my love to her & Bettie both when you see them. I hope you all are not so unfortunate as we are out here about our wheat crops, all through the country the crop is almost ruined with rust, & falling down. John is trying to cut his, but tis all he can do; John has a very bad sore throat right now, it is so painful he can scarcely swallow. Jimmie has been very sick with scarletina (brother J called it). It was 7 days & nights that his fever dident cool on him, he is a good deal better today, & I'm in hopes he will get well, we've had very little sickness in the neighborhood this spring, I think it a wonder; we've had so much rain. But I must tell you about a caper one of our neighbors (he has moved out of the neighborhood now) cut up a few weeks since to keep from going to the war, when he heard of the conscript act, he came near <u>fainting</u>, & immediately got drunk, went home, run his wife & children off, & when his wife came back to see what he was doing, he got his pistol & told her to <u>chop off two of his fingers</u>, or he would shoot her, declaring that he would not go to war; she done so, & worse than all, he sent word to his old neighbors that he had <u>shot</u> his fingers off. Did you ever hear the like. I think him a shame to our state, & he ought to be sent out of the Confederacy. I would be glad to see the above account published all over the South. The man's name is Marshall, the same one that used to teach school here, & a few years ago married sis M's neighbor, Mrs. Dupey. He was highly thought of then, but has got to drinking & throwed himself away. Well Ma I recon you will be surprised to receave a letter from me, mailed the other side of the Missippi; well as the yankee's have partly possession of the Missippi, I thought the surest way would be to send this letter by one of our soldiers that was wounded at the battle of Shiloh, & came home on furlough, he returns tomorrow & I will give him this, trusting that he may be successful in crossing over & that you will get it; though you might have rec'd it the usual way. I do so much hope that I may receave your answer to this, which I hope will not be long delayed, for Ma you dont know how uneasy I get about you & N when I dont hear from you in so long, I know you must be so about us out here is the reason I am sending this the surest way. Please write a long letter Ma & tell me what the people out there think of our prospects now for success, out here their opinion is unchanged; though our prospects are gloomy enough just now, but "<u>Tis always darkest just before day</u>" is an old & true saying, & I hope <u>our day</u> will soon dawn out more brightly for the long night that is proceeding it, surely if our cause is a just & right one, (which I beleave it to be,) it cant be otherwise. Give my love to Mrs. H[oward], Rebecca, & all enquiring friends, & to Nealy & Sis Carrie especially. I dont know what is the cause, but I keep dreaming of Neal & Irene coming out to see us, & they are always together, too, aint it rather strange? Tell all the negroes howdy, I would be so glad to see them all now. Sis M & Sally told me to give their love to you & sis C, & Nealy & accept the same from

         Your affectionate daughter,
         Clara Dunlap

*Note: This postscript is written across the top of page 1.

*The soldier that I expected to send this by failed to get off, so I will have to send it by mail from Cam. I do hope you will get it. All well.
         C. D.

Clara Dunlap in Ouachita Co. to her sister Cornelia Dickson in Autauga Co.

June 7th 1862

Dear Sister,

 I receaved your long looked for letter last week as well as one from Ma; & I need not say how truly glad I was to rec them, the more so as it had been <u>so long</u> since I had a line from home, & I'de become so uneasy.
 Yours found all well with us all, except Jimmie, poor little fellow has had a time of it, he had nearly recovered from Scarletina when I wrote to Ma; but took a slow lingering fever after it, & then had one of the worst looking risings on his thigh I ever saw, think it was the result of a fall he got just before he was taken sick, brother John lanced it, & said he never saw such a singular rising in his life, the matter spurted out just like the bleeding of one's arm, & looked the color of milk-whey, he is better now, but cant walk a step yet, he had been running all about the yard since winter until he was taken sick. But oh C that makes me think how much I wish you were here to stay with me. John has volunteered & will soon leave, though it's rather uncertain as to the time, it may be a week & may be a month before the com[pany] leaves Cam[den]; they have formed a camp of instruction there; & will drill until ordered off, neither brother G[eorge] nor [Brother] John have volunteered, or have any idea of doing so yet a while, but what will <u>poor me</u> do, its true I have the promise of a young lady to stay with me, but that aint like 'twould be if you and Ma were out here, I wish it more now than ever, I wouldent feel half as bad about it. John cant get any one to oversee his negroes, but his brother will come down once & a while to direct them; Oh, I do wish this civil war was ended; it just seems like I'll go crazy if it lasts much longer; I tell J now seems like my brain's are addled some times, cant half tend to my house bussiness <u>now,</u> I dont know how 'twill be after a while;
 Sallie was over & stayed all night with me Saturday night; she walked over too (3 miles) I was very much surprised (though agreably) her carriage is broken & it is such a busy time brother J cant stop to have it mended, & so S said she had stayed at home 'til she was tired & thought as she had never stayed all night with me yet, she would come over & stay all night with me & we would go down to Sis Mollie's next day in my buggy; she remained there several days so that Sis M will learn her to weave, she is so anxious to learn, I told S it seemed like old times, her & I sitting down to the table by ourselves (J had gone patroling) & so we slept in the same room.
 Brother J laughed (in reading your letter) when he came to your <u>two tears,</u> wants to know if one wasent a big & the other a little one for, your two sweethearts, & if the big one wasent for Jimmie H[owar]d, you need not deny it, I expect its so; but John says you've outed him at last, in call-

ing the baby Howard instead of Jimmie, says 'twill never do sure enough to call such an uncommon <u>fine boy</u> <u>Jim</u>, he had never thought of his being called Jim. But I must tell you what a strange dream I had last night, of being in Ala., was near sis Carrie's house & I saw a open <u>rockaway</u> or cariole* going up towards Cousin Mary's, I went on to see who was in it & twas a sick man on a mattress lying in there, I went up to see if it wasent Tom [Love]; but 'twasent him but another man; with his mouth turned right black, like twas mortified, I turned then & went in at sis Carrie's, I found Tom sitting up; he told me howdy, & I noticed his hands looked like they were dyed brown; he said twas where they'd rubbed him when he was sick, said he felt pretty well; I then saw sis C sitting in a chair & her baby in a little chair with its legs crossed, & I thought it was the prettiest child she ever had, with fair skin, black eyes, & rosy round cheeks, & every thing looked so natural, I only wish it had been a reality, my being there any how. It seems you all can enjoy yourselves so much better than we, out here. I have never been to Cam[den], yet, to see the soldiers drill or muster or anything else, have not been to preaching this year, our church was burnt last winter & its been such busy & exciting times too, that havent had another built. We've just heard that Memphis had fallen & probably Vicksburg & I am so afraid this letter may not reach you. Brother John wrote to brother Add a few days ago. Do write soon C & stay with Ma more. I am afraid she will get in bad health sure enough if she stays by herself so much, she will just study herself sick. Give my love to all enquiring friends, accept a good share for Ma & yourself & beleave me as ever

Your affectionate sister
Clara Dunlap

P.S. (Tell Mammy & all the negroes howdy)

*A cariole is a small, open, two-wheeled vehicle.

Mary E. Boddie in Ouachita Co. to her sister-in-law, Caroline LaFayette Boddie Love in Autauga Co.

June 21st 1862

My dear Carrie,

I will answer your most welcome letter & trust to chance for running the blockade, but the Yankees have not yet full sway, & I trust & believe never will. If all the late news we hear of their disasters in Virginia are true, I hope our army there may follow them even to New York, & make them realize the misery of homes laid waste & people hunted up like beasts. — Tell Thomas* we are so proud to know of his having conducted himself so bravely, all honour due such true spirit, & may he be spared many years to enjoy the liberty so dearly won. Too many of our good southern boys have

*"Thomas" refers to Tom Love, son of Sis Carrie, who joined the Confederate Army when he was 16 years old.

fallen, so many having passed <u>unscathed</u> through the battles, died from diseases incident to a soldier life, old Lincoln and his Myrmidons* will have a terrible reconing for which to answer. One good boy, a son of Mrs Elliots of Camden died in a <u>dungeon</u>, in <u>chains</u>, at Chicago, he was discovered attempting the escape of himself, & several of his fellow prisinors. 'Tis perfectly outrageous & barbeous for them to imprison women & children. Mrs Walker I hope will be succoured before she is crazed. In North Carolina the yankees have taken the homes, and all & <u>everything</u>, from the people, & there is much suffering there in consequence. The move of our Army from Corrinth every one concurs in believing it to be a good one, away from their gun boats, no one doubts but that the Federals are lost, & in our State they have met with such a check, that we have no fears of their attempting such raids as they committed on the people of Missouri — We have seen so many of the Missourians, who have left their homes, & families, & never even heard one word from them since they joined Price's army, 'twas death to them to stay, & if they ever get back which Price has promised them they should, I assure you there will be <u>no quarters</u> shown a union man in that state. Several thousand Texans are at Little Rock, they camped on our road going up, & some within a stone throw of the house, & among the calvary many of our acquaintance we say, & I would not be surprised if Bert was not with them though we did not see him. We had some of the soldiers at the house all the time, the sick ones, & one staid with us three weeks, he [was] suffering with a rising in the ear. The high waters detained all the down trains, & thousands of horses sent from the army of the dismounted cavalry companies, & they pretty well cleaned out this part of the country of all provisions — Our quartermaster is stationed in Camden. This week a company of 100 & odd soldiers camped by us on their way to the Rock. The company to which John D[unlap] belongs goes in camp next Monday six miles on the opposite side of the river. John I suppose Clara has told you is one of the conscript, that is, he would come under the act, but they all volunteer, except a few who render excuses by pleading physical disability &c. John Stone is in the same company with John D & many others from our neighborhood. Clara wrote to her mother last week & tell Add I know John R[umph] did write to him at the time spoke of, for <u>Sis</u> said so. We all wish Mother D[ickson] could be out here now, I am so sorry C[lara] has to be left, you know no young lady can supply the place of the head of a family, & though C will not suffer for company 'tis not like John was home. Father wrote to me he could not come out at present, but he would try & arrange to come some time, says he is engaged in the tanning business altogether he will never make another bale of cotton. Says he prefers our country for his business, & to be near us, to have our & John's boys to learn them to work, & I am sure I could not wish mine in better hands, & George says if

*A myrmidon is one who executes without scruple his master's commands. The term comes from Greek mythology.

father was near enough to us he might have all his boys. John R has sold his Stone farm now sure, Mr OBannon declined taking it early this year, as John R left it entirely to him to do as he best pleased about it. Mr Elliot has purchased the place for $4000 cash. Unless we have rain soon the prospect for making plenty corn is sad indeed, we had too much rain the spring, & now for the last month not a drop in our part of the country. Out west from here there was rain recently, the past few days have been quite cool, & tis clear again & no prospect at present for rain. The wheat crops are very indifferent, scarcely worth harvesting, & our gardens will soon yield nothing. My beans are bearing finely yet but the cucumbers turn yellow before half grown, beets tough & stringy. Apples are bearing well, the peaches all look gummy except the indian peaches, & we have a fine crop of plums. Some families here are very near out of corn now, I do hope in other sections of the country there will be good crops, if we cant make enough here; more is said about salt than any other article, they have some in Camden $15 the sack. Hindman* has regulated the prices of provisions, & all the cotton is to be collected & made ready to be burned in case the enemy should attempt to get it, but the people were all determined on persuing that course before & those who would not burn their own rather than let the Feds get it, why others would burn it for them. The capture of Orleans does the Fed no good, neither does the capture of any of our cities, the gun boats do all their fighting, & with it all, & the possession of the Miss river from rise to mouth, we'll whip them so badly they'll never try it again. Carrie from the very beginning I never could feel but that the South would be liberated, no reverse we have ever had, shakes my faith in what I believe will be the final results. We hear now that the French have taken possession of the mouth of the Miss river, & Stonewall Jackson is incamped on the ashes of Washington City — I only wish he had Old Abe in chains, & the rest of his advisors too. There is scarcely a family in the south but have suffered from the consequenses of this war.

*Hindman refers to Major General Thomas C. Hindman, Commander of the Trans-Mississippi Department of the Confederate Army. In this capacity Hindman was responsibile for acquiring provisions for the army. He aggressively pursured the course of forcing farmers to raise corn and other food stuffs and not to raise cotton. He was a resident of Helena.

Tell Irene, John is too lazy to write, he has not since he quit school, written five words, if I had time, would take them in hand myself — Geo. has the boys at work most of the time, they are planting peas now. Geo. says he intends to keep on working; he can destroy grass seed if he cant do any other food by plowing. Speaking of economy in clothes &c why, my dresses are worn until past turning upside down & I take for Mary* one of my old dresses to patch all of hers, & the boys clothes you can scarcely tell they are made of anything but patches — I have in a piece now to weave this week, the first made for them this year. The samples are of womens dresses. Sis [Sallie] has a loom up, she has warp & fitting to spin, two women spin all the time. Rhoda spins well, Sis makes Hannah get dinner so Rhoda can spin. I dont know which of the women she intends learning to weave, she is anx-

*"Mary" refers to Mamie Boddie.

ious to weave herself, but I tell her 'tis too hot work for her, this weather. Geo, says I must take pattern from those heroic women who intend filling our army ranks, he told Mrs. Scott she must get married &c, has Clara told you all she is patriotic enough to try again?* So is Lizzie S[tone?]. Lillah Sr. & one lady over the creek whose husband is in the army, has twins, one boy, & one girl, her youngest child next to them cant walk, besides her oldest not much more than a baby. I told Geo. if I had been in Mrs. Howards' place, after resting four years, I would be disheartened to death.

 I am sorry Uncle Clem has so much sickness among his blacks. Tell him Geo keeps a <u>path well trodden</u> across the yard, for when the war news dont keep him under excitment, the state of the crops does, says if he dont get rain wont make bread for us, let alone helping to feed our soldiers, Geo read your letter over three times, said, "well, I wish Carrie had <u>two</u> or <u>three</u> more sheets to fill." How does Mr Davis come on, & what thinks he of the war affairs? Remember me to Mrs Lassiter & all friends, tell her Dee & Ora spent a day with us recently. Dee is 1st Leut. of the volunteer co. recently made up, he & John D run, & Dee beat John two votes. ___(?)_____ has been quite sick at Corinth, but has recovered. I do hope Thomas has entirely recovered, but I would not think it prudent at all for him to go in camp any more this summer, Clem I suppose is at Corinth yet, he & Thomas were in the same Co. The greatest privation to me, will be a stoppage of mail between us. I do hope we may be able to get letters, I feel uneasy about home folks, the last heard from, was fathers letter dated 6th March. John R. has written to Add again. My love to all the family, Mother D & Nealy; you never told me what name Add has given your baby — our little Carrie grows less, I believe, she is the dearest little creature you ever saw, she was sick a day or two last week, from eating plums, something I never allow a baby to eat, but the children want to give her everything she loves. Kiss Fanny for me & accept the love of your affectionate sister.

Mary E. Boddie

[1]I did not get a Lady Banks rose to live, we nursed ours well, it put forth leaves, grew but little & died. Clara lost hers too. The moles she thought run under the roots was the cause of hers dying.

[2]Tell Add I dont send the samples of jeans because 'tis pretty by any means, 'tis wove very well for me, & I promised to send him some, not starched &c. All well.

Mollie

*Sis Mollie must mean that Clara is "patriotic enough" to get pregnant again.

[1]Note: This postscript was written along the left margin of page 1:

[2]Note: This postscript was written across the top, upside down, of page 1.

Clara Dunlap in Ouachita Co. to her sister Cornelia Dickson in Autauga Co.

June 22, 1862

Dear Sister,

I wrote to Ma several weeks since, & will now try & answer yours which I receaved at the same time, you have no idea C how glad I was to hear from you all, it had been so long since I had rec'd a letter, I had to read them over again & again.

All of us are well out here, brother J[ohn] came by yesterday going to town, he has just lost one of his fine carriage mules. We are needing rain very much now; 4 weeks yesterday since I've had a good season. I do hope we wont have a drouth, as the wheat crop has failed, 'twould be still worse to have no corn; you have ere this heard the news about England regonising us, or rather only eleven states, I beleave, if that is all she'll do, she had better not do anything but we heard yesterday that we had whipped out the yankee's in Virginia, from a northern account they had 30 thousand at least, & we heard also that Stonewall Jackson was probably in possession of Washington Cty, or on the grounds at least as 'tis said that the Federals burnt the Cty previously.

John has volenteered & joined a company in Cam[den], Dawson is the name of their captain, they will camp six miles the other side of Cam until General Hindman orders them off. Dee Newton & John run for second Lieut, Dee beat John 2 votes, J did not want to run, but was told by his friends that he would gain, so poor me — what do you recon I'll do here by myself, 'tis true there is a very nice young lady (Miss Vic Proctor*) going to stay with me, but that wont be like John. I know I'll miss him so much; I know 'tis nothing but right that he should do his part but it seems much harder to bear than I thought 'twould be even, he starts tomorrow. Oh C I do wish you was here to stay with me, it seems I would not feel half so bad. Oh C I had forgotten, I did write you a long letter several weeks ago, & I have been so pestered about J's going off that I'd forgotten 'til this minute whether 'twas you or Ma that I wrote too, I wrote to Ma just before I rec'd your's & her letter, & to you just after, I will send this by a soldier going back to Corinth, his name is Marion Hogue one of our neighbors, he will probably mail it at Grand Junction; & so I'll be certain you'll get this if not the others. I would write more, but he is in a hurry to start & cant wait on me much longer. Give my love to Ma, Sis C, & Mrs. Howard, Mrs. Lasiter, & all enquiring friends, accept a good share for yourself & beleave me as ever

Your affectionate sister,
Clara Dunlap

Tell all the Negroes howdy.

*Victoria Proctor was the sister of Martha Proctor, who would become John Rumph's third wife "Matt" upon the death of Sallie in 1871.

*C, that man I wrote about cutting off his finger <u>to keep from going to war</u>, has been sent after by a party of men, & will be made to go <u>anyway</u>, ain't it good for him, every one is glad of it. I do think it the best thing ever happened. Sis M & S told me to give their love to all. Do write soon C & excuse this short letter. I havent time.

*There is a Mr Mike Wilson just gone from Cam to Marion, Ala to bring home two young ladies going to school there, daughters of one of his friends in Cam, I wish he would go still farther & bring you too, he used to live in Milton, Ala, brother George knew him there & recon Uncle Clem did too, he went in a carriage by land.

*Note: This postscript is written across the top of page 1.

*Note: The following postscript is written along the left margin of page 1:

Clara Dunlap in Ouachita Co. to her sister Cornelia Dickson in Autauga Co.

Aug 16th 1862

Dear Sister,

I receaved your most welcome & long looked for letter a few days since, & C you can probably imagine, by your self, how much pleasure it afforded me to hear once more from home; the last letter from you being dated in May. I declare 'tis too bad to think that you & Ma didn't receave those long letters I wrote & neither have I rec'd yours that you spoke of, but C you cant imagine the surprise I felt when I rec'd your last, to see it mailed from Shreveport. I dident know whether to think you were there & probably on your way out here or what was to pay. Sis M[ollie] has not rec'd a line from Sis Carrie in a <u>long</u> time. I've learned that there has been a mail rout established just above Vicksburg, I do hope 'tis so & that we can hear from each other oftener, your letter was all news to me. Some of it surprised me very much; & some I regretted very much to hear; especially of the death of Mrs. Hall, & of the serious illness of Mrs Howard, oh I do hope 'twill not be <u>His</u> will to take her from her family & from you all, it seems that every dear friend of mine is being taken one after another; & Mrs Howard has been such a kind friend to you, I know you could never find such another soon; 'tis true you have other kind friends there, but, somehow Mrs. Howard took such a motherly interest in you, I do trust she will be spared you all; C you spoke of Mary Jones losing a brother, which one was it. I was very sorry to hear it indeed, & Rebecca Caver, isent she Bill Caver's wife. I dident know that he was dead either. Oh, this cruel war has caused & is causing many a desolate hearthstone. And so Rube Underwood is married at last, tell him I congratulate him in his choice & wish him all the happiness, & cc that generally fall's to the lot of us <u>married folks</u>. I suppose Bettie W.'s old man has gone to war, too; poor me; <u>that</u> brings me to myself, John's regiment left two weeks ago for Pine Bluff, where they will be stationed at present. They were

*Luda Post Office was located at Kent.

camped down at Luda P[ost] Office* for several weeks, John got a furlough once a week at least, & come home for a day or so (as 'twas only 3 miles), a good many of the soldiers wives went down in camp to see them, but I dident feel as though 'twas a proper place for ladies & never went. I sent John every thing good to eat, that I could find, while there & as they fared pretty rough in camps, 'twas very acceptable. Col Grinstead detailed him off on business several times while down here; once, to look up all the guns, he could find, fit for service. The Col has, since going to P Bluff, detailed him back to Cam for a wagon load of bacon; at least he accompanied the wagon to take charge of it, & engage the bacon, & so I got to see him again. I tell him the Col must think a good deal of him to detail him on business so often; but I'm glad of it, as I can get to see him once & a while; oh C you cant think how very lonesome it is since he left, the place dont look the same somehow; & it seems I cant settle myself to regular work; 'tis true that young girl [Victoria Proctor] I spoke of is staying with me, & she is such a good girl too, I dont think I could stand it if she wasent here; but that isent like John's being here to see to every thing & to talk to me & tell me about it, I miss all that now. One of his brothers,[Dick Dunlap] (the one that lost his wife two years ago) attends to his business for him; he comes down once a week to attend to the negroes & see that every thing is going on right. He would come oftener he says but it is 9 or 10 miles to where he lives & its a good long ride. You are a little ahead of me C about weaving. I know all about it except drawing it in, & I was sick when my last piece was put in & [didn't] learn; but intend trying it on the next piece, could have had this piece out but my weaver had to go to field to pulling fodder, & the one that's been cooking for me all year has a right young baby, & so the loom is idle just now until the fodder is gathered, old Aunt Katy that used to always cook is spinning, & has been ever since last winter. She is spinning some fine filling for my <u>dresses</u>, I have a bunch of no. 12* & intend having me some nice dresses wove as soon as I get filling enough. The only dificulty is to decide about dying it, though as indigo is the only color that stay's in well, I will have to have them blue & white. I dont need them until next winter, as I bought several calico dresses last winter, & those with what I had will do me all this & next year, with care; but I wanted some homespun dresses to wear about home to save

Dick Dunlap and Wife, Photo courtesy of Sue Martin Russell.

*When Clara says she "has a bunch of no. 12," she is most likely referring to the size of some thread used in weaving.

my others; as there is not a yard of calico, gingham's, or anything else in Cam, except berage* or swiss* & cc. There was an auction several weeks ago, & what do you suppose calico brought, $1 per yd, & some $1.25 cts; did you ever; & hoops brought from 9 to 11 dollars a piece; & as to domestic, there is not a yd in town, but I dont know what the women will do for hoops. I have two pretty good ones, & intend to keep mending them as long as I can before I go without, & I suppose you are going to take a school soon, I hope you will have every encouragement, as 'tis a task at best. I only wish 'twas out here instead of Ala, if you & Ma only lived here, we are needing a school in the neighborhood so much, John told me C, the last night he stayed at home, to tell Ma just as soon as the war ended (in our favor) that if he was not killed; we would go to Ala & sell her out, & move her out here, if she still wished it. He told me to be certain & write to her & tell her; it made me feel so glad, as he had never said he would do it, positively before. Well I am through my sheet & must close; but tell Ma I will write to her soon. Give my love to her, sis Carrie, Irene, & all enquiring friends, accept a good share for yourself & beleave me as ever, Your affectionate sister,

*Barege is a lightweight dress fabric woven with an open or gauze weave.
*Swiss is a fine sheer cotton fabric with a crisp, stiff finish.

C Dunlap

*I have not seen Sis M[ollie] or Sallie in a week or two, I heard from both of them this week, all well, S has a loom now & is having weaving carried on, brother G has got Berry again, he ran away last October, he was caught & brought in several weeks ago. I think brother G will sell him the first good chance. You never said anything about the negroe's at home, I hope they are all well, tell them howdy for me.

*Note: This postscript is written across the top of page 1.

*C I know you will think this a strangly written letter but my mind is so unsettled now, I cant half write, I will try & do better when I write to Ma.

*Note: This postscript is written along the left margin of page 1:

Clara Dunlap in Ouachita Co. to her mother Clarissa Dickson in Autauga Co.

Aug 24th 1862

Dear Ma,

I embrace this opportunity of writing to you, as I feel almost assured of your getting it; I've just learned there is a Mr. Elliot in Cam, who will leave this week for Mobile; I intend sending this letter by him. It has been so long since I rec'd a letter from you; & from what C. wrote still longer since you rec'd one from me; I have written time & again to you & her; & it does seem too bad that you should not have rec'd one of them. I rec'd C's last letter mailed from Shreveport, Texas* ten days ago, & answered it immediately, but am somewhat afraid it wont pass through. I told her about John's being gone, his regiment left 4 week's ago, John has returned once

*Clara has undoubtedly made a mistake in geography here. She surely means Shreveport, Louisiana.

since; detailed back to Cam to engage a load of bacon; since then I've heard from him once, am looking for a letter every day. They have a pretty rough time of it at Pine Bluff (where they are now stationed), have only fresh beef & flour without any shortening, John's health has been good so far, he complains very much of the fare, & having to do without milk & butter, (his principal diet at home); but if he can only keep his health & return home safe, I will try & not complain, but oh Ma you have no idea how much I miss him & how lonesome it is since he left, the place dont look natural somehow. I had no idea, at least could not reallize how other women felt when left in this way, but think I can sympathise with them now. Jimmie keeps well; he has just well recovered from a severe spell with scarlet fever; of which I wrote you, but your not receaving my letter, you've never heard of it. He can speake a good many words, right plain. I do wish you could see him. I was truly sorry to learn from C's letter of the death of Mrs Wm Hall & of Mrs. Howard's low health, I do hope she will recover it would be difficult to find another neighbor that <u>could</u> fill her place; so kind & considerate, & C would lose her best friend, I think. I was sorry to hear of Charley's uncertain fate — do hope he is not killed. We were glad to learn that Tom Love had recovered; we did not know whether he had gotten well or not. Sis M[ollie] & Sallie & children are spending the day with me today; both were glad to hear from you all through C's letter; sis M says tell Sis Carrie, she has never rec'd a line from her since May; & that letter she answered imedially, her & brother G[eorge] both are anxious to get another one of her <u>long</u> letters. I suppose you are burnt up with the drouth as well as we are, we have had several good seasons lately which will do the potatoes & peas some good, but the corn was too far spent, at least the most of it. A great many wont make bread & there were so much planted, too; we will make more than our bread, but nothing to what we would have made; John had 140 or 50 acres planted; I was so anxious to make a large crop as we made such short wheat-crops, & I could not help hoping that maybe you <u>could</u> move out this fall or winter, & we would have plenty of corn & meat, if nothing else, to divide with you but if the war continues, you couldent have come no how. John told me to tell you, Ma, (the last night he stayed at home) that when the war does end we will go out to Ala & sell you out & move you out here, he says he has enough land to spare some, for a year or two, until he could find a place to suit you, he told me to be certain to tell you. Oh wont I be glad to see that time come; it seems I would not mind it half as much about J's being gone if you were out here; Ma, I dont know any news worth writing; we do hear of the Federal's advancing in the state; but we've heard it so often, dont believe it much. We have the <u>telegraphic wires up to</u> Cam now; from Little Rock, it passes within <u>3 hundred</u> yards of our house.* Ma, you must be certain & write soon, maybe it will come through, there is a mail route established above Vicksburg now, & I do hope we can

*The telegraphic lines ran along the Princeton Road, which lay along the front of Clara's home. General Steele used the road as his retreat route from the area, but before that it was used by the troops.

hear oftener from each other. Give my love to all enquiring friends, to Sis C[arrie] & children, to C, & accept a good share for yourself, sis M & S send their love to you & Sis C & all enquiring friends. Hoping this may find all well with you, I am your affectionate daughter —
Clara Dunlap

Clara Dunlap in Ouachita County to her sister Cornelia Dickson in Autauga Co.

Nov 2nd 1862

Dear Sister,

I receaved your most welcome letter some time since, but have been <u>so</u> busy having spinning, weaving, & cc done, besides other things that I have to attend to, that I have put off writing longer than I ought, & now I embrace an unexpected opportunity of sending it direct to the office, to write a few lines, but will have to be brief, as I havent time to write as long a letter as I ought, but promise to do better soon. I recd a letter from Ma this evening, & tell her C, she has no idea how much good it does me to hear from her, its so seldom she writes too, & I will answer it soon, & write a long letter when I do. John has been home on furlough, — came to get winter clothing for his company, his furlough was for three weeks, but it took him over a week to ride around & notify those that had relatives in the co & so they could have their clothes ready by the time he started back, & so he got to stay at home nearly two weeks, & that was a great pleasure to me, you may be sure. I was so glad to have him home again, & so glad to think his Col. thinks enough of him to entrust him with business of different kinds, it shows he has confidence in his ability to attend to it, as tis not every one they detail off that way. John left two weeks ago, with a wagon load of clothing for his co, he is well pleased with camp life so far, that is, as much as he could be, considering he is away from home; but he has not been sick a day & he says as long as he can keep well he will try & be contented, as much so as possible under the circumstances; he had to send Bob, (his negro man) home, when he went back, he found him very sick, & knowing he said, twould be difacult to cure him, & marching all the time, he would send him home until he got well again. John's regiment has been ordered to Yellville, near the Misouri line, I beleave; it is said there is 50 thousand men now on this side of the Missippi River; & they are calling for all under 45, if that goes into effect, there wont be many left I can tell you, but oh wont I hate it so much; John's brother, Dick Dunlap, that attends to his business for him, will have to go, & I dont know what I will do, as I dont know any thing about directing the farm, Dick only comes down once a week, but the negroes all mind him, as well as they did John, & I've had no trouble at all so far, but 'twill be different then. I had me & Vic some nice dresses woven & will send you a sample of them; & of Jimmie's too, & several others to see how you like our homespun; <u>the two in the paper is mine & Vic's</u>; (the lightest is mine) & the other samples are Jimmie's dresses. I think them very pretty. Sis Mollie is going to weave her dress soon, she was up last Sunday, she has just written to Sis Carrie; & receaved a letter this evening from Sis C by Dee Newton, who brought mine. I have not seen him, brother J[ohn] brought me Ma's letter; Dee [had] to hurry on to join his regiment.

  Jimmie is not right well; has never been since he had scarlet fever in the spring, has had chills off & on all fall; — he had a touch of flux* a week or two ago, but is well of that now, but he dont seem to be doing as well as he should; I am giving him bitters*, in hopes twill help him; I dont know what I would do without him, he is so much company since John is gone; but oh C about Mrs Howard's death — I dont think I ever had a friend or relative's death to affect me more deeply; I could scarcely realize that she was dead; nor can I find words to express my heart-felt sympathy for her bereaved family. "God's will be done", but oh we cant always <u>feel it to be the best</u>, when we have to give up our best & dearest friends, & such a friend she has ever been to you, always taking such a kindly interest in all your welfare; I know you must miss her <u>so much</u>. Ma wrote you were teaching school, & boarding at Mrs Holmes. I am glad you have such a kind woman as Mrs Holmes to board with; I always thought her one of the best & kindest of women, & I know she will be as kind to you as she can be; Give my love to her C & my respects to Mr Holmes, how do you feel, C acting <u>school marm</u>, I can almost imagine I can see you in your school room, hearing lessons; dont I wish it a reality & twould be, of that I'm almost certain if 'twere not for this cruel war; Oh, will it never end, so I could have you & <u>Ma</u> out here with me; I dont think I will ever feel satisfied until I do get Ma moved out; it seems so hard to be compelled to wait so long until she can come. Well C, my time has nearly expired for writing, I am so anxious to send this right off. I will write to Ma just as soon as I can do so tell her, & with more of interest than I have time to do now; You must write soon C, & do C give my love to Ma, Sis Carrie & family, to Mrs. Lasiter, Rebecca, & all enquiring friends, accept a full share for your own self & beleave me as ever to be

        Your affectionate sister,
        Clara Dunlap

  P. S. Tell all the Negroes howdy for me. Tell Harriet & Laura to pick out some pretty names for their babies, dont name them no common names. I would so much like to see H[arriet]'s children. I intend to own their <u>daddy</u> some- day, if it is in my power to do so.

        C. D.

*Flux is a term used for dysentery.

*Bitters are medicinal substances, usually gentian or quinine.

Clara Dunlap in Ouachita Co. to her mother Clarissa Dickson in Autauga Co.

Jan. 15th 1863

Dear Ma,

It has been a long time since I recd a letter from you or C[ornelia] either, & I confess a long time since I wrote to you, but I will explain my reasons for so long doing what I should have done a month or more ago, first there was my confinement & subsequent trouble with my breast, which was only prevented from rising by drying it up, which the phycian done by applying bella-donna* plaster to it, & then my nipples were so very sore, much more so than when Jimmie was a baby, it was seven or eight weeks before they healed up one bit. I had to be held every time baby sucked. I thought at one time they never would heal & came near drying up the other breast on account of the nipple, my whole breast would inflame every time the baby sucked, but I am glad now I dident dry it up; but I have written so far & havent told you what the baby was, a girl, & weighed 8 pounds when she was born, but for the last six or seven weeks she has been the sickest baby I ever saw, to live, she was taken with something like flux, & up to this time we have just got it checked on her, after on[e] month hard work, & she has now the worst cough I ever saw a baby have, she is reduced to nothing but skin & bone, & oh such a time I've had, up night & day, until I am nearly wore out, oh Ma I never needed you so much in my life as now, unless 'twas when I was baby myself, but I know tis impossible for that to be, from what Dee Newton told me, he came & brought the sword & other things you sent, tell C I am much obliged to her for the little dress & saque & other mats, the dress came in <u>very</u> good time, the sacque I will have to keep for the baby as Jimmie cant begin to get it on, but you spoke of sending me some stockings. I did not rec any & think you must have forgotten to put them up, I should have been the proudest in the world to get them. I havent named baby yet, think of calling her <u>Lula</u>, but cant find a <u>middle name</u> to suit it, tell C to find one & send it when she writes again, one that will sound right with Lula. I think Ma if I ever have another baby I will try & get to you, if I have to go by land, I cant but feel that me & baby both would have got along so much better, she is a little better this morning; & I do hope will begin to mend now, every one thinks her prettier than J[immie] was. I miss John so much now, his regiment has been ordered to Little Rock, & I'm in hopes he will get a furlough then, he says in his last letter to tell you he would come after you, but cant even get to stay at home, he has been promoted to ordinance Sargent for the regiment, the Col seems to think a great deal of him, John has fallen off a good deal, he wrote, but keeps well all the time though; has been in one battle at Cane Hill, escaped unhurt, he gave a dreadful ac-

*Belladonna is a drug made from the leaves and roots of the belladonna plant. It contains atropine and related alkoloids and is used to check secretions and spasmas.

count of the battlefield after the fight, says he never imag[in]ed anything so heart-rending as the groans & cries of the wounded & dying, tis awful. We have killed our meat, over 4000 lbs I think, & have nearly as much more to kill, to sell, pork is 15 cts [a pound] now, & John's brother Dick Dunlap, says he would rather bacon it all, & sell the bacon, as 'twill be much higher, just think of it, how much meat we have to sell, & you needing it so much, how I do wish you lived out here, so I could divide with you. I know John would be as willing as myself, too, he bought me enough sugar to do me all this year, before he left, & enough molasses for the negroes, & by saving my coffee until winter, I've had good coffee all winter & enough to last til May. John's brother is very kind, & attends to his [John's] business so well, we made a good deal of corn to sell, too. Sis Mollie was up Sunday, she was well, & is still busy weaving, has woven herself & S[allie] a beautiful dress, & some for Mamie & Carrie, & is now weaving for the negroes, she works hard all the time, Sallie is looking every day to be down, we all took dinner there Christmas, had turkey, cake, & syllabub* & cc., that was all the Christmas I saw as baby kept so sick I could not go anywhere else, it made her worse going there, Jimmie is fatter & healthier than he ever was, says Pa has gone to kill him one <u>yank</u>, talks about his Pa all the time, well Ma the baby frets so much this morning I cant write as much as I wanted to this time, will write again as soon as she gets well, the health of the neighborhood is good, 'tis reported they are fighting at Vicksburg. I do hope we will whip them there, you must be lonesome now [with] C gone from home, tell her to write soon. I am not certain this letter will pass the Mississippi but trust it will, as I know you must be uneasy about us all out here, & I would have written long before this if baby had kept well. I was in hopes I would not have to raise this one on a bottle, but I dont give enough out of one breast for her, do write soon Ma, if only a few lines, give my love to all enquiring friends & accept a good share for yourself & beleave me as ever,

Your affectionate daughter,
Clara Dunlap

P. S. Tell all the negroes howdy. I was so sorry to hear that John Morton was gone, tell Mammy I am so sorry for her, I know she misses him. I send you a pretty sample of homespun to look at.
C.D.

*Syllabub is a traditional southern dessert made from whipped cream with wine and sugar added. It was a standard at most Christmas dinners.

Clara Dunlap in Ouachita Co. to her sister Cornelia Dickson in Autauga Co.

April 22nd 1863

Dear Sister,

It has been some time since I recd your <u>very</u> welcome letter, & I know you are looking ere this for an answer, but C you ought to excuse me, for what with a sick baby & every thing to attend to, (you know John aint here now to help me) I hardly have time to write & loosing so much sleep at night I dont feel well half the time, my baby is mending now, & I'm in hopes she will not be so much trouble at night, I dont think I've had three whole nights sleep since she was a month old. I had given her a middle name though, C, before I recd Ma's letter, it was so long coming I did not know whether a letter could pass through or not, & so I've named her <u>Lula May</u>, though I think Bell a very pretty name, if it had only come sooner; I am glad to say I am doing much better by myself, than I thought I would when John left; have an excellent garden, a good many chickens, & a fine prospect for a corn crop so far; our wheat is much better than we ever had, have nearly 50 acres planted, John's brother Dick Dunlap still attends to every thing about the farm, he is an excelent manager, & having no wife to keep him at home he comes once a week to see how the negroes get along & direct them. I know I shall never forget his kindness. I recd a letter from John a few days since, he thinks he will be at home in a few days, oh C you dont know how glad I will be to see him again, I thought I had told you the name of his Col, Col Grinstead of Cam[den]; they are in winter quarters in Little Rock; but as Gen Price* has come over to take entire command of the Ark troops, I would not be surprised if he did not lead them into Missouri, but I do hope not, it would be so difacult for me to hear from John, if I ever could, & I think his being gone, hard enough to bear, without his being so I never could hear from him. Our hopes have been highly elated all winter about peace being made, but I think it farther off than ever, so it seems anyhow. I was at Sis Mollie's Sunday, all well, but Sis M is like Ma said sis Carrie was, <u>puny</u> & <u>looks weak</u> & <u>feeble</u>, still keeps up though & works hard as ever. I think we will have a fine strawberry crop this spring, mine is finer than they've ever been; Sallie was down at Sis Mollie's also; with her baby, a fine girl, named Martha, after her mother, call her Mattie, the children are all well. I think Ma's dresses pretty & suitable, too. I will send you several samples of homespun that I got in the neighborhood, the green & purple is Mrs Dr Stone's make, the one with yellow stripe is woven (the stripe I mean) with 4 treddle's like four treddle jeans, weave the stripe of yellow; leave off two treddles to weave the plain part; I think it very pretty, the yellow is dyed with paint. Well C I stay at home so close I dont hear much news, & you must excuse this short letter. I will write to Ma soon & try & find something of more interest, than

*"Gen Price" refers to General Sterling Price, a former governor of Missouri, who was the commander of Confederate forces in Arkansas.

this; I know, tell Ma she cant wish to move half as much as I wish her too, & John would move her out if he could only get off, but that seems impossible. My love to all enquiring friends, accept a good share for Ma & yourself.

  Your affectionate sister,
  Clara Dunlap

  P. S. Jimmie is well & hearty & so much company for me now he is learning to talk, tell Mammy & Harriet & all the negroes howdy.
       C.D.

  *John has just come home, looks better than I expected to see him, will stay home two weeks, Jimmie dident know him. Tell Ma I will write in a few days.

  *Sis Mollie & Sallie told me to send their best love to you, Ma & sis Carrie.

> *Note: This postscript is written across the top of page 1.
> *Note: This postscript is written along the left margin of page 2.

Clara Dunlap in Ouachita Co. to her mother Clarissa Dickson in Autauga Co.

June 3rd 1863

Dear Mother,

  It has been a long time since I recd your most welcome letter, which would have been answered sooner, but I was just about to answer Nealy's, & thought to defer writing yours for a while so as to have more news; since then John's going off has troubled me so much that I couldent compose myself enough to write, or do anything else — he had just come home on furlough, when I was writing to C, & I was so in hopes he would get a substitute,* but the man backed out, since then, the brigade John's in (Gen. Tappan's) has been ordered from Little Rock to Cam[den], they arrived here the first of last week, & John hired another substitute, was to give him $4000, but another man offered the fellow more, he backed out, & so J was disappointed again; The brigade recd marching orders a few days ago, for Vicksburg, John came home last night & stayed until this morning about two hours before day, as they were to leave Cam at sun-up, John hated so much to go across the river, & then tis so hot & dusty; I expect many a poor fellow will give out before they get there. They say 'tis about 300 miles. We hear they are fighting in Vicksburg every day. I would not be surprised if all our Ark troops were ordered to Vick. Oh, wouldent I be glad if that fight could end this war, but I know you must be anxious to know how we all are, all all well here, except one of our negroes. She has acute rheumatism, & a very violent attack it was; she is some better this morning, though not able to walk a step, the disease is all over her; the Dr thinks it will be some time before she can walk. I miss her very much as she is my cook, & much the

> *The Confederate Conscription Act allowed a draftee to hire another man to serve his time in the army for him.

best one on the place. Our corn crop looks fine & growing fast, we have 190 acres in corn besides the wheat crop, we cut ours week before last, it turned out finely. John thinks he has made between 3 & 4 hundred bushels, well matured at that. If you were only out here Ma I could keep you in flour all the time and not miss it. I never have been entirely out, have had it all the time & sugar & molasses, too. John bought me over 300 pounds of sugar when he was at home this spring, & I had nearly a barrel on hand, but he said it wouldent be there to get, after a while, & he wanted me to have it, as long as any one else did. I think John is very kind to me Ma, in that respect; he studies more about me & Jimmie & Lula, than himself. I've a first rate garden this spring, though I had no beet seed to plant & I miss them so much, my peas have been better than I ever had, & in a few weeks, will have any quantity of beans. I am trying to raise turkeys this year, have only 10 though, about as large as partridges, the pip* destroyed a great many before I knew what was the matter with them. Sallie was over Sunday & spent the day, all are well at home, she said, she has been weaving some nice shirting for brother J[ohn], woven single slaied; & previously she had woven some pretty checked homespun for the little girls dresses (purple & white). S has a fine looking baby, named Martha, after her mother, call her Mattie. I think she resembles sis Mollie's John; bye the bye, Sis Mollie is off & gone again, (tell Sis Carrie), expects to arrive at her journey's end some time this fall;* she was up last week with Mrs Dr Stone, & it raining in the evening they stayed all night. I told Sis M 'twas quite a treat to have her stay all night as 'twas the first time, too. Sis M is weaving yet, just cut out some dresses for Mamie & Carrie, very pretty I think, she wove some very pretty brown cotton jeans this spring for brother G[eorge] & the boys. I will send you a small sample to look at; & also a very pretty(I think) sample of purple & white that I got in the neighbor hood. I want you to make you a dress just like it Ma because I sent it. Brother G has made sis M a nice pair of cloth gaiters*; stitched them on the machine, & then soled them himself. You could hardly tell them from bought ones. Sis Mollie is very uneasy about her mother, & father, as she has not heard from them since Christmas last. You spoke of everything being so high in Ala, 'tis pretty much the same here, molasses $100 a barrel, sugar (coarse quality) 50 cts, & nice 60c to 70c, & bacon will bring any price you ask for it afterawhile, as the hogs throughout the whole state are dying by the wholesale with hog cholera, they call it. We've lost a good many & still dying. If they keep on we will hardly make our meat for another year.

I beleave I told C that John was made ordnance sargent of the regiment last spring, his Col (Grinstead) seems to have a good deal of confidence in him. Tell Mrs Lasiter that Dee Newton is one of the most popular officers in the regiment, he is first Lieutenant in his co. One of the companys (in the regiment) lost their captain this spring, & they are very anxious for Dee to

*The pip is a contagious disease of birds, especially poultry, characterized by the secretion of a thick mucus in the mouth and throat.

*The journey metaphor is a euphemistic way of saying Sis M. is pregnant.

*One definition for "gaiters" is a high overshoe with a cloth upper.

fill his place, Dee says he hates to leave his co, as he is attached to the boys in it; but Col Grinstead wishes him to take command of that other co, he hasent decided yet. While at Cam, he was adjutant to Col G, done all his writing. Give my love to Mrs. L[asiter] & Bettie & tell B I would be so glad if she would write to me. You said Mrs. Caver intended sending me a letter. I've never recd any yet, but will write to the old lady some of these days anyhow. Give my love to her when you see her. Tell Neal, Jimmie did not recognise John atall this spring when he came home, wouldent beleave twas his Pa. Jim is growing very fast in height, but slender, I used to think he would be like his Pa, but he is more like me. Tell Neal that if I had any way, I would send her enough money to get a pair of cotton cards, (she was saying she had none), but am afraid to send it by mail. You must write soon Ma & tell me all the news about the neighbors. I am looking for a letter from Neal every day. Give my love to all enquiring friends, to sis Carrie, Irene, Mary, & accept a good share for yourself, & beleave me as ever

Your affectionate daughter,
Clara Dunlap.

P. S. Tell Mammy, Harriet & all the negroes howdy. Do wish I could move all of you out here.

Clara Dunlap in Ouachita Co. to her sister Cornelia Dickson in Autauga Co.

July 7th, 1863

Dear Sister,

I receaved your most welcome, a few days since, & cant express how very glad I was to hear from <u>home</u>, home, what a sweet name that is, & how much more sweetly it sounds to me now than it used to, when I was a girl. I did not <u>then</u> know how to appreciate it as I now do; Oh! Would that I were there with you all again, to remain until the war ended. I feel now more low spirited than ever. It must be because I failed to get John off, I sent him another substitute not long since, one of his brothers (Sam Dunlap) carried the substitute down to <u>Delhi</u> where John's reg[iment] is stationed, but his Col refused to take him, said J was too good a soldier to give up. I was <u>so much</u> disappointed, we were to have given the man $4000; but you wanted to know John's Brigadier & Major General. He is in Tappan's Brigade & Gen Walker's division, though I should have said Gen Kirby Smith's* command, but he (Gen Smith) is at Port Hudson now, & Walker is engaged with the Fed's near Delhi, (a small town on the railroad between Monroe & Vicksburg), they have had several fights with the Fed's lately; I recd a letter from J last week, he was well, they have miserable fare now, & the worst of water to drink, but J always write cheerfully, & tells me not to be uneasy

*General Kirby Smith was the Commander of the Confederate Forces west of the Mississippi River.

about him. From what his officers say, he fills the office of ordinance sargent better than most any man in the reg[iment], & they seem to think a great deal of him. My baby is well at last, & is a good deal better about sleeping at night, Jimmie is well also, is very lively and talkative, & so much company for me. We've had fine seasons now for several weeks & the corn looks beautiful, almost like a cane-brake sure enough, our gardens & cc looks better than they have in years, the fruit also promises to be fine this year. We've thrashed our wheat, we made nearly 300 bushels; no end to flour doins now. I hope you all have had as good seasons. C you fooled me completely by sending that silver-edged envelope on your letter, brother J[ohn] brought it from town, brother G[eorge] had read it, & brother J made out that you were married, & made me guess (ever so long before he would give it to me) who to. I asked was he an old or young man; he said an <u>old</u> one, so there I was guessing old Mr. Ross & I dont know who all, & at last when I got it away from him, I read ever so far before I thought to see if your name was changed, & was much releaved to find 'twas not, for I should be so sorry to have you marry out there, for fear Ma would never move, & its my greatest wish to see her out here; I was at Sallie's Sunday, all well, S has just finished weaving her some dresses. I would send you a sample, if I had one, they are single slaid, purple & white. Sis M & brother G were there. C, sis M told me to tell you to be certain & tell sis Carrie, if she loved her; not to write to her until she, (sis Carrie) heard from Mr. Gildersleeve's family, sis M has not heard from any of them since <u>Christmas last</u>, & tell sis Carrie she dont know, C, how hard sis Mollie takes it; she fears they are dead, but then Harriet* ought to write; something is to pay there; & sis M grieves about it all the time, & she made me promise to send the message to Sis Carrie, & says to do please write to George Houston's folks or some one, & find out how they are, or if they are dead, to write as soon as she gets an answer from there; sis M writes often, but never hears a word in return, she thinks maybe sis Carrie could hear from them some way, & says tell Sis C she will never forget her kindness, in so doing. Well, C, this is a very short letter, but I've just found a chance to send it to Cam & will close, such chances are scarce. My love to Ma, sis C & all friends, & a good share for your self & beleave me

*Harriet refers to Harriet Murley, sister of Mollie and Sallie.

Your affectionate sister,
Clara Dunlap

Tell all the negroes howdy for me.

*Sis Mollie sends her best love to you all; & so does Sallie, brother G never says much, but he is the first to break open our letters & read them, before he comes from town, seems as anxious as any of us to hear from you all. I will make amends for this short letter by writing a long one next time. Tell Bettie to write. C I think your dress is very pretty, & Harriet's first-rate. I have a song to send you, if you've never seen it, I think it very appropriate.

*Note: This postscript is written across the top of page 1, upside down so that the page must be turned around to read it. It continues along the left margin:

Clara Dunlap in Ouachita Co. to her mother Clarissa Dickson in Autauga Co.

Oct 7th/63

Dear Mother,

It has been a <u>long, long</u> time since I heard from you all, & I expect equally as long perhaps since you rec'd a letter from me; though I wrote to you & C[ornelia] both since I rec'd a letter from you; my last one was written a few days after the fall of Vicksburg & I suppose you never got it; I now have an opportunity of sending one by hand across the Miss river, & do hope you may get it, as I know you must be uneasy about us all out here. This leaves all well, I beleave, I saw some of the children yesterday; Sis M[ollie] has another fine <u>boy</u>, about two weeks old, born the 22nd of Sept; she is doing well; brother G[eorge] speaks of calling it Robbert Lee after Gen Lee of Virginia. The three oldest children are going to school in this neighborhood, & also three of brother John's, the school is at our new church about a quarter of a mile from here, the teacher is a young lady, a Miss Vowell, she boards with me; Our new church is named <u>Harmony Grove</u>. We had 4 days meeting there in Sept, there was 12 or 14 joined the church, myself among the number; I think we have one of the best preachers this year that we ever had, a Mr. Colwell.* I expect you all had good meetings this summer & fall at Ivy Creek & other places. Oh what would I give to be there now with you & C__, the more so, since the Fed's have taken Little Rock, & Pine Bluff, & almost every other place in the state that they wanted, we dont know what day they will come down here, would not be surprised to see them any day. I've been frightened so much about them that I dont mind it now, have got hardened to it almost, I expect to remain at home, if they do come, as I've found out they treated the propperty of those that run, worse, than those who remain at home, a good many think that slavery is <u>doomed</u>, but Ma I never can beleave that, without <u>disbeleaving</u> the <u>bible</u>, & that I could never, do, you know. I beleave God intended them as slaves, & nothing else, & they may change <u>masters</u> for a while but we'd regain them again. I cant think but that this war is intended for our good, though we cant see it now, & when we get sufficiently humbled & become a better people in the sight of God, he will restore us to our rights & not before. How are you all coming on nowadays, concerning the war, I have heard that the people east of the Miss. river were much more cheerful, than over this side. I dont know Ma <u>what I would not give</u> to be with you until the war ended or that you could be with me. I have so much more meat, wheat, & corn than will do me enough meat to divide & have plenty to do both of us til spring, we've made more corn than we can house, have to build corn pen's to put it in; if we gather all of it, it will be 4 or 5 thousand bushels; if the Yankee's would only let us alone, we could do so well; we have plenty of hogs to make

*"Mr. Colwell" refers to the Rev. James E. Caldwell.

our meat another year; John was home last week on furlough; I made up his winter clothes for him while he was home; he took one of the negro men of[f] with him so, if the Fed's do come; will try & save one, anyhow; our army is at Arkadelphia now, or was when John left it, he heard they had started on toward Texas. Poor John was lower spirited than I ever saw him, & hated leaving home worse; he said he would give anything if you & C was with me; said he could go off in much better spirits; We heard cheering news (if true) the other day; that Gen Bragg* had whipped Rozencrans* & that the port of Charlston was open. I'm almost afraid tis too good to be true; Well Ma I dont know what else to write that would interest you; more than brother G[eorge] is at home yet; the militia was called out, but afterwards ordered to remain & burn cotton & cc if the Feds did start through here, a good many had sold their cotton; you must write the first chance you have of sending. I would be so proud of a letter from home once more; sis M rec'd a letter from her mother a few weeks ago, the first since Christmas, she said sis Carrie had another baby; I thought she was done. Give my love to sis Carrie, Neal, Mrs. Lasiter, Rebecca & old Mrs. Caver, & all enquiring friends & accept a good share for yourself & beleave me as ever,

Your affectionate daughter
Clara Dunlap

Tell Mammy, Harriet, & all of them howdy for me.
*sis Mollie& Sallie send their love to you all. C.D.

*"Gen Bragg" refers to General Braxton Bragg of the Confederate Army.

*"Rozencrans" is a reference to General William Stark Rosecrans of the Union Army, who battled Bragg several times in Tennessee, especially at Murfreesboro, in 1862 and early in 1863. The outcome of the battles were not determined to be victories on either side.

*Note: This postscript was written on the back of page 3:

*Cornelia Dickson in Autauga Co. to her sister Clara Dunlap in Ouachita Co.

April 5th 1864

My dear Sister,

I have tried in vain to send a letter to you, that you may know our bereavement, <u>Our Mother is no more</u>. She left us the 9th of last February, after a long spell of sickness caused from violent cold. Chronic bronchitus, the Dr. called it, though she often suffered with severe attacks of Asthma. She had been quite feeble for some time when one evening I came from school I noticed she was a little hoarse & complained of headache. She thought it was nothing more than an ordinary cold that would soon wear away, but it gradually grew worse until she began to cough. The Dr. was sent for, but he did not think it was anything serious, at last she was confined almost entirely to her bed. The Dr. tended on her and still thought she would recover. I quit my school that I might be all the time with her. Christmas came but it was a sad time for me, for I saw that she was daily growing thinner and more feeble, but suffered no pain. All the time the Dr. said her disease was more distressing than dangerous, and when the weather grew more

*EDITOR'S NOTE: This letter is a reverse of the pattern that has been established in the previous letters. It comes from Alabama <u>to</u> Arkansas, from Cornelia to Clara, and was in the ledger.

pleasant he thought she would improve, but one night about a week before she died Ma told me she had no earthly hope of ever getting well again, and that she felt prepared to go, which is a great consolation to me. But O! Clara, you don't know what a feeling of desolation came over me when I began to realize that I must part forever on this earth with my dear Mother, the best friend I ever expect to have, and O! how sad and lonely it is for me now. If I could only be with you it would be such a great comfort to me. When I look forward to the time I will be with you all again, it helps me a great deal. Ma died very easy. I don't think she was concious of dying. When asked but a short time before, how she felt, she said she felt easy, and went to sleep. I saw after a while that she was awake and thought I would ask if she was lying comfortably, but she closed her eyes again and in about five minutes I went to the bedside again and saw her gently catch her breath. She never breathed but once more, her eyes were closed as if she was asleep. It was about one o'clock at night. I think the cough, which had become very bad, gradually wore her life away. She had no fever and nothing the Dr. could do for her seemed to do her any good. Her death was unexpected to me for tho I did not think that she could get well, I thought she would get better and would live some time.

She wanted me to live on the place & take care of everything until you could come out. I have Sis Carrie's Willie living with me and Reeny and Mary stays with me a good deal. I have resumed my school. I felt like I must have some employment.

Ma wrote to you last fall as soon as she received your letter. I hope you have received it. She scarcely ever spoke of you or any one of her family, her feelings always seemed to overcome her. She said she wanted to be <u>buried by Grandma</u> back of Sis Carrie's garden and was buried there, Mr. Howard is her executor. I have many kind friends here, but I feel very lonely and sad. I often imagined it would grieve me very very much to lose my Ma, but the reality is far more bitter than I ever thought it would be. O! that this cruel war were over & we could be, together again, but I see no prospect for peace now. Write as often as you have opportunity. I will do the same. Sis Carrie & family are well.

Harriet & Jerry have both had a severe attack of pneumonia, but Jerry is able to be about some now. Harriet is able to be about the yard and her house a little but is very thin and feeble. She was down about four weeks. Mammy has rheumatism very bad at times, but keeps up. The rest are well & send howdy & their love. Give my love to all & accept a share for yourself

From your afflicted sister,
Cornelia S. Dickson

Clara Dunlap in Ouachita Co. to her sister Cornelia Dickson Autauga Co.
July 24th/64

Dear dear Sister,

  I've tried again & again to write to you since I rec'd your letter of the 5th of April, telling me of our sad <u>sad</u> loss, but I've failed in every attempt, the news <u>so</u> unexpected to me came with overwhelming force; it seemed at first to crush me down, & I had neither spirit nor nerve to attempt to write; I have hardly recovered enough to write now, but duty to you requires it, though I shall, I fear, make a poor attempt at best. I rec'd Ma's last letter last Feb, telling me of her feeble health, but oh I never dreamed of anything serious. I answered it & sent her a receipt that brother John gave me, for the diarrhea. I dont know whether you ever rec'd it or not, oh little dreamed I when I was writing then of what a sad loss I had sustained. How anxious she seemed in her letter for the war to end so she could move out here & be with us & seemed at the same time fearful if it did not end soon, she would not live to see us again. I beleave C she had some presentiment that such would be the case. But how little dreamed I of such a thing; I just felt as if she would be out here some day, & I had so many many pleasant thoughts mixed up with you all being out here & how much I would try to help her, &, oh, so many pleasant thoughts every way about it, but alas how little can we read the future. I feel in my heart she is a great deal better off, but oh tis so hard to have to give her up. I can hardly realize it yet, 'tis so hard I feel for you, Nealy, there alone & would give I cant tell how much to be with you there til the war does end, but that is impossible, you & I are alone now, our best friend is gone, never more can we replace her, & we have only to try sister to live, so that we will meet her again in a better world, where there is no more parting, no trouble, no trials, all will be peace & happiness there.

  Your letter found me overwhelmed with troubles of a different nature at the time, you have probably learned ere this that the Federals had been to Cam[den], they came about the middle of April, & at first, they seemed so well disposed, it threw a good many off their guard, so very few of us tried to hide anything atall, we had always heard that it proved a great deal worse for anyone if the Feds found out you had hid anything. I consulted brother J[ohn] & he thought best to <u>not hide anything</u>, & I followed his advice; I had no one to help me but the negroes, & we had heard they could always bribe it out of them, & so I did not try, well to make a long story short, they came & took all of our <u>mules, corn, meat, sugar, molasses, flour, everything</u> in the world we had to eat, (though this was after they had been to Cam[den] nearly a week), they sent their forage train out & with them several thousand men, every day, they even took all my <u>soap, candles, coffee,</u> & every <u>hen, chicken, turkey, eggs</u> & cc on the place except two or three old setting hens, that ran off in the woods; all my cooking vesaels, pans, buckets, & cc, & then searched the house over, broke the lock of every trunk (but one) & took a good many little things, all my good shoes, stockings soda, spirits, & cc, & even, Nealy, took my wedding slippers. I could not tell you all, they treated the negroes the same way, said they done that because they were working for me instead of going to town & being free, talked to them pretty roughly, & that evening, the negroes commenced packing up & left the next day, alas, not one stayed with me but my nurse & I hired her to stay & tend to my baby, & they knew I did not have a mouthful, I've learned since then from other negroes in the neighborhood that ours intended going all the time, but kept it a secret to keep us from running them off, anyway, they left Cam with the Feds & went to the Rock, all of them, (12 in no), we had our three young Negro men in the Confederate service & so we saved them, (they were with John), some of our negroes told the feds that we run them men off to keep them from getting them, & that, I think was one reason they took so many things from me, even took my buggy. Sis M[ollie]'s negroes all packed up to go, but the Feds wouldent take their beds & things for them, & they would not leave them; they captured Henry & took him with them, or I think he would have stayed. Richmond left with his wife (one of Wm Stones negroes) Berry wouldent go with them, he wanted to stay at home & be free, as soon as the Feds left, brother J took him (Berry) to town & sold him, that was all sis Mollie lost. The Feds came to brother J's, took all his negro men (except one) & mules (he had one man, a wagon, & 4 mules in government service), they got all the other men & then sent them back to get their wives & children, said if they did not leave they would kill them. All left but Roda & Hannah, they just told the Feds flat down they might kill away they would not go alive out of that yard, even old Jinny went. Two dutchmen (feds) came to brother J's (before the negroes left) & made him give up his gun & pistol, then told him to give up his gold & silver, he said he had none, one of them shot at him, but missed him. Sallie ran out thinking they had killed him, she gave them such a talk they seemed cowed, they said they would take him off & kill him, as they would not kill him before her face, took him off into the woods & told him to say his prayers, he told them he had none to say, & added if they did shoot to be certain & kill him at once as he dident want to be crippled, finding they could not frighten him they quit, told him he was a brave fellow & left, first telling the negroes if they did not leave, they would burn every house down on the place, (the dutch feds are the worst of them all) The real yankee's I was not afraid of, they treated me gentlemanly enough, but the Kansas jay-hawkers that were most always sent with the wagon trains I was afraid of, they looked mean enough for any thing, & the officers as bad as the men, they took every thing from sis Mollie as they did me, except her cooking vessels. They did not get all of brother J's corn & meat, but would if they had remained much longer in Cam, brother G[eorge] & John being in the <u>rebel army</u>, they said was the cause of sis M[ollie] & myself being treated so bad. After they took everything from me, being on the public road & I could not hear a word from sis M or brother J's families, & having no one with me but a lady friend, Mrs. Williams, that was staying with me, we told the feds the next day when they came out, as they had taken all from me, they must move us to town where we could <u>draw rations</u>, as we did not intend starving if we could help it, the Capt. agreed to do so, & we commenced packing up, just as I got my <u>beds, bedclothes</u>, & all my wearing clothes packed, they had orders from the Col to start, & we had to go. I left <u>two matresses</u>, all my <u>crockery ware</u> (I had a good deal) & my furniture; they said we could come out next day & get the ballance, but <u>old daddy Price</u> threatened an attack on them & they could not come out. The next day after that they came out & Mrs. Williams husband came with them to get our things, but twas a different set & they would not take a single thing, but after he [Mr. Williams] left my place, they took all my <u>crockery ware</u>, broke my <u>bureau</u> all to pieces & tore up every <u>thing</u> they could lay hands on, oh how much since, I've regreted going to town, but at the time I & my children were <u>starving</u>, I thought that Sally & sis M were in the same fix; I was afraid to go to either place as the nasty feds were through the woods all the time, hunting for hidden things, & I was afraid, no one blames me for going to town under the circumstances, but I blame myself, as I lost so much by it, we went & stayed at a friends, Mrs Robert Broadnax's, her husband is a son of old Hal, she was very kind indeed to us, & as she had a guard stationed at her gate, they did not get her provisions, indeed a good many of the town people had guards around their houses, sis M came near starving too, she sent John* early one morning to Mrs Dr Stones & she sent her a little meal, they ate that cooked in hoecakes, without sifting, sis M took the flux in the meantime, in consequence of living so hard, but now for our releaf, Price cut off a large train of 240 wagons the feds had sent out to Pine Bluff, & having no provisions in Cam to do them, the Feds evacuated the place taking with them all the negroes nearly in town, Price persued them on until they came to Saline river, where they made a stand & fought, a great many were killed on both sides, though the Feds lost the most, they threw their dead, (a great many of them, at least) <u>in the river</u>, & we pushed them so close they cut up every wagon they had, & threw the wheels in the river, rushed over, took up their pontoon bridge & passed on, when Steele* arrived in Little Rock, he did not have a <u>single wagon</u>. The river's rising very fast & our army's being exhausted (the infantry were just out of the <u>Mansfield</u> & <u>Pleasant Ridge</u> fight in La.) they fell back to Cam to rest; I am now staying at Sam Dunlap's (one of John's brothers) he kindly offered after the feds left to pro-

*"John" is John Rumph Boddie, Sis Mollie's oldest son.

*"Steele" is a reference to General Frederick Steele, serving with the Union Army in Arkansas.

General Frederick Steele

General Sterling Price
Photos courtesy of UCA Archives.

vide for me until I (we) could make something at home to live on again, our three negro boys have been working at home, & we have a nice crop of corn coming on & enough hogs to make our meat. I am living with S Dunlap's family, his wife is a very kind good woman, though no place is like home to me, & twill be hard living next year, just meat & bread, but if the war will only end, I will take it all cheerfully, it is 9 miles from here to my place, & the Feds did not get up here much (so much further from Cam). I've a plenty of every thing to live on. Mr. Dunlap hid out all his <u>sugar, & molases & meat</u>, & then hid himself when the feds were here, he is in the army but happened to be home on furlough when the Feds came. I forgot to say sis Mollie is living with Sallie, they are well crowded, too, as Sallie has only two rooms; S has another fine girl born <u>just a month</u> after the feds left, brother J got some of his negroes back, <u>got all</u> but 7 & two of <u>them</u> was his sisters, some others got some of theirs back, but the majority went on, ours & some more happened to be in advance of the Feds & too escaped our men at the fight; a few of our men that were taken prisoners & carried to the Rock; says the negroes are more anxious to come back to their owners, than they were to go, but the Feds wont let them. We have great talk of peace now, tis reported Lee is in Washington Cty, but am afraid tis too good to be true. Oh C have I not enough trouble to kill me; I sometimes dont know how to bear it, tis too much, you all dont know any thing about the feds yet. If I could only live over the past 4 months, I would hide everything I had, negroes <u>&</u> all, but tis past, if the war ends soon, we stand a good chance of getting ours again, if not, I dont know, my health is not good, <u>trouble is, I think, the cause of it</u>, the children, <u>Jimmie</u> is well, Lula has chronic diarrhea, my nurse has consumption, & I have now to nurse Lula myself, do write soon. I will every chance. I am so tired, I am compelled to stop, hoping this may find you all well I am

Your affectionate sister,
Clara Dunlap

*Give my love to mammy, Harriet, & all the negroes, I know they feel like they have lost their best friend now, I symphathise with them all, my love to all inquiring friend, if I have any out there, do dear sister write soon.

*Note: This postscript is written at the top of page 1, upside down on the page.

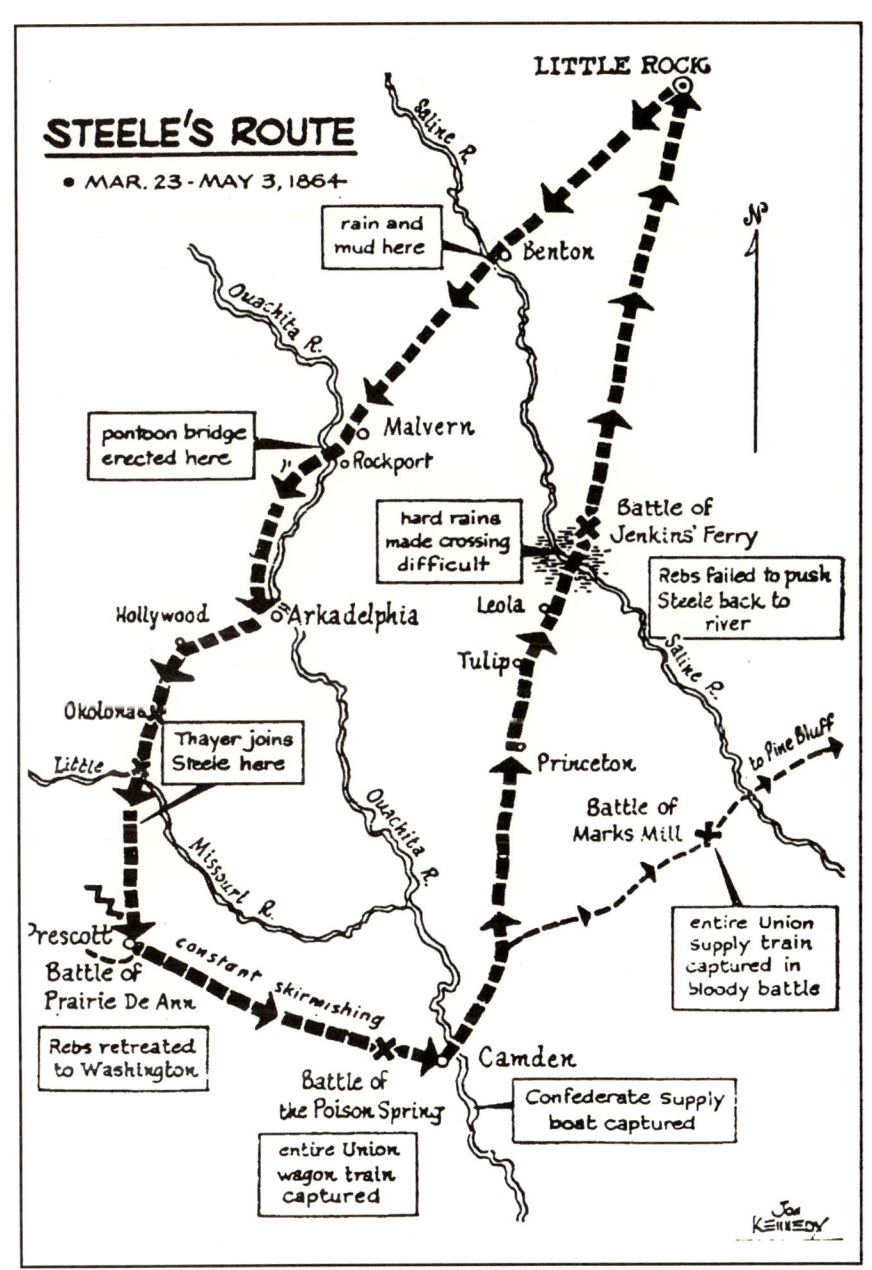

Steele's Expedition into South Arkansas
—Jon Kennedy in the *Arkansas Democrat*

*EDITOR'S NOTE: The letter which follows is one of the very few in this entire collection that is so fragile much of it is indescernible. We have attempted to fill in the blanks with our best guess.

*"Gen McGruder refers to General John Bankhead Magruder, known as "Prince John" because of his theatrical nature, who for a short time took command of the Arkansas regiments.

*The Washington referred to here is Washington, Arkansas, which was established as the Confederate Capitol of Arkansas after the Union forces took Little Rock.

*"Jayhawkers" was a term, used interchangeably with "bushwhackers," and referred to antislavery guerrillias in Kansas, Missouri and other border states.

*Clara Dunlap in Ouachita Co. to her sister Cornelia Dickson Autauga Co.
Nov 17th 1864

Dear Sister,

I receaved your good welcome letter over a week since & have tried in vain to answer it, but every time I make the attempt, I fail. I'm so low spirited & have suffered so much this year with trouble that I dont feel equal to the task of writing. I know this will be a poor appology for a letter. I feel unusually sad to-day, John's command left Cam for red river & I dont know when I will ever see him again, as they will, I think, establish their winter quarters there, they are more strict than ever about letting the men come home since Gen McGruder* has taken command, he is not popular atall with the men, he was having the men shot for almost any offence until Kirby Smith came up to Cam. I think he put a stop to it as there has been no more shooting since, they have camp strongly fortified now & will leave [a small force there] & the rest will go on to Washington* so it is reported, to fortify that place & from there to red river, it seems this country is to be given up to the "jayhawkers,"* Feds, & any other band of robbers that choose to infest it, at least I'm afraid we will be troubled with them again. Sam Dunlap (whose family I am living with), speaks of moving his family to Texas in case the Feds start down here again. I would not be surprised if he did not go anyhow, & although I would rather go any where than meet them again, yet I would almost rather die than go unless we are threatened with them again. I have nothing for them to take this time (unless they take my clothes & bed clothing) with the exception of three negro men which I would be certain to run off to save them, & then I would have nothing, no one to work for me out here. I lost my nurse in Sept. with consumption & have to nurse & attend for Lula myself now, as tis impossible to hire a nurse, Mr Dunlap has but few negroes, no small ones. I let you know I have a hard time of it, C, harder than I ever thought to go through with, if Lula was a healthy child she would not be so much trouble, but she has been sickly & puny since her birth, & no one but those who've tried it know the trouble, she is just recovering from a long spell of fever & she requires more attention than ever, she has had chronic diarhea ever since spring, off & on, & all the remedies I've tried failed, my own health is & has been far from good this summer & fall. I dont feel as though I have any [energy or] life about me to enable me to bear up against so much & no prospect ahead for any thing better. God knows I do [try so] hard & pray to him night & day for strength to enable me [to bear it] better, [but all] seems dark & gloomy, but I will [keep] praying & I know, I feel that "in his own good time" he will [send] relief. He is my only hope now. I feel, C, now more than I ever did, that one must not look for assistance in time of trouble from any other source, you were wishing that I could be with you. God only knows how much I've wished that since last spring. I [thought] I could stand it much better if I was with you all, but 'tis impossible for me to get there now, there is no <u>flag of truce</u> ever crosses the lines now; that is none that [ladies] could go with & no conveyance either. Sis Carrie in her letter to sis Mollie (which she rec'd when I did yours) begged her to persuade me to go. Tell her twouldent need no <u>persuasion</u> to induce me to go. I'm only too ready & willing both if 'twas so I could, but [the] risk would be too great for me to attempt it. I was down at brother John's about a month ago, all was well except a few of the children was suffering from bad colds, sis M was weaving some pants for brother G[eorge], she has wove a good deal this summer. Sallie weaves all her own fine pieces, their cards are getting so scarce now they cant make cloth very fast. S 's baby is a fine fat healthy child; no trouble atall, she calls her <u>Kate</u>, the larger children are going to school now, have a very good school, a young lady teacher, we have not heard from brother G since the cavalry went to Missouri, 'Tis reported that Price is coming back with seven thousand recruits. I only hope tis so, the Feds are still in the Rock & the Bluff, it was hoped a short time since [that our] forces would advance & estabish counter quarters........... & ruin the Fed's................. as the country is eat out so, above here 'twould be impossible to get provisions & forage up there, indeed that is our only hope of the Feds leaving, as tis said they cant get a sufficiency of provisions on the Ark. river, our soldiers are suffering now, a great many of them for clothing, & John says tis sadening to hear them at night as they sit around their camp fires speaking of their families suffering some for the want of food & shoes or clothing, they cant buy a thing for Confederate money, indeed they hardly ever draw any wages nowadays & the soldiers are not allowed to stay at home now long enough to provide anything for their families, where they have a little money, their neighbors (those that maybe are out of the war) wont let them have [anything for money]. Is it not too hard I declare 'tis almost enough to cause many to desert, & the most that do desert out here, do so for that cause. I must not forget to tell you I have recovered my buggy again, it was in Cam all this time just where the Feds left it. John happened to come across it one day, & the old lady that had it did not want to give it up atall & said the Fed <u>officer's</u> made her a <u>present</u> of it. You can guess what kind of a [character] she was. I have one mule, but he is so wild, will have to exchange him for a gentler one. We've never even heard from our negroes that went off. I've heard from several, that have stole off from the Feds & got back, [say] that a great many that went off would give any thing to [be] back, a great many are hoping for peace in case McCelland* is elected, & some think the war will go on any how. Tell Mrs. Clark that her aunt, old Mrs. Stone, died last week. I've not learned what [was the] matter with her ... has been bad for years. Well C, I've filled up my sheet & have not I know written anything worth sending but you [must] excuse it & when, [if ever our country] is at [peace] I can promise

*This comment on McCelland is a reference to George Brinton McClellan, a Union general, who was nominated by the Democrats late in the summer of 1864, to run in November against Abraham Lincoln, who had been renominated by the Republican or National Union Party. The Democrats espoused cessation of hostilities, led by a faction known as "Copperheads." Lincoln was re-elected.

[you a letter]. You cant think how much I wish to see & be with you, Jimmie speaks of you so often (I've told him about you so often), he says he does want to go to Ala & stay with Aunt Nealy so much if I could go, he begs me nearly every week to lets go. I do wish you could see him C, he is such a fine healthy boy & is so good to wait on me or his little sissy as he calls Lula, he was four years old yesterday & is large to his age. You spoke of sending a letter to me by a soldier. I've never rec'd any except the one you wrote last spring until this last by Virgil Lassiter. Sis Mollie has written several times to sis Carrie. Tis strange that she does not receave them, my love to sis C[arrie], Mrs. Lassiter, Betty, & all enquiring friends, accept a good share for yourself & beleave me as ever,

Your affectionate sister,
Clara Dunlap

P.S. I send you a sample of [a] dress I had wove before the Feds came last spring. Poor Ma I thought to send it to her thinking she would fancy it. Tell Mammy I want to see her worse than I ever did & all the negroes. Give my love to them all. I do hope & trust you may not have to experience any of my trouble from the Feds. Write soon & every chance. You dont know how much good your letters do me.

Clara Dunlap in Ouachita Co. to her sister Cornelia Dickson in Autauga Co.

Dec. 15th 1865

Dear Sister,

It has been so long since I had an opportunity of writing to you I hardly know how to commence, I think the last time I wrote to you I was staying at Sam Dunlap's, & thinking of going to Texas, but by the time they got ready to start I gave it out, & remained with Dick Dunlap's family, as he was the only one that remained, about the 7th of Feb my baby was born, you will be surprised I know to hear that I have another child. I have named her <u>Mary Alice</u>, after sis Mollie & one of John's neices. I call her Mollie. Every one says she is the pretiest one of my children, she has beautiful bright dark hazel eyes, though I dont think otherwise, she is remarkably pretty, she is the best baby I ever had, my breast did not rise this time & I nursed my baby altogether, did not use the bottle atall. As soon as the war ended we moved home, & such a place, as it was dirt & filth & trash, no garden or fencing or anything, but we've <u>worked</u> early & late, & have got it in pretty good order now, built a new garden &c, we had no vegetables this summer except some squashes & peas, & cucumbers; that we planted after we came, which was the second week in June, we had also a nice water & mush-melon patch, & then what hope more than any thing else we had 8 cows, with young calves

& made from 3 to 4 pounds of butter a day, through the summer, & about 2 pounds a day all the fall, until recently, I dont make any now, tis so cold, & we have nothing to feed the cows on. While I made it, I exchanged it all along for sugar & coffee, & have supplied my table with a nice set of crockery ware, besides buying some winter clothing for the children, John intends hiring hands & making a large cotton crop next year, we had 3 negro men left, but they quit us last summer, to work for themselves, did not seem mad atall, just quit so. We've had to hire hands ever since, to help work, sowing wheat &c. We have 20 acres in wheat & 9 or 10 in rye & oats. John has bought 3 large fine mules, & will have to buy some more, as he wants to tend a good deal of land. Brother G moved home this fall, his place is to fix up too; Brother John has commenced practicing again, gets a good deal to do too, every one seems to think so much of him as a phyciacian, he is so kind and attentive to his his patients, he sent Mittie to Kentucky to school, the name of the school is Nazerith, it is about 3 miles from Bargtown; Mit has written back several times; she likes [it] <u>very</u> well (it is a Catholic school) says the sisters of Charity are so kind, & good, I expect George R[umph] will go this winter, Sallie R[umph] met with a most severe loss this fall in November, her two oldest girls Sallie & Mattie both died, within 3 days of each other. Mattie first with congestive fever & erycipalis* combined, & Sallie with croup, her death was very sudden indeed, only sick <u>one day & night</u>; brother G called it inflamatory croup, Mattie was sick 3 weeks, poor S[allie], it like to have killed her; it was hard enough to give up <u>one</u>, but <u>2</u> in one short week, she hasent got over it yet, she has only one child living, her youngest, <u>Kate</u>, she is about 18 months old, all of brother John's negroes have quit him, but Hannah & Roda, & Polly, & Ben. Sis M has Julyann & Marinda & old Bill. I've talked to brother G & J both about your coming out here, brother George says times are so uncertain, he dont know what would be best to do, but brother John says you could get a good large school C, right in this neighborhood, the schoolhouse is only a quarter of a mile from here, just a nice little walk, he says you could make a plenty by it to support you well, but he says if you dont wish to come out here, & could get a good school there, twould be as well, though he would do all he could for you if you came, you could come easily when the boats get to running. My advice Nealy, would be to <u>come any how</u> in the world, I do want you with me <u>so much</u> & I know from what Sis Carrie wrote you are not <u>satisfied</u> there. I think if you could sell those <u>3 bales of cotton</u> you spoke of, it would pay your expenses out here, & if you should not like [it], after teaching a session, you could have enough then to take you back. <u>John says</u> it should <u>not cost you anything to stay with me</u>. I would only be too glad to have you here with me, & I think we have such good kind neighbors, you would be pleased with them. I would not sell the <u>place</u> though Nealy, just let the negroes live on it & pay you such rent as its worth. I was very glad to learn

*Erysipelas is an acute, febrile infectious disease, caused by a specific streptococcus, characterized by diffusely spreading deep-red inflammation of the skin or mucous membranes.

that they had behaved so well towards you, & I thank them for it. Give my love to all of them, tell them I dont expect ever to see them again now, as I am not able to go out there, I hate it so much too. I always though I would be <u>fixed</u> if I could get Mammy & Harriet around me. Tell Mammy I have learned to cook & do everything else, but milk the cows. I've had a cook hired most of the time but I would cook & help do myself to learn how. We have a good cook hired for next year. Well Nealy I dont know what else to write, only it is a <u>bitter cold day,</u> & I must let <u>that</u> appologise for <u>bad writing,</u> as my hands are so cold I can scarcely write atall. I've just finished drying up <u>lard, making sausage's</u> &c yesterday. We killed hogs the first of the week, & I hired three negroe women to come & help me, we finished yesterday, have a nice lot of meat & plenty of sausages. I intend saving <u>you some,</u> in hopes you will come, do come this winter Neal. Come by water, if you sell that cotton for a good price it will pay your way out, & once here, you wont be at any expense; <u>only come.</u> brother G & J will get you a <u>good</u> school if you should wish one, if not you could just stay & visit amongst us at your leisure. I will write again the first opportunity I have of sending a letter. I send this by a gentleman going to Clarke Co., near Mr Gildersleeve's. You must write soon & often as you can, Give my love to sis Carrie & family, Cousin Mary Love & family & all enquiring friends. Sis M & S send their love to you all. My love to all, accept a good share for yourself & beleave me as ever

       Your affectionate sister
       C. Dunlap

 P.S. Jimmie is a great big boy, says tell Aunt Nealy to come & he will learn to read, & <u>write letters to his sweetheart,</u> says he wants to go to school to you so much.

THE BODDIE WAR LETTERS
(From home to the field)

Mary E. Boddie and her children spent most of the war years in the home of her sister and brother-in-law Sallie and John Rumph. As Clara described to Cornelia, the treatment of the lone women at the hands of the Yankees was devastating. Like Clara, Mollie sought refuge away from her home. John Rumph was the only family man left at home, so he became the head of George Boddie's family; thus the references to his going up to the homestead to see to the crops and stock.

Mary E. Boddie at home to her husband, George Boddie

March 23rd, 1864

My dear George,

  Yesterday was a week since your left me, and I felt as though you had not been at home two hours. I do miss you so much darling; and am anxious to hear how you got on & if you are well. We have had such cold disagreeable weather, ice, sleet, & some hail fell on Sunday night. On the Camden side of the river the hail was much heavier than here. We commenced planting corn last Thursday evening Bill has been sick two days, they have finished planting the spring cut, & half done the piece of ground they had prepared. On Monday 'twas too cold, & wet for ploughing. To-day tis warm & pleasant, I have Julia Ann & Beck at work in the garden, am not planting any more seed yet, except mustard. The rabbits served my peas so badly, & then commenced on the potato beds, & I put some strycnine for them, & killed four in one night. I am very particular with the poison, John brings to me every piece of the potato, I've put for them, early in the morning, which I lock up till night again. The fruit I expect will all be killed, the large June apple tree in the garden George, is the prettiest you ever saw, <u>every limb</u> & twig on it is filled with blossoms. You recollect the lad I told you of, Geo, my giving him two rose slips, & some tulip seed for his mother, his name is McDonald, & his mother sent me ten papers of pink seed, by a neighbor of hers going to Camden, the gentleman staid here night before last. I had the ground manured & sowed the pink seed today. The severe cold made some of the pink Hyacinth look as though they were scalded. The Tulips look fairly & some of them budding to bloom. I had both your beds cleaned & worked over. The school closes tomorrow with an examination, & I intend going with the children. Miss Cattie will commence "teaching" again in one month. Maima has been sick since you left us, she had a chill last Friday evening, & high fever all night. I gave her a dose of oil on Saturday which acted well, then gave her quinine until noon on her chill day, & she had no return of chills, & is quite well. I thought so much about you darling all that bad weather, fearing you would be sick, you were not well when you left home. Shall expect to hear from you, anyhow this week. Mr Broach called to see me Friday morning, told me he would return as soon as he could travel to the command & return. We have heard that there had been a fight at Monticello also, that the Federals were approaching Camden in three directions, but we place no credence in such a report. I cant help though feeling very anxious to hear if the Federals have been at Monticello. I have not seen sis [Sallie] or John R. since you left, sis sent me a note by the children yesterday, all are well with them. Helen Williams is very low, I went to see her one evening last week, Mrs. Wilson sent me word she did not think Helen could live, there was no one with her at the time except Mrs Wilson & Mrs Ponder. Helen's mother got there Sunday to stay until H. got better. On yesterday I learned that she was no better, she has Pneumonia, & is reduced to perfect helplessness. Maima says I must tell Pa she has found his comb, you dropped it in the front yard. Carrie is well of her cold, & little babe is the sweetest boy in the world Pa. The boys have been studying hard this week for the examination, John went to bed last night forgetting he had to write a composition, got up, dressed & wrote a page, he can memorize a lesson quicker & with less trouble than any child I ever saw.

Darling, when I count the days, & know you have been gone but a week, I can scarcely believe it, as I seem to have <u>lived months</u> in that time, bless your precious self, may you soon return to stay with me always. The children all send dear love to Pa & darling, may God in his goodness, care for & bring you safely home is the prayer of your
             devoted wife,
             (good night)
             Mary E. Boddie
(we have three little lambs now)

Mary E. Boddie at John Rumph's to her husband George Boddie in the field with the Confederate troops.
                                                                  July 6th, 1864

    My dear Husband,

I rec'd your dear letter the second one since you left me, one week ago, & I need not assure you George of how much comfort they afford me, & yet I am in constant dread to hear of your being ill, so badly is your fare & so much impossible hot weather, if you get to be much thinner in flesh darling. I hope there will be less danger of taking the camp fever. I never sit down to a meal Geo. but I wish you could share it with me, we have so many wholesome vegetables & apples too now in abundance. The crop of corn is fine considering the hinderence of working during so much rainy weather & John bids me tell you 'tis <u>very grassy,</u> he is plowing it yet, the boys have quit field work, as there is no necessity for it & 'tis such hot weather. They work the potatoe garden &c in the pleast [pleasant?] part of the day. Our school was to have commenced last week, but Miss Cattie has not yet come, she will board with Mrs. Shaddock if she comes, all interested in the school fear she is going to get married. If she does not come this week, I presume we shall hear from her. I would be so glad to have the children at school as much of their time as possible. The boys are cured of the itch at last, but they are deprived of the pleasure of bathing on account of having used so much sulphur. All the family have kept well so far darling save Sallies little babe, it was taken ill nine days ago, with brain fever, & I never saw anything equal such suffering as it has undergone, day & night during six or seven days. The babe had spasms all the while, & continued & high fever. I never thought to see it any better, but strange to tell there is hope for its recovery. Yesterday & today it has had no spasms, & the fever is very near abated entirely. We sit up with the baby yet. Clara is staying with us this week, & for the past two nights we have had company to relieve us in sitting up. If the baby does recover I will never dispare of any other case of the like. John R. is much troubled with a rising on his knee, he can scarcely get about, he told me to say to you he had written two letters to different parts of Texas to ascertain if he could learn ought of any of his negroes & Henry. I think he wrote to Mr O Banmore & Mr Marks. John has had some news papers recently, the Chicago Times &c in which the Yankees admit of no advantage gained & great loss in their battles in Va. They speak of their armies being held in check in every part of the Confederacy & even in Ark. The dignified Steele had to make a hasty retreat from the Rebel Army. Dockery's command has left for the Saline or there abouts & Churchill's divisions are in Camden. Price's Infantry are encamped in seven miles of Camden. The soldiers belonging to the wagons with their teams are grazing them on our side of the river at Mr. Piles, our home, John, & Wm Stones. They talk very fair, say they will disturb nothing & that they are not allowed to go in the wheat fields, but you are aware George of how much damage they can, & will do. I do wish 'twas in my power to be at home, I do so much dislike to have everything go to rack & be destroyed at our dear home, but I will not complain if in the end I may have my darling husband once more with me, never to part. This time seems long, very long, darling that you are away, & I do pray you can come to see me before you have to go across the Arkansas river. I never rec'd your letter wherein you recounted the trip to Pine Bluff. The one Mr. Cummins brought came safe to hand. I dont have so good an opportunity of sending you letters from here as I did when at home, have to depend now on mailing them in Camden & would have written to you last week but for the babys being so sick. Wm S is threshing his wheat this week, we sent our John down to see about our home, & he had to assist Mr. S. in starting the thrasher. Mr. S. said he would be there all the while he had threshing done, to attend to it, & prevent the soldiers as far as was in his power from destroying any of our grain. John R. will attend to ours as soon as he is done plowing the corn, the soldiers are at present at John S's place. John Dunlap staid at home only two days the last time he came. Jeff Hogue was at home a day or two last week.

The clock is striking twelve darling, & I wonder if you are asleep & whom you are with & what you are doing, Oh! darling how much would I give to see your dear self. I have sit up so much I never get sleepy now until 2 or 3 o'clock. Sis & I do not work but nurse, & rest alternately, I have not wove any in near two weeks & I want only two days weaving to get my cloth out. If you & the children only keep well I shall be thankful. Robert is the greatest boy in the State Pa, & Ma kisses him twenty times a day thinking of her dear absent husband. Do write as often as you can, I have found my gold pen you gave me darling, & am writing with it. I had hid it away to keep the Federals from getting it, & forgot all about it. The children all send dear love to Pa & want to know when you are coming home, I cant help looking for you, though I know the opportunity of your doing so depends on a mere chance. My heart is with you dear George as always, & I pray God to bless you & care for you my own one. A letter full of kisses from your own dear wife.

Mary E. Boddie

Sis & family send love & kind greetings - good night - Clara says she had rather see you than any person in Ark. except John.

Mary E. Boddie at John Rumphs to her husband, George Boddie, in the field with the Confederate troops.

July 31, [18]64

My dear Husband,

I am heart sick for want of a letter from you, & I should have written ere this but Maima was quite sick & I could not feel like writing, she had fever one week, with slight chill nearly every day. She is quite well now, but I have not started her to school yet. Miss C. commenced teaching last week, I expect she will have a very full school. The way through the field that our children walk is so wet with dew early in the day is the reason I dont send Maima yet, I am so fearful 'twould make her sick & when anything is the matter with our children in your absence darling, I feel as though my all was gone, feel more confident in your skill in the treatment of the sick than in any person. You have been gone so long this time darling, I dream of your return nightly, & in my last dream of you, thought you told me you "had not been very well", & I am so anxious to hear from you, do pray that you may be well, & let me see you as soon as possible. John tells me he has no idea you can get off for some time yet, but every passerby I look to see if 'tis not George. John D. came by Saturday eve & took supper with us, he returned to his command today. The last order out from Gen'l Steele we hear is to have everything that man or horse can eat be totally destroyed between the Arkansas & White rivers, we are still hopeful of our cause in Va. though we hear many conflicting rumours of how the battle goes. I feel sometimes darling as though this war will never end, but 'tis only when I get disheartened from your long absence from me. I have been down home once, Mrs. S. sent the buggy for me one Saturday & I returned to Sallies on Sunday eve. We spent the Saturday eve at home, the officers I told you of are there, they have two tents in the yard & occupy the barn. All is nicely cleaned up, but my garden made me cry to look at, previous to the men going to our place, horses had been running in the garden, & not even your seed tulip [red] was clear of hoof prints. It rained so that evening I could not go to the orchard, or fields as I intended. John R. goes over every week, he is much pleased with the Officers, stays all night with them occasionally & takes a hunt. They have killed two deer down there, very large & fat.

 Our grain is all brought up here, the rye I did not ask J. how much there was of it, the wheat turned out 47 bu. Wm. S[tone]. & Mr P. assisted him at the gin house until all was done. We used Mr P's hand & I had your cotton all hauled up & put under the gin house & when he gets through with his own wheat (which they are threshing now) I intend to try & have our garden cleaned up & attended to. The Officers at home wont permit anyone to go in the garden or orchard for fruit, but 'tis too late now almost, when so much damage has already been done. They have one cow & young calf up, & they say, there are more to get up, & as John says they take good care of them, I am willing they should use them.

 Lizzie L., Mrs Portiss & Maj. Monroe spent one day this week with sis, I was perfectly astonished when Lizzie told us of Buck Peter's death which took place last week, she did not know of any particulars of his illness. Maj Woodland also died recently, there is a painful rumour afloat of Maj M.s intimacy with Miss L. Wm's & her having left Camden one night for Eldora[do], at which place she was delivered of a boy babe, which has since died. None of the family we hear give credit to the report, though Miss L. did certainly leave Camden. — Well darling want of space compels me to close, your dear children all send love & kisses to Pa, little Robert isn't very well, his bowels are deranged & he looks badly, but is lively & playful, & Ma kisses him a thousand times for you.

 John & sis send love to you, John is going to town tomorrow. I do hope

to get a letter from you this time. John will remain in Town all night as Mr Garland is to make his speech to the citizens & cc at night. good night, God bless my dear husband & care for him ever is the prayer of your true wife
Mary E. Boddie

Mary E. Boddie at John Rumph's to her husband, George Boddie, in the field with the Confederate army.
September 3rd [18]64

My dear husband,

I felt so disappointed that you did not return the evening after you left. I began to realize then that you were indeed gone for a long time, I feared that such would be the case when you were making preparations to leave but dreaded to speak of it, oh darling, I dont know where you are, only that Gen'l Fagan's Division* is with Gen'l Price, & I thought all the while too that the State troops would not have to leave the State. I know you will perform your duty wherever you are called, but O darling 'tis so hard for me to bear your long absence. I feel myself so incompetent to act without your guidance in all things, you are a dear good husband George to me in all things. Bless your loving heart, I feel that I could enfold you to mine & keep you there forever. Your letter written August 17th I rec'd on Monday last. I will entrust this to the courier hoping you may get it. There are posts established on this road, the couriers stay at the Abe Stones' & Mr Toneys'. Dockery's command* is at, or near Monticello, the Regt. to which John D. belongs are at Princeton. Everything is quiet at present & no news, we do hear occasionally that the Federals have evacuated Little Rock, & I dread daily to hear of battles fought in this State, yet I would that they were driven out of this & every other State in the Condederacy, & our people blessed with peace once more.

We have such extremely warm weather, I fear the clothes you have with you will be burdensome, take good care of yourself & be certain to come to me the last of this month if you can darling to stay with me two or three months if possible. I miss you daily & all the time, though I try to be cheerful & hoping under all circumstances. Willie has been sick all this week, he is up a day then has slight chill, & fever which lasts a day & night, he has had fever all day. I keep him in my room all the time, & he sleeps with me. Maima is not well, has fever every day or two, but as soon as it goes off, she is up & playing about. George R. is sick nearly all this week too, he had chill this evening. Tommy & Betty are on the sick list they are up though today. John R[umph] gave Maima some medicine tonight, he said if we had given Willie a little more medicine, he dont think Willie would have had another fever today. John has been bothered some, had his horse stolen from

*Gen'l Fagan refers to Confederate General James F. Fagan

*"Dockery" refers to Thomas P. Dockery, Colonel of the 19th Arkansas Volunteer Infantry.

the stable one night this week. He started in persuit next morning & was fortunate in getting him, found the horse running loose near Wm. Stones', he thinks some negro rode him down there, whoever it was took the horse soon after dark, they let the lot fence down to the ground. The mules were in a separate lot. Sis & John have traded the carriage to Maj. Hill for a horse & buggy. John will not bring the horse home until he builds a secure stable to keep him in, he was so pestered about Tom S's horse being stolen. Little Tommy Duprey is dead George. He died at Mrs Dion's, & William Duprey has been very sick, but has recovered. Well darling my paper is nearly out, do pray write to me as often as possible. I will write every week, hoping you may hear from us, & let us pray to God my husband that you may be spared to me & your children, & trust in Him that all will be well with us in His good time. Sis & John send kind greeting & our dear children send love & kisses to Pa & ask him to come home. Good night darling husband,

Your Mary

*Sunday night, Dear George. The children are all better, all of them up & about all day except Geo. but he is much better this evening. Willie was clear of fever this morning, — I hope wont be sick any more, shall give him quinine now. John went down home today, the cattle come up to be salted now, but John has not seen any of them both the times he went in the bottom. Our sheep were sheared last week. Wm. Stone was kind enough to let Joe shear them for me. Our Bill assisted. There are 22 of them, 12 old ones & 10 lambs. All bid good night to Pa. God bless you darling good boy.

*Note: This postscript is written at the top and along the sides of page 2:

Mary E. Boddie at John Rumph's to her husband, George Boddie, in the field with the Confederate army.

September 12th, [18]64

My dear Husband,

Again 'tis my pleasure to write to you, but not one word from my dear absent one yet. I know you have written to me, & I still keep hoping day after day to get a letter from you. I am happy to tell you that all are well with us at this time. Willie is not strong enough to go to school yet, he had fever two or three days after I wrote to you last week, but he is mending fast now, though he has the same pale look that Mamia had after her recovery. Mamia is looking much better now, & is going to school this week. Our baby's head is broke out all over in sores, it looks badly, but he is as lively & playful as can be. I do nothing for it but wash his head daily, he is a smart boy Pa & Ma talks to him so much about you & feels like crying at the same time to think you cant be with us, & never have been with us since his birth long enough for him to know & love you. Oh! darling I do so long for the time when we can be together in our own home once more, yet I am as happily cared for as I ever could be anywhere without you darling, for Sis & John are as kind to me & our children as 'tis possible for any one to be, yet no place is home when you are absent, & the love of kindred can never fill the great void in my heart for my dear husband, for you are all in all to me, & I did not know how dear you were till deprived of your presence & society. You are in the path of duty George, I know it, & I feel so proud of you darling, that you tread it so unflinchingly, knowing too that you are sacrificing the greatest happiness to you on earth, that of being with your family.

Our place is deserted again Geo. Maj. Hill left today, Gen'l Magruder compels him to stay in Camden to be in the office from early morn til 4 oclock in the evening. I am sorry they have to leave, for all straglers kept away from the place so long as they were there, & they took good care of the premises, which will all be turned out of doors again now. The cow & calf they had up, John sent for, & had drove up [here] tis a young heifer with first calf, & they look in fine order. Maj. Hill was up here yesterday, he told me some twenty or more of our cattle come up every week or two, to be salted which he had attended to, as I carried salt down there for that purpose. We have news of reverses to our Army in Georgia. Atlanta has fallen into hands of the Feds, great loss on our side. No pariculars yet respecting the battle, Gen'l Hardie* killed. Fort Morgan too was surrendered to the enemy with some 500 men. 'Tis sorrowful to think of, but we must expect some reverses in the fortunes of war, where such numbers are against us, but I seek solace in the Great & Good who says "The battle is not always to the strong." The troops here have been sent from Princeton to Camden, & from the latter place to Monticello again. Logan's reg't only are at Princeton. I wish darling I knew where you are, I know where your heart is, precious one, & we are both in the kind care of a Merciful God, & I pray he may bless you my dear husband.

Your loving wife Mary E. B.

Sis & John send kind greetings to you & our dear children send dear love & kisses to Pa & bid him come home, they want to see you. Carrie & Maima say "good night Pa," & I kiss my babe a thousand times for you darling. I cant help hoping you may come home the last of this month. good night dear George.

*"Gen'l Hardie refers to William J. Hardee of the Confederate Army. He died in the battle for Atlanta.

Mary E. Boddie at John Rumph's to her husband, George Boddie, in the field with the Confederate army.

April 26th [18]'65

My dear husband,

I recd your dear letter of the 12th (the only one) and hasten to answer it, 'tis so very seldom an opportunity offers that I can write with any probability of your receiving it. We are truly water-bound here now, no person passing at all as the bridge has been entirely dislodged by the high water & left floating. John D. spent the day here yesterday, says he is compelled to leave in a day or two (expects to swim the creek), & he proffered to take a letter as he will pass within some fourteen miles of your encampment, & I am in hopes he will see some one to whom he can entrust it to you. For three weeks now the river bottom's been impassable except in boats, so you may judge to what an extent it has been raining, had four days fair, & now 'tis raining again, John R. finds it impos[sible] to plough, & he is not yet done planting all the corn he wishes to. John R. & the boys went out hunting, & John B[oddie] killed two deer, from the same stand at which you killed one when here. The boys are very busy preparing their various hides & skins to be tanned, & John B. has been making them a halter & one for you too. John B. says he has everything complete now, except the horse, he says too, tell Pa to come home, he wants to see you, & so do we all darling, & your poor wife has been looking, & hoping, & praying — for you to come so long, for like you, I feel as though this separation is longest I've ever experienced. I feel thankful to hear you are well darling, & keep in good cheer, the end may be nearer than we think & then, O! then we'll live our young days o'er again, & I feel as though I could wish for no greater happiness than to have you, George, always with me. Tomorrow would have been the birthday of our Little Angel, she is blooming in Heaven, & I would not wish her here, I love to think of her there, as one link from our household band to draw us nearer to God.

The last news from the East side of the river is that Lee & Johnson have surrendered with their Army to the enemy, but we cant believe it to be true, no more than I can bear to think for a moment of your going to Missouri again. I do pray it may not be a necessity, or that it will be required of you. I mentioned in my previous letter to you that John R. wished to send Geo. in camp with you (as in August he would be compelled to go in the Army) & we have been expecting you home daily, thinking a furlough would be readily granted, to come home for that purpose. Sis & I are busy making cloth, so soon as we weave out one piece, have another ready to put in. I can work and think of you all day long darling. The children are all well, & send love & kisses to Pa. Sis & John ask to be remembered to you. May God bless & protect you darling is the prayer of your

                Loving wife,
                Mary E. Boddie

LETTERS FROM THE FIELD TO HOME

George Boddie with the Confederate troops in a camp near Warren, Arkansas, to his wife, Mary E. Boddie.

Feb. 2nd, 1864

My Dear Mary

Knowing you to be as anxious to hear from me as I am to hear from you - I embrace every opportunity that I have to let you know how I am getting along - You see by the date of this that we have been over the Saline & are now at Warren. I do not think that we will remain here long - the country is too poor & too many people have moved away hindering the Support of the Army for any length of time rather precarious - Though we have plenty yet, both for man & horse - There is an abundance near Monticello - especially pork - which is now being hauled to Warren & I Suspect Some of it will go to Camden - The direction we will take from this place I suspect will depend upon the movement of the enemy for I now believe that our Gnls will not fight unless forced to do so - We have made more enemies than friends by the indiscriminate <u>pressing</u> or rather <u>Stealing</u> pursued by our Rulers in the country Bordering on the Arkansas & Bayou Bartholemew - The people say we have nearly ruined them & are now going to leave them at the Mercy of the foe - When we first arrived they were really glad - but that is all changed now. Some are Selling out to move away - more are sad - & others think there is no difference between us & the Feds - How is it possible for us to prosper when we pursue Such a course - ruining our own people when we were welcomed by them as their friends & defenders. It has had a bad influence upon our soldiers. They ask one another how long it will be before they will be Served the same way & a great many of them if they had the opportunity would vote to go back into the Union upon any terms. So much for imbecility & bad management on the part of <u>our would be great men</u>.

I received your letter Dearest - & wrote you immediately & one previously - I hope you have received them - The person carrying them promised me to Stop & deliver them - They may have neglected to do So & dropped them in the office at Camden - Rest assured I will not neglect to write you - whenever I can - It is very trying to be forced to Stay away from you & our dear little ones So long - I will come when I can & am in hopes It will not be long before I can do So - God Bless your <u>Wifely</u> & <u>loving heart</u> - You are more near to me than my own hearts blood, My Mary, - write me Soon direct your letters - when you dont Know where I am - just to Crawford Regnt- 25t[h] Ark Cavelry - care Capt. Wilkinson & be Sure & always to name My Regiment when you direct them to any P. Office - Respects to John & Sallie & family - Kiss our little ones for me & dont let them forget Me

& Darling Your Soldier boy will <u>Kiss their Mother</u> to her hearts content - when he returns - Good bye

> Your affectionate husband
> George Boddie

George Boddie with the Confederate troops at Monticello, Arkansas to his wife, Mary E. Boddie.

Feb. 12th, 1864

My Dear Mary,

 I received your very affectionate letter by the hands of Mr. Green & was made glad by again hearing from home & my loved one - Mr. Cummins' son leaves in a few minutes & I hasten to send you this - letting you Know that I am well & have been here about a week - Where we will be tomorrow or the next day none of us know - The Feds Keep close to their <u>den</u> - though we hear of them occasionly - They are - or pretend to be scared almost out of their lives at our appearance in this Section of the country - just about as bad as the Camdenites were afraid of them - Our Scouting Parties range within five to twenty miles of Pine Bluff - There is a plenty of Provisions up here enough tis Said to last us a year or more - The News we get from the East of the Mississippi is favorable - The Feds have Signally failed in their repeated attacks upon Charleston & our people are in good Spirits & confident of ultimate Success - How different is the Spirit manifested on this Side - Everything appears to be going to ruin - Army demoralized & nearly every one looking forward to the time when he will have to resort to Stealing to Support himself & family - Many men here have taken their last horse from home - & some of them have the only one the[y] own in the world in Service to prevent their being Stolen - And I am afraid that many of them will desert as soon as the leaves put forth Sufficiently to conceal them - We have as mean men as the Feds dare to own. Men that were once good Soldiers & have been driven to desperation by the failure of our Government to protect their families & property from our thieving Soldiers —

 You mentioned that the negroes got along very Slowly with their ploughing in consequence of having bad ploughs - You will find a box of iron under the passage near water pail - which I think will be amply Sufficient to Make the whole of them as good as new - Keep the ploughs going whenever the ground will admit of it - I am glad you Succeded in getting the cattle out of the Bottom - have them taken care of if you possible can - they may be our <u>Sole</u> dependence for a Support if this war continues a great while longer. I dont See now how we could better ourselves by going to Texas at this time & believe that we had best stand our ground & do the best we can—— You neglected to mention whether your horse was a young or an old one - I am truly afraid Some one will come & claim him as Soon as he recovers a trifle - I need one - but cant stand the prices asked for a good one & run the risk of losing my money at that - I am sorry a claimant has come for J. R. mule - tell him to Keep a close watch on the others - horse Stealing is an epedemic at this time.

May a Merciful & <u>just</u> <u>God</u> Protect you & our children My <u>dearest</u> Mary - Kiss the children for me & assure them of Pa's love - & darling love beyond measure for yourself - Love to John & Sallie & family I remain your affectionate husband

Geo Boddie

*Note: This postscript was written upside down on the top of page 2:

*Dont look for me until you see me - I will come as Soon & whenever I can - Write me often & by every opportunity - G Boddie

George Boddie at an army camp near Warren to his wife, Mary E. Boddie.
May 23, 1864

My Dear Wife

I have just time to write you a few lines by a Soldier going to Camden - I stood the trip to this place very well, much better than I anticipated - Our whole command with the exception of the train & Some of Parsons' Cavalry have gone beyond Monticello, What their object is we cant find out - Sawther's command had a brush with the Feds at a bridge on Bayou Bartholmew - We learned they lost one man & had to fall Back as usual - This is a very poor country & we might eat it out in a short time - I am only tolerable well. Take care of yourself & our children - The Soldier is about Starting - May God Protect you. I will write you to-morrow or next day & direct your letters to Warren until you hear further from me - Kiss the children for Pa. I remain my dear wife your devoted husband

Geo Boddie

P.S. Write me Soon I am anxious to hear from you

G B

George Boddie at an army camp near Warren to his wife, Mary E. Boddie.
May 29, 1864

My Dear Mary,

I received your affectionate letter by Mr Bracie & you can't imagine what Satisfaction it gave me to hear from you once more - I had been very Sick Several days was so at the time your letter [arrived?] so much elated me that I am now nearly if not quite well - I have been so anxious & uneasy about you & our children & if I could only hear from you every day or two & learn that all were well, I could bear our Separation much better & with a lighter heart - Though we are farther & farther Separated my dear wife by every movement of our little Army - Your dear Self is ever before me as near & as loving as ever & I fondly hope soon to return to you & happiness.

 We are now encamped near Warren - Foraging & looking after the Feds - Our Scouts have been within five miles of Napoleon & are now within a few [miles] of Pine Bluff. We learn that the Feds are advancing, how far they intend to come remains to be Seen. Sawther the Temporary commander of this division Says he will whip them or give them a hard fight if they come this way. Marmaduke & Shelby will attend to them if they cross the Saline towards Camden & we have Several Regiments of independent troops East of the Arkansas river & Dockery is South of us about 30 miles with 7 or 8 hundred men - So you See they can pick up a fight in any direction if <u>all hands are willing</u>. It is now believed that the Feds have only 12 or 1500 cavalry in all. Little Rock & Pine Bluff are still being hemmed in with fortifications - We have given them a big <u>Scare</u> if we do nothing else.

 I am in hopes that the children will Keep well - Keep them shod if you possibly can - dont wait on Avera for the Leather if you can get it any where's else dont mind the price, if you can preserve the children you may be able to preserve you own health - for I know it will go hard with you - if you have to wait on them during the night after working as hard as you do all day - If you Should need money Sell some corn to procure it - & if you do not - dont sell any - or anything else that is fit for food - for it may be a bad crop year - even if you are suffered to make one - have the ground broken up where wheat was sown last year if it is not already done - Be brave & hopeful - for Surely God will bless & protect you - Oh how <u>near</u> and <u>dear</u> you are to me - My Mary - and if ever we do get through with this war & the arms of the Confederacy are triumphant - I shall try & do all that a husband can do to make the remnant of your life one of happiness & if I Should live a hundred years I will but love you <u>more</u> & more - Kiss our dear children for me - My love to John R, Sallie & family - I wrote you last week when I was sick - I will continue to write you every opportunity - Write often dearest & direct your letters to Monticello - Crawfords Regt of Cavalry care of Capt Wilkinson - May Heaven continue to protect My Mary & my little ones is the heartfelt prayer of your Affectionate Husband

      Geo Boddie

 P.S. Tell Serg* I have his ring made and am wearing it on my little finger -

      G. Boddie

---

*"Serg" was a nickname which George Boddie gave to his son Robert.

*Editor's Note: This letter was not as well preserved as most of the others; therefore there are parts of it that cannot be read. We have tried to insert words that would complete the thought where the writing can not be deciphered.

*George Boddie in a camp near Florence [in Drew County] to his wife, Mary E. Boddie.

June 5th 1864

My Dear Wife

I have written to you once since I reached my command & as yet I have heard nothing from you. I am truly anxious to hear from you & that very often - I am aware that your opportunities are not So good to send me letters as they were formerly from Camden yet you Must write Me often My Mary - hearing from you that often is My best medicine. I believe I can become accustomed to almost everything except being absent from you. I want to see you now & wish to be with you always - I am becoming tired of the Army - too many acts of injustice pirpetrated daily to be borne with patience by an honest man - Our Mules cavalry have just been dismounted & the men Scattered in the different commands of infantry & the mules taken possession of by the Govt - frequently the Mules with best price of property [will be taken by men at the headquarters?] - We are doing nothing at this time toward molesting the enemy - Col Slommans with about [100] of us made a raid toward Pine Bluff last week. We went within two miles of the Bluff & our advanced [men] followed the enemy [to] P. Bluff getting Sight of their fortifications & then fell back hoping to draw them out but they were to smart to follow - So we had to take the back [way to] our camp again - So here we are eating beef- corn bread & drinking the meanest of water - We have had floods of rain here & a good deal of wheat injured - Corn crops are good where they had been cultivated early & camp fever prevailing in camp - I hope you all May Keep well & Mary Should you become Sick let Me Know as Soon as possible & I <u>will come to you</u> - Keep our children for Me. My love to all & for yourself. My dearest & the best of wives I shall always pray for heavens Most choice blessings - Write me often & direct to Slemmins Brigade - Crawford Regt Co D - I remain My Dear Mary your affectionate husband.

Geo Boddie

George Boddie in camp near Tyro, Drew County, to his wife, Mary E. Boddie.

June 11, 1864

My Dear Wife

I reached here in Safety after a tiresome Journey of two days & a half - tired and everything wet from the heavy rains encountered on the way - Have good health - & am in hopes that I am now So far weather proof that I can endure both heat & cold with impunity - I found the men all lively &

in good Spirits with a plenty of Beef for themselves & corn for their horses - The crops that I saw on the way both wheat & corn were generally <u>fine</u> - I came by the Battle grounds & witnessed the disgusting Sight of Hogs & buzzards dragging the remains of <u>Feds</u> & Negroes from their Shallow graves appearing to contend with each other for the <u>choice</u> pieces - Our dead were better cared for - having pole pins placed around the graves - I could hear nothing of John's Negroes or of Henry - nor could I find anyone who had seen a dead Negro woman - but Several Negroes told me they [had] seen several loads of Negro women & children going to <u>Shreveport</u> & - <u>Texas</u> - captured in the Swamps after our men had left. A man by the name of Word living near Marks Mills having captured eight - Mostly fellows - Sold his claim to Macon of Warren for 4000 - who run them to Texas - I Shall not have any Scruples in helping Myself to the property of people of a certain class here after - I firmly believe that most of the missing Negroes from our neighborhood are in Texas. We have no news from the army - It is about commencing to rain again. Write Me Soon- <u>My dear [Miss]</u>. All My <u>love</u> for you & our children - Present My Kindest wishes to Sallie, John & family - Here it comes - good by -

                Your husband
                Geo Boddie

George Boddie at camp near Florence to his wife, Mary E. Boddie.
                                                        June 27th 1864

    My Dear Mary

        I wrote you a few lines on the day before yesterday & as Mr. Cushman is about leaving this morning for home I hasten to write again for fear I will not get to write again I am well though more thin than you ever Saw Me - I manage to Swallow a little Beef & Bread each day - you know it takes but little to do Me - <u>lucky for Me</u> - Mud Larks* & Bacon have made their disappearance from these parts - We get plenty of Corn yet by crossing Bayou Bartholmue for it - The plantations are all abandoned by their owners & being now occupied by poor people more for the purpose of taking care of things than anything else - Several of our company [have been] talking about _____ the company nearly broke up owing to the government taking mules from the men - <u>They wont Stand for it</u>- We hear nothing from the Feds - I wrote you about our trip to Pine Bluff - I was in half a mile of the place. Since I saw you I should not be Surprised if we crossed the Arkansas Shortly - I Should like to come home to See you before crossing - that is, if we have it to do - but I see [no] chance of doing So - Write Me often My Dear wife - I have not received a line from you Since I left home - You cant imagine how I wish to See you & our little ones. I will write you as often as I can

*The *Dictionary of Slang and Unconventional English* lists eleven definitions for "Mud-lark"; the eighth one seems to best fit the context of this sentence: A Hog.

concerning My poor Self - My best to John & family. Be assured of My love & devotion for yourself & children - <u>My More than life</u>
>your husband
>Geo. Boddie
>Direct yours to Crawford Regt Co C Stimmins Brig Calvary Division

George Boddie in camp on the Arkansas River to his wife, Mary E. Boddie.
>July 29th 1864

My Dear Wife

I received your long looked for letter by the hands of John Stone & a load of [uneasiness] is taken from My Mind in consequence - When I [dont] hear from you I imagine a thousand things - all [evil] - that may have befallen you & our little ones, & you dont want to distress me by letting me know [of] them. Do write Me often my dear Mary - You can [imagine] how precious are your letters to me - to see the [paper you] have folded - to read the words you have [written] remind Me & bring near to me My dear [wife] & our babes - I Scarcely have time or opportunity of [writing] you often - and always as now Making use of My Saddle Bags for a table - & a soldier just [leaving] for Camden for a conveyance - it is always safe to trust the courier but we dont know if they will have more mail matter than they can carry - When Such is the case the Govt Mail always have the preference - I am not well darling though yet able [to] do duty - We have been some time on the Arkansas River. It is truly a rich country Surpassing My expectations. The bottom is broad & level intersperced with numerous lakes - any of them as large & most of them Larger than Pine lake & the best Stock range I ever Saw - Those acquainted with the country Say that this, the West, will hardly compare with the East Side in fertility & worth. Very few White people are living here on these extensive plantations - only a few negroes to take care of Stock. The best of old corn we are now gathering from fields where the hog Weeds are 3 & 4 feet higher than the Corn Stalks. We are I Suppose some fourteen miles below Pine Bluff frequently Scouting within Six or Seven miles of the Enemy who Keeps close within his fortifications - I have no news to write you & Scarcly time - it is growing So late to Say much more. I am in hopes John will Succeed in Saving all the grain - I am apprehensive that all our cattle will be destroyed or go wild - are they ever Salted or looked after - I will try and come to See you as Soon as I can - but few furloughs are granted now. I am Sorry our homested has been So devastated & as a general thing our men are as mean as the Federals - My best regards to J.R. Sallie & family - & the love of a devoted husband & father to yourself & children - May God Bless you good night
>Your husband
>Geo Boddie

George Boddie in camp near Mount Elba to his wife, Mary E. Boddie.

Aug 17th 1864

My Dear Wife

This is Wednesday lacking a day of being a week Since I left you. I am well & reached my command in Safety which I found encamped in about nine miles of Mt Elba having left the Arkansas bottom for the purpose of fitting up preparatory to a move towards Missouri - Our wagons are leaving today with all extra Baggage for Camden & will return with guns & ammunition for our Army. We also learn that the infantry & cavalry from Louisana & Texas are on the march northward - which begins to look like doing Something at last - The expectation is that we will move the Feds from Pine Bluff & Little Rock before proceeding northward - The men living South of this have pretty long faces in consequence of this contemplated movement - Not Knowing when they will be allowed to return - All wish to go home & bid their families farewell - but the privilege is denied them - well it may be for the best as many of them if Suffered to leave would never return & we need & want every man at his post - The programme is as yet kept a Secret from us though I feel confident that we will be able to drive every Fed from the State if our Generals [will perform] their duty - Most of us want to get through with this war as Soon as possible & if fighting will do it we are willing and ready - Time flies fast - yet the days are long very long My dear Mary that I am absent from you. Every Morning I look at the ringlet you gave me - it brings you near me & it Shall Serve me my dear wife as a talisman & ever remind me that I Should do nothing that you would be ashamed of in your husband - I wish I was more worthy of you though there is none that can appreciate you more highly than I do - I may be absent from you a long time - but be assured you have my utmost confidence & love & whatever you May do in the Management of our children & affairs will Meet with my approbation. Take good care of yourself & pray to God we May be Spared to each other - for the world to Me would be a desolate waste without you - You are as you have always been Miss Mary to me, time can make no change Give my love to & kiss the children for me - I Know you will not let the little ones forget Pa - My love & best wishes to John R. & Sallie & children - Receive the assurance & dear Mary of My heartfelt & Sincere prayer to God - that he will spare me to return to make you happy - Farewell until we meet again My dear wife

Your affectionate husband
Geo Boddie

P. S. John Agee was instantly killed by the fall of a limb from a dead tree while the army was on the move from the Arkansas bottom on the 10th inst G.B.

George Boddie in camp in Rusk County, Texas, to his wife, Mary E. Boddie.
May 10th 1865

My Dear Mary

  As a courier leaves on tomorrow for Marshall, I hasten to write you - acknowledging the receipt of your precious favor of April 26th, being the Second I have received from you Since I saw you last. How glad I am to hear once more that you were all well & have not as yet been disturbed by the Enemy - I hope & pray they may never come near you again - Just the thoughts of their visiting our Section of the country again gives me more uneasiness than anything else & <u>perhaps</u> is the only thing that would induce me to leave the army as a <u>deserter</u> - The very word is hateful without commiting the act itself - Yet if I know myself - I should try & get to you as Soon as possible & if I Knew of their coming should try to anticipate them - The crimes worse than brutal commited by them in the Northern part of Ark will forever prevent my leaving my post voluntarily as many have done & are now doing for the purpose of ingrating themselves in their favor - The Suffering they caused you to undergo I Shall never get over & never forgive - & will pay with interest whenever I have opportunity - We are now in Texas & making for <u>Navarro</u> county where we expect to find a plenty of provisions for man & horse. This country here & out toward Shreveport is poor, - as to a plenty of provisions - A good many plantations laying waste - owners with <u>Skillet heads</u>* gone to a Supposed place of Safety - further west - Confederate Money not worth a dollar in the hundreds here - But it makes no difference with us. Cribbs* are gouged & emptied with as much unconcern as if we were confering a favor upon the owners - dinners are eaten & tobacco lifted - Confederate Money offered in return - it is refused - We return our money to its hiding place & march off leaving them grumbling - I have no idea how long we will remain in this State & will come to See <u>you dearest</u> whenever I can - Be cheerful - be <u>hopeful</u> - the Same God has charge of us now that provided & cared for us in the past - in whose hands I leave you My More than Wife - I shall write you as often as I can have an opportunity of Sending you a letter - Pay Postage on your letters the Soldiers get more that are post paid than any other way. I am well & have enjoyed very good health so far - An Army has to Keep moving to Keep healthy - The men continue to desert - 45 on one night & 56 on another left previous to our crossing Red River & they are continually leaving in Smaller Squads. They are principally men that were hunted out of the Brush. They Never were & Never will be of any Service - It would be well if they were all <u>Shot</u> - for out of Such Material are robbers made & are our worse enemies on the approach of the Feds - I have met no acquaintances Since I have been in the State with the exception of Mrs Agee & Mrs. Broughton. Met them near

*While references contain nothing about the term "skillet heads," the use in the sentence indicates an uncomplimentary name for people with shallow minds.

*The term Cribbs, although misspelled by our standards today, refers to corn cribs in which farmers stored their harvested corn.

Shreveport going trading in an old wagon. Mrs Agee complained bitterly of the old citizens in Texas & wished the War would end So that they can go back to Ark - I learned while near Marshall that a man was <u>hung</u> a short time previous to our arrival on Red River for <u>horse Stealing</u> - What a fate & record - first disertion - then horse Stealing- there were others concerned with him - But I did not learn their names - I could write you pages of camp News - but there is no credence to be placed in them. The loss of Lee has had an injurious effect upon our Army - Reaction will take place after a while - It is a difficult Matter to form any idea of the course that will be persued by the rulers in this department - Most of the men believe We are Whipped & are waiting to See what will be done with them - Some are for fighting to the <u>bitter end</u> - Now good by My dear wife for this time, I hope to See you Soon - Kiss & give my love to our children - Kind wishes to Sallie, John R & families - Write Me often I may get some of your letters - I remain as ever your affectionate husband -

    Geo Boddie

[1]*Tommy B. Love in Camp Faulkner at Luka Springs* to his aunt Cornelia Dickson in Autauga Co.*

                Sept 21, 1861

Dear Aunt,

  I now take my pen to write you a few lines for the first time in my life. We will leave here tomorrow evening or Thursday morning. I have been sick two or three days since I began to lead camp life, and find it a pleasant good life only when it is my day to cook. We have to get up so soon to get our little fare of coffee, pork, and biscuits. I have sent you a little song and want you to learn it for my sake and tell me in your leter if you have heard from Arkansas since I left. I know several other songs & will send them to you when we get to our destination. We have one boy in our company that can compose a song on anything & all the pieces I send you will be his own make or home made just as you will have it. I can make just as good a biscuit as any lady can but can't make hash yet & want you to send me a note containing all the cooking tactics that belong to a soldier's camp. I have written to Miss Ella & never thought to give her my best respects. Tell her to excuse me this time. I will do better next. You must give them to her for me. While we were passing through the mountains we saw a large black bear. All the boys were well pleased with their trip. I read my Bible every night now. Tim Limbrish made rice soup out of the old bacon one time. Don't know anything else to write to you. Give my love to all the family & neighbors. Don't believe anything what Mr Wagner says we did in Montgomery

[1]Editor's Note: The five letters which follow come from a Confederate soldier on the eastern side of the Mississippi River, where the actual fighting was much more intense. They are written by Tommy, the son of Sis Carrie, to his aunt, Cornelia Dickson.

*The exact location of Luka Springs is an unknown, but since they went "through the mountains" from Montgomery, it is probably in Tennessee.

& it was about me parching coffee, but not with a ten foot pole. Kiss my sweetheart for me if you know who she is & tell Sis to look out for a letter from me in a few days.

I remain your obedient soldier & nephew,
T. B. Love

SONG
Don't you see the soldiers coming
Don't you see the soldiers coming
Don't you see the soldiers coming
From the Alabama State
Chorus:
We are band of freemen
We are band of brothers
We are band of soldiers
From the Alabama State.

Captain Faulkner is our leader
Captain Faulkner is our leader
Captain Faulkner is our leader
From the Alabama State
Chorus:
We are all from old Autauga
We are all from old Autauga
We are all from old Autauga
From the Alabama State
Chorus:
I will tell you the rest of it in my next letter.
T. B. Love
POEM
TO MR LINCOLN
(written by T. B. Love, age 16)
Old honest Abe, You are a babe
In military glory!
An arrant fool, a party tool.
A traitor and a tory.

Dictator now, and in a row,
A pulling of the trigger;
At all the South with foaming mouth
Decoying off the nigger.

Clouds of War

You know its so, at Fort Monroe
You put them all to labor
Whom you declare are free as air,
Your equal and your neighbor.

Why treat them so? 'Tis wrong you know
When Butler doesn't need 'em.
Some future day, you say
You'll give them all freedom.

What is your plea, to set them free?
They cost four thousand million,
You cannot pay that debt, you know,
You everlasting villian.

But you are boss a mighty horse
A snortin' in the stable,
A racer too, a cangaroo
So whip us if you're able.
Your proclamation to us of late
The ports are all blockaded.
The forts retook at Sandy Hook
And Charleston canonaded.

Thats your intent as President
A curious plan to save us,
But we'll be free as you will see
With Beauregard and Davis.

Old Mr. Link, what do you think
About these Southern Cattle?
What horns you see where'er you go
And whips you every battle?

Your brags you made, you would invade,
And whip the old Dominion.
But you will fail and tuck your tail
Is Beauregard's opinion.

If Scoot and Wool should at us pull
Across the country level
We'll meet them there and fight um fair
And thrash them like the devil.

To Wool and Scoot, we'll never speak
But one thing you'll discover,
That wool will fly and Scoot will die
Before he whips his Mother (Virginia)

Keep on your shirt, nobody hurt,
With us you must not trifle,
Or you'll catch hell with shot and shell
And the Kentucky rifle.

So goodbye, Abe, you are a babe
In military glory
An arrant fool, a party tool
A traitor and a tory.

END

Thomas B. Love at Columbus, Kentucky, to his aunt Cornelia Dickson in Autuaga Co.

Oct. 21, 1861

Dear Aunt,

    Your letter of the 15th has been received and I was glad to hear from you, and that you are well and are able to help the volunteers of your county. I am at a private house at the present. I came down yesterday evening. The lady is named Mrs. Badger. She is a very kind lady and a good nurse. W. Wood and Walter are staying here. There are four more of our company here including our lieutenant. Our company has had bad luck some how. There are 45 of them on the sick list and one of the 45 I think will die. Clem is at the hospital, yet I think he is worse off at present than any of the boys from about Mulberry P. O. I did not think to tell you the difference between a private house and a hospital. In the first place I can have a chair to sit in and a fire to warm by and a table to write on. We can't get any of these things at a hospital, and the next, I have a bed to sleep on, a fine toast of milk, light bread and butter, and a warm cup of tea and anything I want. While I was at the hospital I had plenty of everything that was there, such as it was. Old baker's bread, coffee and ham. I am afraid to eat anything but toast and drink tea for yet a while.

    Walter says tell his Ma he is up but not able to write. I think he will write today some time, he has just asked me for a piece of paper, and I refused him. I have a very bad cough and it looks like I can't break it. That was the reason I came to a private house. Tell Miss Ella not to let Miss Jane know who she gets a letter from, and then I am not so apt to get that mighty scolding you spoke of, but please don't let Miss Jane know I sent such a message to Miss E. Tell Miss E. to write as soon as she can and also Miss Jane. I received your letter. I won't stay here more than five or six days, long enough to gain my strength. I am going to write to Uncle Clem today.

We have not been formed into any regiment yet, and I don't know how long we will stay at Columbus, but don't think we will winter-quarter here. I presented your best respects to enquiring friends and found them to be very numerous. Give my love to Grandma and to all the family and enquiring friends. Accept a good share for yourself. Write soon

Your affectionate nephew,
T. B. Love

P. S. I took a walk up to camp this evening and heard that the yankees gave some of our scouts the mischief. There were ten of our men and about 200 yankees. While our men were riding down a deep defile the enemy orders them to halt, but they took to their heels and the yankees fired on them, killing one horse, wounding four men and crippling 4 more horses. Clem is better but Hedgbeth is worse. All the boys are mending. Dee Lamar came down this evening. I must close with my P. S.'s So good by. Write soon.

T. B. Love

Thomas B. Love near Knoxville, Tennessee, to his aunt Cornelia Dickson in Autauga Co.

Sept 8, 1862

Dear Aunt,

I hardly know how to commence to write to you as it has been so long since we corresponded. It is hardly worthwhile to tell how and where I am as you can see that I am near Knoxville. I am in very good health and have very good water. I do not know exactly when or where I will go. There was a report in circulation yesterday that we would go to reinforce General Price, but it was not creditated by anyone. We have the Austrian rifle. It is a very good gun, will kill a man at _____ yds. We will leave one day this week. I hardly evey get a chance to read a paper up here. There is a paper mill about a mile from here I was at it once. It makes 20 reams a day. There is plenty of fruit of every kind that grows in such climates up here. I wish I had a chance to send you some cuttings of the apple and cherry trees. They are so large and nice. I am afraid to eat any apple or drink cider or milk. There might be a bush-whacker concealed within. Our company has been into another fight. I have not heard the casualties yet and it seems that I never will as long as I stay here. Lieutenant C. Moore was killed in the engagement. I will give you a correct list of the officers that I am under. At the present,

Lieutenant Col. Pressly commands the Brigade. Major Dunkin the Battallion that I am in. Captain OConnor the company. My company is Company B. It is the sharp shooters for the Battallion. We drill in skirmish drill every morning from 5 to half past 7. Battallion drill from four to dark in the evening. Conscription is being put in force in East Tenn. I saw some conscripted yesterday at the spring. You ought to have heard the soldiers bawl out (here's ye conscript). They were taken by surprise while selling apples. The boys wanted to conscript the wagon team and its contents, but could not do it. Afterwards every citizen old or young, the soldiers would yell here's ye conscript. The small pox is not far from Knoxville and they are vaccinating all the soldiers since I commenced this letter. I heard that we would leave tomorrow, but no one knows but the commanding officer. There is the best spring above here I ever saw and the largest. There is a spring that the [water?] turns a grist mill and paper mill. If we leave here tomorrow, I do not expect to write to you in a long time. It will take us until the last of December or spring to catch up with our regiment. The last I heard from General Bragg he was at Camp Dick Robinson, Ky, over three hundred miles from here. I expect we will have to fight before we get to them. Postage stamps is the best money we have or it is the only small change we use. I have not met up with any of our company but two since I left home. I forgot to tell you about my trip. I had a good time until I left Chattanooga and had to ride in box cars and was crowded all the time — had to stand up most of the night. You have the advantage of me in the convenience of writing. You have a desk to write on and I have to write on my lap, and I have no lap worth talking about. You must excuse this letter as it is badly written. I have nothing to write on. They are sending those that are not able to stand the march to the hospital. Breckenridge Co. command are still here. Some of them have been furloughed for 10 days. My love to Grandma and all the family. Accept a share for yourself. My respects to all enquiring friends, to Miss E anyhow. Do not write until you hear from me again.

                         Your nephew
                         T. B. Love

Thomas B. Love in camp near Shelbyville, Tennessee, to his aunt Cornelia Dickson in Autauga County, Alabama.

                                            Apr 7th, 1863

Esteem Friend,

As it has been a good while since we have corresponded, I will endeavor to get one up. I am a little surprised at you, for not writing to me as you promised. You know that I wrote you the last letter, & I hope in the future both will be more prompt. I can hear nothing from the front that you have not already heard. Col. Hannons Battallin is at Tuscumbia. The vanguard of the yankees are in three miles of the place, daily skirmishes occur all along the front, but none of interest has transpired since my last, which was to father. Our cavalry scouts are in 2 1/4 miles of Murfreesboro & report the yankees falling back. There has been various reports about cavalry scouts & fights but none are true so far. I suppose ere this you have heard of the burning of the Court House at this place. There was not much loss & it would not have made much difference if the town itself had been burned, for it is one of the greatest bogs & Union holes in Tenn. The yankees exclaimed when they left here, (This is the happiest place we found since we left home). No wonder they had a cause to say so a soldier may dress himself in citizens clothes & go out & play off Union & he will quickly find out what they are. Some time ago it was reported that we were going to Tullahoma. You might see them coming in town from every direction & winking at each other, as if to say, we will be with our friends after a while, Rosencrans is coming, &c &c. The fair weather still continues & the two armies cannot remain idle long. The trees have at last began to bud & the long looked for spring has set in, in good earnest. We have began to drill every day in Company, Battallion or Brigade & we also have (I am almost ashamed to say) become too mischievous for the good of the army & Gen Polk* had to establish Brigade guards to keep the men in. The speculators* have been so numerous in camp that the market has become dull & they have to sell out at <u>cost</u>. Every thing is scarce up in this country as ever, except body guards & they are more numerous than the soldiers themselves. They are in for the war & there is no getting rid of them. I have just come off of dctail & resume my seat. The mess is getting me finely, have plenty to eat such as it is, corn bread, bacon, rice & now & then a little beef & molasses to make it look more like rations for a soldier. The Post Commissary at this place swaps the sugar off for bacon. Billy Wood is still in our mess & he has to buy his rations from the Brigade Commissary & we have a good <u>chance</u> to slip a ham now & then, while drawing his rations. One of the company by the name of Scott is cooking for Lieuts Hall & Myrick. There was an order prohibiting officers from detailing the soldiers to cook & wait on them, but it seems it has not been enforced, as a great many white servants are still in this Regt. We are looking for Capt. Sawyer back every day. I suppose you read my letters that I write to the home folks & ere this you have heard of the resignation of Lieut. Col. Dennell. Capt. S. will be okay I think. An extension of Dee Leaman's furlough to the first of May was recieved this morning, if he is well enough he will have a fine time fishing with the girls. Speaking of fishing reminds me of the (camp talk) as the boys calls it. It is all they can talk about going fishing with the girls. We go fishing occasionaly but hardly ever catch any thing. I went yesterday, but could not catch any. I saw a fine gang of <u>large ducks</u> in the river, & sent some of the boys back to

*"Gen. Polk" refers to Lucius E. Polk, who settled in Helena in 1853. When the war broke out, he enlisted in the Confederate Army as a private; he rose in rank quite rapidly and was made a Brigadier General in December of 1862. He was recognized for heroic action in the battles of Murfreesboro and Chickamauga.

*"Speculators" are most probably men who sold goods on the Black Market.

camp to steal a muskit & some ammunition to kill them but could not make the ripple. Ben Dun is at Atlanta Ga & was doing well when he wrote last. The boys play ball every day, it looks like they just found out they were living to see them run & play, one month ago you could not see or make one get out of a snails trot, & now enlivened by the warmth of good ole <u>Sol</u>, their faces are beginning to look <u>full</u> & <u>rosy</u>, & our streets are as clean & neat as a garden walk. The camp fires are crowd[ed] around every fair night & the next thing is a song from some of the boys & a love song at that or a tune from the <u>violin</u> & then every one seats himself by the glowing embers to chat with some one of his <u>friend prior</u> to the war, about the fine times he used to have with his <u>love</u> & the <u>future, yes</u> the <u>future</u>, when & what he will do when the war ends. Such is the amusements we have in camp though you need not tell any one what I have written you. if you do the boys will be sure to get hold of it & give me <u>jessie</u> about telling tales out of school. I have just come off of Skirmish drill, this makes the second time I have been interupted & I take my pen in hand to finish my letter. I could get another furlough if I would reinlist for five years & join the regular army & go to Fort Morgan* but I believe I prefer staying here some few of our company will enlist but none of the Mulberry boys. I have no idea how many troops are at this place. I know that Polk Corps is here & there is several divisions besides his corps. I know there is enough to give Rosencrans a shock & such a one that will be disgusting to the whole yankee nation. Gen Polk has had some seige guns planted out on the Unionville Pike & reviewing the Corps the other day looks like some thing was going to turn up. I believe I have told you all the news that I know. I have not seen todays paper & have nothing late from the front, I send you a Guttapurcha* ring in this letter. I want you to keep it & also to wear it. I received a letter from Sis this morning & will answer it in a few days. I want you to send me some pickle by Dee Leaman & a bottle of pepper sauce any thing from home these times is so nourishing that the soldiers will talk about it a month. Tell Annie[?] to send me some pickle & eggs by Dee, as eggs is three dollars a dozen & I will make her a nice ring. She says that I never write or send a message to her only when I want something. It is her, she will not write to me. Tell sis to send me a pair of pants & two pr socks by him. I must close with much love to you. Give my love to grandma also to all the family. My respects to all enquiring friends. You know how to direct your letters. You must write soon & regular. Good bye for the present, I remain yours truly,

Tommie
(Afleigh private. rear rank. Co AFCG 24th Regt Ala Vols)

*Fort Morgan was located on Mobile Bay.

*Guttapercha is a concrete milky juice that hardens into a cement substance. It comes from the gum tree.

From Thomas B. Love in camp near Falls Creek, Tennessee to his aunt Cornelia Dickson in Autauga Co Alabama.

May 27th/63

Dear Auntie

Yours of the 23rd Apr has been received though it was a long time coming. I assure you it was read with the greatest pleasure immaginable, no doubt you are impatient to hear from me, but the delay is not my fault. Your letter was mailed the 16th May & written on the 23rd. There has been heavy skirmishing in front. About 80 of the 1st Ala was surprised & captured at Middletown, also 15 of the 8th Confederate Regt with them. Nothing more from the front that would interest you. Ere this you have heard the news by Telegraph of the banishment of Mr. Vallandigham* from the U.S. I think the time has come when the people of the North to rise en masse & resist the Tyrant & his followers if they profess to be freemen. It is useless to dwell upon a point so well known to the entire white population of America & I will pass on by. Vallandigham is now in town (Shelbyville). We have glorious news from Miss. has been confirmed. I hope Gen Stevinson* will be able to capture or kill Grant & his whole army. From all that we can learn, if Grant dont make a hasty retreat Gen Johnson* will capture his whole army. This unholy war cannot last long if we are as successful in the future as we have been in the last four months past. Our Brigade is again out on Pickett on the Unionville Pike, have no idea how long we will remain here. It is reported that we will (that is our Regt) go to town Monday to guard the town. We have moved our permanent camping ground two miles in advance of our old one & it is on Duck river. It is a beautiful camping ground as I ever saw. I will give you a description of it. On the south & East it is bordered by the beautiful little stream, Duck river, the north by a range of high rocks & on the west it is boundless for miles. We have plenty of shade, the sun never or very seldom has a chance to warm the tents so large are the Beech & Sycamore trees. On the opposite side of the river there is a beautiful spring of the coolest Freestone water which the soldiers were determined to taste of cost what it may, so they commenced constructing rafts to cross on. It was indeed amusing to see them get ducked in the river & have to swim to the bank with half dozen canteens around them. They had no instruments to build with & had to tie the logs together with hickory bark & it would [break] very often. They got ducked. The Breastworks are progressing finely between this & town, the larger forts are very near completed & rifle pitts are almost finished. Let Old Rosy come & we will teach him a lesson never to forget. It has been raining some this evening but not much. I hope we may have a good shower before it is over with. Crops are looking finely especialy wheat. I never saw any finer in my life, it is just beginning to head & needs

*"Mr. Vallandigham" refers to Congressman Clement Vallandigham from Ohio. He was a Peace Democrat and was so outspoken in his criticism of the way Lincoln was handling the war that Lincoln banished him from the Union and sent him under guard to Tennessee. When he began to criticize Jefferson Davis, he was banished from the Confederacy. He eventually went to Canada. Some scholars believe that Edward Everett Hale modeled his novel *A Man Without A Country* on him.

*"Gen Stevinson" refers to Carter L. Stevenson of the Confederate Army.

*"Gen Johnson" refers to Bushrod R. Johnson of the Confederate Army.

rain very much. The apple trees are loaded down with the young apples which promises to yield an abundant crop of the nice fruit. The smallpox has disappeared in the Regt but can't say how long it will be before it may break out again. We had five cases in the camp only one died, a Mr Keys from Pratville. He was a <u>perfect scab</u> from head to foot when he died. I know he must have suffered. All the other cases has recovered (excepting one) & returned to camp. I have written you as much as my paper will allow at this time & must close with much love to you & all the family. I have received Father's & will answer it in a few days. More anon

         (Tommie)

PART THREE

After the War

On April 9, 1865, General Robert E. Lee surrendered his army to General U. S. Grant at Appomattox. When the last command surrendered on June 23, the War Between the States was over; the Confederacy was no more, and the United States of America was once again united. Peace reigned again over the land; as is always the case when the ravages of war cease, the difficult task of recovery and rebuilding begins. The debris of war must be cleared away to make way for new structures. Sherman's March to the Sea had left in its wake a burned South, east of the Mississippi; the physical clean up was of Herculean proportions. However, the most difficult recovery lay not in the physical, but in the mental and emotional arena on both sides of the big river. A new South existed, one that called for changes in basic lifestyles and attitudes. Scorched fields can be cleared and replanted with sweat-producing labor, as can destroyed buildings. Restructuring habits, customs, and attitudes, on the other hand, requires mental anguish and heartrending tears. The economy was in a shambles; the agricultural markets had been closed for four long years, and the only labor force the southern farmers had known no longer existed. Slave labor was a thing of the past, and a new system of farming had to be devised. In short, the world they had grown up in was no more. This was a time of total change: the black people, who for generations had existed in a society of servitude with no personal possessions, indeed with no surnames even, were now free, but with precious little of their own to enjoy that freedom with; the white people had their land, still, but no money to farm it, very little livestock to use for food, and exorbitant taxes to pay. This "time of change" would prove frustrating and disheartening for everyone.

The frustration and disheartenment of the time, as well as the agonizing struggle with change, can be felt in the letters which follow. It is hoped that the reader will remember the milieu of these letters and establish some empathy for the writers and their subjects. While the changes they were experiencing are far removed from our perspective nearly 200 years later, they were very current and real for these people and the society of their time.

Cornelia Dickson finally joined her sister Clara Dunlap in Arkansas in March of 1868. It is Cornelia who becomes our letter writer now and sends epistles back to Alabama. Not only do the letters continue the narratives of Clara, Sis Mollie and brother George, and Sallie and brother John, they allow us to catch a glimpse of Cornelia herself, who could turn a neat phrase and who possessed a warm concern for others, along with a clever sense of humor.

Clara Dunlap in Ouachita Co. to her sister Cornelia Dickson in Autauga Co.

June 14th 1867

Dear Nealy,

I was overjoyed to receave once more a letter from you, the first since last August. Oh! I cant begin to tell you how much pleasure it gave me. We've been wondering all the year what had become of you all, feared you were dead or some of you; & Oh, I cant begin to tell you how uneasy I was, all of us were, brother G would ask every time he saw me & seemed as uneasy as I was, Sis M[ollie] rec'd one from Sis C[arrie] at the same time, she will answer in a few days. She is up at Sallies now, said she wanted to go up & see them so she could write all about them, too. She promised to spend the day with me when she returned, went to stay several days at Sallies.

Well, N[ealy] I've written so often, & now, I hardly know how to commence. We are all well with the exception of myself, & enjoying good health. I'm afraid I will never have good health again. I'm not down sick but just a weak low state of health, been so ever since Molly was born, & she is over two years old. I fear sometime I will have consumption. I've taken medicine repeatedly but to no purpose as yet. I hoped so much last fall to have you with me by Christmas anyhow, & anticipated as much, or more pleasure, than you did (if possible), in your coming. Brother G & sis M gave a large dinner Christmas day & somehow, Nealy, I felt almost certain you would be with us, but was bitterly disappointed. Then, I looked all winter & spring, until I rec'd you[r] letter a week or two ago. Yet, I feel that you did right in staying with sis Carrie. As bad as I wanted you, she needed you worse considering all the circumstances by which she was surrounded. Al-

After the War

though it is like hoping against hope, I still <u>will</u> hope on, that I will yet have you with me. You might at first feel dissatisfied being among strangers. I know your disposition is such that you will soon become acquainted, & I think you will like our neighbors. They cant help loving you, Nealy. I'll trust to that, because they all think so much of you out there in Ala that its impossible for me to get a chance at having you myself. At least, I think that's the case.

John had hired enough freedmen this year to cultivate all of his land, & they work for <u>one half</u> the crop & feed themselves. He finds the team & feeds the team & finds the <u>plows</u> & <u>hoes</u> & all that is necessary to make the crop with. He goes their (the freedmen) security for provisions & what ever they need, & takes it out of their part of the crop.* They are all working well & have a fair crop, corn especially. We have 140 acres in cotton & 75 or 80 acres in corn. John says if the season continue[s], he will make in all 70 or 80 bales of cotton & <u>plenty</u> of corn. I do hope we will have a good crop. Its so bad to buy corn & every thing to eat as we've had to do since the war ended. I've a very good cook this year. She understands her business thoroughly, & better still, is a well behaved negro. I've a house-girl, too. She tends to Mollie & does any little thing about the house. My health's been so bad, I couldent have gotten along without her. We've had a 5 month school in the neighborhood this year. I boarded the <u>teacher</u> & <u>three</u> of the scholars, Bettie Rumph & two nieces of John's, Ella & Joanna Dunlap. The teacher is a Miss Rounsiville, an excellent teacher, very strict. Her school is out <u>today</u>. I dont much think she will take up another school. The scholars are not far enough advanced for her & no wonder as during the war & since we've had no school atall scarcely, through the county. Bettie Rumph says she wish's so much you would come & teach, says she knows they would all love you & learn <u>fast</u> too. We hear from Mittie right often. She is learning fast. Her teacher gives an excellent account of her being so studious, & so good & obedient. She will remain there until she graduates. George Rumph & John Boddie are attending school in Camden. They are boarding at Dee Newtons; they are very anxious to go until they complete their education. They worked <u>so well all last</u> year & the year before. I do hope they can go as long as they wish. Both [are] such good boys, Nealy. You would like them so much. Willie Boddie is his Ma's gardener this year he is a good boy to, will go to school next year. All of sis M[ollie]'s children are smart & industrious & brother J[ohn]'s too. I dont say it to <u>brag</u>, but they really are. Sallie R[umph] has a baby, 8 or 9 months old named <u>Attalee</u>. I do wish you could see it, tis so fat & pretty, too. She [Sallie] has only two living [children]. I was over there several weeks ago. Brother J[ohn] continues to practice & is considered one of the most successful physicians in the country. They are trying the freedmen this year, one half the crop for the other.

*This arrangement came to be known as "sharecropping," a practice that is still in existence today. The tenent's share varies with the crop.

*"Howard" refers to Clara's son Jimmy, whose full name is James Howard.

You asked if I've sent Howard* to school yet. Yes, he has been going all this session, can spell & read very well for a boy his age, knows all the multiplication table[s] & can make figures on a slate. He <u>will</u> cry though whenever he misses a lesson. He is large to his age. Lula is like her Pa, <u>short & fat</u>, black eyes though & red cheeks. Mollie is slender like Howard, fair skin, dark eyes. Brother G & sis M say she is the prettiest of my children. She is a sweet child.

 I have a good garden this year, though late owing to my first planting getting killed by the freeze. I have beans, beets, cabbage, irish potatoes, cucumbers, & will soon have squashes & tomatoes & c. We had nice strawberries this year. I had 5 or 6 large messes off my beds, Sis Mollie & Sally had plenty, too. Their beds are larger than mine. We have a nice watermelon patch planted. I raised 15 turkeys last year Nealy, & saved them until away after Christmas, in hopes you would be here to help eat them, have sixteen this year if I can raise them. They are growing pretty now. I lost 30 during the wet spell in May. I have a great many chickens though some large enough to eat. If the weather had been dry & warm during April & May, I think I would have raised 30 or 40 turkeys. The young ones cant stand wet & cold. I intend, if I raise any, to save them again, for you surely will come this fall or winter.

 I regretted <u>very much</u> to hear of Harriet's death. I was so anxious, & have been ever since the war, to get her & Mammy & their families out here to live with me, because I knew their <u>worth</u> & how <u>faithfully</u> & <u>well</u> they served Ma so long & more than that, I was attached to them more than I ever could be to other servants. I wrote repeatedly last year to you about them, offering them a good home & kind, good attention when sick or well with as high wages as the best of them are getting. I wanted them more because I was attached to them & I thought they were to me, than any thing else. I just felt I would have more satisfaction keeping house & with my children attended too, than with any others I could get. I wanted Harriet to cook & Mammy to help me with the children & wait on me in sickness. I wrote & directed my letters to the care of Eustice Golson as you told me to, but I suppose you never receaved one of them. But Nealy, tell them now, Mammy & Uncle Jerry & John if they can come <u>next winter</u> I can do a better part by them than they can do out there living with strangers. The land is much better out here & Jerry & John Morton, & Tom can make so much more renting the land or working for half. I know just for their past faithfulness to Ma, I could & would be a <u>friend to them</u>, Mammy, & Caroline to help her, could do my cooking, & if Laura & Ellen came, they could work with their husbands in the field, or not, just as they wished. I know one thing certain, once here with me it would not be my fault if they were sorry they came, tell them Nealy for me, I want them to come, tell Mammy & Jerry I want to see them so much, more then they do me.

About selling our place to Tom Caver, I think you did perfectly right & was very well satisfied (if poor Harriet could have lived) as it is I am still satisfied because Nealy, I know you acted for the best you could do; & as to any other matters or business there of ours (about cotton or anything else) just do the best you can, I rest assured I will be satisfied as I am not there to see how everything is, so I cant advise you about what is best to do & you must be your own judge, just do the best you can with everything I leave it to you entirely. I will be satisfied, as I said before you can sell the cotton or hold on awhile as you think best. If you dont know what to do, consult some friend out there that can advise you. I think sis Carrie has a pretty name for her baby. Tell her I want the pleasure of naming her first grandchild, as I've never named any of her children. Tell Reeny, I wish her much joy & happiness. I would like so much to see her now. Give my love to Mrs. Lasiter & Mrs. Land(?) & Bettie when you see her, tell her to please write & I will answer her letter with pleasure. I do wish I could see her & Rebecca U[nderwood]. Also give my love to her too. Tell her to write & I will answer every letter I get from her. Give my love to sis Carrie, Cousin Mary, & all enquiring friends. I've tried to write something that would interest you dear Nealy; but in reading my letter over, I've half a mind not to send it, but I might not do any better on second trial so I will send it any how, hoping you will excuse any shortcomings. Sis M told me to give her love to all, she will write in a day or two. I know will write a great deal more thats interesting than I can. If I possibly could I would have all the children's deguerotype's taken & send to you but you would find them all greatly changed since they were small. Sallie R[ump] would send her love did she know I am writing. Do, Nealy, write as soon as you receive this. Give my love to all the children & accept a share for yourself. Hoping this may find you well, I am your affectionate sister,

Clara Dunlap

[1]John sends his best respects to you all. He is a regular hand in the field this year. [He] has a separate field to himself.
C. D.

[2]Let me know when you write what Mammy & all of them say about coming out here, next winter.

[3]Give my love to Mammy & Uncle Jerry & all the negroes, brother John speaks of going out to Ala next winter if he lives & nothing happens, if you see no other way between now & then, you could come with him.

[1]Note: This postscript is written along the left margin of page 1:

[2]Note: This postscript is written in a box across the top of page 1:

[3]Note: This postscript is written upside down across the top of page 1:

Clara Dunlap in Ouachita Co. to her sister Cornelia Dickson in Autauga Co.

Aug. 14th 1867

Dear Dear Sister,

In vain I've tried for the last 3 weeks to write to you; I've delayed writing until I feel I ought not put it off any longer, as you will have to learn the sad news sometime. For 'tis with a heavy heart I now try to write you a few lines. A heart filled with grief & sorrow, Nealy, for since I wrote you in June, I've experienced a bereavement, a loss, Oh God, that only those that have met with such a one, can realize. On the 18th of July, 4 weeks ago tomorrow <u>death</u> entered our happy home circle & bore off <u>two</u> of our dear children, <u>Jimmie</u> & <u>Mollie</u>, our only darling boy & sweet little Mollie, our youngest child; have gone, dear sister, to dwell with the angels. Yes, <u>they</u> are angels now, while I am almost broken hearted, Nealy, I feel as though I had lost my all, all in life worth living for. <u>Lula</u>, our oldest little girl, is all that is left us. Oh, how little I dreamed this when writing to you June last, telling you how anxious I was to have you out here, & Jimmie, bless his little heart, wanted you to come <u>so much</u> so he could go to school to you. He had went all winter & spring & could spell & read <u>very</u> well. Every one thought him so apt. I had told him all about you & how well you <u>loved little children</u> & that he would love to go to school to you. Nealy, both were taken <u>the same morning</u>, Mollie at 2 o'clock in the morning, & Jimmie at 8 o'clock the same morning, after 2 days, Mollie died at 5 o'clock in the morning & Jimmie at 3 in the evening with congestion of the <u>brain</u> & <u>lungs;</u> each only lived <u>48 hours</u>.

Mollie was taken more violently. She was in a stupor all the time; we never could arouse her. Medicine acted well but never releaved her atall. She never spoke or called my name after the first morning, never seemed conscious of pain atall. Brother John attended on both of them, but he never told me she was dangerous until she was dying. He then told me that Jimmie was affected nearly the same way though not so bad; he stayed with them all he could & done all he could to check the desease, but in vain. But, dear sister, the hardest of all remains to be told. We had sent Jimmie up to his Uncle's, Dick Dunlap's, a few days previous to his sickness to spend a few days. He was so well & hearty; I did not dream of his getting sick. Mr. D[unlap] lives 9 miles from here, & as brother John was attending some patients in Mr. D[unlap]'s family, he saw Jimmie soon after he was taken & gave him medicine. It also acted well, but did not releave him, he continued to grow worse until Thursday evening he died of conjestion of the brain & lungs. They brought his body home that evening, &, Oh, dear sister, you can <u>imagine but not realize;</u> & I pray God you may <u>never</u> feel the deep anguish & grief I felt when I saw them bring him in, cold & lifeless, who <u>4 short days before</u> I had <u>seen riding</u> off with his Pa, so full of health & life & so happy in anticipation of enjoying himself with his little cousins. Oh, sister, to think I could not get to see my boy, my only boy die, could not nurse & wait on him even, for Mollie was <u>so sick</u>, I could not leave her. John went up to try & bring him home as soon as he learned he was sick, but found him to sick to be moved. He remained with him until Thursday morning, when learning of poor little Mollie's death, he came home to see about & make some arrangements for her burial. He then hastened back to Jimmie, but he was too late by half an hour <u>to see him</u>. Brother J[ohn] had remained with him, though, & done all he could, but alas, to no purpose ... John did not see either one of the children die. It nearly killed him. He thought so much of them. John would not tell me how dangerous Jimmie was, said he was very sick, indeed, & took a negro boy back with him so as to send me word how he was. I got ready to start up there, <u>fearing</u> he was worse than they said; & just as I was ready to start, the messenger (one of Mr. Dunlap's sons) came to tell me that he was <u>dead</u>. We had their funeral preached here the next day & burried them both in one grave in our garden. Oh, Nealy, pray for me <u>that I may</u> be able to <u>bear</u> this <u>first great sorrow</u> for I feel all other troubles are as nothing, compared to this. Though I've had a great deal of trouble during the war & since, but it seems as nothing to me now, [it] is nothing compared to loseing one's children. When I heard of sis Carrie's Mary's death, I felt so sorry & felt I could sympathize with her so much, oh but so much more now, can I feel for her & every mother. But then she had so many children left & I have <u>only one</u>. Maybe, tis best, I ought to try to feel it so, but I <u>cannot yet</u> a <u>while</u>. If losing <u>one</u> is so bad; how much worse when two is taken at once, & one of them an only boy. Jimmie was so affectionate & <u>loving</u> in his dispo[si]tion & so obedient, too, especially to me. He seemed to love me & little Mollie better than any one else. I took so much pains with him too, trying to learn him how to be a good boy, & if he would be a good boy, every one would love him & God, too, loved good boy's. He would ask me, N[ealy], how good little boys done & I'd tell him & we would talk a long time about it. It seemed to do him more good than any kind of punishment ever did to tell him that God would not love him if he was bad or disobedient; he would come often to me, after doing a <u>good action</u> or being unusually kind to his sisters & ask me if God loved him now & if that was the way to be a good boy. He was more like a girl than a boy though, loved to stay by me & read & spell & look at pictures. Little Mollie was very much like him in her disposition, very winning & affectionate. It seemed she loved every one that she knew that noticed her. Sis Mollie thought after she died that she resembled her little Sallie that died. John always said she favored sis M's children very much. He would frequently call her <u>Boddie</u>. She was much prettier than Lula. Jimmie was always called a fine looking boy, very fair rosy complection, very bright blue eyes, very lively, cheerful & full of spirits. Dear N[ealy], I've tried so hard to pray, to be & feel resigned to God's will; to feel they are better off & free from care & trouble, but oh I miss their little voices <u>so much, so much</u> it seems if I could only hear them call my name it would give me more joy than any thing in this world. But <u>oh</u>, <u>that</u> can never be again in this world. But our minister told me in his sermon, I <u>can go to them</u>, & God helping me, I will. Oh, if you had only come last winter or spring, you could have seen them & been with me now. In your letter written in April last you told me why you remained, & it was best then to stay with sis Carrie. She needed you very much, but I looked all spring hoping you still might come. I wrote you a long letter in June telling you how much I wished you were here & also to try & get Mammy & Uncle Jerry to come & make their home with me henceforth, & that I would always try & be the friend that Ma used to be to them. Tell Mammy I wish now more than ever for her. She used to console & talk to me when I was troubled. It would not be my fault if she ever regreted coming, I would nurse her in sickness & do all I could to make her contented, & in return she could do the same for me. The land is much richer out here & the men, Uncle Jerry & John Morton could make so much more.

Sis Mollie has had some sickness, too this summer in her family, several of the children, but not anything serious. She had an attack of <u>cholera morbus</u>* last week but is nearly well again. Brother J[ohn]'s family are all well. Sallie has a very pretty baby named Attalie, a very large fine looking child about 10 months old. George Rumph & John Boddie have been attending school in Camden this year & are going to continue this fall & winter. George took the first <u>honor</u> for speaking. Their teacher gave them a great deal of credit for being studious, well behaved boys. They have an excellent male school in Camden, & a very good female school also. Brother J heard from Mittie last week. She was doing very well indeed. She took the first honors in 9 classes out of 11. Well, Nealy, when will you come. I've looked so long & anxiously, & have grown almost hopeless of seeing you out here. Do come for my sake. I am so lonely & sad. Somehow, I feel as though I had lost all energy about my house keeping & every thing else. All interest gone. It seems if you were here with your cheerful spirits I would feel so much better. I would be so glad too, if Sis Carrie could move out here this winter. Nealy, if you could get no one to come with you, tell Tom Love, if he will come, I will pay his expenses out here & back. It should not cost him a cent & I would thank him so much, too, or any friend there that would bring you out. I will pledge my self to bear all their expenses here & back. We have another school here now, commenced last Monday. The same teacher we had last spring, a Miss Rounsaville, an excellent teacher. Her school will be out Christmas. She boarded with me & Bettie Rumph & Ella Dunlap, one of John's nieces board here also. But still I've plenty of room

*Cholera Morbus, or sporadic cholera, is a gastroenteritis, having characteristics similar to those of cholera, diarrhea, cramps, vomiting etc, but caused by a different organism.

for you & a warm <u>welcome</u> now & always for you Nealy. Write soon dear sister.

                          Your affectionate sister,
                          Clara Dunlap

[1] I send you a small lock of Jimmie's & Mollie's hair. The lightest is Mollie's.

[2] It was so strange, Nealy. Jimmie & Mollie were the healthiest children I knew of, never sick, but seemed well & hearty all the time. While Lula frequently has little spells of sickness. Poor child. You would pity her; she looks so lonely now.

[3] The farmers are all making good crops this year; plenty of rain so far. We have the best crop we've had in a long time. John thinks he will make enough corn to do him two years & 75 or 85 bales of cotton, but he seems since the children died to have lost all interest in everything.

[4] Tell Mammy, Uncle Jerry & John Morton howdy, give my love to Mammy tell her I want to see her now worse than ever I did, poor Harriet, I was so sorry about her death.

[5] My best love to you & sis Carrie & family & cousin Mary & family, give my love to Uncle Clem, cousin Ike, & all enquiring friends, especially Mrs. Lasiter, Mrs Land, Bettie, Rebecca U., & all of them. Tell Rebecca & Bettie both to write to me, I will answer all their letters with pleasure.

[1] Note: This postscript is written along the left margin of page 1:

[2] Note: This postscript is written upside down across the top of page 2:

[3] Note: This postscript is written upside down across the top of page 3:

[4] Note: This postscript is written upside down across the top of page 4:

[5] Note: This postscript is written upside down across the top of page 1:

Clara Dunlap in Ouachita Co. to her sister Cornelia Dickson in Autauga Co.

                                                    Nov. 1st, 1867

Dear Sister

     Your very kind letter of the 17th was rec'd a week since. I felt so glad to hear again from you & such a kind affectionate letter, too, so full of sympathy. Oh, you cant imagine, dear Nealy, how eagerly I read & re-read every line. No letter I ever rec'd from you did me as much good, & it comforted me more than any thing has since I've been so sadly bereaved. I thank you again & again & those of my friends out there that expressed such kindly words of sympathy in your letter; sis Carrie, Cousin Mary & Mrs. Lasiter, thank them for me. One never knows <u>more truly</u> how to appreciate kindly feelings from others as when the heavy hand of affliction is upon us. And although it does comfort me, to feel that my darlings are angels now & free from all sorrow & pain forever. I do so miss their dear faces <u>so much;</u> miss the attention & care I gave them. 'Twas always more pleasure to be with them than any where else. Ever since I first had a child, my chief enjoyment was in their society. I cannot help wishing & craving for them yet. The void they've left in my heart cannot be filled. I often go off by myself & study over the many happy hours passed & gone & wish so much I could only see them as angels in their happy home above. One moment only would afford me more joy than all this world, but <u>alas vain wish</u> that cannot be. Yet, is it wrong or sinful to wish it when I loved them <u>so dearly</u>. I'm so glad that Tom has promised to bring you in Dec[ember]. Tell him for my sake not to fail, for I feel 'twould comfort me more than anything on earth now to have you with me. Yet, am I selfish; I'm afraid coming from an old settled neighborhood of old & loved friends to a new country, among so many that will be strangers, you will feel regret at leaving them. But I know you have a disposition that can & will make friends where ever you go. I think you will find kind & loving hearts out here with us all, if not all the advantages you have hitherto enjoyed. <u>Sis M, Sallie, brother G & brother J</u>, & especially the children, are all glad that you are coming. Bettie Rumph is still boarding with me, going to school. She says tell you to make haste & come on; she wishes so much to see you, & so <u>do we, all</u>. Their teacher will board with me 'till Christmas, & then her <u>room</u> is yours now & always. I fixed it (the room) up last winter for <u>you</u> hoping every day you would come.

  I was sorry to hear of sis Carrie & baby's bad health, hope they have recovered ere this, & Mrs. Lasiter, too. I wish so much I could see her & have a <u>long talk</u> & Bettie, too. Tell her to be sure & write, & Rebecca also, give my love to them <u>all</u>. We had a two days meeting at our church about two weeks ago, had excellent preaching. I enjoyed it so much & do wish we could have prayer meetings too, like you have out there. Our school is at the church, only 3 hundred yds from here, just a pleasant walk.

  Having very good weather in the neighborhood now & beautiful weather for picking out cotton, too, dry & warm; had our first frost night before last. The farmers are not making as full cotton crops as expected, the cotton worm destroyed one <u>third</u> & in some fields more; of the cotton, all the young & tender bolls & squares were destroyed, the late cotton suffered most. 'Tis the first appearance of the worm in this country. John thought to have made 80 bales at least, but now, he will be glad to get 50 or 55, him & his freedman. All made plenty of corn & potatoes & some will have corn to sell. John dont intend hiring them again another year. They acted so badly this fall. The freedmen have the <u>Loyal League fever</u> out here, too, & will quit their work at any time to attend their <u>meeting</u> & c; John speaks of renting his land out next year, has about 230 acre's cleared land, all of it good land for producing cotton & corn. If Uncle Jerry & Harry would come out & look at it, they might move their kin folks out & rent it & make a great deal more than they can there. There is 3 good new cabins about the middle of the plantation, & a good well & plenty of firewood & 2 cabin's here, near the yard. I wish Mammy & all of them would come.

Nealy, plese bring me some cuttings of the white Lady-banks rose & some of the yellow. I wish them to plant over my little graves & a few white & pink hyacinths. Please bring me something out of Ma's garden to plant. I want something for old times sake, & wont you plant a white rose on Ma's & Pa's grave in my name; before you leave Alabama? If I could have gone there, I intended having a tombstone over each one of their graves, but it has been impossible for me to go, but do plant some roses for me before you leave please, & bring me some cuttings of the white & yellow Lady banks rose. Mine died that I brought with me. I would be so glad for a few small cedar bushes, say not higher than your hand, to plant over J[immie] & M[ollie]. There used to be a great many in that pine ridge between Ma's & sis, where sis Carrie used to live. There is no cedars in this country nearer than Little Rock. I do hope you will have a safe & pleasant trip out here. I intend to commence looking after the first week in Dec. & keep on looking until you do come. I'll try & have plenty of nice sausages for you, & turkeys, & save all my eggs for Christmas eggnog's. Last Christmas I had a happy time, for then my darling Jimmie & Mollie were with me, & how happy he was Christmas morning to find his little socks so full of Santa Claus's presents. It seems I can see him yet, & the other two, Lula & Mollie with their dolls, cc, all three so happy & myself with them, oh, little dreaming it to be our last Christmas all together on earth. Nealy, if we could see into the future & what is oft times in store for us 'twould kill us, I know. Indeed, we could not bear it & maybe tis better so. Lula was asking me this morning "if Santa Claus would come again." I told her yes. She said, "Poor little Mollie & Jimmie wont be here to hang up their stockings, Ma. I'll have to hang mine up by myself". She spoke it so sadly, too, Nealy, it hurt me so much. Lula so often speaks of them & wishes them here. She says, "Tell Aunt Nealy, I'm going to sleep with her when she comes" says "she wants you to come so bad".

You said in your letter that Uncle Clem had written to us on bussiness, but we've never receaved a letter from him. Tell him [we] should like very much to hear from him. Do write soon & tell me all the news. Give my love to all enquiring friends, accept a full share for your dear self & beleave me as ever

Your affectionate sister
Clara Dunlap

P.S. Please dont forget about the little cedars for me, get very small ones (about as high as your finger will do) you can bring them easier. Tell Uncle Clem, if he wishes, he can settle with you instead of me, or any other way he sees fit & proper. I dont know anything about such things & any way he does will suit me. Goodby —

C.D.

Rebecca Underwood in Autauga Co. to her friend Cornelia Dickson also in Autauga Co.

March 15, 1868
Dear Cornelia,

It troubles me a great deal to give you up. I know of no one that is not related to me that I love as I do you. Although you are ready to leave suffer me to beg of you to remain with me this year or for as long as you like, and I will do all I can for you, do get your consent to come and stay with me. Tom and I will take care of you as far as we are able.

I cannot go to sleep for thinking about you. Do remain with me this year. If you can get your consent, I do not believe you will regret it if you stay. You feel like a relative of mine. Tom and I would have proffered you a home with us long ago but was afraid you would not like it, but I cannot bear to think of your going off so far and I not offer you a home with me, for I assure you I love you dearly, do stay if you can.

                Your true friend,
                Rebecca Underwood

do not be angry with me.

THE LEDGER

The letters which follow are correspondences from Cornelia after she moved to Ouachita County, Arkansas, following the death of Clarissa Lanier Boddie Dickson, the mother of Cornelia and Clara. These are not the actual letters, which were mailed to their addressees; they are the rough drafts which Cornelia composed in a ledger before copying them onto paper for mailing. We can assume that Cornelia, ever the teacher, wanted the letters which were mailed to be in their best form, so she first put them into the ledger to edit before writing the final copy. The use of the ampersand in these letters rather than the word <u>and</u> indicates that we have rough drafts, for in all the final copies we have seen the word is written out. Also in these ledger letters there is much crossing out, inserted rewrites and additions. Since she had saved all of Clara's letters written earlier, it is possible that she made copies of her own letters in the ledger to save them for posterity. Whatever the reason, we are grateful, for all of these letters would have been lost were it not for the ledger. In this age of oral communication, it is truly astounding to think of someone writing a letter TWICE when we rarely write it once. Cornelia filled the ledger and then turned to whatever paper was available, even brown paper bags at times. And she saved them all — even those written through World War I. What a treasure she has left us!

Cornelia Dickson in Ouachita Co. to her friend Rebecca Underwood in Autauga Co.

May, 1868

Dear Rebecca,

Scarcely a day has passed since I left you that has not brought a pleasant thought of you and many of my friends at home. Home! How sweet it sounds to call it home in Ala yet, and will I not always feel that it is home to me? for does it not contain the dearest association of my whole life & the sacred dust nearest & dearest to me, yes. I feel that no other spot on earth will ever be home to me but there. No doubt you have been wondering why you have not received a letter from me. My excuse, I waited until I saw something of the country. The river rose so very high this spring since I came, there has been scarcely any communication with Camden and I could not get a letter mailed nearer — therefore thought it useless to write until I could have an opportunity of sending a letter off. But oh, I have so wanted to hear from you all. I think of you so often & then I get out your note you wrote me that cold night, you see I have treasured it, & read it, & feel almost like I had heard you speaking to me again, and I wonder if time, that busy traveler, will ever erase your affection & friendship for me. I hope it never, never may. I shall keep it [that note] Rebecca, as an ever green in the case of my heart as long as life shall last. I would be so glad to see you now. I could tell you so much that I cannot write or that would be uninteresting to write, so many little incidents that occurred during my trip and since.

  I formed several pleasant acquaintances on the boats, met with friends all along, in fact had a very agreeable trip, notwithstanding the annoyance of being delayed at N[ew] O[rleans] three days on a boat & no other lady passenger until we were about starting & the clerk a <u>merry widower</u> clever & pleasant & gentlemanly. The way I was detained on the boat was this. The Captain of the lake boat (under whose care I had been placed by the clerk of the "Gertrude") accompanied me to N. O. procured a paper and saw a Ouachita boat advertised to leave that evening, <u>& placed me in the charge of the clerk</u> of the boat, the captain being absent. The boat did not leave that evening, nor the next, until the third [evening] & every evening we <u>expected</u> to start but was delayed & I did not know what else to do but remain on board for fear of being left when she did start, and being alone, too, I was afraid to set my foot in N. O. I had been disgusted with being alone in a hotel last winter & the clerk was very kind, told me if I did not wish to go to a hotel to make myself at home on the boat. I should have every attention & might feel perfectly safe as there was a watch man on both the upper & lower decks all night as in a hotel. He brought me the morning & evening papers, chatted with me occasionally, but you don't know how very badly I felt being alone among strangers. As long as I was moving, I did not feel so lonely. There was so much to attract my attention & draw my thoughts from myself. So many beautiful residences & situations on the Miss. river. If I ever travel the <u>Red</u> & <u>Ouachita</u> rivers again I would like to be asleep all the way except at Monroe & Trenton, for it seemed to be a perfect wilderness covered with water. I often wondered what <u>wild</u> freak seized my relatives to induce them to leave civilization & wander so far into this apparently never ending forest. I have been so agreeably disappointed in Camden & the country around, thanks to Mr. Davis's gloomy picture of the country. Tell him he would find if he should visit now, that it is greatly improved since he was here, in fact I see but little difference in the general appearance of this country and some portions of that around Mrs. Houston's & from her home on to Mrs. Steele's, no hills scarecly around here. The neighborhood is thickly settled. I have formed a good many acquaintances only a qtr of a mile. I think I will like them very much. I have returned only one of the many calls I've received owing to Clara's having been sick for several weeks. She is up now but only moderately well. We can visit half a doz or more of our neighbors on foot, so near and Mr. Dunlap has had every thing so constantly in the farm, but he says we can have a buggy & a mule next week to sail around! I have been to church twice. Considering how completely broken up the people out here were during the war, most every one seems to be doing very well. Nearly all the negroes in this part of the country followed the Yankees off & died or were killed, & those here now have come in since, are working & conducting very well. Mr. D[unlap] pays wages & feeds them & they don't lose a moment's time, he says they are most too fast for him, before he can come in, sit a few minutes & eat his dinner, they have eaten & gone again. C[lara] has a good cook & house girl. Tell Mr. U[nderwood] two of our nearest neighbors are young bachelors, only a qtr mile, & there are three more, one about a mile away & the other two, two miles away! I have been introduced to three of them, but tell him not to tell Mr. Davis, it might make him <u>miserable</u>! I have not been with my relatives a great deal since I came owing to the high waters between them & here, but I think altogether I will be much better satisfied than I ever expected. Every one is so kind to me. I expect to have a lively time attending fish frys as soon as the waters are sufficiently low to catch fish. There have been several appointments but we were disappointed by rain. Clara has a good many young chickens, turkeys, & geese, half a dozen young geese, while she was sick I attended to them all, getting my hand in you see by the time old Mr. Davis comes. Tell him Sis Mollie sends her love to him, would be so very glad to see him if he would pay them a visit. She says her oldest son John* wrote to him during the war, but she never heard if he received or answered his letter. If he would come out now, he would enjoy his visit more than he did when the country was so new & unsettled. There are still a plenty of deer & game of different kinds here & she would enjoy his company so much. Her oldest son is grown now & attending school in Camden. She has a very interesting family of children, six in number. Brother George has changed but little, says the Federals left him his family & his land & not a rail or even a gate post, hardly a house, a few cattle & hogs that were in the swamps was all, but he is making a living now notwithstanding all his troubles, & this is a great country. Mr. Gildersleeve* has written to them to let him have one of the boys to live with him & I believe they have concluded to let the second or third one go to him. Sis Mollie says she feels like it was her duty to give him up one of them, he is so old now & wants one to attend to his business for him. Sallie has lost her three oldest children, one boy named John & two little girls Mattie & Sallie. She has two living, Kate & Attalie and Sis Fannie left five. She [Sallie] has still a house full, tho some are off at school, looks almost as well as ever, Brother John has a good practice, enjoys telling his old courting scrapes in Ala as much as Mr. Underwood, killed two large deer last week.

  Well Rebecca I expect you are tired & ready to draw a long breath from reading this letter but Clara wishes me to send her love to you & says she has been looking a long time for that promised letter. You must be sure to write to me very soon & tell me all the news & everything else you can think of. Remember me in love to all enquiring friends, & accept, dear friend, a

*"her oldest son John" refers to John Rumph Boddie, son of Sis Mollie and Brother George.

*Mr. Gildersleeve is Sis Mollie's father.

good portion for yourself and family. As ever,
affectionately your friend
Cornelia S. Dickson

Cornelia Dickson in Ouachita Co. to her friend Hattie Underwood in Autauga Co.

June 1, 1868

Dear Hattie,

Your time has come at last. I disliked to write to all at once. I have written to Mrs. Lasiter & Rebecca, & I have still several more letters to write before I will be around once. I have just received a letter from Cousin Mary & am expecting another. I was so very sorry to hear of yours & Rubes misfortune in having your gin house & cotton burned. I hope you will yet be able to bring the perpetrators to justice. I think about you so much & wonder if you ever had those photographs taken yet; it would be such a pleasure to me to see you all now. I do so much wish I could be with you again. I think one year in Ark will be long enough for me to be away from Ala and my dear friends there. Though so far, I am very much pleased with the neighborhood out here, some as nice people you will meet with almost anywhere & others not so nice. I attended church yesterday, heard an excellent sermon by Parson Windfield, presiding elder of this circuit. I have joined the Sabbath School here at this place. We have no books yet but have sent off and will get some in a week or two.

People out here are not too particular about riding in wagons, both mule and horned* teams come driving up with its load of gaily dressed, merry looking occupants. Nearly every body lives in hewned log houses but seem comfortably fixed up. Whenever it rains & is too wet to work the land, you will hear a half dozen or more horns blowing, about a dozen or more men meet & have a drive & such a feast of venison will come steaming in the next day. I never liked it before, but now can enjoy it as well as anyone. I know when Mr. U[nderwood] hears this he will think that this is the greatest country in the world. <u>Just the place for him</u>. But now, let me cool his enthusiasm, the lands out here are very little if any superior to his, for his is a good place, except in low places which are generally very sickly, and the people here have to work very hard or they will go downhill, so to speak, and have nothing. But they seem to have a good deal of stock, considering the depredations commited by our army & the enemy's, but then it takes a stirring energetic person to keep up with it and I think the society around Mulberry superior to most places. It is not all partiality that makes me say this but because I know it is so. And then the political state of this country is awful just now, but the negroes are doing remarkably well this year around

*"horned" team refers to oxen, used to pull wagons.

in this neighborhood so far. Farmers generally are much encouraged with their prospects for good crops this season, though there is some uneasiness felt about the early appearance of the army worms in La and some of the lower counties of the state. And the grasshoppers in Clark County above here are destroying everything as they go. Several gentlemen were in an arguement the other day as to whether the grasshoppers could swim, or if they succeeded in swimming the Washita* if they would not get lost in the cane swamp this side of the river. There has been one fish fry on the lake*, but I did not attend. There will be another Saturday week, and I shall probably be there. We have had several fine messes of fish since the waters have fallen. The creeks & lakes around here abound in fish. I expect to have a fine time at fish frys.

The garden affords a good many vegetables now, have had two messes of cucumbers. Strawberries have lasted longer than usual this spring <u>owing to the abundant rain, (I think)</u>. we can get one nice mess yet, huckleberries are ripe now & such quantities as we have. I never saw so many before & just outside the yard too. Mr. Dunlap's is a very pretty place, one of the oldest in the neighborhood. You must be sure to write me everything you can think of. Tell Rob I have not seen as fine looking boy in Ark as he is for his age, but have seen a little girl just his size & not three years old yet. Kiss Minnie and the babe for me. My love to all enquiring friends. Write soon.

Your affectionate friend,
Cornelia S. Dickson

*Washita was one way of spelling Ouachita in earlier days, before the spelling stabilized into its modern form. Washita is still used by some people writing in dialect.

*The lake Cornelia speaks of is Pine Lake, believed to have been formed when the river changed its course hundreds of years ago.

Cornelia Dickson in Ouachita Co. to her cousin Mary Love in Autauga Co.
July 7, 1868

Dear Cousin Mary

I received your very welcome letter seven or eight weeks ago. It afforded me a great deal of pleasure I assure you. I have been anxiously awaiting the other you promised to write in a few days, when cousin Hannah came over, is one reason I have not responded sooner & then I have been busy returning visits and preparing to attend the examinations & exhibition of the male High School in Camden which came off last week, but more of that anon. I was so glad to hear that you were having such a nice garden, plenty of vegetables, strawberries, cc. I have enjoyed the luxury of strawberries this year as much as ever in my life. Tell Cole [Cousin Mary's son] I don't care if he didn't eat any for me as he sent word in Tom's letter to George.* I [am] sorry I told the boys about his wee beard as he takes it so hard. Tell him if he was to see George hanging around Aunt Mollie at her dairy & then John chasing the cat over the yard, he would think someone else wanted to sprout beard.

*Tom Love and George Rumph, small boys and cousins, exchanged letters.

I have been with Sis Mollie a good deal since I have been here. They all asked me hundreds of questions. Brother G & her expressed so much regret that Tom or Uncle Clem did not come out with me. Say they are poor folks it is true, as they were so completely broken up during the war, but they have worked & made enough to eat & have some stock now. They would have been so glad to have received a visit from them. Sis Mollie managed through all to keep her piano & she plays a great many pieces. She had to cook a while in winter. Their garden reminds me of Grandma's so much & when I came to the little peach nursery, 'twas more like it than ever. Willis* is the gardener, & they have a quantity of vegetables, or did have until the drought became so severe & protracted. Brother George & indeed most of the farmers in the immediate neighborhood, are fearful they will not make a support for the next year if it does not rain very soon. Crops are very much & irreparably injured now. Brother George has good children. I think <u>all</u> good looking & <u>some</u> very handsome.

  I stayed a week with Sallie about a month ago. While there, Dee Newton & his family came from Camden, stayed three or four days, brother John & he went deer hunting — I threw an old shoe after them* — & they kill[ed] three fine ones, we had venison plenty. Bob Golson* was spending a week with Mr. Brodnax* & went with them, but he did not get a deer. He seemed to regret it so much, but he always happened to be at the wrong stand. I like him a great deal better than I did. He seems to be almost as clever as Eustice [Golson]. We spent one day at old Mr. Brodnax's. They killed a deer near his house that day. On Saturday of that week, we went to a picnic on Pine lake, & such a quantity of fish we had, but I did not put a hook in the water all day. I had a delightful time notwithstanding. I went in a wagon with a crowd of girls & our driver was a young bachelor. I had a most pleasant boat ride on the lake. The lake is about two & a half miles from brother George's. We first pass through a gloomy forest of pine, then a flat which rises into a field that extends to the very bluff of the lake. Said bluff slopes gradually to the water & is covered with large water oaks which make a pleasant shade & there is a <u>very cold</u> spring bubbles conveniently near. The lake is about a mile & a half in length & about half as wide as the Ala river, perfectly smooth & is said to have no bottom in some places. There were four or five boats gliding to & fro over its glassy surface all day. We had a pleasant crowd & plenty to gratify a keen appetite which a long ride in a jolting wagon had not tended to diminish. There is a chain of lakes. I did wish some of my old friends could have been with me. Mr Bob Golson was there but left for Camden soon after dinner, he said he was obliged to return immediately to N. O. so that Eustice could visit Autauga. I should have written by him, but was very busy at the time. He told me that West passed through N. O. going back to Ala. I stayed another week with Sallie while brother John was gone for Mittie, Sis Mollie & I. Sis M. carried her sewing machine & such a quan-

*Willis is the second son of Brother George and Sis Mollie.

*We can find no documentation on the saying "I threw an old shoe after them," but we are guessing that it was a hunting superstition to bring good luck.

*The Golson's were cotton buyers in Mobile and New Orleans.

*"Mr. Brodnax" refers to Hal Brodnax, a near neighbor of Dr. Rumph.

tity of work as was done that week & with perfect ease, too & we all had such a pleasant time. Sallie is very lively, her two little children are quite pretty, but not as pretty as the two little girls she lost, so they all say. The other children were going to school. Mamie & Gilder were staying there & going also. Bettie stayed from school that week to fix up her dresses to attend the examinations with us. I enjoyed it all so much. George Rumph received the first honor & John Boddie the second honor for speaking. We had delightful music between every speech. Among the different musical instruments was one quite new to me, the zitta*, an instrument of about thirty strings, laid upon a table & [you] pick the strings, something like playing on a piano, the end of each finger encased in a kind of thimble. The music resembles a music box & a guitar combined, and when accompanied with flutes is very sweet. We stayed at Dee Newtons, his wife & he were very very kind. Sallie in full dress was as fine looking as any lady I saw, & I saw a great many at the examinations. Sis M looked as neat as a pin. Bettie & Mamie enjoyed it finely, Bettie caught a beaux. We tease her a good deal. John & George have not come home to stay yet. They are remaining in town to attend the young ladies' examinations this week, brother George says he expects when the boys get home, they will keep the woods awake after deer. The boys seem to be very popular with the girls, John says he has found a little angel, & some accuse George of giving his photograph to one of the girls.

*The zitta she speaks of is what we call a zither.

 Brother John returned from Kentucky last Saturday after an absence of nearly three weeks, brought Mittie with him. He went as far as Louisville, took the fever & was there sick seven days, he dispatched to Bardstown for Mittie & she met him in Louisville, he says when a bouncing big girl come running in his room & gathered him around the neck, he could scarcely recognize her.* She is a half inch taller than I, a beautiful figure, small waist, perfectly easy & graceful, free from all affectations, wears a number two shoe. She is rather dark but clear & rosy. Her face is round & full as Kates. I think her very pretty & intelligent. She draws & paints beautifully & plays well on the piano. Brother J says he will get her a piano next winter if he makes a good crop. Brother John seems delighted with Kentucky, says the political state of the country he thinks is brightening. The Democrats seem confident of electing their president, and the negroes are very humble & polite, it's Boss this & Boss that all around, he says he received the best attention while sick at Louisville. Mittie says she had rather live there than anywhere else, most every body there are doing so well. Her school had three hundred & forty-five pupils & two hundred sisters [nuns]. She says it is the merriest happiest place anywhere. They are allowed to receive gentlemen visitors in the presence of some one of the sisters. Since writing the above, we have had a nice shower of rain. I am in hopes it will continue until there has been a sufficiency. Mr. Dunlap seems low spirited about his crop, he has

*Mittie had been away for two years, attending boarding school in Kentucky.

only two hands now, he hired hands this year for only five months from the middle of Feb. & now he gets them by the day or month, he works hard himself in the Spring. Clara's cook does her cooking more like Mammy's than anyone I ever saw. She looks something like her too only younger. She keeps her children under good control, her daughter is the house girl & milker, is as quiet & respectful as can be. We like them so much, this is the second year that C has had them. She [the cook] was formerly from Missouri. I have seen old Uncle Bill but once, he is in bad health. He seemed so glad to hear from you all. I saw Julia Ann once in passing. She looked well, living at the Piles. Rhody left Uncle John after they were freed. Since then, she & all her children except two have died. Polly lives about & about, has three girl children & one grand child. Hannah is cooking for Mr William Stone. She left brother John this year. Old Ben lives in Camden. Give my love to Mammy & all my old negroes. Tell her I think if she was out here, she would be pleased with this country. But I shall always love Ala the best and I do want to hear from you all so much and you must not put off writing to me, Cousin Mary, but answer my letters as soon as you receive them, for yours is the only letter I had since I came, & I send to town every week. Please mam send me those photographs. Tell Cousin Hannah to break through ceremony & write to me, for I intend to write to her before long & to Julia Howard & the Dr too I hope Mattie & Rebecca has received my letters. Did I direct yours aright, but I suppose I did as you received them. Give my love to all enquiring friends. Tell Kate I intend some day to write to her. Give her my love and to all your children. Tell Dick & Ann they will soon be grown & they must study very hard & learn all they can for they will feel the need of it some day. Has Ell ever written, I wish he would write to me, I feel so anxious to hear from him. Give my love to all enquiring friends & accept a good share for yourself. Clara wishes to be remembered in love to you all. She says tell Mammy & all our Negroes howdy, her health is not good at all but something better than it was in the spring. She has a little house arranged with a shower bath bucket in it, thinks taking the bath is very beneficial to her. Sis Mollie says she intends writing to Sis Carrie shortly. (Be sure & write immediately) Tell Uncle Jim howdy & we would all be glad to see him. I think if old Uncle Jim Boddie were out here, he could make a support fishing. I never saw as much fish in my life.

Your affectionate cousin,
Cornelia S. Dickson

*Note: This postscript is written across the top of page 1:

*Write soon as yours is the only letter I have received since I came.

Cornelia Dickson in Ouachita Co. to her friend Julia Howard in Autauga Co.

July 22, 1868

Dear Julia,

    I have long thought of writing to you but it seems that thinking was all, owing to indolence or something else, have put it off from time to time until lo it is now mid-summer & I have never written you a scrip. Verily, procrastination is the thief of time. Said time has been very pleasantly passed with me until recently. I have mourned the death of a very dear little girl, daughter of Dr. Rumph's who after two or three days illness was called to part her sweet spirit from the little form we all loved so well.

    I have often felt so much agrieved that I never saw my sister's two little ones, but now I feel reconciled that I never knew them for I know now that I should have been so much more distressed had I known them. Little Kate Rumph died the eighteenth of this month, it was the eighteenth of <u>last July</u> that Clara lost her two little ones one year ago. Strange is it not and it was heart rending to see poor Sally. Kate is the fourth child she has lost, all near the same age at the time of their deaths, between three & four years old. She has only one left, a sweet little creature about two years old, called Attalie.

    I would be delighted to see you all, ... I could tell you so much to interest you, but would be too tedious to mention by pen. My trip out here was not the most pleasant in the world, though I was treated with courtesy by all with whom I was thrown in company, and most of the scenery was new & interesting to me, but the truth was coming up from N. O., after leaving the Miss. river, I felt as though I were going into a perfect wilderness, two thirds of which was covered with water & the remainder as bad as an unhealthy imagination could present, but I am glad to say an agreeable surprise awaited me at the completion of my tedious journey which had been enlivened the last few days and nights by an occasional shock, a crash against trees where the bank ought to have been, sometimes leaving a few small timbers of the boat where the crash took place. Not so pleasant, was it? But Camden is a nice picturesque place, has quite a business air, may well be called a city of hills, or <u>mountains</u> if you chance to <u>be walking</u>.

    I attended the examinations of the male high school at that place several weeks ago, twas very interesting indeed, the oratory part of it particularly had very sweet music between each speech. The Zitta a musical instrument quite new to me, somewhat resembles a music box and guitar combined, when accompanied with the flute is delightful. The young men acquited themselves surprisingly well. I do wish you could have been here. I know you would have enjoyed it. I did not attend the young ladies' examinations. There are a great many in Camden, but I saw very few pretty ones. Tell Jimmy it is the place for him as there are two girls to one boy and by

CAMDEN HIGH SCHOOL,
FOR MALES.
HENRY O. STANLEY, A. M., Principal.

The next Annual Session of this Institution will commence on MONDAY THE 30TH DAY OF AUGUST, 1869. The Session is divided into two Terms of twenty weeks each.

While it is earnestly desired that pupils be entered on the first day of the Session, still they will be received at any time. All will be charged from the day of entrance to the end of the Term.

One-half of the Tuition must be paid upon entrance, and one-half at the beginning of the second Quarter. No deductions will be made except for protracted sickness.

RATES OF TUITION:

First Class	$15 00	Per Term.
Second Class	20 00	" "
Third Class	25 00	" "
Incidental Expenses	1 25	" "
Board (washing and lights excepted) per month	15 00	

This School has been in successful operation, under the management of its present Principal, for the last three years. During that time there has been but one death, and no other case of serious sickness among the pupils. The design of its establishment was, by affording the means of acquiring a finished education at home, to obviate the necessity of sending young gentlemen beyond the limits of the State.

Those who do not desire to pursue a classical course, will be prepared for business by thorough instruction in Penmanship, Book-keeping &c. The Principal will, during the session, deliver a course of lectures free of charge to the students, on Commercial Law, and upon the law bearing upon all business transactions. Special attention will be paid to the cultivation of the morals and manners of the pupils. For further particulars, address the Principal.

CAMDEN, ARK., July 10, 1869.

School Flier
Courtesy of Sue Martin Russell

the way, if he was out here now that George Rumph & John Boddie are at home, he could have the nicest time deer hunting & fishing frequently in hearing of the house too. The boys keep the woods awake and seem to enjoy their vacation. They received the first and second honors in oratory, and nice handsome boys. They are spirited, full of life. I <u>know</u> you would like them <u>so much</u>. I do wish it was so you could set your cap for one of them. Tell Emma I gave her to George this morning, he says he intends going to Oxford Miss College soon & probably he will make a visit to Ala next summer. I am very much pleased with the country & people around here, they are so social & pleasant, we have some young bachelor neighbors very near, only a qtr of a mile, but they are bashful, but who's afraid? (think the old neighborhood where I was raised is or was the most pleasant neighborhood I was ever in, and the country too is preferable to this,) When you write, tell me about everybody. Tell Ella if she fancies an Indian name, to call her baby <u>Lotawana, pronounced Lo-tah-wan-ah</u>, the name of <u>a very pretty little girl In Camden</u>. They call her Lotah or Lottie for short. What has become of the young doctor, tell him one of my nieces out here claims his photograph for a sweetheart. My love to Amanda, & Kate, & all the children. Present my warmest regards to your father, tell him I intend writing to him. My respects to all enquiring friends & believe me as ever

Your affectionate friend
Cornelia S. Dickson

Cornelia Dickson in Ouachita Co. to her friend Eliza Clark in Burnsville, Alabama.

September 1868

Dear Mrs. Clark,

In one of Tom Love's letters he said that you wanted me to correspond with you & that you would write to me regularly. I would be <u>so very glad</u> to have you for a <u>regular</u> correspondent as I don't believe I have <u>one</u>. Sis Mollie says she is interested too as she knows you have not forgotten her & it affords her so much pleasure to hear from her old neighbors & friends. I shall endeavor to give you all the news that will interest you & if I fail ask me questions about any one that I may neglect to mention. I am staying at brother George's, have been here two months. Sis M has had several spells of sickness since I came to spend a <u>week</u> or <u>two</u>, which has kept me from leaving. She is able to be up a little now.

Mrs. Dee Newton received a letter from you some time since, told me to tell you she had commenced as many as three letters to you, some of them two or three pages long but something else called of her attention & they would get destroyed, but says she intends writing yet. She has no house servants except a cook & consequently has a great deal to do besides attending to her three little children, her baby is a boy, a very fine large child & so good. They say looks like Mr Isaac Newton. She calls him <u>Eustice</u>. Miss Jennie Word* stays with her nearly all the time. Mrs. Word lives in Camden, also. She is looking well now. Speaking of Dee & Mrs. Newton reminds me of the dining or rather infair* we attended together about two weeks ago. The groom was old Mr. Pile (father of William Pile who married Mrs Dr Wm Wood), his bride the widow Jordon. Mr. Pile was her fourth husband. She appeared to be about forty. There was a large crowd & they danced all day. That night, the string band from town came out, & they danced nearly all night. The bride is a fine looking lady, was as gay as a girl. Everyone thinks he did well, if he had only waited a little longer. His wife had been dead only three months. There are some fast people out here, especially widowers. Dee Newton's half sister is a widow, Mrs. Brown living with her father [Mr. William Stone]. The old gentleman is one of our neighbors & is improving his place with some new buildings, says he wants to make his place comfortable for his daughter so she may be induced to remain with him, she has two very pretty children, a son & daughter & I think her a very pleasant little lady. Her brother Robert lives nearby, his wife looks & talks enough like Mrs Bob Perry to be a sister. I like her very much. She was a Miss Avery, daughter of Mr. Sam Avery from Ala. They have but one child living, a girl, have lost two oldest, both boys. Her little girl is very delicate. Mr. Robert Stone accidently shot a hole through his hand about a year ago. The leaders were torn out & wrapped around his hand. He came very near losing it, but I believe

*Miss Jennie Word was the niece of Ora Stone Newton.

*An infair is a party or reception for a newly married couple.

it is well now with the loss of the middle finger. His general health for a long time was impaired from it but he looked well Sunday. They spent the day with us. Clara & Sallie Rumph spent the day with us also that day. Clara has but two children living, girls. Sallie has another daughter, calls her Eugenia. She has only two children living, girls, has four children dead. Sallie is a very large, fine looking lady, very much like her father.* I suppose you have heard ere this of the death of Mrs. Gildersleeve. She died in Jan last. Harriet is a widow with six children, is living with her father. Sis Mollie says when you write don't forget old Mr Davis & Mrs Stewart & all the neighborhood.

Mr. Wm Stone's sister Mrs. Cole lost her husband last winter. She has three daughters, one is married & living in sight of her, another is a widow living with her & the other has never married, is almost blind. They are all neighbors to us. Mrs Dr John Stone's three children live on their little place about two miles from here, none of them married, the two oldest are grown, Mary has several beaux. Mr George Stone's widow & family live in town. It is rumored that her only daughter Tommie is to be married soon. Mr Abe Stone left here last Spring with his two children. There are a good many marriageable young ladies & men out here, but few that will do to tie to. We had a pleasant serenade night before last. Yesterday evening went after muscadines, had a lively time gathering them among switch cane*. We preserve the hulls & make jelly out of the juice. I never work with them now but memory brings to mind the time that Hattie Underwood & I preserved some for her. I think of my old friends so often & if they think of me as often, for you must know I am quite a Pharisee in some things & "love them only who love me." I shall direct this to Burnsville care of Mr Holmes, tell me in your letter if I direct right & if there is a regular P. Office established at Mulberry yet. My respects to all inquiring friends, with kindest regards to yourself & family, I am as ever

your friend,
Cornelia S. Dickson

*Sallie Rumph, John Rumph's wife, was Sallie Gildersleeve. Harriet was her sister, as was Sis Mollie Boddie.

*Switch cane is a small, bamboolike grass native to the southern U. S.

Cornelia Dickson in Ouachita Co. to her cousin Mary E. Love in Autauga Co.

Jan. 18, 1869

Dear Cousin Mary,

It has been a long, long time since I received a letter from you, in fact only once since I came. I know you are so much averse to writing a letter that it is a task to you, but with a little exertion I think you might write to me oftener. I have looked in vain for a letter from you for several months, & did I not know what a bug bear it is for you to write, I would not be writing to you again without receiving an answer to my last, which was written last summer in July sometime. I have never heard whether you received it. So much has happened since then, I scarcely know where to commence. I have had a very pleasant time with all. It scarcely seems that I've been here three months until I look back at all that has happened since my coming. I was quite sick several weeks last summer & then in the fall had a short spell like I had at Sis Carrie's. I kept house a while for Clara. She was sick & fancy I am quite adept in that line. Clara is in good health now & her little babe grows very fast, is as fat as a pig. She says tis not like her other children, those she lost, but it looks a little like Lula, weighed <u>thirteen pounds</u>. She calls her Cora Lee. I call her Jackie to tease Mr. Dunlap. He has a very large fine mule named Jack that he loves to brag about. Mr. Dunlap has a niece & nephew from Ga living with us now. The young lady is named Miss Howard Garmany, her brother is about thirteen years old. We find them a pleasant addition to the family. They were orphans. They have three more sisters at Mr Sam & Mr. Archie Dunlap's. They came New Years Day. Mr Sam Dunlap went on & brought them out.

Mr. Dunlap [John] is in good spirits since cotton is advancing in price so rapidly as most everyone is. He made forty bales this year & corn enough to do him, not withstanding the drouth, had only sixty-five acres in cotton, says he run his place, (what was not rented out) with a thousand dollars, had eleven hundred owing to him that is good, & will have his crop clear & out of debt. When he came home after the war ended, had comparatively nothing but his land and that without a fence, did not even have provisions except what he got from his brother, & was in debt about eight hundred dollars. Brother George was as bad off if not worse, had a large family to support, & if it had not been for the assistance he received from brother John, could not have done anything. But says now if he can get thirty cents for his cotton, will feel nearly clear of debt to his merchants in Camden at least, a man by the name of Hill who was very kind to him & advanced him provisions, cc, but his children are getting large enough to be at school now & he feels able to send only one at the time. John is clerking in a store & Willis will start to school at Camden in a few days. Mr. Bracy, a druggist & very clever man, has applied to brother G for Gilder to stay in the store as assistant clerk, for his board & clothes. Brother G says he is not able to send him to school yet, & he thinks he will be learning a good deal in a drug store under Mr. Bracy, intends to let him go. Gilder is very anxious to go, too. George Rumph is clerking, too & Bettie is at School in Camden. John & George get their board & fifteen dollars a month for the first three months work, after which their wages are raised five dollars every three months. The boys are such correct gentlemanly boys they found no trouble in getting employment.

How have you spent Christmas? How I wished I could have given you another surprise. We have had a lively time with eggnog & syllabub and attending sociables nearly every night during the week after Christmas day. <u>The Program:</u> dined at brother John's Christmas Day, had a merry time with fireworks that day & night, Saturday evening went to brother George's having social there that night, Sunday evening home, Monday night a sociable at Mr. Dunlaps, Tuesday night at brother J, Wednesday night at Mr. Proctor's, Thursday night at Mr. Robert Stone's, Friday night at Dee Newton's. I did not attend the two last, nor any the next week for I was tired of parties, for once, & the weather was so unfavorable & waters nearly over the country, for here when the water is up people <u>in some places</u> visit in boats. It seems that so much water would make the country unhealthful, but I dont hear of any more sickness out here than in Ala. Chills and fever are more prevalent than anything else.

 I have thought for a long time I would write to Kate, but thought she might treat my letter as she did Jimmie Jarrots. Do you ever hear from Ell & cousin Hannah & Clem, & Dr Peebles family? How are they?

 Tell Sis Carrie I received her letter, would have answered it ere now, but am gathering items to write her a <u>London Times</u>. I will also write to Hattie soon. When you write, tell me all the news about home as well as neighborhood. The bale of cotton that Tom Caver is to pay this year will you be so kind as to ship it immediately to Eustice Golson in N[ew] O[rleans] to sell and the proceeds to be subject to the order of Dr. Rumph & write to Eustice to that effect. If you will do this favor for me cousin Mary I will be so much obliged. Brother John intends to go to N. O. about the last of Feb or the first of March. If you have collected any of the accounts I left with you, you can pay the expense of shipping with some of that money. I should have written to Uncle Clem to ship it for me, but when I asked him something about it before I left, he did not make any reply, so I concluded he did not want to be troubled with it. If I conclude to have my bed sent, I could receive it in the same way almost any time, but I have a hope to pay you all a visit next winter.

 How are you getting along about your crops, freed men, cc. Write me a long letter. Tell the children I very often think of them. Mamie says she wishes I had brought Kate with me. Have all photographs taken & send me please maam. I dont want to send mine until I have some more. How is Tom Caver, & Mammy, & all of them getting on? Tell them all howdy. Clara's cook & house girl that she has had two years left last week and she has another very nice girl to cook, but no house girl. Mr. Dunlap has nearly enough hands to cultivate what land he don't rent out, brother George has same he had last year, brother John wants a few more. Clara joins me in love to you all. Sends howdy to our negroes. Write soon & a long letter if it takes you a week.

        Yours affectionately,
        Cornelia S. Dickson

Cornelia Dickson in Ouachita Co. to her friend Rebecca Underwood in Autauga Co.

Feb. 4th, 1869

Dear Rebecca,

"Better late than never" as the old adage goes. I hardly know where to begin to make excuses, in fact, I dont believe I have any to make unless it is procrastination. (I was so in hopes of receiving a letter from you notwithstanding) Julia wrote that you were so troubled with your finger. I was in hopes it would be better soon and you would still write. I can hardly tell how the fall & part of the winter have slipped by (it seems but the other day that I received Julia's letter). I have been doing a little of everything in the house keeping line. Clara's health was very bad all summer & fall, in fact has been for two years. She is a great deal better now, has relieved me of the keys.

Last summer I put up about five gal. of brandy peaches (<u>by your recipe</u>). You may know they are nice, every one who tries them, likes them. I have also learned to make those nice ginger cakes like yours & tell Cousin Mary I can <u>make</u> and <u>bake</u> light bread now, have never failed in a single instance & for a while had to make it every week. How have you spent Christmas, we had quite a lively time out here, attending socials, cc, but I have found no one as yet who suits me as well as myself. I like the people a great deal better than I at first expected, but not at all as well as in my old home. There is not as much refinement here as there. The church even out here is used by travelers to camp in & traveling shows & panoramic exhibition & such like which I think is sacrilege, the ceiling torn off by them & used for firewood. So little attention is paid to such things. Everyone seems engrossed in making cotton.

This is indeed a good country for produce, but takes an energetic man to make much as I suppose it would anywhere. With the present price of cotton, most everyone feels easy about money matters. The waters are up now & boats come up to C[amden] nearly every week. I have a pleasant time visiting my relatives.

Brother George has but three children at home now, his oldest son is clerking, the next is at school, & the third son is assistant clerk in a drug store. He has only two daughters, [Carrie and Mamie], brother G's health is not very good, he has chills. Sis Mollie enjoys fine health & is as lively as any of the girls, she recently received a letter telling her of the death of her mother who died the 11th of Jan. The last letter she received from her, she [Mrs. Gildersleeve] expressed the wish that she might be relieved of her suffering. I have not seen her since she heard it. Harriet [Gildersleeve] Murley is living with her father. She lost her husband last spring. She had six children living, all girls but one, the youngest. One of her stepdaughters is married, the other two are living with them. Mr G[ildersleeve] speaks of coming out here on a visit shortly. Sis Mollie & Sallie are very anxious that he should move out, but he tells them he is too old now to leave his home for another. Sallie has but one little girl living now, has lost her four oldest. She is a very large fine looking lady, reminds me somewhat of Mrs Sarsby. Have you seen Mrs Sarsby lately? Write me all the news about my old neighbors & the neighborhood. Clara joins me in love to you & family, says she would be so glad to see you & your children, says it seems strange to hear of your having three old enough to go to school. She too has been looking for a letter from you. How does Mr U[nderwood] stand the politics & freedmen or does he take matters as easy as ever. I use to think he had a great deal of patience. Give my respect [to] him & all inquiring friends. Write soon.

Affectionately, your friend,
Cornelia S. Dickson

Cornelia Dickson in Ouachita Co. to her sister Caroline Boddie Love in Autauga Co.

March 9, 1869

Dear Sis Carrie,

It is raining today and I am not at school so I will embrace this opportunity to reply to your letter which I received some time since. I was sorry to hear of your suffering so much with neuralgia and sickness in your family. Your letter contained a great deal of news to interest me ... I was sorry to hear of so much sickness in our old neighborhood. Brother George says he thinks there is more sickness out there than here. He has never had but two or three spells since he came to this country, and Sis Mollie had her first spell last summer. The children have chills occasionally. Brother George has been having chills occasionally all fall, there has been several overflows & he has exposed himself a good deal while getting his stock out of the river bottoms every time until the chills seem to have taken firm hold on him. He says he can't stand to see the stock go. They are so valuable to him. Sometimes they milk as many as fifteen good cows at once. He has killed enough meat out of the woods to do him that were raised with scarcely any corn. They grow fat on the mass such as acorns in the woods. He says if he can keep them he has a fine lot of hogs for another year that will be two years old. But he has to keep a sharp look out after them. He has the same hands that he had last year and on the same terms. He made twenty bales of cotton but not enough corn to feed his stock as he wished. Sis Mollie is very lively, dances about like a girl. All the children dance at the parties except little Carrie and Bobbie[Robert Lee]. They are very sweet children and I love them so much. Johnnie is clerking at Luda, a branch of the house in Camden in which George Rumph is clerking. I believe he likes it very well. Will is going to school in Camden and boarding with a Mr Winfield. He is much pleased with the boarding house and the school, but he is so timid and shy but one of the best boys in the world. I believe Johnnie is the most mischevious, Gilder is assistant clerk in a drug store and is delighted. I believe Mr Bracey, the druggist, is well pleased with him. Brother G says he is not able to send more than one at a time to school. Mamie and Carrie are studying at home and Sis Mollie is giving Mamie music lessons. Mamie and Johnnie came up to church Sunday and took dinner with us. I have not been down there in two or three weeks. I commenced teaching school about two weeks ago and I can't visit them as often as I did. I went to Camden last Saturday and saw George R[umph], he was well. He says he has written to Tom L[ove] two or three times since he received a letter from him. I was at Brother John R[umph]'s about two or three weeks ago, were all well. Brother John, Sallie, and Mittie are lively. I always enjoy myself so much with them. Tom [Rumph] looks so much like Sis Fannie [his mother]. He is Mittie's gallant now whenever she wants to visit. George (Rumph) is gone and Brother J has his practice to attend to. I think Florence will be real pretty when she gets grown. She is quick to learn, sings well for a little girl. Mittie is at school in Camden, boards at a Mr. Powell's, who married Mrs Mallard's* first cousin, a Miss Tarrant, so you see they are kin-folks of Brother John. Bettie is very well pleased with school. She is a very pretty girl. Tommy and Florence are at home. The creeks around Brother John's are up nearly all winter, he says tis too expensive to have them ride [to school]. Brother John made between thirty and forty bales of cotton. He has bought up a good deal, near a hundred bales, I believe. I think a good many men were owing him and he took cotton at the market price in payment. When the war ended, he had some cotton that he had saved, & there were a good many of his neighbors [who] were completely broken up. Instead of taking advantage of their condition as many would have done, he loaned them money and assisted them to rise in various ways and waited with them until last year, [it] being a good year, a great many were able to pay him up, not only the money borrowed but doctor bills. He has a great many friends. He says he can say with a clear conscience he has yet to take the first advantage of any one. He has been buying some town property lately, says now it will probably be a week or two before he goes down to N[ew] O[rleans]. Eustice Golson was up about two weeks ago. I saw him only a few minutes while in Camden, he received a telegraphic dispatch from Bob Golson that he had received a letter from Clem Love and that my bale of cotton was on the way to N. O. Brother J told him to hold on to it until further orders.

 The new boat, the Governor Allen, makes weekly trips from Camden to New Orleans. Now leaves Camden every Saturday night, arrives in N. O. on Wednesday, and leaves there again in a few hours. Believe she is the fast-

*Mrs. Mallard was John B. Rumph's mother

est boat ever on this river. I could travel now, if I had the greenback. I have not told you about my school. I am employed to teach five or six scholars at a salary of thirty six dollars per month, and all who come in after that I get three dollars per month apiece. I have two over already and I hear there are several more wanting to come. Brother George and brother John would send [theirs], but they say they are not able to board their children out, and three miles through mud and water is too far. This is decidedly the sloppiest country I ever saw. Today, for instance, we could almost visit in boats.

I expected to go to Brother George's next Saturday, but Mr Dunlap says the country down that way will be overflowed about that time from the rain. If the boys were at home, I would like to go down there to take boat rides. Brother G has two boats. I was there once this winter while the river was up. It came up nearly to [his] back gate. We had a short boat ride one evening, Mitt & Mamie and I went with Gilder, caught on a snag, came near upsetting before we got off. We then went with Will a short distance down the road to get the boat that Brother George had been using intending to go down to Luda to pay Johnnie a visit but when we got there some young men had just taken the boat and gone across & left their mule fastened close by. Mitt & Mamie mounted the mule, took a long ride, then carried it to Brother George's and hitched it in the yard. The young men were somewhat disconcerted when they came back for they had brought over some bagging and ties. They soon traced their mule to his hiding place much to our amusement. The next day the water was too low for us to ride. It is reported there are to be several weddings in the neighborhood. I hope to get an invite if it is so.

Mr. Dunlap is very busy stirring, preparing to make another crop, bought two young mules the other day, has hands enough, all croppers*, but one that will work with him. He made a very good crop last year, forty bales of cotton & enough corn. Clara enjoys good health now, is busy setting hens, turkeys, and geese, cc and gardening, has the fattest best little babe. We hardly know she is in the house, so quiet. Lula is a little harem scarem though and an incessant talker. I don't believe I ever told you about giving little Carrie the dress you sent her. She was very proud of it and told me to tell Aunt Carrie "Thank you Mam." She knit her Pa a pair of sox not long ago. He bought her a pair of gloves. She has commenced him another pair, says he told her he would get her a hat when she finishes them. Sis Mollie received a letter about a month ago telling of the death of her mother, who died of typhoid pneumonia. She & Sallie were very much distressed, though her death was not entirely unexpected. She had been suffering some time with rheumatism & neuralgia of the head. Mr G[ildersleeve] wrote that he was coming out to see them but did not say when. Harriet lost her husband last spring & is living with Mr Gildersleeve. She has six children of her own living, her stepchildren one is married & the other two are living with her (the married one), her stepson died in the army.

*"Croppers" refers to "Sharecroppers." When the Emancipation Proclamation freed the slaves, many of them remained on the land of their former owners and farmed under a plan which allowed them to rent the land. They paid 2/3 of their cotton crop and 1/3 of their corn crop to the owner, thus the term "sharecroppers."

I wrote to Rebecca about a month ago. I hope she has received it. I expect you have moved ere this to your new home & the children are going to school. Tell Bess I will be certain to bring her a doll and George some marbles when I come. I had like to have forgotten to tell you Brother George says the next time you write, draw a picture where you commence so he will know where to begin to read. Sis Mollie says, "No, don't. Fill it all with writing."

Affectionately, your sister,
Cornelia S. Dickson

Cornelia Dickson in Ouachita Co. to her cousin Mary Love in Autauga Co.
About the middle of August, 1869

Dear Cousin Mary,

I have waited nearly a year for a letter from you. During the time have written several letters to you; Thinking that probably you have never received them as I have received no reply to many others that I have written induces me to write again, & Cousin Mary you must write to me even if you don't receive my letters regularly; Sometimes I am inclined to think you have all forgotten me, or now that I am gone, that you do not think enough of me to want to hear from me, but I can never forget you all or your motherly kindness when I was left so <u>alone</u>, alas! <u>that</u> is a sad lot, but I have been very fortunate in meeting with friends. The last letter that I received from Ala was from Clem, <u>a mere little note</u>. I replied to it immediately & have been looking for him ever since, or I should have written sooner. I wanted to let you know that Eustice Golsan had received & sold the bale of cotton that you shipped, but it only weighed <u>324</u> in N.O. & the bale that was to be paid to me by Tom Caver ought to have weighed <u>500</u>. It was sold at 28 1/2 cts which makes quite a falling off in the sum that I was to receive last year on the place. Will you please see to it for me & write to me immediately.

I have been very busy ever since my school was out in July. I don't know yet whether I can get another there are so few small children in the neighborhood. This seems to be a fatal country for children, so many die of conjestion and most of them that are large enough are sent to town. They have free schools over there, but the board is high. Brother George has sent Will[is] this year. I have been staying at Brother G's for five or six weeks, Sis Mollie has been very sick during the time, but is well now. I have attended to her dairy nearly all the time & fancy I can make butter nearly equal to the Western. Her cows range in the canebrake, brother G is in low spirits about his cotton crop; he was in hopes in the spring that this crop would put him out of debt & on his feet again, but now says he won't make anything, he will have corn enough to do him. Mr. Dunlap is making a fine crop again, his land is different from that of brother George's or brother John's. Brother John could get no hands scarcely this year & consequently some of his land is idle, what he has in I believe is only moderately good. Sallie has another fine daughter, named Eugenia. George named it I believe; I have not been up there in two weeks. Clara's baby [Cora Lee] is the brag baby of the neighborhood, looks very much like Clem's little Maud when I last saw her! She is as good & sweet as she is pretty. Clara never had a nurse for her, has three or four teeth, can almost walk. Lula is well again now, has been puny ever since last fall. Miss Howard Garmany* is living with us & is so much company for Clara that I can visit brother George & John's & stay as long as I like. You must write me a long letter cousin Mary, tell me all about Clem [Love] & cousin Hannah [Clem's wife] & Kate [Cousin Mary's daughter] & all the children, and about all the neighbors, none of you ever mention Mr. & Mrs. Wallace. They were kind neighbors to us. Give my respects to them. I have just heard the sadest of news to me, the death of Mr L. Howard, & Mrs Houston. I considered Mr Howard one of my very best friends & I do so much regret to hear of his death, I sooner thought of hearing of the death of any one else as him & Mrs Houston's so unexpected. I look back a few years & I see smiling faces beaming with warm friendly feelings & now were I to go back to Ala, I should so much miss them that are gone. What a great change a few years can make. I wrote to Ella Herrmann about the time I heard of Archer's death but have received no answer to my letter. I have not as yet seen Tom Love's letter to George. Brother George told me about it. Do you ever hear from Ell*, if he is in Marshall, Texas he is not a great way from here.*

*Miss Howard Garmany is the daughter of John Dunlap's sister.

*"Ell" refers to Eldred Love, son of Cousin Mary.

*Note: This letter was found on a loose page in Cornelia's journal, and no more of it was found, thus the abrupt ending.

*A Ferrotype was a photograph made on a thin iron plate by a process in which collodion was used as a vehicle for the sensitive salts. A Daguerrotype was produced on a silver plate or on a copper plate covered with silver.

Cornelia Dickson in Ouachita Co. to her cousin Mary E. Love in Autauga Co.

November 1, 1869

Dear Cousin Mary,

Your most welcome letter of the 17th was duly received and perused with great pleasure. We are all well at present. Your letter was almost as interesting as a good chat with you. When I get such a letter it makes me feel like I am not so very far off from you all. My love to Kate & Dick. Tell Dick and Ann they must study very hard and learn all they can, for an education will be worth more to them than anything else. I would like so much to see little Maud. Tell Clem to have her likeness taken and send it to me. Cousin Hannah promised to send me hers and Clem's too, for that Daguerreotype I would not have given it to her on any other condition . . . I believe I like Phareotypes* best. I have had one taken for you as promised.

Mittie and I went up to Holly Springs last week to have Sallie's little

Attalie's picture taken. Sallie had been so distressed at not getting her other children's and feared she might lose Attalie. We made two trips up there before we succeeded in getting it. It [Holly Springs] is about fourteen miles. Reminded me of our trip to Kingston only no sand beds, the country up there is high & rocky. I did not expect to have my picture taken that day and wore my old traveling dress, but the artist insisted my dress would take well. I let him try it & I had only two taken & exchanged one with Mitt for hers.

I spent that week with Sallie. Brother John and George Rumph went up about ten miles on a camp hunt of a week's duration. They hunted about four & half days & killed thirty-three deer. Half a dozen neighbors and about half a dozen from town comprised the company. Dee Newton was with them, George says they had a <u>merry</u> time playing jokes on each other. One evening several of them brought half a dozen deer heads near to camp and fastened them to some trees so they could shine their eyes at night. After supper, some one proposed they go "fire" hunting. Some of the <u>knowing ones</u> led the uninitiated ones near the deer heads. One of them became excited and commenced a rapid and deadly fire upon what he supposed to be <u>deer as thick as hops</u>. He then rushed upon the fallen prey and lo! his mistake. His companions had disappeared and on his return to camp was greeted with peals of laughter.

George [Rumph] intends leaving this week or next for N. O. to attend a commercial college. Brother John wants to give him every advantage he is able in that line. Johnnie [Boddie] is not decided yet what he will do another year. He says if his employer will pay him enough he will remain where he is. He wanted to study law, but brother G tells him that all the Boddies who amassed fortunes did it merchandizing and Johnnie has a mind to grasp almost anything.

Last Saturday was Johnnie's 21st birthday. Sis Mollie prepared a very nice little supper for him and some of his young gentlemen and lady friends. We had a nice time. Sis M said she wished Tom Love if he is coming would have been there. Gilder is home now picking cotton for one of the neighbors at $1.00 per hundred [pounds] and boards at home. He has bought himself a Sunday suit and several things besides. Says he is picking now for a rifle and will soon have it. Brother G intends starting Mamie to school in Camden after Christmas. Bettie R[umph] is in Camden at school. Tommie and Florence are going from home. Tommie killed his first deer about two months ago, a very large, fine one. He was so proud, says he <u>grew three inches</u> that day. He has killed a fawn since.

Brother G has had quite a time trying to entrap a bear that is in the habit of visiting his corn field, but says he fears he has frightened Sir bruen off by catching a coon in his steel trap in that field. He would catch it with dogs, but there are none near here that will run a bear. Brother G's crop is turning out better than he expected. Soon after the drouth, has gathered enough to do him. Mr. Dunlap is also making a good crop of both corn & cotton. I don't know how brother John is. He has sold his place for <u>ten thousand dollars</u> on time, but has reserved the house, garden, and orchard & will live on the place until it is paid for and take a deed of trust to secure himself. He could not get as much labor and such as he wanted and his practice kept him from home a great deal. He sold to a company of freedmen who have agreed to his terms. With all the trade is considered a good one on his part and a good [one] on the freedmen's [part] if they will work and do right.*

*Evidently the sale didn't work out, for John Rumph kept the place.

Speaking of this reminds me to tell you that I have sent Mr. Tom Underwood a power of attorney to act as my agent, you may think Cousin Mary that it was want of confidence in you that made me do it & feel hurt at it. But I assure you it is nothing of the kind. I thought Mr. U was a gentleman & knew more about such things & could get about & see to it with more ease than you could & then I knew you would feel a delicacy in contending with freedmen when anything went wrong. I disliked very much to impose such on you when I left, though you were always so kind, but I felt almost like I had no one else.

Mitt says she intends sending her Aunt Carrie one of her pictures. Says she intends writing to her too. I told her I knew she would be glad to receive a letter from her.

Mr. Dunlap has been so unfortunate. Several months ago he got the middle finger of his left hand so badly mashed as to lose the first joint. It happened while he was assisting at a gin-house raising. Clara tells him he has not worked in so long now that he has outgrown his clothes. He is very fleshy. So is brother George. I tell him if he keeps on he will be as large as Uncle Clem.

Sis Mollie is very thin and looking badly. She was in bad health nearly all summer. Brother John looks about the same. Both he and Brother G wear <u>specks</u> when they read. Sallie has been having chills, something very unusual for her. Her babe looks very much like her and is so good, fat as a pig, calls her Eugenia. Clara's babe [Cora Lee] is walking now, has six teeth and is as pretty as ever. Mamie will be fourteen in Dec. & weighs one hundred and sixteen. We tell her she will be as large as her Aunt Sallie.

Affectionately, your cousin,
Cornelia S. Dickson

Cornelia Dickson in Ouachita Co. to her friend Eliza Clark in Statesville, Ala.

Nov. 29th 1869

Dear Mrs. Clark,

Your most welcome epistle was received in due time and read with much pleasure. You doubtless think me delatory in replying to your letter, but there were several questions to which I was unable to reply without some delay. First, Mrs. Pile* is living in sight of brother George's. She has one child a daughter about twelve years old called Blanche. I have heard that Mr. Pile drinks very hard. I suppose she too has her troubles, for I never hear of her visiting any one.

Mr. Albert Stone's wife died in 1863. She left three children; one has died since. His daughter is a mute. I have not heard anything of them lately.

Mr. and Mrs. Avery are living about ten miles the other side of Camden. I know she would be glad to hear from you, for Mrs. Bob Stone told me that her mother wanted very much to see you, to enquire about her friends in Ala. I asked brother John something about the estate you mentioned. He says he believes Mr. McGraw's estate consisted chiefly of negroes and that after they were freed, there was little else.

Ora Newton says she intends to write to you. I saw her about two weeks ago. Mrs. Cole and her daughter, Mrs. Williams, send their best love to you. I have not seen her sister, Mrs. Nancy Williams, in some time. Her daughter, Mrs. Robert Brodnax, lives about a mile from here this year but I seldom see her. I saw Mr. Frank Brodnax night before last. He had just heard from Ala and that his niece, Miss Emma Stone, was dead. I had heard Julia Howard speak of her as being very pretty. Mrs. Mary Ponder lives in sight of Mrs. Cole. She has four children. Mr. Ponder is a mechanic.

Mr. William Stone, Mr. Bob Stone, brother John and several others in the neighborhood have gone on another camp hunt, the third this fall. They all seem to enjoy themselves very much.

We had a candy stew at brother John's last week. There were about fifty persons present, nearly all young folks. We had a very lively time. Sallie and brother John send love to you. I spent last week with Sis Mollie. All down there are well.

The little folks are having a merry time gathering hickory nuts and saving eggs for Christmas. Will their second son, was staying home that week, is a great duck hunter, and the lakes near there abound in such game this time of the year. Sis Mollie received a letter from Harriet Murley several weeks ago. Sis M read your letter with much interest, and pleasure. We are all so glad to hear about our old neighborhood. She and brother G send their love to you.

*"Mrs. Pile" refers to Eliza Stone Wood, sister of Ora Stone Newton, Dee Newton's wife.

Clara joins me in love to yourself and family & my love to Betty Whetstone. Tell her I intend to write to her before long. Write soon.

Your friend,
Cornelia S. Dickson

Cornelia Dickson in Ouachita Co. to her friend Ella Herrman in Autauga Co.

December 10th 1869

Dear Ella,

Your most welcome letter was received several days ago. It was longer on the road than I hope this will be. Mails are so uncertain since the war. I never knew before what your babe was named. I think [it] a sweet name. You must be sure and send me her photograph. She was a nice little one when I saw her. I am always glad to hear [of] my old home & people. Well Ella I scarcely know what to write that would be interesting to you.

Clara is as busy as a bee with her housekeeping and trying to get through with <u>everything</u> before Christmas. Her babe is walking now and one of the sweetest best babes you ever saw. Lula is just seven years old and is a great deal of company besides the help she is to look after her little sister and keep her out of mischief. She seems to feel very important whenever she gets the keys in the evening and goes to the hen house to gather eggs for the Christmas eggnog. She is making a quilt, says wants to have a quilting before long and have all the young ladies to come and quilt it, don't want any children to come as "they would just be in the way and couldn't quilt." She has no children for playmates and consequently her notions are rather mature and it often reminds me of the appellation you used to give your sister Lula, <u>Grandmother.</u>

Mr Dunlap is [away] from home today. I believe he has made arrangements to have his farm cultivated another year by tenants, reserving only a small part for himself. Miss Garmany, his niece, is a good deal of company for me when I am at home but I stay at my brother George's and at my brother-in-law Dr John Rumph more than half my time. I enjoy being with them all. The young folks are a merry set and nothing seems to stop them, when they set their heads to have a frolic. Indeed the older members of the family enjoy a sociable now and then.

I think altogether we have a pleasant neighborhood. People do not all seem settled here, for some are moving off and others coming in every year. I never in my life saw as many movers <u>going to Texas</u>. We live in sight of a public road and hundreds of wagons have passed in the last few weeks. We have had some to stay all night with us this week who were from Texas going to the north western part of this state, to Washington County. They say the lands where they are from are very rich, but the water is bad and they have no health. The lady had consumption and appeared very feeble. It made me feel sad to see her so ill & think that her stay on earth seemed so limited, but if she is prepared she will be better off.

The river has been so low all summer that we have had no boats. But the heavy rains recently have swelled the river considerably and we hear the boats daily, a most welcome sound as the people out here have to depend on the rise in the river for shipping their produce and for getting fresh groceries, are always glad to see it rise before Christmas, somewhat different from what it is in Ala. But, the railroad is already commenced that will connect Camden with the Miss. river, and as it were, the outer world, for I have felt ever since I have been here as if I were "pinned up in the backwoods".

I will close by wishing you a Merry Christmas and a Happy New Year. This leaves all well. Write soon. With the kindest regards to you and your family, I [am] as ever

Affectionately your friend,
C. S. Dickson

Mary Elizabeth (Mamie) Boddie attending school in Camden to her aunt Cornelia Dickson at home across the river at Harmony Grove.

Feb 26th 1870

My Dear Aunt

I havent heard from home but once since I left. Pa comes to town nearly every day, and never thinks of coming to see me. I think you all have forgotten me. I wrote to Cousin Fannie last week and I dont know where to direct it to. I though[t] I would wait and see Cousin George* he has been to see me once since I came. Johnny* has not been to see me yet. I surpose he is like the rest of you dont care any thing about me, all of the girls gets letters except I. Jinnie Harrice got two last night. I have got one frind left I <u>regon</u> — I can hear from her and she will tell me how you and Uncle Jimmie get along. I know that is the reason you will not write to me, and that is not all. Cousin Bettie said she got a letter last week for the first time in a month. Ma has forgotten me too. I wrote to her two or three weeks ago and havent received answer yet. Mrs Taylor said she would write to me if I would write to her first, if you fail to write to me, I will, Aunt Nelie. Mrs Moor was here this morning with her darling little babe's corps. She was in New O. when it died, it has been dead a week. She would not have it open, it was in a matalic coffin. Oh! you dont know how hard she took it, we would all have gone to the burying had it been clear. There was a ball at the court house last week. I dont think their was any of the school girls there. Mr Browning gave the young men strick ordors about the girls, the little girls had a

*"Cousin George" refers to George Rumph, son of brother John.

*Johnny refers to John Rumph Boddie, brother of Mamie and son of brother George and sis Mollie.

show at the school room one day of last week, and will show again next week, they dance and sung & did a great many little things that no one would have though[t] of. I am getting along very well in my studies now. Mr Browning has the strictest rules I ever heard of, and very few of the girls that keep them. I have been to church every Sunday since I came. I havent commence going to Sunday school yet. I have been to see Mrs Brown and Mrs Newton. I havent been out to call on any of the girls yet. A great many of them have been to see me and Miss Leulia Gray has been to call on me. Tell Bud* when you see him, I would have fallen in love with her to if I had been in his place. I think she is so pretty. Aunt N I am so well please with my boarding place & busy with my studys that the weeks seem like day[s] to me. Mrs. Hamilton is so kind to me she has six boarders & some very noisy ones. Mr H. is like Pa he dont like noisy children, give my love to all my frinds if I have got any, and tell Cousin* that all the girls thinks that she is agoin to get married, and tell her if she does get married & dont let me know any thing about it, I will never speak to her again. Aunt N. I will write you a longer & better letter next time. Please excuse all mistakes and write soon & all the news and a <u>long letter</u> tell Miss Howard to write to me. Aunt Nealy dont let no one see this if you please.

*"Bud" refers to Mamie's brother Robert.

*"Cousin" refers to Mittie Rumph.

       Your loving niece
       M E B

Cornelia Dickson in Ouachita Co. to her cousin Mary Love in Autauga Co.
                March 2nd 1870

Dear Cousin Mary,

  Your most welcome letter of the 14th ... was received yesterday. They always give me so much pleasure. I expected that you received mine about the time they were all leaving for Texas & I knew how you would be feeling then. I thought so much about you & wished I could be with you, indeed it would have given me so much pleasure. I was surprised at your letting Dick go. I saw in a N.O. paper an account of their arrival in that city & was much surprised to see Dick's name among the others. It will doubtless be a great advantage to him, he will see something of the world & learn to depend more on himself. Children cannot be raised <u>now</u> as they used to be under a parents care all the time & he will no doubt appreciate home & a mothers care much more from leaving both awhile. I have heard the land where they are is splendid, but is the water good? I have heard not, but I suppose there is no place a Utopia. I have thought a long time that I would write to cousin Hannah [Murley]. When you write again let me know her POffice. I would like so much to have another Photograph of Ell you know the one I have is very indifferent & he promised to give me another when he had some taken. Brother G wants to know is Tom L[ove] not laboring under a slight attack of cholera when he had his Photograph taken. Tell Andrew to be sure & send me his. You never said a word about mine that I sent, if you thought it like me. Tell Kate <u>I will write to her if I live,</u> & cousin Mary cant you possibly make a way to have yours & Kate's Photograph taken for me. Sis Mollie says tell Kate to be sure if she has any taken to send her one. She is so anxious to see her. Mamie wants to see her too. She is at school now in Cam. I received a letter from her last Saturday. She is delighted. She wrote that she had written to Fannie. Tell sis Carrie I have looked a long time for a letter from her or is she so well content to hear from Ark through yours & Tom's letters that she don't care to write. George [Rumph] told us about meeting with them all in N.O. Says he thinks Tom fine looking & likes cousin H. very much. I knew he would like her but he saw Clem to disadvantage, he had lost his trunk & I imagine he was <u>upset</u>. Bob Golsan was to see me while he was in the neighborhood & told me they had found Clem's trunk & sent it on to him. About my bale of cotton cousin Mary. Mr Underwood wrote me to excuse him from attending to it. Therefore I will have to call on you to take charge of it & send it to E. F. Golsan N.O. subject to the orders of Dr. J. B. Rumph, I am sorry to have to trouble you again cousin Mary but I see no other alternative. Please ascertain the weight before it is shipped as I think that is best.

    I was very sorry to hear of the death of Mrs Wallace. She was a kind neighbor & I think a good woman. Mort is young to be married. Does Red improve any in hearing. You told me so little about Kate, does her hearing improve? How does she wear her hair. Mittie & Bettie wear chignons* tis rather a stylish arrangement but not very becoming. Mamie's hair is short. She wears a bandeaux* & roaches* & crimps the front. Cousin Mary I expect you think this silly chat but it will maybe give you an idea how they look. (<u>You told me so little about Hattie & the children. My love to her tell her not to forget she is due me a letter).</u> I know your old place is beautiful now, you would see no such looking places out here or in any other new country. Brother John's is the prettiest place that I know of here but he has sold, will continue to reside on it until tis paid for. I am at brother G's now, have been for three weeks, Sallie was down to see us, staid four or five days about two weeks ago. All the older children are from home now except Mitt & Florence. Brother J speaks of going down to N.O. soon. I saw Mr Dunlap several days ago, he said all were well at home except Lula, she had a slight fever. Brother G & family are well. Sis Mollie has one of her former servants cooking for her, Lucy's daughter Becky. She looks very much like Mary Jane. July Ann died about a month ago. Bill is still living but is very feeble, is living at Mr. W. Pileses. Hannah is cooking for Sallie this year. My love to Mammy how is she getting on? Do you ever visit the graveyard now. How are the plants around them doing? Who is living at Sis Carrie's

---

* A chignon is a large, smooth twist, roll, or knot of hair, worn by women at the nape of the neck or the back of the head.

* A bandau is a headband, especially one worn about the forehead.

*Roaches means to clip or cut off.

old place now that she has moved?

The health of the neighborhood is very good I believe at present. Brother G heard some time ago that Mrs Wright, formerly Ellen Peters was dead, also Mrs Bob Stone's mother Mrs Avery died of pneumonia about a month ago.*

*Note: There is no signature for this letter in the ledger.

Cornelia Dickson in Ouachita Co. to her friend Eliza Clark in Statesville, Ala.

March 22nd, 1870

Dear Mrs. Clark,

I thought that I would have responded as soon as I received your most welcome and interesting letter, but it seems there is always some unforseen circumstances prevented our accomplishing many things we purpose. Do not think it less appreciated. Sis Mollie has been quite sick but is up and well again now. Then the cook's mother came and took her off, but she ran away and came back, so household occupations have resumed their old channels. It is with pleasure that I can now have a little chat with you. I will first reply to your questions. Mrs. Pile had three children, has but one living. I have heard since I wrote you of her visiting some of her neighbors and relatives. They all visit her. You would never know her. She looks so old and hasn't a tooth in her head. They have a good little farm and are living very well as far as I know. I believe I told you her daughter is going to school in Camden. Sis Mollie and I spent the day with Annie Stone about two weeks ago. Bob had just bought her a Grover and Baker sewing machine, and she wanted Sis Mollie to learn her how to use it. She told me to write you that she had lost her mother, Mrs. Avery*. She died about the middle of January with typhoid pneumonia. She was sick only a week and her death was very unexpected. She and Annie and Ora Newton spent one day here during Christmas week and she looked so well. She was large and fleshy. Mary Pace was very sick at Annie's at the time of her Mothers death & neither of them got to see her before she died. Annie went over the day she was buried, but they would not tell Mary until Annie returned. Mr Avery's son, who is married, is living with him. Little Lula* is staying with Annie. Dee Newton came while we were at Bob's, was just from N. O., is very lively, speaks of going down again shortly and taking Miss Jimmie Word with him and Mr. Ross also and two of his daughters. Brother John expects to go with the crowd. They anticipate a gay trip. I wish I could go with them, too.

Dee's youngest child* is beginning to walk, is a fine little fellow. His oldest goes to school. Mrs Word has been sick. Julia Brown and family are well, I believe. She & her children have been nearly sick with something like hooping cough. Her father sent by Dee and bought her an elegant piano

*"Mrs. Avery" refers to Sarah Avery, wife of Sam F. Avery.

*"Little Lula" refers to the youngest child of Sarah and Sam Avery. "Annie" is Mrs. Robert Stone.

*"Dee's youngest child" would be Eustice Jay Newton, born in 1869.

(Webers). Does Mary play much yet?

Sis Mollie says her piano seems a part of herself. Tis so much pleasure to her. I know how fond of music you used to be & now that your health is bad I should think it would be a source of much pleasure to you. I am sorry to hear that your health is not good, hope ere this you are well again.

I am sorry to hear that Mrs. Lasiter's health is failing. Give my love to her & Sallie. Miss Knox had a strange wedding day, didn't she? I don't think I ever heard of anyone marrying on Monday before. I did not know that Lewis Kirkland was a widower. What in the world possessed as nice a girl as Mary Ellen to marry such a man, was it mother's conduct? I felt real sorry to hear it. I had never heard that Jim Clay was married, but I expected she would marry John Burns. I have [not] written to Bettie W. yet, but I have not forgotten her. My love to her when you see her.

Clara's children, and Miss Garmany (Mr. Dunlap's niece) spent Sunday here. All well. I have not seen any of brother J's family lately. I hear they are all well.

Brother G and Sis Mollie join me in love to yourself and family and kind regards to Mr Davis. We are always glad to hear from you all. You must write soon.

Affectionately, your friend,
Cornelia S. Dickson

Cornelia Dickson in Ouachita Co. to her cousin Kate Love in Autauga Co.
May 2nd 1870

Dear Kate,

I have been out here now two years & one month and this is the first time I have attempted to write to you. Believe me Kate it is not because I do not think of you very often & wish I could see you. But I had so many to write to at first & I knew I could hear from you through Cousin Mary's letters. I have often thought of what you said to me before I left there. "Cousin Nealia, I bet you will write to everybody & never think about writing to me." I hope you will not treat my letter like you did Jimmie Jarrot's. By the way, have you ever answered it yet? You must write me everything you can think of. I know anyone who talks as much as you do can write a long letter. All you need is a little practice. I know that you will be liable to make a good many mistakes too, but never mind that. I will know how to overlook & excuse them all & keep your letters to myself as though you were my sister. I wrote to cousin Mary some time ago, am looking for one from her and Mrs Clark too.

I am at brother John's now, have been staying here four weeks. The first one Sis Mollie, & Carrie, & Bobbie were here too. We were helping dress cakes & cc for a wedding that took place about a mile from here; Mr. Wiggs to Miss Victoria Proctor. I must tell you about the wedding. When the night came, it rained hard all the evening, we could not think of being disappointed so we wrapped up in blankets, oil cloths, overcoats, shawls, & everything we could make available & went anyhow, had no umbrella & had to go in a wagon, would have done finely but had to dismount at the bridge, twas so slippery the mules could'nt go up. I stepped in some mud half over my shoes. Mamie, Bettie & Miss Garmany were here & went with us, also Johnny and George. We had a merry crowd, had a very lively pleasant time. Twas as nice wedding as I ever attended. Mittie was a bridesmaid, the bride & maids were all dressed in white. The bride wore a wreath & long veil. When the bride's cake was cut, Bettie got the dime, but she won't own it, says the young man that cut for her got it. I wore my poplin. I made it according to prevail[ing] mode. I take <u>Arthur's House Magazine</u>, Sally takes <u>Godeys Ladies' Book</u> and Mit[tie] <u>Peterson's</u> so you see we have as many new patterns as we want & more than we can use. I like Godey's best for I believe both fashions & literature. <u>Peterson's</u> next best, though the moral tone of Arthur is good.

    Brother John has been gone two weeks last Saturday to N. Orleans. We will look for him home tomorrow. Florence, Attalie, & the baby Eugenia have the whooping cough. Tis an eppademic through the country and the worse form I ever saw. The two little ones are nearly well of it, but Florence still has it very bad. Brother George's children except John & Willis have had it, too, but are nearly well. Lula* has just taken it. Nearly every Negro baby that takes it, dies. I suppose tis for want of attention. I heard that fifteen were buried near Holly Springs in one week.

    Gardens are beginning to look flourishing, notwithstanding the cold late spring. I expect cousin Mary is having irish potatoes every day now. She used to have them the first of May. Springs are earlier there than here. Have you ever planted the rose cuttings for me? How are the plants at the graveyard doing. Every plant I brought with me died except one little cedar* which is growing finely at the head of Jimmie's & Mollie's grave. Who is living at sis Carrie's old place.

    Write soon. My love to all, accept a share for yourself.
                          Affectionately your cousin
                          Cornelia S. Dickson

*Lula is Clara's daughter.

* The cedar tree is still there, 120 years later, at Sue Martin Russell's home

235   *After the War*

The Cedar Tree brought out from Autauga Co. Ala. in 1868 to plant at the heads of the two children who died the same day in 1867. Photo courtesy of Cora Russell Rogers.

Mary Elizabeth Boddie in Ouachita Co. to her sister-in-law Cornelia Dickson, also in Ouachita Co.

May 8, 1870 [approximate date]

Dear Nealy,

I have been thinking about you all ever since Uncle John left, & wanted to have gone over to see Sis*, but Sunday was such a bad day & I was afraid of the creek's being over the bottom — I deeply sympathize with Sis & the dear little children in their ailments & do hope Atalie is not so bad as Sis thinks. Their cough is at the worst stage now & if we could only have warm pleasant weather there would be doubtless a change for the better. Myself & children were nearly well of the cough previous to this last cold rainy weather. Bobby's eyes though are not all right yet, one of them, tell Sis, is as red as 'twas when we came home. Tell Sis the sore throat is not very pleasant but if she does take the "hooker, hookes"* she will wish she <u>hadn't</u> sure — miss you so much, Nealy, but I did not expect you to come home while Uncle J[ohn] is away. Sis needs you, I am glad, you are there, wish I could stay with her too, & if the creek dont get up again I will try and go one day. Carrie is having the third day fevers again — Mrs. Taylor spent three days with me last week & she is here now. We are making Mamie's Percale dress. Geo says tell Cats his <u>beans</u> are doing finely & that he has just brought in a fine <u>cat</u>[fish] weighing 28 lbs. & a smaller <u>kitten</u> which weighs 3 1/2. He set out his hooks yesterday eve in the river. I send Sis Hattie's letter I rec'd yesterday. I must get to work, Nealy, haven't time to tell you all the news. Tell Mit I am entirely in the dark about "the boat" & want to be enlightened. With dear love to you all, remain

Yours affectionately,
Mary E. Boddie

Tell Sis if the creek is so that I cannot go Sunday do try & send me word how she & the children are.

*Sis refers to Sallie Gildersleeve Rumph, sister to Mary E. Boddie, and Dr. John Rumph's second wife.

* A "hooker, hookes" is a drink of strong liquor.

Mary Love in Autauga Co. to her cousin Cornelia Dickson in Ouachita Co.

May 24th 1870

Dear Cornelia,

I exspect you think I am very negligent about answering your letters, when I received your last letter Ike Lanier & family were here, his children were sick & I had a great deal to do. Tom Caver promised me to haul your cotton off from week to week, I depended on him & he deceived me, since then the negroes on the plantation have been down with the measles, & it was impossible to get a team, I have made arrangements to ship it next week according to your directions, I am sorry, for I know you will be disapointed anything I can do for you, will be a pleasure.

Kate received your letter yesterday. She is staying with Hattie, I sent it to her this morning, she will be delighted, also one from Beck Peeples, Beck is going to school in Garden Valley, is much pleased, Neil we get some very amusing letters from Dick, his description of the people, the Texas Girls, & old Mrs Harvell, would make you laugh. Neil you must write to Hannah she would be so glad to hear from you, she speaks of you in every letter, sayes, "Mother be sure to send us all of Cousin Nelia's letters we want to hear from her so much." Oh, I forgot to tell you Hannah has a fine son, calls him William David, for his grandfather, Clem writes that he takes the shine off of Maud, but I cant think so, Clem sayes Ell is very much improved, Carrie Love & family are quite well, Irene left this morning with Ada. She will spend some time with her, I will have the children's Photographs taken for you as soon as I can, <u>many thanks</u> for <u>yours</u>, I neglected to mention it in my last. Crops look very bad, every thing is suffering for rain, the gardens are burnt up nearly. I dont think I will get more than two messes of peas, they are fired to the top, the cold has killed nearly all the fruit, Irish potatoes was cut down by the cold, wont yield but very little, Well for the neighbourhood news, Mrs Magness was sick a long time this spring is now recovering, Dick Holmes & Miss Ella Howard of Dallas are married, Dee Holmes & Mary Clark, dont you think they were a long time finding out they loved each other, Mag Houston & Dr Green Tompson will marry shortly, there has been a good many deaths among the old settled people, more than I ever knew in so short a time, Mr Jorden[?] is dead, his life was insured for five thousand, took out his polisy the day before he was taken sick, Old Preacher Dentoles & wife are dead, old Mrs Houser & Mrs Pierce Houser are dead, also George Stontamire, Col Sam Stontamire & Edmond Bickness. Amanda Howard lost a child recently, Hattie Underwood sends her best love to you, says you must write to her, she has four little children & no nurce, she calls her youngest Clarance Cole after the present Mrs. Andrews, she alwayes speaks of you so affectionately, I have not seen Mrs Clark in some time & understand she is in feeble health, Uncle Clems old Harry is dead; you wanted to know Hannahs post office, it is Garden Valley, Smith County, Texas. Lucy Souls is married to Mr William Powell, formerly of Lownes. Cousin Sarah Pickett & family were well the last I heard from them. Martha Woods has a daughter. Eliza Banks & Mary Gindrew are keeping boarding house. Fanny Darden's son & Austin Prickett are at college togeather in Tennessee, Neil look over mistakes & write soon, give my love to all the relatives, what a pleasure it would be to see you all, tell George I often think of him & Molly, indeed all of you, dont show this letter I cant hardly make the pen mark,

      Your affectionate Cousin
      M. A. E. Love

Cornelia Dickson in Ouachita Co. to her friend Mrs E. S. Clark in Statesville, Ala.

Sept. 9th 1870

Dear Mrs. Clark,

  Your most welcome letter of the 19th of June, I received in due time. It always gives me great pleasure to receive letters from my old home. I have been so much engaged with my school, & too, we have had company staying with us nearly all summer & I know you have been expecting a letter from me. Today is the first day in a good while that we have been alone. My school has been dismissed a week.

  I was not much surprised to hear of Dee's* & Mary's marriage though they were a long time finding out that they loved each other to be such near neighbors! Present my compliments & warmest congratulations to them. Julia is the one left chicken, & the hawks are after her. I think anyone would do well to get Julia if she is as amiable & industrious as she used to be. I often think of her & Mr. Holmes. Brother George speaks of Mr. Holmes as an esteemed friend. Soon after I came out here, I heard of a Mr. Howard who was murdered near Selma, Alabama. Was he of the family living at the Perry place? Homesteads have changed hands considerably since I left there, How does it happen that Phil Wood owns the De Bardelaben place? I think there was a law suit pending between Mr. Dick Morton's heirs and some of the purchasers of the land. How did it terminate? I believe Rube Underwood was interested, too. Who is Miss Laura Thompson? Have you ever paid your visit to Mrs. Stewart?

  Sis Mollie joins me in warmest love to Mrs. Lasiter. How is Mrs. Lane & where does she live now? Nearly every time I get a letter, some places have changed hands.

  I saw Ora Newton soon after receiving your letter. She seemed so glad to hear from you and asked me to beg you to come out & spend the winter with her. I know I would be so glad to see you, too. I think the change would be beneficial to your health. You can leave your household affairs with Mary and Dee. Probably, you will never have a better opportunity, & then, too, you can see all your relatives. Ora and Dee have a nice large roomy house. He has lately had it fitted over, papered & painted. They seem to live well all the time! I want you to think about it. You might catch a beau!

  I saw Annie Stone the other day. She says she was born in Alabama, but that she was called Martha Ann there. Her brothers Henry & Bob died in childhood. Her brother, William Avery married a Miss Ora Livingston Mary married Mr. Billy Pace. Lula, the only single one, is about ten years old. Mr. Henry Ross married Mrs. Avery's sister. Sis Molly saw her in town day before yesterday, says she is a fine looking lady.

  I spent a night at Cole & Julia Brown's last week. Mrs. Cole and her

*The Dee referred to here is Dee Holmes in Alabama, not Dee Newton of Ouachita County.

afflicted daughter are living at Mr. William Stone's now. Her daughter, Helen, is married again for the third time, to a Mr. Frank Jones of Camden, a widower with three children. Mrs. Cole is always glad to hear from "Cousin Eliza". I saw Mrs. Pile several weeks ago, she sends her love to you. Mrs. Williams lives in town with her daughter, Mrs. Holmes.

Clara has another addition to her family, a wee little girl. All her children are girls, Lula, Cora Lee, and the wee one. She has not named the baby yet. Lula the oldest, is a very bright child and so much help to Clara.

I have not seen Sally for some time. She sent down yesterday for me to come & stay with her a while, but I could not go. I intend going before long. Mittie has been having chills. Sally & brother J[ohn] ask me about you frequently and send their love to you.

I must close, insisting that you come this winter.

Your affectionate friend,
Cornelia S. Dickson

Editor's Note: Inserted here are two letters, concerning the efforts of brother John to recover some of his losses at the hands of the Union troops when they occupied Ouachita County during the war. In one of her letters to Cornelia, Clara described in detail the actions which resulted in extensive losses to many of the residents of the area. After the war Congress passed legislation establishing the Southern Claims Commission which enabled Southern Unionists a means of recovering some of their losses. He is pursuing legal steps to file claims against the government. The first letter is the response of a Washington lawyer to Rumph's inquiry; the second is a letter of recommendation from one of Rumph's friends to Powell Clayton, who was then governor of Arkansas, asking for his support of Rumph's claims. Also included is the list of losses as compiled by Dr. Rumph.

Letter from Washington Attorney R. T. Merrick to Dr. J. B. Rumph in Ouachita County

Washington D.C. May 20, 1871

Dr. J. B. Rumph
Dear Sir:

I am in receipt of your letter of April 20th in reference to your claim against the government for supplies used by U. S. troops. I will agree to prosecute your claim for a contingent fee equal to 25 percent of the amount that may be recovered, in case you can not pay any retainer or other fees in ordinary suits. Otherwise, I would charge a retainer of about $100 and a fee of about $400 or $500 after or upon trial. Most Southern claims come to me upon contingent fees, and while I do not prefer contingencies, such arrangements are generally most convenient to the Southern people. You can select for yourself which will best suit you. Even in the case of a contingent fee the claimant is, of course, expected to defray all the necessary expenses of testimony, witnesses, &c which at present are heavier than they need be, as in most cases this commission insists upon having the witnesses produced here before it, instead of having their testimony taken by special commissioners at their place of residence, as has been the rule in the Court of Claims. It would be impossible for me to tell what these expenses will be in your particular case without further data, as to the residence of the witnesses, the facility of getting them to Washington, &c. We might, however, have the testimony of some of them taken by special commissioners. In any case, a small retaining fee of $10, $15, or $20 is desirable to cover preliminary expenses of printing and other incidental matters.

If you will send me a detailed statement of your claim, including the specific amount, quality, and value of the articles supplied or used, the time when, and the circumstances under which the various articles were taken, as nearly as you can now determine, or ascertain, the names and residences of the witnesses who are to prove your loyalty, and the names and residences of the witnesses who are to prove the taking of the property, together with any other matters bearing upon the subject, I will fill up a regular Petition in form and send it to you to be executed before a Justice of the Peace and returned to me for presentation to the Commission. It is desirable that you send to me all papers on the subject in your possession, retaining copies for yourself as a matter of necessary precaution.

Upon hearing further from you, your claim will receive prompt attention.

Yours respectfully,
R. T. Merrick
per M.F.M.

Letter from H. A. Miller to the Hon. Powell Clayton regarding Dr. J. B. Rumph Camden, Ark.

Sept. 7th, 1871

Hon. Powell Clayton
Little Rock
My Dear Sir

This will be handed you by Dr. J. B. Rumph of this County. Dr. is a thorough going loyal citizen; having taken the oath of allegience to our government when Gen. Steele occupied Camden in 1864. He has since thoroughly and concienciously observed its provisions and in all other respects deported himself as a thorough gentleman in private life, and the good citizen in all his public relations. Genl Steeles Command took from Dr. Rumph property to a considerable extent for the subsistance of the same and for which he has put in a claim, as a loyal citizen before Commissioners of Claims in Washington City. His record for loyalty is clear and unmistakable; he is my personal friend as well. Therefore any personal assistance you may render in the matter will be appreciated by him and will also place me under renewed obligations.

Very truly yours,
H.A. Miller

LIST OF DR. J. B. RUMPH'S LOSSES TO FEDERAL TROOPS

50 loads of corn - 25 bu to load, @ $1.50 per bu	$1912.50
5000 lbs fodder @ $2.00 per 100 lbs	100.00
1000 lbs flour @ $6.00 per 100 lbs	60.00
300 lbs short. @ $3.00 per 100 lbs	9.00
1000 lbs HydSugar, yellow clarified @ 12 ½ cts per lb	125.00
4000 lbs bacon, hams, side, & shoulder @ 18 cts per lb	720.00
2 brls - 80 gals. molasses @ 50 cts a gal	40.00
100 lbs lard @ 20 cts per lb	20.00
12 head of pork Hogs - $8.00 per head	96.00
1 black mare mule, large, six yrs old	150.00
1 brown horse mule, " five " "	150.00
1 sorrel " " " " " "	150.00
1 Bay pony horse eight " "	100.00
1 sorrel mare five " "	150.00
20 bushels of wheat @ $2.00 per bush	40.00
100 lbs tobacco @ 50 cts per lb	50.00
	$3872.50

Cornelia Dickson in Ouachita Co. to her cousin Kate Love in Autauga Co.
May 28th 1871

Dear Kate,

Your most welcome & highly appreciated letter of the 22nd was received & read with a great deal of pleasure several weeks since, I am sorry that your other letter did not come to hand, for I always think I miss a great deal when a letter from Ala and particularly one from a dear relative or friend miscarries. I do not know the cause but would not be surprised if the cause lay with the post office in Camden, a set of stupid radicals have command there, I believe. My letters to Mrs. Clark and hers to me come & go regularly. She directs to Luda P. O., Ouachita County.

Brother John had come for me the day that I rec your letter. I went & stayed nearly two weeks up there. Since coming home, have had a chill, thought I was rid of them entirely, have not had one since before last winter. I enjoyed my stay at brother John's very much, had not been there to stay any since last Christmas, have had so much rain all winter & spring with half a dozen or more overflows, the roads most of the time were almost impassable. Sis Molly says it is a beautiful story to write back to Ala that we out here who live so near dont get to visit sometimes more than once or twice in six months.

Mit[tie] was very anxious to see your letter, says she thinks you might let her see them, asked me if I thought you might write to her. Mamie says she intends writing to you anyhow. Says send her your photograph & she will send you one as soon as she has some taken. Now Kate you know I *must* have one of yours without any excuse, have been waiting a long time for some photographs from Ala. It would give me so much pleasure to have all of my relatives & friends. Very often I am asked "Who does such & such one resemble?" Mit received a letter from Tom Love while I was there, with his Nubs & Adas pho. Nub looks very natural. Ada I should not have recognized. She looks almost exactly like Irene at her age; Brother John & George & sis Mollie says it is just like Sis Carrie when a girl. Ada has certainly inproved wonderfully in looks. May 29th, Was interrupted yesterday with another chill have been quite sick all the morning. Sis Mollie gave me a dose of oil & turpentine & oh, such a dose! I feel much better now dont mind having one or two chills but they generally get worse. This is a great country for chills & I can sympathize with Dick & Fannie. Tell cousin Mary I congratulate her on her good fortune, when it comes to pass & wonder if it is Mr. A. The old gypsy ought to have told her his initials. Of course I wont tell if you will tell me yours name. Be sure to tell me in your next. The 16th of May is past, of course you have seen him, describe him to me. You did not write me anything about Sis Carrie's fortune. Kate did you ever save me any strawberry seed, Mrs Tyuses kind. They are entirely different from these. The strawberry crop was almost a failure this year, we had three hailstorms about the time they commenced ripening, had two in one day & one a week after, the largest hail I ever saw & more of it. The other fruit is not materially injured, we have been feasting on apples, & raspberries, & currant pies some time, to mix the apples & currants or the apples & raspberries make the nicest pies. Brother G's May apple trees came from your Ma's garden. I wish we could get some of the Steele apples. I have not seen one since I left. Did you ever set me any cuttings of the Victoria Lamark &

Lula Dunlap, daughter of Clara & John Dunlap

Creole rose. I have not seen either since I came out here. The garden is rather late owing to the wet spring, is much better in Summer than Spring. Brother G plants all the seed & cultivates the garden this year. All the children are going to school to a Mr Alston from South Carolina, an excellent teacher, also a Methodist preacher. The children are delighted with him. Seven are from here. Have Sabbath School every Sunday at the schoolhouse, have preaching twice a month. So far, our neighborhood is improving. We do not visit much only when we can walk. Brother George lost his nag several months since. She fractured her hip bone & in exerting herself to get up smashed it all. Brother George never knew what was the matter with her til after she was dead, & tended to her faithfully for three weeks he was so attached to her, from this circumstance, When in battle his horse was shot from under him just as a retreat was sounded & the enemy were pressing him. Fannie, (his last nag's name) came dashing up to him, quick as thought, he seized the bridle, mounted & was off in time to overtake his company & made good his escape. He has had very bad luck with his cattle, too, in Feb lost five or six hundred dollars worth in one overflow, the water was freezing & they grew numb, could not swim out, had engaged to sell some of them as soon as they come up. Some of the finest milk cows, and then the chickens took it into their heads to die with cholera, more than half of them & all the turkeys. I attend to them this year, have had a great many hatched but so many have died, I have quit setting any more eggs. I can't tell you anything about going to see you next winter. I am out of a school on account of so many large boys to be sent to school the patrons want a gentleman teacher. But I would be so glad to see you all again. I often think of you all & wish I could visit you. Why dont cousin Mary write to me. I have not received a letter from her in nearly a year tell her I bet I can guess who she will marry. ... Who is living where Sis Carrie lived when I left? How does Sis Carrie & her children get on in their new home? What has become of Cousin Ike and family? What does Uncle Clem do with himself these days? We all think he might pay us a visit. I think he would enjoy a visit out here very much. So many neices & nephews desirous to see him & they are truly a merry crowd. Brother J & Mr. D[unlap] both have horses & buggies & he could ride around at his leisure. Mr D sends his horse & buggy down to Sis M & I whenever we want it now. Clara's babe is a large fine child, resembles Mr D more than the others. She calls it Estelle, but I think <u>Cora is the sweetest of them all.</u> Lula is old enough to be at school but has such an old head they don't want her to study for several yrs. She attends Sabbath School but

Cora Lee Dunlap aged 3 years, daughter of Clara & John Dunlap
Photos courtesy of Sue Martin Russell

* A safe was a kitchen cupboard used to store food in. The term was used in rural areas well into this century; indeed it may still be used by some of the older people today.

can't read, her Ma repeats her lesson to her about twice & she generally knows every word perfectly. Brother J says if she is properly trained will make a brilliant woman. Brother J's youngest, Eugenia, is the merriest little tomboy you ever saw, climbs up the back of her pa's armchair & turns a summersault in his lap, climbs up on top of the bureau to comb her hair, on the top of the shelf of the safe* to find goodies, on her Ma's machine to ride on the arm, scrambles out of the yard into the duck pond, (about waist deep to her), & tries to do like the little puddle ducks, & in just such mischief all day unless her nurse is with her all the time. She is not two years old yet. Mit[tie] is trying to learn her to dance. Attalie has grown to be very quiet & reserved, but a very sweet affectionate child. <u>Mit</u> is looking for a letter from Sis Carrie. Sallie grows larger every day, weight over two hundred, is very lively. Mamie wants to write to you, but dont know whether you will answer her letters, (Commenced one to you the other day but did not finish it) Johnie [Boddie] says George [Rumph] & Will [Boddie] are doing their best to cultivate a moustasche, but he keeps a long way ahead, says if you will send him yours he will send you a picture of the finest looking man with a <u>mouse colored</u> moustache you ever saw. He is the life of the house when at home, has several months respite now & at home most of the time. I get some rare jokes on him at times, he is so impulsive & impetuous. Sis [Mollie] says he grows more like her father every day. (He is such a figure as Mr Calhoun only larger. Says tell all his <u>girl</u> cousins to send him their photographs)

Kate, you must <u>be sure</u> to <u>answer all</u> my questions & write me about Clem, Ell, Dr P, the neighbors, too. I would like so much to see Dick & Andrew now, who are their lady-loves? The boys here have been sending boquets some time & are very fastidious about the arrangement of the flowers, & they must be appreciated too from the amount of little notes received in return. Well dear Kate if I keep on writing you will get tired reading. Sis Mollie sends love to all. My love to all the family & all my relatives & friends with a large share for yourself. Write soon. I never recd but one letter from you before this & replied to that.

Affectionately your cousin,
Nealia

W.G. (Dick) Love, son of Mary E.A. Love

P. S. Tell cousin Mary to write to me & let me know what Tom Caver did about the cotton last year, how is he getting on & how are Mammy & Jerry doing? Remember me to them. Old Billy asks me frequently if I ever hear from Aunt Flora & Mary Jane; sends howdy to them & wants to hear from them, has joined the church, was rejoicing that his fellow freedmen allowed him to join, he is very feeble.

C. S. D.

Cornelia Dickson in Ouachita Co. to her friend Hattie Murley, sister of Sis Mollie and Sallie, in Sunny South, Ala.

July 20, 1871

Dear Hattie,

Sis Mollie says she will write to you in a few weeks. Would have written when she first received your dear letter but brother John was working on her eye & she was up there most of the time, it is apparently cured. She is up there now & will remain several days longer. But you are wondering why I am writing to you. Ah! how shall I tell you & her father of our sad sad loss! Who of us had so much promise of a long life as our dear Sallie. Alas, that death should have claimed her for his own!

She was taken sick last Thursday evening, the 13th, on Friday morning, fever set in & continued until Monday, the 17th; at sunset, she breathed her last, sick only 4 days, died of conjestion. She slept nearly all the time Friday & Saturday. I asked her if she had taken an opiate that caused her to sleep so. She said she always slept a great deal when she had fever. We did not think her at all dangerous, though brother John had began to get uneasy about her, but did not tell us. Sunday, Sis Mollie came up. (I had gone up there Wednesday to spend several weeks) & Sallie seemed so much better but very weak, had been in a profuse perspiration every day, but her pulse never abated at all. She was very cheerful & said she thought she would be well in a few days now, told Sis M she had rather she would go home that evening & make arrangements to come & stay several days with her. Sunday night she was very restless & brother John was up all night but would not waken any of us, said we could do no good. About day, she said she wanted to go to sleep & turned on her side, brother J lay down by her & went asleep, but did not sleep more than a half hour & asked her if she wanted some cool water. She did not answer & oh what a shock it was when his fearful cry called to us that he believed she was dying. Alas, we were fully awaken to her situation when too late. Several physicians were immediately summoned and she revived somewhat through the day, but painful to tell, she could not speak to any of us, was at times fully concious & called the name of many who were around her & tried, O so hard to say something to each one but could not. I believe she knew that her time had come but seemed perfectly calm & signed that we must not weep for her. But it was hard to realize that we must part from one who [a] short time before was so full of life & spirits, So merry & joyous all the time. Ah, how we will miss her.

What greater consolation can I offer to her Father and Sister than to say that she lived a Christian, and though not a member of any visible

Andrew J. Love, Son of Mary E.A. Love
Photos courtesy of Sue Martin Russell

church, would have joined had there been a Presbyterian, the church of her choice, in the neighborhood. Let us trust that she is happily united to her little angels and dear Mother gone before, and that we all may meet again in that bright spirit land. She is buried by her little Kate & at the feet of Sis M's little Sallie.

Brother G[eorge], the children and myself except Bobbie came home yesterday evening, left all well except Bobbie who had a chill the day before, but was up running about. Sis Mollie says she will write to you in a few weeks, and that you must not wait, but answer this as soon as you receive it. She is so anxious to hear from you all.

Cornelia S. Dickson

Cornelia Dickson in Ouachita Co. to her friend Mrs E. S. Clark in Statesville, Ala.

Sept 6th 1871

Dear Mrs Clark,

I received your kind & highly appreciated letter of April 6th, I have been delayed in answering. We have been called upon to pay our last tribute to some one near and dear to us. Our dear Sallie Rumph was taken on the 17th of July. She was taken sick on Thursday evening. Her fever rose on Friday & continued until Monday evening at sunset when she breathed her last. I had gone up on Wednesday and expected to spend several weeks. She was very lively until Thursday evening. She did not seem seriously sick. Even on Sunday she spoke cheerfully about getting up in a few days. Another physician was sent for, but it was too late. Oh, what a dear, kind sister friend I have lost.

On the twenty-third of July, Millard Garmany, Mr Dunlaps nephew who lived with him departed this life after a long and painful illness, first caused by inflamatory rheumatism. He was a very promising boy about fifteen years old.

Then on the third of August, Clara's sweet little babe drew its last breath. It had been sick for some time but would revive, be clear of fever several days. Then without seemingly any cause, would relapse again. Clara has been sick, too but is now well.

Sally's two little girls, Attalie & Eugenia, have been sick since she died. Attalie is still having chills occasionally. I stayed several weeks up there while they were sick. Sis Mollie is there now and will remain several days longer. She is helping Bettie get ready to start to school next Monday. Bettie is going to Memphis, or near there to school.

Dear Friend, do not keep me waiting as long as I have you. My love to all,

Your affectionate friend,
Cornelia S. Dickson

Cornelia Dickson in Ouachita Co. to her cousin Kate Love in Autauga Co.
October 18th 1871

Dear Kate,

 Your most welcome & highly appreciated epistle of the 26th of Aug. was received last month. I assure you it was perused with great pleasure & I embrace this leisure hour to reply. I could have answered it ere now but Clara carried her children to town to have their pictures made & I waited to get them to send one but when they were brought home were so indifferent She would not have them & intends trying again. Mamie says she dont know when she can go over to have any, it takes all of her time Saturdays to write compositions & get her lessons. She feels the importance of improving every hour & I think is progressing rapidly, as are Will & Gilder also. They have a most excellent teacher. He married last month Mrs Julia Brown, Dee Newton's half-sister, a widow with two children, a very pretty, sweet little lady & they seem perfectly happy. I tell you what, Kate, when a widow sets her head to catch a beaux, she will gobble him up before anyone else can think about it. Mamie wrote to you soon after I rec yours, Sent it this time. Mittie wrote to you while I was up there about two weeks. I received a letter from Sis Carrie last month will answer it in a few days. Kate you ought to by all means have sent <u>me</u> one of your pictures. I think hard of you that you did not. Certainly I want one of Maudies, would prize it so highly. I feel so sorry for Clem & cousin Hannah, would have written to cousin H long ago but heard they had moved from Garden Valley, and did not know until the reception of your letter where they were. Tell cousin Mary if she ever has any pictures taken be sure & send me one & tell An[drew] he must not forget his promise.

 You have heard of the death of our dear Sallie, but you don't know what a sad loss it is to us all. Oh! how we miss her merry laughing jest, her kind & loving heart which made its influence felt wherever she went and at home with her loved ones more than anywhere else. It was a happy inviting house with her pleasant face ever ready to greet all who came near her. Mittie's is a severe trial, but she struggles bravely with her household duties, & shows that dear Sallie's example was not all in vain. She is a loving sister to the two little ones & they seem devoted to "Sis Minnie"*. Sis Mollie was very anxious to take the children, but brother John said he could not part with them, too, his home would feel more desolate still. He intends going on a camp hunt next week to be gone a week. Will & myself are going up to stay with Mittie while he is gone. Will will go to school in the day but [will] be there [at night].

 Brother George is preparing to recover his house & is making some alterations in the small rooms, says times are too hard to build a new one, is living in the same house he built when he first came out here.

---

* The small children probably called Mittie "Sis Minnie."

*Sideboards was a popular name given to whiskers in the late 19th century. Johnnie is John Rumph Boddie.

*A benedict was a term used for a married man.

Johnnie says his "sideboards"* are not quite long enough to venture on a picture & can't trust his face without it rather too lean he don't weigh more than a hundred & sixty, five feet & eleven inches in hight, wears a no. eight boot, says a gent who wears a no. four is not worth <u>a chew of tobacco</u>, says pick out a sweetheart for him in Ala, but be sure she is not already engaged; Says he intends to be a benedict* next November year if he is living. Says be sure & send him your picture when you have some taken.

I expect Mamie wrote you a glowing description of some of her beaux. She has one who wears a no. 5 & one who wears a 4. She says they'll do to talk to, but not to tie to.

You surely have a convenient memory Kate that you forgot the name of one of the gents who were present playing cards. Will you permit me to refresh your poor memory? You forget I have more than one correspondent. So you had better tell me all about it or your reticence may create suspicion.

Give my love to Rebecca Pebbles when you write to her. I would like so much to see her now. I often think of the pleasant weeks I spent at her fathers, will send her a photograph if I ever have any taken. Tell her to send me hers & cousin Leons too, where does she live since she married. My love & kindest regards to her & all the family. I am always glad to hear from them all & Ell too, would like to see him now. My love to Mary H & Julia, would send them & Willie my picture but have none at present. Tell them I would be delighted to have them send me theirs. Mr Dunlap says times are too hard to get a suit fine enough to have his picture taken & he is so large he cant borrow & so you must wait till he has to get a suit to attend a wedding. Clara says her health has not been good this year & is too thin to have a picture taken now. We had a good deal of fatal sickness last summer & you know C[lara] lost her little babe. Mr D[unlap]'s nephew who lived with him died also. I was very sorry to hear of Walter Wagners death, it is so sad to see a young man full of life & hope cut down so early. There was just such in-

*Hematuria is the presence of blood in the urine.

stance occured in a mile of us last month. A Mr Leattle had hematuria* and fever that terminated in something like yellow fever. His noble qualities rendered his death a sad loss to our neighborhood. To what part of Texas did Mr Wagner move.

It was I who sent the collar to Cousin Mary. I made it like one that brother J bought Mittie. Sis Mollie sent Sis H[attie] brother George's picture & I wanted to send cousin Mary some thing too. I am glad she likes it. Did you call on Sallie Nixon? I understand that Miss Nealie Newton had gone home with Sallie. I liked them both so much.

Little Carrie wanted to hear your letter read. I read it to her. She says, "Well, cousin Kate didn't say one word about me".

My love to all & accept a good share for yourself.

       Affectionately, your cousin,
       Nealie

Cornelia Dickson in Ouachita Co. to her sister Carrie Love in Autauga Co.
Jan 16th 1872

Dear Sis Carrie,

 At length I have taken my pen to reply to your long neglected letter dated Sept 3rd. I really thought that I should have written long ago, but on account of having so much sewing to do & constant interruptions, have put it off from week to week waiting a more favorable opportunity until a much longer time has elapsed than I intended or even was aware of until seeing your letter today noticed the date. Sis M & I worked early & late in order to get all the sewing done before Christmas that we might have ample leisure for enjoyment afterwards. We succeeded but alas short sighted mortals! The cook married & <u>left</u> New Years day very unexpectedly to us & left us at the cook pot & you know there is not much enjoyment flying round that. We spent Christmas week very pleasantly had a Christmas tree at the School house which afforded great delight to all participants, visited, entertained company, & attended several parties.

 In your letter you mention having written me several times. I have never received but one letter from you since I came out, until I received this, replied to that. I expect they go like some that I have written back to Ala. to different friends, I never hear from them again. Your letter contained a great deal of news to me. Some sad & some that surprised me very much, the most astonishing was that concerning your Demopolis property. — I remember when as a child of hearing brother Add & Ma talking something about it but what it was or how it concerned any of the family I never knew or thought to enquire. As to Ma's leaving any papers to you, I never saw or heard of that before & you are entirely mistaken about my ever telling you anything of the kind. All the papers that I ever saw were some old store accounts before the war, (those only I burnt) and some old recepts from Uncle Clem & others, and some old letters from Pa, Grma, & others all of which I have now & brother G has seen them all.

 Pa left a great many papers which were burnt after Ma had looked over them & found they were concerning his commission business & no use & she didn't want them thrown around and sent them out to be burnt up. It must be that circumstance that has become contorted in your imagination with the help of a Gipsy fortune teller that caused you to write all this absurd story to me. I am astonished at you Sis Carrie, you know me better. The idea that I would have done the least toward defrauding you of property is simply absurd & entirely foreign to my principles. It rather would have been my greatest pleasure to have had the power to aid, advance & promote you & yours for then you were dearer to me than anyone on earth. Besides if there had been papers that affected <u>your</u> interests, would it not have affected <u>mine</u> through Ma. You say that you forgive me. I have a clear concience that I have never wronged you or yours. I felt & knew before I left Ala that you were angry with me for some cause, but what it was I never knew, nor ever could have guessed. When Brother George read your letter, said he thought you were surely going to marry again. Brother John says as you believe in the fortune teller, & that you will be in affluence in two years, why not sit down & make yourself happy until that time comes. And I greatly fear I shall never have the happiness of being your bridesmaid.

About my feather bed that I left with cousin Mary. I do not wish to sell it. I had rather she would keep it til I can get it. Of course I expected her to use it as she does her own.

Mamie has just received a letter from Kate, will reply in a few days, is writing now. Says she has five letters on hand to respond to immediately, recd one from Hattie Murley several days since. All were well out there. The children have holiday now for two weeks when they will commence again, a subscription school this time, have the same teacher, Mr. Alston. Brother G will send only four; Will wanted to farm this year. Suffers with incessant headaches when confined to the schoolroom.

Carrie is enjoying a tea party tonight with some little friends at Mr W[illiam] Stone's given by Mrs Alston. Mamie came home all in a flutter this evening with the news that Mrs R[obert] Stone will give a party next week. Will be one of the elite parties of the season. Our boys & several other young men from town will be out and the band from Camden will discourse sweet music for the dance.*

*Note: There was no signature on this letter but there was a notation that read "I signed it."

Cornelia Dickson in Ouachita Co. to her niece Bettie Rumph, attending school at the State Female Academy in Memphis.

Mar 1, 1872

Dear Bettie,

I know ere this you have despaired of receiving an answer to your dear missive & have thought, "Aunt Nealie don't care anything for me" but indeed you must not think that for I have thought of you almost daily & with regret that your little heart would be wounded at my silence. I could have written immediately, but Sis Mollie said I must wait and let her write first as she had received yours to her several days previously. I complied with her request, & last month she told me that it seemed impossible for her to find an opportunity & that I must write to you. Since then I have not had a leisure hour until now, for this <u>cooking</u> business exhausts me entirely. You are probably aware that Becky has left us at the cook pot. Brother George has ordered a stove, but it has not yet come, will probably get it next week. He went to town today & I received a letter from Kate, Mamie one from

Jennie Weaver, Sis Mollie one from Mr. Davis an old friend in Ala. & Gilder one from his cousin Miss Hattie Murley. Kate's letter was quite interesting as it gave account of three or four marriages in my old neighborhood. All relatives were well. I have never heard of Tom Love's receiving your picture. Did you send one to him sure enough? I think Bet you slighted me, you must not do so again. I should be so glad to have one of you. Well, what shall I write next.

You have heard of all our Christmas festivities. How I missed you! Everything seems settled to the old routine of country life. Nothing new, yes now I have it. <u>Miss Piles</u> is to be married tomorrow to Mr <u>Walter Jenkins</u> So says Madam Rumor. Mr Marvin Moseley speaks of going to Ky. sometime next month. Says he would be delighted to call & see you if admissable as he expects to spend several days in Memphis. We tease him about <u>Miss Archer Hayes</u>. She spent four or five weeks at Mr Robt Stone's this winter, is very lively. Are you acquainted with her? She went up to see Mittie during her stay. Mittie, George, & Mr. Powell from New Orleans dined with us last Sunday. I expect you have had a description of the latter from Mamie as we formed his acquaintance at the party at Mr. Stone's, suppose you have heard of the death of Mrs Word* & W[illiam] Piles removal to town. Mamie says Jennie Weaver is at school in Camden, (bids Mamie send much love to you & says please send her your picture.) Mamie has been weeding among the flowers today, many have raised their dainty heads & are shedding their fragrance to our special delight. I sent Johnie a small bouquet this morning, he sends word that he will lend us the light of his countenance tomorrow. The saucy fellow, You ought to have seen him while he had the mumps several weeks ago. I told him he was a perfect <u>swell</u>. One day he ate an unusually large bait* of pudding for dinner & later in the evening ate some more, that night seemed to be quite uneasy, said he feared the mumps was extending toward the region of the heart, but appeared quite relieved when I suggested that it was the pudding.

Bobbie & Carrie speak often of cousin Bettie & count the months that you have been gone & before your return. Florence was quite sick night before last, but is up today. Says she has not written yet, but intends to write soon. Mr A keeps them very busy with their school studies is her excuse. Have not heard from your Father's this week.

All join me in love to you & your friends,
    Affectionately your aunt,
    Nealie

*"Mrs Word" refers to Amerial Stone Word, sister of Ora Stone Newton.

*Bait was a railroad term for food, especially on trains that provided Pullman service. However, Cornelia's usage would indicate "portion."

Bettie F. Rumph, attending State Female College in Memphis, Tenn. to her aunt Cornelia Dickson in Ouachita Co.

March 17, 1872

Dear Aunt Nealie,

I was very much surprised and also delighted a week or two since in breaking open a letter and seeing your name signed at the bottom. I can assure you that its contents were perused and reperused with the greatest pleasure imaginable. I was very glad to hear that you all were still enjoying good health with the exception of cousin Johnie and be sure and say to him that the next time that he eats so much pudding that he must think of me.

Oh Aunt Nealie how I do long to get home. We had blackberry pie today for our desert, and I declare you can not know how much they reminded me of home. Aunt Nealie, I am sorry that Becky left Aunt Mollie and yourself at the cook-pot, but I expect when Uncle G gets Aunt M a cook stove that she will be so proud of it that she will prefer doing the cooking herself, for a while anyway.

Aunt Nealie, I received a letter from cousin Tom, a very interesting letter giving me a description of the "wedding" and said he deserved a "twenty trinity." He wants me to come and spend the summer with him and his bonnie bride! But I thanked him for his kindness and told him that it has been so long since I had seen any of the loved ones at home that I was afraid I would catch a dreadful disease, "home sickness," and for him and cousin Julia to come and spend the summer with us.

Well, Aunt Nealie let me tell you how smart my room-mates and I were yesterday. First, we gave our room a good cleaning. Then Lucy Paxton wrote a letter and made the skirt of a dress. Lizzie Rogers and I made an apron apiece, and Fannie Atkins darned about a half-dozen pair of stockings, and she and I wrote a composition each. Do you not think we are smart for school girls?

Aunt Nealie, tell Willis, Gilder, and Carrie to write to me. I would be most happy to hear from them. Love to all and a share for yourself and a kiss for sweet little Bobbie.

Your affectionate niece,
Bettie F. Rumph

Cornelia Dickson in Ouachita Co. to her cousin Kate Love in Autauga Co.

April 12th, 1872

Dear Kate,

Your kind and affectionate letter of the 13th of Feb was received about a month ago. There were four letters sent out, but only one for me. Sis Mollie received one from Mr Davis, Gilder one from his cousin Hattie Murley, Mamie one from a Schoolmate & mine was from you, which was very interesting & gave me great pleasure. All have been replied to long since except yours. I have been having chills again & this time they served me worse than they ever have. I did not recover any strength for several weeks. I have fallen off in flesh fifteen or twenty pounds for you know I was very fleshy, weighed a hundred & forty-five. I did not feel that I could interest you. Am well now & take pleasure in replying to your letter, tho' I don't know when I will have the opportunity of sending it off as we are surrounded by the high water now. Gilder*, Carrie & I have just come in from a boat ride, the water is near the back gate, has been in the edge of the yard, but is slowly receding. Brother George succeeded in getting most of his cattle out this time, had'nt lost in any of the overflows this spring, but it keeps him busy & very much worried when the water begins to rise to get them up. They have such a splendid cane brake range, are loath to leave until sometimes they have to swim nearly a mile without finding a spot to rest upon. Had the water been a few feet higher we could have visited in boats. Such is life in Ark. Brother George is complaining this evening, thinks he had a slight chill, he had several last week. He says if I were to go back to Ala I would not be satisfied there now. Says he couldnt live in such a country. I doubt if it is any more unhealthy out here than there, for your letters at times contain sad intelligence of the death of some one that I used to know in days gone by and then again of the marriage of some who I think of as mere children, forgetting that four years, with its many changes, its burden of joys and sorrow have rolled into eternity. Well, we have a stove at last, brother G had quite a time getting it as the first orders were lost. It is the Philanthropist, there were none in town of that make & had to send to N. O. I never heard of so many different kinds of stoves. Clara has the Olive Branch; Mrs. Patterson Philanthropist; Mrs. Alston Charter Oak; Mrs. Annie Stone, Pacific; Mrs. Moseley Bucks Brilliant; Mrs. Norris our nearest neighbor the Star. Some others I don't know the make. But nearly all different. But they don't all do their own cooking. So far, I like ours best in several respects. We have concluded not to get a cook this year & don't mind cooking at all now. Sis M gets breakfast, I clean up the house & get dinner & supper. When we have company, the negro women on the place are very obliging & offer their services. I tell you, Kate, we had a laughable time learning to cook on the stove. Brother George said the Lord provided provisions but Old Scratch* provided cooks. Such are the failings as the coffee pot coming on the table at breakfast with boiling water minus the coffee & bread at dinner that looked like white mud baked in the sun. But we are learning fast, can bake a bird pie to a turn or anything else in the flour line, have not tried light bread. Carrie says tell you she cooked dinner one day while at home from school on account of rain. She & Florence are very fond of experimenting, cooking little knick-knacks.

*Gilder, George Gildersleeve Boddie, is the third child of brother George and Sis Mollie.

*Old Scratch was a colloquial term for the Devil in the 19th and early 20th centuries.

If they are as successful as Bettie R[umph], they will be quite expert.

We are unfortunate with the chickens, they have cholera again. We succeeded in raising a great many last year notwithstanding the fatality among them, had fifty odd to begin with, but they are dying fast, have about a hundred & forty little ones. Mamie says I hardly ever talk about anything that I don't finish with something about the chickens. I tell her my sentimental days are over. I can enjoy something more practical. I attend to the chickens. We are without milk or butter, something very unusual, lost so many of the best cows last Spring. Have a good many left, but they dislike to come through so much water to get home. The garden looks beautiful now. I counted 176 tulips in bloom yesterday, three double ones which resemble those large double poppies that Grma used to raise, have had no vegetables yet, the spring was so late did not plant until recently, will have radishes in a few days, Strawberries in full bloom. Kate did you ever save me any Seed of Mrs Randolph Tyus'es kind. Brother G is anxious to have them. Will you please save some & send in a letter. I would be so much obliged & any other little seed that you may please to send. Of all the plants I brought out here, only one little cedar lived, it is planted at the head of Jimmie's & Mollie's graves. I saw it last Sunday & it is up to my shoulders now, looks beautiful. We all dined at Mr. Dunlap's, had a large turkey gobler for dinner, was very nice, had lettuce & radishes. The high waters have prevented any passing from brother John's for several weeks.

Well, Kate, you will see something of our home life from this letter, if it should not prove very entertaining. I have an excellent picture of Johnie to send or I would send Andrew one of my gems tho they are very indifferent. We have been waiting patiently for yours & cousin Mary's, Kate. I also will send Rebecca Peebles one when I write to cousin Hannah. I think every day or two that I will write but have never done so yet. I wish she would write to me. I am always so glad to hear from her through your letters.

Johnnie bids me ask you if there is anyone in Ala as fine looking, but says you must not compare him to <u>boys</u> who wear no. 4 boots, says his weight is 174 lbs height 5 ft 11 inches, wears no. 8 boot & 7 1/8 hat. In love "knee deep". Says you must see <u>the</u> "sideboards". Mamie regrets she has'nt another picture to send you.

In Sis Carrie's letter, she said she wanted to buy my feather bed. I wrote her that I did not want to sell it. You know I may need it if I keep house for that entertaining widower, there is no probability of it now, but who knows what might happen, "While there's life, there's hope" you know. As it is I

John R. Boddie
Photo courtesy of Ruth Boddie Farmer

don't care to risk selling it, & cousin Mary will please keep it for me & use it as she does her own until I can get it.

Give my warmest love to Hattie Underwood, tell her to write to me. I know she can find enough to write about with so many interesting little ones. I am always so glad to hear from all my old friends & acquaintances. You must write me about everybody & everything you can think of. Your letters are read & reread by me every few days with so much pleasure. Tell cousin Mary to write. I cant excuse her. I have not received a letter from Mrs Clark in a very long time, is she sick or moved away? She was such a regular co-respondent. Give my love to all the family & all enquiring friends & accept a good share for yourself. Write soon to

Your affectionate cousin,
Cornelia S. Dickson

*I rec an interesting letter from Bettie R several days ago. She is well but getting a little home sick I think.

*Note: This postscript was written across the top of the last page.

Cornelia Dickson in Ouachita Co. to her cousin Kate Love in Autauga Co.
July 7th 1872

Dear Kate,

I have just returned this morning from a week's visit to brother John's. The girls came down last Sunday & insisted on my returning home with them, & as Mamie has vacation now & promised to do my part of the work while I was gone, I consented & a very pleasant time I've spent. But the pleasure would have been enhanced had I found leisure to respond to your most welcome epistle of the 28th of May received only several days previously. I suppose it must have been delayed on the route. Your letters always afford me so much pleasure Kate, for everything connected with my old home, friends & associates possess a charm more attractive than anything else, not even excepting Mittie's old widower beau she has been trying to palm off to me. By the way we passed his house on our way to a fish fry the Fourth of July, (not to celebrate the day but because convenient).* We all went in a wagon about six miles over the roughest, rootiest, stumpiest road imaginable, away down in a wilderness on the banks of a stream about a mile from a lake, near the end of the journey we entered a perfect <u>tunnel</u> formed of trees & vines enterlaced over head in some places so low, we had to bend under, this continued about a half mile when we emerged into a large grove & found horses, wagons, & quite a crowd gathered to enjoy a day in the woods & what little life there was left in me after my jolting found a lively interest in the surroundings, fished about five minutes, caught one little fish, but enjoyed watching others catch the little scaly tribe & others angling for bipeds* not scaly. Some of the gentlemen went over to the lake & brought

*Cornelia's parenthetical comment on convenience, not celebration makes one curious. Perhaps the Confederate States were not ready just then to celebrate Independence Day.

* A biped is defined as a two-legged animal; Cornelia makes a clever play on words, implying that the ladies were "angling" for the gentlemen.

fish to the camp by the bagful, we had an abundance of everything eatible & a large tent stretched to protect us from a shower of rain which lasted just long enough to freshen vegetation & cause dame nature to don her brightest robes to greet the sun as he rolled from behind the trancient cloud.

July 8. Well Kate I anticipated having a pleasant chat with you yesterday but was interrupted with company, but will now renew it. Bobby has been trying all evening to persuade me to go with him "just across the branch" to see a bear track made by "Sir Bruin" since the rain Saturday, says "Aunt Nealie let's go & carry the dogs & maybe we can have a race". I tell him <u>I feel most too tired to go "bear hunting"</u>. They [the bears] have not begun on the corn field yet, only prospecting to see where tis finest. Indeed the corn crop is very fine this year, has not suffered at all for rain. Brother George says he never knew a more favorable season on crops generally. I am so glad for he & Will have worked very hard this year, some times they seemed almost exhausted with fatigue. Since Mr Alston has given vacation, Gilder is assisting them in the farm & brother George now finds leisure sometimes to catch us a mess of fish when he goes down on the river to look after his cattle, every now & then he brings up a cow with a young calf, have five up now, Mamie has taken a notion that she must do the milking. I don't know how she will hold out but is doing finely now but will have to engage the services of our old milker again if many more comes up. Mr Alston's vacation is happily enjoyed watching over his <u>wee little heiress</u>, will resume school duties in Sept. Mamie's principal theme of conversation these days is education. Says she has learned enough to conclude that she don't know anything. She reads & studies hard, seems so anxious to be educated for a teacher. I can sympathize with her for I know just how I felt at her age. I craved an education more than anything in the world & I fear that Mamie like myself will taste the bitter dregs of disappointment, for brother George is not able to send her off to school, & Mr A will scarcely teach longer than Christmas. If I only had an education now I would be so independent & do so much good, it would be a fortune beyond the reach of desperation, but I must not suffer myself to repine for I have many many blessings for which to be thankful. And here Kate permit me to say how glad I am that you have improved so much since I saw you; for considering your great misfortune you write me very very interesting letters. Brother G would take your last from me & read it — now don't be angry, for he paid you quite a compliment — Says "Why Nealie she must be a very smart girl, has a good mind to write such a letter with so few advantages." And always write me about Clem, cousin Hannah & Ell. I am so glad to hear from them. I think every week I will write to cousin H but something happens to cause me to put it off from time to time & I have never written yet. I would be so very glad to see her & her dear little ones. In fact to see you all, so you must write me about all & then I can imagine I can see you & be sure & send me your photograph & cousin Mary's. Tell Dick he must have a picture taken for me.

Johnie says he was a little surprised at Uncle Clem's compliment as he had been told that he was growing like him. Says you did not say any thing about rending him one of your pictures & you must not forget that he is entitled to one. Mamie bids me say to you that she replied to your letter of Jan 6th long since & if she had another picture would send to you, but you must be content to wait 'til she can have some more taken. Says she's much obliged for the sweetheart you gave her which will be agreeable provided he will wait until her education is complete, which according to her <u>calculations</u> & <u>aspirations</u> will take four yrs, & in the meantime permit her to have as many out here as she choses, says what has become of Mr Holmes. I fear, Kate, Mitt is irrevocably wounded with you that you have never answered her letter, the more so as you solicited her correspondence. I was very much pleased with Mr Wadsworth's choice, for Tonie is a sweet girl & one whom I loved very much. You must write me all about the wedding, that is if you attend & about every one there that I know.

George is taking a holiday now & we had the pleasure of his company when he was not in the woods hunting or fishing or in the blackberry patch gathering berries for Mitt which she made into pies, jam, cordial or wine as suited her. Tommie worked at home in the farm this year but raised only corn & as his crop is nearly made he has some leisure to hunt, killed three deer in one day not long since. Brother John had only one or two patients & he & George were in quite a musical notion & every night would accompany Mitt or I at the piano with their flutes, discoursing sweet music "to while away the time." Bettie & Florence seem to enjoy very much being at home again & the little ones make the house alive with childish glee.

I regret very much to hear of Mrs. De Bardelaben's death. It is so sad to see a mother taken from her little ones. A man can replace a wife, but children can never replace a mother.

Well, Kate, it is growing late & I believe every one is in bed & asleep save myself, & if you remember, I was never fond of sitting up alone even when so pleasantly employed as writing to absent friends. So good bye this time. All join me in love to you all & accept a good portion for yourself. As ever,

      Affectionately your cousin,
      Cornelia

Cornelia Dickson in Ouachita Co. to her cousin Kate Love in Autauga Co.
Sept. 8th, 1872

Dear Kate,

Your most welcome epistle of the 10th was received several weeks ago, creating sensations of pleasure ever enjoyed on the advent of one of your dear letters. You no doubt think that I am tardy in replying but this is the first leisure hour that I have enjoyed since its receipt, (Will has just returned from the church saying there is no preaching today. We did not go because the mules are running in the cane brake & failed to come up, they generally come up once a week & we all go in the wagon, which seems to be the most popular way of locomotion here.) bearing tidings as they always do that afford much interest to us all, for they all want to hear your letters read, & brother George passed another compliment on your letter (he will read them, Kate) Says they are just the kind he loves to read, pleasant & without gossip, for that is one thing he can't endure. I was so glad too, to hear from all my old friends, notwithstanding they all seem too much occupied with the pleasures & duties of life to write to me, tho I have written time & again. I often think of Dr. Howard's prophecy in regard to corespondents, "That they would be numerous at first, but only for a short time & then they or myself would become negligent & from one or another cause we would cease altogether until I would become indifferent about hearing from any of them." Now I don't think the latter will ever be the case, if the former has come to pass to a certain extent.

Sept 12th Well Kate just as I commenced was interrupted with company but will now proceed. Mittie & George & Eugenia left this evening. They came day before yesterday eve. Yesterday George carried Mamie over to town as Johnie wished to have some of her teeth plugged, they returned this morning. Mittie & Little Pink (as we call her [Eugenia]) remained & we enjoyed so much having them with us. Mittie is very lively, accomplished in music. Eugenia is one of the most winning, sweet & interesting little mischievous witches imaginable, & now that they are gone we miss them so much. School will commence again next Monday, & then we will have a quiet time indeed. Mamie says she will write before long. She has been quite sick since she rec yours, but is well & looks as fleshy as ever. Carrie is the antipode of Mamie in flesh, says give her love to cousin Kate. Mamie keeps chattering so of her visit to town that it is in vain I try to keep an ear open to her & my pen on paper & as it has already become quite late will wait til tomorrow.

14th Bettie & Florence Rumph, Miss Nellie Elliot, & Miss Mollie Quillen spent yesterday with us & a lively, merry set they all were, teased Bet, calling her Mrs Tin-Cup, from this circumstance. When she was going off to school she met one of her old sweethearts from Louisville on the stage.

He was very polite & attentive. At one of the stopping places they found some difficulty in getting water or rather something suitable to drink out of. This gentleman said the next town they came to he intended to buy a tin cup, & if Miss Bettie would stop crying he would give it to her. Bet said she could'nt cry anymore after that for every time she commenced, she would think of the tin cup & the idea seemed so ludicrous, she would laugh. The young man was as good as his word, and when she came home, among other things, told Mittie of the incident. Mittie teasingly told her that "if <u>her</u> sweetheart could'nt give her any better present than a tin cup she would'nt have him." They always have some joke on first one & then another. Miss Elliot is spending vacation at home after two years absence at school in Shelbyville, Ky.

They had not been gone long before Johnie came to spend several days with us. We were all glad to see him for it is not often he gets leave of absence to come over now. This morning Messrs. Robbert & Slaten Stone came by & Johnie, brother George & Gilder went out to drive. This is the first time brother G has been hunting since last summer when his riding mule being lame he rode a little short gaited pony which gave him such a jolting as threw him into a spell of fever, the effects of which in the form of dumb chills lasted him several months. He says "deer hunting don't agree with him," has just come in; says the others had run the deer <u>clear</u> off & he was'nt going to stay by himself so came home, Said I threw the wrong old shoe at him when he started. I told him I was so intently watching them get off that I forgot to throw it at all until they were out of reach.

Mrs. Robbert Stone is in town to remain several weeks, their house is being plastered & tis not prudent for them to occupy it til it becomes dry. Mr Stone told me this morning that she & babe were both sick with having chills. I feel very sorry for her because of her misfortunes. On the third of this month she lost another interesting little girl which makes four children she has had to die. Strange, they all die when about two years old and all such sweet interesting little creatures. Little Iva, the last, was one of the brightest sweetest merry little fairy as ever lived & I loved her dearly. I stayed with them during her sickness nearly a week. We poured water on her head night & day & she was blistered on the spine from her head to her waist & on the stomach also. She was conscious most of the time too, poor little sufferer but all to no purpose, her sweet little frame was too thoroughly diseased to be relieved by medical aid & she sank without a struggle. It was conjestive fever that most fatal destroyer of children in this country. They have but one child now, a baby boy, about four months old.

I don't believe I ever told you about the death of Mrs Amerial Word. She died some time last spring. (The hunters have come in minus of venison). In my last letter to you I forgot to say anything about Clara or her family. She is in good health now looks fleshier than I ever saw her, has a fine boy born the 1st of August. Mr. Dunlap is so proud of him, says they hav'nt book's enough to find a name; Lula & Cora have had several light attacks of fever this summer, but I believe are well now. C[lara] sent us a fine treat of scuppernongs about a week ago, they have a very fine arbor. Brother G's are rather small.

Shall be delighted to receive the pictures but have been expecting them so long am afraid to anticipate for fear of disappointment. Why don't cousin Mary have some taken from herself instead of ambrotype*. I would like so much to see her now, in fact all of you. I would be delighted to visit Ala. for many reasons, but it is of no use to think about it. Mr. Dunlap speaks sometimes of going out there this winter, but it is uncertain. I would be so glad to see Andrew & to know that he thinks enough of me to come to these backwoods to see me. Sis Mollie says to tell him to come by all means. She wants to see him. Says she has despaired of ever visiting her father. Crops are so very short. Corn, I believe is very good, but cotton & every thing else is a failure due to the exceedingly dry weather, even the garden yields only irish potatoes and okra. The winter apple trees have all shed their fruit, even the figs fall off before they ripen, peaches, the few the frost left, almost dried on the trees; we had watermelons about the first of Aug by the wagon loads, but they did not last long.

Notwithstanding the excessively hot weather, we have all save Mamie enjoyed excellent health, in fact brother John says the neighborhood is distressingly healthy. *

*An ambrotype is a picture made by placing a glass negative against a dark background, a technique that is now obsolete and apparently was growing out of fashion in the 1870's.

*Note: There is no signature on this letter.

Cornelia Dickson in Ouachita Co. to her cousin Mary E. Love in Autauga Co.

October 4th, 1872

Dear Cousin Mary,

I have waited and waited a long long time in hopes of receiving a letter from you and in every letter from Kate she would say "Ma says <u>she will write before long</u>", but it seems you <u>never will</u>, content to hear from us through Kate, but that don't content me, Cousin Mary & if you only knew how delighted I am to receive your letters, how much they are appreciated you would not put off writing to me from month to month & <u>year</u> to <u>year</u>. I wrote to Sis Carrie last January but have never heard if she received it.

Well I wrote to Kate about two or three weeks ago, hope she has received it ere this. Was delighted to receive Dicks & little Maudie's picture last Sabbath, tell Dick I am so much obliged to him. I think he resembles uncle Clem's picture taken when he was young. Brother George says it is just like himself. Will says so too, Mamie says she thinks he is so handsome (by the way, she has commenced another letter to Kate). Brother G thinks

Andrew favors your father. And little Maudie. O what a sweet little creature she must have been! I could look at her beautiful shadow all day. I am so much obliged to you cousin Mary for sending it to me. I hardly know how to write to cousin H[annah]. I do feel so sorry for her & Clem. Send my love when you write to them.

 Clara & children spent last Sunday with us, all well, her babe grows very fast, have not named him yet. Brother John spent Tuesday with us. Said all were well. Was brimful of <u>political</u> talk. Indeed Radicals are carrying a high hand in Arkansas, but I'm in hopes their reign is nearly over. Since white men are allowed to vote, Brothers John & George seem to be very hopeful about the election. Attend Greely Club* meetings every Monday night at the school house. The radicals have Grant Club meetings every Thursday night at the negro church.

 Brother George says his crop will be short this year from the severe drouth, and I hear that you all are suffering from the worms so it seems that all are alike unfortunate. Speaking of crops brings to mind my object in writing to you at this time. I hate very much to trouble you cousin Mary. It is in reference to the cotton due me from Tom Caver in payment for our place. You know the terms of the contract and by <u>that</u> he was to pay me four bales of cotton, each weighing five hundred pounds, for the place & to have four years to pay it in, and if cotton went up as high as thirty-five or forty cents, I would let him off with less, but you know cotton has never been near that high. The contract was made the latter part of 1866, nearly five years ago, and the last bale of the four was to be paid in <u>Dec</u> 1870. The first payment for the year <u>1867</u>, he complied with. The second bale that was received for the year <u>1868</u>, weighed only three hundred & twenty four (324) pounds, as shown by E. F. Golsans receipt, which sold for 28 1/4 cts, So there was one hundred and seventy-six pounds due on <u>that</u> bale equal to $49.72 cts without interest. The third bale which was for the year <u>1869</u> was not received until in June 1870, and according to E.F. Golsans receipt, before me, weighed 488 pounds, sold for 18 3/4 cts. The fourth bale which was due in Dec 1870, I have never received, or heard of. Please see him about it cousin Mary for me, & read and explain this portion of my letter to him. I thought that if he <u>was</u> a negro he would try to do what was right and what he agreed to. I thought he surely had honor enough not to deceive me & make me lose by his neglect. I have trusted and waited this long because Clara nor I didn't need the money then, and for the sake of the kindness and good wishes I used to have for him & his family. I hope he will <u>make it right</u> and not <u>deceive me</u> for I should be sorry to be disappointed in him. Urge him to be explicit in what he intends to do. Be careful and talk to him in the presence of witnesses, write it down, and write to me forthwith. Keep this to yourself cousin Mary please until after you write to me. If you will confer this favor cousin Mary you will so much oblige me. I am sorry, very sorry to have to trouble

*The Greeley Club was a political group supporting Horace Greeley in the race for president against U. S. Grant. Greeley was nominated by a faction of the Republican Party, known as the "Mugwumps", and also by the Democratic Party. He was defeated.

you, but then I place myself in your position & you in mine & I know I would do it for you.

I have not much news of importance, have not much variety in the regular routine, visit occasionally, no weddings or deaths, has been but one death in the neighborhood this summer.

George Rumph & partner will be receiving their new goods next week. Sis Mollie & I seldom go to town, save on a shopping expedition. Mamie went home with brother John to spend the week. I don't know when she will finish her letter to Kate. She commences one about every two weeks. There is a <u>probability</u> of school commencing next Monday. It was to commence the first Monday in Sept, but has been put off from time to time in consequence of Mr Alstons bad health.*

*Note: This letter in the ledger ends abruptly at this point.

Cornelia Dickson in Ouachita Co. to her cousin Mary E. Love in Autauga Co.

Nov 7th 1872

Dear Cousin Mary

I was exceedingly rejoiced a few evenings since on receiving your kind letter and to hear that you were all well. Hope Andrew is entirely recovered in this time. Was glad to hear from Clem, cousin Hannah & Ell. Thanks for your prompt attention to my request. It was like you have ever been cousin Mary and I felt sure you would do it for me. I hope Tom Caver will hand the money to you. When the money is paid to you, you can send it to Lewis Golsan of Autaugaville, or his agent John Herman & get a check from him on the Colson brothers New Orleans, subject to the orders of <u>Cornelia S. Dickson</u>, & then send the check to me and I can very easily get it cashed by their agent with whom I am acquainted in Camden.

Tell Tom Caver I will make out the title & get Mr Dunlaps & Claras signature with mine and for him to place the bale of cotton in your care, in <u>trust not to be sent off until I send you the letters & he gets them</u>, then you will please send the bale to Golson brothers, subject to the orders of Dr Rumph, as before, but be sure & see that the bale weights five hundred, please, and let me know when you get the cotton that I may send you the title forthwith. I hope this arrangement will be satisfactory as I want to do only what is right & fair. And cousin Mary if there is any expense about hauling &c I don't wish you to bear it, for you have been so very kind in the matter. You can deduct it from the money before you get the check, &c &c.

I am glad to find I was not mistaken in Tom Cavers character and I believed that if I could explain the business to him he would be willing to do right, for as long as I knew him before he was free he always seemed to be disposed to act right, a virtue that should be commendable in him. I don't blame him for trying to be particular & honorably taking care of his interest. So I hope he will agree to this arrangement, and when he gets the titles he will feel satisfied and I wish he may do well.

I felt assured that Mr Tom Underwood had certain reasons for not granting my request though I was not acquainted with them. And had I never known them my confidence in his friendship to me would not have been lessened, for he & his family will ever hold a prominent place in my record of friends and am always glad to hear from them cousin Mary. My best wishes to Dr Howard. I sincerely hope he will be elected Senator. Do you ever see his family? I very often think of them & wonder why Julia ceased writing to me, let me hear from the elections. Do you ever see or hear of Mr Jack Davis, Sis Mollie received a letter from him sometime last winter. She was so glad to find that the old gentleman remembered her; & wrote him a long letter in reply, but has never heard whether he received it. She says she esteemed him next to her father and is always delighted to hear from him. Heard from Hattie. I was so gratified in getting yours & cousin Williams picture, both seemed so natural and in looking at them I was carried back into the depths of the past & again beheld you all as in the days of yore. Brother George, Sis Mollie & brother John said they would never have recognised yours at all, but cousin Williams was perfect. Clara too asked me who yours was. It seemed strange cousin Mary and you appeared so natural to me. Sis Mollie says she wants to see you[1] now worse than ever & see if she cant trace some resemblance to the Mary she used to know, Sends love to you all. Clara had named her baby Walter. Mr Dunlap's selection, I believe. I wanted her to call him Hugh.[2]

Cornelia Dickson in Ouachita Co. to her cousin Mary E. Love in Autauga Co.

Nov 11th 1872

Dear Cousin Mary

You will no doubt be surprised to receive another letter from me so soon, but I forgot to mention in my letter to you of the 7th inst the time of the sale of the cotton there alluded to. It was sold the 10th of April 1869 & to the 10th of Nov 1872 the interest at 8 per cent on the $49.72 would be $14 and some cents, tho I am not particular about the cents. In case you have

Mary E. A. Love, wife of Wm Love—mother of five sons and one daughter, Kate.
Courtesy of Sue Martin Russell

[1] Inserted here is apparently a set of notes which Cornelia made of subjects as they came to mind that she wished to detail later in the letter: Bear hunting & den &c. Protracted meeting & results. Johnie joined church, Camden. Visit to brother John's. Scenery Autumn &c. Am looking for a letter from Kate, love to Hattie & babies

[2] Note: We have another truncated letter in the ledger, which leaves us wondering if, in the mailed letter, she developed the subjects noted above.

not rec that letter, I will again mention how you can send me the money &c if Tom Caver hands it to you. Send it to Mr John Herman of Autaugaville. I fear you may think me over careful Cousin Mary, but when you remember there is a probability of your never getting my letter of the 7th you will excuse the repitition. As so many of my letters seem never to have reached their destination.

There is not much news. Mr. W Stone came by last Saturday in his double seated buggy & carried Carrie & Bobbie with his two little grandchildren, Effie & Coleman Brown to the Big Show. Mrs Annie Stone's little sister, Lula Avera, went with them also, & a bright pretty merry crew he had with him. They remained all night in town & had a great deal to tell when they came home. There was a negro shot during the day of the show & the negroes in town & country are very much incensed. Tis thought they may attempt to break the jail and lynch the man who shot him. They are somewhat disappointed in the County elections and seem consequently in a very ill humor. Both negroes on brother George's place voted the Greely ticket, but not by any persuasion on his part. Said wanted to do like white men, as they had heard both sides. I am real tired of politics, so we will leave it all to the men.

Brother John called this evening on his way home from town. Says he wants to start day after tomorrow on a Camp hunt. They seem to enjoy those hunts very much. Will be gone over a week. Mrs. Alston came over today and invited Sis Mollie and I to a sewing at her house day after tomorrow, but made me promise to come tomorrow & help her cut out her work, a promise tonight I feel very much inclined to break. Have a severe cold, been almost sick today. Seems to be a prevalent epademic through the neighborhood for nearly all the family are affected with it, and there was a young man here this evening who could hardly talk for Snivilling & Snuffing. I would like to write more but tis so late will close with love to all. Give my love to Mammy when you see her. Tell her I shall never forget her. Write soon. As ever

      Your affectionate cousin,
      Cornelia S. Dickson

Cornelia Dickson in Ouachita Co. to her cousin Mary E. Love in Autauga Co.

                  Jan 28th, 1873

Dear Cousin Mary,

Your long expected & kind letter was received week before last. I was delighted to hear from you all again. Tho sorry that you were compelled to wait so long on Tom Caver. I feel disappointed that he failed to fulfil his promise, thereby giving you so much trouble. I would have replied to your letter immediately but was from home, at brother John's & did not get to see Clara or Mr Dunlap until last Saturday. Please tell Tom Caver, cousin Mary that I will wait another year for the bale of cotton if he will send the Sixty-five dollars immediately. I am sorry to hear of his short crop, was in hopes of being able to settle the business this winter, hope he will make a good crop this year and be ready to settle for the titles by next January. You say he has rented Mrs Lassiter's land. On what terms? His boys are large enough to be a great help to him now. Poor Harriet. I often think of her and her faithfulness to my dear ma.

Tell me of Mrs Lassiter & Bettie, do they enjoy good health. I have not forgotten the little scamp that went to school to me. Give my love to them all. Is Jallie Mixon married yet.

Well cousin Mary I scarcely know where to begin to tell you any news for fear of its being stale, for Mamie wrote to Kate about three weeks ago, and Mittie wrote to Fannie while I was at brother John's, Said she would write to Kate before long & not knowing what they wrote about you may be wearied with a repitition, conclude though that they have given the details of our Christmas festivities, weddings, &c.

Bettie R[umph] returned from Camden day before yesterday having officiated as bridesmaid at the most brilliant wedding ever celebrated in Camden. That of Miss Mattie Milnor to Mr. McMahon. The bride's trousseau as well as the greater portion of the supper was ordered from New Orleans. Johnie was one of the groomsmen & he & Bet were rapping at each other all day about their appearance. Bet said anyhow, she & her attendant were said to be the handsomest couple on the floor. "Pshaw" said Johnnie. "Cousin Bet, you looked very well, but it was Miss Berric & I that was said to be the finest looking couple!" Bettie says she had two beaux while in town, but she did not know whether to take the one that <u>Lide</u> or the one that <u>Bragg</u>-ed."*

I came home last Saturday having spent over three weeks at brother John's. The first week, Mittie was just recovering from severe cold contracted while in town before Christmas acting as bridesmaid to Miss Mamie Winfield who married Mr. T. C. Powell. The next week was one of confusion & bustle getting Bettie ready to attend Mattie, & the third week, brother John was quite sick threatened with pneumonia. Says now he thinks his disease is very similar to that affecting the horses. Mittie and the children were similarly affected & I have not been able to speak in a natural voice since the second day I went up there, from cold. Mr. Dunlap & Clara & children too have had it, C is not at all well yet. All well here except Bobbie has cold from running out in the snow so much.

Mamie says I must not forget to tell you about the snow. She is eating a large piece now. I told her I would scarcely forget to mention the largest

* Bettie has created a wonderful pun here. The Lides and the Braggs are two of the oldest and most respected families in Camden.

snow I ever saw, it fell last Saturday <u>six inches deep</u>, has not melted any at all & commenced snowing again today, is several inches deeper. Brother George says it is the severest winter he ever experienced in this country — more continued cold weather. The Washita river was frozen over nearly half an inch thick during Christmas week.

Tell Kate I have been long expecting a letter from her. Will tell her what I think of her picture when she sends <u>me</u> one. I think Julia L. has selected a pretty name for her babe. I am always glad to hear from Hattie and all my friends in Ala. Tell Kate to please ask Julia Howard by whom is the <u>Russian March Duette</u> that she & Emma played. Also <u>The Captive Knight</u>, a song. The first Carrie & Mamie want & the latter for Mrs Alston. What has become of Mrs Clark. I never hear from her now. Tell her I have a beaux selected for her out here, in view of her making us a visit. Sis Mollie received a letter from Hattie last week. All well. Mattie is at school but I forget the name of the place. She is Primary assistant as well as pupil.*

*Note: We have another abrupt ending. Perhaps Cornelia started leaving off the final paragraph and signature in the ledger because of lack of time. Certainly such omissions are understandable, for she is an enthusiastic letter writer.

Cornelia Dickson in Ouachita Co. to her cousin Mary E. Love in Autauga Co.

April 5th, 1873

Dear Cousin Mary,

Your most welcome & long-looked for letter was received about a week ago, and as it was dated the 8th of Feb, [I] see that the long delay was owing to the mail, for it was due in ten or twelve days from the time it was mailed. I am glad to hear that my letters are always cheering, only wish that it was so that my traveling expenses were as light as theirs, that I might enjoy being with you all again, but it is no use to wish. Your letters always afford me, & in fact all of us, a great deal of pleasure and if we can not have every thing as we wish we have much for which to be thankful. Truely health is one of our greatest blessings and as long as we are favored with that we should not repine.

Tell Kate she must not throw my letters aside because you write to me, for she can find a great deal to write about to me, besides what she writes to Mamie. I recd a letter from Tom Caver prior to yours, he wrote telling me of what he had done in regard to the place & his reasons &c & wanted me to inform him by personality what I intended to do about the titles. Seems that some one has been making him believe that he would never get them & prejudiced him about receiving them from a lady, & you know, in their want of knowledge they are very easily influenced against those who would befriend them. I wrote him that I wished him to pay the money to you to send to me. And here cousin Mary let me say how sorry, yes, how very sorry I am that you should be so annoyed with my business. I had no idea at first that there would be so much trouble to you in getting the money.

And Ellen is near you. I should like very much to see all my old servants. How many children has she! Brother George says he can't blame the negroes for leaving the poor red hills of Ala. I tell him there is some as good land in some portions of Ala as there is in Ark, those old red hills are no criterion. He knows it too but loves to brag on Ark, & indeed most of the land in this bottom is very productive, but considered by some to be sickly. Mr Robt Stone, for instance has a good deal of land that he says produces nearly a bale to the acre. I am boarding at Mr Robt Stone's now teaching school, have a doz pupils, walk nearly two miles. From brother George's was too long the walk.

Sis Mollie received last Tuesday the sad intelligence of the death of Mr Gildersleeve, who departed this life the 19th of March after an illness of about ten days. He had erycipelus* in both legs below the knee, but this had been checked and was getting well, but his age was such that the drain upon his system in his feeble state of health was too much. He passed away with little pain. We were rather expecting to hear of his death from the tone of Hattie's last letter. She wrote that her father was growing more feeble every day & Sis Mollie said she was almost afraid to hear from him again. And if you know anything of the deep affection she cherished for her father, you may know how very hard she takes his death. Indeed, she has scarcely been the same since dear Sallie died. I wished to go & spend tonight with her. Mrs Stone was quite sick last night & this morning but seems much better now, and I think I will go. Last Saturday & Sunday was the first that has passed without my visiting them, but Mamie & Florence spent Sunday eve with me. The latter is one of my pupils. I have a general review the first Friday in every month, the patrons are invited. Yesterday was review day. I saw Clara. She sends her love, her babe is the finest boy (so Mr. D thinks) in Ark, weighs about thirty pounds & as lively as a cricket.

I was glad to hear from my old friends & pleased to learn that Louis Whetstone was so promising. I know it is a great satisfaction to his mother's heart to have such a boy. And Tallie Mixon is married! I guessed as much but was surprised to hear of George's marriage to Tony, had either heard or thought she was married to some one else. I am always glad to hear from Hattie. Give my love to her. I guess Rob & Minnie are large enough to go to school. I have been thinking, ever since I received your letter, that now that cousin Hattie was settled, I would write to her. I am always very much gratified to hear from them all in Texas.

I have not seen Mittie or Bettie in three weeks, met Tommie going to town last week, said all were well. Brother John stays closely at home nursing his garden I suppose as that is his pet every Spring. By the way, we had a snow & freeze the 25th of March that killed all the vegetables except peas & radishes. We had our first mess of radishes today. I fear nearly all the fruit

*Erysipelas is an acute, febrile infectious disease, caused by specific streptoccous, characterized by diffusely spreading deep-red inflammation of the skin or mucous membranes.

is killed. I would so much enjoy eating fruit with you all this summer. Tell Dick & Andrew they must think of me when the fruit ripens. My love to them & all enquiring friends and accept a share for yourself. As ever

Affectionately, your cousin,

Cornelia Dickson in Ouachita Co. to her friend Bettie Lasiter Whetstone in Autauga Co.

June 7th, 1873

Dear Bettie,

The letter accompanying yours I received about a month since, and I know you have been expecting long ere this to receive a reply, but with my school & other duties always on hand, I have postponed writing, waiting when I could devote a large portion of time in replying that I might feel as if I were talking to you, and though not a day has passed that I have not thought of you, a much longer time has elapsed than I had intended. Indeed time now does not seem as it used: for day after day, week after week, & month after month flies away before I am aware and I find it useless to wait a more favorable opportunity. I had heard of your mother's feeble health through Mrs. Clark's letter. I am so very sorry, hope she may recruit* again now that pleasant weather has commenced. You have no idea Bettie how it distresses and arouses my sympathies to hear of the sickness or troubles of my old friends and your mother & your family have always held a prominent place in my affections.

Have you any children besides Louis, Annie & Minnie? I would be glad to see them all. I hear that Louis is very promising. You don't know how rejoiced I am. I know he must be a source of comfort to you. A noble boy is such a blessing to a parent. Clara, too, was glad to hear from you, sends her love. She also has her little world at home. Her youngest is a son, calls him Walter, is the best babe you ever saw & Mr Dunlap thinks there never was such a boy except their oldest who died the summer before I came out. Their little Cora is a plump little darling, loves dearly to be petted by aunt N. Lula is more delicate, very studious, & ambitious at school, was perfect in almost everything in her last months report.

I went down to brother George's Friday evening, did not get back until Tuesday evening, was sick with flux, which seems to be an epademic in the country, though not very malignant. Since then I hear that Sis Mollie has no help at all, the girl that she had became so trifling that she sent her off, and she & Mamie do all the cooking, house, & dairy work now besides sewing. They have a milker, washer, & ironer, but the family is large & with so much to do, I fear Sis M will not be able to stand it, more on account of her eye which threatens to inflame again from constantly going over the stove.

*The *Random House Dictionary of the English Language, Unabridged Edition* cites as its 10th definition of *recruit* "to recover health, strength, etc."

There has been so much rain that nearly all the farmers are "in the grass." Brother George works again this year with his two boys, says "work goes very hard with him in hot weather, with so much grass." Vegetation is of very rapid growth here and what is done in the farm has to be done speedily, or crops will be a failure, I met brother John & Mittie yesterday morning going over to Camden to be present at the young ladies' concert & exhibition last night. The examination has been going on since Tuesday. The annual picnic is to come off today. I had an invitation & should have very much enjoyed attending all, but my school could not be neglected. Mamie was preparing to go over but unfortunately had been vaccinated the week before and was suffering with her arm, had fever several days.

I believe your relations out here are prospering & enjoying good health. Dee Newton spoke of writing to your mother shortly. Give my warmest love to your mother tell her I want to see her very much. My love to all enquiring friends and accept a good share for yourself & family. Write soon and a long letter and be assured of the kindest regards of

Your affectionate friend,
C. S. Dickson

Cornelia Dickson in Ouachita Co. to her cousin Kate Love in Autauga Co.
Sept. 1st, 1873

Dear Kate,

I have three letters on hand waiting replys, but as yours came first will proceed to reply to it first. It was during my school term that it was received & my time so much engrossed with those duties, days warm & tiresome nights short, I put it off until my school was dismissed & what with company, picnics, cooking, sickness, &c I have not been able to fulfill my intentions until now. I have had several attacks of fever this summer, besides chills, in fact have not enjoyed good health this summer. The first week after school, I spent at brother John's & on the fourth of July, attended a picnic & fish-fry on Tulip [Creek], the same place we spent the day the year before. The road was not quite so rough. We had a lively time particularly when after dinner in gathering up the dishes several ladies, including Mitt, were in a romp with old Mr Brodnax. The old man is about eighty years old but is very lively & full of mischief. He commenced throwing pieces of bread & bones at the girls which they returned with a good will & for a while it was quite diverting to see the dodging on both sides. But the most amusing thing that happened Mitt pretended to aim at Mr B with a ham bone, but it landed plump on the enormous <u>bread basket</u> of her <u>old</u> widower, nearly upsetting his dinner & causing him to send forth a prolonged <u>grunt</u> which startled Mitt almost as much as the bone did him. She hastened to ask pardon, said she "really aimed at Uncle Hal," but he took good care to watch the flight of her missles after that, & dodge all that came near him. Soon after dinner, all proceeded to a neighbor's house & spent the evening dancing. <u>We have had several picnics since,</u> but I presume Mitt has told you of them. The last neither Mitt or I attended. She was just recovering from an attack of fever not able to be up & as I was there remained with her that Bet & Florence might go. It was quite a success save the music. I remained with them two weeks.

Brother John was, and is still very much occupied with his practice. There is a great deal of sickness in the neighborhood this year. He remarked about three weeks ago that he had already done more practice this [year] than he did all of last year. The health of this portion of the neighborhood has been very good so far tho. I came home yesterday a week ago & found Mamie sick. Her fever lasted until Wednesday evening. She is up now, speaks of going to town this week to spend several days with some of her schoolmates. She is looking for a letter from you. She wrote & thought she had sent it off but had really laid it in a book she had been reading. She went to spend the next week with Mitt, & while absent I found the letter & sent it off. Mitt wrote to you about three weeks ago. Mitt has an idea that you intend to marry soon Kate, but I do not share [that idea]. In your letters to Mamie & Mitt you ask why don't cousin Nealia write. I must ask the same question about cousin Mary. The last letter I received from her was dated the eighth of Feb. I received it the last week in March & replied the fifth of April. I have been expecting every week to get a letter from her.

In one of your letters to Mamie, you said that Mims Howards called his son Lamar. I had never heard that he was married again. Whom did he marry the second time? I believe Mamie forgets my messages as soon as I cease telling her, I very often ask after she has dispatched her letter if she wrote such & such to hear her exclaim "Dear aunt Nealie I forgot all about it! I was thinking of so much. You write." I surmised as much from never receiving any replies.

Gardens this year are "run away" with grass & weeds, from so much rain in the spring. All available force was kept in the fields that the crops might not be a failure, as it is corn is not very good, cotton only tolerable, though it may produce well, if not attacked by the worm*, which I hear has made its appearance in the neighborhood.

The most exciting theme in the neighborhood is the Ouachita Valley Railroad from Arkadelphia to Camden, the surveyors passed down several weeks ago & run the line about two hundred yds in front of brother John's house & about thirty steps from brother George's front gate. Brother George don't like its coming so near, says he expects he will have to move.

Sis Mollie sends her love, says if you do get married, include old Rackensack in your bridal tour. She & Will, Bobbie & Carrie returned yes-

* Cornelia refers to the "boll worm" which punctures the boll before the cotton makes.

terday from several days visit to brother John's. Clara was there also but not very well, had a light chill & fever but not sick enough to be in bed. Her children were all well. Her "big boy" is considerably reduced from teething & an attack of fever about a month ago. Well Kate one Scriblers a month is quite enough I think so I will not trespass on your good nature any longer. Write soon, & remember your promise. My love to all the family & all enquiring friends. As ever,

      Affectionately, your cousin,
      Cornelia S. Dickson

Cornelia Dickson in Ouachita Co. to her friend Eliza Clark in Statesville, Alabama

                 Oct l8th, 1873

Dear Mrs. Clark,

  It seems that every letter that I write to you must needs contain a list of excuses or apologies, for my tardiness in answering your dear letter. I always have so many things to prevent a prompt response that you must "take the will for the deed," for indeed it would be such a great pleasure to me if I could be always expeditious in replying; that I might the oftener receive yours; But there is so much as company, picnics, sickness & household duties to engage my attention that time flies very rapidly, weeks & months slip by ere I am aware.

  Your kind & interesting letter was received in due time & read with much interest. And I was deeply grieved to hear of the death of one of my best friends. In the common course of nature, I did not expect her to live a great while longer, but I was unprepared to hear of her death so soon. I had hoped to rec a message from her in your letter. Ah! if I should visit Ala I would miss her so much & the warm greeting that I should have been sure of receiving. But away with my selfishness when she is now enjoying the rest of the blessed, & we can all hope to be united when our probation on earth is ended.

  I have received Bettie's letter, will reply to it shortly. I have resumed my school again, a free school this time. I walk from brother George's, was feeling so well this fall, I concluded not to board out.

  You will be lonely indeed if Callie & Austin leaves you & you remain at home. I do so wish you could come out here, but I can find no situation for you or C as school teacher, probably might get you a situation as <u>housekeeper</u>, if you say so, though I believe the salary is only <u>board</u>, & <u>clothes</u> & with <u>some</u>, a <u>grumble</u> about the <u>pin money</u>. There are <u>some</u> widowers around here wanting housekeepers, & I hear that several has succeeded in <u>engaging young ladies</u> to take charge in the course of a week or two. Now, don't think that I mean Mr Avera or Mr Stone, for I do not know of either of them waiting on any lady whatever. Probably they think they are too near their grave to again commit matrimony. I have not seen Mr A in several months. I called at Mr Stone's yesterday evening. Mrs Julia Alston [his daughter] came down to spend several weeks with him & see if the change would not benefit her little Yaidee who has been sick & declining several months. She is reduced to a literal skeleton. This morning they sent for Sis Mollie with news that she was dying. Mrs Dee Newton is spending several days over there, has her two youngest children with her. Little John Boddie [Newton], her baby, is running about now, is a beautiful child, so rosy and merry. Mrs N is looking very thin but enjoys good health. I stayed but a short time & forgot to ask her if she had written to you yet. She attended several of our picnics in the summer & said then that she intended writing to you shortly. I have not succeeded in getting any more pictures for you. Mr Ross, whose picture I sent you, was shot and killed last summer by a Dr Mixon. Mr Ross'es sons & Dr M were in a dispute about something when Mr Ross drew his pistol & ran up to Dr M. The Dr who saw that Mr Ross had been drinking, tried to get him to desist, and backed fifteen paces but Mr Ross followed him and fired, when Dr Mixon immediately shot him down, after which there were several shots fired, by the different parties and a young man who ran to a window to see what was going on received a shot through the head that killed him. Mr Ross'es sons are said to be the most profligate young men in the country. Dr Mixon was a young man of high standing, was justified and acquitted, and what makes the matter more painful was engaged to Mr Ross'es second daughter. Mr Ross having met with many reverses, losing nearly all his property, and trouble about his sons, is said to be the cause of his drinking.

All of Mrs Avera's brothers & sisters are living. She is the only one that is dead. Mr. John and Albert Stone are the only living brothers Mrs. Newton has & Mrs. Piles the only sister. Mr & Mrs Livingston are living fifteen miles beyond Camden. I think some day I will write to Mrs Ora Avera to procure you the likeness, for I have concluded that old Mr Avera is a slow coach to depend upon. I would be so glad to see you now & always & feel much gratified to hear from you & all my friends in Ala. Tho sometime won't you please have your picture taken & send to me. I would have one taken for you but seems to me I grow uglier every day. Tell Callie I would like so much to have hers & Austins.

All my relatives are well. We are expecting brother John's family tomorrow. He is still having a good many patients owing to the changeableness of the weather. Harvesting is again at hand, but the cotton has lost one half on account of the worm. Corn is moderately good. Will has been trying to get a shot at the bears that are frequenting the fields but has not yet succeeded. We had quite a railroad excitement several months ago. The

Ouachita Valley Railroad to run from Arkadelphia to Camden. It passes in seventy yards of brother George's gate. After working about a month, clearing the track & grading, the contractors fell out & all work ceased. Some say that it will yet be built. Brother George thinks not. Some[one] will decide.

  Give my love to all enquiring friends. Sis Mollie, Clara, Mrs Newton & Mrs Annie Stone join me in love to yourself & family. Write soon to
      Your ever affectionate friend,
      C. S. Dickson

Cornelia Dickson at home with the George Boddie family in Ouachita Co. to her nephew John R. Boddie, working in Camden.

               Early in 1874

Dear Johnie,

  Enclosed you will find two dollars. Will you do me the favor to send for a lottery ticket for me from Denison, Texas, also one for Will. I also send you two letters to mail. If Mr. Avera is in town, you need not mail his. Please hand it to him. By complying with my request you will much oblige me
      Yours truely,
      [Aunt Nealie]

Cornelia Dickson in Ouachita Co. to her cousin Hannah V. Love in Mineola, Texas.

          Sometime before August, 1874

My dear Cousin,

  Such a long long time has elapsed since I have heard from you. It has been over a year since I heard from cousin Mary & nearly that long since I received a letter from Kate. I could hear from you occasionaly through their letters. I have been thinking a great deal about you all of late & am so anxious to hear from you. I have despaired of your writing to me first. I intended writing long ago for I felt that I must do so, But it was then that I heard of your sad loss, I deeply sympathize with you & Clem.

  You have no doubt been posted through letters from Ala in regard to my movements since I came to Ark. I am teaching a subscription school about two & half miles from Brother George's, have only ten pupils but they are very interesting children. My school is small. I taught a three months free school last fall at fifty dollars a month, but I understand that all the salaries of the free schools are to be paid in State Script, so I will not receive as much as that for which I was employed. Of course, it is not right, but we have to

*Note: This note was found among the letters in Cornelia's ledger, undated and unsigned. We know only that it was written early in 1874. It is included because it shows a side of Cornelia that we have not seen before; she was not afraid to try something different. It is a bit surprising, however, to think of her as a gambler, albeit a small one.

Sisters, Seeds, and Cedars 274

Martha Hodge "Matt" Proctor Rumph
Photo courtesy of Susan Fiser Taylor

* Florence is 17 years old. When Cornelia says "Florence is nearly age," we assume that she means of the age to begin thinking of marriage.

* Dr John Rumph, whose two previous wives, sis Fannie and sis Sallie, had died, was married a third time to Miss Martha Proctor, a young woman of the Harmony Grove community.

submit to everything ordered by radical rule. All the free schools in Camden & country around are broken up in consequence of the Act. Brother John sent Florence & Tommie to Camden last week, but they will attend an independent school. Florence is nearly age!* Gilder is in town also, clerking in the same house with his brother John but in the hardware department. We will miss them all very much from the home circle.

You have doubtless heard that brother John is again a benedict. He was married last Oct to a young lady about twenty two years of age.* We have no news of interest save an occasional marriage. There is a rumor that our railroad the Ouachita Valley, has resumed the forward movement again, if so we will soon have the cars running near our front gate, and then provided we had the means, we could go & see why some of them in Ala don't write. Have you heard from there lately? How far do you live from your father's & where does cousin Tom live? My kindest regards to them all. The pleasant weeks I spent with them will ever be a bright spot in the memory. How do you all stand Texas? How does Clem look now, is he as lively as ever, & your little ones, cousin Hannah whom do they most resemble? I have never forgotten your promise of those photographs for Clem's daguerrotype, have you? Do you ever hear from Ell? Write me a long letter cousin Hannah as I know you can. Sis Mollie joins me in love to your self & Clem.

Affectionately, your cousin,
Cornelia S. Dickson

SIS MOLLIE AND CORNELIA VISIT ALABAMA
CORNELIA'S NOTES ON 1874 TRIP BACK TO AUTAUGA COUNTY, ALABAMA.

Aug. 10, In Camden - Went shopping, bought
2 neckties for $1.85
1 pair gloves for 40 cts
1 Jar pickle 40 cts

1 box Lilly White 5O cts

Had pin mended 25 cts (Total $3.40)

Sis M[ollie] bought a corset for M[amie] 75 cts

Weighed at B. Sis weighed 101 lbs. I weighed 127 lbs.

Dined with Mrs. Newton [Mrs. Dee Newton] Spent several hours with Mrs. Bracy. Went back to George's [George Rumph] at four o'clock. Found the Babe no better.

Bade goodbye to all and left C[amden] at eight o'clock p.m. in company with Mrs. Winfield and little son, Edward. Mrs. W and sis M occupied the back seat, E[dward] and myself the front. Ed. was soon asleep with my lap for a pillow. We had a pleasant time chatting until about one o'clock when we began to nod our good-nights to each other. Mrs. W sat down on the floor and tried to sleep by resting her head on the seat, but declares that the next time she travels on the stage, will bring a pillow.

The rout[e] seemed long and tedious, & when daylight made everything visible, vegetation seemed parched & withering as if a fire had passed over it. At the last stage stand, we arrived at Prescot at half past eight (a.m.). Dr Winfield met us there, conducted us to the residence of Mr. Hawkins where we washed, shook some of the load of dust from our garments, drank a cup of coffee, felt ready to go on board by the time the train came in sight which was ten o'clock.

We enjoyed our ride on the cars, the more from having bumped about all night on the stage. The cars are very nice indeed. Dr. W bought a watermelon on one of the stations & treated us to a slice.

Arrived at Little Rock at half-past one. The conductor, Mr. Clay, a very clever [man] procured us through tickets and rechecked our trunks to Selma, Ala, at $26.50 each. He then saw us aboard the Memphis train where we secured sleeping cars as we feared that we would not feel so well if we attempted to remain awake another night. Paid $1.00 each for sleeping car.

Arrived at Memphis at 3 o'clock Wednesday morning. The conductor showed us every attention, saw us aboard the omnibus for the Peabody House. We rode about a mile, was met at the bus door by the porter, who conducted us to the reception room where the clerk politely attended us, gave us all the necessary information, procured us a room of which we immediately took possession, shook off some of the dust of travel, bathed, and was soon in the land of dreams. By the by, there are few mosquitoes in Memphis.

We arose at eight the next morning, breakfasted at nine. The clerk accompanied us to the table. The appoints are all in first class hotel style, but I can not say so much for the breakfast. We informed the clerk that we wished to leave on the morning train at half-past ten instead of waiting for the six o'c[lock] train, prefering to travel by daylight that we might see something of the country and lie over at Decator instead of at Memphis as we were compelled to wait at one or the other place. At ten o'[clock], he had the bus of the house to call for, and convey, us to the Memphis and Charleston depot, the porter of the house taking charge of our bundles & finding us seats on board the train, where again, we met our fellow travelers, Mr. Yarbrough and his sister, Mrs. Verner, who by the way, we found to be very pleasant company and friends. They are from Smith Co[unty], Texas, on their way to near Birmingham, Ala, to visit relatives.

The appearance of the country from Memphis to Decator is very different, in many respects, from that between Little Rock and Memphis, of which, by the way, I neglected to make a note. After leaving Little R[ock], crossing two or three rivers and running, more or less, on trestle portions which was rather elevated, produced somewhat the feeling of sailing through the air, we reached the prairie which sight was novel [and] picturesque, & toward night, rendered fearfully grand as we came to that portion which was on fire.* At this time the train seemed flying, running at the rate of twenty-five miles an hour. The stations now appeared but a short distance apart so rapidly did we pass them. Being in the sleeping car, after night set in, it was to be expected that I would see and hear no more of passing events, but not so, for every whistle of the engine, I was wide awake, gazing about "to see what I could see." I suppose that delicious cup of coffee drank at the supper station was the cause of my sleeplessness, while Sis Mollie who would not take a cup, was sleeping as soundly as if she was home in her own room.

Well, I believe, I was on the Charleston-Tenn train from Memphis when I last wrote. The country seems rather monotonous, generally level near the railroad, the crops suffering greatly from the drought. We arrived at Decator at ten o'clock p.m. The conductor called to a porter of the Polk house, a first class hotel. The porter conducted us to the house which was crowded, & we had to wait until twelve o'clock before there was a vacant room, it being occupied by two ladies who left on a twelve o'clock train. We were very tired and sleepy, and dozed on the divan until we could get our room, when we both retired and slept soundly until breakfast next morning.

Decator is rather a delapitated place in appearance near the station, tho it has three nice hotels near by. The principal residences are some distances off. The people seem to be wide awake as they should be, as there is about twenty trains pass there during the day. We counted thirteen telegraph wires that branch off from that place. There is about a half-doz[en] stores near the station. We visited several but found them rather indifferent.

We left Decator on the Louisville North and South train at two-thirty p.m., sped southward over plains, now around a mountain, then over a deep ravine then through another mountain, alternately, mountains & plains & over creeks, ravines, cc. Every little available track of land was under cultivation with its owners hut perched on some nook close by. Vegetation rank and luxurious. Altogether, the scenery between Decator & Galena, at which place we arrived at ten p.m., is the most beautiful, grand, and impressive in

*Cornelia is most probably referring to the sunset on the Little Prairie, along the tracks in the Lonoke area, not to be confused with the Grand Prairie, which is in the Stuttgart area. Or the prairie could have actually been on fire; sparks from the trains often started such fires.

the whole route.

We remained in Galena until five o'clock the next morning when we ate breakfast & went on the Selma train. The country from Galena to our journeys end seemed in fine order, having had an abundance of rain, the crops were, with very few exceptions, the finest we had seen.

Friday, the 14th, at ten o'clock, we reached Clay's Station, our destination. Before stopping, the conductor, who by the way was very clever, came for our check, & when we landed we were greeted with a sight of our trunk which we had not seen since we left Little Rock. We had, previous to our arrival, wrote out a dispatch which the conductor kindly took charge of & said he would go immediately to the office when he reached Selma and send it. As soon as the train left us at the station, we looked around and found a messenger who carried a note about four miles to our friends to let them know of our arrival, as we had not informed them of our proposed visit which was a complete surprise to them all. After giving our baggage in charge of a trusty porter who, by the way, was recommended by Mr. Jeff Clay whom we met at the station. We walked about half a mile to the house of Mrs. Jack Clay, an old acquaintance of us both. Mr. & Mrs. Clay recognized me, but did not at first know Sis M, as they had never met her since her marriage. But, when I mentioned her name, they remembered her and seemed delighted to have met an old friend. We spent several hours very pleasantly at their house. After leaving them, we called to see my very aged friend, Mrs. Betsy Clay, who hearing of my arrival, had just started to see me. I was glad to meet her again, for when I bade her good-by six years ago, I never expected to see her again. She seemed equally rejoiced to see me, but is not enjoying as good health as formerly, having entered her eightieth year.

We then began to climb the hills, or rather mountains, which lay in the four miles road to my uncles. There we met with a most cordial reception. We remained with them all night. The next day, we went on about eight miles to the vicinity of my old home.

ITEMIZED EXPENSES OF THE TRIP:

    For ticket from Camden to Prescott (by stage) $6.50 each.
    Number of baggage check from Prescott to Little Rock-8440
    For ticket from Prescott to Little Rock by train-$4.5O each.
    (I paid $4.50 for Sis Mollie's trip to Little Rock)
    Our through ticket from Little Rock to Memphis, Grand Junction, Corinth, Decator, Galena, Selma-$26.50 each.
    Number of baggage check from Little Rock to Selma-2161
    Sis Mollie paid $1.00 for me a sleeping car and $2.00 at Peabody House, and gave me $1.75. She owes me five cents.
    I paid 30 cts for a cup of coffee at station between Little Rock and Memphis

The 12th of Aug. At Memphis, I spent 70 cts for lemons and lemon sugar

I paid $1.00 omnibus fare to Memphis and Charleston Depot. Sis Mollie now owes me 55 cts.

On the Charleston Train I paid 25 cts for grapes and 10 cts for the APPEAL.*

Aug. 13 At Decator, I spent $1.00, 45 cts for Sis Mollie and 55 cts for myself. Sis Mollie now owes me $1.00. Paid!

Aug. 13, Paid $2.25 each at the Polk House, Decator. Paid 25 cts to the chambermaid.

Aug. 14. At Galena, paid $3.00 for lodging and breakfast, $1.50 each. Sis Mollie now owes me $1.50.

Sis Mollie paid 75 cts for sending dispatch.

At Clay's Depot, I paid 75 cts for sending note and for baggage.

LATER-

Monday, Aug. 24. Passed through Selma. Paid 25 cts for water melon, 25 cts for velvet, and 90 cts for 1 1/2 yards of alpaca. Sis Mollie paid $9.00 for 15 yards silk alpaca.

Sept 25 went to Mrs Underwoods. I loaned Sis $1.10. I paid 50 cts at toll bridge and Tuesday morning paid $5.00 bill for lodging & Friday morning paid $3.00 to boys to take them home. Sis now owes me $6.85.

Sept 10th paid $12 for Hattie, Sis M & self fare to Selma onboard the L_____ 50 cts porterage. Sis now [owes] me $15.10.

Sept 19th paid $1.00 for _____ & $1.00 for candy. paid $1.00 fare for Sis & Hattie & 50 cts for self. Sis now owes me $16.10.

Number of checks - 47 & 78

$5.30 to Galena

$46.70 Tickets through

3.00 bill at Polk house

50 cts dispatch

40 cts coffee

1.87 ½ sash

20 cts for strings

50 cts candy

4.00 bill at Memphis

1.00 omnibus charge 10 cts cup coffee

25 cts grapes

9.60 to Prescott

2.00

<u>12.00</u>

2(87.42 ½

<u>1.97 ½</u>

<u>2(86.45</u>

43.22 ½

*APPEAL most likely refers to the *Memphis Commercial Appeal*.

Cornelia Dickson in Ouachita Co. to her nephew Tom Love in Autauga Co.
Nov. 9, 1874

Dear Tom,

I had no idea when I left Ala that this much time would have elapsed ere I complied with my promise to write to you. But time flies so. I have written but one letter & that to Kate since our arrival home. I wrote to Fannie & Onie from Memphis. A day or two after we came home, Sis Mollie was taken very sick, worse than she ever was in her life. It was two weeks before she was able to be up. Then the first week after she was up, I spent at brother Johns. Expected to write while there, but had company all the time & Since have been afflicted with very painful risings on my right arm & wrist. Brother George says it is Ala <u>malaria</u> that the Arkansas climate is clensing from our systems. And now sis Mollie is well & strong again, She has rheumatism in her left arm & shoulder at times so painful it is almost unbearable, or She would have written to Sis Carrie. We often sit and rehearse the many pleasant days among you all. How are you all and what are you doing? Is little Annie as lively as ever, hope she is able to keep uncle Clem stirred up, that is, if the political state of the country has not already made him feel like cutting the pigeon wing, as did old uncle Hal Brodnax at our Democratic picnic on Pine Lake since we came home. We had a splendid time boating, music, & dancing. The brass band from Camden echoed sweet music for miles through the surrounding woods, and big, little, old & young rallied to the sound. And you would have thought from the bounty, and delicacies of the dinner that the people had forgotten their poverty. I will enclose you a ticket for county election. You will see that brother John is again in the list. He left yesterday for Little Rock, will be absent three or four months, Will make us a short visit Christmas. As soon as the returns of that election was received in Camden, the Democrats were almost wild with joy. Some laughing, Some shouting, some crying & tossing their hats, Some shaking hands & embracing. The band the while sending forth its merriest gladest notes, & the cannon bursting forth in thunder tones until midnight, to let those in the distance know that their nine years bondage was drawing to a close. You can imagine how blank the radicals appeared. But they rallied and made a great effort to elect their congressmen Clayton on the third inst., but they have again been defeated, the Democratic triumph being complete here & elsewhere in the U.S.* There were greater demonstrations than ever in our little city of hills. The cannon again belched forth the glad tidings, & last Saturday night, the houses were illuminated and a grand-torchlight procession with transparencies*, headed by the band, paraded the streets, interspersed with speeches from prominent men until a late hour. Even some of the young ladies were so enthusiastic as to accompany the young men who had charge of the cannon & applied the match several

*The jubilation and celebration Cornelia describes here followed the General Election of 1874 in which the conservative Democrats gained control of Congress from the Liberal Republicans, sounding the end of Reconstruction in the South.

*A transparency is a picture or the like, as on glass, viewed by light shining through it; hence, a framework covered with thin cloth or paper bearing a device for public display.

times. Some young men from this side the river went over & participated in the jubilee; among them Will. Mamie & I would like to have gone over to witness the demonstrations, but did not think about it in time. We do regret so much now that we did not go. But enough about politics.

When we came home [from Alabama], we found a Grange* established in the neighborhood and a good many of the neighbors members, brother George & Mr. Dunlap among them, we have not yet joined. We are having such a dry fall that many of the farmers have not been able to plough & plant small grain & those who have planted are uneasy for fear theirs won't come up. And the country will suffer want indeed if we make no wheat, the corn crop having failed.

Tell the boys that we came very near being at home in time to eat bear meat. The negroes on the place started one from the field, Will joined them & they succeeded in killing four, an old one, three cubs nearly grown.

Clara & children spent the day with us about a week ago. All well at brother John's. Brother G was there yesterday. Mamie was so proud of Ada's picture that she said she intended writing to her & thank her, herself, but I don't believe she will write for she said she would write to Kate when we first came home and she has not done so yet. Tell Ada, Bettie sends very many thanks for her nice present and wishes very much to receive a letter from her. Sis Mollie says among so many girls she thought some of them would think enough of her to write to her & not wait for her to write first.

We have been assailed with hundreds of questions since we came back, and Johnie says the first day we arrived home was as good as a show. So many here, says he could not get in a word edgeways. Nearly all talking at once and among the Babel, Clara's voice above all others, "Sis Mollie! So & so, Nealie! so & so" & drawing up a chair "Now Sis Mollie, I have not had a chance to talk to you any today" to be interrupted by a louder key "Ma so & so, Aunt Mollie or Aunt Nealie so & so " all day long; and we talking all the time. We have so often wished that Ada could have come with us. We would have felt our enjoyment was more complete if some of our relatives could have come with us. We met Howard Jones at Memphis & enjoyed his company very much until we left the cars at Prescott. How is Mr Davis? Sis Mollie has not been able to write to him yet. Johnie wrote for her, I hope he has received the letter, for I know the old man will be anxious to hear from us.

And now that the novelty of getting home is over, we want to see you all worse than ever, & if we ever have the means, we may surprise you again, but that will be when times are more prosperous & business less dull than now. Many are leaving Camden, going up on the railroad, out to Texas, to Hot Springs, or St. Louis to get into more lucrative employment. Johnnie says all the young men of his "set" have left him alone. Tell Cousin Mary to let us know how they all are in Texas when she writes. Tell Dick Miss

* Granges were political groups of farmers throughout the grain-producing Midwest, which wielded considerable power during the election campaigns of the Fall of 1874.

Anna says she agrees to all propositions. But I think he had better come & negotiate for himself & he will have to be a granger too. Tell Andrew I want to see him so much, that he must send me that promised picture. Tell Will we will look for him this winter. Sis Mollie and family join me in love to each & all our relatives.

      Yours affectionally,
      Cornelia S. Dickson

Cornelia Dickson in Ouachita Co. to her friend Mrs. E. S. Clark in Statesville, Alabama.

                Dec 11th 1874

Dear Mrs Clark,

  Your very welcome missive was a complete surprise to me & as a young man remarked several days since "A serenade is doubly sweet when a surprise." So it was with your dear letter. I am truly glad that you did not wait for me to write first, for I have not felt fully settled since my return from Ala, or rather we have had such a whirl of excitement from first one cause & then another & then too I have been so busily employed with household matters, for since our return Sis Mollie has played out of all the cooking. She used to cook breakfast when we prepared every thing the night before. I have spent several of my, rest to me, weeks at brother John's & tried to write some letters while there but was so often interrupted with company that I have never succeeded in writing but two letters, One to Kate & the other to Tom Love. I remarked to Sis Mollie the other day that if any one had told me that I should go to Ala and not visit you while there I would never have believed it and that I did not have the opportunity of doing so has been to me a source [of] sincere regret.

  I was truly sorry to hear of your family's afflictions from sickness. Sis and I have both had similar misfortune. She was confined to her bed several weeks with fever while I suffered somewhat after the manner of Job on both right & left arm. Brother G says it was the Ala malaria being cleansed from our system by the purer atmosphere of Washita bottom. The idea! I rejoice exceedingly in your good fortune, the more so as it will enable you to visit us, will certainly begin to look for you next Summer. I have not had an opportunity of going to Camden but sent your letter to Capt Newton. Mr Stone says he had money it is true but it was loaned out and times are so hard that he could not get a dime of it & he thought that Ora had written to tell you long ago, and that Dee was no better off than himself, & he seemed rejoiced to hear of your visit. I have not heard from Mrs Newton but think she has written to you, since I sent your letter to her to read. I do not think that Morton would be able to get a situation as clerk in Camden for so many merchants there have failed that clerks are at a discount & many who were there are seeking employment elsewhere & next year will be a very trying year on the farmer, owing to the total failure of the crops this year.

I was very much grieved to hear of the death of Lula Howard. She seemed to have promise of a long life when I saw her last summer. I was with her but a few moments but as I recall, her features, I feel that another link that restored her dear mothers face has passed away, never again to gladden my mortal vision. I trust that she is now rejoicing in a happy reunion in the abode of the blest.

Our section of country has been remarkably healthy this year. The young folks are looking forward to Christmas holidays with less avidity than formerly on account of hard times, though that does not seem to affect the matrimonial fever, as there is to be several weddings in & around the neighborhood, but none that you would know. Sis Mollie is spending this week at brother John's, Mat* has a sweet little babe about three month old, they call it Maude Jessie. Brother John was elected to the legislature, in Little Rock. We expect him home Christmas. This leaves us all in good health. The family what are here join me in love to yourself & family. Mamie says if all the young people here were as gay as you are, we would disperse some of the gloom created by that bugbear Hard Times. My love to all friends. Hoping you may have a merry Christmas, I am as ever

Your affectionate friend,
Cornelia S. Dickson

I received a letter from Onie Love yesterday, will answer soon, Yours & her letters are the only ones received since we came home.

*"Mat" refers to Martha Proctor Rumph, Brother John's third wife.

After the War

John B. Rumph in Little Rock, attending the Arkansas Legislature Session to his wife of one year, Matt Proctor Rumph in Ouachita County.

A copy of the Legislative letterhead taken from the original letter.

December 13th 1874

My dear wife and children,

Again I have to acknowledge the receipt of another letter from my sweet wife. You can't imagine how much I appreciate your and the children's letters. I feel, whilst reading them, just like I was at home, and listening to your dear familiar voices, and after I finish reading them and awake from my momentary reverie, I get right vexed with myself for having left my home with its happy social and domestic associations to come here as a servant of the people. My bump of patriotism will have to grow wonderfully from its present status, if ever I am persuaded to be a legislator again. I am glad to hear you and the children are all in the enjoyment of good health. May you all long continue so is my ardent and sincere hope. I am glad to hear that my dear Boy* is managing everything so well in my absence. I feel so proud that I have such a dutiful and good Boy that he will not disappoint me in the trust I have reposed in him. I regret so much to hear of the death of my old dog Highflyer. He was a good dog and a true and faithful friend to his master. He was always ready and willing to join in the exciting sport of the chase -- was ever true in finding the trail and pursuring the antlered monarch of the forest, was ever in at the death, and attested his joy and gladness by the wag of his tail and deep toned bay. He fell over the prostrate form of many an old Buck. May he be wafted to happy hunting grounds beyond the valley of death. On Friday evening last, in company with a number of the members of the Legislature, I visited the Blind Institute. It proved to be a very interesting and instructive visit to all of us, and although designed as a pleasureable excursion for recreation, it filled many a heart with gloomy sadness. It was truly heartrending.*

* The "dear boy" is Thomas Lewis Rumph, son of Dr. Rumph's first wife, Frances "Sis Fannie."

*Note: The extant letter has only two pages; the others have been lost apparently.

Tom Love near Burnsville, Ala to his aunt Cornelia Dickson in Ouachita Co.
Dec 14th 1874

Dear Auntie,

I received your welcome visitor some time ago and ought to have been more punctual in replying. Fannie and Onie received your letter from Memphis but I do not think they have answered yet.

We have about got through with this year's crop that is the gathering, ginning,and the packing. The selling part was done last spring. A pretty fair crop was made notwithstanding dry weather, cc. Freedmen worked very well but stole much better. Since the crop was gathered, they have done but little else than steal and burn. Mr Parker's gin house with ten bales of cotton; James Murry's with fifteen bales; Thomas Northington's with ten and Mr Roundtree with twenty bales are among the incendiary works of the negroes. Aunt Mary's with five bales and 1000 bushels of cottonseed was also burned a short time since. Matches in the cotton. None of the whites of the vicinity by the latter fire except Dick and Cole. They lost about a bale between them. All hands lost about all the cotton seed they had.

I hope Aunt Mollie has recovered from her rheumatism and you from your boils. Say to Uncle George that it is anything else except Alabama malaria — just the reverse. Arkansas malaria stirred up by the trip to Alabama.

We too have had a grand Democratic Victory and much rejoicing in consequence the county is radical and represented in the legislature by J. E. Boseman, Uncle Clem did not cut the "pidgeon wing" <u>but took Uncle George's symptoms</u> of cholera over the result. Ask Uncle George what that is. We were proud to learn that Uncle John Rumph was again in the Arkansas House of Representatives. Hope ere this you have become a Granger and will persuade Uncle John to banish his bad opinion of the only protective organization the farmers have.

I have delivered all your messages. In fact they got the letter before I did, and all hands read it, so eager we were to hear from you.

There is being a good deal of small grain planted, wheat and oats especially. We can raise cotton but it is too expensive and then we cannot compete with Texas, Arkansas, Louisiana, and Mississippi.

There has been a good deal of sickness this fall. Some few deaths. Mr Anderson, second husband of Mrs Roseman, and Mr Callin, second husband of Mrs Amy Cole are the deaths from this vicinity. Mr Dunn is very sick at this time. No marriages on the docket for this season and prospects are gloomy for a merry time this Christmas; I hope it is different in Arkansas.

Ada is going to school and boards at home. Mr Davis was well when last heard from. Report says he will remove from the PO and live with Mr Ross. I learn that two of the Houston girls, Ella and Emma, are living with

Aunt Hattie, making three in all.

We have made no arrangements for another year, save the planting of small grain. No one has contracted with any hands to this time. Notwithstanding we made good crops in comparison to several years back. There will be some suffering another year and want will hover over many a little home where all should be happy unless the money men come to the rescue. If I could get a fair money consideration for what effects we have I would leave here and go west. Lands are very low, from fifty cents to three dollars per acre. All of the family can do very well another year, but it is all due to Uncle Clem. I do not know what we would do were it not for him.

Aunt Mary is greatly troubled about the loss of her ginhouse and wants to go west. We do not hear from Clem [her son in Grand Valley Texas] often. They were all well when last heard from.

All join me in love to you and relatives. Little Annie often asks, "Where is Nealie and Mollie?" They gone to Burnsville she will say. She can talk well now and keeps stirred up as you say. She is always wanting candy and apples. I have finished my sheet and so will bid you adieu for the present. Tell cousin Mitt, I have "laid my crop by."

        Yours affectionately,
        Tom Love

Cornelia Dickson in Ouachita Co. to Onie Love in Autuaga Co.

                January, 1875

Dear Onie,

Your most welcome letter was received some weeks since & read with a great deal of interest, it being the first letter that you had ever written to me. I appreciated very highly. It brought to mind the many pleasant hours spent with you all last summer & memory pictured each and every one of you & the many pleasant faces of all our relatives and friends who contributed so much to our enjoyment while with you. We often talk it over, Sis Mollie & I when some of the children will say, "I wish I had been with you".

It seems to have been only two or three weeks since our return, we are so engaged all the time with first one thing and then another that time flies away with our intentions before we are aware. I am surprised that I have not fulfilled many promises given of writing. I received a letter from Tom during Christmas holiday but I wanted to reply to yours first as it was first received. I was expecting a letter from Fannie too, and Kate. I thought sure she would have written & said something about the grape cuttings I spoke of. Capt Newton & family were here yesterday and he inquired if we had heard from Ala or anything was said about the cuttings. Mrs Newton says she is anxious to hear from Mrs Clark and don't know why Mrs C did not answer her letter.

I was so very sorry to hear of Lula Howards death. I saw her but a short time when in Ala but she seemed the picture of health with fair promise of a long life. We were sorry to hear of Mr Davises feeble health. Sis Mollie wrote to him last week & speaks every week of writing to Sis Carrie, but I suppose she is like I am about writing, defers to a more favorable hour.

Every other week for the last two months, I have spent at brother John's & you may be sure we have a very lively time in one way or another. The little girls are as merry & frolicsome as kittens, & the sweet little babe is a perfect model of a baby and so very interesting, will laugh & coo whenever any one calls "little Maude" & we children of a larger growth have a pleasant time entertaining the farmer boys who frequently call in the evenings & sit until late bed time. Moonlight nights are no exception, for <u>dark nights</u> they bring a <u>lantern</u>.

During Christmas we had only three parties in the neighborhood. I attended two, had the nicest kind of a time. The first was a social at brother John's Christmas night, & the other was a dance at Mr. Elliot's. Since the new year, everyone has set to work in earnest and are economizing on a larger scale than ever before, owing to the total failure of crops last year. Every farmer in this community with one or two exceptions are buying corn or will have to buy. Our new school house is so far off and the pupils are too scarce to justify me in boarding out, & I have not been able to get a school elsewhere, consequently, I feel very unsettled for I want to be making money all the time.

Johnie & Gilder come over occasionally, they speak sometimes of leaving Camden to find more lucrative employment. If they should go, we will all regret it so much for we shall miss them sadly. Tommie [Rumph] is working on the farm at home this year, says that life suits him better than any other unless he could study law, and as it is impossible in the present state of affairs for him to do that, he will try farming. He is a noble boy, has a brilliant mind, resembles his mother [Sis Fannie] more than any of the children. We hear from brother John frequently, expect him home next month.*

I have not seen Clara in several weeks, her health is not very good & she remains closely at home this winter. Mr. Dunlap & the children keep well. The health of the neighborhood has been remarkably good this winter with the exception of slight colds. I hope we will all keep well while brother John is gone at least. We are having some very disagreeable weather, first freezing cold, & then sleet & rain, hard on stock, but brother G[eorge] has been fortunate with his, has not lost any this winter. It is raining very hard now, & Mamie went to town yesterday with Mrs. Newton, will remain several days. I fear she will have an unpleasant time coming home. She teaches Carrie & Robert when at home, thereby reviewing her studies with the view of teaching some day. Carrie says she will be glad to write to you if you will

*Brother John is attending the Legislature session in Little Rock.

promise to answer her letters punctually. Sis Mollie joins me in love to you all. Write soon.

> Affectionately yours,
> Cornelia S. Dickson

Editor's Note: For some reason there is a great lapse in Cornelia's correspondence in 1875. She was possibly much too busy with other duties to pursue her normal dedication to letter writing. Or perhaps she had to forego her usual habit of putting letters in her ledger before copying them for mailing. It is possible, too, that the original copies were written on odd pieces of paper which we are unable to locate. Whatever the reason, the lapses do exist for us; to fill in the blanks, we turn once again to Sis Mollie and her devoted correspondence with her son John Rumph Boddie, who early in 1875 went to St. Louis to avail himself of more lucrative employment. In addition to Sis Mollie's letters, we include a few from other family members to John so that the continuity of community activities continues.

Mary Elizabeth Boddie in Ouachita Co. to her son John Rumph Boddie in St. Louis

March 16th 1875

My dear son,

I write not because there is anything interesting to tell you, but for my great desire to hear from you; we know you have everything to occupy <u>your time</u>, yet I cant help being anxious to have word from you often, & it has been two weeks since the reception of your dear letter from St. Louis. Your Pa too, is saying everyday, is it not time we were hearing from John again? says <u>all</u> your friends in Town are enquiring of him about you, & express regret at your absence. You have no idea my dear son, how much we miss you, & nothing will reconcile me to your absence until I know you are satisfied, doing better than you can here, & above all, that your health remains unimpaired in that severe climate, for wanting the latter, all the good things of this transient life are as draught. Your Pa saw Mr N. Richmond in Camden recently and Mr R. thought you would not like the business assigned you at all for <u>he</u> could not endure it, & preferred soliciting custom anywhere except in the City. He has the same opinion of the place that you entertain. Mr R will leave for St. Louis soon, & Son, I beg to tax your goodness to me one more time, will send the Photographs of sis & myself, from which, will you please have two taken, & send by letter, the case belongs to sis Hattie, & I will have to return it to her, dont send that back, until you can send it safely, by some one you know. Heard from sis H. last week, all were *"little Sis" is the family name for Carrie & "Tug" is the name given to Robert

*"Mrs OScuttle" was a name given by the Boddie family to Florence Rumph. "Miss Dickens" must be Aunt Nealie.

*"Old Miss Boddie" is probably a name for Mamie.

well, said she would come to see us this winter, if possible, she has rented her land on good terms this year & to good tenants. Henry is going to work in the tan-yard. Hattie has all five of Mr Johnston's children now; making twelve in family.

Mittie is taking lessons on the Piano, she has a sweet voice, & is very fond of music. She is teaching the children at home, & a few of the neighbours children. Mamie has a gay time with her pupils, little Sis, & Tug,* sometimes, 'tis so hard to keep Bobby's attention to his books, when she cant be in the room with them, he says though, he will be a good boy, & he wants to see Bud Johnnie, & I must tell him that he caught a big snapping turtle, trying to get through the fence, & put him in Ma's water barrel, the rain filled it that night, & the turtle went overboard & run away.

We have had the biggest snow you ever saw in this country, it commenced snowing the evening of the 6th & fell to the debth of two inches, the roads were impassable for a day or two, as the trees were lapped from side to side, & many broken. Pa said trees in the bottom, as his body, were broken.

The snow is completely covering everything, & is a beautiful sight, but I could not enjoy it, thinking of you. Uncle John spent one day with us since he came home, & beside the pleasure derived from his pleasant company he gave us all the particulars of your stay at the Rock, & you may guess how he was plied with questions. Said he would give your remembrance to Mrs OScuttle*, as have not seen her since the reception of your letter, & Miss Dickens is not yet at home, stayed at Uncle J's two weeks, & is now with Bettie at Aunt Clara's, the latter has been very sick, was taken with Neuralgia in the side, & for two days & nights could not lie down at all, & was scarcely able to move out of one position in her chair. She is much better at present, & I hope may soon be well. Hannah has been staying there to care for the baby.

Gilder spent last Sunday with us, he speaks of being so lonely, do write him one letter, that he may feel he occupies a place in the heart of a brother he so highly esteems, for he has taken you for an example he says, & will endeavour so to comport himself. If I were to tell you of all our friends who ask about you, my sheet would be full of names. About my Rheumatism we'll talk, my darling boy, whenever I get helpless, or past working. Tell me on what St., & who is the Pastor of the church you attend, I can think of you on every sabbath my son, & know how you are passing the time, but of week days can form little idea. The whole family ask to be remembered to you with much love. Little Sis says, tell Bud Johnny I weigh 85 lbs. now.

Old Miss Boddie* says, she is drooping for want of a letter from you. Geo. R[umph] & family are well, Gilder says Bleeges'[?] as bad as ever, he has been to Jennie's once since you left. Good bye darling son, I commend

you to the care of Him, in whose hands we all are, & may he bless you is the daily prayer of your devoted mother
Mary E. Boddie

Mamie Boddie in Ouachita Co. to her brother John R. Boddie in St. Louis
March 26th 1875

Dear Brother:

I shall not attempt to tell you how very glad I was to receive such a long and interesting letter from one so dearly loved, and so sadly missed. So much like you, that I could, while reading, fancy you with us. — "O those happy days will ne'er return."

I have no objection to its being jointly written, save for the fact, that only one of us could keep it, and Ma declared her right most potent, <u>because</u> it was <u>from</u> "Johnny."

I dont think she would have relinquished her claim without some demur, had she not been recipient of another, bearing date March 21st, which she would have answered this week had I not begged to write, for I would have written before, but though[t] that Ma & cousin M. had given all items of interest and that I would wait a while before troubling you with my disinteresting scrawl, for such I know it will be, as letter writing is not my forte. It is raining, thundering and lightning so that I am almost tempted to jump in bed and stop up my ears, but I shall try to finish. All friends and relatives are enjoying good health, except Maud and Aunt Clara; they have been quite sick, though much better now. I am transplanting my flowers and I think, I shall have a pretty garden when I finish it. Am still trying to teach Carrie and Bobbie but dont succeed very well in keeping them at their books. Bobbie has been helping them at the field this week and a part of last. Florence is spending this week with us. Is as gay as ever, says tell cousin Johny, that "Mrs OScuttle" is doing finely, gaining a few pounds, occasionally, just enough to keep them from calling her an old maid, for she says when they get to be old maids, they commence drying up, says pity poor sis Bettie.

We all, that is, Ma, B[obbie],C[arrie], F[lorence], Anna, & I walked to church last Thursday. Uncle Billie and Mr Gouning [Gaughan?] accompanied us. Our Minister, Mr Hare is very much liked by all. Is well educated and spiritual in his appointments. Will have preaching again Sunday by one of Mr. Moseley's brethren.* Pa says he is going. There are some coming from Camden too.

I have not seen or heard anything from any of your C___ friends. Pa says every body wants to know when he's last heard from "John." I did hear too, that Mr Lide would marry shortly, but, of course, you know all about <u>that</u>.

*Mr. Moseley's brethren was Peter Moseley from Bradley County.

Cousin Tommie [Rumph] is playing the devoted to Miss Anna [Moseley] on the sly. Comes down by the covered[?] bridge. Anna says I must tell you how much love she returns, for she cant find words to express it. Mr Stone & Mr Marvin [Moseley] went hunting Thursday, jumped a deer and cat but did not get either. Could have shot the deer but had no guns. I am glad you have written to G[ilder], he said he was so lonesome since you left. Brother please excuse all errors. I will try and do better next time, I cant write in any peace, for there are those silk butterflies* in here; they are everywhere. I cant catch them. Write soon and a long letter. Your
     Loving sister

*She is most likely referring to those tiny moths that gather around light.

Mary Elizabeth Boddie in Ouachita Co. to her son John R. Boddie in St. Louis

March 31st 1875

My dear son,

  Words cannot express the great comfort, and pleasure, that the reception of your dear letters give me, & am waiting with what patience I can for last weeks letter, as they <u>always</u> come in <u>Tuesday's</u> mail, but I seldom get them until the last of the week. Your first letter to me from St. Louis was dated Feb.28th, the second March 14th, the third, & last I've recd March 21st. In consequence of not knowing how to direct properly, I dont suppose you will ever get the first letter I wrote to you, after receiving yours from Hot Springs, & Little Rock. You are a dear good boy to write to home every week, & I love to think of the time when you are so engaged, & I listen too, for the Church bells' chimes, for with every Sabbath it brings me nearer in feeling to you, & minds me of the many times you were wont to respond to those sweet tones, & but a few miles intervened between us then. I feel so much better satisfied about you now son, that you express <u>yourself</u> so <u>well pleased</u> in your present situation, for, as regards those with, & for whom you are working, I've no doubt whatever, but that you'll deserve, & merit their warmest approbation. — Permit me to <u>guess</u> Johnnie that, that "some <u>one</u> who writes to you oftener than those at home" had the <u>earliest</u> information how to direct letters, but I am not at all jealous darling, for I can love her too, which will be a natural consequence, if, &c &c, and is she the <u>one</u> from whom the distance is too great to send a boquet. Speaking of flowers, reminds me to tell you that Maime has sent to Mrs Lee a basket of fine bulbs, Tulips, & some of every variety of Hyecinths she has. Mrs L. wrote a note profuse in thanks to yourself & sister. Both garden & field work progresses slowly, in consequence of so much rain, & I've heard of no one of the farmers, on our side, except Mr Gwhoin [Gaughan] who has finished planting all their corn crop. Yes, Mr Greening finished, before many others commenced. The river has overflowed the banks twice, & a big one is anticipated now, as the water is approaching our road, & still rising.

We went to church last Sunday, & just escaped a wetting, no Preacher came, as the creeks were all up, heard our Minister Mr Hare on Thanksgiving day, 25th* & I like him better & better every time he preaches. You must accompany Messers Lee & Wood some time to their respective churches, if you have not already done so. Did not see any of Uncle John's family Sunday, heard from them this week, all were well, Florence has spent two weeks with us, since you left, says, tell cousin Johnnie, <u>Mrs O'Scuttle</u> entertained half dozen boys at one time last Sunday. Cousin Bettie says, tell cousin J. have gained just a <u>little</u> bit, but if she could live as high, on such good fare as you have every day, knows she would get fleshy. Did Maime tell you she & Mit[tie] made a compromise about their joint letter, both want it, & Mit is to copy it for Maime, & keep the original, as 'twas addressed to her. I cant help telling you that, that letter was a source of greatest pleasure to each one of the family. Be assured son, if I do not write to you oftener than once a month, 'twill be for want of materials at hand all the time. Am glad to know you will write to Gilder, he has been to see us but once since you left. Your guns shall be taken good care of. Pa has had the fine one out one time, but saw no game that day. Willie says tell you they have had another <u>raid</u> after that same <u>old bear</u>, he was seen twice that day, but the dogs behaved as usual, & there was too much water for the hunters to get about through the bottom. Tug says, "I want to write to bud Johnnie myself, & I intend to do it." Little sis says there is no danger of her growing much, for Maime wont give her <u>time</u> from her books; Bobbie has had to help them some in the field, scattering cotton seed. Uncle J. D[unlap]'s family are well, they speak of naming the baby John. Saw Mrs Elliott, Coralic, & Belle Sunday, Mrs E. made many inquires about you. Miss Nellie was at Mrs Ton[e]y's. Miss Anna told me not to forget to mention her with much love when I wrote to you. I believe son I forgot to ask you to let me know the cost of those pictures, if you can have them taken, & when Mr Goddard comes to Camden, please send the frame back, that I sent to you by Mr R.

Nealy says, tell you she has hunted up her <u>lottery ticket</u>, to be <u>ready</u> for the <u>big prize</u>, as the drawing takes place to-day, & she is very patiently awaiting the denoument. Maime says she has not wilted any, but has quit drooping, because of that letter. Am all right now for this week, your dear letter of 28th has just been handed me by Mr Michel. I cant imagine why our letters from here are so long reaching you. Maime & Mittie have written more than a week since, letters superscribed according to directions. The case I sent you belongs to Sis Hattie, & contains a likeness of sis Sallie, & myself, from which you will please have <u>two copies</u> taken in photograph on paper, (or any other style you may think proper). Every time I see Mrs Annie S[tone] she says Bob talks every week about writing to John, so he will give

* In 1729 George Washington proclaimed that there should be a day set aside for giving thanks, but he set no particular date. In 1855 the state of Virginia became the first state to adopt the custom, still with no particular date. Abraham Lincoln, in 1863, proclaimed a National Thanksgiving Day on the last Thursday of November. The South obviously did not recognize that date, as Harmony Grove celebrated on March 25.

you all the hunting news. <u>Pa says</u> dont get to <u>liking</u> Miss <u>Lucy too much</u> — bad stock &c &c. Bro. Will is renovating things generally, when too wet to plow, & his bees come in for their share of attention. Miss Mollie S[tone] stayed with us Saturday night, said she could not help being glad everytime it rained for only then would Bud work on the <u>house</u>. State [Stone] & Pa have not been hunting recently, so the pigs have escaped so far.

I will be, if living, very happy when the time comes darling for you to enjoy yourself hunting, & in the companionship of our (dear) "little Pink," so be as equinomical as you please, but allow yourself some recreation from the cares of business. Do wish I could enjoy a walk with you on that bridge—

Each one of the family send dear love to our absent one, & your many friends desire remembrance. My daily prayer to the Giver of All Good is, for your continued good health & happiness.

Lovingly Your Mother,
M.E.B.

*I have not space to tell you all the good wishes, good words, &c sent by the blacks to Mr John Boddie.

*Note: This postscript was written upside-down along the top of the last page.

John B. Rumph in Ouachita Co. to his nephew John R. Boddie in St. Louis

April 2, —75

My Dear Nephew,

I wrote you some two weeks since, in answer to your note to me asking my advice in regard to investing $150 more in State Script and neglected to address your letter to the care of Tyra Hill & Co, and am affraid you did not get it. In that letter I advised you to invest every spare dollar you did not need in Script, as I could not foresee any possible chance of loosing, and every reasonable probability of doubling your money in less than three years.

The Script itself bears 5 percent interest and the faith and credit of the State is pledged to redeem every dollar of it. It is now being absorbed in taxes, and will continue to appreciate in value as the amount outstanding diminishes. It is now worth 35 ½ @ 36, and will gradually advance to near par in less than three years. The $100 you already have invested is now worth $122 if put on the market. If you wish to invest further, deposit your money with Tyra Hill & Co of St Louis, and draft on Tyra Hill of Camden, and I will do the best I can for you, for above all earthly things I desire to see you succeed financially, as I have no doubt you will succeed morally and socially no matter where you may cast your lot.

I have not been in very good health since my return home, I have stayed at home pretty closely — have been to Camden only twice. The heavy rains have kept up the creeks, and prevented getting about in the neighborhood. The woods are so full of water that I cant get about very well Turkey hunt-

ing. Tom and I went out this morning, both got after the same old gobbler — another old Seigle — he hushed up gobbling as soon as we commenced yelping, strutted around awhile and then retreated in good order, leaving me in no very amiable mood, wet up to my stern and hungry as a wolf. Will write you again more at length when I feel all right and have anything to interest you.— All well — All send much love, My best wishes for your health and happiness, My Boy; as ever your devoted uncle —
J. B. Rumph

Mary E. Boddie in Ouachita Co. to her son John R. Boddie in St. Louis
April 16th '75

My dear Son,

 Your favors of 5th and 11th April rec'd & appreciated more than I can express, for with all your promptness in writing, it seems <u>to me a long time between</u> letters. I read one daily till the next one comes. Your sister <u>is</u> getting impatient for a letter, & I can speak the same for cousin* too, as she sent word to know why I did not send her <u>my letter</u> from you, & as I had the opportunity, did so this morning , also <u>yours</u> to Uncle John.

*Cousin is what the Boddie family called Mittie Rumph.

 My greatest comfort, Son, in your absence, is to hear of your continued good health, & am pleased that you & Mr R[ichards] have made boarding arrangements, both satisfactory & pleasant. Pa said, he did not think you would like private boarding, for the very reasons you gave. Capt. Newton came to see us the week I rec'd your letter, wherein you spoke of boarding with Mrs. Hearn, said he was acquainted with & thought you would be pleased with her. He made many inquiries about you & desired to be particularly remembered & said little Johnny [John Boddie Newton, his son] could not yet realize your being gone as he insists on going to Sunday School to see Mr John Boddie. Frank B[rodnax] stayed with us last night, has heard through letters from Ala. that they are having just such weather as we experienced in Ark. last spring, continual rain for the past three months, & small pox had broken out in Selma. I have not heard from sis Hattie [Murley] since Feb., sent her the <u>duck</u> curls as you requested. Pa killed a fine turkey not long ago, it weighed when dressed 20 pounds. He is too busy now to hunt any. Mr R[obert] Stone as usual hunts every spare time, declared he intended sending you his last trophy, a big cat tail, but I have not seen him since & dont know if he did or not. Will says he will be glad to get a good bear dog & your Pa indulged in a hearty laugh at the idea.

 I am almost persuaded, son, that you are inhabiting a much pleasanter clime than ours, & but for the beautiful appearance of everything in nature we would not know that spring <u>time</u> had come, have such cool weather, & frosty mornings, fires are necessary early, & comfortable nearly all day. That

I take good care of myself, darling, witness, having taken a big dose of castor oil & it quite cured me of a severe cold. I dont intend to work too hard, & exercise you know is good, & don't expect any of us need to complain unless it be Will, for between his farm work & the bees is kept very busy all day, & works on gums, bee shelter &c late at night, & at noon time the bees keep him trotting fast, as that is the favored time for swarming, two or three generally come out at the same time, sometimes after being hived they go back to the old gums that hived since that are working, & Nealie hived one swarm. Willie went to the top of the big black gum in front of the hives this morning & bagged a swarm that settled there yesterday, after hiving two others. All hands run after them with bells & clattering instruments when they start off, as one swarm tried to do yesterday. Will was offered ten cents for his nice honey in Camden this spring, he was anxious to sell some to buy lumber with which to make gums.*

*Gums is the name bee keepers give to their hives. Originally hollow logs were used, but apparently Willis was going to build his out of lumber.

The bees are swarming <u>now</u> & I must send Becky to the field to plow in Will's place, for him to come & hive them. Becky is going to live with Seymore again, & we are all sorry to lose her services. Geo. has persuaded her to remain until he gets through planting cotton, which she has promised to do.

Afternoon — Has hived two swarms, & all hands gone to work. It would be pleasure without alloy to accompany you in a walk on the great bridge. I would not be surprised if it takes you the entire year to visit all the places of interest in, & about St. Louis. Sister M[amie] says, O how I would like to go with brother to Shaw's garden, better than to go shopping, though the display in such a store, the number of ladies, & even the very street, is something greater to be seen in City life than we ever imagined. I sent you violets in a previous letter, knew you loved them darling & I never look at them but think of you. Maimie & Carrie tended their boxes with such care, & saying so often, am saving these for brother when he comes over. So soon as Carrie found I was writing to you, ran & got some violets, "Ma, tell Bud Johnnie I send these." Tug commenced a letter to you but he is so anxious to run round when he gets through reciting, dont know when he will finish it. We have no good pens, & he makes a terrible looking scrawl. Maimie says he dont love a single study except <u>History</u>. He is improving well in grammer. I told you in my first letter about Aunt Clara's babies, twin boys, born 23 Feb. one only is living. They speak of naming him for you. Nealie & I are going to see Clara tomorrow. Nealy says tell Johnnie I would like the best in the world to see him, but when I get the (Uncle Sam) prize* will go to St. Louis & for the purpose of hunting up a lunatic Asylum, for know I would need to be in it." Gilder came over to see us last time in a boat, he & Marvin M[oseley]. G. has rec'd your letter, says 'tis lonely times over there. Am in no haste to get the pictures, Son, suit your own time & convenience about them. I cant answer all your <u>interesting</u> letters, Son. Your friends desire re-

*The Uncle Sam prize must be the lottery.

membrance. This leaves all well. Love from each one of the family. Good bye, darling. God bless you is the prayer of

>your devoted mother,
>Mary E. Boddie

John B. Rumph in Ouachita Co. to his nephew John R. Boddie in St. Louis.

>April 24th 1875

My Dear Nephew

Your favor containing check on St Louis for $200 came safely to hand a few days ago, and I hasten a reply acknowledging its receipt. I will invest it in Scrip for you after a little while, as it will be lower owing to less demand because of the tax paying time being over. About $500,000 of it will be payed into the Treasury this year — which will be <u>cancelled</u> and burned —leaving about $1,500,000 still afloat. Next year another $500,000 will be absorbed in taxes, and so on until it will appreciate in value in <u>four years</u> to be worth as much as <u>greenbacks</u>.*

No news of interest in the neighborhood. The country very healthy — crops in good condition but corn looks badly and very small for the season owing to cold, frosty weather. Negroes are working very well this year, and if Providence will only smile upon us once more and give us a good season we will come out all right yet. Will write you when I have anything worth writing. Write with pencil as we are out of <u>ink</u>. Love of all to you,

>Your affectionate & sincere Uncle,
>J.B. Rumph

*As in several other Southern states which suffered severe revenue shortages during Reconstruction, Arkansas had issued this scrip to fund various public projects. While it was legally accepted at face value for tax payments, the general public refused to accept it at that rate for the settlement of private debts. Consequently, speculation occurred especially as tax payment times approached. "Greenbacks" was the term used for legal tender, or dollars, issued by the United States Government.

Mary E. Boddie in Ouachita Co. to her son, John R. Boddie in St. Louis

>April 27th, 75

My dear Son,

I need not assure you of the heart felt gratification your dear letters afford me, & I count the days that intervene between each one, thinking them long. Have recd yours of the 18th & I generally write every two weeks, though there is little variety here in our farm life, save the fluctuation of the weather & the fears & hopes entertained regarding its effect on the crops, fruits, & etc. The present prospect for a fine crop for the latter was never better, but 'tis very cold & rainy, & we hear that all the fruit in the Northern part of the state is killed, & there has been considerable snow at Little Rock. Our corn crop, your Pa says, is coming on slowly. The ground was too wet & cold for it to come up well, has finished replanting it & has planted one piece in cotton, the field in front of the house. Mr Wm Stone is the only one who has cotton up, but it looks badly, thinks he will plow it up, & plant again. Worse than all, Son, the rust has made the appearance in the wheat. Mr Wm S's, Bob [Stone]'s & Mr Moseley's. Pa says there is none as yet in his, but he don't know how soon it will be, his wheat is not quite so forward as theirs sown later. Pa brags on his irish potatoes, planted a barrel & judging from the looks of the patch, not one failed to come up. We have some pretty sunshiny days, not withstanding the cold, the trees are nearly in full leaf, & everything about your "dear old home" looks so very pretty. I wish every day that you could be here.

There is much to be enjoyed in a city life, & of all the amusements afforded, the Theater was my favourite, & you can attend it just often enough Son to make it more pleasurable. Am not surprised at the amount of your expences. I can give you a little item which will remedy the bother of sewing on buttons so frequently, just get a set of shirt studs,(you need not buy costly ones) if you are not addicted to the bachelor habit of leaving them in to go in wash, but having only one set will remedy that difficulty. I guess you & Mr R[ichards] have a nice time together & I will be so sorry when he has to leave, how far is your sleeping room from the hotel? When you become acquainted with some of the young ladies, I expect you'll believe them to be not only pretty, but sweet too, if you are not thinking too much about our little "Pink", & I would not have you, not to cherish some little Pink for all the world. The fourth Sabbath was our preaching day, but we could not go, as Pa wanted the mules to rest, after plowing so hard all the week. Cousin Mittie, Bettie, Tommy [Rumph] & the children spent the day with us after attending church. Mit said Mr. Hare did not preach as good sermon as usual, but I do enjoy his preaching so much, & would walk to church if Pa did not object. Walking does not fatigue me in the least, have been up to Clara's twice in that way this spring. Lula D[unlap] was here Sunday, said "tell cousin Johnny, the baby is already named John Boddie."* Eugenia & Attalie grow very fast, Mit is teaching them now, & the first thing Eugenia said when she came in "O, cousin Carrie, I can spell your name "C a r r y." Mit asked Maima, "What shall we do with Cousin Johnny for not writing to us! Cousin, if I had hold of brother would make the"spirit move" him. Tommy said 'twas well John was out of reach. Nealy went home with the girls. Have not seen Gilder since writing to you, had a note from him Saturday eve, wrote that he had been indisposed for several days, but was feeling well that evening. Though he enjoys nothing so much as spending a day at home, yet he comes very seldom.

We heard that Mr Milton B. in a difficulty with a negro was severely cut about the breast & one arm. The blood gushed out with every breath & Dr. B[ragg] thought him badly, though not fatally wounded. The affray took place on the farm. The freed men in our part of the country are striking for

*This is the twin who lived, son of Clara and John Dunlap.

higher wages, all Mr Patterson's hands have left, one of Uncle John's, & one or two of Mr. Davis. The blacks have what they call a Grange, club together, & decide for what wages they will work. $1.00 per day for men, 75cts for women, including rations for both, & whoever breaks the compact by working for less is to get so many lashes inflicted by one appointed for the purpose.

Little Sis [Carrie] recd a letter from her cousin Fay last week, telling us of the death of the last one of brother's children, Mrs. Green (whose home was in Miss.) Linn left an infant, & she had the care of George Johnston's one child, a boy. Hattie's family were well.

Mr. Bob [Stone] & Annie were to see us not long since, he says "tell John I've got my little dog home, & it's a beauty, named Willie." Do wish you could have heard him laugh, when I told him what a mistake I made in telling you "he intended sending the cat "tail" instead of the foot. State & Willie [Stone] stay pretty close at home working. Sissy [Agee] comes to see us occasionally & always makes inquiries about you, also Mrs Elliott, she & Billy spent a day with us not long since. Return the compliment to Tommy L[ove] for me when you write. I would be glad to hear of his doing well. Did he say anything respecting his brother Dick? Our vegetable garden is coming on slowly, will have some strawberries, most of my beds had to be reset this spring. The Ala. plants are living & my grape seed are up. Kate [Love] wrote that she sent the grape cuttings as directed, but Capt. Newton has never recd them. Tug says he wants to tell bud Johnnie about the bees & Mama's chickens &cc. & I guess he will finish his letter before long. He has many unavoidable interruptions from his studies & so does "little Sis" but they are making some progress.'Tis such a great pleasure to me son, to know that your dear letter is due tomorrow, because of your punctuality in writing. With much love from each one, I am as ever,
    Your devoted Mother,
    Mary E. Boddie

Spenser begged me to tell you such long items about Mr Graham's hunts & catching cats & cc, & how the bear scared him so bad he threw his hat at it, (had no gun with him at the time) that I have not time to write it, but must tell you, Spenser sends his "special respects," & wants you to send a name for his girl baby. Aunt Panina (as Pa calls her) always asks "how you come on, & tell him we are doing mighty well" &c, &c.

Mary E. Boddie in Ouachita Co. to her son John R. Boddie in St. Louis
June 4th 75

My dear son,

Your dear & most welcome letters of May 23 & 30th rec'd in due time, I need not assure you of the great pleasure they afford me. They always contain something new & interesting to me. Pa was very glad to get the papers, he foregos his usual noon nap to peruse them — he is entirely well of lameness occasioned by the fall, but complains occasionally of pain in his leg. The weather here is very hot too son, but we have the pleasant shade, & cool breezes to mitigate the excessive heat. No rain for the past five weeks (except two small showers) & in consequence the farmers are getting to be discouraged about the corn crops, I believe all of them in our vicinity are getting on well, & with good prospects save the need of rain, though Mr Greening told me to tell you, he was heartily tired of farming operations, had many discouragements (not knowing how to manage) & dont think he will ever try it again. Dr. Brown is to send him hands this week to chop out the cotton, in which the whole place is planted, except the field by the house. Mr Norris & family are living in a house on Mr Moseley's place. Uncle Billy sends a hand to work for the old man occasionally, & takes Mr N. fishing with him. All in the neighbourhood have cut their wheat, save George, his will be ready next week, your Pa thinks none of the wheat will turn out so well on account of the drouth, but if all make a sufficiency for bread will be content. Will says, if he fails to make corn we can live on flour & honey. They are plowing the corn again, & planting peas still hoping to get rain, though "all signs fail in dry weather." None of their cotton put to a stand, except the fields in front of the house which looks very pretty. Pa said Mr Hill told him not to bother about his cotton, that he would send hands to chop it out, but I believe Mr H. finds it difficult to procure hands for his own crop. Uncle John is much discouraged, says we wont make anything if it dont rain soon, all his hands left, no one but Tommy at work, but says they are getting on well, exchange work with Steve, & dont need any hands at present. Tommy took dinner with us last Sunday, we all attended church. Mr Robinson preached (Hardshell) dont like his preaching much. The substance of his discourse was well enough, but the delivery was almost ludicrous, more <u>rapid</u> than you ever could imagine any one to speak. I often wish I could be <u>with you</u> Sabbath mornings, & little sis says "I wish I could see the pretty ladies, & I've a mind to ask bud Johnnie how the dresses are fashioned." When Gilder left here Sunday eve, had sick headache, have heard since, that he is well. He looks to be taller, but pretty thin in flesh. Mit is splurging in town the past week, & will remain a week or two longer. Maima could not get ready to go yet, we have to economize this year, in the way of renovating old garments to answer the purpose of new ones, & I guess she will have her wardrobe in readiness soon. Neely is cook this week, expects to make her advent in Town the coming week. Cousin Bettie & Florence are at home receiving beaux whenever they call, but dont think I'll call the "grape vine" in requesition soon, for any of the Hardscrabble residents, unless the widower succeeds in making a favourable impression. Mr Lide has sent best respects &cc to the girls several times, & wished to know if they will have any picnics this summer? 'Twill be merely fish fries, if anything this season, in consequence of hard times but "small sis" [Mamie] says she dont want to have any at all, if she cant have a nice basket. Uncle Billy insists we shall have several fries.

Such excursions as you tell me of must be very pleasant indeed, & I wish you could have participated. All the young folks of the neighbourhood were here last Sunday eve, including Miss Dolle B. & Miss Martha Kellum. Capt N., Mr Bracy & Mr K. came over to church. Ora came over but staid with Mrs Annie S. & I did not get to see her. Mrs Cole has returned to Old Ouachita, stays in Camden with Ora & Julia A. Many at church made inquiries about you, & Mr Goodwin (or Gooding) & Lady to whom I was introduced mentioned being well acquainted with, & glad to hear from you. Uncle John & Mit took dinner with Clara that day, her boy grows, & does finely. I tell Uncle J[ohn] D[unlap] its all attributable to his name, he says his boy cant be beat. There goes the bell, must stop for dinner — 1 o'clock. Well darling have dined, helped wash dishes, set table, fed chickens &c. On yesterday we had pudding & raspberry sauce. Today pea soup, fried meat, bread, milk, & irish potatoes. Our garden needs rain so much, & there is some indication of it now, but I fear the clouds will pop round us, as has been the case so often of late. Our river has been out of the banks, & still in boating order.

Mrs Mitchel bade me give you her best respects, & tell you they have been expecting to leave for Hot Springs the last three months, they did start once & go two days journey, but returned for want of corn on the route, she & the Capt. have set a day time & again since to leave, but they are here yet. Expect to move, cattle & all, says the milk she will have to sell is already engaged, if it amounts to thirty gallons per day. Have not heard from sis Hattie in a long time, my last letter to her must have gone astray, & we get no letters from any of Carrie's family, I wrote to her soon after you left home, & Nealy has written to several of the family. The three months of your absence has been as so many years to me my son, though time flies fast, think of the "absent one," why darling I dont do anything else, & if wishes could waft you to us, would have been here many times, but Pa always says, John is best where he is, & we try to think so too. Take good care of yourself, for who is to nurse you should you get sick in bed? 'Tis vacation in all the schools here now, & the same with Carrie & Bobbie, though Maima has him to write some every day, requires him to copy history. Tug says, tell bud

Johnnie I am going to write to him next week. Sister wrote last week, that is the reason I did not write until now. State & Miss Mollie L. ask to be remembered to you — Tune stays close at home, says he's <u>coming out</u> Christmas, & if they have any picnics this summer he's determined none of the crowd shall <u>enjoy it for he's not going</u>. I forgot to tell you that young Mr Mitchel's wife has a fine son, also one to Mrs John Norris. I must bid you good bye, & get to my churning. <u>All</u> send love to our dear absent one. With prayers for your welfare, I remain as ever,

      Your devoted mother,
      Mary E. Boddie

  P.S. Spencer says Lotta Neilson is the name, but he could not remember it till he got home. Aunt Nina says I can <u>member</u> it, what's it Miss Mary? & she would repeat it several times, <u>yes I can member,</u> but she didn't only the Lotta, so Liddy came over this morning, says tell you she's much obliged, & likes the name very much — All of them send howdy.

Robert E. (Tug) Boddie in Ouachita Co. to his brother John R. Boddie in St. Louis

              June 26th 1875

  Dear bud Johnie

  I was so glad to get a lettar from you. I did not think much that you would answer my letter. I could read nearly all your letter with the help of mama. I could not tell the u's from n's. Carrie and I dont say my lessons now but I have to write some evry day, you must not think that I dont do any thing because I dont study they all keep me busy.

  I help bud Willie hoe some and work in the garden. pa has finer wheat than any of them and his oats the finest kind. We had the finest kind of a rain last week but pa says the corn wont make a full crop. I went fishing the other day with uncle Billy and we caught a string of fine fish two brim [bream] three white pearch four goggleies* one trout one buffalo and cooked as many at lake as we could eat. I had much rather live in the country than in the city where there is no beggars. I think I should not like to see them. I wish I could have seen those big turtles. I dont hunt rabbits much now, the dogs started something in the field w[h]en I was helping bud Willie plant peas, w[h]en they treed, I went to them and found two minks. I killed them both. bud Johnie when Mr Winston and Mr Marvin Mosely was coming from town last Friday evening they saw a big bear run across the road.

                 July 2nd

  bud Johnie we all had such a nice time at the lake yesterday fishing. uncle Billy Mr R Stone, Miss Lula[?] and Carrie and Bobbie Dee [Newton] Colie* we caught a good many fish, we had three boats to ride in. In the

*"Goggleies" are a kind of small fish known as Goggle-eye.

*"Colie" refers to Coleman Brown, son of Julia Stone Brown Alston.

evening Miss Lula, Carrie and Colie went riding on horseback. uncle Billy, Bobie Dee and I fished and caught some to carry home. they were the finest white perch you ever saw. Bud Johnie I try to be a good boy. I say my prayers every night. all send love to you. We are all well.

     Your affectionate brother,
     Robert Lee Boddie

                 Tues night

My dear son,

 This was my week to write, but as Tug wanted to write to you, deferred answering your dear letters until next week, & must say that I enjoyed the perusal of your letter quite as much as you did the participation in that beautiful garden, amid all the perfections of Nature & Art. Your sister came home today, delighted with her two weeks sojourn in Town, will give you an account of her dilatoriness in writing herself. Cousin Mittie said, I waited till after my trip to have something about which to write, & I rather guess she had considerable — in case she left out the most important item, I will tell you that the <u>Widower</u> [Edmund Rucks] was indefatigable in his attentions, & I believe success will crown his efforts — he makes it convenient to come over often to look after his farm interest on this side of the river. Mit spent one eve with me this week, said she had something to tell me, but as we had other company, did not learn what it was. Saw Uncle J. at church Sunday, told me to tell you he had been so hard at work in his garden, he was too tired to write. I did not commence darling with the thought of writing only a word or two, in fact cant write at night, so must close before I indulge to excess. good night & may Our Father in Heaven guide & care for you is the daily prayer,

    of your devoted Mother—

Mary E. Boddie in Ouachita Co. to her son John R. Boddie in St. Louis
                 July 15th 75

My dear son,

 Although I had much work on hand last week that I was compelled to finish, would have written to you, if I had not known that Mittie sent a letter to be mailed on Wednesday, & your sister one on Saturday of that week, so thought 'twould be superfluous for me to send one too, & they boasted of having written <u>so much</u> & told you of everything possible & probable. Our quarterly meeting came off last Saturday & Sunday. I was much disappointed in not being able to attend, but after working hard to have things in readiness was too tired to go. Maima, Nealy & Willie went Saturday night, & Sunday morning they had to get breakfast, milk, cook dinner, & was hurried to get to church by 11. I had all the cleaning up to do, so told the girls I would enjoy <u>resting</u> & <u>reading</u> my bible at home better than to go. It so happened that the freedmen's meeting came on at the same time, & we could get no help at all, <u>Aunt Nina</u> our chief dependence (since Becky left) was sick. Several from Town attended the meeting, Mr & Mrs Hallam, Mr Saxon & Gordon, with Miss Ella B. & Miss Mary Curry — Gilder, Mr J. Morgan, cousin Mit & the children dined with us that day. Mr Pope preached the A. M. sermon & Parson Lineas delivered the closing sermon Sunday eve. Miss P. (Mit told me) enquired particularly about you, & asked for your address.

That you have my sincere sympathy darling, in your suffering with the most of all maladies you are well aware, & I cant but <u>fear</u> 'tis more Neuralgia than toothache, & do hope you obtained relief without sacrificing more teeth, as surely so many aching at once, cant be caused from decay. I felt so grateful to you my boy for writing, though it had been just <u>one line</u>, for so surely as the weeks' come, I am expecting your dear message. Many thanks darling for the pretty memento of the very pleasant time you spent in Shaw's garden, your sister gained first possession, (being in Camden) as the letter was superscribed to her, & on opening it, the petals from the flower you sent shattered off.

Our garden is all drying up, very few flowers blooming, though Maima is trying to keep many of the plants growing by watering every evening or two, & my strawberry plants too are wilting & dying. We have a few watermelons, plenty apples, but no peaches as yet. No rain son since the 19th June, so you can imagine how the crops in this vicinity has suffered, in nearly all the adjoining counties have had rain plenty, & in some places in this. Will has quit field work for the past eight or ten days, is very busy getting out timbers for a gin house, pretty severe work this hot weather, he goes out very early every morning to raid on the coons, as they are making sad havoc on the corn in roasting ear, the corn tassels are green yet, but the blades twist & look badly in the heat of the day. Uncle J[ohn] D[unlap] was here this morning, said he would make on his new ground a sufficiency, but thinks the cotton crops will be injured past recovery, it looks wilted, & checked in growth. Three weeks ago your Pa's cotton looked fine, & the piece in front of the house Uncle J.D. said was the best he had seen. Aunt C[lara] is in her usual health, young John B. grows fast, & is a fine boy, so his Pa says.

Carrie spent last week at Uncle John R's had a nice time she & Florence taking horseback rides — she is cooking again this week, "tell Bud Johny I will do my best, but he must not wait <u>so long</u> before he comes, we all think he has been gone a long time now." Nealy went home with Mittie Sunday, told me to tell you, that you had her undivided sympathy in your toothache misery. I have not replied to sis Hattie's letter yet, the weather is so hot that by the time I get through with domestic work am fatigued & think I will feel more like writing another day, & so time passes — Am glad Mr

R is with you again, 'tis so like some one from home, remember us to him with kind regards. Another interuption son, & I cant finish my letter to-day — Sun nearly down —

Friday morning. Tug & I were the happy recipients of your dear favors of the 11th yesterday eve, & need not assure you how glad I am to know you are well again. Were both of those extracted teeth decayed, or did you have the wrong one pulled out first? So Mr R is off again, well I am very glad you have a pleasant companion in his place, I expect you & Mr R feel like one of the family at Mr G's & appreciate their kindness much. Your description of the 4th reminds me of several such spent in New York* & which I always feared the advent of, though I enjoyed seeing the companies parade, & going to Castle Garden at night to witness the fireworks. Tug would like the firecracker fun first rate, for that is all he aspires to having Christmas times. We have him studying some again, he always asks me to read your letters to him, & when he heard that one, said, Ma what does Bud Johnnie mean about President?, told him, you did not want him to grow up in ignorance, that he must study hard, & be as smart as the President. Tug is lazy about studying, but I think if we had more <u>uninterupted</u> leisure to devote to him, would progress faster. He will read History by the hour & ask any number of questions, is at work today, as Willie is hauling the wheat to Mr Moseley's to get it thrashed. Pa has been busy up there all this week, they have fixed up a horse power to his threshing machine, & are cleaning all the wheat crops in this vicinity. Mr Moseley's turned out 95 bu. Mr Bob S[tone] 25. I forget the quantity Uncle J. D. made 45 or 50. Pa has quit buying corn some time ago, Will keeps two of the mules in the bottom most of the time, feeds the others on oats, we do without corn bread, no <u>privations</u> at all, but it bothers me much, to have no feed for the poultry. Dont think the dogs suffer though, they are looking <u>better</u> than when we fed them on bread, boil the pot for them every day, filled with pot liquor, dish water; scraps from the table, potatoes, &c &c besides as much milk as they want — Will says his bees are not doing anything now, weather too dry & hot I guess, he did not intend taking his honey to H[ot] S[prings] before ascertaining if he could dispose of it profitably. Capt & Mrs M are delighted up there, tis their Eureka. Miss Mattie & Jennie speak of going up there soon, if Miss Mattie's beau dont interfere in that arrangement, a Mr Roberson visits there quite frequently. The greatest pastime among them here son, is fishing, altogether at the river now, & with good success. Neither Pa or Will has yet taken time to go. Mr Jimmie M. sent us a fine large fish yesterday. Tommy said he took a deer hunt last week, saw three, got a shot at one, but did not kill it. I guess he will hunt some other "dear" this week, as Miss Anna is visiting at Mrs Proctors & I asked Gilder why he did not write, said he had nothing to write about, & wrote such poor letters, he goes nowhere but to church & Sunday school, though he did call on our girls when they were

*Sis Mollie's family, the Gildersleeves, lived in New York for several years when she was a child.

over there, loves to come home every two or three weeks.

Well darling I must bid you good bye for this time, my letter reminds me of the play "Much Ado about Nothing" a long rigmarole containing very little, but I do love to talk with you thus, & cant express myself in a few words. Your friends, whenever I meet them inquire about you & desire remembrance. The blacks too ask me to send howdy for them. With much love from each one of the family, I am as ever,

your devoted mother,
Mary E. Boddie

I am so glad you called my attention to remissness in addressing my letters, Gilder mails all my letters, even those Pa takes over, & I dont know why he did not tell me. Now I think of it, let me tell you darling boy of one misspelled word in your letter which I wish you to correct, because of your having written it so the second time, is why I mention it —"jem"

The enclosed violet is from Miss Anna, Maima says she charged her particularly to send it, but she hurried so with her letter to get to send it, that she forgot to enclose it. The night Maima was to have finished her letter, had company, is the reason she was hurried.

Mary E. Boddie in Ouachita Co. to her son John R. Boddie in St. Louis
July 29th '75

My dear son,

With pleasure I reply to your dear letters of the 11th & 18th Inst. that you may know how much I appreciate the kind privilege of hearing from your weekly, & that you are enjoying good health. We have been favoured with rain at last; real good season, but your Pa says too late for his corn crop, however it has helped some, & cheered all up wonderfully. Will thinks the prospect much better than last year, & it remains yet to be seen how the cotton is benefitted, & we can only hope for the best. Uncle J. R. is in fine spirits since the rain; we went there last Sunday from church, he insisted on my going, though Geo. was expecting us home to dinner; we always cook dinner before we go, & left him plenty, but he did not like being left alone all day. He used to tell us he was glad when we were gone to leave him a quiet day to himself. Uncle J. had killed a fawn on Friday, & the venison was fine, says he cant kill deer liked he did times agone, that he's always in the wrong place now to get a shot. It seems strange to me yet son, to see Mat presiding there, she looks to be out of place, though she is just as good as can be & they all get on admirably, which I am so glad to know, but I dont enjoy being there now. Maud is a very pretty, interesting child, can stand alone & I am sure you will be surprised to see how much Attalie & Eugenia have grown. I must prepare you too, not to expect "little sis" to be a mite, for she is very near as tall as Florence, & will be I guess by the time she enters her sixteenth year, she will be fifteen the 19th of Dec. if she lives to see it. I can scarcely realize how fleeting is time until reminded of how old the children are, 'tis very near a year, since our pleasant sojourn home, & when Nealy & I talk of it (which we often do) the time seems but a month or two ago. Nealy rec'd a letter from Mrs Clark recently, she wrote us nothing respecting the crops — all were well except Carrie's Geo. was having chills.

Maima is spending this week at Uncle J's & Mit is to come home with her to stay with us next week, she is very gay & humorous, seems to be happy in the contemplation of her future, & her decision in favor of Mr R[ucks], pleases all the family, Geo. R[umph] particularly. I think he will be to her a loving & kind companion, but I did not dream how reluctant I would feel about giving Mit up, she is endeared to me by ties only second to my own dear children. The time is not yet decided. Mr R. told Mit if she would only give him a favourable answer, he would be willing to wait ten years, but of course he talks differently now. Makes his visits every Monday, & goes there all by ways possible, but Mrs Grundy knows all about it, & Mr. R. comes in for a considerable share of teasing, & as I heard, said, "that if some of the good people did not mind, he would give them a knock down." Florence is staying with Anna this week, she & Carrie in company with Uncle Billy have gone to Town today, went for the horseback ride, to see their friends & because they knew Mr. L. would go with them, for it seems to be his greatest pleasure to gratify the young folks. We had a very pleasant party at Uncle J[ohn] D[unlap]'s on Thursday last, 'twas given to his nephew John D.* from Atlanta, Geo. "Cousin Bettie" arranged all the preliminaries. The refreshments consisted of hot coffee, light bread, cake & lemonade, & in garden under the Scuppernong Arbor the ground was covered with straw carpeting, a long table fixed up with benches on each side, & the tabled filled with fine melons, peaches, apples & plums, the Arbor lighted up with candles, & torch stands in the garden & yard. Uncle J. D. gave his nephew to Bettie, but that fact nothing daunted the balance of the girls from trying to captivate the young man. He is 24 years of age, has fair complexion, blue eyes, light hair, is about five feet, five inches in height, heavy built, but dont look like any of the Dunlaps, manners very pleasant & agreeable. Uncle J. seemed quite fond of him; Aunt C, too. Florence says she fell in love with his pretty looking mouth, teeth & mustache. He was severely afflicted with Rheumatism, went to Hot Springs the first of April, could not walk at that time, but has nearly recovered, & came down eight or ten days ago (on his way home) to visit his Ark. relatives. . . . We had a lively time riding home through a hard rain, all hands got a thorough soaking, & bare of head covering too, save a kerchief.

I met with Dr. Bragg at Mrs. Annie's yesterday, he inquired particularly about you, expressed himself very glad to hear from, & desired kind

*Uncle John Dunlap's nephew was John Gaston Dunlap, son of James Cousar Dunlap.

regards &c to John. There is considerable sickness in & about Camden, the prevailing disease flux. Mr. J. T. Elliott died yesterday, intemperance the principal cause. Old Mr. Ellis is very low at this time. Mrs. Annie [Stone] bade me tell you that Bob had been grumbling for the past two month about having no rain &c, & now that he has been favoured with a good season, & has a <u>fine boy</u> to brag on, she hopes to hear no more of his growling soon, thinks he will write to you soon, if he aint too overjoyfull! The name Bob has selected for his boy is Amphlett; what do you think of it? says he is prouder of this child, than he ever was before, but I expect 'tis because he was childless. I do hope they may raise it.

We are luxuriating on peaches & milk, our young orchard is bearing finely, but the fruit is small, pears are ripening, though they are not so large as usual, injured by the drouth.

Pa says he dont care how many papers you send him, is very glad & much obliged for any, but he likes the Republican best. Tug has been hunting in every one that Pa gets now, for the <u>one</u> you promised to <u>send him.</u> Will has started his plows in the cotton again since the rain, has finished getting out all the gin house timber, & has it all hauled up, no one worked at it but himself, Spencer & Jack. Geo. intends to put it up back of the horse lot I believe. Pa has been hunting & getting up his dry cattle this week, & there is some out yet with young calves. Tug wants to tell you about those we have up, says he's going to write to bud Johnnie soon, he helped Aunt Nealy milk this morning, his cousin Attalie came home with us last Sunday, & Mit said she would let Eugenia come with her. Your letter to Maima came this week, I sent it over to her, know "little sis" will bring <u>mine</u> this eve. Gilder did not come to see us last Sunday, he went with Mr. Brown & family to the big meeting on the Camden side of the river, some six miles below. Mr Agee told me that Gilder enjoyed it so much, he was reluctant to leave, was flying round among the girls, something unusual for him to do. Will have to stop right here darling, for Miss Anna has come to spend the night with us, & my letter must be ready to send by Pa in the morning. Mr. Moseley's minister, Mr. Roberson, preached for us last Sunday, he read the 1st Chapt. Paul's epistle to the Ephisians, & Jude, & preached from thoughts suggested &c&c. I dare say every one thought we'd have a wide awake, doctrinal sermon, but was agreeably disappointed, for 'twas quite interesting, & charitable towards all.

Our freedmen all send howdy, & Aunt Nina says tell him "the <u>crop</u> is helped <u>mightly since</u> the rain, & we's all doing well." With much love from each one of the family to our dear <u>absent one</u>, I am as ever,

    your devoted mother,
    Mary E. Boddie

Cornelia Dickson in Ouachita Co. to Hattie Murley in Autauga Co.

August 3rd,/ 75

Dear Hattie,

You will probably be surprised at receiving a letter from me at this late date after promising to write to you soon after my return to Ark. Well I shall proceed to write having no apologies to make save procrastination. But I now promise myself the pleasure of writing to each of my friends who were kind enough to request a correspondence. I have much more leisure now, than formerly as Carrie, Sis Mollie's younger daughter, assists Mamie and I in the culinary department, by cooking one week in every three.

We still have all the cows to attend to, nine in number. But the cooking now is not overburdensome. We have scarcely any vegetables, have suffered severly from the drouth; and gardens as well as crops are again a failure this year, that is, in our immediate vicinity. Some of the adjoining neighborhoods and counties have not wanted for seasons and are producing very abundant crops; but many farmers in this neighborhood will be insolvent this year; not being able to endure a long drouth for two successive springs. They are more cheerful since the rain, and think cotton may yet produce a moderate crop.

We attended church last Sunday week, heard a Hard-shell sermon from the thoughts suggested by reading the first chapter of Paul's first letter to the Ephesians and the book of Jude. I think he was more charitable than most of that sect, and almost everyone was pleased with the discourse. We dined at Dr. Rumph's. They are a very lively family & many of us, when we are all together. Matt, brother John's wife, has a very sweet and interesting babe, who is beginning to stand alone and perform many cunning tricks, taught her by the children who all love to play with baby Maude. We left Mamie with her cousins to spend a week, and Attalie, one of the little girls, came home with us to have a merry time at her Uncle G[eorge]'s. Mamie came home yesterday, Mittie came with her to spend two weeks with us. We enjoy so much having her company. We were recalling this morning "this time last year, when we were all together busily engaged in preparing for our trip to Ala." That visit an event to which we often recur with great pleasure. And how are your little folks? Are Bob & Minnie, George & Crawford, as fond of attending Sabbath School as when we were there? We often speak of them, and wish to see them all again.

Of the strawberry plants that you gave us, we succeeded in saving three. The others just would die notwithstanding all our efforts to keep them alive. The three that we saved are fine and flourishing, with many many little vines shooting out that will make a number of little plants. We gave Clara some of the plants when we came home. She also has three living ones. Sis Mollie wants to know how your plants produced this year. The drouth came near destroying our large strawberry bed this summer. It was almost entirely destroyed last year, had to be reset last Feb. Probably Hattie you will think this a rambling letter of but little import to you, but I scarcely know what to write that would prove entertaining, and write more because of my great wish to hear from you, than for your edification.

 Our amusements for the summer generally consist in picnics & fish-frys, but we have had no large picnics at our lake this summer. Times too hard. All our young folks attended a picnic given at a large spring about eleven miles from here, and notwithstanding the dust, had the gayest time imaginable. There was a large crowd. The amusements on the ground consisted of music, dancing, & croquet, and for the small fry, a large swing. Brother John had killed a fawn a day or two before, and the venison was fine. He says he cannot kill as many deer nowadays as formerly, he is always in the wrong place to get a shot, the fact is, he is losing his hearing in one ear, and cannot locate the cry of the hounds as well as he used to. *

*There is no closing for this letter in the journal.

Cornelia Dickson in Ouachita Co. to her friend Rebecca Underwood in Autauga Co.

August 17th 1875

Dear Rebecca,

 I have at last seated myself to enjoy the long promised pleasure of writing to you. I know that you have ceased to look for a letter from me long since, that is, unless time has sped as fleetly with you, sweeping away the last twelve months, since I was permitted to enjoy your society. Yes, many many times have those pleasant hours been recalled, while pondering o'er memory's tablets, and verily have I wished to again realize that happiness, not the least among them my pleasant visit to your most worthy fathers and tell Beckie I often recall my ride over that shaded road with her appreciated company & with which I have always associated her cheery countenance, frequently thinking of her expression not to forget to associate her with my last ride along that road.

 The promised sweetheart I found, on my arrival home to be so deeply in the snares of cupid, it were useless to try to unfetter the chain which held him a willing captive. Notwithstanding, he admired and highly complimented her picture. He is now located in St. Louis. Clara, too, was delighted to see it and Mr. Underwood's. She, brother George, & brother John said they would recognize him anywhere, asked me if he really looked so young. I know I would be so pleased Rebecca to have yours and the childrens pictures.

 Clara with hers spent Sunday with us. She is enjoying better health now than she has in a long time. Says she will send you hers & childrens pictures when she can have some taken, there is no artist in town, nor has been in several months. I wish you could see Clara's babe, he is such a large fine looking, goodnatured boy. I have so often regretted the death of his little twin brother, they were almost exactly alike. Mr Dunlap is so proud of him, thinks of it as he did of the others; that his boys are prodigies. I earnestly hope they will raise this one.

Mittie and little Eugenia Rumph have been with us two weeks, and we enjoy their company very much. Eugenia resembles Sallie both in feature & disposition; is a perfect little busy-body, "feeding Uncle George's pigs and helping to milk the gentlest cows." She is only six years old. Attalie resembles George Rumph. Little Maud the baby of eleven months is beginning to walk, is a sweet interesting child. But enough about the little people, who are too diminuative to occupy so much of your attention.

The young people in the neighborhood participated in a fish fry today week ago, had a gay time fishing & boatriding on the lake & partook of a bountiful fish dinner. I wish you all could have been with us. I know you would have enjoyed the day. It is the first we have had on the lake this season. Most of the young men are farmers and have all been much engage[d] with their crops to go with us fishing until recently. It is true the drouth caused many to curtail their working the corn & cotton, but the wheat crop though short, came in for a share of attention. At present we are having rain in abundance and it is scared that the cotton will be seriously injured by it & it is a precarious crop at best. The night after the fish fry, we were serenaded by a string band.

Do you ever hear of Hattie Murley & the additional cares added to her household since we saw you? Her oldest stepdaughter died sometime last September leaving five little children which Mr Johnson prevailed upon Hattie to take in charge. The youngest was only three weeks old when its mother died. And we have heard since that Mrs Green, Hattie's last stepdaughter is dead. She left only one child, an infant. Mr Green's sister keeps house for him.

Do you ever see or hear from Mr. Davis? Sis Mollie has written to him but received no reply to her letter, have received but one letter from him since we came home, and brother George lost it before he left town.*

*This is another truncated letter in the journal.

Robert Lee "Tug" Boddie in Ouachita Co. to his brother John R. Boddie in St. Louis

August 26th 1875

Dear bud Johnie,

    I was very glad to get your letter and wanted to write to you before now but all of them at home was sending letters and I had to wait. We have nine pretty calves now, and two fine heifers, that Maima calls Belle and Lee. Belle's calf is named Robert Lee. I can milk any of our cows in the pen now except Old Fortune. We have torn the old gin house down, and hauled the good logs up back of the crib, and are going to build a new one, our cotton will soon be ready to pick. Our pigs are nearly grown, bud Johnie I have to pick up eight buckets of peaches and feed them every morning. I have six sows with 30 odd young pigs. I say my lessons every day and Mama makes me say a catechism lesson once a week. I love to read the Universal History you gave me. The old bear come in the field and Henry got our dogs and his, and Spencers run him to Freo Island. The dogs bayed him two or three times, but Henry said he was afraid of getting lost, and blowed the dogs off, and let him alone. Bud Gilder come over last Sunday and went to church with us. I wish you were in Camden so you could come over and go to church with us too. They all say cousin Mittie is going to get married, but I dont think she will much but she pretends she will, what is your opinion. Bud Johnie the dogs are all well, I never hunt any now. Pa and Mama wont let me hunt by myself with your little gun. Robbie Dee [Newton] and I hunted with it one day, he killed two squirrels bud Willie keeps your gun clean and nice, he goes to see Miss Anna [Moseley] some times, and so does cousin Tommy [Rumph]. All of us send love to you

    Your affectionate little brother
    Robert Lee Boddie

Saturday, Aug 28th

    As Tug has left an unfinished sheet, will send a word or two of greeting myself to my dear boy, though what to write I scarcely know these dull & quiet times. We are all plodding along in the usual way, blessed with good health, & cheerful spirits, & nothing to break the routine of every day life save an occasional visit, & the same from our friends & neighbors. Whenever the girls are together, we have the usual amount of small talk about the boys, sweethearts &c, & now that cousin* has decided her own destiny, she has gone to work in earnest & seems absorbed in making preparations for the event. Maima dont like the idea of her marrying Mr R[ucks], says she likes him very well, but she dont want "cousin" to have him. I tell her <u>that is a case</u> in which everyone must please themselves, & we can only wish, that all the happenings allotted to mortals here on earth may be hers. Your letter of Aug 15th I did not get until the 21st & it seems to me a much longer

* "cousin" is what the Boddie family called Mittie Rumph

time between letters, though you write the usual time. Do you write at the office or in your <u>room</u>, (I love to think just where you are,) as you have given such accurate descriptions of both places, I can imagine just how things look. Am so glad you occupy such a pleasant room, & more so, to know you have the opportunity of enjoying such fine music every eve. 'Tis well the young lady is ugly, for if she was pretty, & possessing such musical charms, you would certainly be capitivated, then, what would our little <u>Pink</u> say? Aunt Nealy is well, & lively as ever, contributes very often to our home pleasures in singing "those good old songs" particularly your favourite, "Bonnie Eloise." Here comes our waggon from town, & Pa with it, now for my letter, "small sis, & little sis" are on the alert too, so here we go. 1/2 past 5. Thanks darling for your letter of 22nd & never mind the half sheet so that the weekly tidings of your own dear self reaches me. I will heed your loving admonition to take good care of myself, for if I were to be sick would miss you very much. Must confess feeling great regret that you cannot come to see us this winter, have been thinking more about it than I was aware of, but will hope on, that such pleasure will be permitted me some other time in the future, feeling thankful that you are well, & doing well. Your sister was delighted with her present of beautiful note paper, something quite new & stylish, told Bud she would have to write notes of compliment to her sweetheart, & matter of fact "Bud" said, if you keep it entirely for such a purpose, it will last you a long time. Pa is in rec't of several <u>Papers</u>, all of which he puts carefully away in his <u>own box</u>, & thanks to you, is furnished with reading matter for all his leisure time. "Aunt Hannah" is quite well, called to see me the last time she went to town, asked great many questions about you, & desired to be particularly remembered to Mars Johnnie. The blacks at home ask to send word for them, whenever I write to you. Aunt C[lara]'s family well, your friends make inquiries about you whenever I meet them & all of us at home send dear love to our absent one —
     Your devoted mother,
     Mary E. Boddie

Mary E. Boddie in Ouachita Co. to her son John R. Boddie in St. Louis
                Sept. 25th '75

My dear son,

 It seems to me to have been a long, long time since I wrote to you, & but for your dear letters dont know what I would do, but at the same time darling, knowing your time to be so fully occupied now, am content with the dear privilege of hearing from you <u>weekly</u> & not tax you with writing long letters, when you should be taking a <u>long walk</u> for exercise & health, after the week's confinement in work. During the latter part of Aug & the first week or two in Sept. we had the hottest weather I've ever experienced, & since then, a cold spell such as you speak of, & I thought of you so much during that time, & was hoping the climate with you was not subject to such sudden changes as with us, so I beg son that you will clad yourself accordingly, which precaution may avert a spell of sickness. Your sister wrote to you week before last, & told you why I could not write,* & as I was recruiting so slowly, Ora N[ewton] & the girls persuaded me to go home with her. I enjoyed the rest, & visit very much, though it ceased raining only one evening during my stay, & that was Saturday eve, which Ora & I spent with Jennie.* Did not get to speak with Geo. at all, as I came home Sunday morning. Jenny asked many questions about you, said she would like so much to see you, thinks her hands full now with two boys to care for, & says "Aunt Mollie what will I do; when I haven't learned yet to take care of one?" told her that experience would soon teach her, & though the responsibility was great, yet the comfort of possession counterbalanced all minor trouble. Eugene is a handsome boy, & very shy of strangers, dont try to talk yet, but can make his wants readily understood. The baby is sweet, & pretty, has a head shaped like Uncle John's, all his features good, prominent nose, which Jennie is proud of, as that was "Bluege's" objectionable feature, the baby is much smaller than Eugene was, & dont favor him in the least. Mit thinks him just like his GdPa. Do you think son, I never learned the baby's name till through your letter, & the same about our Camden merchants being at St Louis. So you see, you send me news items from home, as well as everything else interesting in your dear letters. I was more than glad to talk with Mr Rucks after his being with you, he came over the very next day after his arrival, "Cousin Mittie" was here, otherwise, I guess I would not have had that pleasure. O darling I dont wonder you feel like coming too, we all want to see you so much, but while you are well & happy at your post of work, will let hope be my comforter, & may you darling boy, ere very long be able to realize all that pleasure & happiness, to which you very naturally look forward with your chosen one, & which you so richly merit.

Our protracted meeting closed last Tuesday night, commencing the Saturday previous, had some good sermons, & some very indifferent, the girls all liked Mr Powell's preaching best, there were three accessions to the church, Mr. L. Agee, Fanny Chewning & Lula Dunlap. I did not get to go at all, as Pa was sick, he had two, third day chills,* found him in bed when I came home last Sunday, he's desisted the chill, & had no fever for several days. Uncle John spent one day with us this week, said 'twas not necessary for him to take any more medicine. Pa had the first chill to-day week ago, & the last one on Tuesday, & I did not like to write until I could tell you they were broken. Pa says, he will accept the assurance of his boy to draw on him when he "means business," for the fact is he dont love to write letters, however much he appreciates getting them. Tommey has just come from

*Maima had written on September 17th that their mother had suffered another attack of neuralgia, which plagued sis Mollie for many years.

*Jennie is Virginia Jordon Rumph, wife of George Boddie Rumph, son of Dr. John Rumph and Sis Fanny Rumph.

*Third day chills are intermittent sieges which accompany spells of Malaria.

Town & handed Pa's paper from your dear self, & one too for Tug, which he is so proud to get, says, "tell Bud Johnnie I intend to read it all through." Tommey says, be sure to send the Terrier, he will be very glad to get it, then he will have two little dogs, as he carried one home this week, that he begged of some one in Town. Maima & Anna went to Camden this morning in the waggon with Mr Allis M[oseley]. Nealy was to have gone too, but as 'twas rainy declined, & sure enough there has been a slow rain falling all day, they have not yet returned, went to get some little fancy articles for the wedding outfit. Bettie, Maima, Anna, & Georgia P[roctor] are to be the young lady attendants, Mr J Rucks, Geo. Ritchie, & Lide the gentlemen. Mit thought she had Tommy's consent to be one, but he has declined, & we dont know yet who will take his place. You guess correctly about the "little cousin" of yours, the nearer the time approaches the greater the excitement & flurry. Uncle J. has decided that the marriage <u>must</u> take place in <u>daytime</u>, & that flustrated Mit very much. I dont know but <u>that</u> arrangement will be best considering the times &cc, I did want to give them a dinner, but that will be impossible now. The dining will be at Uncle J's when they will all go to Town, & Mrs Rucks wishes to have a supper &c for the bridal party. The 19th of Oct. is the appointed day, so "cousin" had decided when she was down here. She has three dresses yet to make, Geo. sent over by Maima the one purchased for Mit in St. Louis. 'Tis getting late & I must close, for this evening. "Little sis" says she would much prefer you would deliver the kiss in person, but as you cant will accept it, & return much love to Bud Johnnie.

 Sunday 26th. Well darling you are well I hope & wending your way to church this cool but fair Sabbath morn. "Little sis," Tug & Willie have gone to church. "Small sis" wanted to go but had to get dinner, milk &c. Nealy went over to Uncle J's late yesterday eve as she had to see Mittie preparatory to going to Town for her tomorrow. Pa has shaved, washed & dressed, & is enjoying his paper. Capt Dee N. has just come in, so he & Pa can have a chat while I finish my letter. Am glad to know son you allow yourself some recreation occasionally, & being with your old Camden friends makes it the more enjoyable. Mr Brown has told you I guess that they have Mr Y. Duncan in the store now, I was rather sorry to know it, as I would not have chosen him, for an intimate associate for Gilder, having so little confidence in Y's entire manliness & moral worth. The gin house frame is all nearly put up, but I cant say that it will be completed this year, Willie is very busy picking cotton, with only Spencer in the field, Yes they have Tug too, when we had got him in a good way of studying, but he makes a regular field hand now, told me to tell you he picked 105 lbs last Friday, says the patch in front of the house will make 6 or 7 bales, they have nearly picked over it once. All Hardscrabble folks are well at this time, Uncle Billy has been sick, so has Mr & Mrs N[ewton]. Mr P. Greening says he has enjoyed better health here than ever before, talks of trying the bottom another year.

The Mitchell girls are still at Hot S[prings], are looked for home this week. Uncle J.D.'s family are all well. Lula spent the day with Carrie yesterday, she came by for Carrie to go to Town with her to help select a dress to wear to the wedding, but as the day proved so rainy Uncle J.D. did not take them. Maima & Carrie appropriate my butter money as fast as I can make it, but of a truth "necessity is the mother of invention" for they devise many ways to make a little means answer their needs, & I am not at all sorry that they are learning lessons of economy. Will's outfit, thanks to you, has & will serve him well the entire year for dress occasions. Maima met Mrs Wright at church during the meeting, had all her children with her, & Maima says they are the prettiest <u>group</u> of children she ever saw. Kate still holds you in kind remembrance, & expressed herself very glad to hear of you. Mrs Elliott's baby Coralie is quite sick at Mr Ton[e]y's. Florence, Eugenia, & Attalie have been sick with chills, Mittie & Mat were at church today. Bettie had a severe cold, & did not go. Nealy recd a letter last week from Miss Julia Howard, my good old friend. Mr Davis died about the first of Sept. he was a great sufferer, & prayed to die, was buried by request at Pea ridge church. I cant but feel sorrow that another link of the past is severed, but to be reunited in a better world I hope. Dee asks to be remembered to you, Miss Anna also sends her love. With much love from all the family,
remain your devoted mother —
Mary E. Boddie

Cornelia Dickson in Ouachita Co. to her niece Onie Love in Autauga Co.
Oct 1st 1875

Dear Onie,

Your letter enclosed in your mother's to Sis M was received some time since. I was truly glad to receive it. Was reminded by it of the pleasant hours spent with you all last summer. I do not know when I will be able to repeat that visit, if ever. This last clause makes me feel sad, and I will live in hopes of visiting you all again some time in the future. I dreamed the other night that Sis Carrie was here, paying us a visit. Wish that the dream could be realized. Carrie was delighted to learn that you would correspond with her and wrote to you forthwith, is my reason for not replying to your letter ere now.

Sis Mollie is quite sick, similar to the spell she had last fall, though not nearly so severe. It is the second attack she has had this fall. Brother G has just recovered from chills & fever, was quite ill for a week. In my other letter I believe I spoke of the remarkably good health of the neighborhood. Since September set in there has been a great deal of sickness, principally chills. One or two deaths among children. Brother John is kept busy, besides the attention his own family have required, Attalie, Eugenia, Tommie & Florence have all had chills.

Mittie is as busy as a bee, preparing for "the coming event" as she is pleased to term it. Mamie is spending this week with her & I have promised to remain with her the next two weeks. The 19th instant is the day set. She will do well. Mr Rucks is a merchant in Camden, a widower with one child a little girl about two years old. I have been quite busy for some time helping her to get ready, that is when it was not my cook week, have embroidered her a band & sleeves to match the yoke that Kate gave her, am braiding her a skirt, that has two bunches of tucks with braid pattern beneath & between the bunches.

You say Kate & Ada are making quilts, that is certainly ominous. You may depend upon it they have a notion of a "coming event," in their heads. Mittie was quilt-making last winter.

I was in town last Monday. Jennie's new baby is thriving finely under the cognomen of George Boddie Rumph Jr. Gilder was well, comes to see us frequently. We had a letter from John this week, he still enjoys fine health & likes living in St Louis. All well with us & at Mr Dunlap's. Mr D. has a chill occasionally. Our love to all. Tell Kate I am looking for a letter from her. Affectionately

Your aunt,
C. S. Dickson

Mary Elizabeth [Maima] Boddie in Ouachita Co. to her brother John R. Boddie in St. Louis.

Oct. 10th 1875

Dear Brother,

I am too wearied in both body and mind to collect thought sufficient to write a sensible much less an interesting letter. It has been stitch, stitch, work work, 'till my very senses seem wrought into a chaos that will require time to extricate; so pardon this note, for note it must be tonight. I am very grateful for the letters penned in leisure moments, and shall not always await their coming before letting you hear from home, though their perusal affords the sweetest pleasure, and 'tis from them I gain strength to endeavor to eradicate from mind weeds that have grown rank from want of culture and to fit myself to fill the place of a true and noble woman, and above all, to merit the love of fond relatives. Yes Brother the welfare of my soul is paramount to all other considerations but to preserve it, circumstanced as I am in life, is difficult, Oh! so very difficult that experience in like circumstances can only give you an idea of its full meaning.

Ma's indisposition is caused from that of Pa's. He has not been well for sometime, is grumbling, complaining & sleeping all day, & consequently cannot sleep at night. Bob told him yesterday when he was complaining & saying that he did not know what to do to get well, that all he needed was exertion to make his blood warm! All the rest are well. Aunt N. is still with Cousin & will not return till after the wedding. I shall certainly remember you to your friend Mr. Lide. Cousin is still flurried & excited. Cousin F[lorence] & little Eugenia have had a severe spell this fall. Atallie is sick now, Uncle John is riding all the time, looks very much haggard. I went to town with him Sat. the 1st of Oct. The day you wrote me. I did not see any of your Camden friends, that is young men & ladies, save Mr Collins. He came in at Cousin Geo's & chatted a few moments with me. I think your selection of calico the prettiest any where, but would liked to have purchased a dress but did not, was shopping for Cousin is why I have been to town so often this fall.

Aunt C[lara] & her fine boy was with us Saturday. Uncle J. D[unlap] has been quite sick but convelescing. I suppose you have heard ere this of Mrs Elliott's loss. Little Coralie, she died the 20th [of] Sept. Mr Sasser[?] Pope lost his eldest daughter, was buried in town on the 1st of Oct. Sickness abating, they say, in town. Cousin Geo. & family spent last Sunday with us. Little Geo. is not yet as good looking as Eugene. Cousin Jennie is looking well, but not really well. Anna has been with [us] a good deal lately, & is the same Anna Moseley. Expect a "Times" this week from Mama. Bob is gathering his crop. Gilder was over last Sunday. Mr. Powell preaches next Sunday. We all like him very much, & I tell Ma that I am going to captivate him if I can, & go west. She can't bear the idea of my marrying a preacher. Mr Powell is going to college to fit himself for the itinerary;* will be gone four or five years.

Miss Lotta must certainly be a little beauty from your description & I know you enjoy her company.

"As sunshine broken in the rill
Heart turned astray in sunshine still."

Willcox Pine Hill, Wilcox Co. is cousin Mittie's P.O. when you write her. I am waiting for a letter. Tis late & I must be up by time in the morning. goodnight

Ever your devoted sister
Mamie E. Boddie

---

* The itineracy was the term given to Methodist preachers who traveled and preached on a circuit.

Mary E. Boddie in Ouachita Co. to her son John R. Boddie in St. Louis
                                        October 20th 1875

  Well darling, the event has <u>come</u> & <u>gone</u>, a day of sunshine & shadow, not a cloud though to mar the beautiful token of a pleasant future, but the shadow rested on my own heart for though all went merry & joyous, a crowd of memories beside the thoughts of giving up her, whom I love next my very own, made me feel sad, O! so sad all that day, when all about seemed so happy. I scarcely know darling where to begin, unless at the whole week's excitement & bustle of preparation which was no little I assure you, & the termination was quite a success in <u>every detail.</u> I never saw a handsomer table, & better prepared viands anywhere, everything really good, & set off to please the eye as well as taste. Barbecued beef, shoat, & two fine turkeys constituted the meats, cakes of <u>every sort</u>, custards, candies, apples, raisin, sardines, charlotte russe, syllabub, & many other dishes too tedious to mention, even the finest kind of celery, (from Mr Elliott's garden.) The crowd was pretty dense, Uncle J invited all the young folks of the neighbourhood! outside the whole family connexion. The groom & his brother came over in a carriage, Messers Lide & Richie in buggies, also Gilder in Mr. Brown's buggy. Gilder waited with Miss Anna M., Mr R[itchie] with Miss Georgia P., Bettie & Mr R[ucks], Mr L[ide] & Maima. The girls looked beautiful, they all dressed in white swiss, the Bride was dressed in silk, white trimmings, she looked very handsome as regard dress, but the dear child did not look well in the face, had <u>worked so hard</u> early & late, that I feel really glad 'tis all over, & may <u>every happiness</u> connected with our earthly pilgrimage be hers through life. Mr Allston performed the marriage service. Miss Adelle B. & Effie B. were the only girls there from Town. The attendants all accompanied Mittie home, Nealy & Carrie too, so none of our household at home to-day save Pa, Will, Tug and I. You may be on the lookout for some of the <u>wedding</u> cake for I shall certainly start some on the way to you. You were greatly missed & many thoughts were wafted to your distant home darling. All your friends asked to be remembered to you among them, Mr. & Mrs Toney, Mrs. Broadnax, "Uncle Hal" (who when the congratulations were being offered, sang out to Ed, not to "let them all kiss Mittie to death.") Mrs. Elliott desired her love, & told me to tell you, if she had been <u>quite well</u>, she would have written a list of <u>names</u> for me to send with the cake. She has been in bad health, & was too fatigued that evening to ride home. Mrs. Wright & family had left some two weeks since for home, consequently I did not get to see her. Miss Ellie went home with her.
  I dislike to tell you son that I've been quite sick again, & that is why you've had no letter from me before this, but I intend to take things easy now, & be careful of myself for the sake of all my dear loved ones. Pa dont seem to rally from a spell so quickly as I, says he's not near right yet, stirs round

but little, seems to enjoy reading the papers you send more than anything else. Your bro. Will requests me to render kind thanks for the circulars sent him, & "Tug" was very proud of his letter & papers. I cant tell you all he had said about "Bud Johnnie" not writing to him, but when I reasoned with, & told him how busy you were, he said "well Ma tell bud Johnie he need not mind about writing <u>to me</u> yet awhile."

I've rec'd all your letters regularly son, & each one is a treasured memento of a good boy, & let me tell you darling, when you & the "Duck" get ready to <u>jump</u> the broomstick may I be there to see, & by the bye I must let you know that your <u>birthday was</u> the date first suggested by "Cousin" for her "coming event" but when we consulted the Almanac found 'twould not do. <u>Make</u> note of how you spend the 30th. You will be remembered at home though too far off now, for "Mama to make a pet of" as you termed it in your kind note to me of last year, dated at Camden. Rec'd a letter from sis Hattie last week, all well, said tell you, she could not listen to any such excuse for your not going to visit them, but would hold you to the promise still. Said Mattie had written & she hoped to hear from you soon. Our old family servant Hager is dead. I cant but feel much sorrow, for with her is associated so much kind care & attachment toward my dearest father & mother, even to the service rendered them on earth. I reiterate your prayer most heartily darling, "that we may love each other here may so live, as to be reunited in the Great hereafter, forever & ever."

Am glad to know Mr R. has recovered, & do hope you may escape having any chills through the season, as you have been preserved so far, for which I am thankful. Am not surprised at your making the comparison between your first & last employers, the same thoughts occurred to me the last time I passed <u>Luda</u> looking at the delapidated building where your first clerkship began, but I shall be sorry to see that old store house tumble to decay, & may you ever be blessed with the happy disposition to be content in any situation in life as 'tis our duty to be thankful for everything we enjoy, & bear the crosses with patience.

Pa did not get to see Mr. Brown for a week or two after his arrival from St. Louis. Mr. B. was sick at that time — Pa talking with him since, said Mr B. expressed his opinion that "John could have done as well in Camden as where he is." neither your Pa, I, or <u>any others</u>, with whom he had conversed, concur with Mr B. in his opinion, <u>omitting</u> the question entirely of whether you are, or are not, benefitted pecuniarily. Well here comes our crowd from Town, Tommy went over in the waggon to take his sisters' trunks, & has brought all the girls back. I will leave it for some of them to tell you of their reception at Mr. R's. Of course Tommy brought <u>my letter</u>, & thanks darling for the same. All had to inspect with wonder, & curiosity the portion of the great giant tree of Cal. Pa made the right guess of what it was, little sis says Bud Johnnie I am ever so much obliged, & "Ma dont forget to send Bud J. the Geranium leaf I've had pressed for him for the past two weeks." She has gone on home with Bettie & Florence to remain until Sunday. Your sister looks as though she had come from a funeral, & wont be consoled, however time will heal the wound, & she must learn to be less selfish, in her great love for "Cousin." It needs no assurance from you darling to your pet cousin of the place she holds in your generous heart, though I too would have been glad if you could have gratified the dictate of your feelings toward her. Nealy said Mrs. Rucks seemed to be much rejoiced to welcome her home, & will I'm certain do everything in her power to make Mittie feel that she regards her as a daughter indeed. 'Tis well darling I guess, my paper is out, & I shall be compelled to close, with dear love from each & all. May God bless you is the prayer of yours lovingly

M. E. Boddie

There has been considerable sickness here this fall, though I believe tis abating. We have cold frosty mornings, & fires are agreeable all day. Will commenced gathering corn this morning, Bobbie will tell you about the bear! What better news can you write to me, than that you are in fine health, & spirits? None, none, none my child, that is so grateful to, your loving mother—

Cornelia Dickson in Ouachita Co. to her friend Julia Howard in Autauga County, Alabama.

Oct 28th 1875

Dear Julia

Your interesting and highly appreciated letter of the 7th of Sept has been claiming my attention for quite a long time. You must not rate my appreciation of the same by the length of time I have taken in responding. Various duties have deprived me, to some extent, of keeping up regularly with my correspondence, for yours though first, is not the only one waiting the first leisure hour. I have had but few spare moments since its reception, and felt that I wanted to have at least a good hour's chat with you & it seemed that the time would never come. It has been a whole month since I first perused the lines you penned, and it seems scarcely a week. Time has passed as fleetly with me as with you last summer. It was <u>very</u> gratifying to me to hear of the so many incidents recorded in your "first book." I imagine Birmingham a pleasant place for summer sojourn & hardly think Emma has become homesick enough to be with you all as yet. I should like to hear her account of her visit to Mrs Lorsby, you know she is one of my old friends. I was pleased to hear that Mr Underwood & Mr Tyers had joined the church. I can readily believe it was a very sympathetic time with you all and knowing Rebecca's devotion am not surprised that her heart was rejoiced to overflowing.

I think you did remarkably well at the organ considering the embarrassing position in which you were placed, knowing too, the responsibility which knowledge always tends to perplex. I think you should take to yourself the credit of some of the selfpossession with which you hand our little friend, who you mention as exhibiting so much, the night she was capsized on her return from church.

Sis Mollie was grieved to hear of the suffering & death of her old friend Mr Davis, though she knew in the course of nature that he would not live long, yet she feels sad to know that he will never greet her again on earth. She has recently received Mr Ross'es letter to Mrs Murley giving the particulars of his illness & death. She & brother George have both been quite sick this fall, as soon as one would nearly recover the other would be taken until I think they have each suffered from three attacks of fever; with this exception the family have enjoyed excellent health. This is the first year I have escaped having chills since I came to this country. I can imagine Jimmie's delight in his family by calling to mind my last visit to George Rumph's. He is married you know & is merchandizing in Camden. Jennie his wife is the merriest little woman in town. They have two boys, Eugene & George Jr.

Since receiving your letter another link of our loved family circle has been removed to fill a new & untried position in life. On the 19th my niece Mittie Rumph & Mr Edmond Rucks of Camden were married, and your letter found me deeply engaged in assisting in preparations for the "coming event" as she was pleased to term her approaching nuptials. The wedding was largely attended by the many friends & relations of both families. Her attendants were Bettie Rumph with Mr. J. Rucks, Mamie Boddie with Mr Lide, Miss Anna Moseley with Gilder Boddie, & Miss Georgia Proctor with Mr. Richie. She was married at eleven o'clock A.M. In the evening the attendants, Florence Rumph, Carrie Boddie, & myself & some young men & ladies from town, accompanied her to her new home where we were welcomed by his mother who had collected a few friends to participate in the nice little "infare"* awaiting the happy couple. We spent a pleasant night, but home duties compelled us to bid her adieux next morning and I have not seen her since.

I was interrupted yesterday evening with company. Brother John came by to bid us good bye, he expects to start to Little Rock this morning, being a member of the legislature, which adjourned last March to meet again the 2nd of Nov. Will be absent about two months. It will be very lonesome with his family now, he & Mittie both gone. I have promised to spend some of my leisure weeks with them and I know I shall miss him & her very much.

Tell Minnie, Gilder says he has had no inclination whatever to fall in love with any other girl since we told him of the disposition we made of him while in Ala simply from our description of her and will she not favor him

*Infare is a chiefly dialectical term for a party or reception for a newly married couple.

with her picture. Says he is earnestly endeavoring to make something of himself & fill a station in life of which his ladyelove will not be ashamed. This end attained he will visit Ala, and it will not be <u>his</u> fault if she remain a maiden all forlorn.

We received a letter from John this week in which he expressed so much regret at being denied the pleasure of attending Mittie's wedding. The press of business the cause, Says that sales this year more than double those of corresponding time last year. We were so in hopes that he could come. I know he would have been "bewitched" at your description of one of his Ala sweethearts. Matrimonial fever expected to rage in Camden this winter. Sis Mollie & Mamie join me in love to you. Mamie says you would be <u>highly diverted</u> to hear <u>her</u> sing Whispering Hope. She has but little idea of either time or tune. It is Carrie that sings. I shall now close and anxiously await the coming of the "Second book" provided you direct as before, as there are Dicksons near Camden who I doubt not have through mistake taken some of my letters from the office. As ever

      Affectionately your friend,
      Cornelia S. Dickson

Robert Lee "Tug" Boddie in Ouachita Co. to his brother John R. Boddie in St. Louis

                  Nov 6th 1875

Dear Bud Johnie

I wanted to write to you on your birthday, and did commence a letter then, but had to stop to do first one thing and then another until a whole week has passed away and my letter is not finished yet, so I have to commence again. Bud Gilder came over Saturday night and stayed until Sunday evening. I was so glad to get your letter, and also I am much obliged to you for the papers. I like them much better than those you sent to me from Camden. I celebratet your birthday by killing the first squirrel I ever had killed hunting by myself. I never shot him anywhere except in the head, when I brought him in they all holla'd three cheers for me. Since then, I have killed two squirrels, one duck and two robins. When Cousin Mittie maried, Carrie ironed my shirt for me. I told her I could beat her, and she said she would not do up my shirt any more, and that I was too proud, I said she ought to allow a fellow to be proud once a year. We had the nicest kind of a time at the wedding. Mr Rucks brought over a carriage and took Cousin Mittie Home the same day. Eugenia would not go in the room to see her married. Miss Mattie Mitchell was married last Thursday to Mr Roberson no one was invited but our family and Mr State Stone, three young men come up with the groom. We had a very nice dinner, and Miss Mattie looked very pretty, they were standing on the floor when the clock struck twelve; all of us were there but Pa and Mama, and they were not well, and it poured down rain all the morning. Bud Willie has done gathering his corn, made only 200 bushels. When we commenced hauling corn, the old bear come in the field every night, sometimes three bear would come in the same night. We could not kill any of them, but we wished we could have, just such a big bear trap like you told us about. Old Bony had eight pupies, we killed three of them, saved five for Mr Proctor, and Mr Chewning. bud Johnie you must send me a Scotch tarier for a squirrel dog. I wish I could have been with you at the Fair to see so many pretty things you told me about. Carrie said she wanted one of those little cows. All of us send love to you and I want to see you very much.

       Your affectionate little brother
       Robert L. Boddie

              Nov 7th

*The composition of the letter is most interesting. Sis Mollie filled the page, and then turned it around, probably because it was her last sheet of paper, and wrote in the opposite direction between the lines; consequently every other line is written upside-down.

My dear son,*

I am sitting up this morning for the first time in several days. Your Pa & I are just like a couple of children playing see-saw, No sooner does one get up, than the other goes down, but I think, & hope that such play as that is done with for this season as Pa seems to be much better than usual this time, & we have a big bottle of bitters compounded of <u>7 ingredients</u> which ought to stop chills & cc, if it dont 'tis so bad to take. I am sorry to hear that Mr. L is sick again, & you must advise, & nurse him the very best you can. 'Tis my greatest comfort, darling to know that you are still blessed with good health, & that is right, dont sacrifice health for wealth, for I can assure you that all the wealth in the world would not compensate for loss of the former. A suit like sample will make up beautiful, but 'tis not as thick & heavy as some you had made in Camden, of which I have some pieces now. We have had a most beautiful fall season, had several hard rains, but the next day would be fair & sunny. Three weddings took place this last week, Miss Saddie B. & Mr Milton E., Miss C. Clifton to Mr J. Merril. Miss Mattie M. &cc. Small sis says dont you think the old maids of H[armony] G[rove] are in <u>fair way of getting accustomed</u> to weddings &cc without having the nerves shocked. I cant imagine why you thought the mention of your "Duck" troubled Mama, why, just the very reverse darling, so write on, whenever the old time habit & associations prompt you. Uncle J left the 30th for Little Rock, he came by from town on Friday to bid us all good bye. You may be sure we all regret his absence, he took dinner that day with Mit, she & Mr R tried to prevail on Uncle J to let the children stay with them during his absence, but could not get his consent. Mittie & Mr Rucks came over, & stayed with us last night, we were as glad as though Cousin had been off to Europe & back again. Mittie looks to be as happy as a bird, & is at her purpose, for they magnify things to the best advantage, & diminish defects. Gilder ~~says, you need not flatter yourself (because you are such a successful manager~~ of bees) by thinking, that he or Tom will get stung by visiting the bee hive. Miss Anna wishes you to know, that for use, subjects that have not become seared, & tarnished by time are to be preferred, for all mechanics like new material best. Have sent your message to 'Mrs. O Scuttle'. Frank B. told me when he came by here on Monday, she & Uncle John were out in the sun at the cow pen, attending to the cows &c. Tommy has one negro man & two boys to work with him, he has not planted any corn yet. Tommy has killed two turkeys this Spring, & by the by Gilder one. Bettie is teaching Atalie & Eugenia, says they learn very fast. Little Maud is talking now, & the pet of all. Our girls have about slept off the effects of the frolic which lasted the entire night, every party over on this side of the creek went, even Uncle J.D. was there with Lula. Miss Georgia P. said that was snow bound at their house, she & Uncle John went there to eat turkey dinner, & as it rained Mat staid, & I don't expect she got home till to day; the sun is melting the snow, but it dont disappear fast. Little Sis says, she danced her gaiters out, & was wondering why a place on her foot kept feeling so cold, & when she came home found a round piece of her hose danced out. — Your guns shall be taken good care of darling boy, in

Sample of Mollie's upside-down composition

old time tricks, teasing Mr R. &cc, sometimes he gets the joke on her. Her "anxiety" about the children is all that appears to give her the least discomfort. Mit said she wrote to you the 30th, but her finger was so sore at the time 'twas "too badly" penned to send, & she intended writing this week. They took Maima off with them to pay Mrs Elliott a visit, are to stay at Uncle J's tonight, & come here to dinner tomorrow. I am glad you enjoyed the cake, but did not at all like your having to pay extra, as I gave instructions, that if it could not be sent otherwise, to send & pay for it at <u>this office at letter rates.</u> Uncle J told me he went with Gilder to the office & that 'twas mailed all right. "Small Sis" is looking for a letter, but write to <u>Mattie</u> first, always excepting <u>my very own,</u> & darling I dont see anything to excuse in <u>any</u> of them & your request is granted as soon as asked. Miss Anna sends the violet with love. Tug talks so largely of hunting. I must tell you we never allow him to go off out of hearing, but he makes opportunities to go from his work as often as possible. Dont pay any attention him about the little dog. If Pa & bud Willie had only said so, Tug would have kept half of Bonnie's pups to raise. This will be almost unreadable this time, good bye darling. May God bless you is the prayer of your loving mother. All send love,

                        Yours,
                        Mary E. Boddie

Aunt Nealy & Little Sis thought to take a horse back ride this afternoon, but they had company. Pa sends many thanks to you for the papers. We heard yesterday that Mr Sam Dunlap was very sick with pneumonia. Dr Bragg is attending him. Mrs Alston has a baby girl & many others has babies that I cant tell you of now. Our Lucy's Eljira was buried today, she died with consumption.

Mary E. Boddie in Ouachita Co. to her son John R. Boddie in St. Louis
                                                        Nov. 23rd '75

My own dear boy,

With much pleasure I write, all well at home this time, & abroad too among relatives & friends, with one exception as f[ar] as I can hear from in our little Burg. Mrs Elliott has not been entirely well since the wedding, Mittie & Maimae said she was very talkative & lively the day they spent with her altho' confined to the bed. We hear from Mit <u>every week,</u> as she & small sis pass <u>notes</u> back & forth, & judging from the tone of the formers, your little cousin is getting on as happily & contentedly as heart could wish, has not been <u>home sick</u> but once, & that was about the children. I guess she has written to you that she has Eugenia with her. Uncle J left word that if Mittie came over she could take one of the children home, to stay a week or two, & she was ever so glad to avail herself of the permission. Mit writes that she has returned twenty of her bridal calls, & would take another day or two to complete the list. Small sis says, now brother is away, cousin gets all the boquets, & she very often speaks of you in connexion with her flowers. I am glad to know you get to see all the Camdenites who take St. Louis in their travels particularly the lady friends, for they can give you more interesting details of events &c &c aside from the pleasure derived from their company. I thought Miss Dollie was to return home ere her sister left for school. It must be a great pleasure to the parents to give their children such advantages as they enjoy & hope they appreciate it. Miss Calie B. is at her bro. Henry's now, & will be in Town soon, when I would like much to see her, as she has seen you, since I was with her. Indeed darling you cant guess how much I would like to see you in any capacity, & that of Dr. I imagine you play the role with better grace than if you were in the patients place, however, hope Mr L. may not need any more ministrations altho' tendered by a sympathising friend. Does Mr G's family intend remaining in St. Louis this winter? should be very sorry if they do not, as you would miss many pleasant evenings spent in their home circle, & with the little folks. Am ever so much obliged for my dear little letter, the same date with Tugs, you know how I look for their coming, & am content be they ever so brief. Am pleased to know you are kept busy, (for half way work would not suit you,) & am glad too, you have the pleasure of enjoying a good play occassionally, for "all work & no play" exetra* — Carrie rec'd a letter from Onie, (one of her Aunt C's girls) recently, they have made good crops in Autauga, all relatives were well except Uncle Clem, he is confined to the bed, has Paralysis in his left hand & foot. Willie L[ove] sent word, if Uncle C. gets well, we might look for him Christmas. One of Carrie's sons (Addison) is farming near Florence Ala. made a fine crop this year, but he is in very bad health, is living in Nathan Boddies' family. By the bye son, I copy below the genealogy sent by the John B. Boddie* at Hot Springs to your Pa, also sent word by Capt M[itchell] that he would come to see him before he went home.

    John B. Boddie of Maringo Co. Ala. son of Oliver B. Boddie of Maringo Co. Ala.

    son of Jack E. Boddie of Maringo Co. & formerly of N. C.

    Bro. of Nathan Boddie of Georgia & claims kin with any one who spells his name "Boddie" & has never yet met one that he was not proud to claim.

    The weather is very unfavorable for gathering the late cotton, so rainy. Will is trying to get through, has had some hired hands for the past week or so, says he has 6 or 7 bales out, & thinks there will be three more, but Pa says there is not that much, so that constitutes the entire crop except Henry's, the corn turned out only half crop, which we expect to make answer all needs, with the grain they intend sowing. Pa commenced having his wheat sown this week. Farmers in HardScrabble & surroundings made some good

* This is an interesting development. For the very first time, we have a word to replace the usual &c.

*John B. Boddie refers to John Bennett Boddie who compiled, with John Thomas Boddie, *Boddie and Allied Families* in 1918.

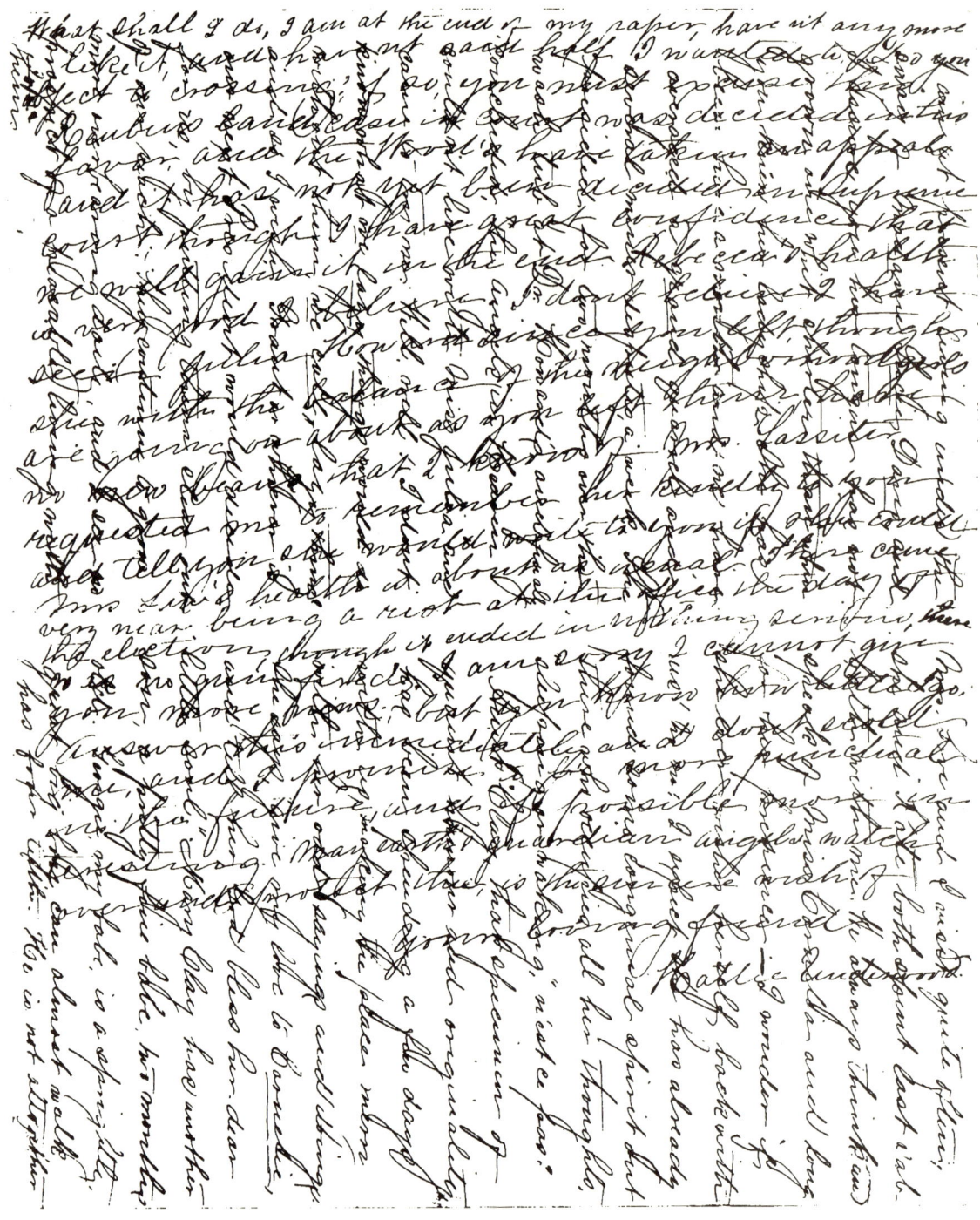

Sample of cross-writing

& some bad crops. Mr Gauhan, Proctor & Chewings turned out fine, both corn & cotton. Mr Moseley failed in corn, good cotton, Uncle J. D[unlap] failed in both, "Uncle Billy"* the same, Robert S[tone] good corn, 20 bales short in cotton, told me to tell you, that he had <u>given</u> up, & come to a stand still, has not been <u>fox hunting</u> but three times this fall, but that <u>his crowd</u> had gone eight times, & killed one everytime. Tommy says, he is kept too busy to go camp hunting. The hunters from the Camden side are off now on a two weeks chase. The Missus Bragg's called by to deliver a package of flower seed to small sis, from Miss Florence B. State [Stone] & Willie are working away at their little cotton patch, State had a spell of fever, which put them back considerable. Miss Mollie says they are <u>camping</u> in the <u>old house</u> yet. They always ask about you whenever I see them. Miss Anna says, you have guessed prezactly right about the red ribbon. She comes down three times every week to take a music lesson. Lula Avera commenced too, the middle of Oct. All the old folks here are plodding along as usual trying to make the best of all reverses. The young ones endeavouring to look their prettiest, for the benefit of the sterner sex I guess, tho' they disclaim any pretentions whatever towards matrimony. Nealy is spending her two weeks leisure at Uncle J's will be home Sunday. Gilder & Mr J. Bustian spent last Sunday up there. Mamie is cook this week, & little sis says, tell bud Johnie my cooking is nothing to brag on yet, have so little variety to practice on, fried bacon, egg bread (minus the eggs) constitute the principal diet, with a chicken pie occasionally. We always have plenty good milk & butter. The girls milk 12 cows, have 14 calves in the pen. Pa let Will have one cow this fall, & has since sold two more, Queen & Redbud. Your Aunt Clara has had two or three bad Neuralgia spells, the young boy is doing fine, have not seen Uncle J. D. in some time, the less he makes the harder he works, is busy now ginning. Tug keeps up with the cotton in the garden, from the seed we brought from Ala. which is turning out well, he thinks he works hard, but his sisters tell him he is very lazy, & make him rise before light, if there is not plenty stove wood on hand. Will gives us an early start every morning by rising before day, we all generally retire before 9, except small sis, & she reads, & sometimes sews till a late hour. Tug reads some every night, he is reading Livingston's travels now, Will reads the papers, & whenever he takes a book, 'tis one of lessons, he works on the frames to go in his bee gums. Pa enjoys reading the papers hugely, they can keep him interested longer than anything else, dont feel strong enough to make exertions of any kind. Lucy has been cooking for Mr Greening all this year, Becky is living with Seymore, they have been picking cotton for Pa. Mr Greening says he has been <u>living on chills</u> all this fall & he really looks badly, his cotton not all picked out yet. Pa says the merchants who have tried farming with freedmen, at present prices of cotton, are satisfied that it wont pay.

 Well darling I will have to close this, hoping you can decipher it. Recd

*"Uncle Billy" refers to William T. Stone.

your, most truly welcomed, of last Sunday eve, before I've had an opportunity of sending this to be mailed. Know you've recd one from Mamie by the time I got yours, & that is why I did not write last week. All send much love. That you may still prosper in health, & all things good, is the prayer of your devoted

Mother

Robert Lee Boddie in Ouachita Co. to his brother John R. Boddie in St. Louis
Dec 2nd 1875

Dear bud Johnie

I was very glad indeed to get your letter. I wish I was there to go with you to the pork packing house to see them kill hogs, and go to the market house too. I think I had better wait for that little squirrel dog, as we have to pay a tax on dogs. We have got rid of our pups, I think we will have to get rid of some of our dogs. The most cotton I have picked out in one day was 104 lbs. and in all 980 lbs. I have killed in all 17 squirrels and 2 ducks, one big hawk, and shot him flying. Bud Willie is sowing wheat. We have picked out all of our cotton except one bale. Bud Johnie you know we haven't had any cats for a long time, but an old cat come here and would stay she had four kitens we gave two away, Carrie claims one, and I claim the other. Carrie named hers <u>Alex</u>. I named mine Corrie. We have some of the prettiest pigs you ever saw. I dont go hunting only a little while in the morning and a little while in the evening. I clean out your gun every week, and rub it off very often. I havn't picked any cotton since we got over the thickest part of it and have all the wood to cut and calves to feed. Pa has not put his killing hogs up to fatten yet,* the peas are to be picked first, so they can go in the field. We have not gathered any hickory nuts this year there are plenty in the bottom, but we have not had time, and Christmas is almost here, and no body talks much about it, only ask if our hens are laying any, we dont get many eggs the hens laid out before Cousin Mittie married. Little Corrie Rucks is spending this week with her grandma Mos[e]ley.* She calls cousin Mittie her new ma. Cousin Eugenia is in town yet. Miss Lula Doer and Carrie went to Miss Mary Ciwning [Chewning?] birthday dinner last Tuesday, they started to ride Mr Robert Stone's old mule but when they got to Uncle Billy's the old mule got contrary and would not go a step and they had to leave him there and foot it. bud Johnie I wish you could come to us. We all send much love.

Your affectionate little brother
Robert Lee Boddie

*It was customary to pen up the hogs that were to be slaughtered and to feed them corn, thus improving the quality and size.

*"Little Corrie Rucks" is the daughter of Edmund Rucks and his first wife Jane Alabama Moseley, sister of Marvin and Allis Moseley. She is the stepdaughter of Mittie Rumph, who was Mr. Rucks' second wife. Corrie Rucks would later, in 1894, marry Walter P. Ritchie.

After the War

                                                                Thursday night

My dear son,

    I cant miss the opportunity of acknowledging the reception of yours of 28th Nov. & the great pleasure it afforded me. Am thankful to say all well with us. Pa says he feels more like himself now, & by this time next week, thinks he will feel like work, or stiring round, that is if the weather is not too bad. We are having a variety of changes from cold to warm vice versa, cloud & sunshine, but mostly the former & all predicted snow, but it grew warmer & rained instead. Threatens rain again daily, but we hope to get all the wheat sown ere it rains again, there is some cotton yet to be picked out, the peas to gather &c. I told you in my letter of last week how Pa's crop turned out, has not had any cotton ginned yet, will have to haul to Mr Stone's or Uncle J. D[unlap].'s to gin and pack. Maima came home from her Aunt Clara's this morning, been there since Sunday, which day we all attended church to hear Mr Hare's last sermon, unless he's appointed to this circuit again next year. We had a small congregation Sunday, the day was so unfavourable. I heard many express the wish for a change of ministers, as Mr. H. is not pleasing to most of our congregation, but we have services seldom enough at best, & will have no more until fourth Sabbath in Jan. Thanksgiving with us darling was spent mostly like other days, the nearest we got to church was hearing the sweet chimes of the church bells. I am so glad you were <u>feeling better</u> when you last wrote, why dont you answer Small Sis's letter? Thus between her letters, my scrawls, & Tug's you might feel all right every week. Have not heard from "Cousin" the past week, Small Sis <u>expects</u> a note Saturday. Aunt Nealy is providing at home this week, says they are all getting on very well at Uncle J's. Florence is as lively, & full of fun as ever. I have not seen her since you [sent] special love to Mrs O'Scuttle* Cousin Bettie is so domestic she seldom leaves home, has promised time & again to stay some with us, but never finds a convenient time. Hannah was to see us one day recently, says "tell Mars Johnie howdy, & tell him I miss him so much. I never cares to go to Town now, haven't been there but once since he left, & wouldn't go to Brown's at all only in Gilder's side of the house, to see him, it dont seem right for Mars Johnie not to be there."

    I regret too Son, that you did not get to see our great Southern Chieftains, perhaps such an opportunity may not occur again. Old man Gaughan* thinks of making a trip to <u>Ould Country</u> next summer, & take the __(?)_____ in his way, & <u>Jimmy</u> to go that far with him. Alis Moseley speaks very often of wishing to go, & thinks probably he will. Little Sis sends a supplement this time because Tug told you about her preferences, & said she would get even with him. I forgot to tell you the message Miss Julia Howard sent in Onie's letter — That <u>you</u> must not fall in love with any of the St. Louis girls but remain loyal to your <u>Ala</u> sweetheart. Tug, & I, hope

*Mrs O'Scuttle was a nickname that only the Boddie family called Florence Rumph.

*"Old man Gaughan" refers to Patrick Gaughan, father of Dennis, Alex, Jim, & Tommy, who are mentioned frequently in the letters.

to have some good <u>pens</u> ere we write again, know you think we need them. Will bid you good night darling. Your friends send kind remembrance. Much love from each one of the family to our dear absent one. Your loving Mother,
M. E. Boddie

Dec 2, 1875

Brother,

You need not believe one word Robert tells you about my cat in his letter, for its name is Fritz. I just said I named it A because he named his Corrie. But he wanted something to fill up his letter. As it was about ironing his shirt, he thought it was so smart in <u>his saying</u>, "I ought to allow a fellow to be proud once a year," he thought he would tell you. Besides you, he told one or two others thinking it was smart. It is a wonder he has not mentioned Everlee Morgan in some of his letters as he fell in love with her the night she spent here with Cousin. At least his actions prove so. He could hardly keep his eyes off of her, and when she started home he came very near giving her all the apples we had gathered, and that is why we have not so many this year.

Much love,
Little Sis*

(My pen is bad.)

*Little Sis is Frances Caroline Boddie, called Carrie.

Cornelia Dickson in Ouachita Co. to her friend Becca Underwood in Autauga Co.

Dec 6th 1875

Dear Becca*

Your very dear little missive was received some time since and should have been duely answered, but making its advent at a time when the matrimonial stampede was raging, which you know must have been an exciting time both mentally and bodily with preparations for first one & then another. I wrote Julia of Mittie Rumphs marriage, Miss Mattie Mitchell our nearest neighbor was the next on the list. I was present at the launching of her bark on the sea of matrimony, Mr Roberson as Captain. The other marriages were in Camden and I did not attend. Have been spending some time at Dr Rumphs during his stay in Little Rock. We are expecting him home about the middle of this month. Since I came home culinary withal I have not felt at leisure to write until now. You must not think your favor the less appreciated, on the contrary; though I was really very much disappointed in not receiving a letter from Rebecca; yet I was delighted that you thought enough of me to write. Tell Rebecca were she not such a dear friend I would hardly

*Becca must be the daughter of Cornelia's friend Rebecca Underwood.

know how to excuse her, and I fear feelings of a rebellious nature may yet prevail did I not cling to the hope of her overcoming her action to this friend and send me a supplement to your next letter. I was interrupted this evening with company, Miss Anna Moseley came to take her music lesson & spent her leisure hour in my room. She is a friend of mine, very lively, and we enjoy some long old chats when we are together. Sis Mollie has two music pupils besides Mamie & Carrie; Mamie is now taking "Caliph of Bagdad," & Carrie "Love's Caresses." Lula Avera takes "Love's Response," & Anna Moseley "Lucy Long with Variations," all very pretty pieces.

 I can readily believe there was great rejoicing when your father and Mr Tyus joined the church. I was glad to hear of it. I was not surprised to hear of Mr Davis'es death. Poor old man. It is to be hoped he is better off. We were grieved to hear of Uncle Clem's ill health, have not heard from him in some time.

 I do not wonder at your uncle Howard's short sojourn in Texas and I am inclined to believe that the bright eyes of one of Ala daughters has more to do with his early return than mere avertion to Texas or its inhabitants. Had he only known it Hot Springs was in much need of a competent teacher at the time he came out. I think he would have been more favorably impressed with Ark than with Texas, had he stopped there, as it is said to be most progressive place in the state. I have never yet been able to fulfil my intentions of writing to Emma. Give her and her mother my love. Tell her I have not forgotten her. Becca, you must not think that _____ treated you mean about that sweetheart. It was a p[ai]r of dark eyes that did the mischief And honor bright from the <u>tone of your letter</u>. I do not [think] though there is any damage done. Tell me the <u>name</u> in your next, please. You surely gave <u>me</u> your picture, & I was merely to show it to <u>him</u>, it never occurred to me to part with it, and it now with many others graces a frame in the parlor. I would send you one of his if I had one that did him justice. I have no idea when I will come to Ala again, were it in my power to do so I would be with you all Christmas, but we should not repine as all things are for the best. Sis Mollie joins me in much love to yourself and all the family. Kindest regards to all inquiring friends.*

                       *no signature

Cornelia Dickson in Ouachita Co. to her friend Emma Jones in Autauga Co.
                Dec 19th, 1875
 Dear Emma,

 When I first thought of writing to you, I expected to fulfill my intentions in a very few days, but various things undermined and the few days have lengthened into many days, even months, but I have never forgotten you, for often memory lends me her aid and I am again with you at your home enjoying the company of your kind mother and yourself as I see you again eagerly culling some of your choicest plants and fruits to lavish upon your friend. The pomegranates produced quite a sensation among the young people when we arrived at home, being the second time they had ever seen any. The plants I carried with safty until I reached Camden, when the night we spent there at Capt Newton's. I placed them on a shelf in the back portico to get the benefit of the dew. The next morning bright and early, a meddlesome old hen completely demolished every plant in my box. I soon found it out and gathered up some of the fragments, carried them home with me and tried by the most careful attention to induce them to grow, but all in vain; I lost every plant. You who are so fond of flowers can imagine my regret at losing them. Mamie, too, was very sorry. She, like yourself, has a flower garden, and I do wish you could see it. She has a great variety of bulbs as well as other plants, and last summer & fall it was rendered even more gay with the beautiful zenias raised from the seed you gave me, though they were not so rich as yours. She sent off & bought a great many seed, some with prodigious names, one of which proved to be "Mullen", another this "briery Careless Weed", and others that were not even so pretty as many of the wild flowers that abound in the Arkansas flats.

The family have all gone to spend the day with Clara save brother George and me. Gilder, (brother G's third son who is clerking in Camden), came over and took breakfast with us this morning. Says the Court house in Camden was burned last night. The fire was discovered about two o'clock and too late to save <u>anything at all</u>. Supposed to be the work of an incendiary. There was no insurance. Many persons will suffer I suppose from the loss of records, cc. It was with difficulty that the houses near by were saved.

I have no news to write that would prove entertaining to you; there you have the advantage of me, for almost anything that transpires in my old neighborhood is interesting to me. Almost everyone is busily engaged trying to accomplish all they can before Christmas. I have finished most of my sewing but will have to devote my time and attention to the culinary department this week, each of us having a cook week. All the domestic work in that department devolves upon me for Christmas, but then I will be free again for another two weeks.

As ever, your friend,
Cornelia S. Dickson

Mary Elizabeth Boddie in Ouachita Co. to her son John R. Boddie in St. Louis.

Dec. 20th 1875

My dear son,

Am in recp't of your ever dear favors of 5th & 12th; and you will know darling how much they are appreciated. Am always thankful to hear that you are well, & though you cant be with us this anniversary, my heart will be with my boy wishing him all the happiness allotted to mortals on earth, & O! I cant tell how much I miss you, how incomplete our family gatherings without you. Uncle J's family, Clara's, George & family, Mr Rucks & Mittie will dine with us Christmas day. We spent yesterday at your Aunt C's. Mr R. & Mittie came over Saturday, & spent that night at Uncle J's, they were to have dined with Clara yesterday, but could not get off in time. Florence went home with them. The young folks anticipate a pleasant time during the holidays, but I dont hear, or know of any parties, that is to be on our side of the river. The school girls give a Party at the Academy tomorrow night. Gilder says he considered one among the young ones, and has an <u>invite</u>, little Sis too, but 'tis uncertain about her going unless her brother can take her over. Gilder walked over to breakfast Sunday morn, brought news of the sad calamity in Town on Saturday night of the entire distruction of the Courthouse by fire, & <u>everything it contained</u>. Not a single paper, or book saved. You know what a serious loss that involves. Gilder said when the first alarm was given by the watchman, he looked from the window & saw dense smoke issuing from every part of the Courthouse, dressed in double quick, waked Jack, & bid him run for Mr Greening, & he started for Mr Browns, met him coming, ran back to see if anything could [be] done in the burning building, & when he entered, the floor of the Clerks office was entirely consumed, & the smoke so dense 'twas impossible to go farther. Mr Lee with a lighted candle tried to reach his safe, but the smoke drove him out by the first window he could reach, & G. said as nothing could be done there, he ran to the top of the store & went to work. Every blanket in the house was put in requisition, even <u>yours off his bed</u>, & every bucket & stove utensil that would hold water was conveyed to them on the roof as fast as possible. Gilder said the heat was so intense when they went to the edge of the roof to spread the wet blankets, 'twould almost scorch them. Mr Brown said 'twas almost an impossibility to save the house, but they worked on & succeeded, but G. said if the burning Cupola had not fallen in just as it did, they could not have remained up there five minutes longer. Many houses took fire several times, but each one had a posse of men on their roofs to sweep off the burning missile, & put out the fire. The wood pile in Mr Bell's yard was set on fire, at that great distance. You can judge son what an exciting time it was to every resident; the fire occurred about one or two o'clock, no one knows how it originated, 'twas evident it commenced in the Clerk's office, or underneath it. Gilder said Capt Dee N. asked Mr Greening if anyone knew where Bobby D.* was? Mr. G. told him, he was on the roof, working like a Trojan, the Capt answered, all right, I only wanted to know if he was at work.

*"Bobby D." refers to Robert Dee Newton, father of Susie Pryor. He was 14 years old at the time of the Courthouse fire.

I imagine the weather is cold enough with you at this time son, as we have had ice several mornings, but beautiful sunshiny days, & do you know I've always felt that the Sabbath, though rain or snow, was different from all other days, & I am glad you are so circumstanced to everything. How will you spend this Christmas? attend church, partake of the family dinner at Mr G's have a romp with the children &c & perhaps go to the Theater in the evening. Col. Hill told Pa he did not like the St Louis climate at all, could not stand such cold, & was glad to get back to his old Camden home. We were so glad to welcome Uncle J. home again, he is much missed when away. We spent one day up there since his return, he looks well & is the same dear old Uncle John. Tommy's mule was hitched in Hardscrabble (where the bee house once stood) yesterday eve, & Gilder remarked as we passed, I always catch Tom, he's there, I know his riding nag. The fever matrimonial has not yet abated, every two or three weeks we hear of another consumation of the nuptial tie, the last was Miss Julia Junior to Mr Henry Gosset, Miss J. was Mr Ed Brodnax's sweetheart, Mr Frank [Brodnax] visits round yet among all the girls. Mr Jimmy G[aughan] confines his attentions I believe to Miss Georgia [Proctor]. Mr Morris' family will move to Calhoun Co. next year. Uncle J. D. says he's made his 70 bales, the products of his home farm, the Hogue place, & by ginnings & will have 2 in his pocket at the winding up. John B. D[unlap] is a fine, hearty looking fellow, & the pet of the family. Yesterday was Little Sis' fifteenth birthday, she is running up like a reed, but looks plump enough now. Mittie looks well & hearty, says she fares fine, & nothing to do. Will[ie] will finish gathering all the cotton in a day or two if it dont rain. Those who have cotton stored in Town express some uneasiness regarding its safety, since the Courthouse has been burned. Pa's health & appetite continues good, takes his usual tramps now to the bottom once or twice a week, always carries your gun, told me to tell you, that until recently one barrel was loaded just as you left it & I always remind him that it must be rubbed off & kept in good order. Tug dont hunt much, but I see that he takes good care of his gun as he terms it. Will has not had his in his hands but two or three times only to clean it up since you left. This will be a very busy week with us darling, all have more or less sewing work to finish off, & ironing, cooking, &c. This is Aunt N's week to preside in the kitchen, we'll have no Turkey to grace our Christmas table, but the "bill o fare" will be Roast Pork & turnips, Cabbage, English peas, Irish potatoes (if we can find them in the garden), stewed fruit Apples & Peaches, Ducks Chicken pie, Chicken salad, baked & candied sweet potatoes, Cress &c Dessert — Pumpkin pie, Potatoe custard, Transparent custard, Cake

Syallabub, & Pudding with Strawberry sauce, the same that was canned <u>for you</u> last spring thinking you would be here to eat them before strawberries came again. Gilder talks about going to Texas, just like you did about this time last year, but I cant think he will, because I feel so averse to it. The prospects here are poor indeed, but I would prefer his remaining a year or two longer. I am sorry too, that Mr G's suit in Court has been so decided. Your Grandpa's expereance with suits in law was to steer clear of them. Pa's thanks to you for the papers, & Tug thinks his last paper always the best. Must bid you good bye darling, & dont work too hard — All join with me in much love, & wishing you a pleasant & enjoyable Christmas.

Your loving mother, Mary E. Boddie

*I always answer Sis Hatties letters promptly, except the last one, & she has been due me a letter now for some time. "Small Sis" says she wrote to cousin Mattie last, but I think Maimia is mistaken about that. I enclose one of your little favorites.

*Note: This postscript was written upside down at the top of page 2.

Dr. John B. Rumph in Ouachita Co. to his nephew John R. Boddie in St. Louis

Dec 23rd, 1875

My dear Nephew,

Your highly esteemed favor came to hand sometime before I left the Rock and found me so immerced in legislative matters that I deferred answering it until I returned home. A new era has dawned upon our good old state, since the inauguration of the Garland government.* Peace and order now prevail on every side, where disorder, disquietude, and anarchy existed under radical rule. Our state credit has rapidly appreciated, confidence has been restored, and a general good feeling pervades all classes of society. The Legislature have worked long and faithfully in the discharge of their onerous duty and seasonably entertain the hope that their efforts may not prove futile, but redowned to the welfare and prosperity of the people and the state. Individually I have, like the "widow of old", contributed my humble mite towards putting our good old state upon her legs again, so that she may walk up beside her Sisters, and take her rightful position. Her onward and upward progress is now an assured fact. Her own sturdy and stalwart sons, native and adopted, have had her in hand, have cleared her decks of all radical freight that impeded her progress, and trimmed her sails so as to catch the breeze that will waft her to the port of glory and renown. We adjourned on the 10th inst. The parting of the members was truly a parting of friends. We had met as strangers to each other a year ago. The circumstances under which we met were most trying, and called for all the nerve and patriotic devotion to principle, of men knowing their rights, and daring to maintain them. Such

* The Garland government refers to the administration of Governor Augustus H. Garland, who served from 1874 to 1877.

a schooling was the ordeal for linking together those who had a common cause at heart, and grappling them together with hooks of steel. We parted with a long and hearty shake of the hand, and mutual blessings for each others welfare and happiness. I returned home in company with Messr Avera, Hill, and Maj Calloway. Found all my family well, and good health prevailing in the neighborhood. Have been to Camden only once since my return. Have had to look after my business so closely, that I have not had time to mingle with my friends and talk politics and state matters. Will have a tight fit to make buckle and tongue fit, and keep the wolf out at the door for the next year as the crop failure of last year left the Doctors out in the cold. Good crop this year, but the merchants will get it all. Hope and look for better times next year. Will endeavor to shove along keep moving by living on thin hoecakes and small rashers of old seed, and restricting the girls to 9 yds of Calico for their pull-backs. By the way, speaking of pull-backs, a young sugar merchant at the Rock, said, he never saw a fashionably dressed Lady, but her dress reminded him of a draw-back on <u>sugar</u>. You have heard of our county's loss in the burning of the CourtHouse. It is truly a sad calamity, all the records of the county were lost. The loss is irreparable. It is thought to have been the work of an incindiary. Some think Ackerbee Jenkins had some hand in it, as he had recently broke jail, where he had been put for stealing cotton. Business has revived very much in our town the present winter. It begins to look like old times again to see the numerous cotton waggons coming in, and going out with fair loads of groceries. We will ship upwards of 20,000 Bales Cotton this season. The merchants all look cheerfull and smiling, and the rusty and sunburned phizs* of the old planters are beginning to assume a broad Santa Claus kind of grin. Confidence and mutual good will seems to prevail on all sides. Hurra for old Ouachita. Since the adjournment of the Legislature, State scrip has gradually tended upward. It is now quoted at 65 @ 70. I look for it to go to 80 by spring, and by next spring year, it will be worth 90 @ 95 — if not 100. You have 730 scrip now worth $511.00. I hope you will have time to visit us this winter. Cant you swap places with Nat for a week or so, if you can and will give us due notice, I will try and have the hams and loin of an old Buck dressed with <u>inguns</u>* to tempt your appetite with. Hoping to see you "vis a vis" before a great while. believe me, my dear Boy, as ever your devoted uncle.

J. B. Rumph

*Phiz is a slang word for face. It is an abbreviation of Physiognomy.

*Inguns was a cockney word for onions.

PART FOUR

Toward a New Century

A decade had passed since the end of that devastating war; the time of Reconstruction was over, and Arkansas was moving forward, looking to the Twentieth Century, in an effort to stabilize her economy and improve the lives of her citizens. The task would be difficult; the future loomed large and awesome, but no one doubted that the outcome would be a stronger hope for the upcoming new century.

Ouachita County entered the last quarter of the Nineteenth Century with the same optimism as did the rest of the state. The city of Camden was becoming more and more a trade center for the county and was developing a cultural nucleus for the arts. Attention was given to opportunities for learning, for social advantages, and for economic advancement. Life was stabilizing, at least as far as it ever can, and the future held promise.

Across the river in the Harmony Grove community, hope and optimism prevailed. Of course there were obstacles in the path, but there was also a strong character and a sense of closeness between families that could overcome or endure the obstacles. There would be hard times yet, and there would be, as there always is with farmers and farming communities, a chance for disaster. Droughts cannot be legislated, and rainy seasons cannot be stemmed; the end result is always the same: crop failures. Seeds are planted, fields are worked, and farmers continually pray that it will or pray that it won't. The biggest gamblers of America are not found in Atlantic City or Las Vegas, but in the farmlands. And yet farmers persevere, take the ultimate gamble, because they are farmers; to do anything else is not an option.

The families of Harmony Grove are changing. Second generations are growing up, marrying and forming their own little families; the young men are seeking better opportunities elsewhere, and the young women look for opportunities to build their own lives. The first generation is getting old, *their bodies feeling the effects of years of hard work, disappointments, heartaches. Their spirits and hearts, however, revel in the joys of remembrance, the pride of accomplishment, and the love of children now grown. All of these things come to light through the upcoming letters, many of which are from Mary Elizabeth Boddie to her son John Rumph Boddie in St. Louis, replete with news of the community, family and friends. Cornelia still corresponds with her friends and relatives in Alabama, but her letters are not as numerous anymore and lack the intimate details of Sis Mollie's.*

Cornelia Dickson in Ouachita Co. to her cousin Kate Love in Autauga Co.
Jan. 1876

Dear Kate,

    It has been so long since I received a letter from you until now that I had concluded from reports that you must be preparing to leave the world by way of a matrimonial leap. I am even now daily expecting that promised long letter to see what it is that engrosses so much of your attention, you speak of leading such a busy life both physically & mentally. I wish you could be with us a while by way of recreation. I would glady accept, O so gladly accept your kind invitation to visit you all again, but I find that it is out of my power at present. You regret not having the opportunity of talking more with me when I was with you, but be assured, Kate, you do not regret my short stay more than I do. Our time there was limited and we felt rather hurried all the while. But the best way that I can think of to help it, is to write me long letters. It seems a long long time since I wrote you last, so long that I scarcely know where to begin to give you the news. I thought of course that you had seen mine [to] Carrie, & Sis Mollie's letters to Onie, but it seems not, as you ask me if Mittie is really married.

    Yes she was married on the morning of the 19th of Oct. last to Mr. Edmund Rucks, had a large wedding. The table was dressed with fruit & flowers & loaded with everything nice to eat and look upon, seated twenty-six at a time. Carrie, Florence, Billy Elliott & Eddie Brodnax officiated as waiters to fly around the table. Mr. Dunlap & Mr. Elliot were carvers at the meat table consisting of ham, turkey, barbecued pig & beef. Her attendants were Bettie Rumph & Mr J. Rucks, Mamie Boddie & Mr Lide, Miss Anna Moseley & Gilder Boddie, Miss Georgia Proctor & Mr George Ritchie. Mitt was dressed in a delicate dove almost pearl colored silk, trimmed with a darker shade, made very stylish with a sash necktie purchased in St. Louis by Johnie. The bridesmaids wore white swiss made with trains, stylish over skirts, & sleeveless basques. Mamie & Georgia wore blue trimmings & white flowers, and Anna & Bettie wore crimson trimmings & white flowers. All looked very pretty. After dinner, the brides cake was cut, & Bettie found the ring.* But it was a sad time when the bride bade her old home farewell, and it was through blinding tears that those left behind saw the carriage that contained one of their loved circle roll away. Carrie, Florence, & myself, with some of the young men of the neigborhood, accompanied her to her new home in Camden; where Mrs Rucks his mother had invited a few of their friends to the nice little supper that awaited the happy couple. We spent a very pleasant night & came home the next morning. I have been to see her once, and she has been to see us twice. Mr. Rucks is a merchant and says he cannot leave the store often or he would bring her over more frequently. She seems perfectly happy, her little step-daughter is named Cornelia and they call her Corrie. She is a pretty child & a most winning little creature, very smart to her age; calls Mittie Mama.

 I stayed with Mittie two weeks before she was married & helped her sew & helped Mat & Bettie bake the cakes &c, we had a merry time. I often wished for you & wondered why you did not write to me. Mittie's dresses were all very pretty, & her underclothing was really very handsome. Your yoke figured conspicously. I embroidered some cuffs for it & a band & sleeves to match. I braided her a skirt that had two bunches of tucks & braid pattern beneath, between, & above the bunches, it was very pretty when completed.

 Well time rolled on and the Christmas hollidays arrived. Christmas Day we had Brother John's & Mr Dunlap's family to dine with us, besides some of the neighbors. We expected George Rumph & Jennie & Mr Rucks & Mittie, but the river rose & they could not come. Gilder came though and we had a pleasant day & plenty of Christmas cheer! Bettie R[umph] remained with us the next week & New Year's Eve, Mamie, Carrie, Bettie, Will & myself went in the wagon to town, Mamie & Bettie to attend a grand holiday ball, & Carrie & I to visit about a mile this side of town, were caught in hard rain, had no protection except shawls. We doffed our hats & took them in our laps, & covered our heads and ears in the shawls. Went up main street in that style. No one knew us, only guessed who it was from seeing Will. We did not get so wet after all. Jennie ran out, delighted to see us; and soon made us comfortable. Florence was with her, had been staying two weeks with Mitt. After chatting a while & fondling her two sweet little children, Mamie, Bettie, & Florence commenced getting ready for the ball. About 9 o'clock, their escorts came & Carrie & I had a quiet time with George & Jennie chatting & enjoying a treat of candies & nuts, wound up with an egg nog & retired. About three o'clock the girls came back, having had a "Splendid time" at the ball. Next day Jennie gave us a turkey dinner. Mittie was with us & we had a pleasant day with the young generation of married folks. We came home that evening & I went home with Bettie & Florence. Mamie stayed in town, remained a week. We heard from her Saturday. She is enjoying her visit & wants to remain two weeks longer. By the

*It was the custom to bury inside the wedding cake a ring, which portends marriage for the one who finds it in her piece of cake. A dime was often buried in the cake also that portends prosperity.

way she has never received a letter from you & often wonders why you don't write.

Well all in all we have had a pleasant Christmas. The weather has been fine, most too fine for this season. Vegetation is being cheated into donning its spring suit. Even now we are having April showers & the frogs are singing as merrily as if it were indeed spring. We spent Monday after Christmas on the lake, boat riding & picknicking generally. Attended two parties. But the holidays days are passed, and everything is fast resuming its old channel. Brother G is ginning his cotton crop, made but little this year of either corn or cotton, on account of the drouth which though not general, fell heavily upon a few in the neighborhood. The potato crop also was a failure, & though he made plenty of peas to fatten his hogs, failed to save seed for another year. Brother G was sick off and on all the fall. Seemed to have slow fever most of the time, something like typhoid & never gained his strength until recently & Will had his hands full to gather what little corn & cotton was made. Thinks he will have meat enough to do him. We are just through with the hog-killing & its attendant greasiness and now reveling in spareribs, backbone bone, souce*, & the like. This is Carrie's cook week, and I tell you she flies around with any of us. Says she wants to copy my recipes, &cc and learn to do every thing.

I wish Kate you could see little Maude*. She is undoubtedly a prodigy. She is only fourteen months old & can run all over the place, tries to dance Shotische, waltz or anything you show her, is a perfect enthusiast over music or a picture book & talks as plainly as many children over two years old. I think she will be a brunette, resembles Bettie more than anyone else. She is the pet of all the family, even brother John notices her more than he did any of his other children. When Mat has her picture taken will try & send you one. They were all well when I was there. Mr Dunlap & family were well also.

Well Andrew is married at last, the dear boy, may his & Fannie's sunlight of happiness never be less bright than now, may he never know Adversity & frown but may his little bark float on over the tide of life wafted to the haven of rest only by the gentlest breezes.

You are mistaken Kate about Dempsy Underwood being a beau of mine. He is younger than I. It was Miss West that repeated poetry to him to which he replied, "Pick up chestnuts, gal." Whom did he marry? Tell cousin Mary it would be a treat to receive a letter from her & she must write to me herself whenever you are tardy in writing. About my bed Kate I do not wish to sell it as feathers are so high out here. I would be unable to replace it. They [feathers] are a dollar to a dollar & a quarter a pound, while there, they are only 75 cts. My bed has 76 lbs of feathers in it and I would not like to take less than $50 dollars for it at least, and that seems like asking you too much for it. I still hope to get it out here some time, as when I come again, will

*Souse is a pickled & congealed hog head cheese.

*Maude is the first born child of Dr. John Rumph and his third wife Martha "Matt" Proctor.

probably return by water. In the meantime Kate, knowing that you will take good care of it, consider your request to keep it in your room until I can get it, granted. I expect to ask any one else 75 cts per pound for it. Well I guess you are tired reading. Probably much that I have written may already be stale to you, had best close wishing you all a happy new year. Sis Mollie joins me in love to you all. I dreamed last night that you and Willie Holmes were married, and I was delighted at the match, for you know I consider the Holmses good blood and our inferior to none. Give my love to Mammy. Tell her I often think of her & Uncle Jerry. I wish that I could see them. I was sorry to see him so reduced; and felt that if negros had not been freed, he would have been better provided for in his old age. How did they all succeed last year in their crops. How did our old place do. But Uncle Clem has that in hand for us, & will let us hear. I hope ere this he has fully recovered his health.*

*The journal copy of this letter ends here.

Mary Elizabeth Boddie in Ouachita Co. to her son John R. Boddie in St. Louis.

January 2nd, 1876

My own dear boy,

'Tis my happy privilege to greet you this beautiful morning with many wishes, that the present New Year may be to you replete with happiness. That we missed you at our Christmas board you well know, tho' all our expected guests (that I told you of) were with us, save "Cousin" & Geo's family. Uncle John occupied your old time seat at the table. Gilder came over Christmas morning, tho' not in time for eggnogg & breakfast, said Mr R[ucks] & Geo could not possibly leave, were too busy, a boat having landed the eve previous & one that morning, & you know what the arrival of a SteamBoat means at the Camden warf. All the young folks have had a very pleasant time during the entire week, we have had such unprecidented warm, pleasant weather, with an occasional shower of rain, & fair & sunny immediately after, that the rain did not discommode them much in their arrangements for visiting round. Bettie stayed with us all the week, & Florence expected to come over with Mittie, as she had been at her sisters, & with Jennie for the past two weeks. All the girls attended a Party at Mrs Agee's Thursday night, & Friday eve Willie took them all to Town, Mamie & Bettie to attend the Holiday Ball, & Nealy to make Mit a visit, & Carrie to see Miss Delle B. Pa & Will went over to mill, & to bring them all home yesterday. The whole crowd dined with Geo. & Jennie, except Pa & Tommy. "Small Sis" remained in Town to make her first, & long promised visit to "Cousins" & others, said she would write to you from there, so I leave her to tell you about the Ball &c &c — as Bettie & "Mrs OScuttle" talked both at the same time, & so fast, did not glean much, only that they looked O so pretty, & "Sis Jennie fixed my hair" so & so, so & so, I learned from "little Sis" however that our girls really looked very nice. Nealy went on in Tommy's waggon with the girls to spend the coming week at Uncle J's. Will went too, as Mat has her big dinner today. Pa intended going up there this morning, but could not get his riding mule out of the field without wading the sloshes, so declined, & he, little sis, Tug & I are having today to ourselves. The church bells rang out so clear & sweet this morning, bringing sweet memories of you, in your far off home, & I am with you in thought each Sabbath morn darling, as you wend your way to the Holy Sanctuary. I imagined you would go to the different churches Christmas morn to see the beautiful & appropriate decorations for the great holiday. I was truly edified by reading a description of the same in the papers you sent Pa, & thought if I only could have been there to see. "Little Sis" was so much surprised, as delighted to receive a letter from Brother, said she did not think you would notice her little note, & that you had so many to write to, she ought not impose on your loving kindness again. Mamie's letter was recd the same day with mine of the 26th & I assure you was happy to know you had recovered. I hope son you will never neglect such attacks, for severe colds lead to all the ailments to which suffering humanity is liable. Am glad Mr R. came in time to be with you during Mr L's absence. Tug was very much amused at the idea of Bud John's hanging up his stocking, says Old Santa never comes down our chimney now. Pa told him the old fellow broke down in the bottom, & could get no farther. You guess right about Tug's impatience for a letter, for the very first mail rec'd after he has sent one, asks for his letter. I tell him he should be more prompt in writing, he loves so well to get a letter. Tug got his paper with Pa's last week, & this week the Paper's containing the engraving, & description of the New Temple of Commerce, with the opening ceremonies, speeches &c, is very interesting.

Another marriage came off in Camden recently, Dr Hudson & Miss Berenice W. The next spoken of is Miss Ella R[itchie]. tho' I guess you know about that, if 'tis, as rumor reports, that Mr C.[harlie] G.[ordon] is to be the happy man.

Monday 3rd Was interrupted by company yesterday, Mrs Annie [Stone] & Julia A. came, the latters babe of two months is as fat, & sweet, as babies usually are, they have named it Helen, for Mrs Cole's daughter. Annie's boy is so pretty, dont look like any of her other children. Both the Ladies inquired particularly about you, & Annie says tell John, Bob has gotten well over the blues, has had such a good time hunting, & seated himself to write to you all about it, & found he was out of ink. They run a cat all day Christmas, caught it, & one too the day previous. A fox hunt to come off next Friday night. State took supper with us Saturday, gave Pa a humorous description of a six hours' chase after a cat afoot, through the cane &c. Willie

L. & Miss Mollie took dinner with us Christmas day, she has been in Town since visiting, & attended the Ball. Mrs Annie & Bob [Stone] spent one day in Town, were at the young folks Party at Capt D's. Gilder was on hand, escorted little Miss Beardon, have not learned with whom he went to the Party at the Academy, he would not tell us, so you perceive he is interesting himself with the young ladies at last, I must tell you of Bro Will's Christmas present from Miss Anna, a pair of <u>specs</u> to enable him she said, to <u>see better</u> than to <u>call Miss Nellie E. pretty</u>. Mrs E[lliot] is well, & enjoying this Christmas at home, with her relatives from Camden. Nellie is at Pine Bluff yet. Mrs Annie & Bob have invited the young folks to their house tonight, none to go from here, but "little sis" & Will, & she is busy fixing up some button hole boquets for Bud, Mr Allis, Anna & herself. "Small Sis" has had flowers the entire winter so far, & the white Hyacinths are beautiful, her box of Pansies are very showey with their rich purple tints. <u>I have pressed one</u> to send you. It dont seem as though we'll have any winter weather sure enough. Will has gone to work to-day cutting & hauling wood, as neither Uncle J[ohn] D[unlap] or Mr Wm S[tone] will be through with their ginning for a week or longer. Pa & Will talk as though they will hire no freedman this year, as it takes all they make to pay their hire, & no profit, but some loss to the employer each year. Mr Powell G. has moved over to his Pa's, says he's fairly sick of housekeeping & farming alone. Well darling my paper is out, & must close hoping to hear that you are well, & with much love from all at home, with kind remembrance from your many friends.

Your devoted mother,
Mary E. Boddie

*Old Mr Gamble died this morning, had been confined to the bed for the past three months.

*Note: This postscript is written upside down across the top of page 3.

Cornelia Dickson in Ouachita Co. to her friend Hattie Underwood in Autauga Co.

Jan 17th, /76

Dear Hattie

It was a most pleasant surprise on returning home from visiting a friend, one evening several weeks since, and opening a letter from home to find your signature. I knew that you had not forgotten me and felt sure that duties of several descriptions prevented your replying to my letter immediately, for I had looked and hoped so long in vain for a letter from you, I had come to the conclusion that you would write whenever you felt at sufficient leisure. I can tell you Hattie I never did think there was much pleasure to be derived from marrying and raising a house full of children, at least I never felt that I was fitted to fill so responsible a position in life. Though I suppose if my hard heart had ever been pierced by an arrow from the "little god," I might have felt that I was fitted for any position to which he pointed and derived great pleasure at times from being surrounded with "little blessings." Let us do as we will, we, none of us, can escape the trials and vexations that inevitably lie in the path of this life, and we are only able to rise above them by "Living in the hope of a better day dawning."

If I greet you coldly in your dream you must remember that dreams always go by contraries my dear. But if the dream was an incentive to writing to me, dream again, very soon. I commenced a reply to your welcome & interesting letter the 21st of Dec but was interrupted with company & then was so much occupied with preparations for the holidays. It being my cook week all devolved upon me. Well all was ready at last and we have been blessed in being permitted to spend another Christmas on earth and partake with our friends & relatives of the bountiful Christmas cheer. We have had a good deal of company. Attended a picnic on the lake. On New Years eve Bettie Rumph, Mamie & Carrie Boddie & myself went over to Camden, were caught in a hard rain, presenting a most forlorn condition as we went up main street. Arriving at George Rumphs, Mamie & Bettie commenced making their toiletts for the ball. Carrie & I went over for a visit, remained with George & Jennie & enjoyed a nice treat of nuts & candies, &c, finishing off with an eggnog. The girls came in about <u>three o'clock</u> reporting a "Splendid time" at the ball, and said they were only able to leave after the leap year set. Next day Jennie gave us a turkey dinner, Mittie came round and we all enjoyed our first family dinner with the young generation of married folks. That evening we came home, bringing Florence & leaving Mamie to spend several weeks. I went on up to Brother John's & spent the next week, came home to fill the duties of my cook week again last week, so you see I have been flying around ever since before Christmas. We heard from Mamie Saturday & she wishes to remain in town two weeks longer, is having a lively time, I suppose. Last Thursday evening Mr Charlie Gordon & Miss Ella Richie of Camden were married. The ceremony took place at church.

It is useless for me to attempt to portray the feelings & memories that rush upon me in reading the gleanings of your pen, and when you again get to the "end of your paper" please do not wait until next time, but get another sheet, & write on. Do not think that I am greedy, but your letters are so interesting I am sorry when they come to a conclusion. I was so glad to hear that Mr Underwood made a good crop. We regret to hear that Mr Abe Lanier has been so unfortunate, but if I mistake not, he has too much energy to [succumb] to advirsity. Our love to Tom, Kate, Emma, ____, when you see them. Do your surmises prove correct about the "old widower" & have the young men elbowed him out of his walk. I have just received a letter from Kate telling me of Andrew's marriage, also one from Julia Howard giving the particulars of Dora's wedding. It seems that the young folks out here are still infected with the matrimonial fever, as since Mittie's marriage, have averaged about three weddings per month in Camden & vicinity. Hoping this may find you all enjoying blessings of health I shall close by wishing you a happy New Year.*

*The letter ends in the ledger at this point.

Mary E. Boddie in Ouachita Co. to her son John R. Boddie in St. Louis
January 18th 1876

My own dear boy,

Your cherished letters of 2nd & 9th ult. came to hand in due time; & if you knew how dearly I appreciated the privilege of hearing from you <u>weekly</u>, would never "upbraid" yourself for any imaginary remisness, when to me, <u>each one</u> is a little volume of love from my dear son. Am glad to know darling, my letter contributed in the least to your pleasure, for I love to write, though there is so little of interest to communicate, as we plod on in the same beaten track each day, varied only with pleasant thoughts, kindly feelings towards each other, & occasional intercourse with neighbours. Pa remarked yesterday, that a rainy day always made him feel sad, & lonely, but I oftener enjoy a rainy day than otherwise, feel a content, & calm retirement within myself, which is so enjoyable, & then after the dark clouds & rain, come the pleasant sunshine. I think the smokey atmosphere of St. Louis must be its most objectionable feature. Am glad you sometimes enjoy one eve of sunshine & fresh air, & wish you could indulge in such recreations oftener. Pa was in Town Saturday, saw Mr G. at the store, had but a short time to talk with him, reported all well & that his stay here would be short, expect he will be back home ere this reaches you, & if it could only <u>be you</u> to make a flying visit, now & then, but that is too good to talk about. Your "Small Sis" has been in Town since the 30th Dec. has written to me only once, begging I would not send for her, from all I can learn Jennie & Geo. claim most of her time, as she has staid at "Cousin's" but one or two nights. She sent "little sis" word to cook for her next week, & she would return the favor when she came home, that cousin Jennie would come with her & spend several days, if I would let her stay one more week, making the fourth. I miss her greatly & want to see her. "Little Sis" accused me of making almost as much to do about seeing Mamie, as about "brother." Tug says I must tell bud Johnie "I'm much obliged for my paper, & Pa reads them too, I wanted to write to him last week but had to drive the gin." They have finished ginning & packing Henry's cotton (three bales) & Pa & Will had to go in the bottom to-day, as the river is rising very fast, & if there has been as much rain above as we had, there will be an overflow. Rained two days & nights & still continues warm, everything here has more the appearance of Spring than

Winter. Pa & Will availed themselves of the first <u>cold days</u> (Tuesday & Wednesday of last week) to kill hogs. Mr Moseley killed before Christmas, & <u>lost all</u> but the sides, has only three more to kill. We killed fourteen, averaging 130. Pa sent one to Mr Bracy, & Will sold two at 8cts & bought one of Capt. Mitchell's two months old Berkshire's, & Tug has been trying to trade him out of it ever since, he says he owns more hogs now than bud Willie has, keeps up pretty well with his claim, & can give account of each one. Pa has made no arrangements with the freedmen yet, but wont employ them in the same manner as heretofore. Jack intends making another trip to Hot S. & Geo. thinks Spencer wants to go with him. Mr Moseley has dispensed with the services of Marinda & children, as she required more than he was willing to give. Mrs M. & Anna are doing the cooking, hire the washing & ironing. Marvin M[oseley] has been working at home ever since Mr Rucks married, has much better health than when confined to the Office. The last Party of the holidays came off at "Uncle Hal's"[Brodnax] last Thursday night. Nealy, Carrie, Miss Anna, Miss Lula A[very], Mr Allis M[oseley], Mr A. Norris went from our Berg, a jolly waggon load. Will did not go as he said he did not want to lose half days work, however pleasant it might be to make one of the crowd. The girls, & Tommy [Rumph] went from Uncle John's, Atalie too. Tommy was to have spent last Sunday with us, but it rained all day, & Gilder has not been to see us since Christmas, I guess because Mamie is over there. Nealy has rec'd letters from Autauga recently, by the bye, we have not sent your message to Miss Julia yet, about the Photo &c. She writes that her sister Miss <u>Dora</u> was married 23rd Dec. to Mr Joe Wilkerson, had a fine wedding, twelve attendents &c &c. Andrew Love (Mary's son) was married on the 15th to Miss Fannie Zimmerman. They are living with his mother. No letter from sis Hattie yet. Well darling have come to the end of this little sheet, which I had to get from Nealy this time. Miss Mollie Norris is very sick from severe cold neglected too long. Mr N. is trying to get a little place on the Camden side. No other rumors to, or from the neighborhood that I know of as yet. Pa said he rode from Town with Mr L. Elliott Saturday, he begged for Cowper* until Pa told him he could send for him. So there will go the last of my pets. This leaves all well, & hoping to hear the same good report of you this week, close with much love from each one of the family.

*Cowper was a hunting dog.

        Your devoted Mother
        Mary E. Boddie

"Aunt Mary" R[umph] says, <u>please</u> tell cousin Johnie "they killed my poor little piggee, for the wedding, the same little piggee that went in the parlor for you to see, cousin Johnie, & I could'nt eat a morsel of it, it like to killed me."

Cornelia Dickson in Ouachita Co. to her friend Julia Howard in Autauga Co.

Feb 1st 1876

Dear Julia

    Your most welcome letter of the 7th inst was received several days since & perused with interest. I was much gratified at your giving me the particulars of Dora's wedding and I could see you all in my mind & eye passing through the different preparations until the final leave taking. Present my best wishes to them. May they realize all their dreams of happiness. Sis Mollie joins me in my congratulations and says tell you that one wedding is the forerunner of others. I had heard of Andrews & Fannie's marriage in a letter from Kate. I believe the girls out here are rather slow in improving their leap year opportunities. The 31st of Dec there was a Grand Holiday Ball given in Camden. The dancing lasted until four o'clock new years morn. Mamie, Bet & Florence left at three after participating in the first leap year set, in which the ladies sought partners for the dance. They enjoyed the novelty particularly, as some of the gentlemen were exceedingly <u>timid</u> & <u>bashful</u>. Carrie & I went with them to Camden & spent a pleasant evening with George & Jennie. Next day Jennie gave us a New Years dinner. Mittie was with us. We enjoyed our visit very much.

    We are having some very fine weather, for this season of the year. It is entirely too fine. Vegetation is being cheated into donning her brightest robes, but to be doffed again ere the winter months have rolled into the past. We have had an abundance of rain - enough to swell the old Ouachita far beyond its banks. A week ago, it even extended to within a few feet of our back yard gate, causing great destruction of property to many who had stock ranging in the extensive canebrake bordering either side of the river. Some lost as many as twenty head of cattle besides hogs, sheep & about two miles above us four mules were found drowned that had been hemmed in by the swelling waters. Brother George was more fortunate this time & lost only two head of cattle. It is really exciting to us all when the water begins to rise so rapidly. After the labor of getting up the stock is over, we generally have a lively time boat riding & regattas with some of the young people of the neighborhood. We find it delightful exercise and sometimes very amusing. Gilder was to see us, came in a boat all the way from town. Says he will avail himself of Miss Minnie's delicate hint & permit her to behold the shadow of a hoosier boy as soon as he can have one taken. Tell Minnie not to attach too much importance to Gilder's professions of constancy, as there is a little blackeyed Minnie in town about whom he seems a little nervous. Mamie is still in Camden. She, Mittie, & Jennie with children expected to come over yesterday, but the water has not subsided sufficiently to allow them to cross.

Well Julia this letter seems uninteresting & disconnected to me, but I have had half doz or more interruptions since commencing. The last of which was rather an agreeable surprise, an invitation to a quilting day after tomorrow, & a candy stew at night.

I was pleased but not surprised that old Mulberry came near bearing off the palm at the Granges State fair. You speak of Mr Sham Jones marrying Miss Fannie Hall, a neice of Mr Andrew Hall. Who is her father & I was not aware that he had a neice bearing his name old enough to marry. Present my kind regards to Mr A. Hall & Albertine, also to Col & Mrs Wilkerson. I am always gratified to hear from them & Tell me something of Ella's whereabouts. I never hear from her now. I was glad to hear from Jennie, bless her heart, with her name Memory wakes from her slumber once more, and in bright dreams of the feast. I regret to hear of Mr Jones' illness, hope ere this he has recovered and may be enabled to do much good even in the "eleventh hour." . . . We have a pleasant neighborhood and I anticipate an enjoyable day. Sis Mollie joins me in love to you & all, and bids me send John's message to you in reply to yours to her through Onie Love's letter. There is no danger of his falling in love with any St Louis girls unless they had chink enough to cover their prodigious ugliness.

> As ever
> Your affectionate friend
> C. L. Dickson

Mary E. Boddie in Ouachita Co. to her son John R. Boddie in St. Louis

February 1st 1876

My own dear boy,

Your dear letters of 16th & 23rd at hand, & am so thankful to note your continued good health, & cheerful spirits through the gloom of such "rainy," "sloppy" &c weather. We have had just such, minus the "smoke" & "smut." To-day is <u>very cold</u> with high wind, & yesterday was too warm for fires. The overflow come sure enough, doing more damage than usual to owners of stock, the water rose so fast, that it took many by surprise, rose two feet in one day, & that night six. Pa & Will was three days getting our cattle out, lost one of the half breeds, & has since heard that a yearling of his was drowned that had strayed over the river. Mr Jim Toney, Dickerson, Mackey, L. Dunlap, & others lost nearly all they had. Mr A. Tait had 40 head drowned. Mr Norris lost one of his horses, & State S[tone] his mule, the one he purchased last Spring, said he "got it out on the ridge next to Burns's but the fool of a mule went back & drowned itself." State bewails his loss, says when a poor fellow starts down hill every thing bad happens to keep him rolling on, he had sold two fine pigs, for a good price, but had not delivered them, & the old sow ruined one by biting it through the loin. Will's pig (Dixie) looks to increase in weight daily. Tug is bragging much on his eight young pigs, & is so indignant at the Buzzards for eating up a whole litter from his best sow, that he wants to kill every buzzard he sees. Says it takes all his money he made picking cotton to keep him in ammunition, but he intends to have a squirrel dog sure. Talks largely of having a cotton patch of his own this year to work, told Pa he wanted him to let him have the seed from the cotton raised in the garden last year to plant, & has selected his ground too, "Bud Willie's" patch that he enriched last year, & grew most of the corn on that was made. Pa & Will, after so many interuptions will finish up the cotton this week, when they get through. Henry will move to "Uncle Billy's" who is very anxious to have a tenant to take Tolberts' place who ran off during court & did not stop this side of Georgia. Lucy was about to have him arrested, as she believed he was instrumental in causing Elzira's early death. Henry is averse to leaving us, but Geo. convinced him 'twas impossible he could run him this year, as Henry cant provision his family except with meat. We female portion are sorry indeed to see "Aunt Nina" go, she is so good to help us with the rough kitchen work. Spencer proposes to work for Geo. six months, if at the end of that time Pa will give him a quit claim for all his old indebtedness, which Geo. is willing to do, but dont much believe Spencer will fulfill his part. Mr Moseley says he dont intend to plant but one acre in cotton this year, & "Uncle Billy" talks of letting a greater portion of his plantation be out, but Pa says he'd be willing to bet the latter will plant more cotton than ever. Bob S. will plant as usual. Mrs Moseley & I spent one day last week with Mrs Annie [Stone]. Bob says, tell John I hunt small game now, such as possum, rabbit, but I dont let my dogs out after such game. Uncle John called an hour or so yesterday on his way from Town, made particular inquiry about you, & read your letters, said he expected to get one himself, & wanted to know if you had written to him. I told him you mentioned in your letter to me of the 9th your intention of writing that week, says he has rec'd the papers you sent. Tommy spent Sunday with us, & of course called on Miss Anna that eve, & "Bro Will" thinks she has convinced Tom, if not himself, that she is the prettiest Pink of all the fair ones. Miss Anna seems to be a general favorite with all the boys. "Miss Dickens"* bids me tell you "never fear that any old maid will grab you, but see to yourself that some idle butterfly dont gobble you up this leap year A. D. 1876." Also that she received some long, & very interesting letters from Miss Julia that she wishes you were here to read, & one from Miss Becca U. who complained of being badly treated in not getting your Photo, when you had the benefit of seeing hers. Aunt Nealie says though, "dont be afraid she wants to gobble you up", as Becca has a host of admirers, & cant imagine why she wants it except to excite the jealousy of some of them by exhibiting it occasionally, & will leave you to judge if it could be done or

*"Miss Dickens" was a Boddie family name for Bettie Rumph.

Patrick Gaughan
Photo courtesy of Dr. Dan Daniel.

*"Mrs. Gaughan" refers to Sarah Caroline Patterson Gaughan, wife of Patrick Gaughan.

not. "Small Sis" is still in Town, & I want to see her so much, Jennie & babies, Mittie & Corrie, were to have come home with her to spend this week, but the high water prevented, & 'tis uncertain now when they can get over. Some waggons went in yesterday, though the bottom is still under water, rising again from the rain here, & up the river which fell last week. Gilder came over home last Saturday eve, not to return, he has not yet decided what he'l do. Mr Brown wanted him to remain there untill summer, go to the Centennial, & perhaps next year he would be able to do better for him. Gilder says he cant work there any longer for only board & clothing, & his Pa approved of his leaving. Dr Brown is going to the Centennial & Geo. B. intends going if possible. Many in Camden speak of it, but I believe the Ouachita Guard Co. will be a failure. Am so glad to hear that you can go son, dont think you'l ever regret having availed yourself of the opportunity, but if you should happen to live to the good old age of some of the Centenariaist I read of in Scribner you'l have another chance. Pa rec'd his papers, & Tug his, which he is so proud of, asked Miss Lula A. if she would not like to read his papers, "the last one I think is best, our new Editor is out." Today is Wills' birthday, & he will dine at the ginhouse on cold rations — Gilder's will be the 12th. The childrens' birthdays come so fast, it makes me feel that I'm growing old, but more thankful each day, that such children has been given me. I appreciate more than I can tell darling, your loving kindness in sending me such a present, but you must not heed the dictates of your generous heart at such promptings, as 'tis against your interest to do so. Thank you too so much for the kind offer to get for me anything I need, & will avail myself of it. Mrs. O'Scuttle has been pretty close at home since her visit in Town, guess I shall meet with her at the quilting given by Mrs Gaughan* to which we are all invited on Thursday next, if nothing prevents my going. Mrs G. gives the young people a candy stew that night, after the old & young ladies get the quilts out. Our new minister Mr Alchley preached his first sermon at our church last Sunday, but the bayou was too high for any one to go from this side. Your friends all desire remembrance, & the blacks at home send howdy & good wishes. With much love from the home ones, I am as ever

Your devoted Mother

Toward a New Century

Mary E. Boddie in Ouachita Co. to her son John R. Boddie in St. Louis

February 21st, 1876

My dear son,

Your ever welcome, & interesting letters of ... 6th & 13th Inst. duly at hand & am thankful that you still enjoy good health, a contented mind & cheerful disposition, in which respect you remind me so much of my dear father, & if you can always keep in good heart darling boy, "For every Fate," the fast fleeting years will have but little trace of old age in your brow, & better than all, is His promise to all, who are faithful Unto the End. You have had one years' experience of a city life, & I dare say will profit by it, was not at all surprised at the state of your finances at the experiation of the year, but did hope the firm could have done better for you the present year, I did want to see you so badly, yet I have cause to be thankful for so much that is good allotted me, wont repine at the inevitable. Well Son, Pa's & Will's cotton crop is off hand, & delivered at Camden, 9 bales (several though weighed 600) & from which they realized so little owing to the low price of cotton that Pa gets almost disheartened, & but for the profit arising from his stock of cattle & hogs would give up. They have a fine lot now of 60 pigs, if they can take care of & raise which is doubtful, owing to the partial failure in the corn crop. Pa says, he feels greatly relieved to be rid of his freedman, all are gone. Spencer & family too, went to "Uncle Billys." Pa says he cant make it pay to keep them, & deal justly (which he has always done) towards them, their familys were so large & expensive, that he can do better without them. I too son, felt sorry for many reasons, that Gilder left Brown & Bro. but am so glad he wishes to work at home this year, dont intend to make farming his profession, but that he wont go off among strangers this year I am truly glad. Wants Pa to let him have twenty acres of land, a mule to work, & for which he will pay all expenses &c. Pa will charge him no board in consideration of his services in assisting Will with cutting & hauling wood, repairing fences, feeding & watering stock &c &c. Gilder has been at work ever since he came home, & but for him I guess Pa would have missed Spencer greatly, as Willie could not use his right hand for a week or more, sprained it badly striking old Moll mule with his <u>fist</u> to make stand still before the waggon. All laughed at Will

Sarah Caroline Patterson Gaughan, wife of Patrick Gaughan Photo courtesy of Bettie Lu Gaughan Rogers.

*Corrie is Corrie Rucks, Mittie's stepdaughter.

so much at the idea of his hitting a mule with his fist, & his hand is not entirely well yet. The boys & Pa have repaled the garden & such weather as we have had is pleasant enough to cheat one into the delusion that 'tis planting time, yet the ground is too wet to admit of hauling out manure, in the field. Plum & Peach trees have been in bloom some time. Mittie & Corrie* came home with "Small Sis," spent a week with us, & at Uncle John's, I enjoyed her visit very much, seemed so much like old times, could scarcely realize that she was married. Mit looks so well, & is as lively as can be. George & Jennie spent yesterday with us, the baby is very sweet, & pretty, but I dont think quite as handsome as Eugene. There was a grand Ball at Kellum & McGill hall, St Valentine day, "Small Sis" begged her bud Gilder the whole week previous to take her over, & thought she was going until Pa objected (after seeing some names on the ticket) which disappointed her greatly. Gilder went with Bettie & Florence, they, as usual "had the nicest kind of a time." Florence says "tell cousin John, Mrs OScuttle is going to make some desperate efforts to get off this year, will give some of the boys a big scare anyhow, & tell him I've got a new beau, very tall, large foot, & small hand." Cousin Bettie sent you many messages, most of which I've forgotten, but a part was, that she was glad you have not entirely forgotten her, & you had better keep a bright lookout that she did not make her advent in a City too one of these days, & be a Star among the city folk. She did not practice much after her sister married, thinking to be without the Piano every week, but as Uncle John had deferred sending it to Mittie until Spring, she keeps up her practice. If you could hear the almost daily drummin[g] on our old Piano, you would not think the musical interest at all abated, indeed 'tis our most pleasant recreation & amusement. Long time ago your "Small Sis" said to me, Ma please dont say anything to brother about my music, he generally laughs at me anyway, but he might be led to expect too much, or more than I can accomplish. I hardly know why, but she has never done herself justice when trying to play for you. Little Sis is getting on very well with her music, & has confidence plenty. Miss Lula A. has been taking lessons again since Christmas. Mrs Annie & I went to see Mrs Elliot last Wednesday, spent a most pleasant day, Mrs Scales makes her home with her brother Lute n[ow], the ladies enquired particularly about you, & Mrs E.

St. Valentine's Ball.

You are respectfully solicited to attend a Grand Ball to be given at Kellam & McGill's Hall, on the evening of February the 14th, 1876.

COMMITTEE ON INVITATION:
R. E. KALLE.   GEO. W. STONE.   ROB'T TUNSTALL.
EZRA D. HILL.   H. HIGENBOTHAM.
J. D. LOCKHART.

COMMITTEE ON ARRANGEMENTS:
R. E. BELL.   E. W. JORDAN,   JNO. A. BROOKS.
J. F. BUSTIN.   H. A. MILLEN.

RECEPTION COMMITTEE:
A. V. BRAGG,   JAS. F. HOLMES.   J. V. COLLINS.   JAMES RUCKS.

FLOOR MANAGERS:
GEO. W. STONE.   DR. J. N. BRAGG.   L. ROGERS.   J. T. CHIDESTER, JR.
W. G. RYAN.

The St. Valentine's Ball invitation.

sends kindest regards. Belle is the [usual] wee bit Belle, looks to be very little taller. Mr E. was in Town that day. Mr L. Pope & family have moved to the Hogue place, he & Mr L. Elliot will cultivate that farm this year. Mr Norris has rented, & moved to the Deato farm. Rec'd letters from Ala. last week, Carrie one from her cousin Onie, all well, no news. Sis Hattie says the sale for a settlement of the estate would take place the 17th. Mr Geo. Johnston is to be married next month to a Miss Mattie Dickson of Blader Springs, Ala. So you admit at last, that some of the young ladies of St Louis possess charms, & Nealy says, she intends to tell your Ala. girls what a dear modest young man, <u>you be</u> in regard to leap year privileges, & "Miss Dickens" wants you to know from her, that waterfalls* are a thing of the past, & not at all the present style in Ark. therefore, will be fully satisfied with a <u>picture</u> of that <u>moustache</u>, wants to see if St Louis polish has added anything to its Walruss appearance. "Small Sis" is looking for a letter, "Little sis" & Tug are invited to a candy stew at Aunt Clara's this eve, & they are in a <u>stew</u> to go, but Pa thinks the weather too unfavourable, been raining all the morning. Uncle J. D. says young John B. thinks himself a man now, can go on all fours everywhere they'l permit him, he's the smartest boy out. Speaking of Mr Lowry's heir, reminds me to tell you that Mr J[ohn] H. Dunlap has one, also a son to old Mr Avera, of which they are so proud, cant decide on a name. Perhaps you have not heard that Mrs Winfield has a granddaughter, Mr Powell was in Camden this winter, his wife is at Little Rock with her mother. The Brides made their advent in Town on Wednesday eve, had no attendents at the double wedding,* Mr Collins & Miss Fannie R. accompanied the grooms down to Mrs Graham's in a coach & four. Miss Jennie Toney was to have gone, but was ill with <u>measles</u>. Mr Lide has made his home at the Word place, Mr Toney jun[ior] will live at "the farm" on our side.

  Well darling I've turned to a fresh leaf to conclude my letter, but have a propensity to write on if I could think of anything more to tell you, as though there was not already <u>quite</u> a <u>sufficiency</u>; such as it is. Pa & Tug send many thanks for papers, the latter has not hunted any in some time, says he will write to Bud Johnie next week. None of the girls rec'd any Valentines, said I was ahead of them for I got a letter, & love from my boy, & you cannot know how dearly your weekly messengers are prised by your loving Mama,

Mary E. Boddie

  P.S. I came near forgetting that Gilder asked me to tell you, he had cared for, & brought home everything you left in his charge, the looking glass he says, you did not tell him anything about, & wants to know if it belongs to you. With much love from each one of the family, remain your devoted Mother.

---

*"Miss Dickens" is apparently referring to beards as "waterfalls, although the term was usually used to refer to a woman's hair style."

*The double wedding was the marriages of Laura B. Graham to James B. Toney and Susan W. Graham to S. B. Lide.

Cornelia Dickson in Ouachita Co. to her cousin Hannah Love in Garden Valley, Smith County, Texas

March 1st, 1876

Dear Cousin Hannah,

Again I have commenced to pen a letter to you though I have never received a line from you since you removed to Texas, and I would have never known but that you had treated my other letters with utter silence if I had not seen, during my brief visit to Ala, in one of your letters to cousin Mary that you replied to my letter, but it went back to you from the dead letter office. I cannot surmise the cause as I send to the office regularly once a week & sometimes oftener, unless it was unpardonable neglect on the part of the post master. And Cousin Hannah I really think you ought to have written again, for I have wanted so much to hear from you. There I am selfish, as probably you do not care so much about me, or at least your loving heart has become so filled with home affections you have no room for those not embraced within that immediate circle. I sometimes heard from you through Kate or cousin Mary, but their letters have become like angel's visits. Though I have half a doz other correspondents in Ala & hear from there frequently, but never from Texas at all now. Write me a long letter, tell me about yourself, Clem & children, your parents & family, and Ell, do you ever hear from him now? I should be much gratified to hear from you all, and how [you are] getting on these hard times.

Short crops for two years in succession and high taxes have rendered many in this country very much dissatisfied, which is not lessened by the low price of cotton this year, though I believe the latter cause is a source of depression almost everywhere. Brother George has no hands at all on his place this year; it being election year, he profits by past experience, and expects to hire as he needs them, if at all. Himself, Gilder & Will have started their crop. Gilder has been in a hardware establishment in Camden the past two years, but that place is fast dying out & wages are not sufficiently remunerative to warrant him to stay longer. He speaks of going to Texas, but we are glad that he assented to stay at home this year, as we felt [loathe] to see him go to any untried country. John is in St. Louis in business in the house of Tyra Hill & Company. We hear from him every week.

We do our own work except the washing. Sometimes have as many as fifteen cows to milk, but we get along smoothly enough as there are three of us to take part with Sis Mollie thrown in for good measure. I have been teaching whenever I could get a school, but children are scarce & times are hard and I failed to get a school last year, or this. Will try again next fall provided I do not take advantage of the privilege accorded us this leap year! If I could have kept a school would have been able in that time to have fulfilled my long cherished desire of paying <u>you</u> a visit Cousin Hannah. I suppose you have heard all about our trip to Ala in the summer of '74. That pleasant epoch to which we shall ever revert with pleasure.

 I spent week before last at brother John Rumph's, always have a pleasant time up there. We all like his last wife so much better than we at first anticipated. She has proved to be a very amiable & excellent woman, has the sweetest little girl imaginable, a perfect household pet, about eighteen months old, with black eyes, dark curly hair, rather dark complexion, & the daintiest little form. I had the honor of naming her, and my selection, Maud, suits well the dainty darling. Her mother says now no other name would have so well become her. Mittie was married last October to Mr Ed Rucks, a merchant of Camden. We were all well pleased with her choice. George Rumph is also living in Camden. He has two boys, Eugene & George Boddie Jr. He & Jennie spent last Sunday week with us.

 Well, Cousin Hannah, I will expect you to write very soon, hope I will not be again disappointed. Sis Mollie joins me in love to you all. As ever,
      affectionately your cousin
      Cornelia S. Dickson

Mary E. Boddie in Ouachita Co. to her son John R. Boddie in St. Louis
            March 20th 1876
My own dear boy,

 Your dear & most welcome letter of 12th Inst. is the latest rec'd, & the interval seems very long, though feel assured there is one awaiting me at the office, if I could only get it. None of our family have been to Town in a month, & if you have directed yours to Geo. R[umph]'s care will certainly call him to account for his remissness, though there has been, I expect, but little passing on account of the water getting up again, 'tis rather high to ride in, & too low for boating. Your "Small Sis" is getting impatient for her letter, & even "Tug" is asking me if he wont get a letter from bud Johnie this week? I tell him no, he was too long writing to you, says he would love to write if he had anything to write about. "Tug" did not at all like the accusation that he had forgotten you, says bud Johnie will see now, wont he, when he gets my letter? Pa, & the boys have driven all the cattle out in anticipation of a general overflow again, yesterday it rained nearly all day & we had a quiet enjoyable time indoors, the first Sabbath we've had no company this year, & for many more. When we retired last night 'twas sleeting & during the night Prof. Ice made a visit, this morning everything is enveloped in a mantle of the "beautiful." Of course the young ones enjoy it, & "small Sis", Nealy & "little sis" have a frolic every time they venture out to escape a snowballing from the boys. Tug is greatly discomfited because I detain him indoors, he was little indisposed yesterday, & his shoes are too badly worn for him to run around in the snow. Invitations to a party at the Bob S[tone]'s were sent out last Friday, for tonight, & Bob has sent word again this morning to all parties to be sure to go, & not let the snow prevent. Miss Archie Hays is at Mrs Annie's to spend some time. Bro's. Will & Gilder boast that they have had a leap year call from two young ladies of Camden — Mr J. Bustin, for his mischief sent them a note Saturday week ago, saying the young ladies would certainly be over next day, & their boy would attend them; signed, Miss Adelle B. Miss Zollie B. They came sure enough, & the contents of the note was a subject of much merriment, as our boys feigned to believe the girls wrote, & sent it, & Johnie B. disclaimed all knowledge of it. By the by Mr B. told us he would be off for Texas in a few weeks. All plow work has been at a stand still ever since the heavy rain on Tuesday & Wednesday last, they were just ready to commence planting corn, many in our vicinity have already planted some, Uncle J. D[unlap] was nearly through, & on the McArath farm the corn crop is all up. Dont know to whom Col. Hill has rented this year. Mr Brown keeps old Joe on the Norris farm, & Beown, (our Ann's husband) is living there too. The Henry Brown place has no tenents as yet. Mr. Lute E. it seems could not assist Mr Silas P[ope] so he has moved with his family, on Jimmy Ghaun's [Gaughan?] farm, & is glad he says, to take a freedman's chance. Our first crop we consider gone, strawberry's too, for they had nearly done blooming, had a half grown berry on the Ala. plants. Pa & I are commiserating the condition of the cattle, shut out from the bottom so long, & such cold bad weather, the little pigs will suffer too. We have two young heifers with their first calves. Mabel & Clare — "Little Sis" named them, & the latter proves to be unmanageable as yet, while Mabel is as gentle as can be. "Small Sis" has all the milking to do now & dinners to cook. Nealy & Carrie alternately get breakfast & supper every two or three weeks. The school arrangement* has interfered with the regular practice & music lessons, but I am so glad to have Tug & Carrie at their books again. 'Tis getting late, & so cold will have to defer my chat till another day. — Oh! darling, Frank M. has brought my letter, & I am all right now, good bye —

*In a letter dated March 7th, Tug tells bud Johnie that "Aunt Nealie is going to teach Carrie, Colin and I in Henry's old house."

Wednesday 22nd. I commence again darling with a fresh impetus, so be patient. Bro Will says, tell you we are nearly frozen & drowned out here, & he cant say when the crop can be planted. Pa says he dont know whether to wish the corn was in the ground or not. Gilder went over to Mill yesterday in the boat. Frank B[rodnax] & State [Stone] went with him. Gilder says Camden looks deserted, that the stores had as well be closed, for the amount of business being done. Mr Rucks was at the house & he did not have time to go up there, George was off bird hunting, consequently did not hear from Mit or Jennie. Gilder brought out the papers, & Pa is having a good time reading, Tug too was so glad to get his, for I assure you the arrival of our mail creates the most pleasurable <u>excitement</u> we have. I enjoyed reading your letter as much as you did witnessing the laughable acts of the commedian. Aunt Nealy bids me tell you, she can borrow Will<u>'s specks</u>, they will answer every purpose, for they magnify things to the best advantage, & diminish defects. Gilder says, you need not flatter yourself (because you are such a successful manager of bees) by thinking, that he or Tom will get stung by visiting the bee house. Miss Anna [Moseley] wishes you to know, that for use, <u>subjects</u> that have not become seared, & tarnished by time are to be preferred, for all mechanics like new material best. Have sent your message to "Mrs O'Scuttle." Frank B. told me when he came by there on Monday, she & Uncle John were out in the snow at the cow pen, attending to the cows, &c. Tommy has one negro man & two boys to work with him, he has not planted any corn yet. Tommy has killed two turkeys this Spring, & by the by Gilder one. Bettie is teaching Atalie & Eugenia, says they learn very fast. Little Maud is talking now, & the pet of all. Our girls have about slept off the effects of the frolic which lasted the entire night, every party goer on this side of the creek went, even Uncle J. D. was there with Lula. Miss Georgia P[roctor] said Mat was snow bound at their house, she & Uncle John went there Sunday to eat turkey dinner, & as it rained Mat staid, & I dont expect she got home till today; the sun is melting the snow, but it dont disappear fast. "Little Sis" says, she danced her gaiters out, & was <u>wondering</u> why a place on her foot kept feeling so cold, & when she came home found a round piece of her hose danced out too. Your <u>guns</u> shall be taken good care of darling boy, for I have inlisted Gilder in my service, & had him to examine & rub up the large one, he uses Will's when he goes hunting, & found it in a pretty bad condition. Will had lent it to Spencer several times, & had not used it since. Pa generally uses his rifle or Will's gun, when he goes at all which is but seldom. Will can always find some work to do, rain or shine, he & Gilder have been trying to make rails, but the weather is very unsettled yet, & looks as though we have more snow, or rain. Among the papers Gilder brought out were two for me, sent by our old friend, Mr Tony Marshall, in which I regretted so much to learn of the death of my good friend Bettie M. They were living at Troupe Station, Rusk Co. Texas. Bettie died the 7th Dec. left two children.

I have not seen Clara since last preaching day, little John B.* has been sick, but all are well with them at this time. Send on some more "ado's" about yourself darling, to make the heart of your Mama glad.

With much love from each one of the family to our dear absent one, I am as ever,

    Your devoted mother,
    Mary E. Boddie

Saturday. I did expect to have had my letter mailed ere this, but there's been no passing from this side, had a heavy rain again Thursday & all that night, so you can guess what high water we'll have this time, when 'twas

*"little John B." refers to the son of Clara and John Dunlap.

already over the bottom. Was much shocked to-day to hear that Mrs Rucks was dead, she was taken ill last Wednesday eve, & died that night. Little Corrie will miss her grandma so much, & Mittie too will miss her, the old lady had endeared herself to them so much by her loving kindness.

Mary E. Boddie in Ouachita Co. to her son John R. Boddie in St. Louis
April 13th 1876

My own dear boy,

While I am quite content with the length, breadth, and debth of your dear "weekly's", you are welcome to believe you have the advantage, when I know I have such a kind, good son, who contributed so much to Mama's happiness. Am in recep't of three favors, 19th, 26th, Ult. & 2nd Inst. You should have seen Nelie when I told her the enclosed book-mark was for her, for me, she says, for me, did Johnie send it to me? Tell him I never can express the half of my appreciation, not only for its being the most perfect little jim of its kind, & the prettiest I ever saw, but prize it the more because coming from him. I never thought son, a book mark could be fashioned so beautifully, then the song* too, Nelie says 'twas her Mother's favorite, & I used to play it, for 'twas one that I loved, & carries me back to the long, long age, when I played & sang for my dear father, & you often remind me of him darling in your fondness for music. My pupils are not progressing at all now, Lula has quit, "Little Sis" has not taken a lesson since she commenced studying, & practised very little, the same with "Small Sis", who says she has not time. The nights are getting shorter, & work is the order of the day, but the latter is the last one to retire, sometimes practising, then reading or writing till a late hour. One night in nearly every week the young folks from Mr Moseley's comes down to have a social chat, play a game or two of Pedro &c &c. Will & Gilder have made one (after supper) call on Miss Archie, she is in Town now to spend a week. I believe every wagon from this side has been rolling over to Town since the first of the week, except ours, (Pa & Gilder went in the boat last Saturday) as the water is off the bottom, for the first time in six weeks. The weather though warm & pleasant is threatening rain daily, & the trees are beginning to don their robes of green. I assure you that farmers lost no time the few good days they could run a plough to get corn planted, & I think all are through now. Pa commenced the 30th, & finished day before yesterday, though in the meantime rain stopped them. Mr Bob S. had fifteen hands hired to make sure of his work, ere it rained again, had some hauling out cotton seed, some to drop them, some planting corn, & seven or eight plows running. Bob, Mrs Annie, Miss Archie & Lula spent a day with us not long since to partake of a turkey dinner, all hands, & the cooks have been feasting on turkey's this Spring. Gilder has killed four since

*The song referred to was "The Old Arm Chair." The book mark is made of silk with the words and music printed on it. Sue Russell has it framed and hanging in her living room.

I wrote to you, two at a time, & such fine ones, the last two weighed when dressed, one 20 lbs. the other 16 lbs. Mr Proctor has killed several, Uncle John & Tommie two or three each, but I guess Uncle John will tell you all about their hunts. Frank B. said, he & Tommie camped out one night, nearly froze next morning, & when they started out <u>yelping</u>*, they spied four or five others yelping after the <u>same old gobbler</u>, none of them got <u>him</u> that time. The only time but one that Gilder made an unsuccessful hunt, was one morning he told Will to <u>wake him early</u>. Will had him up three hours before light, (neither of them knew what hour it was) Gilder hurried off, reached the hunting ground, waited & waited, said he thought day light was a long time coming, & he getting <u>colder</u> & <u>colder</u> every second of time. At last daylight appeared, & he had <u>yelped</u> about the third time, out flew the turkey from the tree above him, & away it went. I dont suppose he thought just then that, "Distance lent enchantment to the view." Uncle John went to Town this week, for the first time in six weeks, he did not give us a call. Willie went over there late Saturday eve, & stayed all night, intended coming home next morning, (in case the bees should swarm) but Uncle J. would not let him. "Small Sis" told Will she would go with him, but the thought of having to ride a mule, made her decline. She, Miss Anna & Mr Marvin rode over there on horseback, & spent Sunday evening. Uncle J. told Mamie, Bettie could come soon, bring the children, & spend several days with us. I will be so glad, for I have not had them with me any, in a long while. "Cousin Mittie" was quite well last Saturday Gilder told me, & Mr Rucks was to leave that night for Orleans. George R[umph] will not return in a week or two. Jennie gave Gilder such a sweet, pretty picture of Eugene, 'tis the very image of her dear little self. Had one letter from Ala. recently, from Onie, to Carrie, no news, Uncle Clems' health is very bad, they dont think he will ever entirely recover. You spoke of hearing from Clem Love, Nelie wishes to know if his family are with him, she had written to his wife, & directed to Garden Valley. Did Clem say in what business he was, & how getting on? Is Mr Lowry your roommate yet? I fear that during the hot summer months you'l miss the pleasant quarters from which you moved. "Small Sis wonders if brother never intends writing to her again" told me to tell you that her flower garden dont afford such beautiful boquets as at this time <u>last year</u>, has some Tulips in bloom, & some beautiful Pinks from the seed you gave her, no roses yet, the freezing weather retarded everything, & we dont expect to have any fruit save apples, even the blackberries were killed. Strawberry vines are blooming some, again. Pa says he dont know how we are to have much garden products, for nearly all that work has to be done at noontime, & then they are so tired, Irish potatoes are my chief vegetable, & they are up fine. The boys intend planting watermelons in the old turnip patch. Pa & Gilder have already planted a few in the garden. Whenever the ground will admit of ploughing Seymore makes a hand, his wife Beckey has a girl

*This use of "yelping" no doubt refers to the sound hunters use to entice turkeys into the open. It is called "turkey calling."

baby two weeks old. One good negro son has gone to his long home, & I felt so sorry for his family, & old "Aunt Nina," for Henry was a good son to her, he died the 2nd of April, was ill two weeks with Pneumonia. Uncle John sent medicine but did not go to see him 'twas the severe weather & the creek bottom overflowed. Dr Heney's made him one or two visits. Uncle Billy [Stone] has moved Henry's family in the house with Spencer & Liddy, & hired Paul McGraw to take Henry's place. Clara spent the day with us recently, sends love, & so many smart doings of baby John B. that I cant repeat them, & whenever Uncle J.D. invites us to see them, says, "come up and see the boy" as though "the boy" was all. He told me that Mrs Lucy D[unlap] lost fifteen head of cattle in the last overflow which was nearly all she had, with those lost previously. 'Tis reported that one of Mr Sam D[unlap]'s daughters (Ophelia) will marry soon, but to whom we hav'nt learned.* Capt. & Mrs M[itchell] are absent on a trip to Malvern, after corn will make another trip to Hot Springs with beef cattle, as soon as they return home; Mr Bill Overman is connected with them in the business. The Capt. while at home set out 100 fruit trees all of them grafts, a choice kind. Pa has a lot of young peach trees from the seed, which he selected himself. The clouds were not threating idly, for the rain is pouring down, & dont sound sweetly to us "against the window-pane," yet I always try to think everything is for the best. Willie says his bees were getting on well, previous to that cold snap, he has 43 gums, no swarms yet, but is preparing for them, works some at night, & rainy days. Gilder is making for himself a double patent plow,* & Pa says he's a neat workman with tools. Cant send you Miss Anna's message this time, but will tell you I dont think Tommie is in danger from the "Bee," & had not failed this time on the hunt for his "Dear." Gilder says, "Ye're might right — keep my armor bright, & lightly-buckled on &c &c." I must tell you of some of your boy "Tug's" aspirations. We were all sitting around the supper table chatting as usual, (a habit in which we most always indulge) when "Little Sis" remarked she would like to have as many dollars as the salt sellars had been moved round the table. Tug said he would like to have as many, as the times he had supped coffee, then was asked first one, then the other, what they would do with a great sum. Gilder said he would go to see his sweetheart, & what would you do Bud Willie? Give it to me first then I'll tell you what I'd do. Tug says, Well, I'd buy a bhd [barrel?] of Molasses, a bhd of sugar, & get for Mama four calico dresses, four for Aunt Nelie, Carrie & Mamie, then I'd have a nice fence put up all round, make the land so rich it would make a bale of cotton to the acre & forty bu[shels] corn, hire plenty hands to work, build a nice new house, then I'd marry. We all laughed till the child blushed with confusion. I asked Tug what he thought his Bud Johnie would say, to that. Aunt Nelie told him you'd say, give him a whipping & send him to school. Tug replied O! of course I'd go to college first. Mr Joe Brooks was here not long ago, said Mr

*Ophelia Dunlap married James Proctor, brother of Matt Proctor Rumph.

*A double patent plow almost has to mean a double pointed plow.

Elliott was up & about again, he I am sorry to say was badly hurt, was not thrown from the mule, had dismounted, & as he turned to walk off, the mule reared, & struck him in the back with both feet, breaking two or three ribs & one entirely loose from his back. Dr Folden attended him. Miss Nellie was at church the fourth Sunday, the girls said she was looking pretty as usual, I guess the boys thought prettier, she has been away so long. With many thanks for the <u>papers</u>, kind remembrance from friends, & much love from each one of the family. I am as ever your devoted Mother.
      Mary E. Boddie

Mary E. Boddie in Ouachita Co. to her son John R. Boddie in St. Louis
           May 30, 1876*   *There is no heading on this letter.

  With many thanks darling for your dear messangers of 14th & 21st Inst. I with much pleasure seat myself to have a little chat with you this afternoon, & for several I guess, for the entire mornings are spent in household duties, dairy, poultry, & various things requiring my attention, that the day is half gone ere I am aware of it, so if my pen chat is disconnected & rambling you will know the reason. In about two hours Aunt Nelies's little scholars will be dismissed, when Colie* & Bobbie will have a romp round awhile, then hie to the orchard for apples, make a call in the garden to the corrint* bushes &c, & after Colie leaves, I always have some work for "Tug" until 'tis time for him to get stove wood, but unless I give him my particular attention, dont get it done, unless special work that he knows he cant put off doing. I must say for my <u>little</u> boy though, that however reluctant he is to work, that anything, & everything in his power to do if 'tis "helping Mama" he never refuses, even to wiping dishes, & setting the table. He told me to tell Bud Johnie he would write to you as soon as school was out, & thank you himself for the pretty keepsake you sent him. Pa I am glad to say is quite well at this time, with spirits that ebbs & flows according to the good or bad prospects for the growing crops. The partial failure of his grain is a great disappointment, particularly as he's been buying corn for the past six or eight weeks. He had limited the family expenses this year including everything to $200 & did not want to exceed that amount, but says <u>we have</u> nearly reached the limit, & must stop. The oat crop was very promising, & now Pa thinks the yield will be inconsiderable, they will be ready to cut by the last of the week. Says he wont give up his wheat crop yet, will know in eight or ten days if 'twill be worth saving. Uncle John had his cut, & so has Mr Patterson. Mr Bob S[tone] has given his up to his hogs. Mr Moseley saved a part of his, hav'nt learned if Uncle J. D.'s was worth cutting or not, we will be sorry indeed to lose ours, as in that case we'l have to do <u>without</u> flour as we've already (only occasionally) for a long time, though that is a small

*"Colie" refers to Colie Brown, son of Julia Stone Brown Alston, daughter of William Stone.

*None of our sources offer the slightest hint as to what this is. It could possibly be currant.

privation when we have been blessed so far with such good health to enjoy everything else. I hear there is considerable sickness in Camden from flux, & Mittie said Mr Rucks had had a slight attack, she & Corrie came over with her Pa on Monday to spend a week, will be down here Friday. Mittie looks well, & expressed herself delighted to get over here, said 'twas no use waiting on "Sis Jennie,"* 'twas such an effort for her to get off. I dont believe I told you that Mittie has broken off one of her front teeth, & says when the next one goes, she will have the entire front set put in as they are all more or less decayed. Since the loss of that tooth, her looks remind me of her Mother [Frances Boddie Rumph, "Sis Fannie."]so much. Thursday — Had rain the greater part of yesterday, which stopped the plows, but the boys always find something to be done, & have come to the conclusion that farmer boys who do all their own work have never any spare time. The cotton is up, the prettiest stand they ever had, & expect to be troubled to get hands to assist in chopping it out. Pa says if he can hold out, hopes that he & Willie with Seymore can manage to chop his, but Gilder will need some help. Gilder after working with them until all the corn crop was plowed over, has been working his cotton, Tug assisted him in chopping last Saturday, & this eve Pa has him dropping peas, & will need his services tomorrow & next day, which Tug wont like so well I know because "Cousin" & Corrie will be here. We are having hot weather too, but been favoured with good seasons* so far, & the grass is thriving as well as the crops. Uncle John said he would finish planting his cotton on Tuesday last, he preferred working over his corn twice before planting any cotton, said he wanted to make sure of that crop. Wont have to buy any corn as some of the freedmen owing him, paid up in that commodity. Uncle J. D. is having to buy now, his present prospects, as well as all the farmers in this vicinity for making plenty, is flattering at present. Uncle John told me to tell you, that you must really excuse him for not writing, he's "been so busy & so bothered with freedman &c has not had time; & he wanted to have something interesting to communicate when he does write." Well! I shall have to put in a plea right here, & beg you'l excuse my sending this bloched sheet, a fly dipped himself in the ink & dabbed down, dont [know] what he intended to write, but am sorry <u>I hav'nt</u> the time to rewrite. Uncle J & Mat have not named the baby yet, did talk of calling her Mabel, or Claudia. He says the pictures are fine, but he prefers a plain one, & I must tell you that "Little Sis" had already claimed one of those you sent us, & "Small Sis" insists on keeping one to herself for a while, I told her she might place it in our picture frame. Little Sis says, tell Bud Johnie "I am ever so much obliged for [the] dime of Centennial date, I shall keep it as a memento, & place it among my little treasures." The girls, children, & Tommy [Rumph] spent Sunday a week ago with me, the latter says, he'l soon have his crops in such condition that he'l go fishing &c. "Uncle Billy" has been doing all the fishing as yet, & with good success,

*"Sis Jennie" refers to Jennie Rumph, wife of George Rumph.

*"Seasons" is apparently a term used for rains.

he promises to take the young folks soon, after
going with Mrs Annie & Mrs Moseley first. We
all attended church Sunday, heard a good sermon
from the text in Psalms 34, 11th verse, but dont
compare I know with Dr Tudor's discourses.
There is never a Sabbath morning darling, that
I dont think of you, & of the manner in which
you are spending it. Mrs Elliott, & family were
prevented (by company) from being at church,
consequently I have not had an opportunity to
deliver the picture, but Mrs Annie was here that
evening & said she was expecting Mrs E. to
make her a visit this week, perhaps to-morrow
night, as Miss Nellie & Miss Mollie L. are coming to the last party of the season at Bob's, they
came last Friday, but 'twas a disappointment, on
account of the rain but very few went, our boys
were all fixed up in their best party style, when
it commenced raining, & on till about midnight.
They never quit work until after sundown, which
makes them late getting ready. Mamie spent last
week with her cousin Bettie, the latter is making
preparation to spend some time in Town. Florence [Rumph] & Miss Georgia [Proctor] went
over in the mill waggon last Saturday, & returned the same day. F. showed
me her picture she had taken, which is a very good one, says 'tis for her
beaux, for whom she had it taken, but would not tell me who that was. You
cant make the girls believe you have any idea of being an old bachelor, so
'tis no use making the assertion. We all took interesting note of the neat, &
pretty price list of your house, & I did wish I could have been with you in
that same house, listening to the sweet music of the evening choir at the old
Cathedral. Thanks for the papers darling, & "Tug" is always delighted to get
his. I did imagine you would take a peep at Royalty, & must confess that
you have less curiosity than I should have had. Old Aunt Nina, & Sarah came
to see me last Saturday, talked a great deal about Henry, & "told me to tell
you she was living yet & wanted to be membered when I wrote to you."
Steve Carey lost his wife Emaline last Saturday night under very distressing circumstances. She had been sick a week or two with chronic
Menenigetis, induced by hard field work. Uncle John was attending the case,
& had relieved her so that she had been up for several days, but showed in-
dications of a wandering mind, which (in spite of all their vigilance) induced
her to slip out of the house, & throw herself in the well. There was 12 feet
of water in the well, no curbing, & no means at hand by which the negroes

John Rumph Boddie
Photo courtesy of Ruth
Boddie Farmer

could get her out. Steve ran screaming to Uncle J. who had heard the hallooing & confusion, was wondering what was the matter, & when told, he & Tommy went immediately, & succeded in drawing her out with hooks, but life was extinct. Uncle John said it nearly killed Steve to lose his wife that way.* Well darling I must bid you goodbye, hoping to hear the same good tidings of you in my next, which was due yesterday, if I could only get it. With much love from all at home, I am as ever,

  Your devoted Mother.

*Aunt Nina, Sarah, Henry, Steve Carey and Emaline were former slaves, now freedmen.

Mary E. Boddie in Ouachita Co. to her son John R. Boddie in St Louis.
July 3rd, 1876

  My own dear boy,

  I have been made the happy recepient of five dear & interesting letters, the smallest one of them to me is a wealth of love, & you dont know how deeply I've regretted that from week to week, been prevented by unavailable circumstances from the pleasure of writing, when I knew too you would be expecting word from home & no letter on the way. Commenced writing two different times, but was interupted by company & will try again this eve, amid the hurry & bustle of the last preperations for the picnic, fish-fry & barbecue to come off on Pine lake tomorrow. Half of Camden & all of this side are expected to be there, yet I never felt less inclination to make one of the party, but if <u>wishes</u> could waft you here darling, you would be one in our midst. I recollect your writing that you never wished to spend another 4th July in a City again, but your ideas about fuss & fire works may have undergone a change in this long interval. Know the excitement & demonstrations respecting the great meeting held in your city was highly enjoyed, particularly as the result was a triumph in nominating the peoples' choice. Even us here, in our quiet corner of old Ouachita felt the enthusiasm. When the old time <u>cannons boomed</u> out the welcome news, nearly all the household were astir on the instant, at first 'twas thought to be thunder but the second peel was not to be mistaken, & when we had counted the last round numbering fifteen, Pa said that was just the number of letters standing for Tilden & Hendricks names, & felt confident they were nominated,* so tumbled into bed again well satisfied. Our candidates here for the different offices are exerting themselves with more than the usual zest, but of course some will have to be disappointed, Mr Moseley* has been on the rounds for the past month or two, Geo. R[umph] spent one night last week with us, he & pa were discussing Politics & cc, but I was not by long enough to hear their opinions as who would be the successful ones. You know Jennie & children are absent on a visit to her sister's at Eldorado, Geo. said he could scarcely <u>endure</u> the time at home, but that he wrote to Jennie she could stay

*This is a reference to Samuel J. Tilden who was nominated by the Democrats to oppose Republican Rutherford B. Hayes in the Presidential Election of 1876. Hayes won in a very close election. Thomas Andrews Hendricks, who was Tilden's running mate, was elected Vice-President in 1885 as the running mate of Grover Cleveland.

*"Mr. Moseley" refers to Elijah Moseley, who was elected as a delegate to the Arkansas Constitutional Convention in 1874. He must have been running for a position in 1876.

until she sent word first, that she wanted to come home. "Cousin" Bettie is in Town to spend several weeks, Mr J. Rucks will bring her over to-morrow, Florence spent a day with us recently, said "tell Cousin Johnnie Mrs O'Scuttle returns the compliments with a low <u>bow</u> & courtesy, & Miss Dickens' said ditto." Small Sis bade me tell you, "instead of compliments I want a letter, I do, & if you dont mind will be Bustin again, with little hope of recovery <u>so soon</u>." Little Sis is cook this week, & is flying round as busy as can be, says all the extra occasions falls on her week, but Mamie is helping her to-day. They have baked some cake like "brother loves" a little sad & underdone. Mrs Jim Toney (jun) spent the day with us not long ago, find her to be quite a pleasant & sociable little lady, very frail & delicate looking though, Mrs Lide called by that evening of the same day to go home with her sister, Mrs L. I think the prettier & looks to be in fine health, though Laura says, "Sue permits Mr Lide to get up & cook breakfast every morning instead of doing it herself, & has him to help her about dinner too when he comes in from work." Mrs Stanley* has been over spending a week with Mrs Moseley, came to see us of course, her children are so handsome son, & her little boy is the most interesting child of his age I ever saw. Mat looks dejected, & careworn.

    Well darling I am happy to tell you, that on last Sabbath I joined the Methodist church, twas not exactly that of my preference, but considered well & long time, concluded that I might never have the opportunity of connecting myself with the Church of my choice, & am more than satisfied now, that I followed the dictates of my feeling. Pa was not well pleased that I should join the church, & I have known it for some time, but felt that I could not defer to his wishes any longer in that respect. The quarterly meeting held only two days. Mr Pope preached for us on Sunday, there were no services that night, & we did not get back from dinner in time for the afternoon services. Was told that Miss Georgia, Florence, & Mr Jimmie Gaughan joined that evening. The rain prevented the use of the arbor that had been erected, & our church was too small to hold all the congregation. Gilder said, that Mr Pope told him to tell me, he wished to be remembered with best respects, & kind wishes when I wrote to you. The rain son we had on the 1st was very much needed, the corn crops were suffering greatly, as it had been two weeks since the dust even has been laid, & all were apprehending a drouth. We have not had a sufficiency yet, but the prospects for more are flattering. The weather here has been very hot, but only for a few days at a time, had the cold spell too you spoke of when we donned some of our winter raiment, kindled up fires, &c. Judging from the sample sent your summer suit must be pretty indeed, & I must tell you right here, that "Mama" is <u>wearing</u> a very nice pair of slippers made of the thick cloth left from your pants that she made for you long time ago. Will be so glad darling if you can take a trip North too this summer, think your fellow workers will be willing to do

*"Mrs. Stanley" refers to Martha Virginia Ritchie Stanley. Her children are Ritchie Stanley and Fannie R. Stanley.

*"Johnie M." refers to John Henry Morgan.

double duty too occasionally, & give you a chance to recreate a little. We guess that Johnie M.* will get a little of his shyness rubbed off ere he gets back to old Camden, & if he does 'twill be quite an improvement.

I prise the flowers much darling, & will enjoy reading the papers when I have time. Pa I think peruses them from beginning to end, for he reads every leisure through the whole week until the next papers come. Well darling the 4th July 1876 is a day of the past & gone & not until to-day could I try to chat again with my boy. All of us & everybody that could joined in this, the first anniversary celebrated since the war. There never was <u>any</u> previous occasion such a large crowd as assembled on the Lake the 4th & every thing passed off pleasantly & harmoniously. One young man Mr Joe Powell took an involuntary bath in the lake as he was about to push his boat from the bank preparatory for a ride, I heard several making inquirys as to his whereabouts afterwards & some said he was streched out to dry, but he did not put in an appearance any more. With the seine they caught any quantity of fine fish, the barbecued meat, Beef, Muttons, Shoats, were done to a turn, & the ladies boxes supplied the table (not set on the ground this time) with an abundance of every thing good in the way of eatables, coffee & ice water to drink, with an occasional glass of ice lemonade, the latter a special treat from the gentlemen, as they purchased from Levy who had a tent erected near by for the purpose of vending lemonade & beer. Dancing to the music from the String Band seemed to be the order of the day among the young folks, from the way they seemed to enjoy it. I had the pleasure of making the acquaintance of Mrs Brooks & Lee, & both of them expressed gladness to meet with Mr Jno. B's mother. Nearly every one with whom I conversed asked me about you, & Mrs Bracy wanted to know if I had your letter with me, seemed so glad that you wrote about Johnie M they had not heard a word from him since he left. Will have to send the letter for her to read I guess. Mrs Elliott said, tell you the picture was as handsome as could be, & just like you, that she appreciates the gift very much, but Belle claims it, says 'twas sent to her. Forgot to tell you that the young people went to Mr Bob S's, danced until 1/2 past 10 that night. Three or four of the girls & nine young men took supper here & Miss Nellie is spending this week with Mamie. Our boys took them all to the lake this morning, Miss Anna M. too & they caught a fine mess of fish. Pa says now wife you & I will go soon when I feel right well, he is lolling round to-day resting & reading & I hope wont try to work any more this hot weather. The cotton crop Pa says, is <u>very good</u> & clear too but the boys will have to plow on to keep it so & growing. The rain saved some of the corn from being a failure again & yesterday had another fine shower at the house & portions of the fields, very little on the corn field, when at the same time Mr Gamible [Gammil] did not get a drop on his place. Tommy said, tell John I have no idea that I'll know him when he comes back until I get him off in the woods on a hunt, & State rang out one of his merry peals of laughter saying, well, well, who but John would have ever <u>thought</u> of my old time name "Featy" again. Why I'd forgotten it myself. Tell John I can see my way through now, if I make a corn crop, hav'nt bought a thing this year but what I've paid for. Miss Mollie looked as sweet as a Pink at the picnic, & Tuney has grown to be taller than our Willie. Forgot to tell you that "Cousin" Mittie was sick the 4th, but Uncle John came by from Town yesterday & told me she was much better. Tommy is cultivating the first gin house cut of acres in corn, the other 25 in cotton.* The old negro quarter is Uncle John's portion, planted in corn for table use, potatoes, beets, peas, winter squashes, pumpkins, watermelons, &c. Had wheat & oats in the Freo fields, the land in front of the house turned out.* Florence told me to tell Cousin Johnie "Pa has a long Arbor for <u>beans</u> clear across the garden, built up precisely like a <u>waggon top</u>, just the place under which me & my beau can promenade." Will & Pa has the field in front of the house & the pine flat in corn. Spring cut & five or six acres round Henry's house in cotton, also the lot by the stable yard (we call that the gin house lot now) & the little patch by the entrance gate in cotton. Pa planted his cheatham seed in the garden! Uncle J. planted his in his quarter patch, neither of them got a good stand. Gilder is cultivating 20 acres in cotton back of the big slash. From the look of this pen scratching fear you'l have trouble to english it* but I must tell you that "Tug" was very proud of his little gift, says, now Mama I got some money ain't I, am going to <u>keep</u> it because bud Johnie sent it. I have not encouraged him to write for he always expects a letter right away, & I know the little spare time you have is already taxed. Tug says your little gun ain't rusty one bit, & he wont let it get so, Gilder says your big gun is all right & he will try & keep it so. "Tug" has been hunting some since school was out, but I dont know how much he would hunt if he could keep in ammunition. Oh I must tell you that the merry Mrs Brooks boasted that she had the finest looking <u>escort</u> on the ground, the day of the picnic, & that gent was Mr Jennings. Good bye darling, hope you are well, the family all send much love, "& Miss Nellie's compliments, says we girls are having the nicest kind of a time." All well —

      Your devoted Mother
      Mary E. Boddie

*Farmers generally designate their fields by areas, or "cuts." "The first gin house cut" means the cut where the first gin house was. References to a new gin house have been made in earlier letters.

* "Turned out" means that the land was not cultivated this year.

*One definition of <u>english</u> is to translate.

Mary Elizabeth Boddie in Ouachita Co. to her son John R. Boddie in St. Louis.

August 3, 1876

My darling boy,

  With much pleasure I avail myself of a little leisure this evening to commence a letter, hoping to have it ready to mail in time to greet you on your arrival at your adopted home. Do you know it seems to me to have been a month since I knew of your intention to leave, although, I was so very glad to know you would go & wanted to urge you to extend the trip to New York & Long Island (my happy childhood home for many years) & hope you have done so. Shall expect in every letter you write for the next month or two, to tell me something of your travel & of the Centennial, & what you think of New York, &c & of everything that interested you, for I do hope you have had the pleasantest kind of time, good health, & propitious weather to enjoy the whole of it. Uncle John said he would have given a pretty to have been with you, & I told him I enjoyed your making the trip as much as I did my visit to Ala. You dont know darling how much I appreciate the few lines penned as you were about to leave, 'twas such a glad surprise, for I had been thinking 'twould be two whole weeks before I could hear from you again. We here at home are getting on as usual except Pa, who I regret to say has been sick for near two weeks, he worked just a few days too long during the hot weather, helping to hoe out the potatoe patch which was very grassy. He has had no fever for the last four or five days, but suffers every night or two with neuralgia in his head, which Uncle John thinks he can prevent a recurrence of & I pray he may, for the attacks make him so sick, & he looks worse than after any sickness he has previously had.

  Uncle John took Bettie over to the Barbecue this morning, said they probably would stay with us tonight. Gilder & Mamie went to, as Clara proffered the use of her buggy. Mamie had the opportunity of going over last Friday & remained until Sunday — she enjoyed the visit to "Cousin" & Miss Clara B. very much. Calie is making a short visit to her sister, has been teaching school near her uncle's for some time, will resume the same in Sept. in the mean time will make a visit to Hot Springs.

  "Small Sis" says "Cousin's" baby is just as pretty as can be, & she is a very gladsome matron as I witnessed the day or two I spent with her the first week of the baby's advent. "Cousin" has suggested every name in the whole calendar for girls but has decided on none yet. Florence wants it to have her name. Mr Rucks calls it <u>Polly</u>, till Mittie will decide, Aunt Clara suggested Jerusha Ann.

  Bettie only came home from Town last Sunday, when Tommy* went over for Miss Delle, & Miss Minnie Lee to spend a week with Florence. Carrie is up there too, & they were all here yesterday having a gay time

*"Tommy" refers to Thomas Rumph.

riding around generally on horseback. Old Scott is one of their studs, & from the Toney farm Mr. Steele carried over three horses for their special benefit during the week. Tommy is making them have a pleasant visit, took them all to the lake to-day picnicing he says, Frank came by this morning for the boat key & said Tommy was mad because Miss Anna & her brothers did not go. They are busy yet, & so are our boys. Gilder is done plowing, but has some hoeing, & Willie has some of both to do, to finish up his patches, &c. We are needing rain again, & our corn crop is not so good as 'twould have been, if we had good seasons the right time. Will thinks though 'twill yield a sufficiency for next year's needs.

Nelie has been in Town nearly two weeks, will come home when Tommy returns with the girls. Florence is going over to stay two months at her brother's, as he wishes her to take guitar lessons under Miss Carrie D. he was so much pleased with her improvement in singing. By the by, "Mrs. O'Scuttle" says she has plighted her troth to Mr. Jimmy Gaughan, told us to tell Cousin Johnie, & that she had confided the fact to no one but "Cousin Mamie" & myself, the information was so sudden & unexpected I hardly knew what to say, advised her that her Pa should be the first one to consult, & she said he had given willing permission for Mr. G. to visit her. Florence seemed solicitious to know what Mittie & George would think of it.

The young folks still have sociables occasionally, one at Mr. Elliot's a week ot two since, & a picnic at Scales Spring, & the young men hereabouts are instituting a Society for Mutual improvement, study, &c which they term the Ouachita Lyceum. They have had two meetings at our church, & when fully organized will tell you more about it, & who are members.

6th, I resume my pen again this Saturday eve darling, wondering <u>where</u> you are now & when tidings of you will reach me, one thing I know, this has been the longest week in the year to me. Pa is getting better having missed the bad spells of Neuralgia for two nights, but is mostly confined to the bed from weakness, & has no relish for anything eatable. Uncle J. dont think it necessary to make him any more visits, he & Bettie staid with us Thursday night, said they had an abundant dinner at the barbecue & some excellent speeches, but you will learn more of that from your "Beacon" than I can tell you, also you will note the <u>well-doing</u> in <u>crop</u> line of our friend Mr Bob S. Many of our farmer gents joke Mr Jimmy H. unmercifully about the slight discrepancy in his Arithmetical calculations. Mrs Annie's baby has had one attack of fever, she stays most of the time in Town at Mr Holmes's & will make but short visits at home until cool weather, they think the change beneficial to the baby. During Mrs Annie's absence, Mrs. Williams stays over here with Lula.

Tommy's crowd had the nicest kind of a time at the Lake, had more fish than they could eat, & Frank said, Carrie caught more than any two of them. "Small Sis" said she would not have missed being in Town Thursday for all the fishfries, enjoyed such pleasant chats with so many of her friends, & yours, particularly Dr Brown & Johnie M[organ]. Says she intends to write to brother again, in fact, set apart one night two weeks ago to do so, but found she had no paper, & I was out too at that time. Tommy, Eddie, Bethel, & Shady Proctor accompanied Florence & her company to Mrs. Steward's to a sociable last night, which I guess will wind up their weeks' frolic. Mrs Elliot, Scales, Belle & Mr Joe Brooks spent last Saturday night with us, the ladies enquired particularly about you & send kind remembrances.

I always feel glad darling to know you meet with so many Camdenites in your City home & that you have some pleasant home circles in which to visit. I dont suppose [I] would know Mrs A. or children if I were to meet them, never having met her since they moved from Camden the first time. Everyone here that can seems to be imbued with a spirit of recreating, if only a few miles off. One or two families in the upper neighborhood have traveled camp style to Hot Springs to spend a few weeks. Mr Jimmy G., Shady P., & Miss Georgia P. have just returned from there, & all of Mr S[am] Dunlap's daughters have gone.

Clara told me that John says she must go this month, & remain until the last of Sept. Uncle J[ohn] D[unlap] & Mr Chewning have made two trips to Malvern for corn, will make another next week, when Uncle J. intends sending Tommy, as one load of corn would be all he needs until his would come in. At Malvern they purchase corn at 30 & 35 cts. per bu. Wish Willie could go with them as he says 20 bu. would suffice for us, & here, Pa pays $1.50 for every bu. Will finished all work in the cotton this morning for this season, has the peas to plow, fodder to pull, &c. Gilder is hoeing in his yet, says he expects to work on till picking time. All the cotton crop is very promising so far. Bro. Will is the same quiet taciturn boy as ever, only smiles at all the innuendoes respecting him & Miss Anna, neither assents to or denies anything. Pa says nothing but a <u>bear chase</u> excites Will to animation, & I must leave it for "Tug" to tell "Bud Johnie" of the latest, & successful raid upon old Bruin. Speaking of Miss Anna reminds me to tell you that she & Tommy have been engaged for ever so long, but from some cause, a lover's quarrel has broken the pledge. Anna says Tom flirted with her, & <u>he</u> says 'tis just the reverse. I think Tommy has always been, & is, Anna's favourite of all the boys.

Frank [Brodnax] will commence teaching the Free School next Monday, we will send Carrie & Bobbie, & I wish Pa would permit Mamie to go, she is so <u>anxious</u> to be advanced in Grammar & Arithmetic & three months application would render her competent to teach a school or at least instruct her brother & sister at home. Pa thinks we cant do without her services at home, but she was willing to stop <u>one day</u> every week to do the washing, which work she has been doing for a month. There are no negro women near us who wish to hire for doing the family washing. Becky is willing, but her hands get too sore to keep it up. Marinda lives on Mr Bob S[tone]'s place, works for them, & does Mrs Moseley's washing. Lucy is too old she says & physically unable, she sent me a bucket of nice figs yesterday, which was quite a treat. Hannah has been staying with Mittie for the past three weeks, she is not near so fleshy as she used to be, but looks well, & like myself turning grey fast. Attalie & Eugenia spent the day with me last Sunday, told me to give their love to Cousin Johnie, they are growing very fast & keep healthy.

John Dunlap is walking & can jabber a little to be understood. I have seen Mat & baby, & although it has dark complexion think she will be much prettier than Maud. Did I tell you it was named Hattie, I believe Bettie suggested the name, & Uncle J. & Mat both liked it. How much longer I could chat with you darling, if I had time dont know, but must close now with much love from all the family to our dear absent one. That God's blessing may be yours, is the prayer of

your devoted Mother,
Mary E. Boddie

Robert Lee Boddie & Mary E. Boddie to their brother and son John R. Boddie in St. Louis.

Sept. 10th 1876

Dear Bud Johnie

I know that I have not written to you in a long time but it is because I know that I write such poor letters, but I do love to get a letter from you. You Say you are getting impatient to know about the bear hunt. I can give you but a poor discription of it. Mr State Stone saw the old bear track in Mr Norris old field near the rail road he went on to Mr Moseley's and told the boys to get redy to give the old bear a chase then went to Mr B Stones to get him and his dog's and to get a horse but Mr S. was not at home he rode back home got his dog's and put them on the track. Mr Marvin [Moseley] come by our house for our dogs, they would not follow him, by that time all the dogs were started good and they beyed it between Mr State Stone's field and uncle John Dunlap's in a little thicket Mr Stone crept up to it the bear was so busy engaged with the dog's that it did not see Mr S. as it ran out at one of the dogs, in turning to go back Mr Stone shot him in the head just below the ear he wheeled and ran off. The dog's ran him about a mile all of them come back except Bragg by that time Bud Willie got there with his dogs and they all went back after the bear. The shot that Mr Stone gave him proved fatal although he ran three miles before he gave out he fell at the Bridges place and then the dog's covered him and when the hunters came up the bear got up and Mr Allis shot him through the neck. They sent to Mr

Bob Stones and got a waggon and carried him to his house. We all had some of the meat it ate very well although he was not fat Mr State got the hide bud Willie brought home one of his feet and his uper and lower front jaws his teeth are Scary looking things it was a big old fellow and Bud Willie says it would have weighed 500 if he had been fat. We have not heard of a bear in any of the corn fields since. Bud Willie's hog Dixie liked to died with choking quinsy. Capt. Mitchel helped him doctor it they cured him with two or three doses of coaloil and rubbing him with it. Bonnie had the prettiest kind of a puppy we gave it to Seymore. Mr Elliott says Cooper cant be beat for being the best kind of a dog. One of Mr Moseley's fine hounds went blind from the distemper and they had to kill him I have been quite sick since I commenced this letter Bud Johnie, two weeks ago but I am well again now and Mama is sick again seems like she cant get strong when she gets up. Bud Gilder has been right sick too but is up now. Miss Anna is sick and Uncle John had to go to see her and he and cousin Bettie came to see Mama this evening. All send much love. I want to see you very much.

       Your affectionate little brother
       Robert Lee Boddie

               Sept 11th 76

My own dear boy,

  Although quite feeble, I cant defer any longer writing to you a few lines to try to express my great appreciation & loving thanks for your most satisfactory & beautiful Centennial* letter. It is replete with interest from beginning to end darling, & we enjoy reading it again & again. Every one who has read it the first time want a second perusal, & Tug had to know, & ask ever so many questions about every Historical name or incident mentioned.

  Uncle John took it home, promising to return the next day or two, when he came back said "I <u>could not</u> bring John's letter, want to read it again, & when I am at perfect leisure to enjoy it, & I declare Aunt Mollie it ought to be published." He brought my document (as Uncle J. calls it) home yesterday, & Mr Bob & Annie are waiting to get to read [it], when I intend to send it to Capt D[ee] N[ewton] & relatives in Town. I derived as much pleasure from the perusal darling as you did the realization & am so glad you went for the cost was a small item in comparison to the benefit & pleasure derived. The description of, & experience of your swimming bath at Long Branch amused the boys, & indeed all of us very much, & very many thanks darling for the pretty little pebble, a memento I shall ever cherish as connected with your first sight of the "Mysterious ever-sounding Main." The Arborvita sprigs are much appreciated too darling, & we were ever so glad to get the Maps, for every one wanted to know by what route you went & returned. Tug studied the Maps a long time & asked many questions till he

*This is a reference to the New York Centennial Celebration of America, which John Boddie attended in the summer of 1876.

understood how & which way bud Johnie traveled. He as well as Gilder look badly since their spell, & I trust this will be my last, for I do, & will try to take good care of myself. If you could hear your sisters scolding me, you would think they intended I should never do any work whatever, & often say "Ma if you dont quit, I'll set right down & write to brother just how you do." They well knowing that, that threat, stops me. I feel so thankful darling for the many blessings that are granted me, that I bear with patience the little ills allotted me. Learned yesterday that George R. had gone to St. Louis, & I am so glad for I know you will enjoy a talk with him more than any other person in Camden. Rec'd a letter from sis Hattie recently, & cant but feel sorry for her disappointment, she spoke so confidently of <u>seeing you</u> either when going or returning. The sale of the personal property of Father's estate took place the 10th of July. Hattie bought in everything except the Barouche* The sales amounted to $1029.35. Land & personal property together $1679.35. Well darling I must bid you a goodbye for this time, & pray you may keep well & give yourself no uneaseness about us here at home, keep a good heart & know that all things are for the best. Each one of the family send much love to our dear absent one. "Cousin Betty says give my love to Cousin Johnie; & [wasn't] his letter <u>interesting</u> Aunt Mollie." I never meet with any of our friends but they dont enquire about you. Aunt Nelie is not very well, neither "Small Sis" but they wont give up I know till obliged. We are having very cool nights & mornings. Pa & Will are at work on the gin house. Gilder has been working with them until to-day he is preparing to commence picking cotton. Uncle J. D. commenced last week. State had a pretty severe spell the same time Gilder was sick, he has been to see me several times recently, & looks hollow eyed & gaunt. Take good care of yourself darling, & believe me as ever,

your devoted Mother.
M. E. B.

Will try & write a little more legible next time.

* A barouche is a four wheel carriage with a convertible top, two passenger seats facing each other, and a raised seat for the driver.

Mary E. Boddie in Ouachita Co. to her son John R. Boddie in St. Louis
Sunday Eve October 22nd 76

My own dear boy,

With much pleasure I devote this short evening to replying to your truly appreciated letters of 8th & 15th Inst. & you may rest assured darling when you do not hear from me, only at long intervals, that illness of any of the family will not be the reason, for in that case I promise you shall be informed, so you need not feel any uneasiness at any time on that account. Regret to hear you have "severe cold", & hope that you'l take good care of yourself, for I feel that you wont sacrifice health by persistance in hard work when unable. The weather here has been so cold as to require winter suits too, had frost a month earlier than usual, & ice one or two mornings, but the past week has been quite warm, & rainy for a day or two. We expected to attend church this morning, but was disappointed, Mrs [Annie?] had persuaded us to go with her & Jimmie W[ord] & when she sent Pete to get our waggon not a man or boy was on the place to put the body on.* All had gone after the bear whose track Pa had discovered early this morning quite fresh all over the potatoe patch & through Seymore's premises. Gilder had his mule ready intending to go to church, so off he went for State & his dogs, they had a chase to the bottom after the bear, when the dogs got after a <u>cat</u> which they caught & killed.

*When a wagon was used to haul logs, the body or bed of the wagon was removed.

Well darling, "Cousin Mitties'" pleasant weeks' visit terminated in great grief, not because our Heavenly Father saw fit to take our little Fannie to Himself, but sorrow for the mother bereft of her little darling, for you knowing Mittie so well, can imagine how her very heart strings were entwined round her baby, & it seemed almost as taking her own life. Mittie & I went over to her Pa's on Thursday, & the baby was taken sick that night with croup, which Uncle J. relieved, but she had fever that night, & next day. On Saturday was apparently clear of fever, & Uncle J. went to Town that morning & I came home, Mittie was to stay at her Pa's until her baby got well, (as Dr Pace was absent) but she grew worse rapidly during the day, & night, Uncle J. pronounced the case Pneumonia, & which terminated fatally at 4 oclock Sunday morn 15th. Little Fanny was just three months, & two days old. She was laid beside Mittie's mother, & you will never see the little Angel till in that Better Land where I trust we may all be permitted to meet, & sorrow no more. Mittie made many good resolutions beside her dead baby which I pray she may remember, & endeavour to fulfill. Florence went home with her sister on Monday, & staid until yesterday. Geo. & Jennie were to have spent to-day with us, but he sent me word on Friday they could not come, was moving again, & said he hoped 'twould be the last time soon, Jennie says they do nothing else, & she's quite reconciled to it. Clara has been quite sick with Rheumatism & Nelie went up to see her yesterday, rode on the cotton waggon with Gilder as he was hauling the last load he had ready to be ginned at Uncle J D.'s. Gilder has two bales ready which he intends taking to Town to-morrow. He has been so equinonical* this year that <u>patches</u> is hardly a name for the shirts & pants he's been wearing, & even his old hat which he had me to enlarge to a sun down (we call it) is patched. Pa & the boys will be ready for the cotton patch again next week, as all the odd work, housing the corn, potatoes &c is done with, the latter crop turned out well, Will says they have about 300 bu of corn, Pa never will tell me when I ask him about the crops, most always says he dont know. Mrs Annie [Stone] says Bob has made a splendid corn crop, but his cotton will fall far short of his anticipations. Miss Jimmie W. has been spending two or three

*"Equinonical" is the word Sis Mollie uses, but the pure definition does not really apply here; we feel that she is making a pun on the word <u>economical.</u> Gilder's financial status certainly depended on the seasons, and Sis M. was learned enough to create the pun.

weeks with Mrs Annie, they came to see us Friday. Bob & Miss Lula have gone to Princeton for a few days, he has been sick twice this fall.

Tuesday 24th

Well darling, as usual I seldom finish a letter the day I commence it. Miss Anna & Miss Jimmie came Sunday eve, & as "Small Sis" was entertaining Mr Allis M[oseley] "Little Sis" & I had to give our attention to the young ladies, & I was too busy yesterday to write at all. By the by, "Small Sis" requests you to give her your <u>opinion entire</u>, of a recent acquaintance of hers who wishes to make his visits special. The gentleman is Dr E. G. Coleman, whom she thinks you may know more about than she does, at any rate she wants to know how you like him. He saw Mamie for the first time at the camp meeting, though expressed himself as having known her for a long time, hearing his relatives speak of her so often. Soon after she came home he wrote to her, & not receiving any reply, wrote again, & before she had an opportunity of having her letter mailed, he came himself. Staid a night at Uncle J's, called to see "Uncle Billy" [Stone] next day, & that evening came here & staid all night. Pa told Mamie he wished to read that letter again, & asked her when Dr C. was coming again? His parents reside in Arkadelphia, & he is attending to the farm near that place, & practicing. Tell brother please write what he may wish to say on a <u>separate sheet</u>, as I dont want the <u>whole family</u> to know it, & moreover, tell him there is no danger of my getting the matrimonial fever, or "Bust," as I dont care to relinquish my <u>freedom</u> for several years yet. Nelie has gone over to Uncle J's to spend the remainder of the week. Uncle J. with the usual hunting crowd have gone off for a week's sport. "Cousin Bettie" told me to tell you about her new beau, but neglected to impart the most important item, his name. Mrs OScuttle says <u>hers</u> is worth [all] the boys she saw in Town, also that maybe she will go up to <u>see you</u> next Spring. "Tug" told me not to forget to tell Bud Johnie that our old Shake is dead — he had no apparent ailment. I missed him only twice at feeding time, & the next morning found him in the garden lying dead beside the palings. This is the last week of the school session, & Mamie did not go, we have so much work & all the winter's sewing to do. Am anxious for my next letter, & O I cant tell you darling how much I want to see you, for I know you cant come. Soon your absense can be counted by years, & yet time flies so very very fast. Many thanks for the papers; Pa & the boys enjoy reading them so much, but I have not read one for the past two months, — You know I cant read at night, & Sunday's when not privileged by company read my bible. Must bid you good by with love from each one of the family & kind remembrance from your friends who always ask me about you —

Your devoted Mother,
M. E. Boddie

Mary Elizabeth Boddie in Ouachita Co. to her son John R. Boddie in St. Louis

Nov. 17th, 1876

My own dear boy,

I am more than glad to hear of your good health, & must thank you again & again for sending me tidings every week. Am in recpt' of four precious letters & assure you no matter how "brief" some of them may be they receive the same welcome. Your telling me of the probability of coming to see us ere another six months, has given us a never tiring theme for every day chat. "Small, & Little Sis" say brother will come about Christmas I know. Tug says no bud Johnie ant' coming at all." Pa & the boys tell us 'twill be very uncertain when you can come, but anyway 'tis something pleasant to think of & hope for in the future, & we dream of it too, yet dreams are not to be compared to what the realization will be. We were talking of you on your birthday, & the girls laughed heartily at the idea of my saying that in two more years you could get married, yes darling that is the age at which your Granpa wed, & to a young miss of fourteen too. I can imagine how you fly around among the young ladies, & being in the prime of life, you need not dub yourself a bachelor, for many years yet. Do wish you could enjoy an 'old time hunt' with the boys. State says tell John "Gilder can out yell anything I ever heard in a cat chase, & until with him thought I could do some tall whooping myself." They went on another hunt recently during the moonlight nights, but J. Mitchels puppies bothered so the dogs lost trail after a long & exciting run through brush & came over the bottom. Bob S. says "I would give the world if John was here, why we need him all the time, there's nobody in Town now worth a cent to stir up the balance, & keep things lively." All are waiting now in painful suspense the issue of the election, Pa says if the Republicans perpetrate the fraud he has all the while believed they would, there is no use for the people ever to have any more elections, & in the face of all the good news we've heard Pa has doubted they would <u>permit</u> Tilden to be elected. We can only hope for the best till the worst comes. We thank you much for the <u>papers</u> son, & also the interesting account of the World's prodigy in Music, such extraordinary genius displayed in the person of a blind negro, is truly wonderful. "Tug" says, tell Bud Johnie I've read <u>my paper</u>, & will wait till he can write to me. "Small Sis" bids me say, she would be most glad to receive a letter, & that she intended writing to you this week, but 'tis her cook week, & she is trying to make herself a calico dress. She is expecting Dr C. next week as he wrote to that effect. They keep up a pretty brisk correspondence for one, & more frequently two letters come weekly.

We too darling have had a most beautiful fall, & it has always been my favorite season of the year, at present the weather is cold & cloudy, & all hands are busy trying to get the cotton out. Pa has two hired hands, gives 6/* & they feed themselves. Gilder has had a little help too, says he has only five or six hundred to pick, now, guesses his whole crop will amount to four bales. "Tug" is helping Pa & Bud Willie, & he is the only one I hear speculating as to how much cotton Pa will have, & he makes it nine bales. Picking cotton is the only <u>work</u> he <u>loves</u> to do he says, but I notice he loves to get off as often as possible to squirrel hunt, & his love of that work is to induce Pa to keep him in ammunition. Your big gun darling is in good order, & as Pa used it the Sunday they went after the bear, I asked Gilder if he had cleaned & rubbed it up since, when he assured me it was all right. I often dust the cover, & that is as far as I dare go. "Tug" uses the little gun often enough to keep it bright. On Tuesday of this week (after a rain the previous night) Gilder went duck hunting, & brought in a fine turkey, killed some ducks but could'nt get them, he met up with Pike B[ragg] in the bottom. Mr Author is in the camp hunt, Uncle J. too, expect to be away two weeks this time. Gilder was at Uncle J's last Sunday, all well with them. Clara had quite a sick spell & is just able to be up & about again, Johnie is a fine boy, has learned to talk well, is very shy of strangers. Uncle J. D. says, he & Lula do most of the cooking & milking. Gilder took the girls up to Mrs Elliots last week to a candy pulling, said they enjoyed it finely, 'twas a very pleasant evening, they danced till twelve, & came home that night, had peanut candy, pop corn candy, lemon candy & candy straight. Although Willie would have liked very much to see Miss Nellie, he would not spare the time that eve to go. Nelie is staying at Uncle J's this week, & Miss Anna is spending the week with Miss Georgia, I have not seen either Cousin Bettie, or Mrs O,S[cuttle] in several weeks, <u>Tommie</u> gave me some message for you about dogs, & hunting, but I have been so long writing have forgotten it. Little Sis has had her first offering of Autumn in press for you for the past three weeks, thinking I would write, but darling these short days pass very rapidly, & we have much work to do.

Trust your new quarters may prove to be quite pleasant in every respect as regards a convenient, & comfortable room, but from the price, including everything you mentioned, I very much doubt it. In a private house you'l have the advantage of feeling secure against <u>borrowers</u> of good suits, & particularly when one winter suit was all you had. Am glad to know you have good company with which to room & beg you will tender my best respects to Mr. B. thank him for me for his kind intentions towards you, though I have every confidence in my boy; keeping himself straight. Where are Mr B's family living? would like ever so much to see my old time school mate, his wife.

Pa has just returned from Town (Saturday) & tells me that Mats* mother, Mrs Searls is dead, he also rec'd a letter from Tom L[ove] informing us that Uncle Clem died the 12th Inst. He has been an invalid for more

*"6/" probably means 6 cents per pound of picked cotton.

*The identification of this "Mat" is unknown. It is not to be confused with "Matt" Proctor, third wife of John B. Rumph. Her mother was Mary Patterson Proctor and is buried in the Rumph Cemetery in Harmony Grove.

than a year, & may his rest be with the blest. Left the bulk of his property to Carrie & Mary & Tom said when the will was made public, he would write Pa all the details. Well darling must bid you good bye for this time, & reluctantly lay aside my pen for the darning needle. "Small Sis" has about finished her dress, & Little Sis is busy ironing, & Pa is deep in his <u>papers</u>. With much love from each one to our dear absent one, I am as ever,

Your devoted Mother,
Mary E. Boddie

Mary Elizabeth Boddie in Ouachita Co. to her son John R. Boddie in St. Louis.

Dec. 19th, 76

My darling boy,

I imagine you are wending your way to Sabbath school & church this blessed Sabbath morning, while I, hearkening to the sweet chimes of the Camden Church bells, am carried back to the time, when you were wont to make one of the happy throng on the way to our Master's Holy Sanctuary. 'Tis a privelege for which to be thanked, & may you ever be circumstanced to enjoy it. That I am gratified to the fullest extent to be assured of your good health through all the past seasons of extreme heat & cold, you well know, & your letters darling are a <u>continual</u> source of pleasure to me, & of which I would not be deprived for <u>naught</u> save your presense, & the blessed <u>hope</u> that I may be fitted for a home in "Our Father's House" where I pray to be with, & meet all our loved ones' when His Will is served with us in this world. Am surprised to find that four weeks have flitted by since I wrote to you, & your "Small Sis" has been saying almost daily she intended to "write to brother," but we have much work (besides the daily routine) which this season, & the advent of Christmas almost makes imperative, then a long epistle is sent every week to the "<u>Highland beau</u>" of whom she brags "that he is as good as brother about writing", persuades herself that he reminds her of you in many other respects, which amounts to the <u>fact</u>, that he is gaining much in her estimation. His last visit was one of several days, came on Saturday eve, remained until Monday, went to Town returned on Tuesday & stayed until Wednesday eve, when he went to Uncle John's & left for home the next morning. Florence was spending that week with us, & at Miss Anna's, the former & "Little Sis" made the old logs ring with music vocal & instrumental on Piano & Guitar, & by the by our old music box has <u>much</u> of its old time sweetness of <u>tone</u> restored by a Mr Puckett who served his apprenticeship in a Piano Manufactory at St. Louis. He renewed the felts on all the keys, replaced the 15 ivories that were off, & put the instrument in good tune for $10. I rather persuaded Willie not to have the work done knowing his very limited means, but he insisted that such an opportunity might never occur, besides the assurance that Mr P.'s work on the Piano's in Town gave entire satisfaction. Am glad to say the cotton crop is all gathered, Gilder has the remainder of his (three bales) packed & in Camden, took it over yesterday week, has not sold it yet. He went over yesterday, said he wanted to go calling last night, & attend Sabbath school & Church this morning. Gilder took your little gun over to have a new tube put on the left hand barrel, says he will try & kill a turkey for Christmas. "Tug" went over with him yesterday, & rode the mule back, he accompanies "Bud Willie" nearly every time he goes to mill, & thinks he is quite "Au faite" in all Town doings, stayed one night recently with "Cousin Mittie", & since purchasing some shot of "Cousin Ed" whom he said gave him the best bargain he ever made, declared he intended giving "Cousin Ed" <u>all his trade</u>. Tug told me he priced some "<u>real good </u>goods for pants at Cousin Ed's" & he would let him have it at cost 75 per yd. & he wanted me to let him get a pr. for Christmas, wanted to know if I could not make them &c &c. Tis as you say darling, we are all counting & counting, I count each day a blessing that I am permitted to live, be it in sunshine, or shadow. "Small Sis" says you guess quite right about her counting, & "Little Sis" says, tell Bud Johnie I'm counting the days to my birthday which will soon be here (19th) & tell him I'm glad he appreciated the little bouquet, for it seems the flowers <u>bloomed purposely for him</u>, & not another little violet has peeped forth since I culled those for him. Uncle John said to me, after reading some of your recent letters, Aunt Mollie a[i]n't you afraid you are going to lose John? told him no, I would gain a daughter, & as <u>your "Duck"</u> lives somewhere down our way, 'twas sure we'd see you one of these days, although you write very suspiciously of some of the St. Louis beauties, & darling I am always proud to know of your visiting among, & enjoying the company of the fair sex. You have quite a companionable little crowd at your cheap boarding house (as you term it) & am glad to know you are better pleased than at first, & that Mr R. has "dumped his carpet-bag" among you. Old Winter has reigned supreme with us here too, & the close "nestling among our big log fires can scarcely keep us from shivering with cold" & but that the weather moderates a <u>little</u> between times dont know how we would endure it. I always think of you during the freezing weather, & am happy to know that you are warmly clad. Pa has treated himself to a new coat too the first since the war, & he still clings to the same old home spun coat that I wove just after the war. Since gathering the cotton, Pa & the boys have been getting the gin house & gin ready to try & gin the cotton at home to save expense, they have all complete except the lint room for which they have been getting out boards &c for the past two weeks. I think they expect to get all that is necessary to put up a rough one out of the woods, & a portion of the old screw timbers. We women folks' most necessary & disagreeable work is over for this season, the work incident to hog killing. Pa has turned all the hogs over to Willie to manage as he thinks best. Will has given us ten for family use, intends selling the balance, of course reserving his stock hogs. There is but little talk of, or much preparation for Christmas, only every one seems anxious to get all work done up before that time, & the young folks anticipate a pleasant time somehow, just because 'tis holyday season I guess. They are minus one merry lass from their midst, Miss Anna has gone to her sister's in Hopkinsville to remain until next Spring — Mr Fisher* came on a visit, spent four days, & persuaded Anna to go home with him. Uncle John & Mat spent all of week before last in Camden among relatives, & Mittie & Jennie promise to spend Christmas day at Uncle J's & a day with us, but I think it uncertain about their coming over at all unless the weather moderates considerably. Mamie & Mittie exchange notes weekly. All of us [were] asked to dine at Uncle J.'s that day, & the young ones may go, but I prefer to stay at home with Pa. Nelie is absent so much, seldom being at home only her cook week, that I came near forgetting to tell you she went to Uncle J's three weeks ago, in a great pat, saying, Mamie ordered her leave, but I will try to tell you the particulars. Fourteen weeks last Spring while Nelie was teaching school Mamie milked, & got dinner every day, & one week Carrie got supper & breakfast & one Nealie, so when Mr Brodnax taught, Mamie told N. that she would call on her to return the favor that was to get dinner on her (M's) week to cook, (I was then having the milking done for all of them) & which Nelie seemed perfectly willing to do when she saw that M. was decided on going to school, but when it was not N's week to get supper & breakfast she would very often go visiting to spend the week, & sometimes two, leaving Becky to get dinner for her, but as I was sick most of the time Mamie would have to stay from school, & one week Nelie was sick & M. had to cook for her, but Mamie did not complain, or say anything until the last week of school which happened on M. week to get supper & breakfast. As sewing work has so accumulated from my having been sick, & M. & Carrie trying to go to school I told M. to stay at home & N. knowing that M. intended doing so, went the Friday before to see Clara (as she was sick) saying she would return home Sunday. She stayed with Clara until Monday when she went to Uncle John's & spent the week. I persuaded M. not to say anything to N. but let it pass, for I knew there would be a rupture if she did, but in a week or two afterwards Mamie asked Nelie to return the work, which N. flatly refused to do & would listen to no reason whatever, & M. finally told N. she would have to do her duty or one or the other would have to leave, as she did not feel desposed to be imposed upon any longer — Nelie replied, that she did her duty, & moreover she would not cook any more unless I or Pa said so. That evening, (it being Saturday) N. went to Mrs Moseley's, came back next morning was getting ready to go to Uncle J's when I told her I thought she ought to stay & cook that week, but she refused, saying she felt under no

*"Mr Fisher" refers to Harry Clay Fisher, who in 1862 married Mary Arkansas Moseley, Anna's sister.

obligations whatever to cook a single day for M. & that she was going off, as M. had given her orders to leave. I cant regret Nelie's leaving, only that Uncle J. has as many as he can well care for already unless he needs, & wants N's services as teacher for the children. Well darling I have exausted my sheet on a disagreeable subject, & am sorry. Regret to tell you that "Uncle Billy" is very sick, Pa went to see him this morning, Mr A[lston] & Julie are over. Uncle B. has never been satisfied since Colie's* death unless Julia is with him. Mr A has quit teaching some time since, he is the regular Minister now at the Camden church. Mrs Annie sent me word today that her Pa is very ill, not expected to live, he has Pneumonia. Pa thinks that to be Uncle B's ailment. Uncle J. is attending him. Mrs Annie always reads your last letter when she comes to see me, sends her love, says that Bob is always talking about writing to John. Must tell you that Willie in looking after [the] bottom hogs came upon a bear, & such a chase he had, but the bear got away of course, & Will came out worsted with pants torn to pieces, no hat save the crown, shoes torn, & worse still, a snag in the foot. Gilder has been <u>possum</u> hunting once & caught the largest one I ever saw. Know 'twill bother you to read this, so will bid you <u>good bye</u> wishing with all my heart, that you will spend a very pleasant Christmas. With much love from each of us, I am as ever,

*Coleman Brown evidently died during the "summer sickness." We know he was attending school with Robert and Carrie Boddie in May in "Henry's old house" with Nealie as the teacher.

      Your devoted Mother
      M. E. Boddie

Please remember me to Mr A. & Mr B & excuse this blocked sheet, as twas the only one on hand.

Mary Elizabeth Boddie in Ouachita County to her son John Rumph Boddie in St. Louis

            January 9th, 1877

 My darling boy,

 If all the tender thoughts & loving heartfelt wishes are wafted to you in your far away home, then will you realize all for which you are "thankful, life, health, strength from on High" to aid in your good purposes; & my heart thrills with love to Him who gave me such a boy, may His choicist blessing rest upon you darling through this, the New Year & always. That you were thought of, spoken of, & wished for during our pleasant Christmas time you well know, & your letters are to me a source of continual happiness, we were all so happy to know you spent such a merry Christmas with young, lady friends — guess Uncle J. will say that you are a gone case on the "Foxhunts", they occur so frequently, but "Mama" has not forgotten what her boy said about his "Ark. Duck," though Uncle J. thinks 'twill be a St Louis girl, & Pa says "Who in the world is it in Camden that John would have?" Well, we'l see, we'l see, &c —

Am happy to respond darling that we all spent as merry Christmas as the company of a party of gay young folks could make it — Christmas eve Tommie & Will went over for Mittie & Jennie, the latter declined coming, (as 'twas so cold) Mittie, Corrie, & Miss Delle B. came, & all our home folks with Mr Johnie M[organ] went to Uncle J's to dine Christmas day — Pa, Tug, & I dined all alone at home, had a big nogg that morning & <u>goodies</u> for dinner, (but no turkey) Tuesday, Mamie, Corrie, Will, Gilder accompanied by Mr Johnie came home — Wednesday, the latter brought Miss Minnie L. over, & all attended a Party at "Aunt Clara's" that night, which was a complete success in the way of enjoyment. Misses Braggs were there, enquired <u>particularly of you</u>, requested "Small Sis" to remember them to, & tell you 'tis well you are not here, for all the folks are dead in Town. They all returned from the Party through the sleet & snow, which by morning had clothed all outdoors in robes of "beautiful white," & the elastic spirits of the young folks rose accordingly. The girls & Mittie from Uncle J's were to have come down on Thursday, but the snow fell thick & fast all day, & we were a little surprised to see Dr Coleman drive up. He & Miss Calie B. arrived at Uncle J's Wednesday night but not in time to attend the party, they drove down from Arkadelphia that day, starting at 1 oclock. Friday & Sat. were two pretty days of sunshine, but too cold for the snow to melt, & Saturday morn Tommy [Rumph] brought Mittie, Corrie, Miss Delle, Calie, & Bettie down, & such a merry time as they all had snowballing &c &c. They purposed going to Town next day, (Sunday) but it commenced snowing again that eve, & all night, all day Sunday, so we had them all to remain with us until the following Wednesday. Tomny went home Tues. said he regretted to leave the crowd, but knew his Pa needed him & thought he could pull through with an <u>empty</u> waggon, & <u>Sis</u> Bettie. They all never seemed to mind the cold or snow, but made merry all the while & I had to caution Mittie several times, when she would say "O Aunt Mollie I cant stand, & see the boys get the advantage of the girls, I must snowball them" & away she would go. The boys had to shovel out wide paths from house to Dairy, kitchen, smoke house, well, lot, & woodpile, & you can imagine what a lively time they had, cutting & getting wood to keep up four good fires, & run the stove too, when the woodpile was covered with snow to the debth of nearly two feet.

Gilder left home New Years' morn to work in Dr Pace's drug store, Dr P. gives him 15 per month & board. I was so glad Gilder accepted that situation instead of going to Texas as he spoke of doing. We all miss him very much at home, he occupied your seat at table darling, & now 'tis empty again — have had but two <u>"tater"</u> puddings this season, plenty nice potatoes, but minus the sugar, we economized all last year to the extent of Coffee but once a day, & <u>no sweeting</u> (except we had company) no flour since the wheat gave out last Spring, (untill Will got us some for Christmas time) & I assure you we enjoyed what we had, plenty of nice milk & butter, for we had <u>appetites</u> to relish any diet, & I felt we were blessed when perhaps hundreds were suffering from actual want.

"Uncle Billy" has just recovered sufficiently to ride out for the first time last Sunday, which was a beautiful day, warm & sunshine, & nearly all the snow disipated, but it rained at night, & when we rose yesterday morn 'twas freezing cold, & the ground all covered with snow again. Pa & Will can do nothing but make up fires, & try to keep warm, they are getting impatient to commence work again, put up the pick room,* get the cotton off hand &c. "Bud Willie" says he has forty odd pigs when he should have had 100, but the weather has been so severe on them, & he had to wade through the deep snow every morn to attend to them. Pa attended to the cows turning them in & out feeding the calves (17). "Small, & Little Sis" have not done any milking for the past three weeks, but had plenty cream on hand for syllabub, & Ice-cream, & butter for cake & table use beside selling 3 & 4 lbs. every week for the past six months up to this week, — Tug says, he did not have any hole in his socks, but Old Santa put a coconut in his <u>shoe</u>, & Tommy told it in presense of Mr Johnie M. that Old Nick could'nt put anything in his for 'twould have dropped out at the toe, which assertion teased Bettie very much, & for whose benefit T[ommy] designed his mischief.

*A pick room is where cotton is stored until a full bale has been picked.

I forgot to tell you, that they all attended a Party at Mr Blacks, & one at "Uncle Hals," from which latter Florence came home with them, & spent the balance of the week with us. Bade me tell "Cousin Johnie" "Mrs OScuttle" is flourishing & having a gay time, but is thinking about commencing preperations for the <u>great event</u> which she dont know yet at what time will come off, & moreover tell him I've recd more presents than any of the girls, a silver cup, finger ring, & a bottle of "meeting-house drops." I must tell you son, the cream of the joke about the latter, Florence told it on Mamie, that her beau had given her a bottle of <u>drops</u> (which was not so) a few days afterward Mr G. made F[lorence] a present of very nice perfume, which she denied <u>his</u> giving to her, to everyone but myself, telling me not to let "Cousin Mamie" know it. Dr Coleman gave Mamie a beautiful copy of Campbell's Poems & her new year's present was a gold pen & pencil, which F. attributed to you, & "Small Sis" let her so believe.

Miss Mollie S. was here last Sunday, also Misses Moseley's, Tommy, Shady P[roctor] & Gau[g]han. Miss Mollie asked to be remembered to you & with kind wishes for a happy New Year, wanted to know when you were coming to see us &c. Tommy reports all well at home, & Mat & Uncle J. intend coming to spend a day & night with us, so soon as the weather will permit. "Little Sis" went home with Florence Sunday, & this week our old habitation makes me think of the "Banquet Hall deserted" so lonely & quiet since all the guests departed.

I dread to imagine the time when I shall have to give up one daughter of our house & heart — yet I will accept things as they come & not murmer. "Small Sis's" chief has gained his suit, & he never stopped till he had a talk with Pa & obtained his sanction to their engagement. We cant but acknowledge that he improves on better acquaintance, & each member of the family seem to like him very much, & I am so gratified that from all you've learned about him, deem him to be a "clever fellow."

Must say darling, I admire your good taste in the beauty, as well as chase design displayed in your complimentary cards of the season, & the visiting card is just as neat, & pretty as can be. Thanks for sending them. Must tell you my boy, that "Mama" does hope press of business will preclude the impossability of your attempting the dangerous feat of skating, recollect your experience at the Rink. Learn sometime on a smaller scale than the "Great Miss." Our little Ouachita has been frozen over too, & crossing was made quite difficult.

*"Mr. S Avera" was Mrs. Annie Stone's father.

Aunt C. spent one day with us last week sends "ever so much love, & says are you never coming to see us?" Young John B. is a stalworth fellow for his age. Mrs Elliotts family all well, Misses Nellie & Mollie attended two of the parties, but did not dance. Have not heard from Sis Hattie in several months, do you write to "Cousin Mattie" now? Neither Nelie or Carrie have had any letters from Autauga in a long time. Pa has not recd the papers as regular as usual, he attributes it to the Mails, & thanks you much for your kind intentions in so contributing to his pleasure. Small Sis wishes to enclose a brief letter with this, you may know I am out of paper, by my making use of these tiny sheets.

You have probably heard of Mr S. Avera's* death, & about a week afterward Mr Wade L. died so tolls the knell of the departed year, passing away, passing away. Your friends white, & colored always ask about you. Good bye darling, & with much love from all the family,

Yours devotely
M. E. Boddie

Mamie Boddie, "Small Sis," to her brother John R. Boddie, and enclosed in her mother's letter of January 9, 1877.
Dear Brother

Uncle John staid with us last night and intends going to C[amden] if the water admit, so can't help stealing a march on Ma by opening & slipping in this, to beg of you, not to mention any thing about my affairs to any one, not even Uncle J., for all want to see them & do. I

Mary Elizabeth "Mamie" Boddie (Small Sis)
1855-1929
Photo courtesy of Ruth Boddie Farmer

am not certain of <u>anything</u> and if I was, could never bear having every one speaking of my private affairs. I'm sorry that you forgot, that I wrote confidentially, when I spoke of that "young goat" as you term him. I would never have married him, even if I had loved him & as he is a friend of mine, I will ask you, if you love me, not to speak of him again. I <u>don't confide in all relatives.</u>

 Write when you have time Your sister
Mamie

Mary Elizabeth Boddie in Ouachita Co. to her son John Rumph Boddie in St. Louis

Feb. 4th '77

 My own dear boy,

 As you said of last Sabbath I can respond, that this is truly another beautiful, sunshiny, pleasant morn, even the little birds are twittering away their delight after the unceasing rain for the past two days & nights, & I avail myself of the quiet leisure it affords to write you some word of home, & home-folks. That there is a dearth of anything interesting in these parts you are well aware, but I know darling you do want to hear from home, & 'tis a great pleasure to me to gratify that wish, & to tell you again, & again how much pleasure your dear letters afford me, & indeed all of us, for their advent is the great speciality of the week with us. My "unworthy chap" can attribute it to what he pleases, when I know he is deserving the fathoms of love that is his.

 Pa has gone to the Lake to secure the boat in case of high water, "Tug" is reading <u>his paper</u>, & "Bro Will" is interesting himself with a reperusal of your Centennial letter. "Small Sis" intends copying that letter in her ledger, also the one you wrote to her, & "Cousin M." jointly, & as 'twas addressed to the latter she claimed ownership. "Little Sis" <u>claims</u> the <u>whole lot</u> of my letters from you, & having promised she reminds me of the fact quite often. You may be sure I shall try & <u>keep her</u> heart whole, for many years yet, for I could not promise but that she would be satisfied to make just such a match as Florence has chosen, as Carrie is not as ambitious as her sister, to study, & improve herself, she is a dear, good, amiable child, & studied well enough when going to school, but cant be persuaded by either Mamie or I that she could accomplish something by her own efforts. Told me be sure & tell Bud Johnie "all right I will <u>keep house</u> for him, just suit me exactly."

 Let us know the impressions made after reading "Reverses of a Bachelor." Have no idea that memories of the pleasure spent with your young Lady friends will <u>suffice</u> for all the year, & hope not, for hard work would then lose half its zest. Am sorry to hear you have been troubled with such painful boils, "they never did come in the right place", as Uncle John said when he was afflicted with one on each wrist at the same time, he could scarcely use his hands, for near two weeks — That was a terrible fall you got darling, & I breathed a prayer of thankfulness that 'twas no worse, & it may be you'l be more careful in future, & avert a greater calamity. Trust the ice season with you is over, our river rose 7 feet yesterday, & Small boats have been coming up the past week or two, & if the recent rain has been general the largest class can come very soon.

"Small Sis" came home last Tuesday, left all well, said Gilder could not come to see us for a month or two yet, he is very busy, & studying hard to fit himself for the business in which he intends to permanently engage. Expresses himself as being very well pleased with his situation, but very ignorant of all details of the Drug business. Mamie says he looks thin, studies till 12 every night after the store is closed at 9. Since I wrote to you Willie has been confined to the house for near two weeks, with severe cold, & the worst cough he ever had, of which he['s] not yet entirely relieved, though he has been at work all the past week. Pa commenced ginning Thurs. & finished up all the cotton they had at hand, the rain preventing them from hauling any yesterday. Seymore is working here again this year, Lucy has parted from Joe, (cause mistreatment) & is staying with Becky, Joe keeps Phillis with him. Old "Aunt Nina" Sarah & Jack are living at Uncle J. D.'s this year, Sarah is cooking for "Aunt Clara." Spencer & Lydia remain at "Uncle Billie's." Lula D. is going to school to Mrs Hodnet, boards with Mittie. Misses Della B. & Minnie S. have gone to the College at Florence Ala. to complete their education. The girls staid a day & night in Memphis with Mrs Daniels, Delle wrote to her Ma that if she told her all she had seen since leaving home, she would be like the girl at the Centennial, exclaim Oh! Oh! Oh! Oh! — Mr Allston went on with them — The first letter Mamie rec'd from Miss Calie B. after leaving here she begged her, "tender many thanks to Mr Boddie for his kind remembrance, & sincerely hope I may realize his kindest of wishes." Miss Calie is one of the assistant teachers in the school at Arkadelphia this year.

Our young people frolick on yet, when the[y] have the opportunity, Mrs [Patrick] Gaughan gave them a very nice party recently, Bob S. danced himself in the humour of going to another, which they speak of having at Mr Chewnings, Florence & Nelie were on this side of the creek nearly all last week, visiting at Mrs Patterson's, Clara's, Gaughans, Proctors &c.

Mr Steele is working at Mr Bob S[tone] this year. Had a letter from Sis Hattie [Murley]at last, they are all well, but she is troubled about her financial affairs, they made on the place only 7 bales of cotton, which with the low price left her in debt over 200 dollars for supplies &c, says she will not try to furnish any more freedmen, & will have only two families on the place. Has concluded to sell out her stock in the Tan Yard to Phil, to enable her to get out of debt, as she cant make it profitable to carry it on in the slow way they've been doing for some time. Poor Hattie she thinks they are so economical, but she will learn somewhat when they do as we do, make the supplies last as long as possible, & when used up, do without, she says they killed only six hogs, & will have to buy meat again, but were I in her place would certainly do without rather than go in debt. Mattie spent Christmas & New Year' day in Mobile with Mrs Watkins.

Hav'nt seen any of Uncle J's family (except Tommy) since I was over there just three weeks ago to-day. Last Sunday was our preaching day but no minister came. We have the same one that preached for us last year, Mr Ashly. Tommy said tell John I'm not flying round any of the <u>fair ones</u> in particular but <u>all</u> in general, & Willie ditto. State wishes John to be informed that he never did have any notion of going "Ashore" Ha! ha! I wonder who told John that." How do you get on with the bird trial? am anxious to know, for <u>I have</u> <u>read</u> that it cant be done, & <u>wondered</u> why, if you dont succeed am sure you'l tell me what's the difficulty. Pa said, he thought he could finish up two or three a day, & Will said he would like very much for some one to offer him the same contract.

Nelie rec'd a letter from Tom L[ove] in which he informed us, that his sisters Ada, & Onie were both married the same night, 19th Dec. (Carrie's birthday) Onie married Mr Northington, Ada, Mr Dunn. They are looking for Clem L. out on a visit [from Texas], & he intends taking Kate home with him. As for marrying time here darling, cant specify it, the preparation necessary is quite an uphill business, & I can speak for "Small Sis" that she seems in no hurry (though Dr C. is) June is the earliest time spoken of, & not at all certain then, so darling, please dont mention about it in any letters you may write to relatives or friends here. Florence told me the last time I was with her, she <u>actually did not know</u> when she would step off, told Carrie long time ago that the 19th Jan. 77 was the appointed time, so dont be scared but just come whenever it suits your convenience, I will be sure to post you in time to ward off any danger from catching the "Epidemic" — Your friends all desire to be remembered, everybody asks me when you are coming, I guess that <u>time</u> is as uncertain as the other affairs. — Kind regards to Mr B & much love from each one at home to my darling boy. May God bless, & care for you is the prayer of

your devoted Mother
Mary E. Boddie

Dr. John B. Rumph in Ouachita Co. to John Rumph Boddie in St. Louis
Feby. 5th 1877

My dear Nephew

    Your highly appreciated favor of the 26th ult, was recd on last Saturday whilst in Camden. It was the 2nd time I had been to Camden since Christmas, and took the pain at that, to get there. We have had the coldest weather this winter within the memory of that sage individual the "oldest inhabitant." Snow 18 inches deep and remaining on the ground two weeks, Old Prof Tice will have to be suppressed or he will turn our temperate zone into an arctic region in a few more years. I have been afflicted the past six weeks with Job's comforters, in the shape of blood boils or carbuncles, old Mike (Rhodas husband) used to call them <u>cow bumpers</u>. I am now just able to use my wrist and hands as they were the points of attack — two cowbumpers, on each wrist at a time. I am truly glad to learn that you have had your salary increased, it was nothing more than I expected, but not in accordance with your honest deserts. The amount but poorly pays you for your services. The only chance now for you is to practice the most rigid economy and spend nothing but what is absolutely necessary to live on decently and like a gentleman. Times I hope will be better from this time on, as the prospect is much more favorable to seat Tilden peacibly than it was. Business of all kind will revive under a good administration of National affairs, and once confidence is restored I look for good times again. In regard to the investment of your surplus monthly earnings, I would suggest a deposit in a savings Bank, where it would pay a small interest. I do not think it would pay very well now to invest in the Ark State Scrip, as the most of that is held by Brokers and they ask from 78 @ 80 for small sums. From the Auditors report we have outstanding about 1,200,OOO State Scrip. The taxes now being collected will absorb nearly half of that. The taxes to be collected by 1st April 1878 will absorb nearly or quite all of the ballance, consequently it is reasonable to expect by that time Scrip will appreciate to 95 @ 100; unless the present Legislature takes a fool notion to issue more scrip, which I do not think likely, although it has been suggested by some of the Representatives. Your Scrip is securely locked in George's safe — about half of it, bearing 5 per cent interest, it can be sold now for about 78c. When you come down this summer we can talk over our financial matters much more satisfactorily than I can write. There are other <u>matters</u> that you hinted at in your letter that <u>must also</u> be satisfactorily discussed viva voce, that "could not be did" with a pen. I'm all curiosity to see her photo, or a charcoal sketch of her surpasing loveliness. Can't you manage to send me a half dozen photos of your lady friend, with a private "dot" on the photo of the "charming Mary Ann," You must not disappoint us this summer in making your proposed visit — I am <u>chug full</u> of Turkey hunting and camp

hunting to interest you for a long sitting — which I cant think of telling only in a regular "Cousin Sally Dillard" stile, that is, to begin at the beginning and wind up at the e'end. Now, my dear Boy, dont fail to put in your appearance some time this summer when you can best spare the time, and we'll all try to make your visit as pleasant as possible. My paper is nearly out and it is all I have, so I must make room for the kind regards of all the family. I am dear Boy your devoted Uncle
      JBRumph
Write me occasionally when you can spare the time

Mary E. Boddie in Ouachita Co. to her son, John R. Boddie in St. Louis
                March 9th 77
  My darling boy,

  Many, many thanks for your <u>precious letters</u>, four of which I've rec'd since writing to you, & fully intended doing so last week, but was deprived of the pleasure from various causes, & on Sunday Misses Cora & Nellie E. with Messers Brooks & A. Agee spent the day with us, the former is living with Mr Agee this year who is farming Bachelor style, professes not to like such a way of living at all, & hopes to better it, if he can persuade some one of the gentler sex to take pity on his forlorn condition. Mrs L. Elliott has taken a school at Holly Sps. & was to commence teaching on Monday last. Mrs Scales is in Town where she expects to remain most of the time, so I guess Miss Nellie & Miss Mollie S. are the housekeepers at home. Miss Cora is over to spend a week or two with them. Seeing her reminded me of what you say of the St. Louis girls "livelys". I think Cora to be the handsomest young lady I've ever seen in this country, & appears to be as amiable as pretty. Both the girls asked about you, & to be remembered with best respects & Small Sis thinks Miss C. & Mr H. Smith are engaged, judging from the devoted attention paid her at the Party they all attended at Mrs Agee's last week. The last party of the season, at least 'tis for our girls, for Pa let them go very reluctantly, & told them they need not ask him any more, for that must be the last. I would like much darling if our girls could go to see <u>one</u> such <u>sociable</u> as you attended at the old Englishman's. Miss Georgia P. gave one several weeks ago, Uncle John & whole family went, (except Atalie Eugenia & Maud) had a very <u>nice supper</u> no dancing, music on Guitar (by "Mrs O S.") violin accompaniment, by Mr Willie Stone, they play well together, & Florence sings ever so many songs. She was down here during the late pretty moonlight nights, & insisted on going serenading, commencing at "Uncle Billy's" & on down through Hardscrabble, said they had a gay time, & quite surprised the natives. State, Tune, Small Sis, Will, Miss Mollie S. Mr W. Chewning composed the crowd. "Mrs O['Scuttle]" said "tell cousin

Johnie the cinnamon drops has all evaporated like his love, & we've had a big smash up, wrote me a scorching note, & I replied, ditto." — Since which time they met at the late party, & affairs are all "gauging" smoothly again I presume, as Small Sis told me they promenaded long enough that eve, to adjust all previous misunderstandings. Bettie has been in Town a week tomorrow at Jennie's, will spend next week with Mittie, & one with us before she returns home, & then wants Mamie to go with her, Nelie is teaching Atalie & Eugenia at home. Yes darling, the children all have grown much since you saw them, two long, long years, & yet how rapidly time flies.

I little thought when you left, 'twould be two yrs. & longer ere you could come to see us, but I'm so glad you are better & better pleased with St. Louis, & City life for I know you never would be content to live here again. We talk, & talk, of "brother" & "son's" coming, but dont look for until we see you. Small Sis says she has perforce to be patient until you will be "spirit moved" to write. Tug says "tell bud Johnie I'm plowing, Tom Abbott is my mule to work, & I ride him too," he rec'd his paper this week with Pa's for which accept thanks. Gilder was to see us last Sunday week, for the first time since he left home. Mr Frank B[rodnax] & Miss Clem [Proctor] organized a Sabbath school at our chruch, have a good attendance so far, Pa is unwilling for Carrie & Bobbie to go walking, & they have no other way. I sent "Tug" last Sunday on "Tom" as they had not been plowing for a day or two, & when he cant go, will have him read & say his lesson at home. The Minister sent word that he could not preach for us only every fifth Sunday, & that will be five times during the year.

Am sorry to note in your last that you have a cold & however "slight" darling dont neglect it, but take good care of yourself. Also regret you will be, without roommates, but hie to your couch earlier (when not "on the War path") & forget in natures' sweet repose that you are alone. Would like much to see Mr B. when he comes. Dr C[oleman] was down last month, spent several days, expect he will come again, though the time appointed for the marriage is the 5th June, nothing Providentially preventing. 'Twill be a family affair, as we are not able to do more. "Small Sis" says, "tell brother, the very night he was thinking of the ring & date, Dr C. & I, were looking at the same, & surmised that "thereby hung a tale." Mamie wishes she could send you a boquet of her pretty Hyacinths, says she has almost forgotten how to arrange them since you left. Intends sending a boquet to Miss Ruth B. soon. Little Sis regrets there is not a single violet in bloom to send bud Johnie. Pa & Will have not commenced planting yet, (except oats), been plowing some, hauling out manure, cleaning up, &c just as the weather admits. We have had some fine weather to work, some rain, & now 'tis as cold as Jan. for the past few days, plenty ice & the peach trees in bloom too. Pa has been much bothered winding up his affairs & making arrangements for this year. Col Hill made a compromise of 1/2 on all the notes, & after turning over to him all the cotton made (8 bales, 10 1/4) & paying $665. Pa is released from <u>all</u> indebtedness to Col. Hill & that house. Pa has now the control, & disposal of his stock as he deems best & hopes with them, & by making a fair crop, to be able to pay the interest & a part, if not all the $665. borrowed money. I went to Town with Pa one day last week, to sign a deed of trust on our place, given to Mr Charley Gee from whom he obtained the means to pay Col. Hill.—Willie wants to plant all cotton, & only sufficient corn for bread, crop of peas for the hogs &c, but Pa has not yet decided about it.

Must close darling as I want my letter mailed tomorrow, pardon sending you soiled sheets, 'twas done before I commenced writing on it, & my last — This leaves all well, nothing new in Hard Scrabble save a baby, 11 lb boy to Mrs Alston named William Stone A. Mr A. says it is his valentine, the boy. With much love from all at home, & hoping you are quite well ere this, leave you in the Hands of Him who careth for us all.

Your devoted Mother
Mary E. Boddie

Cornelia Dickson in Ouachita County to Mrs. Howard Garmany Dunlap in Tulip, Arkansas

March 13 1877

Dear Howard,

Your kind & sympathizing letter of the 4th of Feb. was received in due time, bringing with it the balm of friendship to a wounded spirit for

"Tis sweet in hours of untold grief
To know one steadfast friend
Stands near to offer us relief
And friendships hand extend."

I should have replied to it ere this, believe me, it was not want of appreciation or respect that prevented, but in the first place I was out of envelopes & then circumstanced as I am, for I am still indebted to brother John for a shelter, I cannot at all times do as I feel inclined; but I guess you know all about it. Yes I am still at brother Johns, have failed to get a school, am teaching Attalie and Eugenia, & though it is a pleasant task & occupies a good portion of my time, it is impossible for me to feel at all satisfied, unless it was employment sufficient to pay my board & make my clothes besides. You speak of my trying matrimony to break the monotony, who on earth is there for me to marry. Howard if I felt inclined, that my condition would be bettered thereby. I am sure I do not know any one. There would have to be a decided change in my views, as I should feel that I was doing any man a <u>wrong</u> to marry them merely for a change of name & occupation.

If I only had some lucrative & lasting & agreeable employment would be perfectly satisfied, and teaching seems to be my part, as I can adapt myself to that better than to anything else, matrimony not excepted, though I have never tried the latter. Howard I am somewhat of a predestrinarian and find a little consolation sometimes in the thought that each one has their part to fill in this life & do as we may we can only do what is assigned us, & therefore whatever is, is right, and yet reason as I will, my rebellious spirit <u>will not</u> feel satisfied circumstanced as I am without a home.

  Well Howard, I guess you think, from the space I have occupied, when Self is at hand, I am not wanting Self for a subject, but the subject I know interests a friend. I sent for the picture of your boy Howard, kept it two weeks before I had an opportunity of returning it. He is indeed a beautiful bright little fellow, has a very expressive face & solid look for a child of his age, answers well to your description of him. I think he resembles Eura very much in feature. I saw Ada, Ophelia, & Eura at the party at Mrs Agees. They created several remarks in my hearing by their easy graceful bearing, particularly Ophelia. Eura unfortunately tripped & fell, owing I think to the unpardonable awkwardness of Mr Joe Brooks, who had I guess <u>imbibed</u> most too freely, to keep his feet in proper bounds. Eura seemed much gratified when I told her I thought your babe resembled her. She said yes she was of the same opinion and that Rosa had sent them a picture of her babe also. I am very anxious to see it, Give my love [to all and tell them I wish] to see you all for I miss you very much, though I did not get to see you often while you were living here. How do you like living up there Howard, much better than in this bottom. We all are so glad whenever I receive a letter from you. Besides the family, Miss Clem & Georgia [Proctor] send their love. I scarcely ever see any of brother G's family. Miss Clem received a long letter from Mrs Hogue several weeks since. They are in west Texas, Brown County I believe. She is very much pleased, enjoys fine health but says it is pretty rough, as the country is thinly settled. Bettie Rumph is spending a week or two with Mitt & Jennie. we expect her home next week. Florence received a nice treat, in the way of a wild turkey from Alex Gaughan, this morning. I wish you were here to help us partake of it. She says you must not listen to rumor, for she is really more partial to blue eyes than any other.*

*The letter ends at this point in the journal.

Mary Elizabeth Boddie in Ouachita Co. to her son John Rumph Boddie in St. Louis

April 2nd, 1877

  My own dear boy,

   'Tis my pleasant privilege to acknowlege the rec't of three precious letters, & endeavor to tell you something of home & home folks in return for the great comfort, & pleasure, your loving kindness accords me from week to week. So you have changed houses darling! & I was much gratified to note in your last, that you were very "well pleased with the new business, & succeeding so far, much better than you expected" but the latter is no more than I anticipated, for I know you try to do your whole duty with a thoroughness, that is most always rewarded with success. Though not acquainted with Mr & Mrs Goddard personally, towards them I feel a nearness, & most kind appreciation, because of your long association with, & their uniform kindness to my boy, & Mr G's high recommendation was no more than you merited darling, though I value it none the less. The most pleasing item in the change of business is, that you can come to Camden once or twice a year, & I do hope you may succeed so well, that ere long you will have attained a sufficiency to settle down to home life, & its enjoyment, as I think that kind of life would suit you best.

 Aunt Clara spent one day with us last week, & told me to tell you, that you were a suitable "bluebeard" having your "Dulciema Deltobosas" in St Louis, & your "little [one] as sweet as a peach in Camden." "Cousin Bettie" attended the <u>Bride's</u> reception in Camden, & gave a glowing description of the same, & enjoyed it to the utmost, as she "felt herself dressed equal to the occasion, sis Jennie giving the finishing touch to my toilet of course." I think you might have consoled Mr R. by telling him the "new", & "young sweethearts" were as sweet as the "old ones," thus reconciling him to his fate. Bettie staid with us week before last, said "tell Cousin Johnie I am getting <u>weightier</u> fast." Mamie did not go home with her to spend the promised week, as she had no certain way of getting home. "Small Sis" was so proud to get <u>her</u> letter, that she intended answering it that night, but I asked her to defer writing then, as I had just sent one to you, & since which time she has not had leisure. Is very busy sewing as you may infer from the short time she has to remain with us, & so much other work claiming her time, with many interruptions from company &c. She & "Little Sis" are busy now with the weeks' washing & the latter often says, whatever are we to do Mama when Mamie leaves? I tell her, I dont love to think of <u>that time</u> only as a long, long way off & to the domestic part I never give a thought.

 Mat & children spent yesterday week with me, the Baptist Minister preached that day, but I had one of Uncle J's <u>cricks"</u> in my back, (as he terms the like effection) & could not go. "Small & Little Sis," Bettie, Atalie, & Willie went, "Tug" staid home to play with Eugenia & Maud, the first time he had missed going to Sunday School since it commenced. Miss Lula A. stayed with Carrie Saturday night, & "Tug" went home with her yesterday to go to Sunday School, as Pa wanted him to let his mule rest. Lula & Carrie have made them each a <u>green riding habit</u>, & we tease Little Sis about providing a habit, & <u>nothing to ride</u>, says, never mind she has lost several opportunities of a good ride for want of one. Bob S. tells them that nothing less than a ride through Town will satisfy their ambitions to show off their fine (as they think) habits, trimed off with various rows of <u>pasteboard</u> buttons covered with blk. Alpaca.*

*Alpaca is a fabric made from the wool of the Alpaca animal.

Bob did not sell his cotton until the past week, waited, hoping for a rise which did not take place, the river has been too low for large boats for a long time, & until Saturday night much need of rain, the ground being almost too hard to plow. We have had some very cold weather too Son, for the season & great fears that the fruit blossoms would be killed, but am glad to say, that so far the prospect for fruit is good. Had some hail with the rain on Saturday night, but not sufficient to damage anything so far as heard from. My strawberry bed is white with blossoms, & would look so pretty but for its foul state. My being sick so much last fall prevented me from having kept it clean & in order. All the flowers will be done blooming darling, (except roses) before you come. I <u>was</u> thinking you might stop in any day, but now, 'tis way off, "July or August."

The Sabbath (11th Ult) that you were wondering what we were all doing here at home? was quite cold, but not raining, as with you, & "Cousin Mittie," Miss Florence B., Bettie, India B. & Mr Johnie M. spent the day with us, the first time I had ever seen Miss F. B. she's as lively, & merry as a cricket, asked many questions about you & expressed much pleasure that you would come this summer, & so do all your friends darling both white & black. Mr & Mrs Bracy, & children came over that day, but went on to see Miss Annie & Julia, said their crowd was too large not to divide. All came over in a waggon (11 with the driver) except Mr B. who rode horseback, & <u>two</u> of his little boys behind him, said they created quite a sensation coming through Town.

Mr Buchanan is safe at home with his family, would like much to see him. Pa has not been over since he came, but Uncle J. told me of the long chat <u>he had</u> with Mr B. Uncle J. has been killing ever so many turkeys this Spring, Mr Proctor too, & I do wish you could be here to enjoy the sport, Pa has not been but one morning, which proved to be too cloudy for success, says, hard work, & hunting dont tally very well for him. Will never hunts, but I believe he loves it as well as any one, but wont indulge, we miss Gilder in that, as well as every other respect, he has been to see us twice this year.

Pa & Will have finished planting corn, & have half the ground they intend planting in cotton plowed over. "Tug" says they have made the ground rich enough that is planted in corn (<u>six acres</u>) for it to make 4 or 500 bu. Pa often asks "Tug" if he dont talk too much? if his little tongue dont get tired running? & such questions generally stops him for a time — by the by, he said to me recently, (since he's been plowing pretty hard) "Ma why didn[t] Pa try for the Presidency, perhaps he might <u>have won</u>, I intend to, a[i]nt going to make my living farming." Pa has given him the piece of ground back o[f] the smokehouse to plant in potatoes & he's made several calculations as to how much it will make, what price he can get, & how much money he'l make, & what he can get with it, &c. Pa says, "never mind about <u>the papers</u>, he'l miss them, but is thankful for past favors," he expresses himself as being much pleased with your present prospects, & whilst I am too darling, dont like the idea much of your having to travel most of the time, & then can I hear from you as heretofore? Nelie was here one day last week, overhauling her trunks for summer clothing preparatory to going off to take a school. Mrs Norris has procured one for her of 25 pupils in that neighbourhood. They live 12 miles from Camden this year, dont know if they have purchased or renting. Mollie & Mr B. live with the old folks yet. Expect Nelie will board with Mrs N. Told me she had rec'd a letter from Kate recently, no news save Maj Tyus's death, & a birth in the family, a son to her brother Andrew & his wife. Nelie begged me for the card of your house, said, Kate asked so many questions about, & seemed so anxious to hear from you, she wished to send the card when she answered Kate's letter. If convenient Son, please send me another, we all love to look at the semblance of your present location, & think it to be a fine looking structure. "Tug" wonders which room bud Johnie is in, said he guessed there was one man for every room, & we too, could scarcely grasp the fact that such a bevy of young men could be employed to advantage in one house. Miss Anna, Mrs. Fisher & children are expected home this month, will leave Hopkinsville about the 15th accompanied by Mr F. as far as Prescott.

Well darling, we'l see <u>you</u> when you come, take good care of yourself for the sake of those who love you, & may you be blest in every relation through life, is the prayer of

Your devoted mother
M. E. Boddie

*Dont think I told you in my last that Ada & husband were living at Uncle Clem's place, & Onie & Mr N[orthington] at her Mothers, Tom L. wrote to Nelie asking if she would sell her place, & what take for it. Uncle J. D. told her to tell him she would take 200. All send much love — Goodbye.

*Note: This postscript was written, upside down, at the top of the previous page.

Mary Elizabeth Boddie (Mamie, also called Small Sis in letters) to her brother John Rumph Boddie in St. Louis

Tuesday night, April 16th 1877

My Dear Brother,

It seems an age since I last wrote you, however, I shall offer no excuses, as you once said that you detested nothing more than a page of apologies. I suffice to say, that with company & <u>pressing</u> work, I have but little time to spend in the pleasant task of letter writing. I love it, because tis the only diversion in my monotonous life. Tis needless to say that your long looked for letter, was welcomed cordially, I freely forgive you for not writing, as I well know your time is wholy given to business & then — well <u>dainty missives from else where</u>, have to be answered. I hardly know what to write to interest you for everything is <u>so dull</u>. The bees are the most attractive feature of home at present; they claim all of Bud's [Willie] rest time, & frequently they become quite elevated in their notions. Bud shot two swarms, that came out together, out the white oak at the garden gate. They seemed content to remain & have gone to work. Pa & Bud are planting cotton but dont know when they will finish as tis raining off and [on].

The thunder and lightning was as terrific to my equlibrium as the accompany[ing] rain to farmers. Pa got his cattle out today & will go back tomorrow to be sure. I was at Mrs Annie's this evening. Mr. Stone is sick in bed. Mrs. A said if twould quit raining, he would [get] well. Mrs. Fisher and Anna have come, the former, with their children, will remain all Summer. Anna is the same Anna except in appearance, a little larger. I have not met her yet, as <u>we</u> dont speak. Nellie Elliott spent last week with Mrs. Annie, was with me several days. Lula Avery went home with her to spend this week. Cousin Bettie is at Aunt Clara's spending this week. Cousin Tommie calls on his way from C[amden] has not payed us a visit in three weeks. He went up to Mr. Elliot's Sunday. <u>I think</u> to aggravate Anna, for tis generally believed that she loves him yet not-withstanding his indifference. I hope that Cousin T. will not visit her again, & if he <u>does not love her</u>, which [he] declares is true. I know he will not. He has told me from first, to last, that he never intended to marry her. Bud, [Willie] I am sorry to say, like[s] "Miss Anna," will talk of her whenever he finds someone to speak of her in favorable terms. Gilder is free from the wounds of Cupids dart. Does not visit much if any though I think he is preparing for the future, by sending bouquets. He is studying very [hard] to fill a druggist place. I sent Johny Morgan a boquet, & received a real nice note in return. He will be over before long. Sent Ruth one also. I hear from the girls through Cousin as you, to, are recipent of her little budgets of news will say nothing more of them. My roses are blooming and my garden though almost bare, is pretty. I seldom make bouquets but always think of you. I am expecting Dr. C. this week, but hardly look for him, as tis said that all of the water courses are up. The fifth of June was the time set, but I think now of postponing it till the last of June. Cala will come down with him to spend some time with Mrs. B. All relatives are well. Excuse all errors & bad writing for I write but little,
      Ever Your Devoted Sister
      Mamie Boddie

*Ma wrote you nearly three weeks ago.

*Note: This postscript was written, upside down, across the top of page one.

Mary Elizabeth Boddie in Ouachita Co. to her son John Rumph Boddie in St. Louis

May 22nd 1877

My own dear boy,

  Did not receive your dear letter of 6th Inst. until 12th, & would have written immediately, but Pa wished to write, so had to defer mine till I heard from you again, thinking you would prefer not getting two letters from home the same date. I can never thank you enough darling for the satisfaction & pleasure your precious letters afford me, & the indulgence you promise to accord me even when "on the wing." Did so hope you could be with us before your sister leaves, 'twas her expressed desire, but business before pleasure, & of course you will make a little detour, & visit her at her own home, if you cannot be here by the 5th June, the day on which the marriage will take place, nothing Providentially occurring to prevent.* We expect to give a dinner (as the ceremony will be in the morning,) & to which all relatives will be invited, (few others) which will make up a crowd of about 50. Miss Calie & Bettie, Mr Williams (from Arkadelphia) & Gilder are the only attendents. Mamie was anxious to have her sister [Carrie], but we could not afford the outfit necessary for "Little Sis" to occupy that position, so Mamie decided on having only two, instead of four, as she first desired. You can never know darling boy how much the help to your sister is appreciated, & it suffiseth to say, we are most grateful. I have scarcely seen Mamie for the past three weeks as she has been at home only twice during that time, & then with a crowd, she & Mittie will come Thursday, the latter to stay until the affair is over.

  Last Saturday eve Florence gave a sociable & besides the young people of the neighbourhood, Tommy invited a waggon load from Town. Misses Cala, India, B. Jordan, Mamie & Mittie, Mr J. Rucks, Johnie M. & Gilder. They came by, & insisted on "Little Sis" taking passage too. Tug rode his mule, Pa let him go, as "Cousin Florence" sent him an expressed invitation. They all enjoyed the trip & Party highly, had a delicious strawberry supper &c, when our crowd returned Sunday eve I had another strawberry treat for them, & the callers that evening Messers Bracy, Newton, & Paschal. Dee said they were the finest & best berries he had had this season. I think Son, we have gathered as many as three bushels, & they are not quite gone yet. Little Sis & I would have preserved several gallons, if we'd had the sugar, tried to fill all the jars you gave me, but fruit having been frozen in them (that cold winter), none but two stood the test of being boiled to expel the air. "Bro. Will" did not go to the Party, wanted to take some honey that night, his bees have kept him entirely occupied all his noon time, & nights too since they commenced swarming 8th April. Often, three & five swarms came out at the same time. He has 75 gums in all, & I believe they are about done

*The marriage Sis Mollie refers to is the marriage of Mamie, "Small Sis," to Dr. E. G. Coleman of Arkadelphia. The marriage license, issued in Ouachita County, listed the ages as Mamie 20 years old and the doctor, 28.

swarming now, no, Little Sis has just this moment come from the cowpen, & asked me what I let that swarm of bees run off for?

Pa has to attend court this week as juryman, said he would try to get off to day, they seem to be getting on well with the farm work, weather has been so fair, no rain save slight sprinkle since 27 April. The corn looks very fine, though a season would benefit it — Pa commenced planting cotton 2nd May, & has 15 acres yet to plant, though in the meantime has been working the corn, & other patches &c, this week they are planting peas. Uncle John has not planted his cotton yet, waiting for rain. We would be glad to have some of the sloppy weather you speak of though not of such long duration we experianced just such all through April, & the overflow <u>inconvenienced</u> us as usual, but Pa lost no stock, & Will gained five fine hogs that had not been seen for a year or longer. His fine hog Dixie has been broken down in the loins for the past three months, & all the remedies Will has used, (& they were many) hasn't materially benefited him. All the farmers in our vicinity are in fine spirits, & getting on well because minus of grass, some few commenced chopping cotton, heard Pa tell Willie this morning the cotton in front of the house was large enough to commence chopping.

Was so glad to know darling, that although you changed board [and] do not occupy a room at the hotel. I felt thankful too that you did not witness the terrible scenes of that nights' great disaster, never heard, or read of a fire that made such an impression on me, & like Uncle John, I think laws should be passed, & enforced to provide means for the safe exit from every room in all large Hotels. Can sympathise with you much darling with your sore nose, as mine was in just such condition for two weeks, & until yours gets well know you'l be deprived of the usual pleasant visits to your lady friends, but hope ere this you may be well & "flourishing like a green bay tree &c." I do feel so sorry for Mrs Smythe, & trust that time may smooth her grief, & her heart even cheered, by the thought, of meeting her darling in that better Land, submitting hopefully to that All Wise One whose Will, not mine, but "Thine be done." Have not yet heard of Mr N. R's arrival, Mr B. said nothing to Pa about the bundle, & of course Pa will not mention it to him. Mrs Annie sends love, & says, <u>do come along</u> before "Brama's* & Shang's" get too tough for a pot pie, & Bob says he'd rather see John than any one in the world. Mrs J. Toney called to see me recently, told me to tell you <u>be sure</u> to come & <u>see her</u>, though she had no grown up girls round now, had plenty young ones <u>coming on</u>. Mrs Fisher & Anna arrived in due time, the latter is the same Anna of old, Mrs F. is a sweet lady, & has three interesting boys. With the oldest Freddie, "Tug" would spend half his time if he were not at work. While I think of it will tell you that Mr B. Lide has an addition to his household, a nice girl baby. Mrs Roberson also (formerly Mattie Mitchel). By the by did "Cousin Mattie" send you one of her pictures? she sent "Small Sis" one, & Uncle J. fell completely in love with it, the

*A Brama was a slang term for a pretty girl. Brama and Shanghai were actually types of chickens

sweetest expression he ever saw &c &c said he must send Tom to see her. "Cousin Bettie" went to Town yesterday to remain a week with Jennie & make her dress for the occasion. Nelie did not get the school I told you of, & only returned from that side of the river two weeks ago. She has a school here of seven pupils with the probability of more. Is boarding with Julia A[lston] at "Uncle Billy's," they were not pleased with Effie's progress in Town, & preferred sending her from home. About the garden I came near forgetting. We have had all your Market afforded when you wrote save cucumbers, but I can tell you we dont have vegetables (like in the long) in abundance, as most of the garden is planted in corn, one square vegetable & berries, & one in flowers, which latter is getting to be pretty grassy, as "Small Sis" attentions are engrossed in other things. May apples, raspberries, & currants are ripening, & "Tug" says there are thousands of whortleberries*, but millions of mosquitoes, to prevent you from gathering them. Pleasant anticipations makes one very happy darling, but I would prefer the reality of your being here. With much love from each at home, & kind regards from your many friends remain,

*Whortleberries are blueberries or huckleberries.

Your devoted mother
Mary E. Boddie

"Little Sis" wants to know if it smokes much near Arkadelphia? & that you must remember smoke envelopes bodies sometimes—*

*Little Sis' reference to smoke in Arkadelphia is a clever play on words, since Bud John has romantic interests in a young lady, Cornelia Smoker, who resides in Arkadelphia. John Boddie would soon announce his intentions to marry Miss Smoker.

Mary E.[Mamie] Boddie in Ouachita Co. to her brother John Rumph Boddie in St. Louis

Thursday Evening May 31st 1877

Dear Brother

It seems so strange for you to be flying all about home & yet never stop to see us. We hear from you every where and you may imagine Ma's state of feeling when she heard a young ladies name mentioned with yours. When I tell you that she has requested me more than once to be sure and write immediately my first impressions of Miss Smoker. Your visit to her, created quite a sensation in the little city of Arkadelphia. I flatter my self that I will certainly win a place in her good graces, if she thinks as the most of your Camden friends do, that "You are just the very image of Mr. Jno Boddie". I hope she will, for in that way, they tell me that I'm handsome, fine looking & all that sort of little talk, that never fails to tickle our vanity. No, Brother, 'tis not the idea of being admired, but of being loved, as I know you are. Well maybe I will improve, & yet be a blessing to brothers sister, father & mother.

Cousin & cousin Bettie came out yesterday, both are in the kitchin displaying their skill as cooks. I'm completely exhausted in mind, but none are aware of the fact. Mamma is worrying herself to death about having to give me up. I wish I was really worth half the sorrow my departure will cause. It all seems so strange, for any of them to speak with regret of my leaving, that can hardly realize the fact, that I am going.

Cousin says if cousin Jno would only come would'nt we be glad. All old friends in Camden send love.

Pa & Bud are chopping cotton, have five or six extra hands. I believe their crop in both corn & cotton, is good. Needing rain very much at present & little or no prospect of having any. Oh I do wish you were here to enjoy currants & raspberrys. We have not time to gather them. Strawberrys not quite all gone.

Aunt Hannah is here helping us, she says she will be sure to marry in Sept. Pollas, I believe, is his name. You would enjoy talking to her, about him. I never thought an old person could love so hard, but I believe she really loves him. All are well. I must stop as all are calling & hunting for me.

Good-bye & write to me when you feel like it, as ever

Your loving sister
Mamie

*Ma sends much love & all of them. They are anxious to know what I have written to you. I tell them wonderful things.

*Note: This postscript is written upside down across the top of page 2.

Cornelia Dickson in Ouachita Co. to her niece Virginia Love in Autauga Co.
July 1, 1877

Dear Jennie,

Your very welcome missive was received several weeks ago, it was delayed in rout, I suppose, as it was dated the 13th of May. I should have replied to it immediately, but school duties and various other things claimed my attention so closely, that I just put it off until I could have a more favorable opportunity, but it seems that the opportunity I seek will never approach near[er] than at present. I thought to have devoted to you & several others, but just as I commenced writing, received a note that caused me to lay aside my writing until tonight, & then I was obliged to write to Florence. She is in town, and as it was today decided to have a picnic on the fourth, I have to send her a note in the morning. We have company again tonight too. But I appreciate your letter so much, it being the first you have ever written to me, that I take pleasure tonight in writing.

Carrie was here last week, a night & two days, says she received your letter, but had never answered it, had been so very busy, that she had not even answered her Aunt Carrie's. She & Mamie have had all the house work to do, or rather Carrie had to do the most of it; as Mamie was preparing her bridal wardrobe and spent some time in Camden in order to obtain Mittie's assistance. Carrie is usually very prompt at letter writing & I think she will write before long. She thinks of attending the free school next month. I suppose Sis Mollie intends getting a cook then, it is impossible for her to attempt to do anything of the kind. My subscription school will be out shortly, and I had thought of getting the free school, but there are several advanced pupils who plan to attend, and I have concluded to take a school about ten miles above here if I can make suitable arrangements. I feel sorry to leave this neighborhood, as I have many warm friends here, but it has been my good fortune to meet with friends wherever I have been, considering I was a good teacher too. I only hope that I may always merit their regard. I very often think of those I have left in Ala. and whenever you write, let me hear about them as well as my relatives.

The neighborhood has concluded to have a picnic the Fourth of July on Pine Lake, & Bettie Rumph, as one of the ring leaders, was flying around today preparing something nice. I did not see her, but Clara who I went to see at noon, told me that Bettie had just gone from there. Clara has been quite sick for several days, was better today. She lives about two hundred yds from the school house. All were well except her. Cora goes to school to me. Lula has vacation now. Her school, in Town, closed the middle of June. I think she has improved a good deal. I saw brother John yesterday, he said all were well.

The farmers are all in high spirits with their promising crops, have had such fine seasons for the last month. Is a better crop, and fruit year, than we have had in some time. Some of the neighbors had ripe peaches a month ago.

I was so glad to hear that you were attending school, Jennie. I hope you will improve every moment of your time, if you do not, you will regret it so much hereafter. What you study, learn it thoroughly and think of the relation one lesson & one study, bears to another; do not permit yourself to think of any thing but your studies, and I know you have the talent to be inteligent and should you ever be thrown upon your own resources for a support, will be able to command a competency.

Tell Bessie, George & Crawford* to study hard and be first in their classes. I never want to hear of one of them being "imperfect." I have a little boy in my school, who is twelve years old, and has but one imperfect mark for the past month. He has seven studies besides reading & writing.

It is growing late and I shall have to rise early. So good bye for this time. Write again whenever you have leisure and I will take pleasure in replying. With love to all I am as ever

    Affectionately, your
    Aunt Nealie

*Jennie, Bessie, George and Crawford are nieces and nephews of Cornelia in Alabama. It is interesting to note the encouragement adults offer to the young people in the matter of learning and especially in maintaining a correspondence with their cousins. Many of these people never saw each other, but they enjoyed a closeness of family through the art of letter-writing.

Mary Elizabeth Boddie in Ouachita Co. to her son John Rumph Boddie in St. Louis

July 26th 1877

My own darling boy,

 Can reply to you as I did to "Tug" some weeks ago, when he said, "Mama bud Johnie has forgotten me, he has never said anything about me since he quit writing long time ago," told "Tug" he realy did not think any such thing, & neither do you darling, think for one moment that "Mama" has forgotten her boy, or not ceased to think of him <u>daily</u>, & almost hourly since the day she parted from him, nearly three years ago. I wont tell you how heartsick I've been at each disappointment of your necessarily long deferred visit, because 'twas my duty to keep cheerful, & set an example of patience to all at home, whose impetuosity would often make them say "I dont believe he wants to come at all." The very week you were sick darling, I was thinking that <u>such was the case.</u>, & felt relieved when your letter came to dissipate my worst fears. In each of your letters after returning to your St. Louis home, spoke of <u>leaving again very soon</u>, & did not say if a letter would reach you there, is the reason I did not write. Was so glad to know you had such a nice time, the short time you stayed visiting old lady friends, "Dulciema's" "Ducks" &c. Cousin Bettie says, "I do wonder if Cousin Johnie is like Mr Richmond, <u>not spoiled at all</u>" somehow she has an idea that you take upon yourself City airs &c. She spent yesterday with us, came with Tommie as he was going over to mill, & to bring Jennie, if she would come, & sure enough Jennie came to remain over until Saturday week. The <u>boys</u> are scarcely <u>big enough</u> for pants yet, & not as handsome as they promised to be, yet I know Geo. will be proud to show <u>his boys</u> to "John", & you cant tease Jennie much for Tommie never lets an opportunity pass without indulging his mischievous propensities. Florence is at home, Bettie says, she is as lively as a cricket sometimes, & then for days mopes round half sick, she claims Mr Gee now for a sweetheart I believe. Jimmie G[aughan] is flying round Miss Anna. State & Will disclaim all pretentions to laziness, & say, they <u>needs must</u> abide their time, & worship from afar yet awhile. Willis as usual never indulges in a holiday by going to any of the picnic's &c but work, work, is the order of the day with him, he has been sick too, had one chill, & fever one or two days, is at work on the road this week. "Tug" has had two chills, & unable to work for a week. The free school commences next week (Frank teacher) want Carrie & Bobbie to go two months of the time Sept. & Oct. & Pa is trying to get through with the plowing by the date of your coming, & O! darling that time seems very long to me. "Small Sis" is coming then too. I miss her more & more each day, heard from them last week, all well, & dont suspect 'twould take a <u>Yankee</u> to <u>guess</u> that you will see her again now before I do. Of course "Mamas" so glad <u>all health</u> did'nt drive you to that "powerful" healthy town, but very glad 'tis <u>your pleasure</u> to be near "Small Sis".

  Mrs. H. Wright is on a visit to her Mother, hope to meet her at church Sunday. Mrs L. Elliott is still at Holly Sprs. teaching. I met with all her family save herself, & your <u>little</u> sweetheart, (Belle) at the picnic at Scales' Spring 14 Inst. 'Twas a cool pleasant day, & had a very enjoyable time with the old folks, & seeing the young folks "swing" &c. Mr Gee, Young Revis, & Gilder came over with Florence, they came home with us, & stayed until Sunday eve. So many asked me about you, did wish you could have been there, Mrs Earle said I must be sure to tell you to <u>go to see her</u>. Bob S. was there of course, Julia & Mr A[lston] also, when I told Bob your last message "tell John to come along", & gave vent to one of his merry he, he, laughs. Mrs Annie said, she would be glad enough to see you to give you a kiss. She has been sick with chills recently but is up at present. Mrs Fisher left for home with her little boys, was afraid to risk staying here through the sickly season, she improved much in looks, & health, but the children did not look so well. Was sorry to hear of Mr Goddard's family being sick, & hope Mrs Smythe is well in both body & mind as you said nothing to the contrary. Julia told me that her sister Mrs B. apprehended she would lose the latter. Who do you think has made us a visit? Why Old Ben, & he told me about seeing you at Hot Sprs. The old man talked as though he had a notion of coming back here to stay, but I think he had best remain up there, for he dont <u>look</u> to be <u>any older</u> than when he left here, & if anything, much better. You can judge how stirring times are in Camden when the old man remarked that "they are all dead over there, or might as well be, got so little to eat." We've been having some nice fruit, apples, peaches, no b. berry pies, but any amount of roasting years.* Uncle J. has fine watermelons & cantelopes, but ours are not yet in. Bobbie & Seymore went coon hunting one night this week, halted one in a tree too large to climb, & "Tug" did not have his gun, he's been rubbing up your large one, but says he knows you are <u>not coming</u>, yet until you specified the time. I've noticed him paying particular attention to the little gun, as though he was expecting you any day — "Little Sis" is as busy as a bee, & has but little time to run round. India B. writes to her, two or three times every week, & begging Carrie to spend a week with her. The Misses Clara & Lizzie Carlston's are at Mrs B's on a visit from their home in Tex. they have been to see Mamie too. Nelies school is out here & Mr Scales has employed her to teach his children, she expects to go up there shortly —

  You see darling I've nothing but scraps to write on this time, (but half sheet is better than none) & your "Times" must be perforce curtailed. Weather cool & pleasant, with much rain, which is not so good for the cotton, the weed is larger now than it has been for years on our place, but 'tis uncertain how the yield will be. Corn already made, & fine, what there is of it.

*"<u>Roasting</u> years" was a colloquial way of referring to ears of corn, suitable for eating on the cobs.

Forgot to tell you "Aunt Clara" has been sick, & Johnie too. Uncle J. has but few patients as yet, & those mostly Freedmen, though every one apprehends much sickness this fall. Dr Folden's wife died the 6th Inst. All send much love darling, & may God bless you ever, is the prayer of
>Your devoted Mother,
>M. E. B.

Mary E. Boddie in Ouachita Co. to her son John Rumph Boddie in St. Louis
>15th Sept. 1877

My darling boy

I too can scarcely realize that you have been home, & it all seems to me a dream, yet a very sweet one, to think over till you can come again, & be assured my boy you'l be welcomed with <u>many smiles,</u> & I will conquer my weakness sufficiently to bid you good bye, cherily & hopefully. I am gratified beyond expression darling that you will, "God willing" take to yourself a wife, & may you doubly realize all the happiness to which you look forward, & may she love you more, & more, as time rolls on, then naught can mar the peace & happiness of such a union cemeted by love. Bless her dear little self I love her already, & if you can, & will, bring my little girl to see us, feel that I can welcome her as a dear child, & part of your dear self.

I never regretted anything more my boy, than being sick the little while you were with us, but such occurrences are beyond our control, & we have to submit. And "Little Sis" did not get to play the first piece for you, when she had been practising so long with a view to please "brother." Your "friends" darling I think rather exagerated the case "of its being more like a funeral than a marriage feast on the occasion of your sister's wedding," 'tis true, I could not restrain my feelings during the impressive ceremony, but after that, no one knew by <u>outward</u> expression of <u>any kind</u> that I thought of anything save the comfort & pleasure of our guests. Have written to <u>my little girl</u> long ago, & would have written to you ere this, if your sister had not done so, & although up & about, have not felt quite well, & strong yet. But for Mamie's assistance here at home, would have had to stopped "Little Sis" from school, which I should much regret to do. We are looking for Dr C. every day now, & I feel very grateful to him for permitting Mamie to stay with us this long, which he was good enough to do because we were all sick. Pa I am very glad to say is improving daily, & the greatest trouble now, is his diet, as we cant cook anything to suit his taste, & wants. Mrs Alston & Moseley are well, Miss Anna has a young lady friend visiting her Miss Ella Bonn from Warren. Mamie has gone to see Mrs Annie for the first time since she came down, will go to see Julia [Alston] to-morrow.

Bro Will commenced picking cotton to-day, & the weather is so very hot for such work fear 'twill make him sick, he always said he'd rather do <u>any</u>, & <u>all kinds</u> of farm work in preference to picking cotton. Gilder came to see us last Saturday night & remained till Sunday eve, he sent me the <u>notice</u> that the death of D. W. Bell would effect no change in the business transactions of the house, which assurance relieved me of much apprehension, for I feared perhaps you might lose the situation & be frustrated in your arrangements at this particular time. Of course darling, I will respect your wishes in regard to <u>that letter,</u> & all others you may write, & I cant but reiterate again, & again, loving thanks for my <u>weekly messengers</u>. Hoping <u>you</u> & <u>yours</u> are well, close with much love from each one at home to our absent one.

      Your devoted Mother
      Mary E Boddie

Son, how long is Mr Reeves to keep your gun? & what instructions did you leave about it? I miss it every day from the accustomed place —

<u>Hannah</u> is to be married next Sunday, did you see her when here?

Mary E. Boddie in Ouachita Co. to her son John Rumph Boddie in St. Louis
                  Oct. 11th 1877

Darling Boy,

  Knowing you would like to hear from home, 'tis my pleasure to acknowledge the rec't of your precious letter, & assure you that all's well with us at present. Last Sabbath proved to be a day of rain with us too. Gilder was at home, walked over Saturday night, & returned next evening. "Tug" always takes him as far as the river. "Tug" is going to school again, but "Little Sis" insisted that if she went, I would get sick again doing all the work, & I regret very much that she could not continue the full term. Those of the patrons who are able to send wish Frank [Brodnax] to continue with subscription school, but he has not yet decided, dont suppose there will be a sufficient number of pupils to justify him. Rec'd a letter from "Small Sis" recently, told me "she remained over at Rock Spring on their way home on purpose to see the dearest little girl in the world, & went away more in love with her than ever." I cant express to you darling <u>how great</u> the pleasure & gratification would be to us, did circumstanses permit all, or anyone of us present on the most interesting occasion in your life, but I fear 'twill be almost next to an impossibility, however I'll be with you both in all, all, everything, save in person. My little girls' letter to me was <u>sweet</u> & <u>modest,</u> just like her own dear self, "Little Sis" said "why Mama I want to write to her myself," but we were out of both paper & ink at that time, & neither of us has written, thought probably 'twas best not to do so at present, as her time & thoughts are particularly engaged with matters more momentous, & interesting. You have chosen the month in which we were married, & now I am curious as to date, & most solicitous respecting your business relations, (if you make a change) can you come to see us once or twice during the year? I do hope so my boy, if 'twill be to your interest, but I love you well enough to sacrifice my heart wishes to your well doing. Am sure Bob S. Tommie & Capt Dee all regret not having visited the "Future Great" during the Fair. Tomie did not say why he could not go. Bob said, he could not without a pocket full & Mrs Annie told me Dee was very anxious, she believed would have gone, if Bob had gone with him.

One more household pet to Bob, & Annie, boy (not yet named) born 8 Inst. Julia A & Mrs Scales spent last Saturday with us, asked to be remembered to you, Julia has been urging me time & again to make a trip with her to visit her Uncle House Coleman, Bro. Henry, & Mamie talked of it previous to Mr. A's last illness, & I promised thinking there was so little probability of her doing so, but recently she asked me again, & I thought to myself, what a coincidence 'twould be if I could only happen to be there just at the right time. O how happy twould make me, but that if is an obsticle too stupendous to get over, & I can only indulge in thoughts, pleasant thoughts about it.

Atalie has been spending the past three weeks with us, sends her love to "Cousin Johnie," says she dont want to go home & hopes they wont send for her this week. Hav'nt seen Uncle J since the reception of your last, think he'l be going to Town about Sat. "Cousin B[ettie]" can say that was me at R. S. but I cant say if she own to catching a beaux, or not, have not seen her only at church since she came home. — This in confidence son, & make no mention of it in any of your letters — Mr. J[im] Gaughn has not prepared his cosey cot in vain, as Miss Anna has consented to share it with him, she told me "he had asked, & got Pa's consent" so nothing remains but the all important trousseau to be complete. Think all the family are well pleased with the match, & the marketable boys will have to hie out of this region to find a fair lassie. Florence is going up to Tulip on a visit with one of Mr L[on] Dunlaps daughters. Willie went to mill this week, all relatives well. He has some six or seven hands now picking cotton, & Tug says he'l make one next month. I came near forgetting Carrie's commision, which is, to beg you will please price some cloth suitable for a waterproof* & the number of yards 'twill require to make one for herself. Not the finest quality (as that would contrast too greatly with her other apparel) & the color to suit your own taste. As to the quantity necessary, you can consult some of your lady friends (Mrs S. probably) as that depends entirely on the width of the cloth. She thinks you can get a good article, & cheaper than she can in Camden, if you can do so, please let her know in my next letter, so she can send the money by Post Office order. "For all of which trouble to Brother says she'l

*The *Random House Unabridged Dictionary* lists in its third definition of this word as "Chiefly Brit. a raincoat or other outer coat impervious to water."

be greatly obliged."

I was so glad to hear of our dear little ones' visit to your city as you were darling to have her company, for I knew how greatly you would enjoy it, bless her heart, wish I could see her too. Times here are quiet & lovely, weather pleasant as can be, the forest trees beginning to assume the beautiful hues of Autumn, & I do think it to be the most lovely season of the year. Am happy & thankful too darling that you are enjoying such fine health, & with much work, & all the leisure hours spent with your lady friends the <u>time</u> will <u>speed</u> rapidly till you can claim your "better half" for all time.

With kind regards from the girls & boys, & much love from all the family,

      Your devoted Mother
      Mary E. Boddie

Mary Elizabeth Boddie in Ouachita Co. to her son John Rumph Boddie in St. Louis.

                    Nov 5 '77

My own dear boy,

I know you will wonder what "Mama" means by making use of <u>such paper</u>, so will tell you it means business, & having no other, & no opportunity for procuring any in time to reach you by specified date (10) hope you excuse it. Will enclose in this Post Office Order for $5.75. Carrie rec'd the goods all right, & is the proudest child you ever saw, being well pleased in every respect, quality, color, & price, & returns loving thanks for your kindness. Says she will send Bro a bunch of his little favourite (violets) as a peace offering token, if he will say no more about the <u>flowers</u>. Am happy to hear that you had a day of leisure to spend with <u>some one</u>, knowing how well you enjoyed it, & you need not boast so independantly of having, "some one" to pet you for I am as proud of the fact as you are & 'twil depend somewhat on your own good behavior old darling if <u>she pets</u> you much or not.

I spent nearly a week in Town recently, for the purpose of seeings friends & making preperation to be with you, & <u>my</u> little girl by the 13. Gilder handed me your letter of that week advising me of the postponement, which news was rather favorable than otherwise, & giving us more time but the weather has proved to be so unfavorable, water courses up, & bad condition of the roads in consequence of so much rain, has marred the prospects considerably, & will I fear prevent us making the trip at all, which I shall very much regret, Julia too will be as greatly disappointed for she is very anxious to go. Have not seen her since rec'ng your letter, as I was in Town, & all last week, she was over there.

Constant application to sewing work caused my weak eye to inflame

& it culminated in a rising of the duct leading from the inner corner of the eye. The inflamation, swelling &c have all subsided, & my eye is nearly well again, though Dr P. says that eye will always be a weak, & weeping one. Should not be surprised at all if in the press of business, & the greater press of <u>happiness</u> just now that you did not <u>forget</u> your <u>birthday</u> this time, well I did not, but thought of, & wondered where you were &c all the while sitting here in the corner nursing my eye which was at its worst that day. Did not think for a moment that you would forget me darling after being made "the happiest of men" & would not have grumbled to have been deprived of my <u>weekly treasures</u>, but the assurance from you that I will not is doubly dear, & appreciated more than I can tell you.

Dont know if Geo. R[umph] has told you that Mittie has <u>a boy</u>, that he is a fine <u>one</u> I bear witness, & Mr R[ucks] is as proud as can be, "Cousin" too. They propose to call him Louis Taylor or Geo. Kellam not yet decided. <u>Miss</u> Anna has named Annie's baby Claude. Aunt Nelie is with Anna, to stay until the consumation of her marriage which is appointed to be 20 Dec. Another one of Mary Love's son's is to be married this month Dick L. I forget to whom, none of the girls that I know.

Well son about the farm work, have picked out seven or eight bales, & packed two. Too wet to haul any from the field, & if the present rainy weather continues dont know when the balance can be gathered. Uncle J. says we've never had such [a] fall season since 58 when he had only 5 days picking done during the month of Oct. Uncle John & Co. expect to start on a camp hunt next Friday. Bob S. is going this time. Little <u>Junior</u> has called me John Boddie ever [since] you were here, 'tis realy amusing to hear him he talks so plainly now. Pa & Will are busy looking after the stock, the bottom is under water & if 'tis raining up the river will have a big overflow. Will have to beg you excuse paper writing & all as I have the use of one eye only, the other being bandaged yet. With much love from each one, & mine especially to <u>my</u> little girl, remain

Your devoted Mother
[Mary E. Boddie]

Mary Elizabeth Boddie in Ouachita Co. to her son and daughter-in-law John Rumph and Cornelia Smoker Boddie in St. Louis

Dec. 6 1877

Darling children,

My not being witness of the ceremony which united my first born, & his <u>precious one</u> will <u>ever be</u> a life long <u>regret</u>, but the past cannot be recalled & we wont talk of it. May your lives flow on in one continual stream of unalloyed bliss, with hearts of thankfulness to Him who so blessed you, &

should sorrow ever come may it be borne without murmur, remembering that none of all His creatures are entirely exempt. Pa sends love & congratulations to you both, is more than pleased that his boy has secured the wife of his heart, & we all rejoice in your happiness darling, <u>could not</u>, if we would, help loving one so dear to you, & who has reposed such great trust in our boy who we believe will merit it.

We found all well in our arrival home Monday morn, staid at Uncle J's Sunday night, he expressed much regret that he did not go, came off the camp hunt 23rd & was sick several days with cold. 'Twas <u>our</u> intention to have gone on to Mamie's first but did not recieve your letters in time, both the one from Hope & Arkad[elphia] reaching me by <u>same mail</u> 20th & Gilder sent them over immediately but 'twas then impossible for us to have started a day earlier than the following Sunday, <u>as all the creeks</u> were overflowed & impassable. We went out to Mamie's the eve of the day you & my little girl left, & just imagine, if you can her <u>great disappointment</u> when told that you were married & gone. Never rec'd your letter till after our arrival there, a most unfortunate occurrance, for she & Dr C. would certainly have been "on hand," then, the greatest of all mishaps would not have occured. Your dear letter of 3 Inst. has just been handed me, & I rejoice in your happiness darling, feeling assured that my little daughter will take the best care of you, love her ever so much for telling me so. You have the love & trust of a precious little wife now my boy, & to contribute all in your power to her comfort & happiness will be your greatest pleasure. Am glad that you board with Mrs S. & can imagine how contented & happy you both look in your cosy little home.

Must tell you I am quite relieved that you did not write to "Small Sis" about her being absent, feared you would censure her unjustly, as <u>in</u> my letter of 26 Ult. Told me she "never heard from brother except through mine & Gilder's letters." Please darling [do] not think too hard of Judge C. & connexion, as I dont think, & would not like to believe they erred intentionally. Must write to "Small Sis" by same mail I send this, & am very busy with household affairs &c.

"Little Sis" managed admirably during my absence, considering she had every thing to do, cooking, milking, house work, &c &c. Know son you will be very sorry to hear that our helper & esteemed <u>family servant</u> is <u>no more</u> but for her death Carrie could have been gratified in the dearest wish of her heart, that of going with us to see brother & sister. Becky was taken sick 24th Oct. & died 14th Nov. with Typhoid fever, we all regret her death so much, & indeed to us her place can never be filled.

Had quite an unexpected call this noon, Geo. R. on his way home from a short trip on this side. Of course <u>you</u> & <u>little darling</u> were the principle topic, said Jennie spoke of writing you a congratulatory letter &c &c - recollect how you teased her when here, so look out. They rejoice in a girl baby this time, & Geo. says 'tis ugly, & have decided on no name yet, as it must be pretty due to redeem its ugliness, Mabel, Annie Louise, is spoken of & cant you suggest half dozen or more from which to select?

Guess Uncle J. will tell you all about the hunt, & deer slain, the farmers are very busy now trying to finish up cotton picking, had so much rain & cold weather that not one are through, & the advent of Christmas is not spoken of, only amoung the young folks. Miss Anna will be married 20th. Miss Nellie E[lliot], Miss Lula A[very], Mr Allis M[oseley] & Mr L. Proctor are to be the attendants. Mr & Mrs G[aughan] a dining the next day. Mr Moseley is in Texas on business for Merril & is not looked for home till after Christmas.

Have a letter to answer from Sis Hattie, & wont she be surprised to hear that you are married. By the by Bro Will said he <u>wanted</u> to <u>claim</u> a <u>kiss</u> from his sister C.* but <u>so many were kissing</u> her feared to ask. "Tug" asked many questions, said he did wish he could see Bud Johnie & his wife. Good bye my children, all send much love to you both

Devotedly your Mother
Mary E. Boddie

*Willis Boddie apparently was the only family member to attend the wedding of John R. Boddie and Cornelia Smoker. It seems there was some mix-up in the mails which accounted for the other family members not attending.

George Boddie Rumph in Ouachita Co. to John Rumph Boddie in St. Louis
Dec. 23rd, 1877

Dear John

I had hoped to find a favorable opportunity to write you a long and dear old letter upon this the most important epoch in your life, but it seems the fates combined have willed otherwise & been against me, to ennumerate would be too tedious & unreadable at this time. Think not therefore that I feel, or have felt any less interest in your happiness because I have not spoken before & sooner. My best wishes & love has ever attended you through the long years of childhood & youth & manhood & now that you have assumed new duties & a new life in which your highest expectations & dearest hopes, are that you have bettered the old, & made yourself a happier man. My solicitude is increased, for you, that you have indeed done wisely & for the best. I know your little angel of a wife will indeed do her part. Although I have not as yet the pleasure of her acquaintance, friends - mutual - have glowingly represented her many virtures of mind & heart. So nothing surely remains but that exercise of good sense. You have shown yourself possessed through the past to bring about that real happiness of which you have each so fondly dreamed. Jennie asks me to send her greetings of love & wishes for your happiness. She desired to write you one letter, at least upon this occasion, congratulating you upon snapping the cord that had led you so near to the threshold of bachelordom, but the cares & duties of attending three angels, — but now thoroughly disguised — in the form of two uncompromisingly mischeivous boys & a small baby girl, — have not granted the time to do so.

We have not named our baby girl yet — can not find a name pretty enough as a matter of course. Some of the family suggests letting you name it. I gave them your name for it, without consulting you but they seem still dissatisfied, the name of Cornelia. Anyway the names canvassed for the "coming lady" are Mable, Virginia, Alice, Miriam &c.

We are having gloomy weather today raining, steady & slow. Christmas promises but little enjoyment ahead, for the party going & merry making members of our community. In town a grand ball given by the Social Dance Club, comes off at their hall. Elliott Block, Uncle George & family take dinner this year at Fathers. Several are going over from town also, and the girls over the river will visit their friends in Camden during the holidays & stop with us & partake of our Christmas offering during the time. Rucks & Sister Mittie are to dine with us Christmas day, as we are not going over to home. How very delighted we should all be to have you & cousin Cornelia with us then. Cousin Mamie will not be down from Clark [Co.] either I presume.

Christmas comes now as it did long ago, but with all its preparations for enjoyment it comes, to me with sadness. We find ourselves doing the honors our fathers done then, our flock gradually resettling & scattered.

Growing older, growing wiser, as we linger in this vale trusting too, that we are growing better. As we're nearing to the grave, I know you will regret to learn that Mrs. Bracy is not expected to live. She thinks also that she cannot survive her illness and wanted to talk with Mr. Bracy about dying, but he was so overcome with anguish that she could not.

Business is assuming quite a hopeful aspect. Camden has been crowded with cotton wagons since 1st Dec. A greater part already received is cotton that has heretofore gone to the railroads & other points. I have to work at night to keep my books up. Anticipate for January & Feby. the largest we have had since the Rail Road was built. Dr. J. T. Shannon has decided not to move from here, has bought out the brick store occupied by Paschal Bros & Co. from Jno I Silliman & settled himself down for all time. Collections although somewhat late will be good. As I have about spent the evening writing sundry letters, & it is growing dark, will have to cease.

We send much love from wife, & little ones to cousins Nealie & yourself. With often & believe me ever

      Yours truly
      Geo. B. Rumph

George Gildersleeve Boddie in Ouachita Co. to his brother John Rumph Boddie in St. Louis.

January 3rd 1877

Dear Bro.

There is no subject which I dislike more to name to you, than the one I am just about to enter upon; for it seems that I cant write to you only on business — But nevertheless I hope you wont think hard of me. Dr Pace is closing out his business in Camden & going to Memphis. And the probability is that I'll be thrown out of employment, or at best I would be able to make more than a bear support even if I stay where I am. Several parties are negotiating for the Drug-Store, but no definite settlement yet. I dont think whoever buys him out will be able to keep more than one clerk and of course they'll give Buddie Smith the preference as he is an old druggist & has had Dr Pace's business in his hands for the last five years. However, there is nothing like trying to find out whether or not I can better myself. If you are not too busy & will oblige me by writing me a letter of advice I'll be very glad. You know my business qualifications, ability &c. Therefore what prospect is there for me in St Louis? I think I am competant to take a traveling position, or any other position in any good Drug Store & give perfect satisfaction. I dont mean to say that I am proficient in Pharmacy or a chemist by any means. I can prepare any of Dr Pace's prescriptions or any that comes to Camden. I am not perfect but I can say I am not like I <u>use to be</u> afraid to take hold. I believe in the old saying or song, "You'll never get rich until you learn to paddle your own canoe," which is now my style. I may be employed here through this month, but cant reconcile myself with uncertainties of staying longer. I would dislike very much to give up the idea of being a Druggist, but if I cant get such employment I am willing to do any thing in the mercantile business than to till the soil, for I think it is the hardest way of making a living. Well I guess you are tired of this. I spent last Sunday at home the first time in over a month, found them all well. We are having quite a dull Christmas dont think I ever spent a duller one. Didnt go to any of the parties over the river or to the ball, which, I guess you see an account of in the Beacon. Beautiful weather for now, but I cant say any longer for its been snowing all day, but melts nearly as fast as it falls. Business was a little flushed before Christmas but very dull now. Nothing more of interest in the way of news to write. Let me hear from you as soon as possible. Give my <u>best love</u> to Sister Cornelia.*

I remain as ever,

Your brother,
G. G. Boddie

*This reference to Sister Cornelia, John Boddie's bride, makes the date of January 1877 most suspect, since they did not marry until just before Christmas in 1877. Possibly Gilder suffers from the time lapse which many of us suffer from at the beginning of a new year.

George Gildersleeve Boddie in Ouachita Co. to his brother John Rumph Boddie in St. Louis

Jan 16th 1878

Dear Bro:

Your kind letter 10th inst, I assure you gave much satisfaction in regard my welfare. I feel under m[uch] obligations for your kind advice.

Dr Pace sold out to Dr Bragg and I am, as I expected, left on the wing for a new employment. Dr Bragg wanted me two months only, & wont give me the least inducement even for that short time. Only offers me the same I was getting, which was $16 2/3 & board per month. I think it was an imposition, as I know my business well enough to be of good service, & I [did not] accept. I'll go over home this eve or tomorrow.

I want to go up to Arkadelphia & so see Sister Mamie the first of next week, if possible. Is there any probability of my meeting you that I am down, if so dispatch, at my expense, to me at Camden in care Buddie Smith. I think you are right in regarding my being competent or experienced enough to act as traveling salesman. I'll be willing though, to try any thing rather than farm or do nothing. I am as the old saying is, "Jack of all trades, & good at none" but it seems to me if I keep trying I certainly will strike my talent after a while. I couldnt have been treated better by any body than I have by Dr Pace & Family. I havent any doubt but what I would have staied with him if he had remained in business. I certainly would accept your generous proposition in regard to Cr[edit] but unfortunately I havent got that much capital to begin on. I think it would be the most profitable of any thing I could do. No news of interest to write. I would like so much to see my new Sister Nelia. Ask her to send me her picture. Cousin Mittie's baby has been very sick with Pneumonia, but considerably better now. Hoping to hear from you soon —

Your brother
G. G. Boddie

P. S. I dont mean to quit the Drug business if I am so unfortunate as not to get a position in that line, but will study it in connection, if possible with what I am doing. Excuse haste & cold hands.

G.G.B.

Susan Morton, called Mammy by Cornelia and Clara, in Autauga Co., Alabama, to Cornelia Dickson in Ouachita Co.

January 25, 1878

Dear Miss Cornelia,

  I received your letter a few days since. I was glad to hear from you. I am living with Mr. Dave Caver and doing very well. All my children have left me. I have two of Leamus children and one of Ellen's, Susan, Harriet, and Johnie. Laura is cooking for Mr. King in Dallas City. Ellen is living on Linsey Davis old place. Levi lived with Ira Nunn at Mrs. Love's place until he died last August with brain fever. He was trying to make money enough to carry him to Arkansas. Paten is married and living with Dick Love on the Steel plantation. Ellen has only three children. Her health is good, sends her love to you. Jerry and Charity have bought a place in the Piny woods. His little daughter by Lucy Watson waits on him. He has been sick a long time. Caroline has married and lives on the old Kirkland place. She was sick with fever all summer. She has no children. She is doing very well. All your old friends among the colored folks are well. Hannah Lassiter sends her love to you. Give my love to Miss Clarissa and kiss all her children for me. I would like to see them all so much. I would come to Arkansas if I could get all the children to go with me, but I hate to leave my children. They are all I have to wait on me when I am sick. Little Tommie is in North Alabama. He is not satisfied and wants to go to Arkansas and live with you. Bosie has run away from his father. He is trying to get to me. I want you to send me their ages so that I can get them from him. Tom drinks and is not good to them. I have a bad cold and cough. You must write to me as soon as you can and tell me all about you all and how much I could make if I came out there. Tell Hannah, Judy, (Ephrain daughter) is married and living in Summerfield. Her husband is mean to her. She is not doing well since she left Mrs. Lavender. Give my love to Henry's wife and children and July Ann and all of our old black ones. Give my love to Miss Mollie and Mars George and all their children. I want to see them all. John sends his respects to you and Menses too and wants to be remembered to you. Write to me soon and I will write you a long letter next time.

      Yours truly,
      Susan Morton

*"From Susan Morton, my Black Mammy".

*Cornelia wrote this note on the envelope containing Susan Morton's letter.

Mary E. Boddie in Ouachita Co. to her son John Rumph Boddie in St. Louis
Feb. 2nd 1878

My dear boy,

If your trip in old Ark. could only extend this far how happy it would make me, but your dear letters are a source of unfailing comfort to your old "Mama" and I'm certain you fully appreciate the feeling, now that you are seperated from your darling Pet with only that dear privilege accorded you. I would write to my dear little daughter every week of your absence my boy, if I thought 'twould detract one iota from her loneliness, but apart from such, an assurance of her mother's love, know I could not make them interesting, or even worthy her perusal.

Have you rec'd no word from Uncle J. yet? He staid with us a night the week I wrote to little daughter. Said, "The fact is, I'm out of pens & paper. can't keep any for the girls, have told Geo (B) to write, as he could do it better, & told him what to say to Johnnie for me." Before he left next morning asked to see your letter, & after reading, "Well the fact of the business is Aunt Mollie I must write, will get another supply of pens, paper, & I must write."

"Little Sis" went home with Florence last Sat. & staid until Mon. The latter is as lively, & full of chat as ever says Sis Bettie don't despair now, but is quite elated with the hope that there's a chance for her, since Miss Julia Clark has married. Miss Anna is surely wed and rejoices in the title of Mrs. All the boys express themselves to be quite willing to follow your precept & example, i.e. "trot double" but sorry to say they can scarcely trot in "single harness" at present. They make all the amends they can in enjoying the young ladies' company as often as possible by getting up parties. I have had four since Christmas, & one was to have come off last Thurs. but for the high water. Bettie's and Floy's has been postponed too owing to the bad weather.

What do you think when I tell you, that I attended a party at Clara's last week? Well, I did, & enjoyed it "muchly". Had not seen Clara since I saw you & as she expressed it was nearly dead to see "Sis Mollie" & that occasion was the first opportunity I had of going. Clara's health is not good & has no buggy horse now is the reason she could not come to see me as usual.

Pa and Will packed their last bale of cotton Thurs. eve. 20 & that staple* has tumbled down, down, & with it our hopes down to "Zero" but we'l be up and doing again. Having the cotton to haul off to be packed detered them from finishing up the crop weeks ago. Bob S. made 64 got 10/ is behind $300. "Uncle B[illy]" says he dosn't understand it and Bob ought to quit farming, ie not employ such a large force.

Know son you will do all in your power to assist Gilder to a situation. He is very loathe to give up the business in which he embarked, but says,

*Staple refers to the length and fineness of cotton fiber. The price of cotton is gauged according to the staple.

will go to the cotton patch again before he'l remain idle. 'Twas his misfortune that the house changed hands, & as only one clerk was retained, of course Mr L. had the precidence. Pa thinks Dr. B. is keeping the place open for his bro Milton, & that is exactly what he should do. That Dr. P[ace] leaves Camden is a source of much regret to his host of friends.

Your bro Gilder spent one week at home, then hired a horse from Town & started 23 Ult. to see his sister. The eve of the first day's travel his horse was taken sick, & died, now if that was not the acme of all misfortunes, don't know what would be. Will enclose the note he wrote to me, for you to see what he says.

Have heard from Sis Hattie only once since I came from Arkadelphia, she did not then know of your marriage. All were well with them except our old time servant, Henry. His illness is caused from general debility & old age. Don't believe I told you that Hannah married, yes & lives in a distant neighborhood. Old "Aunt Nina" says, "I's comming to see Marse Johnie & his wife when dey comes, & you must let me know."*

*There is no signature on this letter.

Mary E. Boddie in Ouachita Co. to her daughter in-law Cornelia Smoker Boddie in St. Louis

February 5th 1878

My dear little daughter,

How do you do, & how are you getting on since our old darling left? lonely much? Yes! what with a house full of pleasant company, your music, books to while away these short days. Yes indeed all, & more than that dont compensate for his absence. Well little darling he'l soon return. Providence pemitting, then in the joy of his presence you forget the past loneliness, & all will be well with you both, for he found it to be very hard indeed to leave his little wife, & I felt so sorry for him. "Little Sis" & I are alone, most of the time, an occasional suitor now & then to vary the everyday routine, & it is a multiplicity of work which keeps us very busy, yet she finds some little time to devote to her music, says, ask sister what pieces she plays; what songs she sings; & often wonders "if brother keeps you at the piano half a night playing for him as he used to do Cousin."

Gilder had the pleasure of hearing the extraordinary performances of "Blind Tom" who gave a musical exhibition in Arkadelphia last week, says such rendering of music he never expected to hear & to give a description of it is utterly impossible. Mamie & Sis Carrie* were [there to]. I dont suppose there were many, lovers of music or not, who did not avail themselves of that opportunity of seeing & hearing the "musical prodigy." Gilder spent two days with his sister & Dr. C. dont like the country at all & cant conceive how they can content themselves to live in such an out of the [way]

*This "Sis Carrie" refers to John Boddie's Sister Carrie, not to Sis Mollie's "Sis Carrie," as is usually the case.

place. Dr. Coleman purposes moving to Spoonville this Spring, & give his attention entirely to his profession. Dr. McCollum has moved to Arka[delphia]. During the short time Gilder remained there said he had the pleasure of making the acquaintance of your father & bro's. was very much in hopes to have met his brother but was disappointed.

 Well little darling this is a dull region from which to glean anything to interest you therefore just excuse this duller communication. I only write because I love you & our old darling drew largely on his imagination when he said write to my <u>Pet</u> Mama she will be so lonely as though any letter but his could make amends for his absence. Little daughter's letter to me has not yet been rec'd. This leaves all well.

 With much love from each of us,
     Your devoted Mother
     Mary E. Boddie

Cornelia Dickson in Ouachita Co. to her friend Rebecca Underwood in Autauga Co.

              February 11, 1878

Dear Becca,

 Your most welcome message was received about a week ago. I had begun to think I was completely deserted by everyone in Alabama. I had heard something of a report out there of my death! but did not credit it for an instant and supposed no one else would. My health is greatly improved since last summer, and I assure I have no idea of dying while I see anyone else living! I have always had a horror of that last act on the stage of life. Life may lose some of its "bloomingway" but I accept it and cling to it with a tenacity of human nature. Becca, I have missed your interesting scrolls although I have been pleasantly engaged in the interim.

 At the close of my three month's schools, I employed myself assisting Miss Anna Moseley, a friend of mine, in preparing for her wedding, which happy event took place the twentieth of December. She married Mr. James Gaughan, a staunch young farmer in the community. I have visited them once and spent several days. They seem perfectly happy in their new relation. The wedding and reception were succeeded by several Christmas sociables, enjoyable, particulary so since the neighborhood has credit for possessing the "prettiest and nicest girls and most moral and refined young men in the country."

 It seems the Texas fever is not confined to Alabama. Several from this neighborhood have gone to seek their fortunes in the Lone Star State. Some who went out prospecting came back content to remain where they are. I sincerely trust that Ella Hermann may realize her bright expectations. To what portion of Texas have they gone?

I was pleased to hear that the school at Ivy Creek is in flourishing condition. I am at Dr. Rumph's now, teaching his two little girls, Attalie and Eugenia. They are sweet and learn rapidly. Tell Rebecca they are Sallie's* children. Clara is not enjoying very good health. I have not seen Sis Mollie in over a month. Carrie came to see us several weeks ago. We have had so much wet weather this winter that a portion of the time, the roads were impassable. They are still in a rough condition.

Your letter contained a great deal that was interesting to me. You need not be afraid of writing too long ones.

All join me in sending love to you.

Cornelia S. Dickson

*"Sallie" refers to Sallie Gildersleeve, second wife of John B. Rumph.

Cornelia Dickson in Ouachita Co. to Susan Morton, her black mammy, in Autauga Co.

March 1878

Dear Mammy,

I received your letter several weeks ago, was very glad to hear from you all and that you are doing well. Hope that you are well of your cough and Uncle Jerry has recovered his health by this time. But you are growing old and cannot expect to be as well as formerly. I was very sorry to hear Levi died and know you grieve to lose your only son.

I have been waiting for an opportunity to go to see Clara before writing, but it seems that something always happens to prevent, so I will not wait any longer. She has a new baby girl a month old now, and I have never seen it. She has been sick too having chills & trouble with her breast. Last week Mr Dunlap was very sick also. He is subject to cramp colic & came near dying with it a week ago yesterday, before brother John, who was from home, could get to him. The children are all well.

I was sorry to hear that Tom Caver is doing so badly, am afraid he will come to some bad end. If Harriets children will stay with you it would be the best for them and you, for you could raise them up right, and see after them, while they are old enough now to support you well, and take the place of your own sons. Their ages were set down in Ma's bible and I left it with Cousin Mary, or Sis Carrie I forget which. Tommie is nineteen years old as well as I remember and Bose is two years younger & Harry two years younger than Bose. Why Mammy you are too old to do much toward a support yourself, but with those boys if they are smart & steady would make you a support anywhere. I would be the gladdest in the world if you lived out here, if you could feel satisfied but I am afraid you would not be at first anyhow & could not get back; if I had a home of my own it would be different and I would be anxious for you to come and I would not want you to leave Uncle Jerry behind sick. Provisions are cheaper now than they have ever been but money is scarce. Yet everybody seems to be doing well. <u>Good hands</u> are offered thirteen dollars a month and some get more. A great many good clever colered people live all around here on their own land, drive their own wagons & teams to Camp meetings & fishfrys, ride good horses & pay a three & four hundred dollar store account every year. Brother John's Ben Franklin are among that number and he had three hundred dollars left over after settlement. But you did not know him. He is a Carolina negro. Old Uncle Ben Boddie is living yet, but his memory is almost gone, he hardly remembers living in Alabama. He makes a support waiting about the stores in town & working gardens &c. I have not seen Hannah since she married. Will tell her about Judy when I see her. Polly, old Aunt Jinnys daughter is doing the washing for brother John's family this year. She has eight children, But is rather trifling & lives "from hand to mouth," her husband left her. I do not know what ever became of Henry's wife, but his only boy died several years ago. July Ann has been dead a long time.

Sis Mollie spent a night & day with us last week. Was glad to hear from you. Sends her love to you. I am staying at brother Johns now teaching his two little girls with two others of the neighborhood. They learn rapidly. Bettie has been in town six weeks, will not be at home until May I guess, as George has gone to New Orleans to be gone several weeks. Mittie named her boy Tom Louis, calls him Louie. Jennie calls her girl Ethel Annie. Mittie is coming out to spend a week before long, her baby is not in good health.*

*Note: This letter is unsigned in the ledger.

Mary Elizabeth Boddie in Ouachita Co. to her son John Rumph Boddie in St. Louis

March 27th 1878

My own dear boy,

Though writing seems to strain my ailing member, even more than sewing work, yet I would fain pen a few lines myself to assure you of my excellent health in every other respect, to thank you again & again for your <u>precious</u> letters. If I requested it, Gilder would willingly write for me, but he looks to be so tired after plowing all day that I dislike to ask him, "Little Sis" refuses because <u>she knows</u> her bud Gilder would write, 'twould require a powerful incentive to induce Pa to do so, & Willie <u>loves</u> to write about as well as little daughter. I awaited your letter of last week with much anxiety, & was so glad to learn that little daughter was well again, & since the ability of both of you have been tested in the capacity of nurses, sincerely hope that the occasions will be very infrequent for either of you to acquire any more experience in that line. I could but smile my boy at your expression "playing nurse," but was not at all surprised that little daughter pronounced you an <u>excellent</u> one, for love can accomplish wonders. "Little Sis" takes the kindest care of me, & indeed they all vie with each other in kind offers when anything is the matter with "Mama" which tends greatly to mitigate the pains of illness. I hear from "Small Sis" every week or two, told me she has commenced a letter to her sister two or three times but somehow she could never finish one, that "if brother had <u>answered</u> my <u>two last</u> to him 'twould have been a pleasant duty, but dont know when I shall hear from them unless bro. writes."

Dr. C. & Mamie are not living at the farm this year, & she expresses much content for the present that they are domiciled in a little "Log Cabin" (but not "in the lane") about 9 miles from Arkadelphia, 5 from the farm, & 4 from Spoonville. Am very glad to know that Mamie has a neighbour (Mrs Malcolm) living within call, as Dr C. is attending to his practice altogether, & she will not be so lonely during his absence feeling that some one is near by. I guess little daughter thinks that such a life in the woods would be insupportable, & you such an absentee, as it is dont blame her for rebelling.

I have not been in town since your flying visit home, hear from there every week or two. Mittie's boy still has spells of croup, & Mr Rucks told Pa Tom was so accustomed to the sight of spoon he would laugh, & <u>open his mouth</u> the moment one was presented. Bettie has been spending the past four weeks with Mittie & Jennie, & having a pleasant time generally. Florence spent a week with Mrs Anna G[aughan] not long ago. Nelie is teaching at Uncle J's & has two other pupils Mittie Patterson & Amanda Head, who board there. Uncle J's time is divided now between gardening & turkey hunting, has killed one, he as well as many others regretted very much not seeing you when here, & please tell me son <u>when</u> you can make that other promised visit, as Dr C. purposes coming for me to go to see Mamie, & I would not be away when you & little daughter [Cornelia Smoker Boddie] come for anything in the world. Her Father's & little Mamie's visit was very opportune, made her forget all about chills & chill time too I guess.

We have had, & are still having the most beautiful Spring weather, the trees fast donning their robes of green. Apple, peach, plum, pear trees &c all blossomed out & not a frost as yet to mar the prospect for a fine fruit crop. Cant help but think that you & little darling miss so much of the beauties of nature pent up among brick walls this delightful season of the year. One or two farmers have corn up & nearly ready [for] the plow, Pa & Will are through planting & are preparing cotton land, I think their experience of last year is inducing them to plant more corn, & less cotton, the latter is a very expensive crop to make at present prices & having to buy corn appears to me to be a very unprofitable way of farming. "Tug" & his Abbot mule is in <u>harness again,</u> he says his appetite gains on him every day, thinks Bud Johnie would want more than a lunch for his dinner if he had to plough all day. Gilder has taken Pa's place for the present, & the latter is working in the garden. Know Gilder prefers other employment, & I regret so much you can give no encouragement in respect to obtaining a place, as I should regret still more his leaving this country for any other save near you.

We will have preaching at our church next sabbath for the first time this year, & only every fifth Sunday thereafter. I spent one day recently with Clara, Uncle J. D. was suffering with pain in his side, grumbling much because incapacitated from work, John B. D. grows fast, & his Pa says will soon be big enough to work. Uncle J. calls the baby Rachel, as Clara has'nt decided on any name yet, the baby is three months old. Mrs. Annie is spending this week with her sister Mrs Pace, Bob is busy on his farm. Mr Steele is living there again this year. "Uncle Billy" [Stone] has very few hands, & is not cultivating all his place. Maj Moseley* & boys are getting on as usual & Capt. A[llis]'s mania (everyone calls it) for propagating fruit trees &c is unabated.

"Little Sis" & I have a lively time trying to manage the unbroken cows & young calves, both are afraid of them so you can imagine how we progress. Pa sold two to the butcher last week. Carrie was rejoiced to see the one go that Becky could never break. Willie lost a few of his pigs in the last overflow, had to go in the bottom four days in succession to get them out, has 50 in all. We are needing rain the farmers say, had a slight shower last night, but I always dread an overflow & hope not to have sufficient for that. Well darling boy there is not anything new or interesting to tell you so will bid you good bye hoping that you & little daughter may always enjoy the greatest of His blessings — good health. With much love to you & yours from each one of us,

*"Maj Moseley refers to Elijah Moseley, father of Miss Anna, Mr Allis, and Mr Marvin.

yours devotely.
M. E. B.

Know you will excuse this scratching my boy, yet doubt if I could do any better with such pens as I have, tried the one Carrie uses but 'twas no better. Forgot to tell you that many of our friends ask about you, & to be remembered with kind regards. I have Gilder to see to your guns, that they are in order, & Pa persuaded him today at noon to try the turkeys tomorrow betimes. goodbye.

Cornelia Dickson in Ouachita Co. to the daughter of her friend Rebecca Underwood in Autauga Co.

May 3rd 1878

Dear Becca,

Your very dear letter was received a week since, not however, before its arrival had been eagerly anticipated and each time as the answer from the office "No letter from Ala" greeted me, I would think, well, next week I will surely get one. You speak of your Style of visiting being comical. That style is quite common out here, you & Julia were more fortunate than Anna [Moseley] & myself. Your ride calling ours to mind. The horse scared & springing to one side, Anna lost her equilibrium, going over backward & as she went threw her arm across my shoulders, turned me such a complete summersault from the saddle that set me on my feet while she rolled under the horse. I had never released the bridle & when she sprang up unhurt, the woods rang with peal on peal of laughter; as good luck favored, no one saw us, & with the assistance of a convenient stump we scrambled up again & continued our ride. Florence says "If you want to behold grace pictured, see two large girls on a little mule, and it trying its best to double up & let them fall, but finds it is laboring under dificulties, and concludes to race out in an old field, & regardless of whip or rein show indifference by quietly grazing. Why Miss Becca don't know anything about grace on horseback." But you must not think that our only mode of locomotion. Wagons are the principal conveyances & with spring seats being most convenient & durable.

May is here again in all its lavishing beauty and fragrance, not least among her treasures is the profusion of fruit. On the first we enjoyed our third mess of strawberries. Brother John has taken great care to procure a delicious variety. They are very large, rather long, of a bright pink, & so mellow that they melt in your mouth. But not quite so early as Mrs. Brodnaxes. She brought us our first mess on the 22nd of April, it being Florence & little Hattie's birthday. We had baked a cake, whipped up some sillabub & invited a few friends to dine with us. Oh Becca how I wish for you & Julia sometimes to be with us, But altogether I know you would not enjoy being out here unless you could adapt yourself to any & all circumstances. Sometimes I become very discouraged and am almost tempted to "commit matrimony." Just for a change you know, provided always I could find someone else in the same mind.

Your letter was very interesting to me Becca and your mistake I thought merely a lapsus lingue* that you wrote Bonaparte instead of Wellington. Particularly as Bonaparte figured so signally in the defeat. I should have mentioned it to you but feared you would feel mortified & think I was inclined to critasize & knowing my own imperfections, I feel more ready to overlook the errors of others.

Bettie is still in town — will probably not get home in several weeks. I do not remember that I told you that Proctor & Rumph had dissolved co-partnership. George expected to remove to some other locality, but was offered great inducements to remain in Camden. So he is now established in a new firm Rumph & Gee, & Bettie prolonged her stay to be with Jennie during his absence in New Orleans at the same time.*

*Lapsus Linguae is a Latin phrase meaning "slip of the tongue."

*The ledger abruptly ends this letter at this point.

Cornelia Kimball Smoker Boddie in St. Louis to her husband John Rumph Boddie, away on a business trip.

July 11th 1878

My dear dear Husband:

Received my letter this evening, don't know what would become of me darling if you did not write to me. I had rather have my letter than my breakfast any time. Am glad you are enjoying yourself so well, but it seems to me as you did not do any business in Camden you have stayed very unnecessaryly long. You told me when you left you would not be gone longer than three and <u>perhaps</u> four weeks, and under the circumstances I think you might have dispensed with so many friendly visits knowing how very much I needed you. You are wondering how your darling is I know, she has not been feeling so well today, have been trying to sleep but could not the weather is so warm not quite so hot as it was when you were here but still is <u>very warm</u>. I have the heat broken out all over me and at times feel like it will run me crazy. I will spend tonight in the big chair by the window — I have received only one letter from home since you left and I have written to Pa and Lucie* both and sent Lucie things, have never heard whether she received them or not, it seems like I am forgotten by every one, just at the time I need to be remembered most.* I guess My Darling will think I have not written him a very cheerful letter, forgive me my dear kind husband. I don't feel so well this evening. Don't be uneasy about me, I will let you know if I get sick. Good night. May God protect and bless you is the prayer of

your devoted wife
Nelia

*"Pa and Lucie" refers to Cornelia's father, Captain Smoker, and her sister, Lucie Smoker Hunt.

*Cornelia is pregnant with her first, and only, child.

George B. Rumph in Ouachita Co. to his cousin John Rumph Boddie in St. Louis

July 15th 1878

Dear John,

Your last commmication to hand. The letter I am due you would have been attended to but you left S. Louis before I concluded to answer, & thinking you would be constantly on the road, & perhaps even pay us a visit before your return home, omitted it entirely. I intended giving you a call at Arkadelphia — on my return from Little Rock Convention, but learning in Hot Springs that yourself & wife had passed through on your way back to St. L. only a few days before. So that for my programme was cut short. I have been quite unwell for several days, and cannot somehow get the relief that is usual from fever medicine taken. The returns of the Primary Election are all just in, except perhaps Freeo Township. Lee, Ramsey, & Bearden, Greening & Ike Newton are the nominees. Others having no opposition of course go in. Can not ascertain what our Republican "friends"? are going to do. A ticket is presumed for them about Thurs, John Ritchie for Sherff. Tufts for Clerk, & the remainder unannounced. Business is decidedly duller, & sales short of any previous year. I can not tell about what we will need until quite late in the fall, unless things change greatly. Others I presume are very much in the same attitude, consequently you can promise yourself light sales when you come in August, "for he that expects little" &c. I am partially inclined to visit St. Louis in person this fall, but have not fully decided upon that. I should like to look at North Arkansas, stop off at Batesville anyhow. I am told it is just the place now to locate. Long profits, & long time I am heartily tired of. Crops are fluttering at this time. Corn never better. Cotton will not do to trust until it is gathered & marketed. My family are well except colds. Excuse a short letter, as I am not feeling well enough to write at all. Enclosed you will find a photo to grace the album. Am very sorry its not better one. All join in love to yourself & Cousin Nealia

               Yours
               George

Jennie Rumph, wife of George B. Rumph, in Ouachita Co. to John Rumph Boddie in St. Louis

               Sept. 11th 1878

Dear John

!little dreamed that my first letter to you would be one of condolence.* I use the word, yet I know consolation for a sorrow like yours must come from a higher source than mine. If I could only offer one word that would be of comfort to your aching heart how gladly would I do so. You will not sorrow as those who have no hope, for an angel wife awaits you in heaven. She has left to your care a dear little babe — may the thought bear you up, and cause you to want to live. You have nearer & dearer relatives than I, but none who would more gladly take your sweet babe, if you were willing to trust me with it — you know that I am perfectly healthy, and could nourish it. There would be no risk, for I have the physicians' word for it & another child could be no nearer to me than yours, I will come after it if you will consent. George regrets that he can not meet you in Arkadelphia — he is quite sick — he sympathizes deeply with you, and prays the God of Comfort be with you in your affliction. We sent the telegram to your mother and father. I am certain they will go to you. Dr. Rumph has'nt yet recovered, has been sick for sometime — something like sunstroke. If I have failed to convey to you how sorely grieved we are, I trust you will attribute it to want of

*John R. Boddie's wife, Cornelia, died in childbirth on September 10, 1878. Her baby, a little boy, survived and was named George Kimball Smoker Boddie.

language and not the heart. Believe me that I mean sincerely & truely about your babe. Write to us when you have mental strength. We will be so glad to hear from you.

Your cousin
Jennie Rumph

George B. Rumph in Ouachita Co. to John Rumph Boddie in St. Louis

Sept 12th, 1878

Dear John

    I indeed feel the poverty of mere words, when I attempt to offer you consolation in this your hour of deepest sorrow and affliction. My heart is sincerely with you in sadness. For my hopes had gone forth that in a few brief weeks more at farthest, and I would be permitted to meet your lovely wife, and see you joyous and happy together in your St Louis home. But alas! We know not what a day may bring forth. To Him who transfers the mind to the Shorn Lamb, thou alone canst look to sooth thy grief or heal thy anguish. An Angel wife has but gone before, to that bright celestial home, where your life efforts too have been aimed. She would bid you bear up under this brief separation for the sake of a darling Babe committed to your keeping, tenderly guide his footsteps in the path that will unite you all in Heaven. I would meet you in Arkadelphia, but am too unwell to attempt the trip. I sent your telegrams to Aunt Mollie yesterday. Some of them will go if it is possible. Father's health is very poor, had an attack some time since — similar to sunstroke — or slight paralysis. Jennie writes you also, by todays mail. We would be glad to take your little babe & have the care of it. Will with your consent to this come for it. We have been so fortunate with our children feel that its life & health would be assured in our keeping. Write when it is pleasant for you. I will be in St. Louis about the 25th inst.

Yours truly in sorrow
Geo. B. Rumph

Coralie Rumph Rucks (Mittie) in Ouachita Co. to John Rumph Boddie in St. Louis

Sept. 12th 1878

My dearest cousin,

    You do not know how my heart aches in sympathy for you in this your first great sorrow. Oh! with what feelings of sadness did the dreaded message reach our little household. I am too full of grief to write but wanted you to know that we had not forgotten you in the hours of affliction & do deeply sympathise with you. All seems "shadow" now — but remember that He doeth all things well & the "Sun will shine again." How comforting to know you have still a <u>little</u> heaven left that was also hers. You cannot imagine with what deep affection we cling to such little innocents as you have left & do deeply sympathise with you — Already my heart yearns to number it as one of our household — may'nt I? if you can trust it to me I will by the Grace of the Most High be as a mother to the little motherless boy — Do not think I wish to take it from you always. I will keep it until you wish it, or until it is large enough to follow you about — If you have not made other arrangements think of what I have written, you know me — & believe me always & remember me in the hours of need is my earnest prayer.

Cous. Mittie

P. S. Present my respects to the bereaved family. I do sympathize them also.

Mittie

George Gildersleeve Boddie in Ouachita Co. to his brother John Rumph Boddie in St. Louis

Sept 16th 1878

Dear Bro:

I am happy to inform you that Ma and the dear little "Baby" reached home all safe & well, & doing as well as could be wished so far. Uncle John thinks it could be raised on concentrated milk, but would rather have wet milk* if it could be had. Dr Bragg thinks very diferent, and says procure wet milk by all means, if possible. We think we can procure one in town of the right sort; and if not we'll let you know immediately. Rest assured the Baby will be takened the best care of; and you shall hear from it every opportunity. I close deeply sympathizing, as a loving brother, in your grief and sadest of all misfortions.

Your bro,
G.G.Boddie

*Having "wet milk" means providing the baby with a wet nurse.

Mary Elizabeth Boddie Coleman [Mamie] in Clark Co. to her mother Mary E. Boddie in Ouachita Co.

Log Cabin Sept. 18th 1878

Dearest Mamma

Not until <u>this</u> night did I hear of you being in Arka[delphia] last week What day I do not know nor do I yet know on what day Sis Nelia died Thursday noon we heard indirectly that Capt Smoker had rec'd a telegram that some one of his relations was very sick. Of course, I knew it must be Sis Nelia. Friday we heard directly, through a neighbor that Mrs. Jno R Boddie was dead. Saturday we heard that she was buried in Arka[delphia] & that her father had taken her little infant daughter. Sunday morn & Saturday night I planned & fixed, & planned but all to no purpose, for as there was protracted meeting at Palestine & Had I known for certain that Bro. would have been there or <u>was there</u> I should have gone on horse-back. My object was to get the baby. I could not write to Bro. for I know not where to write, & then too, I heard on Sunday, that the baby died & was buried with its mother. But <u>tonight</u>, Dr. C. told me that "Ma" had recd a letter from Cousin Ada, stating that the baby was a boy & that you would take it when a month old. Now Mamma, I want it, & if I had a <u>settled</u> home, I <u>should insist</u> on having it, but as our stay here, depends on my getting the free school next year, I will insist on having it until Christmas, & then I will know if I can keep it. We will remain in this neighborhood, if not here, any how. I think it would thrive better for me to keep it a while. I have a plenty of nourishment for two & I know Bro would consent, if he would see Godfrey.

 He is such a fine boy. Has <u>fully</u> regained all he lost, laughs & talks as big as any one, can sit alone a little & almost pull up by his dress skirt, will get it around his feet & pull for life. Poor little Darling, Dr. C. lanced a large boil under his chin this morning, & will have another on his breast. He has the thrash* though tis nearly well now. He did not seem to know he had a boil & did not fret with his mouth any worth speaking of. I carried him every day & at night too, to church, he behaved beautifully. Would sit up and look about, until tired, then go to sleep. Every one thought him a perfect beauty, but I still think him not pretty, but handsome.

 Mama please write to Bro & ask him to let me have it, at least until Christmas. <u>I will treat it just as I do Godfrey,</u>, there shall be no difference. Poor Bro. <u>God alone</u> can sustain, & comfort him in this, the greatest trial of his life. I'm so glad, he has something yet to lavish his aff[ection] on. Mamma don't be selfish, but think what will be best for the little Darling, & that, let us try to do. Dr. C is perfectly willing for me to take it, & I <u>will</u>, immediately, if you and Bro. think best. I wait impatiently your decision. Would go to see it but Dr C cant leave. Lecila Malcone (the baby 19 months old) is not expected to live, has been sick all summer.*

*Thrush is a yeast infection that occurs inside the mouth of nursing infants.

*NOTE: The remaining pages of Mamie's letter to her mother have been lost, but what we have were included to indicate still another offer to take and raise Brother John's orphaned baby.

George Gildersleeve Boddie in Ouachita Co. to his brother John Rumph Boddie in St. Louis

Sept 19 /78

Dear Bro,

Your darling Baby is still doing well. Havn't yet procured a wet nurse, find it very dificult matter to get one of the right sort. Dr Bragg says he'll know by tomorrow evening whether or not he can get one. I havn't yet been to see the darling little fellow, but will go to see him sure Sunday. Mr Bracy stays out to his farm all the time & I have a very rough time of it, keeping store by myself. Nothing hurts or pains me more than to hear and know of your grief. Is there not help for the distressed! Is not God merciful! It seems to me even that sometimes He is not merciful, but oh! according to His teachings & for our own good, He is <u>always</u> merciful: which ought to be remembered by us all & at all times.

May God bless you & every thing be for the best.

Your bro.
Gilder Boddie

Mary Elizabeth Boddie in Ouachita Co. to her son John Rumph Boddie in St. Louis

20th [Sept.] 1878

My own dear boy,

Seated by our little darling while he is sleeping so sweetly, will write a few lines to tell you that so far he is doing exceedingly well, & under God's providence hope he'l continue so to do. I feel that you already know he shall [receive] all the kind, & loving care that a Mother can bestow, & I do wish you could see Pa's devotion to our little darling, 'tis as though he was living his young days over again. Said he was expecting to see me with the baby for he knew John would want his mother to care for it, & Little Sis thinks there never was such a baby, comments on every little movement he makes, asking me if ever I saw anything so sweet. Dr Brown came over yesterday asking for our babe to take to his wife, she was confined this week, & her baby lived only two hours. At first I thought 'twould be <u>best</u> for our baby that I should comply, but son; after serious thought of Mrs B's feverish condition &c &c, & particularly when Dr B. told me that his wife's health did not admit of her ever having nursed any of her own children longer than two or three months, decided immediately not to give up my trust, knowing he was doing well so far, & so soon as your sister gets word think she will come to stay until Christmas or longer —. Pa is very anxious for her to do so, for he is decidedly opposed to letting the babe have nourishment from any but

a pure, healthful source. We have decided to adopt Uncle John's & Dr Bragg's advice that is, to use the milk from a good young cow, & keep her up, & feed for the purpose, but by return dont fail to send me 1/2 cans concentrated milk, in case I should need some. "Uncle Billy" cant stand the lonely isolated life he leads, & will take the children home tomorrow. Aunt Nelie is to live with & care for them. I did not neglect to thank Dr B. for his proffered kindness, & indeed son <u>all, every one</u> sympathise with you sincerely, & may God in His mercy, pity & mitigate your great grief until you can feel, & say "Thy will be done." With much love from all
your devoted Mother.

Mittie Rumph Rucks in Camden to her cousin John Rumph Boddie in St. Louis

Sept. 23rd 1878

My dearest Cousin

I wrote you a short letter several days since but thinking you would like to hear from home, write again. I spent Saturday & Sunday with your Mama & Pa & you do not know with what joy I gazed on your sweet & beautiful little boy — Oh he was so lovely & you may rest assured in the tenderest care possible on earth. I will tell you just how things looked when I walked in; you remember the large rocking chair — Well it was near the safe* in the sitting room all bedecked with spreads & wraps — Carrie was over the fire with a little bottle of milk & your Mama was making ready to treat the little darling & interest of the household in his morning's meal, while your Papa with elastic step & smiling face said Just come here Mitt & (<u>went to the big chair</u>) if you want to see our little pet lamb, & Oh with what, saddened love did we all caress him — not that he looked pitiful tho — for he seems in his innocence to be happy as a King with all in his power, asserts his <u>will</u>, by brandish his big fat hands & feet in all direction until he gets his bottle & he actually grabbed the neck & held it until his appetite was satiated when he let go & gave a significant smile turned his head away as if to say — now go about your business — & off he went for nappies house — You talk about a "wet nurse" — Now just let me say right here (tho you may think otherwise) You let well enough alone — Your little Treasure is doing as well as heart could wish on the nourishment proscribed by "Uncle John" — He's <u>growing</u> & getting as <u>fat</u> as a little pig — & your Mama says is never sick & is as regular in his habits as any healthy baby she ever saw, then why do you wish a change to a "wet nurse" such as can be picked up about here, Can not pick one without the taint of some disease surging in her bones if not in her flesh & admitting all that, they take you in their power do just as they please, give as much impendence[?] as they want & as filthy

* A safe was the name given to any kind of chest used for storing articles. All kitchens had "safes" for storing foods, for example. The "safe" in the sitting room no doubt stored linens, etc.

as they wish — & yet you have to put up with it or they threaten to leave just at the time they are most needed. No! No! No!! My advise is to let <u>Wet</u> nurses alone — (<u>many children have been raised on the bottle</u>) if you can do <u>so well without them</u> — I cite you to Mrs. Smythe she perhaps can tell you <u>something</u> of what Mrs. Bragg had to <u>go through with</u> Well <u>my boy</u> is calling me or I could write a long long time to you but must go for the present — Will write again soon, May He who doeth all things for the best be your Guide & Comforter is the prayer of our little household. With much love I am as ever Your loving Cousin

      Mittie

P. S. Excuse writing as my time is limited

      M.

Mary Elizabeth Boddie in Ouachita Co. to her son John Rumph Boddie in St. Louis

Sept. 25th '78

 Yes my own dear grief stricken boy, Mama will take the kindest care of our precious little darling, & leave nothing undone for his comfort, & health. He is already endeared to me by a thousand loving ties, let alone his being <u>your boy</u>, & take comfort to your desolate self that our precious one is well & thriving so far on his cow milk with which I've been feeding him for the past five or six days. I bought all the <u>cans</u> home that they gave me, & have two now on hand, yet Pa insisted I should send to you for more, though I dont expect to have any use for it, if this milk continues to agree with him. Pa went to Town yesterday, saw Dr Bragg who said 'twas impossible to procure the right kind of a wet nurse, & your Uncle J. who was here Monday said he <u>would not have</u>, that "not <u>one</u> in a thousand should nurse that baby, & if I could talk with Johnie five minutes, he would not be willing to risk <u>any</u> either." Will send you part of your sister's letter rec'd yesterday as I hav'nt time to rewrite. Am sure she'l come when she gets my letter, & if she has no means, or way to come will send for her. We have not been able to get any assistance with our work, Pa is riding again to-day, but the women all prefer picking cotton to cooking, house work &c. When we do succeed in getting help, will need 12 or 15 dollars per month, & not that much, <u>after</u> I procure some little necessaries for our baby's comfort, should he live & continue to do well. Little Sis waits on us through the night, & answers readily every call little darling makes for his bottle. She discovers some new perfection in him daily, & you may think, but dont know <u>half</u> his <u>sweetness</u> & how much we all love him. We have such miserable washers here that I have baby's garments done up in Town, as I did not feel willing but that such neat handiwork should have good usage, when every stitch was consecrated with a mother's love for her expected little one. Bless his little heart I cant count the kisses he gets daily, Grandma never kisses him but with thoughts of her sorrowing one, & you & only you my boy can feel the anguish of many lonely, lonely hours, & think it so hard, yet God knows best, & "loveth whom - He chastenith."

Mrs Anna G.[aughan] & Mrs Jim Toney both have girls, Mrs Mitchel a boy, & only from 10 A. M. to 10 P. M. difference in the age of hers & our little darling, (Mrs M's), but there is no comparison in the babies, hers is as large, but looks so hard & thin that it excites my pity to look at it.

Could write more, but my time belongs to our little precious, who is kissed time & again for his only parent in this life, whose sorrowing heart may, by the goodness of God be healed by his only earthly treasure. Each one at home send much love to our stricken one, & may God bless & care for you ever, is the prayer of

your devoted Mother.
Mary E. Boddie

The articles you sent by express had not come yesterday, Gilder came over last Sunday to see baby, told me he would send them immediately upon delivery, as I need the napkins* much, & had to substitute some to make our babe comfortable. The Machine will be a great help with our work, & rest assured it shall be taken good care of.

Your Mama,

Thursday,

*"Napkins" was used to mean diapers in the 19th century.

Little darling is well & sends ever so many kisses to his own dear father, he does look so sweet this morning, we all nearly devour him with kisses. Will write as often as 'tis possible to send letters to the Office.

Devotedly yours

Mary Elizabeth Boddie in Ouachita Co. to her son John Rumph Boddie in St. Louis

Sept 30th 1878

My own dear boy,

Pa has just told me he would ride over to town this eve, therefore will send you sweet kisses from your precious little darling, & the good tidings of his continued <u>well doing</u>, for which you cant think how <u>thankful</u> I feel. May the precious gift be some consolation in your affliction darling, & that you place all your trust in Him, who alone can heal, is the best evidence that your prayers in time <u>will be</u> answered, for He never designed that all of life should be living death for those who love, & trust Him. May he bless you darling is the prayer of

your loving Mother,
M. E. B.

Pa says I've never told you what a good boy our darling is & that even we who are with him constantly can see that he is growing fast. Guess the little fellow feels the increase too, for he has called for increase of rations, & makes his wants known as regular as two hours roll round through each day & night. Is getting to be too big for the great arm chair in which he sleeps in day time, & I do wish you could see him when he first wakes each morn lying in bed, & seemingly to be taking a survey of his surroundings, & the old log cabin. All of us cant enumerate half his sweetness, & how much he is endeared to us, but kiss him again & again for his poor lonely father, good bye,

Mama

A boy to Mat & Uncle John on Thursday last.

Rec'd Carns Napkins &c Sat. Shirts all right should they be large enough by the time my boy will need them

Weather quite warm —

Mary Elizabeth Boddie in Ouachita Co. to her son John Rumph Boddie in St. Louis

Oct 9th '78

My own dear boy,

I am perfectly willing to adopt any plan for the welfare of our precious one that is satisfactory to you, & as you deem it to be all important to have a wet nurse am glad to tell you that Ann T. has promised to come on Monday next. Though I have some doubts son of its being altogether the better plan, will have the satisfaction of having him under my own eye, & particular care. Our darling is very hearty, & I fear will not get all the nourishment needed. Why his big cousin Godfrey comes much nearer being satisfied with one breast than Smoker does, & he takes all he can get from Aunt Mamie, & the bottle too to satisfy him. Granting that Mamie had all sufficient for both I could never let her take our boy unless I went too. She came to stay with us only two months but if 'twere necessary would stay longer. We'l see how our darling gets on with his black Mammy, & if she brings her own baby to care for too, & in either case I have no idea she can do any cooking, (admitting she had the leisure) because I cant have her nurse my baby if overheated or wearied in the breast, & if she can assist Little Sis with the cleaning up, & ironing will be satisfied. Dont propose for Ann to have anything to do with my baby, that is washing, dressing, & other attention, save only to let him nurse when hungry, for 'tis my greatest pleasure to attend to him myself believing no one can contribute so much to his comfort, & cleanliness as Grandma who loves the precious one beyond expression. Grandpa & Uncle J. are furious about his having the nurse, but I tell them you must be gratified, & I will see to the balance. The latter spent yesterday with us bade me tell you, that notwithstanding all your Physician may say to the contrary, your boy will not do half as well as he's doing now, no, not even when teething, or passing through other ill's to which babies are liable.

I was in Town Sat. saw & talked with Geo. rec'd the thirty dollars ($30.00) sent me, & will advise you each time I'm obliged to procure any means from Geo. & the amount rec'd. Dr Bragg told me he had secured Ann's services for $20.00 per month. Our little darling looks small beside Godfrey, but we can see that he is filling out, & growing every day, just the sweetest & dearest little fellow in the world. Sends his Papa & Angel Mother kisses daily with petitions to the Almighty One from Grandma, that love for him will fill the aching void in your heart, & the memory of your Angel Wife be your sweetest solace. The picture of our loved one is a gift we most highly prize, & should our little darling be spared to us, will be taught to know the semblance of his Mother in heaven. When I asked Geo. R. if you had not sent one to your sister, said he knew you must have intended one for her, & knowing how Mamie would feel about it gave one to her without letting her know but that you had so intended it, & but for my baby would rather send Sis Hattie ours than not give Mamie one.

Cornelia Kimball
Smoker Boddie
Photo courtesy of Ruth Boddie Farmer

All send much love darling boy, hoping you are better in mind & body
                    Your devoted Mother
                    Mary E. Boddie

Mary Elizabeth Boddie in Ouachita Co. to her son John Rumph Boddie in St. Louis

Oct. 18th '78

My own dear boy,

Company this morning prevented my writing when our precious baby was taking his longest nap, so your share of Grandma's time will be limited. Want to tell you about our nurse, that we like her first rate, but she has not been able to fill the most important of all requirements, that is, giving our boy a sufficiency, but we are patient & hopeful that a generous diet & constant nursing will induce a greater flow of milk. At present Aunt Mamie supplies the deficiency, nothing to the detriment of our darling big boy Godfrey, who is just as sweet & good as can be. Grandpa has a great time with his boy babies, is prouder of, & notices them much more than he ever did any of his own, in fact it seems as though he felt years younger, since he's had them to pet.

Ann is, so far, willing & obliging in all things, & though her baby does little better than at first, cries much to be fondled, consequently her time is well employed between the two. Our little precious one <u>never cries</u> only when <u>hungry</u>, & if she can get to satisfy his <u>needs</u> in that respect I will be perfectly contented. Rec'd a letter from Mrs Hunt this week, which I will answer as soon as possible.* Little Sallie has been sick, & Capt. Smoker had been confined to his room two weeks with Neuralgia of the eyes, which I was very sorry to hear. I had intended writing to Mrs Hunt anyway, though she did not request me to do so when I left. Say to Miss Joe A. that the <u>neat pretty</u> shawl rec'd from her hands has already graced one of the sweetest & dearest of babies, & he sends her a sweet kiss for the same. 'Twas so kind & thoughtful in you dear son to send me such <u>nice comfortable</u> undershirts, & I hav'nt words to tell you my <u>appreciation</u> of Little daughter's cloak, for I felt as though I would like so much to have some garment that <u>she her dear self had worn</u>. Rec'd our little darlings shawl too, & having the one I brought him home in, think he has wraps sufficient, without a cloak, as I dont expect to take him out in cold weather knowing I can much better care for him at home. Nurse Ann is talking already of wanting to go to town every month or two to see her other children & 'twill puzzle me much how to acquiesce in such an arrangement, though Dr B. told me I had better allow her to go occasionally. If she <u>will consent</u> we would much prefer sending for the children to come to see her.

 I think it best & am <u>glad</u> my dear boy, that you have changed your place of residence, & if you could only see your precious boy daily am sure you would feel better, & I know not so lonely. If you had been keeping house I would have gone to you, & cared for him where you could have been with him. O son you cant realise half his sweetness, & know what a treasure he is to all of us, his own darling Mother could not have loved him more than I do. He is waking now, & I must close with dear love from each one of us, & kisses many to Papa from his darling's babe. Forgot to tell he begins to notice a good deal, but wont smile for us yet, & "Little Sis" says he has the <u>sweetest prettiest</u> mouth in the world, & could not be otherwise for 'tis like his Mother's. Aunt Clara thinks he favours you the first time she ever saw you. Good bye my boy, may God help you to bear your great loss, & bless you, is the prayer of

        your devoted Mother,
        Mary E. Boddie

*"Mrs Hunt" is "Lucie" Smoker Hunt, sister to John Boddies late wife.

Mary E. Boddie in Ouachita Co. to her son John Rumph Boddie in St Louis.
Nov. 1st 1878

My own dear boy,

  If possible you shall hear from your darling baby twice a week, for I deeply sympathise with, & commiserate your bitter loneliness, knowing too your only balm of comfort is tidings of our precious boy. Bless his dear little heart, he is fondled, loved & kissed for his angel Mother & Papa's sake more than ever any babe in this world who has been so bereft, yes! for his own precious self too, he is such a sweet endearing little fellow.
  Aunt Carrie thinks he has the sweetest and prettiest mouth she ever saw, & Tug thinks the world & all of Bud Johnie's baby, says he gets prettier every day. Bud Willie & all hands come in for their share of petting, & Grandpa says a looker on would call him & I a foolish old couple in our eagerness to elicit a <u>smile</u> & a coo from our little darling, but I can assure Papa <u>his</u> notice is all the world to us. Grandpa is little jealous too, says Smoker wont even look at him when he can get his eyes on Grandma. Sometimes little darling wears a frown, & then the expression of his features (not the frown) reminds me of his Grandpa Smoker, but he has unmistakeably a nose like his angel Mother, & his mouth I believe will be an exact copy of hers. He has round cheeks, deep, dark blue eyes, & a forehead not yet fully developed. Grandpa Boddie claims that his <u>long</u> limbs, toes, & fingers are like his, & I do know that altogether our little darling is just the dearest & sweetest babe living. I thought of, wanted so much to get his picture to send to you, even before you requested it, but the weather was too variable for me to risk exposing him in a tent in which the Artists do their work, & I regretted it the more because they take such good likenesses. Mamie went over to have Godfrey's taken but the day proved to be very cloudy & windy, & the dear little fellow has had a very bad cold ever since. No matter how the weather is, Grandpa never lets the fire [go] unreplenished day or night in our nurse room. Am so happy to tell you that Ann gives plenty milk now, & it <u>agrees well</u> with our little darling, so he has nothing to do but grow fast, but you must not imagine him to be half the size of Godfrey, who is as fine looking child to his age as I ever saw. As you spoke of leaving for Ark. about the 25 Ult. was expecting you home is the reason I did not write last week, & would not even trust our little darling's hair in Mamie's letter for fear you would not get it, but as you advise me to write on until further notice <u>will send</u> it in <u>this</u> with unnumbered <u>kisses</u> for dear Papa's angel Mother, praying that God in His mercy may comfort, & bless you now, & ever.
devotedly your Mother
Mary E. Boddie
  Each time when writing forgot to tell you that Uncle John gave our boy a gold dollar, says he always keeps some in reserve for all his boys. I guess

his last boy will come in for a double portion, he is so proud of him. They have not yet decided on a name. All well & send much love.

Cornelia Dickson in Ouachita Co. to her friend Becca Underwood in Autauga Co.

December 1878

Dear Becca

Several days has necesarily elapsed since I received your dear letter, and, Becca, I had become so anxious to hear from you, was thinking of writing, before I rec. it. I was really glad you were "Skeered" that time about the "pedagogue." I am satisfied that you don't "care for him". Particularly if you continue to write punctually, I shall not think that he engrosses all your time, and shall look forward to your <u>next</u> with lively interest. I have at last succeeded in securing the children's pictures for Rebecca, and Clara says she shall expect Rebecca to send <u>her</u> children in return, & tell her she must remember me in the distribution. Tell her, to get her picture, would be next to seeing her, and I know she is not more anxious to see <u>me</u> than I am to be with her again. When she sees Dr Bush, she may say to him; that I "do not seem to be getting married <u>yet</u>." I would like to see him too. I have ever thought it would seem better to be an "old maid" than inflict some man with a lifetime of trouble. Probably if I had ever loved anyone I should have thought differently.

You ask me what I think of youthful marriages. I think they are as often productive of happiness as any, where the parties are sensible & amiable. It all seems a game of chance anyway. Again Becca we have been made very very sad. John Boddie has lost his sweet little wife. She died about the tenth of Sept. and left a wee baby boy only a few hours old. John, poor boy, for a time, was utterly inconsolable, for he loved her to idolatry. The babe survives and was brought from St Louis to Arkadelphia where its mother was interred, the next day after its birth. Sis Mollie met them there, and brought the poor little waif home with her. The first time I saw it, Becca, it was only six days old & had traveled from St Louis, I was to see Sis Mollie yesterday and the "boy" has grown to be an eighteen or twenty pounder, & seems perfectly well & hearty. Has a wet nurse.

Lula Dunlap 1862-1919
(Facing photos courtesy of Sue Martin Russell.)

Carrie has gone to spend some time with Mamie, (Says the yellow fever quarantine prevented her writing to Eula, but she will write now. Effie has just read me a letter from her).

I have been established here at Mr. Stone's Becca since the later part of Sept. and very busy time. Of course I could not do otherwise than engage in household & kitchen duties until we are able to do better.

We are not anticipating a lively Christmas. About a month ago one of our neighbors was shot by one whom he had wronged, and a week ago, one of my warmest friends & near neighbors Mrs. Patterson died of pneumonia, sad occurances have cast a gloom over —*

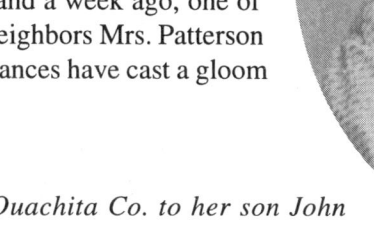

Cora Lee Dunlap
1868-1941

*This letter ends abruptly at this point in the ledger.

Mary Elizabeth Boddie in Ouachita Co. to her son John Rumph Boddie in St. Louis

Dec 20th 78

Dearest Papa,

We were so glad to get your dear letters of 8th & 10th Inst. & I do wish you could have seen our little precious one how intently he scanned the pages all the while Grandma was reading them, & almost seemed to understand from Grandma that they came from his dear Papa's hand. The bouquet is carefully put away because 'tis the first he ever rec'd, & from his dear Papa.

Grandpa says I must tell you he has learned to pull his beard & with both hands, & I dont know which is most delighted, little darling to pull & laugh, or Grandpa to <u>have him do it</u>. He & Smoker have a big frolic & tussel every morning, as Pa invariably gets himself ready to nurse our pet while I go to breakfast, & every night before little darling's sleepy time gives him a promenade, & Uncle Will & "Tug" too comes in for their share since he has gotten to be so playful. Just know if Pa can only succeed in having our baby <u>cry</u> for <u>him</u> to <u>take him</u> will have accomplished the acme of his desires. Gilder came to see us last Sun., was surprised to see how much little precious had grown, said "why Ma he is getting so pretty too, & how knowing the little chap looks." When you see Mrs. Hendreison again give her my love, for I feel a nearness to those who loved your Darling, & tell the dear old lady I gave our little darling a sweet kiss specially for her.

I regret more than I can tell you dear son, that I fear the opportunity is gone this time for having our baby's picture. The same week in which you left town saw a notice in the Beacon that the Artist would leave the following Mon. & only learned to the contrary, since the weather has been too bad to risk taking him over. Believe I could go, & come with him even a cold day safely, but being exposed in a tent without wraps long enough for a setting is too great a risk, & I would fear the consequences. The weather has been, & is at present terrible cold, & it's all we can do to try to keep comfortable by the fire, which Pa keeps up at night too for our little darling. Bless his precious little self, he fills our hearts, & home with life, light & happiness, & that he may grow to be a comfort & blessing to you my son is my earnest prayer. I kissed your Darling's baby, many, many times to send his dear Papa, & with much love from all at home, am as ever,

Your devoted Mother,
Mary E. Boddie

Came near forgetting to tell you, that in selecting baby's undershirts, remember to get them high in the neck, & <u>long sleeves</u>, two will be sufficient, & three prs. infant socks. No news of our absentees since I last wrote to you, did think that my Little Kitten would write often. Ann says, she knows Miss Carrie will almost eat Smoker up now when she comes home, she thinks he's getting to be so smart. Uncle J's family all well, hear from, though I've not seen any of them since you left. Goodbye.

Mary Elizabeth Boddie in Ouachita Co. to her son John Rumph Boddie in St. Louis

Jan. 10th 1879

My own dear boy,

Am in recpt' of your dear, & most welcome letter of 3rd Inst. & think it to be the very date on which I wrote you last, for we have not missed a single week to send you word of your Darling's baby & precious boy. We will be so glad to have you <u>come</u>, Papa for only in seeing can you know how very sweet & interesting our little darling is, & how smart he is getting to be. Grandpa thinks he would like to see his Papa keep his little man's hands covered when he is not a mind to let them. Uncle Will tells him, his Papa had better come, else he is sure to get a <u>spanking</u>. Pet cried this morning for Pa to walk him, & you should have seen Grandpa how proud he was to gratify him. Little precious has such a sweet winning way that no one can withstand his baby pleading. He draws the <u>beam</u> now to 19, but I deduct 1/2 lb for his clothing. Uncle J. says he has got two weeks the start of his boy Garland, & keeps it. We enjoyed Uncle J's visit very much, it had been a long time since he had spent a night with us. Our baby's cloak is the handsomest we ever saw & so becoming to the little darling, the shirts splendid, just the kind & quality I wanted, his hoods & sacques just as pretty as can be, & the right fit, but his <u>boots</u> Papa are <u>too</u> small, can only make two pr. answer at all, & have to keep close watch for he kicks them off continually

I can challenge anything of his size to beat him jumping in the States. That 'tis <u>cold</u> here to us you need not doubt, & wont if you come. Pa says our house never seemed to have so many cracks before, & we'l be so glad when winter is over, have not had such continued cold since 55, there has been no crossing at our ferry for several days on account of ice until last Thur.

We understand that Geo. R. had, or was trying to sell out his interest in the store, says he can make a <u>living anywhere</u>, & that's all he's doing here. I should regret much for them to leave, there are so few of us together anyway, our families have always seemed as one. Pa went to see Bob S. Thurs., he is in bed yet but not dangerously ill. Mrs Annie was in bed too with Neuralgia & chills. Bob had Dr Meek from the first of his illness but sent for Uncle J. this week. Our neighbours all well, with the above exception, but Uncle J. said he had had a good many cases on his side of the creek. I dont look for "Little Sis" now, until I see her, the weather is so bad, & the roads worse I guess.

We do on two meals per day, & lunch between times when hungry. Will gets the first meal, they cant finish ginning until the weather admits of Mr Mosely's getting through with their packing, &c at "Uncle Billy's." Will keeps busy attending to the stock, hauling wood &c "Tug" cuts it for the house & kitchen, & Pa keeps us with good fires, & loves to come in for his share nursing our precious little baby. "Tug" says "now wont Bud Johnie be proud of him." yes indeed, for we all think every little motion of his the sweetest & smartest in the world. Bless his darling little self, sends Papa kiss upon kiss, & we hope to greet him soon. May God bless you my boy. With much love from each one at home,

Yours devotely,
Mary E. Boddie

Saturday eve,

Well my dear boy, failed to get this off to-day, & regret it much because of the delay in reaching you. Been <u>pouring rain</u> all day, & no one could go to town. 'Tis a cold rain too, not melting ice or snow. Pa & Will are apprehending an overflow, in which case 'twill be impossible to get all the cattle out, cant even get the boat from the icelocked lake. Pa was very glad to get the Papers you sent. We are much gratified to know that your employers justly merited their appreciation of your services. Hope you may have occasion to be kept as busy as heart could wish. Goodbye, I kiss your Darling's baby again & again for dear Papa.

Yrs. Mama

Cornelia Dickson in Ouachita Co. to Mr. William Lea in Princeton, Arkansas

Jan. 11th 1879

Mr. Lea, Sir,

Pardon the liberty I take in writing to you. I regret to trouble you, but remembering the kindness you once showed me in procuring for me a school, am induced to solicit a like favor of you. I would be much obliged if you would inquire and let me know if I could get a school in, or near your neighborhood, as I should not in that instance, feel among strangers. If you will confer this favor please let me know all the particulars. How many pupils, the terms, when I can begin, about board, &c I would prefer to board with you if convenient.

The general health of the neighborhood, I believe, is good. In consequence of the very cold disagreeable weather we have had but little communication with anyone recently. I saw Dr. Rumph several days since. He reported all well at home. You have probably heard that I am at present living at Mr W. T. Stones, caring for his orphan grandchildren, but he seems unsettled in his plans and speaks of making other arrangements, and I shall do likewise, though I shall regret to part with my little charges, who seem greatly attached to me.

With kindest regards to yourself & family. Hoping to hear from you at your earliest convenience,

    I am as ever.
    Respectfully,
    Cornelia S. Dickson

Mary Elizabeth Boddie in Ouachita Co. to her son John Rumph Boddie in St. Louis.

Jan. 17th 1879

My own dear boy,

We rec'd your dear & most welcome letters of 9th & 11th Inst. yesterday eve & most gladly welcome you to old Ark. once more hoping to see you before long. Little precious & I have a chat every day about Papa's comings, & what a question for him to ask <u>to be sure</u> he <u>can talk</u>, though not with tongue, his <u>eyes speak</u> volumes, & are the brightest, prettiest, & most expressive, ever placed in human head, & then <u>his motions</u> are <u>worth</u> more than mere words. We all do know, there never was such a child, & I'm afraid will love him too dearly, yet I try not to forget Him who has implanted such feelings in our heart trusting that He will permit us to realize all the cherished hopes for our precious darling. You must know that Ann cant keep from kissing his little hands nearly every time she nurses him & this morning kissed him on the forehead, he has such a sweet cunning way of looking up at her, will draw a little while, then stop, look up, & spread his sweet mouth in a broad smile, as though expressing thanks for his tea. Bless his dear little heart, never looks at his "Grandma" without a smile of recognition. Grandpa is always making his brags that he'l get his little man yet, & Smoker gets frequent <u>promenades</u>, greatly to his delight. He knows Will & Bob too, who have a talk & play with him every night, generally about 9 when he's put to bed, & wakes at daylight. Frequently wakes during the night, if he has to beg for his tea before I can rouse Ann, but after nursing goes to sleep again, & never cries to be taken up.

 The pleasant moderation of the weather is grateful to all, but if the rains continue the threatened <u>overflow</u> will be a certainty. Pa & Will made a boat, & launched it in the field bayou Mon. next day took a run over the bottom to find the whereabouts of the cattle, said they had to break the ice to make way for the boat in the lake.

 Since writing last have'nt seen any neighbours except State, told us Bob S. was up, but yesterday Mrs Annie sent to me for bluemoss, saying Bob was sick again. State said "Uncle Billy" wanted him & sister to live there this year, Miss Mollie to do the cooking, house work, sewing &c & State to work in the field, the latter said "Uncle B." would have to make it to his interest, or he would not go, for he thought Lissy would have a much harder time there than at home, & Uncle B. thinks to the reverse. He wanted us to take the children again, but Pa could not accede to his terms. Dont know why he is dissatisfied with Nelie & wants a change. Pa rec'd a letter from "Little Sis" of 12th Inst. is coming home just as soon as the weather admits, never speaks of wanting to see any of us but Smoker, has enjoyed her visit very much. Godfrey had been sick, & was much reduced, he's one sweet little boy, wrote to his Grandpa, & said he was going to write to his Uncle John Boddie, & thank him for his pretty hood & cloak. Mrs Wm Coleman has a 9 lb boy, have named him Ed Haws.

 Well my boy time out, & little precious wants me, bless his little heart, tell Aunt Lucy I do wish she & Grandpa Smoker could see him, yes Uncle Will S[moker], I know wants to see him too, indeed all of them, they cant begin to think how very sweet, pretty & interesting your Darling's baby is. Remember me to them all with kindest regards.

 Forgot to tell you Pa thinks he will succeed in getting us a cook, & we cant express to you my son our appreciation of your loving kindness. Goodbye. Love from all, & kisses without number from your precious boy.
      Devotely your Mother
      M.E. B.

 Sat. Morn All well — sun rising clear, & the promise of a pretty day had only two of sunshine since Christmas — Little darling sends Papa a good morning kiss.

Mary Elizabeth Boddie in Ouachita County to her son John Rumph Boddie in St. Louis

Jan 27th 1879

My own dear boy,

 Have a few moments in which to write a little note, as I did not send you any word the usual time, was expecting you, & the high water preventing any communication during the whole week, until Sat. when I sent word to Gilder to let you know that all were well with us. We thought the time very long dear Papa between letters, & felt sure you were coming. Yes my boy, you will see one of the sweetest & smartest little darlings ever born, & I do wish his dear relatives every one of them could see him. Grd. Ma Kimball may claim, & love him too. Gd. Ma Boddie will kiss him for her ever so much, but after all he's Papa's & my very own precious boy. Grd. Pa says "tell Papa, dont send him any <u>spurs</u> for my little man gets away with me now." Pet gets both hands good hold on Grd. Pa's whiskers, then tucks his little face down to keep Grd. Pa from bearding him. O I could write all day if time permitted about our little darling & then not tell you half his endearing ways, & sweetness. Willie is nearly ready & I must close, he is going over to take some pork. They did not lose any stock that they know of. Pa is a little credulous still about the R. R. but I will be so glad of such convenience, because I want you to get to see your Darling's baby as frequently, as possible. Good bye, love from all, & kisses morn, noon, & night for dear Papa.

      Devotedly your Mother
      M. E. B.

 Dont get the mits, but a toy rubber of some kind for him to bite on, he loves now to rub his gums, & keeps his little fists wet nearly all the time, so you see 'twont do to trammel his little hands.

Mary Elizabeth Boddie in Ouachita Co. to her son John Rumph Boddie in St. Louis.

Feb. 7th 1879.

My own dear boy,

 It seems rather strange to be writing when you just left town yesterday yet the time seems long since you left us, & just to think of you being so near & not paying us one more little flying visit & if my little darling had been <u>quite well</u> when you left would not have written to you for another whole week. Am so happy to tell you that <u>he's well</u>, & just as <u>playful</u> as ever, & I did want you to see him so much when he's all right. Aunt Mamie & Carrie say he is the sweetest babe in the world, & was <u>quite astonished</u> at his size. Godfrey has fallen off very much, looks taller & is prettier too I think. They left for home to-day although I would not be at all surprised if they return on account of high water. The river is rising again & there will be no passing after to-morrow. Carrie has a dreadful cold, & sore throat, was in bed all yesterday, is up to-day, but not at all well. They regretted not seeing you, but for the detention by high water would have been here two days earlier.

 Well dear Papa we only write this time to relieve your anxiety & send you ever so many sweet kisses from your precious little darling. Good bye, let us hear from you soon & often. With much love from all at home,
      Your devoted Mother
      Mary E. Boddie

Mary Elizabeth Boddie in Ouachita Co. to her son John Rumph Boddie in St. Louis
             Feb 12th 1879

 My own dear boy,

 Rec'd your most welcome letter of 10th Inst. today, & as Willie goes over in the morning will write to let you know that our precious boy is well, & just as lively & frisky as a little lamb. Like you son, I would not have him to take the chickenpox* for anything, but <u>rest assured</u> if he does, he shall have all the loving care & attention for his comfort possible. Uncle J. shall be consulted too, & Dr B. if necessary, our Medical Work speaks of the <u>disease</u> in very light terms, but I dont want our little darling to take it, <u>unless</u> he should be subject to it when older, for I know from experiance 'tis less hurtful at his age, & before teething than at any other time. Dont borrow trouble son, & make yourself miserable thinking about it, if he should get sick will write to you <u>every third day,</u> if 'tis possible to get the notes posted. Willie will finish hauling this week, has one more bale to pack making 18 in all. I wrote the Sat. after you left town c/o Smoker. Carrie is still ailing much but is up most of the day. She will nurse our pet some, & it annoys her greatly for him to cry for me when she has him. Says he has the <u>handsomest eye</u> & <u>mouth</u> she ever saw, & is always calling to me to look at some of his sweet doings, as though Grandma did'nt know them all, & know too, that he is the darlingest of all darlings. Good night, for I must not write longer. I kissed <u>your Darling's</u> baby all day for you & talked to him about his Papa too. Grandpa actually thinks <u>his little man</u> can <u>most talk.</u> Weighed 20 the day he was five months old. Ann will go to see her children Sat. is not willing to defer any longer, & unless the weather is fine I will not take little precious, the road is so bad. Will get Willie to call on Geo. R for the amount due Ann as she wants it, & I will have to get $5.00 to settle with

*The baby did take the chickenpox. According to a note which we did not include he was "very sick" and covered with eruptions.

hirelings for work I've been compelled to have done.
With much love from all at home
Your devoted Mother
Mary E. Boddie

Mary Elizabeth Boddie in Ouachita Co. to her son John Rumph Boddie in St. Louis.

March 6th 1879

My own dear boy,

  Now indeed we can greet you with glad tidings, for your Darling's boy is entirely <u>well</u> yes, well dear Papa, & sweeter & more interesting if possible than ever with his smart doings. "Tug" often remarks, why Mama, Smoker is so smart, he gets away with us all now dont he? I guess his Papa would think so too, could he witness some of little darling's capers. The weather is so pleasant have been out in the yard & garden with him, & with that he's perfectly delighted, looking about as though he would like to embrace everything at one glance. Has <u>two teeth</u> now, can his little cousin Henritta beat that? The hoarseness is <u>all gone</u>, & he gives orders now in such a way that we cant mistake his meaning. Will answer to name with eyes, mouth, & <u>hands</u>, & you have no idea how <u>expressive</u> the latter is, his Aunt C. is always saying look Mama, just look at his hands, & she thinks his mouth the prettiest she ever saw, says 'tis his handsomest feature. Well Papa you must come & see for yourself, bless his precious little self. I can never tell you the half of his smartness, & it gladdens my heart to know that he so loves Grd.Ma will cry to go to her from any of them. No news of interest, all the sick have recovered, & I hear of no new cases. Pa is busy repairing the garden palings, Will planted the lot in front of the house yesterday in corn, & is preparing ground to plant more. Everything out doors begins to put on a Spring like appearance, birds singing, peach trees blossoming &c — No letter from you since the 24th Ult. No word from Mamie since the note enclosed in yours. Little precious is uttering "ha ha" as much as to say, <u>I'm awake Grd.Ma.</u> & <u>ready for you</u>, so good bye, & he sends his dear papa kiss upon kiss. With love from each one, remain as ever
Your devoted Mother.
M. E. B.

*Note: This post script was written upside down on page one.

  *Aunt C. says tell his Papa Smoker has white hair. The enclosed slip contains a good suggestion for the <u>best</u> method of irrigating plants, therefore send it to you, to make use of or not, as you may think proper. I think it would keep <u>violets</u> flourishing through all the heated term, by having <u>many</u> cans, & filling once in two weeks. "Little Sis" has set out a nice bed to increase by the time you want them. Aunt C. will have me enclose the flower — says tell you Smoker <u>pulled</u> it with his own dear little hands.

Mary Elizabeth Boddie in Ouachita Co. to her son John Rumph Boddie in St. Louis

April 18th 79

My own dear boy,

We are more than glad to hear from you at all times, so whenever you dont feel like writing otherwise, send on the "little notes" they are as much appreciated as any coming from dear Papa. Am happy to hear that you are well, & I guess your precious little one was glad too when I told him that Papa was coming to see him, for he laughed & looked so pleased. Ann says he is getting to be <u>too smart</u>, she has to watch him nearly every time when nursing to keep him from biting, & can tell exactly when he's going to do it by his looks & actions, says Will & I learned him to bite, but indeed we all have to laugh at him he is so sweet & cunning, & Ann cant keep from laughing herself. Uncle Will has been bit so often when he had only two teeth, wont venture a finger in his mouth now. Gilder was home last Sun. & we all wondered if our Pet would be afraid of <u>you</u> as of him, he dont at all fancy any one <u>strange,</u> but Gilder soon won him over, for he would take him anyway, & kept him so amused that little darling forgot who had him until he'd spy a familiar face. Willie thinks he favors you now, Gilder said he dont look like John one bit, is more like Godfrey or Mamie, & Pa thinks so too, but one thing we all <u>do know,</u> that he's the sweetest & prettiest boy in the world. Willie & "Little Sis" have had bad colds, Ann had one too, but all are on duty, & little precious seems to be taking cold too, but he is just as lively & playful as a kitten, is a perfect little fidget, with so much curiosity about everything. Weather cool enough for fires nearly all day, & vegetation is not coming on fast. Had our first radishes & mustard salad this week, dont believe the S[trawberry] bed will yield a good mess this season, they all appear to be seedlings, & one year old plants. Our boys have no time to [go] fishing, so Willie is trying how a set lines* will do in the Lake, attends to them at noon & I send his dinner when the others return to the fields. They will commence planting cotton next week. We learn that a survey for the R. R. is commenced from <u>Prescott</u> to Camden, & we'l be so sorry if the route is decided on instead of one this side to Arkadelphia. Gilder told me that Master Smoker's buggy, &c would be in town tomorrow eve but we'l have to wait another week for them I guess, as Uncle Will wont have to go over this week. Uncle J. generally goes to town every Sat. but I have not seem him in a long time, all well with them. Tommie has had your gun some time to turkey hunt, had not killed any the last time I saw him, said there were too many out each morning <u>that he went</u> & all after the same old gobler. Well my boy there is nothing new or interesting in these parts save our precious little One, who is the life of our house, & just the dearest little darling ever born. Sends his dear Papa a bushel of kisses, & with love from each

* A "set line" would be a trot line.

one at home, I pray God to bless you.
>Your loving Mother.
>M. E. Boddie

Mary Elizabeth Boddie in Ouachita Co. to her son John Rumph Boddie in St. Louis

>April 25th '79

Well dear Papa, this is our day to write, & a very rainy one it is & we dont know when we'l have the pleasure of a ride out of doors. Uncle Will brought the carriage & ponies home yesterday. Little darling just waked from his evening nap, by the time the rocker was ready for his inspection, well, he <u>almost</u> talked, & certainly looked his <u>delight</u>. His little toes barely touch the footboard, & he dont yet exactly understand how to travel by himself, but he has learned already to hold fast with both hands while we keep him rocking, just know if he had good foot hold would go it himself. As soon as Pa, & all hands, got his carriage ready, & let him see it, gazed with <u>mute astonishment,</u> & all exclaimed why he likes his ponies best, but when seated & riding, looked a perfect little king, & "Monarch of all he surveyed," & for two hours, or until time to undress for bed did I get him out of it. GrdMa was as highly pleased to ride her little darling, as he was to be rode, for evening is his time to be wearied of all ordinary amusements, & fret to be walked, so the change was very agreeable to both of us. O Papa you could not have pleased your precious One more than by sending such a handsome present, & GrdMa & I can have a nice time now & visit the neighbours too when we wish to. Uncle Will says "Little Sis" must make our boy a hightop hat to put on when he's driving his dappled greys, does look so consequential, & cunningly sweet with head thrown back, a broad smile on his face, & mouth wide open, stops occasionally to lean over the side & examine the equipment of his ponies. We enclose the hair dear Papa, & send it with a kiss to Grdma Kimball, tell her when he gets to be a little man in pants will go & see her. If you could stay with your Darling's baby a few days, he will love you to nurse & play with him, & it occurs to me that he wont be afraid of you, as of all others he's not accustomed to see, but you may expect to get your whiskers pulled, for he governs Grdpa entirely with them. Mamie writes that Godfrey can go with a chair all over the floor, & walk some too without, & in all sorts of mischief generally. She had to put him in short clothes (he tumbled over, & got so many falls trying to get about.) Contrary to the looks of our Strawberry [patch] "Little Sis" & "Tug" did gather a nice little mess yester eve for dinner today, so hope we'l have some when you come.

Must tell you that Aunt C. is teaching little darling to kiss when asked.

sometimes he will, ever so sweetly, then again will make her scream out with a bitten lip, says she does know that if he got good hold would take a piece out. Grdpa says, the carriage is going to make his little man independent of him, & he most wishes his Papa had not sent it. Pa does so love for Smoker to cry for him to take him, cuts as many capers about it as a school boy, but if you could only stay with little precious one week, would not wonder that he is all & all to us. The cold I told you he was taking last week, <u>did not</u> make him sick Papa, but Grdma did, giving him some turtle soup, 'twas too rich, gave him sick stomach, & caused him to lose one nursing of milk, after that, he was <u>all right</u>, but I dont guess I'll give him any more. Will caught the turtle & a fine cat fish on his set hooks. Has Mrs Hunt returned home? & how is Capt. Smoker? I will write regularly <u>every Fri.</u> unless incapacitated from illness, in which case some one of the family will let you hear from Darling's baby boy, & our precious Pet. I prefer writing Friday'[s] because Saturday'[s] are the only days on which I'm <u>certain</u> of getting a letter to town. Good bye, all's well dear Papa, & your little darling sends you ever so many kisses.

      With love from each one,
      Your devotedly
      M. E. B.

Susan Morton in Autuaga Co. to Cornelia Dickson in Ouachita Co.
                 June 12, 1879

 Dear Miss Cornelia

  I thought I would write to you. I have not heard from you in a long time. I want you to write to me and let me know where you are staying and how you and Miss Clara are getting along. I am living with Mrs Dave Caver, renting land. We have Susie and Harriette, Laurie's children and Johnie, Ellen's boy. I have none of my children with me. Laura is living with the Kings in Dallas [County, Alabama]. Ellen and Meuses at the Linsy place. Caroline at Kirklands. They are doing very well. I heard from Harriet's boys Christmas. They are not living with Tom Caver but near him. I look a little older than when you were here. I have good health except Rhumatism. Brother Jerry died last September, he was sick a long time, his children were living with him when he died. Hannah Lassiter sends her love to you, also old Aunt Judy. You don't know how bad I want to see you. I pray for you often and I want you to pray for me, if I never meet you in this life, I want to meet you in heaven. I think you might come out to see us and bring some of the young folks with you. Write me a long long letter, and I answer it in kind. I am writing now to let you know I still living. We have fine crops this year. My grand children are going to school to Mr. W. Adair. Emma, Ellen's girl can write her name, her boy name Squire is very smart. Ellen has only 3 children and Laura 3. Do write soon.

> Your old affectionate mama,
> Susan Morton

Mary Elizabeth Boddie in Ouachita Co. to her son John Rumph Boddie in St. Louis

June 13th 79

My own dear boy,

Had the pleasure of rec'ng your dear letter of 9' Inst. yester eve, & be assured, I sympathize with you most sincerely in your loneliness, & sad feelings, when nearly every place to which you go, brings reminescences of the short & happy past, in forceble contrast with what now is. — Your God, & time is the only Healer son, if you school yourself to think, only of your Darling, as being safe & happy in her "Fathers' House," you can await with patience His summons to join her, who has left you to love & cherish the most sacred pledge of a wife's love. Our little darling is a part of her dear self & if God spares him to you I know that he'l be good. Bless his dear little heart — he's growing sweeter & sweeter every day, & can almost talk now with jestures, as plain as speech. Makes his <u>ponies go now like everything</u>, in the first place, he throws everything out of the box with a wink & a squint, then rises to his feet, <u>starts</u> the rocker, then sits back, & makes his ponies travel with a vim. In all his plays, his movements are very quick. Can sit alone on the floor first rate now, moves forward, & slides along somehow, but has not yet attempted to get about on his hands & knees, & as he dont like a position on his stomach, hope he wont learn to crawl in that way, ie on hands & knees. I can tell you Papa he has rubbed his shoes white nearly all round, except the toes. Aunt C. wants me to let him go barefoot 'tis so warm, but I prefer not, & am afraid he would get splinters in his feet off the rough floors. Pa has been about half sick for the past week, but rest, & a good rain I think will bring him all right. No rain yet, & no prospect for any at present. Ann has been sick with bad cold, a dose of oil relieved that, but she now has nettle rash, to which she says she has always been subject. We try every day to teach little darling to love to eat, yet make slow progress. He will take a few sups of milk, then turn up his nose, laugh & make blubbers in it. Carrie & I tried him with his bottle this morn, but he wont begin to stand the rubber stopper, dont like the taste of it at all. Mashed potatoes, he seems to love, yet, two or three tastes is all he'l take at one feeding. Did Geo R. have to send off for the <u>chair</u>? Willie has been to town twice with the waggon since you left, & he has not sent it. Trust you have rec'd my letter ere this, will be sure to write every week.

Hope that you may keep well son & in good spirits, trusting all to Him who doeth all things well. Little darling is so very sweet, Papa that I cant kiss him half enough for you, & do wish you could enjoy being with him oftener. Aunt Mamie says, she cant help looking for us every day, she wants to see her boy so much, yet entertains but little hope of seeing any of us this summer. No news, Uncle J's family, & all relatives well. Your Darling's precious baby is well, & sends dear Papa a thousand kisses. All send much love.

Your devoted Mother,
Mary E. Boddie

Cornelia Dickson in Ouachita Co. to her friend Julia Howard in Boiling Springs, Alabama

July 2, 1879

Dear Julia,

Many months have come and gone since I last wrote to you, and I at first felt grieved that you neglected to reply. But since knowing you as I do, I cannot but think that the fault lies in the mail, and that probably you may even now be upbraiding me in the same manner. For since I wrote to you, I have heard that you were with your dear Aunt Jane in her last illnes, about the time that I wrote and the circumstance induces me to think that my letter never reached you. Heaven forbid that I should wrongfully censure any one; especially one whom I appreciate as a dear friend. I should have written long ago, but pride my besetting sin would whisper Why not wait for her to write. I have thought of it many times and at last better feelings have prevailed and I feel real pleasure tonight in again holding communion with you, I fear you were never very well entertained with my efforts. But I have sadly missed your pleasant messengers, seeming as they did a small part of your very self. Often I have regretted that it is out of my power to repeat my visit of five years ago, for sometimes I do wish to see all of you again.

I am still teaching Dr. Rumphs two little girls. If I had a large school to engage all my time, would be better satisfied.

Our neighborhood is on the increase. We have a Sabbath School established again. The young men have a debating society in full blast, meets every two weeks. Singing School will open next Saturday, I have not yet decided to attend but Florence, Attalie and Tommie have joined. The young people met here last Friday night, had a real lively sociable. We are invited to attend another next Friday night, But I do not feel much inclined to engage in anything of the kind, while we are suffering with drouth, it has been eight or nine weeks since we last had rain, and crops are cut off one half already. One of the neighbors has just come around, getting up a barbeque for next Thursday, they will meet in the grove in front of this house.

      Affectionately
      Cornelia S. Dickson

Mary Elizabeth Boddie in Ouachita Co. to her son John Rumph Boddie in St. Louis

                 July 7th '79

  My dear boy,

   If I hurry & write a little note can get it off today but know you will be disappointed anyway in not rec'ng by this time some of your precious little darling's pictures, yet you cant be more so than I was when Mr Goe told me, that when he went to work on them was not satisfied with the negative, & determined to wait for another setting. Mittie thought he must have cracked the glass or damaged it in some way, for we all decided that, that negative was first rate. Well! he had little darling to sit <u>six times</u> again, ere he thought one would do, & I doubt now, if he has succeeded as well as we wished. Did not try to get the nude ones that day, believing 'twould be imprudent to strip my baby as so many children in town were ill with croup, accompanied with sore throat, & Dr. B[ragg] said 'twas getting to be an epedemic, with both old & young children, & I wanted to get away with my baby as soon as possible. He is <u>quite well</u> Papa, & just as lively as a cricket, & as Grdpa says, gets away with us all. We have many reasons to suppose that he <u>did miss</u> his Papa, & if you dont stay away too long believe he will know you when you come. He beats anything you ever saw when in his rocker, & loves too to be led about, <u>steps grand</u> & <u>high</u>, but I think 'twill be sometime before he learns to walk, & indeed he's not old enough. That other little tooth is in sight, yet not quite through. Mittie is going to her Pa's today to stay a week or two, the neighbourhood will have a barbecue at Uncle J's spring the 10th Inst. Little Godfrey is walking now, he had a rising which prevented Mamie from coming, as she expected to be here by the 4th. O Papa your Darling's baby delighted Bobbie, & I so much a day or two ago, by saying Ba, ba, ba, over & over again, when I was showing him your picture, & telling him to say Papa. Tug says, Why Mama! he is saying it. Little pet often says Mam Mam now, & his voice is sweeter than music. We rec'd your letter of 30 Ult. not until last Sat. was very glad to know of your good health & safe arrival home. No rain for us yet. Good bye, little precious sends you ever so many kisses, & O Papa you dont know how very sweet & interesting he is unless with him. All send much love,

         Your devoted Mother,
         Mary E. Boddie

Papa, Aunt Carrie says, <u>my shoes</u> were not numbered, but she thinks they were four's. Ask Mrs Goddard, dont like to send the measure as seldom ever fit when taken by measure —

Cornelia Dickson in Ouachita Co. to her friend Julia Howard at Boiling Springs, Alabama

Aug 4th, 1879

Dear Julia

Your most welcome letter of the 19th Ult was received last week. I was delighted to hear from you again too much so to censure you since hearing the cause of your not writing. I can sympathize with you in your attendance in the sickroom having have had considerable experience and by the way what has become of your aunt's little grandchildren she had in charge. What changes, what sad changes a few years have wrought. So many that I numbered [as] friends have passed away never never to meet us again. Brother John and I were speaking last night of the number of men who had died in our old neighborhood since he lived there. Your Father, Uncle Lonnie, Mr Red Jones Jr. and Mr. Tho[mas] Underwood were the only men he could call to mind that are left of the large circle who used to gather around old Mulberry. You see I have wandered into a sad restrospection.

Your trip to Wilcox recalls mine & Sis Mollie's to Marengo. We were two days on the road and enjoyed it most of the time. Cole and Will Love were very kind. How far are you from Rehobeth? I seem to associate that neighborhood with your locality. I am glad to hear from all the young people, particularly Dora & her interesting little family. I would be delighted to have the honor of naming her wee daughter but scarcely anyone fancies my favorite name. It is <u>Jewel</u>. There are many others very pretty, but I think this the sweetest. Bettie Rumph suggests Eugenia, Virginia Pearl and Maude. Jennie, George Rumph's wife, says be sure and call her "Ethel Annie," for her little fairhaired beauty.

Jennie went home Saturday, having spent two weeks with us. I wish you could know her, Julie, she is such a merry good soul. Mittie & Florence are spending several weeks about twenty miles up the country, visiting Mr. Ruck's relatives. I have not seen any of brother George's family recently except Carrie & Will at Church. Sis Mollie will be glad to hear from you. She is a most foolishly fond grandma now. Mamie's son is a year old. You probably heard that she married Dr Coleman of Clark Co. And John Boddie's wife died in St. Louis last Sept. leaving an infant son a few hours old. He immediately brought it to his mother and she has been most successful so far, in raising it. While she lives, it will never know its loss. They call him Smoker, his mother's maiden name. Johnie is a most devoted father, is still commercial agent in Ark for a house in St Louis.

Clara and family have enjoyed unusual health this summer. In fact there has been no sickness in the neighborhood this summer. Crops here, corn crops are almost a failure, owing to a twelve weeks drouth. Cotton is somewhat injured, but the young people have had an unusually lively summer, until recently the weather is so excessively warm. I believe the mania for barbecues and picnics has somewhat subsided.

I regret to see that the yellow fever has again broken out in Memphis. Bettie Rumph lost a great many of her school friends last year during the epidemic there.

I am anxious to know who that sweetheart is, have been waiting a year now for communication. Do you not think my patience truly tried? I am afraid you hav'nt any since the pedagogue subsided. I always entertained a very high opinion of Mr Cory's family, judging them from their parents standing & example, for they were mere children when I left Ala. But there is no accounting for the queer actions produced by matrimonial fever. The most selfish I believe will, in time, become in a measure subdued. I was glad to hear from your Aunt Hattie again. How many children has she now? quite a number I imagine. How many has Mary Smith? I remember her well but I guess she scarecely remembers me. What has ever become of her sister, Mrs Pink Law? We were old friends.

Your affectionate friend
Cornelia S. Dickson

Cornelia Dickson in Ouachita Co. to her friend Julia Howard at Boiling Springs, Alabama

Oct 20th 1879

Dear Julia

I came home last Friday from a two weeks visit to Camden. Spending most of the time with Mittie & Jennie. While over there replied to a letter from Mrs Clark inquiring about her relatives, the Stones. Several of whom live in Camden, met a good many of my friends & enjoyed my visit exceedingly. I would like to go over again in December to attend Conference. I often think of the annual Protracted meetings at old Ivy Creek, and would enjoy visiting Ala again but am unable to do so. Since I last wrote you, we have had a revival in our neighborhood. The most interesting meeting I ever attended. Thirty-two new members were added to the church. Twenty-seven of whom were baptised. Florence & Attalie Rumph among the latter. Brother John's wife, & Sis Mollie's youngest son, Robert, were, and Clara's two daughters joined. Sis Mollie joined several years ago. I had never united myself to any church since I left Ala until during this meeting, for I never felt settled.

You ask about Sis Mollie. She lives six miles from us and as the facilities for visiting are not very favorable & she is almost a recluse since the care of John's baby devolved upon her, we see her but seldom. I saw her about a month ago. She inquired after you and said I must send her best love to you when I wrote again. We never meet that we do not recur to our pleasant visit in Alabama.

Several marriages have taken place in the neighborhood since I last wrote. Miss Mary L. Stone to Mr Walter Richardson, & Miss Lula Avera to Mr T. J. Steele. I attended the first, had a delightful time. Florence Rumph & Carrie Boddie were attendants. Mary Stone, who is a daughter of Dr. J. Stone, is named for Mrs Mary Wilkes. Lula Avera was one of my former pupils, had no wedding, only a marriage.* I met both at church yesterday. They seem very devoted but not quite as much so as another couple I heard of a day or two since. The lady, who was very youthful was exceedingly fond of fishing, her husband who was correspondingly old, would accompany her and would prostrate himself for her to sit on while she enjoyed her favorite sport. Mr. Dunn our minister preached a fine sermon, on Regeneration. He reminds me very much of Mr Axford, Julia. Clara was not out. Lula told me she was quite ill with neuralgia, produced from cold. Your kind letter altogether was very interesting to me, and while they continue I shall not feel the <u>need</u> of a paper from Autauga. However I should be pleased to receive a copy at your earliest convenience.

I had not heard until from your letter that Mims possessed Cedar Grove. I was truly glad to hear of his prosperity. I think your Pa has cause to be proud of his children. He has many to be proud of, fifteen or sixteen is it not. I hope they may all prove a blessing.*

*Cornelia must mean that they did not have a big wedding to which people were invited. Perhaps they just went before a minister or Justice-of-the-peace.

*Note: This letter was unsigned in the journal.

*There is no date, but the following notation was attached by John R. Boddie

*Verses from Cornelia Smoker Boddie**

The verses on the sheet were composed and written by my precious Wife on the fly leaf of her Bible —
Jno. R. Boddie

O! Give me grace to come to thee
Great Father of us all.
Open my eyes that I might see
My sin before I fall ——

Give me strength to turn my heart
From this world of sin
Merciful and strong thou art
O! make me turn within ——

Guide my erring feet along
The straight and narrow way
Put into my mouth a song
To praise thee night and day

Why should I care if all the world
Should mock me as I fast
Derision, scorn should at me hurl
So I reach heaven at last.

Help O! help me ere I fall
To come O Lord to thee
Teach me to obey thy call
And worship only thee.

Mary E. Boddie in Ouachita Co. to her son John R. Boddie in St. Louis
Jan 2nd 1880

Dearest Papa,

  We were so glad to get your dear letter, for the time seems very long since you were here, though the days pass swiftly, & we are enjoying ourselves finely, little darling & I, & every night he & Uncle Will have a big romp, Bob joins in too, & even Grdpa gets on his all fours, which appears quite funny to all hands, but you must know that our little darling is King, & the pet of the household as none can withstand his sweet ways. I do wish that you could see him eating oranges, to say that he enjoys them dont begin to express it. Uncle Will was his Santa Xmas, & Grdpa got more for him New Years' day. Uncle Gilder brought his Xmas box over Fri. & little darling was very much pleased with its contents, but he dont seem to think anything worth a cent that cant stand the test of his <u>mallets</u>, consequently his waggon is minus the wheels already, but he loves to drag it around better I believe without them as it makes more clatter, he turns the wagon body bottom upwards, & you can guess how it delights him to stand on, & step over it time & again.
  I often think son perhaps 'tis best, that you cannot be with your little darling always, for should he be taken, the void would be more poignant. I know that I dearly love my children, & not a care for them was ever considered any trouble, but my love for this precious little one exceeds all, yet

I try to school myself for any ill that may befall, & feeling my dependence placing all trust in Him the Father of all. O Son your darling baby more repays us for all the care we can ever bestow, making our old hearts rejoice as it were in the presence of an Angel, beside appreciating no little your confiding trust that we would care for your precious baby for his father's sake.

    Must tell you what our baby did recently, Pa was reading his papers, & little darling asked him (with motions & grunts) for his <u>specks</u>, put them on his own head, then deliberately turned & asked for the paper, & holding it up before him as he had seen his Grdpa do, pretended to read. Now dont you know he looked sweet, smart & cunning? When in the humor for pratling can say pa, pa, pa, fast enough, & has said anpa (when told say Grdpa) several times for us. Aunt C[arrie] gives him an apple every day, & every time she comes in the house, her presence is a reminder of them, & 'tis ever new, & amusing to us to see his capers, & hear him say ap ap. Our winter apples are better than the imported ones, though not as large, the drouth last summer caused them to be smaller than usual. Aunt C. got two Xmas boxes, one containing a neat little set of jewelry from her Bud Gilder, the other a beautiful box of stationary, (sufficient for the year) from Mr. Allis Moseley, & last but not least — Tug's present to her of a silver thimble which was highly appreciated because one dollar was <u>his</u> all that he had to spend. I am so glad that you went to see Mamie, have not heard from her since my return home — think they will have a very nice little place when improved, & hope you liked it. We all took Turkey dinner with Uncle J[ohn] last Sun. enjoyed the visit very much. Mat remarked that Garland was'nt noticed much when Smoker was about — Mr Wiggs expressed himself very glad to meet the young man, said he had not heard of <u>any other baby</u> for a long time, & thought he did indeed merit much notice. His wife is at Miss Clem's to stay during her confinement. Perhaps you learned of Mr Jim Proctor's marriage to Miss Ophelia Dunlap? I did not hear of it until several days after my return home. Tommy & Gilder were at Uncle J's Sun. & staid with us that night. We've had two boats up recently, & a prospect for more rain to keep the river up. Pa is looking after the stock, & Will & Bob are busy splitting rails. Tug has blistered his hands, & says he has not worked hard for so long a time it makes him sore all over. Little Sis is chief cook, milking, ironer, & guess I shall have to draw on you for cook's wages to keep her in heart, as we were disappointed in getting Ann, she had engaged to cook for Mrs Sales thinking we did not want her as I did not send for her immediately. With much love from each one will close, wishing you a happy New Year. Little darling sends you a big New Year kiss, & each day Grdma kisses him o'er & o'er again telling him 'tis for his dear Papa, & she does know that he is just the sweetest little darling in all the world.

                Devotedly your Mother,
                Mary E. Boddie

Cornelia Dickson in Ouachita Co. to her friend Rebecca Underwood in Autauga Co.

Feb 13th, 1880

Dear Becca,

    Your dear letter came to me so full of the life and enjoyment among those in my old home that I felt while reading it that I was seemingly with you all again and rejoicing in the pleasure and prosperity that "sweeten life and lighten labor." But Becca when I came to that portion of your letter telling of your father's severe cold & cough, I felt very uneasy, and a gloomy sadness I could not dispell seem[ed] to envelope me, as I thought of the great anxiety of your dear mother on his account. They Becca I have ever considered among my truest, best friends.

    Since receiving your letter on the 7th of Jan, we have been deeply afflicted. Our dear Bettie has been called from this changing earth to an eternal home and we are left to grieve that her bright face & winning smile will greet us no more, no more on earth. She was in town, and at the time, was with Mittie, was taken with severe cold, but as she was always so very healthy, paid but little attention to it until the fourth day, not being able to be up, Mittie insisted upon calling in a physician; Bettie still objected & declared she would not take medicine but Mittie becoming for the first time much alarmed, had a physician called, but even then Bettie persisted in telling him that she had only a slight cold & her sister was too scarry, was so very lively that the M.D. was <u>completely deceived</u>, But her sister was not, as her symptons were then developing very dangerously and told Bettie that in the morning she would send for her Pa. But ere a messenger could be procured congestion had done its work. On the 27th ult. our beautiful lovely one breathed her last at about ten oclock next morning without a struggle or even a sigh. That morning early her brothers George & Tommie having heard that [she] was "a little sick" having called in to see her. She was talking & laughing with them, and when George threatened, in case she did not take her medicine to send up a young physician she protested, & said she "would not see him as she would run & lock herself up in the closet" when she saw him coming. Poor child she had no idea how very sick she was. She was not a member of any church but for a long time had been striving to live a Christian life, and the night before, when Mittie in remonstrating with her about throwing off the cover (as she complained of great heat, while her hands were cold) told her, she might get very sick & even die, Bettie replied, If her time had come she was ready to go. You may know Becca it was a great shock to us all for we did not even know that she was ill, and brother John was at the time attending the bedside of my dear friend Anna [Moseley] Gaughan, who on the fifth of this month went to join our dear Bettie in that Better Land. Yes Anna was a true good friend to me, and her loss is a severe prang to my already aching heart. She leaves a devoted husband, [James Gaughan] and a wee babe, who will never know aught of its mother's love. Her death was caused from pneumonia. On the 7th of Jan. Mrs Wiggs of Hot Springs, (a sister of brother John's last wife), died. She had come to spend several months with her mother, Mrs Proctor and sisters. Only a mile from us. Contracted severe cold during the Christmas holidays, and medical aid seemed of no avail. You see Becca our whole neighborhood has been enveloped in the deepest gloom almost since the dawn of the New Year, and I sincerely trust we may be spared further sorrow.*

*This letter is unsigned in the ledger

Cornelia Dickson in Ouachita Co. to her friend Julia Howard in Autauga Co.

Feb 28th 1880

Dear Julia

So many sad changes have occured since I last wrote to you. Indeed I fear I am too sad to write now, but do so in order to solicit one of your interesting missives. I was truly glad to hear of your enjoyment of the Christmas holidays. We too had a most pleasant Christmas, But what an awakening from the too little appreciated happiness.

Four deaths have occurred in the two months that have filled our hearts with deep sorrow. When our dear Bettie passed from earth the 27th of Jan. & my friend Anna so soon followed her, the 5th of Feb, I felt bereft. The other is a sad story. Last of all Florence Rumph was betrothed to one of our most superior young men in the neighborhood, Mr. Ed Richardson. They were to have been married the 19th of Feb. but her sister Bettie's sudden death caused them to defer it until the 25th of March. She had her outfit nearly completed, and a handsome one it was, and she was incessantly picturing to me how very happy she would be, how dearly she would love his motherless sisters & little brother; & they loved her so much, & I rejoiced in her happiness. But alas! a week ago death laid his ruthless hand upon his noble, manly heart, & stilled its pulses forever. She, poor girl, was wild with grief, & would not be comforted, but clung to his lifeless form & prayed to die. He was a most zealous Christian, a devoted son, brother & friend, and a more loyal heart never beat. Just before he died he sang in a clear strong voice, "There is a Fountain Filled with Blood". He had Typhoid fever, Pneumonia, and died in a week from the time he was attack[ed]. Medical aid was not called until the disease was to thoroughly seated to be removed. Florence was taken quite ill a day or two after Bettie's death and we were very uneasy about her then. She seemed to be utterly prostrated, from that shock, for we did not know of Bettie's illness at all, until we heard she was gone. She was spending some time in town with her sister & brothers, and the morning she died, was talking & laughing as usual. Now Florence seems a mere shadow of her former self, and we all feel so distressed about her. She is spending a week in town. Will she ever become resigned? Oh I trust she may. Dear Julia pardon my confiding so much of my grief to you, but I cannot but feel that your sympathy will be very grateful.*

*This letter is unsigned in the ledger

Carrie Boddie [Little Sis] in Ouachita Co. to her brother John R. Boddie in St. Louis

March 17th, 1880

Dear Brother,

Your letter did come unexpectedly and I can never <u>never</u> thank you sufficiently for your kind advice, nor can I express my full appreciation for the deep interest you feel in my welfare. Now that you will care for me, I shall be your dutiful "Little" girl, and <u>be assured</u> will never wed a "Lord of Creation" that you would be ashamed to recognize as a brother; but you ought not to expect too much of me, you well know my advantages have been more than limited: consequently am dull and awkward. Yes Brother, I am young in years, but very <u>very</u> much older in thought and feeling, have never had any girlhood but a complete old woman of nineteen years.

You spoke of taking me to St. Louis next year. Have a care should I be thrown among your friends you might be ashamed to own little Sis. She is such an ignoramus! — though I shall do all in my power to please you. 'Tis you to advise, mine to obey. What more can I do to repay your goodness.

Your Affectionate
Little Sis

Frances Caroline
"Carrie" Boddie
1860-1892
Photo courtesy of Ruth Boddie Farmer.

Florence Rumph in Camden to Cornelia Dickson in Harmony Grove

Mar 26th 1880

My dear aunt;

This beautiful morning, I seat myself with pencil in hand, to assure you that I have not forgotten one who has proved everkind and true, to this sad and broken heart; and never will I neglect you, my dear aunt. It seemes that you, and sis Jennie are the only ones of my relatives that feel and <u>nearly</u> sympathise with me. The beautiful sun shiny days that we have had gladdened and cheered many gloomy feelings, and brighted many sad hearts; but my poor broken heart can never more be gladdened; for it misses and sighs for that sweet voice and cheerful heart which now are silent and cold. Oh! can I ever realize, that my dear Eddie is no more on this earth? there is nothing to cheer me; though I see and are with many bright faces and warm hearts, yet they can not make me feel happy. I can not content myself. I am surely lost without the darling boy. Today, I might have been his happy wife, and he, my loving husband. I can not stand it, it is too much for me; if I just could find relief. Aunt Nealie, my eyes are scarcely ever dry, why, I <u>pray</u>, and read my <u>bible</u> yet still I grieve, it is real hard grief. I do believe that I shall go stone crazy. Surely I can soon follow my loved one. I am as you know in delicate health, and grow weaker every day. I have palpertation of the heart so severe that sometimes I nearly smother and I have dumb chills every three days, had hot fever for four hours yesterday, and I feel badly and have headache this morning. How I wish I could see Mamie and Maggie [Richardson: sisters of Eddie Richardson] in fact all of Edie's loved ones, for all are very dear to me. I receive letters of sympathy from some of my dear friends nearly every day. I did not know, that they ever thought of me. Brother Monk is very kind to me, also his wife; they express their sympathy to me in many ways. They visit me often, and insist that I must come and stay with them. I love them very much, and I go to see them. Oh, they are so kind to me and they seem to love me. Brother [George Rumph] will leave this evening and will be gone several weeks. I will stay over here until he returns. They let me name the sweet little baby Eddie. The children call him little Eddie, "<u>Aunt Florries Baby</u>." Little George had the croup very severe last night, but up this morning playing. All the others are well. Sis Jennie is rapidly improving, says that I shall not leave her. They all are anxious for me to live with them. They say that they will try to make me happy, and will let me go to see and stay with Eddie's relatives when ever I wish too; as they think that I want to be with them as much as possible, and know that I could not rest, unless I could be with those dear ones. The days just drag by. Aunt Nealie will you please get some flowers and put them on Eddie's grave for me. I will send some just as soon as I can, and send them to you to deck his grave. I wish that his grave was near enough, I would go there <u>every</u> day, and put flowers on it. I must close. Sister's [Mittie Rumph Rucks] family are well. Tell Mamie I will write to her tomorrow. Give my love to all of them, and accept a portion for your dear self. Write soon. I reckon you have heard that cousin Mamie lost her little babe. Love to Mrs. G[aughan]. Goodbye Aunt Nealie, please write. Excuse haste.

      Your loving neice
      Florence Rumph

Cornelia Dickson in Ouachita Co. to her friend Rebecca Underwood in Autauga Co.

April 10th, 1880

Dear Becca

If you judge of your very kind letters nonappreciated by the length of time I have been in answering it, you will be greatly mistaken; for if I had followed my inclination, I should have written immediately. I am teaching again, a small school, & boarding at old Mr. Gaughan's. Mrs G. has Anna's little babe trying to raise it. They have a wet nurse and the little granddaughter is thriving finely. The old people have no daughter living, and they & their three boys* are devoted to the wee little creature, and call it "Our baby".* Last Sunday Sis Mollie spent the day with us, brought her "pet" with her. He is a very fine child, runs about the house & tries to talk and it is Sis Mollie's chief delight to recount his wonderfully smart achievements. Carrie & Robert went on to Mr. Richardson's. Florence is still in town, I read a note from her yesterday. She is in wretched health. George is away on a trip to New Orleans, as soon as he comes home I want her to come out to the country. Everything is fast donning Spring attire, since the cold rainy weather has ceased, and I think she would improve. I was sorry to hear of Emma's poor health. I would enjoy more than anything to visit her and all my friends in Ala. But I can only talk about it, that is all I can do, as yet. Carrie & I were speaking of it last Sunday. She says the next time I go she intends to go with me & that I must not put it off too long. Yes, I used to know Willie Wilkinson — well when he was a boy about fourteen. I knew all the family. Jimmie Wilkinson I used to think was one of Autauga's first young men. I am not personally acquainted with Mr. Mac S[mith] but was under the impression he was a married man. Be sure and send me Tommie S. picture. I should prize it so highly. You never sent me the other you promised. Carrie received Eula's but I have never been down there since & she can't think to bring it. Tell Eula I feel slighted. I shall have to close at present, as I rashly promised some time ago to accompany some of my friends to an old widowers this evening to visit his niece and I wish something, not very bad, would happen to keep me from going. However he will marry in a week or two, and so that settles it or I should forego the pleasure. I saw Clara yesterday. She enjoys moderately good health. Mr. D[unlap] and the children keep well. They have all gone shopping today. Brother John and family enjoy good health. They have been feasting on wild turkeys recently. There seem to be an abundance of them this year. The neighborhood seem to enjoy good health at present except Mrs Robert Stone, she is but little improved. Write again Becca very soon, for I do enjoy your letters so much. With love to all I am, as ever

Affectionately your friend
Cornelia S. Dickson

*The three boys that Cornelia mentions are Dennis, Alex, & Tommie Gaughan. Jim Gaughan was the baby's father.
*Anna Moseley Gaughan's baby girl was named Mary.

Cornelia Dickson in Ouachita Co. to her friend Mrs. E. S. Clark in Statesville, Alabama

Summer of 1880

Dear Mrs Clark,

    I had almost ceased to expect a letter from you, not being able to settle upon any conclusion about it. Widows are so uncertain, I did have a faint idea that you had entered again the "Connubial state." Cut me out of that M.D., Or that probably, the cares of life had engrossed too much of your time and attention, that your were compelled to put off writing for a more "convenient time." I am so prone to that fault myself that I can more readily excuse it in others, though I often grow weary awaiting the advent of one of your long interesting letters. They contain so many local items that I almost feel while reading them I am with you all again, entering through the medium of sympathy, all the joys and sorrows that come like silent messengers of sunshine or clouds upon my old friends.

    My delay in answering has seemed to be unavoidable. I have scarcely had breathing time since spring. My principle occupation, school teaching, since the first of March with about a month's respite, which was spent almost entirely nursing the sick and sewing. My own health has suffered and I am now using "Wilhoft's Tonic" to prevent a return of fever. We have had a great deal of rain, which in this country seems calculated to produce sickness. Most suffering has been caused by flux and whooping cough, but few cases of fever have developed.

    Since the first of July, I have been teaching a Public School about five miles above Brother John's. I am well pleased with my pupils though the neighborhood is rather rougher than ours and having to walk a mile and a half this warm weather, I feel completely jaded all the week, and am scarcely rested by Monday morning. My school will not be out before the first of October. Two of the little chaps had a chill yesterday and I fear there will be more sickness yet.

    Crops are generally fine, but most too much rain for cotton. Fruit is plentiful.

    I have not been able to see your relatives since receiving your letter. Annie Stone is very low with cancer, said to be incurable. I would not be surprised at any time to hear of her death. The rest are all well I believe.

    The last time I saw Ora Newton she was speaking of you. She said she would never die satisfied until she had seen you. Like all of us, money is not so plentiful with them as formerly and they have a large family, always a baby on hand. I have never heard of Mrs. Pile* since she went off. Octavia Word is to marry Sandy Brodnax tomorrow. Give my love to all enquiring friends and write again soon to,

                  Your affectionate friend,
                    Cornelia S. Dickson

*"Mrs. Pile" refers to Eliza Stone Wood Pile, sister of Ora Newton. Octavia Word is a niece of Ora Newton.

Cornelia Dickson in Ouachita Co. to the daughter of her friend Rebecca Underwood in Autauga Co.

Oct 14th 1880

Dear Becca

Your loving messenger was so gladly received, but how little prepared I was for the shock awaiting me in its perusal.* I <u>can</u> deeply sympathise with you all, for our hearts still ache from the void that was created in our home circle last winter. Oh I wish I could say something to Rebecca that would bring comfort to her bruised heart. But that can only be found by "taking it to our Lord in prayer." I would so gladly be with you, if it were in my power, but my circumstances in life are such, it is impossible. It is indeed a sad change in our house on earth when our loved ones are taken away and we never more can listen to their dear familiar voices. But such is the experience of all sojourners here below. We each have our crosses and we are inclined to believe that <u>ours are heavier than others.</u> But we should remember that we have Divine promises from which, if we will, we can derive great comfort. In that good old song "How Firm a Foundation," we will not be called upon to bear more than our strength can endure. The burden may never be lightened on this earth. I do not believe it is so intended. I would not if I could forget the <u>jewels</u> that have been taken away. Such "firery trials" are intended for some good purpose, or it would never be, even though we poor mortals cannot understand it now. We know it is only the "blest early dead" who are <u>spared</u> the troubles of earth. Yet we do not understand why those well fitted to <u>live</u> should be called to <u>die</u>. I feel that we can only find comfort in cheerful submission to a <u>Divine</u> and <u>loving</u> decree.

My school closed several weeks since and I was gratified that all the patrons expressed entire satisfaction and solicited me to take charge again next summer. The people in that section are in reduced circumstances, and their children are required to assist in gathering the crops or they said they would have extended my school by subscription to the close of this year. My children were good & obedient throughout, I never had to exercise severer punishment than to require a few minutes stand on the floor; one more thoughtless little fellow had to stand upon the bench a few minutes. I felt real sorry for him, for he cried about it all evening as if his heart would break but gave me no more trouble during the school. They had previously heard that I was very strict. I suppose is the reason they were so easily controlled Every one was very kind to me & little acts of "kindness" tend greatly to brighten the gloomy paths of life.

I am at home [Brother John's] again & though the family is somewhat reduced in numbers, find them all very cheerful. Florence is much improved in health & spirits. The little brats keep up a stir, Brother John has gone driving today. There are an abundance of deer. He is speaking of joining a Cam

---

* In a letter dated February 13, 1880, to Rebecca, Cornelia expressed her distress upon hearing of the poor health of Becca's father. The "shock" awaiting Cornelia in Becca's letter was undoubtedly the death of Rebecca's husband and Becca's father.

hunt this fall. Attalie and Eugenia are at school in Camden. Mittie has been quite sick & brother John told me last night that she wanted me to go over & stay several weeks with her. I expect to go tomorrow; Carrie Boddie is with her now. She [Carrie] has just returned from St. Louis where she was attending the fair. I have not seen her, but will deliver Eula's message when I do. I have not seen Clara in several weeks. She is not in a good health as usual.

Our protracted meeting commences tomorrow and I am afraid I shall be unable to attend. Mrs. Robert Stone [Mrs. Annie] died last month. She was a great sufferer a long time, and death was to her a happy relief. Write again very soon.*

*This letter is unsigned in the ledger.

T. J. Gaughan at St. Joseph College in Bardstown, Kentucky, to Cornelia Dickson in Ouachita Co.

Nov.27th 1880

My Dear Friend

I take pleasure, after so long time, in writing to you. I arrived here safe and well and have been ever since. Of course I felt homesick a few days, but not so much as I expected. There is sixty students that board here, and about twenty-five day scholars that come from Bardstown. They stay in different study rooms from the boarders, but they all recite in the same classroom. Bardstown is a small dirty town. It would be of no importance at all if it was not for the college and the churches. The weather is very cold. The snow has been on the ground for the last two weeks. We have had three snows in that time. The boys have been skating several times, and it is truly surprising to see the antics of a good skater on ice. There is a young man here from Alabama, he lives near Selma, and his name is William Browder. The bridge of the Arkansas at Little Rock is about as high from the ground as I care to be without wings. I often think of the happy days I used to spend going to school to you, and how you made me study in such a way that I did not mind it. I believe they were the happiest and best spent days of my life, and I think I shall never forget them.

We have a little over twelve hours, out of twenty four, for study, about three and a half for recreation, the rest for sleep. We have friday for recreation instead of saturday.

When did you see "the Baby" and how is she? This is the eleventh letter I have written since I received an answer. This does not speak well for Carrol township in the way of letter writing. I believe I am beginning to grow a little since I came here, at least I have gained fifteen pounds. Write soon and tell me something about all my old school mates, as I cannot write to them all.

Yours truly,
T. J. Gaughan

Cornelia Dickson in Ouachita Co. to T. J. Gaughan at St. Joseph College in Bardstown, Kentucky

Dec 10, 1880

Dear Tommie

It was an agreeable surprise to me to receive a letter from you. Yes I saw you pass Mr McKinneys the morning you started and my first impulse was to run out & bid you goodbye, but it occurred to me that you were looking very sad, and I feared I should only make you feel more so, and contented myself with best wishes for your future. I am truly glad to find that you do not suffer from that dreadful malady "homesickness." I have experienced the suffering, and can heartily sympathise with any one so affected. It was very gratifying to me, Tommie, to know, that my efforts for your instruction, in days past, is so much appreciated. But your happiness was not all owing to my mode of control, but to your own discharge of duty, for I must say you were ever a most cheerful and dutiful pupil. You will always find it so in this life, that if you faithfully discharge your duty, you will surely receive your reward. You wish me to tell you about all of your old schoolmates. Ah Tommie you probably remember most of them were girls. Well, it is natural I suppose. I shall Head the list with Amanda. I have not seen her since last summer. She and Elliott have been staying in Holly Springs until recently. Mrs Heads health is no better. You are probably aware that Mittie's father has sold his interest in the farm to your uncle Joe [Patterson]. Mittie seems in consequence farther removed than ever. Lon R[ichardson] was here last Tuesday. She is growing more handsome. Seemed glad to hear from you, Kate Dunlap also spent an hour with us yesterday evening. She has a real pretty face, was one of my pupils last summer, and an old friend of yours, is she not? Dick* was with her, and was all animation, when telling me how he killed a deer the day previous. Their large cur dog immediately attacked the deer & after a short severe contest, pulled it down. Dick ran and jumped upon it & called to his cousin to bring the ax, with which they knocked it in the head.*

*Kate and Dick Dunlap are the children of Richard Love Dunlap, brother of John F. Dunlap, Clara's husband.

*This letter comes to an abrupt end at this point.

T. J. Gaughan in Bardstown, Kentucky, to Cornelia Dickson in Ouachita Co

Dec. 22nd, '8(

My Dear Friend

I received your interesting letter this morning and assure you it wa appreciated. I was expecting a box or something from home, but was dis appointed so your letter came in good time.

I am well and all right, if I get some Christmas presents. The boys ar all excitement about "the Christmas vacation." All those that have permis sion from their parents, can go home. I think over half of them are going to leave. They will start in the morning and will have to return the first Monday after New Years.

Most of the boys are nice and clever, but I must say there are some that are not. But they only answer a good purpose, as they are an example and serve to prevent others from following in their paths.

My conclusion is that if a boy comes here with the intention of learning he will succeed. I was much surprised to hear of the death of Mr Mosely*, though I had heard it when you wrote. But never was I more surpized than when I heard of the death of Jim Burks. While you are having so many deaths, I find marriages are not forgotten. Tell Brother Jim not to be so selfish as to "step off" and I not there.

*"Mr Mosely" refers to Elijah Moseley II, father of Mr Marvin and Mr Allis Moseley

Miss Neelie I think if you were to come here a while you would not break off pieces of cedar. To see a pine is a treat. There are many rocks here, most of the fences are made of them. What is strange to me here is, that you have to pay toll for riding along a road.

We had a nice time a few weeks ago. The people of Bardstown were invited to the College, and they were entertained by two speeches, two plays, and plenty of music. I think they all enjoyed themselves and I know the College boys did.

I am in the study room writing, and there is very little studying. The boys are to much excited about going home in the morning. Write soon.
              Yours truly,
              T. Gaughan

George B. Rumph in Camden to John R. Boddie in St. Louis
                                            Jany 10th 1881
Dear John,

Your two favors are to hand by last mail. I am obliged to you for the money, have drawn favor of Jim & Gillis for same. As I will not need it before the 1st July place to our credit in N. Orleans. I waited until this morning to see some parties for Young Boddie. Have procured him a situation with Paul Schnedler at $15.00 dollars per month and his board. Paul wants a man to cultivate a small farm, to drive his wagon and do anything required of him. If Boddie is willing to take hold of work with a vim, and suits Schnedler he will give him a situation that will pay him well. You know he does an extensive Sewing Machine business, and intimated he would do a good part by a man of the right kind. There will be no trouble to get work here, among the planters, by any man willing to work and dont expect too much. so if he concludes to come let me know at once. We had a fall of snow last night & yesterday, and the ground is covered. It is bad on the ungathered cotton, and business is certainly going to be poor for some time to come. Whenever you need Tom's [Rumph] services I will give him up; as I intended to try and procure him a better place than I could afford to give him. After he becomes familiarized with commercial business. If Tom will cultivate the gift of <u>Gab</u>, a little, he has the elements of a salesman about him; and will do well enough. I will certainly appreciate, anything you can do for him.

Relations all well. My family joins in love to you. Hope to hear from you as often as you feel like writing.

      Yours as ever
      Geo. B. Rumph

Cornelia Dickson in Ouachita Co. to Tommie Gaughan in Bardstown, Kentucky

                  Feb. 1881

Dear Tommie

I have waited longer than I intended in replying to your last. But circumstances were such that I have scarcely had a leisure half hour since its reception. Some portion of the interim I have spent at your fathers. But you have doubtless heard from home since I was there, and of the proceedings in general during that visit, for it was the week that the young people had a Sociable there and all seemed to have a pleasant evening. I will only mention one circumstance. Robert [Boddie] again waited upon Amanda to the table. I guess he is only officiating in the place of an absent friend.

Your letter was rather longer on the rout[e] than usual. It was near the middle of Jan when I received it. It was perused with much pleasure. While my last chronicled the death of several of your acquaintance, this will mention the marriage of several. But why should I write of them, for I dare say you have already heard through some of your correspondents less delinquent. I have heard that Mrs Agee was highly delighted with her new home, Maggie & Mr Barker will live in Hampton. Since I last wrote you, we have concluded that Miss Mamie Richardson is your bro Jim's [Gaughan] favorite. At the wedding however he seemed rather blue, as Dennis [Gaughan] succeeded in monopolizing most of her attention; and when the ring-cake was brought in, cut for her the slice that contained the ring. Mr. J. Gaughan seems too slow, Alex [Gaughan] paid most of his devotions to Miss Cicilia Smith, a niece of Mr Richardson. She is lately from Ga. Is pretty, industrious, and "sweet sixteen". Lou [Richardson] seems to have eyes and ears for Mr B Black alone. Amanda was not present. She is at school in Holly Springs. The old Ouachita was impassable and those invited from town failed to come out I was sorry it was so, for I wanted very much to see Attalie, Eugenia & Cora The latter is going to Mrs Hardnet, and thinks she has a severe teacher. Bu

I know it is better for her. I wish George would send Attalie and Eugenia there also. They all need disciplining.

You speak of it seeming strange to pay for riding along the road. You allude to the macadamized* roads. We have had so much rainy, snowy, freezing weather this winter that the roads everywhere are wretched. I think it a pity that we have not some like those, for the people this side of the river pay a heavy tax to Mrs Darnell, and the river bottom is almost a continuous mudhole. Matt says Georgia made quite an impression upon Dr Jackson from near Hampton. We had been accusing her of captivating Mr Tobe R[ichardson], judging from his frequent visits. Mr Robt. Stone is to be married tomorrow to Miss Kate Holmes of Princeton. Maggie & Mr Barker seemed as happy as possible. The family were well pleased with the match. I must not close without telling you of her [Matt Rumph] little Charley Ben. He is near three months old. Does not look like the other children, has blue eyes & fair complexion. Today is the most pleasant day we have had in many months. Indeed Spring seems almost ready to burst the wintry girdle and establish her supremacy. One wild turkey has already paid the penalty of coming up into the yard, imagining I suppose that it was one of the tame ones. There is yet another that hovers near the tame drove, but is rather shy. Brother John says he will get it when he wants it. Boasting you see, since he has killed one, but being subject to its natural instincts, failed to establish its identity.*

*Macadamizing is to pave by laying and compacating successive layers of broken stone.

*The letter ends abruptly at this point.

Cornelia Dickson in Ouachita Co. to her friend Rebecca Underwood in Autauga Co.

Spring, 1881

Dear Becca

You have ere now been wondering why I do not write. Scarcely a day passes that I do not think of you & promise myself that I shall certainly write in a day or two, I have hardly had a leisure half hour since its reception. You will be surprised and wonder what has occupied my time so constantly. Well as fast as I get through with one thing, another is waiting to be done and I am constantly trying to get through. But I see it is no use so I shall let everything go this evening and write anyhow, and if you should not respond immediately it will be so long before I hear from you. I believe Julia has ceased to write to me altogether. I have not heard from her since last Spring. Your last letter tells of your being all alone. That is nearly my condition. Florence and Aunt Mary, Brother John's sister, & myself are the only members of our large family on the place, Matt has gone over to her mothers, the first time since the advent of her little Charley Ben, now near three months old. She has four little blessings now, and they make the house lively, when at home. Brother John was called away professionally yesterday evening, & has not yet returned. We have just rec[eived] tickets to a sociable, given tonight at one of the neighbors, but will not attend. Florence & I just returned home last Saturday from a two weeks stay at Mr. Richardsons. Maggie R. married last Thursday to Mr. Charley Barker of Hampton and we had the honor of baking the cake & preparing other dainty eatibles for the occasion. All the young people of the neighborhood were in attendance, many were invited from Camden but the Old Ouachita being on a boom at the time, they failed to come. The bride in white looked beautiful indeed and everything went "merry as a marriage bell." Previous to that Mrs Gaughan sent for me to spend a week with her & assist her in giving a Sociable. I then spent a week with old Mrs Moseley, Anna Gaughans mother. I believe I have not written to you since Mr Moseley's death which occurred the fourth of Dec. of meningitus. He was a good citizen & universally respected. I believe he was a stepbrother to Mr Billy Dunn who died in Autauga last year, and an own brother of Mrs. Goodson's* near Mulberry creek. Mrs Moseley is a good friend of mine and I feel so sorry for her. They were a remarkably devoted old couple to each other. He called her "Marmy" & she called him "Pa." He was a Primitive* I went to Bro George's also. Carrie had just received a handsome present from her brother John in the shape of a new carpet for the parlor. It was a beautiful tapestry. He is anxious for her to go to St Louis again, next time he comes & take lessons in music. She plays remarkably well for her advantages, having taken lessons only from her mother. I advised her to take lessons upon the organ. She says she has been expecting a letter from Eula for sometime. I had been gone from home in all four weeks and now Matt has left us to keep house, which embraces everything to be done in kitchen, dairy, house, & yard. Our cook has taken it into her head to visit around. It is a hard matter to keep one long when there is such an abundance of provisions as was raised last year. They grow very independent as long as it lasts. Negros out here are doing finely anyway. Those that work well make plenty of corn & meat & drive their own teams. Command ten to twelve dollars per month wages.

Mr Robt Stone married yesterday Miss Kate Holmes of Princeton, Mrs Annie Stone his former wife has been dead only about five months.*

*"Mrs. Goodson" refers to Nancy Moseley in Alabama. She was a sister to Elijah Moseley, who died December 4.

*Elijah Moseley was a Primitive Baptist preacher.

*This letter ends here in the ledger.

Cornelia Dickson in Ouachita Co. to Miss Howard Dunlap at Tulip, Arkansas

March 15, 1881

Dear Howard,

 I have delayed writing much longer than I intended, but have thought of you so often and sympathized with you in your lonely condition and wondered how you were getting on. I have thought so much about you, Howard, now that you have three little ones to care for, and provide for. It used to be that you had only yourself, and I felt sorry for you then, but now so much more responsibility is resting upon you. I would I had the power to help you. If I could only see you sometimes it would be a treat, but must be content with writing. Yet you know in this time that I am a very poor correspondent. It seems that I have so many many duties to occupy my time & attention. While I am teaching school it is school duties that engage all of my time, and when at home besides my own work, there are so many home duties that I feel bound to lend a helping hand. We have had such a very severe winter but strange to say I have not had a cold even of any note, until the last few days have been almost choked with sore throat. I have been so busy this winter have actually not had time to catch a cold until recently, was not at home all the time though.

 Florence has come home to stay a while. She has been gone ever since Christmas visiting her own & Eddie's relatives. Her health has not been good & she is often low spirited. Matt has four little ones now, her last, little Charlie Ben is three months old and very sprightly to his age. But I think not so handsome as Garland. Mat thinks it resembles Florence. Brother John has several patients with measles. Mollie Stone Richardson and her baby are very sick, the baby dangerously so. Little Smoker Boddie also has it, but he is improving.

 We have had several marriages in the neighborhood this winter. Mrs Sissie Agee to Mr. Leonard York of Johnsville, Miss Maggie Richardson to Mr Charlie Barker, Mr Ed. Brodnax to Miss Kate McLaughlin of Camden. I heard sometime since that Alice Garmany is married, but to whom, or when, I have not learned. Mr Robt. Stone to Miss Kate Holmes of Princeton. Let me hear from you soon, Howard. I shall have to close or will miss the opportunity of sending this to the office. As ever

      Your sincere friend,
      Cornelia S. Dickson

Cornelia Dickson in Ouachita Co. to her friend Rebecca Underwood in Autauga Co.

March 15th 1881

Dear Becca

I was exceedingly gratified to know that you cared enough for me to write again before receiving my tardy messenger which no doubt has ere this reached its destination. Your note was mailed in Jan. Yet it was near the middle of March when I received it. The exceedingly cold weather of the past winter seems to have retarded our mail routs, judging from the dissatisfaction expressed in some of our local papers. In the course of several months we will have a railroad to Camden, a branch of the Iron Mountain, which will greatly facilitate travel to that point. Speaking of the cold weather, you will see from my letter that I have kept too busy this winter to even "catch a cold." My health is splendid. Many old settlers say they never experienced such bitter cold as we have had. I believe we are several degrees above you, but have the advantage of heavy timber as a partial protection against the piercing winds, that penetrate the older & more open States. Spring is fast assuming her supremacy now, but it is not too late for grim winter to give us a parting salute. Several years ago we had a heavy snow on the 26th of March. I was glad to hear from your Uncle Howard and of his felicity in his new treasure. Tommie Rumph spent last night with us, he will leave for St Louis in a few days. He has a situation in the same establishment with John Boddie, Wear Boogher and Co. We feel very sorry to have him go so far, but he thinks he can do better there.*

*The letter ends at this point in the ledger.

George B. Rumph in Ouachita Co. to his cousin John Rumph Boddie in St. Louis

May 17th 1881

Dear John,

Your letter & postal both duly to hand. I trusted to intercept you at Hope by a letter in reply to your first, but find I was too late to do so, as you traveled faster than I had anticipated. The dog came in by express safe, and is a fine specimen of the setter. Eugene & George are delighted with him and can scarcely talk of anything but that dog, and what he does. They say he is the laziest puppy they ever saw, as he sleeps all night & part of the day. Eugene says he likes him fine, but would rather have a mad dog to bite folks when they come in our yard. They think however everything will be all right when their pup has puppies. As they have discovered three teats, for the puppies to suck.

I visited New Orleans since I wrote you last. Had a good time generally. Found business dull & plenty of the boys idle enough to loaf with me. The pleasure resorts of the West-End & Spanish Trail are delightful places, and extensively patronized by the people of the city in the afternoon. I also took in Texas on my return trip. Sojourning a day in the City of Houston; there I met our old friend Tom Archer; who was glad to see me & treated me to a ride over the city of Houston in the afternoon, pointing out all the places of interest to the sightseeing traveler. His Father is editing a paper at Crockett and he tells me his sister Mary & her husband separated. She is living with her father, has two children, both with her. Dr. Archer is doing well in the medical profession in H. Tom says his law earnings have barely supported him, and thinks he missed his calling. Business dull here in the extreme. I hardly think much can be done here before the fall trade sets in. Would be glad to have you come down anyhow, and see us all. Our merchants have all about visited N.O. & returned.

Things seem to be settling down for our usual summer enjoyments of loafing, fishing &c. The overflow of the River has cut off all communication from the other side for several days. All well and asked to be remembered to you in love. Write soon. Yours truly
George

Cornelia Dickson in Ouachita Co. to her friend Rebecca Underwood in Autauga Co.

Summer, 1881

Dear Becca,

I was not at all surprised at receiving your letter, but had been anxiously expecting it for a long long time. So you see I still thought of you constantly, I believe it is so every summer that you are deterred by anticipations of the "summer campaign" from writing in due time. Though I missed your pleasant chatter, I will not complain, as you have sent me a most welcome & long expected souvenir. Accept my warmest thanks. He is indeed fine looking. I can scarcely realize that he is the same little fellow I knew so well. I had thought he would resemble your uncle David more than he does. Bless his heart. I hope he is as good as I used to think he would be. If I were to show it to Carrie she would think it Mr Alex Gaughan, the resemblance is so very striking. Mr G. is a great favorite of C's. He also is large, weighs 175 to 180 pounds.

You want to know how I have employed myself this summer. When I wrote you last I was teaching school in our neighborhood. The hooping cough broke up that school the last of May. The first of July I opened the Public School about six miles above brother Johns up in what is called "the dark corner." Tis true the people are somewhat rougher & more illiterate than our neighborhood but I find them very kind and I have a full school. Thirty-five pupils registered. Some of them really interesting. But there is a great deal of sickness, and some have to work in the crops so there are only sixteen in attendance today. Several of the patrons wish me to take a subscription school as soon as this term expires, but I am undecided. I had already applied for a situation elsewhere, and must hear from that first.

I have not seen any of the home folks in several weeks, but hear occasionlly. All were well. Mittie [Rumph Rucks] & Jennie,[Jordon Rumph, wife of George B. Rumph] George & Tommie [sons of Mittie & Jennie] have each been out spending several weeks. And Florence [Rumph] has recently returned from a visit to Bradley Co. I am anxious to see them all.

I spent a night with Carrie [Boddie] about three weeks ago. She says she has not heard from Eula in a long while & wanted to know what had become of her, and if she & Tommie were not going to fulfil their promise this fall. Says she shall expect them. How I wish they would come.*

*The letter ends at this point in the ledger.

Cornelia S. Dickson in Ouachita Co. to Mr. George Stinson, a jeweler in Camden.

Sept., 1881

Mr. Stintson

On the 14th of August I left my pin with you to be repaired and handed Mr. Marshall twenty-five cts to pay for the repair. He said as you were busy, it would be probably a week before I could get it. Several weeks ago, I sent for the pin by Mr McKinney. It was sent to me without having been repaired at all. I suppose it was an oversight and send it back. You will oblige me by repairing it today if possible.

Respectfully,
C. S. Dickson

Note: For some reason there is a dearth of letters from 1882. We have searched through all the originals available and find only one short note which follows. It is inconceivable that Sis Mollie did not write her weekly letters to son John in St. Louis for a whole year, or that Cornelia dropped her correspondence for a year. However, there is nothing in the ledger, nor any letters to John R. Boddie. We can only assume that such letters have been lost over the years.

George Boddie in Ouachita Co. to his wife Mary Elizabeth Boddie in Clark County visiting their daughter Mamie Coleman

Sept 16th 1882

My Dear Wife

I received a letter from you day before yesterday & was glad to hear that you were all well & that you would be home soon — I havent seen a well day since you left, — Same old complaint — slow fevers — night sweats & general noaccounteness — Our boys, & Carrie keep their usual health. Been some sickness in neighborhood no fatal cases as yet — we have had but little company — though Carrie says she will have some girls next week to stay with her — Tell Smoker I have no little boy to take his place & he must hurry home & bring Godfrey with him. Tell him Auntie learned to dance a new boonpipe yesterday in the dairy when a mouse tried to find winter quarters under the skirts of her dress — Gilder is in Hot Springs or Little Rock — when he left said he did not know when he would return. Love to all — I shall look for you every day, Miss Mary — the thought of your coming Home so soon — has helped me wonderfully. Make haste & hurry along to See your old Boy —

Geo Boddie

George Kimball Smoker Boddie-Age 4
Photo courtesy of Ruth Boddie Farmer

Cornelia Dickson in Ouachita Co. to her friend Becca, daughter of her friend Rebecca Underwood in Autauga Co.

Jan 8th 1883

Dear Becca

Your very dear letter was handed me last night and oh how it cheered my sad heart to hear once more from one whom I love so much. Yes, though, I have been with you so little since your were quite small, your cheerful loving letters have kept bright and glowing the flame of warm affection with which I have ever regarded the child of one of my dearest friends, and you may know I have missed their nonappearance no little. The Merry Xmas has come & gone once more, and the old year with its joys & sorrows, has passed into eternity.

Since I wrote you last we have been so sadly bereaved in the death of my brother George. He died the 19th of last October of Hermaturia, was sick only four days, but you have probably heard all about it as I wrote to Sis Carrie the particulars at the time. I at times feel so very sad it seems impossible to overcome it.

The young folks of the neighborhood have not participated in as many Sociables as usual. Seem rather at a loss for something new. We did not have a Christmas tree this year. The terrible overflow last spring came near ruining so many people. Fifty thousand dollars would scarcely cover the losses of this neighborhood. Three thousand would not cover brother George's losses in that flood, the water rose a foot or two deep in his yard. At Mrs Moseleys & Robt. Stones, skiffs were run through the houses. But it all did not stop the railroad and we now have a road running right through the neighborhood near Mrs Moseley's back-yard, a quarter in front of Brother George's place. Regular trains have not yet been put on as the road is not completed. Its coming at the time has caused people to be vastly more cheerful, as lands are considerably enhanced in value and Camden is on a boom with her two railroads.

I know your Xmas tree must have been a merry affair. Wish that I could have been with you all. But what use to wish. If I could only keep a good school, would soon feel able to go to Ala. But there are so many teachers, and some underbid me & then the system of three months public schools have caused many to depend upon them to educate their children, which is just scarcely any education at all, & a teacher has no chance in so short a time, to thoroughly instruct in anything.

Well do I remember Mittie Cary, & thought when I saw her last that she would make a beautiful woman. Hope she has married one who will never cause a shadow to cloud her fair brow. I regretted exceedingly to hear of the deaths mentioned in your letter. According to the law of nature it was to be expected in the aged, but to see the young & joyous stricken in the morning of life, is indeed at all times a source of sorrow to me.

Yes, I have your Fathers obituary. Would have sent it when I last wrote but wanted Sis Mollie & Clara to read it, and expected to send it the next time I wrote. But your letter never came & I had forgotten that I had it, until reminded in your letter. I have copied it in my Scrap Book, a beautiful description of the life & death of one of my most esteemed friends. And send the original in this letter.

You speak of the ground there being covered with snow on the 29th of Dec. while here it was perfectly fair & brilliantly beautiful weather until Sunday night. Mat, her children & myself spent Sunday with Sis Mollie. She & Carrie were very cheerful, as all were well once more and John was spending the holidays at home. He came home with us that night and next morning took New Years nog with us. He is so pleasant & entertaining Becca I do wish you could see him. But then he is a poor boy, yet, Becca, though his salary is twenty four or five hundred a year, and expenses paid. He is such a liberal whole soul fellow that he manages to get through with it all. George Rumph, on the contrary, though he has a very expensive family and they live well & have every thing that a kind loving husband and father can supply, just saves money and makes all the time. He has recently bought out the firm of Rumph & Gee and is now entire owner of that establishment. Florence spends most of her time in Camden with her brother [George] & sister Mittie. She has such a gay pleasant time over there, has almost deserted home. Gilder Boddie has gone to St. Louis to live. Since he was burnt out in Camden concluded to try the Shoe business in that "Future Great." Tom Rumph is well pleased with that city having now been there two years. How time flies!*

*The letter ends at this point in the ledger.

Cornelia Dickson in Ouachita Co. to her friend Julia Howard in Boiling Springs, Alabama

March 14th 1883

Dear Julia,

Your very dear & interesting letter was received several weeks ago. It had been so long on the way and indeed so long since I had heard from you, had almost despaired of ever receiving another letter from you. I know that you have a great deal more to occupy your attention and time now than a few years ago, and I feel sometimes that it seems selfish in me to think of hearing very often from Ala and while there is but little here to interest you and that little is appreciated. How much greater the pleasure I derive from your letters you can judge. I commenced a letter to you soon after receiving yours but was interrupted from time to time with company, & sickness in the family. All are well.

Becca had written me of your sad bereavement in the death of dear little Milton and I can truly sympathise with you in your loss. Yet it is his gain. That is a blessed hope. The 19th of the same month that filled your home with so much sadness, brought a heavy shadow to our hearts in the death of dear brother George. He had been in bad health for some time, had chills occasionally, was taken with a chill which proved a death stroke, for when the physician saw him, the next morning, Said he saw no possible chance for him to recover. You cannot imagine our feelings Julia when we found that we were so soon to part with him forever on this earth. He was freely conscious of his situation, Said he did not fear death, & we trust he is saved.

I had gone down there to spend a week, my home is now at brother Johns, and was so glad that I happened to be there, I remained a month with the family, what few are left, John is still in St Louis, Gilder is there also now, in the Shoe house of Bryan Brown. Mamie still lives nine miles above Arkadelphia. Carrie & Robert are visiting her at present & only Sis Mollie, Willis & little Smoker are at home now. Eugenia Rumph has gone down to spend several weeks with them. I was so glad to hear from them all Julia and would be delighted to see you all, would visit if it were in my power. Matt's little flock has increased to five since I last wrote you. The baby is called Bessie Jewell & Charlie Ben was two years old last fall, is very much like brother John.*

*The letter ends at this point in the ledger.

J. M. (Jim) Gaughan in Camden to his brother T. J. Gaughan (Tommie), attending college at Springhill College in Mobile, Ala.

July 2d 1883

Dear Tom,

I will not delay so long this time in answering your letter. I was glad to hear from you and was proud to know that you was competing for honors at the examination. I will send you the five dollars that you mention. I regret to say that it will be impossible for me to meet you in Montgomery. Though I want you to come by and see them. I expect I will go out to Texas next week and stay a while. I am going out about Lampasas. Several of the men have gone there from about Camden. Tom Hail & John Rainwater have got employment in good business houses there; and Henry Cliffer and George Proctor are selling furniture together. Shade [Proctor] is there now but don't know whether he will stay there or not. I have got 2 letters from him since he went out there and 1 from George. They are well pleased.

If you go by Montgomery and stay long Ma* will be crazy when you come home; and Mary* has listen at Ma so much that she is nearly as bad; she even knows the day of the month that school will be out. You ought to see her (Mary) now. She is the prettiest, sweetiest, smartest and the proudest little thing you ever saw. We carried her to Holly Springs last Saturday was a week ago & stayed until Monday and she has been wanting to go back ever since, she had a good time with Cad's children *

*"Ma" is Sarah Caroline Patterson Gaughan, who married Patrick Gaughan in 1832

*"Mary" refers to Jim Gaughan's little daughter, who is being raised by Sarah and Patrick Gaughan, following the death of her mother Anna Moseley at her birth in 1880

*"Cad" refers to Cad Patterson, nephew of Sarah P. Gaughan.

I have just been frollicking for more than a week. I carried Ma, Georgia & Miss Linney Green as I said to Holly Springs last Saturday was a week and got back Monday. Then went to a picnic on Woodard Lake Tuesday. Friday night we had a party at my house and yesterday I was at Judge Richardson nearly all day with Miss Mamie on one side and Mis Lou on the other. Now when I tell you what a good time I am having you must not be envious for you are young and I am growing old. I have not got long to run. Alex says that I can happen to more good things than anybody he ever saw. The Missis Schales spent last week at Judge Richardson and I think Dennis got "badly mashed" on Miss Annie. I will have to say we had a nice party, if it was at my house. They danced until 2 o'clock. We had a picnic supper. I got more thanks and compliments than I could bare, all from the ladies.

The health of the neighborhood is very good, and mine is unusually good for this season and I am just as happy as a big sunflower. Everybody has got a good crop and mine is better than it has been for years — corn will not be worth anything if we can get one more rain. Dennis has got the "blue ribbon" cotton, it has the appearance of a bale to the acre.

I had the unexpected pleasure of meeting my unknown brother-in-law Harry Fisher* last Thursday evening. I like him very much, he is very smart. He came by on the L & L. L. R. R. and stopped off two days. Then he went on to Tex. as leaving his son Fred to stay two or three weeks. Fred is about grown. He is not very handsome. He attended our party, but took no hand in the dance.

Hoping to hear from you soon
I remain
J. M. Gaughan

*Harry Fisher was the husband of Mary Arkansas Moseley, sister to Anna.

Carrie Boddie at home to Cornelia Dickson who was apparently visiting somewhere close to the Dennis Gaughan home.

Aug 6th 1883

Dear Aunt Nealie,

I have been wanting to write to you, but actually hadn't time. I am writing now while I wait patiently for Bud Will to come on & eat his supper, and feel that I could write you "lots" if you will only accept it written in pencil. Do wish you was staying with me this summer. It would be mighty nice for me to have such good company. It is real hard to get the girls — they have so much to do at home & can't leave to accomodate me — but I have a good deal of company coming in every day or two.

Bud Gilder was here last week save a few days and will remain this week also — he is waiting orders from his house — and I was so glad to have him with [us] though he is almost as bad as a child — full of mischief and turning every thing upside down — I have done but little sewing since Mama [left]. The household duties keep me busy from morning until three o'clock in the afternoon but let me tell you I embroidered Mr. Allis such a <u>pretty</u> hat band this afternoon, do wish you could see it — the ribbon is delicate pink, the color he admired most among your samples of colors, then the letters of very delicate blue and the filagree (rose buds) of shaded green and red silk — it is so delicate & I think the colors much prettier than those Florence got to embroider her friends — I am going to embroider one for Mr Brodnax, Cos Tom & Bud Gilder — it is such fascinating work I do love to do it — and I did it <u>real</u> well Aunt Nelie for my first attempt — dont mind

I'll learn how to embroader nicely yet—

I was so sorry you did not get to go to the picnic at S[ulpher] Springs — Supper over and dishes washed — was going to tell you about the picnic — I went! and such a day I never before spent — nor never want to spend again — I imagined I was going to have a pleasant day of it — having made an engagement with Mr. Brodnax and he (I thought) to come out in a <u>nice turn-out</u> to carry me to the picnic — well he wrote me to look my prettiest! — I immediately layed aside the lawn dress I was trying to finish to wear that day and said I would don my <u>"finest coat"</u> as was going in a top buggy &c — so the day came! — I <u>too</u> sent to town for nice things for my basket — Effie [Brown] was spending that week with me & she helped me — sent for things also — and we had a <u>nice</u> basket fixed for the occasion — and <u>Friday</u> eve here come Mr. Brodnax in his old shackly open buggy and two old horses that looked like they could scarcely carry themselves much less pull us twelve miles — and me going to wear my best dress in that old buggy to get ruined with dust &c — I was the maddest little mortal you ever saw — said he came the eve before so we could get an early start next morning. Well I was <u>right sure</u> he <u>wouldnt</u> get an <u>early</u> start, wanted the sun to burn him up which I knew it would do, for we had no umbrella my parasol only — and if you remember it was a fearfully warm day — Mr. Allis came down for Effie long before we started to get ready and begged Mr. Brodnax to go in his wagon & leave his shabby turnout here but no he must take me in his buggy — we got off about ten oclock, and Mr. A. & E. rode right behind us all the way making fun & laughing all the time at us — all the boys had heard I was going in <u>fine style</u> which made matters worse — Well my back was almost broken when I got there besides being overheated, riding in the sun — and I thought for awhile I was going to be real sick — am sorry I couldn't be nice to him that day for his trouble — but when anybody takes me anywhere & pretend to go in style I want to go that way or not at all — would never have made the engagement in the first place had he not often wanted to take me out riding before this trip — well you may be sure he will never carry me anywhere in a buggy again — I got enough of this trip & I think he did to because I was not nice at all to him —

Mrs Gaughan (say Aunt Nelie don't mention about my <u>buggy ride</u>) is going to give a sociable Thursday night for Tommies benefit. I do wish you could come — he came home Friday to remain two months I believe — he looks real well — came by this afternoon with Mr. Dennis to see me he said — having paid all the rest of the girls a call, I suppose you have heard that Mr. Jim G[aughan] is in Texas on a pleasure trip — don't guess I'll promenade at the social do you?

Uncle J. Rumph came by this afternoon on his way to see little Eddie [Rumph] who is quite sick. Cos George sent for him this morning — I know they will be glad to move away from Camden — The children are forever sick — E[ugene] & G[eorge Jr.] still at Uncle Johns — The children there have all been sick & Hattie is right sick now Uncle John says. I was amused at Uncle J. Dunlap telling us the other day about Aunt Clara getting snack [snake] bit. — She was in the hen house after a mink & put her hand near enough to the snake to be bitten on the finger. They didn't get to see what kind it was — but Uncle J. made her real drunk on whiskey & he says I just ought to have seen her jumping around & talking — The way he told it was amusing — Lula is coming home in Sept — I will be so glad, know she will stay with me some, let Cora come too — she like myself knows how to manage her work without help. We've never been accustomed to having help — she is visiting in the northern part of Georgia & enjoying it muchly — her Cos. Fannie [Dunlap] is with her.

I received a letter from Mama last week, is enjoying her stay in Shelby very much, she sent me a mighty pretty dress differnt from any dress goods I ever saw — prettier than lawn or calico while it resembles both — it is called Batiste know you will like it — will send a sample. I had a caller last night (Mr. A.) and didn't take a nap today so must bid you goodnight & finish my say tomorrow or when I can but Aunt Nelie I'm afraid you can't read this — will perhaps have time to write with pen next time —

Thursday eve Dear Aunt Nellie — here I am all ready to go to the sociable expecting Mr. Allis every moment I look real nice too. You would tell me so just know — I mean to send this to Mr. Dennis tonight to send up to you. Do come down with Mr. D. soon when he goes to town I would be so glad — must go feed the chickens & close up shop to leave — that is lock up and give Billy the keys —

      Your Devoted niece
      Carrie

Write soon Aunt Nelie if you cant come —
Tube roses in bloom do wish I could send some

Matt Proctor Rumph at her home to Cornelia Dickson somewhere in Ouachita County.

                 Sep 6 1883

  Dear Miss Nealie,

As it is early tonight and all the children have almost gone to bed, I will attempt to write you a few lines. I have been trying to get Attalie to write. She keeps putting me off. I will write but not in reply to her note, and have it ready to send first passing.

We are all very well, except Hattie. She had a chill today, hope she will be up soon. She is so much help to me. She is always wanting to do something. Maud is looking very well now. She has not been sick this summer, yes I believe she was sick some time ago. I keep her busy with Bessie who is walking all around. She thinks she is so smart. She was one year old the 24th of last month. She can get up in my rocking chair and rock. Charlie is fat and full of mischief as he can be. I know you would enjoy seeing his movements and hear his expressions some times. Garland is the same good old boy. He very often speaks of you. It is time to close with children or my note will be composed of them.

Dr. has no patients now. Georgia [Proctor] was his last. She was sick three or four days this week, is up now. We have not had much Sickness in our neighborhood this summmer.

It is so sad to write the death of our good cousin, Jimmie Gaughan. He was sick one week. He was quite sick in Texas and relapsed next day after he got home, then waited several days before he would send for the Dr then it was to late for anybody to do any good. When he found he was going to die, he said he was not afraid to die, left everything in Alex's hands, I feel so sorry for his mother. She feels the loss of him so much.

Lula Dunlap has not come yet, is waiting [for] Mrs Agee. She has not been able to travel on account of her health. She wants to come back to be close to Dr. thinks she will get well. Attalie is busy making her some quilts and other sewing, has not made any nice garments, yet, is soon. I have been trying to hurry her up, you know she will take ten times at every thing. Honey [Eugenia] has just finished Lou Richardson some beautiful ric[k]rack. I think she expects to step off this winter. please do not show this to anyone and excuse badly written note for you know I have not much time to write.

with much love,
Mattie Rumph

Carrie Boddie at John Rumph's to Cornelia Dickson somewhere in Ouachita Co.

Nov 22nd, 1883

Dear Aunt Nelie

When you go down to Mrs Moseleys please mam run down home & get me my cook book for Miss Mat — it is in my room on the mantle — then tell Mama to look in top drawer and get my blk bow of ribbon, if not there look in trunk & everywhere — also my tooth brush — & you please bring them — I am so afraid we can't go in the bottom Saturday — I shall be very much disappointed if I don't get to see Mrs Fisher* again ere she leaves — havn't been with her any at all — don't you think a deal of her — she is so nice & sweet. I really love her — she is so thouroughly womanly don't you think — We are getting on nicely so far with sewing — <u>maybe</u>

*"Mrs Fisher" refers to Mary Arkansas Moseley Fisher, sister of Allis and Marvin Moseley.

we will get through — do wish you could see her gown — I finished it, Monday & it is <u>pretty!</u>, making blk dress this week — Charley is sick — chill & little fever — Miss Mat is going to send for Uncle John if he has fever again today — Give lots of love to Mrs Fisher & Mrs Moseley for me — and — and — somebody else — burn this please mam — & Aunt Nelie do come over here just as soon as you can.

      Lovingly
      Carrie

Mary Elizabeth Boddie in Ouachita Co. to her son John R. Boddie in St. Louis

                Feb 28th 1884

Dear Papa,

  You should have seen, & been with our little darling yesterday eve. when he was made the happy possessor of Ax, pistols & new shoes, Yes! got them at last, & his joy was unbounded. Your dear letter too, & Pet said to me, you can tell Papa, "I hav'nt lost my knife yet, & hav'nt cut my finger but <u>one time</u>" & that is wonderful for he has used it constantly, & thinks more of it than any he has yet had, & Mamma can say that he's been a very good boy not even attempting to cut anything with it that he should not. His shoes fit nicely, not quite as broad as I'd have them, but they'l stretch some, & as they are plenty long, will let him wear them as he's needing them badly.

  Tommie's letter of 20" Inst. only reached me Wed. of this week. Will had to send Billy over yesterday for corn, meal, coffee, sugar, &c but he forgot to get Wills' rubber boots &c that you left with Mr Chidester, & he needs them so much working with the logs these icy cold mornings, & his feet wet all day. 100 of his logs are yet in the Lake, but he intends rafting down the balance as fast, & as long as the water will admit, commencing tomorrow. The boys are delighted with the Engine &c Gilder says, "O it's a beauty, a very daisy I can tell you, & cant be beat & just the very make that Mr Badders wanted," & I am as proud to tell you, as they are of its possession that the whole outfit was safely conveyed to their new quarters, & in one day & a half. They did it with six yoke of oxen, Wills' three, & three of Mr Mains. Bogged down only one time. Gilder says, they are making good progress getting out timber, the <u>raw recruits</u>, himself, Bobbie, & their fireman, got one all over souse in deep water, & although the latter could swim, Gilder said he would have drowned through fright, & exaustion trying to get up on the log, if he had not gone to his assistance in a boat. Told him he wanted no more such work as that, but Gilder said that he left both he & Bob at it again when he came for Mr Mains' oxen. State did'nt get all his timber at the launching place either, says, if he was only worth a <u>few</u>

thousand he'd <u>never float another log</u>. 'Twas very cold yesterday with high <u>wind</u>, same today, which makes the timber much harder to manage. Bobbie Dee [Newton] came over last eve to get the same team our boys had to haul his Machinery from the Gurdon Depot to place. Expressed himself as highly pleased with the Boddie Co's outfit saying he did'nt think there could be any better made than such Machinery as theirs looked to be. The fire in town burned the three houses next to Stinsons, the latter's loss was very heavy from the ruinous handling of his good, the excited populace even breaking out all the glass of the show windows. Recd a letter from Sis Hattie, & am happy to say that Mattie is at home with her, very much better, & Sis H. has great hopes of her ultimate recovery. Says the baby is a fine boy, & thriving well so far on his bottle milk. Sallie has sole charge of the babe, being with her sister, & having the care of him from the first she is too attached to surrender her claim, even to his Grdmother.

Well dear son, you may guess what my little darling is doing right now, Yes, making the pistol caps fly, just as fast as his little fingers can load, & fire. He amused us greatly yesterday with his trials of skill to bring down the giddy robins (with his bow & arrows) which were numerous in the chinaberry tree making themselves sick, with eating the berries. "Oh Auntie I <u>hit</u> one on his tail, & he <u>jes shook it</u> & did'nt fly." The climax was reached this morning when just as he popped away at them with his pistol, a bird fell, & he ran & caught it.

Sat. Mrs Mitchel came yestereve & I could'nt finish this so will have to conclude in a hurry, my little darling is waiting to be dressed. "Tell my Papa I'm much obliged to him for sending me the pistols" & I can add that he is equally obliged for the Ax, it comes in for a big share of his attention. Uncle J. & family are all well except colds. Remember Pet & I to all enquiring friends. I dislike to trouble you, but will have to ask you when 'tis convenient please send me five dollars for my cook. With love from each one, & kisses many from Angel Mother's & " Danpa's" boy, am as ever

your devoted Mother,
Mary E. Boddie

Attalie Rumph Gaughan in Camden to her brother-in-law T. J. Gaughan at Springhill College in Mobile.

March 3, 1884

Dear "little" brother,

As I have not written to you since I was married, will write you a short letter this morning. I am up at Ma's [Sarah P. Gaughan], came Sunday to spend the day, and had a chill and high fever that evening; so I had to remain a few days longer. I am trying to break my chill today.

The rest of the family are well. Mary is as lively as a little cricket, just here and there and everywhere. She is in the other room now contenting herself with two drunk robbins which she has in a cage. Ma is <u>very</u> anxious to hear from you, would like a letter every week, but know you will not write unless some one writes to you. She says it it the hardest matter in the world to get any one to write, says if she could write, would write you a long interesting letter, and explain everthing. Brother Dennis wrote to you Friday night, but forgot the letter Saturday morning when he went to town, and it has not been mailed yet.

I am just delighted with house keeping, as Jim says I am as happy as a big sunflower. I have the nicest kind of a cook, don't have very much to do, only keep house, do my sewing and first one little thing then another, you know when one's cooking is off their hands they don't think they have much to do. I haven't any little chicks yet, it is because my hen will not set. Ma has between sixty and seventy; she says Mary and the chickens keep her busy, says if you were to see her some times, you would not think she had time to give you a single thought, but she thinks of you every day. There was a sale at our house last Monday week. Mr Alex bought the place, and most everything else, except some things people bought from the store; Uncle John D[unlap] bought that little mule they call John. Mr Alex is so much better satisfied since the place belongs to him, says he knows what to do now, and can go to work.

Mr Alex and I went to Holly Springs not very long ago, and had such a pleasant trip. There has been two weddings up there this winter. Ella Proctor and Mr Taylor, Lucy C_____ and Mr Henry Bryant.

Brother George and family has left Camden for their future home in Florida. Mr Tom S[tone] has broken up housekeeping, don't know where he will live, but thinks he will move to the Brown place.

Well Tommie I guess you are getting tired of looking at this badly written letter, but you will please excuse it and all mistakes, as I am not well, and nervous and a little drunk from the effects of quinine.

Write soon, with much love

Your sincere sister
Attalie Gaughan*

Mary Gaughan, "Our Baby," daughter of Anna Moseley and James M. Gaughan.
Photo courtesy of Dan Daniel

*Attalie Rumph married Alex Gaughan probably late in 1883 or early in 1884. We have no specific date.

Alex Gaughan in Camden to his brother T. J. Gaughan at Springhill College in Mobile, Ala.

June 8th 84

Dear brother,

I guess you think I have forgotten you, as you have received no answer from your nice letter. I have no excuse to offer other than neglect. I & Attlie came up to Ma's today, had a nice dinner and had to write a letter to pay for it, so you may not expect an answer from your last as I left it at home & it has been so long since I read it I have forgotten what was in it.

This leaves the family & neighborhood well so far as I know. No deaths nor weddings lately except Henry Chapman. I lernt today that he married last night.

Peaches plums & chickens seem to be pretty plentiful today but I guess Ma will save some for you. Mary is lively as ever & growing fast as she can, you wont know her when you come home.

I know you have already heard of the rain & overflows before now, but I will tell you how long it has been raining so you can imagine the conditions of our crops; it comence raining the middle of April. I have been overflowed twice since that time, fence washed the same no. times, my land is so wet I have not been able to plant it yet & I dont know that I will now as it is getting so late. There are worst prospects for crops this year than I ever saw in this part of the country & I believe it pretty general.

Dennis carried Ma, Georgia & C[ousin] Mat all over to town last week, stayed all night, they say they had a great deal of fun & saw a great many things & had a heap to talk about when they came back.

No picnicks yet Tom, though I reckon it will be a good year. The harder times are the [more] picnicks we have. Tom I have weighed more this spring than I ever did in my life. I reach 197#, imagine its because Attalie & I have plenty of chickings & a pretty good garden, getting along fine, keeping house. Attalie says you may expect a letter from her soon. She is going to ans. that letter shore.

I ask Mary what she want me to write for her. She said to tell you she is pretty little girl & has been troubled with the toothache some, it is still sore.

Ma want you to know that it is not her falt, why you have not got any letters. She says she has been after Dennis all the time to write, but she cant get him at it. She says he is worst than I was about writing, she says she wants to see you mighty bad, but she thinks she can wait until school is out now. Pa wants to know if you got your check, he also wants to know how much money it will take to pay up at the College & to come home by the way Montgomery. Answer this Tom soon as you get it, we have not heard from you in a good while.

Your brother,
A. S. G.

Carrie Boddie in Arkadelphia, visiting the Smoker family, to Cornelia Dickson in Ouachita Co.

July 11th 1884

Dear Aunt Nelie,

I was delighted to get your letter received it yesterday — had been at Mamie's almost two weeks and found it waiting here for me. It is the first news that I have had since I left home — do hope Mama will keep well until I return am having a lovely time and can't say when I will come back —

I am so glad your & Mr Allis' picnic was such a success — and his conduct that day ought to convince folks that he doesn't care anything for me — if he did he certainly couldn't enjoy it so much without me — The time is fast coming when people will quit trying to tease us about each other — Mamie only filled the place that was always hers and I didn't "scotch" forth a cent when I heard it. Do give Mr. Dennis my love — and speak a good word for me. No good pen on the place.

I enjoyed my trip to Hot Springs much better than I expected — we stopped at the Arlington — front room handsomely furnished and on the second floor — They put on a deal of style there but I didn't think the fare was anything extra — We were there two days and two nights and took in the best part of it — I like the place ever so much — some lots are beautiful — Those out of town specially — I do wish you had gone — Lil was not well while there and we didn't go out save with Brother — he took us to a concert & Ball the first night & oh I was never more crazy to dance in my life. The music was grand and the "fellows" so graceful and nice but our valice had been left at Malvern & we didn't feel like we looked fresh enough, though there were a good many ladies in walking suits dancing, and Aunt Nelie we did have so much fun taking our bath together. Yes we found out the woman who waited on us was going to <u>rub</u> us <u>down</u> in a word treat us like infants — & I Just would not hear to such a thing. The idea — she shouldn't stay in or I would not bathe — & Lill was afraid to go in alone so both of us went together & we had it. I came near drowning Lill & ducking my head too. I venture the people in every bath room heard us laughing — will tell you more when I come.

I have not been one bit well but keep up & am feeling somewhat better this morning — We are up every night, so late til half past twelve oclock last night — & The club meets here tonight — Cpt Smoker says I have got to stay with Lill all summer — he is such a good nice old gentleman.

I will write Honey [Eugenia Rumph] this eve — Devotedly,

Carrie

George B. Rumph in Altoona, Florida, to his cousin John R. Boddie in St. Louis

July 19th, 1884

Dear John,

Your valued letter to hand. I exceedingly regret the oversight in not settling the small indebtness due your house. I tried not to overlook any matters of the kind. I now enclose $/exchange on a Jacksonville Fla bank for amount $5.95. I believe Arkansas papers are reporting rather discouragingly of crops. Usually a "bad beginning makes a good ending" especially in Arkansas crops. You have to scare "em up" to make em work. I trust the outcome will justify my predictions and that you and Tom may reap your share of the trade. You should not be discouraged. Wherever you go, you may expect rough sailing. You are doing remarkably well. Stick to it and to Arkansas.

The credit system is the curse of the state whether it will ever be changed or not, God only knows. Common sense ought to teach all their is a better way. But their is always a large crop of fools — in every Country — It does not seem it would be so, but it is the hardest matter in the world to go in Matters of this kind in accordance with your better Judgment. This Country was once equally as bad, strangers and newcomers supplanting the old nations have changed largely the old system. Productions & opportunites offer a way out, and every one is much better off, and happier, and independent for change.

Camden, you say seems dead. I fear she is to remain so. Nothing but Manufacturing industries will ever revive her to her former prestidge among the towns of the State, and this will have to be done, in my humble opinion by her own Citizens. Capitalists from abroad are not going to locate there; when superior advantages are afforded by hundreds of other places in the South. The coal & iron fields, combine with the cotton fields to induce a careful investigation, in the states of Georgia, Alabama and the Carolinas and other points, before an ultimate decision of location is made for cotton manufactures even. The Capital already invested recently; and looking to investment soon is a wonderful factor, surprising alike to all, even those who have looked forward to, and predicted it.

I am glad to know of the encouraging prospect of the boys* in their shingle mill enterprise. I found — when there in April — they had made an irreparable error in employing the time getting up the mill for running instead of rafting out logs during the overflows. I hope they in a measure counteracted the blunder by availing themselves of high waters coming since. Nothing but mismanagement will cause a loss in that enterprise sure.

Well I guess it is in order to say a word or two about my present home. Now that I have had a limited time to pronounce upon it. I think I can freely

*"The boys" refers to Willis and Gilder who have opened a saw mill with a Mr. Badders: Boddie & Badders.

say I am settled for life. At least I feel so, and that with ordinary effort the dream of my life can measureably be realized. The climate is the delightful feature. Summer is unquestionably ten degrees cooler than in Camden Ark. Objections there are but these can more easily be met with money than any place on earth, I have felt — been cramped for money — to carry on in a tolerable way enterprises projected. I was compelled to mortgage my home place for most of the means to commence merchandising on — so as to support myself & family until my orange grove gets better into bearing — I am also compelled to put up with uncomfortable quarters in a residency building until I can do better. I have been called upon to fight my battles alone and unaided — so to speak. Coming among strangers. You will find many seeking advantages for their own pecuniary advancement. It was a stroke of this kind that forced me the other day to buy out the store building I am now and was then occupying, giving Eight hundred dollars therefore when I needed it in my business. I have fortunately enjoyed a paying patronage from the very start in business. Profits are good and I ask but to be able to tide over the first year. Well to enable me to be as solid as the "rock of ages financially." I do a cash business almost to the dollar and propose, so to continue. Should I be pressed in the full on mortgage I may have to sell to meet, and go ahead — Mess. Carter & Tenil bought the Shultz grove. That was the grove I first traded for and when attempting to close the trade Shultz wanted more than agreed on in the presence of a witness. It may seem to you a remarkable assertion but I say in all candor, I would not swap even my place for Carters, if I wanted it to live on. Theirs wlll sell for more money now, but will not in a few years. Nor, do I think this because I own the place. If they comtemplate moving here to live it would be as foolish in them to sell for 25000$ as every one thought it was in Shulze to sell for 15000$. It is a fine profit to close out now, but a better speculation & fortune to wait a few years longer. It will soon yield thrice ten thousand dollars income and go on increasing for almost the balance of time. Others are obtaining similar results — why not they.

I expect 1000$ from my present fruit crop — to double annually — is a reasonably expectation for quite awhile after trees come into bearing. I am enlarging with 600 new trees this fall — Besides I intend growing anything I can on my place. I have had as fine peaches and plums as you get elsewhere — just for fun, or your information, I will enumerate only those fruits that are and can be grown here — are grown here, —— to profit or for home use. These we have, oranges, lemons, limes, Citron, Shaddock grapefruit, Guava, Peaches, Plums, Pecans, Chesnuts, Japan Plums, Japan Persimmons besides the wild persimmon, Grapes, figs, bananas, pineapples — (eating them now) strawberries and blackberries & Mulberries, Huckleberries & dewberries are to be found wild in abundance. Every vegetable known is grown here with success, so far as I am able to ascertain. The lands are poor

> Mr. & Mrs. Geo. B. Rumph,
> request your presence
> at the marriage of their sister
> Florence,
> to
> Edwin Clifton
> Thursday evening, January 17, 1884.
> at 7 o'clock.
> Camden, Arkansas.
>
> Florence Rumph.
> Edwin Clifton.

as a rule — but yield more readily to fertalizing than any I ever saw, and this is commonly concurred in by all new comers.

Ethel has been sick for a few days — but is convalescent. We have enjoyed most excellent health since our coming. Ed had a spell of fever at first is now in better health than I ever knew him. But for the loss of our sweet little babe — Bettie. No family could be found to boast a happier home — Her departure from us — in the wisdom or wish of the Creater and ruler of our destinies. Will leave with us the vacant chair, and the void in our hearts loom on earth, that can never be filled. No sorrow is like it.

Hoping you will find it convenient to pay us a visit some day — and too, fall in love with our orange grove land. The fitful struggles of life, in a tireless search after fortune's fickle Goddess, has scattered us, like chaff before the wind. I trust we may all be together again when He "gathers in the sheaves." I often find myself unconsciously musing over the past of my life — and grow sad, that things "do move" and that changes must yet come to us. How valueless is life, save to those, Who trust in Him. "Who doeth all things well." Who "worketh all things well" for those who love Him.

My little ones think and speak of cousin John often and would be remembered in love to you.

Yours, Sincerely
Geo B. Rumph

Mary E. Boddie at home to Cornelia Dickson in Camden

March 30, 85

Dear Nelie,

I commenced a note to you last Fri expecting to send it to town next day, as Saturdays are almost the only chance time I have to do so, & I was so sorry to [have] been interrupted because I appreciated yours so much, & was truly glad to hear from you. Sorry to hear that you, Florence, & baby had such colds, do believe that I am taking the same, if sneezing, sniffling, &c is any indication, tho otherwise feel first rate. I was thinking of, & looking for you every day until your letter came, as State told me that you would be over in a few days.

Was surprised that the school patrons at Tulip were soliciting the services of Clara Golden after asking you to take the school. Effie told me that she had rec'd a letter from her (C.G.) since you were here, & that she was teaching a school about 25 miles from Holly Springs.

Twas like your own dear kind, thoughtful self to send me your letter from Carrie. I had heard from her only once & <u>was</u> truly glad to hear again, thanks to you for the pleasure. "Bud" rec'd a short letter from her last Sat, too busy to write much.

April 3rd. Was interrupted again right here, dear Nelie, & if I fail to finish & get it off tomorrow will give up; No! "try, try again."

This has been one busyest week with me, consequent on changing cooks, couldn't stand Betty the month out, so had to do duty myself. Will helping some. Been fortunate in getting one that gives entire satisfaction. Melinda, who was cooking for Clara when you were there, — asked me about you, saying she would [like] so much to see you. Melinda has her child with her, a girl about 12 yrs old, & has engaged to do all the work required for four dollars per mo.

Tell Florence that Gilder told me of the woman she spoke to him about for a cook, & I was so anxious to get her at that time, knowing too that I could'nt keep Betty, but Will said he must see Hannah first, Carrie had enjoined it upon him so particularly to get her if possible, & there has not been a day that he could leave home for that purpose.

Times over here are just as quiet as you can imagine, have been to see Mrs Moseley & Effie once, called on both same eve, Clara has spent one day with me & Cora came to see me last Sat.

Do miss Carrie ever so much, & all the time, yet am so constantly occupied don't feel as lonely as I dreaded to be.

Never mind about getting the table cloths, Nelie, if you have not already done so, want to send you the money for some by one of the boys first opportunity, & when I do so, don't bother about the quality, any will do that is not expensive.

The flowers are just lovely, & do wish I could send you & Florence some, but you both know just how the boys are — when they go to town, tis purposely on business & dont like to be bothered. Tell Louis that Smoker sits at his desk an hour or more daily trying his best to learn to write. He is terribly in earnest to have a gun, & I told him that he must know how to write a letter to his Papa first, & his perseverance would come near accomplishing it, if the task was not so great.

Kiss baby Florrie* for me, & whisper in her ear that old Aunt Mollie will get to <u>see her some day if</u> old Auntie lives long enough. Let me hear from you Nelie, & remember me with much love to each one, Mittie's family included.

Ever yours affectionately,
Mary E. Boddie

*"Baby Florrie" refers to Florence's baby girl. Florence married Edwin Clifton on Jan. 17, 1884.

Carrie Boddie in Hollywood, Arkansas, to Cornelia Dickson in Ouachita Co

April 7th 1885

Dear Aunt Nelie,

I was waiting to get settled before answering your letter, business didn't go to suit Bro. Gallie [Dr. Galley Coleman, Mamie Boddie's husband] in Hot Springs, so he thought it best to sell out & come back in time to hold his old practice. So we sent our five boarders to other houses, packed up & left! — got into this little town Thursday, rented what they call the old hotel, it is being repaired & will get moved in this week.

Are staying now with a lady friend and just as soon as we get settled again, I am going to try for a school. There are a lot of ignorant children here, & had I been two weeks sooner would have gotten a good school with all ease, another girl begun teaching then but a great many don't like her — anyway I am going to work for the free school for you & me. There would be at least fifty pupils, but they are just this way whoever is popular with them — They give the school too — good or bad. I would give much to get it, am confident you could keep it after the first term & it is a very agreeable place to live in churches and Sunday schools every Sunday — though somewhat like Holly Springs. They need a good school. The most ignorant children you ever saw — am sure they never had a teacher to control them or teach them correctly —

I can scarsely write with this pencil, tis only an inch long & no ink. If I find it impossible to get a school, guess I will come home — Write me soon & everything — I'll let you know again when I see the trustees of the school — there is a nice place for you to board right near the school room.

Lovingly
Carrie

Mary E. Boddie at home to Cornelia Dickson in Camden at Florence Rumph Clifton's home

April 27, 85

Dear Nelie,

Seeing would be much better than writing to you, & I cant help looking for you all the time, & feel like urging you to come but for the thought that it might probably be the means of your missing some good opportunity that would be to your advantage. What do you think of Carrie's proposition? I was somewhat surprised, & disappointed too, that she proposed <u>remaining away</u>, but will subdue my selfishness <u>if her contentment</u> & well doing is better secured thus. One thing, dear Nelie, I must beg of you, that in case C. does succeed in getting the situation & <u>you elect to go</u>, arrange to stay with me a week or two, if possible, before you leave.

Since writing to you last, we have had one letter from C[arrie]. Fred* was sick with measles, <u>throat</u> complications, &c but they will all get through safely, of course, each of the children will have it, & am glad that C. is there to help nurse them.

Was sorry that Dr. C. was disappointed in his venture, but truly believe it to be for the best that he did not remain at Hot Springs, & am ever so glad that he moved to Hollywood. Will get all his old neighborhood practice & more, & with it all 'twill not be as laborious as living on his farm, & taking part in that kind of work too. Like school teaching dear Nelie, I think that brain work requires absolute rest from all bodily labor, or anything harassing. Would not be surprised that if my little girl [Carrie] has any experience in that line of business, that she dont count it the hardest work she has ever yet done, particularly if she has some such pupils as I dare say that you know would put the patience of most any one to severe test. —

Thurs. 30th You see Nelie that I avail myself of your suggestion, & let me say right here, that I hope that you can come over anyway if we have any strawberries, cant tell even this late, the beds are so foul, but was agreeably surprised that our Pet found a saucer full of nice ripe ones yester eve for his Uncle Will. Says he wants to write to Aunt Nelie now, but I tell him he must wait till he can take her by surprise sure. John sent him copy books of which he's so proud — is making renewed efforts to learn.

Will & Gilder have been very busy since Sat. last getting all the timber out possible on this rise. Gilder stays at the mill. Will comes back & forth, rises at 4, breakfast by lamplight, & dont see him any more till 8 or 1/2 past — eats supper, feeds the mules, then puts on dry clothes from top to toe, & one night had to hive a swarm of bees which occupied him until 11. Allis has been coming the past day or two to hive them for him, as he (Allis) wants a start of stock again in that line. Hav'nt been anywhere since I wrote to you, Uncle J. D. had a severe attack or cramp, or bilious colic last Fri., is up, & well at present. Allis told me that Mat was at church last preaching day.

Tell Florence if I cant get to see <u>baby, can dream about her</u>, & in my dream was getting her ready to run off home, & Mr Clifton was aiding me to wrap her up in a hurry it seemed before Floy should catch us, when lo! just as I was about to be off Florence put in an appearance, & spoiled what it seemed we intended to be a joke at her expense, & was so merry over our failure, & you too laughing at us, that I awoke. Thought to myself, Little Flossie can never be as pretty as I <u>saw her</u> in my dream, but I dare say fully as sweet, & I want to see her now more than ever.

Keep in good cheer child no matter how afflicted, for all things our Master wills is for His own good purpose, & that dear Uncle John, & self are gradually, but surely loosening all hold to things earthly is a providence

*"Fred" refers to Fred Hughes Coleman, son of Mamie Boddie Coleman & Dr. Galley Coleman.

of His very goodness, & tender mercy that is leading us on to resignation to His Will. Many kind, & true friends will be left you, Nelie, but none can love you more than I do, for you always seemed so patient with my shortcomings that I felt as though you <u>understood me</u>, even as <u>my old Darling did</u>.

Good bye, with love from all, & ever so much from me, to each & all kin, & a kiss to the babies.

Yours affectionately,
Mary E. Boddie

Florence Rumph Clifton in Camden to Cornelia Dickson in the country.
Oct 2nd 1885

Dear Aunt Nealie,

I was glad to hear from you and that you were so well pleased. I am glad too, that you keep well. Mrs Clifton and I both have had our summer spell. Flossie* keeps well only teething — four and cutting more — she does [not seem] to mind it. You said she would be walking when you would see her again. You should have said talking. Yes, she can say so many things and speak so plainly too every one has [said] something about it.

She wakes up at night and says "Mama, tittie" and when I give it to her she will yell <u>tittie.</u> You laugh to hear her. She asks for things, says bye bye loudly. She cannot walk alone yet, but will soon. She is as ugly and mean as ever. Mrs. Clifton hurried me so is the reason I never thought of the picture. I have it for you and will send it when I get a good chance. Your other things also.

Yes my machine is a daisy; its just to nice for anything. I do not get time to sew much but enough I guess to do me good. When I can not sew I sit and admire my machine. I prize it more than anything. When you come you may see it. Pa brought me some vinezon. We enjoyed it so much, it was quite a treat. I have learned to make light bread, it just leaves the Bakers bread in the cool. Mr. Clifton says it <u>beats</u> "Clara's," as he has fed so on her bread. I am so glad I won the race at last. I've had two boarders gentlemen. I would not keep them for I took sick. I made some money though. I charged $4.50 per week, and lived high; if I had two backs would keep them all the time. Brother's [George B. Rumph] family are all well. Sis Jennie has had slow fever but up again. Says she will write to you soon. Sister's [Mittie Rumph Rucks] are never all well. Mrs Morgan will move to Tex on the 10th inst. Sister will miss her sadly. Mrs. W. M. Ramsey has been to see me. Dixie has spoken, also Aunt Beckie. Aunt Beckie has [not] seen Flossie yet.* Mrs. Missill has moved to Prescott. He stays here most of his time. Rose Willson has had a baby. Some say it belongs to Mr. Tuftas. They are in Tex. Will

*"Flossie" refers to Florence Clifton, daughter of Florence Rumph Clifton and Edwin Clifton. She was born in 1884, so could be not more than one year old.

*Dixie and Aunt Beckie are former slaves of Dr. John B. Rumph.

Gee[?] has come back. Andsons is going to Tex and take Ella his wife. All the neighbors are well. I will close as I must go to the kitchen. Goodbye. Come when you can.

                Your niece
                Florence Clifton

Gilder Boddie in Austin, Texas, to his mother Mary E. Boddie in Ouachita Co.

                                            Nov. 27th 1885

Dear Mama;

    I arrived here safely. Dr. Wooten says he can cure my eyes but can't say how long it will take him. He is very Clever & seems to understand his business thoroughly.
    His treatment is quite different from Dr. Hudsons.
    Write me at your leasure how you all are and how getting along.

                Your loving son,
                Gilder

Gilder Boddie in Austin, Texas, to his mother Mary E. Boddie in Ouachita Co.

                                            Jan 6th, 1886,

Dear Mama;

    Your last letter received, have been unable to read it up to date. My eyes takened a severe back set on the 24th, and gave me considerable pain and trouble up to the 2nd of this month, since then have been slowly improving and it won't be but a few days before I will be able to see clearly again; its the medicine that prevents me from seeing at present and has been ever since they takened the backset.
    As Dr. Wooten never ceased doctoring the lids to prevent them from going back to where they started when he commenced treating them. The lids are doing well. It was from cold settling in my eyes caused the trouble. They are clear of pain now and improving as rapidly as at first. Have been confined strictly to the house during all Christmas.
    Would be delighted to hear from you all, but am little foolish in getting someone to read your letters for me; however will be able to read it myself by the time you get this. Love to all.

                Your loving son,
                Gilder

Carrie Boddie in Ouachita Co. to her brother Robert L. Boddie, attending Webb School in Bell Buckle, Tennessee

Jan 12th 1886

Dear Robert,

  Your letter came last week — I was so glad to get it and must write you a long one in return. I was sorry to find all the ink frozen. I dread writing with pencil and hope you'll excuse it. You had a better time Xmas than we enjoyed, it hasn't seemed like Xmas and New Year to me — and now it is too dreadfully cold for anything — we really had some chickens to freeze to death and ice everywhere that will hold a mule up. I do hope I will not live to see another winter as cold — The young people have had but one party given them — that one through the kindness of Mrs. Amanda Patterson of Holly Springs & we did enjoy it. She invited us up New Years night but the rain begun to pour that morning early and continued that night & next day — We were so disappointed you may be sure — Cora was with me, and in spite of the rain, we were all ready thinking the boys would come in a covered wagon as Mr. Dennis had said he would if the weather was bad. They did come Messers Allis & Dennis through the rain in the afternoon and brought with them a large bag of oranges to put us in a good humor they said — so we enjoyed the fruit and played cards the rest of the afternoon — Mamie* cooked supper for me & afterwards, I gave them some music & all passed quite a pleasant evening —

  But on the next Wednesday night we had the party over — I went with Mr D[ennis] & we started Wednesday about noon — it was quite a nice party — met several nice girls & boys — <u>your girl</u> was not present, she is a member of the church now & will not attend dances. I got a glimpse of her however — on our return home she came out in the hall as we were passing & bowed to us — She & her Mother were to move down home this week but it has been so cold, I dare say they did not —

  And we liked to have had another party on Monday night after Xmas — Mr. W. Stone invited us up to Mr. Martin's (Uncle Billies old place) to a dance — he was then on his way to town after Cora Holmes, Willie Jordon, & Emma Brodnax, and I expecting a crowd of bad boys from over there, charged him particularly not to bring any one else from town — no no he said it would be a <u>nice party</u>. Well Cora was here & crazy to go, so she & I walked up there with Mr. Allis. Bud W[illie] was too tired to enjoy it and wouldn't go. Before we reached the house, heard voices laughing & talking & I begun to think it was a lively crowd we were to join — and also thought of what was best for me to do — Well we were met at the gate of the little yard by Mr D[ennis] & Mr. Mitchel. The former walked on in the house with me & whispered there was whiskey in the house & would be drinking before it broke up & wanted to know what to do — I told him I

*Mamie Boddie Coleman's husband, Dr. Edwin Gallie Coleman, died June 6, 1885 at Hollywood, Arkansas, and Mamie has evidently moved back home with her three children: Godfrey, Fred, and Mary Gilder.

would manage it — at least for myself & Cora & the rest could follow or not — We went on in & I stopped at the parlor door with all of my wraps on & surveyed the crowd to see who was there — while Cora had gone on in the dressing room, taken off her wraps & was returning to the parlor — as she passed me, I told her that I would send for her in a few moments to go home — She was shocked of course & I suppose told all in the parlor, for soon everything & everybody was in a great stir & hunting me up to beg me to stay & to know what was the matter. All that time I hunted up Mrs. Martin, told her I did not care to stay & begged her to excuse me that I knew she had nothing to do with getting up the party & that I didn't care to have Cora dancing with the boys that were there & would go home — it was all right with her so I sent for Mr. A. & he for Cora & we come home & left the madest set of boys that you ever saw. Mr D. carried his girl home just as soon as we left — in <u>fact</u>, the <u>whole thing</u> broke up —

You wonder what boys were out on a big time with the country green horn girls. Mr. Frank Killam, Will Holmes, Jim Elliot, a barber, & one fellow I did not know. Just the meanest set in town. Since Will Holmes' disgrace, he is not received at all in town, & they thought they would be all right among us country folks — but they find they are mistaken — All the old gentlemen in town & country say a better thing never happened — that I did exactly right — I found out after that, that Will [Stone] could not keep them from coming — don't know when we will have another social or party. I hope you can read this — all well. Bud Willie is getting out boards &c. — they will move the mill soon to Mitchel Station to saw lumber. I don't know their arrangements. Mr. B. has come back, Fred Fisher is here for a hunt will return Sunday — he is coming to see me Thursday night —

      Much love,
      Carrie

Tom G. is in town studying under Col.Brown.*

*Thomas J. Gaughan had returned from Springhill College and was studying Law in Camden.

Gilder Boddie in Austin, Texas, to his mother, Mary E. Boddie, in Ouachita Co.

              Jan. 30th 1886

Dear Mama;

I have been thinking every day I would reply to your last dear letter received some few days ago, but the weather has been so bad on my eyes could not get out for paper, stamps and envelopes. This is borrowed. Received a letter yesterday from Willis, also one from Mr. Baddans. Will write to them soon.

My eyes are still improving gradually, think the doctor intends they shall take no more back sets — I judge from his mild treatments. They are bound to be well or worse within twenty more days.

Small pox — plenty of it in 75 miles of this place and spreading. No one here seem to care or seem in the least alarmed — say they have a few cases here every year. Love to all,

> Your devoted son,
> G.G. Boddie

Matt Proctor Rumph at home to Cornelia Dickson, visiting in Princeton, Arkansas

Feb 14th, 1886

Dear Miss Nelie

Your letter of the 6th has just been received and perused with much pleasure I had not seen Dennis untill yesterday evening he came over and spent a few hours. I had heard of your trip soon after he came back, he seems to have taken cold, has a severe cough. I guess he does not suffer much, he was able to ride across the overflow yesterday eve. I am glad to say Hattie is up and looking better than she has this winter. She got up a few days after you left. I came very near having pneumonia. I took fresh cold after you left. I do not think I ever had such a time. I have not been able to do any thing hardly. Eugenia, Maude, Hattie does the work. I have begun to improve the last few days. I have not been confined to the bed. Dr. says it is more like Catar fever*, had inward fever all the time. I was quite like I was when Lillian was young only worse, had severe pain in my right side, when I cough my side hurts yet. I am so much better now, it was two days I could not raise my hand to my head. I think we are all getting strait once more. Dr's. health has not been good for a month or more, he does not sleep well at night, he said he slept better last night than he had for some time, he expects to go to town tomorrow. He has not been to town since you left. Maude and Hattie says tell you they are anxious to go stay with you and go to school, up there. I do not know how I could let them go so far from home. Garland and Charles are out playing and cutting wood and pine. They are looking very well. Bessie had a light chill Saturday. She has been very well since. Lillian has a cough. I think she has taken a little cold although she is as merry and jolly as can be. She gets around like a little Duck. John Boddie spent last Thursday night with us. He was very lively. Dr went to see Mrs Moseley Friday. She was a little puny not sick enough to be in bed. The health of the neighborhood is very good, at present. Eugenia and myself have not been off the place since you left, Carrie was coming here last Sunday had the water not been over the bottom, we will look for them next Sunday. Mrs D[unlap], Cora and Lula spent one Sunday with us since you left. Mr Lon Dunlap was here yesterday. His family are all well. He said Mamie

*Matt probably means catarrh fever, which is an inflammation of the resperatory tract.

Coleman had applied for the school in their neighborhood. He did not know whether she would get it or not as there was one lady ahead of her over the creek, it would be left to a vote. Miss Nelie I will fix your lamp up in a little box of Cotton seed and send it out to Aunt Carolines,* the first one goes to Camden in a wagon, you get them to call for it, it is the only way of sending it. I will send your umberella which was found a few minutes after you left. Louza Lock found it. I send you some white knitting thread. It will be easy knit and I can dye it afterwards. You can knit for any of the children. Please excuse this badly written letter. Write soon. With much love to you.

*"Aunt Caroline" refers to Sarah Caroline Patterson Gaughan, wife of Patrick Gaughan.

      Mattie Rumph

Maude and Hattie say they are going to write to you soon. They all send love to you.

Robert Lee Boddie at school in Webb School in Bell Buckle, Tennessee to his brother John Rumph Boddie in St. Louis

                Feb. 20th 1886

  Dear Bro.

  Your last two letters duly received. Accept my sincere thanks for the money, it was sufficient. Would have answered sooner, but waited to see if my shoes would fit &c. but as they have not come I could not wait longer. I am gratified that my report pleased you, and will do my best to make my next one still better. Another boy was accidentally shot last week in the heel. It is a very ugly, and painful wound, but I hope not a dangerous one. The boy who got shot was Carneal Murchison, the boy with whom Charley P. & myself roomed, the whole of last year. And is a very near friend. The muzzle of the gun was not more than two feet off. The charge entering the heel just below ancle, and ranged down towards the toes, and lodged near half way the foot, which had to be cut open, pieces of wadding, leather, and bones, with the shot were taken out. He seemed to be in good spirits when I called this evening, though was suffering much. Mr. Webb has prohibited the boys from using their guns any more.

  Wiley Boddie and Walter Stooks are our next Public Debaters. Mr. Soney Webb has not yet returned. We are having some beautiful weather. Had a splendid lecture on The Ruins of Pompeii last Friday by a Mr. Harris of Nashville. We had to write an essay on it. I do not know how I came out on it, for it is the first I have ever written on a mans speech. Am going to send it to Mamma if Mr. Webb will let me have it. Am getting on finely. Time flies so fast I can hardly realize how it does go. Good night.

         Your loving Bro.
         Robt*

*Robert Boddie was called Tug by the family when he was a small boy.

Carrie Boddie at home to her aunt Cornelia Dickson at Princeton, Arkansas

March 11th 1886

Dear Aunt Nelie,

    I should have answered your nice letter two weeks ago and can scarcely tell why I did not — I was getting through with some pressing work to be all ready to visit Cos Attalie when it came — & I meant of course to write while at her house last week but all were against my sparing the time. Mr. <u>Dennis</u> specially — Eugenia came on Tuesday and oh we did have a glorious time. We sewed some too — partly made a quilt, put it in and quilted it out, then some flannel & a dress for the baby — I enjoyed my stay <u>very</u> much and Mr. D[ennis] is just the smartest and most meddlesome fellow I ever saw. Yes he is very thoughtful — we had <u>lots of fun</u>. Attalie looks for Alex home Friday.

    Don't you know Cora is beside herself — this her first glimpse of a big city — I went home with Aunt C[lara] from church Sunday and Uncle J[ohn Dunlap] seemed so proud that Cora had gone to New Orleans. Lula had a new beau that day Mr. Kinch Norman — Mr S[tate] Stone also dined there and I entertained him until Mr. D. called for me in the afternoon — I don't much like Mr. Normans looks, do you hear of him in that neighborhood? Lula has broken off entirely with her Texas sweetheart but you have heard it I presume. I'm going to be left inspite of everything — Honey [Eugenia] and Mr. E[arle] are the best of friends — Mr. D. says he is waiting for Miss Cora to come home — is going to spend Sunday with her, but I don't care, Mr. A. is coming to see me Saturday night, by the way he told me he had begun a letter to you last week and you can imagine my astonishment when he told me it was to thank you for his nice present and that he wanted to hear from you anyway — I asked if he wasn't going to send it — well no — but that he was going to start another that suited him better — said he did appreciate your gift most truly & thought to thank you often but when he saw you it was awkward for him to do so — then after he still put it off — I do wish he would write to you to let you see how beautifully he composes — Mr. D. too says he is going to write to Au[nt] Nelie.

    I heard from Cousin [Mittie Rumph Rucks] the other day, all save John were well, he was suffering with a rising on his head. Mr. Clifton had gone to New Orleans and, from there to see Cos George [Rumph]. Little Florrie is talking & unusually bright for her age — I heard today that Mrs. Leer gave her oldest child morphine for quinine & it died from the effects — was buried Monday and Mr. Snow killed himself the same day with a pistol — dreadful wasn't it —

    Please write me another letter like your last, it would have done you good to see how much I enjoyed it — especially the part where you told of your nose being such a running fountain the day you went up to take charge of the school.

Smoke sends his love to you and says,"tell Aunt Nelie I have got a nice dog". His papa sent it a Scotch Terrier just the ugliest and cutest little thing you ever saw. S. calls him Clevie for Cleveland — Aunt Nelie write soon & a long letter. Bud G[ilder]'s eyes improving slowly. Robert [will] be home in June — is getting on nicely — reports good —

Lovingly,
Carrie

Smoker Boddie with Dog
Photo courtesy of Ruth Boddie Farmer

Gilder Boddie in Austin, Texas, to his mother, Mary E. Boddie in Ouachita Co.

Mch 16th 1886

Dear Mama;

Your most welcome letter of the 9th inst. to hand. Do not worry yourself, dear Mama, about my wellfare at any time, for I am getting along about as well as could be expected under the circumstances. My eyes some[time] give me considerable pain other days are easy owing to the treatment. The doctor says they are healing as fast as he can hope for as it requires time. He is now treating the balls — old ulcer pits he calls them — been there from time immemorial and now opening up again.

For the want of exercise I suppose and a sudden change in the weather, I was taken with a chill last week and fever which lasted me two days, am now as well as usual.

Tell Smoker to train his dog to tree squirrels and I will take him and Godfrey squirrel hunting when I come home —

With much love,
Your son,
G. G. Boddie.

Gilder Boddie in Austin, Texas, to his mother, Mary E. Boddie in Ouachita Co.

April 3rd/ 86

Dear Mama,

Your letter of few days ago to hand but I am unable to read or write. Nothing serious the matter, though my eyes are no better and the doctor is using atropin* in my eyes which prevents me from seeing.

Ulcerative eye balls is the trouble now, which gives me a good deal of pain. They get better for 3 or 4 days then worse. My general health is improving and am tired of taking medicine too which has been an every day business for sometime.

Hope all are well. Tell Willis to ship to me by Ex. the first time he goes to town, my summer shirts and socks if any in my trunk — its getting hot weather here; Enclose key to my trunk, which take care of.

With love,
Gilder

*Atropine is a generic name for Belladonna, which is used to dilate the eyes.

Mittie Rumph Rucks in Camden to Cornelia Dickson in Princeton, Arkansas

April 16th 86

Dear Aunt Nealie,

As I promised to write to you tonight, I am now seated to try & do so — notwithstanding the little folks are keeping such a racket in the dining room, I can scarcely hear my ears — they are having a Sunday School meeting & such songs — John is preacher & Florrie & Ed are singers & shouters — Corrie is in there washing dishes, Louis is in bed — Mr Rucks & Bro E[dwin Clifton] are in parlor trying to solve an illegible letter of business the latter received.

I was real glad to go down town for you today & as Mr. Rucks is home all day now I find much more time to go — Barbara too is with me yet — Sometimes I think I ought to cook myself — but just dread to commence — Mr. Rucks came out very well this winter managed to save enough out of his wages after living expences to pay Dr. Bragg $100.00 & $150.00 back that he borrowed the summer, besides several other smaller debts & gave me $50.00 to get the children clothes & household things, so we feel quite independant.

I did not get to see Mr. Mann as I expected, hence did not remit you the change left — as I sealed my note thinking I would hand it to him —

The mothers are very busy now preparing for the Examination — I do wish you could attend — it will be week after next — important nights will be Wednesday & Thursday — Corrie has a real funny piece & recites it real well too the title of it is "Poetical Courtship" & you would just break down laughing at Emma Bergs, 'tis "Cure for Rheumatism by the Application of a <u>Bee Sting</u>" — in fact all the girls have excellent pieces — Do wish you were here to go with me —

I have weaned Ed so I am all right about leaving him now — (Didn't <u>have</u> to though) am not as smart as Attalie — & Mary Benson — & a doz others, — Mary Puryear has been real sick with pneumonia but is now getting convalescense. Mrs Simmons too is very sick. Am afraid she will never leave her bed any more has rheumatism in her hips & knees — [_____] Pace & little Walter Meek are very sick with pneumonia. I suppose you knew Mrs Cambell died after a long illness — & Marvin now has his baby — don't know what he is going to do with it as they seldom come about us — I did hear that Mrs. Fisher would take it but don't know — He took Lizzie to nurse it as twas so spoiled that <u>she</u> was all the one could manage it — Trudie goes to school so Louie says — is at large, dependant on charity — & stays with whoever will let her — poor little thing. I feel so sorry for her. I do think Marvin might have taken her too but I guess three was <u>one</u> too many —

I have not heard from home in a long time do wish I could go over there but feel that I've too many brats now to go anywhere — Pa has been sick & does not look well so Bro E. & Mr Rucks says as they saw him down town the other day — Now I will have to close & lie down with Eddie as he is sleepy & I know I will get so too so good night & write soon. Give my regards to Mr & Mrs Lea

      Affectionately yours
      Mittie

Carrie Boddie at home to Cornelia Dickson in Princeton, Arkansas
                April 16th 1886

My Dear Auntie,

I was so tired & not well yesterday when your letter came and it did make me feel <u>so much</u> better though I could not write last night was too worn out — and now I have put breakfast on the table and have come to my room for that most pleasant task writing to you — but you'll excuse me using a pencil it is scarcely light enough for me to write at all — and I'll have to iron like "old rip" to get through today after I answer your letter. I had begun wondering if you had recd my letter & would have written again but had no paper — your last was written on the last paper I had and I am still out — tore this from my journal —

I heard from you through Eugenia last Sunday, she and Miss Georgia came in the afternoon on horse back — They were all well & had dined —

<u>all hands</u> at Miss Clem's that day — <u>turkey</u> dinner. The hunters had been on another hunt the week before, Mr. P[atterson] kill one & Mr. D. two — Uncle John don't seem to have good luck with his new gun — Lula & Cora came too Sunday and done me a lot of good to see them. They are so full of life — L. seems a new creature — Yes mam! I do think her Alanta sweetheart the best of all & told her so but he has quit corresponding with her now — Mr. D[ennis] seems to like C[ora] right well and I hope she can captivate him — or go to Atlanta to fit herself for a teacher or something else — Last Sunday a week ago Cos Attalie & Alex spent the day with me. Mr. Richardson and Mamie also — Then Lula Steele, her little folks Amanda and Elliott came in the afternoon, so we had a jolly time. Mr. R. would have us to sing — he joined us and it was real nice —

Every last one of my foil flowers died Aunt Nelie — I am so sorry to lose them but most every one froze or were injured more or less from the severe cold last winter — my hyacinths did not do well either. I reset a good many — the tulips are very sweet — in bloom now and I must send you a few —

We are going to have a May Day picnic and I do wish you could be here to attend — I think all will enjoy it havn't had anything of the kind in so long — Were to have a candy pulling at Aunt C[lara] while Miss Hood was there but it rained — by the way that is a nice girl — Eula Hood — she is real pretty refined & real well educated judging from her language & easy graceful manners — she only stayed one week — & one night and day with the me, she & Lula walked down. I liked her ever so much — had Mr. Allis to call that night and he <u>tried himself</u> by way of being agreeable and they seemed to enjoy their visit very much —

Smoke asked lots of questions about the little dog up there & said tell you "his pup is smart & that it got its leg hurt at the mill but is most well & that he sends a hug and some kisses to you" — our sewing will come soon, then I'll have to work — made Smoker & G[odfrey] some pants this week 4 pairs & Mary a dress — rather altered and made over an old one which is more trouble —

It is right lively down here now. The mill has started up — will have to stop. Write soon & a long letter —
       Lovingly
       Carrie

Miss Clem Proctor at home to Cornelia Dickson in Princeton, Arkansas
[April] 20 [1886] 12 O'clock

Dear Friend,

 I have been thinking of writing you for some time. Am now determined. Am sorry to have to tell you that Dr Rumph is in such a sad condition that he nor any other physician can tell what the matter is. They have deferent theories. Dr Folden & the Camden Dr are to meet here next Monday to Council as to the best course to pursue. Dr R says if it is necessary he will go at once to St Louis to be treated Surgicaly. I suppose you have heard that the trouble is the stomach. Dr R fears it is a tumor. Some think it a displaced spleen probably growing to the stomach. He is gradually growing weaker and suffers more to move. Is worse tonight than ever before though we have worked with him until he is resting real well, though he had to take chloroform. Indeed that is the only relief he has at night for the last week. He eats the least morsel and yet at times is very hungry but dares not to eat. You know dear Miss Nealy how it hurts his family to see him in this condition. Mat* says she would rather it was her suffering. Oh!, how I wish you were here. Everybody is kind and so sorry for Doctor.

 Dear Miss Nealie this is written under difficulty have jumpt to Doctor often am afraid he will take too much Chloroform. Am almost determined to slip out and send for Dr Folden. May do so before day. Doctor is having such a bad night of course he will not let us do so but I can send Steve. If this is mailed at Holly Springs you may know I did so. Mat rarely ever sleeps an hour. You know we are in trouble. She says tell you she has not had time to write that she could not explain anything if she did.

 Miss Nealie I am convinced that Doctor could not stand the best car trip to St Louis and if he could, he could <u>not</u> survive a surgical opperation.

 You know we are in trouble. Hope you are well.
   Goodbye
   Clem

 Friday Morning - Doctor is now quiet and resting well. But I know it will not last all day. Pray for us and come if you can.
   Clem

*"Mat" refers to Martha Proctor Rumph, sister to the writer of this letter, Miss Clem Proctor.

Gilder Boddie in Austin, Texas, to his mother, Mary E. Boddie in Ouachita Co.

April 23rd 1886

Dear Mama;

I received your last letter not long since and have been waiting a few days on my eyes as they are improving again and I was afraid of straining them in attempting to write.

The doctor is now working on my lids again but very slow and carefully. The express pkg came ok. Tell Willis that I am not allowed to smoke ... as thats not too good for a sore eyed man. Am always glad to hear from home. With love to you all,

Your son,
G.G.Boddie

Mittie Rumph Rucks in Camden to Cornelia Dickson in Princeton, Arkansas

May 18th/ 86

Dear Aunt Nealie,

I do not feel at all like writing to you as I have been in bed a week with rheumatism of the heart & am now just creeping about. I received your most welcome letter but feel too sad to answer it as I would — I only write now for fear you have not heard that ere long we will be called upon to give up our dearest of earthly friends, our Father. Oh, Aunt Nealie, I do hope it not so, but the Drs made an examination over here last week — & Dr. Hudson told Mr. Rucks that he had a tumor in his upper bowels & unless an opperation is performed it would soon prove fatal — They are going over again tomorrow & meet Dr. Folden there & have another consultation — I do hope they will convince him what they fear — & succeed in overcoming his horror of them using the knife — I think tis because he is so weak — looks just a shadow — & nothing agrees with him — Will write you more after tomorrow — Much love Yours
Mittie R.

Carrie Boddie at home to Cornelia Dickson in Princeton, Arkansas

May 28, 1886

My Dear Aunt Nelie,

You must think that I am a careless girl not to have answered your letter sooner and your inquiry about the steam washer — for I could have written you a post in regard. That which I ought to have done immediately but I didn't have time to write a long letter, and just put it off —

I like the washer splendidly, it does the work all right, but you are compelled to use it on a stove, & we have so many in the family and I have three hands besides to cook [for] and my kitchen so small that we had to quit using it — the wringer is good too for the price but Mamie says tell you there are some later that are better & says don't get no 99 —

I've had a good time since my last to you — We had our picnic but it wasn't enjoyed by many of the party — but few present, and Miss Georgia bolted off for home about 3 o'clock, and the crowd all followed save myself & two beaux Messrs Allis and Dennis. I had to soon follow, of course, but I'll tell you how come me to be so fortunate — Mamie R[ichardson] and Amanda [Head] were to go in Mr. D's wagon also — then Mr. A. & myself but all declined going save myself and I did have a nice time.

They had another on Woodard [Lake], but I didn't go — am in a great hurry now to get my sewing done so that I can go fishing on Pine Lake every few days — Mr. A. is going to take me he says when Robt comes home — he will be here Saturday — Brother [John] also, the latter spent a day with us this week and Aunt Nelie, Robert's leg was not broken — Some of the bones misplaced and cracked. He is well though limps badly — it was his ankle or slightly above it and did it wrestling with one of the boys —

You have heard of Uncle John's condition ere this — We all feel so sad over it — he has been such a good friend to us all — Brother hurried back to town to spend his last night home by his bedside & Uncle John left the next morning (Wednesday) for St. Louis to have an opperation performed Bro. told us it was impossible for him to live through it — if the Doctors undertook it at all. I think he settled all of his business before he left and has taken it all so coolly — Mama & Mamie & Bud W went to see him Sunday — and Aunt Nelie, Cousin A[ttalie] & Honey [Eugenia] went to church Sunday & dined with Aunt C[lara] and E. had an escort too — Mr. Earle, but Mr. D. told me it was not his (Mr. E.'s) intention to take E. to church, he had an engagement with her but knew of her Pa's illness & only went to stay a few moments when he found that E. had no idea of not going — Well, I reckon they [the girls] don't realize that he [their father] will not recover — he left home Monday morning & Bro. says they have seen him for the last time — he has talked with the Doctors — it is so hard to have to lose our friends and dearest —

We had a letter from Aunt <u>Hattie</u> * tonight, all were well — Stevie is getting on nicely — Dr. Easterling talks of moving to Texas this fall and <u>Cousin Fay</u> is <u>married.</u> She took her a partner on the 2nd of Feb & did not go home to marry, she said it was a useless expense that she and her fellow — (a Mr. Charley Crouse) could ill afford — I thought it a sensible idea as her husband is employed where she is — Aunt Hattie says C. is a moral

*"Aunt Hattie" refers to Hattie Murley, sister of Mary E. Gildersleeve Boddie.

energetic clever boy and Cousin Fay is very happy. I was so glad to hear it and believe from what she says about it that it is a real love match —

The fleas a[re] so bad I can't set still a moment we never did have so many — They nearly eat me up — I am going to enclose samples of my dresses so you can see how pretty [they are] — I've only made one up, the small check — just finished three for Mama & have still another <u>nice</u> one to make — I ought to have made it this week, but I have so much to do couldn't get it all to save my life — but I'll soon get done with all — made Smoker dress suit last week — and Aunt Nelie how about your coming in vacation — Mr. D. asked me to say something to you about it, he did not say exactly or near enough for me to say more — only he wanted to know "<u>what is what</u>" — those boys are awful good to me —

We had church last Saturday night and will have this [Saturday night] — Aunt Mattie asked about you and sent love — Mama also —
       Yours Lovingly
       Carrie

Tell me which dress you think prettiest also something more about the widower — I do wish you would captivate some good fellow — please do — I'm in earnest Aunt N. You would be all right then —

Mittie Rumph Rucks in Camden to Cornelia Dickson in Princeton, Arkansas

                May 31st/86

Dear Aunt Nealie,

I promised to write to you again, but I've been so low-spirited & sick besides I was unable to do so — in hopes of better news from our dear Father to you — but alas! tis all the same — heart rending fact that there is no hopes given us by those wonderful surgeons of St. Louis — where he was accompanied a week ago by Dr. Hudson — & tonight Mr. Rucks, Cos John Boddie & Mr Proctor will meet him at the Depot — returned to us, to soon leave us again — Oh how hard to see him dieing by inches & can do nothing for him — the surgeons of St. Louis, so Bro. Tommie writes, pronounced it a cancerous tumor of the bowels — about the size of a cocoanut — I don't think I can go & see him tonight as he will stop at Mr. Proctors — It hurts me so & I am so weak can hardly walk. Do come & help us cheer his few remaining days —

All rest of us well I reckon — they have written all other particulars from home — Good bye, I can't write more.
       Yours,
       Mittie Rucks

J. S. Mann in Princeton, Arkansas to Cornelia Dickson also in Princeton.
May 29th 1886

Miss C. S. Dickson,

You can do as you think best as far as I am concerned, can you see some of the other patrons of the school. I know you feel like you ought to go and see Dr. Rumph. I shall not think hard of you, let us know when you can take up the school again. My wagon & team has to go to Malvern, & can not assist you in going home.

Yours, &c
J. S. Mann

Gilder Boddie in Austin, Texas, to his brother John R. Boddie in St. Louis
June 23, 1886

Dear Brother:

I have been sick since the 18th and Dr. Wooten left the 21st. He pronounced my case "typhoid fever". I will go to the hospital this evening for treatment. My bill there will be $1.50 per day for room, board, medical attention, nursing, &etc. I received the $20.00 too late to give to Dr. Wooten, reserving same toward paying my fare at the hospital until I hear from home. I owe Dr. Dupree Five Dollars for two days attendance since Dr. Wooten left and Capital Hotel Two 5/100 Dollars on board due July 1st.

Hoping to hear from you soon, I remain, as ever,

Your brother,
G.G. Boddie

The Western Union Telegraph Company
Collect 60cts
Received at 10:30 am
Dated: Austin Texas [June] 30, 1886
To Mrs Mary E. Boddie c/o Boddie & Badders
Camden

Gilder is dead What shall we do with the Remains
L. A. Burdette

George Gildersleeve
"Gilder" Boddie

Geo. A. Prochan in Austin, Texas, to John R. Boddie in Camden

July 3, 1886

Dear John:

I cannot tell you [how] grieved and shocked I was at your brother's death. I had seen but little of him for some time, as he did not go out much on account of his eyes and my wife being very ill I was obliged to stay every moment with her that I could spare from the office. While at the Drug Store for the doctor to see my wife, Dr. McLaughlin told me that Gilder was sick with Typhoid Fever and wished to be taken out to the City Hospital. I told him to take good care of him and I would go out and see him as soon as I could. The rooms, bedding, etc. for a private patient are very nice and the doctor said he thought he would do better there than at the hotel.

My wife was so sick that I did not get to see him. Dr. McL. told me that he did very well up to about 24 hours before he died, and Mrs. Wright, the Matron, says he was getting along pretty well but that the heart's action seemed feeble, but for that, thinks he would have recovered.

Mr. Burdette, proprietor of the Capitol Hotel informed me of his death and he and I were making preparation for his burial when your brother's telegram came and Mr. B. made the arrangements to send him to Camden & also sent his trunk &c. Dr. McL. told me that he had $20.00 which Gilder handed him, also his pistol — & that he had been at Hospital six days at $1.50 making $9.00, so he handed me $11.00 and the pistol and I paid Mr. Burdette the enclosed bill of $4.45 & Dr. DuPree who attended him before he went to the hospital $5.00, leaving a balance of $1.55 for which I enclose Postal Note.

I have the pistol & there is, so Mr. Burdett informs me, a small oil stove belonging to Gilder, which I will do with whatever you wish. Mr. Burdette attended to the preparing and sending the body and gave Gilder all the attention he could. Mrs. Wright says he spoke of his mother & wanted to be at home with her. I will see Mrs. Wright again and learn more of his last days & write again.

I sincerely sympathise with you all and wish I could have done more for the dear boy. My own troubles have been heavy but God in his great goodness has preserved our lives,

Your friend truly,
Geo. A. Prochan

Edwin Clifton in Camden to Cornelia Dickson in Princeton, Arkansas
July 25, 1886

Dear Aunt Nealie,

"I feel like one who treads alone, some banquet hall deserted." I feel that I lost a true friend when Dr. Rumph died. The day of his burial, everything I saw & heard reminded me of my own <u>great</u> loss.* Sometimes it is so painful it is almost more than I can bear. I inclose some verses that describe my experience exactly.

I will send some papers to you by this mail. I did not know you had returned to your school until I went over to the funeral.

Mrs. Rucks [Mittie] has not returned yet. I can't write, it is too painful!

Respectfully,
Edwin Clifton

*Edwin Clifton's "great loss" was the death of his wife Florence Rumph Clifton in 1885.

Lula Dunlap in Ouachita Co. to Cornelia Dickson in Princeton, Arkansas
Aug 5th, 1886

Dear Aunt Nealie,

As I have not heard from you since you left, I thought I would write to see how you are getting along teaching and standing the warm weather. We all spent last Sunday at Attalie's. She was well. Alex had gone to see Carrie*. The Dr. (Nurning?) is treating [her]; hope he will benefit her. [He] come by Mr. Proctor's that evening. Miss Matt & children were all up. The children have been sick. Eugenia is with Attalie. Aunt Mollie was here a little while Monday morn, Coz Willis had gone after your trunks to take care of; they were locked up with Miss Matt's things, Carrie [Boddie] said she was going to write. We all miss Uncle John so much. It was very sad although we were all expecting [it]. Aunt Nealie Ma says when school is out you must come and stay with us. She has been sick once two weeks ago, is up now but not feeling well.

Cora & I went up to Bearden last week to a picnic, went up on the train Wednesday and returned Friday morn, the picnic was on Thursday; everything passed off very nice. There was a large crowd; had speaking, from the candidates, a nice dinner, lemonade, and a flying jenny; Mr. Norman and his sister met us at the depot and we went out home, about a mile; they were all very nice; we enjoyed our stay; liked the old folks splendid, and young ones too. I suppose they criticesed* me as much as I did them hope they were pleased.

There is no news in the neighborhood, everyone seems to be enjoying good health, the farmers are pulling fodder this week.

*Carrie is Alex's little daughter who was staying with her grandfather, Mr. Patrick Gaughan. She had polio and was left with a withered arm and leg.

*The use of "criticize" by Lula implies judging of merits. It is interesting to see how the use of words has changed over the years.

Our protracted meeting comes off the fourth Saturday & Sunday in this month, hope we may all be well, and have a good meeting.

Ma & Cora sends love, accept much from myself, and write soon.

Your loving neice,
Lula Dunlap

Carrie Boddie at home to Cornelia Dickson in Princeton, Arkansas

Aug 7, 1886

My Dear Aunt Nelie,

When I wrote you that little note, I had no idea it would be this long before another letter followed — indeed I do not know how long it has been — don't seem to have any memory at all of dates or anything — I have thought of you so much, Aunt Nealie, and wished from the very depths of my heart that I had a nice home to give you — and it is harder still to know that I could have, just by saying the word — only it would be a living death to me. I have thought of it and it may be yet — I leave it with God for a little while — but anyway, Aunt Nelie, I would love to have you stay here as much as you can — your trunks are here. They were left at Uncle J's in the parlor when Miss Mat moved to Miss Clem's, she also left a few of her things in her room — and Eugenia has gone to live with Cousin Attalie — Bud Willie just found out about your trunks being left there yesterday, and this morning he went up there & got them & told me to tell you they would be taken care of until you wanted them — and they now occupy a place on either side of the door in the dining room — a very nice place for them and not one bit in the way — and you won't be either Aunt Nealie so come whenever you want to and stay just as long as you wish. You are not stout enough now to do any hard work & I would not go to any place & start in that way — if I just had a home I could make you so happy — you should have an easy good time just like Mama has had since I've been old enough to take the work & care of housekeeping from her —

I went up to see Miss Mat this morning while Bud W. went over for your trunks. They were all well though Bessie & Maude had been quite sick since they moved — They broke up the Monday after Uncle J. was buried. I think Mr. J[im] Proctor is going to enlarge the house & keep Miss Mat there for fear of her being troubled with Honey [Eugenia Rumph] or you <u>and company</u>! — I used to think right well of him, but since Uncle John's death, ? see what he is, & Miss G[eorgia] is not one bit better — Miss Clem has kind feelings & Miss Matt would be good if they let her — I mean to go to see her whenever I can — but never to a meal — she is going to send Maude & H[attie] to school in town this fall & Mr. Jesse P. wants them all over there but I know Miss G. & Jim [Proctor] will object on yours & Honey's account

— she [Miss Matt] says she don't know exactly what she will do yet —

Cousin [Mittie] spent last week with us & the week before at her old home — That is the reason I did not write to you last week — was completely broken down — so much to do and felt real unwell all the week & am not feeling the best in the world this [week] — just weak and nervous — and last Friday afternoon Aunt Nealie Mr. Dennis brought a horse for me to ride out with him & I felt real uneasy for fear something might happen. I was so weak came near falling several times & my head would swim & I could understand things he would say to me, & I would ask over — I didn't tell him & I don't know whether he detected it or not, though he did say he believed I was not enjoying my ride — I did enjoy it, but was too weak for such violent exercise — he had the kindness to take me up to see E[ugenia] one afternoon the week before, and yesterday he sent me a nice melon & such a nice basket of peaches — he is so good and nice to me.

Mr. Clifton spent a night with us not long since, & next morning he and Robert took a little hunt. Cousin don't like him one bit but the more I see of him, the better I like him — he has moved back to the Morgan place & has Miss Kate to keep house for him — I do not much blame him — I presume it is the best he can do — it was not pleasant for him at all at Cousin's. I saw that when I was there —

Bro. [John R. Boddie] will be home soon — I hope you will write soon, Aunt Nealie. All of your friends ask me about you — was to see Mrs. M[oseley] a few moments this evening — All are well — Please write soon,
                Lovingly,
                Carrie

Carrie Boddie at home to Cornelia Dickson in Princeton, Arkansas
                                        Aug 11th 1886

My Dear Aunt Nealie,

I was glad to get your letter this evening — hadn't heard from you in so long was afraid you were sick — I wrote to you a week ago but Brother has been home since and told me to write again soon so I was going to send another letter this week anyway — he wanted me to tell you to make our home yours, when your school is out — to come right here — and Bud Willie wants you to live with us, too Aunt Nelie — and Mama is delighted to know she can have you if you will come — and I just tell you Aunt Nealie it is no sweet home now but I reckon if I can stand it you can & I will be the gladest in the world to have you — Mamie is the same old Mamie with one additional trouble — Godfrey — she is teaching him to have his way and that is all she & I fuss about — I won't let him control Smoke — I have quit troubling myself about her or the children in any form or shape — she did not appreciate my working for them — sewing, ironing &c — nor for herself either — so I quit & have nothing more to do with them & its the only way to get along — but when you come you will see how things go —

If I just could love somebody I would marry Aunt Nelia but it seems I can't — and I will have to do as you have done —

We have heard but little more of Bud Gilder's illness — Brother saw Mrs. Proctor she is in Ark. somewhere, & she told him that she could not go to see him herself, but sent the children every day to see him, that he had a nicely furnished room, & the matron found him to be such a nice boy nursed him herself & that he was doing well until the day of his death, June 29 in the evening a few moments to 7 o'clock, he asked his nurse to raise him up that he was smothering. She did so & in a little while, he said he felt all right, & she laid him down & just then he breathed his last — she said his friends ask him to let them write to us but he said no he did not want to alarm Mama unnecessarily & that he would soon be well & come home.

Aunt Nealie it is a wicked wish but every day I ask God to let me go next — I ought to prepare to meet him & I do try to be good —

Robert is going back to school first of Sept. I shall miss him now more than ever —

When your school closes, I want to go up after you if I can — Honey & I — & if you have any way come before then. There will be a protracted meeting on the 4th Sunday — Eugenia is going to spend next week with me — Mrs. Brodnax is going to stay with Cousin Attalie — I am making a dress for a darkey this week through with my sewing two weeks ago but I must make some preserves & jelly soon — Write as soon as you can Aunt Nelie — It is late I must close —

                    Lovingly
                    Carrie

Miss Clem Proctor in Camden to Cornelia Dickson in Princeton, Arkansas
                                                August 23rd, 1886

Dear Miss Nealie

Mat is getting baby to sleep Georgia is writing a line or two and I will add a few. I wrote a page or two on a letter to you the day after the dear Doctors funeral, was interupted then and have never found time when I felt as if I could write at all. The rainey days just after the sad funeral it seemed that all the children would get sick, and everything was so gloomy over there and we were all so worn out going and coming, so my brothers & dear Alec thought it best for Mat to come over here untill they could make other arangements, and I do think it the best thing. It did help Mat & the children so much, everything went well until poor dear Cousin Alex [Gaughan fell ill] with that terable disease Malereal hermaturea. Miss Nealie it was just awful to behold the change made in a few short hours in the handsome face of the Strut man and Oh it was melting to the hardest heart to witness the distress of the young wife [Attalie Rumph] in her delicate condition. In the last moments I kept her from him and reasoned and kept her tolerably quiet with closed doors until she heard the last dying groans. Oh! Miss Nealie I could scarcely control my own feelings. She does not think she will survive the coming event.* Write us soon. Out of space.

Clem

*Attalie Rumph Gaughan was pregnant with her second daughter at the time of her husband's unexpected death.

Carrie Boddie at home to Cornelia Dickson in Princeton, Arkansas

August 24 1886

My Dear Aunt Nelie,

Your last letter was a long time on the way — Mr. Earle forgot to deliver it when you told him to so it was posted in Holly Springs some weeks after — he was here to take Eugenia to church Saturday night — Mr. Dennis was to be my escort but was called to Alex's bedside that afternoon and I was sick too so did not go with them. E. didn't come back — stayed with Aunt C[lara] and went down to Alex's next morning — he died that night (Sunday) at 2 oclock Aunt Nelie — was taken Friday & had a chill that night — he was bad sick from the start and Dr. Foldern did not get to him until late Saturday eve — and could not do one thing with the disease — congestion and malaria fever — he left no will or orders about his business affairs — but was conscious except at times — They burried him yesterday in town. I was not well enough to go nor to go to his house —

I do feel so sorry for Cos Attalie & more specially at this time — Mr. Gaughan went after her Monday eve & carried her to his house — Mrs Brodnax too — and Eugenia will go also & remain with her until she is confined and well again. Then she will go to live in town with Miss Mat — Mr. Jesse P[roctor] is going to move her over there. They say in time to start the children to school — She will occupy a house near Col. Lee's — Cousin wants E. she says but I just know she will not live with Cousin if she can help it —

Mr. Clifton brought Florrie over Monday eve to stay with me until he came on back from Alex's next morning but I couldn't get her to stay of her own free will & I was afraid to force her thinking she might cry that night — but if Cousin had not been with her, I believe she would have willingly stayed with me — she is so sweet — I wish she would love me —

We shall miss Alex so much, I believe he was a good friend of mine & oh Aunt Nelie it is so hard to see them all go — I fear Mama will not last a great while — & I do my very best toward taking care of her — but some how she will trouble about the children & wait on them though since several sermons from me there is some improvement in that line — The children are not near so bad as they have been — Smoke is sick now had a chill today & still some fever tonight. I do hope the little fellow will be spared a spell —

I would like ever so much to accept your invite to visit you but it is useless to think of such a thing unless Mama would stay somewhere until I came home — Mamie will just sit down and let her work herself to death if she wants too — That is another of my troubles & if ever I leave home I want Brother to take Mama & Smoke off somewhere to board & she will not want to go either —

You asked me why I should want to do a thing Aunt Nelie that would not secure my happiness — Well by so doing I could secure a home — one for you — and the pleasure of my people — & in doing another — the displeasure of them & probably no home for you. You see in the first instance there is no love on either side & I dare say if united both lives would be wrecked — & in the latter case one life would be saved as there is sincere love on one side — Now I'm going to take your advice and clear my own conscience — I mean to make a confession to the first party that I've already done to a certain extent — You don't know how I have been tempted — but he will forgive me for I have been frank all along — in the last case — will save him from destruction and some of these days if I can make up my mind will gratify his wish — Now Aunt Nelie — it is a secret and I would not have you tell anyone for my life — because they are both good friends of mine & I do appreciate their offers the most in the world — The first Mr. D. seckond, Mr. A. I ought to be true to the latter for more reasons than one he came first & has had his share trouble already — Aunt Nelie it is hard to be placed in my situation when a girl wants to do what is right & if she has any conscience at all.

We have had so much trouble in our neighborhood have we not? Presume some one has written you about the school teacher losing her little daughter of typhoid fever not long since — Am afraid we will have lots of sickness now — Have written in a hurry hope you can read it & will excuse me for sending such a letter — write soon

      Lovingly,
      Carrie

Mr. Allis made me a presant of five quires* of this paper — I needed it so much & appreciated it you may be sure. Mama sends much love to you —

*A quire is a collection of 25 sheets of paper of the same size and quality.

Cornelia Dickson in Princeton, Arkansas to Tommie Gaughan in Camden

August, 1886

Dear Tommie,

    How good of you to write to me, though I know it was so painful to send a message of such sad, sad news. I was shocked and can hardly realize that our Alex, so promising in physical strength and manliness of character should have been cut down, as it were, in his prime and prosperity and at a time when his wife and child were so dependent upon his thoughtful loving care. It is hard for his relatives and friends to give him up and feel reconciled to the most mysterious claiming of our Heavenly Father. All of you have my heart-felt sympathy for I know what you have lost.

    I wrote to Attalie, but feel that Heaven alone can give comfort to such grief as hers. Time will surely roll these clouds away, but one like Alex can never be forgotten. I shall feel very uneasy until I can hear from Attalie again.

                Your friend,
                 Cornelia S. Dickson

Cornelia Dickson in Princeton, Arkansas to Attalie Rumph Gaughan in Camden

August, 1886

Dear Attalie,

    I have just read Tommie's letter bearing the news of the terrible grief you have been called upon to bear. It is terrible at any time, doubly so coming at this time upon you. And your Aunt Nealie feels for you; and your little darling in your great bereavement. So soon after being deprived of your dear Parent. But child bear up. You will bear up & remember that the hand of your Heavenly Parent is in it all. Look to him for strength in your every trial. Oh how my heart aches in sympathy for those so near and dear to him. He was a noble son, and brother; and I have lost a dear friend that I loved. How thankful I am that you have kind relatives around you, whom you will now love more than ever for his sake, and try to comfort them in their burden of sorrow, by a daughter's loving duty.*

*This lovely little note is unsigned in the ledger.

Mattie Proctor Rumph in Camden to Cornelia Dickson in Princeton, Arkansas

August 26, 1886

Dear Miss Nealie,

No doubt you think it very strange of me for not writing sooner, but you must not think, Miss Nealie, that it is carelessness or that I do not think of you often. The children have been sick except Garland and Charlie.

I guess that you have heard through Carrie that I have left my old home and it seemed to me that I was leaving part of my family, for it will always seem so dear to me. Miss Nealie, Brother Jim and Tom moved me over to Ma's until they could make further arrangements for me a home somewhere else. Brother Jesse is thinking of renting me a house in town so I can send the children to school and to Sunday School. I am looking for Jesse out tomorrow. Of course I will do what he thinks best as I was left in his care. I do feel such a responsibility resting upon me to rear the children right.

When I moved I left your trunks and a great many of my things locked up in the house. Willis Boddie came up the next week and got your trunks. I will take care of your little things that I have.

I guess you have heard of the sad death of Alex Gaughan which was so unexpected to every one. He came here Wednesday evening and brought Carrie [his little daughter] riding before him on the horse. He stayed a while and was not complaining any. We did not hear from him until Saturday. He was very sick. Dennis came by. They had not heard he was sick until Saturday morning. It was such a shock to us all. He had malaria and conjestion combined. My sympathies are with Attalie. She seems heart broken. She has not been confined yet, Uncle Patrick carried her to his house Sunday morning. She is looking worse than I ever saw her. Eugenia is staying with her until she is confined. Alex had carried Eugenia to live with them until I went to house-keeping. I expect to do all I can for her. You know I love her and Eugenia next to my own, and I will do anything I can.* It does seem we are all left together. Everyone says that is a sickly place where Alex and Attalie lived.

*Attalie and Eugenia were Dr. John Rumph's daughters by his second wife Sallie Gildersleeve.

If I could see you I could talk so much better than I can write. Miss Nealie, it is so sad to look around and see all my father-less children and to think they are all in my care.

Jesse wants to educate Maud or Hattie for me. Then she could help educate the little ones. I dislike separating them. I know they would do a good part by her and give her all the advantages. I know I could never give the children half the education Jesse could.

My baby is in good health now. At the time I moved, Maud, Hattie and Bessie were all sick. I thought I would have to send for Dr. Folden, but did not. I used the young doctor in the neighborhood, Dr. Murry who board at Henry Broughton's. He has a good practice.

Write often to me. You know the situation. I will write every opportunity. All join me in love to you.

Mattie Rumph

Carrie Boddie at home to Cornelia Dickson in Princeton, Arkansas

Oct 1st 1886

Dear Aunt Nelie,

I must write you a few lines now that I can — should I put it off for more time fear something might happen to prevent me writing this week.

I heard from you yesterday at Sunday School. I inquired of Miss Georgia, as Miss Mat was absent, and she told me the latter had received a letter from you and you had not been well. I was sorry to hear it Aunt Nelie and you must take good care of yourself, for I would not have you get bad sick away from home where none of us could get to you for anything. Poor Bud Gilder had to die among strangers and I pray God it will be the last one of our family taken that way. If you should have a hard spell let me know of it so I can come and nurse you —

We have a right sick neighbor — Cpt. Mitchell — he has a slight attack of pneumonia and our little folks have been having chills again — well enough to eat though you may be sure.

We hear from Robert every week, he is getting on nicely — and Mama had a paper sent her from Ala Aunt Nelie. The Prattville Signal announcing Cousin S[usan] Love's* death. I will enclose her obituary — We don't know who sent the paper, it has W.J. Zimmermon's name writen on the margin & it is dated Sept 24th — I would like so much to know and see how they are all getting on in Ala — but I don't think now you and I will ever get to go out there —

The girls have all been over to town doing their fall & winter shopping and as next Sunday is our Preaching Day presume they will all come out in fall attire. I did not send to Bro. for anything save flannel drawers & skirt — There are so many to buy for & he writes such discouraging letters home — I can do very well in my three year old dress & bonnet & four year old cloak — I don't care one bit. Lula & Cora have very pretty cloaks — short — and hats too right nice —

I reckon you have heard how badly Lula's beau treated her — a flirt out and out — he is to marry soon — a girl in Stevens or some such place — she has such a bad time with the boys — I try to help her out but she will not listen to a word — she is now wearing his ring — I have thought all the while that it was not pure & I'm most convinced of it now —

All the neighborhood boys are good to me, in fact they never let me

*Susan Frances Love was Sis Carrie's daughter in Alabama. She married M. S. Wadsworth, her sister Irene's husband after Irene's death in 1870.

get very lonely. I make Mama go to S.S. every S. and Mamie & I take turns in going — she one S. & me the next — & nearly everytime I have to stay Mr. Allis, Mr. D[ennis] or Mr. S[tone] will call & I don't of course mind staying to keep house — though I would gladly go everytime if there was somebody to keep house so all could go. Our bible lessons are very interesting. Miss C[lem] hears the class but I study it all out myself — We have a little S.S. don't know how long it will last. You didn't tell me when your school would be out Aunt Nelie — I need you to help me sing. I believe they are going to form a choir. Mr J. Mitchell leader Miss C. wants him. Honey laughs so much & don't seem to be interested. I am on alto or second rather.

Lovingly,
Carrie

Mary E. Boddie in Ouachita Co. to her son Robert Lee Boddie at school in Bell Buckle, Tennessee

Oct 4th '86

My dear boy,

Your dear letters ever so welcome found us all well, & getting on as usual. Been having since the rain quite cool weather, needing fires not only morn & eve, but all day, tho' no killing frost as yet. Will is hauling corn from the field in front today. Mamie & Carrie are washing which work they have been doing for the past three Mondays. As Will was having strips hauled from the mill last Fri. we made good use of the chance to get the balance of saw dust for our grass plot. Our little force, Mamie & I, with Cora to help filled 80 sacks by dinner time. They are sawing pretty regular now, but cant ship lumber yet. 'Tis said now that the R. R. will be finished by middle, or last of this month, ie. the change from narrow to wide gage. Mr. B[rodnax] is sick with nettle rash, he was over here yesterday morn, but Will was in the bottom, & he (Mr. B.) did not stay long. Alec has been sick with chills, & Will had to work in the woods when he took Alec's place ox driving. Mamie's garden corn crop turned out 12 bu. that Will has just finished hauling about 60 bu. The big field crop will fall so short Will will have to buy again next year as well as hay &c, am afraid his expenses will about equal all profits in mill business &c. Mr Wadwsworth sent me a Pratsville (Ala) paper in which was his wife's obituary. She was sick only a week with Typhoid fever. All of them to whom she was dear, have my sincere sympathy in their affliction. Clara says, Fanny was her favourite of all Carrie's children. They, (Clara & girls) were here yesterday until after dinner, when we all went to Sun. school, which children & all seem to enjoy the time thus spent, will I trust prove a blessing to all engaged in it. My proud pleasure that you are getting on so well in all your studies is greater than I can tel you dear boy, but at the same time, let me beg you to desist studying at night, whenever, & the instant your eyes rebel, as persistance will surely be fatal, sooner, or later, therefore dont trifle with your Maker's great gifts of health, strength, & mental capacity. Bless your dear heart Mama just wants her dear boy to be perfect, & you must come as [close as] it is possible. I note that he has a loving nook in his heart yet for old Cully (would'nt be my boy if he did not) but it is altogether best but not to change Teachers, particularly such as those under whose tuition you have had the good fortune to be.

It is all right about the coat son, — I have it in my possession for Will who needed it very much. The young man told Will that Mr. B. was to pay him for it, & told Mr. B. that he had paid you $1.00 for it. Mr. B. told me himself that he would pay no such thing, & that I could have it, but I had no thought of causing the young [man] to lose his dollar, is why I wanted to know of you if he had paid for it, or not. After supper that very Sun. night the young man went off Mrs. B. told me without saying a word to anyone, left all his effects tho, which he afterward sent for. Smoker often wishes you were here to hunt with him, I tell him "Uncle Robert" is better employed. Mr Allis came one eve last week to go with him — result — "The squirrels ran so fast Mr Allis had to do all the shooting —" they saw but three, & got those. "Mr Allis put up a leaf on a tree for me to shoot at, I missed the first time, & hit it the second shot" — "My gun does fine, it only shakes me a little, dont kick one bit" — That is the only time he has had any chance to shoot it, & you may be certain that he'l never get to handle it loaded much less shoot unless when under good care. It is a breach loader, single bbl.[barrel] shot gun. His Papa's feat is — that the No. of shells he is allowed to have must be gaged by the many & good lessons he gets. John writes that he will leave on another trip about 10th or 15th & that means he wont be down here until last of the mo. or later. Do hope, & trust you may keep well my boy, & to that end take good care of yourself for my sake. Think I would [give] butter a wide berth the product of any such creamery as you tried to see. We have the article (butter) once a week (Sun. supper) & meat, bread; turnip salad, lots & are thankful for same. When we have it, consume gal Molasses per week, — no joke — Will says he'l be bound to have a lasses patch* next year. We miss the fish Oh but mostly when appetites fail for homely fare. S[moker] never omits his good night kisses for Uncle Robert, & that God may bless you ever, is the prayer of your devoted Mother.

M. E. B.

*A "lasses patch" would be a field of sorghum, used for making sorghum molasses.

Mattie Proctor Rumph at Jim Proctor's to Cornelia Dickson in Princeton, Arkansas

Oct 24th, 1886

Dear Miss Nealie,

    Your very kind letter was received several days ago and was read with much interest. I was fearful that you were sick as I could not hear from you. I am sorry that you have not been feeling well.

    Yes Miss Nealie you may know it was sad for me to leave my old home where I have spent so many happy days in the past. Oh, how desolate and forsaken it does look. I have been there several times since I moved. I always feel like before I get there that I am going to see that dear sweet face of my husband. Everything looks so natural and like him, I would be better satisfied to live there than anywhere if Garland and Charlie were older. It is so inconvenient for school.

    My sisters and brothers are very kind and good and I have a happy home with them. They all thought it best for me not to live there without a protector. Dear Alex Gaughan said it would not do for me to live there alone. He was anxious for Eugenia to stay with him and Attalie if it were always.

    I thought when I moved over home, I would be moving to town the first of October. Jesse tried several places for rent, but he could not get a place near him. He did not think I was able to buy a place in town. It is so expensive to live there in the winter with all the fire wood to buy, so he concluded to wait until he could see further ahead.

    Maud and Hattie are in town going to school. They are delighted with the school and the home. Sister Martha and their Uncle Jesse are pleased with them.

    Tommie Gaughan is boarding with Jesse now, and that is an advantage to the girls. He is so kind to assist them in getting their lessons. He says he has a heap of fun with them. I do appreciate his kindness to the children. He spent last Saturday night with us and had a lot to say about the children.

    Maud and Hattie are going to write to you soon. Their school commenced there the first of October. Garland is going to Mrs. Newgent. He seems to be learning. It was so long before he could get started and learn the sound of letters. Mrs. Newgent's subscription school began the middle of October. I do not know how long the session will be. Mrs Newgent still remains at Mrs Richardson's. She lost her little girl the first of September.

    Miss Nealie how sad it is for me to write you of the death of Cad Patterson. He died with typhoid fever. Old Mr Block died in Camden last week suddenly. Mrs Culbreath is very low. This young Dr Murry is attending to her. Dr. Folden has been to see her too. Dr Murry has been boarding at Mr Broughton's but is going to move soon to Mr Frank Richardson's wh has built an office for him out in front of the house.

I must tell you something of Honey [Eugenia] and Attalie after Alex's death. Uncle Patrick Gaughan carried them to his house and told them to make it their home. Attalie couldn't get along without Honey. She was so much help to Attalie with her baby, her two babies. Carrie is a cripple yet and can not help herself much. Attalie's little baby is growing fast. Its name is Minnie after Attalie's sister, Mittie. Alex had refered to the coming baby as Allie.

I have not been to see Mrs Boddie [Sis Mollie]. I want to go soon, but I have not visited any this fall. We keep busy as we have all our domestic work to do. Bettie [the cook] has left us and we have all the work to do. Clem is not in good health and we have not much time to visit. I am going to see Attalie and Honey soon. I think Honey is preparing to marry this fall. I guess she has written to you about it. If not, do not mention it to her. I told her she must write to you about it. I hope she may be happy with Mr. Earl. You know you and I have advised her so much. I do not want her to hasten into it too fast. There is plenty of time yet. I want her to do just as her dear father said. I regret it is so situated that she cannot live with me. I love her and Attalie as I do my own children.

Attalie is down at her own home now and will remain until Christmas if she and the baby have good health. Eugenia has little Carrie at Uncle Patrick's. Attalie is very anxious to live in her and Alex's home but they won't hear of it. They will try to sell or rent the place this winter. Dennis remains there all the time. He has Sylvester Hawkins working in the store while he runs the gin.

Miss Nealie we have a nice Sunday School at our church. All seem to be interested in it. Mr. Frank Richardson is the superintendent. Clem hears the Bible class, Mrs. George Boddie is Garland's teacher, and Mrs Richardson is Charlies. They think it is so nice to go to Sunday School every Sunday evening.

All of the children speak of you often and think of you as their own aunt. Lillian is growing so fast and can say anything. Her hair curls all over her head. Bessie is growing fast and getting fat.

Jude Richardson is visiting Mrs Newgent and everyone thinks it will be a match.

Miss Nealie I have not moved half the things from my home. They are all packed up.

I am milking two cows. All the others have dried up and have gone back home. They are doing very well. The redbird heifer has a beautiful heifer calf, black all over — a Holstine. Jim thinks it will make a fine cow. Jim and Tom planted my cowpen with turnips, they are very large. I weighed two the other day. One weighed three pounds and the other two pounds.

We are so crowded up that I can not move my things here until rooms are built. I guess you will be worried by the time you get through reading this badly written letter. All send love. Please excuse the pencil. Write often to me. I appreciate your good letters.

                      Yours with much love,
                      Mattie Rumph

Lula Dunlap at home to Cornelia Dickson in Princeton, Arkansas

                                                                Dec 2nd 1886

Dear Aunt Nealie

I received your most welcome letter last week. Was sorry to hear you were not feeling well. We have been very well, Mama has been complaining some with toothache and Pa has had several chills, he is nearly done picking cotton, is ginning now; has gined some for the public this fall, cotten has gone up a little in price.

Last Sunday we had preaching, it was his last time this year. Aunt Mollie, Dr Murray, Mr John Dunn & Mr Jim Dunn from Hampton, taken dinner with us. We had fine looking beans. The two Mr D's come Saturday night and went to church with us, remained all night and accompanied us next day; think they are real nice, although we are not smitten on them.

I suppose you have heard that Eugenia is to marry, Dec 15th at Mr Gaughan's. She is down at Carrie's now, made her nicest suit of underclothes, and is working on her dresses, will be married in white nunsveiling*, gray & garnet are the color of her other two. She has a lovely hat, and in fact is very well fixed up.

We were at Mrs Gaughan's yesterday — they were very well. Attalie's baby is just as sweet as can be, grows very fast. Mary and Carrie look well. Attalie is looking well now, she said she told Eugenia to write and invite you down, but expected will be to busy, come if you can, when your school is out. You must come and stay some with us, dont expect we will have much fun unless we can get to go off some where. Suppose you have heard that I broke off with my fellow in Sept, found out he was engaged to another girl so unless I could be the only one, would not be none. I do not regret it, I think it a good riddance, of such a fickle fellow.

Madam Rumor says that Judge Richardson and Mrs Newgent will marry soon, he is quite devoted. Mr Alex Dortch died Sunday, he was in Camden Saturday and got drunk, lay out all night in the river bottom and when they found him next day was nearly dead, some one carried him to the ferry house and he died there, carried him home Monday & to Holly Springs next day. Eula will go to some of her relatives — his was a drunkard's doom.

Saw Miss Matt Sunday, she was at church, all her children are well. Maud & Hattie are doing very well. There is been right smart sickness this fall but none fatal. Dr Murray had yellow jaundice, is up now.

---

*Nun's veiling is a thin, plain-woven worsted fabric, originally for nuns' veils, but now used also for dresses, coats, etc.

We are about through with our sewing and are glad of it. Ma & Cora send love, write soon and accept much love from me. It is very cold and cloudy today.

                       Your loving neice
                       Lula Dunlap

Robert Lee Boddie at Webb School in Bell Buckle, Tennessee, to his brother John R. Boddie in St. Louis

                                           Dec 19th 1886
Dear Bro.

    Your last two letters, and the express package duly received. For the nice present accept my warmest thanks, and also for the kind letter, for it encouraged me no little. I trust I may be able to repay you in the way you wish. It is my earnest desire, and with Gods help I do not fear, but that I will. Am getting on well, and enjoying good health. We shall have one day Xmas, and you may be sure I shall enjoy it, almost as well, as I could at home. Hopping you will enjoy Xmas as well as you deserve for one who does so much to make others happy as yourself, should have a happy time, and that you will not forget me, when you are all gathered around the old fireside at home. I will close.

                       Your loving Bro.
                       R. L. Boddie

Smoker Boddie, who was eight years old, at home to Cornelia Dickson in Princeton, Arkansas

                                 Some unknown date in 1886
Aunt Nely

    I have not very many words to say to you in this letter but I will try think up something. I wonder why Mr ferguson dont fix his tramway, fix his rails on it because it will reck it and then they would be so much trouble when ther was no use if I wer Mr Ferguson I would fix it, it dont cost them any thing attall. I wish Mr Fergason would let me be the engineer to it, when I get grown I am a going to be the engineer on the pasenger train, if I dont do that I going to St Louce and work like Papa is. Aunt Mamie said she was not going to have no little chickens this year and then we can have peas insted chickens. I like peas much better than chicken and wish Aunt Mamie would not have any more, and then Mama could have some turkeys which I like they are not as troublesome like chickens this about all I have say only about this I think I have about cleaned up the peckerwoods I have killed eight

or ten and now I have not sene any more in the appletrees for a long time and I killed one this morning that was just calling them up and I hear a sapsucer now and if he dont look out he will be dead for I will kill him he had better leave now while I am giving him a chance
         Smoker Boddie

Carrie Boddie at home to Cornelia Dickson in Princeton, Arkansas
                 Feb 13th 1887
  Dear Aunt Nealie,

  Your letter found me just as busy as ever. Wedding preparations sure enough — and I hope this is the last hurried marriage that will take place for a little while. Mr. [State] Stone did come back from Ala and he and Miss Rena [Piles]* will step off on the 23 inst — They will marry at church about 7 O'clock that evening, then go to his house and have a nice little supper — Mama is going to remain that night at his house — Sissie is so angry, she will not go nor help him out in the least — I am going to bake him some nice cake this week and go over there — Mamie and I the day before and see that everything is fixed all right — They were engaged when you were here, but had no time set — She wanted to marry in a gray dress but said that she could find only one piece and that was too high for her purse so she selected a delicate blue Nuns veiling — I am making it real pretty — trimming it with the same and with white natural flowers. I think it will look nice —

  What kind of a Xmas did I have? Well Aunt Nealie I can't say I enjoyed it — It was so cold and I suffered so much with my feet and had to stay in the kitchen from morning until nine or ten at night — with no help at all, and fine company — It liked to have <u>"laid me up"</u>, Brother, George Goddard, and Edgar Reeves stayed ten days and they had very poor success hunting, fear they did not enjoy it much. You didn't tell me what your Christmas presents were. I received only one but it is ever so nice. Two bottles of perfume from Mr. Allis — White rose and sweet violet — 'tis splendid — Mr. Dennis was here last night and I read your letter to him. He told me to be sure and send his love to you when I wrote —

  I expected you were having some trouble about your school the reason you didn't feel like writing to me and I wasn't going to wait any longer and had told Mama the night before yours came that I wanted to write to you

  I haven't been anywhere in some time. The rest go to Sunday school well we did go to see Mamie R[ichardson] before she went to Texas — I am anxious to go to see Eugenia but don't know when I'll have that pleasure — Bud Willie saw Mr. Earle in town yesterday, he said she had had two or three chills & wasn't well then but up — I reckon she will be like Cos Attali

*"Miss Rena" refers to Lorena Elizabeth Conway Pile.

was — do hope she will not have much trouble —

They were coming down to see me last Sunday had it been a nice day. Robt had a hard spell with Pneumonia not long since, but is all right again and is up with his studies — He says the Itch and measels are raging among the school boys — I will write more the next time.

Lovingly your neice
Carrie

Mittie Rumph Rucks in Camden to Cornelia Dickson in Princeton, Arkansas

Feb 27th /87

Dear Aunt Nealie,

I expect you think it takes me a long time to answer your ever welcome missives, but my duties are so numerous I scarcely have an undisturbed moment I can claim as my own. I am like the old hen & chicks — always scratching & clucking & my chicks are continually in <u>want</u>.

I am well once more — though I had quite a seige of it for one level month after my baby came which was next morn after Christmas — would have gotten along well had the children kept up, but having no one to keep up with or control them, run out in the cold & eat ice and snow till both John & Ed were very sick when the baby was too young for me to stir, but I had it to do or see them neglected or perhaps lose them & the very thought divested me of all care for myself — in consequence, came near being lost myself — had fever, rising breast & an awful awful time, but do not regret it now since all of us are well & I have one of the sweetest little girls imaginable — not very pretty though, regular little negro of a brunette — a head full of long black hair & dark steel grey eyes. I have not named her yet — thought of calling her "Lalla" but as she does not look at all poetical, think some sweet <u>pretty</u> name such as Attalie, Mamie Eugenia would suit her better. As uncle John [Dunlap] said when he saw her — "She's none of your little gals, but a regular "Biddie," has large hands & feet & is fat as a pig — the children all think her the sweetest thing that ever breathed, from Corrie* down. Cous. John [Boddie] wanted me to call her Cornelia & promised her many treasures, but as that was Corrie's name could not oblige him — he now wants me to agree to call her for a widow in St. Louis — a recent flame of his, who has a princess name commencing with G & ends with A, containing six letters — I won't promise & he won't tell me her name unless I do — but I guess I'll find out sometime. He was to see me several times this last week — Bro Tommie also was down to see us two weeks ago. I have not seen any others of my family since Christmas although I looked for some of them — Yes — Lula [Dunlap] spent several days with me on

*Corrie was Mr Rucks' daughter by his first wife, Jane Alabama Moseley.

her return from a visit to her cousins in Texas — left for home yesterday. Lula is looking well & reports fine times for herself while out there & had some fun while here — I think she has fascinated some one over here.

I killed my last old Xmas gobbler for her — he weighed when dressed 16 lbs. I had Maud & Hattie besides Lula's New beaux & I tell you all hands had a royal time — Uncle John [Dunlap] too was over & passed his plate several times and he said twas the winding up of the turkey till next Xmas — unless he could get an invite to another wedding such as Eugenia's —

State [Stone] did marry last Wednesday & had a grand Infair over to his home — Carrie & Aunt Mollie did the honors for him & all goes happy now, although Mollie [Richardson] & Will cut up "high bob" at first — I suppose you saw from the Beacon about Miss Florence Bragg's marriage to "Bud" Jenkins — he is several years her junior — it created quite a comment for Camden folks — as usual — just as it would do if you let that widower up there get away with you — I hear "a few things" from up there once in a while — Now you be like Miss Florence — if he is a good catch — if you love him well enough to take him, don't let busy tongues keep you from being independent — though we'd hate awfully to give you up to those Dallas [County] folks. I know we would seldom ever see you —

You asked of Brother [George], he has sold with good profit & bought & moved to Titusville on the famous Indian River & is perfectly enraptured with his move & more in love with Florida than ever.

I wish you would make us a visit soon, could <u>talk</u> over so many things I haven't time or space to write.

Mr. Rucks did as you requested, Mr. Holmes thanked him & said you should surely get the paper.

It is late & I must bid you good night with much love from us all to you.

Yours,
Mittie

Carrie Boddie at home to Cornelia Dickson in Princeton, Arkansas
March 8th 1887

Dear Aunt Nealie,

I heard yesterday that you were married and I tried my best to write to you last night to know if the report true, but I was so nervous, headached and tired that I couldn't do it — don't know in fact what is the matter with me — had the blues awfully when last I wrote you and have had very near all winter — Mr. Earl came after some lumber yesterday evening and he told us about your being married to Mr. E. J. Avant, the old Gentleman — I won't and don't believe it of course but "Oh yes" he says "It come mighty strait" — Miss C. Foldern told her Pa and he told Mrs. Tony, and from her to him then from him to us — If you are, Aunt Nelie I'll pout because you didn't tell me about it before hand just <u>as long as I live</u> — I don't think you would get off and not tell me a word — Mama and Bud W. don't believe it either but Mamie does & told me to tell you she offers her congratulations and she thinks it a splendid match. I would love to hear that you <u>were going</u> to marry somebody that could and would take nice care of you to keep you from hard work — and would make me a good Uncle — but I don't want you to get off and not say a word — I have been prepared a long time to love anybody that you married and you please write immediately and let me know if I have an Uncle —

I was helping Mrs Pile to get ready to marry when I wrote to you last — Well you never saw such a rain as fell on that day! (23rd) wind, thunder and lightning! and all day until about half past five oclock. She dressed here and had to come over in the rain — It came in such torrents I didn't know whether they would have to marry here or how to do — he sent though for his cakes turkey &c — & word that he was going through if it poured down "<u>pitch forks</u>" — so I packed everything nicely in a trunk and made the darkey spread an oil cloth over it — & her trunk also and they went through the hardest of rains safely — Then Mr W. & D[ennis] came about six o'clock & all of us went & left Johney S. with the children — Ann was to come to get supper for the children & six hands but the rain prevented her & I made one of the men get supper, West Brown — & he did splendidly —

There were a good many out at church although the weather was so bad — & had a nice supper & very good time at his house — Sissie was there but Mama stayed too & returned next day —

Lula has returned home — haven't seen her — would have looked for them last Sunday but it was another rainy day — Bud W. thinks we will have an overflow soon. Dr. Murry didn't get to Mr S. house, had a call at Lilly & fell in the creek coming back — Mr. Allis, Dennis, Bud W., Will — Mamie, Cora & myself, Sissie, her husband, & Mama were all — J. Mitchell was to be there, but a boil on his neck interfered — Please write soon & tell me about <u>my Uncle</u> —

      Your loving neice,
      Carrie

Lula Dunlap at home to Cornelia Dickson in Princeton, Arkansas
                Mar 8th 1887

Dear Aunt Nealie,

Your most welcome letter was received about two weeks ago. I have been on a very pleasant visit to Queen City, Tex, to see Cousin Annette's family. Mamie Richardson was with me as far as Texarkana, she went to

*Maggie was Mamie's sister.

Lou's from there, will go to visit Maggie's,* will remain until next fall if she is satisfied. We left home Jan 31st and I remained until Feb 24th, had a nice time, met the young people, attended two socials. Cousin Georgia was at home, and as sweet and good as ever. Cousin Buelah was teaching school about seven miles from there, she come home twice, Hugh & Elijah's two boys are going to school. I arrived at Camden Thursday about three o'clock and stopped over to see Cousin Mittie. She and children are well, has a sweet little baby, and they all are very proud of it. John and Ed say it is the sweetest baby in town. Saw Florrie, she was quite well. Pa come after me on Saturday. Cousin Edwin [Clifton] come out to see us that night and ate dinner at Mrs. Gaugh[an]'s next day. Our preacher give us a good sermon next day, there was a good congregation. Attalie & Mrs. Gaughan both come and Mr G. kept the baby, it had had fever several days before that, but is well and growing fast. They think it is fixing to cut teeth.

Carrie & Mamie are well. Eugenia was down to see us last week. She is fixed up comfortably at her new home, seems to be well satisfied, she had bonefelons on both thumbs, lasted six weeks after her marriage. Miss Matt's children all keep well, they look rosy and fat. The neighborhood has generally good health, there has been very little sickness this winter.

Oh, I forgot to tell [you] Effie Brodnax has a boy, born the evening I got to Camden. I went around to see her the next day. Mrs. Fannie McGill has two boys, twins. They are doing well.

Mr. Stone and Mrs. Piles married Feb 23rd at the church at night, went from there to his house, Aunt Mollie & Miss Mollie Richardson there to receive them, Carrie cooked the cake, he invited a few home, Cora got to go, I had not come home.

*Three Love sisters married Malcolm S. Wadsworth: (1) Irene Lanier Love, "Cousin Irene," in 1866. She died in 1870. (2) Susan Frances Love, "Cousin Fannie," in 1881. She died in 1886. (3) Mary Catherine Love, "Bessie," in 1887 or 1888.

*"Cousin Irene" refers to Irene Lanier Love Wadsworth, daughter of Sis Carrie in Alabama.

*"Johnnie" is Clara and John Dunlap's son, twelve at the time.

I received a letter from Bessie Love Brock, she wrote to find out how we all were, says she and Aunt Carrie are keeping house for her brother Mack Wadsworth, have seven boys to look after and her own girl. Cousin Fannie* died in Sept, left twin boys five months old, Bessie says they are fine little fellows, she did not say anything about our other relatives, she has a divorce from her husband. Cousin Irene's* boy [that] she left a baby wrote to me, says he is sixteen years old, signs his name T. M. W., don't know wether it is Tom or Mack. I received them last week, will answer soon. Also received a letter from Uncle Jim announcing the sad death of our Aunt Rebecca, which took place Feb 8th. Uncle Jim said she died a happy Christian death, told them not to mourn, she would be better off released from her suffering, all her children come to see her, she to[ld] them all to meet her in heaven.

Ma, Cora, Johnnie* & myself went up to Union Church Saturday morning to a quarterly meeting. Mr. Frank Richardson, Mary Elliot, Miss Georgia [Proctor] & Dr. Murry also. We heard a splendid sermon that day from Mr Jenkins, eat dinner at Mrs. Bill Gatling's that evening. Mr. John Gatling carried Cora & I to see Miss Willie & Dollie Murry about five miles from there, it rained all day Sunday, caused the creek to overflow, & we never got to Bearden till Monday about eleven o'clock, found Ma & John had come home with Mr. R. through the rain Sunday evening. She is complaining of being tired but for a wonder it did not make her sick. Dr. Murry come down with us. We had a pleasant visit up there even if it did rain.

Ma & Cora send love, write soon. I have told all the news I know. Hope you are keeping well.

Your loving neice,
Lula Dunlap

Bessie Brock in Prattville, Autauga Co., Alabama to her cousin Lula M. Dunlap in Ouachita Co.

March 26, 1887

Dear Cousin

I received your most welcome letter yesterday. and the sad contents filled my eyes with tears. I had heard of Uncle J[ohn] R[umph] death, cousin Gilder's also; but the rest we have heard nothing, tell Aunt Mollie that Aunt Mary* is dead, died Dec 19, 1884. She died with cancer of the womb which was a paneful death. She was dilearrious four days and nights before she died and she talked with the dead all the time; Grandma, her husband and little girl, all of which has been dead over twenty years. No one but God knows how she suffered. I got a letter from Kate yesterday (that is the only girl Aunt Mary had) and she said that all was well in that part of the world, her two oldest brothers are single. Their names are Elrid and Cole, both live at Aunt Mary's home, and Kate keeps house for them. Dick is next to her, he married Miss Mollie Kirkland, they has two boys and a girl, lives in hearing of Kate. Andrew, the youngest of her brothers married Miss Fannie Zimmerman, they has five children, one girl four boys. Cousin Clem has been dead six years, that is what helpt to kill Aunt Mary, she took his death so hard, her health began to fail and she finely died. I live twenty miles from Kate, but I love her as well as I do any sister I have and better than I do some of them, we write to each other all the time. Ma's family consist of nine only out of twelve of us. Brother Tom has five girls and boy. Nub has two girls, one boy. Ada has one girl, three boys and two baby girls dead. Onie has one girl and three boys, one boy dead which is five children. I have one little girl six years old. Bud married Julia Holmes. Nub Miss Bettie Miller of Ark. Ada to P. A. Dunn and Onie married W. H. Northington. George is still single, Crofford, ma's baby boy has been verry sick for two months we thought that he would die for two weeks. Kate says in her letter, that he was getting well, but his mind wandered yet. Brother Will has just came in, and gives me the sad news sister Jinnie is quite sick, typhoid fever, Crofford has it. Dr. Gee says there is some hope for him now. Ma is with them. I have

*"Aunt Mary" is Mary A.E. Rawlings Love, who handled some of Cornelia Dickson's business after she came to Arkansas.

not seen her in a month. I wrote to her today, to Kate also.

Brother Mack Wadsworth, Tommie's father says that he is ever so much oblige to you for the good advice you gave his son, that Tom is the wildest boy that he has, wilder than all of the rest of his children all put togather, and he is verry much oblige to you for what you wrote to Tom and says please chunk Tom again, he himself lectures his wild boy nearly every day.

Brother Mack says that he has falen in love with you, that he knows that you are a good girl from the way you wrote to me and Tom. Where is cousin Bobbie [Boddie], you did not say anything about him. Brother Will says send him your picture. Give my love to Aunt Mollie and kiss her for me a thousand times. My love to all of her children. Give my love to Aunt Fannie children, my love to Aunt Nelie your Mother sister brother and pa. Tell them all that I hope some day that I will be able to come to see you someday. If I can get half of a chance I will come to see you all. How old are you. Write soon to your divoted cousin

Bessie Brock

Martha Proctor Rumph at Mr. Jim Proctor's to Cornelia Dickson in Princeton, Arkansas

April 2nd, 1887

Dear Miss Nelie,

This is Sunday evening. Clem, Garland, and Charlie have just gone to Sunday School walking. Miss Nelie, I received your kind letter on the 26th which I appreciated very much. I was anxious to hear from you to know how you were getting along. I would have answered it ere this; have been very busy, so much to do. Georgia has been in town waiting on Maude and Hattie. They are just getting up from a spell of the measels. I have been expecting them to have the measels two months ago but did not take them untill the last of March. You can imagine my feelings when they were sick. Maude will be able to go to school next week. Hattie will not be able to go under another week. She had it last just a week after Maude. Dr. Bragg is their physician, he is very kind to them, thinks so much of them, sister Martha and Jessie* are just as good and kind as can be. I do appreciate them so much. Their school will close the 22nd. of this month, they have their speeches ready, for the examination. Georgia has finished their white dresses. She will come home this week. I want to go over when the school closes. Oh if I could be with you I could talk so much better than I can write. Miss Nelie, Tommie Rumph was to see us last week, the first time since his dear Father left us, it seemed to me he looked more like his Pa than ever before, he enquired of you. I love Tommie, think he is a noble boy, how much his Pa thought of him, he seemed very glad to see us, he camped out with Jim

*"Sister Martha" refers to Martha J. Mendenhall Proctor. "Jessie" is Martha Proctor Rumph's brother, Jessie A. Proctor.

[Proctor] and Dennis [Gaughan] turkey hunting one night, killed a turkey but he could not stay with us long enough to eat it. He had to go back.

It does seem that all the family of children are nearer to me than ever. I love them all. Miss Nelie, I have the blues sometimes and if it was not for the children I do not know what would become of me, they keep me busy at first one thing and another, have been trying to teach Garland and Charlie at home this winter, all the children are growing fast, all grow faster than Bessie, the baby [Lillian] is as large as Bessie. She is like Honey in everything. She is interesting after she becomes acquainted, tries to give out the Sunday School lesson to Bessie, it would make you laugh to hear them. Charlie and Garland are very much interested in Sunday School. They attend regular and have perfect lessons, they get a verse and repeat in Sunday School. We like our new minister very much, he is very plain, unassuming, preaches every fourth Sunday.

Mamie Richardson came back home last week from Texas. She has been gone two months. I have not seen her yet. State and his wife were at church last Sunday. She is so much broken, did you ever see her? I guess Carrie told you all about them marrying.

I am at Ma's yet. Jessie has only rented ten acres of the land to Dave Douglas, the upper part of the field, he has tried to rent it but failed so far, he wants to get good reliable hands on it another year. I went over there last week, carried Garland and Charlie with me, they were delighted. We went all over the place, the house looks so delapidated, the garden covered with limbs. I do have such an attachment for the place, my brothers say it is impossible for me to live there now, it is too much gone to rack, it would take so much to fix it and the children could not walk to school, to inconvenient for them every way. You know I would have to depend on them so much. Jim and Tom are very kind to me and the children. Your few things I have with me will keep untill you come, guess your School will be out next month. Miss Nelie, I expect you could get this School here if you would apply for it soon. I do not hear of anyone coming in for the School, hope you can get it if your School is out there. Mrs. Tobe Richardson may try and get it as Mamie* has come back. You send and see if you want it.

Clem has been talking of writing to you but keeps putting off time to

Martha Hogue "Matt" Proctor Rumph
Photo courtesy of Alice Proctor Martin Fiser

*This "Mamie" refers to Mamie Richardson.

time, she scarcely ever writes a letter. You must excuse this writing, the baby and Bessie are around me talking and shaking me. I am ashamed to send it. None of them have forgotten you, love you the same. It is getting late. Clem and the boys have not come yet.

You keep the stockings untill you come down. I can do without them untill next winter, they will come just right, many thanks to you for your kindness. I will have enough to do untill they go bare footed, that will not be long.

I must tell you something of Attalie and Honey. Aunt Carrie* and Attalie went to Town yesterday and came back this evening. They all think so much of Attalie. Honey is very much interested in keeping house. I have spent one day with her. I like Mr. Earl better than I thought I would, he is very kind to Honey, the neighborhood is very healthy now.

Write, all send love. Please excuse bad writing. I know you can't read it, so I close. Write to me I do enjoy your good letters.

Yours affectionately,
Mattie Rumph

*"Honey" is the nickname given to Eugenia Rumph and "Aunt Carrie is Sarah Caroline Gaughan, mother of Mr. Alex.

Carrie Boddie at home to her brother Robert Lee Boddie in Webb School at Bell Buckle, Tennessee

April 6th 1887

My Dear Robert,

Your ever welcome letter to hand — you have no idea how much I miss them when they don't come when due — I would not have waited, though had I been well have suffered lots within the two past weeks with severe cold — but I'm very nearly well now —

I do hope your speech will "come up" all right at the examination I never saw the piece — though know it is good and you must work <u>hard on</u> it — guard against getting <u>excited and put your whole soul</u> in what you are <u>saying</u> — <u>don't</u> think of anything else & you will make a success — Do wish I could be there to throw you a big boquet — .

I think it is the very thing for you to stop to visit your friend on your way home — know you will enjoy the recreation and you need it — so be a nice boy and show them their efforts to entertain you are well appreciated — You remember how C. Morgan use to take french leave* of us when he came over to see you for a few days — I never did like him for that and a good many more things that he treated with indifference —

Lula received a letter from Bessie Brock (nee Love), she sent it down for us to read. She wrote that George L. was at home still unmarried — I presume he and his girl "busted" — they were to have married soon — Crawford is there also & quite ill with Typhoid fever — Jennie also — but

*French leave is a departure without ceremony, permission, or notice.

Cora will write all about them — Bessie has a divorce from her husband and wrote that she was coming out here to see us all. I have been expecting some of them ever since Cos G. was here and told me about their having spent all the money Uncle Clem left — & I told Lula the very first letter she received that it would end that way — & I didn't want her to write to any of them — We use to write and they were silent — & I knew that was the reason we were getting letters now they want to come out — Lula didn't think so — I do feel sorry for those girls & would like to do something for them if I could but they have treated us so mean and are so uncouth & ill tempered — would much rather they would stay where they are — It will not be long now ere you are home again — then I wont feel so lonesome — You are always so much company for me — Bud W. & I use to have a good time but I don't have much chance to be with him now — he is always so busy & J. Stone is in his room at night & you always would stay with me in the kitchen some — Mamie & I are not much company for each other — never was before she married & I believe we are less now — she thinks that I am a scheaming insignifficant pert little piece — has as good as told me so — but it don't hurt me a bit — I just attend to my business & let her go it — I wont be here very long no way — at least I don't think, I will — & what my future will be then I know not — nor care a pin — I mean to do my best & I'll leave the rest with God — Life is short at best & I'm going to quit worrying & just do the best I can. Bud W. began planting corn today — The chickens are crowing — ten oclock only —

      Lovingly
      Carrie

  A letter from Aunt Nelie. She is <u>not married</u> nor <u>even had a beau</u> she says — she wrote me a very lively letter & just begs me to go up there on a visit — to rest she says, and it shall not cost me a cent — I am not going of course. Mamie is too busy with her chickens & strawberries to take my place now — she & Bud W. have done a little work in the vegetable line too & I have seven hands to cook for now besides the family — I'll go after her [Aunt Nealie] when she comes home.

Carrie Boddie at home to Cornelia Dickson in Princeton, Arkansas
                May 3rd, 1887

  Dear Aunt Nealie,

  I have commenced several letters in reply to your last, but each time I was interrupted — and now, I use my pencil that I may be sure of finishing "my say" and Bud Willie will post it tomorrow and you please answer soon — it has been some time since your last letter came, & I'm anxious to hear from you again — All or a great many of your friends were looking forward to the coming of that letter — to settle their curiosity in regard to your being married, or not — some thought it might be true — but were afraid (they said) of mentioning it to you for fear the report was not true & you would get angry — & they <u>knew I had made you mad by writing to know all about it</u> — but they all wanted to know just the same — I do hope Mr Stone will be successful in getting some of the <u>widowers</u> to call around to see you — enough so to make you have a pleasant time — but Aunt Nelie I reckon it would be very tiresome to you to have a lot, what I call friends, around unless they were very intelligent — well read &c.

I have had a hard time with so much company since my last letter to you — it is such a dry time to get anything to cook & Mamie is so stingy with her eggs, & having to do all the waiting on, cooking, & nearly all the entertaining to do — caused me to fall off several pounds — week before last there was some one here <u>every day</u>. Mr. & Mrs. Stone, Mrs. Hawkins, Lula Steele, Mr. Clifton two days & night — one or two near neighbors — & last week Mrs. Moseley one afternoon, Fannie Stanley one morning, Aunt Clara's family & Mr. & Mrs. Newton with two of their little girls — Then Mr. D[ennis] & Mr. A[llis] in between times — Well Mr. D. only called once during that time — Saturday night one week ago — & Cora entertained him — she came out from town with Bud W. & stayed all night — I had gone home with E[ugenia] & Mr. Earle. They came down for me that afternoon — & I was glad to get to go for I was tired out — Corrie [Corrie Rucks, Mittie's step daughter and grand daughter of Mr. and Mrs. Elijah Moseley) is at Mrs. Moseley's now & will be here tomorrow. Cousin & her little folks will be over in a week or two, she told me the other day when I was in town — don't you know I will have a team with all together — You know I have seven regular hands to cook for & sometimes eight we have at least — Mamie has a very good crop of strawberries & I haven't had a chance yet to put some up for you — but I mean to do it if possible & for Robert too.

Will your school be out Aunt Nelie the last of this month or the first week in June or the last in June — I think I can tell you why I want to know in my next letter — Our things came this week yesterday — & I'm at work on Mama's underclothing — have <u>so much to do</u> — all three of us are naked for clothes — I fear you can't read this — I am ashamed to send you such a letter — Brother & Bud W.'s <u>friend, Mr. Badders</u>, left Saturday in the night for parts unknown — owing Bud W. & Mr. Allis a good little sum & several other parties a few dollars. J. Stone met him up in Tulip Sunday morning — or not a soul would have known the direction they took — but if he will just come back when he gets out of money Bud Willis will try him over — all are well — save Bud W. — he has cold & otherwise ailing — mopping around — Brother [John] sent you the calendar, he will be here this month — must close & scratch Robert a line or two.

> Lovingly,
> Carrie

Note: Carrie had something to tell her Aunt Nealie. It must have been that she had at last accepted Mr. Allis's proposal. They married the following December 21, 1887.

Edwin Clifton in Camden to Cornelia Dickson in Princeton, Arkansas

May 5, 1887

Dear Aunt Neely,

I should have written to you sometime ago, & have thought of doing so time & again. I hope by this time your school matters are in a settled & satisfactory condition.

I have been over the river twice recently, & it might have been my imagination, but I felt that I was not altogether welcome at someplaces, anyway, I will try not to trouble those persons with my company again.

Florence* is growing fast. She is pretty, sharp witted, & a very close observer. She loves to attend Sunday School & wear good clothes. Her actions & words are so much like her mother's,* it makes me right sad sometimes to look at her even in her play.

I don't know that you will be much surprised that I should admire Miss Carrie enough to ask her to be my wife. I saw so much about her to admire, and then she reminds me so much of Florence, and I can't help loving anybody like her. But, as I suspected, she is engaged to another — told me she had lost her heart long ago. Of course that put an end to all prospects there, but still I do admire her very much. Then I suppose her aspirations would over-leap such an obscure person as I am. If she <u>would</u> be mine, she would receive as tender treatment as a husband could bestow. A lonely fireside chills me to the core, & I have thought she could make it delightfully pleasant for me. She does not know nor fully understand me, & I have thought that possibly her answer was a pretext for disposing of the question. The woman who is worth having is worth striving for. True, there are plenty other women besides her, but then are never too many of the right kind. Neither will any woman suit — nor can a man love any woman. Don't you think she would make a suitable wife for me? If you have any influence, and can conscientiously exert it in my favor, I will be very thankful.

I am glad I can contribute a little to your pleasure in the way of papers. Will continue to send them from time to time.

Will be pleased to hear from you when convenient.

> Yours truly,
> Edwin Clifton

*Florence is his little daughter, also called Florrie.

*Edwin Clifton was married to Florence Rumph, who died in 1885.

Cornelia Dickson in Princeton, Arkansas, to Edwin Clifton in Camden
May 12 1887

*No heading in ledger.

*I received your letter a week ago, but various things have kept me from replying as soon as I intended. It seems there is always something. At school, I am busy all day, and at home, Well recently old Mr. Lea is steadily and very perceptibly declining. May die at any hour. Is not confined to his bed, nor entirely helpless, but has a distressing heart trouble. He is in his 81st. yr. Seems perfectly resigned, having from his youth been a consistent christian, but his condition is very distressing to his daughter, who save the hired white man, is the only white person on the place, and my return from school in the evenings seems to be greeted with so much satisfaction by both she & her father, that I scarcely confine myself to my room, until bed time which is always late.

I was so glad to hear of your "little folk's" being so sprightly. She surely takes a share of that from her loving lovable mother.

I was but little surprised at what you wrote in regard to your feelings about marrying again. Thanks for your confidence. To be candid I had thought that you would very probably seek relief from your loneliness & sorrow by anticipating a home made cheerful by some one whom you could safely trust, would be a mother to your little one, and, I had thought that if you fancied each other, she could fill that position. I do not know if her affections are otherwise engaged, tho I should not be surprised that they were, since she has for years had several nice worthy devoted men admirers. As to her entertaining any deeper feelings respecting any of them than mere friendship, she has always been very reticent with me. Yet in justice to you, I must say I know she esteems you highly for your moral worth. From mere observations I believe a very short time will decide the true position of things. Am convinced her home is not as pleasant to her now as formerly. I do not think she is half appreciated as she should be by some of her family; and she feels it and would naturally incline to a home elsewhere. Consequently, any demonstration of affection from one she loves carries additional weight. You have my best wishes. Thanks for your confidence.

My school will close the 31st. instant, and I shall be sorry to give up this neighborhood, but the people have voted against free schools and do not want a subscription school this summer. I have applied elsewhere, but have not heard from the parties. Anyway, do not expect to remain here.*

*This letter is unsigned in the ledger.

Lula Dunlap in Ouachita Co. to Cornelia Dickson in Princeton, Arkansas

May 22nd 1887

Dear Aunt Nealia,

As I have been very busy since your letter was received neglected to write, but was glad to hear from you.

We had preaching today. Cousin Henry Garmany and wife and three children, Cousin Lon, wife & children, Lillie & Virgie Justice & Kate Dunlap they all took dinner with us, we had plenty prepared, and enjoyed their visit very much. They told me you had got the school up there, suppose you will be down soon.

There is no sickness in the neighborhood except Mrs Maggie Broughton, she has been very sick all week, has a little boy weighing five lbs clothes & all, it was a seven months child, it is doing very well but she has had fever all week, was better today.

We all went over to Camden last week to see the Knights of Pythias parade, was over two days and saw it all, everything passed off very pleasant, had the Ball Wednesday night, and Banquet Thursday night. The parade come off at 5 oclock that evening, had two bands. The uniforms were lovely; there was a company of soldiers from Little Rock who with swords and uniforms attracted a great deal of attention, there was one U. S. officer, 2nd Leutenient, who rode Mr Cliffords fine mare "Lucy." She kept time perfectly with the music and he rode well, everything was enjoyed by us very much.

Attalie and babies went over, Mr Gaughan carried her, Mary went also but come home. Attalie will come some time next week, staying with Coz Mittie, her children were all well, the baby is very sweet, and fat as a little pig. We was at Effie's too. She was not well but the baby is growing fast. Cousin Edwin was out today with Florrie, he brought Corrie with him, taken dinner with them. Coz John & Tom are both down. I received a letter from Bessie Brock, she married Mr Wadworth Apr 19. Aunt Carrie is staying with them. Coz Jennie died Apr 2nd of typhoid fever. Crawford got well. Aunt C. sent love to you. You must spend a week with us if you have time before you take up the school. All send love, write soon.

Yours lovingly
Lula Dunlap

Edwin Clifton in Camden to Cornelia Dickson in Princeton, Arkansas
June 12, 1887

Dear Aunt Neely,

Your kind letter was received sometime ago. Am glad to know you are going to have employment nearer your old home. Hope we will be able to see something of you occasionally.

I admire Miss Carrie very much, & "Barkis is willin" but I have no encouragement from her & I don't find the least bit in your letter, so I will give up and trouble her no more about it.

When I can't carry out my designs, I accept defeat as graceously as I can & take it as Providential & all for the best. Of course it is none of my business who the successful party is, still I think I could put my hand on him. From words that fell from Florence's lips, (though she hadn't the least suspicion of it,) and something Miss C. said to me, lead me to suspect a certain one. If my suspicions prove correct, I will tell you of it. Like you, I do not think she is appreciated at home. Well, she has as much right to be happy as anybody & I hope she will be in her marriage. She is the one I cared most about over in that country, now I don't know that I'll have occasion to go over that way again soon. I have some friends over there and some who are not friends. It matters little to me, they can wrap themselves up in their selfishness & die hermits if they want to.

My little daughter has not been quite well lately, but seems to be improving now. She is now playing with her little housekeeping appurtenaners. Aunt B. bought her a tea set & she seems to enjoy them so much. She gets more like her mother every day & I am glad of it, only I hope she will be stronger. I doubt my ability to ever love another woman as deeply as I did Florence, because I have lost none of my love for her & never expect to. When I stand by the side of her grave it pains me very much to know that she will never be with me again on earth.

Those two short years were the happiest of my life.

With best wishes for your welfare.

Yours truly,
Edwin Clifton

Allis Moseley at home to Carrie Boddie also at home.

July 15, 1887

My Sweet Darling

I wish I could give you just one hug, for the sweetest note you ever sent me. Am so glad you are in good spirits this week. I did not intend to scold you the other night but hated to see you so blue. When you are happy I feel that nothing could stand in my way that I could not overcome, and if I succeed in making you so. You will find that my old ambition that you are always throwing up to me is not all gone. Of course I will come down Sunday eve and go with you to Mr Stone's. Havn't had a melon this season. This is written worse than usual as I am nervous this morning.

Ever Yours
Allis

Hattie Rumph [daughter of Dr. John B. Rumph and Matt Proctor Rumph] in Camden to Cornelia Dickson in Ouachita Co.

Oct 1st 1887

Dear Aunt Nelie,

The time is near at hand and we all four will start to school; Sis Maude, Garland, Charlie, and myself. As we have not heard from you in so long, I thought I would write to let you know how we like our new home.

We all like it very much. Mama says she likes it better than she thought she would, it is more like the country than town, we have a good large yard and a nice garden spot and a calf lot and a new cow shed, we have several cedar trees in our yard, Mother [would] like so much for you to come over to see us sometime.

Aunt Nelie, we see more here in town than we do in the country. We saw the baloon go up last week, it went up down town and we were in our yard, it lodged in a large pine tree over the river — an Indian swing [was] under it and I thought it was a tassle, it was so far up. Charlie was on top of the fence, and he thought it was acoming down on his head, and he ran in the house.

Aunt Nealie, Aunt Georgia [Proctor] came over today to see us with Cousin Mittie Patterson. You know Aunt Nelie it does us good to see our Aunts come to see us.

Uncle Jesse and Aunt Mattie [Martha Proctor] are just like a good Mother and Father. They let us have butter milk every morning.

Yours affectionately,
Hattie Rumph

Lucie Smoker Hunt in Arkadelphia to her brother-in-law John R. Boddie in St. Louis

Mar 14 - 88

Dear Brother —

Know you think I am very ungrateful — for not having written & thanked you for your kind remembrance of my Birth-day — but as usual my house-girl left me & I had to fill her place for several days — besides waiting upon Pa, who calls me constantly — I haven't words to express my thanks for the <u>beautiful</u> presents — The Pin is just what I wanted — saw & admired Pins of that style while in New Orleans — but knew they were expensive, so passed them by — & to think after all I got one for which please accept my heart-full of thanks & appreciation — will enjoy wearing it this summer & it will look beautiful with my thin dresses. The flowers were grand, & admired by every one, the next day —being Sunday — Pa had a great deal of company — & of course — the first question was — "Where did you get so many beautiful flowers?" I wore several of them to church — in the morning wore all white ones — but — at night, wore the Pink rose — with some of the pink & white Pinks which were too lovely for any-thing — I was crazy to wear the red ones — but concluded they were most too gay for one of my years — however put a few in my pin, Sunday evening around the house & they were real becoming —I use to wear red a great deal when I was a girl — because my sweet-heart thought I looked better in that color than in any other — how foolish girls are sometimes — I expect we will make our Iowa relatives a visit in April sometime probably the first week, as Pa thinks a trip will be very beneficial just at this time & of course I agree with him —I think Mr Ratcliff was <u>quite</u> complimentary about my picture — as he thought I was about twenty-five. I dont see why you <u>dont</u> like it —for I think it flatters — & you will find our Artist <u>cant</u> improve upon it. You want to know what style of picture I like best of you — really I cant tell — think best to leave that to G Grerin dont you? Capt. Scott left yesterday for St Louis — but suppose you have seen him by this time. I wish you would send half dozen shirts for John — four calico or Pecale & two white ones — size 13 boys — & tell Captain to select him a suit of clothes light in weight but not expensive — I hate always to trouble you with orders of this kind, but it seems as if I cant help it. I have decided not to get the Carpet — but to get an Oil-Cloth for the dining room instead but Capt Scott has the order for that — Today is a lovely Spring day & the middle of March — it will soon be summer again — & I will be ready to go to the Blue Grass region to see my friends — The Hunts haven't made their appearance yet — Mrs Hunt was too unwell to start last Saturday — dont know when to look for them now. Pug still continues to be the <u>pet</u> of the house — grows more interesting every day — & we love him very much — seems to know that he belongs to me — & shows his preference — Now let me thank you again & again for the beautiful presents — which dont express half I feel — I believe Sallie has written to you, will send it tomorrow if she has. Much love from all of us —

    Affectionately
    Sister Lucie*

*Note: This letter from Lucie Hunt offers an undeniable hint of things to come. John R. Boddie would shortly marry Lucie, the sister of Cornelia, his first wife and mother of Smoker. "Pug" most assuredly is a dog, another gift from John.

Mamie Boddie Coleman at home to Cornelia Dickson in Princeton, Arkansas

            March 15, 1888

Dear Aunt Nealie

  Rain and other hindrances have prevented our sending for you. If nothing Providential prevents, will come for you next Sunday morning. Bud is at the Ranch and all are busy trying to make up for lost time. Mr. Brodnax took the school. Be sure to be ready. I don't know who may come for you. Someone Sure. Was at church Sun. Mama was not well enough to go but is all O.K. now. All well. Cora & I went to the wedding under Hugh's special care — had a glorious time. Miss Mittie looked lovely & supremely happy, will finish when you come. Have "lots" to tell. Some good for you.

    Lovingly
    Mamie

Mittie Rumph Rucks in Camden to Cornelia Dickson in the country

            Mar 22nd /88

Dear Aunt Nealie,

  I saw Cousin Willie pass a few minutes ago, & thought it would be a good chance for me to write you a few lines ere he returns & thank you a thousand times for those nice little stockings. They were just right & do look so nice & comfortable on her.*

  I have been looking for you to come — & you must be sure and do so right soon as it will be to your advantage. I'll tell you all about it then — want you to be here, too, for our examination. It comes off in April — Mr. Rucks says he's planted plenty of spinach for you. Our garden looks real spring like — & I have about 75 little chicks, cows plenty, and "Barbara" to help me, so do come.

  Matt & little ones are well. Garland is just up from the mumps. I had a note from Attalie — was so glad to hear from her & will answer it soon — have so little time to write — is the reason I do not write oftener.

  What is Aunt Mollie & Cous Mamie driving at? Wish I could see them

*Cornelia must have knitted some stockings for the baby, Attalie Rucks.

& the children and Carrie. I know she feels lonesome without some "brats" around — both Corrie & Louis are scrambling about which shall spend most of their vacation over there. Attalie says I'm to go home with her. I do wish she would come & stay a long time with me —

Some of our school teachers are on taps for matrimony in vacation. They too, like the children, count on vacations. We have no news of special interest, as I see Cous Will coming, close with much love to all & am as ever,

Yours affectionately,
Mittie

Presley A. Crawford in Fayetteville, Arkansas to John R. Boddie in Atkins, Arkansas *

July 31 1888

Dear Friend:

Yours of July 25th regarding the Egg business of this section is to hand. There are 30 dz Eggs in a case 400 cases in a car load or 12000 dz. March is our best shipping month and Fayetteville ships about 8 car loads during that month., or 40 to 50 car loads in a year (this includes all Eggs shipped from this point, Fayetteville alone will ship 2/3 of the lot). They will average near 15cts per doz the year round. Then say we ship 40 car loads of 400 cases each making 16000 cases of 30 dz each equal to 480,000 dz at 15/ per dz = $72,000.00. You may think that you detect a little "green", similar to the color of the girls dress in the old Blue backed speller*(*The Blue Back Speller was a textbook used in the early schools) in this, but I have given you a close estimate as the Rail Road and other records will verify. One day last March I paid out a little over $500.00 for Eggs alone. That was the largest Egg business that my house ever did in small lots in one day. They came in principally in wagon load lots of about 600 to 800 dz each.

I mail you a paper with a notice of Pa's death, it was so sudden that I can scarcely think him dead. Please remember me kindly to all friends in Adkins

Very truly yours
Presley A. Crawford

*While this letter interrupts the narrative momentarily, it is included because of the surprising information it reveals. SMF

Lucie Smoker Hunt in Shelbyville, Kentucky, to her brother-in-law John Rumph Boddie in St. Louis

August 11 - 88

Dear Brother

I should have had a letter at St Louis for you & thought I would but I got too lazy to do any thing, but eat & sleep — as the weather was so warm

Am thankful to say, just now we are enjoying the cold wave, which no doubt you have also — I am sorry you are having trouble with your eye. You have been afflicted this summer equal to Job, if not as patient.

    I will be glad to see you and will promise you my time while you are here if you dont stay too long, my Kentucky friends dont like my Bro-in-law coming so often anyhow, and will grumble more then ever if I go with him altogether, unless it is for a short time only. We are going to a Fair — up on the new Rail-road next week, for a day only, and expect to have a splendid time — have been on several little jaunts this summer, & enjoyed them each time.

    Recent letters from home report all well — except no one says a word about "Pug" — & I feel so uneasy for fear something has happened to him, & they hate to tell me. I hope not for I love my Pug very much — he is so cute & smart. I can just see the little fellow now. Lillie has two beaux with her now, one from New Orleans & the other from Louisville — it is too bad, that they should both get there at the same time, dont know how she will manage it. I ought to be there to take one off of her hands. We are all gainning, Mamie*(*Mamie and John are Lucie Smoker Hunt's children.) weighing 130 pounds — know she will go to 140 before she leaves — I sold my ticket for 12 dollars but am afraid I will have to loose my half ticket — for I find that so hard to sell — wish now I had bought a whole ticket for the children — when I wrote to Pa that I had sold my ticket he wanted to know what I proposed to do this Fall & how was I to get home — forgetting all about my arrangements before I left home to go to Iowa City — so I wrote to him what I intended to do, suppose he will approve of it. My time in Kentucky is <u>flying</u> too fast — I will soon be settled in Arkansas again — much to my sorrow. Hope by the time this reaches you, you will be perfectly well. All join me in love to you.
                          Affectionately
                          Sister Lucie

Lucie Smoker Hunt in Shelbyville, Kentucky, to her brother-In-law John Rumph Boddie in St. Louis

                                                              Sept. 22nd
    Dear Brother

    Now I am going to be "<u>cheeky</u>", and ask you to send me some flowers to wear to an entertainment next Thursday night, it is given for the benefit of the church, and as I am in the Choir will have to appear on the stage. I feel a little queer asking you to do such a thing, but Brothers have to be imposed sometimes —It is too bad about your eye — I know it is not improving as fast as it should or you would have written more about it — You

can sympathize with Pa a little now —

Mamie had a nice trip home — says every body was so kind to her, & when she arrived at Lonoke her "fellow" (excuse the expression) Robt. Eagle got on, & they had a pleasant time all the way home — I started Mamie alone — and of course felt very uneasy about her as she is very inexperienced — she had her picture taken in Louisville, which I think will be very good — looks very much like a young lady as it was taken evening style.

Please find out what time the train leaves St Louis for Keokuk so that will be the way I will go to "Iowa City". I expect now to leave here on the 9th of October — stay in St Louis one day going, — but two or three days on my return. Cousin Sam writes continually for me to come. Good-bye — All join me in love to you — aff[ectionately]
    Sister Lucie

John R. Boddie in St. Louis to Cornelia Dickson in Ouachita Co.

Oct 12th 1888

Dear Aunt Nelia;

Many thanks for your kind and intersting letter. Please take good care of Ma, send for Dr Bragg if she dont improve at once. Also please find out what underwear or other clothing she needs. She has only sent for a pair of Shoes and a pair of ladies pants. My eye is nearly well but for fear of straining it cannot write you a long letter. I carry insurance for benefit of my boy 15000$, for Mama 5000$ and for my estate 2000$ in case I may die owing something, the two thousand for my estate is payable to Tom Rumph who knows all about my business and if I pass in my check owing nothing, he will turn it over to Mama and my boy. Have had all this arranged several years, but never mentioned to any of you before. I also carry an accident policy of 5000$. The way I am feeling now, expect to remain among [the living] several years, but there is no telling what may happen. Love to all.

    Your devoted Nephew
    Jno. R. Boddie

Mary Elizabeth "Sis Mollie" Boddie and Smoker Boddie at age 8.
Photo courtesy of Ruth Boddie Farmer.

John R. Boddie in St. Louis to Cornelia Dickson in Ouachita Co.*

                                                                                                      Oct 31 1888

Dear Aunt Nelia:

    Your kind favor 27th came duly to hand, accept thanks for same: Wrote Mama yesterday and have her letter of 29th by today's mail. Have lost the memorandum for articles for Mama and Smoker, the first one you sent. Please send me duplicate as I must fill this need. Have Mamie's but cant imagine what became of Ma's. Yours hurriedly

                              J. R. Boddie

*Note: This letter is addressed to Mosely, Ark, Ouachita County.

Mittie Rumph Rucks in Camden to Cornelia Dickson in Ouachita Co.

                                                                                              Jan 6th 1889

Dear Aunt Nealie,

    As I have a few minutes to write while Corrie is in suspense for fear Bobbie won't come for her — will thank you for the strawberry plants — Tell Cous Mamie I am so much obliged but think she ought to have sent word how much they were & let me paid for them — she has been so kind heretofore, [I] feel like it an imposition for me to always be a begging — I will get the flowers from her if she wishes — Why haven't some of you been over — Christmas passed very quietly with us — save for the noise & chatter of the little folks — Corrie can tell you all about it — Hope you will come soon — It would be a great pleasure to me to have someone of the homefolks come to see me once in a while at least. If Aunt Mollie & Smoker would come & stay a while — or Cous Mamie would come — Tell her if she'll just come & bring the Boy's & Mary Gilder will have such a good <u>old</u> time. I'll let G[odfrey] & F[red]* go to school with L[ouis] & J[ohn],* she & Mary G & myself will take in the town in This Bright Happy New Year — Let's all of us turn a New leaf — & do better by visiting each other more like kinfolks & not so much like strangers — I'd give anything to see Carrie's fine boy — do hope she won't call him Harry — but George Elijah or <u>Ed Rucks</u> or some such pretty name, or call him Cornelius — * — Well I'll close with much love to all of you

                                  Yours — Mittie

* Godfrey, Fred and Mary Gilder are the children of Mamie.

*Louis and John are the children of Mittie.

*Carrie Boddie, who married Mr. Allis Moseley on December 21, 1887, DID name her first boy Harry: Harry Fisher Moseley

Cornelia Dickson in Ouachita County to Sue [possibly Sue Lea in Princeton, Arkansas]

May 1889

*No heading in the ledger for this letter.

*"Mr Earl" refers to J. Ransford Earle, husband of Eugenia Rumph.

I am expecting Mr. Earl to come for me today or tomorrow. Spent a week with them — they are very proud of their little daughter about a month old [Sallie Kate Earle]. Carrie's boy begins to jump and squeel when he sees his mama put on her hat to go. He is six months old and just as good as can be.

I came home about the first week in May and have nearly worked myself to death, helping Mamie in shipping strawberries — making & filling boxes and cases, getting them off to the depot in time for the train, besides helping about the cooking — Mamie has an acre in strawberries and they have to be gathered and shipped while ripening or they will be lost. Every box has to be culled as the <u>pickers</u> are sometimes inferior. A rushing business but pays well, when well conducted.

That is over with now, but we have had so much company recently that I have scarcely had time to breathe — was up late last night. Several young people came over to play croquet and Mamie had gone to spend the night in Camden. I have been sick too but kept up, feel better today and enjoy writing to you. I received your short letter last week, glad to hear from you. It was kind in you to write again. Wish I could visit your neighborhood again. Yes the girls are growing all the time, fast becoming young ladies — We have but few girls down here but <u>two gay widows</u> that keep the boys lively.

We had a strawberry festival last Friday night at Mr. W. Martins, for the benefit of our minister. I felt too unwell to attend but it proved a success financially as well as otherwise. We furnished only the berries and others furnished cake.

Sue when you write tell me about all the folks in the neighborhood. I love to hear from all of them.*

*This letter has no heading or signature in the ledger.

Mary E. Boddie, visiting in Alabama, to Cornelia Dickson in Ouachita Co.

Sunny South August 6th 89

Dear Nelie,

I must have a little chat with you which I intended should come in before this, but was interupted each time I tried, & tho' it seems a long time since we left home, the days & weeks just fly by, & cant begin to tell you how delightfully we enjoy being together once more. All are busy of course, but there is <u>not ever</u> any hurry or bother attached to domestic duties, but everything is done quietly & systematically making the daily work more a pleasure than otherwise. Sis H[attie Murley] & the girls are as lovingly careful of me now, as of a precious vase too frail to be used, therefore dont any of you say one word about their keeping me from over work &c — A little sweeping & dusting is everything they'l allow me to do & am in danger of getting gouty, or something worse, eating as heartily as I do, so you all had better mind. Sis gets breakfast, Hattie [Sis Hattie's daughter] does the milking at that time, & after the first meal Mattie & I clean up, ie sweep, make up beds &c — Hattie gets dinner, & we have cold supper, hot tea, light bread (<u>You know well how good</u> is Sis H's <u>light bread</u> & <u>rolls</u>) nice butter, milk, preserves, syrup &c. Smoker greatly enjoys his sweet milk at every meal, & if he dont wax fat dont know why — Sundays no hot cooked meals except breakfast — tried to get Sis H. to have cold tea every P.M. but find that it has not been her habit so to do. She has a fine garden of vegetables, & plenty nice chickens. Sis H. says she would have been so glad if Nelie had come, <u>all asked</u> about you, & why you did'nt come? The first thing <u>old</u> lady Williamson, & Miss Lizzie asked after their kind greeting, was about Miss Nelie, & wishing to see you &c, also many others who met us here before, but whose names I cant recall. Oh! 'tis so pleasant to be here, cant help wishing for all of you. Sis H. & the girls talk, & ask me so much about Sis Sallie's <u>children Attalie & Eugenia</u>; forsooth when I have to tell <u>them now of her children's babies</u>. Mother's friends here tell me that I look very much like her, & make them feel almost like being with her. Hattie is ever so much prettier than her childhood promised, & <u>sweet, amiable</u>, is no word to express it, & Mat<u>tie</u> is not a whit behind. Her children Walter, Gilder, & baby Hattie favor Dr E. most, the baby is a perfect pet with every member of the family, & is as <u>good, & sweet</u> as babies ever get to be — except Harry. Mattie's children hav'nt been right well since here, contracted chills at the sickly place at which they have been living. S[moker] seems to be perfectly contented, he & the two boys play together ever so nicely. Dr E. came up Sun. night, & left last night, he is as fine looking, & pleasant as ever, see no change, save a bald spot on the crown of his head, & by the by Sis H's bald spot is some larger, but she looks just the same, & perhaps fatter. Willie reminds me ever of Gilder whom he favors more than any other two of our children ever favored each other. Stevie has been with us twice, he & Dr E. are only 30 miles by R[ail] & Stevy comes home often. He is closing out

Hattie Murley
Photo courtesy of Ruth Boddie Farmer.

his mill business, & has'nt decided if he will engage again in that, or R. R. work. The Dr speaks of keeping his mule teams at work on the Georgia R. R. As he has been strongly solicited to go there. The home here looks as pleasant & natural as the first time we were here, if any change 'tis for the better, & the crop on it (cotton especially) is the finest I ever saw anywhere, & that is the verdict of all who see it, but there's no telling, or surety about the yield of any <u>cotton crop till baled</u>. Tell "Bud" this fine cotton is growing on Father's pet <u>fertalized</u> (<u>from the woods</u>) acres, & in all these years has detoriated but very little.

Presume that you are with Honey [Eugenia R. Earle] as C[arrie] told me that you had gone up the country, & just know that you too are having a nice, quiet & pleasant time. Wish I could see every one of you, yet am thinking my sojourn will pass ever so quickly. Hav'nt heard from home but once, C's. Mr & Mrs Godfrey's letters all rec'd last week, & to reply to, & one to John each week. Have had three from him, & one from him written to Sis H. S[moker] says I promised to write to Aunt Nelie, & you tell her I'm going to do it before long. The trunk came right side up, (will leave it for S. to tell you how it must have been handled), the <u>delay</u> occured from the Agents' having checked it to Marion Junction, instead of Selma, & the mistake was rectified immediately when found out. I did wish often for you to be with us Nelie, the trip was so pleasant, & every way agreeable all through, attributable to the fact of having such restful nights sleep at every stop over, & 'twas so thoughtful of my boy to have us do just that way. All send much love for you, Eugenia, baby & her Papa, I too, & hope to hear from you soon. Did you & Honey go to S.S. last Sun? Who all there &c? & whenever you go, please remember me with love to every one who may ask of me, & to Clara & family, & Attalie <u>anyway</u>. Good by.

Yours Affectionately
Mary E. Boddie

Mary E. Boddie in Alabama to Cornelia Dickson in Ouachita Co.

Sept 9th 89

Dear Nelie,

However it seems quite superfluous to write this morn, yet am so addicted to certain ways that I surely would not feel all right did I not adhere to my self [made] promise of writing home <u>every Mon.</u> (if there was any letter from either or any of you on hand) flattering myself that there certainly would be, between four of you — Mamie, Will, Carrie, & yourself. I cant tell dear Nelie how much pleasure home letters afford me, each one being a bright day in that calendar. S[moker] was certainly moved by his <u>Quaker</u> yesterday for he jumped up from the breakfast table, saying "I am going to write two letters today," & write he did (such as they were) one to M[amie] & one to C[arrie]. I had written to Robt on 5th, but his are not reconed, as 'tis so seldom any of you ever see, or hear from them. Of course Nelie we all enjoyed Carrie's [Love] & Geo's [George Boddie Love] visit here ever so much, & will have to reserve news of our old time Autauga folks till I see you, 'tis not possible to tell it by stroke of pen in my hand. C. would have stayed with us longer, but was necesssitated to be with Ada at this time, particularly as Mrs Dunn's <u>daughter</u> was needing her presense at home. Mrs D. stayed with Ada until C. returned. You just ought to see C., she is so <u>like herself</u>, & <u>yet so unlike</u>, is dumpy, dumpy fat dont look a day older, but imagine if you can, one of her height with limbs & shoulders as <u>large</u> as <u>yours</u>. I intended to have taken her weight, but we all forgot it. Geo. is changed somewhat, but that is to be expected in young folks. S. did'nt recognize him at first sight, & neither did Geo. (know S., said he was not thinking of meeting with S. at the Depot.) To-day is S's birthday [Smoker is 11 years old], & he's been wondering many times if Papa will forget it. He has not as [in] John's letter of Sat. he wrote that I might expect a package for him, but not to tell S. — In reply to Sis Hattie's request that we might stay with her all winter, [John] said, we could remain till frost, & that he would be in Ark. last of Oct. but you may be sure I could'nt begin to entice S. away that long, & I too when the time first set to go comes, would want to go too. Capt S. went to visit his kinfolks last month in Iowa City, Iowa — Mrs H[unt] & children went there later from Shelbyville, & all of them were to be in St. Louis early this month on the way home, & Mamie to go to school at Lindenwood College, St Charles, Mo. only 20 miles from St. Louis. She is to go home first, & return about 15th —

Miss <u>Theresa</u> Williamson has come on a visit to her mother (who has been almost bedridden for a time), Miss Theresa asked about, & said she would like ever so much to see you. Florida clime agrees with her wonderfully well, every wrinkle erased, & her angular figure (like mine you remember) filled out to beautiful proportions, & altogether she is so pretty, & just as kindly pleasant as ever. Expects to remain with her mother as long as possible, or until cold weather, says she could'nt think of making her home in Ala. any more. Sis Hattie & Little H. too bids me say — they will accept no excuse not any whatever for Attalie's not coming to see them, "En passant" to Florida, even if she does have to make a little "detour" to do it. Will she try it alone if she decides to go? Has M[amie] got off to Arka[delphia] yet? Hope she will call on Mrs. H[unt] if she does go. Mattie is so pleased with the effects of <u>Hyper&c&c, wants to know what it is</u>, & you are not surprised one bit I know that I <u>cant remember</u> if Hyperfus<u>phate</u>, <u>phite</u>, or what, so beg you'l tell us, as I wont take any risk whatever guessing about medicine. Mattie has been troubled with boils all over her back, not near so bad tho' as yours were. Wish M. would let me know if she has ever informed (Mrs. A. H. Deseker, Selma Ala. 1100 Ala St. her address) anything about the Wheat &c med., she was so anxious to get for her daughter — (the kind I was taking) — M. has never alluded to it in any way since I asked her about it, & thought perhaps she had written to the old lady for me, as I sent her Mamie's address.

Tell my Gilder girl* she dont want to see Grdma more than Grdma wants to see her, & bless her little heart she'l come before very long. Mattie has a sweet & very smart baby, & all I can hear of my Harry baby, her & him keep pace in all their ways &c. Have only to shut my eyes & the precise looks of he, & his little Mama are before me. Tell her please dont get to be any <u>thinner</u> but let the boy rough it some 'til I come. With dearest love to each one of you all, remain as ever,

     Yrs truly
     M. E. Boddie

Just know I need not ask, for you will take good care of my Willie boy.

Please remember me with much love to C's family, & Mrs S's family, & all while I'm away ask about me, Rena & State especially —

*"Gilder girl" refers to Mary Gilder Coleman, daughter of Mamie.

Cornelia Dickson in Ouachita Co. to her sister-in-law Mary E. Boddie who is visiting in Alabama.

                Sept 20th 1889

Dear Sis Mollie,

  I reached home Wednesday morning, the 18th inst after a ten days visit in Camden, to Mittie. I had rather a quiet time as it rained a good deal of the time & then I was suffering with a <u>sty</u> a while, besides my felon improved so slowly. It was on my right-hand, fore-finger, commenced the very day I wrote to you. I tried every way I could think of to scatter it, but the fifth day I saw it was no use, so I went up to Lilly, on the Local, and had Dr. Murry to split it to the bone. Well, I hope I'll never have another. It is worse than tooth pulling. And yet mine was nothing like as bad as Eugenia's was soon after she married.

All were well at Mitties & Mats save Hattie, & she improves. Mrs Jessie Proctor is now confined to her bed with a kind of rheumatism in her lower limbs & feet, her general health is good, her trip to Hot Springs did not seem to benefit her, like it did Hattie. So she remained only two weeks. Virginia Newton* is just recovering from a <u>five weeks</u> spell of slow fever. I did not go to see her as I did not know of it at first and then other things intervened. I went to see Florrie & Clara Cross (nee Bracy). She is very slowly convalescing from a <u>five months</u> siege with the fever, can get up & about a little now. Old Mrs Simmons has passed away. She was the last of the original band who formed the Presbyterian C[hurch] in Camden. Cash

*Virginia Newton is the daughter of Captain Dee and Ora Newton.

and his family came into possession of all she left.

When I came home found your dear letter waiting. Mamie had read it, however, as I told her to, & wrote to you last Friday. I sent it to Carrie by Allis yesterday morning as she had not read it. Little Harry is getting all right again, he said, though he has been quite sick for several days, they had Dr. Meek to see him. We are all so glad to hear that you and S[moker] keep well and are having a pleasant time. I hope you will remain until frost anyway. It is very grateful to me to know that I am still so kindly remembered by every one.

I received a letter from Sis Carrie while in C[amden] dated Aug 14th. It had been missent to Camden, Ala, is why it was so long coming. I found two other letters at home. One from Sallie Lon Dunlap & the other from Mrs. Taylor near Princton.

Sis Mollie I know you will regret to hear of the death of Judge Richardson. Such a loss to the neighborhood, as well as his family. He had received the comission to represent this portion of Ouachita at the Fair at Fordice in Oct. Last Friday in returning from Lilly he concluded to go through his field. A cornstalk caught in his stirrup at which his horse took fright and plunged around considerably — he did'nt feel any bad effects from it until about a couple of hours and sent for Dr. Murry — failing in all efforts to relieve him, they sent for Dr. Henry, he also failed. Dr. Meek was then sent for, but to no purpose as inflamation then mortification set in, the internal injury he had received closed his useful life. Tis true he was not what he might have been, with his capacity — but he was so greatly reclaimed from what he was when Eddie died, that he was generally respected & regretted. A third time his poor wife is plunged into the gloom of widowhood. Will attended the funeral — Mamie was too busy getting ready to go to Clark [County], and I was trying to keep off a chill. I had one Monday evening was feeling weak & badly but took medicine & did not have any more, yesterday evening Mamie started. Godfrey went with her as far as Camden & returned on the Local this morning. Saw her off on the Guerdon Branch at six. So she is fairly off this time. Mr Roe is to meet her today in Arkadelphia and take her to Hollywood to attend the Baptist Association. So she will have an opportunity of seeing many of her old acquaintances. I know you will wonder how Mamie ever got off. Well you know how it is; I worked button holes & sewed on buttons till nearly train time then all was not <u>quite</u> ready, <u>but just had to go. So</u>, Mrs Jenkins is to do the milking, there are six cows, two have quit coming.

Will has had no more fever, is busy sharpening his saw, preparing to get boards to do some covering to the out-houses. The children are all well, and promised to be good while their Mama was gone.

I saw Cora & Eugenia a while in town. Cora told me that Clara was

*This John was the fourteen year old son of Clara and John Dunlap.

in better health now than for several months. John* arrived safely in Atlanta and is in school. It was quite a trip for a little backwoods boy to take alone. I will show Attalie your letter when I see her.

Sis Mollie, Sis Carrie wrote that Rebecca Underwood was now living in Selma with her daughter Rebecca Hall. Which Hall did Becca marry? And can't you go by and see her on your return? I do wish I could see them all. Whenever I hear about them the wells of affection seems to flow as fervently within me as ever. And Julia is married, will wonders never cease?

The children all join me in much love to you, Smoker, Hattie and all the family.
Affectionately,
Cornelia S. Dickson

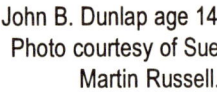

John B. Dunlap age 14
Photo courtesy of Sue Martin Russell.

Hattie Rumph in Camden to Cornelia Dickson in the country.

Oct. 31, 1889

Dear Aunt Nelie,

I fully intended to write to you while in Hot Springs, and first one thing an another prevented so I will write this afternoon and tell you of the nice old lady that boarded with us at the same Hotel, her name was Mrs. Woodson, one day she heard me call your name to Aunt Georgia and she asked me Aunt Nelie who, I told her, and she said that she knew you well, she said you and her, used to board together in Selma, Alabama at Uncle Henry Holmes and her name was Mrs Beckton then. She is very wealthy and stays in Selma in summer and Florida in winter, she owns a very large orange grove in Florida. I fell in love with her, and she seemed to be very interested in me, also. When you come over I can tell more than I can write. I was very sorry I was not here when Aunt Mollie came to see me. Mama and Sis Minnie was going over one day this week on local but my hip has hurt me two nights and mama can't leave. I have been feeling well since I came back from Hot Springs except I have a cold. We would have liked so much to stopped and seen you all Sunday but didnt start from Auntie's [Clem Proctor] soon enough. We went out and spent the day at Auntie's Sunday, and we had a splendid dinner and enjoyed it hugely. Aunt Mattie [Martha M Proctor, wife of Jessie Proctor] is so crippled up she can hardly walk, her feet are getting worse all the time, she is not able to come to see us atall. She seems very low spirited at times. I hope you can come over and stay some with us this fall. All the children are going to school everyday — they have not lost an hour from school this cession. Sis Maud is in Mr. Miller's room and in advanced studies and it keeps her busy at hard study all the time, she does not have any time to write letters now. Lillian is learning to spell at home and she gets very lonely without Sissie. Mama says she has to stir early and late to keep up with these short days.

Aunt Nelie write to me some time when you have leisure. I would enjoy reading some of your good letters. Give my love to all of the home folks and excuse pencil & bad writing. I am ever your loving niece,

Hattie

Corrie Rucks in the country to Cornelia Dickson in Camden

August 27, 1890

Dear Aunt Nealie,

I received your most welcome letter yesterday. I was so glad to hear from home. I am glad you are all well, and having a good time. I am just having a fine time. I will tell you how I have been spending my time. The first Sunday, Aunt Carrie, Uncle Allis, and Harry and myself spent Sunday with Honey. In the evening, we went to Sunday School. On Monday, I went down to Aunt Mollie's and spent the night and next day. I stayed with Grandma [Old Mrs. Moseley] until Thursday and Cora came after me and we rode up to Aunt Clara's on old George. As we passed Mr. Martin's [Mr. W.T. Martin] he just stopped his work and looked with all his might. I think it must have been a circus — two great big girls on one horse. I stayed with Cora Thursday night and I did not get to go down to Grandma's Friday, so I stayed with Aunt Attalie Friday and Friday night and Saturday went to Grandma's. Sunday was a big day over here. They had preaching, dinner at the church, Sunday School and preaching at night. I am dividing my time this week between Cora and Aunt Attalie. I am going up to Aunt Attalie's after church tonight. Aunt Nealie, I just had a picnic last night. It commenced to rain and we had to stay there (at church) about two hours and a half. We sang and laughed and talked until we got tired. Wright [Brodnax] brought Powel Puryear to church last night. Powel and several others are camping down at Pine Lake. They had to ride seven miles last night after church and go back to their camp. They will be up here this evening. Brother Carr and Maud are

The Rumph Sisters (excepting Bettie who died in 1880)
First row (left to right): Hattie, Bessie, Mittie, Lillian
Second row: Eugenia, Attalie, Maude
Photo courtesy of James Harvey Rumph

over attending the big meeting. Fred Coleman has been real sick, but is much better. I think he is up. I saw Aunt Mollie yesterday and she is very well. I will have to close as I am going over to Cousin Lula's to take some sweet potatoes. I am going horseback riding this evening.

Give my love to Rosina and tell her that I am just having a fine time, and also tell her to beware of "Shap". She will understand. You must excuse this writing, but I do not quite understand this pen.

Much love for you and all and a kiss for the "kid" and Attalie [her little half-sister].

I am your niece,
Corrie Rucks

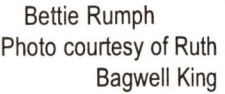

Bettie Rumph
Photo courtesy of Ruth Bagwell King

Mary E. Boddie in Ouachita Co. to her son John R. Boddie in St. Louis

Jan 19th 1892

Dear Son,

Know you will like to hear how we are getting on at this time — Well first rate, considering the weather &c. The coldest we've had for years, & since Tues 12th following your visit to us there has been a succession of sleet & snow to this time & the ground [covered] with ice. Had two days of sunshine which despoiled the trees &c of their lovely coating, but ice still covers the ground nearly solid. Will has been ailing with cold & sore throat, but the <u>like vigorous doctering</u> as in your experience (& I was glad you told us of it) <u>nipped</u> his <u>spell</u> in the bud right away & he's only had to be little more careful of himself than usual. Little Darling has shown himself a very man in being the first to get up these cold mornings & make fires — he begged Will to let him do it in his place some time ago, but never got his consent before. The boys, Gilder girl too have a lively time skating, or trying to, & Pet & G[odfrey] have been hunting some, ie birds. One day Pet killed 16 & G. 5, they went to the dump for birds only once after you left, S. found 5, G. 3, J. 1, said all the [birds] dodged <u>under</u> the wire that eve.

Last Sat. Bob sent our packages over by our darkey here who at present lives in the Henry Jones house. The same freedman who worked for Mrs Mitchel a year, his name [is] Milton Parker.

There has been no passing to town at all except on foot since the ice only occasionally the few who have a well shod horse or mule.

My wristlets dear boy are <u>so nice</u>, & just the article for this cold weather, so comfortably warm. Will's nice present comes in the nick of time, & we're ever so much obliged.

Am so glad to tell you that Little Darling is wearing his braces* — he has always been so averse to putting any on that I was very agreeably surprised that he was willing to do so, but these you sent please him better than any heretofore, & I believe will correct his stooping habit.

*The braces Mollie refers to are suspenders.

Have had no letter from you since you left, but hope to get one tomorrow as we expect to send to the office. I miss my Paper (the Republic) dear boy, the time for which you subscribed for me expired in Dec. "Aunt" Nelie has been at Carrie's since Sun. All well there. Mrs [William] Martin has been dangerously ill again, is better at present. Mr [Cicero] Black sometimes better, then worse, has hired Wright B. as regular nurse. No news — everybody housed in this icy cold weather. The sunshine to-day has'nt made any impression on the ice whatever except in some places a little sloppy, & more slippery.

Good by, with love from all & kisses from Pet "for Papa."

Your devoted
mother,
Mary E.
Boddie

D. Carey (a school mate) and John B. Dunlap (1875-1895) In Atlanta, Ga. Photo courtesy of Sue Martin Russell.

*The "Jonnie" Clara refers to is John B. Dunlap, son of Clara, who is attending school in Atlanta.

Clara Dunlap at home to Cornelia Dickson in Camden

Feb. 23, 1892

Dear Nealie,

Won't you please do me a little favor? Tis this. Could you manage to get me some morning glory seed from some one over there? I mean some of different colors; I have only the pink. And also, a root of white running roses like the one on the front gallery at Miss Jennie Brown's house. Or if you can't get that, a yellow Lady-Banks rose vine (with root). There are some at Mrs. Bracy's old place on Main Street, I think, and also at Mr. Henry Myers. Please try for me, and I will esteem it a very great favor indeed.

My reason for wanting so many vines is that Jonnie* sent home a request to Cora and me to please plant vines all along at the front galery, so they'd run up and shade it from the glare and heat of the sun this summer. Twould be so much pleasanter for him when he came home for vacation.

You know how sunny and disagreeable it is out on our galery in summer. He sent word by Jim M. in January when he returned from his visit to Jonnie. Also that Fannie D. and Jim Watkins, John's cousin would come with him home and give us a visit. So, I would like so much to fix up the yard and house to be as attractive and comfortable as possible for them.

Cora has received her patterns and your Demorest, March No.

I just thought of it. This is Jonnie's birthday. He is 17 years old today, doesn't time fly?

I've suffered a great deal with Neuralgia in my head, face, and ears, too since I saw you. Tis weakened me as much as a severe spell of sickness. I am some better now.

Mrs. Agee has been suffering with risings under each cheek. Dr. Murry has lanced both sides. He says it is her tonsils that are affected and calls it tonsilitus, I believe. I was over to see her yesterday. She seemed to be suffering a great deal, I thought, though she was easier than she had been and was right cheerful.

Sadler* grows and fattens, but still cries a great deal at times.

I have been gardening some. I have radishes, cabbage, lettuce, mustard, and peas up and looking fine.

When will you come out? If you can get the rose vines with roots to them and the seed (any kind of pretty flower seed will do), please send them to me the first good opportunity you have, and I will be a thousand times obliged. Love to Mittie and family,

               Yours affectionately,
               Clara Dunlap

Note: Johnnie Dunlap did spend the summer of 1892 with his family in Ouachita County. He returned to school in Atlanta in the fall. In 1896 the family was informed by telegram that he had died of typhoid fever. Several of the Alabama family members accompanied his body back to Arkansas, and he was buried in the family cemetery at Harmony Grove.

*"Sadler" refers to John Sadler Martin, son of Cora Lee Dunlap and James Walter Martin who were married on January 14, 1891. Sadler is a brother of Sue Martin Russell.

Corrie Rucks in Camden to Cornelia Dickson in the country

               Nov 6th 1892

Dear Aunt Nelie,

I received your note during the Fair. You know what a hubbub we are always in so I would not attempt to write.

All are well again. Mamma [Mittie Rucks] had quite a tight spell of bilious fever and was in bed a week. She is up now, but does not gain her strength very fast.

Well, we have got our cow home at last. She is as wild as a deer and kicks and fights, so I do not take much stock in her. Papa and Milton were trying to get her in the stable. Milton had her by the horns and Papa was twisting her tail (she doesn't have any more than a rabbit) and pulled his finger out of place. Mama and I were on the back gallery and Mama heard it pop and said, "There now. Mr. Rucks has broke the cow's tail," but we soon found out it was his hand and not the cow's tail.

I had a long letter from Harry Fisher. He says that you need not be surprised to see him anytime. Aunt Mollie [Harry Fisher's mother, Mrs Mary Fisher] wants me to come and spend the winter with her. All that I need is the round rocks.*

I have finished Harry's [Moseley] aprons and intended to send them by Cora but she had so many bundles I would not bother her. I saw Miss Mattie about the needles, she sent for hers but they have never come. They will be more than 25cts though.

How is Grand-ma? [Mrs. Moseley, mother of Mr. Allis] Aunt Jane says she is going to make Walter take her over to see her. Diptheria is in town and a good many are scared. Mr. Marshalls child died with it.

I will close. Write when you can. Love to all,
                  Corrie

*Corrie's "round rocks" are most probably coins, money required to make the trip to the Fishers in Kentucky.

Harry Fisher Moseley and his baby brother, George Boddie Moseley, sons of Carrie Boddie and Allis Moseley.
Photo courtesy of Nita R. Moseley Munoz.

PART FIVE

The Twentieth Century Arrives

    The advent of the Twentieth Century, as with any such momentous event, demands a period of reflection on what the past has accomplished and what the future holds. Since the first quarter of the Nineteenth Century, we have been priviliged to establish an intimate relationship with many people. We have observed them as they went about their daily lives and built a community, as they dealt with grief, enjoyment, dreams. We have witnessed a welding of family closeness, a dependence on extraordinary friendships, and the satisfactions of jobs well done. Most of the first generation is gone now; too many of the second generation have also been taken from the family circles. The third generation is growing up, and it is they who will mold the new century into what we know it to be.

    Our concern will rest with only the first quarter of the Twentieth Century. While the last half of our century has made the most startling changes in the world, particularly in the realm of technology, the early decades were quite productive. In 1907 the first highway bridge over the Ouachita River would be opened. Until then one could only cross the river on a ferry or by walking the railroad bridge. Because the bridge made Camden more accessible, trade became vigorous, opening new avenues for business. World War I, while hardly productive, touched the lives of everyone.

Cornelia Dickson in Princeton, Arkansas to her niece Lula Dunlap Martin in Ouachita Co.

Feb 1900

Dear Lula,

How the time flies. Here it is nearly the middle of Feb. I have been so busy since Christmas. My visit to Ouachita seems almost like a dream, a pleasure that was mixed with pain. I often think of your Pa's expression about the many changes in our old neighborhood, in the last few years, "Seemed like a cyclone had passed over it" and I sometimes wonder if there is another neighborhood that has experienced so many changes in so short a time. Though I saw Eugenia married, it all came about so unexpectedly, somehow one <u>event</u> following another in such quick succession that I scarcely realize it is so. While I am off up here leading a busy life of quiet monotony, changes seem to be going on down there all the time. I did not get to talk with Eugenia but very little; been thinking I would write to her. Guess she has a very quiet happy time in her new home. I have not heard from anyone down there since I came back. I neglected to write is the reason I guess. There is but little transpires up here to interest one there, unacquainted with the neighborhood & I have visited very little. Miss Banks is very closely confined at home with her father & I never have anyone to go with me, Saturdays even when I have leisure. The children all live rather far to go home with them. Miss Banks is out today "up to the elbows in greece." Mr Lea finished killing hogs yesterday. People round here with few exceptions seem to have made meat enough to do them. Old Mr Lea sold several cuts at three cents. I have been as well as usual this winter. Let me hear from you soon. With love to you all.

Affectionately,
Your Aunt Nealie

Bessie Love Wadsworth in Prattville, Alabama, to Cornelia Dickson in Ouachita Co.

Aug. 27, 1900

My Dear Aunt,

I guess you will be surprised to get a letter from me, but it looks like Ma* will never write to you. I told her that I recond that you had forgotten me; it has been so long since you had seen or heard from me. Well we all was so grieaved to hear of Aunt Mollie's death. We all loved her so much, but we all have to die, yet it is the saddest thing that could happen in a family. Ma has only eight of us living but she has 48 living grandchildren, and 4 great grandchildren. Now that is a flock to be proud of and in all the 5

*"Ma" is Sis Carrie, Caroline La Fayette Boddie Love.

there is not a one that is afflicted in any way, not even bowleged. The straitest set you ever saw. I have been married twice. My oldest is just 20 years old, Belle is her name. She married in July to a R. R. conductator, a Mr. Hogg. They live in Selma. I have 3 boys & 3 more little girls, 11, 9, & 3 years old. The boys are 12, 6, & 2 years old. Ada has 9 children living. She lives 2 miles on the other side of Prattville, her husband is sherriff of this county & he will be our next tax collector. Onie has 10 living children, she lives about 2 miles from me, her old man runs a dairy. Nub, Bud & Croff lives near Burnsville; Will & George live in Birmingham. Will is excutionner of Birmingham prison, he gets $35 for every man he hangs and he seems to delight in it, he is as bad as ever. George runs a dairy, he has 4 children and a smart wife. Mr. Mac Smith wants to know your post office. He wants to sell your land, you write to him and he can tell you what he wants. Ma send love to you all. Give my love to all of my kin, accept a large share for yourself. Write soon to your loving niece

Bessie Wadsworth

John R. Boddie in St. Louis to Cornelia Dickson in Ouachita Co.

Oct. 2nd, 1900

Dear Aunt Neley:

Brother W. W. Nelson, England, Ark, formerly pastor of our church at Shady Grove will write an obituary of Mama* if you will send him correct data related to her birth, marriage, death &c. Please do so at your earliest convenience —

Hope you and Will keep well. The copper business is booming, and I hope to fix up the old homestead for you and him and Mamie within a year, so you can enjoy living over there to the fullest extent.

Lucie [Smoker Hunt Boddie] and Henrietta [Hunt, Lucie's daughter] are with me this week. I leave for Arkansas by Saturday.

Love to all

Your nephew,
John R. Boddie

Smoker Boddie at Vanderbilt University in Nashville, Tennessee, to Cornelia Dickson in Ouachita Co.

December 30th 1900

Dear Aunt Nelie, —

I sincerely hope that my delay in answering your most welcomed and highly appreciated favor, received so long ago, has not in the least discour-

*Mary Elizabeth Gildersleeve Boddie, Sis Mollie, died on June 27, 1900. It is strange that we can find no details of her last days, since such details of other family deaths were carefully described by Cornelia in letters. Possibly Aunt Nealie was too lonely and too grieved to write her friends and relatives in Alabama of this sad event.

aged you, and that an answer even at this late date will find its way on the road to acceptance.

Would like very much to see you, this dark and dreary night, but alas! too great is the distance which separates us, not so great, however, but what can be gained in the future.

Suppose you all enjoyed yourselves very much during the past week, but it was just the other way with me, and now that Xmas has come and gone, I have had a long rest from my books, and, while I feel that I ought to have studied more than I did during the holiday, am now ready to go to work with a vim, for the fast approaching examinations, and think that I have enough energy in store to last me through them. This is my last night of grace, as the next I hope shall find me at my usual employment.

Hav'nt as yet heard a word from any of you so I take it that you are too much occupied with the pleasure of Christmas, but now as tis over I will have a letter very soon, even my girl has'nt written to me, that's too bad aint it? (never out of hopes though) some day will bring the bright reward for which I have been so long toiling — patience, perseverance and endurance, they tell me, will finally gain the victory;

Wrote to Uncle Will, suppose he has received it ere this, also to Aunt Mamie & Fred, from one of whom I shall expect an answer soon, tell Uncle Will to write also when he can.

Well, Aunt Nelie, must study some tonight so by by for this time.

With much love to you and all, I am as ever
    Your loving Nephew,
    Smoker Boddie

Cornelia Dickson in Ouachita Co. to Smoker Boddie at school in Nashville, Tennessee

Jan 1901

Dear Smoker,

I know you are getting anxious to hear from home again & though I have nothing much to write, you shall hear what is going on at home.

Your Uncle Will recd your most kind letter last week and it does him a world of good to hear from you. Well I am sorry to tell you that I do not see any improvement in his condition. Sometimes he feels much better, walks about & looks after things, then a spell of suffering comes on him that will last maybe a week ere he will begin to improve again. Lies before the fire all the time while suffering, complains all the time, day & night. I moved your lounge in there in front of the fireplace so that he could breathe the warm air and roast his back when suffering. Says he can get no comfort any where else. He is very nervous, scarcely ever sleeps more than two hours at night and as the least noise or movement disturbs him, I am now occupying Mamie's room. Says he thinks his general health is better; and nearly always will get up mornings, start fires & feed, then comes in and eats a light breakfast mostly of rice & butter, soft eggs, or eggbread, sometimes meat & always ready for dinner & supper. Walked down to the mill twice today, seems a little better than yesterday. He and I both had a bad time last week. We have no help at all, only now & then a woodcutter. I was down in my back with something like a "ketch," from lifting something too heavy I guess. I am taking liver medicine now and feel much better. Went with Allis & children* to church last Sunday. We have a good minister again this year — has been to see Will once, inquired after him Sunday. Says he is coming again. Beulah married Pete Sather about two weeks ago. I have not seen her since. I hope she will be happy in her new relation. Sam Earle is off to Tex, so Eugenia tells me, to engage in Merchandising. He is a nice boy and I am sorry to see him leave. Conway is team boss for Bird, on the Eagle train at fifty dollars a month. I have not heard from Godfrey or Fred in some time. Mary Gilder wrote to Will about two weeks ago. Mamie I hear is back in Camden, failed to get the position she sought. I feel sorry about it. Well, this life is full of disappointments to some, while others prosper with all ease, seemingly. Your Uncle Will says his whole life seems to be made up of disappointments. We will probably know some day wherefore the Divine decree, for we are as potter's clay, our lives are shaped by His hand.*

*"Allis and the children" refers to Allis Moseley and his two little boys Harry Fisher and George Boddie Moseley. Carrie Boddie Moseley died in 1892.

*This letter is unsigned in the ledger.

John R. Boddie in Arkadelphia to Cornelia Dickson in Ouachita Co.

Jan. 11th 1901

Dear Aunt Nelie:

Yours recent date received. Glad to hear from you and Will, and especially that Will is improving. I trust and pray he may continue improving. If its [dispepsia?] he is suffering with, he will get well and if the medicine he is taking dont cure him, I know none I think will. All well up here, and jogging along as usual.

I go to St. Louis for a few days and hope to run down to Camden when I return, Love to all

Your nephew
Jno R. Boddie

Smoker Boddie in Nashville, Tennessee, to Cornelia Dickson in Ouachita Co.
Jan 13, 1901

Dear Aunt Nelie,

What has become of you all anyway? hav'nt heard a word from any of you, since about a week before Xmas. I sincerely hope that [it has] <u>not</u> been as a result of sickness in the family. Are Fred and Mary G[ilder] still [at] school in Arkadelphia? if not what are they doing and where are they? and in a word how are you all? and how did you spend your Xmas. How is Uncle Will getting along, and Aunt Mamie with her Postmistresship at Little Rock?* and what is her address. Tell me all the news Aunt Nelie, when you write, <u>no</u> one thinks any more of you all and your affairs than I. Have written you all seven letters, but don't suppose you have received them or I surely would have gotten an answer before now. Am getting on very well at school, but my examinations are near at hand, and I have to work very hard, so must say farewell for this time.

With much love to you and all & hoping to hear soon, I am

Your loving nephew
Smoker Boddie

*The Postmistresship at Little Rock is the position that Cornelia referred to in her previous letter to Smoker, which Mamie did not secure.

John R. Boddie in Arkadelphia to Cornelia Dickson in Ouachita Co.
January 27th, 1901

Dear Aunt Nelie:

Your appreciated letter came some days ago. I was happy to learn Will was improving. I sincerely trust and pray he will soon recover entirely. Write me often how he is getting along, as I feel anxious about him! I spent between trains at Camden Friday but was so pressed for time could not run out to see you, but will run down again in about a week or ten days, to see you. If you and Will need anything let me know. I will send you 10$ by Tuesday or Wednesday.

Mamie is with us spending a few days doing some sewing for [Mary] Gilder, she is not very well, had a chill the day she came, but is up and about. My family keep well, and I am constantly on the go as usually. With love to you and Will I am your devoted Nephew,

Jno R. Boddie

John R. Boddie in St. Louis to Will T. Boddie in Ouachita Co.

3/18/01

Dear Will

Yours 15th received. I mailed you 10$ in a letter just a few days before I was down in Feby. which I hope you received. You acknowledged the 10 sent you in Jan. I enclosed S/D for 10$ which you can use as you like, and let me know if this 10$ a month will answer your needs. Hope you will continue to improve.

    Love to all
    Your bro
    Jno. R. Boddie

Smoker Boddie in Nashville, Tennessee, to Cornelia Dickson in Ouachita Co.

April 5, '01

Dear Aunt Nelie,

Your long and interesting letter of recent date received due time, and wish I was capable of writing an equal to it in answering.

Am <u>very</u> glad to hear that Uncle Will is much better and do hope that he may continue to improve.

Am getting along as usual at school, but have been sick (having chills) during the past week, however, as we got three holidays Thursday, Friday and Saturday. I have not lost much time from school, but have not been enjoying myself either, so you see I have a pretty hard time dont I? and you bet I am anxious to come home and enjoy life a little while.

Well Aunt Nelie don't think hard of me for not writing long letters, for I have to run the same old ruts day in and day out, so you see there is little of interest.

Remember me to all my old friends and acquaintances and you all write when can.

    With love I am always.
    Your loving Nephew,
    G. S. Boddie, '04*

*It is interesting to note that for the first time, Smoker adds his graduation date to his signature, indicating his eagerness to finish.

Smoker Boddie in Nashville, Tennessee, to Cornelia Dickson in Ouachita Co.

May 11th, 1901

Dear Aunt Nelie,

Your long welcomed and most interesting letter of 3rd inst. received some days ago. Aunt Nelie, I appreciate your kind advice and thoughtfulness of me, and think that I might have stopped the chills long before now, had I just taken medicine at the proper time, and it was not either thoughtless or carelessness, as one might suppose, but simply because hated to do it, thinking all the time that every chill was the last one. so it went you know, they will return now and then, but can't hurt me much, and now I am taking tonic prescribed by the Dr and hope to eliminate them altogether. Have not had any now for about a week. Sorry to hear of so much sickness in the neighborhood, and hope for the best results from the Small Pox. . . . Am <u>very</u> sorry to learn that Uncle Will is not doing to well. What does Dr. Meek say is the matter with him? Never worry in the least, Aunt Nelie, as I have no fear of the chills getting the best of me. Will soon be home now, anyway.

You surely have a pretty good job, & if you don't mind you will make yourself sick, trying to do so much. I know what milking is, because I have been there. Glad to hear of Aunt Mamie's success with her strawberries, and wish I was there to help pick some ("not to eat any though!") And Bryant has sold out, professed religion but still is interested in the bottom stock. Well that is Bryant, you know. Am sorry to hear of Uncle Allis being so sick and wish him a speedy recovery. I have about come to the conclusion that it don't pay to worry over anything in the future, but to let the world take care of itself, and go ahead.

Give my love to all, Aunt Nelie. Remember me to all very old friends and acquaintances when you see them, and write me just such letters as the last, when you have time, and they will be most highly appreciated by,

Your loving Nephew,
G. S. Boddie, '04

John R. Boddie in St. Louis to Cornelia Dickson in Ouachita Co.

Dec 20th 1901

Dear Aunt Nelie:

I expressed you today two suits underwear and two pair shoes for Christmas. Will and Mamie some money and she can get what she needs most for herself and Will. Everything frozen hard and fast here, and I am afraid you all are not keeping warm. I told Fred to go down and spend Xmas with you all and get up enough wood to last you until Spring. I am very busy getting ready for next years work, and want to get through and spend Xmas with my family if I can. Hope Will is improving. Love and pleasant Christmas to all.

Your devoted Nephew
Jno. R. Boddie

Smoker Boddie in Nashville, Tennessee, to Cornelia Dickson in Ouachita Co.
January 25, 1902

Dear Aunt Nelie,

Your most welcomed letter of recent date just received. Always glad to hear from home, and especially from Aunt Nelie. Very sorry, however, to learn that you have been sick, and hope that it will not last long.

I am getting along farely well at school, but tis becoming pretty wearisome, as I am anxious to get to work.

I am glad to hear that Uncle Will is improving, and I have more hope now of his recovery than ever before. No doubt everything about home is pretty much as it was when I left last summer, if so, I can almost imagine myself there now.

And Cousin Cora is going to move to town! just a course of time until all of our old neighbors and relatives will be gone from the neighborhood.

Recent letter from Godfrey reports him getting along nicely, but the C. C. Co. [Cornelia Copper Co.?]* have not yet begun work, for some cause [or] another.

My examinations have been in session this week, but am going to take a night off from work tonight, as I don't have any more until Thursday.

Write when you can Aunt Nelie, and give my love to all, I am ever the same,

Your loving Nephew,
G. S. Boddie

*The Cornelia Copper Co. was a mining business in Gila Bend, Arizona, in which John R. Boddie heavily invested. Godfrey Coleman, Mamie's son, was apparently involved in his uncle's business, and eventually George B. Rumph also would leave the orange groves of Florida to become a part of the mining endeavor.

Smoker Boddie in Nashville, Tennessee, to Cornelia Dickson in Ouachita Co.
March 2, '02

Dear Aunt Nelie,

Your letter of 27th is the bearer of some of the saddest news I have had in quite a while: tis impossible for me to express my feelings upon the subject, but I sincerely regret that I cannot be present at the old homestead just now.

I appreciate your giving me the home particulars very much, Aunt Nelie, and never forget that I am <u>deeply</u> interested in all things connected with home. Yes I am surprised to hear of Aunt Mamie's going in the bottom after cattle, and I regret very much that she has to do it. Tis too bad that Jno. Pyles has been taken away just in the prime of his life, and my deepest sympathies are with Mrs. Stone and all the family who have been so kind and neighborly to us. Tis true that a great misfortune seems to have fallen upon the whole community, but let us not mourn but look to and think about the brighter and happier times in store for all.

"On that bright and cloudless morning
When the dead in Christ shall rise,
And the saved of Earth shall gather
To their home beyound the skies,"

I think that I, principally, am to blame for you all not having sufficient wood, for any body ought to have known that what was left there last summer would not last; that is what comes out of putting off, putting off, neglecting to begin work at it until too late; nevertheless I have learned something not only from that incidence, but from many others that have come under my observation. I wish you the best success in hiring hands, and I sincerely hope (in fact I know) that nothing will be free from sacrifice, in order to keep Uncle Will a good fire.

I am glad to tell you that my health is better now than I have had in a long long time before, and both life and work <u>of any</u> kind is a pleasure to me, and you bet I am proud of it too! and never intend to have chills like I had last year again, unless the drug store runs out of medicine.

Write to me Aunt Nealie when you can, and tell Aunt Mamie if she don't write pretty soon I am going to write to her.

With much love I am ever the same,

Your affectionate Nephew
Geo. S. Boddie

W. T. (Will) Boddie in Ouachita Co. to the Dr. Curry Cancer Sanitarium in Lebanon, Ohio

April 7th 1902

I have been suffering with a malignant tumor of the lower bowels, mescenteric, I think the Drs call it & cancerous. Last July Dr Dale of Arkadelphia & Dr Blackman of Camden, Ark performed an opperation (made an inscision) upon me, and were convinced that I was incurable. Said I could live but a few months longer at least. I was very feeble, confined to bed for several months. In the meantime was prevailed upon to try S.S.S.* Contrary to all expectation I am yet living; though at times a great sufferer — at other times, able to be up & walk about the house & yard. I also use constantly Papine [?]. At first, last summer, (after I ceased using morphine) I could allay pain with only a teaspoon of Papine, but now I find relief only in <u>four</u> teaspoon ful, & sometimes five; taken four or five times in twenty-four hours.

You see mine is a desperate case and if you cure me you come near performing a miracle.

*S.S.S. is a high-potency vitamin tonic, made by the S.S.S. Company of Atlanta, Georgia. I can remember as a child my dad selling a lot of this tonic, and was quite surprised to discover that it is still being sold over the counter.

Your advertisement in Dallas Semi-weekly News of March 25 — Sent to me today.

> Yours truly
> W. T. Boddie

The Dr. Curry Cancer Sanitarium in Lebanon, Ohio, to Will Boddie in Ouachita Co.

April 10th, 1902

Dear Sir:

Your request for information as to our method of treatment for cancer is received, and we take pleasure in enclosing herewith our little booklet on cancer, cancerous growths and their cure.

We also enclose our diagnosis sheet which please fill out and mail to us at once. The questions therein are for our information in studying your case from the standpoint of successful specialists in the treatment of cancer. Upon receipt of this blank, properly filled out, we will at once inform you frankly what can be done for you.

We will say, however, that this remedy will positively cure any case of external cancer where the bone is not involved and has cured hundreds of desperate cases which we ourselves looked upon as doubtful at the start. In all cases, however desperate, it affords immediate relief, destroying all offensive odor and prolongs life. We have cured hundreds of malignant cancers where attending physicians predicted death in a very short time and would urge, if you are a sufferer from cancer and have become discouraged by repeated failures in other so-called cures, that you satisfy yourself by writing at once to any or all of those we quote as reference, or in way of testimonials. You will thus learn from those who have been cured that there is a cancer cure that does cure cancer.

It immediately stops all further growth and effectually kills and permanently removes the cancer with all its thousands of tendrils and roots in from ten to twenty days, and our anti-malignant tonic accompanying the remedy removes from the system all the cancer germs that the blood must have picked up and lodged elsewhere for propagation. The treatment is generally accompanied with less pain than patients experience before beginning treatment.

You can use it at your own home, apply it with your own hands and cure yourself as hundreds of others have done and are doing. If you order the Home treatment, we invite you to communicate freely with us, as you may desire, while using it.

If, however, you can spare the time and money and prefer to come to Lebanon for our personal care and attention, you will find here a commodious and homelike Sanitarium with every provision for the convenience and comfort of patients. Here we will treat any case found upon examination to be curable without requiring the payment of a cent for treatment until the cancer is removed, which is the best evidence we can possibly give you of our own unbounded confidence in our ability to effect a prompt and certain cure, and upon these conditions we cordially invite you to come here, if you prefer, and be cured.

The treatment is not expensive as we are placing it within the easy reach of all sufferers, and the cure is positive and permanent.

We hope to receive at once the accompanying blank fully answered, as we know from long experience how dangerous delays are and how much it has to do with suffering unnecessarily endured. It involves you in no expense or obligation and when returned to us we will give your case our careful personal attention and write you fully, honestly and conscientiously our views as to your case.

Sincerely yours,
G. M. Curry, M. D.

Smoker Boddie in school at Nashville, Tennessee, to Cornelia Dickson in Ouachita Co.

4/27/02

Dear Aunt Nelie,

Your most welcomed, appreciated, and long looked for message of 18th inst just received, and I can't resist the temptation of answering it at once, although I will state in the beginning that I hav'nt really anything to say more than "I am well and doing well" (I hope).

Of course <u>anything</u> about Uncle Will or home is most interesting to me, and I hope you will continue, as in the past, to write me all the home news: no doubt you have often wonder[ed] why I dont write more about my daily routine than do, but tis <u>just</u> exactly the same as it was last September, or as it was this time last year for that matter.

There are <u>few</u> men in this world who love to work and do for others as well as Uncle Will aint there? and there are still <u>fewer</u> who would go out and hive bees, when they had to endure what he does.

Sorry to hear of Cousin Attalie's being sick and wish her a speedy recovery.

Remember [me] to all friends, and give my love to homefolks,
Your loving Nephew
G. S. Boddie

Cornelia Dickson in Ouachita Co. to Smoker Boddie in Nashville, Tennessee

May 17th 1902

Dear Smoker

If I had found time to write to you a week ago, should have written you a very cheerful letter for your Uncle Will had just left us for the Medical Institution, Paris, Texas, in care of Dr. Jos Hanby — He seemed to be improving every day, was able to be around quite a good deal. Some days did not lie down at all, made half a doz bee gums, hived a number of swarms. In fact seemed on the "up grade" and we had become so hopeful since he began to use the Pepton aids. He was in good spirits too, But a letter from Dr Hanby this morning has dashed all our hopes. It seems that your papa has had no hope for him before he went to Paris, but was perfectly willing to do all in his power for him. Dr. Hanby says he is growing weaker & will write every day to let us know how he is. Says he keeps his room now, is well cared for, has every comfort, even luxury, that he desires. You know Smoker after Will improved a while here at home he would frequently have a bad spell — could not leave his bed sometimes for several days at a time. I wish I could be with him, but do not feel able to stand the strain of being at the Institute. I want Mamie to go; I know Will would be better satisfied to have some one of the home folks with him. & the Dr said he would pay the fare & board as he has to employ a lady attendant anyway. Mamie has bought her a buggy & is trying to sell butter and milk, Strawberries, vegetables &c to help out her own & M[ary] G[ilder] and F[red] expenses. Has a fine irish potato patch too, & it would be inconvenient for her to leave, but Will if he wants her, must be gratified, for he has devoted his whole life to his relatives unselfishly.

May 19th. We have heard nothing further from Will as had no way of sending to town. Mamie will go over this afternoon, or tomorrow. I have no news of interest.*

*This letter is unsigned in the ledger.

John R. Boddie in St. Louis to Cornelia Dickson in Ouachita Co.

Aug 5th 1902

Dear Aunt Nelie:

I returned a few days since from a visit to Camden and Arkadelphia and found your 22nd Ult. claiming my attention. Mamie told me you were needing some things and I told her to let you to get them at Ruois[?] and charge to me, but I am glad now you did not because its more convenient to send them to you from here, or send you the money that you may select what best suits you and pay for it. So write me what amount of money you need for present use and I will send it to you. You can stay where you please for the present and I will pay your board and supply your clothing. I am at a loss just now whether to sell the old place or keep it. I may have to go there myself some day to keep out of the poor house. I miss brother Will* sadly, but like you, I am thankful he is at rest in our Father's mansions, for no finer man, better man ever lived. Mamie was want to call him her Lilly. I understand now that he is gone, its appropriatness.

Love to you and family

Your affectionate Nephew
Jno. R. Boddie

*Willis Boddie died sometime between May 17 and August 5, 1902, but the exact date cannot be cited with certainty. We do know, however, that he died at home, not alone in Texas as did his brother Gilder.

John R. Boddie in St. Louis to Cornelia Dickson in Ouachita Co.

Aug 13th 1902

Dear Aunt Nelie:

Yours received. Will remit you 15$ in a few days, also send you some dark skirt goods. If you are in a hurry for the money tell Tug to lend it to you, I will return it. The boys pictures also to hand, tell sister Sallie* they are certainly fine fellows and I am thousand of times obliged for them. Love to all

Hurriedly your Nephew

Jno R. Boddie

*"Sallie refers to Sallie Higgins Farley, who married Robert "Tug" Boddie.

Cora Dunlap Martin in Ouachita Co. to Cornelia Dickson, visiting with Robert Boddie and his wife Sallie in Cargile, Arkansas

Aug 18, 1902

Dear Aunt Nealie,

I had intended answering your welcome letter some time ago, but the weather is so very hot, & I have not felt well, so did not write.

I am glad you are having such a nice time.

The tent meeting closed last week — they had a great meeting, say that whiskey is bound to go — A great number of conversions.

Mr. Lynn* was out last week — he expects to move to Camden by Sept — of course wishes to rent a house. Cos Mittie says Bok house is vacant, if he has not already rented — expect Mr. Lynn might like it. His address is M.E. Lynn, Athens, Texas.

Quite a number of the neighbors on the river are sick. Belle Martin for one — Conway Pile was over yesterday for the M.D. — said three were in bed —

*"Mr. Lynn" refers to Milton Lynn, second husband of Lula Dunlap. Her first husband, McDuff Martin, had died in 1890.

Jim & Sam* are doing very well with the market, I suppose.

Mr. Martin* has the house torn up — building & repairing. Cos. Tom Rumph has recovered from his attack of slow fever — I am taking butter from Cos. Mamie now. You must excuse such sorry scribling — Write soon — Love to all — Your loving neice —

      Cora Martin

*Jim is Jim Martin, Cora's husband and Sam is Sam Earle.

* "Mr. Martin refers to William Thomas Martin.

Clara Dunlap in Ouachita Co. to her sister Cornelia Dickson in Cargile, Arkansas

      Aug 22nd, 1902

Dear Nealie,

Yours of the 20th inst just received; will haste to answer it, was real glad to hear from you, as I had not heard since you left Cam. I've kept well so far, all summer, only am more nervous in my hands, can scarcely guide a pen or pencil.

Mrs. McKinney was very sick for a few days, wk before last; something like a conjestive chill; she is quite well now tho, & little Elsie had one chill & fever, is all [over] it now, & have had no other sickness. I've not heard of much, if any, as I go so little & see so few. Little Belle Martin, (old Mrs. Hawkins grand-daughter), was quite sick last week but is much better. I went down to State Stone's Tuesday eve, (Belle Gaughan* came by for me) & found State, his wife, & Nellie all sick with fever. They've had some boarders, for a month past, (men working on the train-road down there). I think it was too hot to cook so much. Conway Pile, who is saw-filer for the Co. down there, had to cook, when couldent get a darkie. All better today.

Our next Quarterly Meeting comes off in Canaan, (at the new church, near Dick Dunlap's) on the 1st Saturday & Sunday in Sept.(By the by, that's your birthday, 6th Sept. you ought to be at it sure.)

Jake Justice married a few wks ago, to Miss Lucy Peterson.

I read your letter to Mr. & Mrs. McKinney & both say you are welcome to bring your things here; will find room for them; as I had rented the house to them (except my room), I thought it only right to ask them, you know; she sends love to you, also Elsie & Bennie send love;

*Belle Gaughan is the wife of Dennis LaFayette Gaughan.

James Walter Martin (1868-1935)
Photo courtesy of Sue Martin Russell

& Eugene, who is here for a few days, says "I must send his love too, to Miss Nealie." Mrs McKinney says tell when you come, to be prepared to stay a wk or two wks; & keep house for her, so she can go to see her daughter Mrs Georgia Smith, once more, says she has not been able to get off to go, in two years, & wants to go so much, says do come. Milking the cows & a little cooking is all you'd have to do; for a wk.

Cora Dunlap Martin (1868-1941) Photo courtesy of Sue Martin Russell.

Well, I've saved my best news for the last. Mr. Lynn was here last week (in Cam) & came out to see me; since he left, I learn that he made arrangements with Stern & Henry Myer to move to Cam, & fatten beeves for them, will have 800 or so; & they will move by 1st Sept, or 15th anyway. Jim [Martin] said the other day, that they've been trying to rent a house for him near the Iron Mountain Depot, as twill be near their big cattle pens out at the Fair Grounds. I'm just swelled up so full Nealie; to think Lula will be near me, if not with me, again. I feel like saying over the old hymn: "And that will be glory for me" &cc. I can see her often & am so glad, so glad. Cora & Emma came over yesterday eve, late, & stayed all night with us; Cora wanted some fine peaches that grew on Jim Tompson's place, to preserve & can that way to avoid the heat (went back soon this morning, with a corn sack of large yellow peaches, will make pretty preserves).

Suppose you've seen, in the Cam. paper, accounts of the big meeting that lasted over 4 wks; 100 conversions & 6 new members added to Methodist church. The others will join churches of their choice. Whiskey abolished in Cam; & of course saloon keepers and Dr. Andrews, the evangelist, who carried on the meeting, put it to a vote; 1200 of 1800 signed the petition.

Well Nealie the mosquetoes have set me wild, & tis so hot too. When are you coming up? There's plenty room for your things always here, much love to Rob't, Sallie & children, & accept same from your loving sister,

Clara Dunlap

Cornelia Dickson in Ouachita Co. to John R. Boddie in St. Louis

Dec 31st, 1902

Dear John

    Both of your letters to me 15th and 18th came to hand the same day and I assure you I was very glad of my Xmas present from you. Harry and George were delighted with their knives, and proud that you remembered them.

    We all fully expected to thank you in person, have been looking for you every day since the 22nd. Mamie says she is afraid you are sick. I hope not.

    Mamie had quite a serious sick spell here one night & day — had several fainting spells before she could call to me. She had exerted herself too much in the boat after her cattle in the bottom that day, trying to save them during the <u>last</u> overflow. <u>Those that escaped the first</u>. Envagination of the bowels, I believe she called it. She had felt a severe pain for a minute while rowing in the bottom and feared something wrong then, but it passed off, and she seemed as well as usual when she came home, ate a hearty supper, retired about ten, awakened at about two in agony & sick stomach, arose & started to the fireplace but fell in the floor unconscious — don't know how long she lay but as soon as she revived vomited profusely & staggered to the door & called me — as soon as I could get to her found her almost unconscious, shivering with cold, and her face wet with perspiration. I applied hot water bag between her shoulders, and hot irons to her feet, and gave her strong salt & hot water, half a glass, then hot water alone until she vomited & purged freely to relieve the painful knot in stomach, then gave her 1/2 teaspoonful of "Quick Relief" when she grew easy & went to sleep. It was then near daylight. She remained in bed all day, but was up the next day, and though very weak and sore, wanted to go to the bottom again, but found the water near on a stand, so gave it up. You see I am giving you particulars John, for I very much fear that Mamie will injure herself for life if she persists in trying to do what is so beyond her strength. Will make a helpless invalid at best, if she don't get something else to do, not so trying to her health strength, for she is usually very healthy, or she would have succumed to that spell. She passed blood from her bowels for several days & is now enveloped in plasters, but has recovered her tone all right. And was delighted this afternoon when five of her <u>lost</u> cows <u>came home</u>, looking fat & well, notwithstanding their swim, but some of her best milkers floated off down the river never to return. She sent off four nice hogs to the mill today that were raised at home, has only one meat hog left, that some one crippled in trying to capture I suppose. It is nearly well but not very fat now.

    I must not close without telling you of my Xmas presents from friends & relatives nearer home. Belle, Dennis, & Tom Gaughan. Clara, Cora, Maude. Garland and Charley, and Harry Moseley, amounting to nine dollars and quarter. Mostly in money for me to suit myself with anything I wished. A very pleasant and unexpected shower of Xmas gifts. We have had a very quiet Xmas, Harry & George with us most of the time. George killed a large fat swamp rabbit on the run, several days ago, says he is getting expert but can't kill a duck yet.

The weather is very cold here, with rain every few days. I have kept closely at home, we have all been well, except Mamie, Maude, Garland & Charley.

Many thanks for your very much appreciated & unexpected Xmas gifts. I assure you it made me feel very happy to be remembered by those I love and in whom I feel so much interested.

I wish you all a happy New Year and hope your brightest anticipations may be realized.

       Affectionately,
       Your Aunt Nealie

Sallie Boddie, wife of Robert L. Boddie, in Dodson, Louisiana, to Cornelia Dickson in Ouachita Co.

                   Feb. 4th 1903

Dear Aunt Nelie:

Your nice long letter received today, was so glad to hear from you. Robert feels very uneasy about Godfrey, said he was afraid something had happened to him. Conway P[ile] is here & told Robert that Godfrey would be home by the 15th & it makes him quite uneasy, but I trust nothing has happened to him.

Cora went up last week, to see about having her things moved out, as the place is sold. I recd quite a nice long letter last week from Cousin Mittie.

We have moved now in a real nice house, five rooms & all painted & papered nicely. I am very comfortably fixed, have nice new shades all over the house (I mean at the windows), a new Grass Cloth in my bedroom, bath[?] & the front room, the old carpet, I am cleaning & fixing for the dining room, will get matting for the boys room, so I will not have so much scrubbing to do.

You must try & come to see us again & tell me how you like this country. I asked Sis Mamie to come, thought maby she could find some thing down this way to do, so as to make money. The Earl boys are down here, Rufus Earl went to work for Robert, Monday driving the wagon, delivering groceries, etc. Received a letter from Mama Sunday, said Hubie's wife expected in April, Mama has a young couple boarding with her, & the lady expects in March, so I think Mama will have her hands full, looking after the babies & the sick. I am O.K. yet and Hubert will be three years old next month. Albert & Eddie* are going to school & doing nicely in all their studies only Arithmetic. I have a time every night trying to get Hubert to sleep and trying to assist them with their Arithmetic.

I would be glad to get that girl, Robert knows her Father; he said for her to come if she will & thinks she will be satisfied, I will give her a good home & treat her well, as long as she behaves herself. You can see her for me & write me if she will come, & when, & I will appreciate it so much.

What will Sis Mamie be doing now? I expect she will raise strawberries. I hope Cora will go in to see you all, and then I will go & see her when she gets back and hear all about you. I would love to see Harry & George. I will get A[lbert] & E[ddie] to write to them, it looks like they have quit writing letters, but they have to help me so much, when they get home from school & do not have much time, Albert is so much better in every way, since he lost Louis Price's company, I never have to tell him to get in his wood, he gets it in, just as soon as he come home from school. I have trouble with Hubert trying to keep him in after a rain, as he will get in the water & then I must change his shoes, or he will cough all night. Robert minds me very well for a little fellow.

Write me again soon,
With love from all

     I am as ever
     Lovingly
     Sallie Boddie

*"Albert & Eddie" refer to Sallie's young sons by her first marriage.

George Kimball Smoker Boddie at Vanderbilt University
Photo courtesy of Ruth Boddie Farmer

Smoker Boddie in Jackson, Tennessee, to Cornelia Dickson in Ouachita Co.
       July 18 1903

Dear Aunt Nelie,

Not having heard from you in such a long long time I hardly know where to send this letter, but will try Camden anyway. When last heard from I believe you were with Aunt Clara, if so, how are you all? you may wonder at first who this can be from, but to save your guessing I will say tis a Friend of yours who has gone astray, but who is liable to come rocking back to old Arkansas sometime or other and hope you all will not forget about him entirely. I am working here now with the city engineer, and having a high old time in general, but am anxious to see you all and am coming down there before middle of Sept. when I expect to return

Fred Hughes Coleman at West Point
Photo courtesy of Ruth Boddie Farmer.

to Vanderbilt to complete my course in engineering, then lumber loose into the world . . .

We are somewhat scattered out now ain't we? Aunt Mamie, Godfrey and Mary Gilder in La. Fred at West Point and me here in Tenn; some day however I hope we shall all assemble again at the old homestead to celebrate the pleasant memories of the past and of our loved ones who have crossed into the great beyond.

Remember me, Aunt Nelie, to all Friends and write to me sometime or other and it will be greatly appreciated by

Your loving Nephew
Geo. S. Boddie

Sallie Boddie, wife of Robert L. Boddie, in Dodson, Louisiana, to Cornelia Dickson in Ouachita Co.
July 26, 1903

Dear Aunt Nelie:

Your nice long letter received a few days past, we always enjoy them so much. We had a splendid rain Friday & it is real cool today. We have all kept very well this summer, a chill now & then, but that is expected at this place. Cora Martin has been sick, & will go to Camden Tuesday & stay until she gets well. Robert says she looks badly. Godfrey was here last night (you know they are about 6 mi from us). They are working so hard, we went out one Sunday & enjoyed it fine, Sis M[amie] said she could not run it, if she finds they are not making enough to pay the three well for their work, & I hardly think she will. Robert sent her word to give it up.

A letter from Mama this A.M. saying she was sick, had two chills the past week. We hear from Smoker now & then; he is well pleased, with his work.

I think it will be so nice for you to spend a while at Mr. Gaughan's & Belle will appreciate it too. Tell Eugenia I would love to see her baby, that I love babies, but do not want any more of my own to love; I am O.K. yet. Hubie's wife has another girl, that is three girls now, too bad, his all girls, & mine all boys.

Albert & Eddie are growing so fast. I had Eddie's eyes examined & he will have to put on glasses, just as soon as the Dr treats his eyes. Robert & Hubert are one size, every one asks if they are twins.

Give all my friends my love. All join with me in love to your dear self.

Lovingly
Sallie Boddie

Smoker Boddie in Jackson, Tennessee, to Cornelia Dickson in Ouachita Co.

Aug 13, 1903

Dear Aunt Nelie,

I write you a little note this afternoon to tell you that I will be down your way before very long; I got sick the other day, making the second time since I have been here, so as my time was nearly up and for fear of a long spell of fever, I threw up my job and will return to Arkansas about the 15th of the month; will come over to see you, Aunt Clara and all kin folks, spend a week or two with Aunt Mamie and then leave again for St. Louis and Nashville; am not at all well now but the doctor said I would be all O.K. in a day or two; so thus endth my first two months of experience. No use in answering this Aunt Nelie, because I can't tell you where to address me.

Received a letter from Cousin Mittie the other day which I answered immediately, and surely am going to see her.

It has been a pretty long time if you think of it, since I left home and am anxious to see the old homestead once more anyway, sometimes I think that I don't want to go back there, but will do so this summer if no more.

With much love I am as ever

Your loving Nephew,
Smoker Boddie

Dennis LaFayette Gaughan (1858-1935) Photo courtesy of Dr. Dan Daniel

Allie Gaughan in Camden to Cornelia Dickson in the country, keeping house for Mr. Dennis Gaughan while his wife Belle was away visiting her family in Indiana.

Sept 14, 1903

Dear Aunt Nelie:

Am sorry I have not written to you sooner but it seems that we have [been] having such a time; Mama [Attalie Rumph] has been in bed since Thursday a week ago & several days was suffering terribly but has no fever this afternoon so is some better. I am still sitting up with my foot in a chair on a pillow. Was in bed several days directly after I came home from over there and all of that time have sat with my foot up, however it is better now. Aunt Nelie, Mama has not been able to make any jelly whatever & wants to know if you will make her some scuppernong jelly. Get them there if you have plenty,

*"Grandma" refers to Sarah Caroline Patterson Gaughan. Allie, born after her father died, is the daughter of Attalie Rumph and Alex Gaughan.

but if not get them at Aunt Clara's. Get sugar & glasses from the store & charge all to her.

How are you & Uncle Dennis & when have you heard from Aunt Belle? We have had so much company since Mama & I have been sick. Grandma* is with us now.

Please excuse scribbling for I am in a hurry & am writing in almost dark. Cannot even see the lines.

With love,
Allie

Cornelia Dickson in Camden to John R. Boddie in St. Louis

Jan 1st, 1904

Dear John

I have been thinking a good deal about you of late, for I have heard that you have been very unfortunate. Indeed that you had lost all, everything that you owned. I cannot think it so bad as that, but should it be, you have my sincere sympathy. I know you are not made of material to give up to misfortune. You have too many avenues open to you and too much pluck and energy to be held in the throes of such misfortunes; which really are <u>sometimes blessings</u> in disguise. We have so many blessings that we can weigh against our troubles if we will. Among the chiefest is <u>health</u> and <u>good friends</u>. And the "Sweet Peace," a gift from above. "Everything happens for the best," was a comforting maxim of dear Sis Mollie's. Mr. W. T. Martin brought the news of your trouble to Clara some time ago. I do not know how he obtained his information. We all have our troubles, John. If I was only qualified to teach, as they are now, would feel so happy & independent, being out of school so long feel now that I must cook or nurse for a living & pray for health & strength to sustain me. I am staying with Eugenia now. She & Mr Earle are very kind to me, have missed my things here, as Clara wanted all of her house room for Mr Lynn & family & Jim Martin & family. Mr Lynn has rented Clara's part of the land and Jim is preparing to build where Duff lived near the Schoolhouse. Mr Earle is a stirring hard working man, makes a good living. Seems to be in fine health, enjoys hunting & killing his wild hogs as much as most hunters do killing deer. There is a heavy mast* this year & some of his hogs weigh over

Belle Ferguson Gaughan (1869-1941) Photo courtesy of Dr. Dan Daniel

*Mast is the fruit of the oak & beech or other forest trees, used as food for hogs & other animals.

two hundred, he sells most of his meat at a good price, and has some gentle hogs to kill for his year's supply of meat & lard. I have had no letter from Sallie Boddie in some time but heard indirectly that the children were down with measles and that Mamie had been quite sick. She & Godfrey were with Sallie, & Robert had gone into business at Felsenthol, but that his family were still at Dodson La.*

*This letter ends abruptly at this point in the ledger.

John R. Boddie in St. Louis to his cousin Mittie Rumph Rucks in Camden
                                                                June 30, 1905
Dear Cousin Mittie:

Brother Robt. wrote me today as per your request, he states, and told me that you and George were not progressing any in the way of health improvement, all of which it grieves me to learn.

I have been wanting to run down and see you all again soon and have some hopes of getting off the last of the present week, if I do will be at Camden about next Tuesday. However, cant say positive until Saturday whether I can leave or not. Business is pretty dull all round. Our copper stock has been on the decline for past few weeks, but will rally in time and then advance, it is the way of all stocks, bears have a day and then the bulls.

Hope Tommie keeps alright? My family on account of hard times will summer in Ark this year, but my Boy* is all run down in health and needs a change, so I have arranged to lend him enough to spend a few weeks by the sea shore in order to restore his health.

*John R. Boddie's "Boy" is Smoker, who graduated from Vanderbilt University.

Tell George the contract to build the railway from Gila to the mines was let last week and it is to be finished by January or sooner. Also tell him that hot air McGahan is here in the ring trying to raise money to erect his vacuum smelters, that has up to date created a vacuum in the pocket books of all who have taken stock in the enterprise. He is not selling stock in any company, I broke him of that in the criminal court at Ft. Smith some years ago, but he has a club organized and you buy a membership and the money goes to promoting various enterprises, chiefly hot air smelters, in other words, McGahan. By this method he escapes the penalty of criminal courts. So wags the world away. Love to all. Your affectionate cousin,
                                            Jno. Rumph Boddie

Godfrey Coleman, son of Mamie Boddie Coleman, in Huttig, Arkansas to his cousin George B. Moseley, son of Carrie Boddie Moseley, in VanDuzer, Arkansas

3-3-1907

My Dear Little Cousin,

Your favor of the 25th to hand some days ago, and would have answered sooner, but so tired at night, thought I would wait untill Sunday, which is today, — I am cutting logs 12 miles from Huttig in La. and am getting on very well, making 2$ per day and board, and sometimes more. — Expect to make more from now on as I have a good partner, and then I got a raise of 5 cents on the thousand, so now I will make from $2.50 to $3.00 in the clear every day that I work. —

Yes George, I would like to be up there with you all for awhile. I would enjoy it fine, but you know there is nothing doing up there for me at the present. I have got to work now and pay for what I have all ready spent, and then work some more and get me a stake, then I will come back for awhile, —

Dont know whether I will get to see State and Harry or not while they are here, for I hav'nt got time to quit work and go in to mill. —

Guess Nat is trying to beat my time at Sid Stone's, but he cant do it if I took any hand in it at all, but I have not heard from any of them since I left home, so I am going to let him go his route untill I get back, then I will put the skates under him. Guess State has got my time beat with Pearl, but then you know I have plenty of time yet to come ahead in that case, hav'nt I? — Say Geo., you tell Annie that I am very sorry that I did not get to make her acquaintance before leaving home, for I am sure from what all the boys say about her that I would fall in love with her at first sight. — Tell her that I think of her often, and for her to wait for me untill I come back home. Tell her that I am still looking for some body to burn my stove wood, but have not found the right one yet. — Say George, I gave my other girl the <u>G. B.</u> since I have been down here, the one that lives down about Robertson's you know. — Well I got one letter from her after that and you talk about your sweet letters but it was one, it was way ahead of any that I ever showed you from her. She certainly did beg me to come back to her and marry, but I never did answer the letter and never will. — Now dont you do to much talking to Annie for yourself and get my time beat there. —

Uncle Robt. and family are all well, except bad colds, the boys are all going to school, — I hav'nt seen any of them since I came out to the woods to work, which has been about two weeks. — I was sick when I left home and came to Huttig, therefore I stayed with Uncle Robt. for about two weeks untill I got able to go to work. I have a bad cold now, but am sawing wood every day, and feel very well. — Poor Rossen, guess he will finally loose out with all of the girls in the neighborhood. You boys must have a little pitty on him. —

Well George there is nothing new down this way, it's the same thing over every day. — There was a boy sawing close to me last week that got his leg broke just below the knee, caused from sawing a tree in too that was fell between two other trees and was binding, and when he had his log half cut off it bursted, struck his left leg just above the ankle, knocked him down and broke the large bone, he hollowed for help, so I and my partner run up and I cut a prize pole and prized the log up while he was pulled out from under the log, we carried him to camp on a log wagon, the dr. set his leg and he was taken the next morning to his brothers in a buggy 30 miles from here. I heard from him yesterday, and he is getting on very well. —

Well old boy I will be glad to hear from you any old time. I hope you all are getting on O.K. with your family work.

With love to all
I remain Your Loving Cousin
E. G. Coleman

George Boddie Rumph in Gila Bend, Arizona, to Mittie Rumph Rucks in Camden

April 18th 1907

My Dear Sister

Your letter of Mch 24th came while I was away at Tucson, Ariz. attending to some business matters for the company. I was very glad to hear from you and about relatives in old Arkansas. I feel thankful that you came through another cold winter alive. I hope we can have you in Arizona next month where the climate is mild & warm with but a few weeks of cold.

The work of opening up the mines has been commenced again, this time along old & well tried lines. It may be late in the summer before we begin shipping ores or metals. There is a lot of work to do, and shipping in and installing new machinery takes time and to us here who have labored and waited so long already it seems a sore trial to our patience. However I am very hopeful now that success is just ahead of us, and our reward will come, and perhaps be all the more appreciated for the trials endured and efforts put forth to attain it. Smoker Boddie is here putting in a leveling plant. He is an intelligent man & hard worker and will make a success in life yet. Outside of his school advantages, he has not had much of a showing, I think a great deal of him as a man socially and otherwise.

I hope that John & Capt. Huie will succeed in landing McGahan in states prison before they get through with him. Fluger & Wirtz ought to be behind the bars with him, as they are, one and all, a set of swindlers & thieves.

*Mildred is the youngest child of George Boddie Rumph and Jennie Jordan Rumph.

You asked about the boys babies names. George's little girls name is Virginia. Eugene's boy — Edward Benjamin. I had hoped to be able to put Mildred* in college this fall but dont know if I can realize on stock to do so. My salary later on will enable me to keep her in school until she graduates. Your George is quite young to go from home to work but as he will be with Edgar Ritchie to look after him it will be safe to do so & I think its better to cast them out of the nest, as the Eagles do & let them learn to depend upon themselves & do their own thinking and planning for success in lifes work. I am agreeably surprised that your daughter has developed into such a tall & <u>mighty</u> young woman, I thought she was destined to be a dainty little Japanese woman, just as Ethel is a type of a little jewess. Mildred is a stout fine looking girl — like Sisters Attalie & Eugenia, so Jennie writes me. I am glad for her sake that she has so grown up. Outdoor sports & a life of physical activity at play has produced this change. Ethel's cared but little for outdoor sports, but loved to dress & play the lady, and a delicate little woman has been the result.

Young parents dont know, always, what is for the best in rearing children. We learn how, when its too late to benefit them. With love to your dear self & family and all relatives

Affectionately Your brother
Geo. B. Rumph

Fred H. Coleman, son of Mamie Boddie Coleman, in Cuba with the U. S. Army to Cornelia Dickson in Van Duzer, Ouachita Co.

April 6, 1908

My Dear Aunt Nealy:

It seems [a] short time since I left you but fact shows a way wrong impression. My last sights around the Community are very vivid because no doubt they are so constantly reviewed regardless of the most attractive life. I find I can't be exactly as the Chambered nautilus: sealed up its idle door and stretched in his newfound home and knew the old no more. Some how my old cow of a mind will frequent occasionally the old salt log and I guess the old stomping ground is the real salt log after all, though it and its people be as silent as the same.

I suppose change has not deserted you and all as I have, it no doubt is ever present with its parties: time at this post of duty, still preparing all matters for the finale.

I would not attempt to describe life in Cuba as its so different to be so real. Very oriental and Pom. Pom. like. Their dances and all: Doves, Chickens, hogs, cattle, dogs, horses, mules, cats, turkeys, sparrow hawks, blackbirds, buzzards and many more animals as goats, sheep, what's in this land the same as in the states.

I have, however, never seen a drunken Cuban. Coffee is the curse of this land, while they drink it in its strongest form from 6 - 12 times daily, it is to be preferred to rum.

Regards to all.

Your loving nephew
Fred H. Coleman

P. S. Seeing this extra page and having a few minutes more thought would add a line about what we are doing:

This is the dry season here and also the season of Cane sugar making, and tobacco gathering. These two are the main industries here. It has rained once since Xmas, and we are taking full advantage of this & do our marches and target practice, we have been on the range now for 2 months and will be for one more. Marksmanship in the army is reaching quite a high degree of skill as with careful aim, a man can be killed or hit every shot 1000 yds distant.

Your loving nephew
F. H. C.

Fred H. Coleman in Cuba to Cornelia Dickson in Ouachita County [Post card]

Jan. 30, 1909

Dear Aunt Neely:

It's funny how long we will go without writing. I don't know why that is the way it goes. You know no one ever writes to me now save Mama [Mamie Boddie Coleman] and Gilder occasionally. Uncle John once in a while. I often take a general review of the good home people, in fact this occurs daily, especially during these long quiet days on the island waiting our turn to be withdrawn, however the home port seems to [be] breaking loose, thread by thread and no doubt in five years when I return, the last will have given away, I will find myself a stranger in my boyhood stomping ground. I have not heard from Smoker in a year, 18 months I should say.

I am plugging along pretty well in the same ruts every day. I have some books along and try to pick up a thing or two while I wait. I will be at Ft. Sheridan, Ill. from now until about April. I expect to be sent to New York for duty there in the Proving grounds. Remember me to all. This carries very best wishes for all.

Your loving nephew.
Fred H. Coleman

Fred H. Coleman at Fort Sheridan, Illinois, to Cornelia Dickson in Ouachita Co.

4/4/09

My Dear Aunt Nealy:

Your letter dated Feb. 24 reached me alright and gave me a great deal of pleasure. I was sorry however to learn that you were not enjoying the best of health just at the time of writing. I trust that ere now well at yourself again.

I am the one to feel forgotten now and then as I scarcely ever hear from any one down in there. Just recently however I have been more fortunate as I not only had a letter from Cousin Attalie [Rumph Gaughan] and little Attalie has had a fine cake from the latter. I think that is doing pretty well for a beginner.

We live in comfortable quarters with electric lights, water works hot and cold and plenty of hard coal right in the house. At present the spring is still in the background and we don't know but what its still winter.

Give my regards to Uncle Allis, Harry, George, and the rest. I don't know when I will be down in those old diggins. Attalie said something about my coming down to her wedding* but I fear there will be nothing doing in this luxurious life of pleasure for me yet awhile with that $184.00 shopper hanging around.

Well Aunt Nealy I'd like to see you all very much, only money and space controll us so. Write when you can. Regards to Miss Belle Gaughan, Aunt Clara, Cousins Lula & Cora and all,

Your loving
Fred

*Attalie married Jim A. Dunn. Her first husband Alex Gaughan died in 1886.

Blanche Fisher, wife of Harry Fisher, in Washington, D. C. to Allis Moseley in Ouachita Co.

May 18, 1909

Dear Uncle Allis,

I have been intending to write to you ever so long, but I guess you know how it is about writing.

Well, to begin with — I like Washington very much: better than any other place I ever lived. Every thing is awfully expensive here though. It takes every thing Harry makes for us to meet expenses & we have to live on short rations at that and you know I don't like that for you know how I love to eat.

I had about made up my mind to be satisfied though and was doing very well til I read your letter to Mother* and Oh how hungry I've been ever since thinking of all that good butter milk and butter and chickens and those

*"Mother" refers to Mary Arkansas Moseley Fisher, sister of Allis and Marvin Moseley, and mother of Harry Fisher, Blanche's husband.

delicious watermelons that are on the way. My, don't I wish I was there to enjoy them with you and to gain 5 lbs a week again, (for I need it).

Well, how are you making it these days? I know you are lonesome without me. What is George* doing and how is he? Give my love to Aunt Nealie and all of Uncle Marvin's family.

Tell Charlie and George I wish I was there to go to meeting with them in the wagon and go thumping and bumping over the road and singing and having a good time. Poor little Gordon* paid up for his visit but it didn't hurt the rest of us. He had chills and fever until we came here and then it ended up in a severe case of pneumonia.

I guess the next thing I hear you will be marrying again. Well, it would be the best thing for you, but don't marry anybody with children. Perhaps it will be Mrs. Coleman.*

Well, Mother and I are making it fairly well together, better than I expected. She hasn't had her rheumatism any since she came here; she stayed in very close during the winter and the house was well heated by steam so she has been better in every way. She looks so much better. She has been quite a good deal of help to me with the children.

I don't see how I have managed to get through this, for Mother and Granville [Blanche's son] both have been talking to me, and I can't hardly hear myself think.

I want you to write and tell me how you are all getting along. And when you are eating those delicious water-melons this summer, think of poor hungry Blanche and eat a piece for me.

Bye, bye, with lots of love to you all and a great big kiss for yourself from,

    Lovingly
    Blanche

Apt. 23 The Savoy

*"George" refers to George Boddie Moseley and "Charlie" refers to Charles Elijah Moseley, eldest son of Marvin Moseley.

*"Gordon" refers to Harry Gordon Fisher, youngest son of Blanche and Harry Fisher.

*"Mrs. Coleman" refers to Mamie Boddie Coleman. Allis Moseley, whose first wife was Carrie Boddie and mother of Harry and George, did marry a second time. His second wife Octavia Word Brodnax lived only 10 months after their marriage. Mr. Allis did not take a third wife.

Cornelia Dickson at Van Duzer to Mamie B. Coleman in New York City
                 Nov 28th 1909

Dear Mamie,

Yours of the 16th inst received several days since and I waited so as to write you a bit of news you were anxious about. Yes Godfrey's & Florence's fine boy* arrived all ok, Friday night. Dr. Rinehart, her mother, and Mrs Annie Stone, backed by Ann Ivins, were the officious parties on hand. Mother & son doing well. Godfrey kinder prostrated, reaction I suppose from mental excitement. I have not been able to go down and see them — am a little better of heart trouble but now have severe cold. Lillie Venable is here spending a week or two with me attending a Singing School, which

*This "fine boy" refers to George Gallie Coleman, son of Godfrey Coleman and Florence Pelt Coleman.

is taking the day here, or rather night, here now. I have not been out to hear them. Lilly is a smart pleasant girl, a good deal of help and company for me. You know Allis has her brother, Rosser, employed since last Spring. The school is at the church & they are out until ten oclock every night, except Sunday n[igh]t. Will close next Thursday night with a concert. They have had exceptionally fine weather for it. We have only had fires night & morning, can sit in the hall in the day. I have scarcely seen George or Ross since receiving your letter. Ross castrated your yearlings when he marked them & says they are fat & nice for beef now, if you want him to kill & sell them, as they are liable to be drowned this winter & he wants to work at the mill in Warren or somewhere. Says Godfrey said something to him about wanting to kill one of them. Uncle John Ivins has a good job down at Warren, comes home occasionally. I will see Geo. about the hogs soon as I can, he came late last night, but left soon after breakfast before I knew it, has not been back. I think he's getting up a "case" with <u>Ruby Stone.</u> Allis is still putting in his time on the road. Cora & Lula called at the gate Friday, all were well as usual up there. Old Mrs. Hawkins has been quite sick but is able to sit up some, George Rumph is at Mittie's under treatment for paralysis or mineral poison. I have not been able to see him. I received a letter from Bessie Wadsworth since I wrote to you. We were expecting her & Sis Carrie to come out to see us this fall. Sis Carrie concluded she could not stand the trip — so they gave it out. I was sorry & disappointed. They are living in Montgomery in winter to educate her children — 124 Martha St. Bessie has three daughters married.

  I received a very pathetic letter from Sallie Lon Dunlap last night. She still wants me to come & spend some time with her. Don't see how I can leave unless Mrs Fisher comes back which I think is probable — As when last heard from were on the eve of removing to Vicksburg; Harry had been given an agency there. Somehow I think being nearer she will probably come. I want to write to Sallie D. soon. If money was <u>plentiful</u> would like to go & see her and Sis C[lara] too.*

*This letter is unsigned in the ledger.

Mamie Boddie Coleman in New York City to Cornelia Dickson in Ouachita Co.

                   Dec 2nd, 1909

  My Dear Aunt Nelie:

  Your letter of 28th & 29th ult. has just been read and enjoyed more than I can express.

  On the night of the 26th I was sitting thinking of Godfrey and trusting God to keep all well, when a tap call[ed] me to the door and my landlady came in with a letter I thought before I took [it], but she instead of mail startled me as something unusual and then to find it a telegram. Of course Florence was my first thought. I could not open it for a few minutes, and Oh how relieved. Yet the shock I suppose, together with the effort required to meet the demands of telegram has kept me real striked [stricken?] all the week. It was from Fred, requesting me to meet one of his West Point young lady friends down town at one of the leading hotels at 10 a.m. Saturday morn, and then meet him at another, at 2 P.M. Well I did it. The young lady was both cultured and beautiful (at times & pretty at others). I played my part well I presume but have only been out 3 times since. Will go to the finest theater in city tomorrow evening, see "Anthony & Cleopatra," played by Mr. E. H. Sothern & Julia Marlowe.

Do you all read any of the New York papers? There are worlds of things here that are educational & don't cost you a cent save time & car fare. I'm so behind in everything that reading consumes much of my time. If I lived here I would live in the Libraries. They are so built and situated that it is a luxury to be seated at a table in any of them. Even if some one take[s] an opposite [seat] or by you (4 at table) they are so refined & quiet that you dont mind it in the least. I must stop. Ask me any thing you wish to call my attention to. I will be glad to give it. Wish I was near enough to give you my magi[z]ens. I have McClure. Current Literature, & Womans Home Companion. Trying to read the paper (some daily). I fail to do any justice.

Can't Lilly keep house for her brother and Mr Allis while you visit "Sallie"? I think it would be beneficial. Wish you [could] imbibe the new thought. Fortunately I always entertained it partially, unconsciously, or else I would never have been here.*

Fred is a noble dear boy. Gives me money every month & between if I need it. Not knowing anyone I need but little. Got another $69.50 dress the other day. But they have sale days here. I happen[ed] to get one of the bargains that day $59.50. Every body attends to their own business. I have a good time any and all the time. Attend lectures, concerts, zoos, Museum of Nat. History & Art, conservatories, & am going to try to get to visit the Observatory. The parks are simply grand & so many of them. I can watch the loveliest babies & children in the parks & streets, see their natural play and then some trying to teach others their kindergarden exercises. All, unconscious of being observed. Again, as this afternoon I went down to 125th St to get some shirt binding, a little miss not more than 5 did notice my observing her Skates (roler). Then she gave me a pleasant [look] as if to say "see", and for two blocks & across 126th St. She kept up her expert tricks on those Skates that would have been a credit to a much older boy or even man. I am glad to inform [you] that in one section of [the] city at least the Catholics failed to get the Bible out of the Public School. They were told that this was a prodistant country and if they wish to patronize the school they could do so, but they could only run their own school. This city is more

* Mamie doesn't identify the "new thought," but one wonders if it could have been the forerunner to "Women's Liberation."

catholic, jew & Irish, though cosmopolic. I have not said anything about my beeves. I hate to kill them so young, yet if Ross leaves I may lose them. I will write G[odfrey] tonight and if he does not let me hear from him, very soon I will write you, but write & not wait for that. I hope I may get something from my hogs, a little is better than nothing. When F. marries I will return (though no prospects now) and it is with that in view that I wish to have a few cents all my own. Again thanking you for that <u>very very</u> welcome letter I close with love to all friends & relatives, would like so much to see Mrs. F[isher] Give her my special love & tell her that her little peanut boy remembers her. Wish she could see him, & especially in full dress uniform.
       With love
       Mamie

Mamie Boddie Coleman in New York City to Cornelia Dickson in Ouachita Co.

Dec. 21, 1909

Dear Aunt Nealie:

How are you this beautiful afternoon? I'm appearantly suffering with cold but in reality it is only coal dust from furneces, as the house is dry heated & when they blow fire in basement if draft is not turned off, your room is filled with dust that can't be seen until it settles but with me I can feel it as well as breathe it. I begin sneezing at once, but don't if nostrils are well-greased with cold cream, suet or anything to catch the dust. I don't feel good today but that is all. I'm going to go <u>all</u> day tomorrow if it is not raining or snowing & every day that I can get out. Wish you all could see Xmas decorations. In fact there is enough here to keep you busy for a year or more just seeing, seeing & hearing. I have not had a paper in two days & must stop & read because I have only two nights in which to finish <u>Faust</u>. It will be played Xmas day afternoon or night & Fred took it to the Hook & just brought it back & of course expects me to read it in a day & quote 1/2 of it. Well, I'm learning to be calm & quite selfpossessed, even when a machine "<u>took</u>" at your heels & fans you as you step from the street. My I believe those monsters of war are coming from the whistles I hear. Must go see them tomorrow if it is. They possess a strange facination for me. I have been over the Navy Yard in Brook[lyn] with F[red] & seen one being built, others in dry dock & others anchored. Gone over them on inspection tour. Talked with the sailors, Looked through their glasses & talked with captains. I may come home by water and again I want to go by Washing[ton], Richmond, Ashville, Atlanta, & Chickamauga to see relatives in Mont[gomery], Sunny South. But I will have to get map and look up my route, but I must see more north of me, Niagra & Don't know when I will return but I'm not making as good use of my time as I should. I have too much reading to do. I am half way inclined to go home & get ready for sight- seeing & enjoy it in earnest. Children don't know what they miss in not reading & studying the maps of [the] country & especially the maps & guides of cities before they ever start out. This kerchief you must use & waft me a kind thought whenever you do. If I only had the money I would have sent something worthwhile. There is so much & so lovely again so <u>much, so cheap</u> but so expensive to send that it is out of reach.

With much love to each of you
>Your loving Niece
>Mamie

Harry F. Moseley in Texarkana, Arkansas, to his father Allis Moseley in Ouachita Co.

April 2 1910

Hello Pop

You must be considerably improved. Able to walk to the barn and back and go buggy riding, and best of all, go to the table and enjoy a good meal of Steak. And they say you have bought you a buggy, well that is the limit, why didn't you get an automobile, they are the latest going. You could have been buggy riding these long years if you had been mind to. Well I hope you will soon be able to navigate without so much fatigue. Hope Geo[rge] is doing well with his crops. Have'nt time to write more as I have got to get back to camp and feed.

>Affectionately,
>Your Son
>Harry

William Allis Moseley and his sister, Mary Arkansas Moseley Fisher on the porch of the Boddie home, 1927. Photo courtesy of Nita Moseley Munoz.

Mamie Boddie Coleman in New York City to Cornelia Dickson in Ouachita Co.

7/31/1910

Dear Aunt Nealie:

    I have wanted to write you so often but the chief reason was knowing that it would be so long before I heard from you, and that very potent element, that is tucked away somewhere in my composition, to let the other fellow wait, prevails at all times, if there is any musical waiting to be done. I do enjoy your letters so much. It is such that I want from you because then I know how all are progressing. . . . Now I'm just back from service, one of the six best I ever heard from any pulpit. What denomination Reformed Dutch Church which is I think the Lutheran or Presby_____. But I would say if I did not know that he is now a Miss[ionary] Bapt. or Present <u>day Christian in life</u>, but Miss. Bapt. in membership. His church is in Brooklin & it is always <u>full</u>, but he is spending his vacations among the Union churches, that is the churches where union services are held every sunday for the summer months. Dr. Randles & family are in Europe (my church pastor of Mt. Morris Baptist Church, a <u>very rich church financially</u>.) & his church, 2 other Presby. churches & one Methodist church, hold only one service at one of the churches each month & one pray[er] meeting at which ever church, at which the 2 services are held on the Sundays of that mo[nth]. July service has been just a few doors from the East corner of 130 St. Next Sunday it will be in the Presby. church on 7th Ave, 129 St.; one blk S. & three W. from me. Though I may divide my time among other sects from now on just for information. All are open every Sunday. I see in yesterdays papers that the Pope is again feeling Uncle Sams pulse on the Catholic question. Poor Spain. May God save Her and us. It is only a question of time when it will have to be settled here.

    Where is Harry? I cant get a hearing from him. I want again his address. I think he must leave by the time you write me & then he of course misses my letter. How [I hope] Mr Allis will someday be brought to know God & Jesus as his Redemmer.

    How is Cousin* & Cousin George [Rumph] & all of them, not forgetting Attalie. Now last but not least if your feet are not cured try my course of treatment & mine were worse than yours but I now walk all day & never tire or hurt. Get a pr. of shoes a no. too large, get a pr. of <u>arches</u> (50 cts pr. will do, <u>not the</u> curved up ones), to fit your instep, plane straight ones, get 3 boxes of acorn salve & a pair of felt soles. Each night rub the hard calous place on your foot with acorn salve, leave on a good coat of it, tie up in cloth & go to bed, next morn take off salve rags (to be replaced that night & every [night] until calous is pulled of & place <u>not</u> sore & soft) then put on hose, then put arch in shoe, & the felt & cork sole on top of it with cork side next

*"Cousin" refers to Coralie "Mittie" Rumph Rucks.

foot or on upper side, & in less than a week you will thank me for telling you this, & Cousin Attalie needs arches too in her shoes. Remember me to all & have a chat with Godfrey before writing me.

With love from
                Your niece
                Mamie

Pardon haste.

John R. Boddie in St. Louis to Mamie Boddie Coleman in New York City
  *NEW CORNELIA COPPER COMPANY
  Successors
  CORNELIA COPPER COMPANY
  Paid Up Capital $3,000,000
  Ajo Pima County Arizona Ter.
              April 7, 1911

*The letterhead of this letter.

Dear Mamie:

Godfrey Coleman
Photo courtesy of Ruth Boddie Farmer

Yours of recent date to hand. Happy to hear from you, but sorry to learn that Fred is not as happy as a young groom should be. He has followed my advice and instructions in all matters except his love affairs, which he consulted me about time and time again, and I gave him instructions had he followed he never would have been in any thing but a happy state. I preferred seeing him wait until 30 or over before marrying, and then get a girl about 25, of good christian character, fine physique, cultivated mind and whose family contained no closeted skeletons. But he followed my instructions in all things but his love affairs, and I know now and did know from the first it was advice wasted telling a man about what was best for him in marrying, but he asked and I gave it, otherwise, should never have said a word. Now, that he has made his own bed let him sleep in it.

    I enclose a copy of the letter I wrote him on the eve of his marriage and in congratulating young married folks, I always take the position that most any kind of a girl is quite good enough for the best man. About 99% of all the meanness and cussedness in life originates with the men. Fred will just have to boss with a quiet iron hand, and the sooner he is transferred to the Philipines, far away from all her relatives, all the better for both.

Am getting along fairly well. Smoker I judge from the way he writes is fast improving. He has been dinging at me for the old home so long and concluded to turn it over to him. What he and Godfrey are up to I don't know and have no time to bother about. S.thinks the sun rises and sets in Godfrey. Love to all,

Your affectionate brother,
Jno. R. Boddie

Mamie Boddie Coleman in Philadelphia to Cornelia Dickson in Ouachita Co.

May 11, 1911

Dear Aunt Nealie:

You will pardon this hasty note. When I tell you that I write under a <u>great pressure</u> that of having too much dinner, strawberry short cake & cream. Yes I am ashamed of having done such a beastly thing and I will not again be guilty of such. I promised to write you today for the strawberry wine receipt or rather Mama's blackberry wine receipt as that is the one I used in making my strawberry wine. Helen [Fred's wife] says strawberries will be 50 cts per quart the later part of this month & Fred is anxious for me to make some wine so please send it to me at once. I have no receipts at all with me. You may send me any others you wish but I wish that one in particular. I would be glad to have a grape wine receipt also, for the preserves & jellie. I think there will be a fine crop of grapes. I certainly am a lady of leisure, but for the life of me I cant accomplish what I wish during a day. I'm trying to get old clothes in shape to wear out. Never again will I have any thing that I cant wear out. I was always too busy with work (household) before to go worn, now I'm free at least for a while. I intend to get to work for a rainy day as this can not always last and I have sufficient time to make a fortune yet.

When I decide what I shall do & where to locate. I would rather stir up & instill life in Ouachita Co. farmers than aught-else, but that is just a bit more than I care to undertake. I see here, all that I advocated at home, relative to planting many crops on same piece of ground. A deep plowing and harrowing in the fertilizer & after that hand plows with drills & all the attachments that go to the single & double gorse plows. One man does as much as 4 at home & work less, that is only 8 hours per day or 10. If the

Mary Gilder Coleman Bagwell
Photo courtesy of Ruth Boddie Farmer

farmers would only systematize their work & keep things under control out of the weather — The South has every advantage over the North & no excuse for not growing rich. I was disappointed that a compulsatory school law was not past in last legislature. If a few of the boys were educated here in these manufactories & mechanical schools & begin work in the South & not wait for Northan capital, things would soon change up. I don't see why the South waits for the North to monopolize the whole world. The South will never know how to make a success of manufactoring until they enter their schools & factories for such & when they once get started it will not be dependent on the North. Just a few days since, I had a clerk to ask me if it was really true, that rice was raised on the same ground or in the same field with corn & cotton. I found out that he wanted to know if the slash land* was that land planted to rice. I told him yes, & he replied that within two years he would own a farm in Ark. The father of Freds wife succeeded his father in the paper business & his son is studying during his vacations in his fathers mill, & the other is in a woolen textile school in Mass. They never do any work themselves after they thoroughly understand every phase of the business, beginning with the raw material & up to the finest finished product of the mill. They employ hundreds of laborers & they are worked harder than any negro in the South ever worked & if compulsory education is not introduced & enforced, also missionaries, right here in these over crowded cities, there will be darker days than the world has ever known, things are bright enough on paper but walk the streets, or travel in either subway, elevated or surface cars & note the class of people from 6 A.M.to 8. & from 4:30 to 8 P.M & you will see how many children are out of school & the class of citizen that will figure in the laws of state & country. I'm not in the least pesimistic but there is a lot of suffering that might be avoided if each would be just a bit less selfish and give more thought and time to helping those that are not capable of helping themselves. I guess you think me crazy but these waifs of poor people, slaves for want of education, appeal to me more than the metropolitan art museum. Human souls starving for human sympathy in a Christian country. If I had the money to help my own I would give my life to helping those that are needing help morally & physically.

Spring is in full sway here and I revel in the beauty of the Arsenal grounds & walks. I seldom stay on the walks. The grass is too tempting. All of the flowers are out doors now, but only a few blooming. Geraniums & daisies, Yes pansies & violets. The whole daffodil family have bloomed, May flowers now, but these are only in the garden & not on beds as the hot house plants. Which are bedded out every Spring & cuttings & plants put back in the fall for the next Spring.

Write me at once & a long letter. I suspect we will be here another year Address me Phila., Pa c/o Gen. Delivery. Love to All
                Your niece
                Mamie

*Slash is defined as a tract of wet or swampy ground overgrown with bushes or trees.

Florence Clifton Boeshear in Columbus, Ohio, to Mittie Rumph Rucks in Camden

April 4, 1913

Dear Aunt Mittie:

Received your letter this P. M. upon my arrival home from the office. Mama [Florence Rumph Clifton] had also received one from Mrs Felsenthal.

I thought of writing you people in regard to the flood, but thought too, that the accounts you would receive through your papers would not be of such a character as to disturb you.

Yes, we've had some dreadful times here. It was so sad & dreadful in many cases. As for ourselves, we live on one of the highest points in town, high as the State House dome, which stands in the center of the city 3 miles to the south of us. The Olentangy river is about 3 or 4 blocks to the west, perhaps 7 or 8 & down grade all the way. The Scioto is still six or seven miles west of us up here. Down town the two rivers flow together & the levee broke in two places. Only one downtown bridge was left & one over the Olentongy at 5th Ave. in the northern part of the city. High St. the main street, is about 100 ft higher than the river downtown & is only three blocks east. The river divides the town. The West side is low for quite a distance west to where high ground commences, which is called "The Hilltop." They have had a number of floods over there where the water came into the lower stories & the people would merely move upstairs until it was over. These have never covered much territory. But when these breaks occurred in the levee, those who had not heeded the warning given were simply caught like rats in a trap. Houses were simply carried away & banged to pieces. This happened Tuesday morning. I had stayed home & knew nothing about it till the man showed up who was doing the papering. The rain kept up almost continually for several days. Tom* came up Tuesday afternoon in the machine* & took us around to different unusually flooded points. Fifth Ave bridge was entirely covered & water several blocks to east. It was worse than anything I had ever seen. Only one house had stood between dry ground & the bridge, however, which was a little green frame cottage. Of course it was gone. We went down several residence streets & saw people coming from their houses across chairs. This was only back water & wading depth. It seemed impossible to me for such a thing to occur on these streets, yet there it was.

We then went to the down town bridges, the Broad St bridge was still standing there. No one could tell what was happening across the river because no one could reach there. But Wednesday people began to do things & the City Hall was turned into a station for refugees. I stayed home that day also. Tom hauled people over the one remaining bridge to the City Hall all day. A great many people with machines did this. People on the other side

*"Tom" refers to Thomas Hess Boeshear, Florence's husband.

*Exactly what Florence calls a machine we are unable to determine. It could be an automobile or a boat.

& the authorities had gotten all the boats possible & reached all they could & brought them to this side. The current was so strong they couldn't reach some people who were marooned in buildings, but they tried in every case to throw them bread & other things to eat. Thursday I went down to the office & the whole building was confusion. I saw people brought in who had not eaten for several days & even wet up to their knees where they had stood in water. It was terrible.

I had several friends on west side. Most of them lived on the high ground but several did not. They all escaped with their lives, however, except a Mrs Wey & her oldest daughter, who were drowned. They were near the levee. Mr & Mrs Wey & two of the girls were at home and moved upstairs but the water wrecked their home & they got out the back window onto drift. The youngest girl & Mr Wey were picked up by boats later. Mr Wey was knocked senseless & later saved himself by clinging to a tree top.

One man & two of his children stayed in a tree for two days. He tied the girl in but she froze to death. The boy died after being rescued; lost his mind. Two of my friends were drowned while trying to rescue people. Edwin Damsel & Probation Officer Sexton. The former, a young man left a wife & three little tots & the latter in his 30's handsome & so nice — leaves a wife. 86 bodies have been recovered so far. Saturday afternoon Tom had a military pass & took me to the Hillrop via the 5th Ave bridge & 14 miles around over Fishinger's bridge over the Scioto — north of the storage dam yet. When we came back we came straight through west Broad St which is the principal street running east & west through Columbus right through the remaining water. People were already sweeping the water out of their houses, hanging out carpets, etc & trying to clean up. It was an awful looking mess, I think I'd move out & leave the whole pile of junk to rot. Some of the houses burned, but only to the water line. Some people on the side streets were still marooned in the upper stories, but were comfortable & seemed satisfied. Everyone we saw seemed cheerful.

Our chief errand was to take a lady over to the Imbecile Asylum to adopt a baby which had been rescued, but his father had shown up, so we came back empty handed. Houses were overturned & piled around in the middle of the streets, but Broad St seemed pretty clear. One Dry Goods Store window was just as it had been arranged except for mud over everything. Other stores looked as though they were piled full of drift.

The Singer Co had over 200 machines unpaid for in the flooded district, over a hundred have been gathered in & they are fixing them up & making them over. The piano stores suffered as did also the installment furniture firms.

Tom brought over one old couple who saved only a pair of new shoes belonging to the wife & to which the husband was clinging for dear life. Oh, there a hundred & one incidents I could tell you, but it would take a book.

It must have been terrible to have seen your neighbors floating down stream & be unable to help them. People knocked holes in the roofs & crawled out on top & even then were sometimes washed off.

The section flooded was not the most substantially built. Mostly cheap frames inhabited by the working class of people. To added to the general panic it was reported Wednesday that the dam had broken & even soldiers & policemen ran up High St warning all stores to close & get out & making so much din & racket with their automobiles etc that everybody down town was in a panic. I was at home, but I heard several say it was a sight to see vehicles & people making for the East & North ends. Telephone girls screamed into every receiver that was taken down & they had people way up on this high ground hysterical.

Tom came home about that time to take down some clothes I'd gathered together for the people brought to the City Hall & Miss Sullivan, a friend, called up & said she'd just heard the Storage Dam had broken & I said I hardly thought it possible but if it did I couldn't see anything to get excited about (I know how high we are & I know how high the dam is). She told me afterwards that I cooled her down more than anything else that had happened.

Mr & Mrs Boeshear & Mr Hull (a Singer employee) appeared on the scene a little later absolutely blue in the face. I thought something terrible must have happened. Finally they managed to gasp, "The Storage Dam has broken" & I said, "Well, what if it has?" Under the circumstances it couldn't possibly do any more damage or cover anymore ground than had already suffered owing to the fall. People didn't think for themselves at all — they just let somebody excite them without grounds. The dam did not break & I dont think it ever will. Its one of the most substantial in America. Tom immediately returned to town & we never let the matter take up any more time or attention. I sent his folks away perfectly contented I think. He came just as they were leaving & they seemed satisfied that everything was O.K.

I heard several ridiculous little happenings. A traveling man at the restaurant Saturday night told us of a woman who was trying on shoes in a shoe store when this dam report came & she rushed out with one shoe on & got into her machine. The clerk followed with the other shoe & went up the street lickity clip. Another woman up north grabbed a suitcase & threw something in it. She later opened it & found a sheet & an Easter egg. Some of the most (seemingly) sensible people did some of the most ridiculous things.

Dayton is a worse sufferer I guess. Their trouble is right in the main thoroughfare & they had so much fire. A neighbor just returned from there (having gone to see about relatives) & said looters were so terrible — were cutting off live people's hands to get rings, etc. Some jumped in water to get away. Dayton was such a pretty town, too.

Everyone seems to have the nerve to begin over & they are cleaning up as fast as they can. The problem of starting them out again with furniture etc confronts the authorities now. There's been no trouble about food & clothing. Money has run short though now.

Sorry I havn't more cheerful things to write about, but of course everyone's time and attention is taken at present with the conditions confronting the city.

Business of course is killed for the time, but everyone predicts that with a little leniency on the part of foreign creditors, things will straighten up in 60 days or 3 mos & there'll perhaps be a boom.

West siders still stick to their little old west side. I wouldn't give them a nickel for the best lot over there. I prefer my own little North End where I'm high & dry. We get all the wind that's coming however, & I hate wind & earthquakes (my chief objection to California.)

Am glad to hear Uncle George [Rumph] has such good prospects of health. Hope he is not disappointed now in the new doctor & his promises. Wish you would strike something good now & perk up & come to see me.

I was somewhat surprised in regard to Maud's baby. Don't understand why hers should receive the extra attention, however, unless its the name. I'll bet he doesn't come up to Dillion's little girl.

Tell Louise Gee I'm safe & sound & trying to help others. Glad to know she thought of me.

What took Allie [Gaughan Barr] to Brazil? You remember you told me of Fred & Helen [Coleman] not going to meet her. I have not heard from them for ages & ages. However, I think it was probably a matter of Helen's choice in the matter. She's a rather — well peculiar disposition you might say. She likes a person or else she doesn't & she isn't long deciding anything. She's somewhat jealous also & I think perhaps — well perhaps I'd better not think anything at all out loud. She's a quiet little girl but is all right when you once win her over. I wish she had gone to meet Allie. They are so similar in some ways. Helen likes "a good sport" as she expresses it & I think Allie would fill the bill. She's very anxious to see Fred's old home [The Boddie Home]. Am afraid she's a little too aristocratic to appreciate it, although she thinks the ferry boat must be grand — never saw one of its kind. She's very lively — Red hair disposition & all. Quite athletic. Can swim & dive & do most everything. Very affectionate. She's quite a combination and hard to understand.

Well must say goodnight. Am getting chilly in here & there's no fire. Think I'll go to bed. Tom is not home yet. Is quite busy now-a-days.

Lots of love to all of you. Tell all the rest of the folks that we're O.K. only suffered from seeing others suffer.

Lovingly,
Florence

Cornelia Dickson in Harmony Grove to Sallie Boddie, wife of Robert L. Boddie, in Camden

Apr 18, 1913

Dear Sallie,

I talked with Carrie Gaughan on the phone* yesterday and she told me that you had been trying to get me several days ago. Well our phone line has been out of business for a week or more & though every one on the line was disconnected no one took time to attend to getting it repaired. But when parties commenced putting in a new line found ours tangled & mashed down with timber that the high winds had thrown across it. It is all right now. Carrie said Robert wanted some of Allis' watermelon seed. Will take pleasure in sending him some. I want to see all of you so much but hardly ever leave home even to visit the neighbors — have so much to do & can hardly keep up. Have not been to see Mittie yet. Clara seems so feeble almost hate to leave home, though I seldom get to see her.

Sallie this is the first letter that I have written in a long time. I feel so sad about Sis Carrie's condition & poor Bessie having so much trouble.* I dread to hear from them. Allis & George [Moseley] are as busy as bees every day, the weather permits, in the crop. Corn planted, realized quite a profit from his peanuts last year. Intends planting again. Prepared his watermelon patch several weeks ago, but has not planted yet. George seems quite popular in the community and with the County officials, as they gave him the road again this year. He keeps an eye on the road, but realizes the needs of the farm to back him and I feel proud Sallie that he is a "little hustler." Has bought four mules & a horse. Allis sold all of his mules except one. So you see the boy has to hustle. He has grown so much you would not know him but for his resemblance to his mother* and to Robert. At times reminds me of Brother George. Our old neighborhood is looking up, <u>some</u> Automobiles passing frequently. Have a social club that meets quite often at the school house. Sometimes a debate or a play or a social function of some kind. I have attended twice and was real well entertained. The last time 'twas a play — and <u>fine</u>. We have a good school. You remember Miss Laura Horn. She is teacher & takes a lively interest in the club.

It was real sad about Cora losing her sweet little baby boy. He was so fine & promising. She & Jim were so grieved to give him up. I feel so sorry for them . . . All they can do is to console them with their blessings, and try to live right.

Clara is up again and seems much better. Lula & Mr Lynn are all right. With love to all must bid you good night.*

*The telephone "party line" has appeared in rural Ouachita County!

*Sis Carrie and Bessie are Cornelia's sister and niece, respectively, who live in Alabama.

*George Moseley's mother was Carrie Boddie Moseley.

*This letter is unsigned in the ledger.

Cornelia Dickson in Ouachita Co. to an old friend Jennie Dowsing in Prattville, Alabama

Feb. 1914

My dear old friend,

Yes, but not forgotten by any means, even though many years, with their joys and sorrows, have come and gone, since we last met. But letters from my relatives around Prattville have often mentioned you as one of my inquiring friends, & so often I have said to myself, "I must write," but each time some intervening incident or care prevailed. My life has been so varied since coming out here & for years I could not hear at all from Ala. though I frequently wrote. My happiest, most satisfactory days were spent in teaching. That was <u>twenty-five yrs ago</u>. Then my niece Carrie Boddie Moseley died — leaving two little boys with a request for me to help raise them, the younger [George B. Moseley] just eleven months old — the other [Harry Fisher Moseley] three yrs old. I cared for them 12 yrs & then their father [Allis Moseley] married again — but his wife lived only ten months & the boys and their father begged me to come back & live with them again, which I did, but my health began to fail last summer. I was very sick several weeks. I spend most of my time with relatives who have been exceedingly kind & nice to me. John B[oddie], my nephew of St. Louis, is at present boarding me with my nephew Godfrey Coleman & wife, who occupy the old Boddie home. With a heart full of love,

    Your old friend
    C. S. Dickson

Write soon.

Cornelia Dickson in Ouachita Co. to Ada Dunn in Prattville, Alabama

Feb. 1915

Dear Ada,

It has been so long since I had a letter from you I scarcely know where to address this to you but hope whoever reads this will forward it to you. I am in hopes you are still in Prattsville. After receiving your last, I was taken very sick with flux, was in bed three weeks, my recovery for a while despaired of. Well I am slowly gaining my usual strength & health. Have moved again — am now living with Godfrey Coleman & wife [Florence Pelt] at the old Boddie home. John Boddie has had the house renovated almost new and comfortable. He said he wanted me to come & live there and he would pay my board to Godfrey & Florence. I was so feeble, felt like I was not able to keep house for Allis and the boys, & as Mrs Fisher, Allis's sister was still there to keep house, I came down here. Godfrey & Florence have ever been nice to me, want to make me feel comfortable and at home. Allis said I could go if I wantd & <u>come back</u> if I should want to at any time.

Last November 19, I lost my sister, Clara Dickson Dunlap. She lived only a few miles from here and was a source of comfort to me. My sister, Caroline Boddie Love, who lived there in Autauga County, Alabama, died June 3, 1913. You probably know that. I am the last one in my family, and at times I am so lonely. But I do have such thoughtful and loving nieces and nephews, and a multitude of faithful friends. I visit around with different ones when I feel well.

Ada Dunn in Alabama to Cornelia Dickson in Ouachita Co.

September 16, 1915

Dear Aunt,

I was so glad to rec a letter from you — but so sorry to hear of dear Cousin Mittie's death — bless her dear soul I have often thought of my visit to her and fully intended going again some of these days — but now she is gone I do feel so sorry for cousin George for in loosing her, I know he feels the best and truest friend he ever had has been taken from him. I do miss my dear old mother [Caroline Lafayette Boddie Love, "Sis Carrie".] so much — life has never felt the same since she died and it was such a comfort to know that I could nurse her in her last helpless days — her mind failed for several months before she died and we had [to] watch her very close for she was very weak, did not seem to suffer, only at times she had rigors, while they lasted her suffering were great — but the dear old darling could never tell us where the pain was, we just had to treat her like a baby. I know it [is] very bad for you at cousin Mittie's home — but dear Aunt think what a comfort you are to Cousin George [Rumph]. What would he do without you. How is Cousin George provided for & did he realize any thing from the mines in Mexico? Crawford was in St Louis last winter but did not see either Cousin John or Tom, said he heard that Cousin Tom had gone back to Camden. You write as though none of Cousin Mittie's boys was at home and you didnt know what disposition they would make of the place — My home too is broken up — my last and youngest boy left for school at Auburn Ala. this week — if he complets his education it will take him four years — he graduated with good honors at our County High School — making a record of twenty over, I

Clarissa (Clara) Dickson Dunlap in later years. (1836-1913) Photos (including facing) courtesy of Sue Martin Russell.

*Editor's Note: The paragraph beginning "Last November 19" is included in the typewritten transcripts, but we are unable to find it in any of the original copies. We include it because of the information contained therein.

*This letter is unsigned in the ledger.

believe the average is fourteen — he will take some engineering course. Annie teaches latin and English in one of our States High Schools, Fannie will teach this winter where she taught last year, a small place called Stony Joint. My three oldest boys farm Lanier farm for the big Smith farmers of this [area]. Gee and Boddie have good positions in wholesale houses in South Ala — both are good Christian boys and fine business men.

Gee is married but has no children — poor Lanier looses all of his — last five all born dead. Perry has one sweet little girl not quite two years old. Nora has four children. She does not live very far from me. Doesn't it seem strange the little rascal you used to spank so much is now grandmother — yes really I am sixty years old. Poor Onie's family is all scattered too — she lives near Birmingham. I seldom see Bessie her troubles have made her so bitter that she seems to care but little for any thing — she lives on one of the river plantations and has the most of her family with her, but they are not a pleasure to her and her life is a hard one. I see Miss Jennie D. right often and we often talk of you. I carried your letter to her last week she seemed so glad to read it. Mr. Jim Howard is tax assesser for our county, asked me for your address, said he was going to write to you did he? Well dear Aunt of all the lovely lives in the world, I think poor Kate Love is the most to be pitied — she lives on the old place yet, seemingly without one soul to love, or one to love her. Everything is so changed around our old home I just cant bear to go there, nothing seems the same. Mrs Tyus is the only living old neighbor that is left, — and most of the younger are dead or gone some where else. Miss Julia Howard lives in Wilcox County. Miss Bettie keeps house for Mr Jim Howard. Fannie's and sisters boys are living on the places that their fathers left them — they are all married and Tom Wadsworth has a large family. Give my love to Mrs. Mitchel and may the good Lord help her to bear the burdens He has seen fit to cast upon her. I have tried to write you a little of every thing that I thought would interest you, hoping you will excuse all mistakes and poor writ-

Caroline Lafayette
Boddie Love
(1825-1913)

John Franklin Dunlap
(1828-1898)

ing. I never write with a pen as I am so nervous. Dont wait until you have sad news to write — but try to write me as often as your time will permit —
With much love to <u>all</u>

        Your niece
        Ada Dunn

Cornelia Dickson in Ouachita Co. to Smoker Boddie in Ashdown, Arkansas

        [Unknown month] 1915

Dear Smoker,

Waitie Butler &
Smoker Boddie
Photo courtesy of Ruth
Boddie Farmer

Your most welcome letter received several weeks since. Should have written ere this but am just recovering from the bad effect of the Grip, was sick about three weeks but not confined to bed more than three days, just up & down. I wanted to write you right away but was not able to.

I wanted to tell you of Sis Mollie's treatment when she had Pneumonia — was up but gained no strength, rather grew weaker. I wrote John of her condition - - for him to send her Phillips'es Phosphate of Wheat, a constructive in Nervous and Wasting diseases. A Nutrient tonic. John had to send to New York for it, but in three days after using it Sis Mollie said she felt a decided change for the better, and continued to improve until she was as well as ever. I felt like you should know this Smoker for I can appreciate your uneasiness about Mr. & Mrs. Butler. Mary Gilder says she keeps this medicine now all the time for her family use. She gave me a bottle two yrs ago that benefited me greatly. She gave me the address. You can send to <u>New Orleans</u> and get it. It is one pt for $1.00 —
    J. L. Lyons
    New Orleans, La.
I hope you & Waitie are still improving. Let me hear from you soon.
    Affectionately
    Aunt Nealie

Smoker Boddie in Ashdown, Arkansas to Cornelia Dickson in Ouachita Co.
                                                            Sept 7, 1915

    Dear Aunt Nelie —

    Your kind and <u>most</u> welcomed letter came this morning. I am deeply grieved to learn of the death of Cousin George Rumph, but of course realized sometime since that he could not get well, but cannot understand why kind heaven should have allowed such a <u>good</u> man to be so afflicted & to have suffered such untold agony. He was certainly a friend to me and <u>true</u> to the great principle of <u>righteousness</u> and <u>morality</u>. Having lived with him so long in an Arizona copper mining camp, I <u>knew</u> him as perhaps few did, and am confident that our Father in heaven has given him a cordial welcome into that great celestial city.

    My dear little girl Waitie has been sick now with Typhoid fever for 24 days, am glad to report however that she is doing nicely and without backset. Am confident that she will pull through O.K.

    I trust Aunt Nelie that you will continue to enjoy good health, which is by far the greatest of all blessings. Your kindness to others who are friends & kindred of mine and especially toward my dear grandmother (& mother) I shall <u>never</u> forget, and I feel that if we are not fully repaid for such deeds here on earth, there is ample reward awaiting us in the great beyond.

    Waitie joins me in love and best wishes for you & all, and we hope to see you some time in the future, when we regain our health.

                     Your affectionate nephew,
                     Smoker Boddie

Cornelia Dickson in Camden to her friend Bettie Dunaway in Appomatox, Virginia
                                                            Oct 8th, 1915

    Dear Bettie,

    I surely do remember you, and often wonder as to your where abouts & prosperity in this ever changing life. Yes! I have sad news for you. George Rumph quietly went to sleep, and in that manner passed to his eternal rest, last Sunday morning, the third of October, a few minutes after ten oclock. His many friends & relatives attended the funeral services and brought beautiful flowers — in token of their esteem and love. We all miss him and Mittie so

                     As ever,
                     Your friend,
                     Cornelia S. Dickson

Cornelia Dickson in Camden to John R. Boddie in St. Louis

Oct 30th 1915

Dear John

I have been wanting to hear from you. When you were here you were suffering with Rheumatism — I have been in that fix myself. Hope you are all right ere now.

Well it flashed through [my] mind this morning, Today is yours & George B. Moseley's birthday. I am sending you something I know you will like to see — "Resources of Arkansas" by the State Historian of the U.D.C. [United Daughters of the Confederacy] Mrs. J. T. Sifford. I enjoyed reading it so much.

I am at Attalie [Rumph] Dunn's yet. Tom R[umph] is all right again, thank God, by a narrow pull this time. Poor boy! All of us are well. I expect to move to Jim & Cora Martin's when I go over the river. Matt & family are all right, Maude is visiting her this week — She expects to go back to Colorado sometime this fall. With love & best wishes for many returns of this day to you —

    Affectionately
    Your Aunt
    Nealie

John R. Boddie in St. Louis to Cornelia Dickson in Ouachita Co.

November 2nd 1915

Dear Aunt Nelie:

Your kind and appreciated favor of the 30th duly to hand and read with great pleasure.

Being written on my 37th (?) birth day, I accept it as a birth day present. These reminders carry me back to the time I first made my debut on life's stage, when the curtain rung up for me to begin my life's stunt. All was rosy then and the future seemed teeming with fruits of great moment and applause. Now, on the last quarter of lifes play, I look back and realize that I have left undone many things I ought to have done and done many that I ought not to have done, as the preacher would say, and the time is near at hand when my stunt will end and lifes' curtain be rung down. I only pray that I may [be] as ready to go as was my sainted Mother, whom I think of every day and who so long as living never forgot her oldest boy on his birthday.

I thank you for the pamphlet, ARKANSAS, gotten up by Mrs. Sifford. It is very interesting, but overdrawn in some instances and not as full as should be in others, then too some errors. For instance she mentioned the founding of the "ARKANSAS GAZETTE in 1818, and that it is still published under that name, which is incorrect, it is now published as the LITTLE ROCK GAZETTE.* Several other inacuracies of minor importance. She omitted to state that the state bears the distinction of being the only one in the union that has had its name pronounced by an act of the legislature. She mentions Kaolin* as being shipped abroad, some samples may of been sent away, but no shipments and the mines are not being worked at all and are not very extensive. She mentions also a cement plant in Little River, there is none there, has been however, but in Little River county and a portion of Sevier adjoining there is the largest known deposit of lime chalk in the U. S. I have had it for sale for the past two years and herewith enclose a description of it.

One other item Arkansas leads the U. S. on and that is that more men have been hung at Ft. Smith, than any other place in the U. S. I presume this was one fact she did not care to publish. But upon the whole the pamphlet is alright and I would like to have one or two more copies if convenient to send them to me.

Happy to hear that poor Tommie is right side up again. How long will he remain that way? For heavens sake try and have his physician impress upon him the danger he is in being liable to pass away on account of his drinking any moment and endeavor to persuade to go off to some retreat where he can secure kind treatment and assist him in breaking off the habit that is surely killing him by inches and very fast ones at that. All hands work on him when he is duly sober and get him to do it. Never give up trying — many a poor fellow has quit in worse condition than he is. My lumbago hung on to me much longer than it usually does, but am about well now.

I may run down again last of present month. With love to all

I remain your affectionate nephew

Jno. Rumph Boddie

*I believe John Boddie is mistaken in this statement. As far as I can determine, the paper always carried the name ARKANSAS GAZETTE until her sad demise in 1991.

*Kaolin is a fine white clay used in the manufacture of porcelain.

Ada Dunn in Prattville, Alabama, to Cornelia Dickson in Ouachita Co.

Nov. 4, 1915

Dear Aunt

It has been sometime since I rec you most welcome letter in the mean time — I rec a letter from Cousin Cora — telling me of cousin George's death — while my heart goes out to you all in sympathy I feel that its best for his long sad life has ended and his sufferings are over, poor fellow it seems that he lived only to make mistakes to benefit those that seem to care so little for him. I have been quite sick since receiving cousin Cora's letter but am going to write to her real soon — have had a severe cold with catarrh and it has left with a very stubborn cough and that with having to break up home is just killing me & it seems that the boll weevil has given our farmers [such a] scare that it has completely demoralized them. My boys are not willing for me to farm under present conditions and my health is not so good. I reckon it is best that I do like my Dr advises — "take a rest" — so I am going to rest a while then go to Auburn to stay with Graham until be completes there and then dear Aunt the allotted time I prayed so earnestly for, fighten[?] long weary years, will be given me. Just to live long enough to educate all my children and see them useful men and women, has been my constant prayer, and I believe it will be answered to the last for with God's guidance I have never tired of the task of leading them on, — only three more years and I will be through. My fourth son Gee has a fine little son born last week, and I am expecting another by Christmas. I tell Miriam it had better be a <u>boy this time</u> too. I want you to send me the recp for citron* yours and Aunt Clara's too. You know the ladies here laughed at me when I told them about the little baskets of citron you used to make, no one seemed to ever heard of muskmelon citron, so I made a little basket for them — they were completely amazed to think any thing could be so pretty, — so much for your jams with me in the long age, but mine did not taste or look as good as yours — in fact it was not firm enough so I want you to send your old time recp — please as soon as you can I have some in brine that I wish to make before I move. I want to know just how long you let them soak in the alum and brime — My fifth son Boddie marries the 24th of this month. I like the girl very much but she is very young, only sixteen. You ask about Bessie's financial condition, Mr. Wadsworth estate owed more than it was able to pay — but his creditors give her the plantation known as the Pope place which would make her a nice support — if her sons would only help her, but they are worthless, consequently she has a hard time supporting them. She has one little girl at school yet that she is trying to educate but I am afraid that will be another disappointment for her, for I dont think the child is much given to study.

Saw Mr. Howard in town asked him about that letter he was to write you — he said he lost the address so I gave another to him. I felt disappointed for I thought I would be razing Uncle Jim by this time — See Miss Jennie right often — she is beginning to look feeble and dont seem to be cheerful by any means, it troubles her to have to live alone, and yet she cant adapt herself to other peoples ways enough to make it so she can live with them. Onie seems to be getting a little easier in the way of making a living. George's oldest daughter, Dixie, has been teaching several years gets good pay — his youngest girl will complete at one of the State Normal Schools this year — his oldest son has given him a good deal of trouble, am glad to see he is doing much better now. His other son is a remarkable fine little fellow, is great help to George and his sister at school. I think I have told you every thing except my troubles, maybe they will turn out a blessing —

*What Ada calls "citron" is most probably what we call "candied lemon or orange rinds," though it is a fruit in its own right.

but I do think some of my children might have spared me this pain in my old age, and come and lived with me, so I could have died in the home I love so dearly, but — God knows best, in him I trust — Goodbye with lots of love to all

> Your niece
> Ada

John R. Boddie in St. Louis to Cornelia Dickson in Ouachita Co.

January 4th, 1917

Dear Aunt Nelie:

Your kind favor of the 23rd received, I deeply regretted not being able to be with you during a few of the holidays. I leave for Arkansas tomorrow to look after my zinc mine in Searcy county, and will try and get down to old Ouachita between now and the 25th.

The history of the BODDIE FAMILY, is at last, about ready to be published, and in our immediate family some records are needed to be filled out, especially Aunt Carrie Loves family so please write me the address of one of her children most likely to be able to give the data on all the Love family and I will forward them the blanks as soon as I hear from you, some of which are already partially filled out. You will also please send me the dates of Cousin Mittie and Georges death, their record was written up a year before their death about a year ago, and it should be changed to the extent of giving their date of death.

> Love to all,
> Your affectionate nephew
> Jno. R. Boddie

Cornelia Dickson in Ouachita Co. to John R. Boddie in St. Louis

Jan 8, 1917

Dear John,

Yours of the 4th inst just received. Am sorry you did not get to come during the holidays. We rather expected you this week or some time soon. Godfrey and family are on a campment this week, Mary is with them. Mrs Pelt & George are visiting her daughter Mrs Kirklin Johnson in La. Harry and I are holding down the home 'til their return Friday.

In reply to yours, I have not had a letter from Alabama since last May, as I was down. Ada Dunn was there at Prattville, Ala. I believe she was to keep track of Sis Carrie's family record. It is certainly immence. Sis Carrie once wrote me that she had 50 grandchildren and 48 great-grandchildren, about five yrs ago. She died. George Love lives at Birmingham, Ala. Onie Northington also. Tom Love's widow & one daughter lives near Burnsville, Dallas Co., Ala. Mittie [Rumph] Rucks died the 4th of July at one o'clock AM 1915. George Rumph died at ten o'clock AM the third of Oct. 1915. Both passed away while asleep.*

*This letter ends abruptly at this point in the ledger.

Cornelia Dickson in Ouachita Co. to John R. Boddie in St. Louis

Aug 14, 1917

Dear John,

I received the paper you sent me all right. Many thanks. I have not been very well for several days.

Tom,* poor boy, succumed on the 10th at last. I went with Mr & Mrs Gaughan over to the funeral. It was just grand. The sermon by Dr. Monk and appropriate music & prayer. I feel that the poor boy is indeed at rest. He told Dr. Monk [several] days before that he was ready to go when his time came. I should have liked to have remained over several days with Attalie & friends but was feeling so badly, came back that morning & took medicine & feel better now. Smoker came with Sallie over to see us that evening and George Moseley came by next morning to bid me good bye.* Harry has been busy with his crop — registered, but has not been called yet. The boys feel very near to me. Harry remembers his mother; but Geo. says he never knew any mother but me. Since I left them say they have a sorry home with Mrs Fisher there.

When are you coming — hope you keep well & prosperous

Affectionately
Your Aunt
Cornelia S. Dickson

*"Tom" refers to Tommie Rumph. "Mr. & Mrs. Gaughan" are Dennis and Belle Gaughan.

* George Moseley left for the Navy Aug. 12th 1917.

George B. Moseley in training with the U. S. Navy at Newport, Rhode Island, to Cornelia Dickson in Ouachita Co.

Sept 8 1917

Dear Aunt Nealie

Guess that you think that I am not going to write but I have been pretty busy and its just lucky that you can write when you have any spare time for the only place we have to write is in the G.M.C.A. and that is always crowded so full untill it is almost impossible to get to write there.

I am feeling better than I ever felt in my life and an appetite such as I never had before. Just seems that I could eat up the world if I could get it in my mouth. Am just crazy for sweet things, cake, candy, pies, anything that's sweet and every one else here is in about the same shape. I don't know why it is unless it is because we get nothing sweet in our meals but just a small piece of cake. All of the cooking is done by steam and does not effect you as home cooking does but I can tell you that it is affecting me the best kind for I never can get enoug[h] altho I have plenty.

Have not had any thing but infantry drilling to do since I have been here and I like it all O.K. We have some of the best lectures, you would like to hear them, all about sea going. Everything is in a big rush and we don't expect to be here longer than the latter part of next week. I don't know where we will go from here but suppose that we will go South where we will train some more. Certainly will be glad to get further South too for it is a little too cool up here for me. We sleep under two blankets every night and you are not to warm then.

Our drill periods are much shorter than when we first came here and does not seem that we have done anything for the past week but pass in Review or go to some kind of intertainment, guess they are letting us have a good time before we ship.

Have not had any trouble and have been getting along just fine.

Got a letter from Fred Coleman today and was quite surprised, wanted to come over to see me, but I was unable to tell him whether I would be here long enough for him to do so or not, but told him to come the middle of next week if he could for I expected to ship some time the latter part.

Hope that everyone at home is well and tell every one that I am getting along fine, but don't expect to write many more letters from here as it always takes 8 days for an answer even if it is answered immediately upon receipt but will write every opportunity I have no matter where I may be stationed next.

This is certainly a wonderful summer resort up here but sure don't want to be here in the winter.

Well I hope to see you some time, maybe Xmas, I don't know, but take care of yourself and give my love to every one of the family and tell them that I think of them often and will write to them every opportunity when I get straightened out.

      Your nephew
      Geo. Moseley

Cornelia Dickson in the country to Belle Gaughan in Camden

Nov 1st 1917

Dear Belle

I often wonder if I will live long enough to do something to show my appreciation of the affection and kindness you and Dennis — and other kind friends, have shown to me.

I often think of it all — and wished that I was able to do something for you in return. I was almost stunned when I saw the very generous check your loving heart prompted you to leave for me, you dear good soul. It certainly lightened my heart — If I <u>can</u> do something for you I shall most gladly do so.

      Affectionately
      Your friend
      Cornelia S. Dickson

Cornelia Dickson in Ouachita Co. to George B. Moseley aboard the U.S.S. Maine

Nov [?] 1917

Dear George

Your most welcome letter of the 25 ult rec several days since. I am always so glad to hear from you George and that you are in <u>good health & spirits.</u> I feel that you are blessed and hope you will continue to feel well. Glad you rec your box in first class condition and enjoyed it so much, & hope I will see you at home Xmas, if only for a short visit, but if otherwise ordered, well, I will have to wait until you can come. Am glad to hear from you if only a few lines — it makes a bright pleasure in my life.

I have not seen your Papa or Harry in some time, your Auntie [Mrs. Fisher] has not been very well but the weather has not been very favorable for me to go to see them since the camp <u>hunt</u>. I guess your Papa has written you about it, as he, Nolan Pelt, your Uncle John, Arthar Puryfoy was included, also Godfrey, Robert, & Hubert

I heard they killed a wild turkey for Thanksgiving and over a hundred squirrels — but missed the deer every time. But had a fine time all the same. Then the next Monday Godfrey, Johnson Pelt, Arthur Puryfoy, who has but one arm, Old Mr Sanders, and his boy Arnold, Florence & her children went on a camp, & returned home Friday in sleet & rain, but were protected by wagon sheet, were just in time to avoid a very cold snap, that has lasted ever since with sleet, ice & snow. Last Wednesday morning Dennis Gaughan came in his auto after me to visit several days with his family, one of the most pleasant visits I ever enjoyed. I spent one morning with old Mr & Mrs

Hawkins — She is 87 and he is near 90. They seemed to enjoy my coming so much. I felt so much younger, only 78. With so many good friends, and relatives, and you and Harry seem so near & dear, now that you are called away. I have been busy knitting for the Red Cross. I <u>knit</u> in the <u>Civil</u> war, but I have not forgotten how, and am glad I can do my mite for the brave soldiers now.*

*The letter in the ledger ends abruptly at this point.

*Cornelia Dickson in Ouachita Co. to Mrs. Mary Lockett, Secretary of the Red Cross in Camden**

Dear Madam

I send in two more pr of socks. One pr of <u>gray</u> & thread left from that, & another pr of white and thread left from those. Also thread of dark gray, left from those sent in some time ago — I send all in as it may be needed by some one else. The last thread you sent me, <u>white</u>, was rather coarse & uneaven with knots now & then, which makes the knitting rather uneaven — I shall be glad to have you send me more thread soon as I wish to do all I can.

*This letter has no date but it can be safely assumed that it was written shortly after the previous one.

Yours truly
C. S. Dickson

Cornelia Dickson in Camden to George B. Moseley aboard the U.S.S. Maine
Nov 19th 1917

My Dear George

Your interesting letter of the 7th inst was duly received at home but as I was in Camden on a several weeks visit, Florence did not send it over until your Aunt Sallie & Attalie went over Wednesday to take your Aunt Mamie over on a visit and brought your letter to me.

I was very glad indeed to hear from you & that you were doing so well &c. Your picture was fine, save that very solumn, little unnatural expression on your face. Well never mind that — was glad to know you were in good health and comfortably situated. Of course I do not worry about you George, but I think of you very often, and hope for the best, and trust in God always, for He makes no mistakes. Feeling this way is very comforting to me. I have a great many blessings for which to be thankful.

I feel very proud that you are man enough to <u>do right</u> under all circumstances. I have full confidence in you and <u>that</u> is <u>one</u> of my blessings. I feel so interested in your letters. You have many warm friends who are always glad to hear from you.

I have spent two weeks with Mrs Rumph & Hattie, am now with Attalie

George Boddie Moseley
World War I
Photo courtesy of Nita
R. Moseley Munoz

Dunn. Mr Dunn has improved greatly in health and is now on a camp over at Webb Lake. Mr. Will Brown who has been here sick joined him yesterday. But so many are outing over there, they propose to remove to Pine Lake next week to squirrel hunt & fish. Garland Rumph was so glad to hear from you, says he thinks a lot of you. He has a new Auto and took me with his family riding last week to Marmaduke's Ford and Devil's Elbow — The river and surroundings looked beautiful, so inviting for picnicing.

Garland showed me the place where you hauled gravel for your road building. Mrs Purifoy says we never have had any good road over the river until a Moseley gets hold of it. Harry was on the road graveling when I came over. We then went to the Rockwell Manufactory establishment which I think is quite an acquisition to this town.

I will deliver your message to Godfrey when I see him. He has been quite successful with his potato crops, both Irish & sweet potatoes, not withstanding the drouth injured his corn & cotton crop. I suppose you hear from your papa & Harry about home affairs — I was not able to go to see them as often as I wished while they were in trouble about your Aunty — at that time I was not well at all — am getting much better, stronger since I came over here, expect to remain about a week longer with Attalie.*

*This letter is unsigned in the ledger.

Cornelia Dickson in Ouachita Co. to Jennie E. Dowling in Florida
Nov 28th 1917

Miss Jennie E. Dowling

Your sweet card came in this morning with your dear good wishes. I was truly, truly glad to hear from you, and that you were recruit again in balmy Florida. Yes, Jennie your dear letter was received two weeks ago & intended writing right away, but was suffering with severe cold and waited to become better of that. Am not feeling very stout yet, but considerably better. I had just come home from a five weeks most pleasant visit in Camden with relatives & friends, but your letters bring me so much pleasure. I love to think of you as one of my dearest friends. (I have been quite busy helping folks off on a camp hunt) I went over to Camden to stay mostly with

Brother John's last wife. If you remember his first wife was my sister [Sis Fannie] — was married to her when I was quite small — & always petted & seemed to me like an own dearly loved brother — when my sister died he married Sallie Gildersleeve. I guess you remember going to school with her in old Mulberry neighborhood. Well she too passed away leaving two little girls — both grew up & since I came out here, married. The younger Eugenia Earle died in 1904 leaving three children. Attalie married, first Alex Gaughan, he died leaving her a widow with two children, girls. The younger of whom married Walter Barr of Port St. Joe, Fla. Attalie married again, J. A. Dunn of Camden, has one daughter, Bessie Dunn. Brother John's <u>third wife</u> Mattie Proctor has 2 sons both married, and four daughters, all married except one. They are all fine characters Jennie, and seem so near and dear to me (now that my own sister Fannie's children have passed away.) I spent two weeks with Mattie & three weeks with Attalie & visited some with the others, and with Robert Boddie's family — the time passed all too swiftly. My home had been with Mattie [Rumph] when not away teaching school before dear brother John's death. She then moved to Camden to educate her children. I was then teaching in Dallas Co. She has ever treated me as an own dear sister & her children all seem to love me as an own Aunt. I have just heard over the phone that one of my friends wants to send for me to come tomorrow morning to stay several days, so will close for this time with love & best wishes. As ever affectionately your friend
       Cornelia S. Dickson

Belle Gaughan in Camden to Cornelia Dickson in the country
              Dec. 24th 1917

Dear Miss Neeley —

 I am sending you this dress hoping it will fit you and that you will put it on and remember it was made to wear and enjoy. Miss Maggie made most of the dress, that is her part of the gift. We could not finish it but it won't take you long to sew the large buttons down the front of hem — and put the fastenings on in front.
 Margaret and Mary send you the sizzors, hoping you will have a happy Xmas and that you can come to see us soon is the wish of your friend —
       Belle Gaughan
 If dress is tight across back let me know at once. I will bring a piece of goods and show you how it can be made more full. Miss Maggie thinks it will fit and I hope so. We didn't have time to even press as we should — We have had a busy day at store.

Cornelia Dickson in the country to Belle Gaughan in Camden
Shortly after Christmas, 1917

Many, very many thanks Bell and Maggie for your thoughtful loving kindness shown me in that beautiful Xmas dress. And Margaret & Mary's most appreciated present. I know I am blessed with some of the best friends an old lady ever had, & they show me kindness and attention in various ways. I feel so grateful, and I sincerely wish them all a prosperous & happy year.

As ever, affectionately
Your friend Cornelia S. Dickson

George B. Moseley aboard the U.S.S. Maine to Cornelia Dickson in Ouachita Co.
May 7th 1918

Dear Aunt Nealy,

It has been some time since I wrote you but haven't had any thing much to write about.

I am in good health and weigh 157#, always have plenty to do to keep me busy, and I guess that every thing is going as well with me as can be expected.

I have not heard from you in some time, but guess that you are well and getting along alright, "hope so at least."

Gee, but we are having some wonderful weather over here, have a nice cool sea breeze most all the time and every thing in shore looks so pretty and green untill it just makes one want to get out for a little recreation every chance they get.

I understand that you people are having quite a bit of rain and high water out there lately, hope that it has not done so very much damage.

Well I haven't any thing interesting to write so will close.

Write me whenever you can and tell me all the news. How Godfrey is getting along with his crop and what you have to eat and how every one's health is &c.

With best wishes for all, I am affectionately
Yours
Geo. Moseley

Cornelia Dickson in Ouachita Co. to George B. Moseley aboard the U.S.S. Maine

July 1st, 1918

My Dear George

Your most welcome letter of the 24 ult. rec in due time, was glad to hear of your good health &c, hope you will always come out all right — I am feeling very well considering the excessively hot dry weather we have had, began to fear the drouth would seriously injure crops as well as gardens — but since we have had several showers vegation seems somewhat revived. Jim Martin just ploughed on through the dust and things are growing right on. His hands seem to work very well too. Succeeded in saving his oat crop, which is a help for his stock. We have vegetables — plenty of milk & butter & eggs for the table — Oliver & Sue are enjoying their vacation, each have a wheel to go for the mail. Sadler has been in Cuba since last Aug, is now rifle drilling, was promoted to 1st Sargent. Cora hears from him about every ten days.

Harry is still in the farm but expects to be called at any time. I am glad he can be a help to your papa who seems so hard pressed with his work. Although so old makes a regular hand, besides the odd jobs that fall to him, says he works harder than he <u>ever did</u> in his life. So you see he is doing his best behind the trenches. And it is just that way all around. So many colored hands have been called from the farms. I heard that Dennis Gaughan is selling out everything. Am afraid he will regret it. Am sorry to hear it.*

* This letter ends abruptly at this point.

Cornelia Dickson in Ouachita Co. to John R. Boddie in St. Louis

July 4th, 1918

Dear John

Many thanks for the check received on July 5th, was in hopes you would write if only a few lines, to let me hear how you are. I am enjoying good health, am very well satisfied. Attended a picnic barbecue on the river near Marmaduke Ford on this side. Something real nice & pleasant, quite a nice crowd. There was also a picnic at Devil's Elbow on the other side above us. And the children about 25 of them enjoyed bathing in the river, seemed to have a lot of fun in their bathing suits, boys & girls. Cora & her two children, Oliver & Sue, went with me. Jim has a buggy & gentle horse, but Jim was sick the night before did [not] feel well enough to go with us. He makes a hand in the field, works hard, says he spent the day resting, Says has a hundred & fifty acres in cultivation and hardly enough hands to keep up with it, besides three acres in sweet potatoes. Saved his oats & sowed the patch in peas, beside peas in his corn, as he has a nice bunch of shoats & pigs coming on. He has several good cows and we have plenty of milk and butter, eggs & chickens. I had a letter from George last week, he was all right. Says has had a little scrap with two U boats* on the coast. Says the whole crew enjoyed the excitement & thinks they got one of them but not certain. Can't tell me every thing. Was in Philadelphia when he wrote.

Sadler is with the Marines in Cuba, is 1st Sargent, is well & all right.*

*"U boats" refers to German submarines.

*This letter ends abruptly in the ledger at this point.

Cornelia Dickson in Ouachita Co. to John R. Boddie in St. Louis

Aug 9th 1918

Dear John

Yours of Aug 2nd enclosing check received on the 6th inst. Many thanks. It comes in as a great blessing to me. Was glad to hear from you, tho so far away. In reviewing my past life, I feel that I have been blessed in many ways. I think I have unusualy good health, for one of my age.

I have certainly enjoyed the nice strawberries, cantalopes, watermelons & peaches this Spring and summer, having been without for two summers past. The hot dry weather has totally ruined the garden, & checked the growth of the Sweet potato crop, am in hopes we will soon have rain, that will greatly benefit peas, potatoes & sorgum. Cotton on the place is not suffering very much at present & well bolled. Corn is somewhat injured and generally matured, but fodder is scorched by the very hot sun we have had in the past two weeks.

Cora and children have not been right well for several weeks, using Vinotone quinine &c. Are up all the time. Sue is a bird full of life, she & Oliver devoted to their Papa when well, but to Cora when sick. Jim has kept up remarkably well, ploughing regularly until yesterday evening, suffered so with heat, said he would be compelled to rest up several days. He went for the mail this morning and has gone to see Henry Hawkins this afternoon, having heard that Henry was very sick. I had a card from Belle Gaughan several days since. She is under treatment at Battle Creek Michigan, for severe Blood pressure. Margaret is with her. She is one of my best friends. Am sorry for her. Dennis has lost both his clerks, Charley Moseley is at Camp Pike bookkeeping & Andrew Lea was sent to <u>Starkville Miss</u> as soon as he was well enough to be in training. Harry Moseley is in the same camp. The board would not call him until he laid bye the crops. Of course was doing his bit behind the trenches. I have not heard from Geo. in several weeks. Through his father I heard he is anxious to be sent to France. I think Will & Louis M[oseley] have gone.*

*This letter ends abruptly in the ledger at this point.

Harry F. Moseley at Fort Barrancas, Pensacola, Florida, to Cornelia Dickson in Ouachita Co.

Oct 8, 1918

My Dear Aunt Nealie:

While I have a little spare time thought I would drop you a line and let you know where I am, but I expect you have already found out from Papa. This post is under quarantine from "Spanish Influenza" and has been for about ten days & no prospects of its being raised real soon. About half the troops are in the hospital, but have only had two deaths so far. Have had an attack of the "Flu" myself, but managed to weather it without going to the hospital. It was something like the Lagrippe only a little more distressing.

I like the place here very well, but am not at all satisfied with my lot. Suppose everything will come out alright in the end. Have been assigned to the Coast Artillery but to no regular organization there-in. They do not give any artillery training here any more, but send them all overseas for that purpose except in a few instances when they send them to stations on the Atlantic Coast. Am anxious to be placed in some battery that is going over seas for I am surely tired of the monotony of the work here. Can't see that we are accomplishing anything worth while.

Fort Broncas is about six or seven miles from Pensacola and right on the Gulf — Very beautiful place — Have a large Naval Training Station just above the Fort, on the Bay, Mainly an Air service station — I have never been through it though because it is so hard to get a pass and have to be accompanied by a guard too. I did'nt care to go to that trouble.

The weather here has been splendid so far, tho it is said, not to be the tipical Florida Climate. I believe the temperature ranges from about forty degrees to about eighty according to the seasons. They say the winters are damp and soggy, a feature I do not like. Had much rather spend the winter in Climate that is dry even if colder.

Had a letter from Papa yesterday, he seems to be getting back to his old self again, but don't expect he will be able to do the work that he has been doing any more. It isn't necessary anyway, but you can't make him believe it. Also had a letter from George a few days ago. He was just back from a three weeks cruise and wrote from Philadelphia, said he thought he would be there for several weeks. Think his vessel is undergoing repairs. Guess you have a letter from him too. When you write tell me every thing that is going on in the neighborhood — What is Godfrey and Florence doing — Would like to write to all of them but looks like I can't keep up with what correspondence I have. How is Cousin Cora and Mr Martin and how did his crop turn out?

          Close with love to all
          Your Nephew
          Harry F. Moseley

Cornelia Dickson in Ouachita Co. to Harry F. Moseley with the U.S. Army stationed at Fort Barrancas, Florida

Oct 13th 1918

Dear Harry

    Your most welcome letter of the 8th inst duely received. I had been a little afraid that you were struglling with this dreadful plague that is going all over the country. Was glad to hear that you were improving, hope you will continue to improve for I have heard there is sometimes danger of relapsing. The schools around here are closed indefinately and Dennis & Belle are very uneasy about Margaret, who is among the 25 girls at Galloway* <u>who have it</u>, and the place is quarantined. Belle is in very poor health. It seems that her trip of five weeks at Battle Creek Mich did her no permanent good. I spent last Thursday & Friday at your Papa's. He has improved wonderfully from that spell of nervous prostration, was able to go with West Roberson Friday to get up his cattle to dip them. Ross Perry came over Thursday & said he would get help to gather peanut hay for him this week. . . . Spent Wednesday last week with old Mr & Mrs Hawkins. Both of them are very feeble and seemed so glad I came. One of the boys have to be with them <u>all the time</u>, both so helpless & the old man is partly paralyzed and the old lady cannot use her broken right hand & arm. Both wanted to hear about you & Geo. I have not seen Godfrey since your Papa was sick. He was so very kind and attentive as long as your papa needed some man to be with him, wait on and care for him day & night, as did most of the neighbor men. Now Mr Earle has been quite sick. Jim went to see him today, found him able to be up. Jim is nearly sick & worried about losing some very fine peavine hay — he hauled in about half of it when several days rain came & ruined the other, but says he has some more to cut if the weather is favorable. Cora is up but not feeling very well, the children are all right.*

*Galloway refers to Galloway Women's College, located in Searcy and operated by the Methodist Church. In 1930 it merged with Hendrix College in Conway.

*This letter ends abruptly in the ledger at this point.

Cornelia Dickson in Ouachita Co. to John R. Boddie in St. Louis

Nov 4th 1918

Dear John

    Yours of the 2nd Inst enclosing check rec. today for which accept many thanks. Yours of the 19th Ult. received several weeks since, and as you spoke of visiting Oklahoma & probably Camden I put off writing. Altho your letter was intensly interesting about that family in Ajo, Arizona, I never heard of such a <u>rush of children</u>, A regular deluge. I guess they feel awfully proud to raise them all, & I sure wish them good luck with them.

    I receive the "New York Times Sunday Edition" all right, and certainly am proud to get it. Thanks. I saw Robert day or two ago he told of your flying visit to Camden & Godfrey's. Am in hopes you can arrange to enjoy your camp hunt & visit to us this month. We have certainly had pleasant weather & Jim has succeeded in saving quite a good deal of hay, has not sold any cotton yet. His potatoes are fine & we have plenty of milk & butter. Mrs. Gaughan & Mrs. Frank Hawkins spent the afternoon with us. School opened Monday — as the flu scare has somewhat abated. We are still cautious about exposure, however. Cora rec. letters from Sadler every week, he is still in Cuba. Enjoying good health, & doing target practice. I believe I told you he was promoted to 1st Sargent. I received a letter from George.*

*This letter ends abruptly in the ledger at this point.

Harry Moseley at Fort Moultrie, South Carolina, to Cornelia Dickson in Ouachita Co.

Nov. 10, 1918

My Dear Aunt Nealie:

I suppose you already know where I am by this time — Should have written you long ago but have just kept putting it off — You know "putting off" is chronic with the Moseleys anyway. Writing is the only thing in the army that I can put off though — nothing else goes and no excuses accepted. Hope it will be of some benefit to me in civil life.

Have been in an overseas outfit ever since come here, and the out-fit is past due in France now but delayed on account of not having a full compliment of men. However, several hundred came in the past week. I think they are still short some.

Am told that we will go over regardless of how things terminate in Europe, but they change their minds so often I don't feel like we will go. Would like to have gone over if I could have gotten there in time to have seen some of the fire but as it is I don't care much about it. Had rather go back home and get busy there. Am getting on in years and if I am ever going to do anything it is time was up and about it. Don't you think so?

This is the first day have had off since coming here and I surely have enjoyed it. Have put in the most of the day walking around mostly up and down the beach and watching the big vessels come in. They are a grand sight too. It is interesting to watch the little "sub chasers" stand off the mouth of the harbor and guide them in.

I enjoyed my trip over here very much, but didn't get to see very much of the country as most of our traveling was at night. Haven't been to Charleston yet as every thing has been under quarantine on account of the "flu" but it [is] all over now and I intend to go the first chance.

Fort Moultarie is on an island about eight miles from Charleston and there is quite a little town here but as it is mostly a summer resort there isn't very many people here — I mean civilians — but there are some very interesting places about here — especially the old fort — It is just as it was originally built and is still in use — about the only change is in the guns — Modern cannon of small caliber have take the place of the old fashion ones.

The large guns of heavy caliber are not in the old fort at all but have modern implacements of their own. I am in a Truck Mortar Battery and haven't seen or had any training with them at all. We are supposed to get our training in France — The truck mortars are better known as the "suicide battery" at least that is what we are called.

Well I wont write any more this time Aunt Nealie and I hope you are well and keeping your health.

Lovingly your nephew,
Harry F. Moseley

Harry F. Moseley at Fort Moultrie, South Carolina, to Cornelia Dickson in Ouachita Co.

Sunday Evening, December 1, 1918

My Dear Aunt Nealie:

Your most appreciated letter of the 24th came to hand Friday. Was so glad to hear from you — as I always am — after so long a time — Was beginning to feel uneasy about you — didn't know but what you might be down with the "flu" and it seemed that I couldn't hear from any one down there at all.

I was sorry didn't write you sooner after coming here, but looked like I just couldn't get to it for I was always too tired to do any thing but go to bed as soon as we got off duty and got our "Chow". We were certainly kept busy up until the time of the signing of the armistice, getting us ready to go overseas but since then we are not so busy. There isn't any probability of our going over now and we are only waiting to be mustered out. How long that will be I can't say. Some think we will be home for Xmas, but I am not of that opinion but am hoping I will anyway.

We had a real nice Thanksgiving dinner such as, Turkey and Cranberry sauce, Oyster dressing, celery, creamed potatoes, English peas, cakes and pies, Bananas, apples, Grapes and nuts, and just <u>all</u> a fellow could stand up to. Had planned a bunch of games for the afternoon but it rained so they were all put on the blink except the football game. We pulled that off in spite of the rain and the Army won over the Navy 13 to 0. Had planned to go to Charleston in the afternoon but it rained me out so I went yesterday afternoon. Saw quite a good deal of the City. It is certainly a dirty place and shows its age, too, to a marked extent. And pretty girls — Gee! never saw so many in one place in my life. And it wasn't paint and powder either but just plain natural beauty. However, I am not going back on Arkansas.

Had a letter from George today, he is well and enjoying himself as usual, but from the way he writes am sure he would like to get back to civ[ilian] life. Well I haven't anything of interest to write so will close, write as often as you can.

     Love to all
     Harry

Cornelia Dickson in Ouachita Co. to John R. Boddie in St. Louis
                 Dec. 1918
Dear John,

  Yours of the 3rd inst, enclosing check received in due time, also paper. Many thanks! I often think of you & what I would do were it not for your continued kindness & consideration. So much like your dear angel mother, who cared for me as an own sister, always. Bereft of the home & property that my dear mother felt she was leaving me well provided for. I was thrown upon my own resources with but a limited education, to make my living. I feel that I have been greatly blessed, all along, with loving friends & relatives, & moderately good health & will to work & do for others, until I am nearing my 80th mile post and am in good health & able to enjoy some of the pleasures of life.

  Last Sunday after attending church, & hearing a fine sermon from our minister, I dined with D. L. Gaughan & family, including our minister, Allis Moseley, Mrs. Fisher, Mr & Mrs Frank Hawkins & son Chester. All enjoyed a regular Thanksgiving dinner. Robert went home Saturday evening to enjoy his first stay at his own home. Sallie & boys having moved. I know they had a proud time.

  You note the time flying. It certainly does fly. I rec. yesterday an interesting letter from Harry. He is at Fort Moultrie, S. C. but has no idea how long he will be there, or where he will be sent. Hopes now that he will be discharged as he did not get to help & mash the Kaiser. He enjoyed a fine Thanksgiving dinner, and had visited Charleston, the one time home of Dr. Samuel Henry Dickson*, who went from there to Philadelphia & was said to be a noted physician.

  I rescued a <u>Montgomery Advertiser</u> when Corrie & Attalie were destroying some old papers & letters of Mittie's after her death. In that old paper was your Aunt Carrie's* life History, as she told it in 1911 to a lady connected with that paper. I <u>found it very interesting</u>. Have you ever seen it? & about her grandfather <u>George Boddie</u> & family & prominent connections in N. C.

  Well I will close as it is growing late.
       As ever affectionately
       Your Aunt Nealie

*Samuel Henry Dickson was Cornelia and Clara's grandfather.

* "Aunt Carrie" refers to Carrie Love, Cornelia Dickson's half-sister who lived in Alabama.

George B. Moseley aboard the U.S.S. South Carolina to Cornelia Dickson in Ouachita Co.

Wednesday night, Dec. 18, 1918

Dear Aunt Nealy,

I hope that this letter finds you well and happy and enjoying the Xmas holidays.

It has been some time since I last wrote you, but there has not been anything specially interesting to write. Everything seems to be about the same with us since the war ended as before and it has had very little effect except every one nearly are trying to get out of the service. You see we boys that came in here after the war was declaired did not come in because they like it or because they were hungry either. We came in here because the country was at war and to do our part; however I will admit that our part in the game has been very little, but we have done all that we could or that they would let us do. We were very anxious to get over on the other side but of course we didn't have any say so in the matter and outside of making one trip as convoy for troops which carried us in several hundred miles of "France" is about all the service that amounted to anything. Of course we had that little scrap with the "subs" in June, but we were on our way to Phila. then or we would not have had that luck and so don't count that anything.

No Aunt Nealy, we are thoroughly disgusted with the whole outfit and very few will stay any longer than they have to. I guess that we will help bring the boys back home, and are quite willing to do so, but after that its civilian life and "<u>Liberty</u>" we want just the same as any one else and we don't see why we can't have it either.

The last letter I received from Harry he was in South Carolina, but I wrote him on the 7 of this month and my letter was returned to me so I don't know where he is now, thought probably that he had gone home as he said he thought perhaps that they would be discharged soon.

We are at present anchored in "York River" and have been during the whole time of the war except the times mentioned above or when we were on target practice or war games, that's what got our goat so bad, where we will spend Xmas; most of the boys are going home on 8 day leaves, but as I don't feel able to do so, guess I will take my Xmas aboard ship where ever it may be; however I intend to come home the latter part of next June, if nothing happens.

Well I can't think of any thing else interesting to tell you so will close. Give my best regards to all, and write me when you can for I am always glad to hear from you. Your letters are very interesting and I like them.

Again wishing you a merry Xmas, I am as ever your nephew,

Geo.

Cornelia Dickson in Ouachita Co. to her friend Margaret Richardson
Jan 22nd, 1919

Dear Friend,

 I certainly appreciate the kind remembrance & good wishes from <u>you</u>, <u>Mary Elliot</u>, & <u>Lucy</u>. I do not remember Mary Elliott's name since her marriage! So I address this to you. I very often think of <u>all of you</u> and the many pleasant days we spent together in the long ago, before you moved away. Our neighborhood has sadly changed in many respects since that time.

 I should have responded earlier but the "Flu" like a cloud seemed to envelope our neighborhood, nearly every home visited by it, more or less. Annie Wright was the first to pass away the 2nd of Jan. Last week Mrs. Robertson a new comer was buried in our churchyard, are the only deaths. Thank God.

 I am boarding with Cora [and Jim Martin] now, and every one of the family, the teacher and the cook were victims for two weeks. Cora, tho sick, was up most of the time & gave medicine to her family. She secured another cook & a man to do the milking, feeding, & getting in the wood. I had a severe cold, but by using medicine freely kept able to wait upon the sick. School suspended for two weeks. We are all right now & able to do justice to the table fare. But some of the neighbors are yet quite sick, not able to be up at all.

 The teachers went to their homes as soon as they were able to be up. Miss Thomas to Fordice, & Miss Owen to Waldo. They will probably return Sunday to open school next week. Both board here & are pleasant companions. I went to see Bell[e] Gaughan Saturday. She has been very sick, but is much better.

 We had a good sermon last Sunday from our new minister Bro. Harwell. Harry Moseley is at home now & looks much improved since he came. George is still in service with the Navy. I am in hopes he will be released soon, that is unless they hold him for future service. Sadler is still in Cuba & well now from malaria.*

*This letter ends at this point in the journal.

John R. Boddie in St. Louis to Cornelia Dickson in Ouachita Co.
February 4th, 1919

Dear Aunt Neely:

 Just a line to mail your check. I went down home to nurse Lucie, or rather to Arkadelphia on the 19th, she was taken with the influenza and wired me to come. Her brother Will Smoker who resides at Arkadelphia had it and she went up to look after him and by time he began convalescing she was taken down. She had only a slight attack and by good nursing and attention she recovered in ten days sufficiently to go home to Texarkana.

I returned a few days ago and sent the Boddie book to Mr. Carr, as you requested. I dont know when I will be able to visit Arkansas again, as Mr. Major will come up soon to be operated on for appendicitis. Guess my time will come next to be carved up in some way.

While I was absent my subscription to the New York Times expired and I have not renewed it is why you dont get the Sunday edition.

Weather very pleasant for the season of the year.

      Love to all,
      Your affectionate nephew.
      Jno. R. Boddie

John R. Boddie in St. Louis to Cornelia Dickson in Ouachita Co.
                  March 5th, 1919

Dear Aunt Nelia:

Here I come again like the cows tail, wagging behind with your monthly allowance.

Your interesting favor of the 8th ultima was duly received and read with pleasure. Since receiving it have been down to Hot Springs and also Texarkana. Last Monday week Mr and Mrs Major and wife all bobbed in on me unexpectedly. They had written Friday previous they were coming, but their letter coming Saturday, a holiday on account of its being the 22nd, was not delivered until Monday after they dropped by my office. Mr. Major has been more or less troubled with his appendix for the past year and decided to come up and have it taken out. He was operated on today a week ago, is doing finely and will return to his business, Monroe, La, in about ten days. His wife would not come unless her mother came with her which accounts for Lucie coming with them. It seems very fashionable to be operated on for appendicitis nowadays, and I may get in line too as I like to keep up with the procession. Unless you allow it to run too long after it becomes affected, it is a simple operation and incurs but little danger to have it removed. But to wait until it becomes badly affected it is dangerous, blood poisoning sets in and up or down you go to another world with but a few hours or days notice.

Weather cold here, but fair.

      Love to all,
      Your affectionate nephew,
      Jno. R. Boddie

Cornelia Dickson in Ouachita Co. to John R. Boddie in St. Louis
March 7th 1919

Dear John,

Yours dated March 5th enclosing check, received this morning — Many thanks from my heart. I hope you may always be prosperous, well, and able to enjoy the blessings of this life to the end of your existance on earth to your final translation to join your loved ones "Over there." Was glad to hear that Mr Major came through his opperation so successfully. I know it was great relief to his family's anxiety. Having that operation is one "fashion" I hope you will not keep up with.

I have been busy several days helping finish up our church "Service Flag." We have fifteen Stars All Blue.* In the ceremony I had the honor of pinning on a Star for George Moseley, Allis Moseley for Harry, J. W. Martin for Sadler. Marvin Moseley for his son Charles, His wife Lucie for Will Moseley & Mrs. Fisher for Louis Moseley. Will & Louis are still in France and George has gone over to bring Soldiers back. Guess I'll hear from him some time soon. Sadler Martin, Sargent, came home on a short leave week before last, but last week joined his Company Marines in N. O. which were immediately transferred from there to Headquarters Detachment U. S. Marines Corps, Marine Barracks, Main Station, Paris Island, S. C.. So you see Sadler was here at the raising of the flag, & was called upon to make a speech, which he did with credit, but owing to a severe cough & cold had to be rather brief.*

*The emphasis on "All Blue" stars is significant. It indicated that none of the men in the church who went away to war were lost. As is still the case, a Gold Star indicated one who was killed in action.

*This letter ends abruptly at this point in the journal.

HONORING THE SOLDIERS MARCH 1919*

The World War I had ended in 1918 and some of those who had served in the armed forces from our Harmony Grove Community had returned home. A program welcoming them was presented in the "big room" of our school house. The program was called a "Flag Raising". Miss Cornelia S. Dickson was asked to make the flag. It was of fine woolen material, rectangular in shape with a border of red and a center of white. Sixteen five-pointed stars of blue were applicated on the field of white.

Mrs. Cora D. Martin had the program. Everyone enjoyed the speeches made and the refreshments served. Parents, friends, and loved ones represented those not yet home from the different branches of the service. . . .

*"As chairman of the committee, I have the honor and pleasure of making the presentation address. First the ladies of the community wished to do honor to our boys, those that have served so faithfully and so honorably during this World War.

*Editor's Note: The following account of the ceremony mentioned by Cornelia Dickson in the previous letter was written by Sue Martin Russell, who attended the ceremony and also had access to her mother's notes.

*Notes from Cora Dunlap Martin

They are our boys. We raised them; we love them; we honor them in this service this afternoon. It affords me great pleasure as chairman to present this flag as a small token of our love and esteem.

ROLL OF HONOR

1. John Sadler Martin - Marines
2. George Boddie Moseley - Navy - The "South Carolina" bringing home soldiers
3. Taylor Henry Earl - Navy Aviation A.E.F.*
4. Carl Lewis Willis - Infantry A.E.F.
5. William Marvin Moseley - Europe Hdw Pts A.E.F.
6. Arch Bryant - Infantry
7. John Louis Moseley - Artillery
8. Garvin McClain
9. Harry Fisher Moseley - Fort Moultrie
10. Claud Gillespie - Camp Pike*
11. Clayton Venable - Camp Pike
12. Charles Elijah Moseley - Camp Pike
13. Aubrey Venable
14. Lucian Martin - A.E.F.
15. Edgar Martin - Spruce Division
16. Richard Hall - S.O.T.Corps

*A.E.F. was the abbreviation for American Expeditionary Force, the designation for U. S. operations in Europe.

*Camp Pike is what is known today as Camp Robinson.

George B. Moseley aboard the U. S. South Carolina docked at Fortress Monroe, Virginia, to Cornelia Dickson in Ouachita Co.

Mar 21/19

Dear Aunt Nealie —

Again it has been some little time since I last wrote you but as usual there has been very little of interest to write.

We just got back from France last Tuesday, with our first load of troops. It taken 28 days for us to make the trip, spending three days at Brest, where the troops were loaded on. While we were there I got to spend a few hours ashore on liberty during which time saw quite a few interesting sights. Some that were very amusing such as wooden shoes; for inst. I thought I was just about to be run over by a bunch of horses several times only to find that it was only a couple of little kids just stepped out of a door behind me with wooden shoes on.

Brest is an awfully old looking town, tho it is not very large, something like 25 or 30,000 population. Its streets are very narrow and are in bad condition. The people — well they look French alright and talk that way too I guess. I know I can't tell anything about what they say when they are talking.

I did not have time to get acquainted very well with the town while I was there but hope to the next time we go over which will be some time next month. We leave here "Hampton Roads Va" about the fifth or about that time.

I have not had an opportunity to see Mr Ross yet. Is he still stationed here at Norfolk? If so I wish that you would send me his address that I may drop him a line. I would like very much to see him.

Well I am still keeping in good health and getting along alright, hope to come home in July but don't know whether I will be able to stay or not. Will close hopeing that all are well and that I will hear from you soon.

Geo.

John R. Boddie in St. Louis to Cornelia Dickson in Ouachita Co.

May 5th, 1919

Dear Aunt Neely:

Will direct this to Vandoozer, as I presume you have returned by now. I only got back last week, stayed longer than I anticipated. After leaving Camden, I went to Texarkana, then to Monroe, from there to Little Rock on some business.

Fred Coleman is now working in Washington, and his family are in Charleston, W. Va. He could not rent a house in Washington, nor Baltimore, nor at any convenient place near Washington. He spends his Sundays with his family and the week at his work. The house he rented is 150 years old and was owned by Charles Washington, brother of the Father of his Country.

It is surrounded, he writes, by spacious grounds, has 22 rooms, running water and gas, many visit Charleston to spend the summers. He has written his mother to come on and live with him, says Helen, his wife, insists on her coming. I know what Helen wants, that is for Mamie to take care of her children, while she spends most of her time in Washington with Fred flying around. I think it will suit all hands better for her to be with Fred, as he can take care of her with less expense. It is pretty tough for her to be living all alone away from her children. She is too old to nurse an idea that she can go over to the old farm and raise chickens, berries and stock, and make a living and get rich.

Weather very pleasant here and we Methodists are having a big time celebrating the 50th anniversary of St. Johns Methodist Church, all its former pastors now living are here, and about all our Bishops. I heard Bishop Moore yesterday morning, Bishop Hendrix will preach Wednesday night and Mouson next Sunday.

> Love to all.
> Your affectionate nephew
> Jno. R. Boddie

Cornelia Dickson in Ouachita Co. to John R. Boddie in St. Louis

May 10th, 1919

Dear John,

Yours of the 5th instant enclosing check <u>received</u> with many thanks. I was on my way to an ice cream and community quilt sale, for Church benefit yesterday evening at 7 o'clock at the club house, notwithstanding the heavy rains for several days and threatening clouds, there was a large crowd.

The quilt was sold for $75.00 and a large handsome decorated cake, made by Attalie Dunn, sold for $75.00 bid in by Van Duzer to Miss Etta Gillespie, a pretty worthy girl. As cake and cream was abundant for the gay crowd of young and old folks from town and villages we sure had a lively time. Wish you could have been with us.

I was glad to hear that Fred and wife had sent for Mamie, for I felt that it was very trying on her nerves to live so alone as she did and it seemed that it could'nt be helped.

I had a very pleasant visit with Mat [Proctor Rumph]. Dr Dale is treating Mr. Dunn seems much better but not able to be up.

Cora's garden affords Irish potatoes, cabbage, & peas, plentifully. I rec a letter from George same time dated April 30. He is still getting along "all right," had unloaded troops at Newport News on Sunday, coaled ship Monday, Cleaned up ship Tuesday, Stood Admiral inspection Wednesday, Expects to leave for France again the last of this month.*

*This letter ends abruptly at this point in the ledger.

*Cornelia Dickson in Ouachita Co. to Maude Dunlap in Texas**

My Dear Maude,

*Date unknown, but the contents of the letter would place it sometime in late May or early June of 1919

Your most welcome letter rec several days since. I was still in Camden when it came to VanDuzer & thinking probably you had left Houston, concluded to wait until you reached Sipes Springs.

I was real glad to hear from you & that you had safely reached your destination. But <u>do</u> wish you could have been with us longer. I told Cora she kept you <u>too busy</u> but, she said she wanted to make you feel <u>at home</u> with us. We have some such very pleasant gatherings of our Club over the <u>beautiful church quilt</u>. Had a regular picnic. The day the Club came here to quilt it out, each one brought a lunch to the table, stretched to its capacity, was loaded with good things to eat. Cora furnished coffee & such a joyous laughing busy crowd you seldom see. Over a thousand names covered most of the border. It was quilted by the piece, & was <u>finished</u> by four o'clock. The Club was called to order & decided to have an ice cream supper & sale of the quilt two weeks later. Each dish of cream & cake for 10 cents and a ticket. <u>Seventy-five dollars</u> worth of tickets were sold. And when Mrs Burke drew the lucky number you should have heard her <u>shout</u>. Yes she actually shouted. There was a large crowd but we had plenty of cream & cake. And a <u>large decorated white cake</u> sold for $75.00, bid in by <u>Van Duzer</u> for the popular girl (Miss Etta Gillespie) <u>against Eagle Mills & Fordice</u>, for Miss Adams of Fordice. The proceeds of quilt & cake went to our <u>Ladies Aid</u>. And the pleasure of it all you would have greatly enjoyed with us.

Am sorry to hear that your Aunt is moving so far away from you. Of course every State has its gains and its disadvantages, and we always hope for the best in a change.

Cora has a fine garden & we have plenty of vegetables, plenty of butter & milk & some to sell. Jim is working very hard with his crop, says the uncommonly cold weather is very much retarding the growth of everything, particularly corn & cotton, the latter is having to be ploughed up & replanted. However oats looking well, and grazing outside is fine for cattle now.

Cora spent last Sunday week with your uncle Knot, he seems to be about the same as when you were there. I guess you hear from him as often as we do. The school here will close the 29th. The teachers are boarding with Mrs. Maggie Hawkins since you were here. When are you coming again. Jim says "Go slow on widowers when there are so many nice boys." Sadler still at Paris Island & George still bringing troops across.*

*The letter ends abruptly at this point in the ledger.

Cornelia Dickson in Ouachita Co. to George B. Moseley aboard the U.S.S. South Carolina

June 2nd 1919

My dear George,

Your most welcome letter of Apr 30 received the 9th of May — I was from home and they did not forward it to me. I came home from Camden that evening — had been spending a week or more with Mat Rumph. She is badly afflicted with Shaking Palsy in her right arm. Can't possibly hold her right hand from fluttering only when she is asleep. It is real distressing to see her in that shape. She has always been a good warm loving friend to me. Garland was so anxious about her. He wanted me to stay with her awhile — took her to Texarkana to Dr. Dale, who examined her thoroughly, & said he found her perfectly sound in body, & is treating her for nervousness. I have not heard of any improvement however since I came home. I was glad to hear of your safe trip. I often think of you, & your responsible position on board ship, & I hope & trust & pray you may allways be successful, not only there but all through your life. I should have written earlier, but knew you would be gone after more troops, ere my letter could reach you.

Garland brought me home in time to be present at our Ladies Aid Quilt Sale — a beautiful red, white & blue quilt, sold by tickets which brought $75.00. Mrs Burk drew the lucky number, and you should have heard her shout. A large white decorated cake was bid in by <u>Van Duzer</u>, against Eagle Mills and Fordice to <u>Miss Etta Gillespie</u> at $75.00. (The Ladies Aid furnished Ice Cream & Cake.) A saucer of cream & a slice of cake and a ticket to draw for the quilt, for 10 cts — There was a <u>large crowd</u> and they bought liberally of <u>cream & cake & tickets</u>.

I have been very well all along and enjoyed the Closing exercizes of our school last Thursday night, but took cold in some way & have not been so well the last day or two, have taken some medicine, & am much better today, on the upgrade again.

Farmers are having a <u>grassy</u> time with so much rain. I heard yesterday that Harry has the road again, I guess you hear from your Papa about home folks. Jim & his hands seem to be getting on all right, except cotton is not so good, has fine oats, good garden, butter & milk plenty.*

*This letter ends abruptly at this point in the ledger.

John R. Boddie in St. Louis to Cornelia Dickson in Ouachita Co.

June 14th, 1919

Dear Aunt Neelie:

I presume you have begun to think I have forgotten you this month, but the fact is that I have just recently returned from a trip to Lynchburg, Va. where I went to attend the closing exercises of Randolph-Macon, to see Sugarloog* graduate. While there I run up and spent a day at Lexington, only 60 miles, looking over Washington - Lee University and its beautiful grounds. I visited the mausoleum where rest Gen. Lee and family awaiting the resurrection morn. Also his life size marble statue in the little Chapel where the students worship, his office desk, books and chairs, just as he left them when he passed away. The house in which he lived and the one in which Gen. Jackson married. It all was most interesting to me. Lexington is a city, not large, but is historic, and when there I felt as if walking on hallowed ground, in fact when in "Old Virginia" I always feel that way. It is a grand old state and its mountains and valleys are picturesque and beautiful. I hope to some day make an auto trip and visit every county in the state, all its old Colonial homes, revolutionary battle fields and also those of the civil war. I wanted to visit Fred's family and sister Mamie, but did not have time,

*"Sugarloog" refers to Frances Major, daughter of Mamie Hunt Major and granddaughter of John R. Boddie.

as I had to hurry back here to look after some matters. Fred writes his mother seems to be improving since her arrival. She landed safe after going wrong, went to Charleston instead of Charles Town and had her baggage scattered all the way from Camden to Virginia.

It is getting hot up this way. My family all keep well and hope to remain home this summer on account of dull stave business and no copper dividends, but when Lucie gets real hot in July, she is liable to break for a cold latitude on short notice. Love to all,

                Your affectionate nephew,
                Jno. R. Boddie

John R. Boddie in St. Louis to Cornelia Dickson in Ouachita Co.

                                              July 3rd, 1919

Dear Aunt Nelia:

Your kind favor was duly received and read with pleasure. All my friends here have left the city for the summer, that is families that I visit, and I am feeling quite lonely these hot summer days. My family all keep well and I believe have about decided to remain home this summer as times are hard in the stave and mining business, that is no dividends coming in. Business is good here in dry-goods and most all lines, and prices still advancing, on account of Europe being bare of goods and also raw material and cotton crops so far not very promising. Hogs are selling at 22 1/2 cents a pound on foot, the lowly hog, he is now coming into his own in the way of values. While I think of it will make a contribution to the church you are all building in the old neighbor-hood, it wont be less than $25.00, and will make it larger if possible. The place selected I think is alright, it can be made a pretty place, plant water oaks around it and make a good lawn also, and fence off the stock from making it a cattle, goat and hog lot.

Fred Coleman is now at Dayton, Ohio, wrote me he would be there probably sixty days. He is checking up and disposing of a lot of shrapnal shell etc. made there for the government. Hope Dennis has recovered from his injury.

Tomorrow will be the Glorious FOURTH, but I do not enjoy it as I did when a boy. We buried brother Gilder on the Fourth of July, and then when Nelia was living here there was so much noise it made her seriously ill, boys shooting fire crackers and guns all day around where we lived. So the day always brings to me sad memories. Will run down to old Camden some time during the month.

                Love to all,
                Your affectionate nephew,
                Jno. R. Boddie

John R. Boddie in St. Louis to Cornelia Dickson in Ouachita Co.
July 31, 1919

Dear Aunt Nelia:

Just a line to mail your check. I was at Camden on the night of the 18th but was too busy to make any calls outside of seeing sis Sallie and Tug. In fact did not know you were in the city until that night late.

I had not learned of Mr. Dunns' death until I arrived there. I was surprised, but knew he was not expected to recover for some little time. Fred Coleman came over last Saturday from Dayton, Ohio, and stayed with me until Sunday afternoon. He finishes his work at Dayton this week and will return to Washington. Sister Mame writes complainingly and worrying as usual. Helen it seems only needs her to play nurse, and act as a kinder of all around house servant while she frolics around. Poor woman surely does have a hard time wherever she goes — no place to call home and be comfortable.

Weather red hot here and then some.

    Love to all,
    Your affectionate nephew,
    Jno. R. Boddie

John R. Boddie in St. Louis to Cornelia Dickson in Ouachita Co.
October 2nd, 1919

Dear Aunt Nelie:

Your interesting favor of the 2nd ultimo was duly received and enjoyed.

As it is again pay day, here I come to mail your allowance. It is small but I hope in time to make it larger.

No news calculated up this [way] to interest you outside of what you get from the papers.

My family as usual. Had a letter from [Mary] Gilder some days [ago] asking the whereabouts of her mother. Said she had been writing to Charleston, W. Va., for months and her letters were all returned marked "unclaimed". I wrote her to direct to Charles Town, W. Va. and she would reach her mother.

Godfrey wrote me some weeks ago that George Moseley was home. What is he and Harry doing?

I see from the papers that Texas is still crazy over oil. Hope Lon Dunlaps family are well greased ere this with bags of cash.

    Love to all,
    Your affectionate nephew,
    Jno. R. Boddie

P. S. What has become of the Dickson book, being published by Mr. Carr in N. C. It is as slow making its advent as was the Boddie book.

John R. Boddie in St. Louis to Cornelia Dickson in Ouachita Co.
November 5th, 1919

Dear Aunt Neely:

I was at Camden last Friday and was told you had just gone home. Was pressed for time, as usually, and only saw Brother Robts. family and cousin Attalies'. They all told me that you were well and getting younger as the years neared sunset.

I enclose your check. I will help out on your church ere long for the sake of other days.

Regretted to learn that cousin Mattie Rumph was not improving much and I fear her paralysis is but the beginning of the end.

It is a great pity that the fall rains have so seriously damaged cotton and fall crops. But such is life, we cannot always have sunshine. It has been all too truly written:

"Into each life some rain must fall,
Some days be dark and dreary."

As soon as I can want to come down and spend several days on that side of the river, and look after the cemetery at Uncle Johns' old place. But it seems as if I will never have the time, and ere I know it I will have to pass in my checks and cross over the river and join the great silent majority.

Love to all,
Your affectionate nephew,
Jno. R. Boddie

Cornelia Dickson in Ouachita Co. to John R. Boddie in St. Louis
Nov 10th, 1919

My Dear John —

Yours most welcome of the 5th inst. enclosing check, received in due time, for which accept many thanks.

If it were not that your Birth-days still come around so regularly, there would be very very gloomy days to me, as well as to your <u>many</u> friends & relatives. And my best wishes are ever with you where-ever you are. As it is I realize <u>your</u> kindness sheds brightness and comfort to my declining years. And may heavens greatest blessing ever abide with you and yours. I hope you will be able to come down and renew your old time hunting days. You are not so old as to think of giving it up.

Our church is fine and I think will be a credit to our community when finished. They are still working on it, though. Farmers have lost most of their crops by the continued rains. Jim [Martin] says he made a thousand dollars last year but lost it this year, paying for labor owed, will fail to save his crop this year, from ruinous rains. Has saved some corn, cotton, potatoes, pigs & cattle, but lost some. Yes, "Some days be dark and dreary." I suppose that is the decree for everyone some time in our existance. I suppose it is all right.

Sadler came in from Paris Island the 7th to the great delight of all of [his] friends & seems full of life as ever.

I look back and see that I was only eight yrs old when Brother Geo & Sis Mollie were married. I well remember being present. Your Aunt Sallie & I were chums then, and we were hand in hand looking on when the bride & groom and their attendants <u>came down stairs</u> and entered the parlor, looking so much like <u>angels</u> I fairly shivered. Remember it all — yes, as plain as ever. The house, family and the <u>big boneless turkey,</u> that ole Mrs Conway who was 70 yrs old had dressed & stuffed, and after the grand supper, the dancing. I shall never forget it and I am eighty years old.*

*This letter ends abruptly at this point in the ledger.

Cornelia Dickson in Ouachita Co. to Maude Dunlap

Nov 15th 1919

My Dear Friend,

I know you have been wondering. Over a month ago [I] went over to Camden to visit a day or two — Shop a little and come home. But found Mrs. [Matt] Rumph not much improved in health and Attalie quite sick in bed with a Dr in attendance. He said she stayed in Hot Springs 10 days, just long enough to stir up the malaria all through her system. Should have stayed at least 20 or more for thorough relief. She remained in bed two weeks. Allie had gone home to Fla. and Bessie had gone to St. Mary of the Woods, a Catholic School in Indiana, left only Attalie and Carrie at home. I of course remained with her two weeks and with Mrs Rumph several days, as Hattie was getting ready to attend the Teachers Convention at L. R. Then as Mrs Rumph's married children claimed her to stay with them, & Attalie was up, I came home with Cora who had come over to do shopping. Attalie came with us & went on to Bearden to see Mr. Earl, who had been stricken with Paralysis the day his mother was buried. So you see, Maude, I'm still in demand if I am past my 80 yr mile post. I enjoy being all the help I can to my loving relatives & friends. But I was very tired when I reached home not withstanding my friends.*

*This letter is unsigned in the ledger.

John R. Boddie in St. Louis to Cornelia Dickson in Ouachita Co.

December 2nd, 1919

Dear Aunt Neely:

Your kind and interesting favor of the 10th ultimo, I found claiming my attention last Tuesday when I returned from a hunting frolic in La. I left here on the 8th for a long contemplated hunt in that state where all varieties of game are plentiful. Owing to delay on account of the engine breaking down on the gasoline launch that took us from Monroe, 300 miles, via water to our hunting ground on the head waters of the Tensas river, we hunted only three days. Killed a fine buck that weighed gross not less than 200 pounds and 225 squirrels. When two days out I had an attack of lumbago, that knocked all my part of the hunt out of me but I enjoyed the good eating etc. as much as any one. Am not well yet but almost, have only slight pains now, and will be all right in a few more days.

Birth days and Christmas holidays come all too frequently to suit me nowadays, too forcibly reminders that I am growing old.

Weather here cold and dreary. Will try to get to Camden some time during the holidays and run over to the old neighborhood and see you all. Love to all relatives and friends,

Your affectionate nephew,
Jno. R. Boddie

P. S. I enclose check for your pin money. It seems so small, but the best I can do for the present. Squirrel headed peanut republican politicians delaying the peace treaty is playing smash with business here and abroad. When the Devil calls for his own, "they will be on his list and not be missed — no never be missed."*

Cornelia Dickson in the country to Mr. and Mrs. Thomas Gaughan in Camden

June 16th, 1920

Dear Tom and Helen,

I feel so shocked and grieved at the terrible trouble* that has befallen you, and <u>many</u> others. My heartfelt sympathy is with all of you. And I sincerely trust that you can feel that your Heavenly Father is with you, that you shall meet your loved one "In the Sweet Bye and bye." Truly " A Flower bloomed to be blighted, A Star that rose but to set."

Lovingly Your friend,
Cornelia S. Dickson*

*John Rumph Boddie's reference to the peace treaty here is the treaty formally ending World War I and the formation of the League of Nations, which the United States refused to join.

*The trouble that Cornelia refers to is a fire that occurred at a gas well near Eldorado, in which the Gaughan's daughter Josephine died. Three other young people from Camden died in the fire, which was called by *The Beacon* "One of the Greatest Disasters to Occur In This Community." The recent opening of oil fields in the area made them an attraction to people, who made excursions to watch the operation.

*Note: Thomas J. Gaughan was the Tommie, who as a former student of Aunt Nealie's, corresponded with her when he was attending school in Bardstown, Kentucky. He completed his legal training and opened what was to become a quite successful law firm in Camden. He was active in politics, as is evidenced by the photograph taken in 1910 at his home. He hosted a visit to Camden by William Jennings Bryan, who was campaigning across the nation for the Initiative and Referendum Constitutional Amendment.

The Gaughan Home 1910 (L-R) Dr. Bragg, T.J. Gaughan, Unidentified man, Helen Bragg (2nd wife of T.J. Gaughan) with a Gaughan daughter, Robert Minor Wallace (U.S. Congressman of the district), and William Jennings Bryan.

Thomas Joseph Gaughan
(1864-1939)

Lula Higgins Gaughan
(1st wife of T.J. Gaughan)
(1866-1896)

Photos courtesy of Bettie Lu Gaughan Rogers.

John Sadler Martin, serving with Marine Corps in San Diego, to Cornelia Dickson in Ouachita Co.

October 10th, 1920

Dear Aunt Nealie,

This is such a beautiful day here that I must write and tell you about it. This morning the old sun came up in a clear, blue, free-from-fog sky and as it came over the low mountains, I am sure that it made a sight worthy of some great poet's ravings, its rays falling on the green lawns, the verdant forest trees in the Park, San Diego Bay, and on out upon the placid waters of the Pacific.

I think it must have been on such a morning that Balboa climbed to the top of the hills on the Isthmus, wiped the sweat from his face, scratched his head and said "Caramba! Es el Pacifico." There is just a faint rustle of wind in the branches of the trees to break the quietness of the Sabbath day, and to give to one a slight feeling of chill, just a reminder that, only a comparatively few miles across the mountains to the East, old King Winter is taking stock of his supply of blizzards, snow northers, sleet and ice: preparing them for his season's distribution. In other words this is the other extreme of the first verse or stanza of Whittier's "Snow Bound".

I am thankful to be here instead of Nicarauga or some cold northern post of the Marine Corps; as Health is paramount; comfort next, and living third in our lives.

The Pacific Fleet made a trip to Honolulu some time since and coming back to this coast a great sham battle was fought in order that efficiency be maintained. When we heard the big guns firing I thought of <u>WAR</u> and all that it means.

There should be enough people in the world with common sense to forever keep conditions and politics from ever bringing on another carnage of slaughter. But all countries are now preparing directly and indirectly for the next one. Am patriotic all right, but cannot see how or why Kings, Emperors and Presidents should be allowed to sacrifice millions of their people to further their greed and avarice. This two years of training will round out my military career so that in case we have a war with Japan I will be qualified to fill some position of trust and command in the Marine Corps. One learns something new every day in the service as well as in civilian life.

Regards to any friends I may have in the neigbborhood and love to all of you in the family.

    As Ever.
    Your loving nephew
    Sad
    J. S. Martin

John R. Boddie in St. Louis to Cornelia Dickson in Ouachita Co.
November 9th, 1920

Dear Aunt Neely:

Your kind and appreciated letter of the 19th ultimo was duly received and as usually enjoyed very much. Am also in receipt of your esteemed remembrance of my 72nd birth day. Will quit from now on, having any birth days, except younger ones, for instance next year on the 30th of October, will be just 71, and so on backward so long as I live. Sorry about George Rucks getting into financial trouble. He knows better and should not have involved himself. Hope he will pay up and get clear of any criminal charges. Am glad cousin Attalie got the place. At $4OOO it is cheaper than she can build. Sell her old lot and pay out the new place on installments, call it rent and it will be paid out in a few short years, or sooner.

Hope that the report about oil at Little Bay will prove true. Regret to learn of cousin Cora's indisposition. I thought old billious fever was out of style in these days of progress. Better give it a new name. In old times when any one died suddenly, it was called a congestive chill, but now its appendicitis.

Fred and Helen [Coleman] stopped over from the evening of the 29th until noon of the 30th enroute home from a four weeks trip out west, chiefly in California. Both looking well. Fred much better than I ever saw him. They left their children with their nurse an old black Mammy. A letter from Fred since their return reports they found them all well and hearty.

From the way the people voted for Wiggly Wobbly Normalcy Harding, it does not seem that good democratic preaching the political gospel of righteousness did any good. All the Huns, Pro-Huns voted against us because we licked their infernal Kaiser. The Italians because Wilson would not consent to allow them Fiume at the peace table. The Irish because he would not help free Ireland. The Reds, Anarchists, I. W. W.'s and all such cattle because they always vote against the party in power. The Negroes and Mormons from habit. The farmers because cotton and wheat has gone down to what they claim is less than cost to raise it. Then many others because the government after selling Liberty Bonds at par to win the war did not guarantee them against any depreciation or decline. This last reason I think good and valid. Canada war bonds are par and so made by the Canadian goverment. Then a lot of fools voted against the democrats because they believed all the lies circulated by the republicans about the Wilson administration. Now they have control, lets see what they will do. If out of their administration any good comes, will get my part, if only bad, can bear my part.

But unless we get into the League [of Nations] and stop the over four billion a year expense to maintain the navy and army, and assist the war ridden nations of Europe to get on their feet financially in order to pay their debts owing us, and be able to buy our surplus cotton, wheat and copper, there is going to be some big smash ups all down the line in next one to two years. Labor wants to continue drawing war salaries, and its impossible for them to think of it. The cotton farmers voted for Harding with the belief his election meant 40 cent cotton and $3.00 wheat. Now watch them take their medicine. Have no sympathy with them whatever.

Love to all,
Your affectionate nephew
Jno. R. Boddie

P. S. Will be able to assist you by and by and I hope it will be real soon.

George B. Moseley in Texarkana to Cornelia Dickson in Ouachita Co.

Dec 30/20

Dear Aunt Nealy:

I am sorry that I did not get to see you Xmas, but I had such a short stay and no way to go any place.

I hope that you had an enjoyable Xmas. I spent a very pleasant day at home, wish that I could have had time to visit all the folks up there but things are so unsettled untill I kinder have to stick close to my job. I am in fairly good health which I certainly am thankful for, and hope that I will continue to be so lucky.

Aunt Nealy, there is no news worth mentioning that is why I don't ever write, but I would enjoy hearing from you once in a while.

Write to me in care of Ark. Road Const. Co.
Texarkana, Texas

Lovingly your nephew,
Geo Moseley

Cornelia Dickson in Ouachita Co. to Eula Underwood Hall in Selma, Alabama

Jan. 17th, 1921

My Dear Eula,*

Your very dear, sweet note of good wishes, & your kind remembrance of dear Sis Mollie & myself came to me this morning, while enjoying a most pleasant visit with relatives and friends in Camden. My home at present is seven miles across the river in the country, with my neice Mrs. J. W. Martin, Who told you of me. I so often recall that most pleasant visit to Ala. and feel that it was too brief. I fully intended at that time to repeat it, but circumstances over which I had no control, caused me to defer it. Then as time

*Eula was the daughter of Cornelia's dear friends Tom and Rebecca Underwood, who had so kindly offered her a home with them when she was preparing to move to Arkansas in 1868.

passed — I failed to carry out my intentions. For busy <u>years</u> passed, & I could hear <u>nothing</u> from my friends or relatives in <u>Ala.</u> and when I finally <u>did hear</u> my heart was so full & sore with sympathy and grief, both <u>here</u> and <u>there</u>, I felt that I must remain here. And mine has been a busy life, altho I gave up teaching to care for dear Carrie's two little boys.* They are grown men now, served their time in <u>army life</u>, came home and have ample employment in road building, so much needed around this & adjacent counties. My nephew John R. Boddie of St. Louis cares for me especially now.

*Carrie's two little boys are Harry Fisher Moseley and George Boddie Moseley.

I feel very thankful that I have many kind friends and relatives here, and I sure do appreciate being remembered by some of my dear Alabama friends.

Write me again dear Eula and tell me all about yourself and your dear mother and family. It has been a long time since I learned of your most estimable father's death. I have written so often without receiving an answer. About a year ago heard that the Mulberry P.O. was changed and of course my relatives & friends, yet living, are scattered, there as well as here.

      As ever,
      Lovingly your friend
      Cornelia S. Dickson

John R. Boddie in St. Louis to Cornelia Dickson in Ouachita Co.
                       June 23, 1922

Dear Aunt Nelie:

Yours of the 21st duly to hand and noted. I have not forgotten you, but the fact is that I have not made a penny in past three years, and only received two small dividends, not sufficient to defray my current living expenses two months. On the other hand am on the borrow all the time. I have interests that should give me an income worthwhile, but as yet not in sight, all out go and no in come. The tide will turn after a while, but when I cant say. The Republican politicians have been playing thunder with business for past three years.

As to Harry, he seems never to collect anything, but always at work for some one who never pays him. I cant understand him. I miss your letters and miss my ability to assist more than you do, but am in fine health, all round, that is physically and mentally and I hope religiously, but as usually "FINANCIALLY DEPRESSED." I say usually, ever since the infamous Republicans killed the treaty and League and began playing politics with the country, killing business all down the line. Will assist you as soon as able,
      With love your nephew,
      Jno. R. Boddie

John R. Boddie in St. Louis to Cornelia Dickson in Ouachita Co.
December 21, 1922

Dear Aunt Nelia:

Just a line to send you a slight Christmas gift. I called to see you when in Camden in Nov. but no one was at home, at least, I could not find any one.

I am in good health and making progress in my business, but am still hard pressed to keep out of the poor house, and unless all signs fail, some of ships will make port one of these days.

Now that my family have moved from Camden, cant say when I will be down that way, but as often as I can.

Am busy early and late. So pardon brevity. You Camdenites are all crazy about oil, and I look for some of you to land in the bug house.

Love to all relatives and friends, and wishing each a Merry Christmas and Happy New Year, am as ever

Your affectionate nephew.
Jno. R. Boddie

Bessie Rumph Brown in Hot Springs to Cornelia Dickson in Camden
Aug 14, '23

Dear Aunt Nealie,

I was so glad to have your good newsy letter Sat. If every thing does'nt go on right now, don't hesitate to tell me. I am a bit home sick anyway and am ready at any time to come, but will stay out the month as had planned, if everyone keeps well. Mildred is having a fine time and wants to stay and Proctor* writes me to by all means stay as its so hot and mosquitoes bad.

Glad to hear of the progress of street paving and that little Frances Usrey is improving.

Tell Mary to keep the rooms nice & clean and plenty of fresh towels, soap and toilet paper. If any of the men want to pay up to leave, see Proctor. He has the list & when their time is up etc.

Tell Mary to water the flowers lots and have them pretty for me when I return. We are having a fine time. Mildred has several admirers. I have a good time with the married couples. Is Carrie up here? Lillian Word wrote Mildred they would be here this wk.

I've met nice people from everywhere. They come and go all the time. Lots of love.

Bessie

*Mildred and Proctor were the children of Bessie Rumph Brown, who was the youngest child of Dr. John B. and Matt Proctor Rumph. Cornelia was evidently attending to Bessie's rooming house while she was away.

Sally Farley Boddie, wife of Robert Lee Boddie, to her sister-in-law Mary Elizabeth Boddie Coleman

Oct 21st 1923

Dear Sis Mamie:

  This is a wonderful day; not too cold, or hot, it does not tire one out, when I walk, or do any thing. I love the fall months, yet they are so sad looking & make me feel sad, if I just let myself get to thinking. I keep busy or get out & go, to keep from thinking; & keep off the blues; you simply would not know Camden, it has grown so much — new houses every place, three new houses below us, just in front of Mrs [Anna Chester] Smead & on down that way. Also three back of me on Greening St. No, Smoker & family are still living here — have bought a lovely new home — up near Meek Birds; right out this st. nearer the Cemetery, in a new street — called Banna [Banner] St., there are 15 new houses up that way; they are fixed up nicely — Bess Dunn's baby has been quite ill — came near having pneumonia, but better now — Attalie and Mrs. Hendricks both have been looking after it — they sat up with it 2 nights — Do tell me what you all find to cook — has'nt Mary Gilder some new dishes she prepares — tell me what they are — my folks has quit eating. Florence & G[odfrey] have a new Ford; she can drive, so she enjoys it, she sure works to help keep it, & buy the gasoline — her boys [Gilder & Gally] doing fine in school, & lots of help to her at home: I think so much of all of them. Allie* is with Walter in Cuba, but she cant hardly stand it down there; is so dissatisfied. Wrote her mother to build a new home & she would come stay a long time with her. Carrie Gaughan has

*"Allie" refers to Allie Gaughan Barr, daughter of Attalie Rumph and Alex Gaughan.

Robert Lee "Tug" Boddie (1863-19470, and Sallie Farley Boddie (1870-1943) with their grandchildren Virginia Lee Boddie Patterson and Mary Catherine Boddie Paul, daughters of Robert Lee Boddie, Jr. (1898-1950.)

been in Hot Springs 2 months, said she would stay away until the streets were paved — so tis near finished — she has an apartment up there, you know she gets $200.00 (two hundred) a month for her store*, now that is for the up & down stairs, so she can enjoy her self — None of A[ttalie]'s children are dependent on her now — so she has it very nice. Aunt Nelie is staying with A. while Carrie is away. My boys are hard at work each day, also my husband & I am kinda lazy — dont do much only keep house. Give all our love & write soon again.

*Carrie Gaughan's inheritance was a store building on East Washington Street in Camden.

       Lovingly
       Sis Sallie

Did you get the papers? I sent a big batch this week.

Cornelia Dickson in Camden to Jennie Rumph [Mrs. George B. Rumph] in Miami, Florida

              Feb. 25th 1925

My Dear Jennie,

 I have been intending to write you ever since Hattie [Rumph] reached home, but if you knew how nervous I have been recently you would excuse me. I thank you ever so much for your present.
 I was so glad that Hattie went by to see you and told me of her happy visit. I so often think of you and always glad to hear from you.
 I suppose Hattie told you we were living in Camden, for a while at least, so that Sue and Oliver can be in school regularly. Oliver will finish this year.
 Cora has <u>four men</u> that <u>room</u> and <u>board</u> besides <u>Sadler</u> and <u>wife</u>, for <u>room & board</u>. She also has a man, wife & child rooming with her. Jim Martin spends most of his time on the farm. Mr. Lynn has given up his house and moved away. Jim has tenant on the place to cultivate it. Cora takes in hemstitching to keep her machine going when she has any idle time. She enjoys fine health, as we all do, most of the time. I spend a good part of my time with <u>Mat Rumph</u>. She is at times almost helpless, but old age I suppose is getting the better of me, keeps me from being more <u>efficient</u>, but she seems always glad to have me come, and keeps help of some kind all the time. Hattie seems to have new life since her visit to Cuba & Florida. Now she keeps pretty busy again and seems to enjoy life.

      As ever, affectionately
      Cornelia S. Dickson

Cornelia Dickson's Obituary which appeared in the Camden Evening News *on November 1, 1928.*

PIONEER RESIDENT DIED THIS MORNING

Miss Cornelia S. Dickson, Aged 89, Died at Van Duzer Home.

Miss Cornelia S. Dickson, aged 89, one of the pioneer residents of this section, died at the home of her niece, Mrs. Cora D. Martin, at Van Duzer, Thursday morning. Burial will be in the family cemetery at Van Duzer at 10 a. m. Friday, with the Rev. Rentz [Reutz], of Thornton, officiating. Proctors' has charge of the arrangements.

Miss Dickson was born in Selma, Ala. on September 6, 1839. She is survived by two nieces, Mrs. Martin, of Van Duzer, and Mrs. Mamie [Boddie] Coleman, of Philadelphia; and two nephews, R. L. Boddie of Camden, and John R. Boddie of St. Louis.

Cornelia Sanderson Dickson

AFTERWORD

The death of Cornelia Sanderson Dickson, Aunt Nealie, brings our narrative to an end. Not because the story of Harmony Grove or Camden or Ouachita County, or even the state of Arkansas and the United States ends here, but because she was our conduit of the past through her correspondence. I am very grateful to Aunt Nealie. All my life I have heard that the life of my grandparents in the country was very hard; now I have witnessed that life first-hand. I have gained a new appreciation for the life I have always known, as well as a lesson in "living" and "coping." I have learned the value of faith and love, and have been given a marvelous study in human behavior.

Aunt Nealie was a remarkable woman who spent almost her entire life in the homes of others, serving them in so many ways. She always went where she was needed, providing assistance and solace to those in need, and she was always a "cheerful giver." Of material goods she possessed very little, but her life was full, as she so often remarked in her letters that she was blessed with many loving and caring friends and relatives. Her staunch faith in a merciful God created her patient and steadfast ability to endure the hardships and grievous times of her life. Her understanding of and sympathy for the human kind gave her the gift of forgiveness and generous love. Her last years were spent in happiness and contentment. She remained active until the very end, reading the Arkansas Gazette *every day and always her Bible before retiring. Her relatives and friends continued their close ties to her, always remembering her on her birthday and at Christmas. She slipped away one night in her sleep, as unobtrusively as she had lived.*

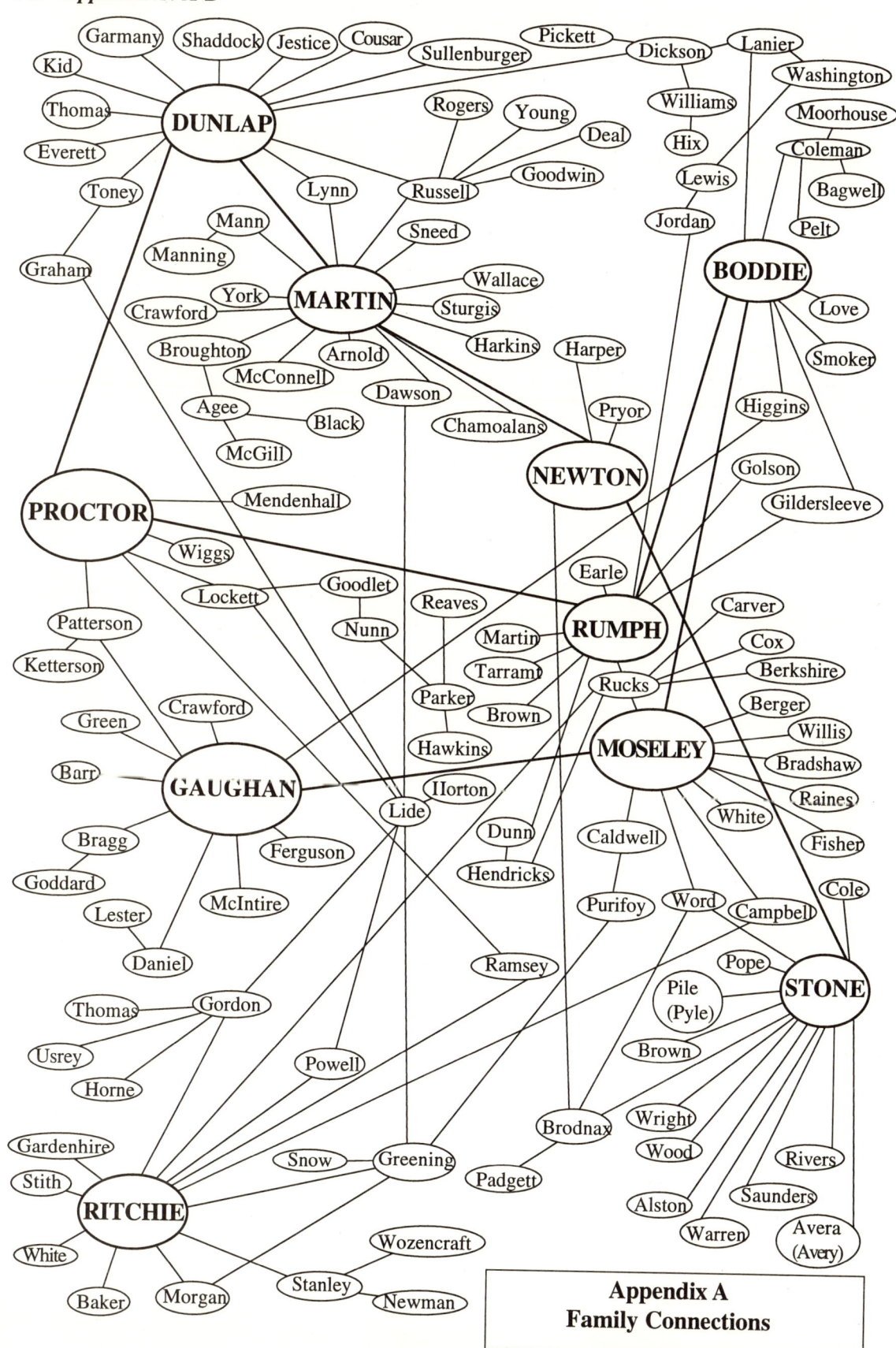

Appendix A
Family Connections

Sisters, Seeds, and Cedars 650

Appendix B
Geneological Charts
in Alphabetical Order

BODDIE

Thomas Hill Boddie ══════ m. 25 Jan 1821 ══════ **Clarissa Lanier*** [see Dickson]
b 12 Nov 1797 Nash Co., NC   b 11 Nov 1801 Duplin Co. NC
d. 12 Oct 1826 Madison Co. AL   d. 1864 Autauga Co. AL
son of George Boddie (1769-1842) and Susan Parham Hill (1760-1798)   She m. (2) Samuel H,N.Dickson

George Boddie* "bro. George" **Frances Pickett Boddie*** "Sis Fannie" **Caroline La Fayette Boddie*** "Sis Carrie" **Thomas Boddie**
b. 12 Nov 1821 near Huntsville, AL b. 13 Aug 1823 Madison Co. AL b. 15 Apr 1825 Lauderdale Co. AL b. 10 Sep 1826
d. 19 Oct 1882 Ouachita Co. AR d. 9 Oct 1858 Oua. Co. AR d. 3 Jun 1913 Auttagua Co. AL d. 29 Jan 1832
m. 11 Nov 1847 "Sis Mollie" m. 25 Jan 1845 Aut. Co. AL m. 22 Aug 1843 Autauga Co. AL
Mary Elizabeth Gildersleeve* **John Benjamin Rumph**, M.D. "bro. John" **Addison Coleman Love*** "Uncle Add"
b. 6 Oct 1824 New Bern, NC [see Rumph] [see Love]
d. 28 Jan 1900 Ouachita Co. AR [see Gildersleeve below]

John Rumph Boddie* **George Gildersleeve Boddie*** **Sarah Catherine Boddie*** "Sallie" **Robert Lee Boddie*** "Tug"
b. 30 Oct 1848 Aut. Co. AL b. 12 Feb 1853 Oua. Co. AR b. 27 Apr 1858 Oua. Co. AR b. 22 Sep 1863 Oua Co. AR
d. 15 Sep 1929 Arkadelphia, AR d. 30 Jun 1886 Austin, TX d. 6 Aug 1861 Oua. Co. AR d. 1947 Camden, AR
m. (1) 27 Nov 1877 Arkadelphia, AR   "Gilder"   m. Sallie Higgens*
Cornelia Kimball Smoker* **Mary Elizabeth Boddie*** "Mamie" "Small Sis"   b. 18 May 1871 d. 1943
b. 7 Mar 1856 Johnson, TX b. 4 Dec 1855 Oua. Co. AR   dau of J.H. and Julia Higgens*
d. 11 Sep 1876 St. Louis, MO d. abt. 22 Sep 1929 Alexandria, LA [while visiting dau.] and sister of Lula Higgens who
m. (2) abt. 1889 m. 5 Jun 1877 Oua. Co. AR   m. T.J.Gaughan*[see Gaughan]
Mrs Lucie Smoker Hunt* **Edwin Gallie Coleman***, M. D. **Frances Caroline Boddie*** "Carrie" "Little Sis"   She m. (1)
dau. of Capt Smoker* [part owner of Miss. son of Judge Hawse H Coleman b. 19 Dec 1860 Oua. Co. AR   **Thomas Farley**
steamboat, "The Robert E. Lee"] and sister d.1885 Hot Springs, AR d. 30 Sep 1892 Oua. Co. AR of maleria
of Cornelia   m. 21 Dec 1887 Oua. Co. AR   **Albert Farley***
b. 11 Mar 1852 **Willis Thomas Boddie*** "Will" **William Allis Moseley*** "Mr. Allis"
d. 28 Jan 1935 b. 1 Feb 1851 Ouachita Co. AR b. 7 Oct 1852 Warren, NC   **Eddie Farley***
                d.1902 Paris, TX [where he was d. 6 Dec 1930 Camden, AR [see Moseley]
                undergoing treatment for cancer]

Ernest Godfrey Coleman* **Fred Hughes Coleman,*** Col. **Edith Coleman*** **Mary Gilder Coleman*** "Gilder"
1878 - 1945 b. 1881 1880 - 1880 b.1884 "Mary Gilder"
m. Florence Pelt* graduated West Point abt. 1904 killed by a train in Chicago, IL
1883 - 1943 m. (1) abt. 1911 Helen Moorhouse* m. Walter Lee Bagwell,* Mjr.

George Galley Coleman* **Edward Gildersleeve Coleman** **Cornelia Esther Bagwell*** **Edith Bagwell*** **Mason Bagwell**
1909 - 1954 1913 - 1954 "Gilder" b. 1906 "Kit" b. 1912 d.14 Jan 1986
m. (1) Mrs. Foster m. (1) Lavern Kauffman d. 1 Aug 1993 d. 1985
    (2) Mable Lewis   (2) Christine Brumbly m. (1) __ Carson **Emerson Grady Bagwell*** **Ruth Omega Bagwell**
She m. [2] Joel She m. (2) Judson Hogg m. (2) Clark Henderson b. 1909 b. 23 Dec 1920
Roberson **Judy Ann Greenwood**   d. Oct 1993 m. Terance King
Jerry Coleman   the artist who painted the Boddie home
m. Mary Elaine Patterson **John Boddie Coleman** **Fred Hughes Coleman** m. Laurane
Chase Coleman b. 1913 b.1916   **John Hubert Boddie***
           Robert Moorhouse Coleman **Mary Constance Coleman**   1900 - 198_
Gaila Coleman **Joyce Coleman** b. 1915   m. Annie Mae Foster
m. Johnny Smalling m. Jack McCormick   **Robert Lee Boddie, Jr.*** 1909 - 1976 **George Gilder Boddie***
Linda Coleman   1898 - 1950   1907 - 1909
                                              m. Virginia Anderson   **John Hubert Boddie**
George Kimball Smoker Boddie*   1905 - 1937
1878 - 1951   **Virginia Lee Boddie**   **Mary Catherine Boddie**
m. Annie Waitie Marie Butler*   b. 1925   b. 19 Jul 1929 d. 2 Jul 1992
1888 -1964   d. 16 Mar 1993 at Denver, CO m. (1) Leroy Paul
                                     m. James Patterson   b. 20 Mar 1926 d. 24 Oct 1968
Ruth Evelyn Boddie **John Rumph Boddie**   m. (2) Mr. Daniels
b. 1918 b. 1920   GILDERSLEEVE
m James Cecil Farmer d. 6 Nov 1993 at Houston, TX **John Gildersleeve*** = m.1821 New Bern, Craven Co.NC= **Martha Jones***
b. 1917 m. (1) Mildred Edwards b. 1791 Huntington, Long Island, NY   b. 1807 New Bern, Craven Co, NC
         m. (2) Marie La Bita d. 19 Mar 1869 Air Mont, Clark Co. AL
                               son of Stephen Gildersleeve

Mary Elizabeth Gildersleeve* **Hattie Gildersleeve*** **Sallie Amelia Gildersleeve*** **John Gildersleeve***
m. George Boddie b. abt 1834 m. M.M.Murley (d. 1868) 1837 - 1871 m. John Benjamin Rumph b. abt. 1842
[see above] He m. (1) __ [see Rumph]   **Linn Gildersleeve***
                                                                         d. 1875
         dau*. m. George Johnson* dau.* dau.* son* died in army   m. Mr. Green* lived in MS
         d. 1874 5 children*   **Infant***

Hattie Murley* **Mattie Murley*** **Fay*** "Cousin Fay" dau* dau* **Steve Murley***
       son b. 1861*   m. Charles Crouse   b. 1869
                                         2 Feb 1886

* Mentioned in the letters.

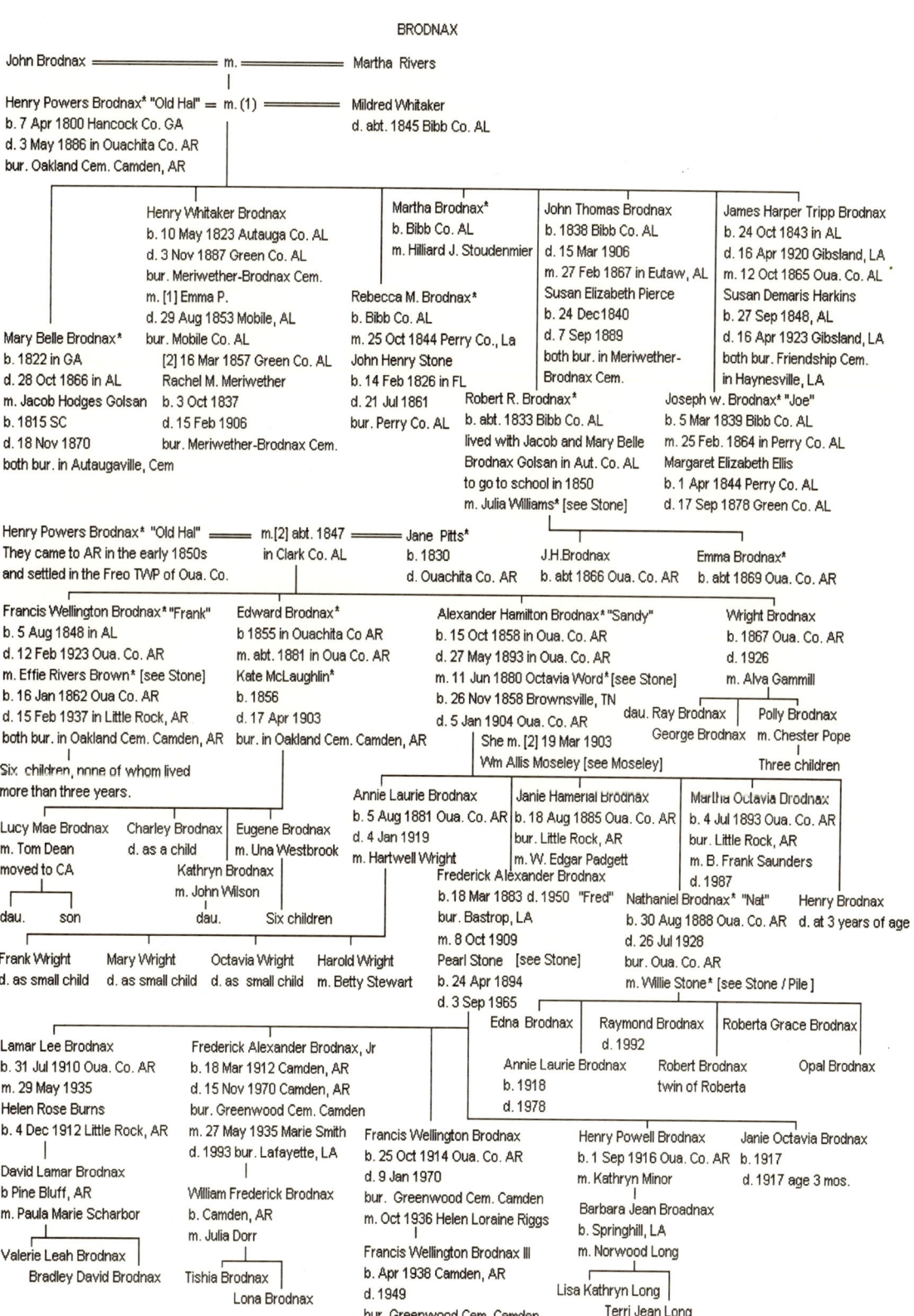

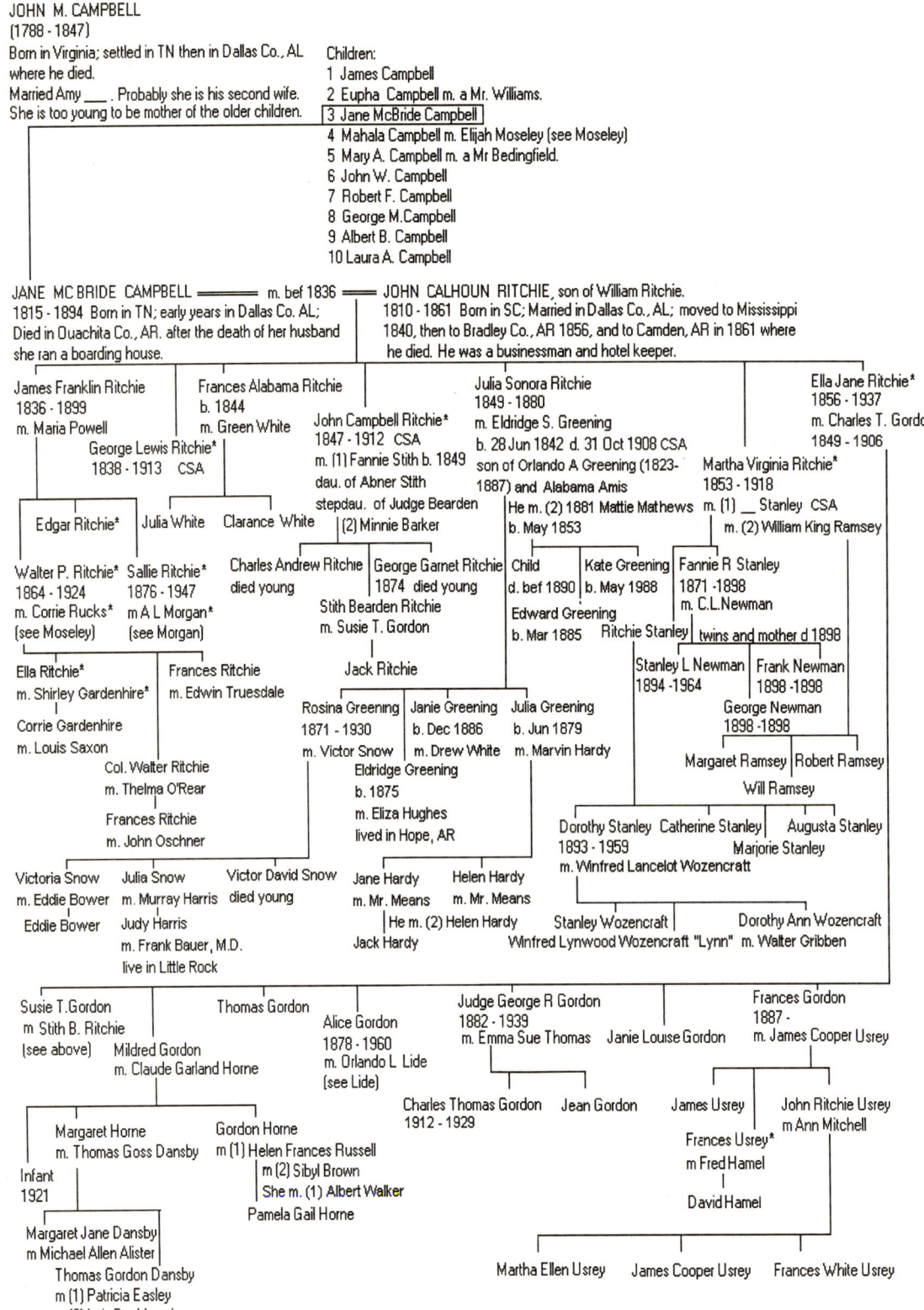

Sisters, Seeds, and Cedars 652

Appendices: A-D

DICKSON

John Dickson — m. — **Ann**
b.1704 Ireland d.1774 Duplin Co.NC
1730 emigrated to PA; abt.1740 to Dup.Co. NC

Michael Dickson
b.1735 Co.Down,Ire.
d.1816 Pendleton Dist,SC
Mjr. in Am.Army in Rev.War
m.1755 Sarah Neeley
1733 - 1830
mother was a Houston.

1 Mary Elizabeth m.Jonathan Fielding
2 Jane Dickson m. Nicholas Bishop
3 John Dickson 1768 - 1831 m. Lydia Tourtelotte
4 Samuel Henry Dickson
5 Hugh Dickson 1772 - 1853; Presbyterian Minister
6 James Dickson

William Dickson
1739 - 1820
m. Mary Hix Williams
dau. of Mary Hix and Joseph Williams

Robert Dickson
served in H of Com.
1774, 1778, 1785-1788

1 Ann Dickson b. 1768 m. Wm Lanier b abt 1763 ,bro. of Isaac. rep. from Anson 1802 - 1806.
2 William Dickson b. 1770
3 James Williams Dickson b. 1772 m. Nellie
4 Joseph Dickson b. 1775
5 Mary Dickson
6 Louis Dickson b. 1778 m. Catherine Hill dau of Thomas Hill and Frankie Smith who was half sister of Burwell Lanier
7 Frances Dickson* "Aunt Fannie"

Joseph Dickson
moved his 8 sons to TN
Dickson Co. is named for Dr. Dickson, his nephew.

Alexander Dickson
unm. established an educational fund

Edward Dickson

James Dickson

Mary Dickson
m. William McGowan

1 John McGowan
2 William McGowan
3 Edward McGowan
4 Robert McGowan
5 James McGowan
6 Michael McGowan
7 Joseph McGowan

Samuel Henry Dickson* liv.in Pendl.Dist. 1798
d. 1836; m. Rebecca Hutton
b. 28 Sep 1773 Abbeville Dist, SC
d. 11 Mar 1836 Mesopotamia, Green Co. AL

Mary Dickson* 1776 - 1861 "Grandma"
m. as (2) wife Isaac Lanier b. 1767. They moved to TN,then Madison Co. AL, then to Autauga Co.
He m. (1) Arabella Clayton. 3 children:
   Burwell Lanier
   Isaac Lanier
   Arabella Lanier m.Dr Brunson

Samuel Henry Neeley Dickson* 1789 - 1860
b. 2 Jul 1798 Pendleton Dist. SC
d. 8 Jun 1860 Autauga Co. AL
m. (1) 1 Feb 1826 Elizabeth Mourning Lockett
b.5 Aug 1810 Putnam Co.GA d. 13 Jan 1829.
m. (2) Mrs Clarissa Lanier Boddie*
[which see]

Dickson Mann C Lanier* "Uncle Dick"
m. Ann Caldwell

Clement G. Lanier* unm. "Uncle Clem"

Isaac D Lanier, M.D.* "Ike"
m. May 1860 Iantha de Jarette

Clarissa Lanier*
b. 13 Nov 1801 Duplin Co. NC
d. 8 Feb 1864 Autauga Co. AL. buried by her mother in Carrie Love's Garden.
m. (1) 25 Jan 1821 Thomas Hill Boddie
b. 12 Nov 1797 Nash Co. NC. d. 12 Oct 1826 Madison Co. AL
m. (2) 20 Jan 1859 S.H.N.Dickson* [which see]

"Mother" "Mother Dickson"

Nancy Lanier*
m. Eldred Rawlings

Elizabeth Ann Dickson
1 Jan 1829 - 20 May 1829

Isaac Lanier Dickson 1835 - 1835

Mary Rebecca Dickson 1833 - 1834

Cornelia Sanderson Dickson* 6 Sep 1839 - 1 Nov 1928

Clarissa Dickson* 4 Nov 1836
b. 14 Apr 1836 Autauga Co. AL
d. 11 Nov 1913 Ouachita Co. AR
m. John Franklin Dunlap*
[see Dunlap]

Frances Pickett Boddie*
m. John Benjamin Humph*, M.D.
[see Rumph]

George Boddie*
m. Mary Elizabeth Gildersleeve*
[see Boddie]

Thomas Boddie
[see Doddie]

Caroline La Fayette Boddie*
m. Addison Coleman Love*
[see Love]

Mary A E Rawlings*
m William Love*
[see Love]

Frances Dickson* b. 1780 Duplin Co. NC m. Wm R.Pickett b.1775/76, Anson NC d.1850 Autauga Co. AL son of James Pickett and Martha Terry; sheriff of Anson Co; mem.of NC Legislature: Tax Accessor. Moved to AL 1818; mem.AL Legislature 1821, 1823,1824, AL Senate 1828 - 1834.

Dickson Pickett

Eliza Pickett* "Cousin Eliza"
Judge L.P. Walker

Eliza Banks Pickett d. 1849
m. Moseley Baker b. 1802 VA
d. 1844 Houston, TX ; buried in Austin. Inscription: Commander Co. D First Reg. of Texas Volunteers at San Jacinto, mem. of 1st & 3rd Congresses of the Rep. & Brig. Gen. of Militia of Texas.

Albert James Pickett* "Cousin Albert"
b. 1810 Anson Co. NC
wrote, THE HISTORY of ALABAMA
m. Sarah Harris* "Cousin Sarah"

Martha Pickett
m. Col. Michael Woods

Eliza W. Pickett*
m. Edwin Banks

Sarah Julia Pickett
m. Robert Carter Randolph

Fannie Baker* "Cousin Fannie"
m. William Darden*
of Galveston, TX
a son*

Eliza Baker
b. abt. 1839
living with Pickett grandparents 1850 died young

William Raiford Pickett
b. 2 Apr 1833 Montgomery, AL
d. 7 Apr 1889 Montgomery, AL
m. Laura Holt dau. of Samuel Doak Holt and Laura Hall

Corinne Pickett
m. Edwin Brett Randolph

Mary Gindrew [Gindrat] Pickett*
m. Samuel Harris
Presbyterian Bishop of Michigan

Albert James Pickett, Jr
m. Eugenia Durden

Austin Harris Pickett*
m. Elizabeth Jackson
gr. gr.dau. of Gov. Bibb

John Gindrat Pickett

---

* Mentioned in the letters.

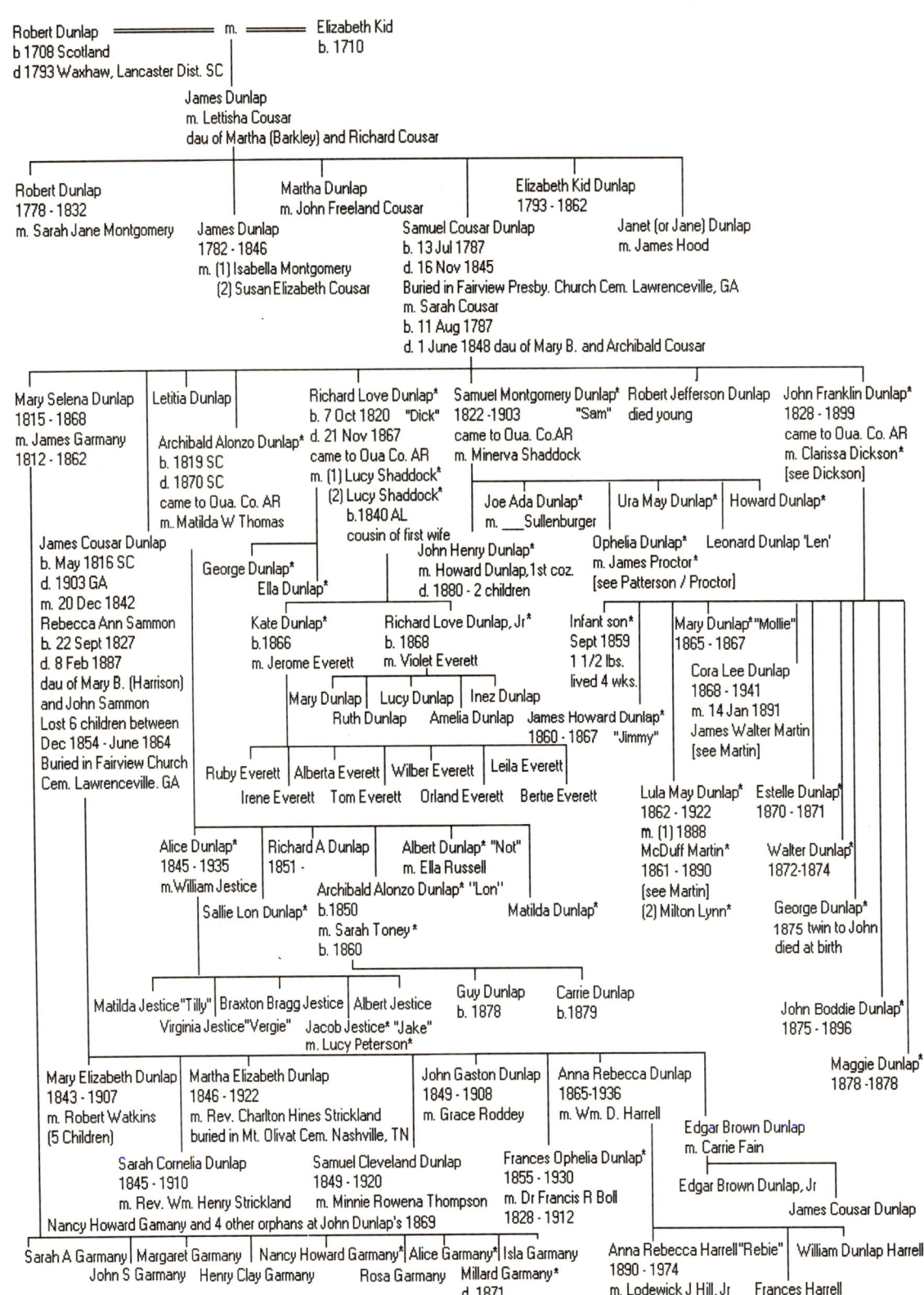

Appendices: A-D

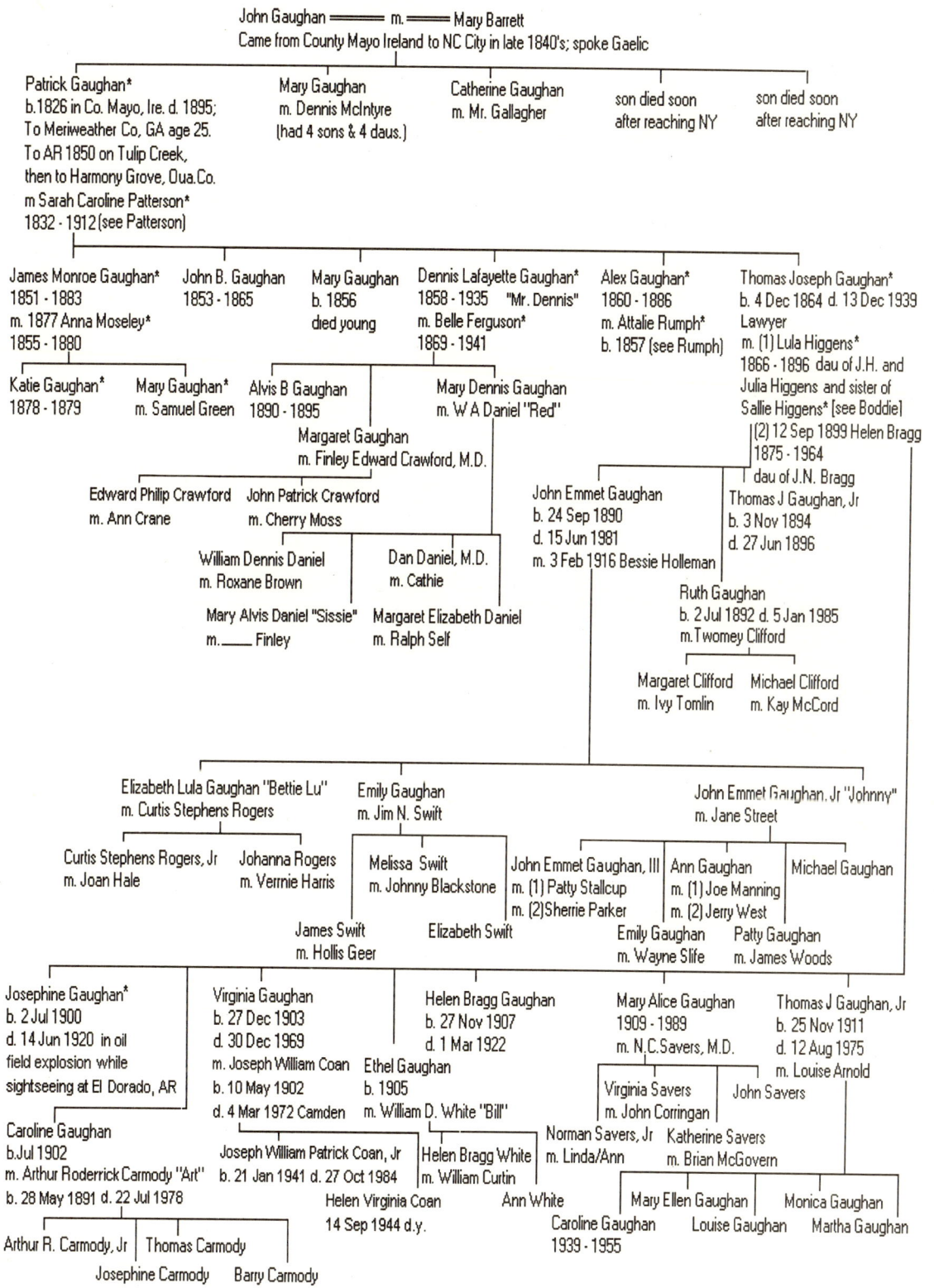

* Mentioned in the letters.

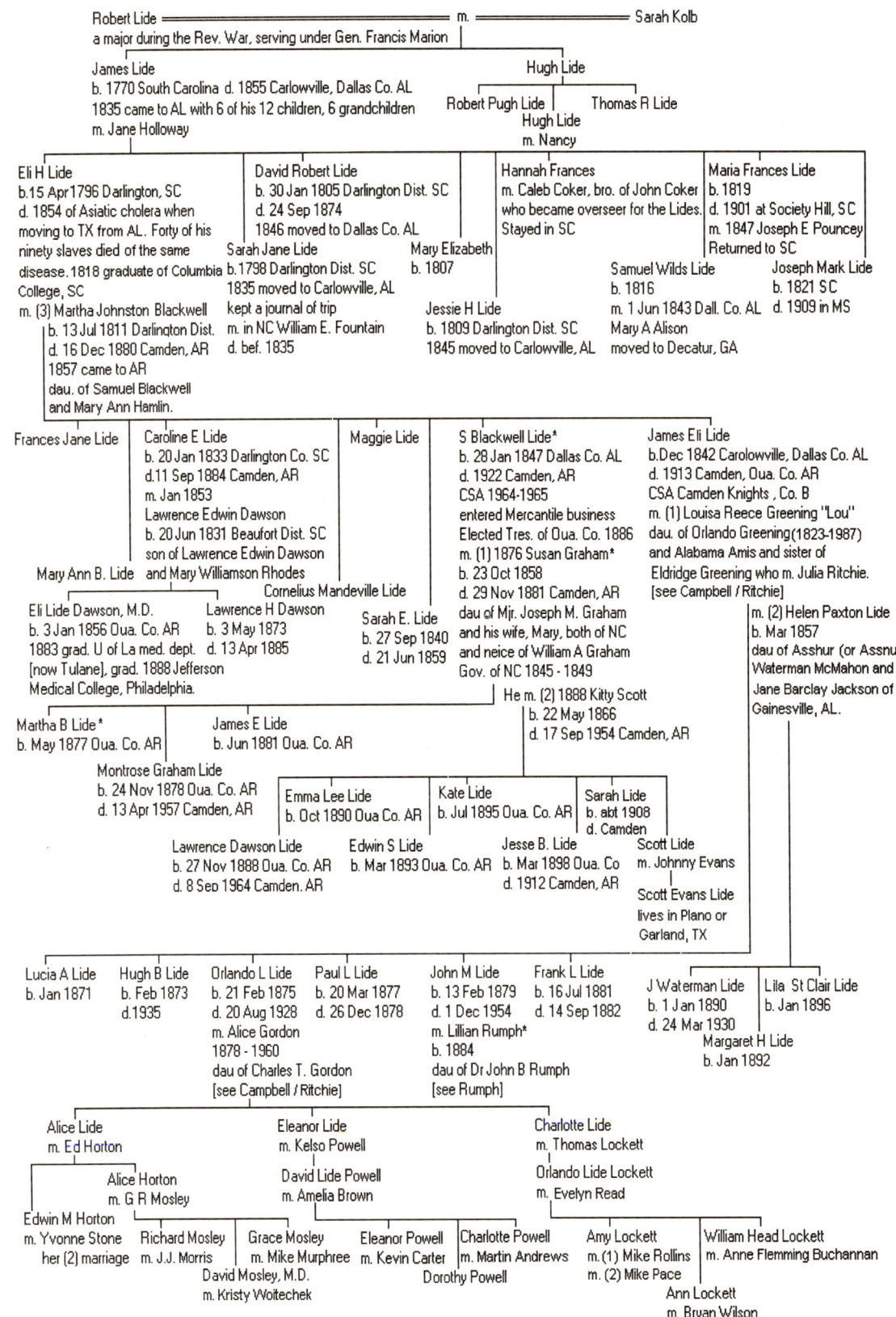

Sisters, Seeds, and Cedars 656

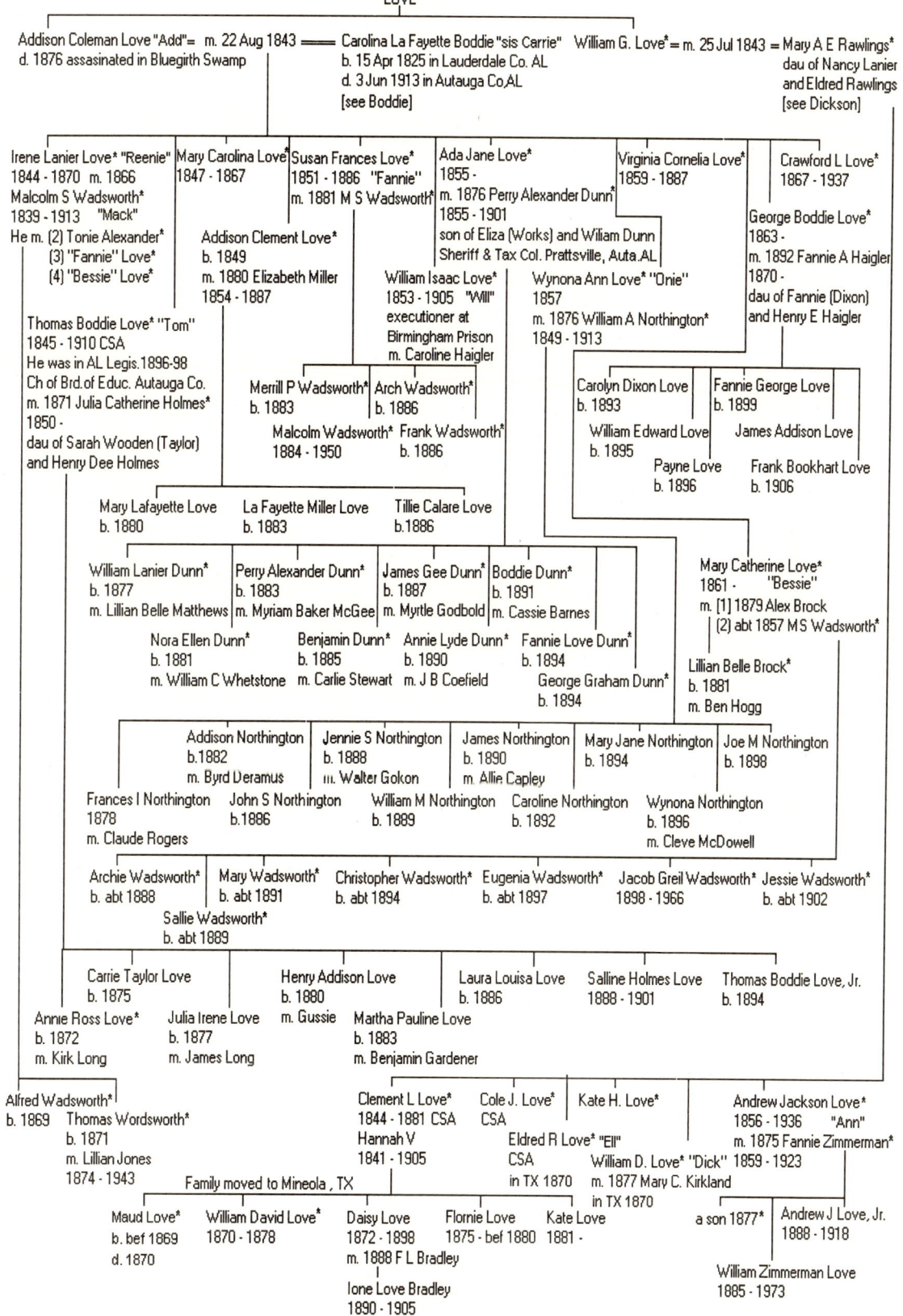

Sisters, Seeds, and Cedars 658

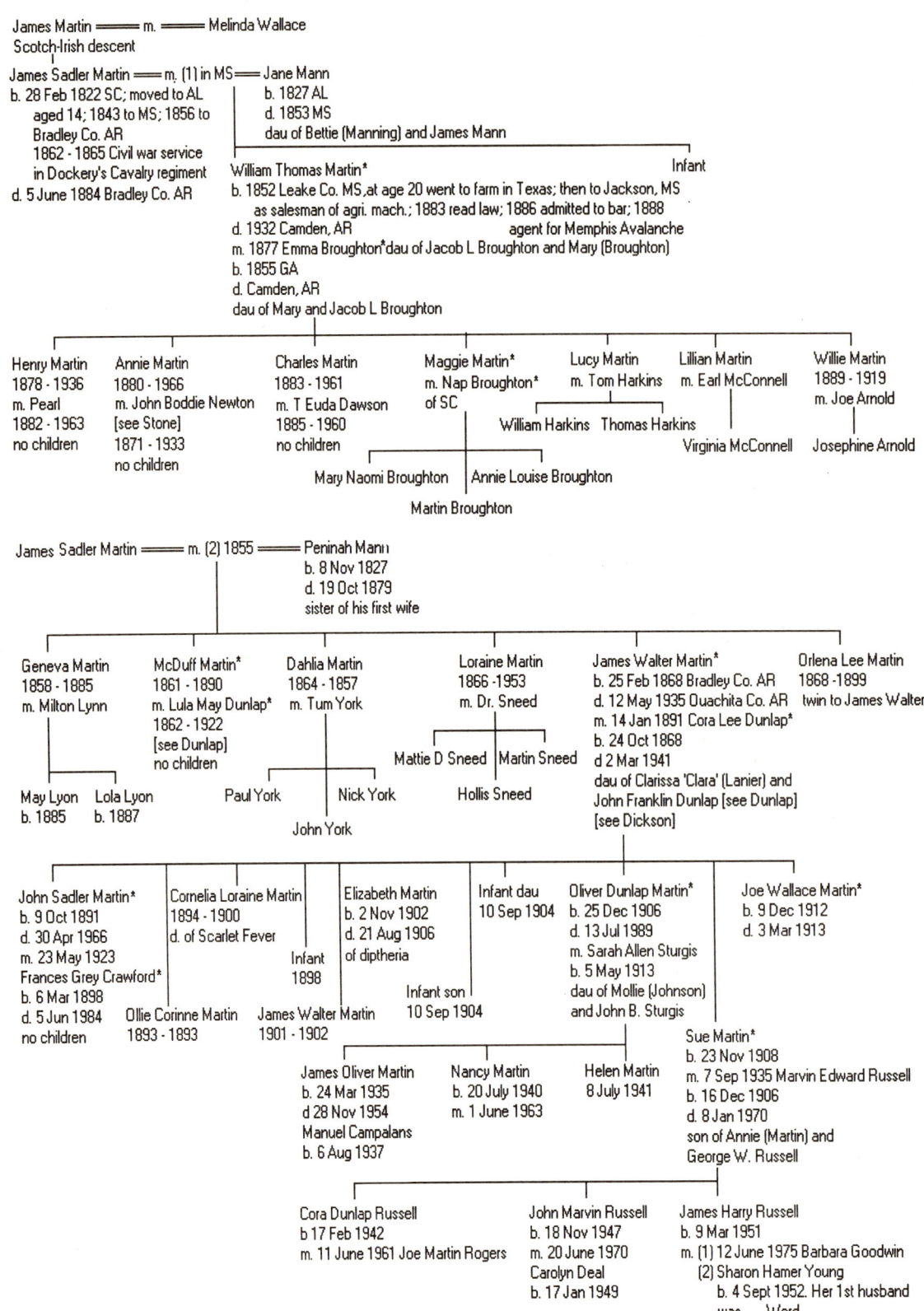

MARTIN

* Mentioned in the letters.

MORGAN

Luke John Morgan — m. — **Ann Brown**
b. Dec 1777 in Wales?   b. in Virginia
d. in Georgia   d. in Georgia?

Col. Asa Stokeley Morgan = m. (1) 10 Jun 1854 = **Eliza Wright**
b. 13 Nov 1825 Macon, GA   b. 19 Aug 1837 Talbot Co. GA
d. 25 Feb 1909 Camden, AR   d. 16 Sep 1869 Mt. Holly, AR
Came to Mt Holly, Arkansas in Jan 1843 with   dau of Mjr. Edward Ward Wright and Martha W. Crowell
Edward Wright when he was 17 years old.   He m. (2) 1 Feb 1871 Martha Julia McRae "Patty"
CSA   b. 14 Jan 1851 Mt Holly, AR
                                                    d. 20 Aug 1889 Mt Holly, AR
                                                    dau of Colin L. McRae and Lydia Ann Chester

John Henry Morgan* | **Edward Wright Morgan** | **Aylmer Lee Morgan "A.L."** | **Charles McRae Morgan, M.D.**
b. 16 May 1855 Mt. Holly, AR | b. 13 Feb 1857 Mt Holly | b. 31 Jul 1864 Mt. Holly, AR | b. 16 May 1872 Mt. Holly, AR
d. 9 Dec 1922 Camden, AR | d. 19 Oct 1868 Mt Holly | d. 15 Nov 1946 Camden, AR? | d. 1923 Camden, AR
Came to Camden 1875; worked | **Stokeley Morgan** | m. (1)1888 Euphemia Graham Newton | m. 17 Jan 1912 Ethel McKay
at Bracy's Drug which he bought. | b. 19 Jul 1859 Mt Holly, AR | b. 27 Oct 1864 Bradley Co. AR "Effie" | b. 21 Dec 1890 Monticello, AR?
In 1882 built a brick building | d. 17 Nov 1900 Roxbury, MA | d. 29 Nov 1904 Camden, AR | dau of Rev. C. W. McKay
at corner of Washington & | Fired the first shot at Spanish Fleet | dau. of Susan Webb Hampton &
Adams. In 1891 established | at the Battle of Manila Bay; took 40 | William Wiley Newton | **Martha McRae Morgan**
Morgan Hardware. | men ashore destroying guns of | m. (2) Sallie Irene Ritchie | b. 18 Jun 1913 Camden
m. 22 Nov 1882 Ida McRae | Cavite Fort; in command of his | b. 17 Sep 1876 Hot Springs, AR
b. 23 Oct 1859 Mt Holly, AR | division at taking of Manila. | d. 5 Oct 1947 at Camden
d. 26 Dec 1919 Camden, AR | m. 1887 Eleanor Williams | dau of James Franklin Ritchie
dau of Lydia Ann Chester & | b. 1867 Roxbury, MA | and Maria Ella Powell
Colin L McRae | d. 1938 Nantucket, MA | [see Campbell/Ritchie]

Stokeley W. Morgan "Lee"
b. 1895 Massachusetts
Diplomat & Banker; ass't Mexican Ambassador; Chief
Counsellor of Latin Affairs, Washington, D.C.
m. 1923 Anne Kupsch
b. in Russia

William Ritchie Morgan | **James Franklin Morgan "Frank"**
b. Feb 1907 Camden | b. 4 May 1911 Camden
d. 1 Feb 1987 Camden | m. 1937 Evalyn Pauline Riley
m. 6 Oct 1931 Hazel Baker | b. 14 Aug 1969 Ft Towson, OK
b. 12 Mar 1914 Warren, AR | dau of Grace Clinton Starnes and
                            Robert Roy Riley

Alymer Lee Morgan, Jr | **Lida Morgan** | **John Hampton Morgan** | **Graham Morgan** | **Asa Stokeley Morgan** | **Mary Morgan**
b. 18 Aug 1889 Camden | b. 5 Nov 1891 Camden | b. 19 Jul 1893 Camden | b. 5 Nov 1904 | b. 19 Apr 1909 Camden | b. 5 Oct 1913
d. May 1955 Strassburg, VA | d. 30 Sep 1979 New Orleans | d. 1954 Hot Springs, NM | d. 8 Apr 1920 | m. 12 Sep 1943 Ann Buford | d. 31 May 1916
m. 1915 Frances Scott | m. 6 Dec 1918 | m. 2 May 1919 Nancy Stuart Beller | | b. 19 Sep 1920 Stephens, AR
 | David Lindsay White | b. 31 May 1898 Little Rock, AR
Alymer Lee Morgan III | b. 2 Aug 1894, d. 25 Sep 1968 | | **Nancy Morgan** | **James F. Morgan, Jr**
b. 22 Sep 1916 Lynchburg, VA | | | b. 26 Dec 1941 Camden | b. 5 Apr 1941 Camden
m. (1) Betty Berry Brumfield | **David White** | **Adam Clarke White "A.C."** | m. Jay Travis Wilson, Jr | d. 7 Apr 1941 Camden
b. 1919 | b. 1923 Natchez, MS ? | b. 5 Nov 1927 Natchez, MS
m. (2) Linda Reed Cuellar | d. May 1935 | m. (1) 1950 Dorothy Lancaster | | **James Hampton Morgan**
b. Lafayette, LA? | **Alymer Virginia White** | m. (2) Jul 1975 Karen Evans | **William Morgan "Bill"** | b. 21 Jan 1957 Camden
 | b. Sep 1925 Natchez, MS | b. 1928 Washington, D.C. | b. 29 Jun 1949 Camden | m. 1979 Donna Gail Smith
Alice Elizabeth Morgan | d. Sep 1990 New Orleans | | m. 30 Jun 1972 | b. 1 Jun 1979 Fordyce, AR
b. 1921 Annapolis, MD | m. James William Barnes "Bill" | | Linda Higman
d. 1980 | b. Apr 24 Bethlehem, PA

John H. Morgan, Jr | **Colin McRae Morgan** | **Robert Wright Morgan** | **David Chester Morgan** | **Sallye Irene Morgan**
b. 21 Mar 1884 Cam. | b. 12 Oct 1887 Cam. | b. 14 Jan 1897 Camden, AR | b. 15 Oct 1903 Camden | b. 29 Jul 1944 Camden
d. 29 Aug 1960 Cam. | d. 1942 Camden | d. 22 Jan 1975 Magnolia, AR | d. 1938 Natchez, MS | m. 1966 George William Sanders
m. 1919 Marguerite Gregg | | m. 25 Mar 1924 Emma Lee Duplantis
b. 7 May 1893 Cincinatti, OH? | | b. 30 Jan 1904 Beaumont, TX | **Charles McRae Morgan** | **Janyth Ann Morgan**
d. 8 May 1981 | **Asa Stokeley Morgan** | d. 7 Aug 1949 | b. 12 Jul 1905 Camden | b. 10 Jan 1946 Camden
 | b. 3 Mar 1890 Camden | | d. 27 May 1987 Cleburne, TX | m. 1965 James Theron
John H. Morgan III | d. 1951 Little Rock, AR | **Emma Lee Morgan** | m. 3 Dec 1931 Bessie Mae Fife | Jackson, Jr
b. 15 Aug 1929 | | b. 20 Dec 1924 Camden, AR | b. 18 Jan 1910 Terrell, TX, d. 28 Jul 1981
d. 27 Jul 1939 | **William Edwin Morgan** | m. 29 Nov 1947 Sterling Smith Lacy III
 | b. 24 Aug 1893 Camden | b. 5 Dec 1924 Eldorado, AR | **Charles McRae Morgan, Jr** | **Mary Linda Morgan**
 | d. 30 Mar 1899 Camden | | b. 19 Jun 1937 Ft. Worth, TX | b. 2 Sep 1942 Ft Worth, TX
 | | | m. 1967 Nancy Jane Choate | d. 26 Feb 1950 Cleburne, TX
 | | | b. 23 Oct 1937 Baytown, TX

* Mentioned in the letters.

Sisters, Seeds, and Cedars

MOSELEY

Lewis Moseley, Jr
b. 8 Jan 1760, d. 5 Dec 1826 in Dallas Co. AL. In Elbert Co. GA 1801, Putnam Co. GA, Dallas Co. AL, m. Elizabeth ___

Elijah Moseley   War of 1812
b. 1767 in NC, d. 14 Sep 1822 in Dallas Co. AL. In Elbert Co. GA 1801, Putnam Co. GA 1810. Moved to Dallas Co. AL 1820. He was a Bap. preacher and farmer, m. (1) bef. 1796 Annie Buckley. She d. bef. 1803.

Eleanor Moseley
m. 18 Jun 1796 in Elbert Co., GA Daniel Parnell, son of John Parnell. moved to Putnam Co. GA, 1818 to Dallas Co. AL

Henry Moseley

Robert Moseley in Elbert Co. 1801

Alanson Moseley settled in Cherokee Co. TX

Benjamin Moseley? in Elbert Co. GA

Jonathan Moseley in Elbert Co. GA 1801

Rev. William Moseley
b. 21 Oct 1796 Ebert Co. GA. Putnam Co. GA, Dallas Co. AL, Jasper Co. GA, Henry Co, AL, Griffin, GA. Elected to Senate 1843, 1851, to House 1847.

Fannie Moseley
m. a Mr Brooks moved to Dallas Co. AL

Lewis Buckley Moseley
b. 15 Jan 1801 Elbert Co. GA
d. Jun 1871 Selma, Dallas AL
m. (1) Susan Lowe
m. (2) Blanche Cathey

Elijah Moseley m. (2) abt. 1802 Susannah Hubbard She m. (2) aft. 1822 Dr. Dunn and moved to Augusta Co. AL
son, William Dunn,* d. 1880 in Autauga Co. AL

David Moseley
b. abt. 1803 Elbert Co. GA Cowetta Co. GA 1830-
m. Elizabeth Spivey
sons Jesse M.Moseley & David Hubbard Moseley settled in Wood Co. TX

Anna Moseley
b. 1807 in GA
d. Bradley Co. AR
m. Robert Parnell son of Eleanor Moseley and Daniel Parnell. ances. of Harvey Parnell, Gov. of AR

John Moseley
b. 1810 in GA twin of Peter
d. 1887 Dall. Co. AL
m. Annie Dean
12 children

Sarah Moseley
b. abt 1814

Nancy Moseley*
m. Mr Goodman*
Autauga Co. AL

Jonathan Moseley
b. abt 1805 in GA
d. in Bradley Co. AR
m. Hildah Jones

Rev. Peter Moseley*
b. 1810 in GA, d. 1887 in Brad. Co. AR
m. (1) 1826 in Dall.Co. AL
Laura Hubbard, m. (2) Elizabeth Beard

Elijah Moseley II,* b. 1812 in Putnam Co. GA, d. 4 Dec 1880 Oua. Co AR settled in Bradley Co. AR 1844, to Oua. Co. abt. 1865. He was merch. and farmer. He rep. Oua Co. at AR Constitutional Convention 1874. m. Mahala Campbell,* b. 10 Dec 1818 in TN, d. 15 May 1898 in Oua. Co. dau of John Campbell [see Campbell / Ritchie]

Charles Moseley
1838 - 1861
d. in CSA

John Campbell Moseley
1842 - 1862, d. Battle of Murfreesboro, TN

Jane Alabama Moseley*
m. bef. 1872 Edmund Rucks*
He m. (2) abt. 1878 Corrie Rumph "Mittie" *
[see Rumph]

William Allis Moseley*
1851 - 1930; m. (1) 1887 Carrie Boddie; m. (2) 1903 Mrs. Octavia Word Brodnax

Elizabeth Susan Moseley
1840 - 1843

Mary Arkansas Moseley*
1845 - 1928; m. 1862 Harry Clay Fisher

Lewis Marvin Moseley*
1850 - 1934; m. (1) 1890 Elizabeth Burger; m. (2) Lucy Willis

Mahala Anna Moseley* "Miss Annie"
1855 - 1880; m. 20 Dec 1877 James M Gaughan*
1851 - 1883 [see Gaughan]

Antoinette A. Fisher
1864 - 1866

Charles Moseley Fisher*
b. 27 Sep 1869 Hopkinsville, KY

Corrie Rucks*
1873 - 1935
m. 1894 Walter P. Ritchie*
[see Campbell / Ritchie]

Katie Gaughan*
1878 - 1879

Frederick Elijah Fisher*
1866 - 1939
m. Daisy ___

Harry Gordon Fisher*
b. 14 Jun 1876 at Hopkinsville, KY
d. 1956 at Miami, FL
m. Blanche Dickens*
b. 1878 at Nashville, TN

Harry Fisher Moseley*
1888 - 1945   WW I

Mary Ann Gaughan*
b. 1880
m. Samuel Green

Harry Gordon Fisher*
b. 1898
m. Grace Eberts

Granville Chapman Fisher,* Ph D
b. 1906
d. 1988 at Miami, Prof. at U. of M.
m. (1) Bobbie Tucker
m. (2) Ijourie Stocks
m. (3) Peggy Adams

Charles A. Fisher
b. 1913
m (1) Ina Farnham

Douglas Fisher
b. 1915
m. (1) Alice ___
m. (2) Vera Highsmith

George Boddie Moseley*
1891 - 1972   WW I
m 1924 Mary Sue Raines

Nita Raines Moseley
m. Charles E Munoz

Frederick Drennan Fisher
m. Agnes ___

Douglas Fisher

April Fisher

Robin Fisher

Steven Fisher
m. (2) Irene McIntosh

Charles Elijah Moseley*
1890 - 1979   WW I
m. 1926 Ruth White

William Marvin Moseley*
1892 - 1899   WW I
m. Mamie Elizabeth Caldwell

Hubert Henry Moseley
1896 - 1968
m. Ethel Hollingsworth

John Lewis Moseley *
1984 - 1960   WW I
m. 1922 Gertrude Bradshaw

Frederick Campbell Moseley
b.1897 ; m. 1939
Mrs. Frances Espy Gunn

Charles E Moseley, Jr.
m. Carolyn Ripley
Sarah Jane Moseley
m. Gordon "Bill" Fountain

Marverine E Moseley
m. Clifford C Rampey
William Caldwell Moseley
1921 -1944 Lt.[Bombadier]
8th Air Force   WWII

Frances Moseley
m. Victor Amdahl
Frederick Thomas Moseley,
M.D. F.A.C.S.
m. Miriam Ann Orr

Edward Moseley
b 6 Feb 1923
d. 6 Oct 1993
m. Odea Lee White

Louise Moseley
b. 4 Dec 1925
d. 6 Jul 1972
m. Herman Ernest Schanzlin
WW II

Helen Lois Gunn
m. Herbert W Hartung, Lt.Col

*Mentioned in the letters.

Appendices: A-D

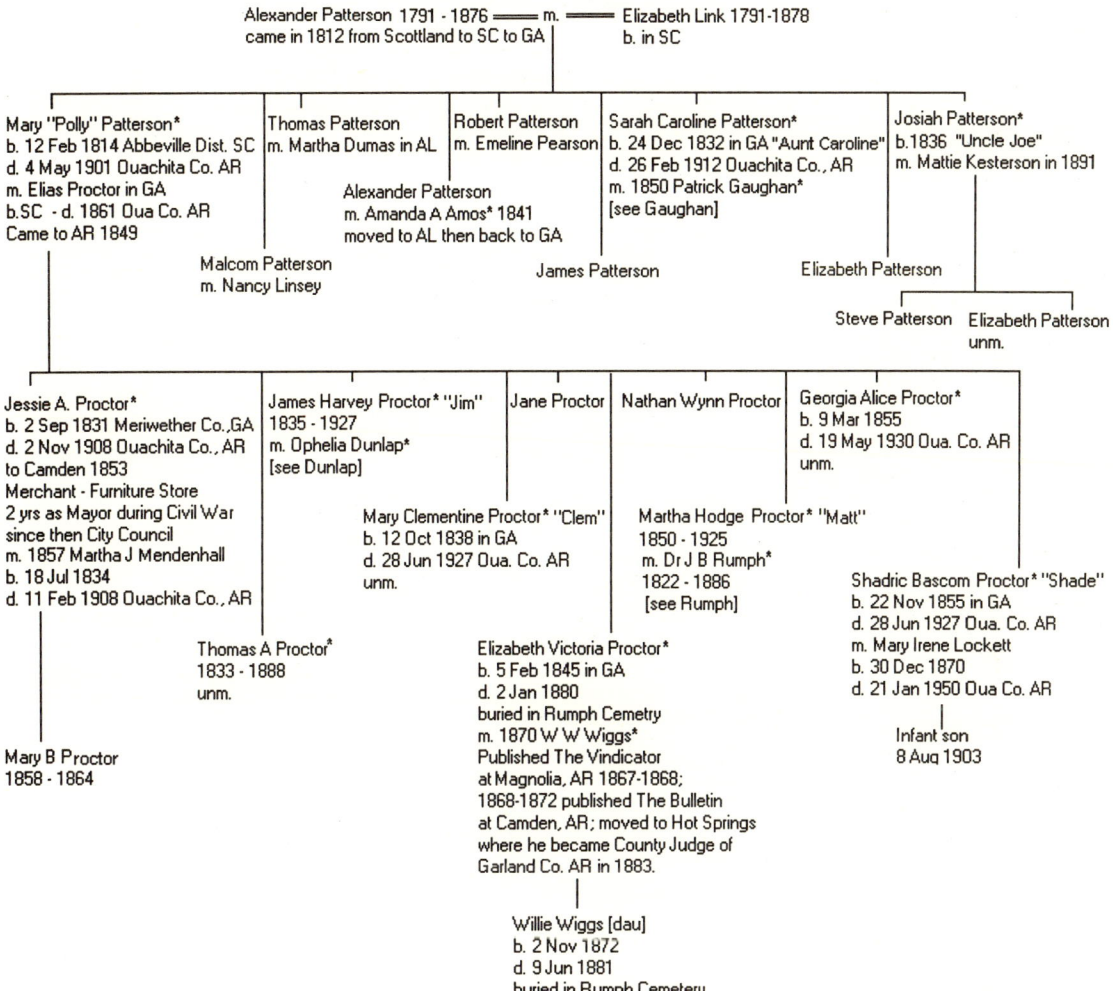

* Mentioned in the letters.

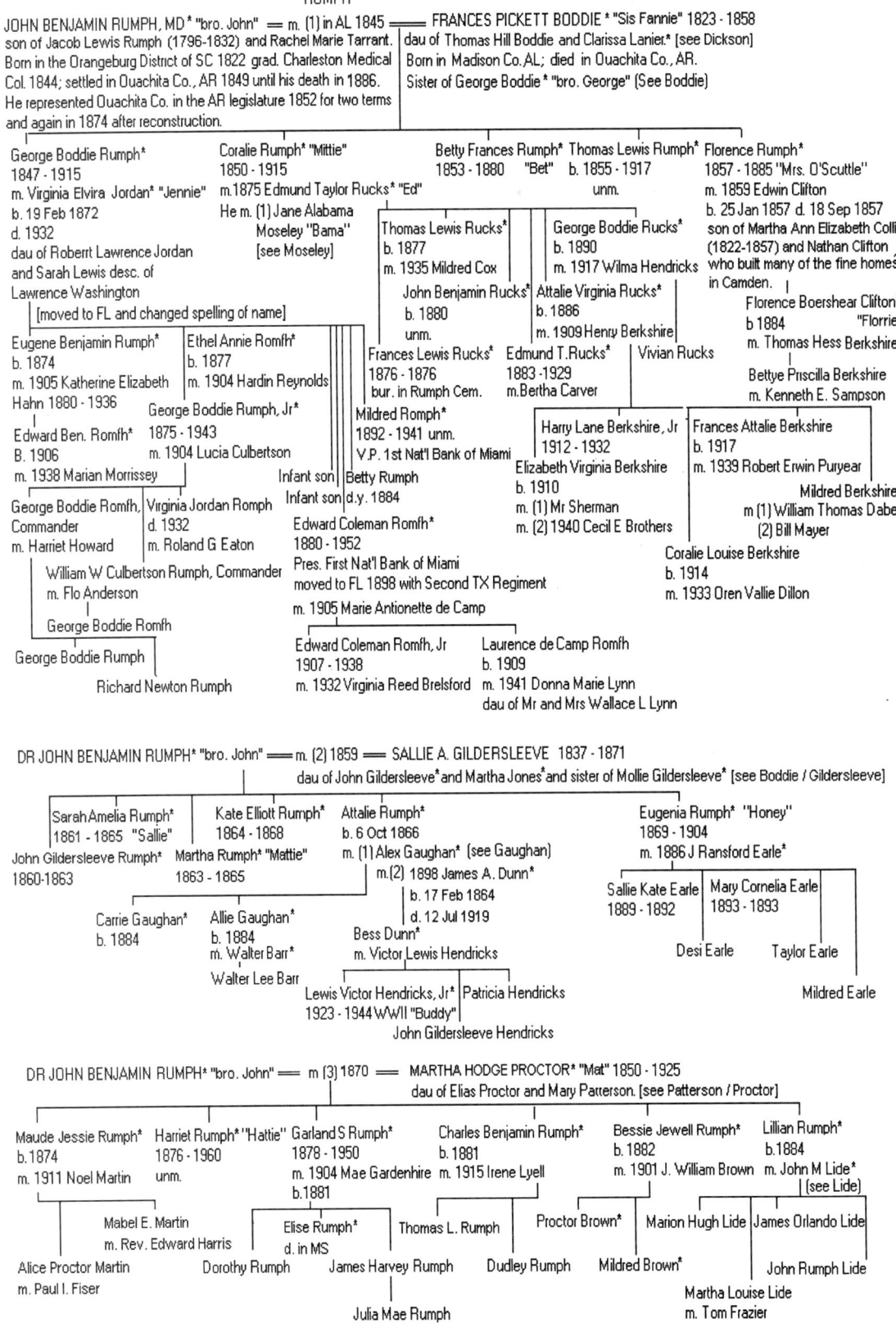

663 Appendices: A-D

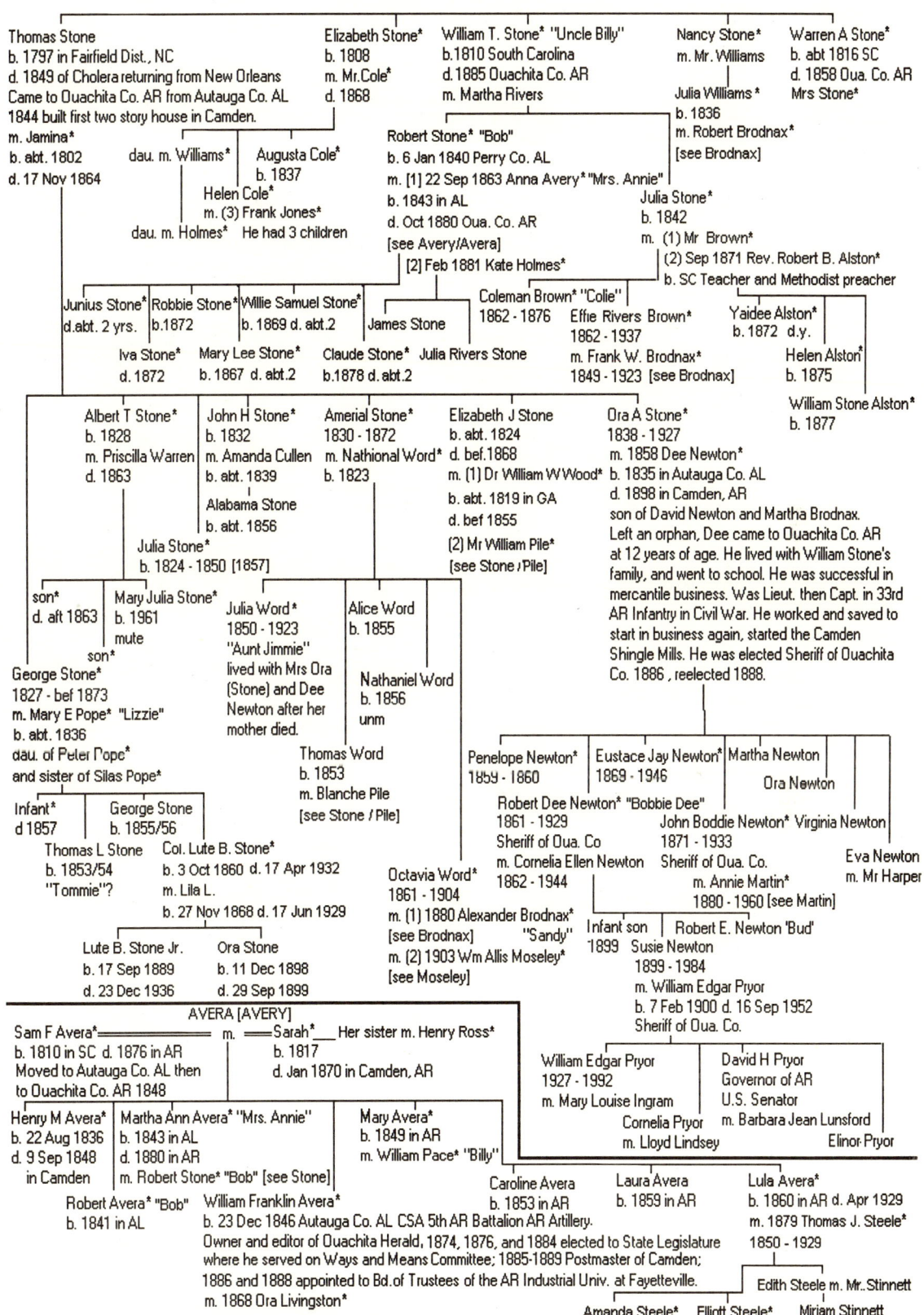

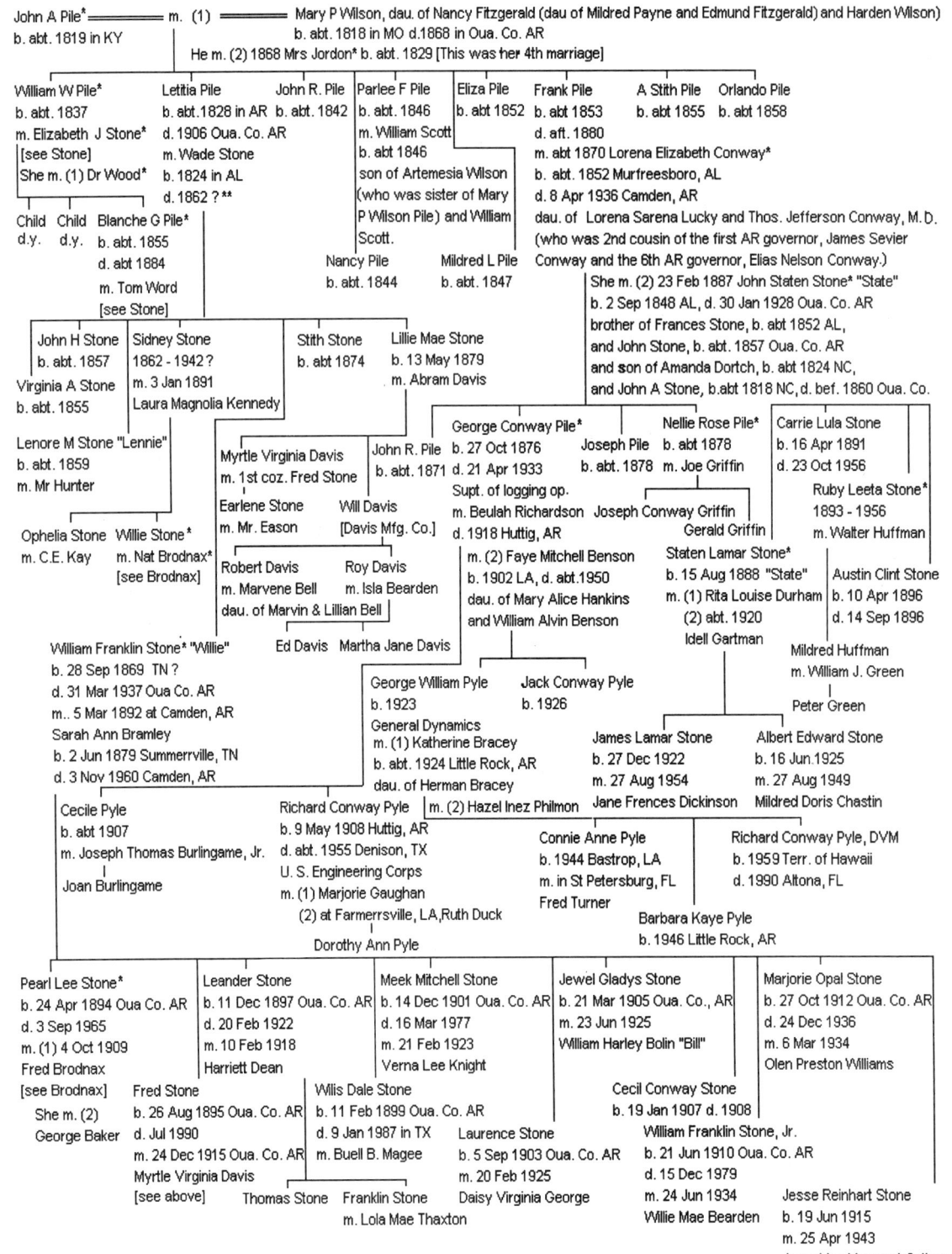

Bibliography of Geneological Charts

Allsopp, F. W. *History of the Arkansas Press*. Little Rock, AR: Parke-Harper Pub. Co., 1922.
Arkansas Gazette, May 11, 1986.
Austin, Jeanette Hellard. *The Georgians Genealogies of Pioneer Settlers*. Baltimore: Genealogical Publishing Company. 1984.
Autauga County Alabama Will, Burial, Estate, Guardian, and Marriage Records. *Bicentenial History of Bradley County, AR*.
Boddie, Caroline Frances "Carrie." Bible records.
Boddie, John Bennett. *Historical Southern Families*. IV. Redwood City, CA: Pacific Coast Pub.
Boddie, John Bennett. *Southside Virginia Families*. IV. 1955.
Boddie, John Thomas and John Bennett Boddie. *Boddie and Allied Families* Privately Printed, 1918.
Bradley County Historical Society, *Views*. 6-2 Winter 1979/1980, 6-4 Summer 1980 and 7-1 Fall 1980. Warren, AR:
Burnett, Gene M. *Florida's Past People and Events That Shaped the State*. Englewood, FL: Pineapple Press. 1986.
Burke's Landed Gentry. London: Burke's Peerage Limited, 1939.
The Camden News, June 30, 1976.
Carr, James O., Esq. ed. *The Dickson Letters*. Raleigh: Edwards and Broughton, Printers. 1901.
Clemens, William Montgomery. *North Carolina and South Carolina Marriage Records Colonial to Civil War*. Baltimore: Baltimore Genealogical Publishing Co. 1881.
D A R Patriots Index. Washington: D A R
Dickson, Cornelia Sanderson, "Pedigree of My Mother's Family, a part of which, is as was told to me by my Gr. mother, Mary Lanier, in 1856."
Dickson, H.N.S. Bible records.
The Duplin Times, 14. April. n.d.
East Texas Its History and Its Makers. III. New York: Lewis Historical Publishing Co. 1940.
Encyclopedia Americana. New York: Americana Corp., 1959.
Genealogies of Virginia Families. IV. Baltimore: Baltimore Genealogical Pub. Co. Inc. 1981.
Georgia Genealogical Records. (Loose Leaf copies of County Records.)
Georgia Genealogical Magazine. 79 Winter 1981; 98 Summer 1981.
Gildersleeve, Willard Harvey. *Gildersleeve Pioneers*. Rutland, VT: The Tuttle Pub. Co., Inc.
The Goodspeed Biographical and Historical Memoirs of Southern Arkansas 1887. Southern Historical Press. 1989
Green, Fletcher M. ed. *The Lides go South and West a Record of a Planter Migration in 1835*. Columbia, SC: Univ. of South Carolina Press. 1952.
Hayes, Louise Frederick. *Rumph-Frederick Families*
Jones, Kathleen Paul and Pauline Jones Gandrud, compilers, *Alabama Records*, 46, Dallas County and 106, Autauga County.
The Montgomery Advertiser, April 23, 1911.
Moseley, Mary Sue Raines, Moseley Chart descendants of Elijah and Mahala Campbell Moseley.
Moseley, Thomas Byrd Moseley, Jr. *A Moseley Genealogy*. Baltimore. Gateway Press, Inc. 1985.
Nelson, W. W., Obituary of Mary E. Boddie in "Arkansasss Methodist 27 Mar 1901.
Ouachita County Homemakers Extension Clubs. *Cemeteries of Ouachita County, Arkansas*.
Ouachita County Marriage Records.
Owen, Thomas McAdory. *History of Alabama and Dictionary of Alabama Biography*. IV. Startanburg, SC: Reprint Company Publishers. 1978.
Pickett, Albert James. *The History of Alabama*. Birmingham: Birmingham Book and Magazine Co. 1962.

Rose, Floretta Purifoy. *Henry Marshall Purifoy Genealogy*. Atlanta, TX: Bowman.

Rumph, Jacob Lewis, Bible records.

Saunders, Col. James Edmonds, with Notes and Genealogies by Elizabeth Saunders Blair Stubbs. *Early Settlers of Alabama*. Baltimore: Genealogical Publishing Co. 1982.

"Southern Standard," Obituary of Mamie Boddie Coleman, 26 Sep 1929

Smith, George Gillman. *The Story of Georgia and the Georgia People 1732-1860*. Baltimore: Genealogical Publishing Company. 1968.

Tap Roots, April-June 1977

Tombstone inscriptions. Greenwood, Greenwood Annex, and Memorial Park Cemeteries, Camden, AR.

Turner, Ida Marie and Adelle Vickery compilers. *Cemeteries of Wood County Texas*. II and IV. Mineola, TX: Adelle Vickery. 1972.

Turner, Ida Marie and Adelle Vickery. compilers. *Marriages of Wood County Texas A,B,C,& D 1879-1903*. Mineola, TX. Adelle Vickery. 1971.

United States Decennial Census Records.

Vital Data From Cemeteries in Dallas County, Alabama. Central Alabama Genealogical Society. 1989.

Wisehart, M. K. *Sam Houston American Giant*. Washington: Robert B. Luce, Inc. 1962.

Note: Much of the genealogical information was found in the letters of *Sisters, Seeds, and Cedars*.

Contributors of Information:
Helen Rose Burns Brodnax
Margaret Horne Dansby
Dan Daniel, M. D.
Ruth Boddie Farmer
Charles A. Fisher
John Gildersleeve Hendricks
Emma Lee and Sterling Lacy
Charlotte Lide Lockett
Cornelia Pryor Lindsey Frank Morgan
George William Pyle
Cora Russell Rogers
Elizabeth Gaughan Rogers
John Harvey Rumph
Sue Martin Russell

Appenix C
PRINCIPAL FAMILIES INDEX

BODDIE
(See Lanier for Clarissa Lanier Boddie Dickson)
Boddie, George ("Brother George') m. Mary Elizabeth ("Sis Mollie") Gildersleeve
    _____,John Rumph ("Brother")   m. [1] Cornelia Kimball Smoker
        _____,George Kimball Smoker Boddie m. Waitie Butler
            _____,Ruth Evelyn m. James Cecil Farmer
            _____,John Rumph m.   [1] Mildred Edwards
                      [2] Marie La Bita
        m. [2] Lucie Smoker Hunt
    _____,Willis Thomas ("Will," "Willie")
    _____,George Gildersleeve ("Gilder")
    _____,Mary Elizabeth ("Mamie," "Small Sis") m. Edwin Gallie Coleman, M.D.
        _____,Ernest Godfrey m. Florence Pelt
        _____,Mary Gilder Coleman ("Gilder") m. Walter Lee Bagwell
        _____,Fred Hughes Coleman m. Helen Moorhouse
    _____,Sarah Catherine ("Little Sallie") died early
    _____,Frances Caroline ("Carrie," "Little Sis") m. William Allis Moseley (See Moseley)
    _____,Robert Lee ("Bobbie," "Tug") m. Sallie Higgins Farley
        _____,Robert Lee Jr. m. Virginia Anderson
        _____,John Hubert m. Annie Mae Foster
        _____,George Gilder Boddie
Boddie, Frances Pickett ("Sis Fannie") m. John Benjamin Rumph (See Rumph)
Boddie, Caroline LaFayette ("Sis Carrie") m. Addison C. ("Add") Love (See Love)

BRODNAX

Brodnax, Henry Powers ("Old Mr. Hal")   m. [1] Mildred Whitaker
    _____,Mary Belle Brodnax m. Jacob Hodges Golson
    _____,Henry Whitaker Brodnax m. [1] Emma P.
                                [2] Rachel M. Meriwether
    _____,Rebecca M. Brodnax m. John Henry Stone
    _____,Martha Brodnax m. Hilliard J. Stoudermier
    _____,Robert R. Brodnax m. Julia
    _____,John Thomas Brodnax m. Susan Elizabeth Pierce
    _____,Joseph W. Brodnax m. Margaret Elizabeth Ellis
    _____,James Harper T. Brodnax m. Susan D. Harkins
                        m. [2] Jane Pitts
    _____,Francis ("Frank") Wellington m. Effie Brown (See Stone)
    _____,Edward m. Kate McLaughlin
        _____,Lucy Mae m. Tom Dean
        _____,Charley (died young)
        _____,Eugene m. Una Westbrook
    _____,Alexander Hamilton ("Sandy") m. Octavia Word
        _____,Annie Laurie m. Hartwell Wright
        _____,Frederick Alexander (Fred) m. Pearl Stone
        _____,Janie Hamerial m. W. Edgar Padgett
        _____,Nathaniel ("Nat") m. Willie Stone (See Wade Stone)
        _____,Martha Octavie m. B. Frank Saunders
        _____,John (died young)

_____,Wright m. Alva Gammill
    _____,Ray
    _____,George
    _____,Polly m. Chester Pope

CAMPBELL/RITCHIE

Campbell, Mahala m. Elijah Moseley (See Moseley)
Campbell, Jane McBride m. John Calhoun Ritchie
    _____,James Franklin m. Maria Power
        _____,Walter P. m. Corrie Rucks (See Moseley)
            _____,Ella m. Shirley Gardenhire
            _____,Col. Walter m. Thelma O'Rear
            _____,Frances m. Edwin Truesdale
        _____,Edgar
        _____,Sallie m. A. L. Morgan (See Morgan)
    _____,George Lewis
    _____,Frances Alabama m. Green White
        _____,Julia
        _____,Clarence
    _____,John Campbell m.   [1] Fannie Stith
        _____,Charles Andrew (died young)
        _____,Stith Bearden m. Susie T. Gordon
        _____,George Garnet (died young)
            [2] Minnie Barker
    _____,Julia Sonora m. Eldridge S. Greening
        _____,Rosina m. Victor Snow
        _____,Eldridge
        _____,Janie
        _____,Julia m. Marvin Hardy
    _____,Martha Virginia m.   [1] Mr. Stanley
        _____,Ritchie
        _____,Fannie R. m. C. L. Newman
            [2] William King Ramsey
        _____,Margaret
        _____,Will
        _____,Robert
    _____,Ella Jane m. Charles T. Gordon
        _____,Susie T. m. Stith B. Ritchie
        _____,Mildred m. Claude Garland Horne
        _____,Thomas
        _____,Alice m. Orlando L. Lide (See Lide)
        _____,Judge George R. m. Emma Sue Thomas
        _____,Frances m. James Cooper Usrey

DICKSON/LANIER

Dickson, Michael m. Sarah Neeley
    _____,Samuel Henry m. Rebecca Hutton
        _____,Dickson, Samuel Henry Neeley m. Clarissa ("Mother Dickson")Lanier Boddie
            (See Boddie)
            _____,Cornelia ("Aunt Nealie," "Nealie/Neelie") Sanderson

_____,Clarissa m. John F. Dunlap (See Dunlap)
Dickson, William m. Mary Hix Williams
    _____,Mary m. Isaac Lanier
        _____,Dickson Mann C.
        _____,Clement G. ("Uncle Clem")
        _____,Clarissa m. [1] Thomas Hill Boddie (See Boddie; Love)
                      [2] Samuel Henry Neeley Dickson

DUNLAP

Dunlap, James m. Lettisha Cousar
    Dunlap, Robert m. Sarah Jane Montgomery
    _____,James m. [1] Isabella Montgomery
                     [2] Susan Elizabeth Cousar
    _____,Martha m. John Freeland Cousar
    _____,Samuel Cousar m. Sarah Cousar
        _____,Mary Selena m. James Garmany
            _____,Sarah A.
            _____,John S.
            _____,Margaret
            _____,Henry Clay
            _____,Nancy Howard
            _____,Rosa
            _____,Alice
            _____,Millard
            _____,Isla
[Nancy Howard and four other Garmany orphans were removed to Arkansas in 1869 by the Dunlap family.]
        _____,James Cousar m. Rebecca Ann Sammon
            _____,Mary Elizabeth m. Robert Watkins
            _____,Sarah Cornelia m. Rev. Wm. Henry Strickland
            _____,Martha Elizabeth m. Rev. Charlton Hines Strickland
            _____,Samuel Cleveland m. Minnie Rowena Thompson
            _____,John Gaston m. Grace Roddey
            _____,Frances Ophelia m. Dr. Francis R. Boll
            _____,Anna Rebecca m. Wm. D. Harrell
            _____,Edgar Brown m. Carrie fain
        _____,Archibald Alonzo m. Matilda W. Thomas
            _____,Alice m. William Jestice
                _____,Matilda ("Tilly")
                _____,Virginia ("Vergie")
                _____,Braxton Bragg
                _____,Jacob ("Jake")
                _____,Albert
            _____,Sallie
            _____,Richard A.
            _____,Archibald Alonzo ("Lon") m. Sarah Toney
            _____,Albert ("Not") m. Ella Russell
            _____,Matilda
    _____,Richard Love m. [1] Lucy Shaddock
                          [2] Lucy Shaddock, cousin of 1st wife
        _____,Kate m. Jerome Everett
        _____,Richard Love Jr. m. Violet Everett

_____,Samuel Montgomery m. Minerva Shaddock
    _____,John Henry m. Howard Dunlap, 1st coz
    _____,Joe Ada m. Sullenberger
    _____,Ophelia m. James Proctor (See Patterson/Proctor)
    _____,Ura May
    _____,Leonard ("Len")
    _____,Howard
_____,Robert Jefferson (died young)
_____,John Franklin m. Clarissa Dickson
    _____,Jimmie
    _____,Lula May m.   [1] McDuff Martin (See Martin)
                      [2] Milton Lynn
    _____,Mary (died young)
    _____,Cora Lee m. James Walter Martin (See Martin)
    _____,Estelle (died young)
    _____,Walter (died young)
    _____,George (twin to John Franklin Jr., died at birth)
    _____,John Franklin, Jr.
    _____,Maggie Dunlap

GAUGHAN

Gaughan, Patrick m. Sarah Caroline Patterson (See Patterson/Proctor)
    _____,James Monroe m. Anna Moseley (See Moseley)
        _____,Katie (died young)
        _____,Mary ("Baby") m. Samuel Green
    _____,John B. Gaughan (died young)
    _____,Mary (died young)
    _____,Dennis Lafayette m. Belle Ferguson
        _____,Alvis B. Gaughan (died young)
        _____,Margaret m. Finley Edward Crawford, M. D.
        _____,Mary Dennis m. W. A. ("Red")Daniel
    _____,Alex m. Attalie Rumph (See Rumph)
        _____,Carrie
        _____,Allie m. Walter Barr
    _____,Thomas Joseph ("Tommie") m.   [1] Lula Higgens
        _____,John Emmet m. Bessie Holleman
        _____,Ruth m. Twomey Clifford
        _____,Thomas Joseph Jr. (died young)
                        [2] Helen Bragg
        _____,Josephine
        _____,Caroline m. Arthur Roderrick ("Art") Carmody
        _____,Virginia m. Joseph William Patrick Coan, jr
        _____,Ethel m. William D. White
        _____,Helen Bragg
        _____,Mary Alice m. Norman C. Savers M. D.
        _____,Thomas Joseph Jr. m. Louise Arnold

LIDE

Lide, Eli H. m. [3] Martha J. Blackwell
    _____,Frances Jane

_____,Mary Ann B.
_____,Caroline E. m. Lawrence Edwin Dawson
    _____,Eli Lide Dawson, M. D.
    _____,Lawrence H. Dawson
_____,S. Blackwell m.   [1] Susan Graham
    _____,Martha B.
    _____,Montrose Graham
    _____,James E.
        [2] Kitty Scott
    _____,Lawrence Dawson
    _____,Emma Lee
    _____,Edwin S.
    _____,Kate
    _____,Jesse B.
_____,James E. m.   [1] Louisa R. ("Lou") Greening
    _____,Lucia A.
    _____,Hugh B.
    _____,Orlando L. m. Alice Gordon
        [2] Helen P.

LOVE

Love, Addison ("Brother Add") Coleman m. Carolina La Fayette ("Sis Carrie") Boddie (See Boddie)
    _____,Irene ("Reeny") m. Malcolm S. Wadsworth
        _____,Alfred
        _____,Thomas m. Lillian Jones
    _____,Thomas Boddie ("Tom") m. Julia Catherine Holmes
        _____,Annie Ross m. Kirk Long
        _____,Carrie Taylor
        _____,Julia Irene m. James Long
        _____,Henry Addison m. Gussie
        _____,Martha Pauline m. Benjamin Gardener
        _____,Laura Louisa
        _____,Salline Holmes
        _____,Thomas Boddie Jr.
_____,Mary Caroline
_____,Addison Clement m. Elizabeth Miller
    _____,Mary Lafayette
    _____,La Fayette Miller
    _____,Tillie Calare
_____,Susan Frances ("Fannie") m. Malcolm S. Wadsworth
    _____,Merrill P.
    _____,Malcolm
    _____,Arch
    _____,Frank
_____,William Isaac m. Caroline Haigler
_____,Ada Jane m. Perry Alexander Dunn
    _____,William Lanier m. Lillian Belle Matthews
    _____,Nora Ellen m. William C. Whetstone
    _____,Perry Alexnder m. Myriam Baker McGee
    _____,Benjamin m. Carlie Stewart
    _____,James Gee m. Myrtle Godbold

_____,Annie Lyde m. J. B. Coefield
_____,Boddie m. Cassie Barnes
_____,Fannie Love
_____,George Graham
_____,Wynona Ann ("Onie") m. William A. Northington
    _____,Frances m. Claude Rogers
    _____,Addison m. Byrd Deramus
    _____,John S.
    _____,Jennie S.
    _____,William M.
    _____,James m. Allie Capley
    _____,Caroline
    _____,Mary Jane
    _____,Wynona m. Cleve McDowell
    _____,Joe M.
_____,Virginia Cornelia
_____,Mary Catherine ("Bessie") m. [1] Alex Brock
    _____,Lillian Belle m. Ben Hogg
            [2] Malcolm S. Wadsworth
    _____,Archie
    _____,Sallie
    _____,Mary
    _____,Christopher
    _____,Eugenia
    _____,Jacob Greil
    _____,Jessie
_____,George Boddie m. Fannie A. Haigler
    _____,Carolyn Dixon
    _____,William Edward
    _____,Payne
    _____,Fannie George
    _____,James Addison
    _____,Frank Bookhart
_____,Crawford L.
_____,William G. m. Mary A. E. Rawlings
    _____,Clement L. ("Clem") m. Hannah V.
        _____,William David
        _____,Daisy m. F. L. Bradley
        _____,Florrie
        _____,Kate
    _____,Cole J. CSA
    _____,Eldred CSA
    _____,Kate H.
    _____,William D. ("Dick") m. Mary C. Kirkland
    _____,Andrew Jackson m. Fannie Zimmerman
        _____,William Zimmerman
        _____,Andrew J. Jr.

MARTIN

Martin, James Sadler m   [1] Jane Mann
    _____,William Thomas m. Emma Broughton

_____ Henry m. Pearl
_____,Annie m. John Boddie Newton [See Newton]
_____,Charles m. T Euda Dawson
_____,Maggie m. Nap Broughton
    _____,Mary Naomi
    _____,Martin
    _____,Annie Louise
_____,Lucy m. Thomas Harkins
    _____,William
    _____,Thomas
_____,Lillian m. Earl McConnell
    _____,Virginia
_____,Willie m. Joe Arnold
    _____,Josephine
[2] Peninah Mann
_____,Geneva m. Milton Lynn
    _____,May
    _____,Lola
_____,McDuff m. Lula May Dunlap [See Dunlap}
_____,Dahlia m. Tum York
    _____,Paul
    _____,John
    _____,Nick
_____,Loraine m. Dr. Sneed
    _____,Mattie D.
    _____,Hollis
    _____,Martin
_____,James Walter m. Cora Lee Dunlap [See Dunlap]
    _____,John Sadler m. Frances Grey Crawford
    _____,Ollie Corinne (died young)
    _____,James Walter (died young)
    _____,Elizabeth (died young)
    _____,Oliver Dunlap m. Sarah Allen Sturgis
        _____,James Oliver m. Manuel Campalans
        _____,Nancy
        _____,Helen
    _____,Sue m. Marvin Edward Russell
        _____,Cora Dunlap m. Joe Martin Rogers
        _____,John Marvin m. Carolyn Deal
        _____,James Harry m.   [1] Barbara Goodwin
                              [2] Sharon Hamer Young

MORGAN

Morgan, Col. Asa Stokeley m.   [1] Eliza Wright
    _____,John Henry m Ida McRae
        _____,John H. , Jr m. Marguerite Gregg
        _____,Colin McRae
        _____,Asa Stokeley
        _____,William Edwin (died young)
        _____,Robert Wright m. Emma Lee Duplantis
        _____,David Chester

_____,Charles McRae
_____,Edward Wright (died young)
_____,Stokeley m. Eleanor Williams
    _____,Stokeley W. ("Lee") m. Anne Kupsch
_____,Aylmer Lee ("Al") m.   [1] Euphemia Graham Newton ("Effie")
    _____,Alymer Lee, Jr. m. Frances Scott
    _____,Alice Elizabeth
    _____,Lida m. David Lindsay White
    _____,John Hampton m. Nancy Stuart Beller
    _____,Graham
        [2] Sallie Irene Ritchie (See Campbell/Ritchie)
    _____,William Ritchie m. Hazel Baker
    _____,Asa Stokeley m. Ann Buford
    _____,James Franklin ("Frank") m. Evalyn Pauline
    _____,Mary (died young)

MOSELEY

Moseley, Elijah m. [1] Annie Buckley
    _____,Rev. William A.
    _____,Fannie m. Mr. Brooks
    _____,Lewis Buckley
    [2] Susannah Hubbard m [1]Mr. Dunn
        _____,William
        _____,David
        _____,Jonathan
        _____,Anna m. Robert Parnell
        _____,Rev. Peter m. [1] Laura Hubbard [2] Elizabeth Beard
        _____,John m. Annie Dean
        _____,Elijah II m. Mahala Campbell
            _____,Charles CSA
            _____,Elizabeth Susan (died young)
            _____,John Campbell CSA (died Battle of Murfreesboro)
            _____,Mary Arkansas m. Harry Clay Fisher
                _____,Antoinette A.
                _____,Frederick Elijah m. Daisy
                _____,Charles Moseley
                _____,Harry Gordon m. Blanche Dickens
            _____,Jane Alabama m Edmund Rucks
                _____,Corrie m. Walter P. Ritchie (See Campbell/Ritchie)
            _____,Lewis Marvin m.   [1] Elizabeth Burger
                _____,Charles Elijah m. Ruth White
                _____,William Marvin m. Mamie E. Caldwell
                _____,Hubert Henry m. Ethel Hollingsworth
                _____,John Lewis m. Gertrude Bradshaw
                _____,Frederick Campbell m. Frances E. Gunn
                    [2] Lucy Willis
            _____,William Allis m. [1] Carrie Boddie (See Boddie)
                _____,Harry Fisher
                _____,George Boddie m. Mary Sue Raines
            _____,Mahala Anna m. James M. Gaughan (See Gaughan)
                _____,Mary K. (died early)2

_____,Mary ("Baby") m. Samuel Green

NEWTON

Newton, Dee m. Ora A. Stone (See Stone)
      _____,Penelope (died young)
      _____,Robert Dee m. Cornelia Ellen Newton
          _____,Susie m. William Edgar Pryor
          _____,Robert E. ("Bud") m. Ora Belle
_____,Eustace Jay
_____,John Boddie m. Annie Martin (See Martin)
_____,Martha
_____,Ora
_____,Virginia
_____,Eva m. Mr. Harper

PATTERSON/PROCTOR

Patterson, Alexander m. Elizabeth Link
      _____,Mary ("Polly") m. Elias Proctor
          _____,Jessie A. m. Martha J. Mendenhall
              _____,Mary B. (died young)
          _____,James Harvey ("Jim") m. Ophelia Dunlap (See Dunlap)
          _____,Thomas A.
          _____,Shadric Bascom ("Shade") m. Mary Irene Lockett
          _____,Mary Clementine ("Clem")
          _____,Elizabeth Victoria m. W. W. Wiggs
              _____,Willie (daughter) (died young)
          _____,Martha Hodge ("Matt") m. Dr. John B. Rumph (See Rumph)
          _____,Georgia Alice

RUMPH

Rumph, John Benjamin, MD m. [1]Frances Pickett ("Sis Fannie") (See Dickson)
      _____,George Boddie m. Virginia Jordon (moved to Florida and changed spelling of name)
          _____,Eugene Benjamin m. Katherine Elizabeth Hahn
          _____,George Boddie Jr. m. Lucia Culbertaon
          Romph, Ethel Annie m. Hardin Reynolds
          _____,Edward Coleman m. Marie Antoinette de Camp
          _____,Mildred
      _____,Coralie ("Mittie") m Edmund Taylor Rucks
          _____,Frances Lewis (died young)
          _____,Thomas Lewis m. Mildred Cox
          _____,John Benjamin
          _____,Edmund T.
          _____,Attalie Virginia m. Henry Berkshire
          _____,George Boddie m. Wilma Hendricks
      _____,Betty Frances
      _____,Thomas Lewis
      _____,Florence ("Mrs. O'Scuttle") m. Edwin Clifton
          _____,Florence Boershear m. Thomas Hess Berkshire
              [2] Sallie A. Gildersleeve

_____,John (died young)
_____,Sallie Amelia (died young)
_____,Mattie (died young)
_____,Kate Elliott (died young)
_____,Attalie m. [1] Alex Gaughan (See Gaughan)
       _____,Carrie
       _____,Allie m. Walter Barr
       [2] James A. Dunn
       _____,Bess m. Victor Lewis Hendricks
_____,Eugenia ("Honey") m. J. Ransford Earle
       _____,Sallie Kate (died young)
       _____,Desi (died young)
       _____,Mary Cornelia (died young)
       _____,Taylor (died young)
       _____,Mildred
       [3] Martha Hodge ("Matt") Proctor
_____,Maude m. Noel Martin
       _____,Alice Proctor m. Paul I. Fiser
       _____,Mable m. Rev. Edward Harris
_____,Harriet ("Hattie")
_____,Garland S. m. Mae Gardenhire
       _____,Dorothy
       _____,Elise
       _____,James Harvey
_____,Charles Benjamin m. Irene Lyell
       _____,Thomas
       _____,Dudley
_____,Bessie m. J. William Brown
       _____,Proctor
       _____,Mildred
_____,Lillian m. John M. Lide (See Lide)

STONE

Stone, Thomas m. Jamina ?
       _____,George m. Mary E. ("Lizzie") Pope
             _____,Thomas L.
             _____,George
             _____,Col. Lute B.
       _____,Albert T. m. Priscilla Warren
             _____,Mary Julia
_____,Julia
_____,John H. m. Amanda Cullen
_____,Amerial m. Nathional Word
             _____,Julia ("Aunt Jimmie")
             _____,Thomas m. Blanche (See Stone/Pile)
             _____,Alice
             _____,Nathaniel
             _____,Octavia m. [1] Alexander Brodnax ("Sandy") (See Brodnax)
                  [2] William Allis Moseley (See Moseley)
             _____,Elizabeth J. m.   [1] Dr. William W. Wood
                              [2] William Pile (See Stone/Pile)

_____,Ora A. m. Dee Newton (See Newton)
_____,Elizabeth m. Mr. Cole
    _____,daughter m. Holmes
    _____,Helen m. Frank Jones
    _____,Augusta
_____,William T. ("Uncle Billy") m. Martha Rivers
    _____,Robert ("Bob") m. [1]Anna Avery ("Mrs. Annie")
        _____,(Six children born ; died under the age of three)
            [2] Kate Holmes
        _____,James
        _____,Julia Rivers
    _____,Julia m. [1] Mr. Brown
        _____,Coleman ("Colie")
        _____,Effie Rivers m. Frank W. Brodnax (See Brodnax)
        [2] Robert B. Alston
        _____,Yaidee
        _____,Helen
        _____,William Stone
_____,Nancy m. Mr. Williams
    _____,Julia m. Robert Brodnax (See Brodnax)
_____,Warren A.

STONE/PILE

Pile, John A. m. [1] Mary P. Wilson
    _____,William W. m. Elizabeth J. Stone (See Stone)
        _____,Blanch m. Tom Word (See Stone)
    _____,Letitia m. Wade Stone
        _____,Virginia A.
        _____,_ John H.
        _____,Sidney m. Laura Magnolia Kennedy
            _____,Ophelia
            _____,Willie m. Nat Brodnax (See Brodnax)
        _____,Lenore ("Lennie") m. Mr. Hunter
        _____,William Franklin ("Willie") m. Sarah Ann Bramley
            _____,Pearl Lea m. Fred Brodnax (See Brodnax")
            _____,Fred m. Myrtle Davis (Lillie Mae Stone)
            _____,Jack m. Harriet Dean
            _____,Jim
            _____,Meek m. Verna Knight
            _____,Lawrence m. Daisy George
            _____,Jewel m. William Bolen
            _____,Cecil Conway (died young)
            _____,Marjorie Opal m. Olen Williams
            _____,Jesse Reinhart m. Josephine Cathey
        _____,Stith
        _____,Lillie Mae m. Abram Davis
            _____,Myrtle m. Fred Stone
            _____,Will Davis
    _____,John
    _____,Nancy
    _____,Parlee F.

_____,Mildred L.
_____,Frank m. Lorena Elizabeth Conway ("Mrs. Pile")
　　　_____,George Conway m. [1] Beulah Richardson
　　　　　　　　　　　　　　　[2] Faye Mitchell Benson
　　　_____,Nellie m. Mr. Griffin
_____,Lorena Elizabeth Conway m. Staten ("State") Stone [February 23, 1887]
　　_____,State
　　_____,Ruby m. Walter Huffman

APPENDIX D
PEOPLE AND PLACES

ALABAMA PEOPLE

A
Adair, Mrs.
Alexander, Mr.
Andrews, Warren
Ann (slave)

B.
Bohanan, Bettie
Baker, Fanny
Baseman, J. E.
Broadwell, Miss
Brodnax, Henry
Brooks, Mr.

C.
Carey, D.
Carey, Mittie
Cater, Mrs.
Caver, Mrs.
Caver, Tom (former slave)
Chester, Mrs.
Clark, Mrs. Eliza S.
Clay, Betsy
Clay, Mr., & Mrs. Jack
Clay, Jeff
Cole, Amy
Collins, Mrs.
Conway, A. A.
Conway, Mrs. S
Crouse, Charley
Cumberland Presbyterian Ladies

D.
Dan (slave)
Darden, William
Davis, Dr. Tom
Davis, Mr.
Deseker, Mrs. A. H.
Dousing, Jennie
Dungan, Tom
Dunn, Ben

E.
Easterling, Dr.
Edwards, Mr.

F.
Fair, Dr.
Foreman, Preacher

G.
Golson, Amy
Golson, Eustice
Golson, James
Grey, Mrs.

H.
Hall, Amy Jane
Harriet (slave)
Harris, Dr.
Hendree, Mrs.
Hermann, Ella
Himble, Mrs.
Holmes, Sue
Holmes, Willie
House, Miss
Houston, Ella
Houston, Mrs.
Howard, Dr. Charles M.
Howard, Dora
Howard, Ella
Howard, James (Jimmy)
Howard, Julia
Howard, Lamon
Howard, Larrant
Howard, Mims
Howard, Mrs. Dr.
Howard, Mrs. L.
Hutton, William G.

J.
Jerry (slave)
John (slave)
Johnson, Old Billy
Johnson, Mrs.

K.
Kennedy, Mrs.
Kent, Miss (Johnson)
Kirkland, Miss F. (Motley)
Kirkland, Mollie
Kirkland, Perry

L.
Lamar, Dee
Lamar, Sarah
Lamar, Burl
Lapsley, Mrs.
Lasiter, Berry (Whitstone)
Lasiter, Dee
Lasiter, Mrs.
Lasiter, Virgil
Leaman, Dee
Limbrish, Tim
Lockett, Mary
Lockett, Mrs.
Lyles, Mr. & Mrs.

M.
McClain, Old Mr.
McCravery, Mr.
McNeal, Sophia (Ware)
Mitchel, Mr.
Mixon, Mr.
Mixon, Tallie
Morgan, Miss
Morton, Mr.
Morton, Susan "Mammy" (slave)
Morton, Tom (slave)
Motley, Dora (Davis)
Murley, Fay
Murley, Hattie Gildersleeve
Murley, Mr.
Murry, James

N.
Newton, Green
Northington, Thomas
Nunn, Mr. & Mrs.

P.
Parker, Mr.
Phillips, Dr. J.
Pickett, Albert "Cousin Albert"
Pickett, Sarah Harris "Cousin Sarah"
Pickett, Eliza "Cousin Fannie"
Pippin, Julia
Pons, G.
Porter, Bill (Phillips)

R.
Roseman, Mrs.
Roundtree, Mr.
Rumph, Old Louis

S.
Simpson, Bob
Simpson, Mat
Smith, Mae
Steele, Mrs.
Stubbs, James

T.
Taylor, Matilda (Mat)
Taylor, T.
Terry, Mr.
Thacher, Mary Elizabeth

U.
Underwood, Becca (daughter of Rebecca)
Underwood, Dempsey
Underwood, Hattie
Underwood, Jr.
Underwood Mr.
Underwood, Rebecca
Underwood, Thomas

Wadsworth, Bessie Love Brock
Wadsworth, Tom
Wagner, Mr. Walter
Walker, Eliza
Wallace, Mr. & Mrs. T.
Ward, Miss
Ware, Henry
Weaver, Cal
Weaver, David
Weaver, Mrs. Cal
Weaver, Phil
Whetstone, Peyton
Whetstone, Betty Lasiter
Wickinson, Jimmie
Wickinson, Willie
Wiggins, Jenny
Wilkerson, Joe
Williams, Theresa
Winter, Bob
Wood, Billy

Z.
Zimmerman, Fannie
Zimmerman, W. J.

ALABAMA PLACES

Air Mount
Alabama River
Autauga County
Birmingham
Boiling Springs
Burnsville
Cahawba
Camden
Clarke County
Clay's Station
Clifton
Decatur
Eutaw
Fort Morgan
Galena
Gaston's Landing
Ivy Creek Church
Jefferson P. O.
Kingston
Lamar School House
Luton County
Madison
Maringo County
Marion
Mobile
Mulberry Academy
Mulberry Post Office
Peachtree
Polk House
Prattville
Selma
Springhill College
Sweetwater P. O.
Wilcox County

ARKANSAS PEOPLE

A
Agee, A.
Agee, Brooks
Agee, John
Alston, Julia Stone Brown
Alston, Robert B.
Ann T.
Arthur, Susan (Peters)
Aunt Nina (Slave)
Avant, E. J.
Avera/Avery, Lula

B
Bacon, Dr.
Badders, Mr.
Becky (Slave)
Ben (Slave)
Benson, Mary
Berg, Emma
Bird, Meek
Black, Cicero
Block, Old Mr.
Bob (Slave)
Bracy, Mr. & Mrs.
Bragg, Florence
Broack, Mr.
Brodnax, Emma
Brooks, Brs.
Brown, Dr.
Brown, Jennie
Brown, West
Brown, Will
Broughton, Henry
Broughton, Maggie
Broughton, Mrs.
Bryant, Arch
Buchanan
Burford, Dr.
Butler, Mr. & Mrs.

C
Carey, Emaline (Former slave)
Carey, Steve (Former slave)
Chapman, Henry
Chidester, Mr.
Cliffer, Henry
Coleman, Ed Harris
Coleman, Mrs. William
Cottie, Miss
Cross, Clara (Bracy)

Culbreath, Mrs.
Cummins, Mr.
Curry, Mary

D
Dick (Slave)
Dion, Mrs.
Dortch, Alex
Douglas, Dave
Duck, Bobbie
Dunlap, Katie
Dunlap, Knot
Dunlap, Lon
Dunlap, Sallie Lou
Dunn, Jim
Dunn, John
Duprey, Mrs.
Duprey, Tommy
Duprey, William

E
Earle, Rufus
Earle, Sam
Elliott, Cord
Elliott, Jim
Elliott, Mary
Elliott, Mollie
Elliott, Mrs.
Elliott, Nellie

F.
Farley, Albert
Farley, Eddie
Felsenthal, Mrs.
Ferguson, Mrs.

G
Garland, Mr.
Garmany, Henry
Garmany, Miss Howard
Gatling, Mrs. Bell
Gatling, John
Gee, Charles
Gee, Louise
Gillespie, Claud
Gillespie, Etta
Goddard, George
Godfrey, Mr. & Mrs.
Golden, Clara
Gordon, Charlie
Greening, MR.

H
Hall, Tom
Hall, Richard
Hallman, MR. & MRs.
Halton, Dr.
Hannah (Slave)
Hare, MR.
Hartwell, Dr.
Hateox, Dr.
Hawkins, Chester
Hawkins, Mr. & Mrs. Frank
Hawkins, Sylvester
Head, Amanda
Hendricks, Mrs. L. V.
Henry (Slave)
Hill, Col.
Hogue, Jeff
Hogue, Mr.
Holmes, Cora
Holmes, Kate
Holmes, Will
Hood, Eula
Horn, Laura
Hudson, Dr.

I
Ivins, Anne

J
Jack (Former Slave)
Jenkins, Bud
Jenning, Mr.
Joe (Former Slave)
Jordan, Willie
Josephine (Slave)
Julia (Slave)
July Ann (Slave)
Justice, Jake
Justice, Lillie
Justice, Virgie

K
Kenenday, Mr.
Killam, Frank
Kinch, Norman

L
Lea, Mr. & Mrs. William
Lide, Mr.
Livingston, Mr. & Mrs.
Lucy (Slave)
Lydia (Former Slave)

M
Macca, Mr.
Madland, Mrs.
Mains, Mr.
Mann, Mr.
Marinda (Slave)
Marshall, Mr.
Martin, Belle
Martin, Edgar
Martin, Lucian
Martin, Mrs. William
Martin, W. T.
McClain, Gavin
McCollum, Dr.
McElrath, Dr.
McGill, Fannie
McKinney, Elsie
McKinney, Mrs.
McMahan, Mattie Malnor
Meek, Dr.
Meek, Lea
Meek, Sue
Meek, Walter
Mitchell, Capt. & Mrs.
Monk, Dr.
Montgomery, Mr.
Morgan, C.
Morgan, John
Murray, Dollie
Murray, Miss Willie
Murry, Dr.
Myers, Henry

N
Newson, W. W.
Newgate, Mrs.

O
O'Bannon, Mrs.

P
Pace, Dr.
Pace, Mary
Parker, Milton
Patterson, Cad
Patterson, Mittie
Patterson, Mrs.
Pelt, Johnson
Pelt, Nolan
Perry, Ross
Peters, Jim
Peters, MRs.

Peterson, Lucy
Phillis (Salve)
Pile, Conway
Pile, William
Polly (Slave)
Ponder, Mrs.
Pope, Silas
Powell, Clayton
Powell, Mamie Winfield
Powell, T. C.
Proctor, George
Proctor, Shade
Purifoy, Arthur
Purifoy, Mrs.
Puryear, Powel
Puryear, Mary
Pyles, John

R
Rainwater, John
Reeves, Edgar
Richardson, Frank
Richardson, Jude
Richardson, Mrs. Toke
Rinehart, Dr.
Ritchie, Ella
Roberson, West
Roda/Rhoda (Slave)
Rounsiville, Miss

S
Sanders, Arnold
Sanders, Old Mr.
Sarah (Former Slave)
Sather, Pete
Saxon Mr.
Scales, Mollie
Scales, Mr.
Scales, Nellie
Scott, Bill (Slave)
Seymore (Former Slave)
Shaddock, Mrs.
Shannon, Dr. J. T.
Sifford, Mrs. J. T.
Silliman, John I.
Simmons, Cash
Simmons, Old Mrs.
Smith, Buddie
Smoker, Lillie
Stanley, Fannie
Steele, Amanda
Steele, Elliott

Steele, Lula
Stinson, George

T
Toney, Jim
Toney, Mr. & Mrs.

U
Usrey, Frances

V
Venable, Aubrey
Venable, Clayton
Venable, Lillie
Venable, Rosser

W
Williams, Helen
Williams, Mr.
Willis, Carl Lewis
Wilson, Mrs.
Wood, Dr. William
Wood, Eliza Stone (Mrs. William)
Word, Miss Jimmie
Word, Lillian

ARKANSAS PLACES

Arkadelphia
Arkansas River
Arlington Hotel, Hot Springs
Bayou Bartholomew
Bearden
Camden
Canian Church
Clark County
Devil's Elbow
Drew County
El Dorado
Felsenthal
Florence, Arkansas
Fordyce
Fort Smith
Freo Creek/ Bottom
Grand Prairie
Gurdon Depot
Holly Springs
Hot Springs
Little Prairie
Little Rock
Lonoke
Luda
Malvern
Marmaduke's Ford
Mitchal Station
Monticello
Mount Elba
Napoleon
Ouachita County
Pine Bluff
Pine Lake
Prescott
Princeton
Rockwell Manufactoring
Shady Grove
Tulip
Tyro, Drew County
Warren
Webb Lake
White River
Woodard Lake

Index

Symbols

2nd City Guards 115
3rd Ouachita Voligneers 115
4th Ouachita Rangers 115

A

Abbott, Tom 390
Abolitionist 109
Adair, Mrs. 55
Agee
  A. 389
  John 181
  L. 312
  Mr 306
  Mrs 182, 341, 389, 392, 466, 480, 556
  Sissy 297, 469
Air Mount 31
Ajo, Arizona 620
Alabama 609
  Burnsville 10
  Clifton 48
  Madison County 57
  Mobile. *See* Mobile
  Peachtree 16
Alabama River 2, 14, 30
Alchley, Mr 350
Alexander
  Mr. 23
  Tonie 257
Al(l)ston
  Julia Stone Brown (Julie) 247, 250, 253, 264, 266, 272, 299, 324, 342, 361, 381, 391, 399, 403, 404, 406
  Robert B., Rev.(Mr.) 243, 250, 251, 256, 262, 317, 381, 386, 403
  William Stone 391
  Yaidee 272
alum 608
Anderson, Mr 284
Andrews
  Dr. 574
  Mrs. 237
  Warren 21
animals, farm (*See also*)
  chickens 71
  cows 72
  geese 71
  hogs 35
  mule 86
  mules 155
  oxen 88
  pigs 97
  pony 94
  sheep 72
  shoat 49
animals, wild
  bear
  deer 40
  ducks 96
  fawn 40
  hawks 84
  partridges 86
  possums 49
  rabbits 165
  squirrels 96
ants 41
appendicitis 626, 640
apple trees 165, 260
apples 3, 19, 21, 32, 57, 73, 75, 88, 111, 136, 166, 187, 188, 192, 242, 285, 302, 305, 317, 330, 334, 359, 403, 420, 455, 622
Arborvita 372
Archer, Tom 471
Archie, Miss 358
Arizona 583, 593, 605, 620
Ark State Scrip 388
Arkadelphia 128, 153, 270, 273, 375, 382, 386, 397, 399, 413, 416, 420, 423, 424, 425, 436, 445, 476, 485, 540, 551, 563, 564, 568, 571, 625
Arkansas 147, 284
  Clark County 57
ARKANSAS GAZETTE 607
Arkansas River 131, 169, 180
Arlington 485
army worms 209
Arrington, Mr 114
Arthur, Susan 36
Arthur's House Magazine 234
Ashville 590
asthma 153
Atkins, Fannie 252
Atlanta 172, 190, 305, 502, 552, 555, 556, 568, 590
Auburn Ala 602
Aunt Flora 244
Aunt Hannah 400
Aunt Mary 284
Aunt Mollie 209
Aunt Nina 302, 386, 416
Austin, Texas 493
Autauga 102, 325, 346, 384, 453, 460, 549
Autauga County, Alabama 70, 114, 602
Autaugaville 22, 262, 264
automobiles 591, 598, 600, 612
Avant, E. J. 526
Avera (y)
  Lula 215, 264, 327, 331, 346, 350, 358, 369, 375, 384, 393, 396, 410, 453
  Mr. 227, 232, 272, 273, 353
  Mrs. 227, 232, 238, 272
  Ora 272
  Sam 215
  William 238

B

B., Dolle 299
B., Ella 302
bacon 140, 142, 146, 149, 179, 183, 189, 241, 327
Bacon, Dr. 47
Badders, Mr. 481, 534
Badger, Mrs. 186
Bagwell, Mary Gilder Coleman 609, 634
Baker, Fanny 8, 9
Balboa 639
Baltimore 629
bananas 487, 622
Banks, Eliza (Miss) 237, 560
Banner 644
barbecue 338, 364, 366, 368, 369, 450, 452
Bardstown, Kentucky 211, 463, 464, 465, 466
Barker, Charlie (ey) 466, 468, 469
Barr
  Allie Gaughan 599, 636, 644
  Walter 615
baskets 68, 478, 608
Batesville 424
Battle Creek Michigan 618
Battle of Pea Ridge 128
Bayou Bartholemew (ue) 174, 176, 179
Beacon 369
beans 36, 43-45, 56, 73, 131, 136, 149, 196, 236, 367, 522

butter 90
bear 39, 130, 183, 225, 256, 263, 280, 291, 293, 297, 300, 310, 319, 322, 370, 371, 372, 374, 377, 381
Bearden 529
  Mr. 424
Beardon, Miss 343
Beauregard, Pierre Gustave Toutant De, General 127
Beck 165
Beckton, Mrs 552
Becky 231, 250, 252, 294, 409
bed 110, 127, 131, 153, 156, 157, 160, 165, 166, 186, 218, 250, 254, 257, 271, 281, 286, 289, 297, 312, 324, 325, 333, 340, 343, 364, 369, 374, 394, 396, 432, 439, 441, 443-446, 479, 491, 496, 500, 501, 504, 536, 547, 550, 556, 568, 571, 572, 575, 579, 592, 593, 595, 599, 601, 604, 622, 636
bedclothes 157
bee-gum 4
beef 104, 142, 178, 179, 189, 338, 360, 366, 588
  barbacued 317
bees 292, 294, 297, 303
beets 32, 82, 127, 136, 196, 367
Bell Buckle, Tennessee 494
Bell,
  John 89
  Mr 333
belladonna 145, 500
Ben 163
Benson, Mary 501
Bergs, Emma 501
Bert 135
Bessie 496, 510
Bickness, Edmond 237
bilious fever 76, 556
Bill 165, 171
Billy 244
Bird, Meek 644
Birmingham, Ala 276, 319, 603, 610
biscuit 111, 183
Bishop Hendrix 630
bitters 144, 322
Black
  B. 466
  Cicero 555

Mr 383
blackberries 39, 359, 487
blacking 3
Blackman, Dr 568
Blader Springs, Ala 353
blankets 68, 234, 333, 611
Block
  Elliott 411
  Mr 520
blockades 121, 122, 123
bluemoss 441
boats
  Cone B___ 30
  Florida 32
  Gertrude 206
  Governor Allen 221
  Miss Le Grand 30, 32
  Soverign 32
  St. Charles 32
  The King 80
Boddie
  Cornelia Kimball Smoker 409, 411-413, 415-417, 419-421, 423, 424, 426, 427, 434, 448, 453, 633
  Frances Caroline 100, 137, 149, 166, 172, 219, 220, 222, 233, 236, 248, 250, 251, 252, 253, 258, 264, 266, 270, 286, 288, 289, 291, 294, 296, 297, 298, 299, 300, 302, 304-307, 311, 313, 314, 317, 318, 320-322, 324, 325, 327-331, 333, 334, 338-342, 344-347, 352, 353, 356-360, 362, 365, 368-370, 375-380, 383-385, 387, 390, 393, 397-407, 409, 415, 416, 418-421, 428-430, 432, 434, 435, 437-439, 441-446, 448, 451, 453, 455, 458, 460, 463, 468, 471-474, 476, 479, 481, 485, 489-491, 495, 496, 499, 502, 506, 509, 511, 512, 514, 516, 518, 521, 522, 525-528, 531, 533, 535,-538, 542, 545, 546, 548, 551, 553, 555, 587
  George (*See also:* Brother George) 2, 7, 8, 12-14, 16,-18, 25, 32, 34, 43, 48, 59, 81, 84, 100, 101, 135-137, 166-171, 173, 236, 242, 252, 284, 291-300, 303, 304, 306, 307, 310-313, 315, 317, 318, 322, 324,

325, 327-329, 334, 341-343, 345, 346, 348-353, 355-362, 364-370, 373-387, 389-391, 393-398, 400, 402, 404, 408, 409, 411, 414, 415, 416, 419-421, 423, 428-433, 435, 437-439, 441-448, 450, 454, 455, 468, 473, 492, 540, 623
  George Gildersleeve (*See also:* Gilder) 32, 71, 97, 124, 211, 217, 221, 222, 225, 247, 251-253, 256, 259, 274, 286, 288, 290, 291, 294, 296, 298, 302-304, 306, 310, 313, 315-317, 320, 321, 324, 327, 329, 332-335, 338
  George Kimball Smoker (*See also:* Smoker) 426, 432, 435, 437, 438, 441-445, 447, 451, 455, 460, 469, 473, 476, 481, 489, 491, 499, 502, 506, 519, 524, 541, 545, 547, 548, 549, 551, 552, 565-568, 570, 578
  Hubert 576, 577, 578, 612
  Jack E. 325
  Jim 212
  John 496, 506
  John B. 325
  John Rumph 41, 54, 58, 94, 109, 116, 136, 157, 165-168, 171, 173, 195, 200, 207, 209, 211, 214, 217, 220-222, 225, 229, 234, 244, 248, 251, 252, 254, 257-259, 263, 265, 273, 280, 286-303, 306, 310, 311, 313, 315, 317, 318, 321, 322, 324, 327-329, 333, 335, 338, 341, 342, 345, 346, 348, 349, 351-356, 358, 360-362, 365-367, 369, 370-373, 375, 376, 379, 381, 383, 385, 387, 390, 393, 395, 398, 402, 406, 410, 415, 416, 420, 423-428, 430, 433, 435, 436, 439, 441, 448, 451, 453, 454, 458, 465, 468, 470, 474, 475, 481, 485, 486, 488, 491, 497, 505, 511, 517, 523-525, 534, 537, 540, 542-544, 548, 549, 554, 561, 563, 564, 567, 571, 572, 575, 580, 581, 583, 585, 594, 601, 602, 604, 606, 607, 609, 612, 617, 618, 620, 623, 626, 627, 630, 633,

Index

634, 635, 637, 641-643, 646
John Thomas 325
Lucie Smoker Hunt 561, 625, 626, 627, 633
Mary Elizabeth (Coleman) (*See also:* Mamie) 18, 25, 35, 82, 109, 165, 168, 170-172, 290, 291, 294, 296, 298, 299, 301, 302, 304-306, 310, 312-315, 317, 324, 329, 341, 343, 345, 350, 352, 353, 355, 356, 358, 359, 362, 365, 368, 369, 373, 375, 376, 378, 379, 382-387, 389, 390, 393, 397-399, 402, 403, 405, 409, 420
Mary Elizabeth Gildersleeve (*See also:* Sis Mollie) 7, 8, 10, 31, 32, 34, 43, 44, 47, 48, 53, 54, 67, 78, 80, 116, 174, 176, 178, 181, 237, 252, 297, 300, 301, 303, 306, 311, 312, 314, 315, 319, 324, 335, 372, 373, 379, 382, 394, 414, 425, 426, 429, 431-435, 437, 439, 441, 443, 444, 446, 451, 455, 473, 482, 485, 510, 553
Nathan 325
Oliver B. 325
Robert Lee (*See also:* Tug) 168, 177, 220, 230, 233, 236, 246, 251, 252, 256, 264, 265, 270, 288, 289, 291, 294, 297, 299, 300, 301, 303, 306, 310, 313, 317-319, 321, 322, 324, 325, 327-330, 334, 335, 361, 370, 372, 390, 402, 452, 454, 455, 460, 466, 476, 481, 489, 499, 505, 512, 517, 519, 523, 525, 530, 532, 534, 545, 549, 554, 572, 574, 576-578, 581, 582, 600, 612, 615, 620, 623, 635, 646
Robert Lee, Jr. 577
Sallie Higgins Farley 57, 80, 115, 117, 246, 574, 577, 581, 600, 610, 613, 623, 634, 645
Waitie Butler 604, 605
Wiley 497
Will Smoker Hunt 625
Willis Thomas 18, 25, 41, 61, 94, 170, 171, 195, 210, 217, 221-223, 227, 234, 244, 247, 248, 250, 252, 256, 258, 260, 270,

272, 273, 280, 291-294, 298, 300-304, 306, 310, 313, 314, 317-319, 322, 324, 325, 327, 328, 334, 339-343, 345, 346, 348-351, 354, 356-360, 362, 367, 369-374, 377-383, 385-387, 389, 390, 393, 394, 396-398, 402, 405, 406, 408, 410, 415, 419-421, 435, 437-439, 441-448, 451, 454, 455, 476, 477, 481, 486, 489, 491, 494, 495, 500, 504, 509-511, 516, 518, 519, 524, 526, 527, 533, 534, 541, 542, 548, 550, 551, 554, 555, 561-568, 570-572
Boddie and Allied Families 325
Boershear
   Florence Clifton 599
   Mr & Mrs 598
   Thomas Hess 596
Bohanon, Bettie 28
Boiling Springs 449, 451, 452
bon-tons 35
bonefelons 528
Bonn, Ella 404
bonnet 6, 31, 32, 42, 517
book mark 358
books 3, 7, 58, 61, 68, 70, 74, 81, 103, 116, 118, 208, 234, 270, 288, 289, 291, 307, 319, 321, 327, 333, 340, 356, 358, 411, 416, 474, 480. 491, 562, 581, 585, 597, 626, 632, 635
Boseman
   J. E. 284
Bracy, (ey) (ie),
   Mr. 176, 217, 221, 299, 346, 411, 428
   Mrs. 275, 366, 394, 411, 555
Bradley County 289
Bragg
   Braxton, General 153, 188
   Florence 526
   Junius N., Dr. 296, 305, 324, 413, 426, 428, 429, 430, 433, 443, 450, 500, 530, 544
   Pike 377
bread 35, 77, 125, 131, 137, 142, 158, 178, 179, 186, 189, 219, 253, 269, 298, 299, 303, 305, 327, 391, 492, 519, 547, 563, 597
Brest 628

Broach, Mr 166
Broadnax, Mrs. 317
Broadwell, Miss 28
Brock, Bessie 530, 532, 537
Brock, Bessie Love 528
Brodnax
   Ed 334, 469
   Eddie 338
   Effie Brown 528, 537
   Emma 494
   Frank 227, 293, 334, 356, 369, 370, 390, 402, 405
   Hal
   Henry (Hal) (Mr.) 31, 43, 48, 53, 83, 157, 210, 269, 279, 317, 346, 380, 383, 477, 478, 518, 541
   Joe 117
   Mrs. 422
   Mrs. Robert 157
   Nat 582
   Octavia Word 587
   Pearl 582
   Robert 227
   Sandy 461
   Wright 553, 555
Brooklyn 590
Brooks
   Joe 360, 370, 392
   Mr. 22
   Mrs 367
Brother George (*See also:* Boddie, George) 31-35, 37, 41, 43, 45, 48, 52, 54, 57-63, 66, 67, 71-73, 75, 82, 84, 85, 87-90, 92, 94, 99, 108-112, 114, 116, 118, 120-122, 124, 127, 128, 130, 131, 133, 141, 142, 149, 151-153, 157, 161, 163, 164, 194, 196, 202, 207, 210, 211, 215, 217-229, 231-234, 238, 242, 243, 246-250, 253, 254, 256, 258-261, 263, 264, 266-271, 273, 279-281, 286, 308, 309, 314, 320, 332, 340, 347, 354, 451, 474, 475, 600, 636
Brother John (*See also:* Rumph, John Benjamin) 29, 30, 33-38, 40-44, 46-78, 80-83, 85-90, 92-94, 98, 99, 109, 112, 113, 119-121, 123, 124, 127, 131, 133, 134, 138, 144, 149, 151, 152, 155-158, 163, 195, 197-200,

202, 207, 210-212, 217, 218,
221, 222, 224-227, 229, 231-
234, 239, 242-245, 247, 248,
250, 254, 255, 257, 260-265,
267, 269, 270, 272, 274, 279,
280-282, 286, 300, 307, 308,
310, 314, 320, 328, 339, 340,
344, 355, 384, 391, 395, 399,
401, 412, 413, 418, 419, 422,
426, 428, 451, 456, 458, 460-
463, 467-469, 475, 476, 497,
507, 523, 615
Broughton
 Henry 517
 Maggie 537
 Mr 520
 Mrs. 77, 103, 182
Browder, William 463
Brown
 Bessie Rumph 643
 Cole 238
 Coleman (Colie) 264, 300, 361, 381
 Dr. 298, 350, 428
 Effie 264, 478, 489
 Jennie 555
 Julia 232, 238
 Mildred 643
 Mr. 306, 313, 317, 318, 333, 350, 356
 Mrs. 215, 230
 Proctor 643
 West 527
 Will 614
Browning, Mr 229
Bryant, Arch 628
Buchanan, Mr 394
buckets 156
buggy 6, 14, 26, 29, 33, 35, 80, 82, 94, 120, 133, 156, 161, 169, 171, 206, 243, 264, 317, 368, 415, 445, 478, 571, 583, 591, 617
Burdette, L. A. 507, 508
bureau 81, 157, 244
Burke, Mrs 631
Burks, Jim 465
Burns, John 233
Burnsville, Dallas Co., Ala 10, 216, 285, 610
Bush, Dr 436
Bussey, Mr. 81
Bustian, J. 327

Bustin
 Johnie 356
bustle 60, 265
Butler, Mr. & Mrs. 604
butter 28, 86, 125, 142, 163, 186, 223, 254, 314, 327, 383, 519, 539, 547, 563, 571, 573, 586, 617, 618, 621, 631, 632
buttermilk 103, 119, 586
buttons 30, 127, 296, 394, 551, 615
buzzards 179

C

cabbage 56, 71, 82, 86, 104, 196, 334, 556, 630
Cahawba 4
cake 305, 334, 383, 422, 611
cakes 317, 622
Caldwell, James E., Rev. 152
calf 169, 172
Calhoun Co 334
Calhoun, Mr 244
calico 126, 140, 141, 316, 336, 360, 376, 479, 540
Callin, Mr 284
calves 111, 162, 306, 310, 327, 328, 356, 383, 421
Cambell, Mrs 501
Camden 7, 13, 14, 17, 31-35, 37, 38, 41, 43, 50, 54, 57, 60, 61, 78, 80, 82, 86, 100, 108, 111, 115, 116, 118-120, 126, 128, 130-136, 138-142, 147, 148, 150, 151, 155-158, 160, 161, 165-167, 169, 172, 174, 176, 177, 178, 180, 181, 195, 200, 205-207, 209, 210, 212-215, 217, 219, 220, 221, 225, 229, 231, 232, 239, 240, 241, 250, 251, 262, 263, 265, 269, 270, 272-274, 277, 279-281, 286, 287, 289, 291, 292, 294, 299, 302, 306, 310, 312, 313, 315, 316, 318, 320-322, 325, 327, 330, 332, 334, 336, 337, 339, 341-347, 350, 351, 353-356, 362, 364, 366, 370, 373, 378-381, 388, 393, 395, 399, 400, 403, 406, 411-413, 416, 422, 423, 429, 445, 452, 458, 463, 465, 468-470, 472, 474-476, 478, 482-484, 486-488, 490, 492, 495, 497, 500, 503, 504,
506-509, 512, 515, 516, 520, 522, 525, 526, 528, 535-539, 541, 545, 546, 550-553, 555, 556, 559, 563, 564, 568, 571, 572-574, 577-581, 583, 596, 600, 602, 605, 606, 612-616, 620, 621, 629-631, 633-637, 641, 643-646
Camden, Ala, 551
Camden Evening News 646
Camden Knights No.1 115
Camden Knights No.2 115
cameo breast pin 30
camomile 21
Camp Dick Robinson 188
Camp Faulkner 183
candies 317
candles 113, 114, 155, 305
candy 10, 15, 22, 83, 227, 278, 285, 502, 611
Candy Party 10
candy pulling 377
candy stew 350, 353
Cane Hill 145
Canian 59
cannon 108, 279, 364, 622
cantalopes 618
Carey
 Emaline 363
 Steve 363
carriage 28, 32, 35, 60, 61, 80, 133, 138, 139, 171, 317, 321, 339, 373, 446, 447
Cary, Mittie 474
Castle Garden 303
cat 20, 209, 236, 290, 293, 297, 328, 330
Caters, Mrs. 11
Cattie, Miss 165, 167, 168
cattle 42, 72, 121, 171, 172, 175, 180, 185, 207, 243, 253, 256, 299, 306, 347, 348, 351, 355, 356, 360, 396, 439, 441, 567, 574, 575, 584, 620, 631, 633, 636, 640
Caver, Bill 124, 139
 Dave 414
 Mr 122, 126
 Mrs. 73, 150, 153
 Tom 124, 197, 218, 223, 236, 244, 261, 262, 264, 265, 266, 418
cedar 203, 234, 254, 453, 465, 539

celery 317, 622
Centennial 350, 362, 368, 372, 385, 386
Champanolle 81
Chapman, Henry 484
Charleston 175, 621, 623, 633
Charleston Train 278
Charleston, W. Va 629
Charleston-Tenn train 276
Charley 142
Charlston 153
Chattanooga 188
cherries 57, 73, 88
cherry trees 111, 187
Chester, Mr. 31
chestnuts 79, 82, 340, 487
Chewning,
  Fanny 312
  Mary 328
  Mr 322, 327
Chicago 135
Chicago Times 167
Chickamauga 189, 590
chicken 155
  Shanghi chick 18
chicken pie 327, 334
Chicken salad 334
chickenpox 443
Chickens 584
chickens 69, 70, 71, 84, 86, 110, 128, 147, 196, 207, 243, 254, 297, 299, 398, 479, 483, 484, 494, 523, 533, 547, 586, 618, 629
Chidester, Mr 481
childbirth
  sore breasts 98
Chills 218
chills 7, 144, 166, 312, 314, 318, 320, 322, 327, 402, 403, 418, 420, 439, 459, 475, 517, 518, 522, 524, 535, 547, 565, 566, 568, 578, 587
chinquapins 94
Chloroform 503
cholera 243, 254, 284
church 202, 206, 208, 219, 221, 230, 244, 246, 258, 261, 263, 288-291, 296, 298, 299, 301-304, 307, 310, 312-314, 319, 320, 329, 331, 334, 342, 344, 350, 361, 363, 365, 369, 374, 378, 379, 381, 403, 406, 421, 427, 451-453, 456, 463, 490, 491, 494, 498, 505, 506, 513, 521, 522, 524, 527, 528, 531, 540, 541, 543, 553, 561, 563, 573, 574, 588, 592, 620, 623, 625, 627, 629, 630, 633, 635, 636
Churchill 167
cider 187
circuit riders 95
Citron 487
Citty Hotell 32
Clark
  Austin 271
  Callie 271
  Eliza Stone Clark, Mrs. 39, 161, 215, 227, 232, 233, 237, 238, 241, 246, 255, 266, 268, 281, 285, 305, 452, 461
  Julia 415
  Mary 237
Clark County 57, 473
Clay
  Betsy 277
  Jack 277
  Jeff 277
  Jim 233
  Mr. 275
  Mrs. 277
Clay's Depot 278
Clay's Station 277
Clayton, Powell 239, 240
Cleveland, Grover 364
Cliffer, Henry 476
Cliffords, Mr 537
Clifton
  Edwin, Mr. 489, 492, 500, 509, 513, 528, 534, 535, 537, 538
  Florence 491, 492, 498, 500, 513, 528, 535, 537, 550
  Florence Rumph 489
  Florrie 489, 538
  Mrs. 492
clothes (*See also* fashion)
  coats 56
  pants 56
coal, hard 586
Coast Artillery 619
coats 56, 59, 125, 379, 406, 478, 519, 522
coconut 383
coffee 22, 126, 146, 155, 163, 183, 184, 186, 253, 275, 276, 277, 278, 305, 366, 481, 585, 631
Cole,
  Amy 284
  Clarance 237
  Mrs. 216, 227, 238, 299
Coleman
  Ed Haws 441
  Edwin Gallie, Dr. 375, 376, 382, 383, 384, 387, 390, 396, 404, 409, 416, 417, 420, 427, 451, 490, 491, 494, 583
  Ernest Godfrey 427, 432, 433, 435, 441, 443, 445, 446, 450, 473, 494, 499, 502, 511, 545, 548, 551, 554, 563, 567, 576, 578, 581, 587, 588, 593, 594, 601, 609, 612, 614, 616, 619, 620, 621, 634, 644
  Florence Pelt 587, 589, 601, 612, 613, 619, 644
  Fred Hughes 491, 494, 545, 554, 562, 563, 564, 566, 571, 578, 585, 586, 589, 590, 593, 594, 595, 599, 611, 629, 630, 632, 633, 634, 640
  Gally 644
  Garland 469
  George Gallie 587, 609
  Gilder 644
  Helen Moorhouse 594, 599, 629, 634, 640
  House 406
  Mary Gilder 494, 502, 545, 550, 554, 563, 564, 571, 578, 585, 604, 644
  Mrs Wm 441
Coles 41
collar 21, 30, 45, 82, 248
Collins, Mr 316, 353
Colorado 606
Columbus 127
Columbus, Ohio 596
Colwell, Mr. 152
composition book 3
compulsatory school law 595
concerts 589
Confederate 147, 156
Confederate Army 136
Confederate States 108, 255
congestive chill 640
conjestion 198, 223, 245, 516
conscript act 132
conservatories 589

consumption 24, 46, 50, 81, 158, 160, 194, 229, 324
Conway, Mrs. S. 6, 70, 636
Copperheads 161
copy book 3
Cor(r)inth 130, 135, 137, 138, 277
corn 14, 15, 17, 38, 42, 43, 45, 59, 62, 75, 80, 84, 87-89, 93, 95, 97, 104, 109, 112, 114, 119, 121, 123, 125, 127, 129, 134, 139, 141, 145, 146, 149, 152, 153, 156, 157, 161-163, 170, 172, 174, 178-180, 183, 185, 186, 188, 189, 195, 201, 202, 217, 221, 223, 225, 227, 242, 259, 260, 273, 294, 306, 311, 315, 316, 318, 320, 321, 324, 325, 327, 331, 336, 340, 349, 351, 356, 357, 358, 360-363, 366-369, 371, 372, 375, 378, 393, 403, 405, 406, 409, 410, 415, 433, 443, 468, 476, 477, 481, 618
cornbread 111, 303
cotton 9, 17, 22, 39, 42, 43, 45, 55, 59, 63, 66, 75, 77-79, 84, 86-88, 90, 93, 95, 97, 104, 109, 110, 112, 114, 117, 120-123, 128-131, 135, 136, 141, 149, 150, 153, 163, 164, 169, 195, 197, 201, 202, 208, 210, 217-223, 225, 226, 231, 236, 244, 260-263, 265, 270, 272, 284, 291, 294, 296, 298, 302, 304, 306, 307, 309, 310, 313, 325, 327-329, 334, 336, 340, 345, 349, 351, 354, 358, 360, 362, 366, 367, 370, 373, 374, 377, 379, 383, 386, 391, 394, 396, 398, 400, 403, 405, 406, 410, 411, 415, 416, 420, 430, 445, 452, 461, 466, 477, 486, 618
  bolls 112
  cards 128, 130
  squares 112
cough 6, 15, 102, 145, 153, 154, 186, 232, 234, 236, 386, 414, 418, 456, 461, 471, 496, 577, 607, 627
Courthouse 332-334
cow 169, 172
Cowan, A.A., teacher 2, 3

cows 58, 72, 103, 111, 162, 163, 164, 220, 223, 254, 307, 309, 310, 322, 327, 354, 357, 383, 421, 521, 541, 551, 574, 575, 618, 626
  milk 243
Cranberry sauce 622
Crawford, Presley A. 542
Cress 334
crockery ware 157, 163
Crockett 471
crops 295
  fodder 140
  oats 163
  rye 163
  watermelons 42
Cross, Clara 550
croup 96, 115, 163, 374, 420, 450, 459
Crouse
  Charley 505
  Fay 506
Cuba 584, 617, 621, 625
cucumbers 39, 71, 73, 88, 136, 162, 196, 209, 399
cuffs 82, 339
Culbreath, Mrs 520
Cumberland Presbyterian Ladies 27
Cummins, Mr. 167, 175
currants 399, 400
Current Literature 589
Curry
  G. M. 570
  Mary 302
Cushman, Mr. 179
custard 317
  Potatoe 334
  Transparent 334

D

daffodils 127
daguerreotype 31
dairy 95, 130, 209, 223, 268, 361, 382, 468, 473, 561
daisies 595
Dale, Dr 568, 630
Dallas Co. 615
dance 215, 220, 230, 244, 250, 286, 340, 347, 357, 366, 377, 384, 386, 411, 460, 468, 472, 473, 477, 485, 494, 522, 584
  Shotische 340

waltz 340
dancing 279, 347
Darden
  Fanny 237
  William 9
Darnell, Mrs 467
darning 101, 378
Davis
  Jack 263
  Jeff 127, 130
  Jefferson, General 110, 127
  Linsey 414
  Mr 21, 206, 207, 216, 233, 251, 253, 280, 284, 286, 297, 309, 314, 320, 331
  Mrs. Ben 14
  Tom, Dr. 8, 9
Dawson 138
Dayton, Ohio 598, 633, 634
De Bardelaben, Mrs. 257
De Bardelaben place 238
Decator 275, 276, 277, 278
deer 40, 94, 97, 118, 169, 173, 207, 210, 211, 214, 225, 257, 259, 290, 303, 304, 308, 410, 462, 464, 556, 580, 612
deguerotype 197
Delhi 150
Democratic Party 261
Dentoles, Preacher 237
Deseker, A. H. 550
Devil's Elbow 614
dewberries 487
diarrhea 112, 155, 158, 160, 200
Dickson
  Clarissa Lanier Boddie (See also: Ma) 7, 12, 13, 14, 50, 53, 97, 101, 129, 135, 137, 249
  Cornelia Sanderson 3-5, 8-11, 16, 19-24, 29, 31, 37, 55, 65, 67, 78, 108, 111, 115, 121, 122, 130, 132, 137, 148, 150, 153, 163, 164, 195, 196, 203, 230, 236, 248, 250-252, 256, 270, 273, 274, 280, 285, 288, 291, 294, 296, 299, 301, 302, 305, 306, 311, 313-317, 319, 321, 324, 327, 329, 332, 334, 341, 342, 346, 348, 349, 353, 355-361, 369, 373-375, 377, 380, 381, 384, 386, 387, 390, 395, 399, 401, 403, 408, 420, 429,

441, 447, 458, 459, 463, 465, 477-481, 485, 488-492, 496-500, 502-507, 509-518, 520-522, 524-527, 530, 531, 533-535, 539, 541, 545-549, 552, 553, 555, 556, 560,-568, 570-574, 576-579, 584-588, 590, 592, 594, 601, 604-607, 609, 610, 612, 613, 615, 619, 621-630, 632, 634, 635, 637, 639-643, 645, 646
  Dr. Samuel Henry 623
  Frances 4
  John 91
  Mattie 353
  Samuel Henry Neely, Col. (*See also:* Pa) 2, 18, 53
Dion, Mrs 171
Dockery, Thomas P. Colonel 167, 170, 177
Dodson La 581
Doer, Lula 328
dogs 36, 291, 300, 349, 371, 374, 376, 377, 584
  fox hunting 36
doll, 77
doll. 82
Donald, J.M. 6
Dorn
  Earl Van, General 128, 130
Dortch, Alex 522
double gorse plows 594
Douglas, Dave 531
Dowling, Jennie E. 614, 615, 616
Dowsing
  Jennie 601
Dr. Curry Cancer Sanitarium 569
drawing 68, 70, 140, 189, 279, 280, 291, 364, 641
dress(es) 2, 5, 8, 9, 11, 21, 24, 29, 30, 41, 46, 53, 58, 59, 61, 62, 79, 82, 109, 117, 120, 141, 144, 145, 146, 149, 151, 162, 189, 211, 222, 225, 236, 252, 314, 316, 317, 336, 339, 376, 378, 399, 427, 473, 478, 479, 481, 498, 502, 506, 512, 517, 524, 542, 584, 589, 615, 616
  Flowing 7
dropsy 44
drought 89, 90, 93, 111, 112, 138, 142, 217, 225, 261, 298, 306, 307, 309, 340, 365, 449, 452,

455, 614, 617
Duck river 191
ducks 96, 97, 189, 227, 244, 321, 328, 334, 377
Dun, Ben 190
Dunaway, Bettie 605
Duncan, Y. 313
Dungan
  Tom 21
Dunkin, Major 188
Dunlap
  Archie 217
  Clarissa Dickson (Clara) 2, 3, 6-8, 10, 13, 14, 15, 18, 22, 96, 97, 99, 102, 135, 167, 168, 206, 207, 212, 213, 216-220, 222, 224, 226, 228, 233, 234, 239, 243, 246-248, 253, 259, 261-263, 265, 267, 268, 271, 273, 280, 286, 288, 289, 294, 296, 299, 302, 305, 307-309, 311, 316, 327, 329, 332, 333, 353, 357, 360, 368, 370, 374, 377, 380, 382, 384, 386, 393, 396, 401, 404, 414, 415, 418, 421, 434, 436, 447, 452, 453, 460, 463, 474, 479, 489, 492, 496, 498, 505, 518, 528, 529, 534, 548, 551-553, 555, 556, 574, 575, 577, 579, 580, 586, 600, 602, 608, 623
  Cora Lee 217, 224, 226, 239, 243, 260, 268, 291, 401, 466, 479, 489, 494-496, 498, 502, 509, 510, 517, 518, 523, 527-529, 533, 534, 541, 551, 553, 555-557, 567, 573-578, 586, 588, 600, 606, 607, 617-621, 625, 627, 630, 631, 636, 640, 645, 646
  Dick 95, 140, 143, 146, 147, 162, 198, 464, 573
  Ella 195, 200
  Estelle 243
  Fannie 479, 556
  Howard Garmany 469
  James Cousar 305
  James Howard (Jimmy) 104, 111, 112, 115, 118, 120, 124, 125, 131, 133, 142, 144, 145, 148, 149, 150, 151, 158, 162, 164, 196, 198, 234, 254
  Joanna 195

  John Boddie 296, 302, 334, 353, 357, 360, 371, 377, 384, 421, 528, 552
  John Franklin 66, 69, 73, 75, 76, 78, 79, 81, 82, 84, 86, 87, 89, 93, 95-99, 101, 103, 108-112, 115-121, 123-125, 127, 128, 130, 131, 133, 135, 138, 139, 141-143, 145, 147, 149, 153, 156, 157, 160, 161, 163, 168, 169, 173, 195, 199, 202, 206, 209, 211, 217, 218, 222-224, 226, 228, 231, 233, 243, 246, 248, 254, 260, 262, 263, 265, 268, 280, 286, 291, 296, 299, 302, 303, 305, 309, 314-316, 327, 329, 334, 338-340, 343, 353, 356, 357, 361, 362, 370, 371, 373, 374, 377, 386, 395, 418, 421, 460, 483, 491, 525, 528, 552
  John Gaston 305
  John Henry 353
  Kate 464, 537
  Knot 631
  Lon 348, 406, 496, 537, 634
  Lucy 360
  Lula May 147, 149, 158, 160, 162, 196, 198, 199, 201, 203, 217, 222, 224, 228, 231, 232, 234, 238, 239, 243, 260, 268, 296, 312, 314, 357, 377, 386, 401, 453, 479, 480, 496, 498, 502, 509, 510, 517, 523, 525, 526, 527, 529, 532, 533, 534, 537, 554
  Mary Alice 162, 194, 195, 196, 198, 199, 234, 254
  Maude 636
  Ophelia 360, 455
  Richard Love 464
  Sallie Lon 551, 588, 589
  Sam 150, 157, 160, 162, 217, 324, 360, 370
  Walter 263, 268
Dunn
  Annie 603
  Attalie Rumph Gaughan 570, 579, 580, 584, 586, 592, 593, 606, 610, 613, 614, 615, 623, 630, 635, 636, 640, 644
  Bessie 615, 636, 644
  Billy 468

Boddie 603, 608
Dixie 608
Fannie 603
Gee 603, 608
George 608
Graham Love 608
Jim A. 522, 586, 615, 630, 634
John 522
Lanier 603
Miriam 608
Mr 284
Mrs 549
Nora 603
Perry A. 529, 603
Dupey, Mrs. 42, 132
Dupree, Dr. 507, 508
Duprey, Tommy 171
Duprey, William 171
Dutch Bend 30
dye 46
dyeing 130

E

Eagle 118
Eagle Mills 632
ear rings 51
Earl(e)
    J. R., Mr. 498, 505, 513, 524, 526, 532, 534, 546, 580, 620, 636
    Rufus 576
    Sally Kate 546
    Sam 563, 573
    Taylor Henry 628
Easterling, Dr. 505
education 256, 257
    (See also)
    books 61
    dictionary 58
    head in class 4
    multiplication tables 196
    spelling 58
    teacher 58
Edwards, Mr. 27
eggbread 563
eggnog 203, 218, 228, 341, 344
eggs 18, 35, 86, 155, 190, 203, 227, 228, 243, 327, 328, 534, 542, 563, 617, 618
Eldorado 364
Ellen 120, 267
Elliot(t)

Belle 352, 366
Billy 297, 338
Cora 389
Coralie 314
Jim T. 306, 495
L. 346, 353, 389, 403
Mary 528, 625
Mr. 136, 141, 286, 317, 338, 360, 369, 396
Mrs. 135, 291, 297, 314, 316, 317, 324, 352, 363, 366, 370, 377, 384
Nellie 258, 361, 389, 396, 410
Ellis, Mr. 306
embroidery 45, 46
entertainment (See also:)
    ball 229
    barbecue 364
    candy stew 348
    candy-pulling 15
    coon hunting 403
    darning 101
    drawing 70, 211
    embroidery 45
    fishing party 26
    fox hunting 36
    Holiday Ball 341
    hull-gull 94
    hunting 257
    infair 215, 320
    knitting 53
    painting 211
    patching 101
    playing piano 211
    quilting 34
    quilting day 348
    sewing 50
    singing school 60
    sociable 228
    spinning 140
    weaving 119
    weddings 24
Eutaw 4
examinations 4

F

fabric
    Alpaca 394
    Batiste 479
    domestic cloth 130
    French cambric 86
    home-spun 82, 128

    jeans 125
    lawn 479
    monoline 32
    muslin 86
    muslin delain 8
    nunsveiling 522
    osnaburg 130
    swiss 141
    white swiss 338
Fagan, James F., General 170
Fair, Dr. 24
Farley
    Albert 577
    Eddie 577
    Sallie Higgins 572
fashion
    band 339
    basque 21
    beads 61
    berage 141
    bishop sleeves 21
    bonnet 31, 32
    brilliants 86
    bustle 60
    buttons 30
    calico 126
    cap 59
    capes 28
    chemise 29
    cloth gaiters 149
    collar 21
    corset 30
    dress, traveling 79
    dress-sleeve 59
    ear rings 51
    flounces 61
    gimp 30
    hair-ring 81
    handkerchief 22
    hoops 54
    indigo 140
    low necked drapes 28
    mantilla 16
    parasol 23
    sack-waist dress 79
    sleeveless basques 338
    sleeves 339
    socks 81
    stockings 71
    trains 338
    underbody, linen 24
    underclothing 339

Index

wedding slippers 156
yoke 339
fat meat 125
fawn 40, 118, 225, 304, 308
feather bed 58, 68, 81
Felsenthal, Mrs 581, 596
Ferguson, Mr 523
Ferrotype 224
fever 2, 7, 14, 38, 40, 42, 43, 45, 60, 63, 76, 77, 80, 85, 87, 88, 90, 94, 102, 112, 115, 116, 118, 120, 131, 133, 142, 144, 154, 160, 163, 165-168, 170, 171, 178, 202, 211, 218, 231, 236, 245, 246, 248, 259, 260, 269, 270, 271, 281, 312, 314, 320, 321, 327, 334, 340, 345, 368, 369, 374, 375, 402, 409, 414, 423, 428, 437, 452, 457, 459, 461, 473, 481, 482, 488, 492, 496, 499, 507, 508, 513, 514, 518, 520, 525, 528, 529, 532, 537, 550, 551, 556, 573, 579, 587, 605, 640
  billious 640
  catarrh 496
  yellow 248
figs 487
finger ring 383
fish 32, 97, 207, 209, 210, 212, 236, 255, 256, 269, 299, 300, 303, 308, 309, 364, 366, 369, 447, 519
Fisher
  Blanche 587
  Fred 495
  Granville 587
  Harry Clay 380, 477, 557, 586
  Harry Gordon 587
  Mary Arkansas Moseley (Mrs.) 395, 396, 398, 403, 480, 557, 588, 590, 601, 610, 612, 623, 627
fishing 26, 86, 96, 189, 212, 214, 257, 298, 300, 303, 309, 362, 363, 445, 453, 471, 505
Fishinger 597
flood 596, 597, 598
Florence Ala. 325, 386
Florida 549, 552, 567, 614, 619, 620, 645
flour 111, 142, 149, 151, 155, 241, 253, 298, 361, 382

flowers 338
  cape jasamine 127
  cedar bushes 203
  daffodils 127
  green ivy 127
  hyacinths 32
  jonquils 127
  Mexican lilies 13
  narcissus 127
  Pansies 343
  purple magnolia 13
  rose 13
  snowball 13
  tulips 32
  zenias (zinnias?) 332
Fluger & Wirtz 583
flute 213
flutes 257
flux 45, 144, 145, 157, 268, 306, 362, 461, 601
fodder 140, 241, 370, 509, 618
Folde(r)n, Dr. C. 361, 404, 503, 504, 513, 516, 520, 526
food (See also:)
  ashcake 22, 28
  bacon 140
  bananas 32
  battercakes 22
  beef 142
  beets 32
  biscuit 111
  biscuits 183
  Brandy 62
  brandy peaches 219
  bread, light 77
  butter 86
  buttermilk 22, 28
  cabbage 32
  cake, iced 30
  cakes 234
  charlotte russe 317
  chestnuts 82
  coconut 30
  cornbread 35
  currant pie 242
  eggnog 203
  English peas 22
  fat meat 99
  fat middling 78
  flour 142
  fresh fish 32
  fruit cake 30
  ginger cakes 219

  greens 78
  gruel 40
  hash 183
  hop-cakes 131
  ice cream 27
  jelly 81
  lard 164
  lemonade, iced 27
  lettuce 32
  lye-hominy 28
  molasses 126
  moonshine 30
  mushmelons 112
  nogs 100
  oysters 32
  pap 40
  pinders 126
  pineapples 30
  popping corn 80
  pork 104
  pork, fresh 104
  pork, pickled 104
  pot liquor 125
  pound cake 27
  radishes 32
  rice 111
  salt 136
  sauer-kraut 53, 56
  sausage 101, 164
  shortening 142
  souce 340
  soup 40
  spare-ribs 340
  sugar 126
  sweet-milk 62
  syllabub 30
  torte 30
  venison 208
  watermelon 73
  yeast-cakes 131
Ford 644
Fordice 551, 625, 632
Foreman, Preacher 8
Fort Barrancas, Pensacola, Florida 619
Fort Henry 127
Fort Morgan 172, 190
Fort Moultrie, South Carolina 621, 623
Fortress Monroe 628
fox 36, 327, 342
France 618
Franklin, Ben 419

freedmen 195, 202, 218, 220, 226, 244, 284, 302, 306, 327
(*See also:*)
Alec 518
Ann, nurse 432-435, 438, 441, 443, 445, 448
Ann T 432
Aunt Jinny 419
Aunt Nina 363
Becky 359, 370, 386
Betty 489
Boddie, Ben 419
Bose 418
Bosie 414
Caroline 414
Charity 414
Eljira 324
Ellen 414
Ephrain 414
Hager 318
Hannah (Aunt) 311, 329, 371, 405, 489
Harriet 418
Harry 418
Henry 310, 325, 416
Jack 346, 386
Jerry 414
Joe 386
John 414
Johnie 414
Judy 414, 419
July Ann 414, 419
Laura 414
Levi 414, 418
Liddy 360
Little Tommie 414
Lucy 324, 371
Marinda 346
Melinda 489
Menses 414
Paten 414
Phillis 386
Polly 419
Sarah 386
Seymore 359
Spencer 310
Tom 414
Uncle Jerry 419
Freeo Bottom 101
French Market 32
fruit 17, 30, 32, 57, 60, 68, 71, 73, 75, 108, 111, 151, 165, 169, 187, 192, 237, 242, 260, 267, 268, 295, 306, 334, 338, 359, 360, 394, 397, 401, 403, 420, 421, 422, 461, 487, 494, 580, 608
apples 57
blackberries 257
cherries 57
chinquapins 94
currants 242
figs 260
grapes, muscadine 73
grapes, scupennong 43
muscadines 216
peaches 83
pears 75
plums 83
pumpkins 125
raspberries 242
Ft. Sheridan, Ill. 585

G

Galena 276, 277, 278
Galloway Women's College 620
Gamble, Mr 343
garden flowers
  jelly flowers 88
  touch-me-nots 88
Garden Valley 237, 247
garden vegetables
  beans 196
  butter beans 90
  cabbage 54
  collards 71
  cucumbers 39
  hops 131
  lettuce 54
  okra 260
  peas, wild goose 43
  radishes 54
  salsify 88
  squash 39
  sweet potatoes 44
  tomatoes 90
  turnips 93
  vegetable oyster 88
Garland, Augustus H. 335
Garmany
  Alice 469
  Henry 537
  Howard (Miss) 217, 224, 228, 233, 234, 391
  Millard 246
Gaston's Landing 2, 32, 63, 72
Gatling
  Bill 528
  John 528
Gaughan
  Alex 329, 392, 466, 471, 476, 480, 483, 484, 498, 502, 509, 513, 515, 516, 520, 521, 532, 580, 586, 615, 644
  Allie 580
  Allis 534
  Anna Moseley 431, 456
  Attalie Rumph 484
  Belle Ferguson 573, 575, 578, 580, 586, 612, 615, 616, 618, 620, 621, 625
  Carrie 509, 516, 600, 636, 643, 644
  Dennis Lafayette 329, 466, 476, 477, 478, 479, 483, 484, 485, 494, 496, 498, 502, 505, 511, 513, 516, 518, 521, 524, 527, 531, 534, 575, 578, 610, 612, 617, 618, 620, 623, 633
  Helen 637
  James Monroe (Jim, Jimmy (ie)) 329, 334, 356, 365, 369, 370, 417, 457, 465, 466, 476, 478, 480, 483
  Margaret 615
  Mary 476, 483, 484, 522, 537, 615, 616
  Mrs Patrick 386, 522
  Patrick 290, 329, 350, 460, 476, 484, 509, 513, 516, 521, 522, 537
  Sarah Caroline Patterson 350, 468, 476, 478, 482, 484, 497, 528, 532, 580
  Thomas Joseph (Tom, Tommie(y)) 329, 463, 464, 466, 476, 478, 482, 484, 495, 515, 520, 575, 637
Gaughan (Crawford)
  Margaret 618, 620
Gauhan, Mr 327
Gazette 118
Gee
  Charley 391
  Dr. 529
  Louise 599
  Mr 403

Index

Will 492
geese 71, 207, 222
Gen. Lee 632
gentian 144
George Rumph 610
Georgia 172, 349, 479
Georgia R. R. 548
Geraniums 595
Gila 581
Gila Bend, Arizona 583
Gilder 338, 339, 341, 343, 346, 347, 350-354, 356- 360, 362, 365, 367-370, 372-374, 376, 377, 379, 381, 382, 386, 390, 394, 396, 397, 403, 405, 407, 409, 412, 413, 415-417, 419-421, 426, 428, 431, 437, 442, 445, 454, 455, 473, 475, 477, 481, 486, 489, 491, 493, 495, 499, 500, 504, 507, 508, 512, 516, 517, 529, 547, 633
Gildersleeve
   Harriet 216
   Hattie 10, 19
   Mr. 13, 47, 49, 50, 52, 124, 126, 135, 151, 164, 207, 222, 267
   Mrs. 77, 78, 79, 80, 216, 219
   Sally 31, 43, 47, 48, 53
Gillespie
   Claud 628
   Etta 630, 631, 632
gin house 78, 94, 97, 169, 208, 226, 284, 285, 302, 306, 310, 313, 350, 367, 373, 379
Gindrew, Mary 237
Gingham Dress 5, 9, 24
ginning 340
gnats 19
Goddard
   George 524
   Mr 291, 403
   Mrs 393
Godeys Ladies' Book 234
gold 127, 128, 156, 168, 383, 435
Gold Star 627
Golden, Clara 489
Golsan (son)
   Amy 33
   Bob 210, 221, 231
   E. F. 231
   Eustice 196, 210, 218, 221, 223
   Jas. 34
   Lewis 262

Goodson
   Nancy Moseley 468
Goodwin, Mr 299
Gordon
   Charlie 344
   Mr. 302
Gosset, Henry 334
Graham
   Laura B. 353
   Mr 297
   Mrs 353
   Susan W. 353
Grand Junction 138, 277
Grand Prairie 276
Grandma 6, 17, 18, 20, 32, 39, 40, 44, 46, 49, 51, 54, 55, 58, 60, 61, 63, 66, 71, 83, 85, 97, 99, 101, 102, 113, 119, 129, 154
Grant Club 261
grape seed 297
grapefruit, Shaddock 487
grapes 43, 73, 95, 120, 278, 487, 594, 622
grass skirt 19
grasshoppers 209
Gray, Leulia 230
Greely Club 261
Green
   Linney 476
   Mary Gaughan 463
   Mr. 175, 309
   Mrs. 297, 309
Green County 5
greenbacks 295
Greening
   Mr. 290, 298, 327, 333, 334, 424
   P. 313
greens 78, 95, 99, 125
Grey, Mrs 68
Grinstead, Colonel 140, 147, 149, 150
gruel 40, 76
Grundy, Mrs 305
Guava 487
Guerdon 551
guitar 211, 213, 369, 378, 389
gums 294, 327
guns 119, 140, 156, 181, 187, 190, 290, 291, 310, 334, 357, 403, 405, 421, 489, 497, 502, 519, 622, 633, 639
Gurdon Depot 482
Gurley, Mr 57

Guttapurcha 190

H

Hail, Tom 476
Hall
   Albertine 348
   Amy-Jane 27
   Andrew 348
   Bill 112
   Eula Underwood 641
   Fannie 348
   Mrs. 139
   Mrs. William 142
   Rebecca 552
   Richard 628
Hallam, Mr. & Mrs. 302
Halton, Dr. 86
ham 186, 189, 269, 338
Hamilton
   Mr. 230
   Mrs. 230
Hampton Roads Va 629
Hanby, Jos 571
hanks 46
Hannah 163, 212, 231, 288
Hannons, Col. 189
Hardee, William J., General 172
Harding, Wiggly Wobbly Normalcy 640
Hardnet, Mrs 466
Hare, Mr. 289, 291, 296, 329
Harmony Grove 152, 274, 458
Harrice, Jinnie 229
Harriet 120, 124, 150, 151, 153, 154, 159, 164, 196, 201, 414
Harris, Dr. 57
harrowing 594
Harry 202
Hartwell, Dr. 34
Harvell, Mrs 237
Harwell, Bro. 625
hats 90, 103, 222, 254, 279, 297, 339, 374, 381, 446, 477, 517, 522, 546
Hattox, Dr 76
hawk 328
Hawkin, Frank 621
Hawkins
   Chester 623
   Frank 623
   Henry 618
   Maggie 631

Mr. 275
Mrs. 534, 573, 588
Mr & Mrs 612, 620
Sylvester 521
hawks 84, 584
Hayes
   Rutherford B. 364
Hayes, Archer 251
Hays, Archie 356
Head, Amanda 420, 464, 505
headache 37, 153, 298, 459
Hearn, Mrs. 293
heifers 310
Helena 136, 189
Hendree, Mrs. 15
Hendricks
   Mrs. 644
   Thomas Andrews 364
Hendrix College 620
Heney, Dr 360
Henry 156, 167, 179, 345, 349, 356, 360, 363, 364, 367, 414, 419, 483
Henry, Dr. 551
hens 155, 156, 222, 328, 525
Herald 118
Herman
   Ella 224, 228, 417
   John 262, 264
   Mrs 59
hickory nuts 328
Hill
   Col. 334, 356, 390
   Maj. 171, 172
   Mr 298
Himble, Mrs. 6
Hindman, Thomas G., Major General 136
Hodnet, Mrs 386
hoecakes 336
hog-killing 340
Hoge, Mr. 83
hogs 35, 42, 54, 72, 101, 149, 152, 158, 164, 179, 207, 220, 241, 328, 340, 346, 347, 351, 361, 380, 381, 387, 391, 398, 560, 575, 580, 581, 584, 588, 590, 633
Hogu, Mrs 392
Hogue
   Jeff 168
   Marion 138
Holly Springs 36, 116, 117, 122, 224, 225, 234, 403, 464, 466, 476, 483, 489, 490, 494, 503, 513, 522
Hollywood, Arkansas 490, 491, 494, 551
Holmes
   Cora 494
   Dee 237, 238
   Dick 237
   Henry 552
   Julia 238, 529
   Kate 467, 469
   Mary 238
   Mr. 144, 216, 238, 257, 526
   Mrs. 144, 239
   Sue 8
   Will 495
   Willie 341
home-guard 113
homespun 128, 140, 144, 146, 147, 149
honey 4, 298, 303
Honolulu 639
Hood, Eula 502
hoops 54, 60, 119, 141
hoosiers 111
Hope 470
Hopkinsville 380, 395
hops 131, 225
Horn, Laura 600
horse 6, 14, 35, 37, 54, 63, 98, 100, 101, 115, 169, 170, 171, 17-176, 182, 183, 185, 187, 241, 243, 303, 306, 324, 371, 415, 416, 422, 427, 501, 511, 516, 551, 553, 554, 600, 617
horse and buggy 6
horses 179, 243
hospital 186, 188, 507, 508, 619
Hot Springs 280, 290, 299, 325, 331, 360, 368, 370, 423, 457, 473, 485, 490, 491, 550, 552, 636
House, Miss 10
household goods *(See also)*
   baskets 68
   bedclothes 157
   beds 157
   blankets 68
   blue stone 46
   buckets 156
   bureau 81
   candles 113
   cooking vessels 156
   counterpin 46
   crockery ware 157
   doll 82
   feather bed 58
   gun 156
   loom 119
   mattress 68
   pans 156
   pillow cases 68
   pistol 156
   sewing machine 84
   sheets 68
   shirt studs 296
   soap 56
   wax 113
   woodpile 52
Houser, Mrs. Pierce 237
Houston 471
   Ella 284
   Emma 284
   George 151
   Mag 237
   Mrs. 10, 206, 224
Howard
   Amanda 237
   Dora 346
   Dr. 258, 263
   Ella 26, 30, 33, 47, 51, 54, 59, 73, 75, 124, 126, 183, 186, 214, 237, 348
   Emma 214, 319
   Jim 603
   Jimmie 320
   Jimmy 109, 133, 213
   Julia 212, 213, 219, 227, 248, 263, 266, 314, 319, 329, 330, 34-347, 349, 422, 449, 451, 452, 457, 467, 475, 603
   Lamar 270
   Lonnie 451
   Lula 282, 286
   Mary 248
   Mims 270, 453
   Minnie 320
   Miss 230
   Mr. 154, 224, 238
   Mr L. 224
   Mrs. 36, 41, 49, 52, 73, 75, 79, 109, 111, 119, 124, 126, 137-139, 142, 144, 391
   Mrs. Dr. 36, 47, 124
   Mrs. L. 47, 51, 70, 91, 96

Index

Onie 329
Tarrant 63
huckleberries 39, 399, 487
Hudson, Dr. 342, 493, 504, 506
Huie, Capt. 583
Hull, Mr 598
hull-gull 94
Hunt
    Henrietta 561
    John 540
    Lucie Smoker 434, 441, 447, 541, 543
    Mamie 543, 544, 549
Huttig, Arkansas 582
Hutton, William G. 92
hyacinths 18, 71, 82, 84, 127, 129, 203, 343, 390, 502

I

ice lemonade 366
Ice-cream 383
illness *(See also)*
    asthma 153
    bilious fever 76
    billious fever 40
    blood boils 388
    bloody dysentery 41
    bonefelons 51
    carbuncles 388
    chicken-pox 118
    child-bed fever 76
    cholera morbus 200
    chronic bronchitus 153
    cold 31
    conjestive fever 42
    consumption 46
    cough 102
    cow bumpers 388
    croup 96
    diarrhea 112
    dropsy 44
    erysipelas 163, 267
    flux 45
    headache 37
    hematuria 248
    hooping cough 232
    itch 167
    measles 37
    meningitus 468
    neuralgia 47
    palsy 42
    Paralysis 325

pneumonia 154
rheumatism 148
risings 48
salivated 40
scarlet fever 38
scarletina 131
small pox 57, 188
sore throat 31
spasms 76
Thrush 427
tonsilitus 556
toothache 302
typhoid fever 45, 94
Imbecile Asylum 597
Indian Nation 93, 95
Indian River 526
infantry drilling 611
insects
    ants 41
    army worms 209
    cotton lice 112
    cut worms 59
    grasshoppers 209
    seedticks 30
    worms 86
Iowa City, Iowa 543, 549
Irene *(See also:* Love, Irene Lanier) 9, 73, 81, 84, 87, 90, 91, 95, 98, 101, 109, 110, 111, 114, 115, 117, 119, 120, 122, 125, 126, 127, 132, 136, 141, 150, 237, 242, 528
Iron Mountain 470
Ivins
    Ann 587
    John 588
Ivy Creek 4, 22, 43, 46, 62, 152, 418, 452
Ivy Creek Church 4, 22

J

Jackson
    Dr 467
    Stonewall, General 136, 138, 632
Jacksonville Fla 486
Japan 639
Jarrots, Jimmie 218
jasmine 19
jayhawkers 160
jeans 119, 124, 125, 128, 129, 137, 147, 149
Jefferson Post Office 4

jelly 81, 82, 83, 216, 512, 579
Jenkins
    Ackerbee 336
    "Bud" 526
    Mr 528
    Mrs 551
    Walter 251
Jennings, Mr 367
Jerry 154, 196, 244
Jimmie 198, 199, 201, 203
John 196
Johnson 173
    Billy 24
    Bushrod R., General 191
    Kirklin 609
    Mr 309
Johnston, George 288, 297, 353
Jones
    Emma 331
    Frank 239
    Henry 554
    Howard 280
    Mary 139
    Mary Ann Rumph 467
    Mr 348
    Red, Jr. 451
    Sham 348
Jonson, Mrs. 15, 22
Jorden, Mr 237
Jordon, Willie 494
Julia Ann (July Ann, Julyann) 163, 165, 212, 231
Junior, Julia 334
Justice
    Jake 573
    Lillie 537
    Virgie 537

K

Kansas jay-hawkers 156
Kellum, Martha 299
Kenerday 83
Kennedy, Mrs. 10
Kent 140
Kent, Miss 24
Kentucky 163, 211
Keokuk 544
Keys, Mr 192
Killam, Frank 495
kindergarden 589
Kingston 225
Kirkland

F. 9
Lewis 233
Mollie 529
Kirkland place 414
Kirklands, Perry 9
kittens 20, 286
Knights of Pythias 537
knit 55, 56, 70, 71, 85, 88, 103, 118, 124, 125, 222, 497, 613
knitting 5, 9, 53, 71, 88, 101, 118, 120, 497, 613
Knox, Miss 233
Knoxville 187, 188

L

Ladies Aid Quilt Sale 632
Lady Godey's Book 74
Lagrippe 619
Lamar
  Dee 187
  Dent 42
  Mrs. 3
  Sarah 15
Lamar School House 15
lambs 166, 171
lanced 99, 101, 102, 103, 133, 427, 556
Land, Mrs. 197, 201
Lane, Mrs. 238
Lanier
  Abe 344
  Burl 57
  Clement 22, 25, 26, 43, 341, 359, 377, 395, 533
  Clement G. 18, 26, 47, 49, 51, 58, 63, 102, 121, 122, 123, 137, 139, 187, 201, 203, 210, 218, 226, 237, 243, 249, 257, 260, 279, 284, 285, 325, 331
  Ike 236
  Isaac 14, 120, 201, 243
  Mary Dickson *(See also:* Grandma) 4, 12, 14, 18, 25, 32, 49, 55, 58, 110, 111, 112, 116, 249, 254
Lapsley, Mrs. 26
lard 164, 241, 581
Lasiter
  Betty 5, 8, 9, 14, 24, 34, 38, 44, 131
  Dee 34, 95, 110, 131
  Dr. 14

  Mrs. 16, 27, 33, 41, 70, 73, 80, 81, 91, 100, 124, 126, 131, 138, 144, 149, 153, 197, 201, 202, 208, 233, 238
Lassiter
  Hannah 414
  Mrs. 110, 119, 137, 162, 265
  Virgil 162
Laura 124
Lavender, Mrs. 414
Lea
  Andrew 618
  Mr. 536, 560
  William 440
League of Nations 637
Leaman, Dee 189, 190
Leamus 414
Leattle, Mr 248
Lebanon, Ohio 569
Lee
  Gen 152, 173
  Mr 333, 424
  Mrs 290
Leer, Mrs. 498
lemonade 305
lemons 487
lettuce 32, 54, 71, 127, 254, 556
levee 596
Lexington 632
Liberty Bonds 640
Liddy 300
Lide
  B. 398
  Mr. 299, 316, 317, 320, 338, 353, 365
  Mrs 365
  S. Blackwell 289, 353
lights, electric 586
Lillian 553
lillies 13, 18, 127
Lilly 550, 551
limes 487
Lincoln, Abraham 97, 108, 109, 110, 118, 135, 161, 184, 191, 291
Lindenwood College 549
Lineas, Parson 302
linsey-woolsey 2
lint room 379
Lisbon Invincibles 119
Little Bay 640
Little Pink 258
Little Prairie 276

Little Rock 7, 55, 110, 111, 118, 130, 135, 142, 145, 147, 148, 152, 157, 160, 170, 177, 181, 203, 240, 275-277, 279, 282, 283, 286, 290, 295, 320, 322, 330, 353, 423, 463, 473, 537, 564, 607, 629
Livingston
  Mollie 300
  Mr. 272
  Mrs. 272
  Ora 238
Lizzie L. 169
Lock, Louza 497
Lockett
  Mary 57, 613
  Mrs. 29
Long Island 368
Lonoke 276
loom 119, 124, 125, 129, 136, 140, 141
Lorsby, Mrs 319
Louis, St 348
Louisiana 181, 284
Louisville 211, 543, 544
Louisville North and South train 276
Love
  Ada 242, 280, 284, 315, 387, 392, 395, 427, 529, 549, 561, 601, 604, 608, 609
  Addison Clement (Clem) 137, 186, 218, 221, 223, 224, 231, 237, 244, 247, 256, 261, 262, 273, 274, 285, 354, 359, 529
  Addison Coleman (Cole) 8, 17, 51, 76, 81, 82, 89, 94, 95, 119, 120, 126, 127, 135, 137, 209, 249, 284, 325, 451, 529
  Andrew 231, 244, 254, 260, 261, 262, 268, 281, 340, 345-347, 395, 529
  Ann 212, 224
  Annie 279
  Bessie 401
  Bud 561
  Caroline LaFayette Boddie *(See also:* Sis Carrie) 6, 7, 8, 13, 15, 17, 33, 34, 42, 44, 53, 62, 79, 87, 99, 101, 109, 115-117, 124, 134, 136, 222, 226, 299, 237, 305, 338, 400, 528, 529, 549, 602, 623

Index

Crawford 401, 529, 532, 537, 602
Croff 561
Dick 212, 224, 230, 237, 242, 244, 257, 260, 268, 280, 284, 297, 408, 414, 529
Eldred 224, 230, 237, 244, 248, 256, 262, 274
Elrid 529
Emma 344
Fannie (y) 5, 15, 125, 137, 242, 279, 285
George 401, 529, 532, 533, 561, 610
George Boddie 549
Hannah Murley 209, 212, 218, 224, 230, 231, 237, 247, 254, 256, 262, 274, 354, 355
Irene Lanier (*See also:* Irene) 9, 73, 81, 84, 87, 91, 154, 197
Jennie 401
Kate 211, 212, 214, 218, 224, 231, 233, 237, 241, 242, 244, 247, 248, 250-258, 260, 262, 263, 265, 266, 269, 270-273, 279-281, 285, 297, 314, 315, 338, 340, 341, 344, 347, 354, 387, 395, 529, 530, 603
Mary A.E. Rawlings 9, 109, 113, 114, 116, 117, 122, 126, 134, 150, 154, 164, 197, 201, 208, 209, 212, 216, 218, 219, 223, 224, 226, 231, 234, 242, 243, 247, 248, 250, 254, 255, 257, 260-266, 270, 273, 280, 285, 340, 354, 378, 408, 418, 529
Maud 224, 247, 260
Nub 242, 529, 561
Onie 279, 282, 285, 314, 325, 338, 348, 353, 359, 387, 395, 529, 561, 603, 608, 610
Susan Frances 517
Tom 58, 95, 96, 134, 137, 142, 200, 202, 204, 209, 210, 215, 221, 224, 225, 231, 242, 251, 252, 274, 279, 281, 284, 285, 344, 377, 378, 387, 529, 610
Tommy 297
Virginia Cornelia 529, 532, 537
Will 281, 451, 561
William 22, 113, 154
William David 237
William G. 263

William Isaac 529
Willie 325
Lowry, Mr 353
Lucy 231
Luda 220, 222, 241
Luda Post Office 140
Luka Springs 183
Lutheran 592
Luton 5
Lyles
  Mr. 22
  Mrs. 16
Lynchburg, Va. 632
Lynn
  Martin 645
  Milton 572, 574, 580
  Mr 600

M

M., Jimmie 303
Ma (*See also:* Dickson, Clarissa Lanier Boddie) 2, 3, 5, 6, 8, 9, 11, 14-16, 19-22, 26, 30, 32, 35-38, 40-43, 45-47, 49-56, 59, 62-64, 66-70, 72-79, 81-89, 91-99, 102-104, 108, 109, 111-124, 126, 129, 130, 132-134, 138, 139, 141-154, 162, 169, 196, 200, 203, 244, 294, 316, 318, 352, 384, 386, 396, 400, 437, 444, 484, 510, 523, 528, 529
Macca, Mr. 83
Madam Oviates 31
Madison County 57
Magness, Mrs 237
Magruder
  John Bankhead, General 160, 172
Main, Mr 481
Major, Mr and Mrs 626
malaria 516
Malcolm, Mrs 420
Mallard, Mrs. 44, 221
Malvern 360, 370, 485, 507
Mamie 124, 146, 149, 211, 218, 219, 221, 222, 225, 226, 229-231, 234, 236, 242, 244, 247, 248, 250, 251, 253-258, 260, 262, 265-270, 280, 282, 286, 288, 289, 299, 307, 311, 313, 315, 316, 320-322, 324, 325,
327-329, 331, 332, 335, 338, 339, 341, 342, 344-347, 359, 360, 363, 365, 366, 368-370, 375, 380, 382-386, 390, 393, 395-397, 399, 400, 403, 404, 406, 409, 411, 413, 416, 420, 426, 427, 432, 433, 435, 437, 442, 444-446, 449-451, 455, 459, 473, 476, 485, 490, 491, 494, 496, 502, 505, 511, 514, 518, 523-525, 527, 528, 531, 533, 534, 541, 545, 546, 548, 550, 551, 561-564, 566-568, 571-573, 575-579, 581, 582, 584, 585, 587-595, 613, 629, 630, 632, 634, 644, 646
Mammy 21, 24, 35, 38, 40, 42, 43, 46, 62, 78, 88, 89, 91, 103, 111, 117, 120, 123, 124, 125, 134, 146, 148, 150, 153, 154, 159, 162, 164, 196, 197, 200-202, 212, 218, 231, 244, 264, 341, 414, 418, 640
Mann
  J. S. 507
  Mr. 500
Mansfield 157
mantilla 16, 20
Marinda 163
Marion 10, 139
Marion Junction 548
Marks, Mr 167
Marksmanship 585
Marlowe, Julia 589
Marmaduke 177
Marmaduke's Ford 614
Marshall 182, 224
  Bettie 357
  Mr. 41, 58, 73
  Tony 357
Martin
  Belle 572, 573
  Edgar 628
  J. W. 627
  James Walter 556
  Jim 573, 574, 580, 600, 606, 617, 618, 619, 620, 621, 625, 631, 632, 636, 645
  John Sadler 556, 639
  Lucian 628
  Lula Dunlap 560, 572, 574, 586, 588, 600, 641
  McDuff 572

Mrs. 646
Oliver 617, 618
Oliver Dunlap 645
Sadler 617, 618
W. T. 553, 580
William 555
William Thomas 573
Martin (Russell)
  Sue 617, 618, 645
Martins, W. 546
Marvin, Mr 359
Mary Jane 244
mattress 68, 134, 157
May apples 399
McClain
  Garvin 628
  Mr. 11
McClellan, George Brinton 161
McClure 589
McCollum, Dr. 417
McCrarry, Mr. 24
McElrath, Dr. 103
McGahan 581, 583
McGill, Fannie 528
McGraw, Paul 227, 360
McKinney
  Bennie 573
  Elsie 573
  Eugene 574
  Mrs. 573
McKinneys, Mr 464
McLaughlin
  Dr. 508
  Kate 469
McMahon, Mr. 265
McNeal, Sophia 24
measles 37, 41, 236, 353, 469, 491, 581
meat 121, 125, 126, 142, 146, 149, 152, 153, 155, 157, 158, 164, 220, 280, 299, 338, 340, 349, 366, 372, 387, 468, 519, 560, 563, 575, 581
Medical Institution 571
medicine 312(*See also:*)
  acorn salve 592
  assafetida 30
  atropin 500
  belladonna 145
  bitters 26
  blistering 37
  calomel 40
  camphor plaster 96

castor oil 294
charcoal 103
coal plaster 103
electric fluid 45
flaxseed 103
hartshorn 98
hot salt 37
hot teas 37
iodine 102
lancing 99
laudanum 98
morphine 76
opium 74
opodeldoc 90
Papine 568
poultice 76
quinine 47
sage tea 85
salts 37
sarsaparilla 102
scotch snuff plaster 115
spanish flies 76
strycnine 165
sulphur 167
sweet oil 98
turpentine 98
Meek
  Dr. 439, 551, 566
  Walter 501
melons 305
Memphis 109, 118, 134, 246, 250, 251, 252, 275, 276, 277, 278, 279, 280, 284, 386, 412, 452
Memphis and Charleston Depot 276, 278
Memphis Appeal 118
Memphis Commercial Appeal 278
Merrick, R.T. 240
Methodist 592
Methodist Church 620
Miami, Florida 645
Michel, Mr 291
Middletown 191
milk 28, 58, 62, 63, 76, 96, 98, 99, 103, 108, 119, 125, 131, 133, 142, 164, 186, 187, 220, 243, 254, 299, 301, 303, 306, 309, 310, 313, 327, 354, 383, 426, 429, 430, 433, 435, 447, 448, 482, 539, 547, 571, 586, 617, 618, 621, 631, 632
butter 539

Miller
  Bettie 529
  H.A. 241
  Mr. 552
Milnor, Mattie 265
Milton 139
Milton, Mr 322
Mineola, Texas 273
mines 581, 583, 602, 607
minks 300
Missionary Baptist 592
Mississippi 6, 284
Missouri 113, 119, 135, 161, 181, 212
Mitchel(l)
  Capt. 346, 360, 372, 517
  J. 376, 518, 527
  Mattie 321, 330, 398
  Mr. 24, 300
  Mrs 299, 360, 431, 482
Mitchel Station 495
Mittie (Mitt, Mit) (*See also:* Coralie Rumph) 12, 13, 25, 35, 40, 41, 45, 58, 61, 66, 73, 80, 83, 85, 89, 96, 97, 163, 195, 200, 210, 211, 221, 224, 230, 231, 234, 236, 239, 242, 244, 247, 248, 251, 255, 258, 259, 265, 267, 269, 288, 291, 293, 296, 298, 299, 301, 302, 305-307, 309, 310, 312-315, 317, 319-322, 324, 328, 330, 333, 334, 338, 339, 341, 344, 345, 347, 350, 352, 355, 356, 358, 359, 362, 367, 368, 369, 371, 374, 379, 380, 382, 386, 390, 394, 397, 400, 408, 411, 413, 419, 420, 425, 426, 429, 430, 450-452, 456, 459, 463, 464, 472, 475, 489, 492, 498, 500, 501, 504, 506, 509, 511, 521, 525, 526, 528, 534, 537, 541, 542, 545, 550, 556, 572, 576, 579, 581, 583, 588, 592, 596, 600, 602, 605, 609, 610, 623
Mixon
  Dr 272
  Jallie 265
  Mr. 81
  Tallie 267
Mobile 2, 13, 21, 31, 32, 49, 69, 80, 119, 141, 210, 387, 476, 482, 484 *See* Alabama: Mobile

Index

molasses 126, 146, 149, 155, 158, 189, 241, 360, 519
Monk, Dr. 610
Monroe 150, 206, 637
Monroe, La 626
Monroe, Maj. 169
Montgomery 183, 476, 484, 588, 590
Montgomery Advertiser 623
Montgomery Mail 118
Montgomery, Mr. 33
Monticello 166, 170, 172, 174, 176, 177
Moor, Mrs 229
Moore
  Bishop 629
  Lieutenant C. 187
Morgan
  C. 532
  Everlee 330
  Johnie (y) 302, 366, 370, 382, 383, 394, 396, 397
  Mrs 492
Morgan place 511
morphine 76, 104, 498, 568
Morris, Mr. 95, 334
Morton
  Dick 238
  John 121, 123, 124, 126, 146, 196, 200, 201
  Mr. 34
  Susan 118
Moseley
  Allis 313, 328, 329, 343, 346, 371, 375, 410, 421, 455, 465, 477-480, 485, 491, 494, 498, 502, 505, 514, 518, 519, 524, 527, 534, 535, 539, 545, 551, 553, 557, 563, 566, 586-589, 591, 592, 600-602, 612, 614, 619, 620, 623, 627
  Anna 281, 289-291, 303-306, 310, 313, 314, 316, 317, 320, 324, 327, 331, 338, 343, 346, 349, 357, 359, 360, 366, 369, 370, 372, 375, 377, 378, 380, 383, 395, 396, 398, 402, 404, 406, 408, 410, 415, 417, 421, 422, 456, 457, 460, 468, 476, 477
  Carrie Boddie 548, 550, 601, 642
  Charles 627
  Charles Elijah 587, 618, 628

Elijah 289, 296, 298, 303, 306, 327, 346, 349, 358, 361, 364, 371, 372, 410, 465, 468, 534
George Boddie 575, 576, 577, 581, 582, 583, 586, 587, 591, 600, 601, 606, 608, 610, 611, 612, 613, 616, 617, 618, 619, 620, 621, 623, 624, 625, 627, 628, 629, 630, 631, 634, 641
Harry Fisher 545, 547, 550, 551, 553, 557, 575, 576, 577, 582, 586, 587, 588, 591, 592, 601, 609, 610, 612, 613, 614, 617, 618, 619, 620, 622, 623, 624, 625, 627, 628, 632, 634, 642
Jane Alabama 328
John Louis 618, 627, 628
Mahala Campbell 253, 349, 363, 365, 371, 380, 383, 404, 468, 474, 480, 489, 496, 511, 534, 553, 557
Maj 421
Marvin 251, 290, 294, 300, 346, 371, 465, 480, 627
Mary Arkansas 380, 477
Peter 289
William Marvin 618, 627, 628
mosquitoes 19, 275, 643
Motley
  Dora 8, 9
  Wm. 9
Mouson 630
Mt Elba 181
Mt. Morris Baptist Church 592
Mugwumps 261
Mulberries 487
Mulberry 186, 216
Mulberry Academy 3
Mulberry Post Office 3, 14, 642
mule 84, 86, 88, 90, 161, 176, 178, 206, 208, 217, 222, 241, 259, 328, 334, 342, 348, 351, 352, 359, 361, 374, 379, 390, 393, 397, 420, 422, 483, 494, 548, 554
mules 138, 155, 156, 163, 171, 178, 179, 222, 234, 258, 296, 303, 347, 491, 584, 600
Murchison, Carneal 497
Murfreesboro 189
Murley
  Bob 307
  Crawford 307

  David 18
  George 307
  Gilder 547
  Harriet Gildersleeve 18, 126, 151, 219, 222, 227, 248, 263, 266, 267
  Hattie 63, 231, 236, 237, 250, 251, 253, 285, 287, 291, 293, 297, 299, 302, 307-309, 318, 335, 373, 410, 416, 433, 482, 505, 546, 547, 549
  Mattie 335, 482, 547, 549, 550
  Minnie 307
  Mrs 320
  Sallie 482
  Stevie 547
  Walter 547
  Willie 547
Murr(a)y
  Dollie 528
  Dr. 516, 520, 522, 528, 550, 551, 556
  James 284
  Willie 528
Museum of Nat. History & Art 589
mushmelons 112, 162
music 14, 19, 93, 211, 213, 221, 233, 250, 257, 258, 270, 279, 288, 308, 311, 327, 331, 340, 352, 356, 358, 363, 366, 378, 389, 416, 450, 465, 468, 485, 494
muslin delain 8
mustard 36, 54, 56, 71, 74, 78, 82, 83, 104, 165, 445, 556
Muttons 366
Myer
  Henry 555, 574
  Stern 574

N

Napoleon 177
narcissus 127
Navarro county 182
Navy Yard 590
Nazerith 163
Neilson, Lotta 300
Nelson, W. W. 561
neuralgia 47, 48, 50, 220, 222, 288, 302, 312, 327, 368, 369, 434, 439, 453, 556
New Orleans 13, 17, 30, 31, 33, 48,

49, 51, 54, 63, 80, 81, 82, 83,
  118, 119, 126, 127, 130, 210,
  221, 251, 262, 265, 419, 422,
  460, 470, 498, 540, 543, 604
 Cathedral 32
 French Market 32
New Orleans Crescent 118
New Orleans Delta 118
New York 134, 368, 372, 585
New York Times Sunday Edition
  620
Newgent, Mrs. 520, 522
Newport News 630
Newport, Rhode Island. 610
newspaper
  Republican 306
Newton
  Dee, Capt. 25, 33, 34, 39, 54, 80,
    91, 100, 137, 138, 144, 145,
    149, 195, 210, 211, 215, 218,
    225, 227, 232, 238, 247, 269,
    272, 275, 281, 285, 293, 297,
    299, 300, 313, 332, 334, 343,
    372, 397, 406
  Eustice 215
  Green 81
  Ike 424
  Isaac 80, 215
  John Boddie 272, 293
  Nealie 248
  Oriana Stone (Mrs. Dee) 137,
    215, 227, 230, 232, 238, 251,
    272, 273, 281, 285, 299, 312,
    313, 461, 534
  Robert Dee (Bobbie Dee) 310,
    334, 482
  Virginia 550
Niagra 590
Nicarauga 639
Nina, Aunt 306
Nixon, Sallie 248
Norman, Kinch 498, 509
Norris
  A. 346
  John 300
  Mollie 346
  Mr. 298, 348, 353, 371
  Mrs. 253, 395
North Carolina 135
Northington
  Onie 610
  Thomas 284
  W. H. 529

Nunn
  Ira 414
  Mr 62
  Mrs. 100
nuts 622

O

O Banmore, Mr. 167
oats 163, 284, 300, 303, 367, 390,
  617, 631, 632
O'Bannon, Mr. 101, 136
Observatory 589
OConnor, Captain 188
Oklahoma 93
Old Ben 212
old Bill 163
old Mike 388
Olentangy river 596
onions 336
opium 74
oranges 3, 30, 32, 487
organ 320
osnaburg 130
Ouachita 31, 108, 110, 112, 114,
  115, 119, 120, 206, 209, 236,
  238, 241, 269, 270, 273, 274,
  283, 285, 289, 290, 292, 293,
  295, 298-301, 304, 307, 308,
  310, 311, 314, 315, 317, 319,
  321, 324, 328, 330, 331, 333,
  335-338, 341, 343, 345, 347,
  348, 350, 351, 354, 355, 358,
  361, 364, 368, 369, 373, 376,
  378, 381, 384, 385, 388, 389,
  391, 392, 397, 399, 400, 402,
  404, 405, 407, 408, 410, 412-
  419, 421, 423-426, 428, 430-
  433, 435-438, 440, 442-452,
  454, 456-458, 460-464, 466-
  473, 475, 479-481, 485, 490,
  493-495, 499, 500, 504, 509,
  518, 529, 537, 539, 544-546,
  548, 550, 551, 554, 556, 559-
  573, 575-579, 584-586, 588,
  590-592, 594, 600-602, 604-
  607, 609, 610, 612-614, 616-
  637, 639-643
Ouachita Co. 88
Ouachita Greys 115
Ouachita Guard Co. 350
Ouachita Lyceum 369
Overman, Bill 360

Owen, Miss 625
ox 88, 518
oxen 90
Oxford Miss College 214
Oyster dressing 622
oysters 32

P

P. O. 4
Pa (*See also:* Dickson, Samuel
  Henry Neely, Col.) 5, 6, 8-11,
  15, 16, 19-21, 23, 26, 35, 41,
  42, 44, 46, 47, 49, 50-53, 55,
  59, 61, 62, 64, 66-68, 70-73,
  75, 77, 79-81, 83, 84, 87-89,
  91, 94, 119, 121, 123, 166,
  168, 169, 173, 203, 249, 289,
  292
Pace
  Billy 238
  Dr 374, 382, 412, 413
  Mary 232, 238
  Mrs 421
Pacific Fleet 639
Palestine 427
pans 156
pansies 595
pantry 95
pants 56, 83, 125, 128, 161, 190,
  365, 374, 379, 381, 402, 446,
  502, 544
pap 40
Paris Island 631, 636
Paris, Texas 571
Parker, Mr 284
parks 589
Parsons' Cavalry 176
Paschal Bros & Co 411
patching 101
Patterson
  Joe 464
Patterson
  Amanda 494
  Cad 476, 520
  Mittie 420
  Mr. 297, 361, 502
  Mrs. 253, 437
Paxton, Lucy 252
pea soup 299
Peabody House 275, 277
peach trees 111, 352, 390
peaches 83, 88, 90, 112, 117, 136,

210, 219, 260, 302, 305, 306, 310, 334, 401, 403, 420, 484, 487, 511, 574, 618
peanut hay 620
pears 75, 306, 420
peas 36, 37, 43-45, 54, 56, 71-73, 82, 83, 104, 110, 125, 127, 131, 136, 142, 149, 162, 165, 237, 267, 298, 300, 328, 329, 334, 340, 362, 367, 370, 391, 398, 523, 556, 617, 618, 622, 630
    Bunch 86
    English 86, 622
peavine hay 620
Pecans 487
peckerwoods 523
Peebles
    Dr 218
    Rebecca 237, 248, 254
Pelt
    Johnson 612
    Mrs 609
    Nolan 612
pens, steel 2
pepper sauce 190
pepperment candy 15
Pepton 571
Perry
    Bob 215
    Ross 620
Persimmons, Japan 487
Peter, Buck 169
Peters
    Ellen 232
    Jim 46
    Mrs. 36
Peterson's Magazine 74, 234
Philadelphia 618, 623
Philipines 593
Philips
    Col. 24
    Dr. J. 24
piano 210, 211, 232, 233, 257, 288, 352, 378, 379, 416, 597
pick room 97, 383
Pickett
    Albert 4
    Fanny 129
    Sarah 8, 9, 237
picnics 308, 452
pies 611, 622
pigs 97, 128, 292, 309, 310, 328,

348, 349, 351, 356, 383, 421, 617, 636
barbecued 338
Pile
    Blanche 227
    Conway 563, 572, 573, 576
    Eliza Stone Wood 461
    Lorena Elizabeth Conway 524, 528
    Miss 251
    Mr. 167, 169, 215, 227
    Mrs. 227, 232, 239, 272
    W. 231
    William 215, 251
pillow cases 68
Pine Bluff 139, 142, 152, 157, 167, 175, 177, 178, 179, 180, 181, 343
Pine Lake 180, 209, 210, 279, 364, 401, 505, 553, 614
pineapples 487
pinks 18, 20, 127, 540
Piny woods 414
Pippin, Julia 4, 5
pistol 132, 156, 272, 482, 498, 508
Pleasant Ridge 157
ploughs 175
plowing 594
plums 19, 39, 83, 136, 137, 305, 352, 420, 484, 487
    Japan 487
pneumonia 115, 154, 166, 222, 232, 265, 324, 360, 374, 381, 413, 437, 457, 496, 501, 517, 525, 587, 604, 644
Polk 276
    Lucius E., General 189
Polk House 278
Polly 163, 212
pomegranates 332
Ponder
    Mary 227
    Mr. 227
    Mrs 166
ponies 446
Pons, G. 34
Pope
    L. 352
    Mr. 302, 365
    Sasser 316
    Silas 100
pork 78, 104, 123, 146, 174, 183, 241, 328, 334, 442

Port Hudson 150
Porter
    Bell 24
Portiss, Mrs 169
possums 49
Post Office 3, 4, 5, 14, 74
pot liquor 125, 303
potato 165
potato crop 340
potatoe 167
Potatoe custard 334
potatoe, Irish 359
potatoes 15, 23, 32, 75, 84, 86, 90, 93, 95, 99, 104, 117, 125, 126, 131, 142, 196, 202, 260, 296, 299, 303, 334, 359, 367, 374, 382, 395, 448, 618
    creamed 622
    Irish 22, 71, 110, 234, 237, 299, 630
    Sweet 618
poultice 76, 98, 103, 115
poultry 361
Powell
    Joe 366
    Mr. 221, 251, 312, 316, 353
    T. C. 265
    William 237
Prattville, Ala 601, 609
Prattville Signal 517
Presbyterian 592
Prescott 275, 277, 278, 280, 445, 492
Pressly, Lieutenant Col. 188
Price, Sterling, General 135, 147, 157, 161, 167, 170, 187
Prickett, Austin 237
Princeton 142, 170, 172, 375, 440, 467, 468, 469, 496, 498, 500, 501, 503, 504, 506, 507, 509-513, 515-517, 520, 522-527, 530, 533, 535-538, 541, 546, 560
Princeton Road 142
Prochan, Geo. A. 508
Proctor
    Clementine (Clem) 390, 455, 503, 510, 513, 521, 530, 531
    Ella 483
    George 476
    Georgia 313, 317, 320, 334, 338, 357, 363, 365, 370, 377, 389, 392, 467, 476, 480, 484, 501,

505, 510, 512, 517, 528, 530, 539, 552
James 360
Jesse (ie) 327, 513, 516, 520, 530, 539, 550
Jim 455, 510, 521, 531
L. 410
Martha 138, 274
Martha Mendenhall 520, 530
Mary Patterson 539
Mattie 615
Mr. 218, 322, 359, 394, 506
Mrs 303
Shade 370, 383, 476
Tom 531
Victoria 138, 140, 234
Proctor & Rumph 422
Proctors, Mr. 506
Pryor, Susie 334
Puckett, Mr 378
pudding & raspberry sauce 299
pudding with Strawberry sauce 335
pumpkin pie 334
pumpkins 125, 367
puncheon 34
Purifoy, Mrs 614
Puryear
   Mary 501
   Powel 553
Puryfoy, Arthur 612
Pyles, Jno. 567

Q

Queen City, Tex 527
Quillen, Mollie 258
quilts 13, 68, 70, 315, 350, 480
quinine 26, 47, 144, 165, 171, 483, 498, 618

R

R., Fannie 353
rabbits 165, 300
radishes 54, 56, 71, 82, 83, 127, 254, 267, 445, 556
rain 403
Rainwater, John 476
raisens 3, 30
raisin 317
Ramsey, Mr. 424
Randles, Dr. 592
Randolph-Macon 632
raspberries 16, 17, 242, 399, 400

Ratcliffe, Rev Mr 116
Rector, Henry M., Governor 110
Red Cross 613
Red River 131
Reeves, Edgar 524
Reformed Dutch Church 592
Rentz, Rev. 646
rheumatism 148, 154, 222, 279, 284, 288, 305, 374, 501, 504, 550, 587, 606
Rhody 212
Rhone, Gen. 130
ribbon 24
rice 111, 183, 189, 563, 595
rice soup 183
Richards, Mr. 293, 296
Richardson
   Ed 457, 459
   Eddie 469
   Frank 520, 521, 528
   Jude 521
   Judge 476, 522, 551
   Lon 464
   Lou 466, 476, 480
   Maggie 459, 466, 468, 469
   Mamie 459, 466, 476, 505, 524, 527, 531
   Margaret 625
   Mollie Stone 469, 528
   Mr. 460, 468, 502
   Mrs 520
   Tobe 467, 531
   Walter 453
Richie
   Ella 344
   Mr. 317, 320
Richmond 590
Richmond Enquirer 118
Richmond, N. 287
Richmond Whig 118
Rinehart, Dr. 587
rising breast 525
risings 48, 55, 102, 133, 279, 556
Ritchie (*See also:* Richie)
   Edgar 584
   George 313, 338
   John 424
rivers
   high water 13
   low water 13
   Ouachita 206
   overflowed 13, 56
   Duck river 191

Mississippi 132
Red 206
Roberson
   Mr. 303, 306, 321, 330
   West 620
Robertson, Mrs. 625
robins 321
Robinson, Mr 298
Rock Spring 405
Rockwell Manufactory 614
Roda 163
Roe, Mr 551
Rogers, Lizzie 252
rose 13, 14, 20, 32, 84, 99, 102, 103, 137, 165, 189, 203, 205, 234, 474, 477, 492, 524, 540, 555, 556
   Creole 243
   Victoria Landmark 243
Rosecrans, William Stark, General 153, 189, 190
Roseman, Mrs 284
roses 6, 14, 18, 36, 71, 73, 127, 203, 359, 394, 396, 479, 555
Ross
   Henry 238
   Mr. 151, 232, 272, 284, 320
Roundtree, Mr 284
Rounsiville, Miss 195
Rucks
   Attalie 541
   Cornelia 339
   Corrie 328, 339, 350, 352, 358, 362, 382, 500, 501, 525, 534, 537, 542, 545, 554, 557, 623
   Edmund 301, 305, 310, 320, 328, 338, 341, 346, 355, 356, 359, 362, 368, 379, 411, 420, 500, 501, 504, 506, 525, 526, 528, 541, 557
   George 584, 640
   J. 313, 320, 338, 365, 397
   John 500, 525, 528, 545
   John Benjamin 498
   Louis 489, 542, 545
   Mr. 312, 315, 317, 321, 322, 328, 333, 339, 408, 451
   Mrs. 313, 319, 339, 509
   Tom Louis 419
Rumph
   Attalie 195, 200, 207, 213, 225, 234, 236, 244, 246, 296, 304, 306, 307, 309, 314-316, 346,

357, 371, 389-391, 393, 406, 418, 449, 452, 463, 466, 467, 479, 480, 483, 484, 498, 501, 502, 509, 510, 512, 513, 515, 516, 520,-522, 524, 525, 528, 532, 537, 541, 542, 547-549, 552-554

Bessie Jewell 476, 480, 531

Betty Frances 41, 60, 61, 63, 71, 85, 97, 170, 195, 200, 202, 211, 217, 221, 225, 229, 231, 234, 246, 250-252, 254, 255, 257-259, 265, 267, 270, 280, 288, 289, 291, 296, 299, 305, 313, 314, 317, 319, 320, 329, 338-342, 344, 347, 352, 357, 359, 363, 365, 368, 369, 371-373, 375, 377, 382, 383, 390, 392-394, 396, 397, 399, 401, 402, 406, 415, 419, 420, 422, 451, 452, 456, 457, 488

Caroline 83

Charlie (ey) Ben 467, 469, 476, 480, 481, 496, 516, 520, 530, 531, 539, 575, 576

Coralie (*See also:* Mittie) 12-14, 25, 40, 41, 45, 58, 60, 66, 80, 222, 225, 226, 231, 247, 257, 269, 270, 285, 289, 316, 321, 329, 341, 345, 362, 368, 385, 396, 399, 400, 408, 416, 498, 511, 513, 534

Edward Benjamin 478, 488, 584

Ethel Annie 419, 488, 584

Eugene 312, 316, 320, 355, 359, 470, 479, 584

Eugenia 216, 224, 226, 234, 244, 246, 258, 296, 304, 306, 309, 314-316, 321, 324, 328, 357, 371, 389-391, 393, 418, 463, 466, 467, 476, 480, 485, 496, 498, 501, 505, 509, 510, 512, 513, 516, 520-522, 524-526, 528, 531, 532, 546-548, 550, 551, 553, 560, 563, 578, 580, 584, 615

Florence 40, 61, 63, 71, 77, 78, 89, 221, 225, 231, 234, 251, 253, 257, 258, 267, 270, 274, 288, 289, 291, 299, 302, 305, 314, 315, 316, 319, 320, 329, 333, 338, 339, 341, 344, 347, 352, 363, 365, 367-370, 374, 378, 383, 385,-387, 389, 392, 397, 400, 402, 403, 406, 415, 420, 422, 449, 451-453, 457-460, 462, 467-469, 472, 475, 477, 488, 489, 491-493, 509, 535, 538

Frances Pickett Boddie (*See also:* Sis Fannie) 7, 12, 16-18, 25, 33, 47, 48, 52, 116, 207, 274, 312, 362

Garland 438, 455, 469, 480, 496, 516, 520, 521, 530, 531, 539, 541, 575, 576, 614, 631, 632

George Boddie 40, 41, 45, 54, 58-61, 66, 73, 80, 83, 94, 95, 97, 102, 125, 163, 170, 195, 200, 209, 211, 214, 217, 221, 224, 225, 229, 231, 234, 237, 244, 251, 257, 258, 262, 275, 288, 298, 305, 309, 312, 316, 320, 333, 339, 341, 344, 345, 347, 350, 352, 355, 356, 359, 362, 364, 369, 373, 374, 388, 402, 408-411, 415, 419, 422, 424, 425, 433, 439, 443, 448, 451, 456, 459, 460, 466, 467, 471, 472, 475, 478, 483, 488, 492, 498, 567, 588, 592, 599, 602, 603, 605, 607, 609

George Boddie, Jr. 315, 316, 320, 355, 470, 479, 584

Hattie 371, 422, 479, 496, 516, 520, 522, 526, 530, 539, 550, 552, 553, 613, 636, 645

John Benjamin, Dr. (*See also:* Brother John) 7, 8, 12, 17, 25, 29, 33, 34, 44, 46-48, 55, 61, 63, 85, 96, 97, 101, 118, 122, 125, 128, 131, 133, 135, 137, 138, 166, 169, 170, 172-174, 176, 177, 179, 180, 181, 183, 213, 218, 228, 231, 239, 284, 288, 291, 292, 293, 295, 298, 299, 301, 302, 304, 305, 307, 312, 313, 316, 317, 322, 324, 327, 329, 330, 333, 334, 341, 342, 346, 349, 352, 357, 359-364, 367-372, 374, 375, 377-384, 386, 387, 389, 393, 394, 398, 403, 404, 406, 408, 409, 410, 415, 418, 420, 421, 424-426, 429, 430, 432, 435, 438-440, 443, 445, 449, 450, 455, 456, 478, 479, 481, 482, 491, 502-506, 509, 510, 529, 530

John Gildersleeve 92, 94, 96, 207

Kate 161, 163, 207, 213, 246

Lillian 496, 521, 531

Louis 30

Martha Proctor 147, 149, 163, 207, 282, 304, 307, 314, 339, 340, 342, 357, 360, 362, 365, 371, 377, 380, 383, 387, 393, 398, 432, 452, 455, 467, 468, 469, 474, 476, 480, 484, 491, 496, 497, 503, 506, 509, 510, 511, 512, 513, 517, 522, 528, 532, 539, 541, 550, 552, 606, 613, 615, 630, 631, 635, 636, 645

Mary 63, 66, 82, 346

Maude 575, 576, 599, 606, 630, 636

Maude Jessie 282, 304, 307, 340, 355, 357, 371, 389, 393, 479, 496, 497, 510, 516, 520, 522, 526, 530, 539, 552, 553

Mildred 584, 643

Sallie 163, 207

Sally Gildersleeve (*See also:* Sis Sallie) 8, 9, 34, 42, 77, 78, 80-83, 85, 89, 91, 92, 94, 96, 98, 101, 102, 109-112, 117, 118, 120-22, 124, 125, 128, 129, 132, 133, 136, 141, 142, 146, 147, 151, 153, 156-158, 161, 163, 166, 167, 169, 172, 174, 176, 177, 179-181, 183, 194-197, 200, 202, 207, 210, 211, 213, 216, 220-222, 224-227, 231, 236, 239, 244-247, 267, 274, 291, 309, 418, 547, 615, 636

Sarah Amelia 125

Thomas Lewis 33, 41, 85, 88, 97, 170, 221, 225, 274, 286, 290, 293, 296, 298, 303, 310, 312, 313, 315, 318, 327, 334, 341, 342, 346, 349, 357, 359, 360, 362, 364, 366-370, 377, 382, 383, 387, 396, 397, 399, 402, 406, 418, 445, 449, 455, 456, 464, 466, 470, 477, 481, 486, 506, 521, 525, 530, 537, 544, 573, 581, 602, 606, 607, 610

Virginia Jordan 315, 316, 320,

584, 645
Virginia Jordon 312, 339, 341, 342, 344, 345, 347, 350, 352, 355, 356, 359, 362, 364, 365, 374, 380, 382, 390, 392, 393, 399, 400, 401, 402, 409, 410, 419, 420, 422, 425, 451, 452, 458, 459, 472, 492
Rumph & Gee 422
Russell, Sue Martin 556, 627
rye 163, 169

S

sacque 5, 9, 13, 145
Sadler 617, 618, 621, 625, 627, 628, 631, 636, 639, 645
safe 429
Saline 157, 167, 174, 177
salt 136, 172, 360, 575, 584
Sanders
   Arnold 612
   Mr 612
sardines 317
Sarsby, Mrs 220
Sather, Pete 563
sausage 101, 102, 164, 203
Sawther's command 176
Saxon, Mr 302
Scales
   Mr 403
   Mrs 352, 389, 406
scarlet fever 14, 38, 85, 87, 142, 144
Scarletina 133
Schnedler, Paul 465
scholars 3, 58, 88, 191, 195, 222, 361, 463
school 1-6, 10, 14-16, 20, 22, 71, 77, 90, 96, 100, 132, 136, 139, 141, 144, 152-154, 161, 163-165, 167, 168, 171, 190, 195, 196, 198, 200, 202, 207-209, 211, 213, 217, 219-223, 225, 229-232, 237, 238, 243, 246, 247, 249-253, 256, 258, 259, 261, 262, 265-271, 273, 274, 284, 286, 293, 299, 303, 307, 325, 333, 336, 354, 356, 360, 361, 367, 368, 370, 375, 377-380, 385, 386, 389-391, 393, 395, 399-405, 417, 418, 427, 440, 447-449, 452, 455, 460-

464, 466, 469, 471, 472, 474, 476, 484, 488-491, 494, 496, 497, 499, 500, 501, 507, 509-518, 520-525, 528, 530, 531, 532, 534-537, 539, 541, 542, 545, 549, 552, 553, 555, 556, 562, 564, 565, 567, 570, 577, 580, 582-584, 587-589, 595, 600, 602, 603, 608, 615, 620, 621, 625, 627, 631, 632, 636, 644, 645
   Sunday 24, 73
   Sabbath 307, 378
Scioto 596
Scott
   Winfield, General 118
   Mrs. 137
screw-builder (carpenter) 77
Scribner 350
Scrip 295
scuppernongs 260
Searcy 620
secession 111
Selma 1, 5, 6, 8, 16, 18, 19, 20, 21, 23, 25, 120, 123, 277, 278, 293, 548, 552
Selma, Ala 275, 552
Selma Co. 117
servant
   Barbara 500
Service Flag 627
sew 50, 53, 54, 56, 58, 64-66, 84-86, 108, 125, 339, 492, 615
sewing 1, 13, 15, 21, 52, 53, 56, 67, 75, 79, 84-86, 108, 118, 125, 210, 232, 249, 264, 268, 296, 332, 334, 375, 380, 393, 407, 419, 441, 461, 477, 480, 483, 502, 505, 512, 523, 564
Sewing Machine 465
sewing society 118, 125
Seymore 294, 359, 362, 372, 374, 386, 403
Shaddock, Mrs. 167
Shady Grove 39, 41, 59, 561
Shannon, J. T. 411
sharecropping 195, 222
Shaw's garden 294
sheep 72, 78, 171, 347, 585
sheets 68, 137, 384, 391, 514
Shelby 177, 479
Shelbyville 259, 549
Shiloh 132

shirt 13, 59, 186, 296, 321, 330, 589
shirt studs 296
shirts 59, 374, 432, 438, 500, 540
shoats 49, 317, 366
shoes 1, 2, 3, 5, 22, 26, 32, 61, 91, 156, 161, 234, 481, 497, 544, 566, 577, 592, 598, 602, 603, 633, 634
shoes, wooden 628
shortening 142
Shreveport 139, 141, 179, 182, 183
Sifford, Mrs. J. T. 606
sillabub 422
Silliman
   Jno I 411
silver 127, 128, 151, 156, 224, 383, 455
Simmons, Mrs 501, 550
Simpson
   Bob 80
   Mat 46
Sims, John 119
sing 12, 14, 17, 19, 98, 108, 321, 502
Singer Co 597
Sipes Springs 630
Sis Carrie (*See also:* Love, Caroline Lafayette Boddie) 19, 34, 36, 40, 45, 51, 59, 61-64, 66, 68, 70, 73, 75, 77, 82, 84, 95, 96, 104, 109, 111, 113, 114, 116, 117, 119, 120, 122, 124, 126, 129, 132, 134, 138, 139, 141-144, 147-151, 153, 154, 161-164, 183, 194, 197, 199-203, 212, 217, 218, 220, 231, 234, 242-244, 247, 249, 254, 260, 279, 286, 314, 418, 474, 528, 537, 551, 552, 560, 588, 600, 602, 609
Sis Fannie (*See also:* Rumph, Frances Pickett Boddie) 33, 35, 36, 37, 39, 40, 41, 42, 43, 44, 45, 46, 47, 48, 49, 52, 53, 55, 57, 60, 62, 63, 64, 67, 69, 77, 104, 221, 615
Ss Mollie (*See also:* Boddie, Mary Elizabeth Gildersleeve) 8, 13, 31-37, 39, 41-45, 47, 48, 52, 53, 57-67, 69, 71, 75-77, 80-89, 91, 93-99, 102, 104, 109-120, 122, 124-126, 128-133,

705   Index

137, 139, 141-144, 146-149, 151-153, 156-158, 161-164, 194-197, 199, 200, 202, 207, 210-212, 215, 216, 219-223, 225-227, 229, 231-233, 238, 242-253, 260, 262-264, 266-268, 270, 272-282, 285-287, 307, 309, 312, 314, 320-322, 331, 338, 341, 347, 348, 354, 355, 374, 397, 401, 415, 418, 419, 436, 451-453, 460, 472, 474, 476, 497, 505, 511, 517-519, 521, 522, 524, 527, 528, 530, 534, 541, 544, 545, 550-555, 560, 561, 580, 594, 604, 623, 636, 641
skiffs 13
Skillet heads 182
skirts 19, 21, 32, 120, 252, 315, 338, 339, 517, 572
slash land 595
slave (*See also*)
  Ann 38, 40
  Aunt Katy 140
  Berry 141, 156
  Bill Scott 45, 116
  Bob 143
  Buchanan 44
  Caroline 196
  Cash 112
  Dan 83
  Derry 117
  Dick 61
  Ellen 196
  Ester 115
  Hannah 37, 48, 136, 156
  Harriet 47, 79, 88, 91, 95, 117, 144
  Harry 237
  Henry 62, 83, 96
  Jerry 13, 29, 55, 83, 91, 117, 197
  Jinny 156
  John 40
  John Morton 122
  Josephine 17
  Julia Ann 45, 58, 59, 119, 124
  Laura 111, 144, 196
  Lucy 47
  Mammy 24, 62
  Margaret 44
  Mark 112
  Phillis 18, 32, 37, 62
  Rhoda 136, 156

Richmond 156
Robert 112
Roda 44, 118
slay 129
Slommans, Col 178
Smallpox 57, 188, 192, 293, 496, 566
Smead, Anna Chester 644
Smith
  Buddie 412, 413
  Cicilia 466
  Georgia 574
  H. 389
  Kirby 160
  Kirby, General 150
  Mac 460, 561
  Mr. 23
Smoker 511, 514, 554, 561, 562, 564, 565, 567, 570, 571, 577, 578, 579, 583, 585, 594, 604, 605, 610, 644
  Capt. 426, 434, 447, 485, 540
  Cornelia Kimball 399, 405, 407, 410
  Grandpa 435, 441
  Lillie 543
  Will 441
Smythe, Mrs 403, 430
Snow, Mr. 498
soap 20, 30, 46, 56, 90, 155, 643
  hard 56
  soft 56
socks 81, 88, 118, 125, 190, 203, 383, 438, 500, 613
sorgum 618
Sothern, E. H. 589
Souls, Lucy 237
soup 40, 76, 183, 299, 447
South Carolina 243
Southern Confederacy 114
sows 310
Spain 592
Spanish Influenza 619
spasms 76, 167
specie 121
speculators 189
Spencer 300, 306, 313, 346, 349, 351, 357, 360, 386
Spenser 297
spinning 140, 143
spoons 25
Spoonville 417
Spring, Scales' 403

Springhill College 476, 482, 495
squash 39, 71, 73, 162, 196, 367
squirrel 321, 322
squirrel dog 328
squirrels 96, 321, 328, 499, 519, 612, 637
St Charles, Mo. 549
St Louis 292, 295, 312, 315, 334, 348, 353, 364, 381, 393, 412, 425, 435, 436, 452, 468, 470, 475, 503, 540, 542, 544
St. Johns Methodist Church 629
St. Joseph College 463, 464
St. Louis 113, 280, 287, 289, 290, 292-295, 298, 300, 301, 304, 308, 310, 311, 313, 315, 317, 318, 321, 324, 325, 328, 329, 333, 335, 338, 341, 345, 348, 351, 354, 355, 358, 361, 368, 371, 373, 376, 378, 379, 381, 385, 388, 389, 390, 392, 395, 397, 399, 402, 404, 405, 407, 408, 410, 412, 413, 415, 416, 419, 423-426, 428-433, 437, 438, 440, 442-446, 448, 450, 451, 454, 458, 463, 465, 470, 472, 475, 481, 486, 497, 505-507, 523, 525, 540, 542-545, 549, 554, 561, 563, 565, 566, 571, 572, 575, 579-581, 593, 601, 606, 609, 610, 617, 618, 620, 623, 625-627, 629, 630, 632-635, 637, 640, 642, 643, 646
St. Mary of the Woods 636
Stanley
  Fannie 534
  Mrs 365
Starkville Miss 618
State Normal Schools 608
State Script 292
Steel plantation 414
Steele
  Amanda 502
  Elliot 502
  Frederick, General 157, 167, 169
  General 142
  Lula 502
  Mr 421
  Mrs. 206
  T. J. 453
Stevenson, Carter L., General 191
Stewart, Mrs. 216, 238

Stinsons 482
stockings 5, 9, 71, 81, 156
Stone
  Abe 170, 216
  Albert T. 7, 100, 119227, 272
  Annie 232, 238, 253, 264, 273, 291, 297, 299, 305, 342, 343, 349, 352, 356, 358, 363, 369, 372, 374, 375, 381, 394, 396, 398, 403, 404, 406, 408, 421, 439, 441, 461, 463, 468, 587
  Billie 289
  Billy 298, 299
  Bob 227, 232, 291, 296, 297
  Dr. J. 453
  Dr. Mrs. 84, 119
  Emma 227
  George 38, 100, 216
  Helen 239
  J. 534
  John 135, 167, 180, 272, 533
  Julia 38, 39, 407
  Mary L. 453
  Mollie 292
  Mr 272, 281, 329
  Mrs. 161, 534
  Mrs. Dr. 125, 149, 157, 169, 216
  Mrs. Robert 250, 259, 460
  Ora Eliza 7, 39, 54, 100, 137
  Robert 94, 215, 218, 251, 259, 267, 290, 293, 300, 303, 306, 316, 327, 328, 342, 343, 349, 356, 358, 361, 363, 366, 369, 371, 372, 374, 376, 381, 386, 393, 394, 398, 403, 406, 408, 415, 421, 439, 441, 467, 469, 474
  Ruby 588
  Sid 582
  Slaten 259
  State 292, 297, 300, 321, 327, 342, 348, 356, 367, 371, 372, 373, 374, 376, 387, 389, 402, 441, 481, 488, 498, 524, 526, 528, 531, 534, 539, 550, 573, 582
  Tom 171, 483
  Tommie 216
  Warren 34, 65
  William 212, 215, 227, 239, 264, 296, 300, 305, 313, 327, 328, 343, 349, 351, 360, 361, 363, 375, 381, 383, 389, 399, 415, 421, 429, 437, 439, 440, 441, 494, 495, 527
  William T. 39, 41, 167, 169, 171, 250
  Willie 297, 389
Stontamire
  George 237
  Sam, Col 237
Stony Joint 603
Stooks, Walter 497
stoves
  Bucks Brilliant 253
  Charter Oak 253
  Olive Branch 253
  Pacific 253
  Philanthropist 253
  Star 253
strawberries 14, 16, 17, 22, 27, 34, 37, 59, 85, 86, 196, 209, 254, 297, 335, 400, 422, 487, 491, 533, 534, 546, 566, 571, 577, 594, 618
strawberry 127, 147, 359, 397, 446
strawberry bed 308
Stubs, James 8, 9
Stuttgart 276
sub chasers 621
sugar 114, 126, 146, 149, 155, 158, 163, 189, 278, 336, 360, 382, 397, 481, 580, 585
  Cane 585
Sulphur Springs 478
Summerfield 414
Susan 414
sweet potatoes 44, 86, 117, 125, 131, 334, 554, 614, 617
Sweetwater P. O. 4
Sweetwater Post Office 4
syllabub 218, 317, 335, 383

T

Tait, A. 348
Tappan, Gen. 148
Tarrant 44
Tarrant, Miss 221
Taylor
  Matilda 14, 49
  Matt 78
  Mr. 16, 483
  Mrs. 229, 236, 551
  T. 14
tea 1, 3, 14, 82, 85, 113, 186, 250, 441, 538, 547
teacher 2, 3, 6, 10, 15, 41, 58, 61, 73, 77, 152, 161, 195, 200, 202, 243, 247, 250, 256, 271, 331, 381, 401, 402, 466, 474, 490, 502, 514, 521, 600, 625
telegraphic wires 142
Tennessee River 127
Tensas river 637
Terry, Mr. 21
Texarkana 527, 626
Texas 122, 123, 128, 141, 153, 160, 162, 167, 175, 179, 181, 182, 183, 224, 228, 230, 237, 248, 267, 273, 274, 276, 280, 284, 285, 331, 335, 354, 356, 357, 382, 387, 392, 410, 417, 418, 471, 476, 478, 480, 493, 495, 498, 499, 500, 504, 505, 507, 508, 524, 526, 531, 571, 572, 630, 634, 641
Thacher, Mary Elizabeth 92
Thomas, Miss 625
Thompson, Laura 238
Thornton 646
thyme 21
Tilden, Samuel J. 364, 376
Tim Limbrish 183
Titusville 526
tobacco 585
toilet paper 643
Tom 196
tomatoes 88, 90, 196
Tompson
  Green, Dr 237
  Jim 574
Toney
  James B. 353
  Jennie 353
  Jim 348, 365, 431
  Mr. 170, 314, 353
  Mrs 291
  Mr. & Mrs. 317
Tony, Mrs. 526
tooth brush 35, 480
transportation
  buggys 31
  cariole 134
  carriages 31
  drays 31
  omnibuses 31
  railroad 229
Trenton 206

Troupe Station, Rusk Co. Texas 357
Truck Mortar Battery 622
Tucson, Ariz. 583
Tudor, Dr 363
Tufts, Mr. 424
Tug 342, 345, 346, 349, 350, 353, 355, 356, 360-363, 367, 370, 372, 375-377, 379, 382, 383, 385, 390, 393-395, 397-399, 402, 403, 405, 406, 410, 420, 435, 437, 439, 444, 446, 450, 455, 497, 634
Tulip Creek 269
Tulips 32, 73, 165, 169, 254, 290, 359, 488, 502, 534
Tullahoma 189
Turkey
turkey 18, 128, 149, 155, 196, 203, 207, 222, 243, 293, 317, 334, 338, 339, 344, 357, 358, 359, 377, 379, 382, 388, 392, 394, 420, 421, 445, 455, 460, 467, 502, 523, 526, 527, 531, 584, 622
  wild 35
turnips 93, 97, 125, 334, 521
turtles 300, 447
Tuscumbia 189
Tyers, Mr 319
typhoid 2, 45, 94, 222, 232, 340, 409, 457, 507, 508, 514, 518, 520, 532, 529, 537, 556, 605
typhoid pneumonia 232
Tyra Hill & Company 292, 354
Tyro 178
Tyus
  Mr 331
  Mrs 603
  Randolph 254

U

U boats 618
U.S.S. Maine 612, 613
Uncle Bill 212
Uncle Cowert 36
Uncle Jerr 196
Uncle Jerry 197, 200, 201, 202, 418
Uncle John 212
underskirt 20
Underwood
  Becca 330, 349, 417, 421, 422, 436, 437, 456, 457, 460, 462, 467, 470, 471, 473, 474, 475, 552
  Bess 223
  Dempsy 340
  George 223
  Hattie 208, 216, 218, 237, 255, 343, 346, 353, 373, 384
  J. 30
  Minnie 209
  Mr. 4, 207, 208, 220, 231, 308, 319, 344
  Rebecca 39, 40, 42, 46, 49, 54, 59, 62, 70, 73, 79, 86, 91, 96, 109, 111, 119, 124, 126, 132, 139, 144, 153, 197, 201, 202, 204, 205, 206, 207, 208, 212, 219, 223, 308, 319, 330, 417, 418, 421, 436, 456, 460, 462, 467, 470, 471, 473, 552, 641
  Rob 209
  Rube 139, 238
  Thomas 451
  Tom 86, 91, 226, 263
Underwoods, Mrs 278
Unionville Pike 191
Usrey, Frances 643

V

Vallandigham, Clement 191
Van Duzer 630, 646
vegetable garden 297
vegetables (See also: garden vegetables) 72, 307
Venable
  Aubrey 628
  Clayton 628
  Lillie 587
  Lilly 589
  Rosser 588
venison 35, 39, 40, 208, 210, 259, 304, 308
Verner, Mrs. 276
Vicksburg 134, 139, 142, 146, 148, 150, 152, 588
vigilante committee 113
violet 379, 390, 407, 444, 524, 595
violin 389
Virginia 110, 113, 134, 138, 152, 186, 400, 411, 605, 628, 632, 633
Vowell, Miss 152

W

Wadsworth
  Bessie Love Brock 561, 588, 600, 603, 608
  Fannie Love 528
  Fanny Love 265
  M. S. 517
  Mack 528, 530
  Mr 257, 518
  Tom 603
  Tommie 530
Wadworth, Mr 537
Wagner
  Mr 183, 248
  Mrs. 95
  Walter 248
wagon 80, 82, 86, 140, 143, 156, 157, 183, 188, 208, 210, 234, 255, 258, 260, 339, 358, 374, 422, 454, 465, 478, 494, 497, 505, 507, 542, 576, 583, 587, 612
Waldo 625
Walker
  Eliza 8, 9
  General 150
  Mrs 135
Wallace, Mrs. 224, 231
Ward, Miss 28
Ware, Henry 24
Warren 174, 176, 177, 179, 404, 588
Washington 586, 590, 629
Washington - Lee University 632
Washington, Arkansas 160
Washington, Charles 629
Washington City 55, 136, 241
Washington County 138, 228
water works 586
watermelon 60, 73, 112, 162, 196, 275, 600
watermelons 42, 43, 44, 55, 112, 260, 302, 359, 367, 403, 587, 618
Watson, Lucy 414
wax 113, 114, 547
weave 119, 124, 125, 128, 129, 130, 133, 136, 137, 141, 144, 147, 173
Weaver
  Col. 21
  David 26

Jennie 251
Mr. 15
Mrs. Col. 15, 16, 19, 22, 23, 30
Phil 27
weaving 119, 124, 125, 129, 130, 140, 141, 143, 146, 149, 151, 161, 168
Webb Lake 614
Webb School 494
Webb, Soney 497
West, Miss 340
West Point 578, 589
wheat 34, 75, 101, 117, 120, 123, 126, 131, 136, 138, 142, 147, 149, 151, 152, 163, 167, 169, 177, 178, 179, 191, 241, 280, 284, 296, 298, 300, 303, 309, 325, 328, 329, 361, 367, 382, 550, 604, 640, 641
Whetstone
  Annie 268
  Bettie (y) Lasiter 41, 44, 46, 50, 56, 57, 62, 67, 70, 73, 80, 91, 96, 100, 119, 120, 124, 126, 139, 150, 151, 162, 197, 201, 202, 228, 233, 265, 268, 271
  Louis 267, 268
  Minnie 268
  Peyton 8, 9
White, Mrs 117
White River 169
whooping cough 234
whortleberries 399
Wiggins
  Jinny 27
Wiggins, Mrs 57
Wiggs, Mr. 234
Wilcox 451
Wilcox County 603
Wilkerson
  Col. 348
  Joe 346
  Mrs. 348
Wilkes, Mrs Mary 453
Wilkinson
  Capt. 174
  Jimmie 460
  Willie 460
Williams
  Helen 166
  Mr. 93, 157
  Mrs. 157, 227, 239
  Nancy 227

Williamson, Theresa 549
Willis, Carl Lewis 628
Wilson 640
Wilson
  Mike 139
  Mrs. 166
Windfield, Parson 208
Winfield
  Dr 275
  Edward 275
  Mr 221
  Mrs 275, 353
Winston, Mr 300
Winter, Bob 27
Womans Home Companion 589
Wood
  Billy 189
  Dr 66, 68, 69, 75
  Eliza Stone 13, 227
  Phil 238
  William 186
  William, Mrs. 8, 215
Woodard Lake 505
woodpile 52, 382
Woods, Martha 237
Woodson, Mrs. 552
wool cards 130
Wooten, Dr. 493, 507
Word
  Amerial Stone 251, 259
  Jennie 215
  Jimmie 232, 374, 375
  Lillian 643
  Mrs 232
  Octavia 461
worms 59, 86
Wright
  Annie 625
  Mrs. 232, 314, 317, 508

Y

Yarbrough, Mr. 276
Yarrington, Mr. 10
yellow fever 452
yellow jaundice 522
Yellville 143
York, Leonard 469
York River 624

Z

Ziglar, Bettie 110
Zimmerman, Fannie 340, 346, 347, 529
Zimmermon, W.J. 517
zinc 609
zitta 211, 213
zoos 589